Acclaim for ROBERT GOTTLIEB*'s*

READING JAZZ

"Fascinating, heroic. . . . [*Reading Jazz* is] a valuable introduction to the practice and history of jazz."

—*The Atlanta Journal-Constitution*

"It's the passion—the passion of and for the music—that matters. No other book on jazz catches that magnificent obsession the way *Reading Jazz* does. . . . [It is] simply a delight."

—*Commonweal*

"An instant classic. . . . If an anthology can be a work of art, *Reading Jazz* is a masterpiece. . . . This terrific book is as vital, surprising, raunchy, beautiful and transcendent as the music it celebrates."

—*Daily News*

"By far the best thing of its kind ever published. . . . If the reportage included in *Reading Jazz* is uniformly excellent, the autobiography is arguably even better."

—*The Wall Street Journal*

"The finest, most informative and colorful writing about jazz . . . probably the most comprehensive one-volume chronicle of jazz ever assembled. . . . Poring through the book, one is struck both by the warmth and depth of the musicians who pioneered the art form and by the caliber of those who chose to write about it."

—*The Denver Post*

"Impressive. . . . [*Reading Jazz*] will provide the jazz-lover not only hours of reading enjoyment but a lasting reference book as well."

—*Richmond Times-Dispatch*

"A feast."

—*The Times-Picayune*

"The last word on jazz as well as jazz writing."

—*Interview*

ROBERT GOTTLIEB

READING JAZZ

Robert Gottlieb has been editor-in-chief of Simon & Schuster, Alfred A. Knopf, and *The New Yorker*. He has previously edited the Everyman's edition of *The Collected Stories of Rudyard Kipling* and *The Journals of John Cheever*.

ALSO BY ROBERT GOTTLIEB

A Certain Style: The Art of the Plastic Handbag 1949–1959

The Journals of John Cheever (Editor)

The Collected Stories of Rudyard Kipling (Everyman's Library, Editor)

READING JAZZ

READING JAZZ

A Gathering of Autobiography, Reportage, and Criticism from 1919 to Now

EDITED BY

ROBERT GOTTLIEB

VINTAGE BOOKS

A DIVISION OF RANDOM HOUSE, INC.

NEW YORK

FIRST VINTAGE BOOKS EDITION, NOVEMBER 1999

Published in the United States of America by Vintage Books, a division of Random House, Inc., New York, and simultaneously in Canada by Random House of Canada Limited, Toronto. Originally published in hardcover in the United States by Pantheon Books, a division of Random House, Inc., New York, in 1996.

Permissions Acknowledgments appear on page 1061.

The Library of Congress has cataloged the Pantheon edition as follows:
Reading jazz : a gathering of autobiography, reportage, and criticism from 1919 to now / edited by Robert Gottlieb.
p. cm.
ISBN 0-679-44251-0 (hc)
1. Jazz—History and criticism. 2. Jazz musicians—Biography.
I. Gottlieb, Robert, 1931– .
ML3507.R44 1996
781.65'09—dc 2069-14219
CIP
MN

Vintage ISBN: 0-679-78111-0

Author photograph © Anne Hall
Book design by Julie Duquet

www.vintagebooks.com

Printed in the United States of America
10 9 8 7 6 5 4 3 2 1

CONTENTS

PART 2: REPORTAGE

INTRODUCTION

Like all anthologies, this one is a compromise. My original idea was to limit it to the very best writing on jazz from whatever source and on whatever subject, from 1919 into the 1990s. But as I read more and more, I kept coming on pieces whose extraordinary interest or historical importance demanded that they be exhumed, even if their actual prose was less than brilliant. Nor did it seem sensible to include half a dozen pieces on one major artist and none on another, simply because the first attracted better writing; a principle of inclusivity began to take over. The same thing happened in regard to writers. As in any field, there are a few masters, and this entire volume could easily have been filled with their work. But I came to feel that in some informal way the book should reflect the history of jazz *writing* as well as the history of jazz.

Reading Jazz is divided into three parts. The first is autobiographical, and I've been surprised and delighted by the quality of expressiveness to be found in so many first-person narratives and interviews—probably a higher level of vitality than could be found, for instance, in a comparable selection of writing from the ballet or opera worlds. The reportage section reflects a broad diversity of attitudes and styles but tries always to provide third-person witness to a subject of real interest. And the criticism has been deliberately chosen to reflect the widest possible spectrum of thinking about jazz itself and its major figures.

I came to jazz late in my life, a disadvantage in some ways, since I had to start from scratch in my reading. On the other hand, I started with no preconceptions about writers or—perhaps more important—about the issues that have torn the jazz world apart for the last half-century or more and have left their mark on much of the writing to be found in this book. These include both the stylistic wars, beginning with the struggle between the "moldy figs" and the "boppers," and the far more unyielding war over race—a war that seems always to be with us, though there has been a radical shift in tone from the relatively sunny narratives of early jazz to the polemical attitudes of so many of the later musicians and commentators. Equally noticeable is a change in the first-person narratives as they progress from the pre-war world of boozing and reefers to the post-war world of hard drugs which devastated the lives and careers of such artists as Charlie Parker, Billie Holiday, Art Pepper, Anita O'Day, and Hampton Hawes.

Another change that this book tries to reflect is that between the earlier criticism, which focuses on trying to place jazz as an art—what *is* jazz, what claims can be made for it as being "serious," what is its relationship to classical music (not unlike the old photography vs. painting comparisons)—and a later criticism that is more centered on specific performers and gradually grows more historical and academic.

THE CONTENTS OF *Reading Jazz* come from many sources—autobiographies, essay collections, old issues of magazines, and previous anthologies, of which many valuable examples have been published, though none on this scale. The literature is enormous, and no one volume, even of these monstrous proportions, can do justice to it. My hope is that readers will be drawn to certain complete texts that could only be excerpted here, and will discover writers whom they can pursue in bookstores and libraries—that this book will serve, in fact, as an advertisement for an entire literature. Some of the material here is, of course, taken from books that remain in print. Other selections—like the extended narrative by Mary Lou Williams, Billie Holiday's blindfold reactions to a bunch of current records, and the long interview with Milt Gabler about Commodore Records—are more or less unavailable elsewhere. And whereas some of our finest critics—men like Whitney Balliett, Gene Lees, and Gary Giddins—have published numerous collections of their work, the work of others, like Dan Morgenstern, is uncollected and unavailable unless one has old copies of the journals they wrote for or the albums for which they provided the liner notes.

My interest in jazz was stimulated and encouraged by Whitney Balliett when I worked with him at *The New Yorker,* and I thank him for that, as well as for the miraculous quality of his work. I've also worked with Nat Hentoff, though never on jazz projects, and his lifelong dedication to jazz has been a factor in my own education—not least through *Hear Me Talkin' to Ya,* his first book (compiled with Nat Shapiro) and in my view the single most valuable book in the field. I've benefited, too, from the encouragement, knowledge, and friendship of Will Friedwald and Gary Giddins. But the book's greatest debt is to two men who in their different ways continue to contribute the most to jazz writers and readers—Sheldon Meyer of Oxford University Press, who for decades has offered a responsible and dedicated publishing apparatus to serious jazz writers, and who has been extraordinarily kind to this tyro in his field, and Dan Morgenstern, whose work at the jazz archive at Rutgers University, together with his encyclopedic knowledge, his modesty, and his unfailing generosity, helps make possible books like this one. Also, of course, I must thank those people at Pantheon who have helped me—Erroll McDonald, my appreciative editor; the firm, patient, organized (and organizing) Altie Karper; Grace McVeigh, senior production editor, who has been generous with her time and talents; and especially Nara Nahm, who consistently has gone beyond her professional obligations to assist me with this project.

1

AUTOBIOGRAPHY

Jelly Roll Morton

Alan Lomax, who sought out and chronicled so many early jazz and blues musicians, induced Jelly Roll Morton to both play and speak at length for a famous series of Library of Congress recordings and for the book Mister Jelly Roll *(1950). Morton's claims about his role in jazz history may be exaggerated, but his testimony about the early days is fascinating and persuasive.*

The first night after my great-grandmother told me to go, I attended the Grand Theatre and saw a play in which they sang a very sweet song, entitled "Give Me Back My Dead Daughter's Child." I thought about how my mother had died and left me a motherless child out in this wide world to mourn, and I began to cry. Fact of the business, I was just fifteen and so dumb I didn't even know how to rent a room. So I walked the streets till morning and then caught a train for Biloxi, where my godmother had her country place in the summer. I knew she would take me in, no matter what happened.

While there in Biloxi I began hanging out with older boys and thinking of myself as quite a man, which I was still just a kid. These guys told me that you could be a real man if you could take a half pint of whiskey, throw it to your mouth, and drink the whole thing down without stopping. Well, I tried that and it knocked me completely out. I lay under the bed at my godmother's house for three whole days before they found me. That finished whiskey and me for that time.

Well, I played in various little places in Biloxi, but I never made the money I had in New Orleans. I worked at The Flat Top until one night the owner was hit in the head with a pool ball, which has made him crazy till this day. Then I moved on to a job in Meridian, Mississippi. Mississippi was always my bad-luck state. I came down with typhoid fever and returned to Biloxi on a stretcher. My godmother fed me for three weeks on a diet of whiskey and milk, which almost ended me with liquor entirely. (I never took another drink, except occasionally . . . Lord, this whiskey is just lovely!)

My next job was playing for a white sporting-house woman named Mattie Bailey. Nobody but white came there, and, as it was a dangerous place, I always carried a .38 Special. Mattie Bailey would keep me behind to close up the place for her, and, because I was always the last man out, talk began to get around that something was going on between the two of us. By her being a white woman, they didn't approve of my being intimate with her, as they thought. One day she told me they were talking about lynching me and right then I decided it was time for me to roll on back to my good old hometown, New Orleans.

So in the year of 1902 when I was about seventeen years old I happened to invade one of the sections where the birth of jazz originated from. Some friends took me to The Frenchman's on the corner of Villery and Bienville, which was at that time the most famous nightspot after everything was closed. It was only a back room, but it was where all the greatest pianists frequented after they got off from work in the sporting-houses. About 4 A.M., unless plenty of money was involved on their jobs, they would go to The Frenchman's and there would be everything in the line of hilarity there.

All the girls that could get out of their houses was there. The millionaires would come to listen to their favorite pianists. There weren't any discrimination of any kind. They all sat at different tables or anywhere they felt like sitting. They all mingled together just as they wished to and everyone was just like one big happy family. People came from all over the country and most times you couldn't get in. So this place would go on at a tremendous rate of speed—plenty money, drinks of all kinds—from four o'clock in the morning until maybe twelve, one, two, or three o'clock in the daytime. Then, when the great pianists used to leave, the crowds would leave.

New Orleans was the stomping grounds for all the greatest pianists in the country. We had Spanish, we had colored, we had white, we had Frenchmens, we had Americans, we had them from all parts of the world because there were more jobs for pianists than any other ten places in the world. The sporting-houses needed professors, and we had so many different styles that whenever you came to New Orleans, it wouldn't make any difference that you just came from Paris or any part of England, Europe, or any place—whatever your tunes were over there, we played them in New Orleans.

I might mention some of our pianists . . . Sammy Davis, one of the greatest manipulators of the keyboard I guess I have ever seen in the history of the world. . . . Alfred Wilson and Albert Cahill, they were both great pianists and both of them were colored. Poor Alfred Wilson, the girls taken to him and showed him a point where he didn't have to work. He finally came to be a dope fiend and smoked so much dope till he died. Albert Cahill didn't smoke dope, but he ruined his eyes staying up all night, gambling. Albert was known as the greatest show player that ever was in existence as I can remember. Then there was Kid Ross, a white boy and one of the outstanding hot players of the country.

All these men were hard to beat, but when Tony Jackson walked in, any one of them would get up from the piano stool. If he didn't, somebody was liable to say, "Get up from that piano. You hurting its feelings. Let Tony play." Tony was real dark and not a bit good-looking, but he had a beautiful disposition. He was the outstanding favorite of New Orleans, and I have never known any pianists to come from any section of the world that could leave New Orleans victorious.

Tony was considered among all who knew him the greatest single-handed entertainer in the world. His memory seemed like something nobody's ever heard of in the music world. He was known as the man of a thousand songs. There was no tune that come up from any opera or any show of any kind or anything that was wrote on paper that Tony couldn't play. He had such a beautiful voice and a marvelous range. His voice on an opera tune was exactly as an opera singer. His range on a blues would be just exactly like a blues singer. Tony had a blues that was a favorite with him . . .

Yes, Michigan water taste like sherry,
I mean sherry, crazy about my sherry,
Michigan water tastes like sherry wine,
But Mississippi water tastes like turpentine.
"Mama, mama, look at sis,
She's out on the levee doing the double twis'."
"Come in here, you dirty little sow,
You tryin' to be a bad girl and you don't know how . . ."

Tony happened to be one of those gentlemens that a lot of people call them lady or sissy—I suppose he was either a ferry or a steamboat, one or the other, probably you would say a ferry because that's what you pay a nickel for—and that was the cause of him going to Chicago about 1906. He liked the freedom there.

Tony was instrumental in my going to Chicago the first time, very much to my regret because there was more money at home. Anyhow he was the outstanding favorite in Chicago until I finally stayed for a battle of music that came up and I won the contest over Tony. That threw me first in line, but, even though I was the winner, I never thought the prize was given to the right party; I thought Tony should have the emblem. We were very, very good friends and whenever he spotted me coming in the door, he would sing a song he knew I liked—"Pretty Baby," one of Tony's great tunes that he wrote in 1913 or 1914 and was a million-dollar hit in less than a year . . .

You can talk about your jelly roll,
But none of them compare with pretty baby,
With pretty baby of mine.

Tony was the favorite of all who knew him, but the poor fellow drank himself to death. Well, I'm getting way ahead of my story.

When I first got back to New Orleans from Biloxi, I had a run of bad luck. I felt sick and bad. Something seemed to be wrong with my hands. When jobs came up in the district, they didn't come my way. One afternoon I was sitting around 25's and wondering if my grandmother hadn't been right after all, when old man Sona walked up to me.

"Son, you are sick."

"That's right, Papa Sona, somebody must have put something on me." I was just kidding when I said that, of course.

"Don't you worry, son, Papa Sona gonna cure you."

I didn't know how *he* could tell I was sick. I had seen him one time before when I was a kid. That day I walked in on a ceremony in a neighbor's house. Papa Sona was dancing barefoot on a blanket, mumbling some type of spell. Afterwards they had a feast of jambalaya rice with some kind of peculiar odor to it and they gave us kids poppy seed to put in our mouths. The seed was supposed to make you highly successful—you could swing people your way.

These operators like Papa Sona did some kind of workmanship with frog legs and boa-constrictor tongues to make somebody fall in love with you, but you don't know how this is done. That's all I knew about Sona, that he operated in this underground stuff I didn't half believe in. He told me, "Come along, son. I'm going to give you three baths and you will be well by the last bath."

He took me to his house. He stripped me and put me in a tub with some kind of grass in it. Then he rubbed me with this grass and mumbled and shook so much it made me very, very nervous, I'm telling you. For three Fridays he gave me this bath and then he told me, "Son, I'm gonna get you a job now so you can pay me. Take me to the house where you want to work, only don't say anything when we get there. Just touch me. In three days you will have that job."

I took Papa Sona past Hilma Burt's house, which was one of the highest class mansions in the district, and did as he had requested. Three days later at two o'clock in the afternoon I was sitting around 25's and a maid from Miss Burt's house walked in and said their regular piano player was sick. "Would I like to make a few dollars?"

Of course, I accepted and you never saw such a well man as I was that night when I sat down at the grand piano in Hilma Burt's mansion. Right away Miss Burt liked my style of music and she told me, "If you think you can come steady, I will be glad to have you."

In a week I had plenty money, but I never thought of paying Papa Sona for what he did, because I never really believed he had helped me. I should have realized that he used some very powerful ingredients. I should have been more appreciative, for I have lived to regret this ungrateful action.

Hilma Burt's was on the corner of Customhouse and Basin Street, next door to Tom Anderson's Saloon—Tom Anderson was the king of the district and ran the Louisiana legislature, and Hilma Burt was supposed to be his old lady. Hers was no doubt one of the best-paying places in the city and I thought I had a very bad night when I made under a hundred dollars. Very often a man would come into the house and hand you a twenty- or forty- or a fifty-dollar note, just like a match. Beer sold for a dollar a bottle. Wine from five to ten, depending on the kind you bought. Wine flowed much more than water—the kind of wine I'm speaking about I don't mean sauterne or nothing like that, I mean champagne, such as Cliquot and Mumm's Extra Dry. And right there was where I got my new name—Wining Boy.*

When the place was closing down, it was my habit to pour these partly finished bottles of wine together and make up a new bottle from the mixture. That fine drink gave me a name and from that I made a tune that was very, very popular in those days . . .

I'm a wining boy, don't deny my name,
I'm a wining boy, don't deny my name,
I'm a wining boy, don't deny my name,
Pick it up and shake it like Stavin Chain,
I'm a wining boy, don't deny my doggone name . . .

Every month, the changing of the moon,
Every month, the changing of the moon,
I say, every month, changing of the moon,
The blood comes rushing from the bitch's womb,
I'm a wining boy, don't deny my name . . .

**Wining* (pronounced with a long ī) is the term Jelly preferred to *winding,* for reasons that Johnny St. Cyr makes quite clear. In fact Johnny was more than a shade embarrassed when asked what the nickname meant, since *winding* also means rotating the hips in dancing or in sexual intercourse. He said, ". . . Winding Boy is a bit on the vulgar side. Let's see—how could I put it—means a fellow that makes good jazz with the women. See, Jelly lived a pretty fast life. In fact, most of those fellows round the district did. They were all halfway pimps anyway . . . Jelly's Winding Boy tune was mighty popular in the early days."

Sidney Bechet

Like Mister Jelly Roll, *Sidney Bechet's* Treat It Gentle *(1960) may not be compulsively accurate, but it represents the voice and spirit of its author and subject, one of the most glorious instrumentalists in jazz. (See p. 49, where Duke Ellington calls him "the very epitome of jazz" and p. 741 for Ernst-Alexandre Ansermet's famous essay of 1919 singling him out as a supreme soloist.)*

People have got an idea that the music started in whorehouses. Well, there was a district there, you know, and the houses in it, they'd all have someone playing a guitar or a mandolin, or a piano . . . someone singing maybe; but they didn't have orchestras, and the musicianers never played regular there. There was Tom Anderson; he had one of those cabaret-like places—saloons. He had practically everything there, card-rooms, bar, a hop-room—and he had music. Sometimes you'd hear accordion, guitar, mandolin, sometimes bass, maybe a violin; other times you'd hear someone singing there. It wasn't a whorehouse but you'd hear *whorehouse* music there. Lulu White, she wanted orchestras; sometimes she'd hire one, but it still wasn't a steady thing. The musicianers would go to those houses just whenever they didn't have a regular engagement or some gig they was playing, when there was no party or picnic or ball to play at. But in those days there was always some party going, some fish fry, and there was always some picnic around the lakes—Milneburg or Spanish Fort Lake.

All that what's been written about you got to play your instrument in a whorehouse, it's all wrong. Just going there for work sometimes, or to one of those cabarets over by Franklin Street when there was nothing else doing, that was all there was. I could pass one of those houses and hear a band and the next night I could pass by again and I wouldn't hear that same band, it wouldn't be there. So how can you say Jazz started in whorehouses when the musicianers didn't have no real need for them? It's just like a man, you know: he doesn't go to a whorehouse unless there's just nothing else for him. He's just letting something bad out, some feeling he isn't wanted somewhere. This Jazz was just like a man. No, it wasn't red-light districts were making ragtime. Musicianers weren't *going* there to make it. The only thing that was holding them back from playing it for everyone was the same thing that was always holding it back. A lot of those houses, sure, they wanted to hear it, they wanted the musicianers.

But Jazz didn't come from a peephole in one of them. You know, you take a woman. Say she's got a light dress on; maybe it's summer—if you look through her dress and see she's a woman, it's not her fault; it's not her fault you're looking to see how she is. And if she moves, and you watch her, all the time thinking about having her, that isn't her fault either. That's your mind putting something else on something very natural; that's a fact and shouldn't be made out of shape. And that's Jazz too. If people want to take a melody and think what it's saying is trash, that ain't the fault of the melody. Sure, there's pieces like "Easy Rider" or "Jockey Blues" that have got lyrics you'd call "dirty." Lots of them, they're exhibition-like, they're for show—a novelty to attract attention. But it's not those lyrics or those blues that really enter into your heart. The ones that really do that, they're about sad things—about loving someone and it turns out bad, or wanting and not knowing what you're wanting. Something sincere, like loving a woman, there's nothing dirty in that.

That's the kind of man he was, my father, back in his young-man days. And about then he took to spending a lot of time along the river. That was the time these riverboats was steaming up and down the river, making a real big splash when they came in to a landing. It was a gay time, the kind of time my father just naturally loved.

These boats used to have contests for music. One boat would line up alongside another and they'd play at each other, not too serious . . . sort of to amuse the people who was paying to ride on the boats. White musicianers they were at that time. There wasn't anything but white musicianers on the boats then, but they'd go along the Mississippi, and they'd hear the singing of the Negroes by the river, and some of it reached them. They'd be the songs of the Negroes working, or maybe just going about their business, maybe just resting . . . there'd be all that kind of music like it was some part of the Mississippi itself, something the river wanted to say. And it had an effect, you know; it just naturally had to have an effect on whoever heard it.

There's been so much that's been written and sung about the Mississippi, all romantic and wonderful somehow. But there's a lot of misery there too, a lot of the bad times and the hurt that's been living there beside the river. And the Negroes by the river, working, singing around, they had to have something to wash away their troubles: they'd let the Mississippi carry some of it for them.

That music was so strong, there was such a want for it that there was no moving away from it. The people on the boats couldn't help listening. Some of them, maybe, they were not showing their liking, not all of them. There were some even who didn't want to hear it at all. But it was one of those things that kind of comes in and robs you; it takes something in you without your even knowing it. And that's the way it was. Pretty soon the people wanted to hear more of it; they wanted to know more about it.

My father, when he wasn't working at his trade or down at the steamboat landing, spent all his time among the Negro musicianers. By that time he'd gotten himself so well known and so liked down at the steamboat landing that the manager of one of those boats had come to depend on him. My father took care of all kinds of arrangements for him. But all the time he could, he was off listening to what the musicianers were doing to those old traditional songs, how they were making a new spirit from them. My father often found jobs for some of those musicianers. Many a time he'd start things going, getting up a dance or a contest. And because he worked down on the river too, and the manager was so fond of him, he got up an idea to put colored musicianers on this one boat . . . put them on and really let them stir things up, let the music show a lot of things what had been happening to it since Emancipation, bring some of the good times to move along the river with the boats.

That's how he got up a band one day, and that was the first colored band that had been put on a boat. That boat, it got started on its excursion and all the people were waiting to have their big time and expecting to hear the old band, when all of a sudden they heard this new music. They'd never heard anything like it . . . at first they didn't know what to make of it. It was something they'd heard about all right, and it was supposed to be bad. *Jass,* that wasn't a pretty word. There was lots of other names for it too, and at first some of those people got mad and demanded their money back—they hadn't paid to come and hear that; it was bad enough when they'd had to listen to some of it, something like it, coming in from across the river. But after a while, you know, everyone, they couldn't help themselves—they were liking it and they were feeling good. The music was coming out to meet them and it got a welcome. Pretty soon they were having a time there. The tunes they were playing . . . "Salty Dog," that would be one . . . just playing on out, coaxing and bragging some, but all natural too, all so warm.

Then another boat came alongside this one. It had heard all the goings on. That other boat, it had white musicianers and the people on her were leaning over trying to hear the new music, and the musicianers were mad. A whole lot of people were feeling mad about it . . . a lot of business was going to be taken away. Negroes, playing on a boat, it wasn't right; mixing that way, it could lead to a lot of trouble. And those people who had been enjoying the music, letting themselves feel friendly to it, all of a sudden they felt they ought to get ashamed. It was just like when you were a kid and you'd been out all day—maybe you were supposed to have been at school, and you came in and your mother was there wanting to know where you'd been. Well, you'd been fishing and you hadn't ought to have been. You just can't come right out and say what you've been doing, so you pull out a string of fish and *then* you say "I've been fishing." Well, those people, they couldn't even feel they could bring out a string of fish. They just felt guilty and they didn't want to hear any more. What was happening was making them feel kind of ashamed, so all they could do was get mad.

But those colored musicianers kept on playing, and pretty soon the people on the boat, even the white musicianers themselves, began to go with the music. They couldn't stay mad. The music, *it* wasn't mad, it hadn't got any threat to it; there was just simple things in it, a lot of moods, a lot of feelings people had inside themselves. And so the white band, it played too, and the people, they gave in and pretty soon there was all kinds of dancing and hell raising, everybody having a whole lot of fun, answering to all that rhythm there, feeling all that melody carry them along.

That's how my father wanted it. He just filled his house with music, and when it wasn't being played at home he'd be off somewhere else where it was being played. Like I said, he wasn't a musicianer, but he really had a feeling for it. He lived right on, too, and died in 1923. I was just hitting New York, coming back from Europe, when it happened. There I was then, a musicianer traveling all over. And there he was dead and I was taking the train back to New Orleans. A long way. A long way home. But that was what he wanted for me, what he'd always wanted for me.

EVERYONE IN OUR house liked music. When they heard it played right, they answered to it from way down inside themselves. If my brothers weren't around the house playing, they was out playing somewhere else. My father, my mother, and me too—we was all the same about music. Even when I was just a little kid I was always running out to where the music was going on, chasing after the parades. Sometimes I'd get into the second line of the parade and just go along.

The second line of the parade, that was a thing you don't see any more. There used to be big parades all over New Orleans—a band playing, people dancing and strutting and shouting, waving their hands, kids following along waving flags. One of those parades would start down the street, and all kinds of people when they saw it pass would forget all about what they was doing and just take off after it, just joining in the fun. You know how it is—a parade, it just makes you stop anything you're doing; you stop working, eating, any damn' thing, and you run on out, and if you can't get in it you just get as close as you can.

In those days people just made up parades for the pleasure. They'd all get together and everyone would put some money into it, maybe a dollar, and they'd make plans for stopping off at one place for one thing, and at some other place for something else—drinks or cake or some food. They'd have maybe six places they was scheduled to go to.

And those that didn't have money, they couldn't get in the parade. But they enjoyed it just as much as those that were doing it—more, some of them. And those people, they were called "second liners." They had to make their own parade with broomsticks, kerchiefs, tin pans, any old damn' thing. And they'd take off shouting, singing, following along the sidewalk, going off on side streets when they was told they had no business being on the sidewalks or along the curbs like that, or maybe when the police would try to break them up. Then they'd go off one way and join the parade away up and start all over again. They'd be having their own damn' parade, taking what was going on in the street and doing something different with it, tearing it up kind of, having their fun. They'd be the second line of the parade.

When I was just a kid I used to get in on a lot of those second lines, singing, dancing, hollering—oh, it just couldn't be stopped! But sometimes you had to watch out: the police, sometimes they did nothing but smile, other times they just weren't taking anything for pleasure.

The police would come by sometimes and, like I say, some of them didn't do nothing to stop what was going on, but others used to beat up the people and break them up and get them moving away from there. You'd just never know which it would be with those police. But somehow they never did touch the musicianers; I never did see that happen.

Once, I remember, Buddy Bolden was out there singing and playing. He was singing a song of his that got to be real famous, "I Thought I Heard Buddy Bolden Say." The words to that, they wasn't considered too nice. A lot of mothers would hear their kids singing when they came home:

I thought I heard Buddy Bolden say,
"Funky Butt, Funky Butt, take it away. . . ."

And if the kids were scratched up at all or hurt some, the mothers they'd know right away where their kids had been, because as often as not someone did get scratched up when they hung around listening to these contests or to the advertising the bands did for some dance hall or something. This time I remember, I was down there around Canal Street somewheres—I was awful little then—and a policeman come along and he looked at my head and he looked at my ass, and he smacked me good with that stick he was carrying. I ran home then and I was really hurting some, I couldn't even sit down for dinner that night; and my mother, she took one look at me and she knew right away where I'd been.

Then there were the funerals. There used to be a lot of clubs in New Orleans, social clubs. They used to meet regular. They had nights for ladies; they played cards, they had concerts—a piano player or two or three musicians; it all depended what night in the week it was. Sometimes they used to have very serious meetings, and talk about how to do something good for members and the club and different things. When a member died, naturally all the members would meet at the club. They would have a brass band, the Onward Brass Band or Allen's Brass Band, and they would go from the club to the house of the member which was dead, and would play not dance music but mortuary music until they got to be about a block from the residence of the dead person. Then the big drum would just give tempo as they approached. The members would all go in to see the corpse, and then they would take him out to the cemetery with funeral marches. And they'd bury him, and as soon as he was buried they would leave the cemetery with that piece "Didn't He Ramble." That was a lovely piece and it's really the story about a bull. This bull, all through his life he rambled and rambled until the butcher cut him down. Well, that really meant that this member he rambled till the Lord cut him down; and that was the end of that.

Sometimes we'd have what they called in those days "bucking contests"; that was long before they talked about "cutting contests." One band, it would come right up in front of the other and play at it, and the first band it would play right back, until finally one band just had to give in. And the one that didn't give in, all the people, they'd rush up to it and give it drinks and food and holler for more, wanting more, not having enough. There just couldn't be enough for those people back there. And that band was best that played the best *together.* No matter what kind of music it was, if the band could keep it together, that made it the best. That band, it would know its numbers and know its foundation and it would know *itself.* And those bands, they could play anything that was wanted—waltzes, shorties, marches, *anything.* Well, the people listening to them, they'd follow wherever they marched along playing, and finally they'd just win out. It was always the public who decided. You was always being judged. It would make you tremble when one of those bands, it came into sight. Say you was somebody standing there, a spectator—you'd be hearing two bands maybe advertising for different theaters or a dance or just being out there. One of them it would come up in front of the other and face it, and you'd hear both of them. There'd be the two. And then you'd start noticing onliest the one. Somehow you'd just hear it better. Maybe it was clearer, maybe it was just giving you a lot more feeling. That band, it would be so gay and fine—the men in it, there was nothing they was depending on but themselves. They didn't have to play after some arrangement. Almost it was like they was playing ahead of themselves. And so they'd have more confidence and there would be a richness to what they were doing. And so you'd want to hear it closer and you'd get up nearer. And then, it seemed it was *all* you was hearing. It was the only one that came through. And the other band, it would get away farther and farther until finally you just didn't hear it at all.

There was another kind of bucking contest too. There'd be those parades of different clubs and often times it would happen that two or three clubs, they would be parading the same day and they'd have engaged these different brass bands. Allen's Brass Band, it was one that was very well known. The Onward, that used to be another. The Excelsior, that was one. And those bands, the men in them, waiting for that parade to start, they'd all have that excited feeling, knowing they could play good, that they was going to please the people who would be about there that day. They had no fears. But the musicianers from other bands, bands that had just been gotten up for that day—they were just a bunch of men who was going to play, and that was a difference; they wouldn't have that sure feeling inside. Bands like the ones I named, they were organized and they had the preference at these club parades.

And those clubs, maybe the Lions Club or the Odd Fellows or the Swells or the Magnolias, the men who were their members, they'd all have their full dress suits on with sashes that would go down to their knees, and they'd have this Grand Marshal who was the leader of the club. He'd have the longest sash. He'd have a sash that would go right down to his shoe tops and it would have gold bangles on it. And on his shoulder, he'd have an emblem, maybe a gold lion. That was his badge. But most of all, the way you could tell the Marshal, it was from how he walked. The Marshal, he'd be a man that really could strut.

It was really a question of that: the best strutter in the club, he'd be the Grand Marshal. He'd be a man who could prance when he walked, a man that could really fool and surprise you. He'd keep time to the music, but all along he'd keep a strutting and moving so you'd never know what he was going to be doing next. Naturally, the music, it makes you strut, but it's *him* too, the way he's strutting, it gets you. It's what you want from a parade: you want to *see* it as well as hear it. And all those fancy steps he'd have—oh, that was really something!—ways he'd have of turning around himself. People, they got a whole lot of pleasure out of just watching him, hearing the music and seeing him strut and other members of the club coming behind him, strutting and marching, some riding on horses but getting down to march a while, gallivanting there in real style. It would have your eyes just the same as your ears for waiting.

And people everywhere, they'd be coming from every direction. They'd just appear. It was like Congo Square again, only modern, different. The times, they had changed. But the happiness, the excitement—that was the same thing all the time.

And so these parades march along. You'd be in the band for this one club, say, you'd be stationed to be somewhere at a certain time, and another band it would be stationed at some other place, maybe somewhere almost on the other side of town. And the time would come you'd have fixed to start both, and you'd move off and start by going to some member of the club's house, stopping off there for a drink or a talk or to eat and have a little fun, and then go on again. The other band, it would be doing the same. Both of you would be moving to the meeting place. And the people, they'd be up by Claiborne Avenue and St. Philip. They know you'd be coming there. You *had* to pass some time. It was a parade and you'd be going to where the people were because naturally if you have a parade you were going out to be seen. And you timed it to reach there the same time as another band. And that's where the hell starts, because if two bands meet, there's got to be this bucking contest.

The way it was fixed, one of the bands, it would stop, face around, and then go up close to the other, go right through it, one band going uptown and the other downtown.

The Grand Marshal, he'd be leading the club and when he got to some corner or some turn, he'd have a way of tricking his knee, of turning all around, prancing—he'd fool you. You wouldn't be knowing if he was going left or right. Oftentimes, the second lines running along after the parade, they'd go complete right after he'd turned left. And that was a big part of it—him stepping and twisting and having you guessing all along. The way he could move, that was doing something for you. He led it.

And people they'd be singing along, dancing, drinking, toasting. That Marshal, he'd lead his club's band up to the other one, and the leader, he'd go through with him. Manuel Perez, for example, he had his Onward Band—other bands, they'd tremble to face him. A brass band, it was twenty pieces, you know. And the leader, he'd take his band right in amongst the other, and he'd stop. You'd be standing there on Claiborne Avenue and the bands, they'd come closer to each other, keep coming closer, and you'd be hearing the two of them, first one in a way, then the next. And then they'd get closer and you couldn't make them out any more. And then they'd be right in together, one line between another, and then it was just noise, just everything all at once. They'd be forty instruments all bucking at one another. And then you'd have to catch your breath: they'd be separating themselves.

Then came the beauty of it. That was the part that really took something right out of you. You'd hear mostly one band, so clear, so good, making you happier, sadder, whatever way it wanted you to feel. It would come out of the bucking and it would still be playing all together. None of the musicianers would be confused, none of them would have mixed up the music, they would all be in time.

And that other band, getting scared, knowing it couldn't go on further, it was finished. It couldn't be trying any harder, it was there still doing its best, but hearing the other band, say some good band like the Onward—it had thrown them off. It wasn't a band any more. It was just some excited musicianers. It would have three or six different tempos going. The men, they didn't know their music and they didn't know their feeling and they couldn't hear the next man. Every man, he'd be thrown back on his own trying to find whatever number it was they had started out to play. But that number, it wasn't there any more. There was nothing to be recognized.

And the people, they just let that band be. They didn't care to hear it. They'd all be gone after the other band, crowding around it, cheering the musicianers, waiting to give them drinks and food. All of them feeling good about the music, how that band it kept the music together.

And being able to play in that kind of band, it was more than a learning kind of thing. You know, when you learn something, you can go just as far. When you've finished that, there's not much else you can do unless you know how to get hold of something inside you that isn't learned. It has to be there inside you without any need of learning. The band that played what it knew, it didn't have enough. In the end it would get confused; it was finished. And the people, they could tell.

But how it was they could tell—that was the music too. It was what they had of the music inside themselves. There wasn't any personality attraction thing to it. The music, it was the onliest thing that counted. The music, it was having a time for itself. It was moving. It was being free and natural.

Louis Armstrong

In Satchmo *(1954), one of his several autobiographies, Louis Armstrong describes the fateful moment in 1922 when he left New Orleans to join his idol, King Oliver, in Chicago.*

Joe Oliver had left New Orleans in 1918, and was now up in Chicago doing real swell. He kept sending me letters and telegrams telling me to come up to Chicago and play second cornet for him. That, I knew, would be real heaven for me.

I had made up my mind that I would not leave New Orleans unless the King sent for me. I would not risk leaving for anyone else. I had seen too many of my little pals leave home and come back in bad shape. Often their parents had to send them the money to come back with. I had had such a wonderful three years on the excursion boats on the Mississippi that I did not dare cut out for some unknown character who might leave me stranded or get me into other trouble. Fate Marable and the Streckfus brothers had made it impossible for me to risk spoiling everything by running off on a wild goose chase.

After I had made all my arrangements I definitely accepted Joe's offer. The day I was leaving for Chicago I played at a funeral over in Algiers, on August 8, 1922. The funeral was for the father of Eddie Vincent, a very good trombone player. When the body was brought out of the house to go to the cemetery the hymn we played was "Free as a Bird," and we played it so beautifully that we brought tears to everybody's eyes.

The boys in the Tuxedo Brass Band and Celestin's band did their best to talk me out of going up to Chicago. They said that Joe Oliver was scabbing and that he was on the musicians' union's unfair list. I told them how fond I was of Joe and what confidence I had in him. I did not care what he and his band were doing. He had sent for me, and that was all that mattered. At that time I did not know very much about union tactics because we did not have a union in New Orleans, so the stuff about the unfair list was all Greek to me.

When the funeral was over I rushed home, threw my few glad rags together and hurried over to the Illinois Central Station to catch the 7 P.M. train for the Windy City. The whole band came to the station to see me off and wish me luck. In a way they were all glad to see me get a chance to go out in the world and make good, but they did not care so much about having me play second cornet to Joe Oliver. They thought I was good enough to go on my own, but I felt it was a great break for me even to sit beside a man like Joe Oliver with all his prestige.

It seemed like all of New Orleans had gathered at the train to give me a little luck. Even the old sisters of my neighborhood who had practically raised me when I was a youngster were there. When they kissed me goodbye they had handkerchiefs at their eyes to wipe away the tears.

When the train pulled in all the Pullman porters and waiters recognized me because they had seen me playing on the tailgate wagons to advertise dances, or "balls" as we used to call them. They all hollered at me saying, "Where are you goin', Dipper?"

"You're a lucky black sommitch," one guy said, "to be going up North to play with ol' Cocky."

This was a reference to the cataract on one of Joe's eyes. The mean guys used to kid him about his bad eye, and he would get fighting mad. But what was the use? If he had messed around fighting with those guys he would have ended up by losing his good eye.

When the conductor hollered all aboard I told those waiters: "Yeah man, I'm going up to Chicago to play with my idol, Papa Joe!"

When I got on the train I found an empty seat next to a lady and her three children, and she was really sticking. What I mean by "sticking" is that she had a big basket of good old southern fried chicken which she had fixed for the trip. She had enough to last her and her kids not only to Chicago, but clear out to California if she wanted to go that far.

I hit the fish sandwich Mayann had prepared for me, but at the same time I was trying my darnedest to think of something to say that would make that lady offer me some of that good and pretty fried chicken. There was no place for colored people to eat on the trains in those days, especially down in Galilee (the South). Colored persons going North crammed their baskets full of everything but the kitchen stove.

Luckily the lady recognized me. She told me she knew Mayann and that she was going to Chicago too. We were both wondering about the big city, and we soon became very good friends. I lived and ate like a king during the whole trip.

Finally, when the conductor came through the train hollering "Chicago next stop" at the top of his voice, a funny feeling started running up and down my spine. The first thing I thought was: "I wonder if Papa Joe will be at the station waiting for me?" He expected me to come on the early morning train, but I had missed that because I had played at the funeral so as to have a little extra change when I hit Chicago.

I was all eyes looking out of the window when the train pulled into the station. Anybody watching me closely could have easily seen that I was a country boy. I certainly hoped Joe Oliver would be at the station. I was not particular about anyone else being there. All I wanted was to see Joe's face and everything would be rosy.

When the conductor hollered "All out for Chicago. Last stop" it looked like everybody rose from their seats at the same time. There was no sign of Joe on the platform, and when I climbed the long flight of stairs to the waiting room I still did not see any sign of him.

I had a million thoughts as I looked at all those people waiting for taxi cabs. It was eleven-thirty at night. All the colored people, including the lady with the chicken, who had come up from New Orleans, were getting into their cabs or relatives' cars. As they left they said good-bye and wished me good luck on my stay in Chicago. As I waved good-bye I thought to myself: "Huh. I don't think I am going to like this old town."

Suddenly I found myself standing all alone. And the longer I stood the more restless I got. I must have stood there about half an hour when a policeman came up to me. He had been watching me for a long time and he could see that I was a stranger in town and that I was looking worriedly for someone.

"Are you looking for someone?" he asked.

"Yes sir."

"Can I help you?"

"I came in from New Orleans, Louisiana," I said. "I am a cornet player, and I came up here to join Joe Oliver's Jazz Band."

He gave me a very pleasant smile.

"Oh," he said. "You are the young man who's to join King Oliver's band at the Lincoln Gardens."

"Yes sir," I said.

Then it struck me that he had just said *King* Oliver. In New Orleans it was just plain Joe Oliver.

I was so anxious to see him that that name was good enough for me. When I told the cop that King Oliver was supposed to meet me here he said:

"King Oliver was down here waiting for you to arrive on an earlier train, but you did not show up. He had to go to work, but he left word for us to look out for you if you came in on this train."

Then he waved to a taxi and told the driver: "Take this kid out to the place where King Oliver is playing." The driver put my bags into the cab and away we went toward the South Side.

As I opened the door to go into the Lincoln Gardens I could hear Joe's band swinging out on one of those good old Dixieland tunes. Believe me, I was really thrilled by the way they were playing. It was worth the price of my trip. But I was a little shaky about going inside. For a moment I wondered if I should. Then, too, I started wondering if I could hold my own with such a fine band. But I went in anyway, and the further in I got, the hotter the band got.

The Lincoln Gardens was located at Thirty-first and Cottage Grove Avenues. It had a beautiful front with a canopy that ran from the doorway to the street. The lobby seemed to be a block long, so long that I thought I was never going to reach the bandstand. The place was jammed with people and Joe and the boys did not see me until I was almost on the bandstand.

Then all hell seemed to break loose. All those guys jumped up at the same time saying: "Here he is! Here he is!" Joe Oliver took his left foot off the cuspidor on which he usually kept it when he was playing his cornet. He had a private cuspidor because he chewed tobacco all the time.

"Wait a minute, let me see him," Joe said to the boys. "Why I've not seen that little slow foot devil in years." He always used to call me "slow foot" whenever he visited me at the honky-tonk where I worked in New Orleans.

Joe began by asking me all kind of questions about what I had been doing since he and Jimmy Noone left New Orleans in 1918. He was tickled to death that I had gotten good enough to become a regular member of the well known Tuxedo Brass Band and that I had played on the boat.

"Gee, son, I'm really proud of you," Joe said. "You've been in some fast company since I last saw you."

The expression on his face proved that he was still in a little wonderment as to whether I was good enough to play with him and his boys. But he did not say so. All he said was:

"Have a seat, son, we're going to do our show. You might as well stick around and see what's happening because you start work tomorrow night."

"Yes sir," I said.

After the show was over Joe took me over to his house which was just around the corner from the Lincoln Gardens. Mrs. Stella Oliver, who had always been fond of me, was as glad to see me as I was to see her. With her was her daughter Ruby by another marriage. They were a happy family and I became one of them.

Mrs. Stella said that I must have a meal with them, which was all right by me. The way Joe ate was right, and there were no formalities and stuff. She fed us a big dish of red beans and rice, a half loaf of bread and a bucket of good ice cold lemonade.

It was getting late and Mrs. Stella told Joe it was time to take me over to the room he had reserved for me in a boarding house at 3412 South Wabash Avenue, run by a friend of his named Filo. As we were going there in the taxi cab Joe told me that I would have a room and a private bath.

"Bath? Private bath? What's a private bath?" I asked.

"Listen you little slow foot sommitch," he said looking at me kind of funny, "don't be so damn dumb."

He had forgotten that he must have asked the same question when he first came up from New Orleans. In the neighborhood where we lived we never heard of such a thing as a bathtub, let alone a *private bath.* After Joe finished giving me hell about the question, I reminded him about the old days and how we used to take baths in the clothes washtub in the backyard, or else a foot tub. I can still remember when I used to take a bath in one of those tin tubs. In order to get real clean I would have to sit on the rim and wash myself from my neck to my middle. After that I would stand up and wash the rest of me. Papa Joe had to laugh when I told him about that.

Filo must have been waiting up for us because she came to the door the minute we rang the bell. She was a good-looking, middle-aged Creole gal. You could see the kindness in her face at once, and as soon as she spoke you felt relaxed.

"Is this my homeboy?" she asked.

"Yep," Joe said, "this is old Dippermouth."

As soon as we came in Filo told me my room was upstairs and I could hardly wait to go up and witness that private bath of mine. However, I had to put that off because Filo and we sat around and talked ourselves silly about New Orleans as far back as any of us could remember. Filo had left New Orleans almost ten years before me, and she had come to Chicago even before Joe Oliver.

The next morning Filo fixed breakfast for me, and just like all Creole women she was a very good cook. After breakfast I went up and took a good hot bath in my private bathtub, and then I dressed to go out for a little stroll and see what the town looked like.

I did not know where I was going and I did not care much because everything looked so good. With all due respect to my hometown every street was much nicer than the streets in New Orleans. In fact, there was no comparison.

When I reached home Filo had the big table all set up and waiting.

"Wash up," she said in her quiet voice, "and come and get these good victuals." Filo had about every good Creole dish one could mention.

After the meal I went upstairs to shave, take a bath and have a good nap. Since I was a kid the old masters had taught me that plenty of sleep is essential for good music. A musician cannot play his best when he is tired and irritable.

When I woke up and was just about dressed Filo came into my room.

"Although you have had a hearty dinner," she said, "you have got a lot of blowing to do and you need some more to hold you up."

I did not argue about that. Downstairs she gave me a sandwich covered with pineapple and brown sugar. Boy, was it good! When I finished that sandwich I started out for the opening night at the Gardens.

I was wearing my old Roast Beef, which was what I called my ragged tuxedo. Of course I had it pressed and fixed up as good as possible so that no one would notice how old it was unless they looked real close and saw the patches here and there. Anyway I thought I looked real sharp.

At eight-thirty on the dot a cab pulled up in front of Filo's house. Filo had ordered it for she was as excited as I was and she wanted everything to go right for the night of my debut with the King. It is a funny thing about the music fame and show business, no matter how long you have been in the profession opening night always makes you feel as though little butterflies were running around in your stomach.

Mrs. Major, the white lady who owned the Gardens, and Red Bud, the colored manager, were the first people I ran into when I walked through the long lobby. Then I ran into King Jones, a short fellow with a loud voice you could hear over a block away when he acted as master of ceremonies. (He acted as though he was not a colored fellow, but his real bad English gave him away.)

When I reached the bandstand there was King Oliver and all his boys having a smoke before the first set and waiting for me to show up. The place was filling up with all the finest musicians from downtown including Louis Panico, the ace white trumpeter, and Isham Jones, who was the talk of the town in the same band.

I was thrilled when I took my place with that grand group of musicians: Johnny and Baby Dodds, Honore Dutrey, Bill Johnson, Lil Hardin, and the master himself. It was good to be playing with Baby Dodds again; I was glad to learn he had stopped drinking excessively and had settled down to his music. He was still a wizard on the drums, and he certainly made me blow my horn that night when I heard him beat those sticks behind one of my hot choruses.

Johnny Dodds was a fine healthy boy and his variations were mellow and perfect. His hobby was watching the baseball scores, especially for the White Sox team. Johnny and I would buy the *Daily News;* he would take out the baseball scores and give me the rest of the paper.

Bill Johnson, the bass player, was the cat that interested me that first evening at the Gardens. He was one of the original Creole Jazz Band boys and one of the first to come North and make a musical hit. He had the features and even the voice of a white boy—an ofay, or Southern, white boy at that. His sense of humor was unlimited.

Dutrey had a wonderful sense of humor and a fine disposition to boot. How well I remembered how I used to follow him and Joe Oliver all day long during the street parades when I was a boy in New Orleans. When he was discharged from the Navy he went to Chicago to live and he had joined Joe Oliver a few weeks before I came to the city. He still played a beautiful horn, but he suffered badly from shortness of breath. Whenever he had a hard solo to play he would go to the back of the bandstand and spray his nose and throat. After that the hep cats would have to look out, for he would blow one whale of a trombone. How he did it was beyond me.

For a woman Lil Hardin was really wonderful, and she certainly surprised me that night with her four beats to a bar. It was startling to find a woman who had been valedictorian in her class at Fisk University fall in line and play such good jazz. She had gotten her training from Joe Oliver, Freddy Keppard, Sugar Johnny, Lawrence Dewey, Tany Johnson and many other of the great pioneers from New Orleans. If she had not run into those top-notchers she would have probably married some big politician or maybe played the classics for a living. Later I found that Lil was doubling after hours at the Edelweiss Gardens. I wondered how she was ever able to get any sleep. I knew those New Orleans cats could take it all right, but it was a tough pull for a woman.

When we cracked down on the first note that night at the Lincoln Gardens I knew that things would go well for me. When Papa Joe began to blow that horn of his it felt right like old times. The first number went over so well that we had to take an encore. It was then that Joe and I developed a little system for the duet breaks. We did not have to write them down. I was so wrapped up in him and lived so closely to his music that I could follow his lead in a split second. No one could understand how we did it, but it was easy for us and we kept it up the whole evening.

I did not take a solo until the evening was almost over. I did not try to go ahead of Papa Joe because I felt that any glory that came to me must go to him. He could blow enough horn for both of us. I was playing second to his lead, and I never dreamed of trying to steal the show or any of that silly rot.

Every number on opening night was a gassuh. A special hit was a piece called "Eccentric" in which Joe took a lot of breaks. First he would take a four-bar break, then the band would play. Then he would take another four-bar break. Finally at the very last chorus Joe and Bill Johnson would do a sort of musical act. Joe would make his horn sound like a baby crying, and Bill Johnson would make his horn sound as though it was a nurse calming the baby in a high voice. While Joe's horn was crying, Bill Johnson's horn would interrupt on that high note as though to say, "Don't cry, little baby." Finally this musical horseplay broke up in a wild squabble between nurse and child, and the number would bring down the house with laughter and applause.

After the floor show was over we went into some dance tunes, and the crowd yelled, "Let the youngster blow!" That meant me. Joe was wonderful and he gladly let me play my rendition of the blues. That was heaven.

Papa Joe was so elated that he played half an hour over time. The boys from downtown stayed until the last note was played and they came back-stage and talked to us while we packed our instruments. They congratulated

Joe on his music and for sending to New Orleans to get me. I was so happy I did not know what to do.

I had hit the big time. I was up North with the greats. I was playing with my idol, the King, Joe Oliver. My boyhood dream had come true at last.

And to illustrate how one man's accounts of the same event can differ, here is Armstrong's recollection of his arrival in Chicago as recorded by Nat Shapiro and Nat Hentoff in their trailblazing and revelatory Hear Me Talkin' to Ya *(1955).*

In 1922, when King Joe Oliver, the trumpet man of those days, sent for me to leave New Orleans and join him at the Lincoln Gardens to play second trumpet to his first trumpet, I jumped sky-high with joy. The day I received the telegram from Papa Joe, that's what I called him, I was playing a funeral in New Orleans and all the members in the Tuxedo Brass Band told me not to go because Joe Oliver and his boys were having some kind of union trouble.

When the Tuxedo Brass Band boys told me that King Oliver and his band were scabbing, I told them the King had sent for me, it didn't matter with me what he was doing. I was going to him just the same. So I went.

I arrived in Chicago about eleven o'clock the night of July 8, 1922, I'll never forget it, at the Illinois Central Station at Twelfth and Michigan Avenue. The King was already at work. I had no one to meet me. I took a cab and went directly to the Gardens.

When I was getting out of the cab and paying the driver, I could hear the King's band playing some kind of a real jump number. Believe me, they were really jumpin' in fine fashion. I said to myself, "My Gawd, I wonder if I'm good enough to play in that band." I hesitated about going inside right away, but finally I did.

When I got inside and near the bandstand, King Oliver spied me. He immediately stopped the band to greet me, saying, "Boy, where have you been? I've been waiting and waiting for you." Well, I did miss the train that the King thought I should have been on. They went into another hot number. In that band were King Oliver, trumpet; Johnny Dodds, clarinet; Honore Dutrey, trombone; Baby Dodds, drums; Bill Johnson, bass; Lillian Hardin, piano, of course she became Mrs. "Satchmo" Louis Armstrong later (tee hee).

When I joined the band on second trumpet I made the seventh member. Those were some thrilling days of my life I shall never forget. I came to work the next night. During my first night on the job, while things were going down in order, King and I stumbled upon a little something that no other two trumpeters together ever thought of. While the band was just swinging, the King would lean over to me, moving his valves on his trumpet, make notes, the notes that he was going to make when the break in the tune came. I'd listen, and at the same time, I'd be figuring out my second to his lead. When the break would come, I'd have my part to blend right along with his. The crowd would go mad over it!

King Oliver and I got so popular blending that jive together that pretty soon all the white musicians from downtown Chicago would all come there after their work and stay until the place closed. Sometimes they would sit-in with us to get their kicks. Lillian was doubling from the Lincoln Gardens to the Edelweiss Gardens, an after-hours place. After our work I would go out there with her. Doing this, she and I became regular running buddies, and we would go to all the other places when we had the time. She knew Chicago like a book. I'll never forget the first time Lil took me to the Dreamland Cabaret on Thirty-fifth and State Streets to hear Ollie Powers and Mae Alix sing. Ollie had one of those high, sweet singing voices, and when he would sing songs like "What'll I Do?" he would really rock the whole house. Mae Alix had one of those fine, strong voices that everyone would also want to hear. Then she would go into her splits, and the customers would throw paper dollars on the floor, and she would make one of those running splits, picking them up one at a time.

I asked Lil if it was all right to give Ollie and Mae a dollar each to sing a song for me. She said sure, it was perfectly all right. She called them over and introduced them to me as the new trumpet man in King Oliver's band. Gee whiz! I really thought I was somebody meeting those fine stars. I followed Ollie Powers everywhere he sang, until the day he died. At his funeral I played a trumpet solo in the church where they had his body laying out for the last time. Ump, what a sad day that was. Mae Alix is still a singing barmaid and as popular as ever.

Speaking of the Lincoln Gardens, I had been playing there about two or three months, when one night, just as we were getting ready to hit the show, we all noticed a real stout lady, with bundles in her hands, cutting across the dance floor. To my surprise it was my mother, Mayann. The funny thing about it is that King Oliver had been kidding me that he was my stepfather, for years and years. When he saw Mayann (tee hee) he didn't know her. We kind of stalled the show so I could greet my dear mother, with a great big kiss, of course. Then I said to her, "Mamma, what on earth are you doing up here in Chicago?" Mayann said, "Lawd, chile, somebody came to New Orleans and told me that you were up here in this North awfully low sick and starving to death." I told mother, "Aw, Mamma, how could I starve when I'm eating at King Oliver's house every day, and you know how Mrs. Stella

Oliver (King's wonderful wife) piles up King's plate, full of red beans and rice. Well, she fills mine the same way. Now, how could I starve?" Mayann said when she asked this man who told her the false bad news, "Why in the world didn't my son come back home to New Orleans when things began to break so bad for him?" this guy told her all I could do was to hang my head and cry. Tch, tch, such lies. I was fat as a butterball.

I took my mother to the house where I was rooming and then went out and bought her a lot of fine vines, a wardrobe with nothing but the finest—from head to foot. Oh, she was sharp! . . .

Chicago was really jumping around that time (1923). The Dreamland was in full bloom. The Lincoln Gardens, of course, was still in there. The Plantation was another hot spot at that time. But the Sunset, my boss' place, was the sharpest of them all, believe that. A lot of after-hour spots were real groovy, too. There was the Apex, where Jimmy Noone and that great piano man, Hines, started all this fine stuff 'yars listen to nowadays. They made history right there in the Apex. The tune, "Sweet Lorraine," used to gas everybody there nightly. I was one of the everybodys.

They had a place on State Street called the Fiume where they had a small ofay band, right in the heart of the South Side. They were really fine. All the musicians, nightlifers, and everybody plunged in there in the wee hours of the morning and had a grand time. I used to meet a lot of the boys there after we would finish at the Lincoln Gardens. That's where I first met Darnell Howard, former sax man with "Fatha" Hines. He was playing the violin at that time with Charles Elgar's orchestra over on the West Side at Harmon's Dreamland Ballroom. Darnell was weighing one hundred and sixty-five pounds then. Of course, he has accumulated a little breadbasket since then, but still sharp.

King Oliver received an offer to go on the road and make some one-night stands at real good money. Ump! That got it. The band almost busted up. Half of the boys just wouldn't go, that's all. The same situation hits bandleaders square in the face these days, the same as then. The King replaced every man that wouldn't go. As for me, anything King did was all right with me. My heart was out for him at all times—until the day he died and even now. The tour was great. We had lots of fun and made lots of money.

At the Dreamland, in 1925, we had some fine moments. Some real jumping acts. There was the team of Brown and McGraw. They did a jazz dance that just wouldn't quit. I'd blow for their act, and every step they made, I put the notes to it. They liked the idea so well they had it arranged. Benny and Harry Goodman used to come out and set in and tear up the joint when they were real young. P.S., the boys have been hep for a long time. While at the Dreamland, Professor Erskine Tate asked me (*ahem*) to join his Symphony Orchestra. I wouldn't take a million for that experience.

Willie "The Lion" Smith

This formidable pianist prefers to refer to himself as "The Lion" in his autobiography, Music on My Mind *(1964; with George Hoefer), an ingratiating account of the life of the competing piano giants of the day and their famous "cutting sessions" in pre-war Harlem.*

Down it, and get from 'round it,
Low it, and you can't owe it,
I'm a poet, and I know it.

Willie "The Lion" Smith

One day in late 1919 I was strolling up 135th Street, at that time the main drag in Harlem (125th Street was then in a white neighborhood), and ran into Barron Wilkins who hailed me.

"Hi there, Sergeant Smith. My brother Leroy is looking for you. He says he needs a good piano man to take charge."

I decided to play it sharp. "The name is the Lion and you tell Leroy to phone for an appointment if he wants to audition me."

Since getting out of the Army I had been doing a little gambling, drinking, and piano playing in the various bars just like I'd been doing before the big mess in Europe had started. After meeting Barron an old saying of my mother's came back to me, "It is far better for the soul to have a crust of bread and plenty of sleep than to have a turkey and a hundred dollars in your pocket." I decided it might be a good idea to settle down somewhere for a while. The vibrations at Leroy's had always seemed good to me.

I was living at the time at Lottie Joplin's boardinghouse. That was where all the big-time theatrical people stayed and everything was free and easy. Mrs. Joplin was the widow of the great ragtime composer, Scott Joplin, who had died back in 1917. She only wanted musicians and theater people for tenants. The place was a regular boardinghouse but sometimes operated like an after-hours joint. She had the entire house at 163 West 131st Street and it was a common occurrence to step in at six in the morning and see guys like Eubie Blake, Jimmy Johnson, and the Lion sitting around talking or playing the piano in the parlor. We used to play Scott's "Maple Leaf Rag" in A-flat for Mrs. Joplin. Before she died she took me down in the cellar and showed me Scott's cellar full of manuscripts—modern things and even some classical pieces he had written.

The Lion decided to have himself a big dinner at the Libya* and then go over and talk to Leroy. The Libya was Harlem's high-class restaurant of the day; it was the dictyest of the dicty. They served tea between four and five in the afternoon and featured dinner dancing until 1 A.M. The music was furnished by a string orchestra made up of members of the Clef Club. They were hidden in a grove of potted palms and were not allowed to rag it or to beautify the melody using their own ideas—they had to read those fly spots closely and truly. We used to kid them about having to read their tails off.

During supper they served the Lion a muskmelon filled with ice cream doused in champagne. These vibrations were too tony for a guy who had just gotten out of the trenches. Leroy's was gonna look good to this piano man.

Leroy's

When I walked in and announced to Leroy, "The Lion is here," he glared as per usual and replied, "You know where the piano is at; go ahead and take charge."

Back in those days "takin' charge" meant the pianist had duties and responsibilities. He played solo piano, accompanied the singers, directed whatever band was on hand, and watched the kitty to be sure no one cheated on tips. That cigar-box kitty was very important at Leroy's, since the boss didn't allow any coins to be thrown around. Everybody's tips, including those given to the musicians, singers, waiters, and bartenders, had to go into the box to be divvied up at closing time. The piano man was *it!* The man in charge.

He had to be an all-round showman and it helped if he could both dance and sing. It was like being the host at the party, you were expected to greet everyone who entered to establish favorable feelings. I used to chat with the patrons at nearby tables in order to get their immediate moods. When I'd run into a noisy, rude one, I'd end the set abruptly, and holler "Man, go get lost!"

The bosses expected you to stay rooted to your stool from nine at night to dawn. Man, if you got up to go to the men's room those guys would scream. Leroy would come up wailing, "What are you trying to do, put me out of business?" And in those days you worked seven nights a week.

---

*139th Street near Seventh Avenue.

Furthermore, you'd rather piss in your pants than leave the piano when a rival was in the house. That was the best way to lose your gig.

Another thing that was different in those days was that you couldn't eat or drink in the joint on an entertainer's discount, yet you were expected to drink all the booze brought to your piano at a customer's expense. To the Harlem cabaret owners, to all nightclub bosses, the money was on a one-way chute—everything coming in, nothing going out.

And that wasn't all. In addition to all this takin'-charge service to the establishment, the tickler was required to build up for himself a big following. It got so that whether or not a place had any business was decided by who the piano man was—and there was no advertising done to help. It was your job to draw in the customers. All the owner had to do was count the money.

For all this, they paid you off in uppercuts. That was a saying we got up in those days; it meant you were allowed to keep your tips, but you got no salary. Sometimes they would give us a small weekly amount—like twenty dollars. That was known as a left hook.

When I started at Leroy's he acted as though he was doing me a big favor by letting me sit at the piano. After I'd been at the club for a couple of weeks I noticed the place was packed. It was time for me to have a little talk with Mr. Leroy. So one night I took time out and sent for an order of southern-fried chicken, the specialty of the house, served with hot biscuits. Instead of the chicken I got Leroy hollering, "What the hell you think you're doin' now, Lion? Ain't you got any food at home? You tryin' to take advantage?"

I looked calmly around the crowded room. "I want a small left hook, man, or else I'm movin' on." It was common practice for a piano player to keep on the go because you weren't considered too good if you stayed at the same place too long a time. It signified you were not in hot demand.

Well, my little move was a success. I wound up with a salary of eighteen dollars a week plus tips—and I was taking home around a hundred a week from the kitty. Old man Wilkins could see which side of the bread had the butter.

At Leroy's they didn't pretend to give out with a fancy show or revue. The show actually consisted of the pianist, occasionally accompanied by several instrumentalists, six or seven sopranos, and a bunch of dancing waiters who also sang.

Our sopranos could sing any kind of music in the book or requested by customers. These gals, like the piano players, worked all the cabarets in Harlem and Atlantic City at one time or another. I recall at Leroy's we had Josephine Stevens, Mattie Hite, and Lucy Thomas, including a cute little Creole girl from New Orleans named Mabel Bertrand—she later married Jelly Roll Morton. All these girls sang at the tables as well as doing their turn on the floor.

On the nights when I had help to keep the music rocking, we had fun. The helpers were usually a drummer, a banjoist, or a violinist. Once or twice we had a tuba player. Most frequently it was just a drummer and we sure had some good ones around New York at that time. Such guys as Carl (Battle Axe) Kenny, George Hines, Harry Green, George Barber, Freddie (Rastus) Crump, Charles (Buddie) Gilmore (the regular drum ace with Jim Europe's Hell Fighters), and a lame guy known as "Traps" (I think his real name was Arthur McIntyre). Traps could make a fly dance with his ratchets. He and Gilmore drummed most of the time in a show band. He was knock-kneed, and like all those people with crazy legs, he was as strong as a bull. Every time one of the girls moved her eye old Traps would hit a lick. The chicks would tell him, "Just brush me lightly, politely, slightly, and get soft—give me that real low gravy." Man, the women sure did love his drumming. When the gals ran out of songs, Traps and I would take over and make up lyrics for them. And talk about blues, we really had 'em, choruses after choruses. It was like Ethel Waters once said over the radio, "I don't care what you talk about. You can talk all about the modern musics, but when it comes down to feeling the music and interpreting it, that we can do. We have the gift to send the message—the blues—Yeah!"

TO GET A SHORT REST from Leroy's, I would sometimes go back to Newark and put in a few weeks at Jimmy Conerton's on Academy Street, Pierson's Hall, or in the dining rooms at the Hotel Navarro or the Robert Treat Hotel.

Several of the times I left to go up 135th Street and help out gambler Jerry Preston, who had just started an upstairs joint called The Orient. I was the first pianist to work for him and talked him into hiring three girl singers to make his place into a regular cabaret. It started him off in the business. I worked again for him years later when he ran Pod's & Jerry's. He was a congenial boss and we always got along. My only complaint was that he hired the damnedest waiters and bartenders—they were a band of crooks. He paid them good salaries but was always firing them for being snooty to the customers. Being a first-rate gambler he had very good connections.

Whenever I would cut out from Leroy's, it was my custom to leave the piano in the custody of a trial horse. In this way I felt I could get my job back when it came time to return. My favorite trial horse was a pool shark named Charles Summers, who had been a pianist at Leroy's before I went in there to take charge. He was a fair tickler, he could only play in three keys, but he made so much playing pool that his piano playing was just for kicks.

But, there came one time when I really goofed and almost lost the job.

That was when I left the stool in charge of a sixteen-year-old fat boy, whose name I didn't even know at the time. He used to hang around wherever there was a piano on 135th Street. I was told they let him play the box at the Crescent dime movie down the street when the regular man was off. (This was long before the time this kid was bugging Maisie Mullins, the pianist-organist at the Lincoln Theater, to let him play the ten-thousand-dollar Wurlitzer pipe organ.)

Yeah, man, I'll never forget how good old Fats, when he was still a stripling, would walk into Leroy's eating one of those caramel-covered apples on a stick. He was never without one.

In Comes Filthy

James P. Johnson brought him down one Sunday afternoon. We were all dressed in full-dress suits and tuxedos and in comes this guy with a greasy suit on, walks down to the bandstand, and says, "Hello there, Lion, what do you say?" He made me furious. I turned around to Jimmy and said, "Get that guy down, because he looks filthy." "Get them pants pressed," I said. "There's no excuse for it." From that day on I called him Filthy.

So he sat down until I got finished and when I got finished he was insistent, very persistent. He insisted he wanted to play Jimmy's "Carolina Shout" and when I got through he sat down and played the "Shout" and made Jimmy like it and me like it. From then on it was Thomas "Fats" Waller. He sat down also and heard me play a couple of strains of something, and then he improvised and the next time I turned around he had a tune called "Squeeze Me."

The Lion was only gone for a few days and when I got back Filthy had built up quite a following for himself. You could tell by the ovation he got when he walked in casual-like. I gave him a listen and made my famous prediction: I said to James P. Johnson, who was in the house again that night, "Watch out, Jimmy, he's got it. He's a piano-playing cub!"

Duke Ellington

This first selection from Ellington's autobiographical Music is my Mistress *(1973) begins where The Lion leaves off—with the appearance of Fats Waller. Then come extended excerpts from a long, revealing self-interview, in which Ellington ranges over a wide variety of experiences and ideas. Finally, in "The Most Essential Instrument"—which originally appeared in the British publication* Jazz Journal *in 1965 and has recently been anthologized in the essential* Duke Ellington Reader *(1993; edited by Mark Tucker)—he talks about jazz musicians who hold significance for him.*

The Big Apple

Fats Waller came to Washington in the spring of 1923 and played for Clarence Robinson in a burlesque show at the Gaiety Theatre. Sonny Greer, Toby Hardwick, and I had gotten to know him well when we were in New York with Sweatman, so now we had a chummy exchange.

"I'm quitting next week," Fats said. "Why don't you all come up to New York and take the job? I'll tell 'em about you."

We jumped at the opportunity and were all on edge until the time came to go. Sonny and Toby went ahead of me by a few days. When I called to find out if everything was straight, they assured me that it was.

"Everything's okay," they said. "Don't worry about nothin', man."

Because I had a gig waiting for me, I felt entitled to travel in style. I hopped a train, took a parlor car, ate a big, expensive dinner in the diner, and got a cab at Pennsylvania Station to take me uptown. With these expenses, and tips in proportion, I had spent all my money by the time I reached 129th Street.

Sonny Greer was waiting, and the first thing he said as he opened the cab door for me was, "Hey, Duke, buddy, give us something! We are all busted and waiting for you to relieve the situation." By "something," he meant money, but it was too late.

"Sorry, I'm broke too," I said. "I blew it all on the trip up from Washington."

Everything had gone wrong, and there was no job. Yet there were friends waiting to help us and to show me the way. Willie "The Lion" Smith was one of them, and Freddie Guy used to let us sit in for him at the Orient and, most important, split the tips.

It was a very hot summer, and I remember how we had to ride that subway every morning to get downtown to audition in the Strand Building, where nearly all the agents seemed to be. We had no luck there and it was Bricktop, the famous Bricktop (Ada Smith), who finally pulled us out of the hole we were in.

The Washingtonians were different in several ways. We paid quite a lot of attention to our appearance, and if any one of us came in dressed improperly Whetsol would flick his cigarette ash in a certain way, or pull down the lower lid of his right eye with his forefinger and stare at the offending party. Whetsol was our first unofficial disciplinarian, and he carried himself with dignity befitting a medical student of lofty ambitions. His tonal character, fragile and genteel, was an important element in our music. As a result of playing all those society dances in Washington, we had learned to play softly, what is sometimes known as under-conversation music. Toby also contributed much to this by playing sweet and straight on his C-melody saxophone. A lot of chicks wanted to mother him, and every now and then he would submit, so over the years he was in and out of the band rather unpredictably. Elmer Snowden was the businessman of the group, and eventually he got so good at business that he went his way, and we had to get Freddie Guy to take his place.

During my first few months in New York, I found out that anybody was eligible to take songs into the music publishers on Broadway. So I joined the parade and teamed up with Joe Trent, a nice guy who was familiar with the routines of the publishing world. He liked my music and he was a good lyricist, so he took my hand and guided me around Broadway. We wrote several songs together and auditioned every day in one publisher's office or another and, as was normal, had practically no success, until one day when we demonstrated a song for Fred Fisher. He was not only a publisher, but a wonderful songwriter himself. He wrote "Chicago," and he was always an inspiration to me.

"I like it," he said, after listening to our song. "I'll take it."

"You know, of course, that we want a fifty-dollar advance," Joe said.

"Okay," Fred Fisher replied. "Give me a lead sheet and I'll sign the contract."

"Give the man a lead sheet," Joe said, turning to me.

I had never made a lead sheet before, nor tried to write music of any kind, but it was 4:30 P.M. and I knew the checkbook would be closed at five. So, in spite of ten pianos banging away in ten different booths, I sat down and made a lead sheet. It was satisfactory. We got the money, split it, and then split the scene. I had broken the ice and at the same time gotten hooked on writing music. (Write on!) The next day, and for many to follow, we were back in our old rut—peddling songs and failing to find any buyers.

One day Joe Trent came running up to me on Broadway. He had a big proposition and there was urgency in his voice.

"Tonight we've got to write a show," he said. *"Tonight!"*

Being dumb, and not knowing any better, I sat down that evening and wrote a show. How was I to know that composers had to go up in the mountains, or to the seashore, to commune with the muses for six months in order to write a show. The next day we played and demonstrated our show for Jack Robbins, who liked it and said he would take it.

"You know we have to get five hundred dollars in advance," Joe said.

"Okay," Robbins said. "Tomorrow."

The true story behind this is that Jack Robbins pawned his wife's engagement ring to give us our five-hundred-dollar advance. The show, *Chocolate Kiddies,* went into rehearsal, after which it went to Germany, where it played for two years in the Berlin Wintergarten. Jack returned to the U.S.A. a millionaire, a lord of music. He published several of my piano solos around that time, such as "Rhapsody Junior" and "Bird of Paradise," which Jimmie Lunceford later recorded after Ed Wilcox and Eddie Durham had orchestrated them.

However, in 1923 we were not exactly thinking in terms of millions, although the engagement at Barron's had brought us to the attention of a lot of people prominent in show business. In the fall of that year we went to the Hollywood Club downtown, at Forty-ninth and Broadway. After the first of several fires, it became the Kentucky Club, and we stayed there four years. It was a good place for us to be, because it stayed open all night and became a rendezvous for all the big stars and musicians on Broadway after they got through working. Paul Whiteman came often, and he always showed his appreciation by laying a big fifty-dollar bill on us.

It was at the Kentucky Club that our music acquired new colors and characteristics. First we added Charlie Irvis, a trombone player nicknamed "Plug" because of the unusual mute he used. Then, when Artie Whetsol went back to Washington to continue his studies at Howard University, we got Bubber Miley, the epitome of soul and a master with the plunger mute. After Irvis left to join Charlie Johnson's band, Joe "Tricky Sam" Nanton came in, and he and Bubber became a great team, working together hand in glove. They made a fine art out of what became known as jungle style, establishing a tradition that we still maintain today.

Sonny Greer was in his element here, and he was known as The Sweet-Singing Drummer in those days. After the band had played the show twice—usually at midnight and 2 A.M.—as well as some dance music, I would send them home and Sonny and I would work the floor. I had one of those little studio upright pianos on wheels that you could push around from table to table, and Sonny would carry his sticks and sing. Answering requests, we sang anything and everything—pop songs, jazz songs, dirty songs, torch songs, Jewish songs. Sometimes, the customer would respond by throwing twenty-dollar bills away from him as though they were on fire. When business was slow, we'd sing "My Buddy." That was the favorite song of the boss, Leo Bernstein, and when we laid that on him he was expected to throw down some bills too.

Sonny always had an eye on the entrance stairway. (The Kentucky Club was a downstairs joint.) He was always ready to give a prosperous-looking customer a big hello, and if he could catch him as he came in, he would introduce him to the manager. "This is my *man,*" he would say. "Take care of him!" More than likely the guy would slip him a sawbuck.

We might leave the club with a hundred dollars each in our pockets, but by the time we got home we would have blown it all, because we had to go from joint to joint to be received, and to find out what was happening. When we walked into one of those after-hours joints, all the chicks would stand up and holler, "Sonny, baby!" When he heard those broads holler, his feet would leave the ground, and he'd say, "Give everybody in the house a drink!"

The Mirrored Self

Let us imagine a quiet, cozy cove where all the senses except one seem to have dispersed. There is nothing to smell, nothing to taste, nothing to hear, and nothing to feel but the reaction to what can be seen. Nearby is a still pool, so still that it resembles a limpid mirror. If we look in it, what we see is the reflection of ourselves, just as we thought we looked, wearing the identical clothes, the same countenance . . .

Ah, this is *us,* the us we know, and as we savor the wonderful selves-of-perfection we suddenly realize that just below our mirror, there is another reflection that is not quite so clear, and not quite what we expected. This translucent surface has a tendency toward the vague: the lines are not firm and the colors not quite the same, but it is us, or should we say *me,* or rather one of our other selves? We examine this uncertain portrait and just as we feel inclined to accept it we realize that, down below this, there is still another mirror reflecting another of our selves, and more. For this third mirror is transparent, and we can plainly see what is going on both before and behind it, and we refuse to credit that here is still another of our selves. But there we are with four reflections, all reflections of us who look at them. We accept the first three, even with the vague and misty overtones, but the fourth, on the other side of the transparent mirror, leaves us baffled and on the verge of defeat. It is hard to believe that we would do this to *me,* but we saw it with our own eyes. Which is the one we love most? We know that *I* am one of our favorite people, but which one? It does not have anything to do with what we are doing to anybody else, but what we are doing to *me,* the thinker-writer, the okayer, the nixer, the player, the listener, the critic, the corrector. What are they all saying? We can't hear them. We can only see them. A ripple in the pool and they all disappear.

Now we can hear, feel, smell, and taste.

Q. What are your major interests?
A. Well, I live in the realm of art and have no monetary interests.
Q. What do you think of people who have monetary interests?
A. I doubt whether art could survive if business and such people did not subsidize it in some form. I do not concern myself with other people's business, because I have enough problems of my own.
Q. Like, what, for instance?
A. I have to answer to my other selves.
Q. Which other selves?
A. My better selves, of course.
Q. What are your better selves like? What demands do they make on you?
A. I have to answer to my better self in music, and that becomes a matter of how it sounds when I write or play it, of its consonance, its dissonance . . .
Q. What about your best self?
A. My best self writes and plays sacred music and keeps me honest to myself. My best self also prays for the health and survival of others—and for the forgiveness of still others.

Q. Do you consider yourself as a forerunner in the advanced musical trends derived from jazz?
A. There were many wonderful musicians who established themselves and the word "jazz" many years before my time. "Jazz" is only a word and really has no meaning. We stopped using it in 1943. To keep the whole thing clear, once and for all, I don't believe in categories of any kind.
Q. In the music you compose now, is there some survival of what was once characterized as "jungle style" in your performances?

A. We write from the same perspective as before. We write to fit the tonal personalities of the individual instrumentalists who have the responsibility of interpreting our works.

Q. How do you regard the phenomenon of the black race's contribution to U.S. and world culture?

A. Regarding the Negro influence on culture generally, I imagine other people too found it agreeable to their senses.

Q. Do you enjoy composing music, or do you prefer performing? And have you a magic formula for attracting audiences?

A. I like any and all of my associations with music—writing, playing, and listening. We write and play from our perspective, and the audience listens from its perspective. If and when we agree, I am lucky.

Q. Do you think your performances in the jazz field can be connected with those of other writers and artists in the U.S.?

A. I try not to conform to vogues.

Q. Do you think jazz is having a kind of revival now?

A. The word "jazz" is still being used with great success, but I don't know how such great extremes as now exist can be contained under the one heading.

Q. Why do so many people, above all abroad, consider jazz intellectual music?

A. We enjoy freedom of expression in presenting our music, and some people prefer to accept it in their own fashion.

Q. When you work with symphony orchestras, what is the greatest hurdle in conducting their musicians and yours? Do the symphony men dig your way easily?

A. There is no hurdle at all in the case of our musicians. The music is mostly all in tempo and the responsibility for togetherness rests in the main with the symphony orchestra. It's more or less a matter of establishing an understandable beat, whether it's in two-four, four-four, or five-four. They can play anything they can see, and the conductor's responsibility is to *know* thoroughly the piece he is conducting.

Q. Can you sense when something special is beginning to happen at a concert or on a record session?

A. When one is fortunate enough to have an extremely sensitive audience, and when every performer within the team on stage feels it, too, and reacts positively in coordination toward the pinnacle, and when both audience and performers are determined not to be outdone by the other, and when both have appreciation and taste to match—then it is indeed a very special moment, never to be forgotten.

Q. Do you work better under pressure?

A. I scarcely do anything without a tight deadline. I work to the last minute.

Q. You are known to work under extraordinary conditions, with the television going, people talking, lights blazing, and telephones ringing. Do you need that kind of semiconfusion, or are you so accustomed to it that you are oblivious to it? Or can you just tune out at will?

A. In the early music publishing houses, there might be as many as ten pianos going at once, and you had to learn to write a lead sheet under those circumstances. If I were making a lead sheet to get an advance, I couldn't afford to let all those noises interfere with the noise I was trying to put down on one sheet of paper. Of course, I don't make the blueprint for coincidences of the kind mentioned, but if and when they happen, I seldom have the urge or fortitude to be a disciplinarian. Nor do I have the impudence to be rude, or the gall or brass to demand *order.*

Q. Do you hear your music mentally first? Does it work out in a pattern from a beginning? And do you hear it in single notes, chords, phrases, or larger, whole parts?

A. Each and all the ways. Acceptance is unconditional.

Q. Do you think a composer will ever be able to figure out mathematically what he wants, feed it to a computer, and let *it* compose?

A. They had the player piano years ago.

Q. An artist is now expected to do many things to "promote" himself and his work. Is there danger in overexposure on television, in radio interviews, etc., etc.?

A. Everybody is different. There is no general rule.

Q. How does the artist keep control and avoid manipulation by agents, managers, and business people?

A. The artist is either a better businessman or a better artist.

Q. You function in triplicate as performer, composer, and conductor. In what order would you put these roles, or does it change according to the situation?

A. Each is different and each must be approached with a different perspective. None is as important as—or more important than—the one being enjoyed at the moment.

Q. How do you rate composition, arrangement, and performance in importance?

A. All are interdependent on each other. Composition depends a great deal on the subsequent arrangement, but neither should burden the performers, for if the performance fails all is lost.

Q. Was there any special reason why you set out to develop a particularly strong left hand at the piano?

A. When I started out, the left hand was considered the first step toward acknowledgment.

Q. When you began composing as a very young man, did you draw from your environment, real experiences, or what you experienced through reading and listening? Where did the initial inspiration come from?

A. The driving power was a matter of wanting to be—and to be heard—on the same level as the best.

Q. Am I wrong in assuming your aural sense is more acute than your other senses? And how strong a part do the other senses play?

A. Composers try to parallel observations made through all the senses.

Q. How does a performer "tune in" to a particular audience, to its receptiveness, reaction, or mood? People in one section of the country may want to hear something completely different to those in another.

A. There is no geographical scale for appraising audiences. When the artist encounters a sensitive audience—jackpot! If he plays to the audience according to geography, nationality, race, or creed, he is condescending, and this is the world's worst social offense.

Q. How does the composer-performer feel when a new work is premiered and there is only a mild audience reaction, perhaps because it is not understood or because the people cannot identify with it?

A. Only the artist really knows whether his performance is good or otherwise. He is the only one who knows what the work or performance was supposed to say or represent.

Q. Who is the artist accountable to?

A. If artist he be, to himself. It is prostitution to sway or bend to money, or to the many other forms of advancement.

Q. What artistic sacrifice would be excusable to obtain monetary success? And do you think this happens frequently, occasionally, or seldom?

A. All kinds of such "sacrifices" have been and are still being overdone.

Q. Do you compose in your head or at the piano? Do you see the piece? Does it have shape?

A. There is no format for the activity of the brain. If it doesn't happen in the mind first, it doesn't happen.

Q. If you were stuck in a mountain cabin for a month without a piano, what would happen? Could you continue to compose?

A. Naturally.

Q. It is sometimes said that young people are the ones with money to spend on concerts and records. Is it possible that our musician-stars have priced themselves out of the range of the average citizen? If so, what can be done about it?

A. I don't understand how or why young people have or get more money more often than older people. There are a lot of things like that being said today without reason.

Q. If the work week of the foreseeable future is appreciably shortened, how do you think the cultural arts will fit into this kind of lifestyle?

A. People who make a living doing something they don't enjoy wouldn't even be happy with a one-day work week.

Q. Is honest apprenticeship a missing factor in performances today, or is a lot of noise made to camouflage the fact that young players don't really know what they are doing?

A. Talent and ability are neither young nor old. Agedness is only vaguely related to chronology. Without know-how, nobody is anything.

Q. Is there satisfaction in knowing that what you have created gives you a chance to live and be known beyond your time? Does gratification offset the rough road you must have had to travel at times?

A. I have no interest in posterity. I have been very lucky and have not had the discomfort of treading the rough road.

Q. At this point in your career, what do you think is expected of you?

A. I don't know, and couldn't care less.

Q. When you travel to other countries as a representative of your own, what do you consciously take to other peoples, and what, in turn, do you take from them?

A. I am neither a tourist nor a sightseer, so what is observed is easily digestible—when I look. I always love to hear the music of my hosts, and hope we shall be in mutual (and total) agreement, so that we can *both* say, "Encore!"

Q. You must get extraordinarily exhausted on your travels. How do you recharge or revitalize?

A. One must always conserve the agreeable or positive. It is not expedient to try to like or enjoy the negative.

Q. When you don't feel like performing, as must sometimes happen, how do you psyche yourself into doing a first-class job?

A. I have no preferred conditions for doing what I do for a living. I love it all, all of the time.

Q. Can any artist ever honestly imagine himself not listening to his muse? Could you accept a blow that would stop your work? Does faith enter at that point?

A. Time entered first, but faith entered next, long ago. One must be aware of possible ups and downs, and try to be in position for one more turn of the wheel.

Q. Is the creative artist like an iceberg? Is a large part of him submerged and only a small part shown?

A. Everyone is that way. Art is a skill.

Q. What do you consider your most important contribution to the music world, to your people, and to your country?

A. There are quite enough professional appraisers around to enjoy that headache. I have no ambition to be a critic or a judge.

Q. Does inspiration come from sorrow, frustration, and disappointment? It has been said that great love songs have followed a broken heart or the end of an affair. Do emotions such as love, anger, loneliness, or happiness affect composition?

A. I think the artist's true position is that of an observer. Personal emotion could spoil his *pièce dè résistance.*

Q. Do you think there is a strong hereditary element in great talent? Or is it, rather, an inherited potential that must be developed? How would you explain child geniuses?

A. The Bible speaks of the first, second, third, and fourth generations being affected by the acts of the fathers.

Q. If you ever questioned your path in life, how did you answer yourself?

A. I like to believe that I do my best to stay in my place on the wheel. I don't think I would want myself in anyone else's spot.

Q. Is there any achievement, outside the realm of music, that you are proud of and happy about?

A. The first social significance show, *Jump for Joy,* in 1941, and its various successors continually since.

Q. The public is always fascinated by details of the private lives of artistic people. Is there danger in the effect of this information on the public's evaluation of the artist's performance?

A. I think these highly publicized private lives are deliberately overdone for the purpose of building "box office." This is a business matter completely unrelated to art.

Q. Have there been special factors that have had an effect on your career and been a cause for concern?

A. Concern, yes. Concern for solving whatever problem faced me, or for curing an illness.

Q. Wouldn't it be marvelous to develop a study center similar to those Frank Lloyd Wright set up in Arizona and Wisconsin for young people to study architecture, so that what you began and accomplished in music may be continued?

A. I am not a teacher.

Q. There can be few musicians so well traveled as you, but do you never tire of traveling?

A. No, it's a constant pursuit, and we just keep going. There is always some place we have never been, and while we are waiting for the opportunity to go there, we just keep circling like airplanes do, until the fog clears. We get in the pattern until we can move to a new level and, eventually, to a new place—by invitation, of course.

Q. Well, do you ever get tired of playing those old perennials night after night?

A. No, this is a responsibility we owe people. Say, for instance, someone comes along who says, "We were married to 'Caravan,'" or "I met my girl at the Blue Note when you were playing 'Mood Indigo.' It's important to them. We were playing one night some place down in Georgia when three people came up. "I met my wife," the man said, "for the first time when you were playing 'Sophisticated Lady,' and we danced together. It's a strange thing that you should be playing in our hometown on our daughter's twenty-first birthday!" Then they introduced their daughter. You have to respect such memories. Of course, when we get requests for numbers that are not in the book from people like that, we just say, "Fake it!"

Q. Would the sound of the Ellington orchestra change perceptibly if you changed personnel?

A. Well, it alters of itself with new music coming in all the time, and we do different interpretations of older numbers, although I suppose you might call that a cop-out. I have had the good fortune to employ several guys who became legends, and other musicians loved them so much that they imitated them. When Paul Gonsalves came in the band, he didn't even have to have a rehearsal. He loved Ben Webster so much, and he knew everything in the book. It was the same with Russell Procope and Barney Bigard's clarinet playing.

Q. How important is discipline?

A. I'm the world's worst disciplinarian. There's too much responsibility in being a *leader!* You have to have the dignity and authority of a leader, and that's all so heavy!

Q. Do you think it is easier or harder for a young musician starting out today than it was when you began?

A. The caliber of musicians is higher today. They have to be better musicians than they were then. In those days, the chief requisite was good personality of tone, identification. If you accomplished that, you didn't even have to read. Nowadays, the same guys play in symphonies, dance bands, and radio and television studios. There's no real problem for those properly qualified, and it can be very lucrative for the guy who gets in the swim of recording, television and movie studio work. Of course, you can isolate yourself to the point of nonavailability, or your timing might be off so that you are not available at the right time, when the juicy one goes by. That's a personal thing with some people, no matter what the conditions. I know when I left Washington that there were half a dozen there who knew ten times more music than I did, but they couldn't leave for one reason or another. I was just in pursuit of the melody, and it carried me to New York where, about a month later, I had a song published. I was twenty-three.

Q. Is there a point where it all becomes mechanical, even with great musicians?

A. It depends on how you relate their mechanical with skill. Skill is needed to operate the mechanical, and then we have to consider the degrees of taste and imagination supplied, but the skill and the mechanical are certainly two different things. The theater, for instance, is a place for skill. Some people say, "I don't see how he can play that part every night without going out of his mind!" It may be a wild, dramatic part, but the actor doesn't necessarily have to throw his emotions into it, because he has studied how to make the people *believe* that he is doing all that suffering. It is one of the arts, and all the arts have similar qualities. Imagine a man sculpting a statue of a crying woman, or a dying man, from a huge piece of marble. He becomes emotionally involved in what he is doing, loses control of his chisel, and louses up the statue. Then our real artist comes along, sees him in his despair, takes him as *his* subject, and paints his picture. Horrible, isn't it?

Q. But isn't there a point ever where the music is coming out of your fingers, and not out of your heart?

A. I don't think it is that easy to define or analyze. If you stop to analyze it, you're going to louse it up real good! Suppose you go out in your garden and cut a flower. "It's a gorgeous flower," you decide, when you come back in the house. So you put it in some water, trim the stem, and give it proper care. Maybe you like it so much that next day you put an aspirin in the water. But if you start to pull it to pieces, and take the petals off, and examine the veins that run through it . . . then you may know everything about it, but you don't have any more flower! Which brings us to another point: I don't think people have to *know* anything about music to appreciate it or enjoy it.

Q. There's probably not a second of the day when one of your compositions is not being played somewhere in the world. Do you ever think about that?

A. No, I never do, and I've never heard it put that way before.

Q. How many are there?

A. Gee, I don't know . . . thousands . . . We write 'em every day.

Q. Where do you get your titles from?

A. You play the tune first, and then turn around and see what the girl's name is, the girl standing down by the bass end of the piano. There's always a girl in the standard original whirl!

Q. Which of all your tunes is your favorite?

A. The next one. The one I'm writing tonight or tomorrow, the new baby is always the favorite.

Q. What does America mean to you?

A. It's where I was born. It's *home.* Its music world has been an extremely competitive scene, and that in itself incites drive. Without competition you wouldn't have it. Then I've been very lucky in America. I've been allowed to live well, and in many instances I've been spoiled. My friends and relatives live well, too. I've learned a lot there, where there are so many great musicians to learn from. Opportunity and luck are so important. You have to be in the right place at the right time. A gambler in a lucky streak can't get lucky unless he's shooting dice or doing what he does best.

Q. Don't you get tired of doing what you're doing year in and year out?

A. You're talking from the perspective either of someone who doesn't love music, or who doesn't do what he enjoys most for a living. To be frank, that question annoys me very much, and not merely because it recurs so often. Millions and millions of dollars are spent building big vacation places for people to escape to from their daily chores, but they are the people who don't enjoy what they are doing for a living. Nobody else does what we do for fifty-two weeks of the year, every day of the week. It's our unique thing. Nobody does anything every day like we do, and nobody does it in so many places as we do. Doctors, surgeons, football players, bankers—you name it—they all take vacations. We go to many countries and we fly more than pilots do! We live in an entirely different climate. Three days ago we crossed the equator. Yesterday we went through a blizzard. Everybody else takes a day off, but not us. We're not captive, but we're built in.

Q. Do you have time for painting now?

A. No, although painting was my recognized talent. When I won a scholarship in fine art to Pratt Institute, I didn't take advantage of it, because I was already involved in what was just beginning to be called jazz. I told myself that that kind of music couldn't last, that I'd give it another year, and then maybe next year go and pick up my scholarship. Sometimes now I buy the materials—paint, canvas, and cardboard—but they only sit in the corner and collect dust. You can't *paint* in planes, trains, cars, or buses.

Q. But you can write music under such conditions?

A. Oh, yes, because when you get an idea, you've got to put it down while you've got it. Otherwise it changes. The notes change places, and the next time you go back in your mind to look for it, you find the third note has become the sixth note, and its value has been altered, and there is actually no resemblance to the original idea.

Q. What is God for you?

A. God? There's one God, and that's all.

Q. Do you believe in God?

A. Oh, yes, and that is why I do so many sacred concerts every year.

Q. What is love for you?

A. Love is indescribable and unconditional. I could tell you a thousand things that it is not, but not one that it *is.* Either you have it or you haven't; there's no proof of it.

Q. What is music to you?

A. My mistress. I love with music.

Q. What is the audience?

A. The audience is the other side of the realm that serves the same muse I do.

Q. While performing, what do you insist on from the audience?

A. I don't insist on anything. I play for the audience, and if I'm lucky they have the same taste I have. It's rather like that word "swing": when two people are together, and my pulse and your pulse are together, then we're swinging.

Q. What do you think of the narcotics problem?

A. Why ask me? You are not a doctor, a detective, or a junkie, are you?

Q. Your house is on fire. What would you grab first to save?

A. I would grab the old Sonny Greer adage: "Feet save ass, ass do feet a good turn someday."

Q. Do you have a favorite season of the year and, if so, what do you specially like about it?

A. Being a chronic indoorsman, it's unimaginable that I should be any sort of authority on this.

Q. What is man's greatest discovery?

A. Electricity. And the telephone is a necessity.

Q. What is your best habit?

A. Prayer.

Q. What is your worst habit?

A. Talking too much.

Q. Apart from your usual meal of grapefruit, steak, and vegetables, what would your next favorite meal be?

A. Room service Chinese food—Cantonese.

Q. What do you think is the most serious breach of trust?

A. Telling.

Q. Is "love" or "like" more important?

A. Love is supreme and unconditional; like is nice but limited.

Q. Do you throw up defense with argument or logic?

A. Sometimes it is necessary to use one to drive the other home—depending on who's home.

Q. Even with the speed of jets, don't you question whether those rigorous itineraries are worthwhile?

A. Or wouldn't it be better, eh, to just sit or lie in one place till you got green first on one side and then on the other as you approached stagnation; till all the slithery slok and slithery slime rolled itself into a tink tank?

Q. Do you think people change as they proceed through life, or do they remain basically the same except for shifts in tempo and purpose?

A. It depends upon who they are. There are no two people alike. If two claim to be, one is a comformist, or most likely both. All are born with different susceptibilities, which are gradually modified by environment, teaching, learning, necessity, desire, etc.

Q. What would be a perfect day?

A. Any day I wake up and look at.

Q. Where do you remember the most beautiful sunrise and sunset?

A. Seconds before dawn from Berkeley Heights, looking west over San Francisco Bay. And then in Bombay at sunset, the whole sky over the Arabian Sea was cerise from the horizon all the way up.

Q. Do you have an actual fear of anything, like heights, storms, or reptiles?

A. The snake catches the insect that would have injected you with a deadly poison. (That makes the snake a jabber-grabber.) Either one could save your life, and either one could kill you.

Q. If you were confined somewhere, all alone, what books would you want?

A. Only the Bible, because all the other books are in it.

Q. Do you think men have a tendency toward polygamy and women toward monogamy?

A. Definitely. It depends upon their minds, not their sex.

Q. What human shortcoming irritates you most?

A. Underestimation.

Q. Did you ever imagine yourself a reincarnated royal genius?

A. When I was a child, my mother told me I was blessed, and I have always taken her word for it. Being born of—or reincarnated from—royalty is nothing like being blessed. Royalty is inherited from another human being, blessedness from God.

Q. Do you think you have a more highly developed degree of anticipation than most people?

A. Some people have sensitivities in directions they never have an opportunity to use, because they have been drawn away from them for monetary reasons. They would be surprised to discover how rewarding it is to pursue the natural tendencies and become a Number One yourself rather than a Number Two somebody else. Heaven is a place where you get an opportunity to use all the millions of sensitivities you never knew you had before.

Q. Who is the most sensitive and gentle person you have known?

A. Daisy, my mother.

Q. If you could make one sure bet, what would it be?

A. Gray skies are just clouds passing over.

Q. How do you live now as compared with earlier stages of your life?

A. Since I have been out on my own, I have always lived rather expensively, but I shall never live as well as I did in my mother's arms.

Q. What has been the most valuable thing in life for you?

A. Time.

Q. How many hours do you sleep a day?

A. I try for eight, and some days I'm luckier than others.

Q. What has been the reason for your continued success?

A. The grace of God.

The Most Essential Instrument

I am delighted you have recently had the opportunity to hear Willie The Lion. He has been such a very strong influence on anybody who ever listened to him. Seriously, I mean that! Art Tatum was influenced by Willie The Lion, and anyone who can influence Art Tatum has to be *really* something, for Tatum was the greatest. And I know that is right, because Oscar Peterson says so; and so too, for that matter, does Billy Strayhorn.

Yes, Willie The Lion was the foundation. He not only had his own natural inclinations towards piano devices, but if he thought you worthy of instruction he would demonstrate and show you the varying styles of his predecessors and their ways and means of playing the piano. To spend an evening with The Lion was really something to experience. If you troubled to hang around for a while and listen to all that was said and played (or should I say, played and saved—that doesn't quite rhyme, but you know what I mean) you'd learn something. Those beautiful tunes and melodies he wrote, they go right back, back to the school of ragtime—the real old jazz piano players. The Eastern piano players, they all played beautifully, melodically. They would swing all the time, but they also played beautiful piano—nothing ugly, grotesque, awkward, ungainly, or ungraceful about anything ever played by those who were known as the ragtime piano players. What they called whorehouse music was the most beautiful, full of the most lovely melodies; the "Bulldiker's Dream" and things like that. Of course, I was never in one of those places, but that is what the big boys used to tell me. Jack The Bear, Sam Gordon, and Jess[e] Pickett, who wrote "The Dream"—the things they and The Lion used to play, was really beautiful music. Also it had a tremendous beat, tremendous pulse. Yes, those piano players were really on the pretty kick. Pity I wasn't around in those days, for I would probably have been a great patron of those whorehouse artists' music. That music hasn't been carried on, hasn't been bettered because you can't beat pretty—when a thing is pretty, it's just pretty. It can of course get prettier, but can you develop pretty? When something is definitely pretty, just how far can it be taken? To what degree can you develop it? If something is absolutely pretty, can it be improved upon? Or is that just gilding the lily? In other words if you find a beautiful flower, it is probably better enjoyed than analyzed, because in order to analyze it, you have to pull it apart, dissect it. And when you get through you have all the formulas, all the botanical information you need, and all the science of it, but you haven't got a beautiful flower anymore. And so as Mr. Strayhorn has said, "Pretty is absolute!" In other words, when something is absolutely pretty it is its own square root—having been compounded to the nth degree. Yet as Mr. Strayhorn so kindly tells us, "square root" is hardly the word for people like us to be using, tho' one part of the word almost modifies the other, if you see what I mean. We are not squares, or to bring Mr. Strayhorn's intellectual language down to the level of the man in the street, there is no such thing as a square root, for one cannot be a square and be a root—a foundation.

But back to music: Of all the musicians Bechet to me was the very epitome of jazz. He represented and executed everything that had to do with the beauty of it all, and everything he played in his whole life was completely original. No matter what he called it, even if he did a chorus on "Clap Hands, Here Comes Charlie" it was like no other version of that tune—it came out as a Bechet original. He was truly a great man and no one has ever been able to play like him. He has his own ideas and nobody could execute the music from the same perspective, accomplish the same musical ends. There have been other great musicians, Louis [Armstrong] was a great trumpeter and so-and-so was a great something else (we shouldn't compare artists ever!), but Bechet was a unique representative. I honestly think he was the most unique man ever to be in this music—but don't ever try and compare because when you talk about Bechet you just don't talk about anyone else. You understand, if I were talking about Bechet, I wouldn't talk about Hodges. Hodges plays soprano too, but Hodges learnt from Bechet, and Bechet taught Hodges who used to play closer to Bechet than anyone else ever has played. They had, in fact, somewhat of the same sort of perspective, I think, at the time that Hodges was blowing soprano. It was the same when Bechet played clarinet—no one played clarinet like him—no one! No one had the same timbre—completely wood.

Now let me make this very clear, I am talking about sounds. When you ask me about musicians, you are talking about stars; I am talking about sounds, not stars. You know Guy Lombardo had it pretty rich too—he had a jazz band called The Royal Canadians, the first time I heard them, they were a jazz band, with a rich sound—and we were a jazz band too. Paul Whiteman had a jazz band, didn't he? [Vincent] Lopez, Coon-Sanders, a whole lot of cats at that time had jazz bands. But there were only a small handful of individuals who were really unique—to my mind anyway. But we are getting too close to this comparison thing again, and I don't like to discuss it that way. Because if they are artists they can't be compared, and if you compare them, then they are no longer artists, they become something that some managing outfit has built from something. The thing is that directly you say Bechet, you get a picture—in the same way you say Armstrong you get a picture, or [Dizzy] Gillespie and you get a picture, or you say Hawk [Coleman Hawkins] you get another picture.

And then, referring to the pianists, there is Tatum, Willie The Lion, Fats

Waller, James P. Johnson, and of course Earl Hines, yes, definitely Hines. And that cat out in New Jersey, Donald Lambert and The Beetle [Stephen Henderson]—they were in that bracket as well. It is impossible to tell you how the Beetle played, if you haven't heard him. If you say he played "good Lion" then at once he becomes not eligible, but he played wonderful piano. He never played anywhere in particular, he didn't play regularly, or in other words he didn't have good management, like some of us have been lucky enough to have. A whole lot of great talent has been channeled down the drain, you know, because of lack of management. Of course some great management has also gone down the drain for lack of talent, but that is another story. Another person you should have heard about forty years ago was Turner Layton—he played piano in those days. Luckey Roberts was another and Dollar Bill. I never heard Dollar Bill, but I have heard The Lion's impression of what he played. Did you ever hear Strayhorn? Hardly what you'd call a jazz pianist, he is strictly from the Strayhorn school. The first and the last of that school. Have you ever heard Ben Webster play piano? No? Well you should. Ben knows The Beetle by the way. He doesn't play what you might call professionally; piano that is, of course.

A great man, Ben, a great personality. Another of the great personalities in our jazz realm was Bubber Miley. Strayhorn doesn't like that word jazz, but this was when the word was ripe. Sometime around 1926, and that was when Bechet was with us too, and played in our band. Bubber Miley and Bechet used to sit side by side, and Bechet would blow ten choruses and then Bubber would get up with his plunger and blow another ten choruses. And so every time one would get through the other would take over while the other was resting. Then he would go back and have a *taste* and then come back fresh and full of new ideas. Oh what a pity some of those things weren't recorded! The invention, the soul invention, the musical emotion ran high. Bubber was one of the great men, in fact Bubber was the first man I heard use the expression, "it don't mean a thing if it ain't got that swing." Everything, and I repeat, everything had to swing. And that was just it, those cats really had it; they had that soul. And you know you can't just play some of this music without soul. Soul is very important. And first to play this music, you have to love music. So if you love music, then it follows you love to listen to it, which makes the ear the most essential instrument, the most essential musical instrument in the world.

Sonny Greer

From Stanley Dance's The World of Duke Ellington *(1970)—and also to be found in* The Duke Ellington Reader*—an appreciation of Ellington and an account of the early Ellington years, written in 1965 by his great drummer, Sonny Greer.*

From the moment I was introduced to Duke, I loved him. It was just something about him. He didn't know it, but he had it then. I've never seen another man like him. When he walks into a strange room, the whole place lights up. That's how he likes people, and how he impresses them.

I had been working in the dining room of the Plaza Hotel on the boardwalk in Asbury Park, in a trio with Fats Waller and a violinist called Shrimp Jones. The same hotel employed a string ensemble called the Conway Boys, and when I struck up a friendship with Sterling Conway he invited me to Washington for a weekend. So when the season ended, I went there for three days and stayed several years.

I was a very good pool player at that time. Pool is like the violin—you've got to play an hour every day. There was a poolroom right near the Howard Theatre in Washington, which was then owned by A. J. Thomas and Louis Thomas. Except for the pianist, the drummer and the leader, Marie Lucas, all the musicians in the pit band were from San Juan, Puerto Rico. The drummer had a little alimony trouble, and rather than pay he ducked out to Canada. A half-hour before the show was due on, they came rushing into the poolroom, frantic. "We've got to have a drummer," they shouted. My financial position was such that I answered them, "I'm the guy." And that was how I came to play the Howard Theatre the first time.

I struck up an acquaintance with Toby Hardwick. He played string bass then, no saxophone, and he and Duke were pals. When I was introduced, Duke wanted to know all about New York. I was an authority, because my two aunts lived there and I had spent a good part of my schooldays in the city. I painted a glowing picture, a fabulous picture. We sat around drinking corn and telling lies, and I won the lying contest.

When I got through at the Howard Theatre, about eleven o'clock at night, I'd go right around the corner to the Dreamland Café and play there from midnight to about six in the morning. Claude Hopkins was on piano and Eddie White—Harry White's brother—on violin. There were about ten waitresses and they could all sing—blues or whatever you wanted. When I say blues, I mean the authentic material, and they sang so well it's a pity they were never recorded. Bootlegging was a big thing in Washington then and tips were flying. They brought in corn from Maryland and the bootleggers would often stack a deuce table with bills and tell the entertainers to help themselves. That's how the times were—come easy, go easy.

Duke wasn't a professional then, but he would come in and play his "Carolina Shout." He was a great admirer of James P. Johnson, and he had got his Q.R.S. piano rolls down fine. He really idolized James P. and he was the only man I ever knew who could play "Carolina Shout" equally well. But Uncle Ed, his father, didn't want him to go into the music field, because he had a degree in art illustration and was already in partnership with Ewell Conway in commercial illustration. But he knew which direction he wanted to go and, as we say, he followed the swallow.

In those days, they would have piano contests as an attraction to get people to go to dances. Cliff Jackson was around and so was Claude Hopkins. Claude's father was a professor and his mother a librarian at Howard University, and he was born and raised on the campus. He was ahead of Cliff Jackson then in terms of finish and experience. Thanks to me, Duke had a cheering section of seven or eight with their noisemakers. So Duke would be all set to play his "Carolina Shout," and I would be there to play the drums, and Toby the bass, so we couldn't lose. We won all kinds of things—suitcases and I don't know what. We'd keep them overnight, sell them next day, and go have a ball again.

After some adventures, we got to New York and opened as the Washingtonians at the Kentucky Club on 49th and Broadway in 1923. We were there five years and the club was so popular that it became a rendezvous for all the musicians. It was owned by Leo Bernstein and Frank Gary. We had six chorus girls in the show and they ended up as star dancers at the Cotton Club uptown, which at that time was known as Jack Johnson's De Luxe Club. The floorshow also included Johnny Hudgins, then the foremost colored comedian and an international star. His act was all pantomime. He never opened his mouth. Joe Smith, the trumpet player, worked with him, and Joe did the talking on trumpet, using his hand as a mute. The M.C. was Bert Lewis and in between the shows he would come out and do an act with Fats Waller as his accompanist.

We went to work at eleven o'clock at night and nobody knew when closing hour was. We usually didn't get through till seven or eight in the morning, but it was beautiful. So many things happened. All kinds of people mixed there—show people, socialites, debutantes, musicians, and racketeers—and everybody had a lovely time. It was still Prohibition, of course, and nobody could get a drink of booze in the place unless I gave an okay. In the whole time we were there, we never had a raid or a pinch. We had an elaborate system and I had a good memory for faces. Any stranger was carefully screened.

The club held only about 130 people, but after all the other clubs closed the musicians would come to ours, and often you would see forty or fifty name musicians in there at a time. There was just a small dance floor and there wasn't much dancing, but everybody could sit in. At three or four in the morning, you would see Bix Beiderbecke, Tommy Dorsey, Miff Mole, Paul Whiteman, and musicians like that. Whiteman had the band at the Palais Royal around the corner for a time. The bandstand was small, cramped even for the six of us, so when they sat in they played right from the floor, from a chair by their table. Bix and I were friends, and we would often go from one place to another, drinking Top and Bottom, but people who never knew him—and writers—have painted a picture of him that did him more than justice. They made him an invincible trumpet player, but he wasn't that good. You could never have put Bix up on a bandstand with Louis Armstrong, Joe Smith, and Bubber Miley when they were at their peak. The competition was pretty fast then, and he was never in life a legend.

Because of the small stand, we couldn't use a bass player and we couldn't expand the band, but there were no small bands so well rehearsed as ours then. Most of them played stocks, which we never did. Duke wasn't writing so much, but he would take the popular tunes and twist them, and Toby was doubling on C-melody and baritone, so we would sound like a big band, but soft and beautiful.

When Arthur Whetsol went back to Washington, we got Bubber Miley. We had heard him in Harlem at the club where Willie "the Lion" Smith was playing. Bubber was a great man with a plunger, but Charlie Irvis had an old tomato can, smashed in at the bottom like a cone, to get the same effect, those low notes and the growl. That was what Charlie was famous for, and everybody in the music business knew him as "Plug."

Word spread among the musicians about the fantastic sounds this trumpet player with us—Bubber Miley—was getting with a plunger. Red Nichols was playing a club not far from us and curiosity must have drawn him to hear Bubber perform. Lee Posner was writing a newspaper column then called "Harlemania" and he asked Red what he thought about using a plunger with a trumpet. Red said he would rather drop dead than be caught using one of those so-and-so plungers.

Sidney Bechet came in one night and pulled out his soprano. Right away, he, Bubber, and Charlie Irvis got to jamming against each other. It was wonderful. So then we hired him and he played with the Washingtonians, clarinet and soprano. He fitted our band like a glove.

After Paul Whiteman, Ross Gorman had a band at the Palais Royal and this was the first time we had seen a band all with gold instruments. Gorman had a terrific band then, and it looked so good with all those gold horns. One night, all the bands went up there for some kind of charity affair. Leo Bernstein, our boss, was a very aggressive guy from Chicago, and he insisted that we play before we went off to work. When we started playing, the house fell in. About the third tune we got into was one of those jam numbers we had then, and Bechet, Bubber, and Charlie came down front. Bechet had taken a table napkin and he held it in his mouth so that it hung down, and you couldn't see his fingers as he played his soprano. He cut everybody, Ross Gorman's band, everybody. When he had finished, the manager of the place came up to Gorman and said, "Play waltzes. Don't play any more jazz." That was our seven pieces.

THE BAND THAT came closest in terms of competition, in my opinion, was Jimmie Lunceford's. He had class, talent, and variety, and his band was full of terrific stars. Count Basie's and Chick Webb's were top bands, but they never had the variety of material and presentation. Jimmie Lunceford was a good man; he believed in discipline, and he never caroused. Duke, on the other hand, would always get down and fraternize with his men, and he had a reason for doing that. He'd go out with them or sit down and play cards with them. He'd never let them lose confidence in themselves. He'd sit up and ball with them, and he used to be able to drink them under the table. He doesn't do that now, but that's how you mature.

Duke Ellington earned his success. He worked at it. The band was getting bigger and climbing all through the thirties, and that was when he began to express some of his dreams by putting different guys into special showcases. Each guy in the band was an individual artist. No two of them ever played alike, and that applies even today. As a team, they're unbeatable. The backgrounds Duke wrote for individual talents not only showed them off to the best advantage, but also made them feel comfortable. The art of presentation is ingrained in him, and when musicians moved out on their own, or into another band, they soon found out it wasn't the same.

When we started to go abroad, that was something else. I always remember the concert we played at the Trocadero in London in 1933. It was a huge place, packed and jammed, and half the people were musicians. We had played a show at the Palladium, but we played *us* there. It was wide open, and we looked sharp, too, in those white suits and orange ties. That was years before other people began giving jazz concerts. They used to say Duke was twenty-five years ahead of his time, and you can see how true it was now. He's still ahead. The other guys never caught him.

Leora Henderson

Again from Hear Me Talkin' to Ya, *Fletcher Henderson's wife—herself a "hot" trumpeter—vividly recalls her husband's flourishing band, and its eventual collapse.*

It's so long ago, it's like a dream. I first met Fletcher when we were playing a dance on a Hudson River boat. It was a gig. (We called jobs like that gigs then.) I was playing trumpet and he played piano. At that time, during the day, he had a job downtown at the Black Swan record company as a sort of recording director and band leader. Fletcher was on all of the Ethel Waters' records for Black Swan. He was her accompanist.

Before I met Fletcher, I could only play classics or else only what I saw on paper, and Fletcher said, "You better learn to jazz or you won't make no money." Then we heard somebody playing "Lady Be Good" on the radio and it had just the *prettiest* trumpet chorus! And that's how I think Fletcher started writing. He went right to the piano and wrote out that chorus for me. From then on, he did that for me many times. Later on, when Louis Armstrong came to the band, I used to sit and watch him, and Louis taught me how to make riffs. Oh, after that, I played a regular hot trumpet and got all the work I wanted.

Fletcher had a band at the Club Alabam for about a year, and in 1924, I think, went into the Roseland Ballroom. The band played there on and off for seventeen years, most of that time as the regular house band. Of course, they would go out on tour for a few months each year, and, do you know, in all that time he never had a contract!

It was considered an honor to get in that band. It had the hardest book in the business, and many a musician just couldn't play those arrangements. Why, there were times when there was an empty chair on the bandstand. Jimmy Harrison couldn't make it. Fletcher turned him away and he went out and studied before Fletcher would take him back. The same thing happened to Rex Stewart. They rehearsed 'most every night, and while there were drinkin' men in the band, I don't remember when any of them was ever drunk on the job. And, at that time, I don't think that there was any of that reefer smokin'. At least, if there was, I didn't know anything about it.

My! Some of those rehearsals were a pleasure to watch. They would have some real battles. "Cuttin' contests," you know. I would set off in a dark corner and watch while Charlie Green (we called him Big Green) would be playing something wonderful and then Jimmy Harrison would say, "Huh, you think *you* done somethin'," and then he'd try to cut him. It was that way with the whole band. I'm telling you, it was just thrilling!

And that would get them all prepared for the Battles of Jazz with the bands that were playing at Roseland—the Dorsey Brothers, Casa Loma, Vincent Lopez, Jean Goldkette, and there was one band that they called The Buffalodians that had a little kid playing piano. He was the boy who wrote "Stormy Weather." His name was Arlen . . . Harold Arlen.

But nobody could beat our band, not with people like Don Redman and Louis, Bobby Stark, Joe Smith, Coleman Hawkins, Buster Bailey, Benny Carter, John Kirby, Big Green, and all the rest of the fine musicians that Fletcher had in those years.

Just before one of those band battles were about to start Fletcher would say to the men. "Come on—let's take charge!" And they would *play!* But, you know, those other bands didn't mind at all. They'd be listenin' and getting ideas and inspiration.

On his tours, Fletcher would see or hear of some musician who would qualify for the band and then later on he'd send for him. And Fletcher wasn't like some other bandleaders. The men liked to work for him. He'd exploit their names and bring them out so people would know them. And he had an easy disposition and a nice way about him. In fact, I never, in all the time I knew him, knew him to get real mad about anything.

Many of the musicians would come up to the house then. The only time any of them ever sat in with the band was during the last set, and afterwards they'd come home with us. Bix Beiderbecke would come all the time, and Joe Venuti and Eddie Lang and many more. Musicians seemed much nicer then. You didn't mind having them in your home. But mercy! I don't know about today. I wouldn't have all that reefer smokin' in my house!

For a while, a rage came along for blues singers—everything was blues, and Fletcher did a lot of work for blues singers. There was Bessie Smith and Clara Smith (she used to rehearse right here in this house) and many others whose names I don't recall. Sometimes Fletcher would work under different names because he was under contract, but it was so long ago, I guess it don't matter if I mention it now.

Around that time Paul Whiteman was called "The King of Jazz" and so people began calling Fletcher "The Colored King of Jazz." Whiteman would be playin' all those novelties and semiclassical numbers and Fletcher would turn right around and swing them. I recall that Don Redman even did an arrangement of *Rhapsody in Blue,* but later on they stopped the band from playin' it.

After the band would finish playin' at Roseland about 1 A.M., they'd sometimes play for dances in Harlem, till about three-thirty in the morning. There'd be a band on before Fletcher got there, but when he and the men arrived, everything would stop. Folks would get out of the way, and then Fletcher would start off with "Sugar Foot Stomp" and the crowd would go wild.

And there were no singers then like there are now. We didn't need 'em. Oh, Louis would carry on with a lot of foolishness—jump up and down and shout like a down-South preacher. And Jimmy Harrison was all fun and comedy too. He'd act like Bert Williams and sing "Somebody Loves Me" just like Williams—and things like that.

Joe Smith was wonderful too. He drank heavy and got real sick and passed later on. But, you know, I didn't know about any drinkin' or carryin' on in the band. The boys would keep that from me—and me being Fletcher's wife, there were *lots of things* I didn't know.

But about Joe Smith. (I used to call him "Toots.") I knew Joe before he could even play trumpet. He was always botherin' me to use my horn. But I used to get real mad. I didn't want anybody blowin' on my trumpet. I used to worry him about going out and finding himself a job . . . maybe learning to play drums or something.

Then he went away for about two years, and one day I found a note under my door. It said, "Back in town" and it was signed "Toots." At that time I was playin' in the pit of the Lafayette Theatre and he came down to see me.

He came in sly-like and said, "I learned to play clarinet." And he picked up a clarinet and started to play.

"That's not so good, Toots," I told him, and started to tell him again about settlin' down and gettin' a job. But when the time came to do the show, he came into the pit with me. I didn't know it, but he had hidden a trumpet there, and when some blues singer (I just can't remember her name) began to sing, Joe played. And the people started to howl. I'm telling you, I couldn't play another note that night!

He came to the theater every day after that and I helped to make him read and he really could play anything. That is, except that Spanish music. But finally he conquered that too. Joe had such a big soft beautiful tone. Bessie Smith was just crazy about his playing and he was on lots of her records later on.

There was one other musician I'd like to mention. He was *so* good. That's Hilton Jefferson. I don't know why people don't appreciate him—one of the finest saxophone players I ever heard. His record of "Who Can I Turn To?" with Cab Calloway is so beautiful.

Believe me Fletcher was never the same after he had that automobile accident down in Kentucky. He was going to Louisville to see my mother in that big open Packard he had, ridin' with Big Green, Coleman Hawkins, Bobby Stark, and Joe Smith. Some woman wouldn't pull over and the car went off the road and fell fourteen feet and turned right over. Fletcher was the only one who got hurt. He had an awful hit in his head and his left shoulder bone was pushed over to his collarbone. You know, it was the left side that got paralyzed later on. That was the only accident he ever had, and after that—why, he just changed.

Everything would seem comical to him and he never achieved to go higher than he was. He never had much business qualities anyhow, but after that accident, he had even less. And worst of all, he would get careless. He had a wonderful ear and if a bell would strike somewhere in the street, Fletcher would tell you what note it was. But one day I went to rehearsal and the boys were blowin' and I said, "Fletcher, can't you tell, one of them horns is out of tune." But he didn't seem to care much. It was the men in the band that kept up the morale then.

Then the managers of Roseland lost confidence in him too. The band was broken up and one day John Hammond came over and asked Fletcher to do some arranging for Benny Goodman. I'm telling you that nobody could have done more than John and Benny. Benny did everything he could to build up Fletcher's name and would tell people that his band was nothin' compared to Fletcher's on those arrangements. Later on Fletcher worked with Benny's band and when he got sick and John arranged that special broadcast, Benny got some of his old men together and made that record so we could get the money.

The last job that Fletcher had before the stroke was in the *Jazz Train* show that played in that place on Broadway, Bop City. He worked so hard on that. He was really trying to make a comeback—workin' days and nights on arrangements and rehearsals. But all of it was for nothing.

The day Fletcher died he had one of his biggest audiences out there on the street what with the ambulances and the oxygen tanks. Louis Armstrong sent the most beautiful floral piece I've ever seen—shaped like an organ, pipes and all. Louis and Joe Glaser came to the funeral—and, you know the people from Roseland sent a man up here to see how I was gettin' on.

Art Hodes

Hodes, who lived into his nineties, collaborated with Chadwick Hansen in 1992 on Hot Man, *the autobiography from which this passage is excerpted. Here he recalls early traditional jazz piano in Chicago—the kind of piano he went on playing and encouraging all his life—as well as fellow musicians like Louis Armstrong and Bessie Smith.*

Learning Jazz: The South Side

It was after I returned from Delavan Lake that I had my first encounter with the great Negro musicians. I was to become very well acquainted with Louis Armstrong, and to see quite a lot, and what was more important, hear a lot, of Earl Hines. I was to become friends with Zutty Singleton. Let me tell you about the Wingy Manone days.

I was introduced to him at our union in Chicago. I'd made friends with a lot of musicians who congregated at the union hall three or more nights a week. There were at least three pool tables and sometimes as many as thirty card games going on at the old union, and leaders hired their men there. There was a real good feeling in that place, although at times the boys got to arguing a bit. Well, I fell right in and was doing all right at about the time someone introduced me to Wingy. He immediately started talking big about who he was and what he'd done. I was very much unimpressed and left him with one of those "glad to have met you" routines that people go through with. But we met again.

This time he was looking for a pianist, and Ray Biondi [the guitarist] was trying to help him find one. They finally fell into where I was working. They stood in the basement underneath the band and listened, and Ray tells me that when Wingy heard me play he said, "That's the man I want."

And so started a most important period in my life. In a short time we were roommates, then buddies, the best and closest of friends. We lived every minute of each day, and each day was a complete life in itself. Wingy and I moved in together first at a Near-North-Side hotel, where we did it up right. Wingy would get on the phone and call all over the country. The Ford had to be washed, greased and delivered. We ate the best. Louis Armstrong was at the Savoy, playing in Carroll Dickerson's band, and we were steady customers. We lasted two weeks at that hotel and they wound up holding our bags.

And then we moved to the North Side proper, Lawrence Avenue, around some kids from New Orleans that Wingy knew, and in no time at all, I knew. And the tales I heard from them about New Orleans, and Mardi Gras, and the musicians! In me they had a real listener. Anybody from New Orleans had a beat, could feel the music. I'd been led into a completely new world than the other I'd known at the union floor.

Wingy owned a Victrola and a half-dozen records, all by Louis, which he played and replayed. Anybody who was somebody stopped at our apartment at some time. The list would sound like a *Who's Who* in jazz. The main reason, the only one, was Wingy—his personality. He was a funny man and good kicks were plentiful around him.

In the two years I lived with Wingy I don't believe I read one book. Our day was so packed with listening to music and playing music and going to see people from our world, mainly Louis Armstrong, that we had no time for reading. We didn't miss it; we didn't know books existed.

Each day was about the same, except for the people we'd run into. Wingy had such personality, could be so funny, and above all could really play then. He had a beat you couldn't get away from. If we had two blocks to walk, we'd walk it in time. Wingy would sing some song as we walked along and we'd both swing along in time. Those couple of years I lived with Wingy, we lived with a beat. Our mistress was music; we worshipped her as a god. From the morning when we'd start in on the Vic till late at night when we were exhausted and had to go to sleep, we had but one desire—to play, to play better this minute than we had the last, or to hear something played that would knock us out. I'd wake up with Louis's "Muskrat Ramble" on the Vic, and immediately I was back in time, walking to the music, dressing to it, and being walked out of the house.

We didn't see people who would break the spell. Out to the Savoy Ballroom to hear Louis. At that time Louis Armstrong could have been elected Mayor of the South Side; he was loved. I can still see him being carried clear across the dance floor of that huge Savoy Ballroom by his cheering fans. Tell me, when's the last time you saw a jazz musician carried on the shoulders of his fans? When Louis picked up his trumpet and blew he was "callin' his children home." That man could blow no wrong. And what a warm person to be around.

The joint was always packed and it would take us minutes to get to the back where the bandstand was. But Louis would see us at once, and his face would light up and we'd feel warm inside. And right after the set we'd go back with the band into the band room. We hung out there like groupies. Most likely Joe Oliver—King—would come in for his visit and there'd be a lot of good feeling in the room. And somebody would say something funny, and that would give Louis an opening and you couldn't beat Louis at being funny—not even Wingy. And we'd laugh through the whole intermission, and then slowly walk Louis back to the stand. And then we'd wait for the band to begin playing again, and for it to be Louis's turn to play. Man, the guy could really blow then. How we wanted to be in the same league. Not the formula, just the feeling. To be able to say the same things, just for the pleasure of saying them.

Wingy had a big bear coat that we took turns wearing. Louis used to greet us with "Who's the bear tonight?" The boys in the band kept a flat especially for themselves, to be able to drop in at all hours and relax. You know the conversation that takes place on the record "Monday Date" where Louis says to Earl Hines, "I bet if you had a half pint of Mrs. Circha's gin . . ." (and I'm spelling her name the way it sounds; I've never seen it in print). Well, that was the name of the woman who kept the flat for the boys. For a half-buck you got a cream pitcher full of gin, which was passed around as far as it would go. In those days that was what the boys drank.

Louis, knowing I loved blues, took me and Wingy to a barbecue place on State Street near 48th where the primitives, the pianists that came up from the South, hung out. They'd fall in there looking for a bite to eat, or a buck to pick up, because they had a kitty there, and if you played you'd pick up something. That's when my real jazz education started. The place itself was a wooden shack, badly in need of repairs, really not much to look at, but to me it couldn't look better. It was everything I could wish for. That place and its people taught me about the blues.

After that first time Wingy and I went there with our gang—Krupa, Freeman, Tesch, and the rest. Wingy didn't go that much. He was a trumpet player, and what a trumpet player wanted to hear was Louis. But I never lost the habit of going there. Often I'd go there alone. One night on entering the barbecue I heard a three-piece band playing: sax, piano, and drums. I got acquainted immediately. That rhythm impelled me to say hello. The drummer's name was Papa Couch. I forget the sax player's name. The piano player was Jackson.

A few days after I'd met him I happened to hear him playing alone and I was startled. He could really play the blues—they flowed out without an effort. I can't begin to tell you what that sound did to me. This was the first time I had heard the blues really being played. I found out later on that he'd just been released from a hospital. Been laying there with a broken leg, thinking about that wife of his who'd left him. When he got out he had the blues. He was really down. When he sat down at the piano those notes would tell all that.

Art followed many pianists on the South Side. Little Brother Montgomery said to him a few years before he died, "You know you used to follow me." But it was Jackson who taught him the most.

I followed Jackson for days. After a while I noticed that he wasn't playing the blues so much. He bought a new suit; I met his new girl. Soon he stopped playing the blues altogether. He would play popular music. Well, I played popular music better than he did, so I would ask him to play the blues. Finally he said to me, "Man, what you always asking me to play the blues; you know, I ain't got the blues." That's how I learned the blues was more than music.

There were no schools where one could go and learn to play jazz. These people were my teachers. I went among them, lived with them, absorbed their music, and came away enriched. Every night that I was free and had some money I'd go down to the barbecue joint, eat, and then sit around putting my nickels into the player piano, with the rolls that were made by black musicians. They also had a jukebox of sorts, which had records by pianists who were blues pianists—Hersal Thomas, Pine Top Smith. I heard those people on that juke box, and they were tremendous, and this was the real fine blues of that time. And of course I heard Leroy Carr.

The part about the barbecue place that was so tremendous was that it exposed you to a bit of the life that these people lived. I mean after they got used to you, so you was part of the furniture. They knew you were there but they could still act themselves. I still recall the time I came in there alone and about a dozen colored folks were sitting and singing and I sat down and they kept on singing and I felt good, and it sounded good. I came to be accepted by these people as one of them, and believe me I never abused the privilege. I never messed with their women. I was just plain music hungry.

There was a grandfather there, or a very elderly guy who had to carry a cane to walk, and he would do a dance with that cane and knock you out. The music would get going and he'd get up there and do this little shuffle thing, and somebody would drum and somebody would sing, and all this would go on any one evening that you were there listening.

Many times they'd ask me to play. I was kidded plenty. Someone would holler, "Play the blues, Art," and when I played they would laugh. Not mean, but they would laugh. That hurt, but I couldn't blame them. I hadn't as yet learned the idiom. I was entranced by their language but I hadn't learned to speak it. The next night I was there again, putting my nickels into that piano.

That music did something to me I can't explain. I had to hear it. That's one feeling that never left me. Jackson would say to me, "Art, I'll show you how to play the blues; just watch my hands." And I'd answer him, "No, don't teach me, just play." Because I knew I couldn't learn that way. I knew that I had to feel the blues myself and then they'd flow easily.

Eventually, of course, people stopped laughing. Art remembers especially a time when he visited Jackson

at a cabaret on West Division Street. After climbing about twenty-five stairs and knocking on a door, an eye would peer out at you from behind a peep-hole. If you looked OK you got in. Jackson got me in the first time. After that they knew me. Inside was a lunch counter, farther on a gambling room, with the piano going. Jackson insisted that I play the piano. Well, the crap game was making a lot of noise, but some time after I started playing it got quiet. Those gamblers had stopped playing and were listening. Man, it's like no other feeling I can describe. Everyone with you, and you're it. It was like graduating. Jackson took me home with him and I lived at his house for days.

Most of us Chicago lads learned from the great Negro players who went there from New Orleans and elsewhere. They inspired us; we came, we listened, we learned. If piano was your instrument you dug Earl Hines or Teddy Weatherford. Trumpet? Louis Armstrong. Clarinetists followed Johnny Dodds or Jimmy Noone. Drummers paid extra attention to Baby Dodds.

So it went, with most of us not falling in love with the music but with the Race too. You could get lost out on the South Side. It was a new world, with so much to see and oh, so much to hear. I heard more music then by accident than I do today on purpose. Just walking down the street early in the morning, and hearing some brother whistle a greeting to another on his way to work.

I would bring two or three people at a time to the barbecue place. I brought Benny Moylan; he played sax. I brought Johnny Lane; he played clarinet. Two fine white pianists came later, George Zack and the late Frank Melrose. I don't know how many others they brought. It became a place to go, a hangout.

A couple of doors from the barbecue was a storefront church, a black church. And many times as you walked by you would hear them having religion, and the beat going on, and the after beat. People singing—shouting. A church with that sound coming out of it. Right across the street was a flat, and a drummer lived there, Papa Couch. Papa and Mama Couch. I don't know how schooled he was. I know he owned a set of drums, and I know I liked the way he played. It was a simple style, not far removed from those small bands that played for nickels and dimes and quarters anywhere on the streets of Chicago. Sometimes you'd catch them on the bridge on Michigan Avenue, just by the river. You'd catch these little bands playing, you know, with a washtub [bass].

Papa Couch had a player piano, and you could drink gin, which was illegal, of course, and smoke tea. That's another high that came from New Orleans. So many times we'd go across the street. Dave Tough came along one night. Dave was a little under the weather, and he needed help. And the squad car happened to go by and saw a black and white helping a white across the street, and that looked suspicious. So they followed us into the apartment moments later and arrested everybody because they were drinking gin.

The police put them all in a cell together until court opened in the morning. Tesch's wife was along that night. Art doesn't remember who else, except that there was a group of them. They didn't have a bad night of it; they talked and smoked their tea. In those days the police didn't recognize the smell of marijuana, because so few people smoked it.

Next day I heard a judge dismiss us by saying, "Why don't you stay in your own neighborhood?" And of course if everybody stayed in their own neighborhood there'd be no enrichment. What if Columbus had stayed in his own neighborhood?

On the South Side the music was everywhere:

It's summer, 1929, 35th and State, a record shop. The turntable spins and the music is being heard outside: the curb is occupied with listeners. It's the same record being played over and over. I ask the clerk, "Ma'am, what is that?"

"That's Leroy Carr; it's 'That's All Right for You, Baby.'" I must have a copy, and she sells me the only one she has, the one spinning on the turntable. As I leave, the curb listeners disperse. That record has been like medicine to me at times. It's a bit of greatness. He played himself inside of me.

Or there was the time Art was walking the South Side, "probably high."

It was dead of winter. Cold, man, like it only can get cold, icy, in dear old Chi. Not that it made any difference. I still made my merry way, looking, seeking out all the colored music I could find. Night time, of course; whoever went looking for it in the day? So I found myself alone, walking the streets of the South Side. Just to hear a colored man whistling a blues paid off. Not like today, with some Tin Pan Alley tune coming from the lips. No, man, this was still the real thing. But look here; isn't that Stepin Fetchit advertised at this theater? Darned if it ain't. But that below it; man, I'm in luck today. If I ain't dreaming that's Bessie Smith. Let's go.

Inside, it was the picture that was on. Not a damn thing about it I can remember. All I know is I waited it out. There it goes, finished. And now the orchestra climbs into the pit, the overture, and that was a honey; and there's Stepin Fetchit. There's a guy that surprised me. I'd always pictured him as a guy that moves slower than slow. That was his Hollywood character. This must be a different guy. Funny? He had me roaring. But I was in for a treat. Evidently I had caught the first show of the week. The band and the actor weren't exactly together, but Mr. S. sure straightened that out in a hurry. Talk about a guy doing his act and rehearsing the band at the same time, this guy was it. How he improvised. Instead of blowing his top when the music went wrong, he called loudly for a phone and the prop man brought it out. He got on the phone and called—guess who?—the orchestra leader, and in a sweet professional way, yet never losing his audience, he straightened him out on what had to be, and what wasn't. It was my first and most impressive lesson in stagecraft. And that audience was right with him; they didn't miss a trick. It was sure something to hear.

Now comes the big hush. Just the piano going. It's the blues. Something tightens up in me. Man, what will she look like? I ain't ever seen her before.

Now I hear her voice and I know this is it . . . my lucky day. I'm hearing the best and I'm seeing her, too. There she is. Resplendent is the word, the only one that can describe her. Of course, she ain't beautiful, although she is to me. A white, shimmering evening gown, a great big woman, and she completely dominates the stage and the whole house when she sings "The Yellow Dog Blues." Ah! I don't know, she just reaches out and grabs and holds me. There's no explaining her singing, her voice. She don't need a mike; she don't use one. Everybody can hear her. This gal sings from the heart. She never lets me get away from her once. As she sings, she walks slowly around the stage, her head sort of bowed. From where I'm sitting I'm not sure she even has her eyes open. On and on, number after number, the same hush, the great performance, the deafening applause. We won't let her stop. What a woman. If she has any faults, like the big head, the prima donna, it doesn't seep through. You just don't get that feeling from her. You just know you're listening to the greatest blues singer you've ever heard.

Outside it's still cold. I don't know when I get up to go and I'm sure I'm not sure where I'm going; just walking. But there's a record playing back something that was recorded, recorded in my head. There's that one woman's voice, "Oh, you easy rider, why don't you hurry back home. . . ." So help me, I still hear it.

Besides Louis Armstrong, besides Jackson, besides Bessie Smith, there was Earl Hines, whom Art used to hear at the Grand Terrace. "The first time I heard Earl Hines," says Art, "it made me want to take my hands and throw them in the lake." And there was the Dodds brothers' band (Johnny on clarinet and Baby on drums; both former members of the King Oliver band), who impressed Art most for their tight ensemble, so different from "the players that only hear themselves. When their chorus is over, the music has ceased. Like the guy who's thinking about what he's going to say while you're talking." The Dodds brothers played

at a club on the Near North Side, Kelly's Stables. It was a two-story building. Nothing on the first floor but a cleaned-out stable. You went upstairs to a big room (I'd guess two hundred people could get in). Red table cloths, no decor, swinging waiters who sang on occasion. Plus music. When you walked in, you pulsated. Every number was an entity. Yet you were recognized as you came in their club. They smiled, nodded, but it kept coming out so good. A six-piece band, stretched straight across the bandstand, the drums at one end, the piano at the other, in between absolute togetherness. Everybody listening to each other. What one played was important to the other.

I think we were all listening, and to the same thing. I'm still listening, and I'm still hearing it. It's part of me, as if we were married. I hear what's going on today. You play the blues well in any language and I'll like it. You don't have to wear a 1920s costume to catch my eye. But to begin with, I do have a music. I have a heritage. This isn't just something that can come unglued from a sheet of music. This is something that goes on inside of me.

And you want to know if I still practice? That's the least I can do for what I've gotten. As my doctor once told me, "I haven't arrived; I practice medicine." Me too. I haven't arrived. Just making the trip daily.

Buck Clayton

These excerpts from Buck Clayton's Jazz World *(1986; with Nancy Miller Elliott) both suggest the warm and sympathetic qualities of this celebrated trumpet player and give us a highly personal glimpse of Louis Armstrong.*

One day I read a poster that said the George E. Lee band of Kansas City was coming to Parsons and was going to play for a dance about a month from the time that I read the poster. Everybody was excited. That was the biggest band to play Parsons as far as I knew. I couldn't dance very well. I wasn't interested in dancing. We were all one hundred percent boys, you know, into football, baseball and basketball, and we had just started to like girls. There was a little girl, Sarah Bright, who lived across the street from me and, knowing that we were going to the dance, we decided to practice on how to dance two or three weeks before the band got there, so we could dance a little bit at least. We practiced for days, one-step, two-step, waltzes and all the dances of those days. Hour upon hour. Finally the big day came. George E. Lee rolled into town in a fleet of beautiful automobiles. Cords, I believe, were the names of the cars.

We all went to the dance and as soon as I entered the hall I saw all of those beautiful instruments standing on the bandstand and I flipped. In the band was a saxophonist, Clarence Taylor, known professionally as Tweety Taylor, whose father and family had lived in Parsons. There was also Baby Lovett on drums, Herman Walder on alto sax, George Lee and his sister Julia. The rest of the band I didn't know. I stood in front of this band and watched them as they began to tune up. I became rooted right to the spot. I didn't see anybody as all I could see was the band. I didn't know what people behind me were doing and cared less. I didn't dance one single dance during the whole four hours that the band played. I didn't even see the little girl, Sarah, that had spent so much time learning to dance with me. All I could see were trumpets, saxophones, trombones and all the other instruments while listening to this beautiful jazz music. When the band left town Sarah didn't speak to me for weeks because I had sabotaged all of her dancing plans, aside from it being very embarrassing to her. Some of the songs that George sang that night I still remember, although it was my first time hearing them. He sang "Chloe, if I could be with you," "Eleven-thirty Saturday Night," and

"Mississippi Mud." He looked so sharp in his Oxford-gray coat, pearl-gray vest and gambler striped pants. When he sang he snapped his fingers. He had a beautiful voice, a strong voice, that could fill up the hall without a microphone. He used a megaphone. He was really sharp.

During the dance, however, I talked with one of the trumpet players in the band, Bob Russell. He was one cool cat and so sharp. He had four or five different kinds of horns in front of him. He took me under his wing a little bit and told me how much money they made, what nice times they had, and how he enjoyed playing. He had just joined George's band and was a well-known trumpeter among the "territory bands," as they were called. The territory bands were mostly southern and midwestern bands that were nearly always on the road. I think Bob later moved out to Seattle or Oregon.

After talking to Bob I said to myself, "This is it! I'm going to get a trumpet." I'd not yet heard of Louis Armstrong nor Duke Ellington. My Dad wanted me to get a trumpet too because he wanted me to play in his church orchestra, which I couldn't do playing piano. I couldn't join my high-school band because I only played piano. I finally bought a trumpet and I was so happy with it. With a trumpet you can carry it with you, take it to bed with you if you feel like it, polish it, keep it clean and tune it up, whereas with a piano you can't tune it yourself unless you happen to be a piano tuner. Sometimes you play on a piano that can cut all of your fingers up because the ivory on the keyboard is broken and jagged. With a trumpet you can take it out on a field and play it out there all by yourself. So I got the trumpet and, boy, was I happy. The first song I learned to play was "Five Foot Two, Eyes of Blue."

I began practicing with my Dad, who taught me the scales. There was another kid in Parsons who had been playing a few years and also played with my Dad's chapel orchestra—Clarence Trice. Between Clarence and my father I learned all of the scales on the trumpet. Clarence later played with big Kansas City bands, notably Andy Kirk's great band. By having played piano I could already read music. That was no problem. I just had to learn the fingering to the trumpet. I practiced and practiced while all the time doing other little jobs around town. I set pins in a bowling alley for an Italian guy, John Delesega. I shined shoes, I sold papers.

About the time I was seventeen a band came through my home from Cherryvale, Kansas: Hoot and Stomp Bailey's band was nothing like George E. Lee's band as there were only about seven musicians. They had one trumpet player and he had taken ill that night and couldn't play. They asked all over town. "Do you know anybody that can play trumpet tonight in our trumpet player's place?" Naturally everybody said, "Yeah, get that little Clayton boy. He's learning to play cornet." So they hired me as there was no one else around that could play anything at all. All night long we played four songs because that was all that I knew: "Five Foot Two, Eyes of Blue," "Hard-to-get Gertie," "'Deed I Do" and "Dinah." We played these four songs over and over again, but just the same I made five dollars for that gig. It was the first time that I had ever made any money playing trumpet in my life.

ABOUT THIS TIME Louis Armstrong made a return trip to California. This time he was to play again at Frank Sebastian's Cotton Club, only this time he was to play with Les Hite and his orchestra. Broomfield and Greely headed the revue. Les Hite had a good band. There were only two big bands in L.A. at the time, our band (Charlie Echols) and the Les Hite band. The first time I heard Louis play was on a recording coming out of a shop window as I was walking down Central Avenue. I just stopped still and stood listening to that golden tone. I had never heard anyone play with such soul. I really had expected to hear Louis play "hot jazz" and I didn't know that he could play with so much expression. My first hearing of Louis's playing was on "I'm Confessin' That I Love You." The wonderful introduction that C. L. Burke made on guitar knocked me out even before the recording had got to the first chorus. Then Pops came in and sang it and played it so beautifully. I guess I was spellbound. I said, "Gee-zus, that's who I want to play like." Pops was the highlight of my career. I listened to other recordings such as "Ding Dong Daddy from Dumas," "Sweethearts on Parade," "Just a Gigolo" and "Body and Soul." Now there was a beautiful piece of work. "Body and Soul" happens to be my favorite ballad and Louie did it so beautifully. When Louie sang the vocal to "Body and Soul" there was a trumpet solo behind him, just a straight melody played by George Orendorff of the Hite band. The way he played that solo so straight and muted was also a highlight of the record. I began to gather all of Louie's recordings that I could get my hands on, and I would listen to him every night when he would broadcast from the Cotton Club.

One night he did something on the radio program that I had never heard anyone do before on a trumpet, which was to make a gliss. A gliss means to slide from one low note to a high note without any in-between notes, in other words like a trombone would do. But a trombone is made with a slide so it's only natural, but to hear a trumpet do that with three valves, I just couldn't understand how that was possible. I thought to myself, "Louis has got to be playing a slide trumpet, because I don't believe he can be doing that with an ordinary trumpet." And then I had seen some pictures of Pops actually playing a slide trumpet. I talked with some fellows who were working at the Cotton Club with Pops—the famous Berry brothers. Nyas Berry was a good friend of mine and I asked him, "Is Pops playing a slide trumpet?"

He said, "No, Buck, he's playing a trumpet just like yours."

I said, "But how does he do that? How does he make a gliss like that?"

He said, "I don't know how he does it but he does. His horn is exactly like yours."

I said, "I don't believe it."

So then Nyas and James, one of the other brothers, said, "You meet us here tomorrow at six o'clock and we'll take you out to the club and you can see the show and talk to Pops."

"Beautiful," I said, "I'll be there."

I was there at five o'clock waiting for them to show up at six. They came and picked me up and took me out to Culver City. I was impressed by the Sebastian Cotton Club. It was a huge green and white club and Frank was very nice also, a nice-looking Italian guy. I went with the Berry brothers to their room first. Then they said, "Now come on, we'll take you to Pops's dressing room."

When they took me in Louis's room it was so full of admirers and fans that I could hardly find Louis in there himself. Finally they got to Pops and said, "Pops, here's a little young cat that wants to play trumpet and he wants to talk to you." Louis was so nice, he said, "Oh that's nice, nice, nice."

I said, "Mr. Armstrong, will you show me how you do this on your horn?"

He said, "Do what?"

I said, "Well, how do you make it sound like a soprano trombone? How do you make it slide up and down?" He took his horn out of his case. With all these people making noise in his room he says, "Now, this is my horn." And he showed it to me. He had a Conn horn at the time, a gold Conn trumpet. He showed me his mouthpiece and he also pulled out a picture of himself and autographed it to me and I was so thrilled. Then he said, "I'll show you how I do it, but if we were down in New Orleans, I wouldn't. In New Orleans whenever I did it, I'd put a handkerchief over my valves so nobody could see how I did it, but you follow me and I'll show you."

He left the room with all the noise and the bunch of people in there and walked down the hall. I followed him, right behind him, and I found out later after I got in the hall that he was going to the john. We went to the toilet and Louis sat down on the stool to do whatever he had to do. He had a white handkerchief tied around his head and he said, "Now I'll tell you." Then he said, "Wait a minute. Here." And he gave me a cigarette. It was a brown cigarette, not the kind that I had been used to seeing. I looked at the cigarette and I guess he knew that I didn't know just what it was, so he said, "Here, let me have it." So he sat on the stool and lit it. He puffed on it and then he said, "Now I'll tell you." Then he puffed again and handed it to me, kinda grinnin' like. I took it and I puffed on it too. I thought right away of my mother who used to talk about dope fiends and coke heads and everything that she didn't want me to be. She had impressed so much on me about taking narcotics, but with Louis Armstrong I would have done anything. So I puffed on it again and give it back to Pops, he puffed on it again and gave it back to me. This went on until the whole cigarette was gone. Then Pops said, "Now here's how you make the gliss." He told me, "You push your valves half way down, not all the way down. All three valves. You push 'em half way down and tighten up your lips, then you'll be able to make the gliss." I later learned to do it. I did it very well after Pops showed me, but when Louis finished with the toilet and we went back into the room again with all the noise and the people, I didn't see him too much more that night because he had to run out and do his show.

That night I went home and I got down on my knees and I prayed to God. I said, "Oh God, now that I'm a dope addict, please forgive me. Please don't let me become a real habitual dope addict. I just did it one time, please stop me now. Please God, please stop me, I don't want to end up being a junkie." I just knew that I had done the worst thing in the world, which really it wasn't because I found out from later use that pot never affected me in any kind of way except that it makes one feel elevated. It never affected Louis either. It's not like being drunk where you may develop into being an alcoholic. With pot you just smoke it without it becoming a habit. If you have it, OK, if not, OK. It never did anything to me. Sometimes I'd take it like a drink or cocktail just to perk me up, and it usually made me more attentive to what I was doing.

Hoagy Carmichael

*The famous songwriter/singer published two versions of his autobiography—*The Stardust Road *(1947) and* Sometimes I Wonder *(1965; with Stephen Longstreet). Both are nostalgic, and both depend upon an extraordinary recollection of decades-old dialogue—or perhaps in the case of* Sometimes I Wonder, *on collaborator Longstreet's novelistic talents. Both books, of course, focus on Carmichael's early, close friendship with Bix Beiderbecke.*

The Stardust Road

Christmas Eve in New Castle, with the little maimed tree, was somewhat different from the night I went up to Chicago to see Bix. It's the summer of 1923. We took two quarts of bathtub gin, a package of muggles, and headed for the black-and-tan joint where King Oliver's band was playing.

The king featured two trumpets, piano, a bass fiddle, and a clarinet. As I sat down to light my first muggle, Bix gave the sign to a big black fellow, playing second trumpet for Oliver, and he slashed into "Bugle Call Rag."

I dropped my cigarette and gulped my drink. Bix was on his feet, his eyes popping. For taking the first chorus was that second trumpet, Louis Armstrong. Louis was taking it fast. Bob Gillette slid off his chair and under the table. He was excitable that way.

"Why," I moaned, "why isn't everybody in the world here to hear that?" I meant it. Something as unutterably stirring as that deserved to be heard by the world.

Then the muggles took effect and my body got light. Every note Louis hit was perfection. I ran to the piano and took the place of Louis's wife. They swung into "Royal Garden Blues." I had never heard the tune before, but somehow I knew every note. I couldn't miss. I was floating in a strange deep-blue whirlpool of jazz.

It wasn't marijuana. The muggles and the gin were, in a way, stage props. It was the music. The music took me and had me and it made me right.

Louis Armstrong was Bix Beiderbecke's idol, and when we went out the next night to crash an S.A.E. dance where Bix was playing with the Wolverines, I learned that Bix was no imitation of Armstrong. The Wolverines sounded better to me than the New Orleans Rhythm Kings. Theirs was a stronger rhythm and the licks that Jimmy Hartwell, George Johnson, and Bix played were precise and beautiful.

Bix's breaks were not as wild as Armstrong's, but they were hot and he selected each note with musical care. He showed me that jazz could be musical and beautiful as well as hot. He showed me that tempo doesn't mean fast. His music affected me in a different way. Can't tell you how—like licorice, you have to eat some.

THE COURSE OF a wandering mind and an unreliable memory is erratic. The path of this piece is helplessly jagged from an absence of chronology.

However, there is a time. There is *one* time, a little fraction of an era, to which my mind reverts. I can remember that time clearly.

That is the spring of 1924.

I expect that Bix brings this about. He of the funny little mouth, the sad eyes that popped a little as if in surprise when those notes showered from his horn.

The spring of '24. Seems like the moon was always out that spring . . . seems like the air of those nights was doubly laden with sweet smells. The air was thick and soft and pale purple. Grass was greener . . . moon was yellower.

Of course it helps to be young, and I was young.

Take a drink of whisky that tastes like kerosene in your mouth and a blowtorch going down. "Best I ever tasted."

"Wonderful. Have another, Hoagy, and turn the record over."

The Wolverines had played a dance on the campus—one of ten dances I had booked for them—and Bix and I were lying in front of the phonograph early in the morning. We were playing the "Firebird" music of Stravinsky.

"Wonderful. Have another slug."

"What's wonderful?"

"Music."

"Sure. Whisky too."

"Guy used to be a lawyer."

"Who?"

"Stravinsky."

"Naw, Rimsky-Korsakov touted him offa the law."

"Touted him offa the torts, huh?"

"I dunno who he slept with."

"I said torts."

"Hell, I've slept with tarts myself."

"It's wonderful. Wonderful. Let's have another drink."

"Sure is. Turn the record over."

There was a long silence. "Why'nt you write music, Hoagy?" Bix asked softly.

"Naw, you're the one that writes the music. Every time you put that horn up to your mouth you write music."

"You write music, Hoagy," Bix said again like he hadn't heard me.

"You write yours different every time."

"What's wrong with that?" Bix asked. "I like it different. Like Rimsky-Korsakov. He heard this Stravinsky, told him to give up the law . . ."

"The torts . . ."

"Leave that crummy joke alone," Bix said. "I got that crummy joke."

"Stravinsky study law?"

"Sure. Young guy like you. He studied law then Rimsy—ah, hell, you know who I mean—he told him to write music. So he wrote his. They dance to it."

"Dance to it?"

"Sure." Bix got up and did an entrechat, fell down and lay where he fell. I turned the record over. "Ballet," he said. "Hell, it's wonderful."

"Sure is," I said. "Give me another drink."

We lay there and listened. The music filled us with some terrible longing. Something, coupled with liquor, that was wonderfully moving; but it made us very close and it made us lonely too. With a feeling of release and a feeling of elation . . . and a feeling of longing too.

Silence. The record had come to a stop. A long silence and I was afraid to speak; afraid I'd spoil something. I can see Bix now, lying there, the music still playing in his head and me knowing it . . . afraid to speak; afraid I might spoil a note.

Finally I spoke. A little shyly. "I'm learning to be a composer."

"Who's teaching you?" Bix asked idly, rolling his head on the floor so he could look at me.

"Everybody," I said. "Everybody's teaching me to be a composer. I learned to be a composer a long time ago. Every time I see a pretty girl I learn more how to be a composer. Every time I play a Bucktown dance I learn how to be a composer."

"Nothing wrong with you," Bix said, "except you're drunk."

"So're you."

"I never said I wasn't." He stopped. "Music kind of hits together in your head. Hurts you across the top of your nose if you can't blow it out . . ."

"But you can't blow it all out."

"You can try."

"Bix," I said.

"Yeah."

"Like what . . . kind of like with a girl . . . ?"

There was another long pause. Bix started up the phonograph and we lay there and listened to the music. Bix wasn't thinking about what I had asked him.

He was feeling something, though, and I was, too. It was the same thing but we couldn't put the words to it. It disturbed us. Ours were a medley of moods.

"Kind of," he said, but he hadn't thought about it.

"Like going first to school when you are a little kid and being scared?"

He nodded, narrowing his eyes and looking at me.

"Like a quick storm comes up on the river . . . and a horn . . . Maybe Armstrong or Oliver, and the storm . . ." he said.

"Put on the next record, let's have a drink."

"Like playing a steam calliope on a riverboat with it hot as hell and the people dancing, all wet with sweat. Like blowing a horn," Bix said. "Like blowing a cornet. Like blowing a cornet."

"Bix," I said, "I'm gonna play a cornet."

"Sure. Everybody ought to play a cornet. Fun. Let's have a little one."

We had a little one and the sound washed over us as we lay there . . . two kids, kind of drunk, full of something and not able to put the words on it. But together, awfully together.

"Funny little horn," I said. "I'm gonna play me a horn."

IT WAS NEARING the Christmas holidays. Bix blew into Indianapolis and asked me to go down to Richmond with him to hear him make some records. He phoned me at my house and I hurried down to pick him up, in my new Ford, a Christmas present to myself.

When I found him he told me that he was on his way to make some records for Gennett, the same outfit that had made our record in the fall. I was delighted to go.

Remembering my own nerve-racking experience, I thought it would be doubly pleasant to be there with no worries of my own. I asked Bix who was going to be with him on the date.

"We're going to make some records in 'slow-drag' style," Bix said, "and I've got some guys who can really go. Tommy Dorsey, Howdy Quicksel, Don Murray, Paul Mertz, and Tommy Gargano. They are going to drive down from Detroit and meet me."

"Boy," I exclaimed, "that's really gonna be somethin'. What are you gonna make?"

"Hell, I don't know. Just make some up, I guess."

"How about me driving you over tonight?"

"That'll be swell," Bix said. "The guys are bringing three quarts . . ."

"When do we leave?"

"Oh, three or four," Bix said, the idea of sleeping never entering his head. He looked at a clock that showed midnight. "Let's go over to the Ohio Theatre and jam awhile."

"Now you're talkin' . . ."

We got to the theater after closing and took our places at the grand pianos in the pit. There, all alone, we banged out chorus after chorus of "Royal Garden Blues." And each interpretation was hotter than the one before. First one of us would play the bass chords while the other played hot licks and then we'd reverse the process. When we finally wore out it was time to leave.

We started for Richmond. And that night I reached greatness.

Bix is dead now, and you'll have to take my word for it, but on that night I hit the peak. We were halfway to Richmond, of a cold dark morning, when we stopped and for some reason Bix took out his horn.

He cut loose with a blast to warn the farmers and to start the dogs howling and I remembered that my own horn, long unused, was lying in the back of the car. I got it out.

Solemnly we exchanged A's.

"'Way Down Yonder in New Orleans,'" Bix said.

He had hit one I knew pretty well and I was in my glory.

And then Bix was off. Clean wonderful banners of melody filled the air, carved the countryside. Split the still night. The trees and the ground and the sky made the tones so right.

I battled along to keep up a rhythmic lead while Bix laid it out for the tillers of the soil. He finally finished in one great blast of pyrotechnic improvisation, then took his horn down from his mouth.

"Hoagy," he said thoughtfully, "you weren't bad."

I had achieved greatness. We drove on into the night.

Sometimes I Wonder

Traveling with a big band is like being an inmate in a traveling zoo. Gags, ribs, girl trouble, money trouble, just trouble, bull sessions, card games, taking over the spare upper. Socks are traded, shirts stolen.

Chicago ran wide open. The Capone mob liked show folk. Whiteman, a powerful drinker in those days, had target practice with pistols, and beer drinking contests with some of the gang chiefs; at least, he often told the story.

In the Uptown Theatre in Chicago, where Whiteman's orchestra was playing, I stood in the wings and watched the boys go. Bing was often late. Between shows we gathered in the small basement rooms backstage and played hot jazz. Bix and Jimmy Dorsey were almost always in on these sessions. I also practiced what, for lack of a better word, I called my singing. I had a good deal of it to do in "Washboard" and the damn recording date was approaching.

Bing came around while I was rehearsing once and stood there, hands in pockets, smoking a pipe.

"Mind if I glom on to the words, Hoagy?"

"No—but why?"

"I'd just like to learn it," Bing said, expressionless.

"What for?"

"It's such a swell number, chum, I'd like to learn it."

"Well, sure."

I didn't realize until later that Whiteman wanted some voice insurance in case I bombed. He wanted somebody there who could do it if I didn't. Bing was being kind to me. He didn't hint to me I might flop. They wanted to make a good record whether I was on it or not. Bing was always kind and calm, but he was more given to living it up before he became an American institution.

So I exercised my voice and observed life backstage. Crowds of jazz followers flocked to the stage entrance to see Bix. Many were musicians. They'd crowd around him and urge him to play.

"Come on Bix—just a few bars."

Bix didn't like meeting so many people. "It's driving me nuts. I try to remember them all, to keep them straight in my mind and not offend anyone."

"That's fame, Bix," I said.

"It's bad for my nerves. I get the heebie-jeebies."

There was always a bottle in his room. I would hear Whiteman ask, "How's Bix *feeling* this afternoon?"

Bix was Whiteman's pet. He loved Bix as if he had been his own boy. But the bottle stayed.

The side of "Washboard Blues" was made at the Victor studios, with "Among My Souvenirs" on the other side. I was so nervous I ruined a half-dozen master records and the best of a double-time trio arrangement. I had a lot of vocalizing to do and the piano solo I had done for the Gennett record was included in the arrangement. It was, for me, nerve-racking, jumping from one act to another. Whiteman remained calm.

"We'll get it all on this one."

I looked at Bing to step in for me. He looked away.

The control man said, "Recording—side six."

The opening notes began. Finally we got a master that was approved. When Leroy Shield came out of the control, I thought I saw a tear on his face. We were emotional slobs about music in those days.

I was a limp, wet, wreck—so relieved I was still alive and now *silent*.

Paul Whiteman was the biggest thing in bands. His father had been a classical musician who had a high school named after him in Denver. But Paul never practiced his violin properly, became a packing house worker (our early jobs crossed here), then a taxi driver. He drifted into popular music and soon had it organized.

As the King of Jazz, he was the big name in the business, taking a fatherly interest in his men. He was a powerful liver, drinker, and worker. My being with him far exceeded anything that had happened to me musically so far. How much more it meant than the acquisition of an LL.B. college degree! College men would soon be peddling Hoover apples on street corners.

Any inner contest between Hoagy the musician and Hoagland the lawyer never bothered me from that day on. I would be forced into mundane work and might even have deep indigo periods of doubt and discouragement about my ability to succeed as a hot composer, but it was now certain that the basic pattern of my life and work was set. It was not a turning point, it was a break-through, all troops committed.

I left Chicago after the recording session in a burst of jubilation hardly comparable to anything I had known before.

Eddie Condon

More tales of early days of fun and poverty—this time from Eddie Condon, the indefatigable Dixieland guitarist, entrepreneur, and jazz propagandist; from his book We Called It Music *(1947; with Thomas Sugrue). The cast of characters includes Jimmy McPartland, Bud Freeman, Frank Teschemaker, Gene Krupa, Jack Teagarden, Mezz Mezzrow, and Joe Sullivan.*

We checked in at the Forrest Hotel on Forty-ninth Street west of Broadway. It was a Sunday night in May 1928. McKenzie took me to the window and pointed to St. Malachy's Church across the street. "A very historical place," he said. "They held the Rudolph Valentino funeral there." I was impressed, but I wanted to see Fifth Avenue. "It's folded until tomorrow," McKenzie explained. "It hasn't any joints; just stores." I made him take me anyhow, and we looked at St. Patrick's Cathedral. McKenzie regarded it with awe. "That's Saks Fifth Avenue," he said, pointing to a building on the next corner. "It's a clipjoint for dames."

On the way back we stopped at a speakeasy. "Pick any place without lights and knock at the door," McKenzie said. "It's a saloon." I was surprised when the bartender put the bottle on the bar and walked away. "Are we allowed to pour our own?" I said. In Chicago under the Capone system the bartenders and waiters did the pouring. "This is a gentleman's town," McKenzie said. "Very honorable."

Next morning I noticed garbage cans on the street; Red explained that New York has no alleys. "Everything is right out in front, very honorable, like I said. In Chicago all this stuff is put in the alleys. You never know what kind of a town you are living in." We walked up to the Mayflower at Sixtieth Street and Central Park West to see Jimmy MacPartland and Bud Freeman. They were surprised to see us, and glad. Their unpaid rent was up to their ears; Pollack's band was idle, waiting to open at a Brooklyn theater with Bee Palmer, the singer, and her husband, Al Siegel. The Whiteman band was in Brooklyn at the moment; we jumped in a subway—it was my first ride in a sewer—and went to visit Bix. We found him in his dressing room. Three hundred dollars a week hadn't changed him; he still needed a suit that would fit him. We had a few drinks and played a little—Bix found a saxophone for Bud and a cornet for Jimmy; I played drums on the dressing table with two empty pint bottles until one of them exploded. "That was a wonderful effect," Bix said.

We went back again to Brooklyn to hear Pollack and the boys with Bee Palmer. "She's heard our records," Bud told us. "She thinks they're sensational. She wants us to work with her." Bee was a Chicago girl; I had met her at the College Inn. She was a beautiful blonde, sang superbly, and had the advantage of a husband who was not only an accompanist but a fine vocal coach. Backstage we talked with her; she had a plan.

"Lou Schwartz is opening a new nightclub," she said. "He wants me to go into it. I'd like to take your band with me. I'll introduce you to the audience and explain your music. Once people hear it they'll like it."

That night she took the four of us—McKenzie, MacPartland, Bud, and myself—to the Club Richman. We sat around a table and watched Schwartz become aware that he wasn't going to get Bee without accepting us. Every time he talked about the new club, the Chateau Madrid, Bee countered with a eulogy of our records. George Olsen's band played background music while she talked. "You've heard these records?" she said. "Yes," Schwartz said, as if admitting he had beaten his wife. "Aren't they wonderful?" she demanded. "Wonderful," Schwartz said sadly. "You see," Bee said, turning to us.

The deal was set. Freeman and MacPartland left on tour with Pollack, prepared to return to New York in time for the opening. We were to use a New York bass player; I went to Chicago to get Teschemaker, Sullivan, and Krupa; McKenzie went to St. Louis to see his wife and son. Panico was amiable when I asked him for Sullivan without the customary two weeks notice. Nothing had bothered Louis since he learned to play the cornet in Italy. His instructor held needles against his cheeks; if they puffed out as Louis blew, the needles went into them. "Those needles hurt like hell," he told me once. "Naturally I learned to blow the right way."

"So you want my piano player too?" he said, when I turned up unprepared to return to work. "Have you got a brother to replace him?"

"I'll send one of my sisters," I said. "Can Joe leave right away, without notice?"

Louis waved his hand toward the band. "Take as many as you like," he said.

Teschemaker was working at the Triangle Club with Floyd Towne's band, which included Muggsy Spanier and George Wettling. The Triangle boss was Mickey Rafferty, who used to stand by the rail in front of the stand and do a dance. Once Mickey wanted Muggsy and Wettling to take a rest without pay. They protested mildly, so Mickey took them for a ride in his automobile, closed the windows, and exploded a tear-gas gun—a small weapon disguised as a fountain pen. After that the boys needed a rest, and they didn't care whether they got paid or not. Towne was as amiable as Panico; he agreed to let Tesch go without notice. Krupa was working at the Wilshire Dance Pavilion with Eddie Neibauer's Seattle Harmony Kings; I got him off too. Then I heard the news. Al Siegel had left Bee Palmer and joined the De Marcos, a dance team, as accompanist. He was in Chicago with them, at the Palace Theater. Bee was also in town at the Sherman House, visiting her mother and obviously hoping for a reconciliation with her husband.

The Palmer-Siegel marriage and business partnership had been through separations and reconciliations before; there had even been a divorce and a re-marriage. With four tickets to New York in my pocket I found myself backstage at the Palace pleading with Siegel to talk to Bee. The De Marcos were opposed to the idea, naturally, but I managed to persuade Al and between shows we went to the Sherman House. Bee was cordial and things went smoothly. At what I considered the psychological moment I withdrew and rounded up the boys. "Everything is set," I said. "They'll be in New York in a week." I wired McKenzie in St. Louis that we were leaving for New York. We stayed up all night at the Fullerton Plaza Hotel, packing, talking, and celebrating our success. In the morning we took the train. In New York we registered at the Cumberland Hotel, across the street from the Chateau Madrid on Fifty-fourth Street, just off Broadway. McKenzie came back from St. Louis. MacPartland and Freeman called us long distance from some road stop to ask how things were going.

"We're ready," I told them. "Come on in."

"Fine," Bud said. "By the way, would you like to hear the greatest trombone player in the world?"

"Put him on," I said. "What's his name?"

"Jack Teagarden," Bud said. "He's from Texas. Wait until we get some blues going; then Jack will play for you."

I listened for a while, then handed the phone to McKenzie. He passed it on to Tesch. Tesch gave it to Krupa. When we had all listened and Bud was back on the other end of the wire I gave him the consensus. "He doesn't bother us," I said. "Put a brand on his stomach and bring him in." "I can't get him now," Bud said, "but we'll snatch him later."

In a few days Bee arrived in town. Siegel was still in Chicago with the De Marcos. The panic was on again. "I'll show him," Bee said. "I've signed up Frankie Signorelli." Signorelli was a fine accompanist and we all felt better. He went to the Mayflower, where Bee was staying, and rehearsed with her. Every day before leaving our hotel we looked across the street at the Chateau Madrid, which was being decorated for the opening. We felt that we ought to talk to Schwartz but our orders were specific—stay away and let Bee do the negotiating. Then one day she said, "I'll show him"—she still meant Siegel—"I won't open without him."

We were sunk, but at least there was no reason now for us to stay away from Schwartz. We walked across the street and asked him if he would listen to the band. "Why not?" he said gloomily. He knew what he wanted, and it wasn't us. The plumbers, carpenters, and decorators were hard at work when we set up our instruments. "He'll have to admit we're good," Bud said hopefully. "It's a free country," McKenzie said. "He can like Leo Reisman."

Schwartz sat at a table and listened. We played "Clarinet Marmalade," "Jazz Me Blues," and "Nobody's Sweetheart." The noises of the carpenters and plumbers didn't help. We could see Schwartz hadn't the slightest idea what we were doing. He didn't have to tell us we weren't hired; we knew it. The Chateau Madrid opened with a fiddle outfit and was a success. We sat in the Cumberland and watched the crowd go in on opening night.

We didn't realize then how little chance we had in New York. Violins and soft saxophones were the fashion. Leo Reisman, Emil Coleman, Pancho, Meyer Davis, Mike Markel—these were the prosperous bandleaders. The only place we could play was in our rooms, at our own request. Krupa set up his drums and we played every night until the complaints began. Don Voorhees had a big band down the street at station WOR; many of his men dropped in to see us and to hear us play. They liked our music. One of them was Vic Berton, the drummer. Red Nichols was another. When we saw Vic listening with admiration to Krupa, our faith in our future rose. If musicians agreed we were good, how could the public resist? Something would break soon; Bee Palmer was sending us to agent after agent—one of them was certain to get us a job. Bee was also taking us to parties, where we were introduced as celebrities from Chicago. "But we're still loafing," McKenzie muttered. "How long can we live like gentlemen and work like bums? Breakfast at Dave's Blue Room for two dollars! We're nuts!"

One day Pancho called and said he was sending Jolly Coburn to interview us about a job. McKenzie was worried. "What does Pancho want with us?" he wondered. "What will we do in the middle of those fiddles and accordions?" Coburn arrived and seemed glad to see us.

"Pancho is going to Newport to play for the debut of Princess Miguel de Briganza's daughter," he said. "He'd like you to come along as an alternate band; he thinks it would be an interesting novelty."

"I think it will," McKenzie said. "It will be the most interesting novelty Newport has ever had."

The eastern seaboard must have been drained of blue blood for the Briganza party. Every name was a foot long; I was surprised that anyone ate with his own hands. The affair was held in the country club; the only common things there were champagne, caviar, and musicians. Even the servants were pedigreed. "Well," McKenzie said, "what are you guys looking at? Those mugs have five fingers on each hand and one head apiece, haven't they?"

I remembered the out-of-town doctors at Mayo's in Rochester. The Briganza guests were all out-of-towners; those born in the United States were pretending it was a sordid mistake, an unhappy mischance. The musicians were supposed to help the pretense with Viennese waltzes. I looked around; Krupa was adjusting a tom-tom. The artillery was ready. "Well," I said, "let's give out with some of that old world atmosphere—'Clarinet Marmalade.'"

Eight seconds later everyone in the room was staring at us. Pancho was smiling; he liked it. So did his boys. The guests automatically began drinking more champagne. They couldn't talk because we were playing too loud; between sets we pushed them out of the way to get at the champagne. "Extraordinary demonstration of the freed libido," I heard one matron mutter. "Lady," I said, "will you hold this glass while I get some caviar?" "Extraordinary creature!" she said, but she took the glass and held it while I got some eggs.

After the party a truck was sent from the hotel to pick up the instruments. I was placed on top of them and driven to the Viking Hotel. Next day I met Pancho in the lobby. "How did we do?" I asked. "You were a hit," he said. Then he smiled. "One of the ladies told me it was just like having the Indians in town again.

"She was old enough to know what she was talking about," he added.

Back in New York our money ran out. Musicians came to see us and brought liquor but never food. It was then I discovered a simple truth about modern society; you can drink yourself to death on your friends except for one thing—you'll die of malnutrition first. When you're broke you can get all the whiskey you want almost anywhere you go, but don't ask for a sandwich; it lowers the social tone of friendship. The important thing is to have enough money to buy a can of tomatoes the next morning; they feed the body and break the hangover.

We discovered the Automat. We walked up and down Broadway, listening to the music coming from commercial bands in dime-a-dance halls. We went to see more agents. We lived on the olives from Martinis and cherries from Manhattans at the cocktail parties to which we were invited. We opened a charge account at a delicatessen for canned tomatoes, to be kept on ice until we called for them in the morning—or in the afternoon. We heard from Pancho again. Barbara Bennett had just left Maurice, her dancing partner, and was forming a new team with Charles Sabin. Sabin was from society; his mother was fighting prohibition. The team was scheduled to go into the Palace, and Pancho recommended us for background music. We auditioned for Barbara and she offered us the job. "Are you sure you know what you're doing?" I asked. "Is this the kind of music you want for your class act?"

"It will be something new," she said. "I'm delighted. We'll start rehearsals tomorrow at Steinway Hall."

By then it was July. We rehearsed for ten days in heat that melted everything but our hunger. One of the dance numbers, a waltz, required a fiddle in the orchestra. Tesch had begun his career on the violin; we borrowed an instrument from Joe Venuti and handed it to him. After one rehearsal we took it away from him and gave it back to Venuti. We got a violinist from the Meyer Davis office, a nice guy named Charlie Miller. Then MacPartland and Freeman were offered a job on the *Ile de France.* They considered taking it.

"You mean you would rather play on a frog ferry than at the Palace?" McKenzie said. He was incredulous. "Thousands of men and women have died of old age on the road trying to make the Palace, and you guys want to sell your chance for a doily and a *crêpe suzette*!" he roared.

MacPartland fidgeted. "I was only thinking about it," he said. "I'll stay."

"So will I," Freeman said, but he looked unhappy. Bud loved culture.

We opened at the Palace on the 16th of July. We were nervous and hot; the fiddle sounded strange and embarrassed in the middle of our mob. When Barbara and Charles ended their waltz they stepped back and bowed; Barbara's legs were shaking worse than mine. Here we go, I thought, she's going to fall on her face—what are we doing here anyhow? While the team was changing costumes we played "I Must Have That Man." When we finished there was silence. Then two, three, and finally four people applauded. "Musicians," Tesch whispered. At the end of the act the dancers got a good hand.

Barbara and Charles waited impatiently for the reviews to appear in *Variety* and *Billboard.* We didn't care if we never saw them. When they appeared Barbara was ecstatic. In *Variety* she was chosen as the "best dressed woman of the week" by The Skirt, Jr. The Skirt described in detail the clothes worn during the act. Barbara read the piece to us. . . . "She appears again in a stunning orange chiffon gown with ragged hem reaching to the floor on one side with a huge spray of coque feathers on the other side and on one shoulder. This is for a weak blackbottom. After a pause in which their rather dreadful orchestra plays an off-key selection. . . ."

She stopped. "Don't mind us," I said. "Go right ahead."

"I'm sure that's just meanness," she said. "There's a review here of the show itself, not of my clothes. Let's see what it says."

It was bad for all of us: "The class act was Charles Sabin and Barbara Bennett, nite club dancers. The nite club they were in may have had a steady trade of 750 people. Of these 600 are now out of town. And of the 600 not

50 would care to see either of the dancers anywhere other than at their homes or in a club ballroom. . . . The couple are no stage dancers of any kind, with the poorest 7-piece orchestra on earth. . . . As a side remark, Mr. Sabin and Miss Bennett neglected to bow to their musicians when exiting. No one could blame them, but it is customary."

"That does it," Tesch said.

"Local boys make good in big city in large way," Joe Sullivan said. "I can see the headlines in the *Chicago Tribune*."

"Well, at last I've played the Palace," I said. "Now I owe Cliff for my banjo."

The next day Krupa turned up with a copy of *Billboard*. "Look at this," he said. "Maybe we're not as much a failure as we think."

The review said: "Charles Sabin and Barbara Bennett closed the first half in an exhibition of ballroom dancing, assisted by a commendable 7-piece musical unit . . . the act was heavily applauded but the hurrahs were not for the terpsichorean talents. They are both graceful, but far removed from being world beaters."

"Who wrote that?" Tesch asked. "The man is a genius." Krupa read out the name—Elias E. Sugarman. "He'll go down in history," Tesch said.

At least the musicians were with us. Johnny Powell, the drummer, went twice a day every day during the week; in the general applause we spotted isolated patches of enthusiasm for our numbers. But we were about as far from being a popular success as it was possible to be. Jazz was still a special taste.

In the middle of the week Bud announced that he was going to take the job on the *Ile de France*. It was sailing the next day. McKenzie was in favor of violence. I told Bud that if he went we would collect his pay at the end of the week and split it among ourselves.

"I don't care," he said. "I'm going to France."

"I will also not pay you that fifty dollars I owe you," I said.

"I still don't care," he said, and he went.

When we finished the run Sabin refused to pay us for Freeman, contending that Bud had forfeited his salary by deserting the act.

"I have had enough trouble, Charles," McKenzie said, "but if necessary I will make some more, all by myself, and give it to you. If you don't pay Freeman's salary I will really louse you up at the union—remember we rehearsed with you for ten days without pay."

"Oh, Charles, shut up!" Barbara said. "Let's not quarrel about trifles." She reached into her stocking, took out a roll of bills, and handed McKenzie Bud's money. We used it to cut down the bill at the Cumberland. McKenzie went to St. Louis to see his family again.

There were five of us now in the two rooms; Mezzrow and Josh Billings, a jazz fan, had come in from Chicago. Very quickly we were back on the olive and cherry diet, with canned tomatoes for breakfast. One day the clerk handed me our bill and added a meaningful look. We owed an interesting sum, ninety-nine dollars. We had to do something.

The Jimmy Noone records were out under Brunswick's Vocalian label and were selling well. I took one of them and went to see Tommy Rockwell at Okeh.

"See how you like this small ensemble group," I said. "I can get you one like it—Teschemaker, Krupa, and Sullivan."

Rockwell listened to the record and nodded agreeably. "Let's make a date," he said.

"Let's make it for tomorrow morning," I said.

"I think we ought to have a vocal on one side," Rockwell said.

I swallowed hard. "I'll sing," I said.

We were at the studio ahead of time. We set up and made "Oh Baby," from *Rain or Shine.* The second side was "Back Home in Indiana," and I sang a chorus. Before the wax was cool on the master I was in Rockwell's office.

"Tommy," I said, "do something about this."

I gave him the hotel bill.

"Why didn't you say something about it before?" he said. He took a wallet from his pocket and handed me two fifty-dollar bills.

"There will be fifty dollars more," he said. "I'll send it to you."

I walked out of the room eighty pounds lighter than when I went in. Back at the hotel I paid the bill. The clerk gave me a dollar.

"What shall we buy with it?" I asked the boys. The vote was unanimous—canned tomatoes.

Mary Lou Williams

The unique pianist / composer / arranger Mary Lou Williams—by far the most important and influential woman in jazz history—published an extensive autobiographical account (almost complete here) in the British magazine Melody Maker *in 1954. She had been everywhere, known everyone, and seen everything, and was still looking forward expectantly as well as back nostalgically.*

I have been tied up with music for about as long as I can remember. By the time I was four I was picking out little tunes my mother played on the reed organ in the living-room. We lived in a big, timber-framed building: what we called a shotgun house, because if you fired through the front door the shot passed through all the rooms and out into the backyard, likely ending up in the privy.

Quite a few musicians came to our house. And my ma took me to hear many more, hoping to encourage in me a love of music. But she wouldn't consent to my having music lessons, for she feared I might end up as she had done—unable to play except from paper. Soon I was playing piano around the district, though I was so small I had to sit on someone's lap to reach the keyboard.

There were two children, me and my older sister Mamie. My father I had never seen. A year or two later, the family moved to a neighborhood in Pittsburgh which brought me my first experience of interracial feeling. This entire section was "white" for five or six blocks, and for a while somebody was throwing bricks through our windows. There was nothing to do but stick it out in silence. Pretty soon the people there were tolerating us.

Then my mother married a man called Fletcher Burley. As a stepfather he was the greatest; and he loved the blues. Fletcher taught me the first blues I ever knew by singing them over to me.

Now it happened he was known as a professional gambler, and he sometimes took me with him at nights—to bring him luck, he said. We had moved again, to Hamilton Boulevard in East Liberty (a suburb of Pittsburgh about six miles from the main drag), and I went with him into a variety of smoke-filled gaming rooms, most of which had an upright against one wall. The game was generally "skin"—the Georgia skin game—and the players would all be men, for women weren't allowed in these places. I was kind of smuggled in, and before the cards began I used to play a few things on the piano. Often I received as much as twenty dollars in tips, which my stepfather had started rolling by dropping a dollar in his hat. This "pound" had to be returned to him as soon as we got outside. Still, it was a fair deal.

We also visited Saturday hops and parties given at someone's house to raise money for rent and other bills. These functions were known as house-rent parties or chitterlin' struts. The windows were kept shut and the atmosphere was stagnant, but I was always fascinated by the boogie pianists and shuffling couples dancing on a spot. Sometimes they'd hire me at a dollar an hour for three hours. I would bring out all the blues and boogies Fletcher had taught me. Should I attempt a popular song or light classic, my stepfather would ask why didn't I play some music.

I had now been attending Lincoln School for a couple of years, learning music and playing college teas and such. Outside, I had earned a local reputation as "the gigging piano gal from East Liberty." I was playing quite a bit of jazz now, and beginning to give it my own interpretation. Of course, my playing was influenced by favorite pianists: principally by Jack Howard, Earl Hines, and Jelly Roll Morton. Of all the musicians I met in my childhood, one who stands out: Jack Howard, who played boogie-woogie so forcefully that he used to break up all the pianos. For those days, he was one of the grooviest, but never made the name he deserved. Jelly Roll I dug from records, and his composition, "The Pearls," was then my number one solo. Many years later I recorded it for Decca at the instigation of John Hammond.

Offers for me to play dances, society parties, even churches, were now coming in regularly. For most dates I was paid the sum of one dollar per hour, and they always tipped me at the end of the night.

And there was usually something worth hearing in town those days, even if Pittsburgh was not one of the jazz centers. One Saturday night I went to a theater on Frankstown Avenue where all the Negro shows were booked. But I hardly noticed any part of the show, for my attention was focused on the lady pianist who worked there. She sat cross-legged at the piano, a cigarette in her mouth, writing music with her right hand while accompanying the show with her swinging left! Impressed, I told myself: "Mary, you'll do that one day." (And I did, traveling with Andy Kirk's band in the thirties on one-nighters.)

The lady turned out to be Lovie Austin, who was working with the pit band and making all the orchestrations. It so happened that she was behind time, and hurriedly arranging a number for one of the acts further down the bill.

Another week, the fabulous Ma Rainey came into a little theater on Wiley Avenue. Some of the older kids and I slipped downtown to hear the woman who had made blues history. Ma was loaded with real diamonds—in her ears, around her neck, in a tiara on her head. Both hands were full of rocks, too; her hair was wild and she had gold teeth. What a sight! To me, as a kid, the whole thing looked and sounded weird. When the engagement ended, and Ma had quit the scene, rumor had it that the jewelry was bought hot and that Ma was picked up and made to disgorge—losing all the loot she had paid for the stuff.

Of our local characters, one of the most famed was Lois Deppe, the popular baritone singer who had been around since 1918 or earlier. His band was the talk of Pennsylvania, and at that time included the great Earl Hines—a local boy from nearby Carnegie—and Vance Dixon on saxophone and clarinet. Wherever Deppe's band appeared, the kids from all around were sure to go—and when Vance started to slap-tongue on that saxophone they really went wild. Numbers I remember the band doing were "Milenberg Joys," "Isabelle," and "Congaine." The last two were recorded by Deppe in the early twenties. "Isabelle" I made as a solo for Columbia around 1935; I once asked Hines about it, thinking he might be the composer, but he did not remember it.

I must have been ten or eleven when I was taken to the Saturday afternoon dances at the Arcadia Ballroom where Deppe was playing. These dances ran from noon until 4 P.M., and shortly before break-up time the biggest fight would invariably commence. Half the kids in Pittsburgh could be seen running from the hall, grabbing the backs of streetcars to get away.

We had groups of kids from the different districts—East Liberty, Soho, the downtown district, and so on—who were considered very tough. If an East Liberty kid was caught in Soho, or downtown, he would either be assaulted or chased back to his own district.

I was at high school when my first big chance came along. *Hits and Bits,* a traveling TOBA show, had just hit town, and the pianist had failed to show up. "Buzzin'" Harris, the owner, was frantic for a replacement. "There's a girl in East Liberty could play your show," he was told. He drove over to investigate, found me playing hopscotch with some kids, and thought a gag had been pulled on him. Reluctantly he agreed to hear me, and I must have proved something, because he started humming the show tunes for me. Within a few hours I had them off, was about ready to play the shows. That night I opened, and during the week Harris was over to the house to talk my mother into letting me leave home.

It was just before the summer vacation, and after a little argument my mother agreed. But she was backstage next day with the public notary, signing papers for me to go with the show for two months. My salary was to be thirty dollars a week, and mother fixed for a friend to go along with me. So I left Pittsburgh with *Hits and Bits* and traveled west to Detroit, Chicago, Cincinnati, and St. Louis. In the Windy City I again ran into Hines, who introduced me to Louis Armstrong. Both were working at the Vendome Theatre with Erskine Tate's orchestra. In fact, so far as the audience was concerned, they *were* the orchestra. Specialties were played from the pit, and I saw Louis stand up, wipe his mouth in preparation for a solo, and break up the place before he'd blown a note. That's how it was with Satchmo in Chicago then. After the show the boys took me over to the Sunset cabaret—owned by the now famous booking agent, Joe Glaser—to hear King Oliver. I was impressed no end by Oliver's kicking combo, and by his own expressive, tale-telling cornet.

I also looked up Lovie Austin—by now making a name in Chicago—at the Monogram, another house on the TOBA circuit. The initials stand for Theater Owners' Booking Association—or, to us who had to work it, "Tough on Black Artists."

Next stop, St. Louis: and there I met Charlie Creath, the riverboat king, who was known all over the Middle West for his crazy growl trumpet playing. Besides being a top jazz performer, Charlie was a most handsome cat.

In St. Louis, our show picked up a young blues singer named Irene Scruggs (now in Paris with her daughter, dancer Baby Leazar Scruggs). Irene had not long settled in St. Louis, and was starting out to become one of St. Louis's finest singers.

Then on to Cleveland, where I met John Williams, later to become my husband. He was working at the theater where we appeared, leading a five-piece combo known as John Williams and his Syncopators. John played alto, soprano, and baritone saxes, also clarinet. Acknowledged to be one of the finest baritone players, he was much in demand. We named him "Bearcat," on account of him being wild on the big saxophone, and it was this nickname which led in later years to the Kirk instrumental number, "Bearcat Shuffle."

The Syncopators were strong in all departments. A man called Martin, a friend and schoolmate of Coleman Hawkins from St. Joseph, Missouri, played tenor. Shirley Clay, from St. Louis, was already blowing good trumpet (we used to call him "Hoggy"). The drummer, Edward Temple, was a showman, but also a solid, subtle rhythm player. Then they had a banjoist whose name has got away from me. They didn't carry a brass bass. John Williams blew a slap-tongue two beats on baritone, when he wasn't taking a solo, like a bass horn would play. It eliminated the need for a tuba.

I played in the pit with this band, doubling on stage in the second half with a specialty that was slightly sensational. Spreading a sheet over the keys, I did a version of "Milenberg Joys" mostly with my elbows, winding up by taking a break while spinning around on the piano stool. I perpetrated this novelty until an older musician came to me one day and said he had detected something nice in my playing. He explained how ridiculous the clowning was, and there and then I decided to settle down and play seriously.

The piano had done well enough by me, but I wasn't going to be hung up with it without trying some other instruments. And at Westinghouse Junior High School the opportunity existed for every pupil to study a variety of instruments. I was back at school after my eight weeks' tour with *Hits and Bits,* having said good-bye to comedian Buzzin' Harris and his wife, Arletta, and parted from the show in Pittsburgh.

At Westinghouse we had some of the best music teachers in the world (I guess). Under their guidance, I tried out most of the instruments—last but not least being the violin. Right after the first fiddle lesson I played "Sheik of Araby" on one string. My teacher advised me to forget it and stick to piano; which I did.

In later years, both Billy Strayhorn and Erroll Garner attended that same school and class, receiving tuition from the master I was with. One day I pinch-hit for a tuning fork the teacher had lost, and it was discovered I possessed perfect pitch. Rumor of this oddity spread throughout the school, and pupils would drop pots, pans and other loud objects, asking: "What note, Mary?"

At this point in my career a very fine jazz orchestra came to Pittsburgh: McKinney's Cotton Pickers, with Prince Robinson on saxophone and Todd Rhodes at the piano. Todd became a friend and adviser to me, used to take me out jamming, and on one date let me sit in with the band. Some nights we jammed all the way from East Liberty down to Wylie Avenue, then a notorious section of town which was held in dread by so-called decent people. We always wound up in the Subway on Wylie, a hole in the ground to which the cream of the crop came to enjoy the finest in the way of entertainment. For me it was a paradise. Visiting musicians made straight for the place to listen to artists like beautiful Louise Mann, and Baby Hines, Earl's first wife.

Until this time I had paid little attention to singers, but the feeling in Baby's singing made the strongest impression upon me. Baby is still working, I believe, for I saw her in Jersey City in 1952: but she never received the recognition she merits. Those days, when she began a number like "You're an Old Smoothie," the customers showered tips on her in appreciation—and I've seen fifty- and one-hundred-dollar bills among them. Her torch songs brought real tears to their eyes—as you can guess, for that kind of dough!

At this same spot I heard a lot of Prince Robinson, and have never forgotten his excellent tenor. He was one of the outstanding jazz players of the generation. Prince would refuse to jam with inadequate musicians, waiting until he could round up some other out-of-the-ordinary players to make the session inspirational or at least worthwhile.

One way and another I was having a ball—playing gigs, jamming and listening to fine musicians. Then came a crisis at home. My stepfather fell sick, and it meant I had to support the family. Finishing up at high school, I went back to Buzzin' Harris'. John Williams still had the band, which by now included trumpet player Doc Cheatham. Doc came from a long line of medicos, was studying himself when he decided to follow the call of music. He was a very accomplished musician.

For a time the tour went well, taking us to different theaters on the TOBA and Gus Sun circuits. Suddenly we found ourselves stranded in Cincinnati—350 miles from home and short of gold. Just as we were feeling dragged, Fate stepped in—in the shape of a telegram inviting us to join the celebrated dance team of Seymour and Jeanette to play the Keith-Orpheum theaters. It was practically the rags to riches routine. We were on our way to one of the top theater circuits direct from TOBA, one of the toughest. At that time, Keith's were booking only one other Negro act besides Seymour and Jeanette (I think it was Bojangles), and we felt justified in saying "at last!"

Right away John sent to Kansas City for banjoist Joe Williams. On trumpet there was a guy called Max. Doc Cheatham's uncle, a St. Louis dentist, had reclaimed him for a while. On trombone we had a fabulous Sylvester Briscoe, who could and did play more horn with his foot in the slide than most cats can with their hands.

Seymour and Jeanette had previously worked with pit bands. But Seymour was now a sick man who could no longer dance flat out. He was famed for a wild strut, which he performed with cane, and it was said that the dance had stretched his heart to the size of a saucer, which seemed likely to anyone who had seen him strutting. He needed a supporting attraction, and it was our job to accompany and provide a couple of specialty numbers.

When Seymour saw me seated at the piano at that first rehearsal, he shouted: "What's that kid doing here? Call your piano player and let's get started."

"She is it," replied John, smiling.

"We cannot have a child in this act," Jeanette put in. "Especially a female child. We'll have to put pants on her, or something."

By this time, the boys were falling out. John told the dancers not to worry but just to listen. We ran through one or two of our showiest things and we were in.

The band went over well: so well, in fact, that Seymour kept changing our spot. We thought at any moment we might lose the job because of the way the public was going for our "Tiger Rag." This featured Briscoe's crazy act of playing trombone with both hands behind his back, the instrument somehow wedged between his mouth and the floor. This may sound impossible, but it is the truth. I never knew how he did it, and never saw anyone who could imitate him.

"Tiger Rag" was the last number, and needed to be. The applause even stopped the movie that followed us, often a Rin Tin Tin picture. After our show, the house would be blacked, then the dog appeared on the screen. Some nights they had to cut the picture for us to take another encore, and the guys would say: "Don't look like Rin Tin Tin will bark tonight."

Seymour's death cut short this engagement, and the group was disbanded while Jeanette looked for another partner. By this time drummer Temple had gone and been replaced by a good but heavy footed Kaycee man named Abie Price. Trombonist Briscoe had also split.

My travels had not taken me to New York until now, when we played the 81st Theatre on Broadway and a few weekend gigs. To someone who lived for music, this was it. Jeanette did a stint at the old Lincoln Theatre, off Lenox Avenue, and not being able to afford five pieces, she just took me in with her. I played the entire show in the pit, then went on stage to accompany her act. That week was the most exciting of my life thus far. I was working with some of the boys from Duke Ellington's Washingtonians—Sonny Greer, Bubber Miley, and Tricky Sam Nanton among them, and never had I heard such music before. The two growlers, Bubber and Tricky, were the nicest to me. Though they invariably took their jugs into the pit with them, they never got too juiced to play or to respect me. Coming downstairs for the show, I sometimes overheard Bubber warning the guys: "Be careful now, the kid's coming down."

I stayed in New York, eyes and ears open to all the attractions Harlem had to offer. Like most other pianists I revered the amazing Fats Waller, who had lately made a splash wailing on organ at the Lincoln. When he quit New York, his admirers wouldn't let anyone follow him on organ, and those frantic kids were likely to throw most anything if you tried. Naturally it was a great day for me when some musicians took me across to Connie's Inn on 7th Avenue to meet Fats, working on a new show. The way Waller worked was anything but slavery. The OAO (one and only) sat overflowing the piano stool, a jug of whiskey within easy reach. Leonard Harper, the producer, said: "Have you anything written for this number, Fats?" And Fats would reply: "Yeah, go on ahead with the dance, man." Then he composed his number while the girls were dancing. He must have composed the whole show, with lyrics, while I was sitting there—ears working overtime. Meanwhile, he bubbled over with so many stories and funny remarks that those girls could hardly hoof it for laughing. The girls, thirty- to forty-dollar-a-week chorus beauties, were loaded with enough ice around their shapely ankles to sink a battleship, for these were generous days in New York.

After the rehearsal, one of the boys—knowing my memory—bet Fats I could repeat all the tunes he had just written: a bet Waller snapped up at paying odds. Falling apart with nerves at having to play before this big name,

I was prodded to the piano, but managed to concentrate and play nearly everything I had heard Fats play. He was knocked out, picking me up and throwing me in the air and roaring like a crazy man.

Not long afterwards, Harper asked me how I'd like to work at Connie's Inn. I would, and I began playing intermission piano while the band was over at the Lafayette Theatre, just up the Avenue near the Tree of Hope, where musicians used to exchange stories and await work. In these later months, I ran into many great artists: luscious Florence Mills, Bill Robinson, Adelaide Hall, comedian Johnny Huggins, and Nina Mae McKinney (then about sixteen), who wished me to accompany her.

I was glad of the chance to meet Clarence Williams and Jelly Roll Morton. I had admired Williams's compositions for some time, and I found him a kindly man who seemed to like me, and who was reassuring about the things I played him. I have never seen Clarence again, though he lives in New York to this day.

Mr. Jelly Lord was a more frightening proposition. He was considered a big deal then, and he had me scared. When the guys dragged me into his office downtown we were surprised to see him playing duets with an ofay piccolo player. At a convenient break, they introduced me and told Jelly they would like for him to hear me. Indicating that I should park my hips on the stool, Jelly gave over the piano and I got started on my favorite Morton piece, "The Pearls." Almost immediately I was stopped and reprimanded, told the right way to phrase it. I played it the way Jelly told me, and when I had it to his satisfaction, I slipped in one of my own tunes. This made no difference. I was soon stopped and told: "Now that passage should be phrased like this."

Jelly Roll had a mouthful of diamond and spoke with a stammer when he got excited. He was what we call a "big mouth," and the sound of his voice had me shaking in my boots. Any minute I was expecting to get up off the floor because I had played his "Pearls" wrong. That's how they trained you in those days (half those chorus girls had black eyes!), and Morton had the reputation of being a demanding taskmaster. Musicians—they really have it easy now!

My first real experience of the South came about the year 1927. In my earlier tours I had not crossed the Mason-Dixon line; now, domestic business rather than music took me there. John Williams and I decided to get married, and it meant going to Memphis, Tennessee, to meet his parents. Apparently they had saved for John to go to college and study law, and they didn't approve of his musical career. I could understand their disappointment, because I saw that education meant everything to the Southern Negro then. A teacher, lawyer, or doctor was regarded almost as some kind of a god down there, while musicians were more often looked on as undesirables.

We were married very quietly, and decided to spend some time in Memphis. John set about forming a band of local musicians of whom there were a good number, though not many who could read music well. Now John was a smooth talker and a shrewd character. He soon maneuvered the new combo into clubs and hotels that ordinarily never employed a colored outfit, and dug up a job at the Pink Rose Ballroom, where we made quite a name. One thing I have to say for John: he knew how to talk up salaries. Memphis musicians were getting a dollar and a half or two dollars a night when we went there. John kept working on it, and by the time we left they were making five and seven bucks, and I was making ten.

Through the neighborhood grapevine we heard one day that a young man was in town looking for work as a teacher. We heard he was shabbily dressed, and that the "fay" board of education were going to interview him to determine if he was capable. In no time they found out. In fact, he knew more than they did, was answering so fast he had them baffled. The scholastic young man was Jimmie Lunceford, later to take America by storm with a very hard-hitting orchestra, but then an unknown saxophone player out of Denver, Colorado. He became a close friend of John's, and they spent hours playing checkers together. Usually John won the games, but Lunceford used to say he'd get a band and beat John with that. He was for ever kidding about building up a combo that would make ours look sick. Finally he started out to do it—not an easy job because we probably had the pick of the men in Memphis then, yet they were not top class. Still, Jimmy went ahead, and we had to admire the way he taught the young musicians in his school.

Drummer James Crawford was one from the school; perhaps bassist Moses Allen was there, and others whose names I have since forgotten. To begin with, Jimmy had a small group like ours, even to the girl pianist—talented Bobby Jones. Then, unable to get the band sounding right, Jimmy went off to Nashville and returned bragging with pianist Eddie Wilcox and saxophone player Willie Smith. By the time we left Memphis we must have had twelve pieces.

Our leaving was caused by a telegram from Terrence Holder, a bandleader in Oklahoma City, offering good money for John to go out and join him there. John went first, leaving me in charge for the rest of the dates we had contracted. This made me a bandleader at the age of seventeen. I had no alto player, so had to ask Jimmie Lunceford to play the remainder of the dates with us, which he consented to do.

Though we didn't meet too often while I was on the road with Kirk, I remained friendly with Lunceford. Later, when I lived in New York, he once came to my house at four in the morning, asking if I wanted to fly to Pittsburgh with him. I said: "What are we going to fly in?" and Jimmie said: "Didn't you know I had a pilot's license and my own plane?" I hadn't known, but refused to go anyway, saying: "It's too foggy there." Pittsburgh with its hundreds of steel mills makes its own fog. Not for nothing is it called the Smoky City.

To get back to Memphis, though: I worked off the outstanding engagements, then set out to join John in Oklahoma City, 700 hard miles away. He had left our Chevrolet for me to make the journey in, and with John's mother and a friend I hit the highway. The Chev wasn't much of a "short" to look at. It looked like a red bathtub in fact, but ran like one of those streamlined trains on the Pennsylvania Railroad, and was the craziest for wear and tear. Unfortunately, we had miles of dirt and turtle-back roads to travel, and these excuses for highways were studded with sharp stones. To top all, it was August and hot as a young girl's doojie. Every forty to fifty miles we stopped to change tires or clean out the carburetor. As my passengers were strictly non-drivers and non-fixers, I was in sole command. We got along somehow, and after what seemed like weeks of blow-outs and fuel trouble we fell into Oklahoma City. Considering it was surrounded by every description of oil well, the place was a beauty spot. But the smell of gas . . . wow!

John was anxious to show me off musically, for he was proud of my ability. Though out of my mind from the journey, I went without sleep to make rehearsal the next morning. Holder's boys rehearsed two days a week, beginning 11 A.M.; and I was in the hall by nine. I don't know what Holder's band made of me, but I thought them the handsomest bunch of intellectuals I had seen so far. They looked liked collegians, all had beautiful brown complexions and wore sharp beige suits to match. Going out, they sported yellow raincoats with the instrument each man played illustrated on the back. Most came from good families, and their manners were perfect. I could hardly wait to hear the music. As I suspected, it was out of the ordinary. They had a novel arrangement of "Casey Jones" featuring Claude Williams, who was strong on both guitar and violin. Tenorman Lawrence "Slim" Freeman supplied the show stuff by playing bass clarinet while lying on his back. For the rest, they played jazz numbers and the better commercial things. They were all reading like mad, and I had to admit it was a good and different orchestra: smooth showmanship (minus the "Tom-ing") coupled with musical ability. No wonder Holder had held this one job for more than two years. And at high money for a no-name band.

As I shall explain, this was to be the basis of the Andy Kirk combo. Kirk was a tuba player with the band, and he also played alto and baritone saxes. Bill Dirvin doubled guitar and piano, and Harry "Big Jim" Lawson was on trumpet. Holder conducted and didn't play an instrument. I guess he was the most musically ignorant one in the band, but a fast talker and a sportsman who took chances. He liked to gamble, and I was told he had more than once lost the payroll in this way. There was talk about bad management, and one day the boys got together and arranged a change. They put Andy Kirk in charge of the band, incorporated it, and renamed it Andy Kirk's Twelve Clouds of Joy. I reckon the year would be 1928.

We moved to Tulsa, and I went to live over an undertaker's. Apart from natural deaths, there was a killing every other day, with weekends the best for business. I was not working, and to break the monotony I'd got permission to drive for the undertaker. In those days they had to go after work, racing to the scene as soon as a killing was reported. Whoever got there first took the body.

Apart from this, I had no way of passing the time. I couldn't see myself getting ahead in music, and the life was getting me down fast. Then a letter from home said my stepfather had passed away, and this broke me up. Inveigling the fare out of my husband, I made for Pittsburgh—not sorry to escape from the oil fumes of Oklahoma.

While I was at home the Kirk band began to shape up nicely. An offer came for them to go into the Pla-mor Ballroom in Kansas City, Missouri. The Clouds of Joy accepted, were held over several times, and took the first stride towards the nationwide success they won in the mid-thirties.

I FOUND KANSAS CITY to be a heavenly city—music everywhere in the Negro section of town, and fifty or more cabarets rocking on 12th and 18th Streets. Kirk's band was drawing them into the handsome Pla-mor Ballroom when my husband, John Williams, had me return to him in Kaycee. This was my first visit to Missouri's jazz metropolis, a city that was to have a big influence on my career.

With two sisters, Lucille and Louise, who knew every speakeasy in town, I began to make the rounds from "Hell's Kitchen" on 5th Avenue to a club on 18th where I met Sam Price. Sammy was playing an unusual type of blues piano which I thought could hardly be improved on. I had the luck to hear him again when we were both in New York during 1934.

One night, we ran into a place where Ben Pollack had a combo which included Jack Teagarden and, I think, Benny Goodman. The girls introduced me to the Texas trombonist, and right away we felt like friends. After work, he and a couple of the musicians asked us to go out, and we visited most of the speaks downtown. One I remember particularly, because it was decorated to resemble the inside of a penitentiary, with bars on the windows and waiters in striped uniforms like down-South convicts. In these weird surroundings, I played for the boys and Jack got up and sang some blues. I thought he was more than wonderful. While they stayed in Kaycee, Jack and some of Pollack's men came round every night, and I was very happy to see them.

Now at this time, which was still Prohibition, Kansas City was under Tom Pendergast's control. Most of the night spots were run by politicians and hoodlums, and the town was wide open for drinking, gambling and pretty much every form of vice. Naturally, work was plentiful for musicians, though some of the employers were tough people. For instance, when Kirk moved from Pla-mor, the orchestra went to work for a nationally feared gangster. He was real bad: people used to run when you just mentioned his name. At that time, Andy was playing tuba, and the band was conducted by our singer, Billy Massey. Billy was a man not easily scared, and one day at the new job he ran off his mouth to the boss. The hood concluded he was crazy (which was not far wrong), and told all the band to pack and leave—but fast. The rest of the guys were too nice, he said, for him to think about killing Billy.

I heard that Count Basie later worked for the same Dracula, and also had a slight misunderstanding. As a result, Basie had to work two weeks without pay.

So for the Clouds of Joy it was more one-nighters. After a few, short trips, we headed east to New York to open in the Roseland Ballroom, that spot made famous by Fletcher Henderson. Kirk was on his way up. By now, I had graduated to composer, arranger, and first-class chauffeur for the organization. I was not playing in the band but was doing their recordings for Brunswick, and sometimes sitting in to try things I had written.

In Kansas City, Kirk had liked my ideas, though I could not set them down on paper. He would sit up as long as twelve hours at a stretch, taking down my ideas for arrangements, and I got so sick of the method that I began putting them down myself. I hadn't studied theory, but asked Kirk about chords and the voicing register. In about 15 minutes I had memorized what I wanted. That's how I started writing. My first attempt, "Messa Stomp," was beyond the range of half the instruments. But the boys gave me a chance and each time I did better, until I found myself doing five and six arrangements per week. Later on, I learned more theory from people like the great Don Redman, Edgar Sampson, Milton Orent, and Will Bradley.

The Clouds of Joy had a long run at the Roseland, playing opposite a bunch named the Vagabonds, then opposite the Casa Loma Band (later led by Glen Gray). From the Roseland, they moved to the celebrated Savoy Ballroom, where they faced Chick Webb's orchestra. The Savoy was a place of tremendous enthusiasm, a home of fantastic dancing. And Webb was acknowledged king of the Savoy. Any visiting band could depend on catching hell from little Chick, for he was a crazy drummer and shrewd to boot. The way I made it out, Chick would wait until the opposition had blown its hottest numbers and then—during a so-so set—would unexpectedly bring his band fresh to the stand and wham into a fine arrangement, like Benny

Carter's "Liza," that was hard to beat. Few visiting bands could stand up to this.

Kirk must have played a couple of months at the Savoy, during which time I often sat in, playing either "Mary's Plea" or "Froggy Bottom," and doing quite well with the kids who liked a good beat for their dancing. From there, we toured Pennsylvania and the eastern states, and after what seemed like a year of one-nighters, returned to Kansas City.

Kaycee was really jumping now—so many great bands having sprung up there or moved in from over the river. I should explain that Kansas City, Missouri, wasn't too prejudiced for a Midwestern town. It was a ballin' town, and it attracted musicians from all over the South and Southwest, and especially from Kansas.

Kansas City, Kansas, was right across the viaduct, just about 5 or 6 miles distant. But on the Kansas side they were much snootier. A lot of their musicians were from good families who frowned on jazz, so the musicians and kids would come across to Kaycee to blast. In Kaycee, nothing mattered.

I've known musicians so enthused about playing that they would walk all the way from the Kansas side to attend a jam session. Even bass players, caught without streetcar fare, would hump their bass on their back and come running. That was how music stood in Kansas City in those years around 1930.

At the head of the bands was Bennie Moten's, led by pianist Bennie, and featuring his brother, Buster, on accordion. Then there was George E. Lee, whose sister, Julia, played piano in George's band and took care of the vocals.

From Oklahoma came Walter Page, with a terrific combo named the Blue Devils. Page, known as "Big One," was one of the very first to use the string bass as well as tuba, and he also doubled on bass saxophone. For a while he had Bill Basie on piano. Count had come to Kansas City with the Gonzele White touring show, and dropped out of it to join Page. Later, Basie returned to the roadshow, again leaving it in Kaycee to go into Moten's band on second piano.

Singing with Moten then was the lovable Jimmy Rushing, "Mr. Five by Five." Unlike the run of blues shouters, Jimmy could read music, and he could be heard ten blocks away without a microphone (they used megaphones then, anyway). Jimmy was big brother to me, and some of the other band wives. I remember him playing piano and singing wonderful ballads to us; other times he would keep us laughing with his *risqué* stories, getting a kick out of seeing us blush.

Yes, Kaycee was a place to be enjoyed, even if you were without funds. People would make you a loan without you asking for it, would look at you and tell if you were hungry and put things right. There was the best food to be had: the finest barbecue, crawdads, and other seafood. There were the races, and swimming, and the beautiful Swope Park and zoo to amuse you. There were jam sessions all the time, and big dances such as the union dance given every year by our local. As many as ten or twelve bands participated in this event, and you were sure to hear at least eight original styles there, as well as one or two outfits trying to imitate Duke.

For private entertainment we had our hot corn club every Monday, at which the musicians and wives would drink and play bridge, "tonk" or "hearts." At these meetings the boys drank corn whisky and home brew—in fact, most anything with a high alcohol content—and they got laughs out of giving me rough liquor so strong it would almost blow the top of one's head off.

One of the regulars was Herman Walder, brilliant tenor player with Moten and brother of saxophonist Woodie Walder. Herman asked me if I'd like a cool drink one night, and not knowing the taste of corn I gulped down a large glassful. The next thing I remember was people putting cold towels on my head. Being stubborn, I thought: if they can take it, so can I. So each Monday I tried to drink, with much the same result. The boys took to betting that I'd be high within ten minutes of entering—and they always won.

It was in the winter of 1930–31 that the breaks began to happen. Andy Kirk's band had hit the road for another string of one-nighters, leaving me in Kansas City. Then came a wire, telling me to meet the band right away in Chicago. It said that Jack Kapp, the Brunswick record man, wanted to hear me play. This looked great. I knew they wouldn't send for me unless something was in the wind, so by next day I was on my way to St. Louis, where I changed trains for Chicago. When I arrived I was cold and tired, but went direct to the studio and sat down and played.

I had been in the habit of making up my own things when asked to play. Out of this training, and the way I was feeling beat, came two originals titled "Drag 'Em" and "Night Life"—the first a blues, the other a faster piece. These were the first solo records I ever made. So far as I can remember it, the session took place in 1930. I know the record was released early in '31 and I never received a recording fee nor any royalties from it, though the record sold quite well. I tried to get some loot, but was fluffed to Mayo Williams, then a kind of artists' manager and connected with some publishing house or other, who in turn fluffed me to the executives. Many years after, I threatened to sue, and stopped the sale of a record that had been reissued ever since 1931 and was even included in the forties in an album of "barrelhouse piano."

That record didn't make my fortune, but it made my name in a double sense. I had been born Mary Elfreda Winn, and had played as Mary Winn until I became Mary Williams. It was Jack Kapp laid the "Lou" on me. Perhaps he figured plain Mary wasn't enough for a recording artist, whereas Mary Lou was right on the beam. Anyway, Mary Lou went on the label, and Mary Lou it stayed. Until today, few people knew I wasn't born with that name.

Being still broke after the session, I moved in with Mary Kirk, Andy's wife. The Bear (as we call wintertime) was in Chicago and it was very cold. Mary provided food and clothes and was the kindest to me. Once again I traveled with Kirk, and it was at the Pearl Theatre in Philadelphia that I joined the band full-time. Kirk had decided to use two pianos, and I was to play the second—a small upright.

Over the two pianos Kirk had a shed-like enclosure built. On top of the shed stood the drums, now presided over by Ben Thigpen, whom we had picked up near Toledo, Ohio. It was tough going; I was used to a large piano, but our regular man, Jack, had the Steinway and I was doing my best with what seemed like a two-octaves "Tom Thumb." And I could hear practically nothing but the thunder of drums overhead. This routine had lasted about a week when Jack failed to make the show one night. I graduated to the grand—and solo honors—and it seems my playing surprised everyone in the theater, including Sam Stiefle, who owned the place. Jack later had hot words with Stiefle, ending in his taking two weeks' pay and a ticket home. I stayed on as the orchestra's pianist and arranger and must have gone around the world (or the equivalent distance) a thousand times a month on one-night dates.

These things happened in 1930, and Blanche Calloway, Cab's sister, was fronting the band at the Pearl. Blanche behaved like Cab on stage, and I heard that she was the originator of his style. Though Blanche was short on voice, she had personality to spare, and I got a kick from her versions of "Let's Do It" and "I Need Lovin'." Stiefle secured Victor recording dates for Blanche and the band, and we cut those two songs with her, also "Sugar Blues," "Casey Jones," and some original things. I always wondered what became of the check for these dates; none of it came my way, but I was getting used to that by now.

We played at the Pearl for many months with Blanche, meeting such top Negro performers as Ethel Waters, Bill Bailey, and Butterbeans and Susie. Eddie Heywood, Sr., was accompanying the Butterbeans act, and he gave me plenty of constructive advice.

After parting from Blanche Calloway, we returned to Kansas City to open the Winnwood Beach Park Ballroom with a somewhat altered personnel. On trumpets we had Irving "Mouse" Randolph, great musician from St. Louis, and Harry "Big Jim" Lawson and Earl Thompson. The trombonist was Floyd "Stumpy" Brady, and the reeds were John Williams, Johnny Harrington, and Slim Freeman. Andy Kirk played tuba, Ben Thigpen was on drums, myself on piano, and Bill Dirvin on guitar.

It was one of our great bands. With Randolph leading the brass, no music was difficult to read. I could pass out arrangements on the stand during the evening and they'd be read right off. Our engagement was a riot, causing the rival Fairyland Park to employ Bennie Moten in self-defense. Kansas City in the thirties was jumping harder than ever. The "Heart of America" was at that time one of the nerve centers of jazz, and I could write about it for a month and never do justice to the half of it. Lester Young, who had worked with Walter Page and Bennie Moten, was blowing cool sounds at the Subway on 18th Street. This was a small place with only one entrance: really a firetrap, yet groovy. The first time I heard Lester I was astounded. It took him several choruses to get started—then, brother, what a horn!

A wild 12th Street spot we fell in regularly was the Sunset, owned by Piney Brown, who loved jazz and was very liberal with musicians. Pianist Pete Johnson worked there with bass and drums, sometimes with Baby Lovett, a New Orleans drummer who became one of Kansas City's best. Now the Sunset had a bartender named Joe Turner, and while Joe was serving drinks he would suddenly pick up a cue for a blues and sing it right where he stood, with Pete playing piano for him. I don't think I'll ever forget the thrill of listening to big Joe Turner shouting and sending everybody night after night while mixing drinks.

Pete Johnson was great on boogie, but he was by no means solely a boogie player. It was only when someone like Ben Webster, the Kaycee-born tenor man, yelled "Roll for me . . . come on, roll 'em, Pete, make 'em jump," that he would play boogie for us.

In the summer Kirk's band worked only from nine to twelve at night, and afterwards we would drive by the Sunset—John Williams and me and the five or six that rode with us. Pete might be playing something like "Sweet Georgia Brown" or "Indiana" when we got there. I'd go home to bathe and change, and when I got back, ten to one Pete would still be jamming the same tune, and maybe some of the guys wailing along with him.

Hot Lips Page was the life of many a Kaycee jam session. After a soloist had blown nine or ten choruses, Lips would start a riff in the background which the other horns picked up. Not many arrangers could improve on Lips when it came to backing up a soloist.

Of course, we didn't have any closing hours in these spots. We could play all morning and half through the day if we wished to, and in fact we often did. The music was so good that I seldom got to bed before midday. It was just such a late-morning occasion that once had Coleman Hawkins hung up. Fletcher Henderson came to town with Hawkins on tenor, and after the dance the band cruised round until they fell into the Cherry Blossom where Count Basie worked. The date must have been early 1934, because Prohibition had been lifted and whisky was freely on sale. The Cherry Blossom was a new nightclub, richly decorated in Japanese style even to the beautiful little brown-skinned waitress.

The word went round that Hawkins was in the Cherry Blossom, and within about half an hour there were Lester Young, Ben Webster, Herschel Evans, Herman Walder, and one or two unknown tenors piling in the club to blow. Ben didn't know the Kaycee tenormen were so terrific, and he couldn't get himself together though he played all morning. I happened to be nodding that night, and around 4 A.M. I woke to hear someone pecking on my screen. I opened the window on Ben Webster. He was saying: "Get up, pussycat, we're jammin' and all the pianists are tired out now. Hawkins has got his shirt off and is still blowing. You got to come down." Sure enough, when we got there Hawkins was in his singlet taking turns with the Kaycee men. It seems he had run into something he didn't expect.

Lester's style was light and, as I said, it took him maybe five choruses to warm up. But then he would really blow; then you couldn't handle him on a cutting session. That was how Hawkins got hung up. The Henderson band was playing in St. Louis that evening, and Bean knew he ought to be on the way. But he kept trying to blow something to beat Ben and Herschel and Lester. When at last he gave up, he got straight in his car and drove to St. Louis. I heard he'd just bought a new Cadillac and that he burnt it out trying to make the job on time. Yes, Hawkins was king until he met those crazy Kansas City tenormen.

Off and on, I was with Andy Kirk right through the thirties and up until 1942. Enough characters passed through the band in that time to fill a book. And if I could set down everything that happened, it would probably turn out a best-seller. Tenormen, as I have said before, were in good supply in Kansas City. We certainly had our share of them. After Slim Freeman, we used Buddy Tate, Ben Webster, Lester Young, Dick Wilson, and Don Byas.

It was when we returned to Kaycee for a summer season at Harry Duncan's Fairyland Park ballroom that Ben Webster was added. What a wild cat! I remember him first as a spoiled youngster from one of the company's most respected Negro families: a family of lawyers and other professional people. From the moment I met him I was fascinated because he was always up to something. Then, too, I liked his tenor. If he felt overanxious, Ben would play roughly, distorting a style which was already full of vitality. It seemed to me he played best when he was either sick or tired.

Ben was really bad boy pick, always wrong. Sometimes John Williams yelled at him on the stand to stop experimenting and play. But after being around with the guys a while Ben became less boisterous, which made me like him better. We used to walk for miles together, and he always took me to jam sessions. At one place, called Val's, we ran into Art Tatum. Art had a radio program, also a job in a dicty private club, but preferred wailing at Val's after hours. It was Val's every night then. Whenever I wasn't listening to Tatum I was playing—Art inspired me so much. Chords he was throwing in then, the boppers are using now. And his mind was the quickest.

Art usually drank a bottle of beer while the other pianists took over, and didn't miss a thing. For instance, there was a run that Buck Washington showed me. (Buck, of the Buck and Bubbles team, played a lotta piano, especially when out jamming. Everything he did was unusual.) Now Art heard me play this run, which consisted of F, E-flat, D-flat, C; (octave up) C, B-flat, A-flat, G; and so on all the way to the top of the keyboard. When he sat down he played it right off. Other pianists had heard and tried, but taken time to pick it up.

I can remember only one man who sounded good following Tatum. His name was Lannie Scott, and he was the most popular pianist in Cleveland, until Tatum came to Cleveland. Then Lannie lost his popularity.

In Kaycee, though, we had a kind of counterpart of Tatum, an ear man called Sleepy who played almost as much as Art, and in the hard keys—A-natural, B-natural, E-natural. Another unsung piano player was Lincoln, known as a three-chord man. His harmonies were the worst, yet he was terrific with the beat. Martha Raye, then eighteen, stopped in Kansas City on her way to California and got hung up listening to Lincoln's nasty beat. She stayed close on two weeks, and was down at the clubs digging the music and singing like mad night after night. Martha hated to leave, nearly missed doing her picture. That was how Kaycee would get you, for there were always places open and music to hear.

Besides the players I've mentioned, and Bennie Moten, Count Basie, Pete Johnson, Sam Price, and Clyde Hart, there were three girl pianists apart from myself. One was Julia Lee, who took little part in the sessions; another I recollect only as Oceola; the third was known as Countess Margaret. Countess was a friend of Lester Young, and when I was sick for a time, Kirk sent for her to take my place for a month. The tour got her, I fear, for she died of tuberculosis before she had done very much, though I hear she was quite good.

Two other pianists I met in Kaycee during the mid-thirties were Tadd Dameron and Thelonius Monk. I was to get to know both of them well in New York in later years. Tadd, who came from Cleveland, was just starting out playing and writing for a band from Kansas. Though very young, he had ideas even then that were 'way ahead of his time. Thelonius, still in his teens, came into town with either an evangelist or a medicine show—I forget which.

While Monk was in Kaycee he jammed every night; really used to blow on piano, employing a lot more technique than he does today. Monk plays the way he does now because he got fed up. Whatever people may tell you, I *know* how Monk can play. He felt that musicians should play something new, and started doing it. Most of us admire him for this. He was one of the original modernists all right, playing pretty much the same harmonies then that he's playing now. Only in those days we called it "Zombie music" and reserved it mostly for musicians after hours.

Why "Zombie music"? Because the screwy chords reminded us of music from *Frankenstein* or any horror film. I was one of the first with these frozen sounds, and after a night's jamming would sit and play weird harmonies (just chord progressions) with Dick Wilson, a very advanced tenor player.

But this is getting ahead of my story. Our next added attraction was Pha Terrell, a good-looking singer who helped to make Kirk's band the hot proposition it soon became, though he never got recognition for doing so. Pha was naturally lucky with females, as all of them—from schoolgirls to schoolmarms—drooled over his smooth, pleasing voice.

As for Ben Webster: he stayed with us two or three years—longer than he'd stuck with anyone—then quit to join Cab Calloway. Until he had gone I didn't realize how much I would miss him. Then I lost twenty-five pounds, as I could not eat for some time.

Lester Young replaced Ben, and sensational as he was, never fitted the band like that big Webster-sound had. In truth, Ben could blow more in two bars, so far as soul and "story" are concerned, than most men can in a chorus. Of course, being accustomed to the big tenor tone, I thought at first that Lester's sound was anemic. But soon I learned to appreciate what he could do, for he was a master at improvising solos of five or fifteen choruses, never repeating.

Lester wasn't with the band too long before he left and went over to Basie, with whom he had worked previously. Basie had, some time before, quit the Moten band to form his own small group. Then along around April of 1935, Bennie died. It seems that a young intern operated on him for removal of tonsils, but something went wrong and the operation killed Bennie. So Basie drew several of Moten's men into his outfit and built the band that blew up a storm at Kaycee's Reno Club.

While the Count was getting this group together, he sent out for Jo Jones on drums. I loved to see Jo teaming with Walter Page, the bassist. Page showed Jo what to do and when to do it, and it was really something to dig these two great musicians. I have caught Basie's orchestra at times when there was no one on the stand except Page and the horns and, believe me, "Big One" swung that band on his bass without much effort.

Meanwhile, we continued our one-nighters, working our way back East to Baltimore, Maryland, where we landed in a beautiful little club called the Astoria. Joe Glaser caught our band and promised to do something about it. He had us come to New York after the engagement, securing a record date on Decca for the band. Never have I written so many things so quickly in my entire career. I must have done twenty in one week, including "Cloudy," "Corky" and "Froggy Bottom" (both new arrangements), "Steppin' Pretty" and "Walkin' and Swingin'."

For nights I could not leave my room, having my meals brought in to me. And at 7 A.M. I was up again for another session.

I had begun to think my arrangements were not worth much, as no one ever wanted to pay for them, and Andy, I knew, could not afford a proper arranger's fee. But the work paid off in the long run. Whenever musicians listened to the band they would ask who made a certain arrangement. Nearly always it was one of mine. "Walkin' and Swingin'" was one of those numbers musicians liked to play. I had tried out trumpet combining with saxes to make the sound of five reeds, and this was different and effective. So other bands took up the arrangement. Our band paid three dollars for the arrangement, Earl Hines ten, and the Casa Lomas fifty-nine; which totals seventy-two dollars—wow!

We made these records in 1936, with the new and superb tenorman Dick Wilson, who had joined us before the tour. We had Booker Collins on bass (Kirk having finally decided to use string bass), and wonderful Ted Brinson on the guitar. In between band sessions, I cut my first Decca solos, including "Isabelle" and "Overhand." We were still supposed to be incorporated, but after our first big record we were no longer that way (smile). The more I asked about it, the dumber everybody got.

Glaser put us in a Cleveland ballroom, where we broadcast nightly over a national hook-up with America's top sports commentator. What power and money can do! We stayed until the name of Kirk was ringing from coast to coast, also three of his stars—Pha Terrell, Dick Wilson, and (let's face it) Mary Lou Williams.

After our first release, "Froggy Bottom," which was a fabulous seller on the juke boxes, we were booked into Harlem's Apollo Theatre. At this time I met luscious Billie Holiday, then just catching on like mad with her early records. She and Teddy Wilson's combo, with Ben Webster's crazy horn, really went together. Pha had a crush on Billie, but was too bashful to visit her alone, so I was made to go along with him. I have been fond of Billie ever since, for I have always felt tremendous warmth and kindness in her.

By now, Dick Wilson had become my special buddy; perhaps tenor players were my weakness. He was a handsome cat, and when we weren't jamming in his room it was generally full of girls. One night, scuffling around

Harlem, Wilson and I fell in the Savoy. After dancing a couple of rounds, I heard a voice that sent chills up and down my spine (which I never thought could happen). I almost ran to the stand to find out who belonged to the voice, and saw a pleasant-looking brown-skinned girl standing modestly and singing the greatest. I was told her name was Ella Fitzgerald, and that Chick Webb had unearthed her from one of the Apollo's amateur hours. Later I learned that Ella never once forgot Chick for giving her the break when others turned their backs—others who wanted her when success came.

By the time we returned to Kaycee, to Fairyland Park, all that could be heard on the jukeboxes was "Froggy Bottom." That particular tune was being played all over the country, and as a result our band started hitting like mad on one-nighters.

I OFTEN WONDER what an agent would do if he had to travel with the band he's booking. After the release of our Decca records, in 1936, the Kirk band traveled five or six thousand miles a week on one-nighters all through the South, repeating most of the dates before coming West again. For nearly three years we toiled across Georgia, Mississippi, Alabama, the Carolinas, Tennessee, Louisiana, Oklahoma, and Texas. I shall never forget some of the beautiful stretches of country, nor the many attractions of New Orleans.

We got little chance to hear the local musicians, though, for we arrived in most places in time to play, and left right afterwards. I have gone to sleep with my fur coat on, near to freezing, and woken up in the car hours later wet from perspiration in the subtropics of Florida.

Our sidemen were making only eight and a half dollars a night, and paying two or three bucks for a decent room. Since they had gone through hardships to keep the band intact, I thought they deserved at least fifteen dollars. I made seventy-five a week, with arranging, and think Pha Terrell got even less.

This didn't make me feel any too good, and I began to lose interest in the project, particularly as we repeated in so many mosquito-infested states. Sometimes I sat on the stand working crossword puzzles, only playing with my left hand. Every place we played had to turn people away, and my fans must have been disappointed with my conduct. If they were, I wasn't bothering at the time.

By now I was writing for some half-dozen bands each week. As we were making perhaps 500 miles per night, I used to write in the car by flashlight between engagements. Benny Goodman requested a blues and I did "Roll 'Em" and several others for him. One week I was called on for twelve arrangements, including a couple for Louis Armstrong and Earl Hines, and I was beginning to get telegrams from Gus Arnheim, Glen Gray, Tommy Dorsey, and many more like them.

As a result of Benny's success with "Roll 'Em" (I received recognition as the composer), our band had to start featuring boogies. One I wrote was "Little Joe from Chicago"—dedicated to Joe Glaser and Joe Louis—and this turned out a big seller when we recorded it in 1938.

I guess our group and Lunceford's did more one-nighters than anyone. Jimmie's trumpet man, Paul Webster, once played with us, and bet me they had traveled more miles than we had. I'd show him either the itinerary or the speedometer and win the bet. That itinerary I have kept for when I want to look back on the impossible!

I remember jumping from St. Louis to Canada: over 750 miles in one day. We played St. Louis until 3 A.M., slept and left for Canada around 11 A.M., and arrived at ten at night—one hour late for the job.

Eventually we worked our way round to Pittsburgh. As soon as I reached my hometown I was told about a great young pianist just coming up. When I asked my brother-in-law who this was, he said it could only be Erroll Garner, then going to Westinghouse High School with my niece. I arranged to visit a friend's house to hear Erroll, and was surprised to find such a little guy, playing so much. And he did not even read music. The next few days were spent just listening to him. He was original then, sounding like no one in the world except Erroll Garner.

At one point I tried teaching him to read by giving him first whole notes, then halves, then quarters. I soon found he didn't want to bother, so I skipped it but tried to guide him any way I could, as others had guided me. I realized he was born with more than most musicians could accomplish in a lifetime.

Our tour took us to Oklahoma City again. Jack Teagarden had given me his family's phone number, so I called Norma Teagarden and she came to our dance. Norma talked about a remarkable guitarist named Charlie Christian, who played electric guitar and was raised in Oklahoma City. Norma is supposed to have taught Christian music, and she told us he could play everything from jazz to the classics. His favorites were "In a Mist" and "Rhapsody In Blue."

Our guitarist, Floyd Smith (who replaced Ted Brinson), considered he could improvise with the best of them, and the guys in the band were anxious to see what he'd do after hearing Charlie. So after the dance everyone tore out to the club where Christian worked. I rode there with Pha Terrell, and when we got in the two guitarists were down with it: Floyd playing his head off for two choruses, then Charlie taking over—very cool.

For a while it was a close call, then Charlie decided to blow. He used his head on cutting sessions, the way Chu Berry used to do, taking it easy while the other musician played everything he knew, then cutting loose to blast him off the map. Never in my life had I heard such inspired and exciting music as Christian beat out of his guitar. Poor Floyd gave it up and walked off the stand. Charlie played for us till daybreak.

I knew many leaders, including Benny Goodman, had tried to get Christian. Up to now he had refused to leave Oklahoma. But feeling that he and jazz should have a break, I asked him would he leave to join B.G. if I wired New York. Finally he said: "Okay, if you say so, Mary." I wired John Hammond right quick, and John (who had heard Charlie previously) got together with B.G. In the summer of '39 Christian made the move, and Benny thanked me on one of his broadcasts for getting him for the band.

At this time I was feeling really dragged so far as Kirk's outfit went. I could not play or write my best for thinking about my share of the loot, and my sacrifices before we made a hit. All my piano solos I turned over to Floyd. I had gotten sick of playing the same ones long ago. Our repertoire consisted of recorded hits, and the solos had to be exactly like those on the records.

I had plenty of offers to leave, but turned them down. Though dissatisfied, I still felt loyal to the band. All the same, Pha and I caused so much annoyance through asking for raises that the "Golden System" decided to add more stars and oust us completely. Henry Wells, who played fine trombone and sang a fair ballad (though he was no Pha Terrell), joined a little later. And the next star to be added was sensational June Richmond who could break up the coldest audience. How I enjoyed her act.

Don Byas came into the band, and now we had two great tenorman—Don and Dick Wilson. I think it was these two who kept me in the band, for I got real kicks out of jamming with them. I began to feel better.

We were booked into the Grand Terrace in Chicago, the place made famous by Earl Hines with the best band he's ever had. Omer Simeon was on clarinet, George Dixon and Walter Fuller on trumpet, Budd Johnson on tenor, Quinn Wilson (bass), and the late Alvin Burroughs on drums. Earl had gone out on the road, and we went in with twenty-five chorus girls and a big floor show. The engagement was sensational. We must have stayed there six months, and I jammed night after night, Chicago being second only to Kansas City for inspiration. Even those chorus girls swung like mad while dancing!

Going to session upon session with Dick Wilson, I became ill and was carted off to the hospital. At least fifteen young interns visited me daily, and I had a radio, record machine, and so many flowers they were lined up along the corridor. I did not get much rest there. The interns offered to pay for my board and room if I stayed another week. I went home to Pittsburgh to convalesce, and after a time rejoined the band.

We must have repeated on our Southern dates about 100 times. Practically everyone was ill from traveling when we got an offer to go into the Cotton Club (on Broadway), by now operating on its last legs. Before this engagement, Harold Baker joined us on trumpet. It seemed our brass section was wilder than ever . . . with Harold, Big Jim Lawson, Howard McGhee, Henry Wells, and Theo Donnelly. Every section hung out together and tried to outdo the others. On the stand, the rhythm was always pushing and telling each other to get on the ball. After the date, we'd say: "We were really going, but you guys . . . huh!" Of course, when a new arrangement was brought out we found time to help each other.

At the end of the Cotton Club deal, John Williams decided to stay in New York and go into the barbecue business with Mary Kirk. He made a few more dates and left the band. He and I were nearly through, anyway. Don Byas also left and was replaced by Edward Inge.

I began to notice that Dick Wilson was looking ill. Then he started disappearing upstairs during intermission. When I took him a drink, I'd find him stretched out on a divan. One night Wilson stayed home, and Harold Baker and I decided to visit him. He was in bed ill, too sick to eat. I ran across the street and got a doctor, who said he should be in the hospital. When Dick heard this he wanted to get out, said it would be the end if he went into the hospital. He must have known he was dying.

The band left New York shortly after for a Southern tour, and the next we heard was that Dick had been taken to the hospital. In a couple of days, they said, he looked like a skeleton, and soon afterwards died. This happened towards the close of 1941, when Wilson could not have been older than thirty.

The next months were my last with Andy Kirk. For twelve years with the band I'd known swell times and bad ones, but barnstorming and the "New System" of management were bringing me down. Looking back, I can smile at our life on the road. Towards the end, though, there was no more brotherly love. I had lost so much through thefts that for a solid year I had to sleep with everything I owned. When someone broke in my trunk and took earrings, Indian-head pennies, and silver dollars which I cherished, I decided to leave.

Dragging my trunk off the bus, I drove to Pittsburgh. Within two weeks, I heard from Harold Baker, who said he'd be coming through Pittsburgh and would stop by and see me. He stopped by all right. The band did not see him any more. Next thing, we both received letters from the union. I countered this move by stating that I would make it very unpleasant for the "New System" if I answered. Nothing further happened to me. Baker was fined a few dollars, I think.

So ended my long association with the Kirk orchestra. Harold and I stayed in Pittsburgh, forming a six-piece combo which had Art Blakey on drums and Orlando Wright on tenor. While rehearsing, Art told us of a terrific singer over on Wylie Avenue. I visited the club and was taken off my feet to see a guy who could sing so pretty and look so handsome. Girls were swooning all around the place, which was packed. Billy Eckstine was the handsome cat, and when I had a chance to meet him I found he lived near me out in East Liberty. It was a pleasure to talk to such a nice cool gentleman.

We rehearsed the new outfit every day, Harold Baker and myself, and through John Hammond contacted some people who were able to find us work. Our first job was in Cleveland, at Mason's Farm, and the combo went over well enough for us to be kept on from August to October—way past the summer season.

Tadd Dameron and most of the musicians around came out to hear us. When Duke Ellington hit Cleveland, all the guys dropped by Mason's Farm. And they liked Harold so much they hired him. Later I learned why he decided to go. There had been a little dissension because he was not from Pittsburgh. It seemed my guys wanted all Pittsburghers in the combo, and had almost come to blows about it. So Harold went to Duke, and I said nothing though I thought plenty.

After he had gone, Art Blakey and the rest had me stop by Pittsburgh to pick up the greatest (they said) on trumpet. We arrived in New York with "The Greatest." He couldn't even blow his nose! I must have auditioned every good trumpetman in NY. No one had realized the value of Harold Baker. He could play ten choruses solo and fall back into a fast-moving ensemble without splitting or missing a note. The new trumpetman would split anything. We were playing tricky arrangements that called for a bit of reading, and I could not even find a sound reader on trumpet. I felt depressed and made up my mind to join Harold as soon as I could.

Duke's band was in California. When it came to New York, Harold and I went off to Baltimore and got married. I traveled with Ellington, arranging about fifteen things for the orchestra. They included "Trumpet No End," my version of "Blue Skies," which I suppose was written early in '42 but not recorded until some years later.

I hope Duke always keeps a band, for he is a genius who gets the best results out of musicians. And what strange guys they were: half of them didn't speak to each other. Too many stars, I guess. When they were speaking, and felt like playing, they'd rearrange some of the band's oldies spontaneously right on the stand. Basie's is the only other band I know capable of doing this.

I moved around with Duke's orchestra until we reached Canada, and I came close to freezing. Then I caught the first train out to New York leaving Harold with the band.

Now I want to write what I know about how and why bop got started. Monk and some of the cleverest of the young musicians used to complain: "We'll never get credit for what we're doing." They had reason to say it. In the music business the going is tough for original talent. Everybody is being exploited through paid-for publicity, and most anybody can become a great name if he can afford enough of it. In the end the public believes what it reads. So it is often difficult for the real talent to break through. Anyway, Monk said: "We are going to get a big band started. We're going to create something that they can't steal, because they can't play it." There were more than a dozen people interested in the idea, and the band began rehearsing in a basement somewhere. Monk was writing arrangements, and Bud Powell and maybe Milt Jackson. Everyone contributed towards the arrangements, and some of them were real tough. Even those guys couldn't always get them right.

It was the usual story. The guys got hungry, so they had to go to work with different bands. Monk got himself a job at Minton's—the house that built bop—and after work the cats fell in to jam, and pretty soon you couldn't get in Minton's for musicians and instruments. Minton's Playhouse was not a large place, but it was nice and intimate. The bar was at the front, and the cabaret was in the back. The bandstand was situated at the rear of the back room, where the wall was covered with strange paintings depicting weird characters sitting on a brass bed, or jamming or talking to chicks.

During the day-time, people played the jukebox and danced. I used to call in often and got many laughs. It is amazing how happy those characters were—jiving, dancing, and drinking. It seemed everybody was talking at the same time: the noise was terrific. Even the kids playing out on the sidewalk danced when they heard the records.

That's how we were then—one big family on West 118th Street. Minton's was a room next door to the Cecil Hotel and it was run by Teddy Hill, the onetime bandleader who did quite well in Europe, and who now managed for Minton. Henry Minton must have been a man about fifty who at one time played saxophone and at another owned the famous Rhythm Club where Louie, Fats, James P., Earl Hines, and other big names filled the sessions. He had also been a union official at Local 802. He believed in keeping the place up, and was constantly redecorating. And the food was good. Lindsay Steele had the kitchen at one time. He cooked wonderful meals and was a good mixer who could sing a while during intermission.

When Monk first played at Minton's there were few musicians who could run changes with him. Charlie Christian, Kenny Clarke, Idrees Sulieman, and a couple more were the only ones who could play along with Monk then. Charlie and I used to go to the basement of the hotel where I lived and play and write all night long. I still have the music of a song he started but never completed.

Sometime in 1943 I had an offer to go into Café Society Downtown. I accepted, though fearing I might be shaky on solo piano since I had been so long with Andy Kirk's band and my own combo. I immediately made some arrangements for six pieces to accompany piano. At my opening people were standing upstairs, which I was glad to see. Georgia Gibbs, who was just starting out, was in the show with Ram Ramirez (composer of "Lover Man"), playing piano for her. Pearl Primus was also in the show, and Frankie Newton had the small band. I was sorry to hear of Newton's death just recently. He was a real great trumpetman, always very easy on the ear.

During this period Monk and the kids would come to my apartment every morning around four or pick me up at the Café after I'd finished my last show, and we'd play and swap ideas until noon or later. Monk, Tadd Dameron, Kenny Dorham, Bud Powell, Aaron Bridges, Billy Strayhorn, plus various disc jockeys and newspapermen, would be in and out of my place at all hours, and we'd really ball. When Monk wrote a new song he customarily played it night and day for weeks unless you stopped him. That, he said, was the only way to find out if it was going to be good. "Either it grew on or it didn't."

I considered myself lucky having men like Monk and Bud playing me the things they had composed. And I have always upheld and had faith in the boppers, for they originated something but looked like losing credit for it. Too often have I seen people being chummy with creative musicians, then—when the people have dug what is happening—put down the creators and proclaim themselves king of jazz, swing or whatever. So the boppers worked out a music that was hard to steal. I'll say this for the "leeches," though: they tried. I've seen them in Minton's busily writing on their shirt cuffs or scribbling on the tablecloth. And even our own guys, I'm afraid, did not give Monk the credit he had coming. Why, they even stole his idea of the beret and bop glasses.

I happened to run into Thelonius standing next door to the 802 union building on 6th Avenue, where I was going to pay my dues. He was looking at some heavy-framed sunglasses in a shop window, and said he was going to have a pair made similar to a pair of ladies' glasses he had seen and liked. He suggested a few improvements in the design, and I remember laughing at him. But he had them made in the Bronx, and several days later came to the house with his new glasses and, of course, a beret. He had been wearing a beret, with a small piano clip on it, for some years previous to this. Now he started wearing the glasses and beret, and the others copied him.

Out of that first band Monk formed grew people like Milt Jackson, J. J. Johnson, and Bud Powell. No one could play like Bud, not until he recorded and the guys had a chance to dig him. And even now they cannot play just like him, for I believe he is the only pianist who makes every note ring. The strength in his fingers must be unequaled. Yet I am forced to the conclusion that Monk influenced him as a kid. He idolizes Monk and can interpret Monk's compositions better than anyone I know. And the two used to be inseparable. At the piano Bud still does a few things the way Monk would do them, though he has more technique.

Yes, Thelonius Monk, Charlie Christian, Kenny Clarke, Art Blakey, and Idrees Sulieman were the first to play bop. Next were Parker, Gillespie, and Clyde Hart, now dead, who was sensational on piano. After them came J. J. Johnson, Bud Powell, Al Haig, Milt Jackson, Tadd Dameron, Leo Parker, Babs Gonzales, Max Roach, Kenny Dorham, and Oscar Pettiford. Those men played the authentic bop, and anybody who heard the small combo that Dizzy kept together for so long in New York should easily be able to distinguish the music from the imitation article.

Often you hear guys blowing a lot of notes and people say: "They're bopping." But they are not. Bop is the phrasing and accenting of the notes, as well as the harmonies used. Every other note is accented. Never in the history of jazz has the phrasing been like it is in bop. Musicians like Dave Brubeck come up with different styles which may be interesting. But they are not bop. Personally, I have always believed that bebop was here to stay. That's one reason I tried to encourage the original modernists to continue writing and experimenting.

Right from the start, musical reactionaries have said the worst about bop. But after seeing the Savoy Ballroom kids fit dances to this kind of music, I felt it was destined to become the new era of music, though not taking anything away from Dixieland or swing or any of the great stars of jazz. I see no reason why there should be a battle in music. All of us aim to make our listeners happy. . . .

ONE DAY I heard that Erroll Garner was opening the following week at a place on 52nd Street. I could hardly wait to hear him again, and got away between shows to catch his opening. He was playing more than ever before, yet seemed to me to have got on a Tatum kick, playing fast runs and all. I reminded Erroll of his own original manner of playing which I had admired so much when he was working in Pittsburgh. Before very long I was glad to hear him back on his old style.

In those times, Garner made a habit of going over to Inez Cavanaugh's apartment, an inspiring spot for musicians where Erroll used to play and compose all day. She told me he once sat gazing at a subdued table lamp of hers, then composed something to fit the mood, which he titled "Lamplight." Often he gets ideas for his pieces from some object or scene that happens to catch his attention.

Some unpleasantness came up on the job about this time, so Erroll went out to California for two years or so. When he returned to New York he was astonished by the reception he got. He had thought of the Three Deuces as just another job, he told me later, and was surprised to see it full of people like Robert Sylvester, Barry Ulanov, and Leonard Feather for his opening. Garner had not realized the impact made by his best-seller, "Laura," in the East. And to back this up, he had dozens of sides with small companies, all of which released his stuff at one time in an attempt to cash in while "Laura" was still hot. So far as jazz pianists go, I guess Erroll has become the fastest seller on records in the world. And he surely deserves this success, for he is a fine and distinctive player.

Unknown to Erroll, I often won small bets on him. You see, many people have the idea that he lacks technique and cannot execute difficult passages. I have been able to prove them wrong. Garner is modern, yet his style is different from bop. He has worked out a sound of his own, doing four beats in the left hand like a guitar. He often uses bass and drums but can play alone and still promote a terrific beat. I like his playing for several reasons, primarily because it is original and has more feeling than almost any pianist I can think of. To me he is the Billie Holiday of the piano. Some musicians put him down because he does not read music nor indulge in a lot of senseless modern progressions. But these are not the important things in jazz.

What would jazz piano have done for inspiration without Earl Hines, Teddy Wilson, Bud Powell, Monk, Tatum, Garner, and the older giants like Willie The Lion Smith, James P. Johnson, and Fats Waller? Without these individualists, many of today's pianists wouldn't be playing anything, for they lack the power of creative thinking. Garner has been an asset and inspiration to the jazz world.

Teddy Wilson I would call a genius. He has studied a great deal, and it is reflected in his playing, but the study has not been allowed to impair his individual style. Many people forget that jazz, no matter what form it takes, must come from the heart as well as the mind. Regardless of what technique he may have, a jazzman must be able also to tell a story. I can never admire a robot pianist whose runs flow straight from his studies instead of his feelings.

For short periods I would be out of the Café, on concert tours and such, and then go back. I had become like one of the fixtures, and was treated like a member of the boss's family. On Sunday nights we had a little party, just the staff and a few musicians. Hazel Scott, Thelma Carpenter, Billy Strayhorn, Aaron Bridges, and Lena Horne and friends would come by and we'd have the most enjoyable time.

The only drag in New York was the many benefit shows we were expected to do—late shows which prevented me from running up on 52nd Street to see my favorite modernists. Sometimes Johnny Gary (the valet) and I would dig a boogie character coming to take me on a benefit. We'd tear across the street to the 18th Hole and hide real quick under a table till the danger was past.

All this time, Minton's Playhouse jumped with cool sounds. People had heard about Monk and were coming from all over town to see what was happening. Teddy Hill had named Monk the "High Priest of Beebop" (at first that spelling was often used), and this title attracted disc jockeys and newspapermen. I cannot remember who gave bebop its name, though it was explained to me that the word was derived from the sound of the modern drummer dropping bombs. Klook Clarke was one who developed the bop method of drumming, and Art Blakey was bombing away very early. Sometimes Art's moving so fast you cannot see his hands: he's a crazy drummer.

Some players, like Art and J. C. Heard, seem to have been born bopping. J. C. played so much drums when he was with Teddy Wilson's great band that they had to hold him back in order to get a good solid bet going. And Art was about the same when I met him—we had a difficult time with him on ballads and straight dance things. He was a real eager-beaver.

Few creative artists can explain or analyze what they write or play because musical ideas come to them spontaneously while they're playing. I have heard Garner and others, listening to a playback on a record date, say: "I didn't know I made that passage." Jazz is created in the mind, felt in the heart and heard through the fingertips.

My reason for feeling that bop is the "next era" music is that it came about spontaneously in the same way as our blues and classic jazz, or any other music that a race of people produces. And I contend that bop is the only real modern jazz, despite the contentions of the copyists of Stravinsky, Hindemith, and Schoenberg. The swing era produced smooth eighth notes which many of our theoreticians are still playing. The phrasing and timing of bop puts it in a different category altogether. The American Negro musician of today is born to this new phrasing, just as in the past he was born to the rhythm and phrasing of ragtime or boogie and naturally played those styles of music.

Bop has become a powerful and, I believe, permanent influence on our native music. The guys who originated it were as gifted as the creative musicians of the thirties and the eras that came before. I have known older musicians discourage them, speak badly of the music. Perhaps these older players feared for themselves and their positions. If so, they were being ridiculous. If some of them were to add a few modern changes here and there in their own work, it might revive their inspiration and help them avoid the danger of artistic stagnation. The sooner the older players and fans accept the new music the better it will be for everyone concerned with jazz. It does not mean that Duke, Louis, Count, Teddy Wilson and the rest will lose out completely. Without a war in music we can all survive. For, regardless of whether the music is bop or something else, it will have to have the jazz foundation—a beat!

Cab Calloway

*From the autobiography of the unsquelchable jazz entertainer Cab Calloway—*Of Minnie the Moocher & Me *(1976; with Bryant Rollins)—another happy account of a performer coming into his own.*

I never will forget coming into New York City. I had never been there before, nor had Betty, though a few of the musicians had. On the road we had all listened to their stories about how hip New York was and how big and jazzed up the nightclubs were. By the time we got to New Jersey, I was a bundle of nerves. We drove up through New Jersey to Fort Lee, where we had to wait for the ferry to get across the Hudson River. The George Washington Bridge hadn't been built yet. I never will forget standing there in the late afternoon. We could see big, bad old New York across the river. Of course there wasn't as many skyscrapers as there are now, but we could see the enormity of the city. I was scared to death and excited as hell. We all stood there, five or six carloads of people, waiting for the ferry, with that wide, beautiful Hudson River all that separated us from New York. Finally the ferry came, and we got on and made that long, slow trip across the river to 125th Street. We drove around Harlem for a while, awestruck by the whole scene. I had never seen so many Negroes in one place before in my life. Finally we started to break up. Various guys in the band had made arrangements to rent rooms with families, and the guys went their separate ways. Betty and I dropped off the musicians who were traveling with us and then drove up Seventh Avenue, the glamour street of Harlem in those days. It was beautiful. Just beautiful. People out in the streets, and nightclubs all over, nightclubs whose names were legendary to me. Then we drove to 139th Street, where we had rented a room with Fletcher Henderson. One hundred and Thirty-ninth Street running from Lenox Avenue across Seventh to Eighth Avenue was called Strivers' Row then because it was the most beautifully kept up block in Harlem. The people who lived there—maids and butlers and postal clerks and cab drivers and mechanics—had saved their pennies all their lives to buy a house. Fletcher's house, between Seventh and Eighth avenues, was three stories and nicely furnished with soft old couches and rocking chairs and lace doilies and fine, flowered wallpaper.

The place was so lovely Betty and I nearly flipped. We had a room on the third floor. Several other musicians and entertainers also rented rooms there. Usually Lee, Fletcher's wife, would cook dinner and the whole "family" would eat together before we went our separate ways to our gigs. That included Lee, because Mrs. Henderson was a fine trumpet player in the pit orchestra at the Lafayette Theatre.

I was damned impressed by Fletcher. He was around thirty years old, a handsome, thin, fair-skinned man with a mustache. He had been born in Georgia, attended Atlanta University, and then came to New York in the early 1920s. He said he had come to do graduate work, but some of us suspected he really came to play jazz. He joined up with W. C. Handy, and before anyone knew it he was leading his own band at the Club Alabam. By the time I came to New York, he was at the famous Roseland in midtown Manhattan, playing a style of music that was strictly his and that later came to be known as "swing." Years later, of course, Fletcher joined up with Benny Goodman and wrote and arranged many of Benny's hit tunes.

Fletcher's band at Roseland was something else. His lineup included himself on piano, Coleman Hawkins on clarinet and tenor sax, Bob Escudero on tuba, Buster Bailey on clarinet and alto, Benny Carter on alto and soprano sax and clarinet, Kaiser Marshall on drums, Russell Smith, Elmer Chambers, and Joe Smith on trumpet, and Charlie Dixon on banjo and guitar. It was a hell of an outfit. When I arrived in New York the first thing I did was go down to Roseland with Fletcher to hear what kind of music he was playing. Then I went over to Connie's Inn to see my old buddy Louis Armstrong, who was the star of Carroll Dickerson's big orchestra and was also featured with Leroy Smith's band in the revue *Connie's Hot Chocolates* playing down at the Hudson Theatre on Broadway. It was in that show that Satchmo introduced "Ain't Misbehavin'"—his first big hit. Thanks to Louis I later joined the show.

As I made the rounds of New York jazz clubs and variety shows, I began to realize that my little band was in for trouble. We had come out of the Midwest playing old-time, unhip, novelty tunes with a little weak Dixieland jazz. Compared to the jumping jazz they were playing in New York, we were strictly from the sticks. I had seen the problem coming and I had argued with the guys all summer. I tried to get them to loosen up, to expand their repertoire, to include some straight-up jazz and swing numbers, but they fought me all the way. We had some pretty strong arguments about it, but it was a corporate band and I was outnumbered. We didn't change, and it was a disastrous mistake.

About a week after we hit New York, we opened at the Savoy Ballroom on Lenox Avenue near 140th Street in Harlem. Now, the Savoy Ballroom was strictly big-time. There were always two bands alternating sets of twenty minutes each, and the crowds were used to bands like King Oliver and Chick Webb, the drummer who had influenced me in Baltimore. It was in 1934 at the Savoy that Chick first played "Stomping at the Savoy," written for him by Edgar Sampson, and it was there that Chick created what came to be known as the "Savoy tempo," a semi-quick, two-four rhythm good for dancing. Dancing was the main activity at the Savoy. The place could hold hundreds of people and the dance floor was huge. The crowds were 90 percent colored at the Savoy.

We opened at the Savoy in November 1929, barely a month after the crash. By the end of the year, investors had lost $40 billion and more than 6 million people were out of work, 5,000 banks had failed, and 32,000 businesses were bankrupt. There were breadlines everywhere and near-riots in New York. Everybody was angry with poor old Herbert Hoover. Everybody except people in the entertainment world, I guess. It's a funny thing, when things get really bad, when the bottom falls out of the economy, that's when people really need entertainment. It's just as true today as it was in 1929. During the great depression of 1974–1975, when 8 million people were out of work, the entertainment business was booming. The movie industry was making a mint, Broadway was having its best season in years, the record industry was cleaning up, and the number of concerts increased. I suppose that people figure, what the hell, let's go out and have a ball. It's one way to get away from the gloom.

That's the way it was in 1929. Jazz was swinging, the theaters on Broadway were cleaning up, and in Harlem the nightclubs, speakeasies, and jazz spots were packed every night. Everybody was making it. Everybody, that is, except the Alabamians.

We went into the Savoy opposite Cecil Scott and his band. Cecil, a saxophonist, and his brother Lloyd had brought their band to New York from Springfield, Ohio, in 1926. By 1929 Cecil had developed his own style and was running the band himself. He was a bitch; those guys played gut-bucket-stomping, gutsy New York jazz. Cecil was one of the most exciting and fiery horn blowers in Harlem . . .

In addition to playing up a storm, Cecil and his band would put on a hell of a show. Old Cecil would get to honking and march down off the bandstand and half the band would follow him, winding through the crowds on the dance floor just blowin' away. Man, the people would go crazy behind that, jumping and dancing and carrying on all over the place.

After Cecil and his band finished their first set, we came out. Man, we looked like a million dollars. The guys were eleven pieces of pure gold, dressed sharp as a tack—black Prince Albert coats and straight trousers, ascots, and black Oxford shoes spit-shined so you could see your reflection in them. Then I jumped out cool as an ice cube in a white tuxedo with a white baton. And of course the Savoy was such a pretty club, lights and colors all around. Man, we were beautiful—until we hit our first lick. Brother, when we started playing that dipsy-doodle music from the Midwest—"Come Up and See Me Sometime" or "Are You Home, Josephine," or "Bye, Bye, Blues"—the damned dance floor cleaned out. You could feel the place go cold. Cecil had damn near set it on fire and we just cooled it off. We were an absolute flop, bust, zero, nothing. Our music didn't suit those jazzed-up people worth a damn.

We got our notice that first night. Charlie Buchanan, one great tough guy who later became one of my best friends, was managing the place. He came up to us after the show, scowled, and said, "I'm sorry, fellas, but you had your chance. You've got to go." We had a two-week contract and on the first night we got our two-week notice.

I was furious with the guys in the band. "Dammit," I hollered, "I tried to tell you this jive music wouldn't make it in New York City. This ain't Toledo or Mendota, this is New York. You've got to come into New York swinging! I'll stay with you through the end of this gig, but after that, I'm splitting. You all can go back to Chicago or wherever you want, but that's it for me." They were all angry and upset, too, but there was nothing they could do. I wanted to make it in New York and I knew that those guys didn't have the stuff to get over. It was time for me to split.

The Savoy didn't know quite what to do. They had a two-week contract with a weak band and no way out. Then Charlie Buchanan whipped up a Battle of the Bands for our last performance and crowds started coming in, in anticipation of the great war that was to take place between the Alabamians and the Savoy's house band, the Missourians.

The Missourians had quite a band. They couldn't compare to Chick Webb or King Oliver, to Duke Ellington or Jimmie Lunceford, but they were a hell of a lot better than the Alabamians. And on our last night in the gig, the place was packed. The idea was that each band would play a couple of sets, trying to blow the other band away, and the audience would clap and cheer to decide which had won.

The Missourians ran us off the damned bandstand. We had tried during rehearsals to add a little swing to our sound, but it hadn't worked. We were blown away. The audience hollered for the Missourians. After we played, there wasn't a sound. Then the M.C. asked the audience which bandleader they preferred. I was holding my breath. I knew I had developed a style, and was known in the Savoy as quite a character. I would run across the stage, directing the band, singing along with it into my megaphone, leading the guys in call and response, and the audience loved it. Now, when the M.C. pointed to me, the audience stamped and screamed and whistled. I knew I had won and it felt great. But it didn't help my situation. The Alabamians left town and I was stuck without a job like millions of other guys across the country. I had enough money to get along—for a while—but I damned sure needed some work soon.

I was too young to know it at the time, but I learned an important lesson from that experience. Never make so many compromises that you end up doing somebody else's thing and not your own. I was too anxious to keep the band. I disagreed with the kind of music that the Alabamians went into New York with, but I said to myself, "Well, hell, they're not the best thing around, but they're the best I've got right now." I was young and looking for a start, so the only thing I could do at the time was swallow my pride—and my judgment—and stay with them. It may have been a mistake, but I learned from it. Since then I've rarely made compromises of that sort. When I've strongly disagreed with the format of a show, or the music a band was playing, or the way something was being handled, I've gotten out. . . .

I've made compromises in my life, plenty of them. Any person who is successful makes compromises, but when I reach the point where the thing I'm doing has no integrity for me personally, then I say, "Screw it. Let someone else do it." The experience at the Savoy taught me that lesson.

Lionel Hampton

Hampton's own account of how he became the fourth man in the Benny Goodman Quartet. He and Teddy Wilson, already with Goodman, were, famously, the first black musicians to be conspicuously integrated into a white jazz group. From Hamp *(1989; with James Haskins).*

When Benny Goodman arrived in L.A. for a two-week engagement at the Palomar Ballroom, Hammond told Goodman that he ought to hear me. Before Benny got around to coming by, two of his guys, Hymie Schertzer and Pee Wee Erwin, dropped in, and I guess they told Benny he ought to come and hear me, too.

Benny had just come off a gig in Denver, Colorado, where his band didn't take. In fact, I heard that after that Benny was thinking about breaking up his band because he wasn't having any success. It was John Hammond who thought he should get a more exciting sound—and who decided my sound might be what Benny needed.

Now, John Hammond knew that I was black, and by recommending me to Benny, he was leading Benny into uncharted territory—an integrated band. Benny did have Teddy Wilson traveling with him, but Teddy didn't play with the band. Teddy only played intermission piano. By recommending me, John Hammond was pushing Benny into a completely different arrangement.

Benny was busy, so he sent his brother Harry out to the Paradise. Harry must have brought back a good report, because the next night Benny came himself. He sat at one of the front tables, and I remember thinking he looked familiar. But I didn't try to place him in jazz circles. With his granny glasses and his business suit, I thought maybe he was a politician or somebody whose picture I'd seen in the papers. Then, during a break, Sam Ervine whispered to me that Benny Goodman was in the audience, and then I knew why the guy looked so familiar.

After the break, he got up on the bandstand with me, pulled his clarinet out of his case, and we started to jam. We jammed all night and into the morning—it must have been about six o'clock when he finally said, "Pleased to meet ya," and left. For me, it was a night to remember. I had all his records and had copied his solos and his riffs. But he was white and we moved in different circles. I was honored to jam with Benny Goodman.

The next night was even more exciting. I'm up onstage playing as usual, and I hear this clarinet player next to me, and I turn and there is Benny Goodman, playing right next to me. He had brought Gene Krupa and Teddy Wilson along, and the four of us got on the bandstand together, and man, we started wailing out. We played for two hours straight, and Benny liked the sound we made so well that he said, "Come on and join me at a recording session tomorrow at RCA Victor, out in Hollywood."

Well, I was so excited that I couldn't sleep. I didn't get to sleep until about seven or eight o'clock the next morning. Around eleven, Gladys's mother shook me awake and told me that a Mr. Goodman had called and he was waiting for me at the RCA Victor studio. I was wide awake in an instant. I jumped out of bed and into some clothes and hailed a taxi for the Paradise to pick up my vibes. On the way, I decided I should tell Gladys, so I had the taxi driver stop at her shop. She decided that she should come with me.

When we walked into the RCA Victor studio, Benny gave me a look, but he didn't say anything. Teddy Wilson and Gene Krupa were there. We didn't do much rehearsing before we started to record. We did two numbers—"Moonglow" and "Dinah." I had a great time. I felt as if I'd been playing with those guys all my life. That was August 19, 1936, and I'll never forget it.

I recorded two more times with members of the Benny Goodman Orchestra before they left Los Angeles. About a week later, I played vibes with Teddy Wilson and His Orchestra. Benny was on clarinet, but for that session he was part of Teddy's group. I liked that—Benny was very unselfish when it came to recording, and he had no problem with his guys recording on their own, and even playing in "their orchestras." Teddy had his own deal with Brunswick Records, and we did "You Came to My Rescue" and "Here's Love in Your Eyes." And after that, without Benny, we did "You Turned the Tables on Me" and "Sing, Baby, Sing."

Benny and his band finished their gig at the Palomar and went back to New York, and I went back to the Paradise. A few weeks later, the records I had made with Benny and Gene and Teddy were released. They really took off. Every one of them was a sensational success. When the impact of that success hit Benny, he decided he wanted me as part of his orchestra. One night, a couple of months later, Tyree Glenn tells me that Benny Goodman's on the phone. Now, Tyree was in the habit of playing practical jokes on me, and I thought this was just another one of those. Part of me wanted to believe it, but nobody had ever called me to come east before. I didn't think that was going to happen to me. So I just ignored Tyree. Over the next week or so, Tyree kept shouting "Benny's on the phone from New York," but I thought he was just joking.

Then one night Gladys answered the phone, and she and Benny got to talking serious. After she hung up, she said that Benny had offered me a one-year contract at $550 a week. He also said that she could come along and travel with the band. I couldn't believe it. That was big money. But that was also a big change. Going with Benny meant moving to New York, and I wasn't sure I wanted to relocate. But Benny Goodman had the biggest big band in the country; he had Gene Krupa and Teddy Wilson. Playing with them was like being in heaven. I couldn't make up my mind. I did know one thing: I wasn't going to New York without Gladys.

Gladys never really asked me how I felt about it. She talked it over with everybody but me. She even had her brother, Dr. Riddle, come from Texas to discuss the matter. For Gladys it meant leaving her business, so she talked it over with Beazie DeVaughan, her partner. Beazie agreed, and Gladys and Beazie remained close friends for the rest of their lives. She talked it over with Dr. Chops. She used to like to tell how everybody said to her, "Go, Gladys. This man is going to be a star." She gambled on me. She finally told me, "We're going to New York," and next thing I knew I was on my way to join Benny Goodman in New York City.

We drove from Los Angeles to New York. Benny Goodman offered to pay for train tickets, but Gladys wasn't taking any chances. She said, "No, I'm going to take my car so if anything happens we can get in the car and come back home." So we set out in the early hours of the morning on November 9, 1936. We had a white Chevrolet, and my drums and vibes were in the back. Allen Durham, a trombone player with me, helped us drive. We were going to stop only when we had to, and make that cross-country drive in record time.

One stop we had to make was in Arizona. You see, we had to get married. Gladys's mother wouldn't let us go unless we promised to get married. Said she wouldn't have us living together in New York City. We had to get married, and we had to send her back the marriage certificate. Gladys's mother said, "You don't do it, you come on back home."

Now, Gladys and I had been together a long time by then. We were shacking up. We acted like we were married. In fact, a lot of people thought we were. Milt Hinton thought we were married when he came out to Los Angeles in 1933. But we'd never gotten around to that formality. But now Gladys's mother said we had to. I said, "It's all right with me," and Gladys said the same thing. So we drove until we got to Arizona, where you could get married right away and didn't have to wait, and we got married in Yuma in about five minutes. It was Armistice Day, 1936, and the next stop was the post office so we could send the marriage certificate to my new mother-in-law.

I don't remember much about that trip. We were so excited we weren't worrying about hotels or anything. We just slept in the car and kept on coming. Route 66, Route 80. When we had to stop we went to the black part of town. But we were rushing so fast that we didn't stop much. We had to stay on the road because we were due in New York to play with Benny on November 21, 1936. Gladys drove night and day, and we made it in record time. We even had some time to settle into the Big Apple before my debut with the Benny Goodman Orchestra.

Gladys had a friend from California in New York, who she'd gone to school with. Her name was Hazel, and Gladys had asked her to find a place for us. When we got there, Hazel had a place all picked out. She said, "I'm gonna take you on Sugar Hill. You're with Benny Goodman, you gotta be on Sugar Hill." It was a really nice neighborhood of tall apartment buildings that overlooked the Polo Grounds and the rest of Harlem. The 500 block of Edgecombe Avenue and the buildings right around that block were Sugar Hill, and we lived at 409 Edgecombe. The big shots lived in that building, including W. E. B. DuBois. Paul Robeson lived in the neighborhood. Duke Ellington lived right down the street, and every Sunday when we were off we used to have dinner together with Duke and his son, Mercer, and his sister, Ruth. She lived about a block down, around 375 or 390 Edgecombe, and she and Gladys were very good friends. Every Sunday after dinner, Duke and I and whoever else was around would have jam sessions in Ruth's apartment. She was good to us, a wonderful person.

A couple of years later, we decided we were in New York to stay, so we got our own apartment at the Doris E. Brooks Houses on 137th Street. We stayed there for more than thirty years. In fact I didn't move out of there until after Gladys died.

When I got in touch with Benny to let him know we were in town, the first thing he wanted me to do was go to a doctor so he could get insurance on me. Benny didn't leave anything to chance—he wanted his musicians insured. The doctor checked me out, and afterward he said, "The doctor who operated on your appendix did a tremendous job. Who was it?" "Dr. Jesus," I answered.

The next item on the agenda was a photo session. Benny and Gene Krupa and Teddy Wilson and I all went to a studio and the photographer made pictures of the four of us, in all different poses. By this time the record we cut back in Los Angeles was selling like hotcakes and everybody wanted a picture of the "Benny Goodman Quartet." Well, they couldn't supply those pictures until the fourth member of that quartet arrived.

Then, Benny asked me if I needed an advance, and he handed me two weeks' pay in cash. Since Gladys was the banker in the family, I wasn't used to having this much cash. But I was glad to have it, because I wanted to buy her a wedding present. I asked the guys where I could get some nice jewelry and furs, and they sent me to Seventh Avenue, and I rushed up and down Seventh Avenue, and I ended up buying Gladys a half-carat diamond ring and a secondhand mink coat. When I got back home, I proudly presented Gladys with her wedding gifts. She accepted them, and I could tell she was pleased. But she wanted to know, "How much money do you have in your pocket?" I had about thirteen dollars. Gladys got on the phone with Benny right away and told him never again to give me that much money. Benny promised not to do it again, and from then on, Gladys and Benny wouldn't even talk about money to me.

I made my debut with Benny Goodman at the Madhattan Room of the Pennsylvania Hotel across the street from Penn Station. It was November 21, 1936, and it wasn't exactly the kind of debut I had planned. I found out at rehearsal that I wasn't going to be in the Benny Goodman Orchestra, I was going to be part of the Benny Goodman Quartet that only played for part of every show.

I wasn't the only one who was surprised. So was Gene Krupa. He didn't like that arrangement any more than I did. Gene had been with Benny for a long time, and Benny hadn't even told him. That was Benny—he made these major decisions and forgot to tell anybody else. Gene calmed down when Benny told him that he would be getting a double salary.

Gene had more reason to be upset than me. There were good reasons why Benny couldn't put Teddy and me in the orchestra. I don't know why it hadn't occurred to me before that he was going to have a lot of trouble booking his band into those big white places with two black musicians. Teddy Wilson wasn't part of the Benny Goodman Orchestra, either. He couldn't sit on the stage with the white musicians. He came on for specialty numbers and also played intermission piano. I was going to play under the same arrangement. That's how it was in those days—you didn't have mixed bands.

Sometimes a black musician would be featured with a white band, or the other way around. Louis Armstrong recorded with Jimmy Dorsey the same year I joined Benny Goodman. Later on, after Gene Krupa got his own band in the early 1940s, he featured Roy Eldridge. But they didn't live and travel together.

Benny had Teddy and me traveling with the band, and both of us were on the regular payroll.

I wanted to play with the Benny Goodman Quartet, and Benny was paying me good money. And my name was getting out there. At the Pennsylvania Hotel they had live broadcasts of Benny's music, and so through radio I was getting famous on the East Coast just as I had on the West Coast.

We were still playing at the Pennsylvania Hotel when we went into the Paramount Theater for a gig. Benny planned on doubling at both places, because he didn't hold out much hope for big success at the Paramount. He hadn't usually done very well in theaters. But when we arrived at the Paramount for an early-morning rehearsal, we were astounded to see a couple of hundred kids already lined up at the box office. By ten o'clock that morning there were over four thousand kids. An integrated band was such an unheard-of thing, even in New York in those days, that some people actually worried that there would be a race riot. I remember that *Down Beat* carried the headline, "Predicted Race Riot Fades As Crowd Applauds Goodman Quartet." In fact, we were so popular at the Paramount that we had kids screaming and dancing in the aisles, and parents clucking just like they later did about rock and roll. Something like twenty-one thousand people heard us that first day, and every day after that. It was some kind of record. We ended up leaving the Madhattan Room and just playing at the Paramount for several weeks.

It was with the Benny Goodman Quartet that I became famous as a jazz vibraharpist. There was another guy, named Adrian Rollini, who was a vibes player and had made a name for himself before me. But he played cocktail-lounge music, not jazz. By the time I joined Benny, I had developed my style, and it really hasn't changed much since. With my background as a drummer, it made sense for me to drum on the vibraharp. (By the same token, my famous two-fingered piano style comes from playing the vibraharp—I use my fingers like mallets.) The effect was like a percussion instrument. The Goodman Quartet played things very fast, and that suited me, the fastest drummer in the world, just fine. But something I did that was unique was to make use of the silences—I used long rests between phrases, and that made for some high drama.

Benny also took good care of Teddy and me. After a show, he'd have a limousine drive us up to Harlem so we wouldn't have to worry about getting a taxi. Back in those days, too, taxi drivers would pass by a black man, and would refuse to go to Harlem at night.

But I had an edge when I arrived in New York. Not only did I have a job with the hottest big band of the day, I also had my own following. *Down Beat* magazine named me the most exciting artist of the year 1936, and that was no small bit of recognition in those days. I was with Benny, but I was my own man.

Traveling with Benny Goodman was a lot different from traveling with my own band. We used to cram into a couple of cars. With Benny, we traveled by train. Benny would have a drawing room, and we would have a drawing room. But when I had my own band, we were all black and we knew what to expect, and the audiences knew what to expect. With Benny, touring with two black musicians was a pioneering effort. Nobody had ever traveled with an integrated band before, and even though Teddy Wilson and I were only part of the Benny Goodman Quartet, not the whole orchestra, that was still too much for some white folks.

I don't know how many times Teddy and I were mistaken for servants—Mr. Goodman's valet or the water boy for the Benny Goodman Orchestra. We learned to take it in stride. There wasn't anything else we could do. We knew what society was like.

Benny didn't have to have us in his band, and he put up with a lot. Theater managers would tell him they were getting a lot of mail protesting Teddy and me, but Benny wouldn't back down. He once bopped a guy in the head with his clarinet when the guy told him he should "get those niggers off his show." Meanwhile, he was getting flack from some critics in the black community who accused him of using blacks. That was nonsense. He didn't have to hire Teddy or me; he hired us because we made his kind of music. And this was in the North. Benny knew he was going to have to make some serious advance plans when we went south.

Benny was invited to perform at the Pan American Casino at the Dallas Exposition in the late summer of 1937. We had just finished up some gigs in Hollywood, including the film *Hollywood Hotel,* and were working our way back east, so it fit in with the schedule. But Benny knew that was going to be a rough gig for an integrated band, because no integrated orchestra had ever played in the Deep South before. So Benny took precautions. In fact, he planned that visit like a military campaign.

First, he made it a part of the orchestra's contract that Teddy and I would be able to stay with the rest of the band in the Statler Hotel in downtown Dallas and that we would also be able to use the same entrance and elevators. (You had to dot every *i* and cross every *t* in those days. If he hadn't made that a specific part of the contract, the hotel would have let us stay there but probably in the basement next to the boiler, and they would have made us come through the service entrance.) The hotel people and the centennial committee weren't too happy about signing that contract, but they wanted Benny Goodman. He was the King of Swing, the biggest name in music in the country, and if they wanted him, they would have to take him on his terms.

But Benny went further than that. He had his own car, a Packard, sent down to Dallas by train so Teddy and I wouldn't have to worry about taxi drivers refusing to pick us up. He also hired a guy just to escort us from the hotel entrance to our rooms and back so we wouldn't be exposed to any unpleasantness.

I knew about all these precautions, so I wasn't worried about going south with Benny. People said to me, "Why you goin' down south? Those white folks will kill you." And I'd say, "They'll have to kill Benny Goodman first."

As it turned out, all these precautions except the car weren't necessary most of the time. Both Teddy and I wound up staying with family a good portion of the trip because we felt more comfortable. Teddy had been born and raised in a town about thirty miles outside Dallas, and he hardly ever used the hotel room. And Gladys had her brother, Dr. Riddle, in Dennison, and we preferred to stay with him.

But you can only take so many precautions against unpleasantness. Teddy and I got insulted anyway, once, and then Teddy got really insulted.

The case involving Teddy and me was minor. We had a drink from a water fountain marked "White." I don't remember why we did it now—maybe we felt protected by the name of Benny Goodman and just wanted to test the limits. A policeman saw us and shouted, "You niggers, don't you ever do that no more!" We walked away, and that was the end of that.

The thing with Teddy happened that night when we were playing at the Pan American Casino. A white man who had known Teddy since he was young tried to bring a bottle of champagne up to him on the bandstand. He was just about to give it to Teddy when a policeman blocked his way. The cop knocked the bottle out of the man's hand and said, "No champagne for niggers," he said. When the man protested, the cop called him a nigger lover. Teddy witnessed this, and he got real depressed. The next morning he didn't show up for rehearsal, and Benny went to his room to find out why. Teddy had stayed in the hotel that night, and he was in his room, brooding. He didn't want to tell Benny why, but Benny considered it a capital crime to miss rehearsal and Teddy had to tell him to save his job.

Benny was furious when he found out what happened. I think he called Marcus of Neiman-Marcus. Anyway, somebody who knew an important local police official got the word out about the cop who had insulted Teddy. He came to the hall, grabbed the guy by the shoulder, and told him to get the hell out.

That night, the police commissioner himself sent a bottle of champagne to the bandstand, with a card that read, "To Teddy Wilson, the great son of Texas."

We were probably lucky that that's all that happened. There had been predictions of real trouble. But as John Hammond later wrote on the front page of *Down Beat:* "All along I had the suspicion that if the Trio and Quartet made excellent music the crowd would swallow its prejudices and acclaim the artists."

Benny Goodman was no civil rights activist. He didn't talk much about racism. His whole concentration was on music, but it galled him that something as petty as race prejudice could mess up the music he wanted to hear and play. He realized that America was poorer in music than it should be, because of racism. He understood that a guy like Teddy couldn't concentrate on his music when he had to deal with hate. So Benny saw to it that his musicians were protected. And he also saw to it that a lot of talented black musicians and singers got a chance to show their talent to the white public. Benny had a weekly radio show, and he started featuring black artists on it. The first one was Ella Fitzgerald, who'd just had her first big hit, "A-Tisket, A-Tasket." Benny would always say, "I am selling music, not prejudice," and in his no-nonsense way he did a lot more for black artists and blacks in general than most people give him credit for.

John Hammond

Hammond, the most famous discoverer of talent in jazz—famous for his energy, his taste, his enthusiasm, and his ego—wrote his autobiography, John Hammond on Record, *in 1977 (with Irving Townsend). Not every detail may be strictly accurate, but his championship of Billie Holiday and Count Basie is history.*

My happiest discovery occurred one night about two weeks before the famous Hot Club concert at which the Goodman Trio was introduced. Having heard enough of Benny's music for the evening, I went out to my car, parked across the street from the Congress, not quite decided where to go next. It was cold as only Chicago in January can be, and I turned on the car radio. I had a twelve-tube Motorola with a large speaker, unlike any other car radio in those days. I spent so much time on the road that I wanted a superior instrument to keep me in touch with music around the country. It was one o'clock in the morning. The local stations had gone off the air and the only music I could find was at the top of the dial, 1550 kilocycles, where I picked up W9XBY, an experimental station in Kansas City. The nightly broadcast by the Count Basie band from the Reno Club was just beginning. I couldn't believe my ears.

Two years before, when Coleman Hawkins had left Fletcher Henderson for his celebrated expatriate sojourn in Europe, Smack discussed with me the possibility of bringing in Lester Young as a replacement. He was playing out in the sticks with a small band headed by Bill Basie and probably would welcome a shot at the big time.

I remembered Basie, of course, from that night at Covan's, behind the Lafayette Theater in Harlem, when he was Benny Moten's second pianist. He was a little guy then, weighing about one hundred and twenty pounds, and playing up a storm (as he also did on his first important record as featured soloist, "Prince of Wails"). I had heard Young with King Oliver in 1933, although not enough to form an opinion one way or the other. If Fletcher wanted him that was enough for me.

His band, interestingly enough, didn't agree. They wanted Chu Berry because he had Bean's full-bodied tone, which Lester certainly did not. John Kirby, Buster Bailey, that fine clarinet, and Russell Procope, the tasteful alto who later settled in for a long term with the Duke, they were all groaning about Lester. Fletcher took him on anyway, although it wasn't a happy experience. For one thing, until he found digs of his own Lester stayed with the Hendersons, and Leora made him miserable by constantly playing Hawkins records, evidently hoping that Bean's booming solos would influence Lester's style of playing!

It was not long before Lester returned to Basie.

So, I had known of the Basie band without ever having heard it play. And what I picked up from Kansas City was amazing. Basie had developed an extraordinary economy of style. With fewer notes he was saying all that Waller and Hines could say pianistically, using perfectly timed punctuation—a chord, even a single note—which could inspire a horn player to heights he had never reached before. This inspired economy, the right note at the right place, has always been one of my criteria for fine performance, whether jazz or classical. It accounts for my early interest in Bartok quartets, for my becoming a Stravinsky fanatic, as well as a jazz buff, and perhaps it explains why I have always found excitement in both kinds of music. Somewhere between 1932 and 1936 Basie had discovered how effective simplicity can be.

After that I went to my car every night to listen to Basie. Once I dragged Benny out to listen with me in that cold, cold car. He was less impressed than I'd hoped ("So what's the big deal?"); when I am enthusiastic I often expect my companions to feel what I feel. Just as I could hardly expect Mildred Bailey to pronounce Billie Holiday the greatest jazz singer she had ever heard, I suppose I was asking too much of Benny. There I was in the parking lot of the Congress, telling him that a nine-piece group in Kansas City was the best I had ever heard, while across the street he was enjoying a triumph with one of the smash bands of the country. He made no comment.

I immediately began writing about Basie in *Down Beat.* I talked about the band wherever I went and as soon as possible I went to Kansas City to see for myself. After checking in at the Muehlebach Hotel I walked down to 12th Street to a dingy building with a second floor which must have been a whorehouse, because there were girls lounging on the stairway. On the street level was the Reno Club with signs advertising domestic Scotch for 10¢, imported Scotch for 15¢, and beer 5¢. Hot dogs were 10¢, hamburgers were 15¢, and drinks served at tables were 25¢. There was no cover, no minimum, and there was a show which included chorus girls and the Basie band with Jimmy Rushing and Hattie Noel as vocalists. It was quite a bargain.

The first thing I saw was the high bandstand, at the top of which sat Jo Jones surrounded by his drums. Basie sat at the left with Walter Page and his bass crowded as close to the piano as he could get. In the front line were Lester Young, Buster Smith on alto, and Jack Washington on baritone. Behind them were two trumpets, Oran "Lips" Page and Joe Keys, and the trombone, Dan Minor. Jimmy Rushing, the famous Mr. Five-by-Five, sang the blues, and Hattie Noel, as big as Rushing and dressed in a ridiculous pinafore, was the comedienne and a fairly good singer.

The band played long sets, working almost constantly, and on Saturday nights it played a so-called "spook dance" which lasted from eight in the evening to eight the following morning. I noticed an open window behind the bandstand at which occasional transactions took place; I assumed that "tea" was being passed. And no wonder. Liquor, even at those prices, was too expensive for musicians who were making $15 a week. Basie was paid $18, but he had a day job playing the organ at station WHB, so he paid Lester, Jo Jones, and Walter Page a little extra each week. It was the announcer at WHB who dubbed Basie "Count" because, as he pointed out, there was an Earl Hines, a King Oliver, a Duke Ellington, and Bill Basie deserved to join the royalty of jazz.

But the band! Jo Jones has always been my favorite drummer. His subtle playing with brushes or sticks, and the effects he got with cymbals, particularly the high-hat, were beautiful. There was extraordinary wit in his playing. His foot on the bass drum never pounded, yet the accents were where they needed to be. And the wide smile he wore showed clearly that he felt the lift he gave the band and enjoyed it thoroughly. (Born Jonathan, I shortened him to Jo—not Joe—so there would be distinction in his name, as well as in his drumming.)

Buster Smith was the best lead alto Basie ever had. It was Buster who taught Charlie Parker, and who led Basie's reed section as no one has since. But Buster was a strange man. He would not leave Kansas City with the band because he was sure it would never make it in the big time! Instead, he remained behind, working in the Midwest and Texas. Even when Basie celebrated his twenty-fifth anniversary as a bandleader, no one could persuade Buster to get on an airplane and lend his alto to the occasion.

Lester Young—not yet known as Prez—and Lips Page were the soloists. Enough has been heard of them since their stand at the Reno Club to need little amplification here. I might say, though, that Lester was already at his absolute zenith. He already had that contained, unemphatic tone and legato phrasing; he was phenomenal. Walter Page, half-brother to Lips, was a seasoned and superb bass. Basie, Rushing, and Young had all been with his Blue Devils several years before. Now he was the man on whom Basie depended most. He wanted Walter as close to the piano as he could place him, well aware that the economical Basie style demanded the support and rhythmic line of a great bass player.

Later that night we ended up on 18th Street, where Lester Young sat in with Clarence Johnson, a fabulous boogie-woogie pianist. This was the era of the Pendergast machine in Kansas City, and the town was wide open and filled with jazz. Rachel Maddox, the short-story writer, lived in Kansas City, and one night while I was there I took her to hear Basie. Rachel wanted to return the favor, so she took me to a club called the Orange Blossom in Kansas City, Kansas, where, she said, there was a wonderful girl pianist, Vassie Mae McGhee. Vassie was indeed great, and it was only after we listened for two and a half hours that I realized that Vassie Mae was a female impersonator. Later I asked Pete Johnson about her. "You mean Joe McGhee?" Pete asked. "He's a hell of a piano player." I never could bring myself to look up Vassie Mae again. What would I have done in the mid-thirties with a jazz pianist in drag? But thanks to Rachel Maddox at least I heard one.

WHAT I HEARD in that first nine-piece Basie band was the sort of free, swinging jazz I have always preferred. Fletcher's band had the same elements; so did Benny Moten's, back in 1932, when Basie played with him. To me this sort of unbuttoned, never-too-disciplined band is the foundation from which inspired jazz solos spring. Not everyone agrees. Even in those days many people were more impressed by the disciplined ranks of Ellington's show band, the vaudevillian backdrop which Cab Calloway's band provided, and the parade-ground precision of Jimmie Lunceford. I first heard Lunceford a week after the Basie appearance with Moten. He was tall, immaculately dressed, waved a long baton, and wowed the Harlem squares. The "Harlem Express," they called him. And, in fairness, he always had excellent players in the band—Sy Oliver, Willie Smith, tenor-playing Joe Thomas—and his music was danceable. ("For Dancers Only" was one of his successful records.) But I thought the rhythm section stiff, the squealing trumpet of "Steve" Stevenson flamboyant, and the band as a whole over-conducted. I had one recording session with Jimmie for Majestic shortly before he died in 1947.

But for me there has never been anything like the early Basie band. It had shortcomings. Its sound was occasionally raw and raucous, but you expected it to erupt and sooner or later it did.

I spread the news of Basie's band to everyone interested in jazz, and I went to Dick Altschuler at the American Record Company to urge him to sign Basie for the Brunswick label. Dick agreed, so back I went to Kansas City to sign the band to its first recording contract. Basie said, "A friend of yours was here to see me, John."

"Who?" I asked. "I didn't send anyone to see you."

"Dave Kapp."

Dave, the brother of Jack Kapp, the head of Decca Records, was no emissary of mine, but I knew why he had come to see Basie. "Let me see what you signed," I said, fearing the worst.

Basie showed me the contract. It called for twenty-four sides a year for three years for $750 each year. To Basie it seemed like a lot of money. To me it was devastating—for both of us. There was no provision for royalties, so that for the period when Basie recorded "One O'Clock Jump," "Jumping at the Woodside," and the rest of those classic hits, he earned nothing from record sales. It was also below the legal minimum scale demanded by the American Federation of Musicians for recording.

Back in New York I called Local 802 to protest these outrageous terms, and did manage to raise the per-side payment to scale, but there was nothing the union would do to break the contract. The loss of Basie to Decca was partially my own fault. I had praised the band in *Down Beat* for months. I had talked about Basie to everybody I knew, and in the music business there are no secrets. Every record executive knew about Basie by the time I went out to sign him. Even Joe Glaser, the head of Associated Booking Corporation, had hurried to Kansas City before me, except that he thought Lips Page was the star and that Basie was no leader; so he signed Page and not Basie.

Glaser's mistake turned out well for Basie. We replaced Lips with Buck Clayton, one of the best—as well as one of the handsomest—trumpet players in jazz. Buck joined Basie and you'll just have to believe me when I say Lips was never missed.

WHILE MY ENTHUSIASM for the Basie band did result in the miserable Decca contract, it helped Basie in other ways. One of these was Willard Alexander's immediate interest in the band and his signing Basie to MCA. In fact, Willard deserves as much credit as I for the band's escape from Kansas City to national prominence. Willard accomplished an almost impossible task when he persuaded MCA to represent Basie. Never before had the giant agency taken on such a rough-hewn, still-to-be developed group, or used its prestige with club and theater owners to book an untried band into prime locations. Of course, Willard's persuasive power at MCA had been considerably enhanced by Benny Goodman's success. Now a major attraction, Goodman's earnings were growing, and MCA was getting ten percent of the gross from location bookings and fifteen percent from one-nighters. It could afford to take a chance with Basie.

After playing a final Kansas City date, the Basie band boarded a bus for Chicago and the future. It opened first at the Grand Terrace, the home of Earl Hines and Fletcher Henderson, a nightclub with an elaborate floor show that was a challenge to any band. Although Basie had by then enlarged to the usual dance band complement—four saxophones, five brass, and four rhythm—he had few arrangements. Worse, only about half the band could read music well. Remembering those first nights at the Grand Terrace, I am astonished they were not fired. They struggled through Ed Fox's show arrangements, but the chorus girls loved the band because it was so easy to dance to. Jo Jones, a dancer himself, knew how to play for dancers. Fletcher came to the rescue, allowing Basie to use half his own library of arrangements, one of the generous gestures which endeared Fletcher to so many jazz musicians.

The Grand Terrace engagement lasted long enough for the band to get used to each other and to prepare for the crucial test ahead in New York. After Chicago they played one-nighters, heading east until they reached New London, Connecticut, where they played on the night of a terrible New England storm. Edgar Siskin drove with me to hear the band in a ballroom which normally held about sixteen hundred people. That night there were no more than four hundred.

The band now included Couchy Roberts, a bald, dour man who replaced Buster on first alto, Lester Young and Jack Washington, and an extraordinary tenor saxophone from Texas, Herschel Evans. The trumpets were Carl "Tatti" Smith, Buck Clayton, and Joe Keys. The trombonists were Dan Minor and Rabbit Hunt. Walter, of course, was the bass player, Jo the drummer, and Claude Williams, who played wonderful guitar and an excruciating violin. Claude loved to play his violin, in those days still a rare instrument in jazz played well only by Joe Venuti and Stuff Smith. Basie loved Claude Williams and willingly, if ill-advisedly, put up with his violin.

Storm or not, that night in New London was one to remember. Lester and Herschel, two completely opposite kinds of jazz players, became involved in a battle of saxes. Herschel had the big "Texas sound." Lester's sound was unusually light for the instrument—something like the Frankie Trumbauer, C-melody sax sound. But his inspiration never flagged. He could play sixty choruses, each different from the last, each building from the preceding one. Actually, no one could win a contest against Lester; he could cut anyone in the world. But their contrasting sounds, their alternating choruses, inspired them to play better than either would have without the other. They were totally different personalities, too. Herschel was the banker of the band. He saved his money, and when he made loans to the other players he charged interest. Lester lived in a world of his own, communicating very little with anybody, speaking his own language. He chose to be different and he was. Both men joined Basie in 1936. Herschel died in 1939. Lester left the band in 1940 and died in 1959, a mere fifty years of age.

The New York debut was at the Roseland Ballroom in November. A crowd was on hand, including many jazz critics, to hear what I had been raving about for so many months. One critic, George Simon, whose books on the big-band era are now widely read, could not stand the band. He said it was the most out-of-tune bunch he had ever heard and that Jo Jones rushed the tempos. Well! George soon acknowledged this sacrilegious first impression as one of the all-time critical goofs and, of course, has been a Basie fan for years. The band was far from perfect that first night, but it was the swingingest band ever to play for dancers and it could only get better.

Count Basie

Possibly the most distinguished collaboration in jazz autobiography was that between Count Basie and the educator/critic/novelist Albert Murray (see p. 992 for an excerpt from his Stomping the Blues*). The simplicity, clarity, and transparent honesty of this book,* Good Morning Blues, *earned it an extraordinary reception when it first appeared in 1985. This excerpt gives the other side of the Basie–Hammond encounter.*

I don't remember exactly how long we had been in the Reno when Fats Waller came down there. But he came in there to see me one night, and he just flipped out over that band. He sent back to the hotel to get Ed Kirkeby to come down there and listen to those cats. Kirkeby was his personal manager at that time. Fats was *crazy* about that band. He was in there every night while he was in town. I think he was either on his way out to the Coast from New York and Chicago, or on his way back east, because he did something in the movies out in Hollywood around that time.

He was working in some theater downtown, I think, and as soon as his show was over, he was right back down there at the Reno. He'd come in there and sit down, and he was there for the evening.

"*That's* what I want," he told Kirkeby.

He said he wanted to fire his band and take mine on the road with him. He didn't mean that he wanted to take it away from me or anything like that. He just wanted that band to have a break. He kept saying we ought to come on the road with him.

I don't mean to pat myself on the back, but that band was strutting, really strutting. It was still pretty new when Fats heard it, but we already had all those heads together. I don't think we had over four or five sheets of music up there at that time. But we had our own thing, and we could always play some more blues and call it something, and we did our thing on the old standards and the current pops. We had a ball every night in there.

It must have been at some point during that time that I got Sol Steibold to put an elevated band shell in the Reno. I suggested it to him, and he thought it was a good idea. So I told him that I knew the guys who had built the one in the Cherry Blossom, and that's who did the job in the Reno. That showed the band off very nicely, but it was pretty crowded up there, too, because they also brought a baby grand in there. And we also forgot that the tuba player couldn't quite fit in there, either. So old Big 'Un used to have to go outside and reach in through the window. He'd leave the horn inside, but he was outside, sitting on a stool or something if he wanted. But he didn't mind that at all, because he had his little action going on out there. He could take his little nips. He had a ball out there. But of course, when we used the bass fiddle, he was inside, right next to the piano. It was pretty tight in there. But when we really got into those broadcasts, I'm pretty sure we were beginning to use the fiddle most of the time. I think that's what most people remember on those broadcasts—not the tuba—and he was walking on that thing, too, you can bet that.

That band went on like that in there for quiet awhile. Then I began to get little messages from a fellow in New York named John Hammond. They were not letters or telegrams or phone calls or anything like that. He was writing articles for *Down Beat,* or some magazine like that, and he would put little things in there about picking up our broadcast on the shortwave-radio set he had in his automobile.

Somebody would always let you know when there was something about you in the papers and magazines, and I'm pretty sure somebody also let me see some of those articles mentioning how much John Hammond liked the band, and I thought that was just great, but I really didn't think about it anymore. Even when he mentioned something about how he would like to hear from me and said I should drop him a line or something like that, I didn't really pay much attention. I really didn't know what to think about what he was writing.

Then, in another article, he said he was wondering why I hadn't responded. I think he must have mentioned something about that more than once, because I seem to remember something like "I don't see why Count Basie doesn't answer his correspondence," or something like that. So that's when I finally got together with a friend of mine and wrote to him, and that's when John got word back to me that he was coming out to Kansas City to hear us. But I didn't think about that very much either, because I didn't think he was really coming all the way out there just to hear us. I really didn't know what to make of it. I guess the thing about it was that I really wasn't actually shooting for the top at that time. I was just interested in having something sounding good there in the Reno.

But he did come, and we hit it off all right immediately, and we've been friends ever since. He came in there that night and sat right on the piano bench with me.

It was a Sunday night and we were on the air, and this very young cat just came right on up there and sat on the bench beside me. I didn't pay much attention to him at first, because actually that was something that used to happen very often, especially at the Reno. I was also busy trying to figure out what we were going to do for our next number so I could tell the announcer while we were still playing. After I did that, I looked around, and that's when I saw that the young fellow sitting there was a complete stranger to me.

"Hi," he said with a big, wide grin. "I'm John Hammond."

At that time I was a pretty good gin drinker, and he ordered me a little taste, and we had a ball all through that set, and he stayed through all the shows. And the band played exceptionally well that night too. I don't know, but all of a sudden it just sounded like the guys turned on another button or something. I don't think it was because John was there either, because nobody knew who John Hammond was. It was just one of those good nights when the band was solidly in the groove and could go on and on swinging like that forever. We didn't know that anybody was coming to check us out, but the way those guys played that night surely was a good example of what we were about and what we could do.

And this young fellow really dug it. He stuck around to talk some more after we finished our last number, and we went out to some other spots that were still open, and that was a ball, too. He liked what I liked. He liked the blues. So we took him by the Sunset to hear Pete Johnson and Big Joe Turner, which, of course, he had already heard about; and those two cats damn near killed him because they were swinging so much. He just sat there shaking his head and slapping his hands.

We also went to a couple of more places that he was curious about, and then we had breakfast at Eleanor's and I introduced him to some fried corn and ham and some beautiful biscuits that I think he still remembers.

I was very impressed with all of the musicians that this very young cat was familiar with. He started dropping all kinds of names on me. I mean, there were some names of musicians and names of joints, too, in there that people right up in Harlem and right out in that part of Kansas City probably wouldn't pick up on right away, and some they wouldn't recognize unless they happened to come from a certain neighborhood.

But here was this cat asking about guys and joints in places I had almost forgotten existed. He even told me about what was going on when he first saw me with Bennie Moten at the Lafayette and had actually spoken with me at the bar in Covan's Morocco Club back when he was still just a little schoolkid from down on Fifth Avenue running around up in Harlem and hanging out wherever they would let him in. He was something else.

He must have stayed around for another day or so, because I know we also went downtown to studio KMBC, where some kind of reception or something was going on, and I did a little session on the organ with a couple of cats, and I think he came back to the Reno at least one more time before he left. But I already knew that he was all for us.

So he made his report back to New York, and that sort of started a lot of things for us. It was through him that Willard Alexander at MCA, which was booking Benny Goodman, who was a very big hit at that time, became interested in us. John was also connected with that in some way. As a matter of fact he says that it was while he was in Chicago with Benny Goodman that he happened to go out to the parking lot and turn on the shortwave set in his car and pick us up that first time.

I THINK JOHN must have come back out to Kansas City at least two more times that year. That first time was in the spring. Then he came back in the summer. But before he got back that second time, Dave Kapp from Decca Records came out there and told me that he was a friend of John's and said that John had been telling him all about us and so he had come out to hear us, and he offered me a contract to make twenty-four sides a year for three years.

That was how I came to sign my first recording contract, and I really made a very big mistake on that one. He said something about how Decca was going to provide us with transportation for the band to go to Chicago to record, and at that time that sounded like the biggest deal I'd ever heard of, and I asked him again, and he said, "Oh, yes." And I was ready to go. So I told the guys the good news, and the part about transportation made a big impression on most of them too.

I never will forget what Lester said when I took him aside and told him about that. I think I must have passed the word on to the other fellows before Lester got to the Reno that night. So when he came in, I called him over, got us a couple of nips, and we went and stood outside the doorway to the back alley, where we usually went when we wanted to have a little private sip and a little personal chat.

"Well," I said, "I got some great news. I think we'll take a Pullman into Chicago and do some recording for Decca."

And all he did was just sort of stand there looking into space like he hadn't heard what I said because he was listening to something else or thinking about something else. Then he looked at me again.

"What did I hear you say? Did I hear you?"

"Yes," I said. "We're going to Chicago to make some records for Decca."

And he just stood there and looked at me and looked away and then looked at me again. Then he went into his sweet-talk thing.

"Listen, Lady B, you all right?"

"Oh, yes," I said. "Everything's okay. I got me this contract with Decca."

And he just stood there nodding his head, thinking about it, and then the next thing he said was like he was talking to himself.

"Well, okay. So now we'll find out what happens."

Then he finished his shot and looked at me and mumbled and went back into his sweet-jive thing again.

"Hey, look. I tell you what, Lady B. Let's go back in there and get us another little taste, and maybe you'll tell me that again."

When John came back out there a short time later and saw that contract, he hit the ceiling. Without realizing what I was doing, I had agreed to record twelve records a year for $750 a year outright, no royalties! I didn't know anything about royalties. John couldn't believe it. He couldn't get us out of that contract, but he was able to get Decca to raise the musicians' pay up to minimum scale. I don't think I had ever heard of minimum scale before that, and if I had, I had never paid any attention to it. I guess I just had to learn some things the hard way.

The thing about the whole situation was that the very reason that John had come back to Kansas City at that time was to tell me about a deal he had in the works for me with Brunswick Records. Naturally it was a much better deal, and John had set it up just because he liked us and wanted people to hear us on records. There was no money at all in it for him. . . .

By the way, here's a little something that I don't think is generally known. During the same time that John Hammond began his thing, somebody else was trying to get in touch with me about coming east. It's funny how things can get mixed up. There was a time when promoters used to give the impression that Benny Goodman was the one who discovered us out in the sticks and opened the way for us. Now, Benny and John were close, and I don't know what went on between them regarding me, but it just so happens that the name bandleader who actually offered to sponsor us was Charlie Barnet. Charlie sent me a telegram from the Glen Island Casino saying that all I had to do was just drop him a line.

But when John came out to see me and we got along so well, that decided it for me, and I didn't even answer Charlie's wire, which I think I still have somewhere among my souvenirs. Every time I remember that, I feel like apologizing to Charlie for not acknowledging his message, because later on we became very good friends, and he has always been one of the most wonderful people I've ever met.

John Hammond says that he felt that Willard Alexander was probably the only topflight booking agent in the country at that time who would understand why he was so excited about our band. I didn't know anything about all of that at that time, either, but I do know that once John got Willard involved we had to start making plans for a different scene, and that's when I started building the band up to the standard dance-band size.

WHEN WE STARTED working out the arrangements for the full-size band I was getting ready at the Reno, I knew just where I wanted those two tenors. After certain modulations and certain breaks, I knew exactly which one I wanted to come in, and sometimes it would be one and sometimes the other. Because each one had his own thing. But it was not really in my mind to battle them. Not at first. It was just a matter of using two different styles to the best advantage of the band.

The band was called the Barons of Rhythm. So we were advertised as Count Basie and His Barons of Rhythm. That was the name somebody thought up as a gimmick for those radio broadcasts over W9XBY. So the announcer could say, "And now here is Count Basie and his fourteen Barons of Rhythm." Something like that. I don't know, maybe that is what somebody got mixed up with how I got the name Count Basie. But I was already billed as Count Basie a few years before those broadcasts. There were no Barons of Rhythm before those broadcasts, but there was Count Basie.

BILLIE HOLIDAY

More Basie and Hammond in Holiday's notoriously inaccurate but fascinating Lady Sings the Blues *(1956; with William Dufty). See p. 635 for Holiday's voice in a different mode.*

You can be up to your boobies in white satin, with gardenias in your hair and no sugar cane for miles, but you can still be working on a plantation.

Take 52nd Street in the late thirties and early forties. It was supposed to be a big deal. "Swing Street," they called it. Joint after joint was jumping. It was this "new" kind of music. They could get away with calling it new because millions of squares hadn't taken a trip to 131st Street. If they had they could have dug swing for twenty years.

By the time the ofays got around to copping "swing" a new-style music was already breaking out all over uptown. Ten years later that became the newest thing when the white boys downtown figured out how to cop it.

Anyway, white musicians were "swinging" from one end of 52nd Street to the other, but there wasn't a black face in sight on the street except Teddy Wilson and me. Teddy played intermission piano at the Famous Door and I sang. There was no cotton to be picked between Leon and Eddie's and the East River, but man, it was a plantation any way you looked at it. And we had to not only look at it, we lived in it. We were not allowed to mingle any kind of way. The minute we were finished with our intermission stint we had to scoot out back to the alley or go out and sit in the street.

Teddy had an old beat-up Ford he used to drive to work in. Sometimes we'd just go out and sit in it parked at the curb.

There was a wild cat who used to come around the joint all the time and he drove a crazy foreign car. Every time he got in it to take off, it sounded like a B-29, and the Famous Door management didn't like that. Anyway, we got friendly with him, and he got friendly with us, and it cost Teddy and me our first jobs on 52nd Street. We got our asses fraternized right off the street.

He was a young millionaire living it up and nobody was going to tell him what to do, who to drink with and who not to drink with. He'd come in the joint and listen to me and Teddy and always wanted to buy us drinks. He insisted we ball with him. And as much as they wanted to please a big spender, both the boss and the headwaiter insisted we didn't.

We told him we were under orders not to socialize with the customers, but he'd insist back that nobody was going to give him orders. Finally one night after he'd bugged me so and practically made me feel like a Tom for not sitting down with him, I got fed up and did.

We had a couple of drinks together, and they were my last ones in that joint for a while. When I got up, the boss told me to go pick up my papers, I was fired. He was nasty enough to fire Teddy, too, although Teddy hadn't done a thing. After this big scandal which might ruin him on the street, he said he didn't want any Negroes in the place at all.

I burned. I had to get out, but I hated like hell to go home and tell Mom I'd been bounced again—over something as silly as this. So our millionaire friend tried to cheer us up. We went off with him in his fancy foreign car and drove uptown through Central Park in that crazy-assed wagon in three minutes.

He told us not to worry, he had plenty of money and there were plenty of jobs. And besides, he was a musician and going to have his own damn dance band soon and everything would be fine.

"Yeah," I told him, "big deal. You've got plenty of money, but in the meantime you've ruined my life so I don't even dare go home. What's going to happen to Teddy and me?"

So he said, "Don't go home, let's ball a little." We wound up back at the Uptown House. Everyone insisted I get up and sing. So I did. And they offered me a regular job again back at the old stand.

Our millionaire friend kept his word, too. He pulled a few wires and got Teddy a job in a radio studio band. He also kept his word and ended up with his own band—and a good one. He was Charlie Barnet.

BUT 52ND STREET couldn't hold the line against Negroes forever. Something had to give. And eventually it was the plantation owners. They found they could make money off Negro artists and they couldn't afford their old prejudices. So the barriers went down, and it gave jobs to a lot of great musicians.

I went into Ralph Watkins' Kelly's Stables as a headliner—no more intermission stuff. The typical bill I appeared with in those days would cost plenty today. One time there was Coleman Hawkins' band, me and Stuff Smith, and for intermission Nat Cole and his trio. Nobody in the joint got two hundred a week. I was there for two years at a top of $175 and I was the star. Then there was Roy Eldridge's band, Una Mae Carlisle, Lips Page and his group, and the great Art Tatum playing intermission piano.

Working on the street seemed like a homecoming every night. People I'd met in Harlem, Hollywood, and Café Society used to come in and there was always some kind of reunion. I was getting a little billing and publicity, so my old friends and acquaintances knew where to find me.

ON MY FIRST trip to the West Coast the valley joint had folded up under me and we had an earthquake to boot. My second trip a couple of years later was a little better—but as soon as I got on the scene we had another earthquake. Everybody finds unusual weather out there.

At least on my second trip West I wasn't alone. Lester had left the Basie Organization by then and he went out with me to work at Billy Berg's.

This was a different kind of place—not high class enough to be high class and not low class enough to be a dive. It was out near the valley—but not too far out like Red Colonna's had been. That first place couldn't live without movie people. Some nights you'd get Gable, another night Garland. But they came one at a time, and it took 150 people to keep the joint from rattling. And the trouble with movie people is they've got everything at home. It takes something different or great to drag them out, especially when they got those 6 A.M. dates with the makeup man in the morning. And Hollywood was booming in those days.

It was a crazy group Lester assembled at Billy's place. I can hear them now even though I can't remember all their proper names. We had a little trumpet player who sounded like Buck Clayton, only he sang more; and Bumps Mayers, a California man; two tenors and a trumpet. Lester had his brother Lee on drums and a nice ofay cat on piano and Red Kallen on bass.

We used to rock that joint. Bette Davis came in one night and danced herself crazy. Lana Turner used to come in every Tuesday and Thursday. That girl can really dance, and she did at Billy's. She always asked me for "Strange Fruit" and "Gloomy Sunday." She used to like to dance with young Mel Tormé, who used to win all of Billy's lindy contests. Maybe he couldn't cut the cats at the Savoy in Harlem, but he sure could dance.

He was like me when I was a kid, in a way, wanting to make it as a dancer and not interested in singing. And he was a switch on me in another way. My singing voice is clear but my speaking voice is husky; Mel's speaking voice was clear but his singing voice sounded sort of cloudy and foggy. I tried to tell him he had something different in the way of sound and encouraged him to try singing. He never seemed to want to listen. Maybe a lot of other people told him the same thing, but anyway, I was pleased later to hear he was making it. I always liked his singing, too. No matter what he was doing, he wasn't imitating anybody and he had that beat.

Another raggedy youngster I met at Billy's in those days is a big man today. He was as broke as me and Lester then. We used to sit on a fence out back of the joint, talking big and dreaming big, and then pool our money to go off and buy Chinese food. He had a good mind and loved jazz. "John Hammond thinks he's something," he used to say. "Someday I'm going to be really big, and when I do I'm going to do something for Negro jazz musicians." He got there and he did, and he's been a good friend of mine from that day to this, Norman Granz.

This was the time when Billy Eckstine's band was playing at the Plantation Club in Los Angeles. Lester and I used to sneak over there and catch Billy's group and the new things they were doing. Sarah Vaughan was singing with Billy then and just getting started. It brought back the rough old days with the Basie band to see the way those kids had to work.

All of them, including Sarah, wore some damn uniforms and they were a mess. I used to try to get Billy to get Sarah a couple of gowns, but he wouldn't get her a spool of thread. He had his troubles, I guess, making payroll at the end of the week. But I looked at it from Sarah's viewpoint. If I had to work like she worked, I'd have died of shame.

Even in the worst Basie days I paid the cleaners for cleaning and pressing my gowns before I ate. And I knew what a hassle it was to keep your foot out of your mouth on the road on the salary that chick was making. So when Billy couldn't do nothing to help, I went to see a dame I knew who sold me a beautiful three-hundred-dollar evening gown for a song. I went out to the plantation and gave it to Sarah. She didn't know where the gown came from and I didn't tell her. But the moment she put it on she looked more like a girl who was going somewhere. And she did, and I was happy she did.

During my first Hollywood earthquake I was drinking champagne with Bob Hope. My second one happened while I was balling at Joe Louis' place. There was a mob of people there, but I was leaving early because I had a recording date the next day and I had a helluva toothache.

There was a young cat there who told me he had something for my toothache and asked me to come outside. When we got out, it turned out he had some pot. He gave me some of it, told me to put it in my tooth, and we stood there underneath this big tree and smoked up the rest. I was in the middle of a drag on this cigarette when the damnedest feeling came over me. It came so fast and was over so fast, I didn't know what had happened. But this young cat was smart; he gave me a shove that landed me on the ground a few feet away, and there was a whoom and this big tree crashed over with a wham and a bang.

It just wasn't my time, I guess. Joe had driven off just a few seconds before then in his car with some girl and they didn't feel a thing.

It only lasted two or three seconds, but when we went back in Joe's house every damn glass and dish in the place was broken. Furniture was upside down and people were running around screaming. One of Joe's friends had been upstairs with some broad, sneaking himself a little time, and he came running down the stairs half dressed, and half out of his head screaming, "Joe, save me!"

I stopped this son of a gun and told him to go back up and finish dressing. "Joe needs somebody to save *him* and he ain't even here."

Mezz Mezzrow

Mezzrow, the most fanatically "hip" of all white jazz musicians, gave his colorful (and frequently fanciful) version of his life with Bix, Louis, and just about everyone else, in his autobiography, Really the Blues *(1946; written with Bernard Wolfe).*

The Martinique was right on the highway between Gary and Chicago, so we used to get a lot of transient trade and college kids from South Bend dropping in, besides the local guzzlers. Not long after we opened, a fine youngster named Fats Morris started to come around. He was a student at Notre Dame, a robust Joe-College kind of kid, husky and tall and always dressed in plus-four knickers. Fats seemed to be well off and he had only one passion in life, jazz music. He used to bring along a gang of college kids who just sat around drinking and listening to the band with expressions that showed how much they were wrapped up and down with it. It never struck us funny that these youngsters didn't bring any girls with them, even though they were a pretty manly bunch of guys. Like practically all jazz disciples they really came to listen, not to dance or gumbeat around the table.

That kind of single-minded attitude always strikes a gong in us musicians. A guy who's really serious about this music likes to take it straight, without getting it all tangled up with sex. One thing at a time, as they say. The musicians I worked and ran with never fooled with women either, not enough to amount to anything. When we saw one of our buddies blowing his top over some chicken dinner we pitied him for going tangent and we hoped he'd get himself straight soon. You can't mix up the sweet talk and high-pressure fruiting with blowing jazz music out of your guts. I know, because I've tried it.

One night Fats invited me to have a drink at his table, and he asked me did I ever hear a kid named Beiderbecke play the cornet. He was surprised when I told him I had heard some of the Wolverines' records but never met Bix, because the only musicians I knew personally and cared much about were Joe Oliver, Sidney Bechet, Jimmy Noone, Baby Dodds and guys like that. "You've got to hear this boy," Fats said. "He's playing not far from here, at Gary Beach."

I didn't pay this talk much mind, but it led to my meeting with a cat that became one of my best friends later on. A few nights later Fats walked into the Martinique with Leon Bismarck "Bix" Beiderbecke.

Musicians get keyed-up and complexy when a brother of the same school drops in to hear them get off. Whether you know the visitor or not, you can dig him just by looking at him; you know right away that this cat is hip and that one isn't. When somebody solid is present and makes you know it, it sets all the performers on edge and sometimes they render a very sad solo trying to send him. The night Bix came in that's what happened. I dug right away that this big overgrown kid, who looked like he'd been snatched out of a cradle in the cornfields, knew what the score was.

We were playing when he came in, and he took a seat with Fats in front of the bandstand. When we looked down at him he just smiled in a friendly way, to show he appreciated what we were doing, and went on watching us, his chin resting in one hand and a glass of beer snuggled in the other like it was a second thumb. There was a dead-serious, concentrated look on his face that I got to know later as his trademark—I've never seen such an intense, searching expression on anybody else. With that pokerface mask of his and his left eye half closed, he looked like a jeweler squinting at a diamond to find out whether it's phony or not. He seemed to be looking right through us.

Bix was a rawboned, husky, farmboy kind of kid, a little above average height and still growing. His frog-eyes popped out of a ruddy face and he had light brown hair that always looked like it was trying to go someplace else. In those days he had an air of cynicism and boredom about most things, just sitting around lazy-like with his legs crossed and his body drooping, but it wasn't an act with him. Even in his teens he had worked out the special tastes and interests that he carried all through his short life—his shying-away from things showed that what got most people worked up left him completely cold.

Not that he was dull or sluggish; nothing like that. That kid could get as lively and hopped-up as anybody you ever saw, but it took something really stirring, something really good, to get a rise out of him. Music is what did it mostly. When something got him all tense and aroused he would keep chuckling "Ha! Ha! Ha!" deep down in his throat and his arms would fly around like a windmill. Music was the one thing that really brought him to life. Not even whisky could do it, and he gave it every chance. The kid must have been born with a hollow leg, the way he gulped the stuff down. But he always had a tight grip on himself, until some music came along that made him want to relax and let go.

When I met Bix he was a star member of the Wolverines, and that little white band had already made some recordings that cause record collectors to foam at the mouth today. The music they were turning out, thanks to Bix's head arrangements, was ten years ahead of its time, and two of their recordings, "Copenhagen" and "Riverboat Shuffle," were already on their way to becoming classics. Bix's horn work in those numbers was amazing for a kid of schoolboy age.

That night, as soon as we finished the number we were playing for an entertainer, I called "Royal Garden Blues," our old standby. We had a trick way of playing the breaks in the interlude following the verse and this time we gave it all we had, for Bix's benefit. He sat there like a mummy, not moving a muscle. Then, just as we finished the first break, he jumped to his feet, his face all lit up, grabbed his horn and hopped on the bandstand.

Bix played a cornet that he carried without a case, a short, stubby, silver-plated horn that looked like it came from the junkpile and should never have left there. He stood facing me as he played, because we were the two lead instruments, and the whisky fumes that he blew out of that beat-up old cornet almost gassed me. The music that came out, pickled in alcohol, hit me even harder. I noticed that some of his inflections were like Joe Oliver's and Freddie Keppard's—what he tried to do was to play Joe's half-valve inflections with Freddie's hard drive. All in all, it was more a polished riverboat style than anything else. That style was second nature to Bix because he'd grown up in Davenport, Iowa, and always hung around the waterfront.

I have never heard a tone like he got before or since. He played mostly open horn, every note full, big, rich and round, standing out like a pearl, loud but never irritating or jangling, with a powerful drive that few white musicians had in those days. Bix was too young for the soulful tone, full of oppression and misery, that the great Negro trumpeters get—too young and, maybe, too disciplined. His attack was more on the militaristic side, powerful and energetic, every note packing a solid punch, with his head always in full control over his heart. That attack was as surefooted as a mountain goat; every note was sharp as a rifle's crack, incisive as a bite. Bix was a natural-born leader. He set the pace and the idiom, defined the style, wherever he played, and the other musicians just naturally fell into step.

With his half-valve inflections he produced little quarter-tones, in glissandos that blended into just the right harmonies. He felt his way into those harmonies, groped his way towards them, with a judgment that never failed. In musical chords some notes are supposed to be sharp and some flat, and the whole secret of our music was that in our slurs we instinctively worked towards those notes, without knowing the ABC's of musical theory. A lot of us, including Bix, never learned to read much music until later. Bix had the most perfect instincts of all. He was born with harmony in his soul, and chords instead of corpuscles.

When we finished playing that set we all gathered around Bix and began to pop questions about his recordings. "Gee," I said, "I'd sure like to learn

'Riverboat Shuffle.'" Without a word he sat down at the piano and started to play it, while we stood around with our mouths hanging open. His touch knocked us all out, it was like his horn playing so much in metric pattern. To a man we forgot we were working. So far as we were concerned there was no such animal as a boss or an audience.

"Get your horn," Bix said to me, reaching for his own. Then he started to blow the introduction to "Riverboat Shuffle." "You take this note and do this," he told me, blowing the second harmony part. I played it back for him and he yelled, "That's it! That's it!" All worked up, he turned and played Eddie Long a part on the piano, and one by one the pieces began to fit together like the parts of a jigsaw puzzle. Right then and there was one of the early examples of a real "head arrangement," as the colored musicians call it, orchestrated not on paper but by ear. Everybody got their parts straight and Bix gave us a downbeat with his horn to his mouth. "Ha! Ha! Ha!" was all he said when we finished, and all he had to say. His eyes told us the rest.

Monkey Pollack was climbing all over the stand by this time, hardly able to believe his ears. "This kid want a job, Milton?" he said. "Let him start Saturday night!"

From then on Bix and I were pals. He played with us until closing and came back every chance he got. I never stopped being astounded by the things he could do on his horn; a favorite trick of his that always got me was to grab a sheet of music and hold it in front of his horn, flat up against the bell, to give him what we called a "buzz tone." He'd picked up this twist from the colored boys on the South Side and the musicians on the riverboats.

Playing with Bix was one of the great experiences in my life. The minute he started to blow I jumped with a flying leap into the harmony pattern like I was born to it, and never left the track for a moment. It was like slipping into a suit made to order for you by a fine tailor, silk-lined all through. When two musicians hit it off like that right from the start, a fine glow of ease and contentment creeps over them. They've reached a perfect understanding through their music; they're friends, seeing eye to eye. Maybe there's a parable here for the world. Two guys, complete strangers, face each other, and while one takes off on the lead the other feeds the accompaniment to him, helping him to render his solo and making the solo richer, spurring him on and encouraging him all the way. One feeds harmony while the other speaks his piece on his horn, telling the world what's on his mind, supported every inch of the way by his pal. It's like a congregation backing up the minister's words with whispered "Amen's" at the right places. The congregation never stands up and hollers "Shut up! You're a liar!" while the minister's preaching—that would be discord, the whole spell of being together and united in a common feeling would be broken. That's how it is when you play music with a man you understand and who understands you. You preach to him with your horn and he answers back with his "Amen," never contradicting you. You speak the same language, back each other up. Your message and his message fit together like pie and ice cream. When that happens, man, you know you've got a friend. You get that good feeling. You're really sent.

Even when we talked to each other it was the same way, each guy echoing the other. The words could have been dropped altogether; we might just as well have kept nodding at each other. Once in a while, when business was slow at the Martinique, I would knock off early and Bix and I would pile into a cab, bound for the South Side in Chicago to hear some of our favorite musicians. Bix always had a jug of raw corn with him, and while he guzzled we would talk back and forth.

"What do you think about the longhaired musicians?" I asked him once, as we were riding along.

"Most of them are corny," he said, "but it's the composers I like—that is, the modern ones."

"Boy," he told me another time, "it's such a relief to get to the South Side and hear Joe Oliver and Jimmy Noone and Bessie. I miss those old riverboat bands down around Davenport." He got serious for a moment. "I wonder," he said, thinking hard, "why white musicians are so corny? Hell, you even feel better physically when you get in a colored café. The people all seem to be enjoying everything in a real way. The band always has something that keeps your ear cocked all the time. The dancers all feel the music, and the expression on their faces when somebody takes off really gives me a lift. Goddamn, those people know how to live."

It's hard to put into words, but my friendship with Bix was one of the fine things in my life. It's probably tough for anybody outside of the jazz world to latch on to its real meaning. When you're a kid and your first millennium falls on you—when you get in a groove that you know is *right* for you, find a way of expressing something deep down and know it's *your* way—it makes you bubble inside. But it's hard to tell outsiders about it. It's all locked up inside you, in a kind of mental prison. Then, once in a million years, somebody like Bix comes along and you know the same millennium is upon him too, it's the same with him as it is with you. That gives you the courage of your convictions—all of a sudden you know you aren't plodding around in circles in a wilderness. No wonder jazz musicians have an off-center perspective on the world. You can't blame them for walking around with a superior air, partly because they're plain lonely and partly because they know they've got hold of something good, a straight slant on things, and yet nobody understands it. A Bix Beiderbecke will. He knows where to put the "Amen's."

* * *

WAY BACK THERE the music grabbed me by the stringpost and yanked me off The Corner on Chicago's Northwest Side. Now the same music parked me right smack on another corner, this time in the heart of Harlem where 131st Street breezes across Seventh Avenue.

This wasn't just one more of them busy street crossings, with a poolroom for a hangout. Uh, uh. This corner was a whole atlas by itself—the crossroads of the universe, meeting-place of the hipsters' fraternal order. In this block-long beehive life was close-packed and teeming, a-bubble with novelty, and in its many crannies you could find all the many kicks and capers your heart yenned after. Back on Chicago's street-corner haunts you tangled with gamblers and racketeers and poolroom sharks, and all day long your tongue wagged its way from money to horses to women and back again. There your outlook was plenty hemmed-in, squeezed down to one dimension. But on The Corner in Harlem you stood with your jaws swinging wide open while all there is to this crazy world, the whole frantic works, strutted by. Life was full and jumping in that fantastic place, covered all spots and invaded all dimensions, including the fourth.

Anything you had a yen for—that's no lie. You couldn't see for looking, there were so many things to dig on The Stroll between 131st and 132nd. Dramas and tragedies in your face all the livelong day, till there were more lumps in your throat than you'd find in drugstore mashed potatoes. Happiness and ease too, in such big doses that fine-and-mellow was the play day in and day out. All the emotions, all the time, simmering in one big bubbling cauldron that covered a city block. Most all the great musicians, performers, and entertainers the race produced used to congregate on The Corner, drawn back there by a powerful magnet after traveling all over the world. This place was the central clearing-house for a global grapevine—you could stand under the Tree of Hope without budging from one year to the next and know what was going down all through the South, or in Hollywood and Chicago, or Paris and London and Berlin and Stockholm. Let any of our boys get in a scrape with the pecks down in Memphis or Little Rock, or let them panic the English in Albert Hall or send the Danes in the Tivalis Koncertsal, and the news buzzed back to us on Seventh Avenue quicker than right now.

When good old Buck, of Buck and Bubbles, was driving along down South in his big Cadillac and dared to challenge the supremacy of the white race by passing a couple of white trash in a dinky old rattletrap Ford, he spent the night in jail for his crime and we knew all about it almost before his cell door closed. When Fats Waller was touring the South and kept having his big Lincoln sedan wrecked, with sand poured into the crankcase and the tires slashed, he made his booking agent rent him a whole private Pullman car before he'd budge, and we heard about it before Fats boarded his special train. When a little white girl was out strolling with her mother along a Paris boulevard, and then spotted Louis Armstrong and ran up and threw her arms around him yelling *"M'sieur Armstrong, M'sieur Armstrong, comme il est beau!"* and Louis grinned with delight, we were in on it before he stopped grinning, damn near. We were planted at the race's switchboard there, the listening-post for the whole planet. We had our earphones on all the time.

You had your pick of hangouts on The Corner. Just on Seventh Avenue alone, going north from 131st Street, the line-up was: a barbershop, a drugstore, the Performers and Entertainers Club and under it the dicty Connie's Inn, then the Lafayette Theater, then a candy store, the Hoofers' Club down in the basement, and finally, Big John's famous ginmill. Around on 132nd Street were Tabb's Restaurant, and next to it the Rhythm Club, where you could call any hour of the day or night and hire a musician. And back on 131st Street, soon as you turned into it you found a fine rib joint called the Barbeque, the entrance to a gang of upstairs halls where top bands like Armstrong's and Count Basie's and Jimmie Lunceford's and Cab Calloway's and Erskine Hawkins's used to rehearse, and a speakeasy and nightclub called the Bandbox. Most important of all, there was an areaway running all around the corner building there, a wide alley with entrances from both Seventh Avenue and 131st Street. This alley led to the Lafayette's backstage entrance and also to a special bar in the rear of the Bandbox, and here it was that most of our social life was spent. Louis Armstrong was heading the Connie's Inn show (it was *Hot Chocolates,* written by Fats Waller and Andy Razaff and staged by Leonard Harper, and it was doubling at the Hudson Theater down on 46th Street) and all the cats from the show would come out in the alley and mingle with the other great performers of Harlem who were appearing at the Lafayette, and they would be joined by visitors from all over, including a lot of white musicians that I began to bring up from downtown. I dragged so many cats uptown, I got to be known as the "link between the races" after a while.

And, finally, out in front of the Connie's Inn marquee on Seventh Avenue there was the legendary Tree of Hope, Harlem's Blarney Stone, which the guys would hug and kiss half playfully when they prayed for their dreams to come true. Once a good friend of mine, a fine hoofer who was having trouble getting bookings, ran up to that tree, gave it a big smack, and yelled "Lawd please make me a pimp, any kind of a pimp, long as I'm pimpin'. I'm tired of scufflin' and my feet are too long outa work." Years later, when Seventh Avenue was widened, Bill Robinson had the Tree of Hope transplanted out to the strip of parkway that was built in the middle of the avenue, and there it still stands today.

This was my happy hunting ground. Right from the start I was surrounded by a lot of wonderful friends, the first gang of vipers in Harlem (who I didn't make vipers out of, no matter what anybody says, because they were buying their gauge from some Spanish boys over on Lenox Avenue before I ever came to Harlem). There were some other fine kids too, including Little Fats, who knew everybody and was the key to the grapevine, another youngster named Mark, an orphan boy named Travis, a dancer named George Morton, little Frankie Walker and his dancing partner Dooley, Oakie, Nappy, Brother Raymond of that famous dance trio, Tip, Tap & Toe, and two girls named Thelma and Myrtle. Most all of us were real poor, until some of us began pushing reefer, but we loved each other and we had our fun. We'd sit in the Barbeque, right over the bandstand in Connie's Inn, and wait to catch the first few notes from Louis's horn. Zutty used to really punish those tomtoms when Louise Cook was doing her Salome routine, and the whole building would bump and fishtail right along with her. Soon as we heard the finale we knew Louis was going to start playing for the dancers, so we'd tear out for the street and kneel down on the sidewalk at a small boarded-up window, where Louis came through loud and clear.

Then it got to be wintertime, and the sidewalk was covered with snow, so we'd race into the alleyway and huddle up in front of a huge exhaust fan that was built into a shed. You could hear Louis there too, if you didn't choke first on the smoke and funk that was pumped in your face. Warm air came out of the fan too, so things were groovy. Course, I could have gone downstairs in the Inn and stood backstage to hear Pops, but it wouldn't have been so good that way, with all my friends outside at the fan. I wanted to stick with the gang because those cats enjoyed every note Louis made, and their delight sent me even more. I couldn't sneak down and get those kicks by myself—that kind of selfish quality evaporated when it came to hearing Louis because you wanted the whole world to dig what he had to say on his horn. Roaches were passed round and round, and even though some of those vipers were plenty raggedy they loved Louis like nobody else. We spent most all the winter of 1930 squoze together in front of that fan-shed.

Yes, it was my hunting ground, and it was solid happy. Course, my home wasn't exactly in Harlem—Bonnie wasn't with me all the way on that issue, and she had her son to think of, so I compromised by moving right next door to Harlem, just across the river in the Bronx, on the Grand Concourse. But it was just a quick ten-minute ride to The Corner from where we lived, and all my waking hours were passed down there. . . . My brain would never soak up all the jive my eyes and ears were drinking in. It was really too much.

On The Corner I was to become known as the Reefer King, the Link between the Races, the Philosopher, the Mezz, Poppa Mezz, Mother Mezz,

Pop's Boy, the White Mayor of Harlem, the Man about Town, the Man that Hipped the World, the Man that Made History, the Man with the Righteous Bush, He who Diggeth the Digger, Father Neptune. I don't mean to boast; that's what the cats really called me, at different times. I did become a kind of link between the races there. My education was completed on The Stroll, and I became a Negro. The next ten years of my life were to be spent there, and in a cellar opium pad a few blocks away . . .

Louis had brought his private chauffeur to New York with him, a fellow we all knew from the Sunset and the Nest in Chicago. Anywhere you showed up on the South Side, there was Too Sweet on the scene, ready to act as a guide to the younger boys who came around. Now Too Sweet was about six-foot-two, with a massive body, his playground sticking out in front of him about two feet. With Louis getting so famous, he started to walk up and down The Avenue, posing back with a cane so you almost thought he was Mr. Armstrong himself. One day as little Frankie and I approached the corner, we saw a crowd out in front of Connie's Inn, and we made our way through to pick up on what was going down. It seemed as though Too Sweet couldn't stand Louis's getting all the glory in The Apple, because everywhere you turned the cats were buzzing about Pops, and Too Sweet couldn't get in the play. This night he decided he was going to get some note for himself, so there he stood on The Corner in a pair of bright purple shorts and a yellow top shirt, swinging a walking stick with a knob on it big as an oak tree stump, and on his shoulder was an honest-to-God monkey. Too Sweet stopped traffic that night, and he was happy. He even made the papers.

Louis and I were running together all the time, and we togged so sharp we got to be known as the Esquires of Harlem. Dig these outfits: oxford-gray double-breasted suits, white silk-broadcloth shirts (Louis wore Barrymore collars for comfort when he played, with great big knots in his ties), black double-breasted velvet-collared overcoats, formal white silk mufflers, French lisle hand-clocked socks, black custom-built London brogues, white silk handkerchiefs tucked in the breast pockets of our suits, a derby for Louis, a light gray felt for me with the brim turned down on one side, kind of debonair and rakish. Louis always held a handkerchief in his hand because he perspired so much, onstage and off, and that started a real fad—before long all the kids on The Avenue were running up to him with white handkerchiefs in their hands too, to show how much they loved him. Louis always stood with his hands clasped in front of him, in a kind of easy slouch. Pretty soon all the kids were lounging around The Corner with their hands locked in front of them, one foot a little in front of the other, and a white handkerchief always peeking out from between their fingers. All the raggedy kids, especially those who became vipers, were so inspired with self-respect after digging how neat and natty Louis was, they started to dress up real good, and took pride in it too, because if Louis did it it must be right. The slogan in our circle of vipers became, *Light up and be somebody.*

Every day soon as I woke up about four in the P.M., I would jump up to Louis's apartment and most of the time catch him in the shower. That man really enjoyed his bath and shave. I would sit there watching him handle his razor, sliding it along with such rhythm and grace you could feel each individual hair being cut, and I'd think it was just like the way he fingered the valves on his horn, in fact, just like he did everything. When he slid his fingertips over the buttons, delicate as an embroiderer and still so masculine, the tones took wing as though they sprang from his fingers instead of his lips. The way he shaved put me in mind of the time Louis was blowing and I brushed up against him by accident, and goddamn if I didn't feel his whole body vibrating like one of those electric testing machines in the penny arcade that tell how many volts your frame can stand. Louis really blew with every dancing molecule in his body. He did everything like that, graceful and easy but still full of power and drive. He was a dynamo with a slight slouch.

He was kind of stout then—that was many years before Hollywood made him reduce for that picture he made with Bing Crosby—and he had the most magnetic personality I ever saw. Those sparkling teeth of his, white as a cotton ball, reminded me of the record where Bessie Smith sings "My man's got teeth shine like a lighthouse on the sea." What a warm, good-hearted, down-to-earth gem of a human being was Louis. With all the money and success that came to him, you could still talk behind him because he never said anything he didn't mean and didn't speak any foolishness. He always looked at the humorous side of life and if he saw anybody angry he'd look the situation over and say gently, "Well, he hasn't dug life yet but he's a good cat at heart." He never lowrated anybody, always believed the best about his fellow-man. A lot of people, mostly white, took plenty of advantage of Louis's good heart, but he never once came up evil about it. He was a prince. Hell, he was king of the tribe.

Artie Shaw

The brilliant, rebellious Artie Shaw told his story in The Trouble with Cinderella *(1952), a book that Gene Lees refers to as "not so much an autobiography as an unsparing and soulsearching essay on the life of one troubled man living in fame-crazed America." This excerpt perfectly reflects Shaw's engaging and provocative nature.*

In show business you're apt to hear a good deal about "getting the breaks," but whenever I hear this phrase I wonder whether people have the slightest idea of what they're overlooking when they talk in these terms.

Of course, I understand what they *think* they are saying. I've even heard another and far more colorful expression that covers the same thing. The first time I ever heard it was when a certain agent was speaking of one of his bandleader clients—a fellow named Artie Shaw, that fellow I've already told you a few things about, but definitely *not* the fellow I've been talking about throughout most of this.

What the agent said—and I quote it verbatim—was this: "You're the kind of guy who can fall into a pile of shit and come up with a diamond."

Well, I don't know. My own experience with the only such pile I've ever fallen into—namely, the band business—is that a fellow is far more apt to come up with shit than diamonds; although I suppose there *may* also be some diamonds down there somewhere.

In any case, what I'm getting at is this whole concept of "breaks"—and how inaccurate it is. There is almost no one on earth who could truthfully say that his luck has been so extraordinarily bad, over the entire period of his lifetime, that he has never been presented with an opportunity to prove himself. And as for the old saw about opportunity knocking but once—well, as in the case of most old saws, this one too should be taken with the proverbial grain of salt. Most of us are often presented with opportunities; the difficulty is that most of us are unwilling to take on the actual labor involved in *making* something of these opportunities. Either we are too inertia-ridden, or else we are not conditioned to take on the challenge. For that is essentially what most opportunities—or "breaks"—entail: Challenge.

Then too, there are those times when a man is presented with a chance to do something he wants to do and is furthermore willing to take on as a job—but finds he is not yet *able* to do it. This is nothing unusual, and scarcely the tragedy lots of people try to make it out to be. The chances are the man will sooner or later have another chance—if not for the same thing, at least for something nearly as good; possibly even better. Here, though, the way it works out many times, the trouble is that the average guy who once actually was willing to accept a healthy challenge, may, by the time he gets another chance, have slowed down, become tired, discouraged, or what-have-you; so that instead of accepting a new challenge he has now become inclined to look backward and bewail the "bad breaks" involved in his having once had a good opportunity at a time when he was unprepared; thus indulging an essential defeatism which is the real reason for his not being able to conceive of anyone else being able to get on except through what he calls "getting the breaks."

Now I am not intimating that I don't believe there is such a thing as "a good break"—that would be pretty silly. But the fact is that no "break" can do any more than give a guy a *chance to prove himself.* In other words, given that chance, presented with "the break"—from there on in, a fellow is on his own. He can't keep hoping for "breaks" to go on doing his job for him. If he does he's going to end up right back where he started from before he ever got his "break" to begin with.

Let me illustrate what I mean, by telling you now what my first real "break" was, and what happened as a result of it.

About the time Prohibition was repealed, there used to be a little musicians' hangout over on West 52nd Street called the Onyx Club. It had started out as a speakeasy, and now that it became necessary to buy a liquor license, the fellow who ran it, a man named Joe Helbock, got the idea of taking up a collection among the radio and recording musicians who frequented the place and making each contributor a "charter member" of this new, legitimatized Onyx Club.

At first the place ran strictly as a musicians' club, where we used to drop in after work and sit in and play with other fellows. For a while, a few musicians were even hired to work there regularly, and, since this was a place where other musicians hung out, the musicians employed had to be damn good. But mostly, the best music in the place was made by the actual customers—those same jazz musicians who had to play that musical junk I've already spoken about, that was being played around the radio studios in which they made their living.

Pretty soon, the public began to find out about this little spot, and within a short while after it had opened Joe Helbock found himself with a small gold mine on his hands.

After a year or so, the Onyx Club became a kind of institution—and Helbock became a sort of unofficial jazz authority, merely by virtue of his acquaintance with most of the best jazz musicians around the business in those days.

I don't know how it finally worked out, financially at any rate, but for some reason or other the whole thing ultimately folded up, and the last I heard of Joe he was working at the Copacabana—as a bartender. Which is just about the same job he had when I first knew him, during the old days when the Onyx Club was a speakeasy—making this a rather tidy little example of the full circle type of life; although I can't say how Joe himself would feel about either the tidiness *or* the circle, let alone the life.

In any case, at about that same time the public was beginning to become interested in jazz music—on a large scale, that is—and the word "swing" was being used to designate the aspect of American jazz that later became a national, and even an international, fad.

At this point I can condense what happened, by quoting from an article which appeared in the June 29, 1951, issue of a magazine called *Down Beat*. This piece was written by a young English jazz critic named Leonard Feather, who was also around New York City in those days.

"In the summer of 1935," writes Feather, "Joe Helbock, then owner of the Onyx Club, decided to put on a concert featuring that red-hot novelty, 'swing,' at the Imperial Theatre. Approached to participate along with a bunch of bigger swing names, Artie decided to do something different by writing a jazz piece for clarinet and string quartet."

This was the first time such a concert had ever been given in New York City. The whole idea was brand new, since up to this time American dance music had always been regarded as a sort of bastard child of "real" music—considered as a merely functional kind of music, good enough to be danced to but hardly to be taken seriously as anything to listen to.

Here, for the first time, as I say, there was this rather revolutionary concept—that "swing" music, as an American idiom, was something to be listened to for itself. Not the words, not the tune, not the popular melody—but the jazz idiom, as played by the musician who took the tune itself *only* as a point of departure for his own inventive, improvisational creativeness and embellished the melody, or else forgot it altogether and based his improvisation not on the melody but on the chord structure of the melody. The result was something entirely different from the kind of popular music it stemmed from (to say nothing of the words, which were, of course, completely forgotten, utterly meaningless in this new context), stressing the ability of the improviser, rather than the composer, and demanding an entirely different kind of audience from that which is interested in hearing popular music *per se*.

It's rather difficult to go into all this without using technical language. Perhaps I can leave it at this: Jazz, or Swing, or Bop, or whatever-you-want-to-call-it (since these words are all nothing but labels for something essentially pre-verbal, and no one has yet managed to define them so as to make any sort of sense for anybody who hasn't heard the music itself)—all these are rather complex idioms, musically; and so are the thousand and one factors that go to make them up, historical, sociological, psychological, even anthropological. The definitive treatise about this kind of music has certainly not yet been written; possibly may never be written. That's as it may be. As to what this whole idiom represents in the mainstream of music as an art form—well, that too is a pretty complex matter, far too detailed to attempt to deal with in the scope of such a book as this. For now, then, let's get back to this same "swing concert" of Joe Helbock's and I'll explain a bit more of what it was all about and how I came to get involved with it.

By the time the whole affair was organized, it had resolved itself into a benefit performance for the American Federation of Musicians, Local 802. As a result there was no difficulty in getting just about every big band in New York to appear.

The way the thing was to be run off was this:

In between each pair of big band performances, time was needed to break down one setup and get it off the stage so the next big band could set up. Each performance was to last ten to twelve minutes. In order to kill the lag between big performances it was decided to lower the curtain after each performance and have the audience hear performances by smaller groups fronted by various top-notch instrumentalists. Although these instrumentalists had no "commercial" reputation whatsoever outside the business itself—still, this being the sort of thing it was, the business of "big names" didn't mean as much as it might have under other circumstances.

The whole concert was to be more or less an inside affair, a kind of trade get-together, and even the audience itself was in some way related to the music business—if only in a distant manner, through radio, recording, publishing, etc.

Joe Helbock asked me if I would get together a small group for one of those in-between performances. Since many of these groups were going to be fronted by friends of mine, guys I worked with daily around the radio studios, I could see no harm in it. All it entailed was my calling up three or four musical acquaintances—a piano player, a drummer, a bass player, and maybe a guitar player—going down to the Imperial Theatre the night of the concert, and playing a few choruses of some jazz standard.

All we had to do was to fill in for three to five minutes at the most, Joe told me, so I said OK.

It sounded like nothing very special, and on the whole it might even turn out to be some fun. That was all the thought I gave it, until about a week or so before the thing was to come off. Then one day I ran into a friend who was also going to appear with his own small group. He told me the instrumentation he was going to use; it was exactly the same as what I had thought of. That same day, another fellow told me the same thing. It began to appear as if we were all going to do pretty much the same.

Of course, it didn't really matter. But for some reason I thought it might be a good idea if I were to dream up something just a tiny bit different, just for the hell of it.

So I got what seemed to me to be a rather bright idea.

You see, from time to time during that period, I used to get together with a few fellows who had a string quartet, and spend an evening playing some of the clarinet-and-string-quartet literature—the Mozart quintet, the Brahms ditto, stuff like that. Now if you have heard either of these pieces you'll know they're pretty damn wonderful music of their kind. I happen to like the sound of clarinet and strings, and used to enjoy these little sessions enormously. In fact, it had at times occurred to me to try writing something in the jazz idiom for this combination. Now it suddenly occurred to me that this might be a good idea for this swing concert of Helbock's. At least I felt fairly certain no one else would show up with the same instrumentation.

Consequently, I dreamed up a little piece of music, a composition I entitled "Interlude in B-Flat"—for the excellent reason that it was (a) an interlude, and (be) in the key of B-flat. I got hold of two violin-playing friends, a violist, a cellist, and—adding guitar, string bass, and drums (for the sake of rhythm, since this was to be a jazz piece)—we ran the thing over. It sounded pretty good, and these fellows agreed to appear with me for my little stint at the concert.

The night of the concert we were all lined up backstage, waiting our turn. The longer we waited, the more dubious I became. The place was a madhouse. Those were the early days of this thing called Swing, and if you happened to be around at that time you may recall that such bands played in what could hardly be called dulcet tones. Those were the days when swing bands used to try to raise the roof, and some of them frequently did—or at least caused the roof to do some pretty ominous quivering at times.

By the time we were supposed to walk on stage my knees were knocking together like a pair of castanets. And with good reason. The band that had just finished, the particular big band we were following, was one of the loudest I had ever heard—with the exception of one other I'll mention in due time. And here I was, trying to follow it with nothing but a quiet little chamber piece for clarinet and string quartet—a combination hardly noted for its ability to produce great volumes of sound—plus an attenuated rhythm section, minus even piano, which I had left out for the sake of keeping the rhythmic aspects of the piece down to a subtle minimum.

Well, we got out there somehow, and somehow we managed to get started. And as I heard the first few notes of the introduction, I was pretty sure we might all just as well have stayed home, for all the benefit anyone connected with this clambake was going to get out of our performance. Still, there was nothing for it but to get through with it as best we could, so we went ahead.

There was a hell of a lot of racket going on out in the audience. I suppose all that loud music they had been subjected to up to this point had more or less deafened everyone; and now that they had to try to adjust to the comparatively puny sounds of an essentially chamber music instrumentation, they couldn't get with it immediately.

But in no time at all, much to my surprise, you began to hear people shushing each other all over the place. And in a few moments the whole theater had quieted down. I was vaguely aware of people in the first few rows leaning forward and listening intently. The first few rows are about all you can ever see from a lighted stage anyway, so I couldn't tell what anyone else was doing; besides, I was too damn scared to notice much else, for it was time for me to begin playing, and after I came in and started in on the "jazz" part of the piece it seemed to me I heard some strange noise and it took a few seconds before I realized it was the audience applauding! I couldn't figure out what in hell was going on, for I had only just begun, and the only thing I was really consciously aware of, for my fingers were automatically coming down on the right keys and somehow making the clarinet do what it was supposed to be doing, was that I had to make *pipi* about as bad as I've ever had to in my whole life!

Somehow or other, we managed to get through the piece and all come out together at the other end. At that point the only thing I could figure out to do about it was to get the hell off that stage as fast as I could. I think I tried to make some kind of bow, or something I thought of as a bow; and then I ran. I not only ran off stage, but I was ready to keep right on running, out of that theater and all the way home.

But Helbock was standing in the wings, along with several other people I didn't know. Even if I did know them, I wouldn't have recognized anyone at that moment. The only way I recognized Helbock himself was when he grabbed me by the arm and yelled, "That was *great,* Art—*listen* to them out there. Go on out and take another bow."

I stared at him blindly.

"Go *on!*" he shouted, pushing me toward the stage.

I resisted him. I couldn't feel or hear or see very much of what was happening.

"*Listen* to them!" he yelled at me again.

And all of a sudden I became aware of a noise. It was like thunder. No, not like thunder—this seemed to *spray* the air with a heavy thunderous *hissing* sound. I couldn't figure out what on earth it was, and then all at once I realized it was people still clapping out there. I began to hear shouting and yelling and it sounded like "More, more, more," but I was too dazed to be sure of anything that was going on; then suddenly, the next thing I knew, Joe Helbock had given me a violent shove and I found myself out on the stage again.

The musicians in my little combination were still milling around aimlessly out there. Apparently they hadn't even come off stage at all.

I walked awkwardly out, and by the time I got to the center of the stage, the theater began to quiet down. Then there was a long heavy silence, and I couldn't figure out what to do. I looked over into the wings and saw Joe and those other people grinning out at me, and I wished I could get out of there and go somewhere where I could sit down and be by myself for a while.

I don't suppose I stood there for more than a few seconds at the most, but it seemed like hours before I finally heard someone from the wings whispering hoarsely, "*Thank 'em—tell 'em thanks.*" Maybe it was Helbock, but I couldn't tell who it was.

I looked out at the theater and saw a blur of faces out there, and the next moment found myself talking. I can't remember what words I said, but I remember thanking them and saying something to the effect that this whole thing was a complete surprise to me, that I'd had no idea that they might like the piece that much or I'd have written another one to play as an encore, but. . . .

There was another dead silence after this. I started to make a bow and get off when I heard somebody holler up from the audience, "Play the same one again," and all at once it seemed as if they were all hollering the same thing and I couldn't figure out what to do about that.

I looked over into the wings again. Joe Helbock was grinning all over his face now and nodding, as if to say, "Go *ahead*. Play it *again*. What are you waiting for?" I turned around to look at the musicians up there on stage with me. They were all grinning too. Somehow I must have got across to them that we might as well play the damn thing once more and then get out of there, for we started in once again, and this time we played the whole thing through in a deathly silence.

Not until then could I get out of there and go to the nearest toilet. I don't believe anybody has ever had to make *pipi* as bad as I did at that moment, as well as throughout the whole time I'd been out there on that goddamn stage of the Imperial Theatre!

And all my friend Leonard Feather can find to say about all this is, ". . . Artie's one number 'Interlude in B-Flat,' broke up the show." How do you like that?

Shows you how much you can trust a jazz critic. Why, if I'd had to stay out there for a few minutes more—just long enough to actually wet my pants—that's the time you might have seen a show *really* broken up.

Charlie Barnet

Charlie Barnet seems the exact temperamental opposite of Artie Shaw—a relaxed and happy approach to life permeates his autobiography, Those Swinging Years *(1984; with Stanley Dance). These two excerpts show him first in the early, carefree years and then in the postwar period when his world of the swing bands disappears out from under him.*

We ran out of money in Antwerp. I cabled home with our last buck, asking them to send me some. I knew they'd send it, and they did, but we couldn't find it. We'd go over to Brussels and the people at the cable office would say, "No, it's not here."

We were in seamen's bar right on the waterfront, and we'd run up quite a bill there. They were rough characters in that place and they would have killed us if we had tried to run out, but finally somebody suggested we try American Express. Sure enough, when we went over there, that was where my mother had sent the money, enough to bail us out all the way. I remember when we left Antwerp, Gordon Tully and I were out on deck playing "That's a-Plenty." I had a bottle of Hollands gin in one hand and was playing the clarinet with the other—no easy trick.

Liquor was very much part of the scene in those days. Artie Shaw is credited with having said that jazz was born in a whisky barrel, was reared on marijuana, and was currently expiring on heroin. In that era, just about everybody was a lush, most of the jazz guys around the bands, Pee Wee Russell, Bix Beiderbecke . . . Poor Bix! He and I were rehearsing in Huston Ray's orchestra at the Jane Grey Studios in New York, a place where a lot of bands rehearsed. We made the one rehearsal and were supposed to return the next day, but Bix never showed up. He didn't look well and he had been playing badly. A few days later I heard he had died.

Drinking was like a fashion, the thing to do, but I was also into pot while I was still with Winegar. It had become very common around town and Mezz was a hero. I remember going to his apartment and watching him put it through a screen. This was up on Riverside Drive. But the first person I ever saw smoke marijuana was Louis Armstrong. We were playing at Princeton University. They'd have a band at each fraternity house, and I was there with a group of guys put together for the occasion. During an intermission, we all went over to hear Louis. He was down in the basement rolling the stuff and I know I had some that night. It was easily obtainable uptown, but this was a transition period when it was becoming prevalent in jazz society. Louis had even made a record called "Muggles," a nickname for marijuana cigarettes. There weren't really any laws against them, but if you were caught selling them you could be prosecuted for not paying the government tax. Guys used to light up, go to a cop, blow smoke in his face, and ask, "Can you tell me how to get to such-and-such a place?" Of course, the smell was very like that of the Cubeb cigarettes asthma sufferers used to clear up their lungs. You couldn't tell the difference. Out in California the first big bust involved Louis Armstrong and a drummer named Vic Berton. Louis was working at Sebastian's Cotton Club, and kept on working—though each night he and Berton were escorted back to jail. The cops had no substantial legal precedent, because marijuana wasn't classified as a narcotic then, and they were afraid of being sued if they interfered with performances at the club. But that case was the cause of the subsequent stringent California laws. Of course, the stuff that was around in those days was pure marijuana, not the kind today that is laced with all sorts of foreign substances. It doesn't even *smell* right. In the old days, there was nothing about it that would prevent your going about your business and performing properly. Somebody gave me some of the new stuff a couple of years ago when I was on my boat, and for four hours I was afraid to get out of my chair.

After the Winegar band and my trip to Antwerp, I decided that I wanted to check out the South, where so many talented jazzmen had originated. Accompanied by Scoop Tomson, I headed for Louisiana in my Chevrolet convertible. Gordon Tully was working in the Flem Ferguson band at the Washington-Youree Hotel in Shreveport, and I had enough saved to afford a short wait until an opening in the band came up.

In the meantime, Scoop and I spent a few weeks in Kilgore, Texas, in what they called a "keg" house—a dancehall with hostesses. These places were all over the oil fields, and Kilgore was the heart of the East Texas boom. The manager of the ballroom played drums in the band and the pianist, Slick Rayburn, could play only in the key of F. We played from 8:00 to 3:00 without intermissions. Guys would get off the stand one by one. You couldn't buy anything but sugar whisky, which was about two hours old. It was rotgut made out of fermented sugar with a little coloring, and it sold for two dollars a gallon. The first fight usually started at 8:15.

I got hit over the head in a brawl one night, and I still have the scar. I was talking when I should have been listening, and I was lucky I didn't get killed, because life was very cheap in those oil fields. My mother never knew about the incident. I wound up in jail, one with a dirt floor and a bucket for a latrine. One of my fellow inmates set his beard on fire one day while in a drunken stupor, and another guy picked up the bucket to douse the fire.

The law down there would regularly round up everybody on the street. There was not enough room in the jail for two hundred or so people, so the cops strung a rope from tree to tree to form a square and tied everyone to it. Like animals on leashes, the people waited while the cops processed them. Twenty to thirty known, wanted criminals were usually found in such roundups. I had an offer from one fellow in jail with me to do away with the guy who had clobbered me with the bottle. All he wanted for this service was a bus ticket to Omaha.

When the job in Shreveport came through, we got the hell out of that town fast. The band played at noon and dinnertime in the hotel, and for this we received free room and an allowance of ten dollars and fifty cents in the coffee shop, but no cash. The only way we could get our hands on any money was by playing outside the hotel on Saturday nights, usually at the country club, where they would pay us six or seven dollars. Where was the musicians' union while this was going on? Well, the president and secretary of the local played in the band! That gives some idea of how weak the union was in those days.

There were no great players in that band, but we had a ball and I look back on those days as some of the happiest in my life. We were on the freebie list with all the local ladies of the evening, and marijuana was plentiful and very cheap. But I did have one particularly disturbing experience when a tenor saxophonist from Dallas, the son of well-to-do parents, came through town with Hogan Hancock, in whose band Harry James played a little later. This saxophonist turned the whole Ferguson band on to heroin, but it scared the hell out of me and I've never wanted any part of it since. I guess it was pretty pure stuff, because it hit me like a sledgehammer. My knees sagged; I sat down and didn't want to do anything. A lot of people in the business grew accustomed to taking a diluted dose, but when someone came along with the pure stuff, the same amount was lethal in strength. I understand that when those involved in the trade are afraid someone is going to squeal, they get rid of him that way, by giving him an overdose. One of the trumpet players wasn't as fortunate as I was. He got hung up and had a rough time getting straight.

As pleasant as the life was down there, I got to missing New York and took off for the Big Apple. The depression was really on and jobs were scarce. I spent some time with Beasley Smith, who had a really good band out of Nashville. Beasley played piano and was a great guy. Matty Matlock, the fine clarinetist, had just left the band. We played mostly one-nighters, but we got to sit down a couple of times, once at the Brooklyn Roseland and once at a nightclub up in Monticello which was owned by the mob. Beasley's band was much more jazz-oriented than any I had yet played in, and I had become by now a jazz soloist of minor importance. Unfortunately, Beasley had to break up the band when he began to lose his eyesight. It was disturbing to me because I had been riding in his car with him and his wife Elizabeth, and he had been doing all the driving. He was a real gentleman and we were close friends. He later became a Dot Records executive and wrote several hit songs.

The job situation remained rough, but I got a call from Flem Ferguson in Shreveport. He wanted me back and, if possible, to find him some more musicians, because he had had a shake-up and needed men. It was not easy to find guys who would work for what that job paid, and at one time I think nine out of the ten men in the band had the clap. This was before penicillin and the cure was long and painful.

Bebop music had been getting bigger and bigger in jazz circles, although it never did catch on with the public. The boppers became quite clannish and didn't want to play with anyone but their fellow cultists. This began to destroy the great fellowship that had previously existed among all jazz musicians. In addition, a large proportion of the boppers were into heroin and were literally unmanageable, unpredictable, and thoroughly unreliable. A lot of those guys not only destroyed themselves, they gave the whole music business a bad name. Outside of top exponents of the music like Charlie Parker, Dizzy Gillespie, and a few others, the boppers were a bunch of fumblers who were obviously incapable of handling the new idiom. In conjunction with Stan Kenton's so-called progressive jazz and Petrillo's recording ban, this effectively delivered the death blow to the big bands as we had known them. The music was now undanceable, too loud, and incomprehensible to the general public, whose interest switched to rock (a simpler form of music). The public is always ready for a change when it cannot stomach a situation. We still have a few big bands today, but they are all concert-oriented and scarcely ever play any dance music. The few that do are mostly riding on Glenn Miller's coattails and they offer nothing new, only the tried-and-true.

Duke Ellington never swerved from *his* musical path, continued to produce music in the Ellington manner, and survived 'way past the bop era until 1974, when he died. Kenton was off in left field with a big cultist following that he had mesmerized with his oratory. I personally never cared for his music. The ballads his band played were gloomy exercises, with Wagnerian overtones. Taken at exaggeratedly slow tempos, they seemed to go on forever. The up-tempo numbers were too pretentious, and it seemed as though he didn't want the band ever to swing for more than a few bars at a time. Most of the rare swinging moments were the result of Bill Holman's charts. On the other hand, Duke would surround you with warm, melodic tones and a variety of beautiful colors, all vibrantly complemented by his superlative soloists.

There was always Count Basie, and a world without his happy, swinging sounds would be a much less pleasant place. Whenever I heard his band, it always made me feel good. Tommy Dorsey, too, always presented a thoroughly musical band which performed the arrangements cleanly and intelligently. To me, his was an excellent dance band with enough jazz orientation to make it consistently interesting while pleasing the people at the same time.

Woody Herman, however, had reorganized his band along bop lines and it seemed that was the way things were going. I held out against the bop influence until 1949, but had to go along with it then because none of the younger musicians knew how to approach big band playing except in that idiom. I still thought of bop as a small-group style that allowed unlimited freedom for solos, but not as a big band ploy. Nevertheless, I went to New York and started to put together a band designed along the lines of the new music. This meant that a lot of the guys I had been using had to be replaced with bop musicians. I didn't like this, but you couldn't mix the two kinds, because they were just incompatible.

THE BAND WAS not a very good dance band in this period, I must admit, but we were booked into Virginia Beach to play for dancing. We had been playing for listeners only and the book was loaded with undanceable arrangements that Manny Albam, Pete Rugolo, and Dave Matthews had written for concert use. Trudy Richards and Buddy Stewart handled the vocals. Neither the owner of the club nor the people were happy with us.

During the engagement, a softball game was scheduled with one of the other bands in Virginia Beach. It was to take place on the public playground right outside the city jail. I went out to some of the gambling joints the night before and I had a full head of steam up when I was hauled over by one of the local gendarmes on the way home. He concluded that I was drunk, and he was correct. According to the local law the next step was to have a doctor declare me drunk officially. What was funny was that he rode me all over town trying to find a doctor, and as time passed I became more and more sober. Finally, giving up in disgust, he took me to jail and booked me on a disorderly conduct charge, so that he could hold me until he got a doctor to examine me. It was broad daylight by now and my wife of the time, Rita, had gotten hold of the owner of the spot where we were playing. He came down and got me out on bail. Meanwhile, they had found a doctor, but he refused to declare me intoxicated. He said I had been under the influence of something, but was now okay. I stepped from the jailhouse to the field, where, under the eyes of the frustrated cop, I managed to play a passable game of softball. We lost the game, however, because my guys were all overtrained from the night before. When the trial came up a few days later and I was acquitted, the cop who arrested me threw his cap on the floor and cursed the obvious fix that had been put in. The owner of the private beach club where we were playing had to pass out several free memberships in order to get me off.

A few years later I stayed overnight in Virginia Beach and the big hotel had, in the meantime, unbeknown to me, become "restricted," meaning that no Jews were allowed. I wondered about the lengthy questioning from the desk clerk when I checked in, but I was so tired that it wasn't until the next day that I realized what was going on. Before I left, I went in the men's room and scrawled on the wall with a grease pencil, "My name is Cohen and I have just shit here!" No, Virginia Beach was definitely not my kind of town.

Although the band was in great shape and the quality of the musicians the best I ever had, I felt control slipping away from me as the music leaned more and more to the taste of the band's members. In other words, I was proud of the band, but not happy with the direction we were taking. I still missed the warmth and color of the Ellington approach, and I had a horror of ending up in Stan Kenton's bag.

We were playing in the ballroom at the end of the Steel Pier in Atlantic City, a half-mile out to sea, when I saw quite a sight one night near closing time. Here was a Chevrolet touring car with a chauffeur and rear-seat window shields driving into the room. An elderly gentleman in a straw hat was seated in the back. He turned out to be Nuckey Johnson, the famous boss of Atlantic City, and he had just been released from the penitentiary. He invited me to go with him on a tour of the nightspots. Everywhere we went we were treated like royalty. He was quite a guy and I enjoyed the evening immensely, but why he suddenly decided he wanted my company is still a mystery, for I had played in Atlantic City many times without ever seeing him, let alone being his guest for a night on the town.

Next we had an engagement at Bop City on the corner of Broadway and Forty-ninth Street with Billy Eckstine, who was then very hot. Our band had been attracting a bit of attention, too, and between the two of us we played to standing room only for the whole four weeks. There was no dancing there and the band, while sensational, was slipping further into a concert entity. I have nothing against concerts, but I felt we should try to play *some* decent dance music rather than having just enough to get by. All of the new charts coming in were directed toward a listening audience, not toward dancers. This, plus the bebop influence, made them completely incomprehensible to most people. I thought it was possible to be creative without jamming the unpalatable down people's throats. In any case, we began to get static from music publishers about arrangements like that on "All the Things You Are," which featured Maynard Ferguson in a trumpet frenzy, and one that Johnny Richards had written for us on *Rhapsody in Blue.* We recorded both of them, but they had to be recalled by Capitol on threats of lawsuits from the publishers. Both records went underground immediately, but they are still available in bootleg circles. I liked *Rhapsody in Blue,* but "All the Things You Are" was an atrocity that should never have been committed. Some compensation was a particularly beautiful treatment of "Over the Rainbow" written by Tiny Kahn, an unusual feat for a drummer. Tiny was also a fine vibraphone player, but we never made use of that talent. His tragic death a few years later was a great loss to the profession.

After Bop City, we took off again on a one-nighter tour to the West Coast via Canada, where the band was well received by big crowds. The guys in the band had all bought cap pistols or water pistols, and they had a high old time as the bus went through some of the small towns. They would open the windows and shoot at everybody on the street. I guess they were lucky no one returned their "fire" with real bullets. By this time the band was clear of junkies, because I didn't hire anyone about whom there was any doubt. Woody Herman was not so careful—or not so lucky—and, while he had a great band, he had some guys with serious problems. Woody and I had the Rendezvous Ballroom in Balboa for the summer of 1949. He did the first four weeks; then we played a weekend together; and after that I continued for four weeks alone.

The weekend we were together, Stan Kenton acted as guest commentator. He was about to return to the band business, having regained his health. The Mutual Broadcasting System was airing the ballroom the whole summer, and much attention was focused on that weekend, especially since it enabled Stan to let people know about his future plans. There was a festive atmosphere at this gathering of some of the world's great jazz musicians. When we did the broadcast in the late afternoon for listeners in the East, no charge was made for admission. The people could come in off the beach just as they were, free. That was when I got the message loud and clear. Scarcely anyone showed up. Here we were, Kenton, Herman, and Barnet, and we couldn't get a crowd to come in even for free!

MAX GORDON

The irrepressible producer Max Gordon turned his club, The Village Vanguard, into what was probably America's most famous jazz venue. In these unsentimental excerpts from his memoirs, Life at the Village Vanguard *(1980), he turns his clear eye on some of the formidable talents who played for him, like Sonny Rollins and Charlie Mingus.*

SONNY'S THE GREATEST

Yeah, I know all about Sonny Rollins. He's up in the big time now. I didn't go to his Carnegie Hall concert last year. I was surprised he showed up, that he didn't go off somewhere by himself that night—down to the walkway under the Williamsburg Bridge like he used to do, carrying his horn with him—and blow the night away, alone, and to hell with the mob at Carnegie Hall!

Sonny's into the big money now. I know about that too—that place on Bleecker Street, the Gate: a converted laundry, seats five hundred, and pays him fifteen hundred a night weekends, whenever they can find him.

There was a time when if you wanted to hear Sonny Rollins, you had to come to the Village Vanguard to hear him. He played the Vanguard four times a year, every year for ten years, once as a sideman with Miles Davis but mostly with a quartet of his own.

There's sharp disagreement among critics and jazz buffs about the playing prowess of some jazz musicians, but not about Sonny. He's the greatest—the greatest tenor saxophonist of his generation. Dexter Gordon, Billy Harper, Johnny Griffin, all great tenor men, but Sonny's the greatest of them all—no two ways about it.

Don't ask me why I never book Sonny anymore, why it's been years now since he worked at the Vanguard. It never was easy tying Sonny down to a specific date.

I remember one year I couldn't find him. I had his phone number on Willoughby Street in Brooklyn, where he lived, but every time I tried it, I got his wife or mother-in-law.

He's got to be home sometime, I thought. I kept trying. One morning at 3 A.M., I let the phone ring five minutes, when lo and behold I heard the receiver lifted. "Yah!" It was Sonny's voice. Sonny never says "hello."

"Sonny!" I shouted. I was always afraid he didn't hear me.

"How're you doin'?" he asked matter-of-factly, as if he talked to me every day. "What's happenin'?"

"I got a week open in November," I kept shouting.

"Who's in the joint this week?" he wanted to know.

I told him.

"I'll be down tomorrow night," he said. "Just got back from India." Sonny was always just getting back from Japan, Denmark, or Poland; this time it was India.

It was a year later when he showed up at the Vanguard—just walked in one night. It was Sonny all right, a tall, powerful, black man, with a bull neck, dressed in a flowing white caftan. His large round head was clean-shaven except for a cross-shaped outline of hair on top. "Something religious," the other cats whispered when they saw him.

I knew Sonny was weird, but I wasn't prepared for this vision in white from India. He stood around smiling, countering every question with a benign, tired voice. Sonny was always like that—only now he was more so.

"He's been playing his sax out there in a cave in India—alone, man."

"Who told you?" I asked Al Dailey, Sonny's favorite piano player.

"He told me."

"What was he doing out there in India?"

"Meditatin', man, meditatin'."

(Incidentally, Al Dailey is the only piano player Sonny never fired. That's a record because Sonny never hired a musician he didn't fire at least once, and often right in the middle of a number. He once fired Elvin Jones, probably jazz's greatest drummer.)

When I suggested a drink to him, Sonny smiled a refusal. He didn't touch the stuff anymore. His religion wouldn't let him. And about a gig, he was taking no gigs for the present. He was having his teeth fixed. God knows how long that was going to take. So I crossed Sonny off my list again, hoping for better luck next time.

About a year later, I heard through the jazz grapevine that Sonny was hanging out at George Richard's loft on Greene Street, or is it Prince, and that he was dressed in a suit like you and me, letting his hair grow and playing like a sonofabitch. So I said to myself, "Maybe the bastard is ready to go to work. But what's he doing hanging out in George's place? He certainly can't be getting more money at George Richard's joint than I can pay him."

George ran weekend jazz in his Soho loft. Orange lights, pillows on the floor, broads trying to get picked up, that sort of shit. Unemployed jazz musicians jammed there for peanuts three or four nights a week. Whatthehell was Sonny doing there?

I called up Al Dailey. Al assured me that Sonny wouldn't play in a sink like George's place. "We use the place to rehearse, afternoons—that's all. Sonny wants to get his chops in order after all that work his dentist did on his mouth."

"Who's he using?" I asked.

"A white cat he found in California on trumpet. Paid his fare to New York. Sonny is crazy about him. The cat stinks." Al didn't sound happy.

Another week passed. Al dropped in and told me that Sonny talked about calling me—wanted to get back on the scene. "Hasn't he called you yet? In that case, call him. Here's his new number."

So I started calling that new number every day, twice, three times a day, for a month—no answer!

"Let it ring, man, let it ring—you know Sonny!" said Al.

It was the middle of the night and I dialed the number again. Three minutes, four minutes, five minutes pass; then I hear Sonny's breathy baritone. "Yah!"

"It's Max, Sonny," I'm shouting again.

"What's happenin', man?" he asks as usual.

"I'll give you the three grand—I got a date in April—a Tuesday opening. Al is here now. I'll make out the contracts, and he'll take 'em over to you. It's only a little after three. Sign 'em—I'll wait until Al gets back. OK? A quartet? A quintet? Bring in anything you want."

And that's how it happened that Sonny opened on a Tuesday in April, four years ago—the last time he played the Vanguard. Naturally the place was jammed. It was Sonny Rollins! Everybody was waiting to hear him. He'd been away too long. The critics and their girls came down, the chief executive officer of a record company, and Sonny's first wife, raising hell. But mostly it was the jazz community that had been missing him that crowded the place, some who'd only heard him on records, never in person, and a lot of young cats, graduates from rock, who had heard tell of Sonny and were glad to pay their money to hear him, because Sonny was the greatest.

The lights went down. Al Dailey was at the piano. Beaver Harris, drummer, and the bass player were in their places. Next, up came a blond cat hugging a trumpet—Sonny's newest discovery from California. Then in slow succession, four men carrying saxophones trekked their way to the bandstand.

"How many men are there in Sonny's quartet?" I asked.

That's how Sonny is. He'll pick up musicians on the way, invite them to sit in with him. I thought I knew all the active jazz musicians in the New York area. I recognized Eddie Daniels and Rocky Boyd, but the rest were strangers to me.

Finally Sonny appeared, in a floor-length white caftan (Holy Moses, Sonny is still a Moslem, I thought), his head bald, with only that cross of hair on top. The screaming and applause that greeted him was something.

Sonny seemed oblivious to the crowd. He gave the downbeat, stated the theme on his horn, then cut out to let the other instruments take over. Every man took a turn soloing while Sonny stood quietly listening, the rhythm section maintaining a pulsing, insistent beat.

Now it was Sonny's turn. After a few flourishes on his horn, he launched into a honking, ecstatic solo.

The musicians on the bandstand stayed with him at first but soon dropped their weak, supportive sounds. They seemed stunned by what was coming out of Sonny's horn, the thrusts, the swoops, the soft lyrical descents, the roaring cries. He went on like that for an hour, with every chorus different. He started a number, then segued into another, then a third, then found his way back to the original tune—nothing repeated, nothing trite. Only Al Dailey's piano punctuated Sonny with tentative, searching chords.

If I were a jazz critic like Whitney Balliett of *The New Yorker* magazine or Nat Hentoff or Gary Giddins of *The Village Voice,* I could describe his playing like it should be described. I'll say one thing—he was terrific and playing like the Sonny of old.

At the intermission, in the kitchen where the musicians hang out between sets, I noticed Beaver Harris, sweaty and exhausted, slumped into a chair. "Man, that Sonny's too much. He's too much," he kept saying. "He kills me, man, he kills me."

That's how it was with musicians who played with Sonny. He scared the hell out of them. They were in the big league playing with him. It was a challenge to their musicianship, to their improvisational skills.

The blond trumpet player, looking scared, stood around saying nothing.

The half-hour intermission was over, the second set about to begin. Down went the lights again and up came the blond trumpet player, still scared; then the bassist; then Beaver Harris; and finally Al Dailey. The four saxophone men didn't show up. I guess they'd had it. They probably felt that Sonny's invitation to them to sit in didn't reach into the second act.

Ten minutes passed. The men were in their places, ready to start the second set, waiting for Sonny. Where was Sonny? I went looking for him, in the kitchen, the men's room, on the sidewalk out front, and in the back—no Sonny. He was nowhere to be found.

"Whatthehell's happened to Sonny?" I whispered to Al Dailey at the piano.

"Probably on his way back to India."

"That's not funny, Al. Where's the bastard? Where the hell'd he go?"

And do you know what? Sonny never showed up for the second set. He vanished. And I haven't seen him since.

I was about to lock up for the night. Al was there. He stayed with me to the end. "What d'you think, Al?" I asked him. "What really happened to Sonny?"

"It's that blond trumpet player," said Al. "Like I told you, he sounded great in California but terrible in New York. Sonny couldn't take him."

"Why didn't Sonny fire him?"

"Dunno."

"How can a trumpet player sound great in California and terrible in New York?" I asked Al.

"It's the vibes, man, the vibes!"

"What vibes?"

"Coltrane, Miles, Coleman Hawkins, Bill Evans, Mingus, and Sonny himself, cats who've played here and left their vibes here, man! Know what I mean? The vibes! That's what I'm talking about. That blond cat didn't belong in this company. The vibes scared the hell out of him!"

"Al," I said, "if you hear from Sonny, tell him if he can play his horn in a cave in India, *alone,* he can play his horn here at the Vanguard *alone.* Tell him I'll give him the same bread I pay the quartet."

I understand Sonny clips an electronic gadget to his horn these days—a pickup that will give his horn a bigger sound so he can hear himself above the electrified instruments he likes to surround himself with now.

Sonny doesn't need it; he doesn't need any gadgets. He doesn't need any electricity, not Sonny. He needs his horn. Let him stand up there alone and pour it out. Mark my word, Sonny will throw that gadget away. Because Sonny's the greatest.

I haven't seen Sonny since that night. I still owe him a night's pay.

Twenty Years with Charlie Mingus

The last time I saw Charlie Mingus was in July 1978 on the lawn behind the White House, where President Jimmy Carter was throwing a party to commemorate the twenty-fifth anniversary of the Newport Jazz Festival. Charlie was in a wheelchair, had been in a wheelchair for more than a year, suffering from the same debilitating disease that killed Lou Gehrig, the Yankee first baseman.

George Wein, the producer of the Newport Jazz Festival, introduced Charlie, "the world's greatest living jazz composer," he called him.

Charlie couldn't stand up to take a bow, but a thousand people rose to their feet to give him an ovation. Jimmy Carter walked over to his wheelchair to shake his hand. Charlie sat there, unable to speak, tears streaming down his face.

I remember when George Wein wouldn't hire Charlie for the Newport Jazz Festivals. George didn't think Charlie was good enough or big enough to play in his festivals. One year, 1962 I think it was, Charlie, who felt his band was good enough and big enough, mounted a jazz festival of his own, a rebel jazz festival right next door to George's in Newport, Rhode Island. He got Max Roach and a lot of other jazz musicians who were sore at George Wein to join him. He scared the hell out of George.

I kept thinking, standing there on the White House lawn, how George Wein would be goddamn glad to have Charlie's band play in his next Newport Jazz Festival, if he could get him. But Charlie isn't going to play in any jazz festival anymore, or in any nightclubs or anywhere else.

He was sitting there in his wheelchair, dying. In fact it wasn't long after that White House barbecue that poor Charlie did die.

A MONTH LATER Dannie Richmond, the drummer in Charlie's band, came down to see me, looking for a gig for Charlie's old band, now leaderless and unemployed.

"I guess I'm the leader now with Charlie gone," Dannie said. "I talked to Charlie when he was still alive and told him I was planning to go down to see you one day. 'You know the music,' he said, 'you played it with me for twenty years. And I know the men in the band got to work.'

"Charlie was living on the forty-third floor of a high-rise building on Tenth Avenue. His nurse lit him a cigar and he was puffing on it when he said to me, 'If anybody can play my music, Dannie, you can play it.'

"'How 'bout my using Eddie Gomez on bass?' I asked him." The bass was Charlie's old instrument.

"'Eddie is great,' he said.

"'And I'm going to call the band "Dannie Richmond Plays Charlie Mingus Jazz Workshop Quintet" with Eddie Gomez on bass. That's what I'm gonna call the band. Is that OK?'

"'OK,' said Charlie. OK! He said, OK. What else could he say?

"So when's your first open date?" Dannie asked me.

We were sitting at my desk in the kitchen.

"Without Charlie up there, who's coming to the Vanguard to hear the band?" I asked him.

"Plenty," said Dannie. "The music'll be the same. The men in the band will be the same men who were with Charlie. With Eddie Gomez on bass, the music'll be as great as ever."

Maybe, but who knows Dannie Richmond?

I told Dannie he was no Charlie Mingus. "People came not only to hear Charlie but to see him in action. They'd sit and wait for him to throw one of his fits, stop the music cold, right in the middle of a number, rage and fume at his men because he heard something he didn't like. They'd sit fascinated.

"Do you remember the night he hit Jimmy Knepper, the trombone player, right in the stomach, right on the bandstand? Why'd he hit Jimmy like that?"

"Charlie wanted to hear the number we were playing the way he wrote it," explained Dannie.

Dannie, thin, tall, wearing a large head of hair, spoke in the even, quiet, courtly accents of a black man from the South.

"You're right," he said. "I'm no Charlie Mingus, I'm not going to knock no trombone player's teeth out for striking a wrong note. But there won't be any wrong notes. We're going to play the music the way he wrote it. Dig? God knows, I played it for twenty years.

"Sure Charlie was quick with his fists," Dannie said and laughed gently. "So what? He didn't always get away with it. D'you know Charlie was once in Duke Ellington's band? And the Duke fired him because he punched Juan Tizol, the saxophone player, on the bandstand. When he fired Charlie, the Duke is supposed to have said: 'Had I known you were going to get into a rumble like that on the bandstand, I'd have written an intro to it.'

"Charlie threw a lot of punches, and I've seen him take a few too," Dannie continued. "Sunny Murry laid one on him in the Five Spot one night. And the night the word got around that Oscar Pettiford knocked him cold in a Harlem joint, the cats in the band hearing the news didn't mind showing intense personal satisfaction, as if Oscar had evened the score for them."

"All right," I said to Dannie, "maybe the music will be the same, but the money I used to pay Charlie isn't going to be the same."

"I don't expect it to be the same," he said. "Give me a minimum guarantee, and if we do the business, sweeten it up a bit at the end of the run, right?"

I gave Dannie my hand, and we set the date for his opening.

This was a big moment for Dannie, a sideman becoming the leader of his own band. He sat there thinking about it—thinking about his twenty years with Mingus—twenty years! And now he was going on his own.

"I don't care what they say, I loved Charlie," he said. "He never threw a punch at me. Twenty years together in all kinds of weather! Now he's gone."

So we sat in the afternoon gloom of the Vanguard that hadn't yet opened for the night, talking about Charlie Mingus.

"I remember the first time you and Charlie played the Vanguard, in 1958," I said. "Jimmy Giuffre's trio was here, and Charlie came down to hear them. Jimmy, a tenor saxophonist and jazz innovator, was experimenting with what he called Swamp Jazz. He was attracting a small, intense audience. Don't ask me what Swamp Jazz was. Jimmy wrote The Four Brothers a great number for the Woody Herman band, when Stan Getz was a member of that thundering herd, and gave up that kind of straightahead jazz to probe the mysteries of Swamp Jazz."

Jimmy was from Louisiana and distilled some pretty fancy musical notions out of the Louisiana swamps, which he was offering to the jazz avant-garde at the Village Vanguard in New York.

"After listening to Jimmy's Swamp Jazz for half an hour, Mingus said to me, 'Let me bring my band over next Sunday so you can hear some jazz.' Next Sunday Mingus and the quintet arrived. You were on drums," I reminded Dannie. "I introduced Mingus, and he looked at the small, dedicated Swamp Jazz audience down in front, snorted, gave the downbeat and let go with his first number. The volume, the intensity, the blistering attack of the music made me gasp. I'd never heard Mingus before.

"When the time came for the second set, Giuffre suggested we wait to allow the place to cool down before he resumed his own Swamp Jazz experimentations. I let Jimmy go the next week and hired Mingus. I never heard of Swamp Jazz again. Mingus wiped it out."

"No, Charlie couldn't stand Swamp Jazz," Dannie said. "He couldn't stand the free-style jazz the cats started experimenting with either. 'That's not jazz,' he said. 'You don't have to be a musician to play that crap. Dogs can play it.' Charlie read where some critics called it the sound of the future. 'It's got no future,' he said, 'because it's the kind of music that goes nowhere.'

"Man, he didn't like jazz critics either," said Dannie. "He didn't like jazz promoters, he didn't like jazz record producers or jazz executives of all kinds, and he didn't like jazz nightclub owners."

"No, maybe he didn't like me," I admitted. "Still, one night he walked over to where I was standing at the bar, picked the cigar I was smoking out of my fingers, took a puff and handed it back to me. 'I love you, you bastard.'"

Charlie was funny like that. He felt exploited. If he worked for you, you were exploiting him. The money you paid him was never enough. Maybe it wasn't.

"He once held a knife in front of me," I told Dannie. "So what? I knew he wasn't going to use it."

"What about? Money, I suppose," Dannie guessed.

"He needed a cash draw. I handed him a roll of bills. It wasn't the amount he asked for, so he threw the whole roll up in the air and grabbed a knife."

"I remember that," said Dannie. "I, like a good boy, bent down and started picking up the bills."

"And the night he tore the front door off its hinges," I said, "because the sign outside didn't have the words *Jazz Workshop* on it. 'And it's Charles, not Charlie,' he shouted down the steps. He wanted to be known as Charles Mingus, not Charlie Mingus. I didn't make that mistake again." Then I asked Dannie, "How'd you stand it—for twenty years?"

"It was the music he kept writing. I don't know a greater jazz ballad than 'Goodbye Porkpie Hat,' he wrote when Lester Young died. Do you?

"No, it wasn't always easy," he continued. "Charlie was a ladies' man. He was a handsome bastard before he got fat and weighed three hundred pounds. He'd take jobs as a male model when things got tough. I saw pictures of Charlie, half naked, with three half-naked broads beaming at him in some porno mag. He always had some dame around, running his errands. He married four of 'em. I think it was four. Some he supported, some supported him. Don't ask me how. In the early years, when we had to take gigs—any gig—for peanuts to keep going, it was always good to have a dame around who could bring in a few bucks.

"One night we were closing at The Black Hawk, a hotspot in the San Francisco Tenderloin. Charlie was talking to one of the girls who hung out in the joint. Her pimp came up, saw Charlie talking to his girl, didn't like what he saw, didn't want no goddamn musician poaching on his territory.

"Words passed. Charlie wasted no time. He swung a right. The pimp pulled a gun, fumbled it; Charlie kept swinging. The pimp went down, and Charlie stomped him till he lay quiet in the gutter.

"Charlie's foot swelled up so bad the next day I had to do all the driving all the way back to New York," Dannie said, shaking his head. "No, man, Charlie was no pimp. He was a ladies' man, like I said. It was good to have a broad around who could bring in a few bucks when things got tough. And Charlie had 'em. Dig?

"I watched Charlie step on a scale one day. We were about to board a plane for a gig in London. He weighed three hundred seven pounds. He didn't believe it. 'You can't eat a half-gallon of ice cream at every meal,' I told him. 'I've got to do something about it,' he said.

"Two weeks later, after we got back from London, Charlie went up to Dick Gregory's health farm; Dick, the ex-comedian, and his wife were running it somewhere in Massachusetts. Dick had a strict way of thinning you down: juice in the morning and one lean meal at night. That way you'd lose two pounds a day—guaranteed. In a month, sixty pounds.

"Charlie stood it for a week. Then he heard that Rahsaan Roland Kirk was playing at a place in Boston. So he told Dick he'd drive to town at night, hear Rahsaan, and be back in the morning. Right next to the place in Boston where Rahsaan was playing was a Chinese restaurant. Charlie saw it, hesitated a moment, and walked in. He didn't come out for a week. I mean he didn't get back to Dick's farm for a week." Dannie and I looked at each other for a moment before we started to laugh.

Then I asked Dannie, "What year was it that Charlie retired? Gave up playing jazz, swore he'd never play again? What year was that? '68, '69? That's when he holed himself up in his pad—a couple of furnished rooms on East Fifth Street—had his telephone disconnected, and refused to see anybody. He'd had it: the musicians, employed and unemployed, coming around bullshitting; the kind of joints he had to play in; the jazz buffs, sober and drunk. He was through with all that.

"Nobody saw Charlie for a year. Then I heard from a cat who ran into him one afternoon in a bar on First Avenue. The cat was a filmmaker, had moved to the Village to become a documentary filmmaker.

"'How did, Charlie look?' I asked the filmmaker, and he said, 'Terrible.' And when he asked Charlie where he'd been for a year, what do you think Charlie did? He pulled a piece of paper out of his pocket, a dispossess notice his landlord handed him that morning, and said, 'That's where I've been.'

"So what do you think happened?" I asked Dannie. "This embryo filmmaker gets a bright idea. He says to Charlie: 'Go home, don't make a move. I'll be there in an hour.' So in an hour he's in Charlie's pad with a rented camera. And he starts shooting a documentary of Charlie getting dispossessed, an hour-long documentary of Charlie getting thrown out of his East Fifth Street pad.

"It's all there: the cops and Charlie's six-year-old daughter, Charlie's furniture on the sidewalk, his bass fiddle, his upright piano, his record player, sheets of music strewn all over the street. A city sanitation truck is loading it all 'to take it to a warehouse on Thirty-fourth Street,' the driver says on camera. There's a good shot of the landlord shouting at Charlie: 'Get outta here, you bum!' At the end a television reporter, his microphone stuck in Charlie's tearful face, wants to know 'What's up?'

"'Let people see what happens, what can happen to jazz in this bright land of ours,' says Charlie, or words to that effect."

"You were there," I said to Dannie. "I saw your face in some of the shots."

"Yeah, I sure was there."

"And two years later Charlie won a Guggenheim Fellowship. Fifteen grand!" I reminded Dannie.

"I was there when that happened too. Yessir! Did you ever read Charlie's book he started writing about that time, *Beneath the Underdog?*"

"No, I tried to read it but couldn't make it—because Charlie never wrote it."

"What do you mean, never wrote it? Who wrote it?"

"I know he didn't write it because I once read a manuscript Charlie wrote in longhand, about his early turbulent years in California. He showed it to me. It took me three hours to decipher it. When I got through reading it, I knew it was by Charlie. It was wild, angry and mean, like Charlie. I dipped into *Beneath the Underdog.* It's got Charlie's name on it, but it isn't Charlie. I know the girl who wrote it. Besides, why do I need to read a book about Charlie? I knew Charlie for twenty years. What I want to hear about Charlie is the music he wrote and played all his life."

I told Dannie I had a good chance to hear some again the other night when I got home after closing the Vanguard. WKCR, the Columbia University Radio Station, was running a twenty-four-hour memorial marathon of Charlie's music. I turned on my radio, and the music came pouring out. One number after another—frenzied, heated, rhapsodic jazz music.

Charlie won't be playing those numbers anymore, I kept thinking, sitting alone at four in the morning, hearing the same ones he used to play at the Vanguard on and off for twenty years until I couldn't afford him anymore. "Better Git It in Your Soul," "Love Is a Dangerous Necessity," "Self-Portrait in 3 Colors," "Meditation in Times Square." What titles!

I asked Dannie about one of Charlie's numbers I'd almost forgotten: "All the Things You Could Be Now if Sigmund Freud's Wife Was Your Mother."

"Yeah!"

"Sounds like one of Charlie's love songs," I said.

"It is. Duke Ellington's 'All the Things You Are' inspired him to write it. Charlie loved the Duke. He wrote 'Open Letter to the Duke.' Did they play that one?"

"No, but they played 'Eat That Chicken.'"

"Charlie could be funny," said Dannie.

"I couldn't tear myself from that radio. It must've been six o'clock before I got to bed."

Dannie rose from his chair. Everything was agreed between us: the date, the money, and how the ad announcing his opening was to read:

> Twenty years with Mingus, Dannie Richmond plays The Charlie Mingus Jazz Workshop Quintet with Eddie Gomez on bass.

My phone rang a couple weeks later. It was a woman's voice on the other end telling me she's the secretary of Mrs. Mingus.

"I've heard you're planning to book Dannie Richmond into the Village Vanguard using the Mingus name," she says. "If you do that, Mrs. Mingus expects twenty-five percent of the money you're paying Dannie to be held out, kept for her in escrow. Do you understand? Mrs. Mingus has a lawyer."

Then she hangs up.

When I told Dannie what had transpired on the telephone, he hung his head for a moment. "That's Sue," he said. "I didn't know Charlie was married to her—or is he? Like I've been telling you, there's always some dame around, running Charlie's errands for him. And it looks to me like there still is."

Dannie opened at the Village Vanguard on February 6, 1979. Every night when he came to work the first thing he said to me was, "Sue was on the phone with me again today for an hour. She doesn't want to be left out. She wants me to help her stay with Charlie's music that she loves. Wants to bring back Charlie's men, wherever they are, put a band together and call it The Charlie Mingus Dynasty Band—with me on drums."

"With you as the leader, right?"

"No, man, she wants to be the leader."

"How can she be the leader?"

"That's what I keep telling her. 'Sue,' I tell her, 'I'm the leader. I've played Charlie's music for twenty years. You love the music, but *I've played it* for twenty years.'"

"Dannie," I advised him, "let Sue call herself the leader if that's what she wants. You know and every man in that band'll know you're the leader. Let her stay with Charlie's music. Give her something to do, sign papers, anything, and give her twenty-five percent."

He looked me straight in the eye and said, "When you book The Charlie Mingus Dynasty Band at the Vanguard, brother, if you want to give her twenty-five percent, you give her twenty-five percent. But out of your money, not mine. Dig?"

Anita O'Day

Anita O'Day—still singing after all these years (more than fifty of them)—has been one of the great jazz singers and one of the great jazz drug abusers. Her account of what her habit reduced her to dominates her harrowing and moving autobiography, High Times Hard Times *(1981; with George Eells).*

When I began working at the Starlite again, I'd loosened up a little. I began hanging out with all these characters at the bar. Pushers and users, not even musicians—they were people who wanted to get to know me because they thought I had money.

They invited me to parties where there was a lot of drugging and drinking. Of course, I was boozing. I can't swear to it, but I think I snorted heroin a few times, too.

Anyway, I was a mess. By this time I was so unhappy about what I'd done with my life, I'd become a falling-down drunk. I passed out a couple times on beer cases in what they called my dressing room. Then one day I heard the owner's son, our bartender, bragging, "Yeah, I fucked her in the back room." I knew that wasn't my style. I never completely passed out, and as drunk as I might have been, I'd have fought off that terrible, foul-mouthed animal.

I was fascinated by John Poole. Not because he was tall, slim and good-looking or was a terrific drummer, but what interested me was that he never took alcohol of any kind. I guessed he had a secret I wanted to be let in on. I decided to speak to him. He'd given up trying to talk to me. But the only dumb thing I could think of to do was offer him a drink.

"Thanks, but I don't use liquor or cigarettes," he said.

"Never?"

"It's against my religion."

He was serious. Before getting into music, he'd studied for the ministry at the Moody Bible Institute in Chicago. So I bought him a 7-Up, and he told me how he worshiped Krupa and by extension me, and how I'd deflated him that time in San Francisco during the war when I refused to sign his snare drum and had told him to bug off.

We talked about music and he came at me with the suggestion that we pick up the tempos of the jump tunes so the ballads would have more impact. Most of the squares at the Starlite didn't notice, but a few people paid attention. In the *Los Angeles Daily News,* a fellow named Bill Brown wrote: "Anita . . . [has] got a new sound and it's better than anything she's ever done in the past. The girl is hitting fantastic notes and demonstrating a control that's hard to believe. . . . She has a hushed, almost reverential delivery that scores and all in all is the most exciting voice we've heard for a long time."

I decided then and there that John was a cat who had interesting ideas. So I had two reasons for wanting to get to know him: 1) to talk music, 2) to find out what he used so he didn't have to drink. Because the Good Anita was nagging at me to stop boozing before I got cirrhosis of the liver.

One day I asked why he didn't come to the motel for dinner. It wasn't romance I had in mind. I realized I needed a friend and John was it.

He showed up with a record player, Charlie Parker's "Just Friends"—I guess he didn't have romance in mind either—plus a book for me. I thanked him, but suggested he take back the book. My eyesight wasn't up to reading.

"That's not just any book," he said. "That's the Bible, Anita." Then he told me that he'd been hanging around the club the day I was to arrive, wanting to meet me and scared to death of a repeat of our San Francisco hassle. John tends to idolize people and the fact I'd sung on all those Krupa records made my joining the group a big event for him. What really made him flip was that when I walked through the door with old man Mystokos, John saw this bright-as-sunlight angel at my side. He said he knew at once he had to give me a Bible.

That night at the motel, we played the Bird's record and talked about my days with Krupa. I begged him to give me a taste of whatever he was using, but he refused.

"You're the most 'no' person since my first husband," I kidded. "You don't drink. You don't smoke. What do you do?"

"I don't have sex outside marriage," he said.

"So? That's okay with me. I just want a friend. I have to stop drinking so much. You don't drink. Why?" I have this way of pounding away until I get an answer and I kept crowding him about how he got his kicks.

"I have a pretty good idea that you know," he said.

I did and I didn't, but I kept pushing.

Finally he said, "I don't like anything you smoke or drink. If I can't shoot it, it doesn't interest me."

When he said that, I knew I wanted to try it. I looked at him. He was very together. I thought if I go that route I won't end up in an alcoholic ward or with cirrhosis. Anyway, I've got the name, I'll play the game. At first John wasn't having any part of turning me on. He tried to talk me out of it. I begged. I got mad. I pleaded. At last he agreed that we'd fix. Not then, but after his connection delivered.

The next night we went to a room he had near the club. An old lady rented out two single rooms. She rented only to men, and we had to be stealthy as burglars slipping in because of her rule against female visitors. I always thought that was ironic because sex was the farthest thing from our minds. At first John idolized me and a guy doesn't try to make his idol. As for me, with all my abortions I'd been turned off sex. Later we became so close, it would have seemed incestuous.

Once in the room, John broke out the stuff, got the apparatus and cooked up the shit. He put it in the syringe and tied off my arm. "Believe me, Anita, I wouldn't do this. But the way you're coming on, if I don't, somebody else will. And you're likely to get a hot shot and end up in the morgue."

"Cut the sermon and get on with it," I told him. I looked at him and could see he was really torn about what he was doing. Sweat popped out on his forehead. He hesitated, then plunged the needle into a vein on the outside of my arm.

"Why there?"

"I'm hiding the mark. The first place cops look is on the inside."

What I got was one tiny, diluted drop. "That's it?" I asked. I was waiting for the glow produced by a fast shot of whiskey or something.

Meanwhile, he was giving himself all the rest because he had a pretty big habit by then. By the time he'd finished, I began to feel the glow. I was really getting a ding. Mentally I was into it, thinking now I'm shooting heroin I won't need to drink.

I knew heroin was for me because I didn't feel angry about what had happened to me in Long Beach, and I didn't feel sorry for myself anymore. When I'd come out of jail, I'd had long hair that hung down my back. One day in an orgy of anger, bitterness and self-pity I whacked it off. I did a lot of self-defeating things like that. But after John stuck that needle in my arm, I relaxed. I stopped drinking as soon as I began using heroin, and for the next eight years I hardly touched booze.

JOHN AND I were constantly together. Everyone assumed we were lovers. Carl even called me "Mrs. Poole." He was wrong. John and I were hype friends. Nobody thought of that. One night I left a Kleenex with lipstick on it in John's room. The landlady ordered him out for "having a girl in there." What could we do? Explain it was dope instead of sex?

Anyway, it was a complicated relationship. We loved one another dearly and still do. We admired one another professionally and still do. But we weren't *in love.* John has always carried a lot of guilt about jabbing that needle in my arm. That's made him very protective of me. For instance, the Mystokoses were grossing $14,000 a week and paying me $200. John got in a beef with them over it. "She's the one who brings people in," he told them. "These crowds aren't coming for your drinks or to hear the combo!" He turned to me. "How can you let them do this to you?"

I knew I needed help when it came to handling money. Because suddenly the IRS was after me. Including interest, they said I owed $41,000 for a lot of things I didn't understand, such as withholdings for musicians who had played in groups I'd hired. I didn't have a dime. Most of what I owed came from the 1940s when Carl and I were trying to make money operating clubs. I just assumed I was too *d-u-m-b* to understand about such things as W-2 forms and other government rules. That was Carl's department. If he tried to warn me that we were falling behind in our payments, I wouldn't listen. Anyway, he filed the forms for the guys, but I guess day-to-day expenses took whatever bread there was, so the government just never got paid.

Now, as if I didn't have enough hassles at the Starlite, the Internal Revenue Service swooped down and attached my salary. I couldn't collect a dime for a cup of coffee. So I asked John to go with me to the IRS to see whether we couldn't work something out.

John was terrific. He explained my situation to them—that I didn't have any assets, not even a car. If they insisted on withholding my entire salary, I'd have to go on welfare. Finally, it was worked out that I'd turn over three-fourths of my net salary whenever I had an engagement. Under that setup, it took me over three years to square things.

I remember the day we went for the final payment. I never had any money so naturally I didn't have a checking account. Over those years I'd either take the money to the office in an envelope and get a receipt or send them a money order. Actually, John had usually given them the money and got the receipt, but this time he said, "Here, you go and pay it. You've worked long and hard and done without to pay up. So you deserve the joy of making the last payment."

I trotted up to the desk and told them this was the big day. They didn't smile or congratulate me. This square opened this big book, checked his figures, counted the money, looked up, and said, "You owe us one penny."

I exploded with laughter at the ridiculousness of it. I didn't have a cent.

The square got defensive and said, "Well, if I'm short, they take it out of my pocket. It all adds up."

"How well I know!" I said, calling John over to ask him to lend me a penny. John's not as businesslike as the government. To this day he's never dunned me for it.

* * *

WHILE WE WERE still at the Starlite, John again brought up the subject of the Mystokoses exploiting me and I asked how to change it.

"Free-lance," he said. "Let the guy who can come up with the best deal back you. Your probation officer will go for that."

I confessed to John I couldn't handle these things and suggested we team up. So in June we handed in our notices. The Mystokoses tried to talk us out of it, but he held firm. We got our final checks the day before we were to close and when we took them to the bank to be cashed, the cashier stamped them "Insufficient Funds."

John was half sick, not having any heroin and trying to get by on Dolophine pills, whatever. So he jumped into the car and we went back to the club where he showed the checks to the younger Mystokos. Mystokos tried giving him double-talk. John started yelling and picked up a bar stool which he used to knock the young Mystokos down, screaming he was going to kill him.

Somebody phoned the police.

I tried to keep John from hitting Mystokos again and killing him. Mr. Mystokos came running out of the backroom, shouting for help.

The police arrived and grabbed John. The younger Mystokos got to his feet, screaming John had tried to murder him. The police asked whether he wanted to press charges of assault with a deadly weapon with intent to do bodily harm. The younger Mystokos said he did.

"Go ahead. Have them arrest me," John yelled at him as he pulled our checks out of his pocket. He turned to the police. "Look at these. We'll press charges for passing bad checks. Which charge is more serious?"

Crunnnnnch! That brought things to a halt. The old man pulled out a bankroll and peeled off enough folding money to cover our salaries. "Now get out!" he shouted. "Enough aggravation! You're fired!"

We called Vido to tell him what had come down, got permission to leave the state from our probation officers, piled our belongings into John's Plymouth, and headed toward Detroit. It was summer so we decided to go the northern route which was prettier and would take us through San Francisco. There we got waylaid by an offer from the Blackhawk for me to pick up some extra bread augmenting the Vernon Alley–Cal Tjader combo. Tjader had majored in music at San Francisco State and played both vibes and drums which left no opening for John, although Cal would let him sit in occasionally. Still, the gig did fatten our bankroll. So in his spare time, John found a druggist who sold us 2 cc bottles of Methadrine or speed.

Man, we were really flying. With that stuff, you felt as if you didn't need any sleep. You were sure you could do anything. We could hoard our Dolophine pills. The speed killed our appetites, so we saved on food bills.

While I was working, John had plenty of energy to look for a connection. The trouble with speed was when you came off it, you crashed for, like, twenty-four hours.

When we set out to cross the Rocky Mountains, we had enough little packets of heroin to last us until we got to Detroit, but it was a rough go and we got into those packets pretty heavily.

We didn't want to spend money on restaurants, so we got individual cereal boxes, bananas, and Carnation canned milk. We opened the cereal, poured the milk in and ate out of the box. It wasn't good, but it was cheap, and we didn't know how much bread we were going to need to get a new supply of smack.

By the time we hit Wyoming, we'd run out of everything and were beginning to get sick. John looked around Cheyenne, a city of about forty thousand. He tried to find some musicians who would know somebody. But wherever he turned, he came up empty-handed. Finally he returned to the car and woke me. "Listen, I got a great title for a song," he said, "We Ran Out of Shit in Cheyenne."

Sick as I was, that cracked me up. I still think it's funny. But it really didn't help solve our problem. John decided the only thing to do was to wire $50 to Carol Wills, a hype who was a plumbing contractor he'd met in jail in 1953, and have him send the stuff special delivery to Omaha. It sounded like a great idea.

We finally limped into town and John went to the Omaha post office every two hours for two days. Live entertainment wasn't too plentiful, but John finally met a couple of musicians who had heard of us. A lot of good that did. We were too hot to monkey with because of my Long Beach bust and publicity.

John phoned Wills to ask where the dope was.

"Man, the narcs were there when I came out of Western Union." It seemed they'd been watching all of us while John and I were at the Starlite. There was no way Wills could send anything—not even our fifty bucks.

We flopped back into the car and John drove straight through to Chicago. I passed out and don't remember a thing until we got to my hometown. Then we bought a paper to see what jazz clubs were going.

The Bee Hive on the South Side had a couple of known users advertised.

John didn't want me along in case he got busted making the buy, so he checked me into a fairly nice hotel across the street and went to the Bee Hive. He said when he walked in a world-famous sax player spied him, took a deep breath and pointed toward the men's room. John got the message and went in. A guy immediately got up from the bar and followed him. The door was hardly closed when the pusher asked: "How much do you want?"

John had $17. This cat told him he had a $15 bag and John bought it. The whole transaction was so obvious. If there'd been a narc in the club, he'd have nabbed both of them. But you get careless when you're strung out.

We fixed, got on our feet, freshened up and went over to the Bee Hive to catch the last set. That's how fast heroin can straighten out the chemical imbalance in your body that causes all the trouble. Before leaving Chicago, John arranged with the night clerk at another hotel to special delivery more heroin to Detroit. When we arrived, it was waiting on the dresser of the room reserved for John. That wasn't the smartest thing to do because sending dope through the mail is a Federal rap. But we were into playing cops and robbers in those days.

Our engagement was at the Flame Show Bar for a week, and between the big shows the house band took over. During their set one night, I slipped over to the Crystal Lounge where the legendary Charlie Parker was blowing. I didn't really know him. But in 1950 when I'd been at the Show Boat in Philadelphia with Buddy De Franco backing me, during a number one night I heard this thrilling alto sax solo propelling me. I was too shook to look around but when I finally did no one new was there. Afterward, I asked Buddy who sat in to play the solo. He said, "Oh, that was Bird."

"It sure was," I said, "and he flew out as quick as he flew in."

That first night I visited the Crystal Lounge, Bird told the audience, although he only knew me professionally, "I'd like to acknowledge the presence of my good friend Anita O'Day, but I'm not going to ask her to sing because she's under contract to another establishment in this city."

I didn't sing, but I kept thinking about it all day long and regretted the lost opportunity. So the next night I went back and sang some numbers with Bird and his group. Charlie offered to introduce John and me to some of his *friends* at closing time. Then we'd all be able to buy plenty of stuff. He and John got in the front seat and I was in the back. He had us stop at a place where he picked up three roasted chickens which he ate while we talked.

He'd been to the doctor that day for a checkup. I asked how he'd done. He laughed and said the doctor had told him he had four months to live.

I was alarmed.

"Aw," he said, laughing some more, "those guys are quacks. I don't pay no attention to what they say."

I felt the same way. Looking at him, it didn't seem possible. He was young. We were about the same age, thirty-four, and I had a lot to accomplish before I checked out.

I idolized Charlie Parker because I would say he was one of the great jazz geniuses of all time. He changed the whole face of music. What I mean is that when Louis Armstrong became popular, all trumpet players had to change their styles. Not the rest of the band. But when Charlie Parker became popular with his bebop tunes, everybody had to change his style—the drummer, the piano player, the singer, whoever.

In the car he paid me the highest compliment. He said, "You come from the same branch of the tree as I do when it comes to time." That means my time is in the fourth dimension.

He wanted us to do an album together. We called Norman Granz, who said okay. So it was planned we would do one with strings. But that was not to be. A month later Charlie attempted suicide. He was in and out of hospitals for the rest of 1954 and he died March 12, 1955, eight months after he told us what the doctor in Detroit had predicted.

WE CLOSED AT the Flame on Saturday and I opened at the Orchid Lounge in Kansas City on August 16, 1954.

Now that we were so deep into drugs, we secretly made it a practice to stay at different hotels. I checked in at the Andrew Jackson and John at a nameless dive on East 12th Street. "If they ever come after us, I'll take the heat," he said, and a couple of times he did.

The Orchid Lounge at 1519 East 12th was another black club where Charlie Parker, Miles Davis and a lot of jazz stars played. I was happy to be accepted there. But on opening night after I'd begged off to a real ovation, this red-necked sheriff who was right out of a B-movie stopped me and snarled, "We don't like white girls workin' nigger joints in this town. You know that, don'cha?"

I smiled. "What do I know? I'm from Los Angeles."

That was a bad scene, but when owner Buddy O'Neil came around after closing time and told me I'd set an attendance record that night I cheered up. And we continued to do it almost every night that week. The Long Beach scandal had hurt me in radio and helped in clubs. It brought in people and they liked what they heard.

As soon as we opened, John began trying for a connection. Tuesday night this guy Jimmy—a lot of people had no last names in the dope scene—showed up. He claimed he was a fan but he obviously wasn't into music. After a bit he said he could get some great stuff and suggested he and his hype girlfriend get together with John and me.

He'd lay it on us free because my singing really sent him. We agreed.

Next day he and this chick came to the room where everybody thought John and I were staying. The girl was an addict, but there was something phony about the way the guy cooked his dope. He used a lot of water while an addict tries for a minimum amount. I wondered what John thought, but nothing happened and I decided maybe I was just paranoid.

The minute they were out the door John started going over the room checking for anything they might have planted. "I got a hunch he's a stoolie for the Feds," John said. At that time, the government couldn't bring its informants into court because it would have disclosed their identities.

We agreed not to have anything more to do with Jimmy. We'd try to get by on Dolophine pills and Cosynal cough syrup if we couldn't make another connection. It would be good for our health to clean up a little anyway.

On Wednesday night after the last set, John was covering his drums when this old janitor came along sweeping up. As he passed the part of the bandstand where John was, he mumbled, "Gonna be a big bust! Watch it!"

John and I went to his room after the janitor's warning. We were both a little sick, but I tried to read a paperback called *Hooked: Narcotics, America's Peril,* telling John we didn't want to become case histories in a book like this.

We managed to get to work the next night and during the evening Jimmy showed up. He said he had a packet for me if I'd meet him at the bar across from the East 12th Street room. Even though we knew we shouldn't, all I could think about was getting that stuff into my arm and I agreed. When Jimmy showed up he apologized for being empty-handed, but said he'd have it when this joint opened next morning.

So early Saturday morning, I got up, went over and ordered a beer. Pretty soon Jimmy hit the bar, I was waiting in a booth. He got a drink and sat with me. We talked. He slipped a packet under the table and I passed him some money. He finished his drink and got up. I got up, too. He was a gentleman and let me go first—a gentleman who would kill you for forty cents!

He walked behind me and said, "When we hit the street, you go one way. I'll go to the corner and cross." Then just before he cut out he muttered, "Doan whadayado goatayerroom."

I asked him what he said, but he was gone. What did he mean? I looked around. Everything looked normal—just a Saturday morning's deserted street. So I went to the hotel and told John what had happened.

John went to the window. There was no action outside. Nothing took place in the first five minutes so we decided it was cool.

I made a little space on the table and opened the packet. It was a nice little pile. John was running around getting the paraphernalia. So I snitched a little taste, folded it in another paper and stuck it under the windowsill. I was learning to squirrel away a little for when we were sick and couldn't score because John had a big habit by now.

Someone knocked on the door. I thought it must be the cat coming to tell me something. I opened the door. That was a goof on my part—not asking John. Because here were these two guys with drawn guns. They were both big. The city narc was ordinary big, but the other one who turned out to be the Treasury Guy was super-big, weighed about 270 pounds, all muscle. He had his gun in his right hand. The local narc held his gun in his left hand. They were so nervous, not knowing whether they were going to have to use them, their guns were clacking together. I looked at those guns, walked over, put a hand over each muzzle, and said, "Please gentlemen! Those may be loaded."

If I do say so, it blew their whole act. They were stunned to have anybody make a funny about guns, but I knew the shit was on the table and they had to be distracted. Stalled.

We'd been right about Jimmy and his girlfriend. The narcs had a search warrant. Jimmy's "Jane Doe" swore she had seen us inject heroin into our veins two days before. I knew it was her when they removed my wristwatch to look for needle marks underneath it.

Suddenly it struck me that the guy must have had a change of heart at the last moment. What he'd mumbled was, "Whatever you do, don't go to your room."

To keep them away from the table, John pulled out a hypodermic needle still wrapped in cellophane and held it out. He handed it to the Treasury Guy who said, "There's no law against them in Kansas City."

John knew it, but he also knew he'd get ten years if they found the shit because he'd been busted for heroin in Long Beach before I met him. He began to warm up for what he called his "madman act." If the narcs discovered the shit, he knew my career was down the drain and he was convinced he'd never survive ten years in prison where humiliation, rape, murder and everything else went on. It would be all over.

"Take off your shoes," the city narc ordered.

We did. He examined them and came up empty-handed.

"It's not in the room," John said. "It's down the hall in the john." That was logical because a lot of hypes hid the stuff there. The Treasury Guy stayed with me and the local narc marched John to the latrine where, naturally, they didn't find anything. They continued pressuring us. John said, "Those guns have me all upset, but I think I took most of the stuff. The rest is under the bed."

I began to dig what he was up to. It was all a ruse to confuse the fuzz. The Treasury Guy had a low boiling point. He took his gun by the barrel as if he intended to hit John with the handle.

John was really going to it now, talking one thing one minute and another the next, chattering away, making no sense. The man stepped toward him and as he did John urinated on the guy's lower pants leg and shoe.

The Treasury Guy yelled, "Why you dirty—"

"I'm sorry," John whimpered. "I can't stand violence. Just let me get a cigarette and I'll give you the stuff."

The Treasury Guy was trying to wipe off his pants and shoe. John was at the table, asking where his cigarettes were. He was shielding the shit by placing his body between it and the cops. If he'd been a trumpeter instead of a drummer we'd both have gone to jail. But John's left hand went one way, his right the other, his body was in action, his head bobbed and his feet moved as he pretended to look for cigarettes.

When it was all over, he told me how he maneuvered his body between the heroin and the cops as he flipped the stuff on the linoleum floor. I didn't see it. Neither did the cops. How could we? He mopped up the heroin with the bottom of his wet sock as he walked over to ask, "Cigarette?"

I took one. So did he. He was cool now. In fact, I couldn't figure out why he was so relaxed. He offered the cops cigarettes. I knew he'd succeeded in getting rid of the shit but I couldn't figure out how he could have.

The cops sensed it too. "We've fooled around long enough," the Treasury Guy said. "We're going to find it and we're going to bust your asses. She's on probation. She goes back to jail for five years. This is your second offense, you'll get ten."

Well, all they found was one codeine tablet in John's shaving kit and the empty bottle. Prescription. Not what the warrant described.

"Give up," John told them. "She doesn't even live here."

"Nah, I live down the street at the Andrew Jackson," I said. "I'm only visiting."

"That's an immediate release," John said.

They ordered us to put on our shoes, took us down to the desk, flashed their IDs and found I *wasn't* registered. Out came the handcuffs and we were marched through the streets to the Andrew Jackson Hotel.

At the desk, the cops ignored the fact they had no search warrant. They flashed their IDs, found out from the frightened desk clerk I was on the registry and ordered that terrified kid to take us to my room. The clerk took us.

They really went over that room. The local narc apparently wasn't into deodorants. He unscrewed the top of my Mum, dipped in his pinky, and touched it to his tongue.

Half an hour later, they decided the dope was back in John's room. Still handcuffed, we were marched through the streets filled with pre-luncheon shoppers. I felt degraded which was exactly what they wanted, but I refused to let them know that. If John could pull off his crazyman act, I could play the hard-boiled dame.

Why would they do it? Their search warrant for the East 12th Street address spelled out the heroin and the glacine envelope, the size of the one postage stamps are kept in. Subsequently, it was alleged that—get the *alleged?* I learned about libel during my troubles—their determination to recover the heroin was based on the fact that it belonged to the government. Its strength was estimated at about 84 percent as opposed to the ten percent purity of stuff bought on the streets in Kansas City—pure enough to kill anyone who used it.

For the next four hours, they searched John's room. They ripped off baseboards, tore off molding around the windows, tore up the linoleum where it was loose, opened the mattress, dismantled the bed—left the room a shambles.

What finally came down was that John was charged with illegal possession of codeine and I was held for investigation in connection with narcotics violations. I guess what they hoped was that my California probation would be revoked and I'd have to serve four years in prison.

They told a *Kansas City Star* reporter I'd been tailed since my arrival the previous Sunday and my room had been frequented by known drug addicts. Untrue. I had hardly used my room at the Andrew Jackson myself. They also said I'd been purchasing heroin since my arrival. Half true. I'd bought a packet from Jimmy the Fink which had probably been supplied by them. They claimed to have found several hypodermic needles, syringes, and some burned spoons plus the codeine bottle and some capsules in John's room. Exaggerated, there was only one codeine tablet and (I'm guessing) not all that many needles, syringes, or burned spoons as they hoped readers would believe.

We were held without bail which meant spending part of Saturday and all of Sunday, before our cases came up before Judge Joe W. McQueen on Monday.

Those fifty-odd hours were as near hell as I ever hope to experience. I was first thrown into an overcrowded cell with three drunks, two broken-down whores, and a psycho. The screams, vomiting, and menacing atmosphere frightened me more than my months in prison.

When the shift changed, I asked the new guard whether there wasn't another cell. She immediately transferred me to one with only one other occupant. I congratulated myself on my good luck and lay down to get some rest. An hour later, I was awakened by strange animallike sounds and opened my eyes to see my elderly cellmate on the floor frothing at the mouth. I screamed for help and when the guard came she said the woman was *only* having an epileptic fit. I was so terrified I asked to be returned to the overcrowded cell that I'd thought a few hours before was as close to hell as I ever wanted to get.

After word of my arrest broke in newspapers, Uncle Vance showed up. I hadn't wanted to embarrass him with his new second wife so I'd claimed I had no relatives. But Uncle Vance loved me and through his first wife

Gladys, now an attorney herself, had obtained a high-priced lawyer, John C. Pohlman, who got me released by filing a writ pointing out I'd been held beyond the statutory limit of twenty hours. He also succeeded in quashing the Federal government's request that I be held on bond. Mr. Pohlman brought it to the judge's attention that no charges had been filed against me by the Federal government or the State of Missouri and that my California probation officer had wired there was no intention to press violation of probation charges against me. So I was released. John appeared for his preliminary hearing on possession of codeine on Monday afternoon and was given a Friday arraignment.

I knew I couldn't help John on my own so I went to my old friend Tootie Clarken. Tootie ran the Mayfair. He loved jazz and the people who played it.

At his club, he sold ice cubes and mixes. Each party brought its own bottle. The club was located outside the city limits and to give you an idea of what kind of a guy Tootie was—when the boundary line of Kansas City was expanded to include his club, he had the building dismantled brick by brick and reassembled on Highway 40 outside the city's jurisdiction.

I got Tootie to go bail for John so we could fill a gig at the Mayfair. When we opened, the scandal brought in huge crowds and everything was cool.

A couple of days later we went into the Kansas City post office to the General Delivery window to pick up any mail we might have. As it was handed to us, two plainclothesmen walked up and ordered us to open the letters.

John demanded their court order, reminding them they were city cops and this was Federal property. They didn't have one, but to avoid trouble we opened the envelopes containing work offers, fan letters and notes from friends. There was nothing illegal. When the police saw they'd come up empty-handed, they took John and handed me over to a female officer who took me into a room, made me disrobe and bend over for a thorough search of my body cavities. Finding nothing on either of us, they ordered us out of the post office, warning, "We don't want to see you in here again."

Now John and I weren't innocents, but some musicians who *were* got the treatment. Norman Granz threatened to sue the U.S. Customs for their harassment of Ella Fitzgerald. And as I understand it, Ella is such a straight chick she never touches anything stronger than beer.

Of course, we weren't angels. One night Tootie and John got into a real hassle. John's got a superloud voice and Tootie couldn't understand somebody who could yell as loud and talk as fast as he could. So the next thing I knew the cops marched in, grabbed John off the stage and hauled him to jail. Tootie had revoked the bail bond.

That turned out to be a lucky break. The prison doctor took one look at

John and asked when he'd begun turning yellow. John had a serious case of hepatitis. I had a talk with Tootie, who liked me very much, and persuaded him to go John's bail so he could be admitted to the Veterans' Hospital.

To an operator like Tootie, that's not as unusual as it sounds. He'd dealt with jazz musicians for years and was used to their peculiarities. For example, when Charlie Parker made his debut at Tootie's, his sax was held together with rubber bands and glue. Bird got wonderful sounds out of it, but he wasn't always there. Once when he arrived late, Tootie chewed him out and the Bird flew. Later Tootie hunted him down, apologized, and bought him an expensive new sax. Charlie tearfully thanked him and promised never to be late again. He took off with the sax and didn't show up for a couple of days. Tootie went looking for him again. He eventually located Charlie, but the new sax had been hocked for dope. So Tootie redeemed it and Charlie returned to work. In that perspective, a little shouting match with John wasn't going to keep Tootie from going bail.

For a couple of weeks I visited John every day and worked at the Mayfair at night. Then I got an offer from the Streamliner in Chicago at more bread which would help pay Mr. Pohlman, who was going to defend John. I gave notice. When I told John, he advised telling Tootie I'd be hanging around until the middle of the week because Tootie's family was close to the sheriff's department and some reason might be found to detain me.

So I fooled Tootie and after the last set on closing night, I got into the already packed car, gulped a couple of bennies and took off for the Streamliner.

When John got well enough to appear, Mr. Pohlman got him off by pointing out the search warrant was for heroin and they were prosecuting John for possession of a prescription drug.

John immediately called to give me details on his arrival. I met him at the railroad station and took him to the Streamliner where the boss, a fan of mine, got him a set of drums (John's had joined many of our other belongings in a pawnshop) and we went to work. After our first set, the busboy asked, "What're you doing with just piano and drums when I play bass?"

John took off his jacket for hot solos anyway. So he lent the busboy his jacket for a tryout. And the kid was so good we kept him on.

John's long stay in the hospital and my awkwardness in handling a needle without him meant we were both pretty clean. If our addiction had been only physical instead of psychological, we probably could have stayed that way. But we didn't *want* to give up dope. So we started asking the kid if he knew where we could score. That changed his attitude toward us and when we closed, he split.

Integration wasn't a big issue in most spots I played, but the Comedy

Club in Baltimore was an exception. White clubs and black clubs nestled side by side in the same block, but there was plenty of prejudice. John and I were working a club catering to blacks and no whites were allowed in. And black entertainers could work white clubs, but their black brothers couldn't get in to see them. Coming from the world of jazz where talent had always been the great equalizer, I became even angrier and I was pretty angry to begin with.

Here I was thirty-five years old, the ex-*wunderkind,* drifting like a ship without a rudder. Luckily, John, who'd never got over feeling guilty about putting that first needle in my arm, was like a tugboat giving me direction. We headed for the West Coast, playing here and there for expenses and gas, eating mostly hot dogs and hamburgers.

At one point I got to feeling sorry for myself because I couldn't afford having my hair done, so I whacked it off short as a boy's. I had no clothes. I wore shirt and slacks. Could I blame anyone for looking at me and jumping to the conclusion I was a dyke?

It didn't have to be that way. There are white-collar hypes who hold regular jobs, own homes and live nicely. They don't go out looking for dope. Their dealer delivers it.

We were spending ten to twelve hours a day looking for it and playing games. I couldn't guess how much we spent on cosmetics I'd never wear and sundries John would never use just so we could add, "Oh yes, and hypodermic needles for my vitamin shots."

It was hilarious. Who did we think we were fooling?

Milt Hinton

The superb bassist Milt Hinton recalls working with Louis Armstrong in his autobiography, Bass Line *(1988; with David G. Berger).*

On our next to last night at the Bandbox with Basie, I got an offer to go out on the road with Louis Armstrong. Joe Glaser, who handled Louis, sent one of his people—a guy named Frenchy Tallerie—down to the club to ask if I wanted the job. It was as simple as that.

I was really taken by surprise. I told Frenchy I needed time to talk about it with my wife and that I'd call Joe in a couple of days.

In the old days around Chicago, Joe Glaser had a reputation for being a real tough guy. From what I heard, he came from a middle-class family but he was the black sheep. I think his mother owned the building on the Southside which the Sunset Cafe was in. That's the place a lot of famous entertainers, including Cab, got their start. Evidently, at one point after Joe had gotten in some kind of serious trouble with the law, she'd helped him become an agent and manager.

Louis and Glaser got together in 1935. As the story goes, for years there was never a written contract between them. They shook hands one time and that was it. For some reason, right from the start, they hit it off. Joe had the connections and got the bookings. Louis had that wonderful, friendly personality and, of course, the musicianship. Their careers just took off together.

Louis's name was well known around Chicago when I was growing up. Along with Eddie South, he was one of my two boyhood idols. As a kid I'd seen him perform in theaters, but as I got older and more involved playing music, I was around guys who knew him personally. In fact, I remember watching him rehearse and I can recall many times when I'd run into him talking with a group of guys on a street corner or in a bar. And later, when I worked with Zutty, Louis's close friend, I really got an opportunity to spend some time with him.

Deciding whether or not to go with Louis was very difficult. My month-long commitment to Basie was over, but I was getting good freelance jobs. And even though I couldn't be sure how much I'd be making from week to week, the pay was getting better. When I left Cab, I said I'd never go back on the road for any length of time, but the thought of playing with a legend like Louis made the idea of traveling more acceptable.

I knew I wanted to go, but with my family to support, money became a real issue. Mona and I figured I might earn a little less with Louis than freelancing, but it would be a steady salary. Besides, if I got paid expenses on the road, I'd be able to save much more. We decided if the money was right, I'd take the job.

Everyone knew Pops didn't discuss money. Joe dealt with those kinds of things. But before I called him, I figured I should try and get an idea about what other guys in the band were making.

I got ahold of Cozy, who'd been with Pops for a while. He told me he'd just given notice and was planning to form his own band. Of course, I was disappointed. We were close back in the Cab Calloway days and I'd been looking forward to spending time with him again. He filled me in on the personalities in the band and Joe's people. Then we talked about money.

When Frenchy had approached me at the Bandbox, he'd told me the pay would be seventy-five a night. But when I mentioned that figure to Cozy he said, "That may sound good to you, but I'm makin' one twenty-five and I don't see why you can't get that too."

A couple of days later, I sat down with Joe and Frenchy to talk about money. Joe was a thin, dapper-looking guy with pretty sharp features, who walked pigeon-toed. Frenchy was just the opposite. He was sloppy and fat. He didn't like anyone and you couldn't believe a word he said. Everyone knew he hated Louis and Louis couldn't stand him. In fact, some people said that's why Joe made him road manager. He knew if Louis did something wrong, Frenchy would report him, and if Frenchy tried to steal, Louis would do exactly the same thing.

For some reason, just before the conversation began, Louis walked in. I started out real bold. "Look, I gotta have one twenty-five a night." At that point I wanted the job and I was hoping they wouldn't say no when I gave them my price.

"Get the hell out of here!" Joe screamed, "We don't even know your work."

I kept cool. "Louis's known me for years. He can tell you how I play," I said.

"I don't pay one twenty-five to nobody just startin' out. I'll give you a hundred. If you work out, I'll give you more," Joe answered.

I stood my ground. "No," I said. "I gotta get one twenty-five."

Joe shook his head, which was his way of saying, "Forget it."

There was dead silence for a couple of seconds and then Louis spoke. "I know this boy, give it to him." It was settled, as simple as that.

A week later I went out with the band and for a while we mostly did one-nighters. Cozy was still there along with Trummy Young playing trombone, Barney Bigard on clarinet, and Marty Napoleon on piano. We also had Velma Middleton as a vocalist. At one of those early gigs something incredible happened.

It was at an outdoor concert in Washington, D.C., near one of the big malls, right on the Potomac. The stage and dressing rooms were set up on a big barge which was docked at the edge of the river, and the audience sat on the long, wide grass bank in front of it. I remember we had to walk down a ramp to get on the barge so we could change clothes and get set up. But the facilities were very comfortable.

In addition to us, Lionel Hampton and Illinois Jacquet's bands were on the program. Jacquet was scheduled to play first, from six to seven, and Hamp was to follow from seven to eight. Then, after an intermission, Louis would come out and do the finale.

We had worked in New Jersey the night before and drove down from there in a private bus. We arrived at five-thirty, a half hour before show time. There was about a thousand people in the audience, but no sign of Jacquet's band.

We unloaded our suitcases and instruments and moved everything over to the barge. By the time we'd changed into our tuxedos, it was six-thirty. Jacquet should have gone on at six, but he still hadn't arrived. To make matters worse, Hamp hadn't either.

Standing backstage, we could sense the audience was getting restless. Every couple of minutes they'd start applauding and chanting, "Start the show," and "We want music."

About fifteen minutes later one of the producers went to Frenchy and asked if Louis would go on first. Louis was a star, but he didn't care about billing or protocol. He was usually understanding and cooperative.

So we went out and started playing. After waiting so long the audience gave us an unbelievable reception. They applauded every solo and when we finished a tune they'd stand and cheer for a couple of minutes.

We played about an hour and then took our bows. But the people wouldn't let us off the stage. They screamed for encores and we kept doing them. Louis knew there was no act to follow us. And he was content to stay out there and keep everyone happy until help arrived.

Finally, during our fifth or sixth encore, we saw a bus pull up and unload. As soon as Louis knew it was Jacquet's band, he told us, "This time when we end, walk off and stay off."

As soon as we finished, we headed for the dressing rooms and changed. Then we packed up our instruments and hung around backstage talking to some of the guys from Jacquet's band.

Trying to follow a performer like Louis really put Jacquet in a difficult position. To make matters worse, the audience knew he'd been scheduled to play first and had kept them waiting. So when he came out on stage, he got a lukewarm reception.

Jacquet had eight or nine good musicians with him. They started with a couple of standards, but there was no response. They even featured the drummer, but that didn't seem to rouse the audience either. Then Jacquet must've figured he had nothing to lose, so he called "Flying Home," the tune he'd made famous with Hamp's band.

It took a couple of minutes before the audience recognized the tune and started to react. By then Jacquet was soloing and he gave it everything he had, building, honking, screaming, and dancing. All the moves, chorus after chorus. By the time he finished, he had the audience in the palm of his hand, the same way Louis had them an hour before.

The audience screamed for an encore and Jacquet did another couple of choruses of "Flying Home." But right in the middle, Hamp's bus pulled up. Hearing someone else play a tune he was known for and seeing the fantastic audience reaction must've made him furious. Everyone backstage saw what was going on and knew Hamp would want to somehow outdo Jacquet. Louis was watching and he got interested too. I remember we were set to get on the bus, but Louis turned to a couple of us and said, "Wait, we have to see this."

Jacquet finished and after the stage got set up, Hamp came out. He began with "Midnight Sun," one of his famous ballads. But after Louis's performance and Jacquet's finale, the audience was in no mood for it. He did "Hamp's Boogie Woogie," and a couple more numbers. He even played drums and sang, but he still didn't get much of a reaction.

I was standing in the wings with Louis and a couple of other guys and we could see how hard he was working. But time was running out. He looked frustrated and desperate and he finally called "Flying Home."

The band started playing but there wasn't much response from the audience. Hamp wouldn't give up. He put everything he had into his solo, starting out soft, then building to a crescendo. When he finished, sweat was dripping off every part of him, and a handful of people cheered.

I guess Hamp sensed he was making some headway with the crowd. So while the band continued, he went back to Monk Montgomery, who was playing Fender bass, and told him, "Gates, you jump in the river on the next chorus, I'll give you an extra ten."

Monk must've agreed because when the band got to the next crescendo and Hamp raised his mallets, Monk jumped over the railing. The audience went crazy.

The band kept playing and a few minutes later Monk came out on stage soaking wet. Hamp walked over to him and said, "Another ten if you do it again."

Monk made it back to his bass and played another chorus. Then when the band came to the same crescendo and Hamp raised his hands, he went over the side again.

By this time the people were in a frenzy and Hamp knew he'd accomplished what he'd set out to do. Louis turned to us and said, "Start up the bus. We can go now."

Art Blakey

Art Blakey, the dedicated and influential drummer, talks about his start, his career, and his ideas in this excerpt from a long interview recorded in 1976 in Jazz Spoken Here *(1992; Wayne Enstice and Paul Rubin).*

WE: Art, you've been playing the drums professionally for decades. How did it happen that you chose that instrument rather than something else?

AB: I didn't intend to be a drummer. It's just a means of survival. When I came along I was very lucky. I came along in the time of the depression, and it was very rough. I went to school in Pittsburgh. You know Pennsylvania always had integrated schools, but in our schools, especially in the junior high school, most of the teachers were white, and most of them were bigots, and I couldn't learn anything. I could see right through that. I could see that the teacher wasn't teaching me.

You see, I was sort of an orphan, and I was rejected by my father's parents. My mother died when I was six months old, and I was rejected by his parents. And they even had racial prejudice in my family—on my father's side was mulatto, and my mother, who was very, very black. Her father—my grandfather—and my great-grandfather, who I knew were all descendants of Africa, were very black people. And the part of Africa where they come from was Guinea, West Africa.

My father used to sneak out—because my mother was very pretty, and he used to sneak out and see her. She lived out in the country. So I happened along. They had a shotgun wedding, you see. They had this big church wedding, and they came out and got in the carriage. My mother was carrying me at that time, and he rode two blocks and got out of the carriage and went into the drugstore to get some cigars, and he went out the back door and went to Chicago. And after sitting out there for four or five hours—she was so stunned about it—she was very stunned, very hurt, and really they say she really didn't care. She died of a broken heart. She just gave up [and] took about four or five months to die. Well, my father, he couldn't take me in his family, right? So that left me sort of on the outside. So my mother's friend—well, she sort of looked out after me. She let me stay there, and I always felt that guilt, and I always felt that I had to work. I would work and go to school.

Then I formed a group in school. I always played piano because there was a piano around the house, and I played by ear. I never had the money to get the lessons, and I wouldn't dare ask the woman who was helping me—who I was living with. I called her my mother. I took the band into a club called the Ritz, in Pittsburgh. At that time, Prohibition was on. In them joints you come late at night and knock at the door, "Charlie sent me," and you get in. But I had an eighteen-piece band—we had the best gig in town. And we wore tails. So I had a lot of kids out of the high school band working with me.

We made fifteen dollars a week, which was a helluva lot of money at that time. A room with bath and everybody had a car, and you drive to school, and you hear a teacher talking down to you, and you know better. So I rebelled, and I went to the principal about it and he says, "Well . . ." I didn't like his attitude either, you know, the way he talked to me. I didn't think it was fair. So I was thrown out of school for doing a report—what messed me up, really. I had to do a report in history class on Africa. They told me that Africans go around in grass skirts and they eat people and they're cannibals. So I went and got a thing on Africa and found out that the first university in the world was in Africa, found out that—ohhhh, I found out so many things, you know, so many lies have been told.

And I had stayed in this club about two years with the band, and they brought in a show from New York, called *Tondelayo and Lopez,* and it had some music. It was a lot of piano music, and it looked like some flies had been all over the thing—I couldn't believe it! So instead of being honest with myself and honest with the guys—they all knew I couldn't read music too. But you know I'm not going to admit it, to myself, above all. I'm the bandleader; you can't admit, right? So I come in and run the brass down that part, run the reeds down, run the rhythm section down. I'd run up and show the drummer how to do something, to catch different things, because I had a little experience in the school band about the drums and I always loved them. So I said, "OK, let's play it." So the band run it down, so we got to the piano part, and the band said *pow* and stopped for the piano to come in, and I sat there and look, and I start perspiring, and I looked up and said, "You all know goddamn well I can't read."

So I got up and stormed out. And so the guy that owned the club—Charlie—is sitting in the corner. He had a big .38 on him, and he said, "Hey, Blakey, come here." He say, "What's happenin'." I say, "Nothing." I said, "I got it, I got it." I saw some kid in the corner who was sittin' over there. And he was looking. So he came over, and he says, "Hey, Art, do you mind if I try that?" I said, "Sure, go ahead." He had been listening to the records; and the band come down and played it so beautiful, and it come to the piano part. He played the hell out of it. Like it was made for him. Come to find out it was Erroll Garner.

We were kids at that time. Erroll Garner had such an ear for music, and I said, "Well, damn." This man, he could hear that and played every note, played everything. I said, "Jesus Christ!" I was kinda bugged, so Charlie said, "Come here." He said, "Why don't you play the drums?" So I said, "Hey, Charlie, why don't you mind your own business." He said, "Well, how long you been working out here?" And I said, "Well, a little over two years, I guess." He said, "Do you wanna continue working here?" I said, "*Sure* I want my gig." He said, "Well, you play the drums. You dumb bastard, you go up there and play them drums." I went up there and played. I've been playing drums ever since. I went back to see him one time before he passed, you know. He said, "I told ya, ya big dummy." So that's how I started playing drums—I had to survive.

PR: Soon you went on the road, and you braved the Deep South. Since this was the early 1940s, it must have been difficult.

AB: I was working at night and day and goin' to school. 'Cause I wanted to support myself and I wanted to help the woman who raised me, so I left there. And I took the band, and I went out on the road, and we worked. We had a ten-piece band, and Fletcher Henderson come through and took the whole band because of the war. All the musicians were going to the army, so he just took the whole band out with him. Wonderful musicians. And I later joined Fletcher, because most of my buddies was in his band. And we traveled all over the country. We drove to Albany, Georgia, and I had some problems down there with the police and got beat up. They put a plate in my head. Boy, we fought like dogs down there, and I'm lucky to be alive in Georgia at that time. You know, *very* lucky to be alive. And that time was about 1942, I was down there, and I broke a policeman's jaw. At that time the South was very rough.

And what the people went through in the sixties ain't nothing what we went through, man. We traveled through the South all day and have a pocketful of money and couldn't get a glass of water. And if you did, they'd sell it to you a dollar a glass. And it would be hot as panther piss. This is the way, man, that you had to go and survive. That's the reason I see things always looking better. I always can look back and see where things were always worse than they are today. There is definite improvement in every field, especially in the jazz field. It's a helluva improvement.

Well, after that episode down there with the police, I got very sick and ended up in Boston and met the band there. And I got sick, and I stayed—because of that blow in the head. I stayed there for a year or so.

WE: Then you met up with Billy Eckstine and company?

AB: That was the most fascinating time of my life when I met Dizzy, and I met Sarah Vaughan, and I met—oh my God—all the stars. The band, the whole band, anyone you pick out is one of the big top men—they're the giants. Boy, they could play! I never heard nobody play that. The only big band I ever liked was Billy Eckstine, 'cause everybody in that band could play. There was no first trumpet player, no first alto player, no first tenor player—any part that you get you play. If you make a mistake, you just make it loud. Next time you don't make it, you replace it with another note. Everything was committed to memory. And that was, in my eyes, a helluva big band. That is a *band*. Now, that is a jazz orchestra! I've heard a lot of big bands, and they sound good, perfect, but they sound too clinical, it's too perfect, it's not a good band, it's not good jazz. Jazz is not clinical. It's not like that. Jazz is born by somebody goofin'. So if you feel that band hasn't got that looseness, they're not creating.

In that band it was a pleasure; it was like working in a small combo. But the rest of the big bands wasn't: Lucky Millinder wasn't, Basie wasn't, Duke wasn't. 'Cause Duke was set. He had this certain thing that you do. And if you go to play with Duke, whatever it is, you let the punishment fit the crime. Whatever it is: you don't go into Duke's band and play Art Blakey, you go into Duke's band and play Duke Ellington. You go to Count Basie's band, you play Count Basie. You don't go and try to stick your influence in there. The only way I had a chance to stick my influence is in Billy Eckstine's band, because it was that type of thing. It was like a combo. But the rest of the bands you're the timekeeper. You understand? Like Billy Eckstine's band, I could—like in most big bands, it's like fifteen musicians and a drummer. In Billy Eckstine's band, there were sixteen musicians, and everybody got to play, and that made a difference, and it's the same way in a combo. That's why I like a combo, because every tub's got to sit on its own bottom. And if it doesn't, it shows up.

And they liked me—the style that I was trying to develop—I didn't know why I was trying to develop that on drums, but I was just trying to do something different because I knew one thing: I always wanted to record, and I knew that I was playing what I call a bastard instrument, you know, it's not set—you know the piano's got eighty-eight keys, the trumpet's got three keys, and the saxophone has, et cetera. But the drum you add this, you add that; but . . . I knew I had to identify myself, and I had to play different.

And I heard and I watched Chick Webb, and I tried to take the best of him and Big Sid Catlett. I tried to take the best of these cats and try to incorporate it in what I was trying to do. And the most advanced of all of them—the drummer at that time—was a little young guy called Kenny Clarke. Fantastic drummer! He came back to Pittsburgh, and I just admired him. He sounded different from any other drummer. But I admired him—Sid Catlett and Chick Webb I took in. I heard Ray Bauduc—I liked him. And Gene Krupa came, and I heard him. At that time Gene Krupa was known as the Chicago Flash!

I learned, you know. You pick up things here, and you pick up things there, and you listen and learn. And I tried to just do it a little different. It did pay off by joining [Eckstine's] band. I knew why they wanted me there. Because it was a little different. The attack was a little different, the way I played. I think that's some of the most happy days of my life. And I guess we made about ten dollars a night. Didn't make no difference about the money, I was so happy just to be there. I heard all these great musicians, and I watched this music change the trend of all American music. I watched Bird and them cats change everything.

PR: You've spoken often about how your peers of that era never received the attention they deserved.

AB: My contention is, is to give the people credit who brought forth the idea. Now this is my problem. They never give them credit for it. They never give Louis Armstrong credit for what he did. They never did, man. And they never gave Duke Ellington credit for what he did—or King Oliver the credit for what he did.

They turn around and they name Paul Whiteman the King of Swing, you know, and the only way he could swing is from a rope. I didn't think that was fair. Then they turn around and name Benny Goodman the King of Swing, and he's playing Fletcher Henderson's arrangements note for note. I could walk into Benny Goodman's band and play every arrangement they had, because Smack [Henderson] did it—it's Smack's music. He didn't get the credit for it, see, and that's what hurt. And he died a pauper—up in Harlem—and it hurt. And I didn't understand why that could be.

Don Redman, I mean these great men who've really put it down in music—Charlie Parker and these cats—man! I mean, why should this be—Art Tatum. And I remember when Arthur Rubinstein come to New York—if he had a concert in Carnegie Hall—and I was working in Café Society in the Village with Art Tatum. Well, Arthur Rubinstein didn't make his concert; he canceled it. Sold-out house—he'd cancel and be sitting down there looking at Art Tatum. But yet we had to take money up to bury this man—that hurts.

That hurts, I mean, where is things going? What's happening? And nobody's paying any attention to it. Right now we just found out where Bird was buried, and now they just begin to build a thing over his grave just to show some appreciation; they name a street after him in Kansas City. But what's happened to Art Tatum? He never had a marker for his grave. What's happened to Fats Navarro? I buried him; the union wouldn't even bury him. I buried him in New York. Yeah, I just left his daughter up there in Seattle. She's a grown girl, and her mother's dead, and this girl up there struggling to get through law school. Struggling like hell to get through law school, and you got to pity. Now you know that the records that Fat Girl [Navarro] has made, has made *lots* of money, and it's setting there somewhere. And you know they won't give it to her. That isn't fair. *That is not fair!* We need some kind of legislation going on. The jazz musicians—Fats Navarro, and Eddie "Lockjaw" Davis—those records they made like thirty years ago. They still sellin'!

And this proves to me that this is the music. You know after a quarter of a century and you turn around and hear your own records, I mean, it must be something. Because everything else is gone and flash in the pan is past and forgotten, and every time you turn on one of these records it's just as fresh. You say, "Oh, man," you know—it's just as fresh. So this proves to me that it's right, and I can't understand why these artists can't get their just due—*all* of them.

WE: Art, you are as much a spokesman for the music as you are a musician.

AB: You can't separate rock from the spirituals from the church—that's where it came from. You can't separate modern jazz from rock or from rhythm and blues—you can't separate it. Because that's where it all started, and that's where it come from—that's where I learned to keep rhythm—in church. Because they'd be in there singing and shouting and swinging *all* the time, no instruments but their hands and their mouth and their feet.

You know so that's where it started, so you can't separate it. It's all American music. It's just as American as apple pie, and we got to stop this foolishness. Tell the kids where it's at so they can get a chance to go back and listen to that. Listen to ragtime, listen to Dixieland. And the proof of that is Eubie Blake. Here's a man out there, and he's damned near a hundred years old, and he's playing jazz like he did then, and he's good. And it all come from the same thing. Like Eubie Blake say, he learned—he was playing every night in the house of ill repute. That's where it started.

See, it doesn't matter to me about like Freddie Hubbard and all the cats who work with the Jazz Messengers—they may go off in twenty different directions, but they know where home base is. They know where they got to go—they always turn around and come back to the mother they always know. They know what jazz is all about.

Even the Japanese, even the Africans. Just our [American] kids, man, just don't know. You take those kids over there, they say, "Yeah! so and so and so and so Charlie Parker he was born in so and so and so and so." It's amazing. I say, "How old are you, fifteen or sixteen?" It's amazing. How did they know way over there? At a disadvantage, they knew.

And the Japanese, they weren't even brought into jazz until in the sixties, really. And listen to them. My bass player is a Japanese. The first time he ever heard jazz he was a little boy and I come to Japan. He was a little boy with his dad. His dad is a music teacher, and he said, "I want you to hear something," and brought him in. He was a little boy—eight years old. And he grew up, and he's working with me. You understand?

Same thing with Chuck Mangione's father. When I first met Chuck he was eleven years old—his father brought him. He said, "Mr. Blakey, some day I'm going to play trumpet." And I said, "Yeah, he will." And he did. Because his father said, "Listen to this, listen to that." He's a well-trained and well-rounded musician. And Mangione grew up knowing just as much about Dizzy Gillespie as he did about Harry James, as he did about anybody. He knew all about it because of his parents, you see.

PR: Showmanship seems to be a very important part of your approach. Tell us how you developed your own stage style.

AB: I told you I had this band and was playing drums—I got into this drumming thing. I had an act that I could do, and I always envisioned myself someday just coming out just playing and doing my little drum act and that was it. So I had an act. I had taken the sticks, you know; you put this paint on them and take the black light and shine the light up. Well, I had some gloves you put on and you paint the sticks a different color. I had one stick on the trap-set—at that time we had a trap-table with a table about this big, and the cymbals come up and you have temple blocks on it, call it a trap-table—and I have the stick laying on the trap-table. But I had a black string from the ceiling down to the trap-table and this stick. I'd be playing, and all of a sudden I change sticks and hit a loud rim shot on my left hand and throw the stick out of my right hand, and people say "Oooh!" and it'd come back and I'd catch it.

But all the time this is going on ain't nothin' happening—it is quiet. Everybody is sitting there, so I went back in, and Chick Webb said, "Hey son, can I see you a minute. You interested in them drums?" I said, "Yes, sir, Mr. Webb." He said, "Bring your snare drum back in the dressing room." He said, "Bring your sticks." I come into the dressing room; I set my snare drum up. Chick Webb come back, and he has a Chihuahua and a camel-hair coat and his cap. So Chick Webb say, "OK, kid, the first thing I want to tell ya: The rhythm ain't in the air; it's on the hides." So he said, "You can roll?" I said, "Sure, Mr. Webb, I can roll." He said, "Well, roll." I grabbed the drums and eh-eh-eh-eh-eh. So he eased over to the door, and he looked at me [and] say, "Shit!" Bam! Slammed the door and left me standing there.

I started crying. I was so hurt, I went out there, and he said, "I'm sorry, kid." He said, "You be down to the theater in the morning. Come down to see me. I want to talk to you." Boy, I get up at nine, get down there for the first show at ten-thirty. He said, "C'mon." Went upstairs to his dressing room, and he had this valet set a snare drum up in a room—way up on top where they weren't using. So we went upstairs, and he brought a metronome. He set the metronome down, and he turned real slow. He said, "Now I want you to sit there at that snare drum, and I want you to roll 'til you get to one hundred, and I don't want you to break that roll, and don't think I'm not listening to you." I liked to busted my wrist.

Every day I go down, and he'd say, "Up in the room." I'd say, "I want to tell . . ." He'd say, "Ain't nothin' to talk about. Get up there and play, start rolling." I developed a press roll out of that. I wanted to learn. From that he helped me develop a press roll. Because I couldn't even roll on a drum. And that's what's happening today. A lot of drummers, they can't even roll. And that's the fundamental part about the drum. And that's what hurts: you see the young kids, you don't get a chance to help them. They got seven, eight, ten, twelve tom-toms around, two, three bass drums. What is that, for show? *Play!* Never mind the show. All them drums and you can't even play a snare drum. That's all you need.

WE: Like Webb, you've passed the torch to the younger drummers. That seems to be a major theme of yours.

AB: That's awful important. That's the most important movement there is. Not the modern musician, but the older musicians. What happened during that time from the swing era over into what they call the bebop era—most of the musicians in that time, they got so when they felt that everything they did was right. This is the wrong attitude, because all the music that we have been playing all our lives and what we have done, we only scratched the surface. Just like Charlie Parker just before he passed, he was talking about the only thing he wished in earnest—that the young kids learn how to play the blues, 'cause he was learning how to play the blues. A lot of kids think, "I don't want to play no blues." They don't want to play 'cause they can't. All has not been played yet. And like they asked Charlie Parker, "What's the best record that you have ever made?" He said, "I've yet that to make."

Milt Gabler

Milt Gabler, like John Hammond, is a non-musician who played a crucial role in jazz history. This extensive interview with him, carried out by Dan Morgenstern (with Michael Cuscuna and Charlie Lourie) for Mosaic Records' huge project of reissuing the entire catalog of Gabler's Commodore Records, is a unique piece of jazz history.

Q: You were born in New York City?

MG: That's right. I was born in Harlem, 114th Street and St. Nicholas Avenue, 169 St. Nicholas Ave. I went back to take a picture of it a few years ago, because the address was on my birth certificate.

Q: Let's start with the shop. It was your father's shop, but it wasn't a record store until you got involved in it, right?

MG: That's right. I was in high school. I think I graduated junior high school in '24, and went down to Stuyvesant High School in Manhattan, which was between 15th and 16th streets between 1st and 2nd avenues. First of all, it had shops—liked anything that I could work on with my hands whether it was woodwork or metalworking. And I liked the science courses they had. That was like the number one school in New York City. They had a great football team that year. They had a great runner named Frank Hussey who won in the Olympics. So it had sports, and it had science subjects, and so I went there.

But the real reason was, my father's store was on Third Avenue between 41st and 42nd streets at that time. He had a radio and electrical store, a supply shop. Originally he was a hardware man, and when electrical stuff came in, he took that in. Then at the end of World War I, my Uncle Sid, my mother's younger brother, talked him into putting in radio parts and stuff like that, and they opened their radio department.

Later, a store became available between Lex and Third Avenue on the downtown side of the street, at 144 East 42nd Street, a little nine-foot store. Sid talked my dad into opening a radio shop exclusively on 42nd Street, to be nearer to Grand Central and get the flow of traffic when people walked to the Third and Second Avenue El. They had elevated trains in those years, although the Lexington Avenue was below ground.

Across the street from the store were red brick tenements about three or four stories tall, where mostly the redcaps who worked at Grand Central lived with their families. Where the Chatham Building is now was Manhattan Storage and Warehouse Company. The Commodore Hotel was right there, so my father called the little shop Commodore Radio Corporation.

The schools were so crowded in those years that, especially down at Stuyvesant, they had a morning session and an afternoon session for the students. So luckily, I got into the morning session, where you attended school from 8 A.M. to 12:15, and after 12:15 I would either get on the Third Avenue El and go to 42nd Street, or I'd walk from 15th Street to my father's store with my books, and do my homework in the back, and help him wait on trade. My Uncle Sid then opened the radio department.

Radio was coming in by '26 and '27, especially ham radios. Everybody built their own sets in those years. You bought kits, or you bought parts. You got these radio magazines and learned how to put together a crystal set or a one-tube set. And we sold batteries and aerial wire and all that kind of stuff.

I, of course, went with Sid to the 42nd Street store, and would wait on customers. Acetone speakers came out . . . Cone speakers were invented in those years, where you would get, like a wooden frame and you would stretch airplane cloth that they used on the wings of the airplanes in 1918, like the Wright Brothers and all. You stretched it over this square frame. They had magnetic coil and stuff with a stylus coming out of it, and a gimmick for putting the hole in the cloth, and then tightening on with a thumb screw, and pulling it back. Then you bought this stuff that kids used to sniff later, the glue, and you poured it on the cloth and it would shrink and become taut, and you would have a cone. Now they're made out of paper, but then you did it with this airplane cloth. And we sold all those kits and everything. It had a better sound the little magnetic thing, like a more sensitive earphone in your telephone. Those were the first loudspeakers with a cone on them, a cone diaphragm.

Anyway, I had one of those cone speakers up over the door transom. We used to tune in the radio stations, whatever was on—I don't remember the call letters. Of course, it was before the Red and the Blue Networks. But you did have Schenectady and you had what's now NBC and you had WOR. If it was music playing, some people walked in and asked if I sold phonograph records. I said "No, it's a radio store." Because they heard the music. After a while, there were quite frequent requests for phonograph records. So I told my father, "Pop, I'm getting calls for records in the store and we ought to take in records." He said, "Well, if you're getting calls, get the Yellow Pages [they had Yellow Pages in those years too] and look up the phonograph record companies" . . . Because at home, we had always had a crank phonograph, a Columbia Graphinola that my father bought in 1917 or 1918. So I was familiar with the records of the day, the humorous records, the cantorial records, opera records, and classical records that he used to play.

So I called up and I got the Columbia salesman. He said, "The salesman will come down." So the Columbia man came in and the Brunswick salesman came in. Victor wouldn't send anybody down because two blocks away from us there was a franchise. In the early days, around the time of World War I, or when Caruso was so big, you got exclusive dealerships on records. Even Columbia and Victor . . . If you had Columbia, you didn't have Victor records. If you had Victor they were almighty. They wouldn't let you stock any other label. And if you got that franchise, you had a good shop. So they still had that policy—1926 probably was the tail end of it. We had to wait until the dealer closed up a couple of blocks away. As soon as he went out of business, I called them and we got Victor Records. But it was a couple of years after I had the others.

I started in '26. Of course, you start by ordering whatever is coming out. They used to come in with mimeographed lists. The salesman came every week. That's how I got interested in composers. The looseleaf book they had would have the description of the record. The artists were mostly known artists, but they would give you the composer's name. If it was Irving Berlin, it said "Song by Irving Berlin," and then it would describe it—"This is a ballad." You know, the hokiest descriptions! You didn't hear those things on the air. They were brand new, and they didn't have samples. So you had to go by the description and by the composer. So I soon learned who were the good composers.

Q: You still hadn't become aware of jazz at this point.

MG: Oh, I was aware of jazz right from the beginning, because when I went to dances or I went to a wedding dance, the bands were little bands like Dixieland bands. My favorite band in those early years was Ted Lewis. I wasn't that crazy about Paul Whiteman, who was the "King of Jazz," but he was kind of concerty. Once in a while there would be a good solo on the record. Of course, the radio stations used to have remote wires in all the hotels and on the weekend you heard all the bands that were working. Even the ones from Chicago and the Coast if you stayed up late enough.

I found the part I liked best on the dance record were the solos. If it had a good trumpet chorus or clarinet or a sax or trombone chorus, that's the part that stayed with me the most. When you got a band like a Ted Lewis on Harmony that had the Dixie Stompers, which I later found out, was Fletcher Henderson . . . those were my favorites. I took every Dixie Stomper record. I took all the Ellington records home. Then, of course, when I took in Okeh and I had Louis Armstrong, that was my favorite right away. So I kind of leaned towards jazz. And because I liked that kind of music, I always had them in stock. I never let them run out even if some of those bands did pop tunes. The Original Dixieland Jazz Band even recorded "Margie," which was one of the biggest records they ever made. I used to like certain singers. Bing was the first . . . outside of Louis's vocals on his records, Bing was the first singing voice that I really took to. I tried to keep every record that a company would put out, and kept what I called a library stock of recordings. The store soon became known for having unusual records that you couldn't find in your neighborhood. If you came down to 144 E. 42nd, you could find it.

But jazz was what I really liked. One of my favorite records of all time would be, "There'll Be Some Changes Made" and "I Found a New Baby" by the Chicago Rhythm Kings. I didn't know Eddie Condon, Muggsy, or Teschemaker or any of those people from a hole in the ground. I liked the spirit on that record. They were two good songs.

When I heard Louis Armstrong singing and playing, that was it. You were able, in those years, to get the Louies through Columbia. Some of the stuff came out on Columbia anyway, and that's where I heard it, and then I started to go back and get the early ones. Then I always loved Duke Ellington, and when he was on the radio he used to have a program every day. I think he was on maybe from the Cotton Club, for Moe Levy Clothes, I think it was—a clothing store at Third Avenue and 149th Street that he did a show for. That might have only been a fifteen-minute broadcast, but boy, I wouldn't miss that show with Duke Ellington's band.

Q:. What did records sell for at that time? Did they have two prices then?

MG: Well, Perfects were 25 cents. Harmonies were three for a dollar or 35 cents. Crowns were 35 cents, I believe. They didn't last long, the Crown Company. Later, the Mellotone was an offshoot of Perfect, when American Record Company bought it, and they were 25 cents. Victors and Columbias and Brunswicks were 75 cents. On the 25 cent label you didn't really get name artists. They were all on 75 cent records. The dance orchestras and the singers . . .

Q: Did they use the 25 cent label to break new artists and then move them to the 75 cent label? Did that ever happen?

MG: They changed their name when they sang on a cheaper label! On Columbia it was Fletcher Henderson and His Orchestra. On Harmony he was Dixie Stompers. Duke Ellington recorded under lots of different names. The Washingtonians on a 25 cent label.

Q: Of course. But it was for cheaper labels? It wasn't just to be able to record, because he had a contract with one label and he wanted to record for another?

MG: Well, some of the major companies made the cheap labels. They made them for the five-and-dime stores. In other words, it would be Silvertone for Sears Roebuck and it could be another label down the street, the same master with a different name for the artist. So record collectors had a ball figuring it all out. You would have Harmony in one store and Velvetone in another. So the customers thought they were getting something different.

Q: That's what made discographers' work complicated.

MG: Yeah. I think the printing of *Discography in America* really got record collecting going. Because that was the Bible—to me, it still is.

Q: And that's important because it was Commodore that published it here.

MG: Yes. We published it in America. And we would help them during the years when they were collecting the information. We would cross-examine the musicians when they came in, to see if they remembered sessions. And what you got in those years, you were able to play a record and you knew approximately what the band was—whether it was Ben Pollack or Jean Goldkette or Fletcher or whomever. You knew who probably was in the band. But you got so you could recognize the lead horns, you could recognize the soloists—they all had different styles. Just like the spoken word. The human voice. You can recognize a man by the tone of his voice. You can recognize a musician by the way he blows his notes. And that's what we did. Through trial and error and all . . . Even when *Discography* came out, it had a lot of errors. But it was a fantastic work! It's a definitive work and the reason collecting became what it did.

Q: When actually did people start collecting jazz records? Because you got very much involved in that aspect of things.

MG: The Depression came right after radio hit big. Because as soon as they invented cone speakers, and electronic recording and all that stuff, things went . . . Electronically, the sound was much better than the old acoustical diaphragms on the old phonographs that we used to wind up and play. Although RCA or Victor had the Orthophonic, with a great air chamber in it and all, it couldn't compare to the electric sound that you got by playing a record. You see, they invented the phonograph pickup. So about this time, people could play records through their radio speaker rather than play them acoustically through air chambers.

And the Depression hit at that time, and people didn't have the money to buy records. People were listening to radio.

Actually, I may have been the first teacher to get my customers to get deep into collecting. It was an evolution for me. People found they could come into my store, and I would tell them about a new Louis Armstrong or a Duke Ellington record, that it was out. By musicians coming in, I found out the names of people that played on records. I would say "Who played that great trombone solo on that?" You soon found out, in the '20s, that it was Jack Teagarden or young Benny Goodman on those records. So that's what we would talk about.

Our name in the phone book was Commodore Radio Corporation, 144 E. 42nd Street. The telephone company was very efficient in those years. They called up and said, "We're getting calls for a Commodore Music Shop, and the Commodore Radio Corp. is listed at that address. Why don't you buy a listing for Commodore Music Shop in the phone book so people will be able to find you?" It was obviously a great idea, so we paid for the extra listing. The record part of it kept growing. Every week records would come out. So we changed the name from the Commodore Radio Corp. to the Commodore Music Shop. The record department got so big, we got rid of the radios, we got rid of all the sporting goods and tricks and novelties, etc.

Q: How did it happen that at the time radio was eclipsing the record industry and the Depression hit, your record department flourished?

MG: I wouldn't say flourished. We were way in debt!

Q: So you basically went into records and replaced radios with records not because of any great success you were having, but because of your own personal need to do it?

MG: That's right. It replaced it because it just kept growing! In items. In physical stock. My father used to complain, when we took inventory. Once a year we would take inventory. He would say, "This is a terrible business because you only turn your investment in merchandise over four times a year, and it should be a lot more than that. Besides, what about all the records that don't sell?" He noticed the stock getting bigger and bigger. You had only a 5 percent return privilege based on how much you sold. But he said, "A song is like a tomato in a vegetable market. When a song gets old, you're stuck with it, same as a tomato. In my hardware and electrical business, a lamp is a lamp and a plier is a plier forever. It never gets old!" He still was around the corner in Third Avenue. I was in the 42nd Street store.

Q: Oh, then you already had two stores?

MG: Yeah. And I would try to explain to him that if you have a good singer or a good orchestra, it doesn't get old. People always collect them. There were people that collected every recording of "Stardust." Every recording of "St. Louis Blues." Every Bix record. I think we were the first store that had pick bins by artist.

Q: When did reissues start? Who started them?

MG: Well, I started them.

Q: There was no such thing as reissuing records before you started doing it?

MG: Not really.

Q: And you were the first one to list the complete personnel on the label?

MG: Yes. I put my first records out on the white Commodore label.

Q:. You leased the masters?

MG: Well, you had to press records and you had to go to a record factory to press them. So the obvious thing to do was to pick masters that weren't destroyed of artists you wanted to put out and sell. The first records I put out were the original Wolverine Vocalions.

Q: They were out of print at the time?

MG: Yes. What did I know about making records in those years? I went to Brunswick-Vocalion, and I told them I wanted to order some pressings. They checked. They said they had the masters on these three records by the original Wolverines. They were good titles. I didn't even have a sample of a record. So I ordered them. They happened to be the McPartland Wolverines, not the Beiderbecke Wolverines. But they were little jazz band records . . .

Q: How long had they been unavailable?

MG: They were made in '27 or '28, something like that. And I put them out in '34 and '35. They probably were cut out around 1930. If they didn't sell, they just stopped pressing them. All I did was give them the name and address of the store. The other copy was the same label copy they would have had on a regular Vocalion record under the hole. And they paid the publishers. I paid them four cents extra on a pressing to take care of the copyright royalties or artist royalties, if there were any. Actually, we could buy a record in those years, if you base it on the price of a 25 cent record . . . They were making records profitably, and they charged the dealer 16 cents for a 25 cent record. And 21 cents for a 35 cent record. So they were able to press the records for less than 16 cents. Which I found out later when I worked for record companies. If it was a 25 cent or 30 cent record, they didn't pay two cents a title; they only paid a penny or a penny and a quarter per title.

Q: Did you have any kind of minimum pressing you had to do?

MG: Yeah. I had to buy 300 of each. And I didn't give them a logo for a label. I just said "Make it 'Commodore Music Shop' where it says 'Vocalion.'" So they just took type and put it in whatever label form they had. They put ordinary type in it. The bottom of the label was the same.

Q: Now, were you allowed to sell this elsewhere, or just at the Commodore Record Shop?

MG: I could sell them anywhere. I paid for the records. But it was mostly just the Commodore Record Shop. If a dealer wanted the record, I would give him 40 percent off.

Q: Did you have enough of a following of jazz fans to sell 300 of anything in those days?

MG: I estimated I could sell 300 of a record in a year or two. But by '34, I had a jazz following. I had decided that's the kind of music

I liked, and I was going to try to keep every hot record that was made, and that I could get ahold of.

Because of the 5 percent return privilege, that was supposed to enable you to get rid of your rotten tomato records, and send them back to the company. So there were guys, like Charlie Stinson who later put out Stinson Records. Charles Stinson used to warehouse records and go around the country buying up stock from dealers that were quitting the record business. Of course, the record business when radios came in had dipped, and furniture dealers and people like that who had record departments, were tickled to death to sell him the records for a penny or two apiece and let him cart them out of the place. So he would warehouse all the standard brand records . . . Not numerically; he would just have them on the shelves. When it came time, every six months you had this 5 percent return privilege—he would come around and say "How many records do you need?" I'd say, "Well, this year I can use 200." But I would keep the records that I didn't want to send back for credit because I thought someone might buy them later. He would buy them for a penny or two apiece, and sell them to dealers for a nickel.

So I went down to his place and told him, "Charlie, I'll pay you a dime a record, but I don't want you to dump off 200 records." Now, when it was time for the return privilege . . . Let's say it happened in January and in August. He was just collecting records the rest of the time, putting them in inventory. So I'd say, "Rather than go to Salvation Army for used records I'll go to you and let me pick what I want. You'll never miss them. The dealers you schlock your records to wouldn't care." And I'd say, "I'll pay you a dime a record . . ." And they were clean records.

So I'd cherrypick them for twice as much as he got from others. So he was crazy about me! And I got a lot of great cutout jazz records that way. So because of my relationship with Charlie Stinson, when Columbia dumped . . . When CBS bought Columbia, and they dumped the old Okeh inventory they had up in the Bridgeport factory, the first guy he called was me. He said, "Milt, do you want to go up and cherrypick the stuff in Bridgeport?" I said, "Absolutely!"

Q: Milt, in those days, how did a customer know that a record came out? There were no jazz magazines, and radio was live music.

MG: He'd have to go to a dealer who could tell him, a dealer who handled the labels that Ellington was on, and say, "Are there any new

Dukes?" There were magazine reviews. And the record companies weren't asleep. They had PR departments. They'd print little catalogues and monthly circulars and the people would take them off our counters.

Q: Right. But how did you get the person into the record store?

MG: From '35 on, you had your stations playing phonograph records—even before '35. They started to play records when the electronic records came out. And the little stations found out it's a cheap way to put a program on. You don't have to hire a house band or anything. And sell local advertisers. Which is done to this day. The revolution came when Martin Block became a high pressure, very personable announcer with stories, who got to know all the singers and bandleaders. But that's another story.

Q: What was your first recording studio experience?

MG: The first date I ever watched was a John Hammond date in '33. It was the Benny Goodman date with Coleman Hawkins and Mildred Bailey, "Georgia Jubilee," "Old Pappy," "Jump Man" . . .

Q: He just let you come and visit?

MG: He didn't let me come. You're talking about reissues. We'll go back to reissues. Glenn Gray and the Casa Loma Band came to New York and played the Essex House and opened up in Glen Island Casino. I liked what they did on records. They had some Okeh records. And then they went to Brunswick. Gene Gifford did some terrific instrumentals. And I liked the way Pee Wee Hunt sang . . . I always loved the way musicians sang. Then they left Brunswick, and they went to Victor. And they did two or four sides for Victor—I don't know how many. They did "Lazy Bones," though, and it was a smash hit with a Pee Wee Hunt vocal. I remembered the Okeh Casa Loma records, and I loved one that was on Harmony by Roy Carroll and the Sands Point Orchestra. They had to change their names to sell them for less money. And then they did "Royal Garden Blues."

So the Columbia salesman came in, and I said to him, "You know, you guys own Casa Loma masters. They're on Okeh and on Harmony. You even have 'Royal Garden Blues.' You ought to put that out with 'Casa Loma Stomp' on the back, so it really says Casa Loma, and reissue it on your blue label Columbias for 75 cents, because 'Lazy Bones' is a big hit and the band is catching on." So he said, "I'll tell them to do it." And sure enough, they did it, and it sold! So Harry Crews, who worked for them at that time (later he was at Decca, when Decca was formed), he called me up and he said, "Milt, the record is a success. What can we give you as a reward? Do you want to see a show or do you want us to take you to dinner?" Well, John Hammond used to come into my store, and the first Goodman All Star records that he made were already out. I knew John had another date coming up, and I wanted to watch how the record was made. I had never been in a studio. So I said to Harry Crews, "The only reward I want is, John Hammond is recording next week, and I want to go down and watch the session." So he said, "Absolutely." So they took pictures of it . . . John isn't in the picture. They took a picture of me and Benny.

Q: Were you hooked by the experience?

MG: On making records? That was '33. I didn't dream I was going to make a record yet. It just was interesting, the way they set them up and to watch them make it, and do a second take and stuff like that. I sat in the control room, that's all.

Q: Did you feel like, "God, I'd love to do this someday"?

MG: No. Not at that point. Of course, after that I was hooked on watching record sessions! No, I didn't dream of it. After that, because I was more friendly with the people up at Decca, I went up there and watched the Dorsey Brothers record, just some pop stuff . . . I just went up to say hello, and they were in the studio, so I went in the control room. I knew some of the guys in the band, so I stuck around.

Q: Were musicians starting to come into the store?

MG: Oh yeah! By the thirties, absolutely. I got hooked . . . It was a development. You see, about that time, the first reissue would be that Casa Loma record that Columbia put out. Then Bix died, and we decided there should be a Bix Beiderbecke memorial album. So I called RCA, and they said, "Absolutely."

Then Nappy Lamar, Ben Pollack's guitarist, came in to order "Pinetop's Boogie Woogie." This would be in 1935. When I reordered, the company didn't have it. I had been used to ordering custom pressings for White Label Commodore reissues, so I said, "That's a great record." So I called up and I ordered more, and they said it would be the same 300 minimum. So I ordered my 300, and then when they finally came in on the Vocalion label, a customer came in, or a musician, and I said, "I got in 'Pinetop's Boogie Woogie.' Did you ever hear it? Do you have it?" He said, "Oh, I bought it last week in Old Supporter." That later became Gateway Music Shop in Times Square, 46th Street and Broadway. So I said, "Oh, Supporter has it!" I called up

Brunswick-Vocalion and I got the customer rep, and I said, "You got a hell of a nerve selling Old Supporter 'Pinetop's Boogie Woogie' when I order 300. How did he get it?" He said, "Well, when you ordered it, we figured if it's a good record and you got 300 . . . We have 50 extra copies, and we gave a portion of them to dealers, and Supporter bought ten of them." I said, "Boy that's great. I have to stock a record for two years to get my money out of it, and he gets the benefit of it."

That gave me the idea of having them pressed on a special label. About that point, Marshall Stearns had been coming in from New Haven, Connecticut—he was a student up at Yale at that time. He had what he called The Yale Hot Club. I had my New York guys, which we didn't call a hot club at that point. But there were a hundred people that used to come in. Marshall said, "You know, we ought to do like they do in England with The Federation of Rhythm Clubs. And France has the Hot Club of France. We'll start an organization in America." He loved to write. I said, "Well, if you want to write to everybody, we can make an international federation of hot clubs." He said, "Sure. I'll write to Panassie right away and to England." I think Helen Oakley was in Chicago then; that's Stanley Dance's wife now. We formed a hot club in Chicago. We formed one in Washington. I think Sid Weiss, the bass player, and his wife were down there then. They formed a Washington hot club. They formed a Boston hot club. I think they had one in Princeton, and they had one in New Haven. He said, "How are we going to put it over?" I had my reissues, so I said, "I'll make up a special label, United Hot Clubs of America, and, in order to get the record, you have to become a member." That's how we formed the UHCA, United Hot Clubs of America. I think we had one or two trustee or governors meetings.

Anyway, I said, "I'll tell you what we'll do, Marshall. I will print them up on the special United Hot Clubs of America label. We'll put the information of who plays on the record right on the label. And you can't buy that record unless you're a member of a hot club." So he said, "Terrific!" I said, "And that's how the clubs will grow. Because to get the record, you have to be a member of the UHCA." I said, "We'll charge $2.00 a year to become a member, and that will take care of the postage stamps."

Q: Is that the first mail order record operation, too?

MG: I imagine so. But we didn't go at it like mail order companies do today. It was mail order because if you saw a writeup in *Life* magazine or *Time* magazine and you wrote to me, I would mail you the record!

So Marshall wrote to everyone, and of course they wanted to get the jazz reissues. I said, I'd run jam sessions because Eddie Condon had been telling me "Boy, you should have been at . . ." Every once in a while at the Yale Club on Vanderbilt Avenue . . . Wilder Hobson was an amateur trombone player, and Jim Moynihan, who worked for Henry Luce's March of Time was a clarinet player. So they used to have sessions. Eddie would get his guitar, and maybe they'd find Bud Freeman or somebody, and they would have sessions at the Yale Club or at someone's house. He'd say, "Gee, you should have been in the Village here. He had a great jam session"—he used to call them that. I don't know if they had a place in the back of Plunkett's to play or not, because I never went to Plunkett's.

So he got me interested in this idea of impromptu little jazz groups playing for the hell of it. Oh, and 52nd Street had started to be important. I told Marshall, "We'll run jazz concerts, jam sessions, and I'll get all my people in the magazines and the trades and inform them about it. I'll go up to Jack Kapp and get the use of their studio for a Sunday, and you get the musicians together."

Incidentally, John Hammond, when we formed the club, was in Europe, or Russia or something. So I said, "Marshall, the obvious guy to be president of the hot club is John Hammond. So when he comes back from Europe we'll tell him he's the president." And he was the president. He was the most logical man to be president of a thing like that. I was the treasurer, of course—somebody had to take care of the money. Marshall was the secretary—a corresponding secretary. I don't know who was vice president.

Anyway, Richard Edes Harrison was the prime mover of that organization, too. He was one of the great cartographers. He used to do the covers for *Fortune* magazine. In those years *Fortune* magazine had maps on the cover, and Ricky Harrison did them. He was a great idea man. He never liked phonograph record labels, because when they spun around on the turntable they were all top heavy. They had the main log on the top and the titles underneath, and he said, "When you look at it, your head has to spin because it's lopsided. It's not a balanced thing when it turns." So I needed a label for UHCA and we had to have room for the personnel. The first time in America that they ever put the personnel on the label. Now you put it in your liner notes. But in those years, I was the first one to put the musicians' names on the label—who played on the records. And all the companies copied that. So he had to design the label. The UHCA label to me, today, is still so ornate, with scrolls on it . . . It's really a beautiful label. He had room above the hole and below the hole to put the information. So I put the origin of the record, the company who originally made it, the original record number and the year, and then "dubbed at so-and-so," and then on the bottom we had the personnel and the record titles and all. There was so much copy on some of them, I used to have to have them set and reduced to fit on the record label, rather than just set type in a form. But it was an innovation.

Q: Was Eddie Condon among the first musicians that you became personally acquainted with?

MG: Yeah. Well, Paul Smith, the guy who became his brother-in-law, came in. He found in my stock the Billy Banks Rhythm Makers on Perfect and the Jack Bland records which I didn't know Condon was on. But I liked those two-bit records. They had the same spirit that the Chicago Rhythm Kings records had. Also, on Okeh, I used to like the McKenzie-Condon Chicagoans. These were all the same heart, the same thinking. So when Paul Smith heard a Frankie Trumbauer record that I was playing out over the speaker in front of the store with Bix Beiderbecke on it, he came in and wanted the record. We used to pipe the records from a turntable up onto that transom. Then he found the Billy Banks and the Jack Bland, which he couldn't find anywhere. He knew Eddie. But Eddie still hadn't married his sister Phyllis. So he brought Eddie into the store, and we became fast friends, and Eddie started telling me stories about what he was doing. He was scuffling. It was the middle thirties.

Q: You and Eddie Condon soon started to get some musicians together for the Hot Club jam sessions. You would go to a studio on Sundays.

MG: For jam sessions, right.

Q: Would you invite people to attend those then?

MG: Yes, it was free! I would let all my customers know by sending postcards. We'd invite all the critics and writers. The idea was to get musicians work, and get people to know about 52nd Street.

52nd Street only had two or three clubs going, but the idea was to have it spread out. It started in the Village also. And it worked. They'd do the writeups of the concerts (let's call them concerts, because that's what they became later—I called them jam sessions), and the prime fellows in getting the musicians to play for nothing were Eddie Condon and John Hammond. One of the greatest sessions we ever put together, and it was photographed for *Tempo* magazine, was when John had a small Count Basie Group come in, Benny Goodman played at that and Gene Krupa (because they were working at Times Square with a band, I think), Chick and Ella Fitzgerald were there and played, Artie Shaw played. We had a trio with Ella singing, Chick Webb on drums, Graham Forbes on piano, and I think it was Artie Shaw on clarinet. I have a photo of that somewhere at home. And Mezz Mezzrow played. Of course, all the Condon guys. Frankie Newton.

I remember, the room was jam-packed. We broke all fire laws. I used to rent chairs and pay the super for opening the building, and I would buy club soda, ginger ale, ice, and bring up Scotch and rye, about six bottles of each, to feed anybody that was playing a drink. We weren't paying them. And you couldn't fit in that room. That studio was so jammed. Actually, the big studio we used at that time was when Irving Mills started his label in conjunction with Brunswick. It was really at 1780 Broadway. I think that was the greatest jam session I ever ran for people that played and all.

Q: Then you moved them from the studio eventually to Jimmy Ryan's.

MG: I'll tell you what happened. A session prior to that I ran at Decca when it was at 799 Seventh Avenue. Benny Goodman played at that one also, and I think Bunny Berigan and Teddy Wilson and Eddie's guys . . . I remember, it was at Decca across from Charlie's Tavern. That was the first free jam session that the store ran. You couldn't move. They were packed like sardines in that room. But, it was costing too much, and they were smoking and ruining the floor in the studio, stepping on the butts, and it made such a mess, even though we rented chairs for the crowd, they didn't want to do it anymore. Decca had done it twice. Brunswick did it.

After that, I said, "This is costing too much. We can't handle the people." So I said, "We should have them on 52nd Street, where people can buy booze, the clubs will let us take it over on a dead Sunday afternoon." Then we ran one at the Famous Door. Bessie Smith sang at that one; John got Bessie to come. There were so many people on 52nd Street on a Sunday afternoon that it hung over—it ended at eight to nine o'clock. They stayed on the street. They wanted to hear more music. And by that time, the clubs were opening. And Hickory House had a big restaurant around that block. So a lot of people went in there to eat. Joe Marsala started playing. He said, "What the hell are all you guys doing here on a Sunday?" He said, "Well, Milt had a jazz concert at the Famous Door this afternoon."

So right after that, the Hickory House started to run Sunday sessions. They even got a WNEW wire. Ralph Berton started running them down in the Village. Berton was charging admission! And Pee Wee came in, and he said, "We had a good session down in the Village yesterday with Ralph Berton." The customers that went to it told me that he was charging a dollar. I said, "He got a nerve. Pee Wee, did you get paid?" He said, "No." To publicize the music is one thing. But for him to charge a dollar and not pay the guys, it's against the AFM rules and it's just not right.

So I decided to run my own sessions, and I went over and made a deal at Ryan's, which was across from my 52nd Street store. Because they weren't doing any business at all. I ran them until 1946. Then I turned them over to my brother-in-law Jack Crystal.

Q: That takes us to opening another store on 52nd Street.

MG: I did enough mail order business by 1938 that I said, "Pop, Time-Life moved to Radio City . . ." All the radio stations that I was selling to were around there. Even WNEW. CBS was on 52nd Street. NBC. WEVD. I could walk down Sixth Avenue and deliver the records. I said, "I want to move where the musicians are, on 52nd Street." So there was an empty store on the middle of the block, and that's when I opened at 46 West 52nd Street.

Q: Did you stay open late for the club trade?

MG: Yes.

Q: Your father was still involved in those days?

MG: He was in the store, yeah. He took care of paying the bills. We split the stock, and I moved to 52nd. By that time we were selling dealers. The Commodores were getting writeups, and I was selling records to a lot of dealers that knew enough to write away for a record—L.A., everywhere, all the major cities in the U.S., so I opened an office at 415 Lexington Avenue for the wholesale business, and on 52nd Street.

Q: Aside from so many musicians and celebrated writers and news journalists from Time-Life and *The New Yorker* and so on, you also had lots of jazz fans as regulars who also started their own labels or became record producers.

MG: There was John Hammond, of course, and George Avakian was just a kid. Jerry Wexler courted his wife in my store and Ahmet and Nesuhi Ertegun used to come up from Washington. They all eventually created Atlantic Records.

But soon after I started Commodore, Alfred Lion created Blue Note and Dan Quayle started Solo Art. And Bob Thiele had Signature.

Also Eugene Williams and Ralph DeToledano and Ralph Gleason started Jazz Information in the back of my shop.

Q: When the war came, and Frank Wolff worked for you, were you distributing Blue Notes during the war—through that period?

MG: Yes. We kept the label going. He was able to run it, and also pack and ship Commodores. They didn't have to close up.

I want to go back to the end of the Commodore reissues and how I got to Decca. I got up to 113 on the Commodore reissues. That was "Pinetop's Boogie Woogie." I ran an ad in *Down Beat* which was going to be our next release, and they ordered it from Columbia, and the legal department notified the customer division that they couldn't press it because they didn't own the master. The masters were there, but they belonged to Warner Brothers. Evidently, when Warner's bought Brunswick for a calendar company, it was a separate deal than the ones that went to Perfect and Mellotone and American Record Company. So when Columbia bought American Record Company, they only got the masters after December 1931, and they didn't own any of the early Vocalions. I knew that Jack Kapp was an A&R man up at Vocalion in those years, and I went up to see him, and I told him, "Warner Brothers owns those early Vocalion-Brunswick records." He said he knew that. And I said, "You ought to buy them. Columbia is putting out jazz reissues. John Hammond is putting them out for them. If you get the Brunswicks and the Vocalions back, I will come up and put them out for you." So he said, "Okay." Months later, when he did finally close the deal and get the rights to it, he called me to come and work for Decca to put out the Brunswick and Vocalion reissues. That's how I went to Decca. I started November 17, 1941.

Q: Were you at Decca all day?

MG: No, I was only there in the mornings. I told them I could work for them for half-a-day, and leave at lunchtime to go to the store, because the store got busy at noon.

Q: When did you go to work full-time for them?

MG: Actually, it became full time because I loved the record business so much, and I never got down to the store until later, I'd get so involved up there. They also hired me because I had been successful with the Commodores. And the Billie Holiday record had been a big hit, and they wanted me to produce records for them. Not jazz records. Just any kind of records.

Q: How did you keep the Commodore label alive?

MG: I told them, "I'll work for you for half-a-day, and the rest of the day Commodore's." I'd go to the store and on Saturdays I generally did my record dates—or after 5 P.M.

Q: The Commodores.

MG: The Commodores, yes. Most of them were done on Saturdays or after 5 P.M. during the week. But later, I had a contract with them. In the contract it had a clause which acknowledged that I was president of Commodore Records and I could still record with Commodore. In fact, if I hadn't been able to record for Commodore, I wouldn't have worked for Decca. So that was the only way they could get me. And I loved the record business so much when I got in there and got into the popular end, and how everything was done, and listened to the songwriters come up and play songs and things like that . . . Instead of getting into the store at one o'clock, I used to get there when Decca closed, and eventually was working full-time for them. Then they got me into producing records. It was a whole new world to me.

Q: And why did Commodore discontinue reissues?

MG: As soon as John Hammond went up to Columbia in '37 or '38 and they announced the 50-cent reissues of the Columbias and Okehs, with all the personnels on the labels and all, I said, "That's the end of UHCA." The majors would take their masters back and do it themselves. The only way for Commodore Music Shop to stay in business was for me to start my own label. Because if I had paid the guys to make a record, I would own them for the rest of my life, and never cut them out. They would always be available. So I got my guys together, and we did the first session with Eddie Condon . . . Bobby Hackett had come into New York then from Boston, and he was getting a lot of write-ups as the next Bix—although he wasn't Bix; he just played beautifully. He was working in the Village at the Original Nick's, on the west side of 7th Avenue near 10th Street. It was one of those step-down saloons. And Brunies, and Pee Wee, and Bobby Hackett, and Eddie, of course, were there. Jess Stacy on piano. The bass player was working at the Hickory House with Joe Marsala. Wettling was with Red Norvo and Mildred Bailey. Anyway, the records came out. "Jada" and "Love Is Just Around the Corner" is a classic. Should be in the hall of fame. First independent jazz record.

Eddie, of course, was one of the most hustling promotion-minded men I ever met in my life. And a delightful man. Every writer loved him. Newspaper people adored him. As well as disc jockeys and anybody. He rushed up to *Life* magazine, and he said, "Teagarden is in town." Teagarden was with Paul Whiteman's band. He said, "Teagarden's in town. If I can get Milt to do another record date, will you come and take a picture of it?" So Alexander King was up there then. He was in charge of the photo essays. He was a real character. And he used to hang out in my store. Eddie said, "Will you take a picture of Milt's recording session? It's an important thing, a little record store doing its own recordings. It doesn't like the records that the big companies make. It's got to make its own." So they said, "Sure."

They were across the street in the Chrysler Building. There was no Radio City then. So Alex came down and said, "Teagarden's in town. If you will do another session, *Life* will take a picture of it." I said, "Terrific! Let's set it up." So we set almost the identical band that I had on "Jada," but instead of George Brunies we used Jack Teagarden. I booked the studio up at Brunswick. They sent photographers.

Martin Block was having a big swing concert at Randall's Island Stadium. So they decided to make an essay of the thing. They had some old photos. They did the story of King Oliver, the story of Bix Beiderbecke, and they sent out photographers to take photographs at Randall's Island Stadium, with the people jumping in the aisles and going crazy. They did two pages of photos of my session. Then, the last page of the article, I did like a "Dr. Elliott's Five-Foot Shelf of Books"—I called it. "The Thirty Records to Start a Balanced Jazz Collection With. These are important."

So they ran the story . . . Pee Wee Russell was supposed to be on the cover. He had one of those fantastic Charlie Peterson photographs. Later it ran inside, but it was supposed to be the cover. So what happened? King Edward abdicated in England, and knocked us off the cover. Knocked us out of the issue completely! Of course, King Edward was on the cover. So they held up our story, which was just an essay on jazz music and swing. We ran a few months later. I kept going over. By that time, they had moved to the Time-Life Building. I kept going over there and buggin' Alex King, who was a fantastic guy. What used to amaze me about him was the bill he used to run up on the telephone. He would be calling Afghanistan, Austria, England . . . What a fantastic mind he had! He was quite a humorous individual and a great storyteller. He wound up on *The Jack Paar Show,* as his most famous guest. He's got a couple of good books. He was really a delightful man.

And he loved Commodore. And he finally ran the story. It was August when they ran it. They had some guys diving off a cliff going swimming on the cover, instead of Pee Wee.

But that made Commodore. God, did we sell records with that list of thirty jazz records. I was sure to put in a half-dozen UHCAs and my Commodores. That really enabled me to open the wholesale office and the 52nd Street store.

Q: And you continued to have a good relationship with Time-Life?

MG: Always. They were great people. That was the great thing . . . Someone once asked me, "Who does your publicity?"—as if I had a Madison Avenue agency. He said, "You get more writeups . . ." I said, "I do it myself. They're all my friends"—which was true. Doug Watt . . . Everyone. The disc jockeys, the radio stations . . .

In those years, the radio stations bought their records. They hadn't found out that the publishers and the record companies would supply them with the records to get them played on the air. The industry hadn't arrived at that point yet, because the plugging of songs was all done by contact then, for remote broadcasts and stuff.

There's an interesting story on how I came to sell the radio stations records. Martin Block in 1935 came from California and went on the air with the *Make Believe Ballroom* at WNEW. His show was a hit right from the beginning. I objected to his using "Sugar Blues" as a theme song, the Clyde McCoy record. To me, with the wah-wah trumpet, that was the corniest thing in the world. Because that wasn't swingin' jazz to me. In fact, when the record was issued on Decca . . . It was Decca 381—I'll never forget that number. I refused to order it. Clyde McCoy had made that record for Columbia Blue '78s before Decca was in business. So I knew the record. But then, when Martin started to use it as a theme song, I started to get calls for it! I wouldn't stock it when Decca first issued it. So I started to get calls for it, and reluctantly, I ordered record 381.

Now, one day Block played the Red Norvo record of "Blues in E-Flat," which had a marvelous Bunny Berigan solo. Someone called WNEW and said, "Who is the trumpet player on that record?" And Martin, what did he know about musicians in those years? He said on the air, "If anybody in the audience that just heard that record 'Blues in E-Flat,' knows the trumpet player, please call in." The switchboard lit up and everybody said, "Call Milt Gabler at the Commodore Record Shop on 42nd Street." And that's the first time Martin ever heard of me. So he yelled [at] me. Of course, when the phone call came, I said, "Bunny Berigan," and then I took him to lunch. And I started to tell him what kind of store I had and everything. He said, "Do you want to sell us records?" They had to go out and buy their records, and it was a nuisance for them. He said, "I've got to have new releases. What day do they come out?" I said, "Thursdays." So a dealer would have them for the weekend. He said, "Would you give me every record that comes out?" I said, "Geez, terrific." Then I had to give him a discount, of course. But I thought, "Gee, what a tie-up. I'll get plugs from Martin Block!"

So I made a deal to sell him records at a 30 percent discount. We used to buy them for 40 percent off, so I made 10 percent. He said, "I want you to come up and fill in all the missing records in our record library." I built that first WNEW record library. Sold them all their records from Commodore. I built his whole stock, a tremendous library.

Then, as the records came out, I used to make a route. There were only four companies then, really. Capitol wasn't even in the picture yet then. I used to have to give them the Brunswick-Vocalions, the Columbias and the Victors and later the Bluebirds, and the Deccas. So I would make a route. Decca was 621 W. 54th Street. I would come down with my little Chevy early in the morning, as soon as the record company opened. I had four radio stations to deliver to. I'd pick up the bundle, I'd make four packages, put them in the trunk of my car, and I would go from there to RCA, which was 34th Street and 10th Avenue. There I'd get the Bluebirds and Victors, divide them up. Then I would go to Columbia, which originally was down on 20th Street on the West Side, before Times Appliance had it. In their fire stairwell I would put together the bundles for each station and then I would get to Martin Block at about eleven o'clock in the morning. His program went on at ten. By the time I did all this, it was about 11 A.M., and I would come in there. He used to say, "Here comes the man on the white horse with this week's releases." He was a fantastic announcer. He was really the guy who started disc jockeys as a phenomenon.

Q: This boxed set is going to start with the Cow-Cow Davenport, Fletcher and the Djangos—which you didn't produce. It's pre-Commodore, but it's part of Commodore.

MG: Yes.

Q: How did you acquire those masters?

MG: Well, the U.S. Record Company owned them. That was Eli Oberstein's company. And they went into receivership. The masters that U.S. Record Company had were offered, I imagine, to many other people. The whole catalogue was. I could only afford certain ones, and I only had a limited budget. I really wanted to get the Jess Stacy date with Fazola on it. It was like a Commodore session. So while I was buying those, I bought "Slow Drag," by Cow-Cow Davenport.

Q: How did you get the Fletcher and Djangos?

MG: Well, Fletcher was in there also.

Q: Those were the Crown masters?

MG: They were Crown masters that U.S. Record Company used. The list didn't have all the Fletchers on it. I had to pick out ten records, I remember. So I picked two Fletchers, two Django Reinhardt-Grappelli records, the "Slow Drag" would make five, and the five Stacys I think it was.

Q: One that pops up a little later is the "Teagarden Blues."

MG: Yeah, I bought that also. That's how I got those. I bought them from the receivership of U.S. Record Company. I also had the opportunity to buy Buzz Reeves's General Records. I had been using the Reeves Studio, and we had become very friendly. He was always great on inventions. He developed the acetate disc for recording on it. The audio disc was his. And the war came along, and he made so much money on the audio disc for the government and sixteen-inch and all that stuff, that he wasn't enamored of the record business any longer—and he was always struggling in that; it was a loss to him. I either was up there to record at his studio, or he called me on the phone and he said, "Do you want to buy my company?" He said, "I have such a tax problem this year with all the money I made on audio discs that I am going to take a loss on General Records." So I took over his lease at 1600 Broadway, and his inventory, and all the dopey little labels he had, mainly to buy the Jelly Roll Morton stuff. It was a big investment, but we came out all right because we could sell off the inventory, and I wound up with the Jelly Roll Mortons. I mainly bought it for Jelly Roll's solos. He also made jukebox records called Tavern Tunes. Reeves had Jelly Roll write commercial jukebox type songs, what he thought was R&B, and they were, like, old-timey pop tunes. But they really were made for coin machines in Harlem. They were nothing like Louis Jordan or other people that were recording. Jelly was in a different world.

Q: So all the band sides were made for this Tavern Tunes label?

MG: Yeah, the band sides were made for Tavern Tunes. He has "Panama" and a couple of other good ones in there. But I wish I had been able to make those records. I would have improved on the band. He had some good guys in the band, too. But the producer who was behind the glass didn't know what he was doing.

Q: Did you get to know Jelly Roll at all?

MG: He came into the store a couple of times. It was when he had the feud on with somebody at *Down Beat*—I don't know whether it was Marshall Stearns or someone else. Jelly always said he invented jazz, and somebody had written that the great original jazz band was, I think, the Original Dixieland Jazz Band. I guess that came about the time that Victor was trying to revive the Original Dixieland Jazz Band. They had this whole thing in *Down Beat*. Jelly would write an article on how he started it, and then it would be answered the next week by . . .

Q: They were probably both wrong.

MG: That's when Jelly Roll came to New York, and he came to the store. But it was very early then. If I knew what I knew a little later, I would have recorded Jelly. But then, Panassie came over and made those good Victor sides with him. When I used to make Commodores, I knew I couldn't record everybody that I liked or should have recorded. I only had a limited budget and I figured that as long as someone else was making it, I would be able to sell it in my Commodore Music Shop. I didn't care if it was Keynote or Blue Note or Hot Record Society or Solo Art or Victor or Columbia. If Hammond was doing the boogie-woogies, I could get the boogie-woogies. If Alfred Lion did the boogie-woogies, that wiped them out of my catalogue! I did Albert Ammons later.

Q: Did you guys coordinate that kind of stuff?

MG: No. It's just that, as a dealer, I was the first place they would run to get an order. I would order in solid box lots. And they were so proud of their records, they would run to my shop with them because they were doing what I was doing. And I'd say, "Great, it's more stuff for me to sell retail." So I would stay away from those artists. I never did more with Lester Young because he started with John Hammond, and I didn't want to have a conflict with any of those record producers. There was enough music and enough artists for me to have my own, and not to bother with them—and I was happy if they stayed away from Pee Wee. If I were a real record company I probably would have been more hungry and tried to tie up some of those people that I knew were great. But the fact that I could get product of their work on other labels kept me away from them.

Q: None of you guys really made exclusive deals with artists?

MG: No. They were all just regular 802 single engagement contracts. If a guy was honorable and you had a handshake deal with him . . . Condon, of course, he'd cut for Columbia and other people, but not really when he was doing a lot of work for me. He didn't have to have the extra income. George Brunies, of all those guys, in those years would not work for anybody but Commodore. He did some sessions where he was a sideman, but he wouldn't do any real Brunies work because we liked each other that much. He was great for what he did. What he did was unique and old-timey and nobody played a better bottom in a jazz band than he did.

Q: You also purchased that all-star jam band with Leo Watson.

MG: Yeah. Leonard Feather came in. They only put out two sides on Vocalion. He came in. Where else would he go? He said, "Milt, they don't like the session I did up at Vocalion. There are two sides left over. If you want to buy them, they're available." So I refunded them the cost of the musicians, and I put them out on Commodore for him. Mostly I liked Leo Watson on them. I wanted Leo's scat singing. And Pete Brown I didn't have on the label. But Feather always had the musicians change instruments and everything, and that didn't settle well with me. It's a bouncy little record. But I took it for Pete Brown and Leo Watson, and so that it wouldn't be laying around.

The same thing happened when John Hammond did the Kansas City Five. He did a date for Vocalion also. He was working for them then, I think. They didn't like the date. It was only Buck Clayton and Eddie Durham. Eddie Durham was the leader on the date. And the bass and guitar, and Jo Jones. He said, "They don't want to put it out. They don't think it will sell." I said, "John, anything you make, I'll buy." He said, "There are only three sides." He never told me about the fourth side, "Love Me or Leave Me." He was unhappy with it, I guess, and he never told about it. He said, "There's only three sides." So John only respected those three sides. I said, "Well, I can't put out half a record, John. If you get the guys for me, I will do five tunes, so that I can have four records. But I want to add Lester Young on clarinet." Because Lester Young had made "Blue and Sentimental" with the Basie band. He played that beautiful clarinet solo. And I said, "I think with that combination, with the trombone and the muted trumpet and the guitar underneath, Lester's clarinet would just go beautifully with that." So John agreed, and he said, "I'll get you Lester." I said, "Well, when the guys are available I'll book the studio." And I did the Kansas City Sixes. That's a historical session.

Q: You are responsible for that beautiful Lester clarinet? There's very little of his clarinet on records.

MG: Right. The only sad thing in retrospect now is, that because of my love for John and respect that he was using Lester and the Basie guys, they were his boys . . . I never recorded Lester again until years later, with Joe Bushkin.

Q: You also purchased The Teddy Wilson School For Pianists sides.

MG: Yes, they were made for pianists that wanted to learn how to play swing or jazz—the way Teddy played, obviously. I don't know if you'll put this in your notes, but it's a feeling I had when I heard the records that they were Teddy Wilson's, but he didn't go all out because he knew it was going to be transcribed on sheet music for students to play. I think Jay Marion Cook was in it with him. And a woman named Eve Ross, who used to do a piano column in a jazz magazine that is extinct now. It didn't do any real business, and it closed down. And they owed her money. I have the thing now from the receivership, or the right she got from the court to sell the firm, and the masters and everything. Cook's name is in there, and Teddy's. Teddy and Cook sold Eve Ross all right to it. And she sold it to Commodore.

Teddy Wilson found out immediately thereafter. Then Teddy came in the store after he found out I'd bought them. He said, "Milt, they weren't made as real Teddy Wilson solo records. They were made for students. And I wish you wouldn't put them out." I said, "Well, Teddy, if you don't want them out, I won't put them out." And I held them until now. Now it's history and they're actually quite good.

Q: How did you approach making a record? What was your idea of what you as a producer would do? Did you have to be friends with the guys? Did you have to have an idea?

MG: I guess this is the first time I ever would talk about that. Because now, in these later years, I can reflect on why I did it, the way I did it, and the repertoire I chose. Maybe because I started in the music shop, selling records as they came out at the end of the twenties. And I sold sheet music, and I sold piano rolls. To me, the music was very important. American music. We didn't sell really European music, unless Noel Coward could be called a European. But the point is, I knew the value of songs and songwriters. I came up as a young man at the time from World War I on, when the great music of the twenties and songs of the twenties were written. At the Beach, at Silver Beach where we hung out here in Throgs Neck when I grew up, in the saloon, we would do barbershop singing. I always liked being in a barbershop quartet. I loved that high tenor part and stuff when I was a kid.

I first heard music at Silver Beach. It's still there, near Fort Schuyler. My folks built a bungalow there at the end of World War I. We used to have dances there. It was an open-air dance pavilion. They hired a black band of six men—I would say they would have had to come from Manhattan, from Harlem or somewhere—that played jazz, and they were called The Black Diamonds. And I loved that band. Then, when Fourth of July would come, and they would get the hot guys from the military band at Fort Schuyler, which is right adjacent to Silver Beach, and they would play the parade, and at night play the dance at the pavilion—and they would play like a jazz band. That's where I first heard music. Then in the store, I took in records around

1926. I was all of fifteen years old. So I got to hear the bands that were on the record labels. And as I said before, I liked the kind of music that Louis played rather than the arranged music. Then, when I started to listen to soloists on those records, I started to find Duke Ellington, Louis Armstrong, and the Chicago Rhythm Kings kind of stuff. That was my taste. That's what I liked. I always knew what I liked. "I Found a New Baby," the year I took that record in the store was the year it was written and came out on a record! And tunes of the thirties and the late twenties, they were songs that came out as popular songs. Now, when I started to make records for Commodore, I always loved the good, old-time songs. Like some guys liked New Orleans songs. I liked those pop songs. Now, you'll see the songs in the Commodore catalogue. There are a lot of old pop tunes in there that you didn't hear that much on the radio any more. I knew the songwriters—to me, it meant something. Because when the salesman came in to sell me a record, we didn't have a sample. So I soon learned that I could buy an Irving Berlin or a Gershwin or a Jerome Kern song blind.

So, because I sold music, I knew the people that liked certain kinds of songs. Now I get up to where I am doing my Commodores, and I am saying, "Well, if I go to Nick's and go to 52nd Street, I might hear 'Mean to Me' or one of those kinds of songs, but there are other songs that you don't hear any more. I ought to preserve them." So, in addition to preserving the old Dixieland warhorses . . . which Eddie Condon, by the way, was tired of playing and didn't want to record because he used to say, "They're bleeding, they're bloody, we play them every night." So he really liked what I wanted to do, the old pop tunes of the twenties and thirties. Even in my years at Decca later, if you look at the repertoire I made of pop artists, I always chose tunes of that vintage so that the songs would live. If you do them by a good artist, they could live forever. So to do a Bobby Hackett "Embraceable You" or some of the great things I did with Billie—it preserves the tune, and other artists pick up on it. So that was the idea that I wanted to put in the Commodore catalogue.

Q: In terms of the repertoire, you mention the standards. Of course, there's also a lot of blues in there.

MG: There were two reasons for doing blues. I liked blues, and the customers liked blues. But I always knew, if you get to the end of a date and you're running out of time . . . See, after the three hours you have to pay overtime, and I figured if I'm stuck in the last ten minutes, I could always do a blues in ten minutes, in two or three takes, no problem, to make sure I had four sides. In addition to that, to me, blues were PD, or a Commodore publication, and I didn't pay it to myself, so I would save two cents on the record. And blues is good to have. The guys can stretch a little and blow. It's always an easy way to get in a fourth side.

Q: By the way, Mosaic usually does things, where possible, in chronological order, if you know the chronological order. Now, with the Commodores, you've asked us to do the master take, and then alternate number and alternate number 2, etc. Why is that?

MG: When I started to make the first recordings, there was no tape, and there were no 16-inch safety discs at 33⅓. The guys would make Take 1, and I'd say, "Let's make another one." They'd make Take 2. Etc. But what happened is, if I liked the second attempt, if it was a complete take and better, when it came to the end I would say "Mark that '-1'." And supposing I did it three times. I could only afford to process two of them. So even though there was a "-3", I wouldn't process it; I would mark that "-2." The number 1 then was lost forever because it wasn't processed at the factory, and it disappeared.

Now, you have to realize, when you cut a record in those years, they would send it to the factory to be processed to put the nitrate on or whatever it is, so the silver could adhere, and put it in the electrolytic baths . . . It would take anywhere from two to four weeks for me to get a test pressing back as a customer of the company, to decide on which choice I wanted to put on my release when it came out on a 78. Now, the reason I didn't number them numerically the way I recorded them was because I wanted to have a clue when it came back to me four weeks later, on which one I liked the afternoon I made it. So the one that was marked "1" was the one that I liked on the session. The one that was marked "2" was my second choice. Now, when I wanted to put it out and I got the pressings in, I might have liked a solo in "2" better, or the overall performance might have hit me better, so when I put the record out I used the second choice rather than the choice I marked "1" on the day of the session.

To me it was like, say, your mother baked pies, and the weather was good weather. She would take the pie and she'd put it on the windowsill to cool off, and then she'd put the next one on the windowsill to cool off. You would number them the way I liked them the day of the session, because that's when your memory is fresh from the performances. But sometimes they came back and you liked the other one better. Or you heard a goof that you didn't notice when you assigned the number. Even though it had a good solo, it had a goof that marked it down. So when I reissued them later, when I was putting out alternates, to me, as a record collector, if I remembered "Jada" by Condon and Bobby Hackett the way it came out, by the time I played it through the years I'd know that record cold. All I had to do was play it, and it would all come back to me. Now, when I put out the alternate choice, suppose that was "-1" and the one that came out was "-2." I want to hear the one I brought out originally first so that I could compare the solos and see how they changed. If I play the alternate first, it wipes that out! So I decided, for discographers, to number them. The original I didn't put a number on, but when the alternate came out, I would mark it "#2," and if we had third ones now, the "#3," "#4" or whatever. So it's just a question of how I reviewed them when I made them. But not necessarily the way I recorded them.

Today, of course, when everything is on tape, you have them in the order they were recorded. But still, if the #2 take was used to come out, I think that the alternate, when it comes out, should have after the title "#2." The master number stays the same. It's the number after the title which shows you the order of release. That's it.

Miles Davis

Miles: The Autobiography (1989; with Quincy Troupe) is hardly an ingratiating self-portrait, but it's fascinating in its agenda and compelling in its presentation. *Another excerpt from this book, about Charlie Parker, appears on p. 577.*

Most of what had happened up until this time in small group playing had come down from Louis Armstrong through Lester Young and Coleman Hawkins to Dizzy and Bird, and bebop had basically come from that. What everybody was playing in 1958 had mostly come out of bebop. *Birth of the Cool* had gone somewhat in another direction, but it had mainly come out of what Duke Ellington and Billy Strayhorn had already done; it just made the music "whiter," so that white people could digest it better. And then the other records I made, like "Walkin'" and "Blue 'n' Boogie"—which the critics called hard bop—had only gone back to the blues and some of the things that Bird and Dizzy had done. It was great music, well played and everything, but the musical ideas and concepts had mostly been already done; it just had a little more space in it.

Of all the stuff I had done with a small group, what we did on *Modern Jazz Giants* came closest to what I wanted to do now, that kind of stretched-out sound we got there on "Bags' Groove," "The Man I Love," "Swing Spring." Now, in bebop, the music had a lot of notes in it. Diz and Bird played a lot of real fast notes and chord changes because that's the way they heard everything; that's the way their voices were: fast, up in the upper register. Their concept of music was *more* rather than *less.*

I personally wanted to cut the notes down, because I've always felt that most musicians play way too much for too long (although I put up with it with Trane because he played so good and I used to just love hearing him play). But I didn't hear music like that. I heard it in the middle and lower registers, and so did Coltrane. We had to do something suited for what we did best, for our own voices.

I wanted the music this new group would play to be freer, more modal, more African or Eastern, and less Western. I wanted them to go beyond themselves. See, if you put a musician in a place where he has to do something different from what he does all the time, then he can do that—but he's got to think differently in order to do it. He has to use his imagination, be more creative, more innovative; he's got to take more risks. He's got to play above what he knows—far above it—and what that might lead to might take him above the place where he's been playing all along, to the new place where he finds himself right now—and to the next place he's going and even above that! So then he'll be freer, will expect things differently, will anticipate and know something different is coming down. I've always told the musicians in my band to play what they *know* and then play *above that.* Because then anything can happen, and that's where great art and music happens.

Another thing you have to remember is that this was December 1957, not December 1944, and things were different, sounds were different, people didn't hear things the same as they heard it back then. It's always been that way; every time has its own style, and what Bird and Diz did was the style for that time—and it was great. But now it was time for something different.

If any group was going to change the concept of music and take it someplace altogether different, a new place, forward and fresh, then I felt this group was it. I couldn't wait for us to start playing together so we could get used to what each musician would bring to the mix, get used to listening to each other's voices in that mix, know each other's strengths and weaknesses. It always takes a while for everybody to get used to one another—that's why I've always taken a new band out on the road for a while before I take them into the studio.

The idea I had for this working sextet was to keep what we already had going with Trane, Red, Joe, Paul, and myself and add the blues voice of Cannonball Adderley into this mixture and then to stretch everything out. I felt that Cannonball's blues-rooted alto sax up against Trane's harmonic, chordal way of playing, his more free-form approach, would create a new kind of feeling, a new kind of sound, because Coltrane's voice was already going in a new direction. And then I wanted to give that musical mixture more space, using the concepts I had picked up from what Ahmad Jamal did. I heard my trumpet voice kind of floating over and cutting through all of this mixture, and I felt that if we could do it right, the music would have all the tension up in it.

In this group, everybody had played together for over two years, except for Cannonball. But one voice can change the entire way a band hears itself, can change the whole rhythm, the whole timing of a band, even if everyone else had been playing together forever. It's a whole new thing when you add or take away a voice.

We went out on tour in late December 1957, around Christmas time, starting at the Sutherland Lounge in Chicago. I've always tried to be in Chicago around Christmas so I can get together with my family. My brother

Vernon comes up from East St. Louis, and my children, who live in St. Louis, all get together at my sister Dorothy's house in Chicago, along with some guys I grew up with who live in Chicago.

We'd all get together and drink and eat for a week or so. You know, have a ball. When we first opened with the sextet at the Sutherland, my old high school friend Darnell, who used to play piano, drove his city bus all the way from Peoria, Illinois, and parked it outside our hotel for three days! Every time we would play Chicago he would come on up. My friend Boonie used to get me the best barbecue in town, because being from East St. Louis, which is a barbecue town, I've always been a freak for good barbecue and chitlings, too. I really love great black cooking, collard greens and candied yams and cornbread and black-eyed peas and southern fried chicken—all of it—and with some bad hot sauce off to the side.

Right from the beginning the tour was just a motherfucker. BANG! We hit and tore up the fucking place and that's when I knew it was going to be something else. That first night in Chicago, we started off playing the blues, and Cannonball was just standing there with his mouth open, listening to Trane playing this way-out shit on a blues. He asked me what we were playing and I told him, "the blues."

He says, "Well, I ain't never heard no blues played like that!" See, no matter how many times he played a tune, Trane would always find ways to play it different every night. I told Trane after the set to take Cannonball in the kitchen and show him what he was doing. He did, but we had substituted so many things in the twelve-bar mode that if you weren't listening when it started off, where the soloist began, then when you *did* start to pay attention, you might not know what had happened. Cannonball had told me that what Trane was playing *sounded* like the blues, but that it really wasn't, it was something else altogether. That just fucked him up because *Cannonball* was a blues player.

But Cannonball caught on quick, just like snapping your fingers, that's how fast he picked things up. He was like a sponge; he just absorbed everything. With the blues thing, I should have told him that was just the way Trane played—far out—because Cannonball was the only one in the group who hadn't played with him. But once Cannonball caught on to what was happening, he was right in there, playing his ass off. He and Trane were very different players, but both of them were great. When Cannonball first joined the band, everyone liked him right away because he was this big, jovial guy, always laughing and real nice, a gentleman, and smart as they come.

After he'd been with us a while and then after Trane came back, the sound of the band just kept getting thicker and thicker, almost like when a woman uses too much makeup. Because of the chemistry and the way people were playing off each other, everybody started playing above what they knew almost from the beginning. Trane would play some weird, great shit, and Cannonball would take it in the other direction, and I would put my sound right down the middle or float over it, or whatever. And then I might play real fast, or buzzzzz, like Freddie Webster. This would take Trane someplace else, and he would come back with other different shit and so would Cannonball. And then Paul's anchoring all this creative tension between the horns, and Red's laying down his light, hip shit, and Philly Joe pushing everything with that hip shit he was playing and then sending us all off again with them hip-de-dip, slick rim shots that were so bad, them "Philly licks." Man, that was too hip and bad. Everybody was laying all kinds of slick shit on everyone. And I was telling them things like, "Don't leave that F until the last beat. You'll be able to play the mode five beats more than you would if you would leave it in like four beats. You leave it on the last bar, you know, and you accent the bar." And they would listen. It would be slicker than slick.

Trane was the loudest, fastest saxophonist I've ever heard. He could play real fast and real loud at the same time and that's very difficult to do. Because when most players play loud, they lock themselves. I've seen many saxophonists get messed up trying to play like that. But Trane could do it and he was phenomenal. It was like he was possessed when he put that horn in his mouth. He was so passionate—fierce—and yet so quiet and gentle when he wasn't playing. A sweet guy.

He scared me one time while we were in California when he wanted to go to the dentist to get a tooth put in. Trane could play two notes all at once and I thought his missing tooth was the cause of it. I thought it gave him his sound. So when he told me he was going to the dentist to get the tooth put in, I almost panicked. I told him that I had called a rehearsal for the same time that he was going. I asked him if he could postpone his dental appointment. "Naw," he said, "naw, man, I can't make the rehearsal; I'm going to the dentist." I asked him what kind of replacement he was going to get and he says, "A permanent one." So I try to talk him into getting a removable one that he can take out every night before he plays. He looks at me like I'm crazy. He goes to the dentist and comes back looking like a piano, he was grinning so much. At the gig that night—I think it was at the Blackhawk—I play my first solo and go back by Philly Joe and wait for Trane to play, almost in tears because I know he's fucked himself up. But when he ripped off them runs like he always did, man, talk about a motherfucker being relieved!

Trane never wrote anything down when he was with my band. All he did was just start off playing. We used to talk a lot about music at rehearsals and on the way to gigs. I would show him a lot of shit, and he would always listen and do it. I'd say, "Trane, here are some chords, but don't play them like they are all the time, you know? Start in the middle sometimes and don't forget that you can play them up in thirds. So that means you got eighteen, nineteen different things to play in two bars." He would sit there, his eyes wide open, soaking up everything. Trane was an innovator, and you have to say the right thing to people like that. That's why I'd tell him to begin in the middle, because that's the way his head worked anyway. He was looking to be challenged, and if you brought the shit to him wrong he wasn't going to listen. But Trane was the only player who could play those chords I gave him without them sounding like chords.

After the gig he would go back to his hotel room and practice while everybody else was hanging out. He would practice for hours after he had just got through playing three sets. And later in 1960, after I gave him a soprano saxophone that I got from a woman I knew in Paris, an antique dealer, it had an effect on his tenor playing. Before he got that soprano, he was still playing like Dexter Gordon, Eddie "Lockjaw" Davis, Sonny Stitt, and Bird. After he got that horn, his style changed. After that, he didn't sound like nobody but himself. He found out that he could play lighter and faster on the soprano than he could on the tenor. And this really turned him on, because he couldn't do the things on tenor that he could on alto, because a soprano is a straight horn, and since he liked the lower register, he found he could also think and hear better with the soprano than he could with the tenor. When he played the soprano, after a while it sounded almost like a human voice, wailing.

But as much as I liked Trane we didn't hang out much once we left the bandstand because we had different styles. Before, it was because he was deep into heroin, and I had just come out of that. Now, he was clean and didn't hardly ever hang out, but would go back to his hotel room to practice. He had always been serious about music and always practiced a lot. But now it was almost like he was on some kind of mission. He used to tell me that he had messed up enough, had wasted too much time and not given enough attention to his own personal life, his family, and, most of all, to his playing. So he was only really concerned about playing his music and growing as a musician. That's all he thought about. He couldn't be seduced by a woman's beauty because he had already been seduced by the beauty of music, and he was loyal to his wife. Whereas for me, after the music was through, I was out the door seeing what pretty lady I was going to be with that night. Cannonball and I would sit and talk and hang out sometimes when I wasn't with some woman. Philly and I were still friends, but he was always running down that dope, him and Paul and Red. But we were all close and everybody got along real good together.

Back in New York, Cannonball, who had signed a deal to do a record for Blue Note, asked me to play on the date, which I did as a favor. The record was called "Something Else" and was very nice. I wanted to get my group into the studio, and in April, we recorded "Billy Boy," "Straight, No Chaser," "Milestones," "Two Bass Hit," "Sid's Ahead," and "Dr. Jackle" (listed as "Dr. Jekyll") for the album *Milestones* on Columbia. I played piano on "Sid's Ahead" because Red got mad at me when I was trying to tell him something and left. But I loved the way the band sounded on this record and I knew that we had something special. Trane and Cannon were really playing their asses off and by then were really used to each other.

This was the first record where I started to really write in the modal form and on "Milestones," the title track, I really used that form. Modal music is seven notes off each scale, each note. It's a scale off each note, you know, a minor note. The composer-arranger George Russell used to say that in modal music C is where F should be. He says that the whole piano starts at F. What I had learned about the modal form is that when you play this way, go in this direction, you can go on forever. You don't have to worry about changes and shit like that. You can do more with the musical line. The challenge here, when you work in the modal way, is to see how inventive you can become melodically. It's not like when you base stuff on chords, and you know at the end of thirty-two bars that the chords have run out and there's nothing to do but repeat what you've done with variations. I was moving away from that and into more melodic ways of doing things. And in the modal way I saw all kinds of possibilities.

After Red Garland walked out on me, I found a new piano player named Bill Evans. I wasn't mad at Red, but I had moved past the point where he could contribute what I wanted in the sound of the band. I needed a piano player who was into the modal thing, and Bill Evans was. I met Bill Evans through George Russell, whom Bill had studied with. I knew George from the days back at Gil's house on 55th Street. As I was getting deeper into the modal thing, I asked George if he knew a piano player who could play the kinds of things I wanted, and he recommended Bill.

I had gotten into the modal thing from watching a performance by the Ballet Africaine from Guinea. I was seeing Frances Taylor again; she was living in New York now and dancing in a show. I had run into her on 52nd Street and was real happy to see her. She went to all the dance performances, and I would go with her. Anyway, we went to this performance by the Ballet Africaine and it just fucked me up what they was doing, the steps and all them flying leaps and shit. And when I first heard them play the finger piano that night and sing this song with this other guy dancing, man, that was some powerful stuff. It was beautiful. And their rhythm! The rhythm of the dancers was something. I was counting off while I was watching them. They were so acrobatic. They had one drummer watching them dance, doing their flips and shit, and when they jumped he would play DA DA DA DA POW! in this bad rhythm. He would hit it when they would fall. And man, he was catching everybody that did anything. The other drummers got them, too. So they would do rhythms like 5/4 and 6/8 and 4/4, and the rhythm would be changing and popping. That's the thing, that secret, inner thing that they had. It's African. I knew I couldn't do it from just watching them dance because I'm not African, but I loved what they were doing. I didn't want to copy that, but I got a concept from it.

When Bill Evans—we sometimes called him Moe—first got with the band, he was so quiet, man. One day, just to see what he could do, I told him, "Bill, you know what you have to do, don't you, to be in this band?"

He looked at me all puzzled and shit and shook his head and said, "No, Miles, what do I have to do?"

I said, "Bill, now you know we all brothers and shit and everybody's in this thing together and so what I came up with for you is that you got to make it with everybody, you know what I mean? You got to fuck the band." Now, I was kidding, but Bill was real serious, like Trane.

He thought about it for about fifteen minutes and then came back and told me, "Miles, I thought about what you said and I just can't do it, I just can't do that. I'd like to please everyone and make everyone happy here, but I just can't do that."

I looked at him and smiled and said, "My man!" And then he knew I was teasing.

Bill brought a great knowledge of classical music, people like Rachmaninoff and Ravel. He was the one who told me to listen to the Italian pianist Arturo Michelangeli, so I did and fell in love with his playing. Bill had this quiet fire that I loved on piano. The way he approached it, the sound he got was like crystal notes or sparkling water cascading down from some clear waterfall. I had to change the way the band sounded again for Bill's style by playing different tunes, softer ones at first. Bill played underneath the rhythm and I liked that, the way he played scales with the band. Red's playing had carried the rhythm but Bill underplayed it and for what I was doing now with the modal thing, I liked what Bill was doing better. I still liked Red and brought him back on a few occasions, but I mostly liked him when we were going through that Ahmad thing. Bill could play a little like that Ahmad thing, too, although when he did, he sounded a little wild.

In the spring of 1958, we moved from the Cafe Bohemia where we had played for two years, to the Village Vanguard, a club owned and run by a guy named Max Gordon. The crowds that were coming to see us over at the Bohemia just moved on over to the Vanguard and there were full houses there, too, as long as we stayed there. I moved over to the Vanguard because Max gave me more money than the Bohemia. Before I opened he had to give me $1,000 front money in cash or I wouldn't play.

But the most important thing that happened to me in the spring of 1958 was Frances Taylor coming back into my life. Man, she was a wonderful woman and I loved just being with her. I cut everyone else loose and was just with her during this time. We were so compatible—I'm a Gemini and she's a Libra. I thought she was just outta sight. She was kind of tall, honey brown, beautiful, soft smooth skin, sensitive, artistic. An elegant, gracious, graceful person. I'm making her sound perfect, right? Well, she damn near was. Everybody else loved her, too. I know Marlon Brando did, and Quincy Jones, who was on the scene back then, too. Quincy even gave her a ring, and he still don't know what I know. Frances and I started living together in my apartment up on Tenth Avenue, and everywhere we went we stopped traffic.

I turned in my Mercedes-Benz for a white Ferrari convertible that cost me something like $8,000, which was considered a whole lot of money back then. Now, here we are riding around town in this spectacular car. A real black motherfucker like me with this stunningly beautiful woman! When she got out of the bad-ass car she seemed to be all legs, because she had these long, gorgeous, dancer's legs and she carried herself with that dancer's carriage. Man, it was something, people stopping and looking with their mouths hanging open and everything.

I was sharp as a tack every time I went out in public and so was Frances. *Life* magazine even put me in their international issue as a black person who was doing something good for his people. That was all right. But I always wondered why they didn't put me in the issue that comes out over here.

Frances was from Chicago and I was also from the Midwest, so that might have had something to do with us hitting it off so quick, because we never did have to explain a lot of shit. And she was black and that helped a lot, too, although I ain't never been into a racial thing about the women I am with; if they're cool, they're cool, no matter what color they are. I'm the same way about white men, too.

Frances was great for me because she settled me down and took me out of the streets and let me concentrate more on my music. I was basically a loner and she was, too. She used to always say, "We rehearsed for this for four years, Miles, so let's make it work." I loved Frances so much that for the first time in my life I found myself jealous. I remember I hit her once when she came home and told me some shit about Quincy Jones being handsome. Before I realized what had happened, I had knocked her down and she ran out of the apartment over to Monte Kay and Diahann Carroll's place buck naked. Then she got some clothes and went over to Gil Evans's and spent the night there because she was afraid I was going to knock down Diahann and Monte's door and hit her again. Gil called to tell me that she was there and safe, I told her not to ever mention Quincy Jones's name to me again, and she never did.

We had our verbal arguments just like all couples have, but that was the first time I had hit her—though it wouldn't be the last. Every time I hit her, I felt bad because a lot of it really wasn't her fault but had to do with me being temperamental and jealous. I mean, I never thought I was jealous until I was with Frances. Before, I didn't care what a woman did; it didn't matter to me because I was so into my music. Now it did and it was something that was new for me, hard for me to understand.

She was a star and on her way to being a superstar, probably the premier black female dancer when she went with me. She was getting all these offers to dance when she won Best Dancer for what she did in *West Side Story* on Broadway. But I made her get out of that because I wanted her at home with me. Later when Jerome Robbins personally asked her to do the movie version of *West Side Story,* I wouldn't let her do that. Or *Golden Boy* with Sammy Davis, Jr., who asked her himself when we were playing in Philadelphia. He was doing the tryouts the next morning and he asked her to come down. The next day at 8 A.M., we were on the turnpike in my Ferrari on our way back to New York. That was my answer.

I just wanted her with me *all* the time. But she would argue about that shit with me, tell me that she had a career, too, that she was an artist, too, but I just didn't want to hear no shit that was going to keep us apart. After a while, she stopped talking about it and started teaching a dance class for people like Diahann Carroll and Johnny Mathis. I didn't mind her doing that because she was home with me every night.

Frances had been married before and had a little boy named Jean-Pierre, who was staying with her parents, Maceo and Ellen, in Chicago while she pursued her dancing career. When we started living together, her father called one day from Chicago and wanted to speak with me. He beat around the bush for a while before he got to the point of asking when I was going to marry Frances. He said, "Well, Miles, it seems to me if you settle for something long enough and live with it and taste it, you know how the goodies are, you know whether you want to buy it or not. So what about you and Frances, what y'all gonna do, when y'all gonna get married?"

I liked her father; he was a very nice man. But I knew how he was and we talked man to man. I knew he was concerned about his daughter because that's the kind of person he was, so I said, "It's none of your fucking business, Maceo. Frances don't mind, so what you got to do with it, man? We all grown, you know!"

He didn't say nothing else about it for a while after that, but he would bring it up from time to time and I would say the same thing until we got married, later.

Frances was dancing in *Porgy and Bess* at City Center when I first saw her again, so I went to see that a lot and that's where I got the idea to do the music on the *Porgy and Bess* album that Gil and I did in the summer of 1958. Being with Frances was a big influence on me in another way outside of music; going to see her dance all the time I really got interested in that and the theater because we started going to see a lot of plays. I even wrote a song for her called "Fran Dance" that we recorded on that "Green Dolphin Street" album. After Frances finished with *Porgy and Bess* she was in *Mr. Wonderful* with Sammy Davis, Jr.

By now people were starting to talk about "the Miles Davis Mystique." I don't know *where* that shit came from, but it was around everywhere. Even the music critics had gotten off my back by this time and many of them were calling me "Charlie Parker's successor."

The first important record the sextet made with Bill Evans in the band was the one we did in May 1958, *Jazz Track,* when we recorded "Green Dolphin Street," "Stella by Starlight," "Love for Sale," and "Fran Dance." Philly Joe was gone again by the time we recorded this and had been replaced by Jimmy Cobb, who had worked with me once when he replaced Art Taylor for a minute at the Cafe Bohemia. Everyone was tired of Philly's junkie shit by now and we just couldn't handle it any longer. He finally quit and started his own band that sometimes had Red Garland in it. I would miss that "Philly thing," that "Philly lick" on the rim. But Jimmy was a good drummer who brought his own thing to the sound of the group. And since I played with the rhythm section, played off what they did, I knew Paul and Bill and Jimmy were going to be reacting to and playing off that, off their thing together. I was going to miss Philly, but I knew I was going to like Jimmy, too.

Columbia put all the "Green Dolphin Street" recordings on the other side of the music score I had done for Louis Malle's film, *Elevator to the Gallows,* and released it over here under the title of *On Green Dolphin Street*. But that was the first recording the new group made as a band. After that, in June, I did a guest appearance on an album of the Frenchman Michel Legrand's big orchestra date that he did for Columbia. Coltrane, Paul Chambers, and Bill Evans also played on that album. Then we played around New York at the Vanguard and played up at the Newport Jazz Festival.

I came back and went into the studio with Gil to make *Porgy and Bess.* We started in late July and worked over into the middle of August. I didn't use

Trane and Cannon on this album because they would have been too dominant in the saxophone section. All I wanted was straight tones. Couldn't nobody match their sounds, so I just went with guys who played those plain-Jane sounds for those plain-Jane songs. I also didn't use Bill Evans because we didn't use a piano. But I did use Paul and Jimmy Cobb and I brought in Philly Joe to do a couple of things. The rest of the musicians were mostly studio musicians and one of them, the tuba-player Bill Barber, had been on *Birth of the Cool.* That was real good to do, because I had to get close to a human-voice sound in some places. That was hard, but I did it. Gil's arrangements were great. He wrote an arrangement for me to play on "I Loves You, Porgy" and he wrote a scale that I was supposed to play. No chords. He had used two chords for the other voicing, and so my passage of scales with those two chords gives you a lot of freedom and space to hear other things.

Besides Ravel and a whole lot of others, Bill Evans had turned me on to Aram Khachaturian, a Russian-Armenian composer. I had been listening to him and what intrigued me about him were all those different scales he used. Classical composers, at least some of them, have been writing like this for a long time, but not many jazz musicians have. The musicians were giving me tunes with chords all the time, and at the time I didn't want to play them. The music was too thick.

Anyway, we did *Porgy and Bess* and then we went down to play the Showboat in Philadelphia, and that's where a narcotics policeman tried to bust Jimmy Cobb and Coltrane for drugs, but everybody was clean. One time they even came fucking with me during this engagement, looking for drugs. I just pulled down my shorts and told the motherfuckers to look up my asshole since they couldn't find no shit no place else. Man, them Philadelphia police were a bitch, always fucking with you; they were some of the most corrupt motherfuckers on the planet, and racist, too.

But things were starting to go bad in the group. After about seven months, Bill wanted to leave because he hated all the traveling and he wanted to do his own thing. Cannonball was talking about the same thing, and wanted to get his old group back together again, and even Coltrane was beginning to feel the same way. In Cannon's case, he didn't like being the road manager, paying off the guys and all. But the reason he was doing that was because he had a good head for that kind of thing and I really trusted him. Also I gave him more money for doing this so he was making more than everyone else except me. When he first joined the band, he said he would stay for a year and that year was up in October 1958. I convinced him to stay on for a little while longer and he agreed, but Harold Lovett and I really had to talk to him to keep him.

Some of the things that caused Bill to leave the band hurt me, like that shit some black people put on him about being a white boy in our band. Many blacks felt that since I had the top small group in jazz and was paying the most money that I should have a black piano player. Now, I don't go for that kind of shit; I have always just wanted the best players in my group and I don't care about whether they're black, white, blue, red, or yellow. As long as they can play what I want that's it. But I know this stuff got up under Bill's skin and made him feel bad. Bill was a very sensitive person and it didn't take much to set him off. Then a lot of people were saying he didn't play fast enough and hard enough for them, that he was too delicate. So on top of all this shit was the thing about traveling and wanting to form his own group and play his own music, which was where Coltrane and Cannonball were moving.

We were playing the same program every night and a lot of it was standards, or my music. I know they wanted to play their own stuff and establish their own musical identity. I didn't blame them for feeling that way. But we had the best group in the business and it was *my* band and so I wanted to keep it together for as long as I could. That was a problem, but it happens with most bands after a while. People just outgrow each other, like I did with Bird, and they have to move on.

Bill left the band in November 1958 and went down to Louisiana to live with his brother. Then he came back after a while and formed his own group. After a while he got Scott LaFaro on bass and Paul Motian on drums and he became very popular with that group, winning a number of Grammy Awards. He was a great little piano player, but I don't think he ever sounded as good after that as he did when he played with me. It's a strange thing about a lot of white players—not all, just most—that after they make it in a black group they always go and play with all white guys no matter how good the black guys treated them. Bill did that, and I'm not saying he could have gotten any black guys any better than Scott and Paul, I'm just telling what I've seen happen over and over again.

I asked Red Garland to replace Bill until I could find a replacement, and he stayed three months until he left to form his own trio. While he was with me Red went on the road with us for a while and then we came back and played Town Hall, and even Philly Joe played that gig because I think Jimmy Cobb was sick. It was like a reunion and everybody played their asses off. But now that we were going on the road, I had to deal with Trane, who now really wanted to leave. He was getting comfortable with himself, playing better and with more confidence than he had ever played. Plus he was happy and staying home and gaining weight. I even started kidding him about his weight, but those kinds of things didn't even cross his mind, you know, things like how much he weighed or clothes and shit like that. All he cared about was music and how he sounded playing. I was concerned because he was eating a lot of sweets in place of shooting drugs, so I offered to sell him some gym equipment so he could get his weight down.

Trane used to call me "the teacher" and it was hard for him to bring up that he wanted to leave; I would find it out from other people he had told. But he did bring it up finally and we made a compromise: I turned him on to Harold Lovett as a manager to handle his financial affairs. And then Harold got him a recording contract with Nesuhi Ertegun at Atlantic Records, who had always loved his playing since Trane had first come into the group. Trane had been doing some things for Prestige as a leader, which I turned him on to, but as usual, Bob Weinstock wasn't paying no real money. Harold set up a publishing company for Trane (he kept it until his death, in 1967, and he also kept Harold Lovett as his manager). I had thought if Trane was going out on his own then he needed to learn something about business and be involved with someone he could trust. To keep Trane in the band longer, I asked Jack Whittemore, my agent, to get bookings for Trane's group whenever we weren't playing, and he did. So by the beginning of 1959, Trane was in a good position to get his own independent career on the road and that's what he began to do. If he wasn't playing with me, he was always playing somewhere as a headliner, fronting his own band.

Cannonball was doing the same thing, so in 1959 we had three bandleaders in the group, and things started getting difficult. By now Trane had found his drummer in Elvin Jones, my old friend from Detroit, and he was constantly raving about him; but I already knew Elvin was bad. And Cannon was playing with his brother, Nat, so both of them knew where they were going. I felt good for them and bad for me, because I could see the writing on the wall, and I knew soon it was going to be over. I'd be lying if I said that that didn't make me sad, because I really loved playing with this band and I think it was the best small band of all time, or at least the best I had heard up until then.

I found a new piano player in February; his name was Wynton Kelly. There was another piano player that I liked and his name was Joe Zawinul (he would play with me later). But it was Wynton who came into the band. Wynton was from the West Indies, from Jamaica, and had played with Dizzy for a minute. I loved the way Wynton played, because he was a combination of Red Garland and Bill Evans; he could play almost anything. Plus, he could play behind a soloist like a motherfucker, man. Cannonball and Trane loved him, and so did I.

Wynton joined us just before I was going into the studio to make *Kind of Blue,* but I had already planned that album around the piano playing of Bill Evans, who had agreed to play on it with us. We went into the studio to record *Kind of Blue* on the first or second day of March 1959. We had the sextet of Trane, Jimmy Cobb, Paul, Cannon, myself, and Wynton Kelly, but he played on only one tune: "Freddie Freeloader." That song was named after this black guy I knew who was always seeing what he could get from you free, and he was always around the jazz scene. Bill Evans played on the rest of the tunes.

We made *Kind of Blue* at two recording sessions—one in March and the other one in April. In between, Gil Evans and I took a big orchestra and did a television show with a lot of the music on *Miles Ahead*.

Kind of Blue also came out of the modal thing I started on *Milestones.* This time I added some other kind of sound I remembered from being back in Arkansas, when we were walking home from church and they were playing these bad gospels. So that kind of feeling came back to me and I started remembering what that music sounded like and felt like. That feeling is what I was trying to get close to. That feeling had got in my creative blood, my imagination, and I had forgotten it was there. I wrote this blues that tried to get back to that feeling I had when I was six years old, walking with my cousin along that dark Arkansas road. So I wrote about five bars of that and I recorded it and added a kind of running sound into the mix, because that was the only way I could get in the sound of the finger piano. But you write something and then guys play off it and take it someplace else through their creativity and imagination, and you just miss where you thought you wanted to go. I was trying to do one thing and ended up doing something else.

I didn't write out the music for *Kind of Blue,* but brought in sketches for what everybody was supposed to play because I wanted a lot of spontaneity in the playing, just like I thought was in the interplay between those dancers and those drummers and that finger piano player with the Ballet Africaine. Everything was a first take, which indicates the level everyone was playing on. It was beautiful. Some people went around saying that Bill was cocomposer of the music on *Kind of Blue.* That isn't true; it's all mine and the concept was mine. What he did do was turn me on to some classical composers, and they influenced me. But the first time Bill saw any of that music was when I gave him a sketch to look at just like everyone else. We didn't even have rehearsals for that music—we'd only had about five or six in the last two years—because I had great musicians in that band and that's the only way that can work.

I had Bill playing on *Kind of Blue* in a minor mode. Bill was the kind of player that when you played with him, if he started something, he would end it, but he would take it a little bit farther. You subconsciously knew this, but it always put a little tension up in everyone's playing, which was good. And because we were into Ravel (especially his Concerto for the Left Hand and Orchestra) and Rachmaninoff (Concerto No. 4), all of that was up in there somewhere. When I tell people that I missed what I was trying to do on

Kind of Blue, that I missed getting the exact sound of the African finger piano up in that sound, they just look at me like I'm crazy. Everyone said that record was a masterpiece—and I loved it too—and so they just feel I'm trying to put them on. But that's what I was trying to do on most of that album, particularly on "All Blues" and "So What." I just missed.

I remember when Billie Holiday died in July 1959. I didn't know Billie all that well; we didn't hang out or nothing like that. Billie loved my son, Gregory. She used to think he was cute. I knew that she and her husband weren't getting along because she said to me once, "Miles, I told him he could leave me alone. He could have our house, everything, but just leave me alone." But that was all I remember her telling me that was personal. She did tell me she liked a man built like Roy Campanella, the old Brooklyn Dodgers catcher, because she thought that kind of man had that sexual thrust that she liked when she was making love. She loved those short, wide, big legs, low ass; built like a buffalo. From what she told me, Billie was really into sex when that dope and alcohol didn't kill her sexual drive.

I remember her being a very warm, nice woman, and she had that smooth, light-brown-skinned Indian look before drugs destroyed her face. She and Carmen McRae reminded me of the way my mother looked, Carmen more so than Billie. Billie was a beautiful woman before all the alcohol and drugs wore her down.

The last time I saw her alive was when she came down to Birdland where I was playing in early 1959. She asked me to give her some money to buy some heroin and I gave her what I had. I think it was about a hundred dollars. Her husband, John (I forget his last name), kept her on the stuff so he could control her. He was an opium user himself. He used to be telling me to come and lay on the sofa with him and smoke some opium. I never did it with him, never smoked opium once in my life. He kept all the drugs and gave them to Billie whenever he felt like it; this was his way of keeping her in line. John was one of those slick hustling street cats from Harlem who'd do anything for money.

"Miles," Billie had said, "that motherfucker John done run off with all my money. So can you loan me some to get a fix? I need it real bad." So I gave her what I had because she was looking real bad by this time, worn out, worn down, and haggard around the face and all. Thin. Mouth sagging at both corners. She was scratching a lot. Before she was such a well-built woman, but now she had lost all that weight and her face was bloated from all that drinking. Man, I felt bad for her.

Whenever I'd go see her, I always asked Billie to sing "I Loves You, Porgy," because when she sang "don't let him touch me with his hot hands," you could almost feel that shit she was feeling. It was beautiful and sad the way she sang that. Everybody loved Billie.

She and Bird died the same way. They both had pneumonia. One time down in Philadelphia they had kept Billie in jail overnight for drugs. Maybe it was a couple of days, I don't remember. But I know they had her in jail. So she's in there sweating and then being cold and stuff. When you are trying to break a habit, you get hot and cold, and if you don't get the proper medical treatment, you go right into pneumonia. And that's what happened with Billie and Bird. When somebody gets backed up with that dope—using, stopping, using, stopping—and then when it gets into your system, you die. It just kills you and that's what happened to Billie and Bird; they just gave in to all the shit they was doing. Got tired of everything and just checked out.

Except for that, in 1959 I was feeling on top of the world. The new sextet with Wynton Kelly on piano opened at Birdland to packed crowds. People like Ava Gardner and Elizabeth Taylor were in the audience every night and coming back to the dressing room to say hello. Coltrane went into the studio and recorded *Giant Steps* around this time, about two weeks after the *Kind of Blue* last session, and he did the same thing that I did with the music I recorded on *Kind of Blue:* he came into the studio with sketches of the music that none of the musicians on that date had ever heard. That was a compliment to me. We also played the Apollo Theatre in Harlem, as one of the headliners, then we went to San Francisco and spent about three weeks at the Blackhawk, which was jammed every night with overflowing audiences and lines that wrapped around the corners.

It was in San Francisco that Trane gave an interview to a writer named Russ Wilson and told him that he was seriously thinking about leaving the group, which Wilson wrote in the papers the next day. Then, the guy went on to say who was going to be replacing Trane: Jimmy Heath. Jimmy Heath did replace Trane when he left, but I didn't think it was none of Trane's business to be telling the writer what I had told Trane in private. This made me real mad, and I told Trane not to do it anymore. I mean, what had I ever done to front him off like that? I told him I had done everything for him, had treated him like my brother and here he was doing this kind of shit to me and telling a white boy all about my business. I told him, if you want to leave, leave, but tell me before you start running around telling everybody else that shit and don't be putting it out there who's going to replace you. Everyone was praising Trane now, and I know it was hard on him not to go out on his own. But he was moving farther and farther away from the group. When we played the Playboy Jazz Festival in Chicago that summer, he didn't come with us because he had other commitments. But Cannonball played his ass off, alternating his solos with mine. Everybody was playing great that day in early August and when I got back to New York everybody was talking about how great we sounded even without Trane.

In late August we opened up at Birdland again to standing-room-only crowds. Pee Wee Marquette, the famous midget emcee, who was the mascot at Birdland, was introducing Ava Gardner from the bandstand every night, and she was throwing kisses and coming backstage and kissing me back there. One time Pee Wee came back and said Ava was looking for me out front, wanted to come back and speak to me. So I asked Pee Wee, "What for, why does she want to speak to me?"

"I don't know, but she said she wants to take you to this party."

So I said, "Okay, Pee Wee, send her back."

He brought her back, all smiling and shit, and left her with me. She kidded with me and took me to this party, because she liked me a lot. The party got boring, and so I introduced her to this big black dude named Jesse, sitting there about to have a fit looking at Ava Gardner, who was a stunningly beautiful woman, dark and sensuous with a beautiful full mouth that was soft as a motherfucker. Man, she was a hot number. I said, "Ava, kiss him on the fucking cheek so he can stop looking at you; he's almost about to have a baby." So she kissed him on the cheek and he started talking to her. Then she kissed me and froze him out and then we left and I dropped her off. We didn't get down or nothing like that. She was a nice person, though, real nice, and if I would have wanted to we could have had a thing. I just don't know why it didn't happen, but it didn't, even though a lot of people swear that it did.

The only thing negative during this time was Trane still grumbling about leaving the band, but everybody had gotten used to that. Then something happened, some real jive bullshit that changed my whole life and my whole attitude again, made me bitter and cynical again when I was really starting to feel good about the things that had changed in this country.

I had just finished doing an Armed Forces Day broadcast, you know, Voice of America and all that bullshit. I had just walked this pretty white girl named Judy out to get a cab. She got in the cab, and I'm standing there in front of Birdland wringing wet because it's a hot, steaming, muggy night in August. This white policeman comes up to me and tells me to move on. At the time I was doing a lot of boxing so I thought to myself, I ought to hit this motherfucker because I knew what he was doing. But instead I said, "Move on, for what? I'm working downstairs. That's my name up there, Miles Davis," and I pointed to my name on the marquee all up in lights.

He said, "I don't care where you work, I said move on! If you don't move on I'm going to arrest you."

I just looked at his face real straight and hard, and I didn't move. Then he said, "You're under arrest!" He reached for his handcuffs, but he was stepping back. Now, boxers had told me that if a guy's going to hit you, if you walk *toward* him you can see what's happening. I saw by the way he was handling himself that the policeman was an ex-fighter. So I kind of leaned in closer because I wasn't going to give him no distance so he could hit me on the head. He stumbled, and all his stuff fell on the sidewalk, and I thought to myself, Oh, shit, they're going to think that I fucked with him or something. I'm waiting for him to put the handcuffs on, because all his stuff is on the ground and shit. Then I move closer so he won't be able to fuck me up. A crowd had gathered all of a sudden from out of nowhere, and this white detective runs in and BAM! hits me on the head. I never saw him coming. Blood was running down the khaki suit I had on. Then I remember Dorothy Kilgallen coming outside with this horrible look on her face—I had known Dorothy for years and I used to date her good friend, Jean Bock—and saying, "Miles, what happened?" I couldn't say nothing. Illinois Jacquet was there, too.

It was almost a race riot, so the police got scared and hurried up and got my ass out of there and took me to the 54th Precinct where they took pictures of me bleeding and shit. So, I'm sitting there, madder than a motherfucker, right? And they're saying to me in the station, "So you're the wiseguy, huh?" Then they'd bump up against me, you know, try to get me mad so they could probably knock me upside my head again. I'm just sitting there, taking it all in, watching every move they make.

I look up on the wall and see they were advertising voyages for officers to take to Germany, like a tour. And this is about fourteen years after the war. And they're going there to learn police shit. It's advertised in the brochure; they'll probably teach them how to be meaner and shit, do to niggers over here what the Nazis did to the Jews over there. I couldn't believe that shit in there and they're supposed to be protecting us. I ain't done nothing but help a woman friend of mine get a cab and she happened to be white and the white boy who was the policeman didn't like seeing a nigger doing that.

I had called my lawyer, Harold Lovett, at about 3 A.M. The police charged me with resisting arrest, and assault and battery of a police officer. *Me!* And I ain't done nothing! It's so late that Harold can't really do nothing. They take me downtown to police headquarters and so Harold comes down to Centre Street, where they had me in the morning.

It makes the front pages of the New York newspapers, and they repeat the charges in their headlines. There was a picture, which became famous, of me leaving the jail with this bandage all over my head (they had taken me to the hospital to have my head stitched up), and Frances—who had come down to see me when they were transferring me downtown—walking in front of me like a proud stallion.

When Frances had come down to that police station and saw me all beat up like that, she was almost hysterical, screaming. I think the policemen started to think they had made a mistake, a beautiful woman like this screaming over this nigger. And then Dorothy Kilgallen came down and then wrote about it in her column the next day. The piece was very negative against the police, and that was of some help to my cause.

Now I would have expected this kind of bullshit about resisting arrest and all back in East St. Louis (before the city went all-black), but not here in New York City, which is supposed to be the slickest, hippest city in the world. But then, again, I was surrounded by white folks and I have learned that when this happens, if you're black, there is no justice. None.

At the hearing, the district attorney said to me, "When the policeman said, 'You're under arrest,' and you looked at him, what did that look mean?"

Harold Lovett, my lawyer, said, "What does that mean, 'What did that look mean?' " What they were trying to say was that I was going to knock the policeman down or something. My lawyers didn't put me on the witness stand, because they thought that the white judge and white jury would mistake my confidence for arrogance, and because of my bad temper, which they didn't trust me to keep in check. But that incident changed me forever, made me much more bitter and cynical than I might have been. It took two months for three judges to rule that my arrest had been illegal and dismiss the charges against me.

Later I sued the police department for $500,000. Harold wasn't doing negligence suits, so he got another lawyer, who forgot to file the claim before the statute of limitations ran out. We lost the damage suit, and I was madder than a motherfucker, but there wasn't nothing I could do about it.

The police revoked my cabaret license, and that prevented me from playing New York clubs for a while. My band had played out the last set without me, but the club made an announcement about what had happened. I heard that the band had played their asses off without me, stretching out and playing everything, every tune the way they probably would have played them in their own groups. Cannonball and Coltrane both called off the tunes after I left, so I know the place was popping. But after that shit made the front pages of the New York papers for a couple of days, everything was quiet. A lot of people forgot about it in a second. But a lot of musicians and people in the know—black and white—didn't, and thought I was a hero for standing up to the police like I did.

Around this time, people—white people—started saying that I was always "angry," that I was "racist," or some silly shit like that. Now, I've been racist toward nobody, but that don't mean I'm going to take shit from a person just because he's white. I didn't grin or shuffle and didn't walk around with my finger up my ass begging for no handout and thinking I was inferior to whites. I was living in America, too, and I was going to try to get everything that was coming to me.

Willie Ruff

In these excerpts from his charming autobiography, A Call to Assembly: An American Success Story *(1991), Willie Ruff—best known as the horn half of the duo Mitchell and Ruff—writes of a beginning and a climax to a dedicated life in jazz.*

Tel Aviv or Lionel Hampton?

Shortly after I got my master's from Yale, in 1954, I went to New York with Pete Hodgson, to hear Erich Leinsdorf conduct the Boston Symphony in an extremely moving all-Beethoven program at Carnegie Hall. A few days later, in a musicians' union newsletter, I saw an announcement that the Tel Aviv Philharmonic Orchestra, the pride of the new state of Israel, was auditioning horn players. Leinsdorf would listen to several Americans and would recommend the one he liked best. He was a regular on the podiums of Israel, and he knew the American musical scene and its players as well as any conductor alive. The newsletter gave his phone number.

The more I thought of the Leinsdorf concert I'd heard at Carnegie Hall, the stronger was the pull of the audition. I called the Westchester County, New York, number in the newsletter. Leinsdorf himself answered the phone. I introduced myself and said I was calling from New Haven about the Israel horn position. Leinsdorf said the position hadn't been filled, though he'd heard a lot of fine players. He asked about my background, and when I reported the Yale years, he wanted to know if any of them had been spent making music with Hindemith. I told him I had been taught by Abe Kniaz, and he said he knew Abe's work. After a cordial and warm few minutes, he made a date with me.

I prepared myself for the audition, which would be held at Leinsdorf's home, in every way, including sartorially. I dressed up in a good-quality medium-weight suit Morris Widder had sold me (at cost), shined my best pair of conservative shoes, and stopped by the clothing store to kill a few minutes before the drive down to Larchmont. Morris, I knew, would want to wish me good luck: give me his "mazel."

It was a hot summer day, shirtsleeve weather. As I approached the store, horn under my arm, Morris spotted me and left his customer, who stood in new pants with pins down the seat and in the cuffs.

"Wrong suit!" he yelled to me. "It's summertime. Too heavy. Besides, you're not going to a funeral. Brighten up, man! A well-dressed man *looks* comfortable. Look at you: you're sweating, for crying out loud! Maestro Leinsdorf will take one look at you in that schmatta and say, 'Uhh uhh, another schlemiel schlepping to the Holy Land.' "

"This is the best you ever sold me," I said.

"How much time we got?" he asked as he marked the cuffs and seat for the man in the new pants and sent him on his way with a "Next Tuesday. So long." To me he said, "Gimme ten minutes, and I'll make you a new man. Do you think I'd let you go to Israel looking like *that?*"

"Morris," I said, "I'm not going to Israel today, just to Westchester County."

"Same difference. Don't argue; we don't have much time. You'll borrow a new suit, something right for the season." Manipulating a long broomstick with a hook affixed to its end, he jiggled loose from a high rack a new light-tan linen suit, threw the jacket at me, and plugged in the iron.

By the time he'd pinned and sewn the pants cuffs, the iron was hot, and he sponged and pressed the whole suit. I was ready. I admired my image in his full-length mirror, while he checked and tugged at the jacket from behind. He turned me around to inspect the jacket front and recoiled. "My Gawd," he said. "I *hate* that shirt! You'll never get to Israel wearing that." He was off to the back room, returning with a bundle, the laundry ticket still stuck to it, of his own shirts. Ripping the paper off, he took from the stack a button-down oxford shirt with a quiet stripe, held it under my chin. No good.

"We need something more muted," he said. When I tried a muted one, Morris complained, "Cheez, that tie is a dog!" He ran his hand into his pants pocket and yanked out a bill.

"Here, take this ten bucks and run around the corner to J. Press and buy a four-in-hand rep stripe tie with a little red, green, maybe a hint of yellow. But no blue! Tell em it's for Morris, they'll give you a discount. Understand?"

I pushed the hand with the bill away. "Thanks anyway, Morris," I said, "but I can at least afford a tie." J. Press had the tie, but no discount. When I came back, Morris said, "That's better. You're going to be the hottest shofar man in Jerusalem!"

"Tel Aviv," I said. He followed me to the door, and as I sprinted in the heat for my Ford, he hollered after me, "Slow down. Don't sweat in my suit! Play well, Raggs!"

DRIVING DOWN THE Merritt Parkway, I tried to remember all the pointers Kniaz had offered along the way about playing for conductors.

"Don't be flashy. Don't play horn concertos unless you're asked, but show that you know more than just orchestral music. Remember that the audition starts with the first warm-up notes you play. Be relaxed."

I arrived in Larchmont nearly a half hour early. Once I'd spotted the house, I drove on down the block, found a parking spot in the shade, took out the horn, sat in the car, and warmed up with soft slow scales. I played through the melody of Rossini's *Semiramide,* one of my favorites for the instrument. Everything felt fine. My clothes were comfortable. No more sweating.

Going up the long walkway to Leinsdorf's large house, I could hear a piece of very modern music coming from a piano inside. I guessed it was Leinsdorf though I didn't know he was a pianist. It was one o'clock, time for my appointment, but I waited for the final cadence before pushing the doorbell. A woman answered, I introduced myself, and she asked me in. "My husband just left the piano and went upstairs. He'll be with you shortly," she said. "He said you may warm up there in the music room." Kniaz had been right; of course Leinsdorf would be listening from upstairs. I continued with the easy blowing I'd started in the car, playing a quiet phrase or two of *Semiramide;* it was on my mind.

After a few moments, Leinsdorf came into the music room, carrying a few sheets of an old *New York Times,* extended his right hand to me, and in a resonant, warm, and friendly voice said, "Good afternoon, Mr. Ruff. I'm glad to see you." So far so good. He then spread the *Times* on the floor next to my chair to protect the carpet from the water that horn players must constantly empty from their horns. "He's done a lot of this," I told myself.

Taking a seat on a nearby piano stool, Maestro said, "Tell me some more about yourself." I recited all I thought he would care to know about my military experience and Yale. Then he said, "What have you prepared that you would like to play for me?" Well, of course, *Semiramide.* I played it through to the end this time. "A very nice approach, and an interesting tone," was his comment.

Then I put a book of orchestra excerpts on the music stand and asked if he would like to choose something for me to play. He fingered through the book and asked for samplings of orchestral horn writing from the eighteenth century to modern composers. I had practiced everything in the book; there were no mishaps in the dozen or so excerpts he chose. The last thing he asked me to play from the book was a bit from a Haydn symphony. The part, written before the horn had valves, required transposing. The symphony was in the key of D, not one of the more difficult transpositions a horn player must learn and keep in his professional baggage. I played through the passage, and near the end there was a slip of a finger, or the lip, or of my concentration. Anyway, a note of the melody was not right. Not a *missed* note but a wrong one.

When I was finished, Leinsdorf asked me if transposing was troublesome for me. I said it was not ordinarily. But I didn't want to make excuses for the slip and offered to play other transpositions from the book. He said, "No, I'll take your word. However, you might want to pay more attention to your transposing for future auditions." He then asked if I wanted to play anything else. I thought it was a good time to do as Kniaz had advised: play something that was not from the orchestral literature. Abe had shown me a piece from Schumann's *Carnival* piano suite, in which one movement, a musical portrait of Chopin, elegantly shows off the best of the horn's lyrical qualities. Nobody ever plays the piece on the horn. "Wonderfully effective for encore pieces or auditions. Use it," Kniaz had said. I played the movement once through, not too loud, not too soft, then made the repeat at a hushed whisper. It worked. I hoped that I had made up for the earlier slip. Maestro smiled at me.

The audition was over, and Leinsdorf said some very complimentary things. Then he pulled the piano stool closer to my chair and said, "Would you care to tell me why you, an American, are interested in the position in Israel?" I told him that all my working life in music, from my fifteenth year till then, had been devoted to preparing myself as a horn player. I wanted to play in a symphony orchestra, perhaps not for the rest of my life but for now.

"I am certainly aware that positions in the professional orchestras in this country are not available to Negro artists," he told me. "I know these orchestras and the communities that support them." Then he mentioned an alternative to the job in Israel.

"I'm the music director and conductor of the Buffalo Symphony Orchestra. I can definitely offer you a position in the horn section. It might be a more direct route to your later entry into another, larger American orchestra. The Tel Aviv position would also be good for you, and you would certainly be appreciated there regardless of race. There are no laws that would separate you from anybody else. I suggest you consider both these options, but don't short-change Buffalo."

I thanked him and he saw me to the door, where his wife met us to shake my hand. We would talk by phone in a week.

No matter what would happen as a result of the encounter, I was glad to have had the frank talk with an artist I admired as much as Leinsdorf.

SHORTLY AFTER MY audition, Emma and I sat home one night watching television, the Ed Sullivan show. Lionel Hampton and his orchestra were announced. When Lionel and the band started his theme song, "Flying Home," the camera panned across the full band and stopped on the piano player. He was Ivory Mitchell, from Lockbourne! I raced for the telephone.

Manhattan information gave me the CBS number. I dialed. The CBS switchboard rang through to the theater's backstage. I asked the person on the other end to give my number to Hampton's piano player.

"The band just came off. Hold a second. I'll call him. What's his name?"

"Mitchell," I said.

The next voice I heard said, "Hello, who's this?" It was the same old fall-in-the-ditch Ivory Mitchell's voice. Instead of answering, I sang the deep bass-notes to "All the Things You Are," the way he'd taught it to me for our first radio program back at Lockbourne: "Thum thuuuum thum thum thum thum thum thuuum thuum." At about the third bar, he screamed, "Ruff! Aww man . . . Ruff!"

All of a sudden, he was going, "Kyah . . . Kyah . . . heekh, heekh, wheeeew, huuu—awwwww, Jeeeesuuuus!" I picked up his giggle fit, until Emma, showing serious concern, asked, "Do you two ever talk? Or is it all bass fiddles and guffaws?"

"Your timing was perfect," Mitchell said. "You got me just as I came off the bandstand. But the band is working at Basin Street, here in town, and we're due on now. Everybody is leaving."

"Well, at least I got you, at last," I said. "I will probably be leaving soon to play in the Israel Philharmonic Orchestra."

"Naw, man, don't do it. We got to get together. Israel is a very hip place; we go there often with Lionel. But you ought to join this band, and we can work out that duo we always talked about back in Mr. Brice's band. I think about him all the time, man, God rest his soul.

"Listen, Ruff, we're playing in Bridgeport, Connecticut, tomorrow night, at the Ritz Ballroom. Bring your horn; I'm sure Lionel will hire you. We gotta get our shit together now. I can't wait to see you. Gotta go. Don't forget tomorrow. Later!"

WHEN I ARRIVED at the Ritz Ballroom, Hamp's musicians were about to go on the stage. Mitchell spotted me and tapped Hamp on the shoulder. They came right over. "Hey, Gates"—Lionel's name for everyone, and the one he likes to be called—"Mitchell told me all about you. Just take a seat anywhere and move around in the band. Blow with the different sections. Hell, make yourself at home wherever you think it sounds good." Mitchell and I saved our reunion until later, but I wondered if he knew what he was getting me into. We had spoken again on the phone earlier that day. Would it be possible, or practical, for us to organize our duo and work up a repertoire while traveling on the road? The one thing I was certain of was that I wanted to sound good that night and not embarrass us both.

The opening number with Lionel is always a fast and active piece of pyrotechnics called "Big Slide." Sitting between the two trombonists, I discovered that playing in that band was not so much a musical challenge as one of showmanship, that dominant feature of any Hampton performance. After the intermission, I played a few numbers with the trumpets, then I moved my chair forward to play with the saxophones and finally found music to suit the special character of the French horn. The horn's tone, when mixed with a saxophone section, enlarges and adds color to the ensemble. The lead alto saxophonist, Bobby Platter, sitting in the chair to my left, guided me through the best of the band's library. Platter was a large but quiet and gentle man, who had been the band's assistant leader for many years. He had also composed the great dance-band classic "The Jersey Bounce." As we read through "Midnight Sun," we reached a point where Platter nudged me and said, "Big reed section solo coming up. Double the lead part with me." We began the phrase together, and from the sound of our first note, I could imagine that a midnight sun did break through the smoky haze of the ballroom. Matching Bobby's lyrical tone was even more effective when we played softly, accompanying Lionel's vibes solos. Lionel got inspired at one point, stopped midphrase in his solo, turned from his vibes with a grin, his mallets high over his head, and yelled at me, "Yeah, Gates, blow, blow, blow!"

Platter signaled the other saxes to tune up and to pay more attention to the expressive shadings in the music. "Shhh, way down, man. Don't drown out the French horn!" Almost immediately our blend and balance improved. Platter looked at the saxophonists and said testily, "That's a whole lot better! Yeah. Damn. Why don't you cats play like that *all* the time?" Lionel's chief musician was tuning his section to a level he'd apparently had difficulty sustaining otherwise.

Before we started again, Bobby searched through the music on his stand, trying to find ballads that would show off our new saxophone–French horn mix. We experimented like that for the rest of the night, turning up beautiful ballads to play, which, according to Bobby and Mitchell, the band hadn't touched in years.

During the next intermission, trumpeter Wallace Davenport came to shake my hand. Others followed. Some of the men were interested in arranging, and had questions about the horn: its range, pitch, and mixing characteristics. Lionel asked me to play solos on a few ballads with his vibes during the last set of the evening. I was in horn heaven.

When the night was finished, Bobby, Lionel's main musical adviser, said, "Sign him up, Gates. You heard that sound!"

"Yeah, ain't no other bands got no French horns, except Claude Thornhill and them cats. It's something new. I'll call Gladys and ask her." He went for the telephone booth to consult long-distance with the real boss of the band, his wife.

Gladys Hampton was the force that kept the Lionel Hampton organization afloat. A glamorous and adroit businesswoman, she did all the hiring and firing in the band, made all the business decisions, and supervised the tours. Mrs. Hampton, as she was addressed by band members, controlled one of the all-time-big-grossing packages in the music industry. Arrogantly secure in what she'd had to teach herself about show business, Gladys flaunted her power. The industry was not yet ready for a black woman representative, so Gladys left the hard contract negotiations to the white agent Joe Glaser. Lionel was but one star on the roster of jazz greats the Glaser office booked. Others commanding big money through Glaser's Associated Booking Agency were Louis Armstrong, Duke Ellington, Woody Herman, Sarah Vaughan, Stan Kenton, Billy Eckstine, Billy Daniels, and on down. But from the moment a Hampton contract was nailed down by Glaser, Gladys took over.

Lionel, speaking to his wife on the pay phone, was saying, "Gladys, I just heard this musician up here in Bridgeport. He sat in with the band tonight. It sounded great. We're still short a trombone player, you know, so we can put him in there to bring the band up to full strength." Gladys said something, to which Lionel replied, "Naw, he ain't no trombone player, he plays the French horn." There was a long pause, presumably Gladys giving her husband fits. Lionel broke in.

"I *know* I ain't never had no French horn in the band before, but you oughta hear it. The whole band sounds bigger. It's something *new,* Gladys. It's classy, and the people will dig it! Bobby Platter and Mitchell can tell you. This guy was in the Air Force with Mitchell. . . . Come on, Gladys, can we hire him?" Finally, Gladys gave a tentative OK, but she was going to have to check it out for herself when the band came to Harlem in two days for its annual month-long stint at the Apollo Theater.

The next day, I called Erich Leinsdorf's house to say that I was no longer "in the running" for the job in Israel. I wanted especially to thank him again for his thoughtful offer of a job in the Buffalo Philharmonic. It was a kindness I would never forget.

The news that I would probably be going with Lionel Hampton was a relief to my New Haven family. Israel seemed such a long way from home. My sister Mary had wanted to know, "How the devil are you going to even talk to those people way over there, boy? You can't speak Hebrew!" To them, Hamp's band, no matter how far it traveled abroad, was still familiar territory. And what better place than the Apollo to start one's band career?

The Conservatory Without Walls

Not long after our return from the Central African Republic, I called Duke Ellington. I had an idea for him. I asked if he would bring his orchestra to Yale. I wanted him to play a concert for schoolchildren and then give an evening public program at Yale similar in scope to his 1968 "dream concert" for the Billy Strayhorn Juilliard scholarship.

"Why, we would love to come back to the campus. Anytime. You know," Ellington added, "that yours truly is now among the exalted: Mother Yale awarded us the degree of Doctor of Humane Letters in 1967. We're a Yale man now!"

Well, of course I knew that, but when he reminded me of it I thought of another idea, a lot bigger than the one we had just talked about. "Maestro," I urged, "give me a few phone numbers where I can reach you out on the road for the next week. I have some homework to do before I get back to you."

I went to Dean Phil Nelson and Yale president Kingman Brewster and persuaded them to follow up Ellington's honorary degree with a permanent visiting fellows program at the university bearing Ellington's name. My dream was for world-class artists to come regularly to the campus and give performances and workshops for Yale students as well as children in the public schools. President Brewster was enthusiastic, and everything began to fall in place.

Within a week, forty artists were selected as the first Ellington fellows, and President Brewster agreed to welcome them to the university and present them with a special medal in a gala ceremony. No other university had ever honored so many great names in music at one time.

When I tracked Ellington down, somewhere out on the road, I had the details, the finances, and the convocation worked out. A local foundation headed by Ernie Osborne, a jazz fan I knew from the Playback days, funded the event. I had two concert halls booked at Yale for three days of concerts, workshops, and jam sessions. Ellington's orchestra would be the centerpiece of the convocation, along with the forty artists from across the United States and Europe. Our lineup included Benny Carter, Dizzy Gillespie, Eubie Blake, Joe Williams, William Warfield, Roland Hayes, Marian Anderson, Charlie Mingus, Max Roach, Kenny Clarke, Ray Brown, Clarke Terry, Slam Stewart, Milt Hinton, George Duvivier, Odetta, Mary Lou Williams, Lucky Thompson, and Harry Edison. The remaining names we wanted among the forty would confirm after schedule adjustments.

When I called Kenny Clarke in Paris, he said, "Man! This is going to be the biggest reunion in music." I hoped it would be that. To me it was shaping up as the world's most lavish and prestigious jam session.

A couple of days after my conversation with Clarke in Paris, I called Charlie Mingus in New York. "Yeah, definitely count me in," he said. "Dizzy already told me about Kenny Clarke coming all the way from France, and Ray Brown and Benny Carter and Harry Edison all flying in from California. That's Christmas in October! I'll be there with my bass. Maybe I'll even get to play something with Duke, wouldn't *that* be a gas!"

The classical artists—Marian Anderson, William Warfield, Roland Hayes, and Dorothy Maynor—were equally enthusiastic. Of the entire venture, nothing could have meant more to me than having Miss Anderson graciously agree to come out of her retirement and near seclusion to help me host a press conference at Yale two months before the convocation. Her appearance in New Haven gave me my first chance to meet her. When the day came, I found her powerful aura and quiet dignity so stunning, I couldn't take my eyes off her. At one point I asked her, "Miss Anderson, why did you so readily agree to come out of your retirement to help me publicize this convocation?"

In her rich and serene contralto, she said, "When you called me and said you wanted this university to honor so many pioneering artists of our tradition, it struck me as a very positive idea, and one that is important for the music. I also heard an urgency in your voice that I couldn't ignore. I had to respond, Mr. Ruff, and do what I could."

Paul Robeson, though hospitalized and sinking, assured us that had he been well, nothing could have made him miss the gathering and the music of "my good friend Dizzy Gillespie and all those other lifelong musical favorites of mine." I had almost forgotten what tremendous fans our musical giants are of one another's work.

When Ellington and I began the "dream list" of those he wanted Yale to honor, I knew that scheduling around the availability of so many busy stars and President Brewster's calendar could be a nightmare. I was right. But as the date approached, Ellington went to work on the "impossible to reach" musicians. Miles Davis, for instance, was incognito that year and beyond even Ellington's long telephoning arm; Ella Fitzgerald was out of the country; and Lena Horne, Roy Eldridge, Sarah Vaughan, and Teddy Wilson all had bookings. Sadly, the invitation we sent Don Byas in Europe reached his house the day after his untimely death. Ben Webster, also living in Europe by then, was not well enough to come.

But we were lining up some good ones, and as the confirmed roster of performers grew, so did the considerations for programming: what to have whom play, and when, and with whom. Not since the Strayhorn Juilliard scholarship concert four years earlier had Duke involved himself in so large and varied an enterprise. And even that hadn't approached the scale of the New Haven celebration. But there he was, right on track again, full of new ideas. I had to fly cross-country to some of his concert and festival sites just to squeeze in hurried meetings with him backstage and in taxis, in elevators, airports, and hotel rooms.

"One never knows about time, baby," he said to me one day as room service in his Madison, Wisconsin, hotel spread his dinner before him in bed. "Eubie Blake, Noble Sissle, and Roland Hayes are crowding ninety, and Willie The Lion isn't far behind. They're the ones we want center stage. Tomorrow is, too often, too late. We should honor the greats among us while they can still smell the flowers." I loved learning the ropes from the "master of situations."

Finally, with all our artists' confirmations in hand, I set about ordering forty handsome medals bearing Duke's likeness. Studying the list of medalists at that moment, I realized that this assemblage of musical immortals represented a virtual living conservatory: an informal and uncredited school through which the lifeblood of jazz music had quietly perpetuated itself. Furthermore, I recognized those same elderly musicians Ellington wanted center stage as direct musical descendants of the generations that preceded them—the music's originators. Taken all together, our honorees came very close to spanning the history of jazz music. And the classical musicians—Hayes, Miss Anderson, Robeson, and Dorothy Maynor—had been role models for those of us who followed them on the American concert stage back when that possibility was systematically denied African Americans.

For days I could think of nothing but this invisible conservatory. I reviewed again and again the teaching materials I'd developed for my classes at UCLA, Dartmouth, and Yale; the recordings and films I'd collected over the years, featuring these same artists. I discussed the "conservatory" and its cultural weight with Sidney Fine and Benny Carter in California; with Dizzy, Max Roach, Kenny Clarke, Joe Williams, and Jo Jones. Then I phoned Ellington.

"Maestro," I said, "have you come up with a name for our celebration yet?" He hadn't. Had I?

"Well, what we are really preparing to celebrate here is a real conservatory, a conservatory without walls. Why not just call it that?"

Duke paused a minute. "Conservatory. Hmmn. 'Conservatory without walls'? I think I like it. We do have all those specialties of the conservatory—the instrumentalists, singers, and composers—don't we? The bassists, for instance, with Slam Stewart, Charles Mingus, Milt Hinton, Ray Brown, and George Duvivier. And the pianists: Eubie, a great composer too; and of course Willie 'the Lion' Smith, who was Fats Waller's piano professor and mine, breaking us in way back in our 'kid' days in Harlem. And while we are on the pianists, don't forget the fabulous Mary Lou Williams, also a great composer and arranger. And we have the drummers: Sonny Greer, Jo

Jones, Max Roach, Kenny Clarke. The saxophonists, trumpets, singers . . . I'm out of breath. But I can't beat that title, man. Print it!"

I wasn't through with the Maestro. I said, "And when President Brewster presents the medals, why don't we have all forty of those legends sit there on the stage together; and for each of their instrumental and vocal specialties, let's have a young world-class artist perform something special in their honor. We'll get a young trumpeter to play for Dizzy, Harry Edison, Cootie Williams, and Clarke Terry while they're sitting there onstage. We'll have a saxophonist play for Harry Carney, Benny Carter, Sonny Stitt, Russell Procope, Lucky Thompson, and Paul Gonsalves. A pianist for you, Eubie, the Lion and Mary Lou. A singer for Joe Williams, Bessie Jones, Marion Williams, Bill Warfield, Odetta, Roland Hayes, Dorothy Maynor, and Marian Anderson."

There was a pause. Then from Duke:

"Like I said before: Print it, Willie!"

We printed it. Printed and distributed it in press releases and in thousands of posters and brochures, until the three-day jubilee was upon us.

All day long on Thursday, October 12, 1972, the musicians began to gather. Little cells of old friends and mentors had cropped up all over the campus, in hallways, in classrooms, and on street corners. Musicians who'd been out of touch for decades were hugging one another and reminiscing.

Ellington's drummer Rufus Jones, my seatmate on Lionel Hampton's band bus when he, Mitchell, and I played with Lionel, spent that afternoon in Sonny Greer's hotel room. Greer was Ellington's original drummer, fifty years earlier. Jo Jones and Kenny Clarke also stopped by.

Rufus, a confident man who is seldom flustered, said to me later, just before going onstage to play, "I never saw so many from the generations that came before us! Just having Sonny Greer—who helped invent this band—out there in the audience tonight listening to me gives me goose bumps."

That night, students at Yale and Ellington devotees from around the world were treated to a full concert featuring the Duke Ellington Orchestra. The orchestra strode to the stage without its leader but with its collective chest thrown forward and gave "Take the A Train" a rare fire and celebratory lift. I knew they were playing on the inspiration that surfaces whenever professionals perform for an audience of their peers.

Just as "A Train" was ending, Ellington made his entrance, and his audience stood in a roaring welcome. He went to the side of the stage and brought out Willie "The Lion" Smith and introduced him as his "artistic overseer and custodian of good taste."

I joined several other musicians in the audience, then began to move all around the hall to hear from different vantage points. Mingus, Dizzy, and Sonny Stitt were lined up along a side wall, listening. "Imagine Harry Carney," Mingus said, "after all these years, still playing with that great big sound, making the whole band sparkle!"

Just then, onstage, Cootie Williams eased up out of his chair and, with his plumber's plunger, bent his deep-throated trumpet growls all around the melody of "Concerto for Cootie."

Dizzy Gillespie grabbed his face. "I don't know if I can stand three days of this much excitement!"

THE NEXT AFTERNOON was given over entirely to that jam session I had thought so much about. I directed traffic, putting the various dream bands onstage. Joe Williams had given me some preliminary guidelines beforehand: he wanted to sing with Duke at the piano, Benny Carter at the alto sax, and Jo Jones, and Ray Brown filling out the rhythm section. Dizzy said he wanted to play with his old friends Kenny Clarke, at the drums, Mary Lou Williams, at the piano, Sonny Stitt and Lucky Thompson, playing saxophones, and Slam Stewart, playing bass. Even with such explicit directions, there were latecomers to accommodate, and other surprises, such as Jo Jones moving Max Roach over and himself playing a number with Harry "Sweets" Edison, his old friend and soulmate from their days as stars of Count Basie's band.

The oldest team performing on the bill was Eubie Blake, eighty-nine, and Noble Sissle, eighty-three, giving what was to be their last public performance together; Sissle died shortly afterward. Their young audience, mostly students, gave their songs, from *Shuffle Along,* one of the most heartfelt standing ovations I've ever witnessed. Dizzy, Kenny Clarke, Mary Lou Williams, and Sonny Stitt were backstage, getting ready to play and recalling the spirit of the 1940s Harlem jam sessions they'd had at Minton's Playhouse with Charlie Parker and Thelonious Monk. Kenny said, "Charlie Parker would have loved this whole thing. He used to be around Minton's and other places, talking about the new music he liked. Hindemith was one of his favorites. Bird would really be in his element here today."

At one point the stage filled up spontaneously with musicians wanting to play "How High the Moon," one of the all-time-favorite jam session numbers. From somewhere came the idea to feature solos by all the bass players in the house: Mingus, Ray Brown, Milt Hinton, George Duvivier, Duke's bassist, Joe Benjamin, and Slam Stewart. Duke even asked me to play, but I wisely declined in that company. All I wanted was to be out front to hear it all, and it was something to hear. Had an earthquake at that moment swallowed up Woolsey Hall, jazz would have been very wanting in the bass clef. But I knew I shouldn't even be *thinking* like that.

In fact, in the midst of all that jumping with those bassists, plus Benny

Carter, Lucky Thompson, Sonny Stitt, and the nineteen-year-old Dizzy protégé, Jon Faddis, a police captain rushed backstage. "Clear the hall!" he yelled. "We're on bomb alert! Somebody called in that a bomb has been planted in this building."

My levelheaded assistant, Brent Henry, immediately went to the microphone. "Ladies and gentlemen," he said calmly, "we've just been informed that a bomb alert is in effect in the hall. The fire marshal and the police are searching the building now. Please go calmly to the nearest exit and leave the building. In twenty minutes we expect the building will be safe to reenter, and the concert will go on."

The audience moved easily out the exits, and with Michele and my bass in tow, I watched the huge concert hall emptying itself. Musicians, clutching their instruments, took safe ground across the street. The music was silenced. But not for long. One who hadn't deserted the hall was Charlie Mingus. There he was onstage with his bass, talking on the microphone as the police captain tried to get him out of the hall.

From the door I heard him say to the cops, "You all just get Duke, Eubie, Noble Sissle, Harry Carney, and all of my musical forebears out of here. I'm staying. I'm not moving, do you understand? I'm staying right here! I've got to die sometime, and it ain't ever gonna get better than right now. Racism planted that bomb, but racism ain't strong enough to kill this music; if I'm going to die, I'm ready. But I'm going out playing 'Sophisticated Lady.'"

The bass version Mingus played of the song was so great I hated to have to miss it. My daughter and I walked slowly toward the exit, and we could hear the tune going on, with Mingus's verbal counterpoint hotly expressing his righteous indignation while he played. Ellington, standing among the waiting crowd out on the street, smiled as he listened through the open doors. Mingus was getting hotter, and the police captain's pleas for him to leave the stage couldn't have fallen on deafer ears.

Kenny Clarke, standing near Duke, shook his head. "I wouldn't have believed it if I hadn't seen it and heard it for myself," Kenny said. "Listen to all that music coming out of Charles even while he's raising hell! Charles sure *is* a bitch, bless his heart."

Mingus's indomitable spirit rained on the old devil's hellfire and completely defused the ugly trick.

"False alarm," declared the police captain after about twenty minutes, and the musicians returned to the stage, hell-bent on raising the roof—with music.

We got tremendous press for the whole event—Radio France, the BBC, and German radio and television covered it. At least two major American magazines listed the preconvocation activities and the programs at Yale. But I was disappointed that American network television felt that Duke Ellington and forty of America's greatest musical artists at Yale lacked "audience appeal"; they all passed. Our publicists were shocked, but not Ellington. His stoic serenity was never more biting:

"We learn from our experiences, don't we, Willie?" he said. "We're honoring all those beautiful musicians *because* they have become great *even* in their invisibility. Maybe Fate is trying to tell us something about invisible. Why spoil a good thing, man?"

Sonny Stitt didn't spoil a good thing. As soon as the crowd was seated again after the bomb scare, he marched onto the stage, playing his saxophone with a fire that made Kenny Clarke shout, "It never got *this* hot even up at Minton's!"

Harry Edison responded, "Nothing *ever* got this hot."

I fell back in the spirit of it all and saw my chance to practice what I'd watched Duke carry off so masterfully back at the Lincoln Center Strayhorn concert. Looking over the waiting sea of legends standing backstage, ready primed, I called out to Duke: "Maestro, will you play with Kenny Clarke, Mingus, Dizzy, and Benny Carter now? And oh, yes—Slam, do you want some of this? Mary Lou, how about you and Milt Hinton, Max Roach, and Joe Williams teaming up Lucky Thompson, Cootie Williams, Sweets Edison, and Sonny Stitt." I was hitting my stride as a new master of situations. Mingus had been right: I knew it would never get better than that day.

BUT THAT NIGHT, at eight o'clock sharp, it came close. The stage of Woolsey Hall was filled with forty chairs, and in them sat the artists who were to receive the Ellington Medal. Sidney Fine had come East to help keep me straight. Watching that stage fill up with legends, he, from his perils backstage, passed me a note saying, "Go to the mic. *now* and say, 'I declare this house sanctified.'" When I did, a strange hush enveloped the stage and spread over the waiting crowd.

Kingman Brewster came onstage and presented the medals to the artists individually according to their musical specialties. The trumpeters came first: Dizzy Gillespie, Clarke Terry, Cootie Williams, and Harry Edison. Then young Jimmy Owens, a New York trumpeter of great stature, came forward and played his heart out before the elder masters of his instrument. The effect of such a spirited musical offering was all I could have hoped for. How can I ever forget the prideful look on the great musicians' faces as Jimmy played his musical synopsis of what the trumpet meant to him and his feeling about honoring its place in the history of jazz? Owens's improvised essay covered it all with wit, humor, and style.

Then Odetta, herself an honoree that night, sang a song called "Black Woman," performing without accompaniment. Her singing hushed the hall, and she began building the drama and pulling her audience right along with her, right up to her grand emotional climax. It brought the house down. Ellington led the musicians on the stage in applause, and the audience came to its feet.

I thought it fitting for Odetta's lone rendition to be followed by a solo from the young drummer Tony Williams. About ten years earlier, Tony had, at age sixteen, joined Miles Davis's band. Weeks before the convocation, Max Roach had told me why Tony was the young drummer to play for his elders at the convocation. "Tony," Max said, "of course, is a young master himself. But more important than that, he never stops giving credit to Jo Jones, Sonny Greer, Kenny Clarke, and all of us who came before him. His last album is dedicated to Papa Jo." I hadn't expected that a drum solo could have so much music in it. Max had chosen correctly. Tony showed us all that he was the man for playing drum honors that night.

Mitchell hadn't wanted to play for the pianists. He was nervous. "What am I going to play for all those people on that stage, Ruff?" he pleaded. But several of the honorees helped me talk him into it, and he followed Tony Williams and played the pants off "I Got It Bad and That Ain't Good." Willie the Lion, who had only heard Mitchell the night of the Strayhorn concert, leaned over and whispered to Duke, "That boy has promise." And then it was time for Lucky Thompson's soprano saxophone. As Lucky played, "In a Sentimental Mood" as nobody on the stage had ever heard it, I watched Benny Carter's face shine with pure admiration. The same admiring smile played on Harry Carney's face, and on Russell Procope's. And when Lucky was finished, he spoke eloquently of his debt to the late saxophone masters: to Johnny Hodges, Lester Young, and Coleman Hawkins.

Then Richard Davis brought to the stage the very same bass that the late, great Jimmy Blanton had played in Duke's band in the 1940s. Richard also spoke some admiring words for Ray Brown, Slam Stewart, Milt Hinton, George Duvivier, and Joe Benjamin, and went on to make us all proud with his original improvised solo, which he dedicated to Blanton. I though I saw a tear rise to Ellington's eye.

Now all the departments of our conservatory were honored. But there was still the unfinished business of the medals for those absent heroes who'd been kept away because of illness. I had asked Dizzy Gillespie, who enjoyed a close friendship with Paul Robeson, to accept Robeson's medal and deliver it to him. Dizzy said a few words about what the great Robeson meant to him, then he quoted Mary Bethune's famous statement: "'Paul Robeson is the tallest tree in our forest.'"

Joe Williams accepted Marian Anderson's award, and as he looked hard at the medal in his hand, he, too, had a quote to pass on, from Miss Anderson's past. He said he'd once heard her relate a piece of sage advice her grandmother gave her as she was about to launch her career: "Always remember, darling, wherever you go, and whatever you do, try always to do your best, for someone will be paying attention to what you do and the way you carry yourself, in order that they may pattern themselves after you."

William Warfield stood in for Roland Hayes. Holding Mr. Hayes's medal in one hand and his own in the other, Warfield said to the audience, "I am here tonight because a legend came to Buffalo, New York, my hometown, when I was a boy. I heard the great tenor Roland Hayes sing, and from that magical moment on, I knew that I had to be a singer too."

We still had a screening, the next afternoon, of my film made with Bessie Jones and Dizzy Gillespie in the Georgia Sea Islands, to be followed by yet another jam session.

But now we prepared to cap the concert's magnificence with a party, which President Brewster would host.

As we were leaving, the hall buzzed with high excitement. People like Ray Brown, Benny Carter, Harry Carney, Cootie Williams, and Harry Edison all came over to me with warm words of praise for the event and the role I'd played. But the impact of what had taken place didn't come into sharp focus until Charlie Mingus, with the full force of his nearly three-hundred-pound frame, surrounded me and gripped my hand in both of his with a surprising warmth. "You gave me the greatest gift of my life just by making it possible for me to see Duke and all these great artists get the honor they deserve," he said. I got misty and felt a huge tear begin to blur my vision. Mingus saw it and with a forcefulness that was startling at such a moment, said, "Oh, no. Naw, man. Hold that tear! Call it back. Don't let that one fall. Call that one back. I mean it. Call it *back!*"

It scared and stirred me. I was lost inside Mingus's new tone of voice for a whole symphony of reasons: primarily because I'd always admired him so much, yet I knew his reputation for physical chastisement. But there was no hint of violence in his tone now. Rather, there was that old teacherly manner Mama had used so often to preach at me: "Read between the lines, boy!" Now, a grown man of forty-one then, I was locked in Mingus's terrifying clutches, with him bearing down on me: "Keep that tear. Save it for another time on down the road. You need to keep that one—it's special. Hold it in reserve!"

My vision cleared, and though I would have sworn it was physiologically impossible, I managed to call back the tear.

Art Pepper

One of the most moving and disturbing personal narratives in jazz is Art Pepper's Straight Life *(1979; with Laurie Pepper)—a searing record of a life both tormented and heroic.*

There's a thing about empathy between musicians. The great bands were the ones in which the majority of the people were good people, morally good people; I call them real people—in jail they call them regulars. Bands that are made up of more good people than bad, those are the great bands. Those are the bands like Basie's was at one time and Kenton's and Woody Herman's and Duke Ellington's were at a couple of different times.

There's so many facets to playing music. In the beginning you learn the fundamentals of whatever instrument you might play: you learn the scales and how to get a tone. But once you become proficient mechanically, so you can be a jazz musician, then a lot of other things enter into it. Then it becomes a way of life, and how you relate musically is really involved.

The selfish or shallow person might be a great musician technically, but he'll be so involved with himself that his playing will lack warmth, intensity, beauty and won't be deeply felt by the listener. He'll arbitrarily play the first solo every time. If he's backing a singer he'll play anything he wants or he'll be practicing scales. A person that lets the other guy take the first solo, and when he plays behind a soloist plays only to enhance him, that's the guy that will care about his wife and children and will be courteous in his everyday contact with people.

Miles Davis is basically a good person and that's why his playing is so beautiful and pure. This is my own thinking and the older I get the more I believe I'm correct in my views. Miles is a master of the understatement and he's got an uncanny knack for finding the right note or the right phrase. He's tried to give an appearance of being something he's not. I've heard he's broken a television set when he didn't like something that was said on TV, that he's burnt connections, been really a bastard with women, and come on as a racist. The connections probably deserved to be burnt; they were assholes, animals, guys that would burn you: give you bad stuff and charge you too much, people that would turn you in to the cops if they got busted. Most of the women that hang around jazz musicians are phonies. And as for his prejudice, not wanting white people in his bands, that's what he feels he should be like. He's caught up in the way the country is, the way the people are, and he figures that's the easiest way to go. One time he did hire Bill Evans for his band, but people ranked him so badly and it was such a hassle that I think he became bitter and assumed this posture of racism and hatred. But I feel he's a good person or he couldn't play as well as he plays.

Billy Wilson plays like *he* is. When I knew him, when he was young, he was a real warm, sweet, loving person. And he plays just that way. But if you listen to his tone, it never was very strong; it's pretty and kind of cracking. It's weak. And when he was faced with prison—because he got busted for using drugs—he couldn't stand it. He couldn't go because he was afraid, and when they offered him an out by turning over on somebody he couldn't help but do it. He's a weak person. That's the way he plays. That's the way he sounds.

Stan Getz is a great technician, but he plays cold to me. I hear him as he is and he's rarely moved me. He never knocked me out like Lester Young, Zoot Sims, Coltrane.

John Coltrane was a great person, warm with no prejudice. He was a dedicated musician but he got caught up in the same thing I did. He was playing at the time when using heroin was fashionable, when the big blowers like Bird were using, and so, working in Dizzy Gillespie's band, playing lead alto, he became a junkie. But he was serious about his playing so he finally stopped using heroin and devoted all his time to practicing. He became a fanatic and he reached a point where he was technically great, but he was also a good person so he played warm and real. I've talked to him, talked to him for hours, and he told me, "Why don't you straighten up? You have so much to offer. Why don't you give the world what you can?" That's what *he* did. But success trapped him. He got so successful that everyone was expecting him to be always in the forefront. It's the same thing that's happening to Miles right now. Miles is panicked. He's stopped. He's got panicked trying to be different, trying to continually change and be modern and to do the avant-garde thing. Coltrane did that until there was no place else to go. What he finally had, what he really had and wanted and had developed, he could no longer play because that wasn't new anymore. He got on that treadmill and ran himself ragged trying to be new and to change. It destroyed him. It was too wearing, too draining. And he became frustrated and worried. Then he started hurting, getting pains, and he got scared. He got these pains in his back, and he got terrified. He was afraid of doctors, afraid of hospitals, afraid of audiences, afraid of bandstands. He lost his teeth. He was afraid that his sound wasn't strong enough, afraid that the new, young black kids wouldn't think he was the greatest thing that ever lived anymore.

And the pains got worse and worse: they got so bad he couldn't stand the pain. So they carried him to a hospital but he was too far gone. He had cirrhosis, and he died that night. Fear killed him. His life killed him. That thing killed him.

So being a musician and being great is the same as living and being a real person, an honest person, a caring person. You have to be happy with what you have and what you give and not have to be totally different and wreak havoc, not have to have everything be completely new at all times. You just have to be a part of something and have the capacity to love and to play with love. Harry Sweets Edison has done that; Zoot Sims has done that, has finally done that. Dizzy Gillespie has done that to a very strong degree. Dizzy is a very open, contented, loving person; he lives and plays the same way; he does the best he can. A lot of the *old* players were like that—Jack Teagarden, Freddie Webster—people that just played and were good people.

Jealousy has hurt jazz. Instead of trying to help each other and enjoy each other, musicians have become petty and jealous. A guy will be afraid somebody's going to play better than him and steal his job. And the black power—a lot of the blacks want jazz to be *their* music and won't have anything to do with the whites. Jazz is an art form. How can art form *belong* to one race of people? I had a group for a while—Lawrence Marable was playing drums, Curtis Counce was playing bass—and one night I got off the stand, we were at Jazz City, and a couple of friends of mine who were there said, "Hey, man, did you realize what was happening? Those cats were ranking you while you were playing, laughing and really ranking you." I said, "You're *kidding,* man!" I started asking people and I started, every now and then, turning around real quick when I'd be playing. And there they were, sneering at me. Finally I just wigged out at Lawrence Marable. We went out in front of the club and I said, "Man, what's *happening* with you?" And he said, "Oh, fuck you! You know what I think of you, you white motherfucker?" And he spit in the dirt and stepped in it. He said, "You can't play. None of you white punks can play!" I said, "You lousy, stinking, black motherfucker! Why the fuck do you work for me if you feel like that?" And he said, "Oh, we're just taking advantage of you white punk motherfuckers." And that was it. That's what they think of me. If that's what they think of me, what am I going to think of them? I was really hurt, you know; I wanted to cry, you know; I just couldn't believe it—guys I'd given jobs to, and I find out they're talking behind my back and, not only that, laughing behind my back when I'm playing in a club!

There's people like Ray Brown that I worked with, Sonny Stitt, who I blew with, black cats that played marvelous and really were beautiful to me, so I couldn't believe it when these things started happening. But you're going to start wondering, you're going to be leery, naturally, and when you see people that you know . . . I'd go to the union and run into Benny Carter or Gerald Wilson and find myself shying away from them because I'd be wondering, "Do they think, 'Oh, there's that white asshole, that Art Pepper; that white punk can't play; *we* can only play; us black folks is the only people that can play!'?" That's how I started thinking and it destroyed everything. How can you have any harmony together or any beauty when *that's* going on? So that's what happened to jazz. That's why so many people just stopped. Buddy DeFranco, probably the greatest clarinet player who ever lived, people like that, they just got so sick of it; they just got sick to death of it; and they had to get out because it was so heartbreaking.

But all that happened later on. In 1951, musically at least, I had the world by the tail. That was the year I placed second, on alto saxophone, in the *Down Beat* jazz poll. Charlie Parker got fourteen votes more than me and came in first.

DIANE WOKE ME one morning and said, "You have a record date today." I hadn't been playing. I hadn't been doing anything. I said, "Are you kidding? Who with? And where? And what?" She told me that she and Les Koenig from Contemporary Records had got together. The only way they could do it, they figured, was to set it up and not tell me about it so I'd be forced into it. They knew that no matter how strung out I was I would take care of business if people were depending on me. Even at my worst I was always that way. She told me that Miles Davis was in town, and they had gotten his rhythm section and set it all up with them. They were going to record with me that day: Philly Joe Jones on drums, Paul Chambers on bass, and Red Garland on piano.

I wouldn't speak to Diane at all. I told her, "Get out of my sight." I got my horn out of the closet, got the case and put it on the bed and looked at it, and it looked like some stranger. It looked like something from another life. I took the horn out of the case. When you take the saxophone apart there's the body piece, the neck, and the mouthpiece, and those three pieces are supposed to be wiped and wrapped up separately when they're put in the case. Evidently, the last time I'd played I'd been loaded and I'd left the mouthpiece on the neck. I had to clean the horn because it was all dirty. I had to oil it and make sure it was operating correctly. On the end of the neck is a cork, and the mouthpiece slips over that. I had to put a little cork grease on it. I grabbed the mouthpiece and pulled. It was stuck at first and then all of a sudden it came off in my hand. The mouthpiece had been on the neck for so long that the cork had stuck inside it, and on the end of the neck was just bare metal. It takes a good repair man four or five hours to put a new cork on. It has to set. It has to dry. It has to be sanded down. I didn't have time for that. I was going to have to play on a messed up horn.

And I was going to have to play with Miles Davis's rhythm section. They played every single night, all night. I hadn't touched my horn in six months. And being a musician is like being a professional basketball player. If you've been on the bench for six months you can't all of a sudden just go into the game and play, you know. It's almost impossible. And I realized that that's what I had to do, the impossible. No one else could have done it. At all. Unless it was someone as steeped in the genius role as I was. As I *am*. Was and am. And will be. And will always be. And have always been. Born, bred, and raised, nothing but a total genius! Ha! Ahahaha!

There was no way to fix the neck so I put the mouthpiece back on it with the cork and fitted it where it was. If I wasn't in tune, or if it started slipping or pulling loose or leaking, I was dead. I wrapped some tape around it. I took the reed off. It was stuck on the mouthpiece, all rotted and green. I got a new reed, found one I liked, and I blew into the horn for a little while. Then Diane came to the doorway. She was afraid to come in the room. She said, "It's time for us to go." I called her a few choice words: "You stinkin' motherfucker, you! I'd like to kill you, you lousy bitch! You'll get yours!" Then I went into the bathroom and fixed a huge amount.

I had no idea what I was going to play. Talk about being unprepared! The first albums I'd made, I'd always had something I'd written, a couple of tunes. We drove to Melrose Place, where the recording studio was, and there was Les at the door. He gave me a sheepish grin and said, "Well, how're you doing?" I said, "Uh." He said, "It'll be alright. Everything'll be alright."

Les Koenig was someone I'd met in the early fifties. He'd been a movie producer at Paramount, a good producer with a lot of credits (he co-produced *Detective Story, The Heiress, Roman Holiday*). But right after the war they started a big campaign to rid the movie industry of Communists; I think it was the McCarthy thing. I guess after Goebbels and Hitler they saw what a strong force propaganda was, and they were trying to clean up, rightly or wrongly, the people that started it. Probably they were thinking right, but like anything else that starts out like that it becomes a monster after a while and a lot of people suffer. So the people in the industry were asked to sign a paper saying that they didn't believe this or believe that or had never been a Communist or had never attended a meeting or *would* never attend one and all this nonsense. And the people were called before a committee and asked to name Communists in the movie industry. Most of them signed the paper and named names. They just said, "Well, fuck it—this is my livelihood." But there were a few that were such real people, such honest people, honest to themselves, that they would not cooperate. And Les Koenig was one of these. He wasn't a Communist actually, but he refused to go along with it because he felt that the committee infringed upon his rights. And so he was ostracized and kicked out of an industry where he'd become a producer.

After he left the movies he had to find something to do. Les was a person that liked good things. He liked art; he liked good writing; he loved music. And so he started Contemporary Records. Les was the first to record the legendary Ornette Coleman when no other company would touch him. He recorded many young, far-out people and gave them their first opportunities to be heard. And he recorded Sonny Rollins, Shelly Manne, André Previn, Hampton Hawes, Barney Kessel, and many more. I had made albums for different companies, but I'd never gotten the right shake on my royalties, things like that. (In fact, all the records I made prior to my association with Les are still being sold in this country or in Europe, in Japan, and I don't get a penny in royalties from them to this day.) I just figured that was how the record business was. Then I was approached by Les. He offered me a contract, and his whole operation was very different. I saw that here was an honest man, and I felt very safe with him, and so I signed, and I've never had any regrets. We developed a beautiful friendship over the years. When I was really troubled, I could talk to him. He helped me a lot.

So here he is at the door, and I walk in, and I'm afraid to meet these guys because they've been playing with Miles and they're at the pinnacle of success in the jazz world. They're masters. Practicing masters. But here I am and here they are, and I have to act like everything's cool—"Hi" and "What's doin'?" "Hi, Red, what's goin' on?"

When the amenities are over and Les gets everything set up, the balance on the horn and all the microphones, then it's time to start making the album. Red Garland is looking at me, and my mind is a total blank. That's always been one of my faults—memory. I have a poor memory, and I can't think of anything to play. Red says, "Well, I know a nice tune. Do you know this?" He starts playing a tune I've heard before. I say, "What's the name of it?" He says, "You'd Be So Nice to Come Home To." "What key?" "D-minor."

It came out beautiful. My sound was great. The rhythm was great. And I remember in the reviews, by people like Leonard Feather, Martin Williams, they said, "The way Art plays the melody is wonderful. He's so creative. He makes it sound even better than the actual tune." Well, what I'm doing, I don't *know* the melody so I'm playing as close to it as I can get, and that's the creativity part. It does sound good because I play it with a jazz feeling, and it's like a jazz solo, but I'm really trying to play what I recollect of the song.

Les suggested we try a ballad for the next side, so Paul Chambers said, "You know what would be a nice tune for alto and the way you play? 'Imagination.' Do you know that?" I said, "Yeah, I've heard that. Bah dah dah dahhhh dah . . ." Red said, "That's A-flat." I said "Well, I was just goofing around." We ran through the melody and the bridge and then I said, "What should we do at the ending?" Red said, "Just do a little tag kind of thing. Just make it a free kind of thing." I played the melody and then I blew; Red played; Paul played; I came in and just followed along, a little series of chords; and then they stopped and I played a little ad lib kind of thing and we went into the ending. It was just *fantastic.* "Imagination" on *Art Pepper Meets the Rhythm Section.* It sounded as if we'd been rehearsing for months.

That's the way the whole thing went. We played a lot of things I'd liked but never done. And I really moved them, you know. And that's something. They'd been playing with *Miles!* And me being white! They were all real friendly and said it was beautiful, and they dug the way I played. Diane looked at me, like, "Would I forgive her?" and "Wasn't I happy?" And I was so relieved it was over I told her, "Everything's cool." So that was the session, and when it came out the people really liked it.

WHEN I WAS a kid I played clarinet, and my first influence was Artie Shaw. I heard him play on records and on the radio, and I thought he played beautifully, with a wonderful sound and a great technique. Then I saw a picture of him. He was going with or married to a movie star. She was beautiful. He seemed very glamorous to me and I thought, "Wow!" and I saw an opening for *me* at nine, ten years old. I thought, "Wow, there it is!" And I never doubted for a second that I could be as great as Artie Shaw.

I kept buying records. I remember I got "Annie Laurie" by Jimmie Lunceford's band; it was so swinging. In that band at the time was Joe Thomas, the tenor player. He had a full sound; he kind of moaned through his horn; he growled; he moved me. Playing alto was Willie Smith, and I liked the way he led the section. That saxophone section was the best I've ever heard, even up to now. Later on I had occasion to hear the band in person at the Trianon ballroom: they were more devastating than they were on record. And I was standing in front of the band, listening to them, when all of a sudden this beautiful black chick came up. Dorothy Dandridge. She had furs on, and she stood there listening to the band and looking at Joe Thomas, and after they finished their set everybody fell all over her, and she went to Joe Thomas and started rapping with him. It was so glamorous. I loved not only the music, I loved the whole idea.

I liked a lot of people. I loved Johnny Hodges in Duke Ellington's band, the way he played ballads, and in that band was Ben Webster, who had a rich, full tone like Joe Thomas's but more subtle. Joe Thomas was a shouter; Ben Webster was more soulful. Then I heard Louis Jordan on alto: he knocked me out. I liked Benny Goodman. I liked Charlie Barnet, and then all the Dixieland people—Wingy Manone and, oh, that guy that played cornet, "Livery Stable Blues," what was his name? I liked Roy Eldridge and, naturally, when I got with Benny Carter, I liked him, but I never attempted to play like any of these people. Never. I'd see little books—*Solos by So-and-so,* taken off the records—and every now and then I'd buy one and try it, but it just wasn't me, and it had no meaning to me at all, playing what was written. All these people influenced me, subconsciously, but I didn't feel like any of them and I didn't play like any of them. I'd go to sessions and hear other people playing and think, "Oh, that guy sounds like Willie Smith; that guy sounds like Johnny Hodges." And I used to think, "Well, maybe I don't play good. Maybe I'm on the wrong track." Just before I was drafted I heard Lester Young—he was with Basie's band—and, boy, I said, "That's the one!" But he played tenor and I played alto. I dug the things he did, but I didn't want to ape him. I ran into Zoot Sims; he knew all of Prez's solos and could sound just like him, and he'd hold the horn up at a forty-five-degree angle, just like Prez did. I thought, "Why don't *I* sound like anybody else? What's wrong with me?" Finally, I got with Stan Kenton's band, and then people started telling me, "Man, you sure sound great!" I'd ask, "What do you mean?" I'd want to know why. They'd say, "Man, I can tell it's *you.*" And I thought, "Well, that's what it is. I wasn't wrong after all."

I got drafted. I went overseas and played there, and everybody liked me. I came home three years later and just assumed everything was the same as it was when I left. I'm not home more than a few days when this friend comes over and he says, "Man, have you heard Bird or Diz?" I said, "Bird or Diz who?" "Have you heard bebop?" *"Be-bop?"* I hadn't heard a word, I swear to God. I was feeling good. I'd been playing in England, built up a style of my own.

He put on a record, Sonny Stitt and Dizzy Gillespie. On one side was "Salt Peanuts" and on the other was "Oop Bop Sh'Bam . . ." Ahahaha! " . . .A Klug Ya Mop!" They played these charts—"Salt Peanuts" was so fast . . . Jimmie Lunceford used to have a tune called "White Heat" that was real, real fast, beyond comprehension at the time. These guys played faster than that, and they really *played.* Not only were they fast, technically, but it all had meaning, and they swung! They were playing notes in the chords that I'd never heard before. It was more intricate, more bluesy, more swinging, more everything. They had gone from one decade to another, one culture to another. Straight up! I heard it and I thought, "Oh, Jesus Christ! What am I going to do?" I heard this Sonny Stitt just roaring, flying over the keys, swinging, shouting. It moved me so much—and it scared me to death.

The guy said, "Well, what do you think of that?" I said, "Yeah, well." I had to protect myself so I said, "Yeah, but, boy, it's so . . . They never relax. When are they going to settle back and groove? Where's the warmth and the feeling? Their tones . . ." I tried everything. Anything to justify my own position. He played a thing by Dizzy and Charlie Parker, and I heard Charlie Parker, and I really didn't like his tone. It sounded coarse to me. I finally had something to hang on to. I said, "I don't dig his tone." My friend said, "Well, what about Dizzy?" I had to admit, "Yeah, he's got a nice tone. It's a little thin though."

He left. I got ill. What was I going to do now? I decided the only thing I could do was just practice and play and play and develop my own thing. The tenor was always the more popular instrument. It used to be there was never a solo written in a stock band arrangement for alto. It was all tenor solos—that was the "jazz saxophone." Charlie Parker made the alto popular, and I thought, "Well, that's good. That's good." I noticed that all the tenor players had switched to alto, and they all sounded just like Charlie Parker.

Books came out. Bird's solo on this, Bird's solo on that. They'd copy these things off the records and practice by the hour Bird's solos and his licks. Everybody sounded like him with the same ugly sound. Guys I'd heard before who had had beautiful tones now, all of a sudden, had ugly tones like Bird. Out of tune. Squalling. Squawking. I didn't want to play that way at all, but I realized that I had to upgrade my playing and I had to really learn chords and scales. So I didn't copy anyone. I didn't practice much, but I went out and blew and blew and blew. Then I rejoined Kenton, and I sounded only like me.

Bird had a great ear for changes, a great blues sense, great technical ability. He was able to play real fast, and his lines were beautiful. Everything was thought out and made sense. I never used to like his tone, but that's personal. A tone is like a person's voice. Now when I listen to him I love the whole thing, tone and all. He was a genius. But when I heard Coltrane!

In the late fifties I heard John Coltrane with Miles Davis. I heard the *Kind of Blue* album. On that album he played everything you can imagine. He played more notes than Bird, more involved than Bird, and I *loved* his tone. Everything he played held together and meant something to me, and he really moved me. He's the only guy I ever heard in my life that I said, "I'd give my right arm to play like that."

It happened slowly, but by 1964, when I got out of San Quentin and started playing again, more and more I found myself sounding like Coltrane. Never copied any of his licks consciously, but from my ear and my feeling and my sense of music . . . I went into Shelly's Manne Hole with a group, and a lot of people liked what I did and really thought I was playing modern, and a lot of others asked what had happened to the old Art Pepper.

When I got out of the joint the last time, in '66, I had no horns. I could only afford one horn, and I got a tenor because, I told myself, to make a living I had to play rock. But what I really wanted to do was play like Coltrane.

In '68 I got the job playing lead alto with Buddy Rich. And that day in Las Vegas, after the rehearsal, I was blowing Don Menza's alto in the motel room. I was jamming in front of the mirror, blowing the blues, really shouting, and all of a sudden I realized, "Wow, this is me! This is *me!*" Christine was there in the room reading a book, and at the same time she looked up and said, "Art, that's fantastic! *Alto,* that's you!" Then I realized that I had almost lost myself. Something had protected me for all those years, but Trane was so strong he'd almost destroyed me.

That experience—it lasted about four years that I was influenced so much by John Coltrane—was a freeing experience. It enabled me to be more adventurous, to extend myself notewise and emotionally. It enabled me to break through inhibitions that for a long time had kept me from growing and developing. But since the day I picked up the alto again I've realized that if you don't play *yourself* you're nothing. And since that day I've been playing what I felt, what *I* felt, regardless of what those around me were playing or how they thought I should sound.

THE FIRST NIGHT at Caesar's Palace I sounded good, and everybody congratulated me. Afterwards, Christine and I went with some of the guys and had a bite to eat and some drinks, and then we went to somebody's room and smoked pot and put on our bathing suits and went swimming in the pool. It was fun, and it was great to be accepted into that world. I thought of all the things I'd given up in using drugs. I started feeling good about being a musician and about life.

Every night I got stronger and played better and more together with the band. Me and Al Porcino made the band swing in a different kind of way. I was playing good solos. There was talk about going to Europe pretty soon. We made an album. Then, all of a sudden I started noticing some little pains in my stomach. And when I put my uniform on . . . One night I asked Christine, "Do I look heavier to you?" It seemed like every day I'd feel these pains. I felt bloated. I went to the drugstore and bought all kinds of stuff for gas and laxatives, but they didn't help. I got worried.

We finished the job in Vegas and went from there to San Francisco, to Basin Street West. Christine and I got a room right above the club. The pain got worse and worse, but I kept playing, until one night the pain was so bad I couldn't bend over to get my music out. I didn't want to go to a doctor because I was afraid—afraid of what it might be. I was hoping it would go away by itself. I walked out of the club that night, and Christine helped me up the stairs. I sat on the bed. I couldn't lay down. I started to fall over, and I thought I was going to die. Christine got me back into a sitting position and ran down the stairs and hit on Buddy Rich. He'd heard that my stomach was hurting, but he didn't know it was that bad.

Buddy found out from the owner of the club where the nearest hospital was. He helped carry me from the room and drove me to St. Luke's. They weren't going to let me into the hospital because I didn't have insurance, but Buddy flipped out and forced them to take me. He signed for me.

They didn't know what was wrong so they couldn't give me anything for the pain. They put me in the intensive care unit. They put tubes in my nose and in my veins, and they stuck a tube from one vein into my heart so they could measure the way my heart was pumping. They had two things fastened on my chest that went to a machine that recorded my heartbeat. I remember looking at the screen and seeing it. It made a pattern and a noise, but the pattern would change and drop and the beeping would slow. I think I went into a coma for a little while, and when I came out of it I saw that the pattern of my heartbeat was very irregular and everyone had gathered around me. There had been two or three other patients in this room, and they had died. Now all the attention was focused on me. Then I saw the doctor. He was leaning on me, he had a big syringe in his hand, and I felt it prick my stomach. It filled immediately, completely with blood. He looked at it and at me and shook his head. He said, "Where's Mrs. Pepper?" They'd said she was my wife to make it easier. Christine wasn't there. He sent a couple of people to look for her, and he said, "We haven't got time to wait. We have to operate." I said, "I can't stand to have an operation. I can't stand to be cut." He said, "You've got to sign this paper. You can't live without the operation." I signed my name.

From then on, it was all hustle. They gave me a shot, and I was rolled through a hallway. I was in an elevator and in a room that was very bright. I still had all the tubes; the bottles were still hanging; people were holding them, wheeling them by me. I remember saying to the doctor, "Please put me out!" I remembered the operation in Chino. I can't stand pain and I can't stand to see blood. If I see a wreck on the highway I get sick. I got into this bright room, and they put something over my nose, and, mercifully, from that point I was out.

DURING THIS TIME, I later found out, besides going through the operation I was having DTs because I'd been drinking so much. I dreamed I was in a farmhouse with a gang, and we were selling dope and robbing and hiding from the police. We had piles of heroin. They didn't want us to shoot any, but I was begging for some of it. I was in such pain. Then the police came and started shooting at us, but I kept trying to get the heroin, and finally I got some. But every time I found a way to hide from the rest of the people the needle would clog or the dropper would break, and I could never get it into me. I wasn't hooked at that time, but I was still dreaming about dope.

I opened my eyes and saw the ceiling. I heard somebody say, "He's coming out of it. Call the doctor." I saw Christine standing by the bed. She grabbed me and said, "Thank God." The doctor came in. I was aware of a tight feeling around my stomach and a throbbing pain. He said, "How are you feeling?" I said, "I don't know." He said, "Do you know where you are?" I said, "Yeah, in a hospital." He said, "Where?" I had to think for a while. I said, "San Francisco." He said, "Don't be scared. You've had a bad time. We didn't give you a chance in the world to survive, but the way things look now I don't think there's any danger. First there's something I have to tell you, and I'm going to tell you immediately so you can start getting used to the idea. You can never drink again. We had to cut you open for exploratory surgery, and I noticed that your liver didn't look right, so we did a biopsy. It showed a cirrhosis condition. Your days of drinking are over." Then the doctor asked me if I had been in an automobile accident or a bad fight. I said no, and he said, "Well, when I put the hypodermic in your stomach, you were bleeding to death internally. All we could do was open you up, try to find out where it was coming from, and stop it. I made the incision, and blood just flew out of you, and when we got you cleaned up I saw that your spleen was ruptured. These things usually happen in automobile accidents." They had removed my spleen. I looked at the doctor and I saw that he was the leader of the gang in the dream I'd had.

I started getting pains in my upper back. I had contracted pneumonia right after the operation, and one of my lungs was filled with fluid. The doctor came in. "This is going to hurt, but it has to be done." He gave me a local anesthetic and took a long needle and stuck it through my back and all the way into my lung. I sat on the edge of my bed bent over. He had Christine there and two nurses holding me. The pain was unbearable. He got the needle into my lung and drew the fluid out. When he was done he gave me a big shot of morphine. I said, "I don't think I could ever stand to go through that again." I looked at this monstrous jug: it was almost six inches full of a lightish pink liquid that had been in my lung.

During this period they gave me Demerol and morphine. When they started pulling me off these drugs, I dreamed and I saw things. I was being chased by police—these were dreams I'd had before—I'd be with my grandmother driving on the freeway trying to fix. She'd be trying to stop me and I'd be hitting her with my fist. I'd be running, hiding, and then I'd actually see things crawling around. Little insects.

Christine was very good. She'd stayed up with me for two days while they were trying to find out what was wrong, and when they'd decided to operate and couldn't find her, she was asleep on a little bench in a chapel they had. I kept searching my mind, trying to remember when I'd gotten a violent blow to my stomach, because the doctor said that that was the only thing that could have caused my spleen to rupture. And I remembered those times, just before I went with Buddy, when we were at our wildest, when she'd hit me so hard. I remembered that at those times I was in such pain from those punches I could hardly breathe. The first time I mentioned it to her, Christine really flipped out. I guess she thought I was blaming her. I was just trying to figure out what caused it, that's all. I don't know if she felt bad because she thought she had done it. I don't know what she thought.

WHILE I WAS in the hospital—for about three months—I had visits from all kinds of people and cards and letters. It was amazing to find out how many people cared about me. There was a nurse there, a black girl; her old man dug me. When she told him I was in the hospital he got a TV for me. You have to rent them. He paid for the TV, and I never even met him.

A priest came and asked me if I wanted to talk. I said no. He came when Christine was there, and he inquired and found out she was there all the time. He asked about our financial situation. The priest made an arrangement. He paid for Christine's food, and they fed her and me at the same time in my room. That was a beautiful thing.

I didn't know how we were going to pay for the hospital. The bill was twelve or thirteen thousand dollars. Some people got together in Oakland and had a benefit for me. They rented a club in Jack London Square, and a bunch of musicians played for free. Roland Kirk played, and I had never even met Roland Kirk. It still surprises me that he would do that. They got about thirteen hundred dollars to help me pay my hospital bill. It was the nicest thing that ever happened to me. It was something amazing. I never could get over it.

For a long time after the operation, I was afraid to look down. The nurse would change the bandages, the doctor would check the incision, but I never would look at it. Finally the doctor gave me this long pitch saying, "You've got to accept yourself as you are and be thankful you're alive." He forced me to look. I got sick at my stomach. I had two incisions, one from the middle of my breastbone down to just above the pubic hair and another to the left. My bellybutton was gone. It was the ugliest thing I'd ever seen. When I was young, with Patti, she had to have a cyst removed from her ovary, and I paid a lot of money to a specialist to make a tiny incision where the pubic hair was and then go up to remove the cyst so there wouldn't be a scar. That's how I felt about those things. Now here I was with horrible scars all over my stomach, just ruined. I thought, "How in the world will I ever ball anybody? Have anybody see me?" It got to the point where I'd never take my shirt off. I hated to take a bath or a shower because I couldn't stand to see myself. And I still feel the same way. I still feel the same way.

WELL, WE WENT back to Hollywood, and I was in bad shape but I was healing. Then I got out of bed one morning, and I noticed a pain in the middle of my stomach and saw a little puffiness there. It kept getting bigger. Christine talked me into calling the doctor who performed the operation at St. Luke's in San Francisco. He said it might be a hernia.

I went to the Veterans Hospital in Brentwood, where they would treat me for free. They checked it out and said that's what it was. I was in pain. I'd gotten a bunch of pills from the hospital, and I took them all the time. I drank wine and shot stuff. A guy I knew came around with some Numorphan, pills I'd never tried before. I cooked them up and shot them. It was like shooting heroin and coke, and it took the pain away. Then I got a call from Buddy Rich. They were on their way to New York and wanted me to join the band as soon as I could. At the VA they said I could play even with the hernia. My dad loaned me a corset he wore for his back. I felt strong enough, and I knew that if I didn't get back with the band or do something I was going to get hooked and die. Buddy sent me my ticket. They were opening at the Riverboat. Fortunately, I wasn't strung out yet, so I cleaned up and got on the plane with Christine and joined the band. I'd been playing lead alto before, but now it was too much of a strain. They put me on third alto. I wore the corset; Christine would lace it up. I kept working as hard as I could. I was juicing and taking uppers. We played the Riverboat for quite a while and then started back to L.A. on the road, playing Boston and Philadelphia. We played Chicago. The pain got worse and worse. By the time we got to Texas I couldn't make it anymore, and Don Menza and the guys in the sax section told me to just finger the notes. The last night was New Year's Eve, and the pain was so bad I had to stop playing.

I had a ventral hernia, and my stomach was all puffed out. We got back to L.A., and I ran into this guy again, and he still had Numorphan, so I started shooting it. It killed the pain so I could play. With that and some Percodan tablets I made it through the job we had then.

I went to the VA again and somebody else had a look at me. This doctor said I needed an operation. I told Christine, "I'm so scared I can't stand it. I wish I could die." I wanted us to make a pact—we would kill ourselves. The doctor said he had to make a big incision and then pull the flesh and wrap it around my insides to keep them from pushing out. He said it would be very painful and it might not be successful. I checked into the hospital. I was so messed up from the things I'd been doing it took them a month and a half with food and vitamins to build me up so they could operate.

I had the operation. I got pneumonia again. Finally I went home. I laid in bed and Christine gave me medicine. I couldn't lay on either of my sides or on my stomach. Fortunately we had a little TV at the foot of the bed. The guy came around with the Numorphan, and I bought some heroin, too. I got strung out like a dog. Then one day I noticed the little pain again. I looked at my stomach and saw a swelling. There was a little area right in the middle that was puffing out exactly the way it had the last time. I had the TV by the bed, and I left it on all day and all night.

Christine couldn't stand it anymore. She wanted me to go to her mother's house and stay. Her mother was sick, too. She had had an operation at the same time, and Christine wanted to take care of both of us at her mother's. I was using. I couldn't do it. She had to leave. She said, "You're just going to kill yourself! That's all you want to do! I can't watch it anymore!" She cried and called me every name under the sun. She left. I laid in bed and watched television.

In the icebox was a little lunch meat, a little jar of mayonnaise, and half a loaf of bread. I'd take my medicine. This guy would come with the Numorphan. The guy I was copping stuff from, he'd bring a taste over and lay it on me; I got him to go pawn my horn. Christine came back three days later. She burst out crying when she saw me: "Oh God, Art, you look like you're dead. Look at yourself!" She brought a mirror. I looked horrible. She said, "You've got to do something. Either do something or I'll call the police and have them take you away. What about Greg Dykes?"

I had first met Greg in the federal joint. When I saw him again, later, he said that if I ever got really hung up I could give him a call and go to Synanon. I told Christine, "I don't want to go there. People think that everybody that's there is a rat." She said, "Fuck what people think. *You* know what you are. I can't leave you like this. I'm going to call Synanon or I'm going to call the police." I said, "All right, call Greg and see what he has to say, but I'm not promising anything." She called him, and she was crying over the phone. Greg asked to talk to me. He said, "Art, what's wrong?" I told him I was just ruined physically: "All I want to do is get loaded and die, but I don't have the nerve to kill myself." He said, "Ohhhh, man. Get down here! Come down and we'll take care of you! Please, man. It's your only salvation. I really love you, man. I want to save you. Please come down." I said okay and I hung up. I looked at Christine and said, "Oh God, man, it's the end of my life."

Charles Mingus

Mingus's Beneath the Underdog *(1971), more than a decade in work and written in the third person, remains the most provocative autobiography in jazz—as unrelenting and aggressive and original as Mingus the musician and Mingus the man.*

On a Sunday afternoon in August, before their second son Eugene had begun to walk, Mingus said, "Barbara, find somebody to stay with the baby and get Charles dressed and ready—I got to make it out to a session at Billy Berg's this afternoon and I'm gonna take you and him."

"Oh, honey, he's too young to enjoy anything like that."

"No, he isn't, and I want his opinion. I gotta call Buddy Collette . . . Hello, Buddy? Can you make a gig out to Billy Berg's today? Here's your chance to show me what you're talking about with that Merle Johnson small lay mouthpiece and soft reed, 'cause Charlie Parker's going to be there with his old out-of-tune self like you say . . . Yeah, I heard him with strings. Sounded to me like the strings were out of tune and Bird was bending notes playing jazz regardless of those overpaid motherfuckers—and not one black violin player on the session! Come on out, I want to see you cut him so musicians will start talking about *you,* 'cause I know if you play like you played as a kid, with balls, Buddy, that's what's gonna happen. Later, Buddy."

"Daddy, Daddy!"

"Hey, boy. You and Mama are coming with me to hear some music. I want your opinion today. You remember all the records I played for you, don't you? You remember Buddy?"

"Yes, Daddy."

"You like Duke Ellington?"

"Yes, Daddy. Duke, Duke!"

"That's all I want to know. When I'm up on the stand today playing with Buddy and Bird—that's Charlie Parker, the man with the same kind of horn as Buddy—you come up and stand by the one you like as much as Duke Ellington."

"All right, Daddy."

"Ready, Barbara?"

"Coming."

* * *

"AND NOW, LADIES and gentlemen, the final set for this afternoon. Stan Levy, drums, from Dizzy Gillespie's group. Dodo Marmarosa, piano. Lucky Thompson, tenor sax."

"Who's he, Buddy?"

"Cat cut from Basie's."

"Buddy Collette, alto sax. Charles Parker, a gentleman from Dizzy's group also. And Charles Mingus on bass. And please will all you people give Miles Davis a hand—Miles is just in from New York. Come on now, everybody—Miles Davis! Give him a good California welcome!"

"Okay, Bird. Something everybody knows."

"'Billy's Bounce'?"

"Don't know that, Bird."

"It's just the blues in F. Buddy, gone . . . Take four, Dodo . . . Blow, Miles."

"I done blew, motherfucker. Now you got it, cocksucker. Blow, Lucky."

". . . Miles, why's his head so swollen? . . . He sounds like a subtone Don Byas."

"What was that, country-boy bass-player? Cool it and keep some time behind me!"

"Keep your own time, Lucky, before I start playing your solos back at you."

"What? Dig this cat! With a bass? Come on, I want to hear that."

"Move over and share the mike, big head, so you won't be embarrassed. I'll ape you. Dodo, Stan, lay out. Stroll."

"Whewee! This motherfucker can play! What was that tag you added to my solo?"

"Kiddle lid."

"How the hell you play that sound like you laughing and talking?"

"Bird, you hear this country boy?"

"Yeah, Lucky, did you? The same way we make dah ooh dah down on chromatics from your C to C-sharp to B to C natural, B-flat to B natural, and so forth. He just added a quarter tone glissando, put his heart in it."

"The other night I heard a cat play bass the way Adolphus Allbrook used to. It don't supposed to be possible but they do it."

"Bird, you putting me on? That's the second time I heard about Adolphus Allbrook. Jimmy Blanton told me he carved a wooden pick with one hand, kept playing with the other, finished his pick, and played more than a guitar with it."

"Stone genius, Mingus."

"I'd sure like to meet him."

"Yeah, he's great. A scientist too—physics major. Teaches judo at the police department. Mastered the harp in two years."

"When are you motherfuckers going to stop talking and start playing, instead of just Dodo and Stan over there jacking off?"

"Miles, you're so vulgar."

"I want to hear Bird blow, not all this dumb-ass conversation."

"So gone. One, two, one, two, three, four."

"Yeah, Bird. Play, baby! Go, man."

"Hooray!"

"Ladies and gentlemen, will you all shut up and just listen to this motherfucker blowing!"

"Miles! Careful, man, you can't say that."

"Schitt, man, I put my hand over the mike on 'motherfucker.' Remember Monk calling the club owner in Detroit a motherfucker seven times on the mike 'cause he didn't have a good piano?"

"He had it next night though. If he'd called him 'sir' he'd of had the same old clunker."

"Who's this Buddy Collette, Mingus?"

"My best friend. He used to really play but Whitey scared him white inside. He likes to sound white. He can read fly-schitt scattered on a fly-swatter though."

"And that ain't jazz."

"So tell *him,* Lucky."

"I will. First I'll cut him in his own bag."

"Don't try, Lucky, you'll bleed to death. Everybody in the studio clique tried it. He plays flute, clarinet, everything—just like the white man says you're supposed to play and a little fuller."

"Cat named Paul Desmond up in Frisco plays like that. You heard him?"

"Who's that little boy holding onto Bird's pants leg?"

"That's my son."

"Duke Ellington, Daddy! Duke Ellington, Daddy!"

"What's he mean?"

"He's telling me he digs Bird. Look at old Bird smiling from cheek to cheek. He's sure a beautiful person."

"Go on, Dodo! Man, that ofay sure can play! And that drummer too. What's his name?"

"Stan Levy. He's a Jew. You know them Jew boys got the soul and gone."

"Gone. Take it out."

"Hooray! Yeah!!"

"How about 'April in Paris,' Bird?"

"Sure thing. Sure thing."

"Ming, listen to this!"

"*Good dog!* sounds like millions of souls all wrapped up in that old ragged horn of his. Scotch tape, rubber bands, and chewing gum and they say he squeaks. Haw! Squeak, Bird! He's just holding it listening to it sing."

"Look, he's got your little boy in a trance. He can't even move."

"Sshhh, Lucky! Now I heard him. He's the cat I been hearing in my dreams."

"Let's catch a smoke outside, Mingus."

"I wonder if Buddy still thinks Merle Johnson mouthpieces give a bigger sound. Some teacher's been telling him that colored cats don't get big sounds with open lay mouthpieces."

"Haw haw, Mingus! It takes effort is what they mean. Work. They don't like to sweat. The white man ain't satisfied till they take all the human element out. Like Bird—he made it this far and they give him horns with soft action. He says, 'What for? Too late.' He likes working. He plays an old Conn with a number thirty open lay mouthpiece. I remember some kid telling Bird he heard Negroes used trick mouthpieces to make things easier. Bird reached in his case, said 'Here, try this Berg Larsen, son.' The kid put it on his horn and blew. Wheeee! Nothing came out but air. He turned red and blue in the face. Not a sound came forth. Bird said, 'Give it here, let's see what's wrong with it. Oh, the reed's too soft.' He took out a fifty-cent piece and held the reed to it and burned around it with a cigarette lighter—burned it down almost to the stem. Then he tried it out. 'Plays beautiful,' Bird said. 'Still a little soft but it will do.' If that kid had tried to blow a reed that stiff he'd passed out or died before he got it to play. You know who that was? A kid named Lee Konitz. Ask him when you meet him if you ever get to New York . . . Say, you wanna play with my band, Mingus?"

"No. You wanna play with my trio, Lucky?"

"Ho ho! Mingus, ain't nobody heard of you."

"I'm glad, man. That's why I make three bills a week at home in sunny funny California."

"Three? Who you with?"

"Ourselves. 'Pick, Plank and Plunk.' Me and Lucius Lane and Harry Hopewell."

"Lane?"

"Guitar. The greatest."

"Oh, yeah? You heard of Barney Kessel?"

"Yeah, and Kessel heard of Lane. Lucky, why don't you and Miles rehearse with us? Maybe we can incorporate. We got a *bad* book. Can't too many trumpet players play it. Carl George says he has trouble. He says it's too much movement."

"You heard Diz?"

"Just on records with Bird. Sounds like he's kinda into Bartok. But fuck all that dumb schitt, Lucky. Come and play some of our simple west-coast colored no-name music. We're rehearsing tomorrow at Britt Woodman's. He's with Boyd Rayburn now. Some of the sidemen said no colored could possibly play the trombone parts, so I'm the funny cat that got Britt an audition."

"Boyd's a real straight cat though."

"Yeah, but I can't stand people looking over my shoulder and Harry Babson was standing behind breathing over me so I fucked up Boyd's music. But I told Boyd since he needed a trombone player to give Britt a chance and not judge all blacks by me."

"Want to go inside and hear Ray Brown?"

"If that's the kid with Diz I heard him on the radio the other night—he plays Pettiford pretty well, but I wonder what *he* can do on his own with all that technique. I know when a player is still using standard bass tricks. Bill Hadnot, one of the greatest bass players on earth—and he may not ever be heard—called me to check if I was playing with Bird and Diz. I turned on my radio and wham!—there I was, at least the way I played around 'thirty-nine. It turned out to be Ray. But Ray stays too close to Oscar's ideas. He's thinking bass, which shouldn't be. It's thinking *notes,* sounds you hear, same as a horn. If a cat could *hum* good ideas I'd dig that. Have you ever heard an alto sound like Bird?"

"Not even Buster Smith."

"Well, you watch and see if Bird's sound don't become more or less the pattern for alto, all over the world for anyone who hears it . . . Lucky, I'd better leave. I have to drive my wife and boy home and then out to Venice for the gig."

"Okay, Mingus. We'll talk about forming a group one of these days. See ya."

"Barbara, ready?"

"Yes, if you can get Charles to stop sticking his head in Bird's alto."

"Hey, boy! Come on."

"Bird. Daddy! Duke Ellington. Bird! Bird!"

"Yeah, I know, son. Bird true is something else."

THERE WAS a man named Fats Navarro who was born in Key West, Florida, in 1923. He was a jazz trumpet player, one of the best in the world. He and my boy met for the first time on a cold winter night in 1947 in Grand Central Station in New York City. Lionel Hampton's band had just got off the train from Chicago and Benny Bailey gaily said good-bye and split: he was leaving for Paris, France. The guys all stood around in their overcoats by the clock, waiting for the new man joining the band. A big, fat fellow walked up carrying a trumpet case and asked in the oddest high squeaky voice "This the Hampton crew?" and Britt Woodman introduced Fats Navarro.

Charles felt embarrassed as the band walked out. There were strangers, women and children, all around, and the guys were laughing too loudly and joking and words like motherfucker and cocksucker echoed through the station. They took the shuttle to Times Square and another subway to Pennsylvania Station and boarded the train for Washington, D.C. It was my boy's first trip to the Apple, but all he saw of it was underground.

Next day they rehearsed at the Palace Theatre in Washington. Hampton had a nine-brass book. The trumpets were Wendell Cully, Duke Garrett, Walter Williams, and the high-note player they all called "Whistler." Navarro just sat there placidly with his horn on his lap waiting for his solos while the rest of the band played arrangements. When Hamp pointed to him, Fats stood up and played, and played, and played! played! played! One of the other trumpet players became resentful of this new star in their midst and started muttering, "Schitt, this guy can't even read!" Fats laughed, grabbed the musician's part, eyed it and said, "Schitt, you ain't got nothin' to read here!" And he sight-read from the score impeccably for the entire last show.

Fats was featured all that week in Washington and then they went on the road. The trumpet player whose part Fats had read with such scornful ease couldn't forget what had happened. He was a man who carried a gun and he was convinced he had been insulted. He was lipping a lot about how he would kill Fats one of these days.

They traveled by bus. The small instruments were in the luggage racks, the basses lay cushioned in the back row. Seats were assigned by seniority and the one next to my boy was vacant and was given to Fats Navarro. Mingus and he hadn't talked much up to now. The first night out the whole band was tired and they settled down to rest as the bus headed west. Later Mingus woke up feeling uneasy. It was past twelve midnight and everything was still, the men were sleeping, but the seat beside Mingus was empty. He heard a voice in the dark, someone pleading, "No . . . nooo . . . noooo . . ." Then a familiar little high-pitched voice squeaked, "Don't *ever* say you gonna cut or shoot somebody 'less you do it, hear? Now if you don't be quiet I might cut you too deep so hold still while I makes you bleed a little 'cause when Theodore Navarro says *he's* gonna cut you that's what he's gonna do." My boy felt the others waking and listening too but nobody made a sound.

Later Fats came quietly back to his seat. After a silence he said, "That wasn't no way to treat a new member, that was old-fashioned jealousy schitt. Me and Miles and Dizzy and little Benny Harris played together and didn't never have no old-fashioned jealousy schitt. Why should any old member of the band be so uncourteous as to uncourteously threaten a new member?"

Nothing was said afterwards about the cat who got scratched and nothing more was heard from him about shooting Fats.

The band played thirty or forty one-nighters in a row, usually arriving in a town just in time to check into their dingy hotel rooms and wash up. Fats and my boy liked to talk to each other and began to room together. It was cheaper that way anyhow.

So this bus rolled on and on across the country, sometimes by day and sometimes at night. And in the crummy hotel rooms with big old-fashioned brass beds that sagged under Fats's enormous weight like hammocks they began a dialogue that continued off and on until the time it had to end.

"YOU LIKE ALL kinds of music, Mingus? I was born in Key West, Florida. My family's Cuban. You play Cuban music?"

"I'm not hip to that, Fats. I know some Mexican tunes."

"Hang out with me and I'll take you to some of the joints. You can sit in, blow some. Do you play any other than bass?"

"I try my best not to but I get my chops up on piano sometimes when I'm scoring long enough. I love to hear it on piano."

"Who'd you work with before, Mingus?"

"Illinois Jacquet . . . Alvino Rey . . ."

"Yeah? I played with Jacquet too. You play with Diz or Bird when they was in California? See, I knowed of you before you knowed of me. Talk to Jacquet or someone else—you ain't so undiscovered. Miles played once with you. He used to tell about the band you guys had."

"He did? He hardly said a word except with his horn. How cool can you get when a cat don't even say hello. That's the system, Fats, the system that keeps the blacks apart."

"I see what you mean—so busy worrying how to make a dime with your horn, ain't got time to make a race. Gotta go downtown and see the man, ain't got time to shake your hand. So we play jazz in its place."

"Where's the place, Fats?"

"Right in their faces. They know we know where it's at. Aw, they own us, Mingus. If they don't own us, they push us off the scene. Jazz is big business to the white man and you can't move without him. We just work-ants. He owns the magazines, agencies, record companies, and all the joints that sell jazz to the public. If you won't sell out and you try to fight they won't hire you and they give a bad picture of you with that false publicity."

"Sell out, Fats? To who? Look at Ellington, Armstrong, Basie—look at Hamp. All big famous bandleaders. You can't tell me that agents and bookers own guys like that!"

"Mingus, you a nice guy from California, I don't want to disillusion you. But I been through all that schitt and I had to learn to do some other things to get along. I learned better than to try to make it just with my music out on these dirty gang-mob streets 'cause I still love playing better than money. Jazz ain't supposed to make nobody no millions but that's where it's at. Them that shouldn't is raking it in but the purest are out in the street with me and Bird and it rains all over us, man. I was better off when nobody knew my name except musicians. You can bet it ain't jazz no more when the underworld moves in and runs it strictly for geetz and even close out the colored agents. They shut you up and cheat you on the count of your record sales and if you go along they tell the world you a real genius. But if you don't play they put out the word you're a troublemaker, like they did me. Then if some honest club owner tries to get hold of you to book you, they tell you're not available or you don't draw or you'll tear up the joint like you was a gorilla. And you won't hear nothin' about it except by accident. But if you behave, boy, you'll get booked—except for less than the white cats that copy your playing and likely either the agent or owner'll pocket the difference."

"But Fats, I know a lot of guys with managers taking a fair cut—fifteen, twenty, maybe thirty percent."

"Who told you that? Mingus, *King Spook* don't even own fifty percent of himself! His agent gets fifty-one, forty-nine goes to a corporation set up in his name that he don't control and he draws five hundred a week and don't say *nothing*—but he's famous, Mingus, hear, he's famous!"

"Nobody didn't hold no gun on King Spook to sign no contract like that."

"You sure about that? One time he got uppity and they kicked him out of the syndicate joints. He had to break up his band out in California. He tried to buck it on his own with nobody but his old lady to help him beat the system. Mingus, that's the biggest gun in the world to stick in a man's ribs—*hunger.* So he sold out again. Now he's got a club named after him but it ain't his. Oh, it's a hard wrinkle, Mingus. Haw haw! I'm thinking when Peggy Lee be appearing in some east side club. Her biggest applause come when she says, 'Now I'm going to do the great Billie Holiday,' and Billie be out on the street and they all be saying she's a junkie. They had Billie so hung up they wouldn't pay the right way, they just put a little money in her hand every night after work, just enough so she come back tomorrow. They drives ya to it, Mingus. They got you down and they don't let you up."

"If you're right, why don't some of the big Negro businessmen step into the picture?"

"'Cause they ain't caught on it's a diamond mine and they too busy scufflin' in their own corn patch and maybe scared. You breaking into Whitey's private vault when you start telling Negroes to wake up and move in where they belong and it ain't safe, Mingus. When the day comes the black man says I want mine, then hide your family and get yourself some guns. 'Cause there ain't no better business for Whitey to be in than Jim Crow business."

"I guess you got something here, Fats. I notice you and me staying in hotels like this one for twice what the white man pays."

"Well, if things don't change, Cholly, do like I tell you, get yourself some heat, guns, cannons, and be willing to die like *they* was. That's all I heared when I was a kid, how bad they was and not afraid to die—to arms, to arms, and all that schitt, give me liberty or give me death! Show me where that atomic power button is and I'll give them cocksuckers some liberty!"

"You said money shouldn't matter to musicians, Fats. What if we all gave up on fame and fortune and played 'cause we love to, like the jazzmen before us—at private sessions for people that listened and respected the players? Then people would know that jazz musicians play for love."

"I thought you had some children, Mingus. Don't they need no ends out there in California?"

"I'm going to write a book and when I sell it I'm not gonna play any more for money. I'll compose and now and then rent a ballroom and throw a party and pay some great musicians to play a couple of things and improvise all night long. That's what jazz originally was, getting away from the usual tiddy, the hime, the gig."

"But Mingus, how about them crumb-crushers of yours when their little stomachs get to poppin' and there ain't nothin' in their jaws but their gums, teeth and tongue, what you gonna do? Play for money or be a pimp?"

"I tried being a pimp, Fats. I didn't like it."

"Then you gonna play for money."

THEN BILLIE HOLIDAY came to town and Fats Navarro—it was the next to last time I talked to him. They were playing a concert for Norman Granz and I went over to the theater to see them.

"MINKUS FINKUS! I heard you was here, I knewed you'd come!"

"I been here awhile, Fats."

"I know, I heared. Come on backstage and meet the folks. You losed a lot of weight too, huh, Mingus? Look at me—I made a record with Jacquet under the name of *Slim* Romero, how 'bout that! Billie, here's Ming!"

"Mingus, honey! You on the show?"

"Just come to listen, Billie."

"Give me some sugar, baby—mmmmm! Want to gig! Norman needs another bass man on the show, you know?"

"That would do me good, Billie."

"How're you doing with your girls?"

"That's all over. It was too much for a man of high degree."

"Solid, baby."

"Remember that song I wrote for you, Billie—'Eclipse'? You never did sing it."

"Go home and get your bass and bring the song with you. You're working, 'cause I'm the star of the show and I say so."

OH, THERE'S NO way to describe how my boy feels when he's all tied up inside digging the mood conjured up by a Lady in Philharmonic Hall singing to an audience that's with her every note and innuendo and someone calls a tune that's great and Lady Soul who has already blessed the entire evening with her presence says, "You got it, Mingus, what's your 'Sophisticated Lady' like tonight?" Just pure music, no funny clothes or trick effects, 'cause that Lady's elegant in dress and manner and mind. She *is* the song and the people are pleased and show it with their Bravos! and Encores! After the last curtain call, a few voices call out on the dimly lighted stage—"Be with you in a moment, hon!" . . . "Who's coming for something to eat?"—and Mingus is feeling at home again, packing his bass and waiting for Fats. Two girls come by that he used to know, their names are Bobbie and Jo. They sit on his knees, hugging and saying, "Come with us to Jimbo's!" He thinks he'll save one of them for Fats but Fats has a different girl on his mind, you take her inside your veins in your arm at night when you're alone and Fats can't wait to get home. So Mingus goes with the two girls who are so completely different from the kind of women he's always liked. Bobbie looks straight out of a Turkish harem, dark and curvy, and Jo is tall and strongly built, brunette and huge-breasted. That night, just hanging out together, the memory of Donnalee is banished, at least for a little while.

NEXT DAY MY boy walked past a man on Fillmore Street whose suit, three sizes too large, hung on him in folds.

"Minkus! Hey, Minkus! Dat-chew, baby?"

"Girl! Fat Girl!"

"Goddamn, Mingus, why you still got to call me Girl? Fats was bad enough. What's wrong with calling me by my name which is Theodore Navarro?"

"I'm sorry, Theodore."

"Well, you can call me Fats now 'cause I'm gettin' skinny and I know you love me, Mingus, you ain't like some them other motherfuckers that don't like me but don't even know it."

"I love you, Mr. Navarro."

"So be sure, 'cause I'm leaving soon."

"Got your bags packed right, Fats?"

"What's the bag schitt you takin' outta, Ming?"

"Well, if I'm going somewhere I pack up the things I want to take with me."

"I'm going to nothing so I'm taking nothing—but I still ain't afraid to die like you, Mingus."

"That's where we clashed before, Fats, when you took those fifty Dexedrines plus a handful of bennies all at once and said 'Fuck God!' You scared me at first till I got it figured out. When you said 'Fuck God' you really said fuck yourself. But since it is the omni-invisible, in order for you to fuck the invisible you have to stick it in yourself 'cause to be fucking nothing but the wind itself is fucking alone by yourself. And since you believe there ain't no God, you're fucking yourself, hurting, killing yourself long before your time. I can't even get you to go see a doctor to see why you're bleeding inside."

"Mingus, I'm bleeding 'cause I want to bleed. I got TB intentionally and I'm hoping there ain't no heaven or hell like you say there is. Think how drug I'd be to get there and find the white man owns that too and it's rent-controlled in heaven and hell's the slums. I'd tell them, 'Kill me, white faggot cocksucking angels, like you did down on earth, 'cause you sure ain't gonna get no work or rent from my soul!' Dig it for yourself: unless you let his earthly white angels schitt all over you, you can't even have your soul cleaned white. Like picture me giving my enemy my coat—not in New York City! Not me! Turn *whose* cheek to be smite on the other side! Schitt! Dig how the white man's black Bible is always gonna make some money and make somebody do something! Jeremiah, sixteenth chapter, twenty-first verse—'Behold, I will this once cause them to know, I will cause them to know mine hand and my might and they shall know that my name *is* the Lord.' See, I remember that chapter and verse 'cause I had a girl named Mary and I got her cherry when she was sixteen years old on my twenty-first birthday. That verse shows you right there God is white, 'cause the white man's the only thing I know can cause, make or force people to do his bid—mostly us. I don't dig nobody making me do nothing. I'm about to let God kill me just so I can meet him. And if he's white I don't dig him in the first place or in my place either. Then soon as the white angels Crow me out of heaven I'm gonna take my shiv and peel the devil in his sleep, put on his black skin suit, horns and tail, and stab the white man's god with old Dev's pitchfork right in his fat rich old ass, find his old lady, suck her cunt and fuck her good, then make her kiss me all over my black ass while I beat her with my arrow-pointed tail. See, Mingus? Aw, you look scared for me. Don't be scared if all you believe in don't exist for me. I'll burn for my sins gladly when I know them white cocksuckers so full of hate gonna burn for theirs. Mingus, I still ain't as scared to die as I am to go home to see my mother and family in Florida. You should see all the churches we got out in Key West. The white man's got 'em too, I heard 'em praying once when I was little in some kind of weird tongue. I later found out it was Latin. Imagine! Nigger-hating Southern white man that can't hardly read or write English sitting up in a church looking holy with his big red turkey neck, speaking in Latin! I snuck in back trying to get some of that white man's God-magic-spirit. The priest caught me and you know what he said? God didn't want no little black niggers stinkin' up heaven! That's why when Mary gave me her cherry I was fuckin' and cussin' right in that priest's church under the Virgin's statue and all over his altar, I got that good red ass white pussy hole condoned by the permission of the Southern Catholic Church of Key West, Florida. I also got myself a picture of the Virgin on a Sunday school card and I peed all over it and put it in the suggestion box and Mary and I split out for New York City . . . Well, Minkus, you gettin' famous back in the Apple?"

"No, no star eyes, Fats, not even for playing there right now. Listen, I asked Max Roach what you meant when we were with Hamp and you said I was helping you carry the stick. Max said, 'Why, Fats was talking about you carrying the cross with him like Simon the black Cyrenian who helped Jesus.' Was he putting me on?"

"Yeah, Ming. Carrying the stick, further than it would go otherwise, that's when you can't get none or you're kicking yourself with no help, carrying yourself dead on your feet without putting that dumb schitt in your arm to make your burden lighter. But it only gets heavier each time you lose your will power and stick yourself again. You're drug with yourself, hate yourself coming and going—you wish you didn't have to get high but you carried the stick so long and so far you know your next sober step alone will be into your grave. After you're high you forget for a while but the time of forgetting gets shorter and shorter and you up to one and a half grains every four hours. Mingus, I'm over twelve grains a day, day and night, twenty-four hours, 'cause I don't sleep no more. That's two hundred and fifty to two hundred and seventy dollars a day."

"Impossible, Fats—you're putting me on, too."

"No, Mingus, I gotta be serious with somebody. You lucky or something, most cats ain't like you—try schitt three, four times and forget it. I wish I could get turned on with some of that God-junk you got so I don't have to buy no more highs . . . Hey Ming, if you gettin' rich back east you sure is cool 'cause you sure is raggedy! You dress like a farmer, a poor farmer ain't got no seeds to plant. Milkman's overalls, old sweaters—what kind of shoes? Oh, I see *dey* do cos' a nice taste of bread."

"Well, I been getting in a lot of rumbles lately and I guess I'm looking like it. Not long ago I went in a club in New York and started drinking, and suddenly everything just turned white. I started to read ofays' minds and challenged the whole joint. Twenty cats at least, I don't know how I did it. I didn't get a scratch on me, I was so drunk. Tore the raggedy joint up and I still went back in after they barred me out. Maybe I want to die, like you, Fats, but I only feel that way when I'm juiced. In a way these clothes are my protest to Whitey, I don't want him to forget that he don't have to dress ragged. Neither do I, right now, but my underdog brothers can't afford to dress like the white man who comes to hear me play. When they see me ragged, I remind them subconsciously of a poor black farmer ain't got no seeds to plant, like you said. Playing in their expensive drinking joints, I dress like this to remind them who I am. They can't tell me how to dress. If they dress more casual, *I'll* put on evening clothes."

"Mingus, they own us and howeverwhichway you dress ain't gonna make de master free de slaves."

"You leaving tomorrow, Fats? When I'm gonna see you again?"

"I be out here in a coupla months for a record date."

"See you then, Fats?"

"See you then, Minkus."

HAMPTON HAWES

Like so many other jazz musicians of his day, Hawes was heavily involved with drugs, and—like Art Pepper, Anita O'Day, and Billie Holiday—he landed in serious legal trouble. His fine autobiography, Raise Up Off Me *(1974; with Don Asher), documents his start down this road (see p. 573 on his relationship with Charlie Parker) as well as this account of his time in prison and his extraordinary Presidential pardon.*

There were so many good people who got busted in that decade between '55 and '65 that didn't deserve it. Friends of mine who were caught in the same dragnet as me and tried to fight it got twenty years. They should have known better because those of our generation who were using and rebelling were getting slammed down hard and the word going around was, It's no use, be cool.

Just before sentencing I was visited by a fine, light-skinned black bitch who asked me how I'd like to pay these white motherfuckers back. I said to her, You work for the blue-eyed man, don't you. She gave me a funny look and split. Next day I pleaded guilty and got a dime.*

I think Jackie still believed I'd only be going to the hospital again—maybe a year for using and come out cured—until that judge said, Ten years. Two mornings later they shot me back before another judge to testify against a supplier in a different case they thought I might be connected with. Offered me immunity. I said to the judge, You can't give me immunity, I just got ten years for the same shit. Should have stopped there but I kept on—You people have had me under your thumbs tryin' to make me tremble, sendin' me out in the street to hunt down friends. Well you can put me in a dungeon and I'll turn into a motherfucking prune, but you won't break me. Fuck you and the Treasury Department and the FBI—

Jackie stood up, shaking. *Hampton, what're you doing?*

Fuck you too, I said.

The judge said, Two years to run concurrently.

The marshal who took me back to the county jail said, You're a stupid son of a bitch, but I'll say one thing, you got a lotta heart.

---

*Ten years.

In the narcotics tank all the federal prisoners had red slips stamped U.S. All the others were state prisoners. Anybody who had a red slip was a bad cat—everyone else looked up to him because he had to have done something far out for the government to bust him; it was a badge of recognition.

On a summer day in 1959 after I'd been locked up for seven months a deputy ordered about ten of us red-slip people to roll 'em up—by which he meant roll up your mattresses and collect your personal belongings. Gonna be some changes made, new scene. Okay, had to be better than this. Only good things I remembered in seven months were the variety of little pies a cat named Oscar brought around that only cost you a dime. We were herded out the back door of the hall of justice, across to the federal building and upstairs to the marshal's office. At the same time streams of other cats from different tanks were all converging on the federal building; it was like a mass exodus except there wasn't going to be any Moses leading us out of L.A. In the marshal's office a platoon of feds who must have mistaken us for Georgia lepers came at us with arm and leg chains. Our hands and legs were cuffed, one leg chained to someone else's, then groups of us were marched to the elevator clanking like Christmas ghosts.

It was in the elevator that I had my final contact with a young chick. We were all jammed inside ready for the descent when the door opened again and two county women sheriffs squeezed in with three fine bitches. They were handcuffed but unchained 'cause never in a hundred years could you mistake any one of these bitches for a Georgia leper. I asked the one standing in front of me as we descended how she'd been busted and she told me she'd been getting twenty-six allotment checks from twenty-six servicemen she was married to. Her hair had a jasmine smell, she was so fine I said to her, "Baby, I wish they'd take these chains off and let me fuck you quick because you in big trouble and so am I." She said, "Well, I can't do that, but I'll back into you." And went ahead and did it, backed her ass right into me and kept it there. Everybody in the car fell out. When the women sheriffs finally pulled us apart I called to her, "Beautiful, maybe that'll hold me for a minute."

Our destination was Fort Worth which was becoming like a second home to me. The train ride took three days. You slept in a bunk with the cat you were chained to and if he had to go to the can you went with him, standing outside with the chain stuck in the door. Most of the first-offense cats were nervous and had a right to be. I tried to set their minds at ease. The atmosphere's going to change, I told them, you'll be more like a patient than a prisoner. They couldn't believe it. No guards, no guns? No armed guards, I said, only thing is your ass is going to be lodged in one continuous tunnel.

The first inmate I saw at Fort Worth was Stymie. I'd met him the last time

I was there. He had been one of the "Our Gang" kids, a famous black child actor when there was hardly any such thing, but nobody has heard of him for a long time. Now he was houseboy to the head doctor, pretty much free to come and go, with access to different departments. No one is supposed to talk to the incoming inmates until they're released into the general population, but Stymie came busting into the medical room where I was waiting for my exam and said, "Hamp, how you doin'? Was it a dime?" I said, "Yeah, it was a dime," and he said, "Well, that was the wire we got." (The grapevine has always been strong in these joints because the same junkies are constantly being shifted around and filtered through the different prisons and hospitals.)

After the physical I was taken straight to the kick ward where the people coming off the streets are held until they're considered clean enough to be turned out into the population. Now having been incarcerated in an L.A. tank for seven months I sure as hell was clean, they could see that, but they started reviewing my records, which by that time had blossomed into a pretty far-out dossier (probably had my army files, all those weird trips) and decided the time wasn't quite ripe for me to be turned out. I was kept in the kick ward for a month on hold. Stymie said he thought they were considering putting me in the nut ward of the hospital or sending me to McNeil Island, which is hardcore and maximum security.

The doctor they sent to interview me looked over the records and said, "You sure have done a lot of crazy things, Hampton." I told him that at the time I did them it didn't seem to make any difference whether I did them or not. He said, "Would you like to stay at Fort Worth?" and I said, What difference does it make, neither me or any of my people are getting shit. I'm locked up, got to stay somewhere, here or outside chained to a tree.

A few days after the interview I was released into the population and assigned to a regular ward. Probably decided this cat's so messed up, been strung out so long, we better keep him here for psychiatric treatment; if he gets too funny we can always ship him out. What they were doing then was leaving it up to me, which was the best thing they could have done.

In an innocent, ungreedy kind of way those doctors were like the jackleg preachers, all robes and ceremony. It wasn't that any of them were dumb or incompetent, but if you start with someone like me who has come out of the haven of the church into the streets, playing jazz and messing with dope, why there's no white psychiatrist in the wide world qualified to analyze me because whatever he would start from, whatever funny little program he tried to work me into, his thinking is going to be alien and wrong. He's going to go into his generalizing bag, and that's the big mistake down front because there is no way he can possibly conceive of where I'm coming from. So it isn't their fault that most of the time they don't know what they're doing.

* * *

THE FIRST NIGHT I was assigned to a ward I could feel the buzzing and electricity through the dining room. The word had filtered through that Hampton Hawes was down from kick ward, and I guess it was inevitable there was going to be a session that night. I hadn't played piano in over seven months. When I walked into the band room after dinner it seemed like every cat in the hospital had a pass, looked like a therapy room the way they were jammed in, sitting on top of the piano, spilling out into the tunnels. Bass and drums set up, a couple of horns. We left the doors open and started playing, drawing in some of the doctors and nurses who dug it and a few funny Texas guards who didn't know what to make of the music, wondering what the hell's going on, what are all these people doing down here? Well we cooked pretty good, no one trying to shoot anyone else down, no peacock feathers in view, just easy blowing on old standards and one cat sitting atop the piano, feet dangling in my face, calling down, "I heard about you before, you a bad motherfucker." Came nine o'clock when the band room was supposed to close, we played right on through and every now and then some old Texas cracker guard would poke his face in, saying, "What are all these people doin' in here after hours?" He had no idea what was going down; heard the music, but it didn't register, *weird* seeing all these people jam-packed in, hardly a breath of air in the room. What the hell's goin' on? Probably thinking, They're shootin' craps or something, big dice game, crazy junkies.

On July 4th I wrote to the Attorney General, told him a dime was a long time for what I did, the days were moving slow, and would he send me some information about how I could get out before 1969. His office wrote back a polite letter saying, Man, don't bother us.

A week later I read in the paper that Billie Holiday had died in New York, her deathbed a hospital cot guarded by city police. They had hounded her right up to the last day. But I knew she would live on, that she had just said Bye for a while.

My first gig was mopping the tunnels with 11 other cats from 10 P.M. to 4 A.M. with a half-hour break for "lunch"—not knowing what else to call it at two in the morning. When I didn't fuck up and they saw I was cool they gave me a day gig in the band room issuing instruments and taking inventory. Had a chair and desk, access to a Steinway spinet. But every time I started to play, cats would drop in to listen, so I had to stop. I wasn't in a performing mood, just wanted to play some shit for myself. My assistant was a big dude with a shiny bald head and bushy beard, looked like Man Mountain Dean. Wore gold hoop earrings and said to me one day, Watts, I have a problem. (Various cats would call me that, knowing I was from L.A.) I said, I'm no psychiatrist, but what's your problem? He said, I think I'm a homosexual. I said, All highways got at least two lanes, and as long as everybody isn't driving on the same one there won't be any crashes. He said, What're you trying to tell me, Watts? I said, I wouldn't be interested in that trip myself, but if that's your pleasure, pursue it.

I fell into the routine: vocational therapy and all the other funny little programs. Little by little I could feel my suspicions and fears of the hospital and the people who ran it slipping away. Some of them understood I shouldn't have been there, not for ten years anyway, and were sympathetic. By letting me know they felt for me and wanted to help, they made me want to try. Probably the most sensible thing you can do for someone in a situation like mine is to forget the psychiatrist-patient relation—our worlds are too far apart, it's like Jupiter trying to do something for Mars—and just be nice to him, allow him his dignity, provide the facilities and let him work out his own shit in his own way.

But I couldn't help looking at the calendar from time to time. October 1959, January 1960 . . . Release Date was 1969, well past my prime. Be hard getting back in the ballgame when you're over forty. I kept feeling in my pocket, but there was no key there.

JUST AFTER MY third Christmas I was watching John Kennedy accept the Presidency on the Washington steps. Something about the look of him, the voice and eyes, way he stood bright and coatless and proud in that cold air . . . I thought, That's the right cat; looks like he got some soul and might listen.

The next day I told one of the medical officers I wanted to apply for a Presidential pardon. He said, That's the root of your trouble, Hampton, you refuse to be realistic. When you leave here you're probably going to go back to dope because you'll still be thinking unrealistic. As I said before it wasn't basically their fault that those doctors' heads were all fucked up.

They put so many obstacles in my path—warning me the effort would be useless and I'd be worse off than before—that it was a year before I even found out the name of the pardon attorney I had to contact. Meanwhile I took care of business, played some piano, watched the volunteers come in on their three-to-six-month commitments, go back out on the streets and be back in the tunnels a week, month, or year later.

Late in 1962 the official form finally arrived: Application for Executive Clemency. Raft of pages in funny type and at the bottom of the first page the date 1923, so I knew nothing in this field had changed for a long while.

Most of the brief was made up of routine information questions. The last page was the heavy one—the place where you explained your reasons. I decided I didn't want to make it a personal cry for help. What I did was send John Kennedy a directive: As you are the Commander-in-Chief it is my duty as a citizen to inform you that an injustice has been perpetrated, one of your people is being subjected to cruel and unjust punishment, and it is your duty to consider the evidence and reciprocate. Made it professional and detached. I wasn't asking for a shoulder to cry on. It was as if I were an officer in battle informing my commander that as things are coming down at present we're getting our ass kicked, might be a good idea to switch to plan B. And then to round it off I added some heavy legal shit in Latin I'd dug up in the library.

Now at the time I was in the honor ward. Established, nonfretting. Cool, docile, and not contemplating escape. Had my own room, unlimited TV privileges, first in chow line, free to walk on the grounds; it was the next thing to the streets. I'd made a lot of friends among the staff and started collecting letters of recommendation to go with the brief. I hadn't won anyone over, no one thought it was any use, thought I was crazy to try, but they wanted to help me take my best shot.

On the afternoon of my fourth Christmas they showed a movie, *The Alamo.* There was a sweet tune on the sound track, "The Green Leaves of Summer," that kept humming through my mind and I told myself I would try to record it if I ever saw daylight again.

In January of 1963 news came through the grapevine that Sonny Clark had OD'd in New York.

By March I had collected eighteen letters of recommendation and made my move: sent the letters with the application to the President and tried to forget about it.

In April I wrote my first letter home to my mother and father . . . *I don't blame you or anyone else for what's happened, you were trying to help. You took a direction you thought was cool so don't dwell on any mistakes, rid your conscience of all that stuff, it's all right, I love you.* Sevener wrote back, You know, your mama had a heart attack a while ago but she's feeling better now.

In May I heard on the grapevine that Bud Powell was down, out, and fucked up in Paris.

In July I was let out for an afternoon to play a jazz concert at Texas Christian University. My first day on the outside in five Christmases. Later one of the musicians said he'd heard Ladybird Johnson was in the audience and that was probably how it all came about. But I was looking inward and didn't see any ladybird there that day or any other kind of bird.

On August 16, 1963, the President of the United States came through.

I woke up in the morning just as I'd been doing for five years, took my little funny case into the can to wash up and brush my teeth, headed for chow as usual, here's another day, man, and was stopped by a security guard. Deputy MOC wants you at the administration building. The guard drove me over.

Doctor Foley, the deputy medical officer, said, "Good morning, Hampton." Cool. Behind his desk were two flags, the American flag and the public health service flag, and between them a big color picture of John F. Kennedy. "I've got some news for you, Hampton." He turned and called through a doorway to another doctor and now his voice was shaking a little—"Would you come in, Bob? I want you to hear this." He showed Bob the paper. "Ever see one of these?" Bob's eyes got wide and he shook his head. "Never." So the two top cats in the hospital told me to my face that my struggle was over, the long five years was over and I wouldn't have to do the other five. Executive clemency granted by authority of the President of the United States. I had my final diploma.

I sat down and asked them to read it again.

That's it then, I said.

Yeah, they said and handed it to me. Saw a blur of Gothic letters on parchment paper, about twenty "whereases," signed with the Man's name.

I said when can I leave.

They said forthwith.

By the time I got back to the chow hall the grapevine was already alive. Stymie whipping it on everyone and the word spreading like flash fire. Nine hundred cats in there eating breakfast and most of them seemed to be jumping up against the rules, crowding around to shake my hand, bewildered and happy—those that liked me happy and the others bewildered. I moved through it all wooden, like a dead limb, hardly reacting to any of it 'cause you can't immediately react to something that heavy. We were moving through the tunnels—chaplain saw me, took a little jump in the air and yelled "Hallelujah!"—aids, security guards, nurses crying, a lot of well-wishers tagging along, all those cats I wasn't going to see any more, taking me to some building to be processed out; records put in order, personal stuff gathered, bags packed, put him in a suit and tie, make a plane reservation.

I haven't shaved yet, I said, dazed.

Hasn't shaved yet! Man's sprung him and the crazy motherfucker wants to shave.

Someone drove me to Dr. Kay's house on the edge of the grounds. Don't know what I was doing there, but I was upstairs shaving in his pink-tiled bathroom, going through the motions looking at myself quiet and stone dumb in the mirror, when his wife busted in so glad and excited she practically jumped on my back, hugging me then backing off and looking at me with shaving cream on her face and tears in her eyes. And the doctor calling up to get my ass downstairs 'cause we had to get to the airport.

Next thing I remember I was drinking a toast with his family downstairs, and now the curtains were parting a bit, clear light showing through, and it began to come in on me what had happened. August, Texas, dig it. Hot as blazes in the little linoleum kitchen. My first drink in five years. Made it. President told them to let me go. Right? Laid it on him in Latin. Some hope left in the world. Nine years strung out, all those hospitals and dungeons, right? Made it, kicked. Standing up with this fine family, tall, straight, not fucked up. Looking good, feeling strong . . . together . . . confident. Never been so confident before. And all these people who'd helped me thinking a miracle had happened. Wasn't no miracle. The only thing that had happened was the most ordinary thing in the world—somebody was watching over the country. President sitting up there in his tower and a small cry for help had come out of the dungeon, filtered on up there. And the powers that be answered back, you don't need to feel alone anymore. Wasn't no miracle. What happened was normal, the kind of thing that's *supposed* to happen if the person on the throne is watching the shop, doing his job. So how could it be a miracle?

American Airlines lifting over Fort Worth. Heading west, thirty thousand feet over the Pecos River. Dig it. Cute little smiling stewardess in an orange cap coming in at me with the first words I'd heard on the outside in five years. "Good afternoon, sir, would you like coffee or a beverage?" I said, "Baby, please bring me a hard drink, any kind at all." And when she returned with it, still smiling, the cute little cap perched just so on top of her hair, she said, "How was your day today?" Like I was coming back from a week's vacation on a dude ranch or visiting my old grandmammy in Abilene. How was your day today. "Just beautiful," I said.

PAUL DESMOND

An amusing writer, Desmond—according to the liner notes for Mosaic's Desmond collection—had intended writing an autobiography to be called How Many of You Are There in the Quartet? *These pages, which appeared originally in the British magazine* Punch, *constitute the only portion of that work known to exist.*

Dawn. A station wagon pulls up to the office of an obscure motel in New Jersey. Three men enter—pasty-faced, grim-eyed, silent (for those are their names). Perfect opening shot, before credits, for a really lousy bank-robbery movie? Wrong. The Dave Brubeck Quartet, some years ago, starting our day's work.

Today we have a contract (an offer we should have refused) for two concerts at the Orange County State Fair in Middletown. 2 P.M. and 8 P.M. Brubeck likes to get to the job early.

So we pull up behind this hay truck around noon, finally locating the guy who had signed the contract. Stout, red-necked, gruff and harried (from the old New Jersey law firm of the same name), and clearly more comfortable judging cattle than booking jazz groups, he peers into the station wagon, which contains four musicians, bass, drums, and assorted baggage, and for the first and only time in our seventeen years of wandering about the world, we get this question: "Where's the piano?"

So, leaving Brubeck to cope with the situation, we head into town for sandwiches and browsing. Since the sandwiches take more time than the browsing, I pick up a copy of the *Middletown Record* and things become a bit more clear. TEENAGER'S DAY AT THE ORANGE COUNTY STATE FAIR, says the headline across the two center pages (*heavy* move, in that the paper only has four pages). Those poor folk, especially the cattle-judge type (who was probably lumbered into heading the entertainment committee), thought we were this red-hot teenage attraction, which, Lord knows we've never been. Our basic audience begins with creaking elderly types of twenty-three and above.

Nevertheless, here we are, splashed all over this ad, along with the other attractions of the day—judo exhibition, fire-fighting demonstration, Wild West show, and Animalorama (which may have been merely misspelled). And right at the top, first two columns on the left, is this picture of Brubeck's teeth and much of his face, along with the following text, which

I'm paraphrasing only slightly. HEAR THE MUSIC TEENAGERS EVERYWHERE THRILL TO, it began. HEAR THE MUSIC THAT ROCKED NEWPORT RHODE ISLAND (an unfortunate reference in that only a few weeks earlier the Newport Jazz Festival had undergone its first riot). HEAR DAVE BRUBECK SING AND PLAY HIS FAMOUS HITS, INCLUDING "JAZZ GOES TO COLLEGE," "JAZZ IN EUROPE," and "TANGERINE."

So, now realizing—in Brubeck's piquant ranch phrase—which way the hole slopes, we head back to the fairgrounds where the scene is roughly as follows: there is a smallish, almost transistorized, oval race track. (I'm not exactly sure how long a furlong is, but it seems not too many of them are actually present.) On one side of the oval is the grandstand, built to accommodate 2,000 or so, occupied at the moment by eight or nine elderly folk who clearly paid their money to sit in the shade and fan themselves, as opposed to any burning desire to hear the music their teenage grandchildren everywhere thrill to.

Directly across the track from them is our bandstand—a wooden platform, about ten feet high and immense. Evidently no piano has been locatable in Orange County, since the only props on stage are a vintage electric organ and one mike. Behind us is a fair-sized tent containing about two hundred people, in which a horse show for young teenagers is currently in progress—scheduled, we soon discover, to continue throughout our concert. This is hazardous mainly because their sound system is vastly superior to ours.

So we begin our desperation opener, "St. Louis Blues." Brubeck, who has never spent more than ten minutes of his life at an electric organ, much less the one he is now at, is producing sounds like an early Atwater-Kent Synthesizer. (Later he makes a few major breakthroughs, like locating the volume control pedal and figuring out how to wiggle his right hand, achieving a tremolo effect similar to Jimmy Smith with a terminal hangover, but it doesn't help much.) Eugene Wright, our noble bass player, and me take turns schlepping the mike back and forth between us and playing grouchy, doomed choruses, but the only sound we can hear comes from our friendly neighborhood horse show.

"LOPE," it roars. "CANTER . . . TROT . . . AND THE WINNER IN THE TWELVE-YEAR-OLD-CLASS IS . . . JACQUELINE HIGGS!"

As always in difficult situations such as these, we turn to our main man, primo virtuoso of the group, the Maria Callas of the drums, Joe Morello, who has rescued us from disaster from Grand Forks to Rajkot, India.

"You got it," we said, "stretch out," which ordinarily is like issuing an air travel card to a hijacker. And, to his eternal credit, Morello outdoes himself. All cymbals sizzling, all feet working. (Morello has several. Not many people know this.) Now he's into triplets around the tom-toms, which has shifted foundations from the Odeon Hammersmith to Free Trade Hall and turned Buddy Rich greener than usual with envy.

The horse show is suddenly silent. Fanning in the stands has subsided slightly.

Suddenly a figure emerges from the horse tent, hurtles to the side of the stage, and yells at Brubeck, "For Chrissakes, could you tell the drummer not to play so loud? He's terrifying the horses."

Never a group to accept defeat gracelessly, we play a sort of Muzak for a suitable period and split.

When we return at eight, all is different. A piano has been found, the stands are packed with our geriatric following of twenty-five and above, and we play a fairly respectable concert.

Even so, we're upstaged by the grand finale of the fair—the fire-fighting demonstration. A group of local residents has been bandaged and made up to appear as if they've just leapt from the *Hindenburg* and their last rites are imminent. But instead of remaining discreetly behind the scenes until their big moment, they mingle casually with friends and neighbors in the audience during the evening, sipping beer, munching popcorn, casting an eerie, Fellini-like quality over the gathering, and considerably diminishing the impact of their ultimate appearance.

After their pageant come the main events of the fair, which have clearly been planned for months: a flaming auto wreck, followed by a flaming plane wreck, each to be dealt with instantly and efficiently by the Middletown Fire Dept. At one end of the oval is a precariously balanced car; at the other end, a truly impressive skeletal mock-up of a single-engine plane, tail up. Midway, at ground zero, is the Middletown Fire Truck, bristling with ladders and hoses and overflowing with volunteers.

A hush falls over the stands. At a signal given by the fire chief, the car is ignited. The truck reaches it in two or three seconds, by which time the fire is roughly equivalent to that created by dropping a cigarette on the backseat for two or three seconds. It is extinguished by many men with several hoses.

A murmur falls over the stands. The fire chief, painfully aware that his moment of the year is at hand, signals for the plane to be ignited, also instructing the truck to take it easy, so that the fire should be blazing briskly when it arrives. The truck starts, at about the pace of a cab looking for a fare. The plane goes WHOOSH!, like a flashbulb, and by the time the leisurely truck arrives, has shrunk to a lovely camp-fire, just large enough for roasting marshmallows.

Later, four pasty-faced, grim-eyed men pile into a station wagon and drive away. It may not be bank-robbery, but it's a living.

Cecil Taylor

From Len Lyons's The Great Jazz Pianists *(1983) comes this characteristically provocative series of encounters with Cecil Taylor. An interviewer's life is not always an easy one.*

What approach did you use for developing finger dexterity, and what would you recommend that younger pianists do in that regard?

You've really asked me two questions. The answer to both is essentially that each player must decide for himself.

You've told me that you have had music students, and I assume some of them were pianists. What did you ask them to do?

I can't really answer the question the way you've presented it. The implications of music are larger than the compartmentalization of technique, form, or content. It's a matter of the ability to express.

What do you mean by musical expression? Expression of what?

What do you mean by it?

The realization, the creation, of what you hear.

If you hear it, why is there any need to play it? It exists as soon as you hear it.

You "hear" it metaphorically—not the way you hear my voice. I often "hear" music that I can't express, or play, on the piano.

Isn't it enough that it exists in your head?

No, it's frustrating, in fact. How did you develop your finger dexterity?

I don't have it. It's all comparative. Music isn't that special. It's just one of those things in the air, something I've done. It comes out of the history, environment, culture we're living in. That determines how we hear, what we hear, and the method we use to create the sound. It also determines the standards, goals, and aesthetic levels we achieve. To talk about technique as anything more than a minimal consequence of a larger order—I mean, civilization—is to give it more importance than it deserves. Music is just another activity of man. Technique is only part of that. The traditions of the civilization shape it.

Yes, we are always building on the past. We didn't reinvent the wheel in order to build the automobile. We're interested in what you built on? Whom did you listen to as a student?

You want me to talk about certain things, but I'm prepared to talk only about the things I think are important. I'm interested in the cultural importance of the life of the music. The instrument a man uses is only a tool with which he makes his comment on the structure of music. That's why the evaluation of what a cat says about how he plays music is not too far from the noninteresting things he does when he is playing. That person wouldn't have too profound an understanding of what has happened in the music and the culture. We have to define the procedures and examine the aesthetics that have shaped the history of the music. That's more important than discussing finger dexterity. We might as well discuss basketball or tennis.

Well, what does distinguish your approach to the music from other approaches?

The history of the people, the culture, even the things they forget consciously. The way they cook, speak, the way they move, dress, how they relate to the pressures around them. What you experience in life informs (in-forms) you. If you work on One Hundred Forty-fifth Street in Harlem and years later in Tokyo, where you are taken to see the sights, you experience . . . the environment, listen to the sounds, watch the movement.

You'll be able to see that there are not these separations between things. There are different aesthetic choices made. What happened in the latter part of the eighteenth century in Africa had a profound effect on painting. The concepts of musical organization now have to be broadened to accommodate the worldwide awareness of music. Things are not that simple. Last year thousands of people came to hear me, [saxophonist] Archie Shepp, and Count Basie in the middle of a town built in the fifteenth century. There were people as far as you could see, and their shapes were just visible in the mist. It was like New York's "Jazzmobile" magnified forty or fifty times. I can't ignore that.

[Our conversation took an entirely unexpected turn, establishing that both of us liked the architecture of Antonio Gaudí, an early twentieth-century Catalan architect. His buildings are highly expressive, complicated, sensuous structures. Taylor especially liked the cathedral in Barcelona and believed Gaudí to have been a fascinating person. It was a typical digression in that it illustrated Taylor's intense interest in all the arts: painting, architecture, poetry, and dance. I was struck by the parallel between the qualities of Taylor's music and Gaudí's buildings, which were also ahead of their time yet classical in form. Taylor then picked up the subject of music again.]

Given the history of America, the phenomenon of black people playing music a certain way is not surprising. If in 1969 I was asked to join a music faculty [University of Wisconsin], then this whole thing is not about music. There's at least a duality of things operating here. I had the largest class at the university—one thousand and eighty students! And only one teaching assistant, by the way. For their examination I asked them to create something: a painting, a dance, poems, or music. The Music Department was outraged. But the students fought for this creativity, so I was heartened and came back for a second year. In that year we formed an orchestra [the Black Music Ensemble] which further outraged the department. The academy is not interested in creating artists. They are interested in making the learning of music into a commodity which can be packaged. Therefore, the creative responses of young people are not encouraged.

Historically the sixties was a time when teaching concepts were being challenged. There was a reexamination of what kind of teaching was "relevant." A few people were also beginning to understand how exclusive a clientele was being informed by the college experience.

When I went to the conservatory, there was one order, a list of the titans of music, which was considered to be absolute. Why? André Malraux [novelist and once minister of culture of France] was considered a very sophisticated man. Yet at an audience he had with Mao Tse-tung he allegedly said, "But of course you read Shakespeare here." Now what could be more provincial than that? There is the absolutism of the conservatory. What must be seen is that there are certain conceptions in music which are never challenged. At least not in the schools. That is a very narrow perspective.

Did you ever work with any individuals in your class?

Yes. In fact, one of the people in the band is someone who came to me while I was teaching at Antioch in Ohio.

Who?

I'm more interested in your response. *Who?* Which one? Why is that important?

I didn't say it was important. I simply wanted to know. [It was trumpeter Raphé Malik.]

Art works in really mysterious ways. [This statement, connecting art with mystery, took on more significance when I learned later that Taylor's book in progress about music is called *Mysteries.*] Do you play an instrument, too?

I play piano, I started playing classical music when I was young and eventually studied improvising with Lennie Tristano.

What was that like?

Finding out what it was all about.

Name something that it's all about—linear dimension, maybe? If you're talking about the top layer of music, which the ear responds to first, there's all kinds of movement, not just linear. I've heard Lennie play many times. What music do you listen to?

That's what I was going to ask you.

I once went to meet Lennie and went through a lot of nonsense just to get in to see him. What did you learn from him?

I remember playing left-hand chords to "You Go to My Head," trying to get a coun-

termelody going with the thumb of my left hand. He had asked me to learn the song from Billie Holiday's recording of it. At one point my countermelody didn't work with the right-hand melody, and Lennie was quick to point out that it was wrong. "Yeah, I know," I admitted. "You only know it in your head," he told me, "but I'm not concerned with what you know in your wig." What I learned was that there are other ways of knowing something in music.

Like what?

Knowing in your hands or ears.

Now you're talking about what works and what doesn't work.

I'm talking about a separate cognitive process, knowing what you're doing musically. Making sense musically. That's not something you can learn intellectually. You can only develop the instinct you already have. . . . Why do I feel like you're interviewing me?

If intellectual cognition isn't enough, what else is music made up of?

Feelings.

What are they?

Why must I define my terms when you aren't willing to clarify your answers. That doesn't seem fair.

Does fairness amount to much?

Yes, it does. What's your concept of technique? . . . Isn't that where we began?

I don't know what language you speak or what you're prepared to hear. If we're going to talk, I need some idea of who you are. You might write anything. How do I know?

I'm trying to tell you.

Well, I thank you.

WHEN I SAW Cecil again, he was chain-smoking, pacing backstage at the Zellerbach Auditorium on the Berkeley campus of the University of California. "I always get nervous before I play," he said. "I practiced four hours today, but that didn't help. Then I played on this Mason and Hamlin downstairs for about fifteen minutes, but it wasn't any good. If you can't play, you can't play."

Taylor was wearing a sleeveless undershirt with a towel draped over his shoulders. It seemed obvious that he exercised regularly. "A body has to stay in shape to play," he commented. As we sat down to talk, he cooled off with occasional swigs from a bottle of imported beer. Taylor's exercise regimen consists primarily of running around his loft in New York City. He does quite a few laps, though he can't say how many because he counts the steps instead.

Taylor is a dance *aficionado.* In fact, he choreographed a work for thirteen dancers while directing his play *A Rat's Mass* in New York. "At least I thought of it as dancing," he quipped, "though I know a few people who didn't." The play had a short run.

Just then the solo playing of Paul Bley, who had preceded Taylor on the bill, became audible through the backstage monitors, a Bley much more romantic than usual. "Sort of a *bluesy* romanticism," Cecil said, correcting me. "I remember hearing Paul play when he first came to New York. At the time I thought he was technically very interesting. Youth demonstrates its strength in terms of its technical prowess. But when players reach their maturity . . . hmmm, you know he [Paul] is playing everything he wants to play. It's interesting how the past has an influence on the music's continuance. The blues flavor . . . those tenths he's playing in the left hand right now—that's Teddy Wilson. It's funny that the roots show more in one's maturity than in youth. Which probably makes me a genius. It's a reflection of a greater understanding of the history of the music."

"How does that make you a genius?"

"Because I've continued to expand the realm of the piano in terms of what I attempt to do."

"How does that relate to the past?"

"Ah, that's the mystery. Anyway, a lot of people feel it doesn't [relate to the past], but the past is always with it."

"I don't think your playing is out of the context of tradition."

"I don't either." He recalled a recent duo piano performance with the sixty-eight-year-old Mary Lou Williams, who personifies the jazz piano tradition. His assessment of these duets was completely ambiguous to me. "One could write a small book about my experience of it," he said.

"What would the title of the book be?"

"*The Wrong Embrace*. Perhaps *The Misunderstood Embrace*. A lot of the critics thought it didn't work. The liner notes to the album [*Embraced,* on Pablo] was my answer to those people." Taylor stood abruptly to prepare for his appearance onstage.

"Why do you have an aversion to discussing the mundane realities of playing the piano?"

"When you get older, you get into the realities because you're trying to survive. One begins to understand what one's limits are."

Several days passed before we met for what I suspected would be the last time, at least in the context of this project. He was now in the midst of a San Francisco club date at the Keystone Korner opposite pianist Randy Weston. We sat on the lawn of Union Square Park. I had decided on a new tactic of quoting statements Taylor had made to other interviewers, and then asking him to defend, explain, or recant them. Naturally things did not go as planned.

* * *

In 1965 you said that "electronic music divorces itself from human energy." You've also told me that many of your attitudes have changed over the years. Has that one changed?

People put their emotions to all sorts of ends. I don't know that I've changed my opinion, but the area of human emotion can be perverted and subverted in a lot of ways. I'm answering your question, by the way.

You once said that musical notation can be used as a point of reference, "but the notation does not indicate music, it indicates direction." Could you explain how you use notation to communicate a piece of music to your band?

I don't know what I meant by saying that. I don't know if I said it . . . you know that old Rita Hayworth song "Put the Blame on Mame"?

Do you have a view on the usefulness of musical notation?

Now who'd be interested in that?

People interested in your music.

Who would they be? They aren't responsible for me making any money all these years. It's all right for them to love the idea of abstract pleasure which they get out of some intellectual preoccupations. Maybe that absolves them of their responsibility.

Do you feel an obligation to communicate what you know of your art to those people who are working in the same art form?

[Taylor laughed and indicated that I should say so. "Damn right I laughed," he added. After a few moments he continued.] That's not what your magazine does. You can't give anyone anything, or make choices for them. It takes long enough to be satisfied with choices you've made for yourself.

Are you satisfied with the choices you've made for yourself?

I accept the responsibility of having made them. I'm talking about the small part I'm playing in the evolution of the music, the gift that has been given to me, to have seen spiritualized the mysteries of the music at an early age. This made my actions predestined. One has to become aware of the force, both realistic and spiritual. It's about hard work, which is about living to the full extent of one's capabilities.

You once said that the recording procedure obscured a musician's sound rather than clarified it. Must it be so deceptive? Is there no such thing as "high fidelity" in recordings today? Are you dissatisfied with your own records?

Of course, I like ninety-eight percent of the records I've made, but that doesn't alter the fact that the engineers don't know how to record the music.

How could they improve their work?

If I had part of their salary, I might tell them.

Is money the only thing that would motivate you to—

Who's giving me money?

Your music and, indirectly, a lot of people who have affection for it.

Affection or curiosity? If they come to hear me play, it's not like coming to hear Bill Evans play. They have to work at it. I don't expect people who listen to Emerson, Lake, and Palmer to come hear me. I accept that reality. They are victims of a situation they don't even know exists. To produce music of this tradition is work, and I should be paid for it. Are the people who love my music responsible for paying my rent? If that's true, they're getting off light because I don't live all that well. Not like Peter Duchin does, although I play four times as much piano as he does.

What I really should be talking about is the cultural discrimination that exists in Europe and America—in the West. That's all right, though. The Third World is coming alive; their art is growing even though Western Europeans are trying to decimate it, like those barbarians in South Africa.

I can understand your being bitter about a lot of things, but not about the genuine affection many people feel for your music. Don't you believe they really feel that?

You say I appear to be bitter. That can't be inferred from anything I say because I don't feel that an audience has any responsibility other than to be there or not to be there. There's nothing personal between me and the audience at all. Liking the music is not personal. They're responding to sounds which they would just as soon dissociate from the person making the sounds. Otherwise, things would not be the way they are historically. They feel about me the way their parents felt about Louis Armstrong, although the nature of the oppression has been more subtle over the passage of time. You seem to think one should be grateful that there are these people who get emotionally involved. I'm also saying that there are certain levels of the relationship . . . well, it's not necessary to speak about them. There's no need to talk about the most important things in our lives, unless you want to write a poem about them. Listen, you can tell if an audience is there or not, or if one or two people are moved. I'm not going to pretend that there is cultural justice in America.

There may not be, but that doesn't mean each and every person is unjust.

You keep trying to defend what is historically endemic—the disease that consumes the vectors, or activity, which determine what people buy.

I'm saying that history is not totally endemic or determined. People can rise above their past.

The myth that there is [social] progress, which makes you comfortable, has no reality. The percentage of unemployed teenagers among blacks is getting larger, not smaller. Benny Goodman was the King of Swing, but he had Teddy Wilson, Lionel Hampton, and Mary Lou Williams working for him. The Beatles and the Rolling Stones were brought over here and made the

Americans give them millions of dollars, but everyone knows who created that music. That's a manifestation of the disease. You know . . . Mick Jagger. Nothing's changed. It's just more subtle.

Obviously my importance does not have anything to do with the nature of the forces that have tried to hinder that development. The ability to sustain myself is made up of things that are not as negative as the things I see when I walk out my door. It's a gift of the knowledge of my ancestors' great accomplishments. I can do without appearing on Johnny Carson's show. I'm perfectly content to do what I do. I have a very interesting band now.

Anthony Braxton

In Forces in Motion: Anthony Braxton and the Meta-reality of Creative Music *(1988), Graham Lock questions Braxton on many subjects, from Paul Desmond to Black Power, and gets stimulating, straight answers.*

Paul Desmond—"Only the Essence Remained"

B: I have eight million heroes.

L: OK, let's take them one at a time. Paul Desmond was your first major influence?

B: Yes, Paul Desmond would open the door of the saxophone world for me.

L: What was the attraction?

B: What *is* the attraction, because I have never stopped loving this man's music. The first thing I recall that struck me about it was his sound. The sound grabbed me. Then, after that, his logic grabbed me—held me in its grip, in fact. I think Paul Desmond's music is widely misunderstood on many levels. He was fashionable for the wrong reasons and he was hated for the wrong reasons. In retrospect, when I look at his life, his is a kind of . . . what's the word? Kind of mysterious music, he's not always there.

L: Enigmatic?

B: Enigmatic, thank you. I understood that better when I met Mr. Desmond. I met him in Paris, though actually I said hello to him in the street before. He turned around and looked at me—I said, thank you very much for your music, sir. He said, well—thank you. And suddenly I understood everything, because while I was talking to him I was aware of the fact that he was way over here. I mean, he was not *there,* in the sense that we talk of there. He had already plotted out five seconds ahead of time what he was gonna do, and you could hear it in his music. It looked like he was a very slow player, but in fact he was making very quick decisions, and because he understood his craft so well his music has this air of easiness about it, as if it's just kind of floating. But, oh, the man is very ahead, a profound thinker. He was far ahead of what you heard: what you heard had been edited completely, only the essence remained. Desmond understood how to get to the point quicker than most players ever learn. This is a lightning-fast improviser, who understood sound logic and how to prepare the event.

The Tightrope of "It"—Masters

B: Desmond too was a very good chess player; I hear it in his music. He actually had his personal language within the style of so-called jazz. He was never afraid to walk the tightrope. It didn't look like he was walking on the tightrope, but he was there—right on the line of invention, the line of *it*. His solo flights fired me up as a young boy, then later as a teenager, as a man, and now as an old cruster. It fires me up because it's all *it*. I'm surprised that people are not able to hear his influence—no saxophonist has put their stamp on me more than Paul. Well, I'd say Paul, Coltrane, and Warne Marsh would put their stamp on me deeper than any other instrumentalists.

L: I know you've dedicated compositions to Coltrane and Marsh; are there any to Desmond?

B: The saxophone piece on *The Complete Braxton,* the overdubbed soprano piece, is dedicated to Paul Desmond. Is that right?—I think it is. I was afraid to tell him that, though, when I met him in the street, I didn't want to bother him. He was a strange man. He became very successful in the monetary sense of the word, but he never got what he wanted. He wanted the respect of the African masters; they denied him that, and they should not have denied him. Duke Ellington didn't deny him, Charles Mingus acknowledged him; but Miles Davis, I think it was, spat on him verbally in public, talked about Desmond's sound insultingly. It was very fashionable not to respect Desmond, but he touched a lot of people's hearts. That's the thing about the masters that's so interesting: you can say what you like, but masters can touch your heart and change your life. In the case of Desmond, I *know* that's true.

L: Do any of your records particularly show Desmond's influence?

B: *All* of my recordings show the influence of Paul Desmond. But remember, I never wanted to imitate anybody because that would insult the masters. What I liked about them was that they found their own way. You have to do that; and the only way you can do that is, you have to know yourself. You have to know what you believe in and you have to set out on a path and develop it. It's the only way. You can't theorize it, even. You can theorize some of it but you've got to live it, and experience it, and you have to be tested to make sure that you believe what you say you believe.

Desmond understood that he couldn't deal with Charlie Parker's dynamic, electric brilliance—he knew he couldn't out-Charlie Parker Charlie Parker—but he also knew he could create the same aura by playing slower. So you go to the opposites. You've heard the old saying, listen to everybody so you know what *not* to play. As soon as I hear the pentatonic scale or the Parker licks or the Coltrane licks, I say, OK—bang!—next! It's the ones who've put together their own language, their own syntax, their own way of being—those are the ones I'm interested in. That's why I love Paul. Plus, he understood how not to let even ruffles and flourishes get in the way of singing from the heart.

Charlie Parker—Talking of the Upper Partials

L: It was later, after Desmond, that you began to listen to Charlie Parker?

B: Yes. Charlie Parker's effect on me would not be so apparent in the beginning. When I first heard Charlie Parker—the record was *Bird on 52nd Street*—that record frightened me. It frightened me, and it was the most exciting music I'd ever heard, and it was also talking of partials that I could not, as a young man, understand exactly.

L: Partials?

B: Spiritual partials, vibrational partials, upper scientific partials—different levels with respect to a given subject. Charlie Parker solidified all of the language dynamics that took place in his time period and, like Louis Armstrong before him, his language would express the—what's the word?—the *brilliance* of the era and all the people who had worked to solidify bebop. I've always disagreed with the concept that Charlie Parker was, like, the only restructuralist, at the expense of Wardell Gray, Lester Young, and Coleman Hawkins: all of those people are part of a continuum.

But Charlie Parker is one of the masters. His work made it possible for the intellectual and vibrational dynamics of African-American creativity to be carried further. It's because of Charlie Parker that we have the lineage moving into John Coltrane, to Albert

Ayler, later to Roscoe Mitchell and Joseph Jarman. There was more in his music than just the notes: I mean, his notes, his ideas, would set the stage for the projectional possibilities of trans-African and world culture information dynamics. His work personified the next juncture of the post-existential African American, vibrationally and intellectually, after the Second World War.

L: What do you mean?

B: Well, Charlie Parker's music and the solidification of bebop would represent many different things. Bebop would represent a serious break between the black middle-class community and the restructuralist revolutionary intellectuals and intellectual thought that was gathering in that period. For instance, bebop would extend separately (in terms of what I call the affinity insight principle) from the Baptist Church continuum that had solidified; I'm thinking of the gospel and spiritual musics that developed as a direct affirmation of, and linkage to, the community and in that context men and women would go to the church and participate in shaping that music. It became a profoundly important music that contributed to the information feed of American culture on several levels. But bebop was different. It emphasized the individual, the solo; and it was existential in the sense that musicians would look for God, for meaning, on a personal level, in the music. Also, bebop took place in the back rooms, the smoke-filled rooms . . .

Of course, the gangster community in America has always had its relationship to so-called "black exotica" in every period. You can't talk about New Orleans, for example, without talking about the political forces that affected, or even caused, the situation where early jazz was associated with the red-light districts, and the separation between the rich blacks and the house blacks. You can't talk about Kansas City without looking at the Pendergast political machine that ran the town, and its relationship to the music's formings. There's a long history to how black culture has been reduced to terms of "black exotica," and black people seen only in terms of their sexuality. It's happening to white women too in the Western media today. The music has always been associated with the red-light district and all of that mentality, as if the music was an affirmation of lower partials, or sin, when in fact in every phase all of the masters had a viewpoint about humanity, and the music that was solidified—the science and vibrational dynamics of that music—held forth the most positive alternatives for the culture.

So Charlie Parker's music would shape the vibrational . . . *bridges* that were operating in his time period, and set those forces into motion. His language especially would be so dynamic that all the saxophonists would be blinded by him for a period of twenty years, and even now many people have not been able to think in terms of establishing their own vocabularies because of the brilliance of his language. Unlike the people who would take his music, Charlie Parker didn't repeat himself. His music was always living, always fresh, always trying to be honest.

The Post-Parker Continuum

L: You've used the phrase "the post-Parker continuum" in the lectures: presumably you're referring to those people still playing Charlie Parker's language?

B: Yes, but let me be clear. When I talk about the post-Parker continuum, I'm talking about a continuum of stylists and I have respect for that continuum. The master stylists who would take Charlie Parker's music as a point of departure and within that vocabulary try to make something special happen, people like Cannonball Adderley—they can still be original. But the music that is now coming from the universities—the assumption there being that the technical solutions and scientific dynamics of bebop are now understood, which I say is completely untrue—those people are fundamentally misusing the music, as far as I'm concerned. They're not really playing bebop, they're playing other people's solutions and other people's versions of Charlie Parker. But Charlie Parker was participating with affinity insight dynamics, with respect to his own life, to what he set into motion, to what he was thinking about. There's a big difference between what Mr. Parker was playing and how his music is currently being used.

"Black Exotica"—The Concept of African Inferiority

L: You said in a 1984 *Cadence* interview that you felt the *intellectual* content of Charlie Parker's music had been completely neglected. Could you explain that a little?

B: Well, what has happened . . . This is part of the misinformation that African Americans are dealing with, and the position of powerlessness that we are in as regards having the possibility to make our definitions stick. Charlie Parker's music is separated from his actual thoughts. It's as if the notion they're trying to perpetuate—they being the power structure and the collective forces of Western culture—is that this man is sticking all of this dope into his arm and just playing, without making any kind of intelligent decisions about the music.

L: You mean the glamorization of pain? Like a kind of intellectual pornography?

B: Well, it's all a part of what I was just talking about, "black exotica"; that being the notion of separating the results of the music from what the person was thinking, and portraying the person as a dope addict or as incapable of establishing a thought that's valuable enough to be respected, that comes with its own value systems. What the Europeans have done, I think, is to undercut trans-African, even world culture, value systems; and this is not separate from the moves that have taken place in the last 300 years to justify what has happened in Africa, and to justify the present notion of human beings . . . the idea that a person's IQ is a justification for saying he or she is a better person, or not a better person, and from that point to say that some lives are better than other lives, and then to say let's get rid of those lives which are not as good as the other lives . . . the concept of African inferiority.

I'm sorry, we're getting away from my eight million heroes (*laughs*). But all these matters are connected. . . .

African-American Intellectuals—The Left

B: Here we are, you and I, sitting in this room because you're interested enough in my music to do the book. So OK, that's great. For those African-American intellectuals who look at this book and say, "Well, Graham Lock is white" . . . Ted Joans, for instance, put down Ross Russell for *Bird Lives*—that was ten years ago, we're still waiting for Mr. Joans's book! I can name—I won't do it, but I could—fifteen African-American intellectuals, so-called, who would protest to the heights if they see an article or a book on Benny Carter, say, written by a white American intellectual. They would cry out—and rightfully—that a black guy could have written this too. OK, but where are these people? I see only a handful of African Americans at my concerts—well, Braxton's the so-called White Negro, I'm not a good example—but I don't see many at the Art Ensemble's concerts, I don't see many at Dexter Gordon's concerts. Are we gonna blame this on white people too?

The African-American intellectual is great at being able to point out how the Europeans have fooled us and suppressed us, but they're not so good at explaining why they haven't documented some area of expertise themselves. I would love to judge Mr. Russell's book on Charlie Parker against some of those African-American writers Charlie Parker hung out with, to look at the differences and see what there is to learn. But it's the age-old problem that it's better to talk about it than to do it.

L: Well, I'm talking only as an outsider, but surely there are some African-American writers who are functioning?

B: Oh yes! For instance, Dr. Yosef ben-Jochannan: this is an African-American intellectual who is like a shining tower in an ocean of despair, an ocean of negligence.* There are a handful of African-American scholars who are functioning on Dr. ben-Jochannan's level, but why is it that in 1985 there is so much ignorance in black communities across America with respect to history, to documentation, to understanding the political machinery that's been set into motion? The rivalries and separations that happened in the sixties between the Garvey and DuBois vibrational sectors of the community—why did they occur? Why is it that African Americans have not only not supported my music, but all of the musics after Charlie Parker? No one wants to say this, but the turn-out of the black community for the music is a sign of real danger; and this is not only true for music, but for theater, dance . . .

What has happened, in my opinion, is that African Americans have been profoundly shaped and manipulated by the media, by the Top Ten mentality, *and* by a persuasion of nationalism that seeks to establish Europe as the only source of the illness we're dealing with, as if we have had no part in creating the sadness that's taking place in this time period.

Why have African Americans not been able to mobilize? Of course, we are dealing with overwhelming forces, very sophisticated forces, in so far as how our suppression is maintained *still;* but the fact is that there is no jazz magazine from African-American intellectuals, no jazz record company, no art music record company . . . Yes, we can blame it on Europe, blame it on white America, that's fine with me, blame it on white America for the next 5,000 years—but the only way something's gonna get done is for someone to do it.

*Dr. Yosef ben-Jochannan, writer, historian, Egyptologist, was a student of George G. M. James and has since done extensive research into James's theses that ancient Egypt was a) a black African civilization, and b) the primary source of much supposedly Greek classical philosophy. Dr. ben-Jochannan has also written about the black roots of both Christianity and Freemasonry; his numerous books include *Black Man of the Nile and His Family* and *Africa: Mother of "Western Civilization."*

L: How do you relate this malaise to the hope and promise of the sixties? I know a lot of black leaders were assassinated or imprisoned, but—what's happened, say, to the notion of Black Power?

B: If we look at the young nationalists, the concept of Black Power, in the last fifteen years we've seen a robust, dynamic movement, full of hope—young people thinking about world consciousness and change—be reduced to rubble, where all that's left is a twelve-hour handshake that isn't even used any more.

L: But how did it happen?

B: Oh, it's complex, Graham . . . I believe there were many levels of dishonesty associated with the left. Historically, the left have constantly run to the black community when any kind of . . . mmm . . . diversion is needed, but they've never dealt with the music with respect to its own definitions. The reason I indict the left is that, at every point of the way, the left could have tried to teach people about what was happening, but they chose only to take those areas of information that were conducive to their own interests. It was very fashionable to talk about black power, black rage, the music as screaming, etc., etc.—a concept of nationalism that made it impossible to talk about fundamentals; but, in fact, everybody knows that at some point fundamentals, the concepts of information and evolution, are laws which are manifested in every period. There *are* universal fundamentals, and to respect them does not imply no commitment to Africa.

The Black Power movement came to a stop because it was based on unhealthy premises, one of those being that all the problems African Americans are facing can be reduced to European-Americans. It's more complex than that: African Americans are dealing with divisions between themselves—particularly the dichotomy between the Marcus Garvey and the W. E. B. DuBois intellectual forces—just as Europeans are dealing with the war between the technocrat and the European mystic. If we look too at what's happened to the feminist movement, we can see that it's gotten bogged down in the same *distortions of essence* that the black community fell to. I see all of these things as being part of the central problem—not having the power to define your own terms.

"Put the Mystics in Charge"

L: You said in 1967 that you thought we were on the eve of the fall of Western values: do you still believe that?

B: Well, as a young man I might have overstated it (*laughs*). Looking back at what took place in the sixties and seventies, especially in the black community, I've had to come to terms with that and integrate it into my understanding. I might not make the same statement today, although I wouldn't disagree with it either—I just wouldn't be the person to say it (*laughs*).

L: Isn't there a contradiction between your critique of Western values and the sophisticated level of technology that, say, your projected multi-orchestral works will require?

B: Where's the contradiction?

L: Well, in current Western value systems, technology has a high priority and is allocated enormous funds. The change we would both like to see involves reshuffling those priorities so that first everyone is fed, clothed, housed—which would mean less funds available for technological research.

B: Oh, I don't agree. I think there's enough money to do whatever we want to do. The U.S. military budget alone is so outlandish that we could not imagine what the figures mean in real money: just the budget for the army bands, the money to buy those guys saxophones and stuff, is greater than the *entire* National Endowment of the Arts in America. The money's there, but the value systems are not, nor the awareness of the people.

The divisions in present-day American society are tragic. The fragmented left, you know . . . It's like everybody broke up into little factions and sat in front of the television. Now we're all wondering how we ever got to this point in time. I say, give the musicians a shot! They can't make the planet any worse (*laughs*). Put the mystics in charge! You know, *do something.*

The Pentagon has shown that they are not morally capable of dealing with the consideration of war, let alone that of peace. Hmm, I like that idea—put the creative people in charge . . . I don't know though, let me stop and think about this. I wouldn't want some of the musicians I've known to be in charge (*laughs*). No, take the creative people out! (*Laughs.*)

How to Live?

L: Could you say a little more about the ancients, how you became aware of that information?

B: I'll say it *again*—for every thought you think, there is information related to that thought. What do I mean by that? I'm only saying that all of us are dealing with the wonderful experience of living and no one knows what this is—but then maybe someone knows what this is. OK, from there I'll go to here. I believe very much in God; and in the last ten years, which have brought me and my family to our knees because of the intensity of our struggle and the poverty that we've been dealing with, this has only increased my convictions about the oneness of . . . wonder, and how fortunate it is to exist. And when I say I believe in God, by that I'm only saying that I believe in God. OK, from that I'll go to this. I'm very interested in trying to understand for myself how to live, how to be the best person that I can possibly be—whatever that means. And I'm trying to understand what it does mean.

This kind of information can be obtained in many different directions (though it seems to me that they all go back to the Negative Confessions),* and, of course, whatever level of understanding you want from that information depends upon what you're walking with, what your thoughts are, and how serious you are in applying your forces to understanding better what it is you say you're interested in.

L: And encoding this information in music will set forces for good, or for change, into motion? You've said that you hope your music will help to bring about world change.

B: By that I just mean . . . My hope is to establish a body of music that will represent my potential, my aspirations, in terms of how I see music and sound logic. I stated before that a force sets its operatives into motion; by that I was talking of the power of music to set given forces and values into motion. I can say for a fact, based on my own life, that John Coltrane's music has helped me to be a better person, that Arnold Schoenberg's and Karlheinz Stockhausen's music has made me work harder and want to be a better person. I could also say that the body of musics I've been trying to deal with . . . the thoughts it brings me are not in the zone of trying to hurt anyone, I don't walk around in a perceived negative space.

I believe music has much more power than we generally associate with it, but at the same time I don't mean to say, "listen to my music and you're gonna be a better person" or that my work is going to change the world. Even though, of course, I think it has its

*The Negative Confessions were an ancient Egyptian code of ethics which Dr. ben-Jochannan has traced as the likely source of the Ten Commandments.

place: I think everything has its place. You do the best work you can do and it will set into motion what it sets into motion.

L: You said earlier that, on one level, it didn't matter if your music wasn't performed so long as you were free to compose it: but, surely, if music has this power, it's vital that it be played.

B: Oh yes, but I don't want to confuse *me* with music; I'm just one person on the planet. I think it's important so I'm dedicating my life to my work, but whether Anthony Braxton succeeds or not is not even the question. Music is important and we have to find a way to bring people back to true information, real information, that can really help in this experience; but it's not dependent on any one person. A lot of creative people have gone down the tubes, down the drain into poverty: if that's my fate, I'm not unique. Many jazz musicians, as you know . . . Coltrane never got to fifty years old, Booker Little—so I'm fortunate to be on the planet.

2

REPORTAGE

King Oliver: A Very Personal Memoir

Edmond Souchon, M.D.

Dr. Souchon was born in New Orleans in 1897. In 1901, at the age of four, he was—in the words of Martin Williams—"captivated by the music, soon to be called jazz, that he heard in the city streets." Williams published this piece in his superb anthology Jazz Panorama *(1962).*

This is a memoir about a great musician, Joe Oliver. It begins in the molten period of a magnificent American art before Oliver's star had begun its ascent. It is written by a surgeon who, by the fortunes of birth, came to life within the citadel of Southern white caste privileges and who has reached middle age following the main course of the wonderfully proud, prejudiced, and all too human oligarchs (the books have called them so) who were his forebearers. But it also springs from a turbulence of honest feelings from the heart and mind of one who, regardless of birth, luck, privileges, place or time, was fortunate enough to hear the great Joe Oliver blasting the heavens and shaking the blackberry leaves in funeral parades through the fringes of his neighborhood.

A rather pampered and sheltered child I was, arrayed in the ridiculous trappings of that Little Lord Fauntleroy era of "Southern aristocracy" which now seems unbelievable. So I was dressed—in about 1901–2 at the age of four or five—when my Negro nurse first took me walking into the dense Negro neighborhood to hear Joe Oliver play. The impact of this experience—the power and beauty of that music—has never left me. I followed the career of this New Orleans artist with a fidelity at least as great as that which I gave to medical faculties or to the gentle pomp and circumstances of my privileged world.

Surrounded by my corduroy breeches, knee-high leather leggings, stiff starched Lord Fauntleroy collar with soft flowing tie, I suddenly found myself relegated to the care of Armotine. All that was missing from my picture was a foreign governess who spoke several languages. In her stead was Armotine, Tine to me. Thank God she was colored, or this story could never have been.

Tine was many-faceted. She was my boss, my instructor, and my protector. She was also the most interesting person to cross my life up to that point. Undoubtedly, she was one of the finest cooks in the city of New Orleans. When starting to prepare the evening meal, she would keep her eye on my play in the side yard beneath her kitchen window. The ritual of a spicy *fine herb* sauce or the preparation of a *roux* for *grillarde* was accompanied by hours of never-ending song. Her deep contralto was clear and soft, with a rhythm that often made me stop playing to listen and pat my foot. Her songs were an admixture of Creole folk songs, church hymns, and up-to-date hits of the late '90s or early 1900s. One refrain she repeated so often that I remember the words perfectly. It went:

Ain't that man got a funny walk,
Doin' the "Ping-Pong" 'round Southern park.
Nigger man, white man, take him away,
I thought I heard them say.

There were innumerable verses to this song. Tine would shush me if I started to sing any of the less refined ones along with her. And there was another song which she seemed to like almost as well as the first. I always sang it for people if I was certain they would not go tell my mother; I knew I could always get a laugh, although I hadn't the slightest idea of its meaning.

I have learned many verses to this song since then, but I still like the one Tine taught me the best:

I'm Alabamy bound, I'm Alabamy bound,
I'm Alabamy bound,
And if you want my cabbage patch,
You gotta hoe the ground.

Every afternoon, Tine would take me for a walk, either up or down St. Charles Avenue, seldom on the side streets. Occasionally, when she fancied she needed something very special for preparing dinner, Mom would grant me permission to accompany Tine to Terrell's Grocery on First and Dryades. By coincidence (or was it?) a thrilling thing happened every time we went to Terrell's Grocery; Tine's intuition, or the grapevine, passed the word along. Invariably, the most exciting parade went by. And always Tine and I marched along with a long black wagon, accompanied by men in tinseled uniforms, plumed hats and sabers. A hundred kids my age skipped along. There were plenty of grownups too, following on the sidewalks and in the streets. I never got tired, even when I missed my afternoon nap.

Someone mentioned that the heavy man playing that short, stubby instrument at the head of the band was working for a family a few houses down the street from ours. He was their butler-yardman, and only played music on his time off. I did not understand all this at all. Everybody seemed to love this man. Somehow I thought that possibly I did too. That man was Joe Oliver.

By 1907, I had grown to the point where I was taking streetcars all by myself and making my way around the city, and a few months before Tine's death, I heard one of her friends tell her that "Joe Oliver was playing at a cabaret down in the district." My heart beat fast. I had not heard him in a long time, and I missed his music. I knew that the "district" was spoken of vaguely and in whispers. It was a place where no "nice people" went. Maybe I heard mention of it because my mother's sister had married an alderman who had passed the law restricting a "certain element" (the prostitutes) to this area.

I learned that kids were never allowed in that section of the city, but that newsboys were an exception, tolerated "along the fringe" but not in the main streets. Afraid to venture on my escapade alone, I prevailed on one of my more venturesome pals to accompany me. We dug up the oldest clothes we could find, tore them in many places, and rubbed them in the dirt; a half dozen copies of *The Daily States* or the *New Orleans Item* under our arms, and the disguise was complete.

The "Big 25" where Oliver was playing was just one block from Basin Street, and about three quarters of a block from Canal. The time was just after dusk. Our objective was reached without so much as a side glance of suspicion from the grownups along the way. The streets were practically deserted. But our hearts were in our throats! When we arrived, not one sound was issuing forth. We were crestfallen: the music started at 9:00 P.M.

A couple of Friday nights later we were at it again, this time after dark. Except for faint red lights that shone through half-drawn shutters and the sputtering carbon lights on the corner, there was not much illumination. We could see strange figures peering out through half-open doorways. A new cop on the beat immediately tried to chase us, but the peeping female figures behind the blinds came to our rescue. They hurled invective of such vehemence—"Let them poor newsboys make a livin', you ——" — that he let us go. We told him we were only going as far as Joe Oliver's saloon to bring him his paper. It seemed to satisfy him.

We could now hear that music from half a block away; it probably would have taken more than one policeman to stop us. The place was twice as long as it was wide. It was one-story wooden frame building at sidewalk level, lengthwise parallel to the street. There was a bar at the Iberville end, and a sort of dance hall to the rear, nearer Canal Street. Quick glances through the swinging doors showed us that the inside was fairly well lighted. But outside the building there were many deep shadows, and the sputtering carbon arc-light on the corner was out more than on. Gutters three feet wide and almost as deep ran alongside the sidewalk. A tall telegraph pole stood just in front of the dance hall, across the gutter. In its shadow we sought refuge until someone discovered us and told us to move on. After listening to the music for almost an hour and a half, with reluctance we turned homeward. That trip was just the beginning. We came there many Friday nights. They got to know us and hardly noticed that we were there. We sat on the gutter's edge, our feet dangling, and drank in that sound.

Sometimes Oliver would come outside for a breather. We wondered how we might approach him to get him to say a few words to us. Finally, I ventured, "Mr. Oliver, here is the paper you ordered." I'll never forget how big and tough he looked! His brown derby was tilted low over one eye, his shirt collar was open at the neck, and a bright red undershirt peeked out at the V. Wide suspenders held up an expanse of trousers of unbelievable width. He looked at us and said, "You know damn well, white boy, I never ordered no paper." We thought the end of the world had come. Suddenly, we realized that he had not spoken loud enough for anyone to hear us! Then he went on, much more friendly, "I been knowin' you kids were hanging around here to listen to my music. Do you think I'm going to chase you away for that? This is a rough neighborhood, kids, and I don't want you to get into trouble. Keep out of sight and go home at a decent time." We were *in!* We had really made it!

But gradually, the city law agencies and police began to adopt a tougher policy in the district. We thought it best that we quit. But we tapered off; we couldn't stop all of a sudden.

Ten fast years went by. Then came Tulane University from 1913 to 1917. None of us had forgotten Oliver and the memory of his music. We were invited to the regular Saturday night "script" dances at the Tulane gymnasium. For one dollar, you got yourself and your best girl in from eight to twelve. On the bandstand, surrounded by his entire band, was Joe Oliver! My bunch, jazz lovers all, scarcely missed a Saturday night for the next four years. There were seven of us who hardly danced at all but surrounded the bandstand the whole evening. In retrospect, it's hard to believe that we were so lucky. Gradually, we learned the players' names, and they learned ours. We got special kicks out of listening to the little drummer who quietly sang risqué parodies on the tunes the band was playing. A bunch of white boys in the deep South, second lining with utter rapture to a Negro band! In those narrow times, such a thing was unheard of!

We were so imbued with the music that as soon as the dance was over, and we had absorbed all we could, we'd go over to somebody's house and attempt to imitate on string instruments what Oliver's band had been doing on brass and woodwind. The fact that fifty years later, four of that same group still play together many of the old tunes which Oliver featured is evidence, I think, of how deeply the experience imbedded itself. It is also proof—to ourselves and to others—that we were actually there; it was no figment of our imaginations.

Then World War I. The district was closed by order of the Secretary of the Navy, and all the good musicians moved away. For us, France, back to America, and, for me, medical school. On graduation, I was in Chicago to finish a two-year internship. It was late 1924, I believe, that my passing all final exams called for special celebration. A party began to shape up. Someone heard us bragging about the great bands to which we had danced in New Orleans and informed us that in a black-and-tan joint on the South Side the greatest jazz band of all times was currently playing. There was no further discussion.

Prohibition was at its maudlin height. The place was far from inviting from the outside, dingy and needing several coats of paint. Ancient paper decorations and faded flowers hung dejectedly from unpainted walls and peeling columns. A long, winding ill-lit hallway seemed to take us back of some large hotel or building. The place smelled of last week's beer. But the closer we got to the dance hall, the more excited we became. No one had mentioned the name of the band playing there, but it was only necessary for a few musical strains to meet us for us to realize that something familiar was greeting us.

A rather pretentious floor show was in progress as we made our way to our table. A brilliant spotlight followed the performers on the dance floor, but gloom made the faces of the musicians undistinguishable. The bandstand supported about ten chairs, and the musicians were decked out in tuxedos or dress suits (I am not sure which) with much tinsel and fancy braid. A heavy man was their leader, and he was following the cues of the dancers and singers. The floor-show star that night was Frankie "Halfpint" Jackson.

Suddenly we realized we were looking at someone on the bandstand who greatly resembled Joe Oliver. We could hardly wait for the floor show to stop, so the lights would go up for dancing.

It was Oliver all right. But his was a much more impressive figure now. The transition from the red undershirt and suspenders of Storyville's "Big 25" to the clean white shirt at the Tulane gymnasium to the formidable figure he now presented, was almost too much to believe! He was now "King," the most important personage in the jazz world, surrounded by his own hand-picked galaxy of sidemen. His cordial welcome to two old New Orleans friends almost made us ashamed of the lumps in our throats—the same lump I had had when, in newsboys' clothes, we offered him a newspaper. His affability that night equaled his kindness to us youngsters who had braved the terrors of Storyville to hear him play.

The turmoil and excitement which was going on around us in that speakeasy was nothing compared to what was going on within our hearts. The realization of the very privilege which had been ours over these thirty years suddenly burst on us. Joe Oliver is long dead. His body lies in an almost unmarked grave. I have all the records he ever made. These are brittle and fragile. The "Big 25" has been torn down. I've taken pictures of that, but these too are perishable. What remains for me is the *sound* of Joe Oliver. Perhaps auditory memory is better than visual. It is easy for me to recall many, many tunes which the Oliver band played in the very early days at "Big 25." Maybe when our first venturesome escapades into Storyville were going on, we were too excited—perhaps not interested—we do not recall one name at "Big 25" other than Joe Oliver. But the tunes, yes!

At Tulane, it was different. Every man in the band was known to every one of us. Names such as Johnny Dodds, Sidney Bechet, Johnny St. Cyr, Kid Ory, Baby Dodds, Pops Foster, Tilman Braud, Armand J. Piron, Clarence Williams, Steve Lewis. There were many others, too, in Joe's Tulane groups, for personnels varied from week to week. But the sound of the band remained just as thrilling with each group. And Joe Oliver was always there, or the band wouldn't have been hired. And the tunes they played were always the same.

I believe without fear of memory-tricks that by the time Oliver was playing at Tulane gymnasium, he had acquired a technique that was much more smooth, and that his band was adapting itself to the white dances more and more. At "Big 25" it was hard-hitting, rough and ready, full of fire and drive. He subdued this to please the different patrons at the gym dances. It is easy to recall this when I recall a transition which one of jazz's most popular tunes underwent. Sometimes, when Joe would be playing for a private party at a home or a ball, a midnight supper would be served to the guests. In order to get the couples into line and stop the dancing, Oliver was requested to play a march to which no one could dance. He would use "High Society." It was played at a very slow marching tempo, the same tempo his band used in marching funerals and processions. It was a shuffle, easy to walk to. And the first part seemed interminable, before he broke into the chorus which has immortalized Alphonse Picou. You couldn't even do a "slow drag" to it, as it was played then. Gradually, the tempo of this tune was quickened, and it was converted into a dance tune, almost the same as we know today; the transition probably took three or four years!

Historians have often said that the early New Orleans bands played an ensemble style almost entirely, with few if any solos. I am afraid that I must disagree. However, the manner in which solos began finding their way into such bands as Joe Oliver's was without plan from the leaders or of the sidemen. Early New Orleans groups *were* trained to play ensemble almost entirely, with occasional breaks for a particular instrument. But during parades and at dances the cornet or trumpet might get tired and without warning simply drop out. Or maybe he had blown a few bad ones, so he simply stopped playing and blew saliva out of his horn. Immediately, as he stopped, either the clarinet or the trombone took the lead—sometimes both instruments did this, playing unison lead. When the trumpet man decided his lip was rested, he resumed playing at any time and at any place in the piece. It was not those Chicago musicians, or the New Yorkers who first started passing it around; New Orleans did it, long ago.

The Chicago Oliver group was a magnificently drilled band. Each member was a star, intent on making the overall sound of the band good. Each, too, was a fine soloist in his own right. But Joe Oliver saw to it that nobody outshone him. The sidemen's solos were few and shorter than those Oliver appropriated to himself. It was without doubt the very best music in Chicago at that time, and they still had that beat.

The records which I have, made during the Chicago stage and afterwards, seem to be collector's items, a yardstick by which the neophyte judges other bands, and which many attempt to copy. I disagree sadly that these are representative of Oliver at his greatest. By the time Oliver had reached Chicago and the peak of his popularity, his sound was not the same. It was a different band, a different and more polished Oliver, an Oliver who had completely lost his New Orleans sound.

Regressing in our discussion, and trying after fifty years to conjure up as fairly as a sexagenarian can do, I had these thoughts:

In Chicago Joe Oliver was at his most popular and polished, but he was already on the way out. Instead of realizing the treasure that was his in playing New Orleans music, he was trying to sound like a big white band!

Even at Tulane Oliver's style was beginning to change. It was still very great music, but something in the inner feeling of the band was shaking itself loose from the roots from which it had sprung. Perhaps playing together too often is the reason, for who can dispute that head arrangements, repeated night after night with the same musicians, can become just as deadly as the written score can? Perhaps it was a desire to "improve" (let's not use the word "progress").

There are no bands playing today whose sound faintly resembles that of

Oliver's band at "Big 25." Jazz histories have many times told me whom I had been listening to in that bistro and possibly I now call up the sound of these men by suggestion; I doubt my own memory. We kids were not interested in who was playing in the band, as long as it was Joe Oliver's band. Even if I readily admit I knew the name only of Joe Oliver, I still have my complete and honest belief that this first Oliver I heard was the most thrilling. It was rough, rugged, and contained many bad chords. There were many fluffed notes, too. But the drive, the rhythm, the wonderfully joyous New Orleans sound was there in all its beauty. This is what the recordings made in Chicago missed. Those records even miss conveying the way that Oliver was playing in Chicago when I heard him.

A Music of the Streets

Frederick Turner

In his book Remembering Song *(1982), Turner records his relationship with an old-time New Orleans trombonist, Jim Robinson, and through Robinson's life and death convincingly re-creates a jazz world going back to the First World War.*

For all the great players to come out of [New Orleans] we have scarcely a handful of full-length autobiographies, and my view was that the more we could get, the better our chances of understanding the cultural significance of the tradition, its place in our common history. I made several stabs at this project over the next couple of years, interviewing in brief various players. Perhaps I was searching for *the* right subject; perhaps I was only screwing up my courage to ask someone to commit himself to so major an investment of time and privacy. However it was, eventually I could see no one so remarkably suitable as Jim Robinson, the featured trombonist with the various bands at Preservation Hall. Robinson was friendly, even ebullient; he was certainly old enough to have direct ties to the tradition; and his open, big-toned playing spoke of one of the happiest aspects of the city's musical heritage. I asked him one night at the Hall if I might call on him at home. He agreed, cheerful and casual as ever, and the next afternoon we sat in the front room of his St. Philip Street home, the tape recorder picking up the sounds of clinking glasses and the random street noises that sifted in through the open door. There was a bottle of I. W. Harper and a mixing bowl full of ice cubes and talk of old bands and their players, styles, and of his own style and musical philosophy.

The project was thus well begun, but it was never completed. Over the succeeding years I got down to New Orleans whenever I could to interview Robinson, but over that same span of time it became clear even to me that Jim wasn't interested in this work. It also became clear, to my surprise and delight, that he enjoyed my company, so that eventually the visits came to be just that, and I never bothered anymore to bring the recorder or the camera.

In those days Jim's wife, Pearl, was still alive, and the three of us would sit in the close, immaculate living room with the heavy plastic slipcovers of the chairs and davenport rustling when we moved, the walls covered with crisped brown photographs of musicians and bands with which Jim had played. Above the television there was a large photo of a young and strikingly handsome Jim with his horn held aslant his chest, looking casually conscious of his youth, looks, talent: the player in his prime. The picture served as a combination reference point and standard joke, useful to date something from, to measure aging by, or to suggest his ways with women.

Our talk was of such random things but especially of the past—into which I still tried to lead him. He and I would drink slowly, and Pearl would content herself with an occasional beer. Sometimes she would disappear into the recesses of the house and emerge later at the far door of the bedroom to tell us she'd fixed a meal which we'd then eat at the kitchen table—red beans, rice, and hamhocks, maybe.

When properly warmed Jim would play some of his favorite recordings which usually had to compete with the seemingly eternal *American Bandstand* the grandniece Tammy attended on TV. He would point out particular passages he wanted me to listen to, especially his own ("Just listen to what I do here: some of these fellas, all they can play is melody!"), and after one of these that roused him he would strike his knee with a long, limber hand and wag his head in affirmation, gold-capped teeth sparkling out of the Indian-wide face.

Gradually, in this no longer systematic way, Jim's life details emerged, the rambling talk striking here and there against some fact of place, name, or time. In such a fashion I learned one evening that Jim's given name was Nathan, and that "Jim" was a shortened version of a boyhood nickname, "Jim Crow," some old joke, maybe, that even he had forgotten.

That boyhood was spent about thirty-five miles downriver at Deer Range Plantation where Nathan Robinson was born on Christmas Day, 1892. I had always planned to sometime rent a car and drive Jim down to his old home until one day he told me it wasn't there anymore: the big river had washed it all away. His father had come down there from Richmond, Virginia, perhaps as early as the 1870s. There he met a Louisiana woman, married her, and stayed on to work as a teamster and breaker of mules and horses. Jim recalled trailing the plantation's dusty roads and paths behind his mother, using her long dresses as both handkerchief and security blanket; recalled too the omnipresence of the mules and horses and tack his father worked with; and, of course, the river the other kids would swim in. "I never could swim," he laughed. "Other boys, they'd say, 'Do this-a-way, Jim.' But I'd go right to the bottom like a stone." What schooling there was he had here, and though I had seen him sign his name in a slow, neat hand, I came to suspect that he was illiterate.

There was another, more native, sort of schooling to be had there, however, and this was the music of the country bands. Deer Range was just up the river from the old Magnolia Plantation, and on Saturdays Jim and his friends would go down there to hear Professor Humphrey's boys play a dance. Once he scoffed at me when I confused Louis Keppard's Magnolia Orchestra with this rural outfit that had thrilled him in his youth. "Naw, naw, naw," he said, flapping his hand dismissingly at me. "This was a *country* band. Man, I'm tellin' you, them fellas was *tough! Hogs!*"

One of Jim's three brothers played valve trombone in such a band, and Jim told me he had started on that instrument, though on another occasion he remembered that he'd really started on guitar. In either case, what seems important is the strength of the influence: there was the music right there in the parish and there were immediate models for those who aspired to play it.

In 1910, like a lot of country kids, he came up to the city. Here the music was in its most gorgeous effulgence, dozens of good bands, each with outstanding players, reputations in the making, and more work for a player than he could easily handle. Yet in all this Jim Robinson had no part. In those days he was a longshoreman and might have remained one had he not entered the army in 1917.

In France, where his segregated unit worked at building and repairing the roads of war, "They was some fellas was gettin' up a jazz band, you know. And they needed a trombone. Well, I had been foolin' with my brother's trombone—back in the country my brother had a trombone, but it was a valve trombone and this here was a slide. Trombone is a tough instrument. It's a guess instrument.

"Anyway, he [the bandleader] says to 'em, 'We'll take Bob here'—he called me Bob—'and we'll teach him, and he can play the trombone parts.'" So, while the band practiced at a YMCA building, Jim would practice by himself on a slope behind it ("They didn't want me around playin' all them bad notes") until he could get along in the ensemble unnoticed.

"Pretty soon, maybe two, maybe three weeks, I was doin' pretty good. Six weeks, why, I could play right along with 'em. We'd have a special car, the back all fixed up, you know, like a truck, with a red cross painted on the side, and we'd play all over." Then, lowering his voice conspiratorily, he winked at me: "Nurses travelin' with us, too."

In 1919, when Jim got back to New Orleans, the great flowering of the music was barely past. Many of the big names like Keppard and Oliver and Morton had gone north; others like Armstrong were out of town on the boats; and others like Bunk Johnson were drifting into the country. The District that had provided so many jobs was closed. Still, it was a fine place for a musician and would have been called "great" were it not for the scale of comparison. Indeed, there were so many accomplished musicians still in town that Jim hooted when I asked him once whether on his return he had started in playing with some local group. As he subsequently explained, he was far from good enough to cut it in New Orleans, and so he went back to work on the docks. But still the music called, not only from all around him but now also from within. He had the taste of brass in his mouth, and when the time came for the call to play, he was ready with his response.

"I was livin' then down on Marais and Iberville, and I could hear them fellas playin' trombone right next door. When I was on the day shift, I could come out at night and just sit on my back porch and listen to them fellas playin'—*dat-dat-dat*—in that hall. Sometimes I'd sit out there all night long and listen to 'em play, and I'd think, Shucks! I could do that! I could do what they doin'! Sometimes they'd play till six in the mornin'.

"Well, my sister—I was livin' with her then—my sister, she got this player piano. You ever seen a player piano? Got all them great big rolls on it? Well, she got this player piano, and when I'd be on the night shift, then during the day I'd just sit there and work them pedals and figure out the trombone. And that's where I learned my stuff.

"I'd come home seven in the mornin', sleep a little, and then get up and just *work* that piano and figure out the trombone. Sometimes my sister, if she was at home, she would pedal for me."

The call came from Kid Rena who needed a trombone on an advertising job. Jim's friend John Marrero, who played banjo in the band, brought Jim around so that Rena could audition him. The leader was surprised and impressed, and when the band played later that day at a street corner, Jim remembered that someone had gone to the house of the regular trombonist, Maurice French, with some bad news. His voice rising higher toward laughter, Jim reconstructed the message: "He say, 'Maurice! Maurice! You better come out here. They's a new trombone player, Maurice, and he sound *real* good!' Maurice, he come out to see who was playin' that way, and if he thought he was sick before, you should have seen him when he seen me!!"

That was the breakthrough. Rena used Jim occasionally thereafter, as did the Tuxedo Brass Band, so he was now a member of the fraternity, even though he continued to work regularly as a longshoreman. Then he wholly entered it by joining the Young Morgan Band led by the trumpet-playing brothers, Isaiah and Sam Morgan. Any time I wanted to get Jim really talking, all I had to do was to mention either the country bands of his youth or the Young Morgan Band. "Ohhh," he would say of the latter in something between laughter and a shout, "them fellas was a tough band!" He said they were known as the "'Time Band,' 'cause our rhythm was so good." Once, he said, the Time Band had been on the river, playing for a day's excursion when they had come alongside another boat with its band going full tilt. First he was serious as he set this scene for me, but then he fell into laughter as he told how quickly his bunch had played the others down. And "them boys that had hired that band, they called out over the side at us, 'Young Morgan Band! Young Morgan Band!' After that they didn't want no other band: 'Young Morgan Band!'"

Here there is supporting evidence. The Young Morgan Band, recording as "Sam Morgan's Jazz Band," made some records for Columbia in 1927. It is indeed a tight, tough group that swings as hard as Jim remembered.

After Sam Morgan's death in 1936, the band disintegrated and Jim gigged around with other groups, mostly in New Orleans. He was still at this when history, in the persons of Bill Russell and Bunk Johnson, found him. Jim was an integral part of the Johnson comeback and the subsequent revival of interest in New Orleans music. He worked regularly with George Lewis's bands in the 1950s and after the Jaffes opened Preservation Hall in 1961, he was a staple of the groups assembled there. Allan Jaffe's announcement that "Jim Robinson will be here tomorrow night" rarely failed to elicit a thrill of anticipation in the hall, and Jim just as rarely failed to deliver.

Thus when I first met Jim Robinson he had more than half a century of playing behind him and an even more remarkable amount of music and life within him, in his laughter, his delight in the ridiculous, in his easy, flowing talk. Some of this seemed to dwindle when Pearl died unexpectedly—though at her age of seventy-six, what can truly be unexpected? It was a different Jim I visited thereafter, and I fancied I could even hear an older, chastened quality to his playing. He was given sometimes to dark moods in which he seemed to huddle within himself and from which not even a stiff glass or two of I.W. Harper could release him. For some time after Pearl's death he continued to speak of her as an active presence. "I get into bed at night," he said once, "and I lie right in the middle. I know Pearl, she around, and this way, if I lie in the middle, she have to squeeze in on one side or the other." And sometimes when the mood struck, he would kiss a heavily retouched photograph of her as a young woman.

For a while Pearl's sister, Viola, came over often from Slidell to help out and keep company, and once I had a magnificent fried fish dinner she fixed, during the course of which I had to make two beer runs to the corner market. But then she stopped coming, and Jim was at home alone a good deal, though his relative Joe was around when not working. Many nights Jim would sit alone behind shuttered windows and bolted door, listening to his music, sipping a glass of whiskey, and going to bed at first light. Occasionally neighbors would visit, especially children, and on warm days Jim, sitting on his stoop beneath a green awning, would be the great-grandfather to the block, waving to the children, laughing at their roller-skating mishaps, pointing out to them a brightly painted mural of himself on the wall of the building facing the vacant lot wherein they played.

And of course the work at Preservation Hall still took him out. Here in the tiny, airless hall, with its splintered floor and massed, sweating tourists, and on the tours the band made throughout the states, he was still the irrepressible crowd-pleaser, the clown, arms flapping, bony butt stuck out, moving in his pigeon-toed circle dance to someone else's solo.

The edge to this act was that he could still play, the crowd's delighted laughter to be followed in the preserved order of things by its admiration as he followed his dance routine with some wide, swinging solo, deep, tremulous reworking of a hymn, or spirited ensemble work, the long slide of the horn glinting out and down, the face intent and wholly serious behind the mouthpiece. Now he was beyond the crowd, his talent and his dedication to it taking him as much out of reach of laughter as of admiration, the artist here entirely himself. This was Robinson's ultimate salvation, this allegiance to his talent and to the tradition within which he exercised it. It was what saved him from both the adulation of his late career and the periodic neglect he had experienced in earlier years. It was, as I finally came to understand through the years of our friendship, that inward place where he truly lived.

ON A SOFT May afternoon in 1976, the history of the New Orleans tradition and the symbol of its passing converged for me in a phone call. A friend's voice on the other end told me of Jim's obituary in the day's newspaper. The funeral was scheduled for the next morning, and as I tried to absorb this news, I could see the sun already well spent in the hills of western Massachusetts. I wondered how I could possibly make it. I wondered, too, about the propriety of making it at all. In the eight years I had known Jim the funerals of New Orleans musicians had been attended with ever-increasing outside pressure to the point where they had almost become media rumbles. Recognizing this situation, Louis Armstrong had decreed the simplest of services for himself, and when he died in 1971 no jazz was allowed. If I went, I would become part of the huge scene certain to ensue. And yet I had to go.

The next morning I walked St. Philip Street up out of the Vieux Carré, beginning to pick up the signs of festivity as I crossed Dauphine. Already, well beforehand, a large crowd was gathered outside Jim Robinson's house. Across the street lay the unfinished park, a mess of dried mud, weeds, and boards with a vacant enclosure just opposite the house where they plan someday to erect a statue of Armstrong. And behind the park, there were the remains of Congo Square with its grand Spanish oaks brooding over the spot and writhing their heavy branches like black snakes over that stretch of ground where so much of this music's history sank roots into American soil. Many a time after the intervening houses had been torn away in another ill-conceived "renewal" project, Jim Robinson and I had sat in the shade of his stoop, chatting and looking across toward that bit of green where once the transplanted Africans had danced and drummed the history of their blood. I never knew how much of all that Jim Robinson had ever heard, his interest in history being rigorously selective.

The day even at so early an hour was already steaming up with opalescent clouds hanging heavily about an unforgiving white sun. Beneath this colors matched the heat. Umbrellas of various shades were already unfurled above bobbing heads, not only black and red ones, but striped and parti-colored numbers that looked as if they might have been gotten up for just such occasions. The crowd's clothing suggested more a fair or a ballgame than a funeral.

Around the corner St. Claude Street was jammed all the way to the funeral home, but these were neighborhood people who had merely stepped out of doors: sleepy-eyed drinkers; clots of chatting women with children at their knees; old men with hands in their pockets and faces shaded with straw hats; teenagers flitting on bicycles through openings in the crowd. A festive air was on a decaying neighborhood Jim Robinson had not seen too much of in his last years. It had become too hazardous now for an old man who might be presumed to have some money on him. As his late wife had once observed, "If you go away without someone to watch, they liable to just run a truck right up to your door and take everything."

Farther on toward the funeral home I came upon a mountainous man leaning against a car with a pair of crutches, their tops padded with torn sheets, resting against his belly. It was Fats Houston, once grand marshal of these parades and whose jazzy, mincing steps and solemn mien I had seen at the head of that funeral procession on my first visit to New Orleans. Now he was clearly but a stranded observer, and shaking his hand I noticed its missing fingers. "They taking us old-timers out, one by one."

In the parlor of the Blandin Funeral Home, as well as in the streets, there was a festive feeling. Laughter tumbled out, there was much visiting between the rows, and watchers singly or in pairs sauntered casually forward to view the body and just as casually returned to their talk and their plans. Meanwhile, right in all our faces the coffin was propped on its Formica catafalque. Under all this buzz Jim Robinson lay squeezed into his box.

Too old to have close living kin, Robinson was attended in this by relatives through marriage: his grand-niece, Tammy, and her father, Joe, who had for the past three years lived with Robinson and had taken on the household duties. There was also a cousin, George, a big, square ex-trucker, now slowly dwindling back into what Big Jim himself became in time—one whose frame was a sort of echoing reminder of old power.

It was hard to tell whether Jim was the victim of a poor mortician's work or of the terrific, wasting disease that took him so quickly. But this clay-colored mummy in gabardine with a wilting rose on what once had been a chest looked like nothing I'd ever known. Especially the lips, sealed and grim like an alien slash across the visage: no lips like those could ever have caressed the mouthpiece of a horn and made it sing.

The finishing touches were an American flag folded into a triangle and propped on the rough pillow at the coffin's head; a floral wreath at the foot with gold letters on a red field spelling FAMILY; a floral cross at the right; and at the left another arrangement in the shape of a trombone ("Preservation Hall"). Behind the coffin hung a large portrait of Jesus.

In the warm and humming room images of Jim and moments with him came unbidden and heedless of their chronology as I gazed at that estranged face or turned away to watch the plaster scallops climbing the heavily painted walls. Then the floral tributes were withdrawn with the inescapable brutality of such ceremonies by two dark messengers in stiff hair and suits, and the lid came down on Jim Robinson, lying now with the flag folded across his chest.

Outside, everything was ablaze, and as the coffin made its careful, jerky descent to a hearse all but swallowed by the crowd, one of the bands, instruments resplendent in the dented and scored glory of many processions, bellowed above the street sounds, "Just a Closer Walk with Thee." As the last of those within emerged into this larger scene, a professional mourner materialized from within the building's innards, adding her broken, runny-nosed lament to the density of sound: "Ohhh, Jeees-us! Ohhh, Jeees-us! Have mercy! Have mercy, Jeees-us!" The mercy at hand was to move beyond this and into the wake of the slowly toiling hearse that seemed almost to sweat beneath the hundreds of hands that caressed its passage amidst them.

Here in the streets was that inevitable confrontation with the world that had done much to render these funerals quaint. Recording devices of varying degrees of sophistication bristled in the sun, and their operators fought each other for position. They seemed about to outnumber the locals as we picked our way through a landscape of glittering glass, burned mattresses, and wasted clumps of cement in weed-grown lots. At every corner turned things coagulated, the backward-walking technicians, the attendant crowd, and the two bands fused yet more tightly as they circumnavigated the old frame buildings with their scrollwork, their crowded stoops, and the dark faces peering from darker doorways that led back from all this light and play.

Our way to the church ended on the strains of a second rendering of "Oh, What a Friend We Have in Jesus," one of several hymns associated with Jim Robinson. Again at the entrance to the church things were tangled and messy, and it was only by a certain brutishness that I got into the building at all. Much of its space had already been assumed by the photographers, soundmen, tourists, and others out for the holiday this provided, and while the coffin was brought in and set up and its lid lifted one more time, the accompaniment most obvious was the measured whirring and meshing of camera gears.

Against a wall at the front three ministerial presences confronted and counterpoised all this with black-capped severity and vestments that seemed out of another, more coherent time. In support of them and of the disposition of the coffin, the organist struck heavily into "Amazing Grace." The majority did not know the words, so that articulation was at first slow and confused but then surging inevitable as a tide, and as the last notes rolled, one of the three dark presences approached his bulwark. Mounted behind it, he took up his incantations just where the sung cadences ceased.

Asking a lengthy mercy for Jim Robinson, he then gave way to the one whose words had ushered the coffin out into the streets, and as this exchange took place the ancillary sounds rushed in to fill the space: people pushing to get in at the doors, muttered altercations, and the unawed talk of spectators at a public event. But once the smallish, skull-capped man had attained his stride this babble was stilled by the menace of his tone.

Sweeping the back of his hand downward toward the coffin, he warned us that he would not repeat the eulogies of last night's wake with all its useless talk of "Robason and what a good man he was. All that"—again, the downward, dismissive wave—"can't do Robason any good now." And here his voice dropped down a bit:

"Last Sunday I had the privilege of attending Brother Robason at Touro Hospital. He wanted to tell me something, but the voice was too weak. *The voice was too weak.* I baptized him in the name of the Lord." Sensing then the right moment, a temporary vulnerability in even this audience, forced to ponder the existential crisis he had raised into view, he shot home his bolt:

"*Don't* make the mistake Robason made!" he thundered, dropping the "Brother" now. "*Don't* wait! God won't be played with!" And then again, finally, "All this won't help him now. He can't hear it."

On this he turned to the last of the ministers, an ancestral figure who had patiently endured the shots of the cameras, impervious to their flickering nuisance. He was the church's pastor, the Reverend Arthur James Alexander, and as he arose and stared a long moment at the crowd there was a sudden hush. He looked like God's inevitable judgment.

This hush—awe, amazement, curiosity—lasted into his opening words which were borne on a voice as dry and raspy as sifted cinders, but then the ground noises rose again, obscuring all but the barest outline of message: ". . . raised together. . . ." ". . . Jim Crow. . . ." ". . . a promise made more than fifty years ago. If he died first, I would bury him. If I died first, he would see to my burial." Then, signifying that he was here fulfilling that promise, he looked in the direction of the coffin and seemed to speak of Jim Robinson's late redemption and its efficacy, his voice rising and filling out on the last words, ". . . because He has never failed, *and never will fail!*" On which affirmation the other two ministers escorted him back to his seat, from which he stared hard and sightless beyond the buzzing crowd.

Jim Robinson's harsh assessor now for the third time assumed command and introduced the final speaker with the preliminary admonition that his speech would be "about two and a half minutes." In fact, the address of the hip young minister went considerably beyond that, and though it ran into clichés, as all such addresses must, still it was heartfelt and knowing, and his voice broke as he remembered Jim's singing of "Bye and Bye." The master of the ceremony relieved him here and guided the audience into the hymn, which began to lilt just a little, as if in involuntary tribute to the man who once so joyously sang it, accompanying himself with a waving white handkerchief.

The respite was brief: our Jeremiah insisted once again on the grim necessities, and where perhaps the service might have been deflected into a group sing, instead he commanded those who would view the body once more to assemble and file past. Whipped by the scorn of his voice and its terrific judgment, we followed one another under his eyes. There was nothing more or less to see than before, and I took this opportunity to escape the remainder of the service.

This was short enough, for I had barely wedged my way out through the crowd on the low wooden steps before a pallbearer emerged behind me, crying at the crowd, "Won't you let the body out? Please! Make way for the body!" Murmurs among us, "Make way," "Make way," "The family. . . ." "The family. . . ." ". . . family. . . ." A path opened and teen-aged Tammy, tearful and uncertain on high platform shoes, and Joe, his hand on her back, passed down it and into one of the limousines. Then the coffin again, borne atop the crowd and lowered amidst umbrellas, heads, shoulders, out of sight until an obscured flash of metal told us the hearse door had closed. The bands, already hushed twice by the grand marshal, now struck up once more into "Just a Closer Walk with Thee," and Jim Robinson had gone on to the last stage.

Once more the cortege took up its wearisome way, inching through the crowd and the tumult, both considerably augmented since the funeral home. Lost in this push and unwillingly carried along by it, I could not even touch the hearse with its dark cargo behind drapes. I was one of those the limousine-borne mourners glanced out at, somber-eyed now and perhaps justly offended by this motley show of strangers who in their turn stared in at them—curious, vacant, suppositious. The car with Tammy and Joe passed me, and in another few minutes the one with Jim's cousin, George, his eyes masked by sunglasses.

The procession moved now through the outer edge of the old Downtown area, past the ranked houses, past the bars and barbecue shacks. The glass-seeded streets sparkled wickedly, dogs barked, and empty cans rolled into the gutters, kicked aside by a thousand scuffed and shuffling shoes.

We were bound for the entrance to a freeway. There the cortege would at last break loose of its shambling retinue, scoop up one of the bands for a graveside service, and hurtle through asphalt isolation five miles out to a newer cemetery on the Airlines Highway where Jim would lie next to Pearl. In the old days the entire procession would have gone all the way to the graveside and then returned with the hot, purgative notes of "Didn't He Ramble" and "South Rampart Street Parade" washing through them. But in those old days there weren't cemeteries five miles out from the center of town, nor were there automobiles to take you there.

We followed as far as we could, but as the freeway entrance loomed and the long cars swung up it, the crowd broke and eddied, uncertain now that the feature attraction was about to be taken from them. But there was yet another band and a "second line" to be formed, and in a few minutes resolution replaced uncertainty and the parade began to generate its own power. With umbrellas waving, the crowd turned back into old Downtown.

I went on alone toward the ramp. Breasting the last buildings before the arid expanse of the freeway, I saw the cortege ahead, balked, stalled, still within reach: one of the limousines had broken down—vapor lock, perhaps. Its hood yawned upward like a patient with a toothache, and I could see that the hearse too had stopped and opened its doors for ventilation. Hot delta sunlight invested the butt of Jim's coffin. Powerless as ever to efface this last misery, I turned back. In the darkness of the overpass the parade raged and swirled.

The Blues for Jimmy

Vincent McHugh

Vincent McHugh was a leading proponent of a school of journalism about whose passing it is hard not to be ambivalent. This account of the funeral of the great clarinetist Jimmy Noone, in 1944, gives us not only a sense of a long-gone era in jazz but a taste of a long-gone era of prose.

All that February it rained, a maddening cold pour that made the royal palms look like draggletail ballet dancers. You walked down Hollywood Boulevard to the white banner with Jimmy Noone's name on it, and down the headlong pitch of the stairs into a big, damp joint like an abandoned automobile showroom, with pillars, a curved bar in the middle, and a bandstand inside the bar. There were always scads of soldiers and sailors dancing with the funny rag dolls they use for girls in Hollywood, and quieter people who came for the music but didn't always have their boots laced up. What with Ida James, Helen Humes, and Gladys Palmer, the amount of bouncing female vitality on the stand warmed the dreary place up a little. But you were waiting.

Then Jimmy, coming out along the far wall, walking easily with a kind of thoughtful composure. His Roman senator's head, the firm, egg-shaped torso in the blue suit, made him look like a good courtroom lawyer. He would climb up on the stand, nod to a couple of friends, play a ripple or two, and stamp it off. The young bass player would mug and twirl his blond fiddle on its axis, the pianist did flashy stuff, and the drummer would get excited and keep tapping a cymbal in a very bad and busy way behind one of Jimmy's choruses.

But the choruses were coming out. The fine choruses—as fine as any on the too-few records from the Apex Club days, and before, to "The Blues Jumped a Rabbit." It didn't much matter what they were: a melodious pop called "My Heart Tells Me" or the signature, "Sweet Lorraine," done all the way through. That mellow, round, easy, warm New Orleans tone, given a slight whiskey-sour edge by the long Chicago influence. The whippoorwill wail, and the whippoorwill double-stopping that was like a trademark. The glide up or down to a note and the deft mixture of melodic phrases with agile runs. The almost classical sense of form that could hang a chorus in the air and give it its own light shape and balance. All the wonderful, unshowy elegance and finesse of the thing. Some of it pleased you because it was so perfectly in the New Orleans clarinet tradition, but all of it was Jimmy.

That Wednesday in April he died. He was happy, except for the usual thing about a contract and a chiseling manager. He'd had it hard, very hard, for a while in Chicago. They said his music was old-fashioned. But now it was coming out all right. He got up that morning feeling fine and said to his wife that he'd either have to get a haircut or carry a violin case to work. Then he went into the bathroom and in a few minutes she heard him thump against the wall. When she went in and touched him he was dead, and after the doctor came and she was sure he was dead she had him carried out so that the children wouldn't know.

But they asked, and at first she told them he'd been taken to the hospital. She took Jimmy, Junior, his son, for a long walk. She said that his daddy had been taken to a hospital but they couldn't do anything for him. Then why didn't they take him to another hospital? Because he's dead, Jimmy's wife said. You won't see your daddy anymore. The boy took it hard. But he was a good daddy, Mrs. Noone said after a while. He left you his diamond ring and his gold watch and his clarinet. Only a good daddy would do that. He wanted you to grow up and play the clarinet like him.

That Wednesday night the band of New Orleans veterans Jimmy had played with moved into the white Lescaze studio on Sunset Boulevard and played the blues for Jimmy. Many people heard Orson Welles speak the grave and tender promises of the Twenty-third Psalm. But only a few people could see Kid Ory's face as he blew the long phrases of lament, or Zutty's big shoulders bowed and crying over the drums. Gone from Iberville, gone from Calumet. Yes, gone from Iberville, gone from Calumet. I won't see you baby, but you know I won't forget.

That Saturday they buried him from the very modern and correct mortuary on Jefferson Boulevard, off Central Avenue. Forty or fifty people in the straight white pews of the Georgian funeral chapel. The music of a Hammond organ flowed through the room and a warm Negro contralto with a silvery vibrato sang "Just A-Wearyin' for You." A young white sailor sat there crying with his face up. Nobody knew who he was. Some of Jimmy's friends got up and said that he had been a good man and a fine musician. The preacher, who had a North Carolina accent, said some musicians didn't talk very well. They didn't need to. They talked with their music, and that was what made people love them. He said David was a musician too.

Someone parted the gray curtains in the front of the room and Jimmy's face lay there. The casket and the wall behind him and the floor all around were covered with the abundant flowers of the Los Angeles spring: roses and lilies, stocks, gardenias, jonquils. People came out row by row—Nappy Lamare, Matty Matlock, Marge Singleton, Joe Sullivan, Gladys Palmer—and went up and looked at him. The last to come out were the bearers in the front row. The boys from Jimmy's band at the club. Tall, gray Papa Mutt and the small, graying Kid Ory. Dooley Wilson and Bud Scott. Zutty Singleton, walking softly. There was the unbearable crying of a woman behind the looped curtains as people went out into the pale sunlight under the glistening pepper trees.

A motorcycle escort led the line of cars to Evergreen Cemetery. An open, sandy slope, pale green, with two or three big palms in the distance, under the warm blue sky. They had hung a tarpaulin on the cyclone fence behind the grave. The eight bearers lifted the coffin, Zutty's big shoulders at the forward end cradling it down in the ruts. People formed up in twos behind, like the second line of a New Orleans funeral. The undertaker prayed and they stood a moment in the listening sunlight. The wind had spilled a few loose flowers off the casket. Some of the women picked them up and put them into their handbags as they walked away.

Jack Teagarden

Charles Edward Smith

Smith, known at one time as "dean of the jazz critics," wrote widely in books and magazines, and was co-editor of Jazzmen *and editor of the* The Jazz Record Book. *Here (slightly edited), in Nat Shapiro and Nat Hentoff's 1958* The Jazz Makers, *he affectionately traces the career of the great trombonist Jack Teagarden.*

"I started up to see Bud Freeman, but I lost my way
An' I thought for a minute I was on the road for M C A."

—*Jack Hits the Road*

Jack Teagarden has been hitting the road since about the age of seven when he walked out on some of his old man's bad notes. He didn't get far, only to the next room, but you might say that that was the beginning of an odyssey. Another significant incident occurred when he was a youngster, studying music. He had heard blues and spirituals and was going off in a way all his own when his music teacher admonished him with creditable severity to return to the beaten track. That was the hardest thing in the world for him to do and, fortunately for us, he didn't.

He is a big man, generally amiable and occasionally moody, with dark eyes and a lazy smile. The laziness is completely disingenuous, reminding one of the friendly panther who, in the interests of a high-protein diet, had just swallowed the Cheshire cat.* He doesn't flaunt his background, and perhaps that's what makes him a real Texan, blood brother to the hard-drinking, hard-living pioneers.

Weldon John Teagarden was born August 20, 1905, in Vernon, not far from the Red River Valley where the oxcart wagon trains of the early settlers came in from the east and only a matter of miles from the famous Red River crossing on the Chisholm Trail. But that most famous of the dozen or

*Who had just swallowed the canary trained at great expense to sing *The Eyes of Texas.*

so cattle trails that snaked north out of Texas was marked, if at all, only by a thinner growth of grass and bush by the time Jack was growing up and the family had moved to Oklahoma. By then the oil fields were roaring with life and he spent some time working around them. He was fascinated with tools and machinery and before long he had a lifetime avocation, an unflagging interest in things mechanical, from power tools to Stanley steamers.

But not a career. That was laid out for him when his mother, who was of Pennsylvania Dutch background, gave him piano lessons at age five and when, at seven, his father presented him at Christmas with his first trombone. By the time he was sixteen he was with Peck Kelly's Bad Boys, and in 1924, when he worked in Mexico with R. J. Marin's Original Southern Trumpeters, he was billed as "The South's Greatest Trombone Wonder." He has always been close in feeling to New Orleans musicians, who took their pet name from an alligator named Al (who, when he smoked his foul pipe—probably thrown overboard by Sam Clemens—blew up a fog on the Mississippi). They got to call Jack *Mr. T.*, and *Jackson,* and sometimes they called him *Big Gate,* after old Al.

With the Teagardens, you might say that the whole family was musical, even though Dad was a trifle on the square side. Not too long ago, out on the Coast, there was a musical reunion with Jack's mother and his sister Norma both playing pianos, Charlie ("Little Gate") on trumpet, and Clois on drums. When Jack was a kid, his father played trumpet and baritone horn but, says George Hoefer, Jr.—that knowledgeable man about records and jazz personalities—"with so many clinkers that two months after Jack got his Christmas trombone he refused to play duets with the old man but instead ran into the next room covering his ears with his hands and shouting, 'first valve, first valve!' "*

While still in grammar school he was allowed to join the high-school orchestra. The first thing he learned on the road to fame and fortune was that his horn was pitched too high and that he had to start all over. George Hoefer snatched for posterity a teacher's ambiguous comment from its fast flight to oblivion. "I can't teach that lad anything," was what she said.

"He used to sit on a fence," wrote George, "listening to the music of the Negroes at Holy Roller meetings. Their spirituals and blues fascinated him, and he began to apply the blues phrases to his trombone playing." No doubt he also heard many an early jazz trombone, born to blow unrecorded, during those early years when (to quote myself) "he barnstormed around Texas, often without a barn to call his own." At any rate, by the time he got to work with Peck Kelly, from all accounts, he sang and played horn with a Western

***Down Beat,* March 9, 1951.

drawl and a fast, Western draw. At one time during those early years he was romancing a switchboard sweetie. The long-lines operators co-operated in conveying messages and, for themselves, maintained a lively interest in developments. Once they were reduced to biting their fingernails when Jack failed to keep in touch. On that occasion, he'd got lost in the wide open spaces, no Texas rangers or telephones in sight and not even the smell of oil to guide him back to civilization.

At the age of fifteen he was working the roadhouse, honky-tonk circuit with a four-piece unit, which gives you a fair idea of where and why his schooling terminated. He was at the Horn Palace in San Antonio (the band had Terry Shand on piano) when three toughs, who hadn't been told that the days of Sam Bass were long gone, shot up the joint and the boss "who got seven slugs."* They were told to stick around and testify but, happily for them, a flood inundated the courthouse; the legal papers in the case got lost and the boys did likewise, fast.

Jack made his way to Galveston where he joined Peck Kelly's Bad Boys. "Peck Kelly played better piano than anyone I'd heard," Jack told Len Guttridge. In later years Peck seemed to be a hard man to pin down. One critic may have antagonized him—at a time when *Jack* was recognized as a top jazz trombonist—by writing that *Peck* was playing typical cocktail lounge music at a place in Houston. Len Guttridge wanted to interview him but, unfortunately, was himself ill on his day in Houston, though he'd been assured that Peck would see him. Said Len, "His phone remains disconnected and he won't answer mail. Last I heard, his sight had just about gone."

"By now," wrote Len Guttridge, "Teagarden had discovered the strange blues flavor which the combination of trombone and water glass could produce. The sound became forever associated with him." In his early years, and on such recordings as "Makin' Friends," he simply took his horn apart and used an ordinary water glass as a mute on the unattached end of the mouthpiece half of his horn. Recently he has used a professional-looking cup-shaped job that he probably made himself.

While with Peck Kelly during 1921–22, Jack made a trip to New Orleans to find a clarinet player for the band. Hoefer reveals that it was on this occasion that he first heard Louis Armstrong—the man who has had the greatest influence in the history of jazz—playing on the upper deck of a riverboat off Canal Street. They met then and there, in the home city of jazz, and have matched horns in marvellous music, off and on, ever since, in jam sessions, on records, and finally, in 1947 and until 1951, on road tours here and abroad, with Louis Armstrong's All Stars.

*Hoefer.

With Peck Kelly at that time were three jazzmen—Pee Wee Russell, Rappolo, and Teagarden—who were to contribute to developments in jazz that, while related to Dixieland, and often interestingly so, were even more significant as establishing once more, vital and living contacts with the bloodline of jazz (Armstrong, Oliver, Keppard, Bunk, Bolden), which was, after all, what the Dixieland musicians had done in the days when they worked with Jack Laine before they branched out on their own. In some bands of well-intentioned young musicians during the revival of early styles in the 1940s, a too-faithful hewing to the Original Dixieland Jazz Band line achieved neither the interesting angularity of that group (which, on some numbers, was more staccato than swing) nor the rhythmic thrust of King Oliver.

In jazz, to borrow a distinction made in another field by the talented American designer, Elizabeth Hawes ("Fashion Is Spinach"), there is style and, since it is related to both folk and popular music, there is fashion. The essence of jazz is not in the blue notes—these often, but not always, indicate the presence of jazz or blues—not in fact in anything that can be written down and played by rote. When one says that it is, in effect, an improvised music, the conclusion might sensibly be that this refers to the melody alone, or the melodic line in relation to the chords on which it is based. However, in jazz, improvisation begins—for the blowing instruments—with the breath, the vibrato; and breath and blowing combine to manipulate—always sensitive to certain canons of unwritten tradition—the tone itself, the rhythm and the instrumental timbre. Some jazzmen have been so from their earliest beginnings, and among them Jack Teagarden is outstanding.

When popular bands imitated jazz, particularly in the 1920s, they pounced upon its most familiar and least unique aspects. The hot musicians called them "ricky-tick," for their plodding ploppity-plop rhythms and cornball tricks of intonation (which escaped jazz intonation by a narrow, bridgeless chasm). Yet, because of the close relationship of rhythmic conventions to dance steps, the hot musicians, masters of style though they were, shared with the Mickey Mouse artistes something of this pandering to rhythmic and melodic fashion. All the more so because hot jazz furnished the root music for the bona fide dance steps, close to folk art, that in turn inspired ballroom conventions—from the Bolden band playing for the *free steps* and the cakewalk in the Quadrille to Cootie Williams playing for rock and roll at Harlem's Savoy ballroom. (In Chicago, that toddlin' town, they toddled, the lucky ones did, to King Oliver and Louis, to the Rhythm Kings and Rappolo; in St. Louis, as elsewhere noted, they did the Charleston to Bix and Pee Wee; at Roseland in New York, they danced *cake*—tight and cool style—or *collegiate*—real gone rococo—to Fletcher, Red Nichols, Mr.

T.; and all over the map and to any number of jazz bands, they did the Lindy Hop.) This is why, when you listen to old jazz records, you often listen to the fashion of the times, the then-popular treatment of tone and rhythm, as well as the style (that worships the beat and wrestles with it at the same time). Some benighted souls have only an ear and a memory for the musical spinach. In Hollywood they seldom show a proper appreciation of either. And though nowadays thousands of musicians have a working knowledge of jazz, surprisingly few, considering the many who play it, have a deeply ingrained sense of style. And no arrangements, no assortment of well-learned *licks,* can substitute for a sound, blues-oriented jazz technique.

Jack has been chided sometimes by critics for a sentimental streak, as well as a sort of maverick genius on trombone. This is liable to show, perhaps, when he does not work too hard on a number, when he is, as they say, coasting, making an honest buck, come what may. No one is always at his best and, with Jack, the soft spot of sentiment is part of his mental make-up; without it, the vocal masterpieces, which are the opposite of *schmaltz,* just wouldn't come through. Though some of the more cynically disposed may not like it that way, jazz—as Nick LaRocca and many other musicians have remarked—is from the heart. The great danger to a present-day vocalist is that he might be ill-advisedly "packaged" out of his métier and learn the hard way about square pegs and round holes. One suspects that Jack's good sense would prevent such a catastrophe. Remembering such lighthearted foolishness as "The Waiter and the Porter and the Upstairs Maid" with Mary Martin and Bing Crosby, the odd thing is that more use hasn't been made of Jack's real and very versatile talents. As Hoagy Carmichael remarked, "He is one of the best things that has ever appeared on the popular music scene. A warm and honest talent like Jack's is a rare thing indeed."

When a concert pianist is influenced by commercial considerations—which influence us all—that nasty word is seldom used. Instead we learn that he has an unusual flair for *bravura* pieces or that he is especially adept at resurrecting the soul of Schumann. Also, to be commercial in the classics is, generally speaking, more in line with one's aesthetic aims (which are colored by non-aesthetic needs anyway) and implies not so much a misuse of musical gifts as an adroit exploitation of them.

The *hot* musician is in a slightly more difficult predicament. Not only must he stand in some relationship to what is currently popular (which may or may not coincide with his personal taste), he is often asked to play or record numbers about which, to put it bluntly, he couldn't care less. Few jukeboxes are serviced by the actual tastes of a locality, except in a most general and haphazard fashion. Radio disc jockeys have one eye on *Cash Box* record ratings, are harassed and flattered and sometimes flummoxed by promoters of this or that band or singer, and often disdain pieces of more than two or three minutes' duration. (Oftentimes the bartender or the candy-store owner leaves it to the jukebox serviceman to fill the slots; this contributes to a sort of mass-media approach to popular taste—reported, it must be said, quite honestly, in a statistical fashion, by *Cash Box*—and reflected in the tendency of most disc jockeys to play only a pittance of the many really fine jazz records issued month after month.) There are exceptions happily, but as Jack expressed it in an interview with John Tynan ". . . they could do a lot to help jazz—all kinds—if once in a while they played a good jazz record.

"For me, especially, this would be important," he went on. "I'm bending over backwards these days trying to please the people with my kind of music, but I don't know if I'm reaching them. It's frustrating trying to fit yourself into this new world of music. You feel so insecure in what you're playing."

Long before coming to New York, Jack made it out to the West Coast with Doc Ross and His Cowboy Band. They were supposed to make a grand entry into San Diego. Saddle horses were waiting for them when they got off the train. The musical cowhands weren't too happy about that, being more accustomed to bar stools than saddles, but they managed to mount and, luckily for them, no riders of the range were around to give them the horse-laugh. As for the horses themselves, they were as nervous as Boppists at a Dixieland jam session. When the band let out a blast of Texas music, the horses promptly dumped the band members, one horse neatly tossing the drummer into his bass drum.

Carson Robison is a good friend of Jack's, and has been for more than thirty years, though possibly the only jazz record Carson is listed as working on is the Hoagy Carmichael disc on which Bix played cornet and Jack and Hoagy sang "Rockin' Chair." (Probably that should be revised to read: *the only one listed in Discography;* it seems to me I've heard him with some small recording groups of the 1920s.) Be that as it may, Jack looks back upon the days with Robison as a happy period, and one that seasoned his style. Frankie Trumbauer had planned to have Jack in his outfit in St. Louis (1926) but local union rules prevented it and, after staying with his friend Pee Wee Russell overnight, he left the next day for Indiana.

Working in a band that had Wingy Mannone on trumpet during that Southwest period, Jack found himself in the company of a New Orleanian who could, when he wanted to, toss off a whacky vocal; who was, like himself, an admirer of Louis, and who was also an entertaining guy to have around. Jack had begun to tote Louis's records in his trombone case. He listened to Louis by the hour and tried to match his ease of phrasing.

George Hoefer notes that, although not a bop musician, Jack made bop possible for trombone, handling the quick changes with the ease of a skilled trumpet player (a fact testified to by top modern trombonists as well, e.g., Kai Winding). And this came, above all, from listening and learning from Louis on "Cornet Chop Suey," "Muskrat Ramble" and other records, most of them now in the Columbia LP series, *The Louis Armstrong Story.* Said Hoefer: "He and Wingy revered 'Oriental Strut' to such an extent they took it out on the desert and buried it." Wingy had heard that, thus interred, it would become petrified and forever preserved!

Jack blew into New York with Wingy Mannone and promptly decided that he'd—

"... rather drink muddy water, Lord, sleep like a hollow log,
Than to be up here in New York, treated like a dirty dog ..."

Not that there wasn't work. There were record dates and society dates or gigs. "They would not play jazz at those social functions, of course," commented Tony Parenti (*Hear Me Talkin' to Ya*), "but they did want a man with them who could play a couple of solo choruses on the up-tempo things." In his first book *We Called It Music,* Eddie Condon referred to this situation and, bemoaning the loss of hot men to name bands, compared it to a jigger of whiskey in a quart of milk. You couldn't even taste it.

"I was having a couple of drinks with Bud Freeman and Pee Wee Russell one evening in a little speakeasy on Fifty-first Street," said Jimmy McPartland (*Hear Me Talkin' to Ya*), "when Pee Wee began talking about a trombone player, the greatest thing he had heard in this life.

"We said we would like to hear the guy, and Pee Wee said, right, he'd just pop over and get him. Two drinks later, Pee Wee was back with the guy, who was wearing a horrible-looking cap and overcoat and carrying a trombone in a case under his arm.

"Pee Wee introduced us. He was Jack Teagarden, from Texas, and looked it. 'Fine,' we said. 'We've been hearing a lot about you, would sure like to hear you play.'

"The guy says, 'All right,' gets his horn out, puts it together, blows a couple of warm-up notes and starts to play 'Diane.' No accompanist, just neat; he played it solo, and I'm telling you he knocked us out. He really blew it. And when he'd done with that, he started on the blues, still by himself. We had to agree with Pee Wee, we'd never heard anyone play trombone like that. We were flabbergasted."

Jack once sang that he was born in Texas, raised in Tennessee, and this is only partly true, the Texas part. Much to his amazement, some writers took him seriously and had him learning his licks in the Great Smokies! There are many anecdotes about Jack that also verge on folklore, like the countless scenes in which he's wearing a horrible cap. Now that caps are once again in vogue, someone truly enterprising should locate the Teagarden model. Who knows? It might replace the beard and beret.

There is one story, heard in slightly different versions, that appears to be reasonably accurate. In this, a musician knocks on Jack's hotel door. Jack mumbles sleepily. The musician comes into the room. Jack appears to be asleep but, having a wide experience of jazz musicians, the visitor speaks in a normal voice, not bothering to raise it, and says, "How'd you like to work in my band?" Jack grunts, in effect, "Go away and let me sleep." The visitor does not act offended as this response is normal for a jazz musician at high noon. "Well," says the visitor, looking dubiously at the drowsiest Texan he'd ever seen, "if you change your mind, just come over to the Park Central. Ask for Ben Pollack." Jack sits up, suddenly less sleepy and even beginning to tingle with interest. "Who are *you?*" he asks his visitor. "I'm Ben Pollack," says Ben Pollack.

NOT LONG AFTER coming to New York, Jack Teagarden worked with Billy Lustig's band at Roseland. On the opposite stand was the band of Fletcher Henderson, with an incomparable brass team that included Jimmy Harrison on trombone, and thereby hangs the clue to a myth, or rather, clues to two of them, both closely related.

The first myth is that Jack was the first person to effectively use the trombone as a solo instrument in jazz. This is a rather careless brush-off of the many fine trombonists who preceded him. One doubts if any knowledgeable jazz collector would agree or that Jack himself would so lightly dismiss his predecessors. To do so would bypass, for example, the great technical facility and far from negligible solo work of Mid Mole, about whom Otis Ferguson wrote in 1939: "He played jazz when jazz was pretty crude; he played on the beat and on the chord and he played with a certain easy bounding zest. . . . He is still so much more interesting in any stretch than all but Jimmy Harrison and Teagarden that I would not guarantee what might now be said of him if he had died ten years ago in rather horrible circumstances."

What distinguished Jack Teagarden in jazz (apart from his scat-singing and vocals) was not that he was the first to employ the trombone creatively in solos, but that he did this in an easy swing with very blue intonation, in a panther style, lazy and lightning-quick. He played with remarkable facility and with no unintentional smearing of notes. His first loyalty was to *hot* intonation and phrasing and to the basic, beat-contending rhythm of jazz.

In *Jazz-Tango Dancing,* a predecessor to *Jazz Hot,* Paris, October 1933, Joost van Praag contributed an allegorical description of *swing* that is particularly apropos in relation to Jack's trombone style. "Imagine a man who is going to catch a train," says van Praag. "He enters the station very calmly, moves toward the train without hurrying and, on reaching his car, enters it sedately with perfect tranquillity. At the moment the train leaves, he closes the door. Anyone else would already have been in his place for a moment or two, or would at least have had the door closed before the train started. But our gentleman is in the habit of getting on the train at the latest possible second, without hurrying himself a bit—in brief, with the greatest of ease."

Where others' preoccupation with Dixieland angularity lent their work the awkwardness of music on stilts, with Jack—as with Pee Wee Russell—it was assimilated, to give style yet another dimension. You can *hear* this in choruses of both men today—Jack in his recent album, *This Is Teagarden.* Weighing all the ponderables and imponderables, the quantitative and qualitative, the measurable and immeasurable, Bill Russo—whose work in jazz and on trombone is rated highly—concluded that Jack "*is* the best trombonist." Explaining further, he says, "He has an unequaled mastery of his instrument which is evident in the simple perfection of his performance, not in sensational displays; the content of his playing illustrates a deep understanding of compositional principles—and this is the true though unspoken ultimate of the jazz improviser."

The fact is, Jimmy Harrison probably blew solos on trombone in New York at about the time Jack was blowing them in the Southwest. That brings us to the other myth, which has some basis in fact. It is that Jimmy influenced T.'s style. And this is a half-truth. The other half is that Jack influenced Jimmy. When Pee Wee Russell says that all the essentials of Jack's way of playing were in evidence back there when the Big Gate was a teenaged trombone wonder, this writer, for one, will take Pee Wee's word for it. As one might expect, it developed considerably and became stronger and surer of itself. (I have yet to hear Jack freshly, after an absence, without realizing that he always has something new and pretty wonderful to listen to.)

The truth is better than the myth or the half-truth. When Jack and Jimmy heard each other play, they were really knocked out, which was not so surprising, seeing how much they had in common. However, they were anything but trombone twins. In some ways, J. J. Johnson seems closer to Jimmy than does Jack. But that's begging the point—what Jimmy and Jack did have in common was a solid, blues-based approach, great technical facility that never obtruded and, above all, an appreciation of how much any jazzman, playing any instrument, could learn from Louis Armstrong.

You can trace the coincidental line of development—and a lot more of interest that we haven't room for here—by consulting the index of *Hear Me Talkin' to Ya* (a most valuable book for homework as well as entertainment)—with the added suggestion that you also listen with unjaded ears to "Mandy Lee Blues" and "Snake Rag" on London's *Louis Armstrong; 1923: With*

King Oliver's Creole Jazz Band (AL 3504). On the records you'll refresh your memory as to how the greatest cornet team in jazz sounded—assuming that you once heard the Gennetts of which these are reissues. And in the book you'll learn that June Clark and Jimmy Harrison "were known as the greatest brass team of that (wonderful) period" (in Harlem jazz, c. 1923–24), and the interesting sidelight that Fletcher Henderson sent Jimmy home to bone up on his reading ability! The latter was admittedly a technical asset but not at all what the Fletcher Henderson Orchestra was famous for.

Kaiser Marshall, the drummer, said of Jimmy: "He liked Jack Teagarden, who used to come to our house often, sometimes staying all night, and we would have a slight jam session with Hawkins, who lived only a few doors from us. So Jack would play the piano, Jimmy trombone, Hawkins tenor, and myself on my rubber-pad I kept at home. Then Hawkins would play piano, Jack and Jimmy trombone. My, what fun we had! Of course, we brought home, in my car, twelve bottles of beer, some wine, whiskey, ice cream, cake, barbecue ribs, and chitlin's, to make our morning complete."

Jam sessions were the lifeline of jazz in the twenties and early thirties and had an intimacy oftentimes (but not always) lacking in the more or less public sessions of later years. Even the ones open to the public in a limited way provided a different environment for the musician since, among the small number of jazz fans likely to be present, there were fewer "tourists"—only an occasional slumming party that got an earful and left. So Jack brought his trombone along to Small's and other places uptown and downtown, and in those places it seemed like home was where you blew your horn.

It was so in Kansas City a few years later, where Mary Lou Williams (talented arranger and first lady of jazz piano) with her sisters made the rounds of the clubs. "One night," she recalled, "we ran into a place where Ben Pollack had a combo, which included Jack Teagarden and, I think, Benny Goodman. The girls introduced me to the Texan trombonist, and right away we felt like friends. After work, he and a couple of musicians asked us to go out, and we visited some of the speaks downtown. One I remember particularly, because it was decorated to resemble the inside of a penitentiary, with bars on the windows and waiters in striped uniforms like down-South convicts. In these weird surroundings, I played for the boys and Jack got up and sang some blues. I thought he was more than wonderful. While they stayed in Kaycee, Jack and some of Pollack's men came round every night, and I was very happy to see them."

OTIS FERGUSON WROTE: ". . . there had blown into town a man from Texas with a trombone under his arm and a fine blues timbre in his voice; a Mr. Jackson, a Mr. T., otherwise Jack Teagarden. Pollack's boys spotted him (playing with a band called Dexter's, I believe); and when they left for Atlantic City, to which Glenn Miller quite understandably did not wish to go, they took him in the band. Later when Pollack decided to stand in front instead of behind the drums, Teagarden got a man still pretty hot from New Orleans in the band: Ray Bauduc."

George Hoefer noted that when Jack first took a chorus with the Pollack band, the boys were still and silent. He thought they were being unfriendly to a Texas trombone, but soon learned that the silence was because they liked him and liked what they heard. Later, as older members quit, the band style came to be built around Jack and he, wrote Hoefer, "brought most of the New Orleans boys into the organization."

While with Pollack, he cut his first, still-famous record of "Basin Street Blues," in February 1931. The evening before the record date, Glenn Miller, who was to do the arrangement, phoned from his apartment in Jackson Heights. "I think we could do a better job," he told Jack, "if we could put together some lyrics and you could sing it. Want to come over and see what we can do? My wife will fix us some supper."

"After we had worked out a first draft of verse and chorus," Jack recalled, "Glenn sat on the piano bench and I leaned over his shoulder. We each had a pencil, and as he played, we'd each cross out words and phrases here and there, putting in new ones. . . . Next day we cut the record. . . . The lyrics were later included in the sheet music, but never carried our names."

In 1933 Jack worked at ninety dollars a week in a band with Sterling Bose at Chicago's Centenary of Progress. "Right outside the 23rd Street entrance," wrote Hoefer, "Wingy Mannone, Joe Marsala, Charlie LaVere and Jim Barnes were playing at a roof-garden beer joint. T. walked in one night and asked the boys to make room, and was again playing for $60 a week and gin."

In the fall he was back in New York and on October sixteenth made four sides with a group led by Benny Goodman, two with Joe Sullivan on piano and two with Frank Froeba. In sequence, these were: "I Gotta Right To Sing the Blues," "Ain't Cha Glad," "Dr. Heckle and Mr. Jibe," and "Texas Tea Party," the last a two-way pun. John Hammond had suggested these sides for Columbia's English label.

In those days pop tunes were usually recorded with stock arrangements but, observes Marshall W. Stearns in *The Story of Jazz,* "Hammond had insisted on special arrangements, and Goodman's first record for the English Gramophone Company . . . was a notable success in England. When the American record executives woke up and decided to issue it in the United States, only Hammond's violent objections kept them from coupling each side with a commercial number by Clyde McCoy or Harry Reser 'to insure the recording's success.'"

Even though it didn't make much of a splash, state-side, at the time, this was one of the most exuberant recording sessions of that period. The rhythm was very much alive (Joe Sullivan, Dick McDonough, Artie Bernstein, Gene Krupa) and the music had a happy sound. Taken at an easy jump tempo, Jack's vocal on "Ain't Cha Glad" is infectiously joyous and his classical vocal and trombone work on "I Gotta Right To Sing the Blues," a superb performance, is in most jazz collections worthy of the name. All four numbers are played in a relaxed manner, to which Jack's trombone contributes an easy, seemingly effortless, swing. Moreover, a sense of humor is discernible in these and, indeed, in many Teagarden performances. Not the brash humor of Wingy nor the sly spoofing of Fats—rather, a casual whimsicality that, oftentimes, could be expressed more deftly with a slur and a slide or an insouciant arabesque on horn than with the voice. T. was one of the few jazzmen who could articulate a coda, in two to four bars, without putting pen to paper.

JACK WAS WITH Mal Hallett for a short time in the New England (Boston) area, and Toots Mondello, Frankie Carle, and Gene Krupa were among his fellow sidemen. But with no reflection on Mal Hallett or his music, Jack did not seem especially happy in that particular name band. For it was a name band and not a gathering of the clan, as Pollack's outfit had seemed at times. Also, in Pollack's band there was, now and again, the excitement of creation and discovery. Corny as some of the stuff sounds today, you can still pick out spots on Pollack's records that showed how the discoveries of little-band, New Orleans jazz were being applied to the then emerging big-band style.

Just as the bands of the thirties learned some lessons from Pollack, Paul Whiteman, in the twenties, appeared not only to have taken the best *hot* men from Goldkette's historic band but took a few pointers from the way Goldkette had used *hot* men. One got the impression that Jack—while not completely happy (what *hot* man could be?)—was at least happier than he had been with Hallett, and more with it, as they say. And this may have been partly due to Paul's determination not to use *hot* men to salt the *schmaltz* (as a gold-brick promoter salts a mine) but to present them in something approaching a congenial musical atmosphere, even though this was a popular—for some years *the most popular*—name band, using for the most part popular arrangements.

It wasn't that Paul's arrangers exactly burned up the bandstand—the Whiteman book would hardly be compared to orchestrations by Edgar Sampson, Jimmy Mundy, Sy Oliver, Mary Lou Williams, and Fletcher Henderson that gave the bands of Tommy Dorsey and Benny Goodman something to sink their chops in during that decade that saw the great boom of commercial swing.* But though the arrangements were not truly *hot*—Whiteman's, that is—neither were they always hopelessly sweet. Once in a while, for a Bix or a Mr. T., they came out clean and uncluttered. And with both Big Gate and Little Gate in there, did the brasses sometimes bite? They did, indeed. It was a wonderful thawing out of the spirit, after a particularly *schmaltzy* number, to listen to the brothers Teagarden set the pace for the brasses. You wanted to get up and shout to the saxophones: *They went that-away!*

On January 5, 1939, Jack Teagarden, as an orchestra leader in his own right, "embarked on seven years of bad luck." He had experience and ideas, but somehow the group seldom shaped up to the stature of its leader. "The first band put him in bankruptcy," George explained. "By the end of the first year he owed $46,000. His second, less expensive orchestra, got gone with the draft, losing seventeen sidemen in four months. His health broke on him several times, his managers got his income tax messed up and his domestic life got tangled up." It was in the early part of this unhappy period that a *Down Beat* interview carried the plaintive headline: "There's No Back-Biting in My Band." There were also an untoward number of auto accidents, hotel fires and other calamities that fall to the lot of jazzmen on the unglamorous grind of one-night stands.

The big Texan had broad shoulders and that was fortunate; the load they had to carry would have broken most. Even when bad luck haunted him like a zombie looking for blood, Jack kept his sense of humor. He could smile wryly at his own misfortunes, and without even thinking about it, you knew the smile was sincere.

In his spare moments Jack reconditioned a museum piece on wheels and thanks to what is known in this line of country as old American know-how (in New Delhi it's probably called old Indian ingenuity) he was the only jazzman of distinction to drive to the job in a Stanley steamer. With or without the vintage chariot, he didn't always make it. Take the time the band arrived, as per schedule, for a booking at Greenville, N.C.—Jack showed up all right—but at Greenville, Carolina South! Once, at a society wing-ding for charity in South Bend, Indiana, the boys waited on the stand for the maestro, no mere jazz band but a symphony in black and white. Our boy Jackson showed up in street clothes. The next date was in Hoagy's old alma

***Commercial swing* was a term used by musicians to distinguish corny imitations from the real article that B.G. and T.D. played often enough to merit mention and that Bill Basie from Red Bank played almost always. *Commercial,* in musicians' slang, has many shades of meaning, however, not all of them altogether derogatory.

mater town, Bloomington, and Jack wasn't going to be caught in his expensive old gabardines this time—he rented a tux. It is well known by thousands of women in these United States that Mr. T. cuts a handsome figure in dinner clothes. There was only one thing wrong on this occasion. The boys were in mufti.

In 1947 all that Jack had left was the band bus, which his manager proceeded to take off his hands. He opened at a West Coast club, the Suzy Q, and Local 47, American Federation of Musicians (Los Angeles area) pulled him off the job for some four hundred dollars arrears in traveling band taxes. His friend Bing Crosby, with whom Jack had appeared in the movie *Birth of the Blues,* in 1941, suggested he build up his name as a single. Writes George Hoefer, "A disgusted Jackson flew into Chicago with his only possession, a new trombone in an old case . . . moaning, 'I wouldn't like California even if the weather was good.'" Yes, that's what the man said. But while on the road the next few years he often spoke with genuine nostalgia of a place where one could settle down and relax—home—California. He now lives in a comfortable house on a cliff in the hills above Hollywood, with his fourth wife, Addie, and a son, Joe, now aged five.

Jack was with Louis Armstrong's All Stars from 1947 until 1951. The All Stars didn't always light up the galaxy but when they did it was extraterrestrial. They were that way when they played the Apollo, in Harlem, and when they played at Symphony Hall, Boston. Nor do you have to take anyone's word for the latter performance; it's ready and waiting on Decca DL 8037 and 8038. Forty-eight inches, all told, of the best.

Once a woman remarked of Jack, "He's profound, isn't he?" No doubt Jack would have been surprised, had he known of this reaction. However, she didn't mean anything complicated or abstrusely intellectual. She only meant that he didn't live on surfaces. But, however deep Jack's thoughts may be, they are voiced in everyday speech, never showcased.

While he likes to talk about sports and the kind of mechanical, modestly scientific stuff that intrigued Ben Franklin all his life—and of course, music—he is also an excellent yarn-spinner when he's in the right mood. (Some years ago Leo R. Herschman, to whom I had been introduced by Dean Shaffner—a friend of mine and a discerning jazz collector, who is with the ABC network—supplied the long-play equipment for a documentary experiment. My typewriter being allergic to ghosts, I wanted to see how much of Jack would come through, if he was allowed to speak, in his own words. Quite a lot did, although the project has not yet been completed. I am East and Jack is West and we haven't met in one hell of a long five years or so. On that occasion, for a few evenings, we sat around a microphone and Jack talked. Once when he stopped for a break, the minutes dragged on and on and Jack didn't return. Finally we went to look for him. He was down in the big basement workshop, having a ball with power tools.)

"There isn't a more musically forward-thinking man in jazz," observed George Hoefer. "He is constantly dreaming of progress. This writer heard him rehearse a French horn, a trumpet, and a couple of saxes, around a table in the kitchen back of the old Panther Room of the Hotel Sherman, after the job. . . ." He has an understandable admiration for men who are highly rated (that is, if they are deserving of it) and this may be one out of several reasons for the losses sustained when he first got into the big-band business:* "Unless I've got good men around me," Jack confessed to John Tynan, "I'm no good. Guess you could call me strictly an inspiration man. Louis is that way, too. He's gotta be in good company. The better the company, the better Pops will blow."

An inspired companion volume to *This Is Teagarden,* previously mentioned, is *Swing Low, Sweet Spiritual.* In the former, he displays his mastery of the jazz vocal and the jazz trombone in a collection of Teagarden favorites; his compositional ideas fully confirm Bill Russo's remarks. And in the second album, he recalls early influences not so widely known to his followers. Before it had been released he was already talking about future albums, perhaps of show tunes, but not the usual run-of-the-mill stuff, and pop tunes that fit his style and moods. In the Tynan interview he noted that many old tunes had been done to death. On the other hand, many haven't—such as Tony Jackson's "Pretty Baby" that might have been written to be sung and swung by the Big Gate, medium drag tempo.

(As you may have surmised, Jack never gets very far away from music. Once I phoned him at a Brooklyn hospital where he was getting over a repeat performance of pneumonia—the first had caught him when he was with Whiteman—and asked if there was anything he needed. [Jack was in a private room, with paperbacks, a portable television set, a friendly hospital staff, and visitors as and when allowed.] He started to say no and then changed it to, yes, there was. He asked if I'd stop at the Hotel Markwell and pick up his trombone. I did that, and brought it along. Almost the first thing Jack did after thanking me was to take the personally machined mouthpiece and rub its edges on the floor. I was reminded of Louis's cornet mouthpiece that I'd seen at the Milne Municipal Boys' Home in New Orleans, which

*Most agency people would appear to be more at home in the popular promotional slant, rather than in the jazz department. The great big-band successes are men who were not only able to think orchestrally but who were also able to take charge of the entire operation and see that jazz was not slighted, from the lowliest band boy to the highest paid arranger. Despite his easygoing ways, Jack has very definite orchestral ideas and is by no means—despite his failures—limited to a one-man, or combo, field.

he'd filed with crosshatches to assure himself a firm mouth-grip, or *embouchure.* Well, Jackson played, not very loud because he wasn't supposed to give his lungs too heavy a workout just yet, and some nurses and an intern paused at the doorway—I thought, to protest, but that wasn't it at all; Jack had already built up a loyal following in Brooklyn!)

"This twenty percent tax is murder," Jack told John Tynan. "Where we're working now, at Astor's in the Valley, I can't sing a note because of the tax. It isn't only that I like to sing, but people come to the stand, wanting me to sing particular tunes. It keeps me busy explaining why I can't."

That should have been a good excuse for a headache, but Jack only has moods, not migraines. Queried on this by Tynan, he laughed and explained, "It goes back to our Whiteman days. On the bandstand Johnny (Mercer) used to sit right above the trombone section. He was, and I guess still is, a chronic sinus sufferer, and always had a headache, it seemed. He'd look down at me and ask, 'How ya feel tonight, Jack?' I'd say, 'Why, just fine, Johnny. How you?' Then he'd moan, 'Man, my head is killing me. Don't you ever have a headache?' And the truth is, I never have."

"Guess I'll be off to Europe in March," he said, "Joe Glaser's setting it up." And though he was no longer in the San Fernando Valley in April 1957, neither was he in Europe. He was at a place on the Strip in Las Vegas. But at least he could sing.

Even His Feet Look Sad

Whitney Balliett

A book could be filled (and many have been) with the work of Whitney Balliett, The New Yorker*'s jazz critic for almost forty years and generally acknowledged as the finest stylist as well as one of the most perceptive writers in the field. This 1962 Profile of Pee Wee Russell is a perfect example of Balliett's art of compression, sympathy, and acuity.*

The clarinetist Pee Wee Russell was born in St. Louis, Missouri, in March of 1906, and died just short of his sixty-third birthday in Arlington, Virginia. He was unique—in his looks, in his inward-straining shyness, in his furtive, circumambulatory speech, and in his extraordinary style. His life was higgledy-piggledy. He once accidentally shot and killed a man when all he was trying to do was keep an eye on a friend's girl. He spent most of his career linked—in fact and fiction—to the wrong musicians. People laughed at him—he *looked* like a clown perfectly at ease in a clown's body—when, hearing him, they should have wept. He drank so much for so long that he almost died, and when he miraculously recovered, he began drinking again. In the last seven or eight years of his life, he came into focus: his originality began to be appreciated, and he worked and recorded with the sort of musicians he should have been working and recording with all his life. He even took up painting, producing a series of seemingly abstract canvases that were actually accurate chartings of his inner workings. But then, true to form, the bottom fell out. His wife Mary died unexpectedly, and he was soon dead himself. Mary had been his guidon, his ballast, his right hand, his helpmeet. She was a funny, sharp, nervous woman, and she knew she deserved better than Pee Wee. She had no illusions, but she was devoted to him. She laughed when she said this: "Do you know Pee Wee? I mean what do you *think* of him? Oh, not those funny sounds that come out of his clarinet. Do you *know* him? You think he's kind and sensitive and sweet. Well, he's intelligent and he doesn't use dope and he is sensitive, but Pee Wee can also be *mean.* In fact, Pee Wee is the most egocentric son of a bitch I know."

No jazz musician has ever played with the same daring and nakedness and intuition. His solos didn't always arrive at their original destination. He took wild improvisational chances, and when he found himself above the abyss, he simply turned in another direction, invariably hitting firm ground. His singular tone was never at rest. He had a rich chalumeau register, a piping upper register, and a whining middle register, and when he couldn't think of anything else to do, he growled. Above all, he sounded cranky and querulous, but that was camouflage, for he was the most plaintive and lyrical of players. He was particularly affecting in a medium or slow-tempo blues. He'd start in the chalumeau range with a delicate rush of notes that were intensely multiplied into a single, unbroken phrase that might last the entire chorus. Thus he'd begin with a pattern of winged double-time staccato notes that, moving steadily downward, were abruptly pierced by falsetto jumps. When he had nearly sunk out of hearing, he reversed this pattern, keeping his myriad notes back to back, and then swung into an easy uphill-downdale movement, topping each rise with an oddly placed vibrato. By this time, his first chorus was over, and one had the impression of having passed through a crowd of jostling, whispering people. Russell then took what appeared to be his first breath, and, momentarily breaking the tension he had established, opened the next chorus with a languorous, questioning phrase made up of three or four notes, at least one of them a spiny dissonance of the sort favored by Thelonious Monk. A closely linked variation would follow, and Russell would fill out the chorus by reaching behind him and producing an ironed paraphrase of the chalumeau first chorus. In his final chorus, he'd move snakily up toward the middle register with tissue-paper notes and placid rests, taking on a legato I've-made-it attack that allowed the listener to move back from the edge of his seat.

Here is Russell in his apartment on King Street, in Greenwich Village, in the early sixties, when he was on the verge of his greatest period. It wasn't a comeback he was about to begin, though, for he'd never been where he was going. Russell lived then on the third floor of a peeling brownstone. He was standing in his door, a pepper-and-salt schnauzer barking and dancing about behind him. "Shut up, Winkie, for God's sake!" Russell said, and made a loose, whirlpool gesture at the dog. A tall, close-packed, slightly bent man, Russell had a wry, wandering face, dominated by a generous nose. The general arrangement of his eyes and eyebrows was mansard, and he had a brush mustache and a full chin. A heavy trellis of wrinkles held his features in place. His gray-black hair was combed absolutely flat. Russell smiled, without showing any teeth, and went down a short, bright hall, through a Pullman kitchen, and into a dark living room, brownish in color, with two day beds and two easy chairs, a bureau, a television, and several small tables. The corners of the room were stuffed with suitcases and fat manila envelopes. Under one table were two clarinet cases. The shades on the three windows were drawn, and only one lamp was lit. The room was suffocatingly hot. Russell, who was dressed in a tan, short-sleeved sports shirt, navy-blue trousers, black socks, black square-toed shoes, and dark glasses, sat down in a huge red leather chair. "We've lived in this cave six years too long. Mary's no housekeeper, but she tries. Every time a new cleaning gadget comes out, she buys it and stuffs it in a closet with all the other ones. I bought an apartment three years ago in a development on Eighth Avenue in the Chelsea district, and we're moving in. It has a balcony and a living room and a bedroom and a full kitchen. We'll have to get a cleaning woman to keep it respectable." Russell laughed—a sighing sound that seemed to travel down his nose. "Mary got me up at seven this morning before she went to work, but I haven't had any breakfast, which is my own fault. I've been on the road four weeks—two at the Theatrical Café, in Cleveland, with George Wein, and two in Pittsburgh with Jimmy McPartland. I shouldn't have gone to Pittsburgh. I celebrated my birthday there, and I'm still paying for it, physically and mentally. And the music. I can't go near 'Muskrat Ramble' any more without freezing up. Last fall, I did a television show with McPartland and Eddie Condon and Bud Freeman and Gene Krupa and Joe Sullivan—all the Chicago boys. We made a record just before it. They sent me a copy the other day and I listened halfway through and turned it off and gave it to the super. Mary was here, and she said, 'Pee Wee, you sound like you did when I first knew you in 1942.' I'd gone back twenty years in three hours. There's no room left in that music. It tells *you* how to solo. You're as good as the company you keep. You go with fast musicians, housebroken musicians, and you improve."

Russell spoke in a low, nasal voice. Sometimes he stuttered, and sometimes whole sentences came out in a sluice-like manner, and trailed off into mumbles and down-the-nose laughs. His face was never still. When he was surprised, he opened his mouth slightly and popped his eyes, rolling them up to the right. When he was thoughtful, he glanced quickly about, tugged his nose, and cocked his head. When he was amused, everything turned down instead of up—the edges of his eyes, his eyebrows, and the corners of his mouth. Russell got up and walked with short, crabwise steps into the kitchen. "Talking dries me up," he said. "I'm going to have an ale."

There were four framed photographs on the walls. Two of them showed what was already unmistakably Russell, in a dress and long, curly hair. In one, he was sucking his thumb. In the other, an arm was draped about a cocker spaniel. The third showed him at about fifteen, in military uniform, standing beneath a tree, and in the fourth he was wearing a dinner jacket and a wing collar and holding an alto saxophone. Russell came back, a bottle of ale in one hand and a pink plastic cup in the other. "Isn't that something? A wing collar. I was sixteen, and my father bought me that saxophone for three hundred and seventy-five dollars." Russell filled his cup and put the bottle on the floor. "My father was a steward at the Planter's Hotel, in St. Louis, when I was born, and I was named after him—Charles Ellsworth. I was a late child and the only one. My mother was forty. She was a very intelligent person. She'd been a newspaperwoman in Chicago, and she used to read a lot. Being a late child, I was excess baggage. I was like a toy. My parents, who were pretty well off, would say, You want this or that, it's yours. But I never really knew them. Not that they were cold, but they just didn't divulge anything. Someone discovered a few years ago that my father had a lot of brothers. I never knew he had *any.* When I was little, we moved to Muskogee, where my father and a friend hit a couple of gas wells. I took up piano and drums and violin, roughly in that order. One day, after I'd played in a school recital, I put my violin in the backseat of our car and my mother got in and sat on it. That was the end of my violin career. 'Thank God that's over,' I said to myself. I tried the clarinet when I was about twelve or thirteen. I studied with Charlie Merrill, who was in the pit band in the only theater in Muskogee. Oklahoma was a dry state and he sneaked corn liquor during the lessons. My first job was playing at a resort lake. I played for about twelve hours and made three dollars. Once in a while, my father'd take me into the Elks' Club, where I heard Yellow Nunez, the New Orleans clarinet player. He had a trombone and piano and drums with him, and he played the lead in the ensembles. On my next job, *I* played the lead, using the violin part. Of course, I'd already heard the Original Dixieland Jazz Band on records. I was anxious in school—anxious to finish it. I'd drive my father to work in his car and, instead of going on to school, pick up a friend and drive around all day. I wanted to study music at the University of Oklahoma, but my aunt—she was living with us—said I was bad and wicked and persuaded my parents to take me out of high school and send me to Western Military Academy, in Alton, Illinois. My aunt is still alive. Mary keeps in touch with her, but I won't speak to her. I majored in wigwams at the military school, and I lasted just a year. Charlie Smith, the jazz historian, wrote the school not long ago and they told him Thomas Hart Benton and I are their two most distinguished nongraduates." Russell laughed and poured out more ale.

"We moved back to St. Louis and I began working in Herbert Berger's hotel band. It was Berger who gave me my nickname. Then I went with a tent show to Moulton, Iowa. Berger had gone to Juárez, Mexico, and he sent me a telegram asking me to join him. That was around the time my father gave me the saxophone. I was a punk kid, but my parents—can you imagine?—

said, Go ahead, good riddance. When I got to Juárez, Berger told me, to my surprise, I wouldn't be working with him but across the street with piano and drums in the Big Kid's Palace, which had a bar about a block long. There weren't any microphones and you had to blow. I must have used a board for a reed. Three days later there were union troubles and I got fired and joined Berger. This wasn't long after Pancho Villa, and all the Mexicans wore guns. There'd be shooting in the streets day and night, but nobody paid any attention. You'd just duck into a saloon and wait till it was over. The day Berger hired me, he gave me a ten-dollar advance. That was a lot of money and I went crazy on it. It was the custom in Juárez to hire a kind of cop at night for a dollar, and if you got in a scrape he'd clop the other guy with his billy. So I hired one and got drunk and we went to see a bulldog-badger fight, which is the most vicious thing you can imagine. I kept on drinking and finally told the cop to beat it, that I knew the way back to the hotel in El Paso, across the river. Or I thought I did, because I got lost and had an argument over a tab and the next thing I was in jail. What a place, Mister! A big room with bars all the way around and bars for a ceiling and a floor like a cesspool, and full of the worst cutthroats you ever saw. I was there three days on bread and water before Berger found me and paid ten dollars to get me out." Russell's voice trailed off. He squinted at the bottle, which was empty, and stood up. "I need some lunch."

The light outside was blinding, and Russell headed west on King Street, turned up Varick Street and into West Houston. He pointed at a small restaurant with a pine-paneled front, called the Lodge. "Mary and I eat here sometimes evenings. The food's all right." He found a table in the back room, which was decorated with more paneling and a small pair of antlers. A waiter came up. "Where you been, Pee Wee? You look fifteen years younger." Russell mumbled a denial and something about his birthday and Pittsburgh and ordered a Scotch-on-the-rocks and ravioli. He sipped his drink for a while in silence, studying the tablecloth. Then he looked up and said, "For ten years I couldn't eat *anything*. All during the forties. I'd be hungry and take a couple of bites of delicious steak, say, and have to put the fork down—finished. My food wouldn't go from my upper stomach to my lower stomach. I lived on brandy milkshakes and scrambled-egg sandwiches. And on whiskey. The doctors couldn't find a thing. No tumors, no ulcers. I got as thin as a lamppost and so weak I had to drink half a pint of whiskey in the morning before I could get out of bed. It began to affect my mind, and sometime in 1948 I left Mary and went to Chicago. Everything there is a blank, except what people have told me since. They say I did things that were unheard of, they were so wild. Early in 1950, I went on to San Francisco. By this time my stomach was bloated and I was so feeble I remember someone pushing me up Bush Street and me stopping to put my arms around each telegraph pole to rest. I guess I was dying. Some friends finally got me into the Franklin Hospital and they discovered I had pancreatitis and multiple cysts on my liver. The pancreatitis was why I couldn't eat for so many years. They operated, and I was in that hospital for nine months. People gave benefits around the country to pay the bills. I was still crazy. I told them Mary was after me for money. Hell, she was back in New York, minding her own business. When they sent me back here, they put me in St. Clare's Hospital under an assumed name—McGrath, I think it was—so Mary couldn't find me. After they let me out, I stayed with Eddie Condon. Mary heard where I was and came over and we went out and sat in Washington Square park. Then she took me home. After three years."

Russell picked up a spoon and twiddled the ends of his long, beautifully tapered fingers on it, as if it were a clarinet. "You take each solo like it was the last one you were going to play in your life. What notes to hit, and when to hit them—that's the secret. You can *make* a particular phrase with just one note. Maybe at the end, maybe at the beginning. It's like a little pattern. What will lead in quietly and not be too emphatic. Sometimes I jump the right chord and use what seems wrong to the next guy but I *know* is right for me. I usually think about four bars ahead what I am going to play. Sometimes things go wrong, and I have to scramble. If I can make it to the bridge of the tune, I know everything will be all right. I suppose it's not that obnoxious the average musician would notice. When I play the blues, mood, frame of mind, enters into it. One day your choice of notes would be melancholy, a blue trend, a drift of blue notes. The next day your choice of notes would be more cheerful. Standard tunes are different. Some of them require a legato treatment, and others have sparks of rhythm you have to bring out. In lots of cases, your solo depends on who you're following. The guy played a great chorus, you say to yourself. How am I going to follow *that?* I applaud him inwardly, and it becomes a matter of silent pride. Not jealousy, mind you. A kind of competition. So I make myself a guinea pig—what the hell, I'll try something new. All this goes through your mind in a split second. You start and if it sounds good to you you keep it up and write a little tune of your own. I get in bad habits and I'm trying to break myself of a couple right now. A little triplet thing, for one. Fast tempos are good to display your technique, but that's all. You prove you know the chords, but you don't have the time to insert those new little chords you could at slower tempos. Or if you do, they go unnoticed. I haven't been able to play the way I want to until recently. Coming out of that illness has given me courage, a little moral courage in my playing. When I was sick, I lived night by night. It was bang! straight ahead with the whiskey. As a result, my playing was a series of desperations. Now I have a freedom. For the past five or so months, Marshall Brown, the trombonist, and I have been rehearsing a quartet in his studio—just Brown, on the bass cornet, which is like a valve trombone; me, a bass, and drums. We get together a couple of days a week and we *work*. I didn't realize what we had until I listened to the tapes we've made. We sound like seven or eight men. Something's always going. There's a lot of bottom in the group. And we can do anything we want—soft, crescendo, decrescendo, textures, voicings. What musical knowledge we have, we use it. A little while ago, an A&R man from one of the New York jazz labels approached me and suggested a record date—on his terms. Instead, I took him to Brown's studio to hear the tapes. He was cool at first, but by the third number he looked different. I scared him with a stiff price, so we'll see what happens. A record with the quartet would feel just right. And no 'Musket Ramble' and no 'Royal Garden Blues.'"

Outside the Lodge, the sunlight seemed to accelerate Russell, and he got back to King Street quickly. He unlocked the door, and Winkie barked. "Cut that out, Winkie!" Russell shouted. "Mary'll be here soon and take you out." He removed his jacket, folded it carefully on one of the day beds, and sat down in the red chair with a grunt.

"I wish Mary was here. She knows more about me than I'll ever know. Well, after Juárez I went with Berger to the Coast and back to St. Louis, where I made my first record, in 1923 or 1924. 'Fuzzy Wuzzy Bird,' by Herbert Berger and his Coronado Hotel Orchestra. The bad notes in the reed passages are me. I also worked on the big riverboats—the J. S., the St. Paul—during the day and then stayed at night to listen to the good bands, the Negro bands like Fate Marable's and Charlie Creath's. Then Sonny Lee, the trombonist, asked me did I want to go to Houston and play in Peck Kelley's group. Peck Kelley's Bad Boys. At this time, spats and a derby were the vogue, and that's what I was wearing when I got there. Kelley looked at me in the station and didn't say a word. We got in a cab and I could feel him still looking at me, so I rolled down the window and threw the derby out. Kelley laughed and thanked me. He took me straight to Goggan's music store and sat down at a piano and started to play. He was marvelous, a kind of stride pianist, and I got panicky. About ten minutes later, a guy walked in, took a trombone off the wall, and started to play. It was Jack Teagarden. I went over to Peck when they finished and said, 'Peck, I'm in over my head. Let me work a week and make my fare home.' But I got over it and I was with Kelley several months." Russell went into the kitchen to get another bottle of ale. "Not long after I got back to St. Louis, Sonny Lee brought Bix Beiderbecke around to my house, and bang! we hit it right off. We were never apart for a couple of years—day, night, good, bad, sick, well, broke, drunk. Then Bix left to join Jean Goldkette's band and Red Nichols sent for me to come to New York. That was 1927. I went straight to the old Manger Hotel and found a note in my box: Come to a speakeasy under the Roseland Ballroom. I went over and there was Red Nichols and Eddie Lang and Miff Mole and Vic Berton. I got panicky again. They told me there'd be a recording date at Brunswick the next morning at nine, and don't be late. I got there at eight-fifteen. The place was empty, except for a handyman. Mole arrived first. He said, 'You look peaked, kid,' and opened his trombone case and took out a quart. Everybody had quarts. We made 'Ida,' and it wasn't any trouble at all. In the late twenties and early thirties I worked in a lot of bands and made God knows how many records in New York. Cass Hagen, Bert Lown, Paul Specht, Ray Levy, the Scranton Sirens, Red Nichols. We lived uptown at night. We heard Elmer Snowden and Luis Russell and Ellington. Once I went to a ballroom where Fletcher Henderson was. Coleman Hawkins had a bad cold and I sat in for him one set. My God, those scores! They were written in six flats, eight flats, I don't know how many flats. I never saw anything like it. Buster Bailey was in the section next to me, and after a couple of numbers I told him, 'Man, I came up here to have a good time, not to work. I've had enough. Where's Hawkins?'

"I joined Louis Prima around 1935. We were at the Famous Door, on Fifty-second Street, and a couple of hoodlums loaded with knives cornered Prima and me and said they wanted protection money every week—fifty bucks from Prima and twenty-five from me. Well, I didn't want any of that. I'd played a couple of private parties for Lucky Luciano, so I called him. He sent Pretty Amberg over in a big car with a bodyguard as chauffeur. Prima sat in the back with Amberg and I sat in front with the bodyguard. Nobody said much, just 'Hello' and 'Goodbye,' and for a week they drove Prima and me from our hotels to a midday radio broadcast, back to our hotels, picked us up for work at night, and took us home after. We never saw the protection-money boys again. Red McKenzie, the singer, got me into Nick's in 1938, and I worked there and at Condon's place for most of the next ten years. I have a sorrow about that time. Those guys made a joke of me, a clown, and I let myself be treated that way because I was afraid. I didn't know where else to go, where to take refuge. I'm not sure how all of us feel about each other now, though we're 'Hello, Pee Wee,' 'Hello, Eddie,' and all that. Since my sickness, Mary's given me confidence, and so has George Wein. I've worked for him with a lot of fast musicians in Boston, in New York, at Newport, on the road, and in Europe last year. I'll head a kind of house band if he opens a club here. A quiet little group. But Nick's did one thing. That's where I first met Mary."

* * *

AT THAT MOMENT, a key turned in the lock, and Mary Russell walked quickly down the hall and into the living room. A trim, pretty, black-haired woman in her forties, she was wearing a green silk dress and black harlequin glasses.

"How's Winkie been?" she asked Russell, plumping herself down and taking off her shoes. "She's the kind of dog that's always barking except at burglars. Pee Wee, you forgot to say, Did you have a hard day at the office, dear? And where's my tea?"

Russell got up and shuffled into the kitchen.

"I work in the statistics and advertising part of Robert Hall clothes," she said. "I've got a quick mind for figures. I like the job and the place. It's full of respectable ladies. Pee Wee, did I get any mail?"

"Next to you, on the table. A letter," he said from the kitchen.

"It's from my brother Al," she said. "I always look for a check in letters. My God, there *is* a check! Now why do you suppose he did that? And there's a P.S.: Please excuse the pencil. I like that. It makes me feel good."

"How much did he send you?" Russell asked, handing Mrs. Russell her tea.

"You're not going to get a cent," she said. "You know what I found the other day, Pee Wee? Old letters from you. Love letters. Every one says the same thing: I love you, I miss you. Just the dates are different." Mary Russell, who spoke in a quick, decisive way, laughed. "Pee Wee and I had an awful wedding. It was at City Hall. Danny Alvin, the drummer, stood up for us. He and Pee Wee wept. I didn't, but *they* did. After the ceremony, Danny tried to borrow money from me. Pee Wee didn't buy me any flowers and a friend lent us the wedding ring. Pee Wee has never given me a wedding ring. The one I'm wearing a nephew gave me a year ago. Just to make it proper, he said. That's not the way a woman wants to get married. Pee Wee, we ought to do it all over again. I have a rage in me to be proper. I don't play bridge and go to beauty parlors and I don't have women friends like other women. But one thing Pee Wee and I have that no one else has: we never stop talking when we're with each other. Pee Wee, you know why I love you? You're like Papa. Every time Mama got up to tidy something, he'd say, Clara, sit down, and she would. That's what you do. I loved my parents. They were Russian Jews from Odessa. Chaloff was their name. I was born on the lower East Side. I was a charity case and the doctor gave me my name, and signed the birth certificate—Dr. E. Condon. Isn't that weird? I was one of nine kids and six are left. I've got twenty nephews and nieces." Mary Russell paused and sipped her tea.

"Pee Wee worships those inchbrows. Lucky Luciano was his dream man."

"He was an acquaintance," Russell snorted.

"I'll never know you completely, Pee Wee," Mrs. Russell said. She took another sip of tea, holding the cup with both hands. "Sometimes Pee Wee can't sleep. He sits in the kitchen and plays solitaire, and I go to bed in here and sing to him. Awful songs like 'Belgian Rose' and 'Carolina Mammy.' I have a terrible voice."

"Oh, God!" Russell muttered. "The worst thing is she knows *all* the lyrics."

"I not only sing, I write," she said, laughing. "I wrote a three-act play. My hero's name is Tiny Ballard. An Italian clarinet player. It has wonderful dialogue."

"Mary's no saloon girl, coming where I work," he said. "She outgrew that long ago. She reads about ten books a week. You could have been a writer, Mary."

"I don't know why I wrote about a clarinet player. I hate the clarinet. Pee Wee's playing embarrasses me. But I like trombones: Miff Mole and Brad Gowans. And I like Duke Ellington. Last New Year's Eve, Pee Wee and I were at a party and Duke kissed me at midnight."

"Where was I?" he asked.

"You had a clarinet stuck in your mouth," she said. "The story of your life, or part of your life. Once when Pee Wee had left me and was in Chicago, he came back to New York for a couple of days. He denies it. He doesn't remember it. He went to the nightclub where I was working as a hat-check girl and asked to see me. I said no. The boss's wife went out and took one look at him and came back and said, 'At least go out and talk to him. He's pathetic. Even his feet look sad.'"

Russell made an apologetic face. "That was twelve years ago, Mary. I have no claim to being an angel."

She sat up very straight. "Pee Wee, this room is hot. Let's go out and have dinner on my brother Al."

"I'll put on a tie," he said.

THE CUTTING SESSIONS

REX STEWART

Fiercely competitive cutting sessions engaged jazz musicians of every kind, as Rex Stewart, the renowned trumpet player, recounts in this selection (originally published in Down Beat *in 1967) from his 1972 book,* Jazz Masters of the Thirties. *Since the most famous sessions involved the piano, this memoir can serve as an introduction to a group of pieces on major jazz pianists.*

Today, fame can come swiftly on the heels of a Top Twenty record, but there was a time when a musician had to prove himself to other musicians in a cutting session. Whether a fellow hailed from New Orleans, San Francisco, Chicago, or wherever, he had to come to the center—New York—before he could get on the road to (relatively speaking) fame and fortune.

There, in the Apple, his skill was tested in competition with the established ones. If he couldn't cut the mustard, he became part of the anonymous mob; capable, perhaps, but not of star quality. However, if the critical, hardblowing jazzmen conceded him recognition, that acclaim would carry him on to bigger and better jobs.

This musical action on the New York battlefield was the cutting session, and the expression was an appropriate one. When a musician picked up his instrument, his intention was to outperform the other man. No quarter was given or expected, and the wound to a musician's ego and reputation could be as deep as a cut.

To a degree, all musicians, white or black, underwent the same test of strength. After arriving in the big town, a player first got squared away with a room. The next thing he'd do would be to ask where the musicians hung out. Downtown and in the evenings, this was usually a bar, say Charlie's Tavern. By day, it was much easier—most of the fellows could be found congregated on the street around the offices of the musicians union, Local 802. But uptown, night or day, Bert Hall's Rhythm Club at 132nd Street, just off Seventh Avenue in Harlem was the main testing ground, and there most of the jamming originated.

As I recall, the process of elimination usually went this way. Whenever a stranger popped into the Rhythm Club, somebody would greet him with a hearty "Hi there, where are you from?" followed by "What do you blow?" If the newcomer was carrying his saxophone, trombone, or trumpet case, he would be invited to blow some, or, as they said in the argot of the time, "to show out."

Some piano man—and there were always a few of them in the place—would amble over to the keyboard and start comping a tune like "Sweet Georgia Brown" or "Dinah." This was the cue for the stranger to pull out his instrument and show what he could do. Meanwhile, the word had gone out all over the neighborhood—"stand by!"—because if this cat was really good, it was the duty of every tub to drop whatever he was doing and rush to the club. And nobody ever did fall into New York City and cut the entire field—some brother always came to the rescue of New York's prestige.

These sessions, as every other aspect of life, had a pecking order. The giants seldom deigned to compete with the peasantry. Instead, they sat around getting their kicks, listening with amusement as the neophyte struggled to justify his claim to entry into the charmed circle of the (for want of a better word) establishment.

The blowing would start, and the pilgrim's status was soon established—he was either in or out. If he was in, he would be toasted at Big John's bar, and friendships were formed that assured his being invited to sit in a session with the big shots, who did their serious blowing at the Hoofer's Club, downstairs in the basement of the same building.

There, in the Hoofer's Club, the cream of the crop in New York could be found—Jimmy and Tommy Dorsey, Benny Carter, Frankie Trumbauer, Buster Bailey, Sidney De Paris, Fats Waller, and just about every other great name in jazz. Almost every night, rain, snow, or what have you, there was a session—nothing prevented the cats from getting together.

I said that no individual ever came to town and carved everybody, but there was one exception—Louis Armstrong. He was so tough on his trumpet that nobody dared challenge him. Come to think of it, I don't remember ever seeing him at a session. He didn't come to us—we had to go to him. I shall never forget the scrambling to get to one tiny window backstage at Roseland Ballroom, just to catch Satchmo putting the "heat to the beat" with Fletcher Henderson.

Nor can I forget the memorable occasion when Jelly Roll Morton swaggered up to the piano in the Rhythm Club announcing that he, the king of the ivory ticklers, was ready for all turkeys (a not-so-flattering way of referring to any possible competition). Making such a proclamation was like waving a red flag in front of a bull.

Jelly's monologue was fascinating as he comped and talked about how great he was, but after a few minutes of this performance, the first of the local piano giants, Willie "The Tiger" Gant walked in. He immediately sensed that Morton outclassed him, and after listening a while to Jelly's Kansas City rolling bass, he phoned Willie "The Lion" Smith to come right down. I don't think Jelly Roll and Willie had ever met, but the air became charged with professional animosity when The Lion hit the scene and snarled, "Either play something or get up, you heathen. The Lion is in port, and it's my mood to roar!" Such an unfriendly put-down caused Jelly to tear into a fast rag, which brought the house down. Morton, hearing the applause, looked up from the piano, sweating and beaming. Evidently he felt that there would be no contest.

The Lion, unimpressed, just pushed Jelly off the piano stool and, without breaking the rhythm of Jelly's tour de force, played one of his own rags with equal skill and just as great an impact on the audience.

The duel had taken on the aspect of a standoff, so the call went out for Fats Waller, but Fats was nowhere to be found. Just then, the all-time boss of the Harlem stride piano players, James P. Johnson, arrived, having been advised of what was going on via the grapevine.

James P., who sometimes stuttered, said, "Jelly, come on, l-l-let's go down to the Hoofers. They have a b-b-better piano there, and I'll en-entertain you."

Jelly agreed, and everybody followed. As I recall, there were about sixty or seventy cats in the "second line" on that occasion. History was made as James P. wiped up the floor with Jelly Roll. Never before or since have I heard such piano playing!

At that time, New York was session-happy. Everybody blew at everybody. Guys were so eager not to miss an opportunity to sit in that many of them had two horns—one kept on the job and the other stashed away at the Rhythm Club or a nearby bar. Some sessions might be held in almost any corner bar, but they weren't the important ones.

One character, Jazz Curry, a bassist, was a familiar sight on Seventh Avenue, trudging up and down the street carrying both his brass and string basses, looking for another bass man to challenge. Bass contests were rare in the Rhythm Club or anywhere else.

A history-making session was the one between Thornton Blue, the Saint Louis clarinetist then with Cab Calloway, and Buster Bailey. That evening, a gang of clarinet players started noodling. I remember Blue, Russell Procope, Carmelito Jejo, Jimmy Dorsey, Benny Goodman, and many others being present (this was in the very early thirties before Benny had his band). After trying out various tunes, they agreed to play "Liza." One by one, everybody dropped out until only Bailey and Blue remained. Blue was swinging like mad, but Buster took the honors as he increased the tempo, chorus by chorus, until you could hardly pat your foot. In those days, the late Buster Bailey could cut every living tub on the clarinet.

This was a beautiful period for the music and the players. There was little jealousy and no semblance of Jim Crow or Crow Jim in the sessions. Musicians were like fraternity brothers, despite their being aware of the distinction that was strongly maintained by white agents, bookers, and the public. The jazzmen were bound together by their love for the music—and what the rest of the world thought about fraternizing did not matter.

Among my memories, I treasure the historic confrontation that took place between the trombone giants, Jack Teagarden and Jimmy Harrison. They first met in 1927 at Roseland Ballroom in New York. That meeting remains etched firmly in my mind, since, on that night, the band was initiated into the sacred rites of what was then known as Texas Muggles. Now it is called by many other names—tea, Mary-Jane, or just plain marijuana. (I only mention this to pinpoint the occasion.) When Mr. Texas met Mr. New York, a mutual admiration society was formed at once. Jack thought that Jimmy was just about the greatest 'bone that had ever come down the pike, and Jimmy felt the same way about Jack, putting him above Miff Mole, who also was a tremendous trombone on that scene. I might also mention that Teagarden was one of the few musicians, except for a few greats like Fats Waller, who ever was permitted to sit in with the Fletcher Henderson Band.

Soon Jimmy and Jack started hanging out uptown, which caused quite a few uplifted eyebrows among those Harlemites who resented Teagarden's Texas brogue and appearance. But Jimmy would declare that Jack was more Indian than Caucasian, which made everything all right, so the two buddies began to be seen quite a bit, especially in the King Kong flats—so named because they featured corn whiskey reputed to be as strong as King Kong. All these flats specialized in down-home "vittles"—delicacies like hog maws, chitterlings, cornbread, and skillet biscuits—all of which Teagarden craved and could not find outside Harlem.

Sallie Mae's pad in the basement on 133rd Street was the setting for an event that was unusual because Jack and Jimmy had great respect for each other's abilities. However, under the influence of King Kong, fried chicken, and good fellowship, they squared away and blew, solo for solo, chorus for chorus, accompanied at first by Clarence Holiday's guitar and John Kirby's bass. When the news spread (as it always did), Sallie Mae's joint became crowded with tooters, and Cliff Jackson took over the comping on piano, along with George Stafford beating out rhythm on an old suitcase.

Actually, this confrontation was more of a friendly demonstration between, as we used to say, "the true bosses with the hot sauce," on how to extract the most swinging sounds out of the trombone than it was a real cutting session. Harrison gave new life to that old broad "Dinah," while Teagarden had the cats screaming their approval when he swung—and I mean swung—in waltz time, "The World Is Waiting for the Sunrise!"

Sometimes the cutting sessions were less fraternal and more competitive. When Coleman Hawkins returned to his Harlem stomping grounds in 1939, after several years' absence in Europe, he was more than mildly concerned about whether the cats had caught up with him, as he put it. At that time, all the hippies hung out in former drummer Nightsie Johnson's joint, which I recall as on 131st Street near Saint Nicholas Avenue. Sunrise usually found the place filled with the cream of the entertainment world: musicians, singers, comics, dancers—Billy Daniels, Artie Shaw, and just about anyone else you could think of, but chiefly Billie Holiday, who, by her presence there every night, actually gave the impression that she owned the after-hours spot.

This was the setting for another of the most memorable cutting sessions. Hawk fell in about 3:00 or 4:00 A.M. without his instrument and just sat and sipped, listening until the last toot was tooted. All the cats paraded their wares before him because he was the big man—Hawkins had become king of the tenor saxes when he recorded "One Hour" and "Hello, Lola" with the Mound City Blue Blowers in 1929. They vied for his attention just in case he planned to start a band or had a record date on the fire—that was the talk among the assorted horn players: trumpets, trombones, and alto saxes.

But the tenor saxophonists had other ideas; they wanted to gain prestige by outplaying the master. They reasoned that Coleman had been away from the source too long to know the hot licks that Harlem was putting down now. But what they'd forgotten was that Bean was a creative source within himself, an innovator rather than a copier. And I guess that most of the men were simply too young to realize how much of an old fox Coleman Hawkins was.

In any case, Hawk frequented the pad nightly for several weeks, and every time he was asked to play, he'd have another new excuse—he was resting from the constant grind of appearances in Europe, his horn was in pawn, he had a toothache, or he just couldn't bring himself to play in front of all these tenor giants. Fellows like Lester Young, Don Byas, Dick Wilson, Chu Berry, and many lesser talents were all itching to get a piece of the Hawk—especially Lester, whose staunchest fan was Billie Holiday.

One night Billie brought the personal element into focus by "signifying," which in Harlemese means making a series of pointed but oblique remarks apparently addressed to no one in particular, but unmistakable in intention in such a close-knit circle.

When Hawk ignored her, she proceeded to bring her opinions out into the open, saying that *her* man (and I figured at that time that she meant "her man" in more than one sense*) was the only tenor saxophone in the world, the one and only Pres, Lester Young, and it really wasn't any use for any tired old man to try and blow against her President.

Hawk took Lady Day's caustic remarks as a big joke, but apparently he'd previously decided that this was the night to make his move. Up to the last minute, the old fox played it cool, waiting until Billie's juice told her it was time for her to sing some blues. Then, he slipped out, returning with his saxophone, and started to accompany Billie's blues, softly. Billie, hearing his sound, looked up, startled, and then motioned to Pres as if to say, "Take charge."

So Lester began blowing the blues, and to give credit where credit is due, he really *played* the blues that night, chorus after chorus, until finally Hawk burst in on the end of one of his choruses, cascading a harmonic interruption, not unlike Mount Vesuvius erupting, virtually overpowering Lester's more haunting approach. When Hawk finished off the blues, soaring, searing, and lifting the entire house with his guttural, positive sonority, every tub began cheering, with the exception of Lady Day, Lester, and her pet boxer, Mister. They, like the Arabs, folded their tents and stole away.

---

*According to several associates, and Lester Young himself, Rex—and others who figured the same—figured wrong.

THOMAS "FATS" WALLER

JOHN S. WILSON

Also from Shapiro and Hentoff's The Jazz Makers, *this appreciation, by the critic and broadcaster John Wilson, of the beloved composer/pianist whose happy music and happy nature continue to charm more than fifty years after his early death, in 1943.*

Both Fats Waller and his principal tutor, James P. Johnson, lived lives of aching frustration. Johnson ached openly because he could find no audience for his serious compositions, but Waller's desire to find acceptance as a serious musician was buried under a heavy coating of pervasive geniality. And while Johnson plodded steadily downhill in puzzled despair, Waller's blithely ironical attitude carried him up and up and up in the material world—eventually to a level that even his enormous energy could not cope with.

He was one of the most massively talented men who has ever turned up in the world of popular music—an inimitable entertainer whose charm has, if anything, grown in the nostalgic decade and a half since his death; the writer of some of the great evergreen songs in the popular repertoire ("Honeysuckle Rose," "Ain't Misbehavin'"); a jazz pianist whose playing was a landmark in the development of that instrument and whose influence on pre-bop pianists was surpassed only by that of Earl Hines; and a section man who could swing an entire band as no one else could. All of these gifts were his and yet, like the inevitable clown who wants to play Hamlet, he had a consuming desire to bring to the public his love of classical music and of the organ. His need to offer this gift and have it accepted was almost childlike and, childlike, the hurt when it was rejected was deep and long.

Gene Sedric, the saxophonist and clarinetist in Fats's little band from 1938 to 1943, remembers times when Waller was so full of his feeling for serious music that he couldn't help playing, even in a nightclub, with all the musicality of which he was capable. But this wasn't the Fats that the customers had paid to hear.

"People in the audience would think he was lying down," Sedric says.

"They'd yell, 'Come on, Fats!' He'd take a swig of gin or something and say resignedly, 'Aw right, here it is.'"

And he'd plod into some tawdry trifle from Tin Pan Alley.

Waller's serious ambitions were all entwined with his love of the organ. The Chicago critic, Ashton Stevens, once observed perceptively that "the organ is the instrument of his heart, the piano of his stomach."

Fats had an organ in his apartment in New York and, later, in his house at St. Albans, L.I. Wherever he went, he sought out opportunities to play the organ. In Paris, in 1932, on an otherwise rambunctious trip with songwriter Spencer Williams, he climbed up to the organ loft of the Cathedral of Notre Dame with Marcel Dupré, the cathedral's organist. His report on what happened there was typically Wallerian: "First Mr. Dupré played the God-box and then I played the God-box."

When he was working in the film *Stormy Weather* in 1943, shortly before his death, he found an organ on the set. He sat down to play and for three hours production was held up as the entire company listened entranced. One of his few opportunities to play the organ for a wide audience, and to play as he wanted to play, came during a year he spent on the staff of WLW in Cincinnati in the early thirties. He had an enormously successful late night program there, *Fats Waller's Rhythm Club,* on which he sang and clowned and played the driving stride piano that was his specialty. And then, a couple of hours later, in the early hours of the morning, the station offered a program of quiet, peaceful organ music. The organist never received any billing. It was Fats Waller, playing with a full contentment that rarely came to him.

There must have been something of the same contentment for him on a day in 1927 when he sat down at a pipe organ in Victor's Camden studios and recorded two fugues by Bach (who ran third in Fats's book as the greatest man in history—Lincoln and Franklin D. Roosevelt were first and second), Moszkowski's "Spanish Dance No. 1," Liszt's "Liebestraum," Rimsky-Korsakov's "Flight of the Bumble Bee" (which, thirty years ago, had not yet been galloped to death by accordionists and Harry James), and Friml's "Spanish Days." None of these recordings has ever been released, but the rumors about them suggest that Waller felt the stern eye of studio expectations burning over his shoulder: he played them through straight and then dressed them up in a hot treatment.

A Chicago musical instrument store often sent a Hammond organ (compliments of the house) to Waller's hotel room when he was playing there. In the small hours, he would lull a roomful of guests with spirituals, Bach, and hymns. One morning, after three hours of music, Fats sat back and suggested to his guests, "Have another glass, and I'll play you my favorite piece." His friends refreshed themselves and Waller launched into his favorite—"Abide with Me."

This was something that came out of the very marrow of Thomas Wright Waller. It was part of the continuing evidence of the enormous sense of loss that he felt when his mother died. He had been sixteen at the time. Adeline Lockett Waller played the piano and the organ and, of the dozen children that she bore, Thomas, her youngest son, was her favorite. Her death was a shock from which Waller never really recovered. Shortly before his own death at the unseemly age of thirty-nine, he composed a melody which "really shook his soul," according to his last manager, Ed Kirkeby. He called it "Where Has My Mother Gone?"

"Several lyrics with different titles were written," Kirkeby recalls, "but none were accepted by Tom. None satisfied him nor adequately expressed the anguish of that melody."

This anguish pursued Waller for the full twenty-three years that he was completely a part of the world of music. It led him, hard on the heels of his mother's death, to an impetuous marriage to Edith Hatchett. It quickly foundered and left him with an unending stream of alimony troubles which, at one point, landed him in jail. But it was his mother's death, too, that led to his real entrance into the music world of Harlem.

He was born May 21, 1904, into a deeply religious family. His father, Edward Waller, minister of the Abyssinian Baptist Church, looked on jazz as "music from the devil's workshop." But young Tom heard sounds coming out of the cellars of Harlem that intrigued him. A brief try at formal piano instruction had little effect on him. He taught himself and quickly gained a reputation as a musical clown at P.S. 89. Later in life he listed his hobbies as "music, music, music and more music." By then he had also acquired abiding interests in food and liquor, but in his school days this listing would have been reasonably accurate.

When he was fourteen he regularly wormed his way into the Lincoln Theatre, a movie house, and battled his way down to a front-row seat right in back of Maizie Mullins, who played piano for the silent films. She let him slide under the brass rail and on to the piano stool beside her and, when she wanted a rest, young Tom was allowed to play along with the picture. When the theater's organist fell ill, the boy filled in for him and later, when the organist left, Tom got his job. He was a professional, making twenty-three dollars a week.

Waller soon had a chance to pass along the kindness that Maizie Mullins had shown him. Just as Waller had sat entranced in the seat behind Miss Mullins, another youngster, Bill Basie, was soon sitting behind Waller, watching him play the organ. One day Waller asked Basie if he'd like to learn the instrument ("I'd give my right arm," said Basie), and invited him to join him in the pit. Basie sat on the floor, watching Waller's feet work the pedals. Then Basie worked the pedals with his hands while Waller played. Then he sat beside Waller and learned the keyboard. And finally Waller found a convenient excuse for leaving him alone and Basie found himself playing accompaniment to the film.

Waller was a big wheel to his schoolmates by now and the next year, when he won a piano contest at the Roosevelt Theatre, playing James P. Johnson's "Carolina Shout," his reputation began to spread beyond the precincts of school.

And then his mother died. His world suddenly fell apart. It no longer had gaugeable boundaries and edges. Shortly after his mother's death, Waller was found disconsolate on the steps of the home of a friend, Russell Brooks, a pianist of some local fame. The Brooks family took the boy in and, through Brooks, he moved into the heart of the hectic Harlem nightlife of the early twenties. Brooks introduced him to the rent-party scene, to such rent-party stars as Willie "The Lion" Smith (his appraisal of Waller: "Yeah, a yearling, he's coming along, I guess he'll do all right"), and, most importantly, James P. Johnson.

James P. was the big man at the Harlem rent parties then and after he heard young Waller play the pipe organ, he told his wife, "I know I can teach that boy." So Waller practiced on the Johnsons' piano far into the morning, until three or four o'clock when Mrs. Johnson would order him to go home. Johnson got Waller his first nightclub job when Willie The Lion decided to quit Leroy's at One Hundred and Thirty-fifth Street and Fifth Ave. Johnson was asked to take over but he couldn't and recommended young Fats. Johnson also took Waller over to QRS, where he was making piano rolls, and introduced him there. This resulted in nineteen rolls by Fats, at one hundred dollars a roll. The next year he made his first record, a pair of piano solos, "Muscle Shoals Blues" and "Birmingham Blues," for Okeh. And 1923 found him on the radio for the first time, broadcasting from the stage of the Fox Terminal Theatre in Newark.

By then, too, Waller had written the first of what was to be a long series of brightly melodic tunes. He based his first effort on a ribald lyric, "The Boy in the Boat." He was in Boston at the time, taking a leave from his organ chores at the Lincoln to accompany a vaudeville act called "Liza and Her Shufflin' Six." So he called his tune "Boston Blues." By the time it was published in 1925, however, Clarence Williams had provided it with lyrics that could be used anywhere, and the title had been changed to "Squeeze Me."

Waller was very pleased with his first composition, and he played it endlessly. Don Redman once visited him at the Lafayette, where Fats presided at the organ after the Lincoln was sold. Redman sat beside Waller, chatting with him while the newsreel filled the screen above them. As they talked, Waller pounded out "Squeeze Me" which at that time was still "The Boy in the Boat" set to music. Glancing up at the screen, Redman noticed with horror that a funeral was being shown.

"Hey, Fats," he whispered, "they're showing a funeral. You shouldn't be playing that."

"Why not?" exclaimed Fats, with a satanic grin, pumping sturdily at the keyboard. Then, beckoning an usher, Waller gave him fifty cents to get him a pint of gin.

The pint was the modest beginning of what was to become a standard drinking set-up for Waller. At a recording session he invariably had one quart on the piano, another in reserve underneath. In his later days, when he was touring with his little band and had switched from gin to whiskey, his dressing-room was supplied with three fifths every day—two for Waller (and *nobody else*) and one for visitors. At the end of the day, there were invariably two dead Waller soldiers while the visitors' bottle, as frequently as not, hadn't been finished.

When he got up in the morning, his regular dosage was four fingers neat ("my liquid ham and eggs"), followed by four fingers after shaving. For excursions (anywhere out of reach of a bottle), he carried a suitcase equipped with collapsible cups and, of course, proper cheer.

Waller's customary procedure on entering anyone's office was to walk over to the desk, pull open a drawer and exclaim, "Where's the bottle?"

One day, with his good friend, Redman, he strode into the office of music publisher Harry Link, examined Link's desk and made his usual request. While Link was sending out for a bottle, Waller fooled around the piano. Redman's fancy was caught by some chords Waller was playing. He took them down and, by the time the bottle arrived, the two had worked out a chorus. Just then Andy Razaf, Waller's most frequent collaborator, walked in.

"Listen to this, Andy," said Redman, and Waller played over the chorus. Razaf immediately picked up a pencil and started writing a lyric. Before the three left Link's office, they had written a complete tune, words and music, gotten an advance and killed a bottle. The tune was "If It Ain't Love."

Waller's speed and facility as a composer were fabulous. When he was writing scores for the shows at Connie's Inn in Harlem, he would be playing piano at a rehearsal when Leonard Harper, the producer, asked him, "Have you written anything for this next number, Fats?"

"Yeah, yeah," Fats would reply. "Go on with the dance, man."

And while the chorus danced, Fats composed the number that they were to dance to.

His delicate "Jitterbug Waltz" was written in ten minutes after he woke up one day with the tune floating through his mind (the inspiration, possibly subconscious, was a finger exercise his son, Maurice, had been playing). In one two-hour session, Waller and Razaf turned out "Honeysuckle Rose," "My Fate Is in Your Hands," and "Zonky." "Ain't Misbehavin'" was created in forty-five minutes. His six-part *London Suite* was composed in an hour to fulfill a commitment so that Fats could leave England. Waller sat at the piano playing while his manager, Ed Kirkeby, described the various sections of London which Waller portrayed in his music.

Waller, in fact, was so fluent as a composer and so eternally in need of money that he was very casual about all but giving away many of his compositions.

There were times when it seemed as though composing was just as easy as breathing for Fats. There was one occasion when it was as easy as eating hamburgers. This was one early morning when he was out with Fletcher Henderson and some of the men in Henderson's band. They stopped in a hamburger joint where Fats quickly consumed nine specialties of the house. He was broke and he offered Henderson one tune per hamburger if he'd pick up the check. Henderson agreed and Waller called for manuscript paper. He quickly wrote out nine tunes and handed them over to Henderson who upped the price per tune from one hamburg to ten dollars. Waller's hamburg numbers included "Top and Bottom" (named after a Harlem drink made of wine and gin) which was later retitled "Henderson Stomp," "Thundermug Stomp" which was changed to "Hot Mustard," and other tunes that were subsequently known as "Variety Stomp," "St. Louis Shuffle," and "Whiteman Stomp."

Another time when he was hard up, Waller tried to peddle an entire folio of manuscripts to QRS for ten dollars (offer refused); and once, in a moment of deep financial desperation shortly after his second marriage (to Anita Rutherford), he offered every song in his possession to Redman for ten dollars (again refused). However, he wasn't always so unsuccessful in his efforts to rob himself. On one occasion he managed to sell his rights to "Ain't Misbehavin'," "Black and Blue," and seventeen other songs for a total of five hundred dollars.

Waller's fortunes started to take a turn for the better in 1932 when he acquired a manager, Phil Ponce, who placed him on the staff of WLW in Cincinnati. His late night *Rhythm Club* program there made his name known throughout the East and Midwest. It was on this program that he was tagged "the harmful little armful," and the Waller personality began to make itself felt beyond the confines of a small group of friends. The personality got even wider exposure when he started recording for Victor in 1934 with the little band called His Rhythm. At the same time, the popular appeal of his sometimes brutal desecrations of the finest flowers of Tin Pan Alley shadowed his talents as a jazz pianist and as a song writer.

Fats, the pianist, had one of the strongest left hands in jazz. This is an important consideration for anyone attempting stride piano, the style brought to an initial peak by James P. Johnson and then polished off by Waller. In stride piano, the left hand plays alternate single notes and chords. Rudi Blesh has aptly described Waller's solid left as rolling on "like heat thunder on a summer day." For Bennie Payne, who recorded some duets with Waller, the high point of the show, "Keep Shufflin'," was the fact that the two best left hands in jazz were playing together in the pit—the hands of James P. Johnson and Fats Waller. Along with his strength, Waller had unusual delicacy, a remarkable lightness of touch which gave his stride playing a romping airiness that Johnson's never achieved.

His pianism, however, became subordinate once the path for his display of personality had been marked out. The system was the essence of simplicity. Fats just relaxed and did whatever came to mind. And the Waller mind had always been wryly direct. During a period in the middle twenties, when he was playing with Erskine Tate's Vendome orchestra in Chicago (Louis Armstrong was in the band then, too), it was the custom for song-pluggers to hand out new tunes to the men in the band and have them play them at sight. Inevitably, this led to some treacherous tangles as the band waded through strange material. One night, when confusion was more rampant than usual in the orchestra pit, Waller leaned down from his elevated piano and asked, "Pardon me, boys, but what key are you all strugglin' in down there?"

There is a claim, made by the late Lips Page, that the term "bop" was created by Fats in one of his offhand remarks. It happened, said Lips, when Fats was playing with a small group at Minton's.

"Late one night some of the younger generation of musicians would bring along their instruments in the hope of jamming with the band," Lips related. "Waller would signal for one of them to take a chorus. The musician would start to play, then rest for eight or twelve bars in order to get in condition for one of his crazy bop runs. Fats would shout at them, 'Stop that crazy boppin' and a-stoppin' and play that jive like the rest of us guys!'"

The interjected comments that became his trademark both on the air and on records were often tinted with blue and his manager was repeatedly asked to muzzle him, to put him under wraps. But there was no wrap that could contain the effusive Fats. If he chose to wind up a recording of "Spring Cleaning" by remarking, "No, lady, we can't haul your ashes for twenty-five cents. That's bad business," there was nothing much that could be done about it because no one, including Waller, had the slightest idea he was going to say it until it popped out.

He went along, as he said, "livin' the life I love," pouring out himself, creating laughter everywhere he appeared. If he failed to find acceptance for the serious side of himself that he wanted to show, it was not through any lack of musical technique so much as his lack of personal discipline. He could never pass up a good time. What should have been one of the high points of his career occurred in January 1942, when he gave a concert at Carnegie Hall. The auditorium was packed. Fats had a few anticipatory drinks but he went out and played the first half of his program in controlled, quiet form. During intermission he found that he had as many friends backstage as he had out front, and he tried to have a drink with each of them. When he returned for the second half, he played a medley of Gershwin tunes, including "Summertime," and everything else that he played for the rest of the concert kept turning into "Summertime." It was not a notable performance.

He had been warned a couple of times to stop drinking and once he tried—for a while. But zest alone could not keep him going and finally the 270-pound body gave out. It was on a train near Kansas City in December 1943, when he was on his way home to spend Christmas with his second wife and their two children.

He left behind a legacy of laughter.

"Every time someone mentions Fats Waller's name," said Louis Armstrong, "why you can see the grins on all the faces as if to say, 'Yea, yea, yea, yea, Fats is a solid sender, ain't he?'"

For James P. Johnson, who looked on Waller as a son, his death was particularly hard to take. He went into seclusion, emerging only to play a "Blues for Fats," which he had composed, at a Waller memorial at Town Hall. He came to the concert still shrouded in his sorrow but backstage, as memories of Fats were exchanged, each recollection ended in an uproarious laugh. Soon all the mourners, including Johnson, were chortling with happy memories of an irrepressible spirit whose gift for provoking laughter has given him a form of immortality.

On another level, his memory is kept green in the work of the many pianists who responded to his brightly swinging style—in the playing of Ralph Sutton and Joe Sullivan and Johnny Guarnieri. And in the records Art Tatum has left us. Tatum was particularly proud of his musical origin.

"Fats, man—that's where I come from," he once said. And he added with a sly grin, "Quite a place to come from."

Sunshine Always Opens Out

Whitney Balliett

Another remarkable Balliett profile, this one (from 1965) of the great Earl "Fatha" Hines, whose career as soloist and band leader spanned fifty years and influenced, directly or indirectly, every jazz pianist who followed him.

Late in the winter of 1964, Earl "Fatha" Hines gave a concert at the Little Theatre, on West Forty-fourth Street, that is still mentioned with awe by those fortunate enough to have been there. The obstacles Hines faced that night were formidable. He was fifty-nine, an age when most jazz musicians have become slow-gaited; he had, except for a brief nightclub appearance, been absent from New York for ten years, and the occasional recordings that had floated east from Oakland, where he had settled, had done little to provoke demands for his return; and he had never before attempted a full-length solo recital—a feat that few jazz pianists, of whatever bent, have carried off. He met these hindrances by first announcing, when he walked on stage, that he was not giving a concert but was simply playing in his living room for friends, and by then performing with a brilliance that touched at least a part of each of his thirty-odd numbers. Not only was his celebrated style intact, but it had taken on a subtlety and unpredictability that continually pleased and startled the audience. Even Hines's face, which has the nobility often imparted by a wide mouth, a strong nose, and high cheekbones, was hypnotic. His steady smile kept turning to the glassy grimace presaging tears. His eyes—when they were open—were bright and pained, and his lower lip, pushed by a steady flow of grunts and hums, surged heavily back and forth. He made quick feints to the right and left with his shoulders, or rocked easily back and forth, his legs wide and supporting him like outriggers. Between numbers, that smile—one of the renowned lamps of show business—made his face look transparent. It was exemplary showmanship—not wrappings and tinsel but the gift itself, freely offered.

Not long after, Hines took a small band into Birdland for a week, and he stayed at the Taft Hotel. The Birdland gig had upset him: "Man, that's a hard job at Birdland," he said quickly and clearly. "It's ten to four, which I'm not used to anymore, and it wears me out. I got to bed at seven yesterday, but I had to be up and downtown for my cabaret card, then to a booking agency, then to a rehearsal for the Johnny Carson show. I didn't get to bed until six-thirty this morning, and then some damn fool called me at nine and said [his voice went falsetto], 'Is this Earl Hines, and did you write "Rosetta"?' I won't say what I said. So I'm a little stupid. I'm *breathing,* but I don't feel like jumping rope."

Hines was stretched out on his bed in his hotel room watching an old Edward G. Robinson movie on television. He had on white pajamas, a silver bathrobe, and brown slippers. A silk stocking hid the top of his head. The room was small and hot and cluttered with suitcases, and its single window faced a black air shaft. Hines's eyes were half shut and there were deep circles under them. "I haven't eaten yet, so I just ordered up some chicken-gumbo soup and a Western omelette and plenty of coffee and cream. It'll probably come by suppertime, the way room service goes here. Yesterday, I asked for ham and eggs for breakfast and they sent a ham steak and candied sweets and string beans and rolls, and when I called down, the man said he was two blocks from the kitchen and how could he help what the chef did?" Hines laughed—or, rather, barked—and rubbed a hand slowly back and forth across his brow. "I mean, I don't know what has caused New York to tighten up so. All the hotels—including this one—want musicians to pay in advance. My goodness, it's almost dog-eat-dog. Pittsburgh, where I'm from, is a country town compared to New York, where it takes every bit of energy to keep that front up. The streets are all littered up, and last night I go in the back door at Birdland and three guys are laying there, sick all over theirselves. Next time, I go in the front door, and two guys want a dime, a quarter. I've been all over this country and Canada and Europe, and how clean and nice they are. I'd be ashamed to tell people I was from New York. Maybe I been away from home too long. It's three months now. I finish this recording date I have with Victor tomorrow and the next day and—boom!—I'm off. Stanley Dance set up the Victor date. He's coming by around now with tapes of some records I made with my big band in the late thirties that Victor is bringing out again. He wants me to identify a couple of the soloists. My man Stanley."

There was a knock, and a portly, mustached man walked briskly in. He was carrying a small tape recorder. "Hey, Stanley," Hines said, and sat up straight.

"Did you get a good sleep?" Dance asked, in a pleasant Essex accent.

"Oh, people start calling at eight or nine again, but I'll sleep later, I'll rest later. I'm not doing *nothing* for a month when I get home."

"If it's all right, I'll play the tapes now, Earl." Dance put the machine on a luggage stand and plugged it in.

Hines stood up, stretched, and pummeled his stomach, which was flat and hard. "I haven't been sick since I was twelve years old. In the thirties, when we were on tour in the East, I'd work out with Joe Louis at Pompton Lakes. We'd sit on a fence a while and talk, and then we'd throw that medicine ball back and forth. That's why my stomach is so hard today." He sat down next to the tape recorder, crossed his ankles, clasped his hands in his lap, and stared at the machine. Dance started the tape. The first number, "Piano Man," was fast and was built around Hines's piano.

Hines listened attentively, his head cocked. "I haven't heard that in I don't know *how* long," he said. "That was a big production number in the show at the Grand Terrace, in Chicago, where I had my band from 1928 to 1940. I played it on a white grand piano and all the lights would go down, except for a spot on me and on each of the chorus girls, who were at tiny white baby grands all around me on the dance floor. When I played, they played with me—selected notes I taught them. Just now at the end I could picture the girls going off. Gene Krupa came in a lot, and he used that number for *his* show number—'Drummin' Man.' He just changed the piano parts to drum parts. I told him he was a Tom Mix without a gun." Hines laughed. "What's that!" he asked when the next number began.

"'Father Steps In.'" Dance said.

Hines hummed the melody with the band. A trumpet soloed. "That's Walter Fuller. He was my workhorse." An alto saxophone came in. "That's Budd Johnson, my Budd. He'll be down at Victor tomorrow. He usually played tenor." Hines scat-sang Johnson's solo note for note. "He sounds like Benny Carter there."

"G. T. Stomp," "Ridin' and Jivin'," and "'Gator Swing" went by. "The only trouble with this record, Earl, is there are so many fast tempos," Dance said.

"It was a very hot band. That's why the people were all so happy in those days. Nobody slept at the Grand Terrace. When we went on the road, the only band we had trouble with in all the cutting contests there used to be was the Savoy Sultans, the house group at the Savoy Ballroom, in Harlem. They only had eight pieces, but they could swing you into bad health. They'd sit there and listen and watch, and when you finished they'd pick up right where you'd left off and play it back twice as hard. We had a chance, we ducked them. *Everybody* did."

A waiter rolled in a table and placed it beside the bed. "Am I glad to see you, even if it is almost suppertime!" Hines barked, and he sat down on the bed. "Stanley, could we finish that after I've had something to eat? I only eat twice a day, and never between meals, and I get hungry. Take some coffee.

Did they bring enough sugar? I like a lot of sugar and cream." He opened a suitcase beside the night table and took out a two-pound box of sugar. "I never travel without my sugar bag. I learned that long ago." Hines filled a soup bowl from a tureen and buried the soup under croutons. Dance sipped a cup of coffee and watched Hines. "Earl, you were talking a bit the other day about what it was like to be the leader of a big band."

Hines looked up from his soup and put his spoon down. He wiped his mouth with a napkin. Then he picked up his spoon again. "An organization is no bigger than its leader, Stanley. You have to set an example—let them know *you* know what you're doing. An animal will fear you if you're leading, but you let down and he'll get you. Same thing with handling a big band. For that reason, I used to stay a little apart from the band, so there wouldn't be too much familiarity. But I had to be an understanding guy, a psychologist. I had to study each man, I had to know each man's ability. I'd be serious with one, joke with another, maybe take another out for a game of pool. Once in a while I'd give a little dinner for the band. But I was very strict about one thing. The band had to be on time, particularly on the road. There was a twenty-five-dollar fine if you missed the curtain in a theater, and a dollar a minute after that. It cost five dollars if you were late for the bus, and a dollar a minute after that. We even fined the bus driver if he was late. The fines worked so well, after a while I could take them off. As I said before, I've always stayed physically in condition. The band knew I'd fight at the drop of a hat, even though I had an even disposition. I believe the only time I lost my temper was on the road when a trombonist I had was bugging me and I picked him up and had him over my head and would have thrown him off the bus if the boys hadn't stopped me.

"The Grand Terrace was very beautifully done—a big ballroom with a bar in the back and mirrors on the walls, with blue lights fixed here and there on the glass. Those mirrors were like looking at the sky with stars in it. The bandstand was raised and had stairs coming down around both sides for the chorus girls and the show. The dance floor was also elevated. The Grand Terrace was the Cotton Club of Chicago, and we were a show band as much as a dance band and a jazz band. We worked seven days a week, and how we did it I don't know. There were three shows a night during the week and four on Saturday. The hours were nine-thirty to three-thirty, except on Saturday, when we worked ten to five. The chorus girls—we had fourteen or sixteen of them—were very important. They were ponies—middle-sized girls who were not overweight and could dance. Or they were parade girls, who were taller and more for just show. The chorus line, coming down the stairways, opened the show. Then there was a vocalist, he or she. A soft-shoe dancer or ballroom team came next. Then maybe a picture number, with fake African huts and a big fire and such. The highlight of the show was a special act, like the four Step Brothers or Ethel Waters or Bojangles, and then everyone on for the finale. Sometimes a comedian like Billy Mitchell took the dancers' spot. He had a trick of turning one foot all the way around, so that that foot pointed one way and the other the other way, and he'd walk along like it was nothing and bring down the house. It was always a good hot show, with everything jumping. The girls were its heart, and they really danced. They'd come off the floor wringing wet. They spent a lot of money on their costumes, and we always had two women backstage to put on buttons and fasten snaps and adjust new costumes that sometimes didn't arrive until half an hour before show time. I was a stickler for the boys in the band dressing, too, and we had a costume fund. One cause of my feeling for clothes was George Raft. I'd visit him in his hotel room when he was in town and he'd have three trunks of clothes. He'd tell me not to buy expensive suits—just suits that looked good—and to have plenty of them and change them all the time and that way they'd last. I had shoes made to fit my suits from the Chicago Theatrical Shoe store. They were dancers' shoes—sharp-looking, with round toes, and soft, so that they fitted like a glove. Wherever I went, they'd send a new pair if I needed them, because they had my measurements. A valet took care of my clothes, and there was another valet—a band valet—for the boys."

Hines emptied the tureen into his soup bowl. "The Grand Terrace was always in an orderly place. The audiences were mixed. Segregation never crossed anyone's mind. Friday nights we had college kids and we had to learn the college songs. Saturdays we got the office and shop people. Sunday was seventy-five percent colored, and Mondays were tourists. On Wednesdays we got elderly people and played waltzes. The racketeers owned twenty-five percent of the Grand Terrace, and they always had four or five men there—floating men. They never bothered us. 'We're here for your protection, boys,' they'd say. If they were going to run some beer from Detroit to Chicago, they'd figure the job out right in the kitchen. I'd be sitting there, but it was hear nothing, see nothing, say nothing if the cops came around. There was pistol play every night during Prohibition. No shooting; just waving guns around. I was heading for the kitchen one night and this guy went pounding past and another guy came up behind me and told me to stand still and rested a pistol on my shoulder and aimed at the first guy and would have fired if the kitchen door hadn't swung shut in time. Some of the waiters even had pistols. The racketeers weren't any credit to Chicago, but they kept the money flowing. My girl vocalist might make fifteen hundred a week in tips for requests, and she'd split it with the boys, and they'd put it in the costume fund. The racketeers owned me, too, and so did the man who controlled the other 75 percent of the Grand Terrace. This was something I didn't fully realize until late in the thirties. We were always paid in cash—one hundred and fifty a week for me and ninety apiece for the boys in the band. I couldn't complain. The Grand Terrace was our seat nine months of every year, and we had a nightly coast-to-coast radio hookup, which gave us solid bookings for the two or three months we were on the road. I couldn't afford to hire stars for the band, so I had to *make* my stars. In this way, I brought alone Ivie Anderson, the singer, and Ray Nance, the trumpet player. Duke Ellington took both of them from me. And I developed other singers, like Ida James and Herb Jeffries and Billy Eckstine and Sarah Vaughan, and I had musicians like Trummy Young and Budd Johnson and Dizzy Gillespie and Charlie Parker."

Hines exchanged his soup bowl for the Western omelette and poured more coffee. He chewed carefully. "We had a doctor at home, Dr. Martin, and he always said all your sickness derives from your stomach. I've never forgotten that. I was a wild kid in the twenties and thirties and I drank a lot, but what saved me was I always ate when I was drinking. The music publishers had something to do with my drinking. After we had our radio hookup, they'd come around every night, trying to get me to play this tune or that." Hines shifted into falsetto again: "'I got a little tune here, Earl, and I wish you'd play it and blah blah blah,' and then he'd buy me a drink and another publisher would buy me a couple of more drinks and I'd end up drinking all night and then I'd have to drink some more, if we had a record session early the next day, to keep going. I'd forget where I left my car, and I got so tired sometimes I'd put on shades and play whole shows asleep, with George Dixon, my sax man, nudging me when I was supposed to come in. I never considered myself a piano soloist anyway, so I was happy to just take my little eight bars and get off. It's the public that's pushed me out and made me a soloist. Then one night the owner of the Grand Terrace said, 'Earl, you're drinking yourself to death.' I thought about that and I decided he was right. When we went on the road soon after, I quit. I was all skin and bones. I bought a camera and took a picture of every pretty girl I saw to pass the time, and when I came back to Chicago I weighed one hundred and eighty-five. I only drink now after I'm finished work. But people *still* are after me to buy me drinks, and you hate to keep saying no. It almost agitates you."

Hines pushed his plate away and lit a big cigar. He arranged a couple of pillows against the headboard, leaned back, and swung his feet onto the bed. He puffed quietly, his eyes shut. "The excitement of the Grand Terrace days was something you couldn't realize unless you were there," he said, in a low voice. "It was a thrill when that curtain went up and us in white suits and playing and you knew you'd caught your audience. I bought my way out of the Grand Terrace in 1940 after I finally learned about all the money I was making and wasn't seeing. I kept the band together until 1948. By then it had twenty-four musicians and strings. But things were changing, with the entertainment tax and higher prices and fewer and fewer bookings in theaters and ballrooms. I saw the handwriting on the wall, and I disbanded and went with Louis Armstrong's All Stars. I didn't care for being a sideman again after all the years I'd spent building my reputation. Play some more of that tape, Stanley. Let me hear that band again."

Midway in the fourth or fifth number, Dance looked over at Hines. His cigar was in an ashtray on the night table, his eyes were shut, and his mouth was open. He was asleep.

HINES'S VIEW OF himself as reluctant soloist was surprising, for although he has spent a good part of his career as a leader of big and small bands, he is valued chiefly as a pianist. When he came to the fore in Louis Armstrong's celebrated 1928 recordings, the effect he created was stunning. No one had ever played the piano like that. Most jazz pianists were either blues performers, whose techniques were shaped by their materials, or stride pianists, whose oompah basses and florid right hands reflected the hothouse luxury of ragtime. Hines filled the space between these approaches with an almost hornlike style. He fashioned complex, irregular single-note patterns in the right hand, octave chords with brief tremolos that suggested a vibrato, stark single notes, and big flatted chords. His left hand, ignoring the stride pianists' catapult action, cushioned his right hand. He used floating tenths and offsetting, offbeat single notes, and he sometimes played counter-melodies. Now and then he slipped into urgent arrhythmic passages full of broken melodic lines and heavy offbeat chords. Hines and Louis Armstrong became the first jazz soloists to sustain the tension that is the secret of improvisation. Each of Hines's solos—particularly any that lasted several choruses—had a unity that was heightened by his pioneering use of dynamics. He italicized his most felicitous phrases by quickly increasing his volume and then as quickly letting it fall away. At the same time, he retained the emotional substance of the blues pianists and the head-on rhythms of the stride men. His earliest recordings still sound modern, and they must have been as shocking then as the atonal musings of Ornette Coleman first were.

That night at Birdland, Hines sat down at the piano ten minutes before the first set. The bandstand was dark and Hines unreeled a progression of soft, Debussy chords. He finished, and a couple of spotlights went on, but the illumination seemed to come from Hines himself. He was immaculate; his smile was permanently in place for the evening, and he was wearing a dark suit and a white shirt and dark shoes. His jet-black hair was flat and combed straight back, and he appeared as limber as a long-distance swimmer. Stanley Dance had pointed out that the group Hines happened to have at the moment was the sort of ingenuous, good-time, doubling-in-brass outfit that used to be a part of the stage show at the Apollo Theatre. It was, Dance had said, a surprising group—for Hines and for Birdland. It had a drummer and an organist, a male vocal trio, and a female alto saxophonist who sounded like Charlie Parker and who also sang. The next forty-five minutes were toally unpredictable, and Hines's assemblage soon seemed twice its actual size. The vocal trio sang together and separately; the organist soloed and sang a couple of numbers; the lady saxophonist not only emulated Charlie Parker but sang by herself or with the trio; the drummer took over for a long spell; and Hines, after eight-bar sips here and there, played a fifteen-minute solo medley. All this was executed with the precision of a Grand Terrace show, and when it was over, Hines was soaking wet. "I'm trying something nobody else is," he said, mopping himself. "I've had this group six months and I want to reach young and old. You play Dixieland, you get the old and drive away the young. You play modern, you get the young and keep away the old. A girl asked me last night, 'Are you Earl Hines's son? My mother used to listen to your dad at the Grand Terrace in 1930.' The young don't believe I'm me and the old are too tired to come and see. But I want both, and the manager has told me he's seen types of people in here all week he's never seen before. People have also said I'm crazy to have such a group, that the public wants to hear my piano, and that's why I put that medley in every show. This band is a kind of variation of what I was trying to do in my own club in Oakland, which opened last December. It had an international tinge. I had Irish and Chinese dancers and Italian and Japanese vocalists. I had Negro and Chinese and white waiters. I had Jewish musicians. I had Mexican and Chinese comedians. Then I found out one of my partners wasn't international and that the other didn't know much about show business, and I got out."

Hines ordered coffee, and lit a cigar. He was quiet for a while, then he said: "I don't think I *think* when I play. I have a photographic memory for chords, and when I'm playing, the right chords appear in my mind like photographs long before I get to them. This gives me a little time to alter them, to get a little clash or make coloring or get in harmony chords. It may flash on me that I can change an F chord to a D-flat ninth. But I might find the altering isn't working the way it should, so I stop and clarify myself with an off-beat passage, a broken-rhythm thing. I always challenge myself. I get out in deep water and I always try to get back. But I get hung up. The audience never knows, but that's when I smile the most, when I show the most ivory. I've even had to tell my bass player I'm going into the last eight bars of a tune because he wouldn't know where the hell I was. I play however I feel. If I'm working a pretty melody, I'll just slip into waltz time or cut the tempo in half. My mind is going a mile a minute, and it goes even better when I have a good piano and the audience doesn't distract me. I'm like a racehorse. I've been taught by the old masters—put everything out of your mind except what you have to do. I've been through every sort of disturbance before I go on the stand, but I never get so upset that it makes the audience uneasy. If one of my musicians is late, I may tell the audience when he arrives that I *kept* him off the stand because he needed a little rest. I always use the assistance of the Man Upstairs before I go on. I ask for that and it gives me courage and strength and personality. It causes me to blank everything else out, and the mood comes right down on me no matter how I feel. I don't go to church regularly, because I'm generally too tired from the hours I have to keep. I'd only fall asleep, and I don't believe in going just to say, yes, I go to church every Sunday. One Easter Sunday, I played in the Reverend Cobbs's church in Chicago—a standing-room-only church, he's so popular with his parishioners. I played 'Roses of Picardy.' They had three hundred voices in the choir. I played the first chorus; the choir hummed the second behind me and sang the lyrics on the third. Good God, it shook me up, the sound of those voices. I was nothing but goosepimples, and I stood right up off the piano stool. It was almost angelic."

HINES LOOKED FRESH and eager the next day. He was smoking a pipe and watching television, and he was wearing a black silk suit, a striped tan sports shirt, and pointed shoes trimmed with alligator leather. He had on a dark porkpie hat and dark glasses. Stanley Dance was telephoning. "He's checking Budd Johnson to make sure he's left for the studio," Hines said. He pointed to his glasses. "I wear these to shut out those photographers who turn up at every record session and seem like they're popping pictures of you from right inside the piano."

"Budd's on his way," Dance said. "And Jimmy Crawford and Aaron Bell are definite for drums and bass."

"Fine, fine, Stanley, bring that fake book, please, in case they ask me to play something I recorded forty years ago. Everybody but me remembers those tunes."

Hines leaned back in the cab and tilted his hat over his eyes. It was drizzling and the traffic was heavy. "Coming down in that elevator puts me in mind of Jack Hylton, the English bandleader, and the time he came to Chicago in the thirties. He was staying at the Blackstone and asked me if I'd come and see him. When I got there, the elevator man told me to take the freight elevator around back. Like a delivery boy. That upset me and I refused and pretty soon the assistant manager and the manager and Hylton's secretary and Hylton himself were all there and it ended in my going up in the front elevator. I don't say much about race, but it's always in the back of my head. I've tried to handle it by thinking things out up front and avoiding trouble if it can be avoided—like when I bought my house in Oakland four or five years ago. It has four bedrooms, a maid's room, family room, kitchen, parlor, and a fifty-foot patio in back. It's almost too much house. It was a white neighborhood before my wife and I and our two girls came, and I knew there might be trouble. The house belonged to a guy down on his luck and it was a mess inside and out. It's in an area where people keep their lawns nice, so before we moved in I painted the outside and installed a watering system and hired a Japanese gardener. I painted the inside and put in wall-to-wall carpets and drapes. When it was the best-looking place around, we moved in. We haven't had any trouble. But I've learned those precautions the long, hard way, beginning when we were the first big Negro band to travel extensively through the South. I think you could call us the first Freedom Riders. We stayed mostly with the Negro population and only came in contact with the Caucasian race if we needed something in a drug or dry-goods way. On our first tour, in 1931, we had a booker named Harry D. Squires. He booked us out of his hat, calling the next town from the one we'd just played and generally using his wits, like once when we got stopped for speeding. Squires told us before the cop came up, 'Now, we'll just tell him we're a young group and haven't had any work. So get out all your change and put it in a hat to show him what we're worth.' And that's just what we did. The cop got on the bus and we all sat there, looking forlorn and half starved and he looked in the hat, which had ten or twelve dollars in it, and he let us go. That was our first acting duty. Going South was an invasion for us. We weren't accustomed to the system, being from the North, and it put a damper on us. Things happened all the time. They made us walk in the street off the sidewalk in Fort Lauderdale, and at a white dance in Valdosta, Georgia, some hecklers in the crowd turned off the lights and exploded a bomb under the bandstand. We didn't none of us get hurt, but we didn't play so well after that, either. Sometimes when we came into a town that had a bad reputation, the driver would tell us—and here we were in our own chartered bus—to move to the back of the bus just to make it look all right and not get anyone riled up. We pulled into a gas station early one morning and a trombonist named Stevens got out to stretch his legs. He asked the gas-station attendant was it OK, and he said, 'Go ahead, but I just killed one nigger. He's layin' over there in the weeds. You don't believe me, take a look for yourself.' Stevens got back on the bus quick, and the next day we read about the killing in the papers. They had a diner at another gas station, and my guitarist, who was new and very, very light-skinned, ducked off the bus and went right into the diner. He didn't know any better and we didn't see him go in. When we'd gassed up, I asked our road manager, a Jewish fellow who was swarthy and very dark, to get us some sandwiches. The counterman took one look at him and wouldn't serve him, and my road manager glanced up and there was my guitarist at the counter, stuffing down ham and eggs. We never let that manager forget. It was a happening we kept him in line with the rest of the trip."

Hines laughed quietly and looked out of the window. It was raining heavily and the cab was crawling through Twenty-eighth Street. "We played a colored dance somewhere in Alabama and it worked out there was a gang of white people sitting back of us on the stage because there wasn't any more room on the floor. They'd been invited by the Negro who was giving the dance, since he worked for one of the whites. We'd only been playing fifteen minutes when along came this old captain, this sheriff man, and told me, 'You can't have those white people up there. You get them off that stage.' I said I didn't know anything about it. Fifteen minutes more and that cap'n was back. 'You and these niggers get out of here and out of this town. You have half an hour.' He escorted us personally to the town line. I found out later he knew all those white people, but they were the cream in the town and he was afraid to say anything to them, except to tell them after we'd gone that one of my boys had been looking at a white woman and that was why he drove us out. But I had me a victory in Tennessee. I went into a dry-goods store to buy some shirts. The clerk said, 'You want something, boy?' I told him. He took me to the cheapest section. I told him I wanted to see the best shirts he had. 'Where you from, boy, to ask for things like that?' I pointed at some ten-dollar silk shirts. 'Give me five of those,' I said. 'You want five of *those*?' He started to laugh and I showed him a fifty-dollar bill. After that, that man couldn't get enough of me. Money changed his whole attitude. Money shamed him. I spent close to eighty-five dollars, and when I came out all these local colored boys were looking in the front windows, noses on the glass. They said, 'You go in *there*? Don't *no one* go in there!' Well, those were the days when if you were a Negro and wanted to buy a hat and tried it on it was *your* hat whether it fitted or not.

"But there were good times, too. We were always seeing new territory, new beauty. In those days the country was a lot more open and sometimes we'd run into another band and just park the buses by the road and get out and play baseball in a field. We traveled by train, also, but buses were only twenty-eight cents a mile and you kept the same bus and driver throughout a whole tour. There was always a little tonk game on the bus at night. The boys put something for a table across the aisle and sat on Coke boxes and hung a flashlight from the luggage rack on a coat hanger. I generally sat on the right side about four seats back of the driver, where I kept an eye on things. They played most of the night, and it was amusing and something to keep you interested if you couldn't sleep. Our radio broadcasts made us well known after a while and sometimes we felt like a Presidential party. People would gather around the bus and say, 'Where's Fatha Hines? Where's Fatha Hines?' Fatha was a nickname given to me by a radio announcer we had at the Grand Terrace, and one I'd just as soon be shut of now. I had a kiddish face then and they expected an *old* man from my nickname, so I'd just slip into the hotel and maybe go into the coffee shop, but when these people found out who and where I was they'd come in and stand around and stare at me. Just stand and stare and not say anything, and if I looked up they'd pretend to be looking away in the distance."

HINES IS GREETED at the RCA Victor recording studio, which is on East Twenty-fourth Street, by Brad McCuen, an A&R man of Sydney Greenstreet proportions. Hines goes immediately into the studio, which is bright and chilly and thicketed with microphones. Jimmy Crawford is setting up his drums and Aaron Bell is putting rosin on his bow.

HINES (*in a loud, happy voice*): *O solo mio, o solo mio.* Hey, Craw, man. And Aaron. A *long* time, a *long* time. (*All shake hands warmly.*) We're going to do something today. But just leave all the doors open so we can git out when everything goes wrong.

CRAWFORD: You look wonderful, Earl. Just wonderful.

HINES: I feel like a million dollars. (*He takes off his coat and sits down at a grand piano and rubs his hands together and blows on them. McCuen leaves a list of prospective tunes and a large gold ashtray beside Hines, who lights a cigar. McCuen is followed into the control room by Dance, still carrying the fake book. A round, genial man enters the studio. He is dressed all in brown and has an Oriental face.*) My Budd. Budd Johnson. (*The two men embrace and laugh and pound one another. Hines returns to the piano and plays ad-lib chords, which gradually crystallize into a slow "It Had to Be You." Crawford and Bell join in. Hines has already vanished into what he is doing. His mouth is open slightly and his lower lip moves in and out. His face, disguised by his hat and glasses, looks closed and secret. A photographer comes out of the control room, lies down on the floor near Hines, and starts shooting pictures. Hines finishes two choruses and stops.*) Hey, Mr. Camera Man, would you mind waiting on that? You're getting me all nervous. (*The photographer retreats into the control room.*) You ready, Budd? Tenor would be nice for this. Rich and slow and warm. *Pretty* tenor. I'll take the first two choruses and you come in for one. I'll come back and you come in again for the last sixteen bars.

MCCUEN (*in a booming voice over the control-room microphone*): Ready to roll one, Earl?

HINES: Let's do one right away. (*After the last note dies away, Hines jumps up, laughs, snaps his fingers, and spins around.*) Ooooo-*wee*. Budd, how'd you like that ad-lib ending? I couldn't do that again to save my life. I didn't know if I was going to get out alive or not. Shoo, man.

MCCUEN: We'll play it back.

HINES: No, let's do another real quick. I feel it. Here we go. (*The second take is faster and the ending more precise.*) All right, let's hear *that*. (*The music comes crashing out of two enormous loudspeakers. Hines gets up and moves over beside the nearest wall. His hands hang loose at his sides. He throws back his head, opens his mouth, and listens. He is even more concentrated than when he plays. He doesn't move until the number ends. Then he does a little dance and laughs.*) I'll buy it. I'll buy it. Beautiful, Budd. Just beautiful. You can shut those doors now.

(*During the next couple of hours, the group does "I've Got the World on a String," "A Cottage for Sale," "Linger Awhile," and a fast original by Hines. Two or three takes suffice for each tune. Hines wastes no time, and after each play back he starts playing again.*)

HINES: "Wrap Your Troubles in Dreams." Budd, you rest on this one. We'll do about four choruses. (*The first take is indifferent, but on the second one Hines suddenly catches fire, moving with extraordinary intensity into the upper register in the third chorus and shaping the fourth chorus into a perfect climax.*)

MCCUEN: Let's try another, Earl. That opening wasn't quite right. (*Hines looks surprised, but immediately makes another take. After the playback, he shakes his head.*)

HINES: I don't know. Let's go again. (*In all, twelve takes, including false starts, are made. Each is slightly faster, and each time Hines appears less satisfied. The last take is replayed. Hines is leaning on an upright piano in the center of the studio, Bell and Johnson flanking him.*) You know, I don't feel it, I'm not *inside* that tune. I'm not bringing it *out*.

BELL: Earl, you know it's getting faster and faster?

HINES: Yeh? I didn't notice.

JOHNSON: Earl, you were *cookin'*, man, way back there on that second take, and they never did play it back for you.

HINES (*looking puzzled*): That right? Hey, Brad, can you play that *second* take for me. You never did, and I can't recall it. (*It is played, and slowly Hines's face relaxes. Johnson snaps his fingers and Bell nods his head.*) Budd, you got it, man. You were right. *That's* it, and we wasting all that time when the *good* one is just sitting there waiting to be heard. Man, I feel *young* again.

(*It is now almost six o'clock, and McCuen suggests that they meet again the next day. He thanks the musicians. Hines moves to the center of the stu-*

dio, lights a fresh cigar, and stretches his arms wide. Crawford and Bell and Johnson fall into a loose semicircle before him.)

HINES: Thank you, Craw, and Aaron. Just fine, man. Just fine. Budd, I haven't heard that baritone of yours in I don't know how long. You take Harry Carney's job away he doesn't look out. (*Johnson beams.*) The piano they got here makes it feel good, too. You play on a bad instrument and you want to take just eight bars and get out. *So* many clubs now have cheap pianos. It's the last thing the owners think of. They wouldn't put a well behind their bars and dip water out of it, instead of having faucets, so why do they have pianos that are cheap and out of tune?

JOHNSON: That's right, Earl.

BELL: Yeah, Earl.

HINES: In the forties, we played a place in Texas and they had a *miserable* piano. It was even full of water from a leak in the roof first night we were there. When the job was finished, Billy Eckstine and some of the boys decided to take that piano apart. Man, they clipped the strings and loosened the hammers and pulled off the keyboard and left it laying all over the floor. (*All laugh.*) I just finished four weeks in Canada, and the owner of that club must have had a hundred-dollar piano, it was so bad. And he had this fancy bandstand with a great big Buddha sitting on each side of it and they must of cost a *thousand* dollars apiece. I asked him, "Man, why do you spend all that money on Buddhas and decorations and not on a piano," and he answered blah blah blah, and got mad. Now, that's crazy.

CRAWFORD: Well, you told him, Earl.

HINES: It's the same thing nowadays with dressing rooms. No place to put on your makeup or rest and change your clothes between sets. (*Hines's voice has slowly grown louder and he is almost chanting. His listeners intensify their responses.*) They got one room down at Birdland, one small room, man, and we can't use it when Vi Redd—she's my saxophonist—goes in there, and when she's finished there's no time left anyway. I have to go back to the hotel between every set and change clothes. It's only a couple of blocks and I don't mind, but what if it snowing or raining and I catch my death?

JOHNSON: Earl, I was down to the Copa a while ago and it's the same there. You got to go out and walk the sidewalk.

HINES: That's what I mean. That's what I mean. You remember the old days all the theaters had good dressing rooms and places to sit down? Of course, these young musicians don't dress anyway, so maybe it doesn't matter. The band opposite me at Birdland, led by that young trumpet player—what's his name?

BELL: Byrd? Donald Byrd?

HINES: Yeh. Well, the first night they all dressed in different clothes and have scuffy shoes and no neckties. We come on, all spruced and neat—ties, of course—and you watch, the next night they got on ties and suits and their hair combed and they look *human*. And those young musicians don't know how to handle themselves before an audience. Never look at the audience or tell it what they're playing or smile or bow or be at all gracious. Just toot-toot-a-toot and look dead while the other guy is playing and get off. No wonder everybody having such a hard time all over. No one—not even Duke or Basie—raising any hell anymore. They just scuffling to keep the payroll going. That's why I have this different group, to reach the young people and teach them the old ways, the right ways, not the rock-and-roll ways. I've always helped the young people along, developed them, showed them how to dress and act and carry themselves properly. I've been at it so long I couldn't stop. Well, man, all we can do is be examples. A man can't do no more than that.

JOHNSON: Amen, Earl. Amen.

THE RAIN HAD stopped, and Hines found a cab on Third Avenue. He was still wound up from his oration and the recording session, and he sat on the edge of his seat, puffing at his cigar. "Why didn't somebody tell me I still had these dark glasses on? I wondered why I couldn't see anything when I came out of that building. The reason I've always looked out for the young people, I guess, is because my dad always looked out for me. I don't think there was anyone else in the world who brought up their chlidren better than my mother and dad. We lived in Duquesne, where I was born, and my mother was a housewife. My dad started on a hoisting machine—or histing machine, as they called it—on the coal docks and worked his way up to foreman. He was a loosely type fellow. He never chastised me for the medium things, and I didn't have over four solid whippings from him. I never was brought in at night at the time the average kid in my neighborhood was, and it looked like I was let run helter-skelter and my dad was criticized for that, but he defended himself by saying if you don't chastise your child continually he will confide in you. When I was twelve, he sat down with me one night at evening table after my mother had gone out and told me I was too old to whip anymore and how to conduct myself. 'I'm not a wealthy man,' he told me. 'So I can't get you out of serious trouble.' He told me *everything* that night—about all the different kinds of women and men I'd come up against, and how to tell the good from the bad, about thinking you're outsmarting someone else when he's probably outsmarting *you*, about staying on lighted streets at night, and such as that. It gave me the confidence that's always guided me. A lot of the children of strict parents where I grew up ended in jail. The exceptions were far and few.

"My family was very musical. My mother was an organist and my dad played cornet. My uncle knew all the brass instruments and my auntie was in light opera. My dad was also the leader of the Eureka Brass Band, which played for picnics and dances and outings. I was nine or ten when I was taken on my first outing. We traveled from McKeesport about twelve miles in four open trolleys, which were chartered. The band rode the first trolley and played as we went. After the picnic there was dancing in a hall and the children who were allowed to stay were sent up to a balcony, where they had a matron to watch us. Some of the kids roughhoused, but I just leaned over the rail and listened and watched. It was such a pretty thing to see all those people dancing and flowing in one direction. The men seemed so pleasant to the women and the women back to the men. My mother started teaching me the piano when I was very young. I also tried the cornet, after my dad, but it hurt me behind the ears to blow, so I gave it up. I had my first outside piano lessons when I was nine, from a teacher named Emma D. Young, of McKeesport. My next teacher, Von Holz, was German and pretty well advanced. I was studying to be a classical artist. I loved the piano and I was always three or four lessons ahead in my book. My auntie lived in Pittsburgh, and when I went to Schenley High School, where I majored in music, I lived with her. I was interested in conducting and watched the directors of pit orchestras every chance I got. And I memorized all the music I heard, some of it even before the sheet music came out. When I was about thirteen, my life changed. I had a cousin and an uncle who were play-time boys and they used to take me downtown to the tenderloin section with them. I was tall and they fitted me out in long trousers. The first time they took me to the Leader House, which had dancing upstairs and a restaurant downstairs, I heard this strange music and I heard the feet and the beat and so much laughter and happiness I asked my uncle and cousin could I go upstairs and listen. They put a Coca-Cola in my hand and I did. Pittsburgh was a wide-open town and there wasn't such a ban then on children going into clubs. A hunchback fellow named Toadlo was playing the piano. He was playing 'Squeeze Me,' and singing. His playing turned me around completely. It put rhythm in my mind, and I went home and told my auntie that that was the way I wanted to play. In the meantime, I was shining shoes and had learned barbering and for the first time I had enough money to get around. I formed a little trio, with a violinist and a drummer, and then Lois B. Deppe, who was a well-known Pittsburgh singer and bandleader, hired me and my drummer for his band at the Leader House. It was summer and I talked to my dad and he said it was all right and I went to work. Fifteen dollars a week and two meals a day. Toadlo still worked there, and so did a pianist named Johnny Watters. He was dynamic. He was more advanced than Toadlo. He could stretch fourteen notes with his right hand and play a melody at the same time with his middle fingers. He liked Camels and gin and in the afternoons I'd buy him a pack of cigarettes and a double shot of gin and we'd go upstairs at the Leader House, and he would show me. Then, at a party, I heard a piano player named Jim Fellman playing tenths with his left hand, instead of the old oompah bass. It was so easy and rhythmic. *He* liked beer and chewed Mail Pouch, so I got him upstairs at the Leader House, too, and he showed me those tenths. I got my rhythmic training from a banjoist named Verchet. He was a musical fanatic. He tried to make his banjo sound like a harp, and he had all these nuts and bolts for tightening and loosening the strings, only the damn thing always fell apart when he played. His instrument case was full of tools and he sounded like a plumber when he picked it up. But he was a heck of a critic of tempo. He'd sit there, strumming like lightning and rocking back and forth in half time, and if I got away from the beat, he'd say, 'Watch-it-boy, watch-it-boy.' So I began to form my little style. I still had the idea of the cornet in my head and I would try things that I might have played on the cornet—single-note figures and runs that were not ordinary then on the piano. And I hit on using octaves in the right hand, when I was with a band, to cut through the music and be heard."

The cab stopped in front of the hotel. Upstairs, Hines ordered a bottle of Scotch and ice and glasses. Then he took off his hat for the first time that afternoon and flopped down on the bed. He looked tired but pleased. "That Budd Johnson is something, isn't he, Stanley? He was a playing a fool today. He was in my big band almost ten years. But I've always been lucky in my musicians. I formed my first band in 1924 and Benny Carter played baritone in it and his cousin Cuban Bennett was on trumpet. He was a *great* trumpet player, but nobody remembers him. We went into the Grape Arbor, in Pittsburgh, and stayed there several months. Eubie Blake used to come through town once in a while, and the first time I met him he told me. 'Son, you have no business here. You got to leave Pittsburgh.' He came through again while we were at the Grape Arbor, and when he saw me, he said, 'You *still* here? I'm going to take this cane'—he always carried a cane and wore a raccoon coat and a brown derby—'and wear it out all over your head if you're not gone when I come back.' I was. That same year, I went to Chicago to the Elite No. 2 Club, an after-hours place. Teddy Weatherford, the pianist, was *it* in Chicago then, and soon people began telling him, 'There's a tall, skinny kid from Pittsburgh plays piano. You better hear him.' Teddy and I became friends, and we'd go around together and both play and people began to notice me. They even began to lean toward me over Teddy. Louis Armstrong and I first worked together in the Carroll Dickerson orchestra at the Sunset. Louis was the first trumpet player I heard who played what *I* had wanted to play on cornet. I'd steal ideas from him and he'd steal them from me. He'd bend over after a solo and say way down deep in that rumble, 'Thank you, man.' Louis was wild and I was wild, and we were inseparable. He was the most happy-go-lucky guy I ever met. Then Louis and I and Zutty Singleton, who was also with Dickerson, formed our own group. We were full of jokes and were always kidding each other. We drove around in this old, broken-down automobile we had, and when we got home after work we'd leave it parked in the middle of the street or in front of someone else's house. But there wasn't *that* much work and we like to starve to death, making a dollar or a dollar and a half apiece a night. So we drifted apart, and I worked for Jimmy Noone for a year, and then I went to New York to make some QRS piano rolls. I had a little band rehearsing at the same time, and it was then I got a call to come and open up the Grand Terrace."

The whiskey and ice and glasses arrived. Dance gave Hines a brandy from a bottle on the dresser and poured himself a Scotch-and-water. Hines lifted his glass in the air. "This is for Stanley. If it hadn't been for him, I'd probably be out of this business now. I was ready to quit about a year ago. In fact, my wife and I were talking about opening a little shop out on the Coast. But Stanley kept after me on that long-distance phone, and persuaded me to come here last winter, and then he set up the record session. I was down low again when I got here last week. But something *good* happened today, and it's going to happen tomorrow. I try never to worry. The greatest thing to draw wrinkles in a man's face is worry. And why should I be unhappy and pull down my face and drag my feet and make everybody around me feel that way too? By being what you are, something always comes up. Sunshine always opens out. I'll leave for the Coast day after tomorrow in my car, and I'll stop and see my mother in Duquesne. My sister, Nancy, and my brother, Boots, still live with her. I'll see my mother-in-law in Philadelphia and she'll give me a whole mess of fried chicken. I'll put that on the seat beside me, along with those cigars and my pipe and pipe tobacco and a map and a gallon jug of water. I'll open the window wide and keep my eye on the road. Stanley, let me have a little more of that brandy, please."

The Poet: Bill Evans

Gene Lees

Gene Lees has been a strong presence in jazz as critic, editor, and lyricist. He is equally fierce as advocate and enemy—outspoken, passionate, even polemical. Perhaps he is at his formidable best in his appreciations of those major figures with whom he has been personally involved, one of whom is the unique Bill Evans. From the 1988 collection Meet Me at Jim and Andy's.

It is a commonplace of psychology that people remember very precisely the circumstances in which they learned of certain historic events—for Americans, the death of John F. Kennedy, in China the death of Mao Tse-tung. A great many musicians and other music lovers can recall with comparable vividness their discovery of Bill Evans.

In 1963, in Auckland, New Zealand, a fifteen-year-old boy, hearing piano music emanating from a shop, entered, listened to his first Bill Evans record, and burst into tears. This event changed the course of Alan Broadbent's life. He went on to become one of the finest jazz pianists in a generation of players influenced by Evans. And more than twenty years later, he recalled that moment of discovery as if it had been a week ago.

I recall my own discovery of Evans with similar clarity. It occurred in the early summer of 1959, shortly after I joined *Down Beat.* In the office, I noticed among a stack of records awaiting assignment for review a gold-covered Riverside album titled *Everybody Digs Bill Evans,* bearing the signed endorsements of Miles Davis, Cannonball Adderley, Ahmad Jamal, and others of like stature. I took the album home and, sometime after dinner, probably about nine o'clock, put it on the phonograph. At 4 A.M. I was still listening, though by now I had it memorized.

I remember my amazement not so much at the brilliance of the playing—itself cause enough for wonder—as at the emotional content of the music. Until then I had assumed, albeit unconsciously, that I alone had the feelings therein expressed. His playing spoke to me in an intensely personal way. And as the years have gone by, I have discovered that he had the same effect on many people. Martin Williams, in his annotation to the complete set of Bill's Riverside recordings, reissued by the Fantasy label in 1984, refers to Bill's as "some of the most private and emotionally naked music I have ever heard."

Music is the art that expresses the inexpressible, the language beyond language that communicates what words can never convey, summoning shades of emotion for which we have no words. The Eskimo language is said to contain sixteen or so words for snow, since the people speaking it have need for such refined expression of the conditions they encounter. Our vocabulary for the nuances of emotion is inadequate, though we can somewhat compensate for this by creating compound words such as happy-sad, wistful-joyous, surprised-pleased, and the like. But music can go beyond that. It doesn't and of course can't name these subtle nameless emotions. It can evoke them.

And no one had ever evoked emotions that I feel the way Bill Evans did. Since he has had this effect on so many other people, many of whom are fanatic in their admiration of his work, musicians and laymen alike, one faces the inescapable conclusion that Bill Evans was "saying" something in his music of prodigious pertinence to our era and the people doomed to live in it.

Within a day or two of hearing *Everybody Digs,* I wrote Bill a fan letter. I recall saying that the album sounded like love letters written to the world from some prison of the heart. It struck me even then that to anyone of the sensitivity so manifest in the music, life must be extraordinarily painful—which turned out to be all too true.

I decided to put Bill on the cover of *Down Beat,* and assigned the New York writer Don Nelson, who knew him, to write the accompanying article. I myself wanted to know more about this young man from Plainfield, New Jersey. Bill always gave credit to this exposure for helping to loft his recording career, but I think he exaggerated the value of that article, and the many others that I wrote about him afterwards. His career would have crested inevitably because of that peculiar power he had to move people. To this day, people are extraordinarily possessive about him, so many of his admirers seeming to believe that he or she alone perceives and appreciates his music. This possessiveness is an odd phenomenon, without any precedent that I know.

Oscar Peterson had raised the level of playing the piano in jazz to the proficiency long the norm in classical music. One musician made his apt observation: "It was said in their own time that Liszt conquered the piano, Chopin seduced it. Oscar is our Liszt and Bill is our Chopin." The poetry of Bill's playing compels the comparison to Chopin, whose music, incidentally, Bill played exquisitely. The pattern of chords in eighth notes in "Young and Foolish" on *Everybody Digs,* for example, recalls the Chopin E-minor Prelude. Bill certainly knew the literature. I once saw him, in Warren Bernhardt's apartment, sitting with his head down over the keyboard of Warren's Steinway, in that characteristic posture, sight-reading Rachmaninoff preludes at tempo. Oscar Peterson brought jazz piano to the bravura level of the great Romantic pianists. Bill, influenced by Oscar in his early days, brought to bear coloristic devices and voicings and shadings from post-Romantic composers, including Debussy, Ravel, Poulenc, Scriabin, and maybe Alban Berg. After listening to a test pressing of *Conversations with Myself* that I had sent him, Glenn Gould phoned to say of Bill, "He's the Scriabin of jazz." I had no idea whether Bill was even that familiar with Scriabin, but sure enough, he turned out to be a Scriabin buff, and gave me a soft and enormously enlightening dissertation on that Russian, whose mysticism seemingly appealed to a like element in Bill's own half-Russian half-Welsh soul.

I quoted that remark of Gould's in print, only to have my friend the noted classical music critic Robert Offergeld take issue with it. "More to the point," Bob said, "he was the Bill Evans of jazz. He could produce a broader range of tonal color in thirty-two measures than Glenn Gould did in his whole career."

Bill managed to blend in his playing sophisticated methods with a trusting youthful emotionality, almost like the music of Grieg. I was discussing Grieg with Bill once, specifically the lovely *Holberg Suite.* "I went through a phase of pretending I didn't like Grieg," I said.

"So did I," Bill said.

And, anticipating his answer, I said, "I know what happened to me, but what happened to you?"

"The intellectuals got to me," he said.

The mood of the *Everybody Digs* album is one of springtime lilac poignancy. It is the second Riverside album. *New Jazz Conceptions,* which preceded it, is brittle by comparison. Bill had electrified the profession before that with solos on "All About Rosie," a tune in a record by Tony Scott, and "Billy the Kid" by his composer friend George Russell.

Something happened in the two years between *New Jazz Conceptions* (September 1956) and *Everybody Digs* (December 1958): Bill found his way into the heart of his own lyricism. After that Bill formed a standing trio, with bassist Scott LaFaro and drummer Paul Motian, with which group Orrin Keepnews produced a series of Riverside albums that constitute one of the most significant bodies of work in the history of jazz.

Bill wanted it to be a three-way colloquy, rather than pianist-accompanied-by-rhythm-section. And it was. LaFaro, still in his early twenties, had developed bass playing to a new level of facility. He had a gorgeous tone and unflagging melodicism. Motian, Armenian by background, had since childhood been steeped in a music of complex time figures and was able to feed his companions patterns of polyrhythm that delighted them both.

Pianists waited for their albums to come out almost the way people gather at street-corners in New York on Saturday night to get the Sunday *Times*. *Portrait in Jazz, Explorations,* and the last two, *Waltz for Debby* and *Sunday at the Village Vanguard,* derived from afternoon and evening sessions recorded live on June 25, 1961. These albums alone (which are best heard in the compact-disc reissues from Fantasy, which have superb sound), if Bill had never recorded anything else, would have secured his position in jazz. Indeed, his solo on Johnny Carisis's tune "Israel," a soaring flight of breathtaking melodic invention, which is in the *Explorations* album, would almost have done that. There is a deep spirituality in those Riverside albums, the more astounding when you realize that Bill was at that time sinking into his heroin addiction, to Scott LaFaro's helpless dismay. If you look at the album covers in sequence, you find Bill's face getting thinner.

In the photo taken for the interior cover of *Undercurrent,* the duet album he made with Jim Hall for the UA label a couple of years later, you can see a tell-tale Band-Aid on Bill's right wrist.

WARREN BERNHARDT SAID of Bill in 1963, "Everything he plays seems to be the distillation of the music. In 'How Deep Is the Ocean,' he never states the original melody. Yet his performance is the quintessence of it. On 'My Foolish Heart,' he plays nothing but the melody, but you still receive that essence of the thing.

"Pianistically, he's beautiful. He never seems to be hung up in doing anything he wants to do, either technically or harmonically. When he's confronted with a choice in improvisation, he doesn't have to wonder which voicing of a chord is best. He *knows.* A given voicing will have different effects in different registers, especially when you use semitones as much as he does. So he constantly shifts voicings, depending on the register. And he is technically capable of executing his thought immediately. It's as if the line between his brain and his fingers were absolutely direct."

"It's reached the point," Bill said, "where I'm seldom conscious of the physical effort of playing. I simply think, and there's no conscious transmission to the fingers."

Bill had his clichés, as every jazz musician does. But they were very much his. Many pianists have adopted them, and still more have tried. He was far and away the most influential jazz pianist after Bud Powell. And he used his various configurations in interesting combinations. There were, however, times when he seemed stuck in them. Had I not known of what he was capable, I would doubtless have found these performances marvelous. But his work at such times bored me, a fact I always tried to conceal from him, although he probably knew. Perhaps he too was bored by it.

There was something special in *Everybody Digs* that had been lost. And he seemed to want to combine both qualities.

BILL WAS ONE of those elegantly coordinated people. His posture and his bespectacled mien made him seem almost fragile, but stripped, he was, at least in his thirties, strong and lean, with well-delineated musculature. He had played football in college, he was a superb driver with fine reflexes (who, like Glenn Gould, had a taste for snappy cars), he was a golfer of professional stature, and he was, by all testimony, a demon pool shark.

When he was young, he looked like some sort of sequestered and impractical scholastic. There is a heartbreaking photo of him on the cover of the famous Village Vanguard recordings, made for Riverside in the early summer of 1961. Whether that photo was taken before or after the grim fiery death of Scott LaFaro in an automobile accident ten days after the sessions, I do not know. But there is something terribly vulnerable and sad in Bill's young, gentle, ingenuous face. I knew Scott LaFaro only slightly, through Bill, and I didn't like him. He seemed to me smug and self-congratulatory. But he was a brilliant bass player, as influential on his instrument as Bill was on his, and Bill always said LaFaro was not at all like that when you got past the surface, which I never did. The shock of LaFaro's death stayed with Bill for years, and he felt vaguely guilty about it. This is not speculation. He told me so. He felt that because of his heroin habit he had made insufficient use of the time he and Scott had had together. LaFaro was always trying to talk him into quitting. After LaFaro's death, Bill was like a man with a lost love, always looking to find its replacement. He found not so much a replacement of LaFaro as an alternative in the virtuosic Eddie Gomez, who was with him longer than any other bassist.

In any event, to look into that face, with its square short small-town-America 1950s haircut, is terribly revealing, particularly when you contrast it with Bill's later photos. He looked like the young WASP in those days, which he never was—he was a Celtic Slav—but in the later years, when he had grown a beard and left his hair long in some sort of final symbolic departure from Plainfield, New Jersey, he looked more and more Russian, which his mother was. She used to read his Russian fan mail to him, and answer it. Russian jazz fans, I am told, think of him as their own.

Bill was politically liberal and passionately anti-racist. His speech was low level, but he was highly literate and articulate. He was expert on the novels of Thomas Hardy, and he was fascinated with words and letters and their patterns. The title "Re: Person I Knew," one of his best-known compositions, is an anagram on the name of Orrin Keepnews, who produced for Riverside all Bill's early albums and was one of his first champions. Another of Bill's titles, "N.Y.C.'s No Lark," is an anagram on the name of Sonny Clark, who Bill said was one of his influences, along with Nat Cole and Oscar Peterson and Bud Powell.

Bill's knowledge of the entire range of jazz piano was phenomenal. Benny Golson says that when he first heard Bill—they were both in their teens—he played like, of all people, Milt Buckner. One night late at the Village Vanguard in New York, when there was almost no audience, Bill played about ten minutes of "primitive" blues. "I can really play that," he said afterwards with a sly kind of little-boy grin. And he could.

He had a big technique. I doubt if anyone in the history of jazz piano had more. Yet he never, never showed off those chops for the mere display of them. He kept technique in total subservience to expression. But he assuredly had it.

One of the greatest glories of his playing was his tone. Trilingual people will often be found to speak their third language with the accent of the second. I suspect this phenomenon may carry over into music. Oscar Peterson learned to play trumpet almost as soon as he learned piano, which may in part explain his brilliant projecting sound. Bill was a fine flutist, although he rarely if ever played the instrument in the later years.

The level of his dynamics was often kept low, like his speech. He was a soft player. But within that range, his playing was full of subtle dynamic shadings and constantly shifting colors. Some physicists have argued that a pianist cannot have a personal and individual "tone" because of the nature of the instrument, which consists of a bunch of felt hammers hitting strings. So much for theory. It is all in how the hammers are made to strike the strings, as well of course as the more obvious effects of pedaling, of which Bill was a master.

Bill's was a comparatively flat-fingered approach, as opposed to the vertical hammer-stroke attack with which so many German piano teachers tensed up the hands and ruined the playing of generations of American children. Bill used to argue with me that his playing was not all that flat-fingered, but I sat low by the keyboard on many occasions and watched, and it certainly looked that way to me. On one such occasion, I kidded him about his rocking a finger on a key on a long note at the end of a phrase. After all, the hammer has already left the string: one has no further physical contact with the sound. "Don't you know the piano has no vibrato?" I said.

"Yes," Bill responded, "but trying for it affects what comes before it in the phrase." That is more than a little mystical, but he was right. Dizzy Gillespie and Lalo Schifrin were once in Erroll Garner's room at the Chateau Marmont in Los Angeles. Erroll was putting golf balls into a cup against the wall. Dizzy asked if he might try it, took Erroll's putter, and sank one ball after another, to the amazement of Erroll and Lalo, who asked if he had played a lot of golf. He said he had never done it before. How, then, was he doing it? "I just imagine," Dizzy said, "that I'm the ball and I want to be in the cup." He with a golf ball and Bill with a vibrato influencing events in time already past were, deliberately or no, practicing something akin to Zen archery.

Bill did not always have that sound, or more precisely that astonishing palette of colors. Sometime before he recorded *Everybody Digs,* he took a year off and went into comparative reclusion to rebuild his tone, with which he was dissatisfied. I doubt that he consciously sought to be flute-like, but some ideal derived from playing that other instrument surely was in his conception. Whatever the process, the result of that year was the golden sound that in recent years has often been emulated though never equaled.

And that year was typical of him.

He made absolutely no claims for himself. Orrin Keepnews had a hard time talking him into making his first album as a leader, *New Jazz Conceptions,* in late 1956, when Bill was twenty-eight. It is, incidentally, a remarkable album even now, a highly imaginative excursion through bebop, in which we hear strong hints of the Bill Evans that he would within two years become. When Orrin gathered those testimonials from Miles Davis and the rest for the cover of *Everybody Digs,* Bill said, "Why didn't you get one from my mother?" But what he was—an emergent genius—was apparent to every musician with ears. Credit for the earliest discovery goes to Mundell Lowe, who heard him in New Orleans when Bill was still an undergraduate at Southeastern Louisiana College. (He was graduated as an honor student with two degrees, Bachelor of Music with a piano major, and Bachelor of Music Education.) Mundell hired him for summer jobs during that period.

Bill always disliked formal practice and evaded it in childhood. He would play through a huge pile of secondhand sheet music his mother had bought. It contained sentimental turn-of-the-century songs, marches, and classical music. Because of that experience, Bill was an uncanny sight-reader.

He retained his cavalier attitude to practice even at Southeastern Louisiana. His teachers found his attitude frustrating and infuriating. He would turn up at classes unable to play the scales and arpeggios assigned him but able to execute flawlessly any composition that contained them. "They couldn't flunk me," he said in what for him was an intemperate burst of immodesty, "because I played the instrument so well." And now that same college houses the Bill Evans Archives.

"It's just that I've played such a *quantity* of piano," he said. "Three hours a day in childhood, about six hours a day in college, and at least six hours now. With that, I could afford to develop slowly. Everything I've learned, I've learned with feeling being the generating force.

"I've never approached the piano as a thing in itself but as a gateway to music. I knew what I wanted to play. But I relaxed with it, knowing I would be able to eventually."

Whereas many jazz musicians build solos in sections of four, eight, or sixteen bars, Bill seemed able to think in units as large as or larger than the full thirty-two-bar chorus. He would obliterate the chorus unit, building an entire solo into a seamless whole. To be sure, there was not as much form as one would find in classical music.

"Obviously," Bill said, "you can't find in jazz the perfection of craft that is possible in contemplative music. Yet, oddly enough, this very lack of perfection can result in good jazz. For example, in classical music, a mistake is a mistake. But in jazz, a mistake can be—in fact, must be—justified by what follows it. If you were improvising a speech and started a sentence in a way you hadn't intended, you would have to carry it out so that it would make sense. It is the same in spontaneous music.

"In good contemplative composition, the creator tries to *recapture* those qualities—the trouble is that there are a lot of so-called composers who compose primarily by putting together tones in a logical structure they have set up. But spontaneous material can be worked over and developed, according to the limits of the person's craft. And the result will in some way be in touch with the universal language of understanding in music."

"If," I asked, "through travel in a time machine, you could hear Beethoven or Chopin improvising, would you call it jazz?"

"Jazz is not a what," Bill said, "it is a how. If it were a what, it would be static, never growing. The how is that the music comes from the moment, it is spontaneous, it exists at the time it is created. And anyone who makes music according to this method conveys to me an element that makes his music jazz."

Bill said once, "I had to work harder at music than most cats, because you see, man, I don't have very much talent."

The remark so astonished me that some ten years later, I challenged him on it.

"But it's true," he said. "Everybody talks about my harmonic conception. I worked very hard at that because I didn't have very good ears."

"Maybe working at it is the talent," I said. Like working on the reconstruction of his tone for a year. The bassist Ray Brown remarked once, "They," meaning, I suppose, jazz fans and some critics, "think we just roll out of bed and play the D-major scale." The implication was that major musicians, major artists of all kinds, work very hard at their craft. Perhaps that is what makes the difference, as Bill intimated. He once told me that when he and the late Don Elliott, a friend during their adolescence in New Jersey, were in high school, they knew several young musicians they thought were more talented than they. But those young players to whom it had come so easily all dropped out of music, while Don and Bill remained in the profession to join the ranks of its serious practitioners—perhaps because they had the deeper fascination with its mysteries.

I DO NOT for a moment pretend objectivity about the life and work of Bill Evans. I was much too involved in it, at several levels. It went far beyond that first *Down Beat* cover. One of the most important relationships of his life was with Helen Keane, tall and blonde and Nordic, who became first his manager and later his record producer as well. I introduced them in 1962. The three of us profoundly affected each other's lives. Like many men, I am reticent to discuss personal relationships, but Helen talked about ours in an interview with Linda Dahl for the book *Stormy Weather,* a collection of essays about women in jazz, so it's no secret.

She told Dahl, "Along the way I met . . . Gene Lees. He had just left his editorship at *Down Beat*. After he came to New York, we fell in love and we were together for years. Right away he said, 'I want you to hear Bill Evans . . . You should be his manager.'"

In that summer of 1962 I found Bill's life and career in hideous disarray. Due to an error of the American Federation of Musicians, he had validated contracts with two managers, one of whom was the late Joe Glaser, president of Associated Booking Corporation and Louis Armstrong's personal manager. Glaser was a harsh and rather crude man with known underworld associations. He and his company, which made capital of Armstrong's showboating, were indifferent to an artist of Bill's sensitivity, if indeed anyone in that office was capable of perceiving it. And Bill was in the worst phase of his narcotics habit, borrowing money wherever he could.

He played a gig at the Hickory House on 52nd Street. His bassist on that job was Hal Gaylor, an excellent player from Montreal who had been with Chico Hamilton and Tony Bennett. Hal, about six feet tall, had very large and sinewy hands, full of the strength that years of playing the bass impart.

Bill was late for the job one night.

"I knew where he was," Hal recalled in 1987. "He was down at this guy's apartment in the Village, getting his stuff. I knew where he was because I used to pick him up there. And I used to cop there myself." Hal was at that time an occasional heroin user. Later he became firmly addicted, then kicked his habit and now works as a drug counselor in Monroe County, New York. "I went down there, and the guy had just got in his shipment. And he was toying with Bill, playing games with him. I could see that Bill was sick, and I just wigged. I banged the table, the stuff flew up in the air, and I grabbed this guy. I scared him—scared myself, too. The guy's wife was screaming, it was a bad scene, and Bill was just sitting there, sick. I told the guy, 'You fix him up, right *now!* Or I'm going to blow all this stuff away!' So the guy gave Bill his bag, and we left. Bill did it up right in the car."

One day Bill came out of the office of Riverside Records in midtown Manhattan, having just borrowed some money from Orrin Keepnews. He got into a taxi to head for his connection. Another well-known musician, also an addict, opened the taxi door, grabbed the money out of Bill's hand, and ran off.

I was only too aware of the sordid conditions of Bill's life—of the pushers, including one named Bebop who came to Bill's apartment one day while I was there, and of the loan sharks threatening to break his hands if he did not immediately repay the money he'd borrowed for his habit.

I felt that Helen Keane was one of the most conscientious and capable talent managers in the business. At that time she was Mark Murphy's manager. She had been substantially instrumental in launching the careers of Marlon Brando and Harry Belafonte. I took her to see Bill at the Village Vanguard.

"Oh no," she said, after she'd heard about sixteen bars, "oh no, not this one. This is the one that could break my heart." How prophetic that remark turned out to be. Nonetheless, when we went back uptown and sat in a back booth in Jim and Andy's and talked about Bill, she agreed to manage him, assuming that he was willing to have her do so, which I knew he was.

But there was the problem of his contracts with the two other managers. Bill got copies of the contracts for me. I telephoned the late Herman Kenin, then president of the American Federation of Musicians, with whom I was on cordial terms. I had done some favors for the union and, as they say in New York, he owed me. I asked him to have lunch with me. Toward the end of the lunch I showed him the two contracts, bearing union validations.

"There's no doubt about it," Herman said. "The union made a mistake. Which contract do you want cancelled?"

"Both of them," I said, and Herman Kenin annulled the contracts, opening the way for Helen Keane to become Bill's manager.

BILL FOLLOWED A daily routine at that time. He would go into a telephone booth—the phone in his apartment on West 104th Street was usually disconnected—and leaf through his address book, calling one friend after another. One day Bob Brookmeyer lost his patience and told him angrily, "How come you only call me when you want to borrow money?"

Bill phoned me late one afternoon. I was going through a tough time of it myself. He asked if I could lend him ten dollars. Remembering Brookmeyer, I too lost my temper and said, "God damn it, I don't even have enough money to eat tonight!" and hung up on him.

Perhaps an hour later the phone rang again. I heard that low-key voice. "Gene? This's Bill. I got enough money for both of us. Let's go and eat."

During this period, Bill's wife, Ellaine, of whom I was extremely fond, made a valiant attempt to get them both off dope. In an amazing display of strength, she quit using, and composed a pledge that she tried to get Bill to sign—a promise that he too would quit. One severe winter night, probably in January or February of 1962, I went up to their apartment. The three of us had planned to go to a movie, but it was obvious that Bill had no intention of going anywhere. Ellaine, fiercely angry, insisted that I take her anyway. Bill urged us to go. We went to some movie house on 42nd Street, which had not then been taken over by the porn industry, although it was seedy enough. Afterwards, when we came out of the theater, it was cruelly cold. We didn't have enough money for a taxi. We stood waiting for a subway train in the station under Rockefeller Center. Ellaine was shivering. I opened my raincoat and put it around her and held her in my arms. She was so fragile from the dope; she seemed birdlike. We waited and waited, and at last got a train heading north. I dropped her off at their apartment and walked home in the cold.

All of us who cared about Bill were desperate about his condition. I became part of a conspiracy against him. Some of us reasoned—naively—that if he couldn't get money from his friends, he'd have to quit heroin. So Orrin Keepnews, Creed Taylor, Helen, and a few more of us tried to cut off his money sources. It didn't work. He'd just go to the loan sharks, who would then threaten to break his hands.

Ironically, at this very time, his career, under Helen's management, was beginning to take off. Riverside Records was going out of business. Helen negotiated a contract with Creed Taylor and Verve Records. And Bill began to get money from Creed. One day Helen went to Creed's office to discuss getting Bill yet another advance. She called me. She and Creed wanted me to take a message to Bill: Creed said that he would pay Bill's rent, pay his electric, telephone, and grocery bills, and would even pay for hospitalization if Bill would submit to it, but he wouldn't advance him one more penny in cash.

"Why me?" I said indignantly. "Why is it always me who has to take him the news?"

"Because you live near him," she said. "And he's waiting for an answer."

So again I went up to Bill's apartment. The electricity had been turned off. He had run an extension cord from a light fixture on the wall of the hallway up to and under his door. To this line a lamp was attached, the only one working in the apartment. We went out to a hamburger joint on Broadway, just above the point where West End Avenue intersects it. I gave Bill the news.

He was furious. "You people don't understand!" he said. "I'm kind of attached to shit."

"Bill," I said, "that may qualify as the understatement of the year."

"No, I mean it," he said. "You *don't* understand. It's like death and transfiguration. Every day you wake in pain like death, and then you go out and score, and that is transfiguration. Each day becomes all of life in microcosm."

This capacity of Bill's to be clear about and articulate the nature of his drug habit always mystified me. If he was the ultimate denial of the myth of the jazz musician as a folk artist, he also refuted every popular image of the drug addict. He told me some years later that he did not in his heart really regret his years of the drug experience, for he had learned something even from that: an understanding of and tolerance for his father, who was an alcoholic.

There was a moment, however, when I caught a glimpse of what heroin did for this extraordinarily intelligent and sensitive man. I tore a meniscus in my right knee and was told by doctors that it would have to be removed. The surgery was performed in Roosevelt Hospital. Evidently somebody didn't do something right, because the pain afterwards was terrible. The doctor ordered shots of some kind to relieve it. Bill came to see me. As we talked, the pain returned, gradually growing more severe. Finally I rang for the nurse, who gave me yet another shot. And I began to nod, in a way I had seen addicts do on many occasions. The warmth of the drug spread through my body and the pain dissolved in it, like sugar in tea. I would follow for a while what Bill, sitting at the bedside, was saying, then lose track of it, then return to it. Through a window I could see a steady rain. Somehow I didn't mind its melancholy. And the pain was gone, not only the pain in the knee but that of life itself. I felt reconciled to everything. Looking at Bill, I felt that I truly understood him. I fell asleep after a while, and when I awoke Bill was gone.

The next day I asked a nurse. "What is this drug that you're giving me?" I had noticed that I was vaguely looking forward to the pain in order to get the shot.

"Morphine," she said.

"What? Forget it!" I was terrified of the opium drugs, not only because of Bill but because of other friends such as John Coltrane, who'd been through the hell of quitting. "From here on," I told her, "I'll get by on aspirins."

It was about this time that the late pianist and teacher John Mehegan told Bill that some of his students knew of Bill's condition and were tempted to emulate him. Bill told John to turn on a tape recorder. He dictated an eloquent dissertation against drug use. It's no doubt lost by now. I do remember that he stated firmly that his style was well formed before he ever began using dope.

Orrin Keepnews said once that when So-and-So—he named a famous musician—came around to borrow dope money, it was easy to turn him down because he was an evil son of a bitch. But Bill broke your heart, Orrin said, because of the sweetness of his nature, and his immense moral decency. He would sit there in the outer office at Riverside, waiting patiently, until Orrin would advance him some more money.

One day—probably when Helen first negotiated the contract with Creed Taylor and Verve—Bill received a large advance, something like ten thousand dollars. He came by my apartment in a taxi and asked me to go with him on some errands. We went from one apartment building to another. I would hold the taxi while he went up and paid debts to friends. Then he would come down and consult the file cards he was carrying and order the taxi driver on to the next stop. He'd kept careful track of every penny he owed! He went through about six thousand dollars that afternoon, and at the end of it handed me two hundred dollars.

"What's that for?" I said.

"I hocked your record player, didn't I? And some of your records too."

A few years after this, I mentioned the experience to the late Zoot Sims, himself one of the many jazz musicians of that generation who had broken the heroin habit.

"Yeah," Zoot said. "I remember that time. I was playing at the Golden Circle in Stockholm. Bill walked in and handed me six hundred dollars. I didn't know how much I'd lent him, but he knew to the penny."

IT WAS DURING that winter of 1962–63 that Bill got an idea for an overdubbed album in which he would play three pianos. Overdubbing was by now a widely used technique. It had been pioneered by Les Paul and Mary Ford, then used as a commercial gimmick by many singers, Patti Page among them. But it had rarely been used to serious artistic purpose. Neither Creed Taylor nor Helen nor I had any idea what Bill had in mind, but we took it on faith that he knew what he was doing. In January and February of 1963, the album was made in a series of remarkable sessions that made us all intensely aware of the clarity of Bill's musical thinking.

The album was recorded with the tape running at thirty inches per second. The industry standard was fifteen i.p.s., but the higher speed would more accurately capture Bill's tone. The album was made at Webster Hall, and the engineer was Ray Hall. Bill was playing Glenn Gould's Steinway.

Ray would tape Bill's first track. Bill was particularly fussy about the first one. He said that if that wasn't right, the other two couldn't be. Then, listening in headphones to what he had played before, he would add the second track, and finally a third.

The four of us in the control booth—Ray, Creed, Helen, and I—were constantly open-mouthed at what was going on. On the second track, Bill would play some strangely appropriate echo of something he'd done on the first. Or there would be some flawless pause in which all three pianists were perfectly together; or some deft run fitted effortlessly into a space left for it. I began to think of Bill as three Bills: Bill Left Channel, Bill Right, and Bill Center.

Bill Left would lay down the first track, stating the melody and launching into an improvisation for a couple of choruses, after which he would move into an accompanist's role, playing a background over which Bill Center would later play *his* solo. His mind obviously was working in three dimensions of time simultaneously, because each Bill was anticipating and responding to what the other two were doing. Bill Left was hearing in his head what Bill Center and Bill Right *were going to play* a half-hour or so from now, while Bill Center and Bill Right were in constant communication with a Bill Left who had vanished into the past a half hour or an hour before. The sessions took on a feeling of science-fiction eeriness.

In the acclaim for his tone and his lyricism, it is easy to overlook Bill's time. By this point in his life, it had become extremely subtle. But it was *there*. Bill made several basic tracks on Alex North's "Love Theme from *Spartacus*." Bill had seen the film with Scott LaFaro, liked the theme, began performing it, and added it to the jazz repertoire. He somewhat altered the release of the tune. After he'd made about six passes at it, Creed Taylor pushed the log sheet along the console to Helen, silently pointing to the times he had marked. Though there were retards and pauses in the music, the time on the first take was, say, five minutes and four seconds. The rest of the takes were 5:06, 5:04, 5:05, 5:06—never a variation of more than a second or two. The final take was 5:05.

Warren Bernhardt had said that Bill always played the essence of a melody. But on "Spartacus," he was playing more than the essence of a love theme, he was playing the essence of love itself, the essence of all tenderness. You love a woman with this feeling, or the autumn or a sunrise or a child.

When the album was finished, I found that repeated playing of that track yielded up constantly new beauties. But there was a mysteriously exquisite something, some sense of unfolding discovery, for the four of us who were in the control booth that day that would haunt my memory for years.

Empty Coke bottles stood all about Bill's feet. Bill had that taste for sugar that goes with heroin addiction. He ran out of dope and began to go into withdrawal. He was sweating. We all knew what he was suffering. I couldn't get the image of the final crucifixion in the movie out of my mind. Creed asked Bill if he wanted to call the session off. "No," Bill said. "Let's finish it." And he went on.

He played a lovely rippling figure at the opening, one that turned up again at the end, transformed into some spiritual quintessence. There is a cheerful and jaunty, almost martial, quality to the recording at one point, which makes the memory of the session all the more poignant. When Bill had completed the first two tracks, Creed and Helen and I all thought that he shouldn't do a third—that another one would only clutter what he had already done. We were wrong.

As the end of the track neared, the "third" Bill took the opening figure and extended it into a long, fantastic, flowing line that he wove in and out and around and through what the other two pianists were playing, never colliding with these two previous selves. That final line seemed like a magical firefly hurrying through a forest at night, never striking the trees, leaving behind a line of golden sparks that slowly fell to earth, illuminating everything around it. I think Helen and Creed were close to tears when he completed that track. I know I was.

Bill accomplished another prodigy at that period of his life. Putting a needle into his right arm, he hit a nerve. The arm went numb, becoming all but useless. Bill was contracted for a week's engagement at the Village Vanguard, and he needed the money. So he went to the job on the first night and played with his left hand only. His pedaling was always very skilled. That night he played accompanying chords below middle C with his left hand, depressing the center pedal, which sustains only lower notes, then jumped the hand up the keyboard to execute his fluent running lines. With one's eyes shut, it was hardly possible to tell there was anything amiss in his playing. This went on during the whole engagement. Word of it spread through the jazz community, and pianists flocked to the Vanguard from all over the city to watch this amazing event.

THEN BILL TOLD us he was going to leave New York for a while. He said he was going to kick his habit. He said he couldn't do it in these familiar haunts, where the stuff was so available. He thought he would have to get away from his usual life, at least for a while, if he were to succeed. He thought that the best place to do this would be at his mother's home in Florida. He and Ellaine gave up their apartment, she went home to her parents, Bill gave us his mother's telephone number and left.

After a while the musicians began to be aware of his absence, and a rumor went around in Jim and Andy's that he was dead. When I entered the place one afternoon, several of them asked me with alarm if it were true. I went directly to the phone booth and called the number in Florida. Bill answered. I remember the almost audible sigh of relief that went through the place when I stuck my head out of the booth and said, "Any of you guys want to talk to Bill Evans?"

Bill came back from Florida free, for the present, of his habit, and lived with me for a little while in the basement apartment I had on West End Avenue at 71st Street—right around the corner from Erroll Garner. Bill was nominated for a Grammy award for *Conversations with Myself*. Just before the banquet, he broke a front tooth. "How d'you like that? It's the first time in years I've had a reason to smile, and I have to go and do that."

Turn Out the Stars dates from that period. One night, while Bill was playing a gig somewhere, I was looking for a movie on late-night television, and came across a listing for a film called *Turn Off the Moon*. I didn't know then and don't know now what it was about. But the title stuck. Bill had been after me to write some songs with him—"Waltz for Debby" already bore my lyric. He wanted titles, or complete lyrics, to set to music. But I preferred to work the other way around, putting words to music. When he came home, I said, "I've got a title for you. 'Turn Out the Stars.'" He wrote the melody in the next day or two, and I then completed a lyric which, later, I found almost unbearably dark. "Yesterday I Heard the Rain" also dates from that period. It has music by the Mexican composer Armando Manzanero and my lyrics; Bill got in the habit of playing it, and recorded it in the Tokyo concert album.

That little apartment in the basement of a brownstone on West End Avenue, with a sofa and rumpsprung bottlegreen armchairs, a rented spinet piano and worn carpet, seemed hidden and safe. It was a kind of haven for both of us. Its kitchen and living room gave onto a small cement courtyard from which, if you looked up, you could see a rectangle of sky. Warren Bernhardt used to come by, and Gary McFarland, and Antonio Carlos Jobim. Bill used to wake me up mornings and give me impromptu harmony lessons. "I think of all harmony," he said one such morning, "as an expansion from and return to the tonic."

It was years before the value of that struck me.

"Why does a flat ninth work with a dominant chord?" I asked.

"It has to do with counterpoint more than harmony," he said. "It's the ninth of the dominant moving through the flat ninth to become the fifth of the tonic."

The day of the Grammy awards dinner arrived. Just starting to put his life back together, Bill had very little money, and nothing appropriate to wear. As it happened, I was storing a closetful of clothes for Woody Herman, one of the dapper dressers in the business. There was a particularly well-made blue blazer which, to Bill's surprise and mine, fit him perfectly. So he donned it. Just before we were to leave, I turned somehow and spilled a drink in his lap. Fortunately there was another pair of slacks that fit him. We picked up Helen and went to the banquet. And I managed to repeat the trick: I turned and spilled another drink in his lap. He laughed and said, "Man, are you trying to tell me something?" At that moment, they called his name. Bill picked up his Grammy for *Conversations* in soaking pants and Woody Herman's blazer.

Bill had never met Woody Herman, one of his early idols, and I arranged for the three of us to have lunch a few days later. Bill turned up wearing, to my horror, that blazer. "Do you like the jacket?" Bill said, after the formality of introduction.

"It looks faintly familiar," Woody said.

Bill flung it open with a matadorial gesture to show its brilliant lining. "How do you like the monogram?" he said. It was of course WH. "It stands," Bill said, "for William Heavens." And Woody laughed. Fortunately.

That evening we went to hear the band. Woody tried to introduce a tune only to be interrupted by some drunk blearily shouting, "Play 'Woodpeckers' Ball.'" Woody tried to talk him down but the drunk persisted, "Play 'Woodpeckers' Ball.'"

Finally Woody said, "All right, for Charlie Pecker over there, we're going to play 'Woodpeckers' Ball.'"

"Man," said Bill, who was quite shy, "that takes real hostility. If I tried that, some cat would come up on the bandstand and punch me in the mouth."

BILL HAD REMARKED to me at some point that, despite the obvious differences in their playing, he and Oscar Peterson played alike in that their work was pianistic. The influence of Earl Hines had become widespread, resulting in the phenomenon of so-called one-handed pianists, that is to say pianists playing "horn lines" in the right hand accompanied by laconic chords in the left. It was an approach to piano that reached a zenith in bebop, but for all the inventiveness of some of the players, it was an approach that eschewed much of what the instrument was capable of.

Precisely because it is not inherently an ensemble instrument, Gerry Mulligan had good reason to leave it out of his quartet—and precedent for doing so in the marching bands of New Orleans. Played to its full potential, the piano overwhelms everything around it, and so, in jazz, it must in a context of horns be played with exceptional restraint. The perfect orchestral jazz pianist was Count Basie, who understood this and actually restricted a considerable technique.

If the piano is to be what it inherently is, it must be taken away from the horns, allowed to do its solo turn, like a great magician or juggler. It is not by its nature an ensemble actor but a spell-binding story-teller. It is Homeric. Because jazz is a music whose tradition is so heavily rooted in horns, the instrument is therefore very much misunderstood, which fact results in those strange comments that Oscar Peterson plays "too much," the logical extension of which is that Bach writes too much. Art Tatum so thoroughly understood the nature of the problem that he preferred to play without a rhythm section. If, however, a pianist wants to partake of that special joy of making music with a rhythm section, the logical context is the trio, a format elected by Nat Cole in those too-few years before his success as a singer overshadowed his brilliance as a pianist.

Oscar had changed the nature of jazz piano, Bill was changing it further, and perceptive listeners noticed that if Oscar had once influenced Bill, Bill was now influencing Oscar, at least in ballads.

I was asked to write an essay on Oscar Peterson for *Holiday* magazine in New York. I was musing on what Bill had said about the similarity in their playing. I realized that there were also similarities in personality, including a profound stubbornness. When Oscar made up his mind to something, he was absolutely intractable. And Bill was the same.

I noted that Oscar was born August 15, which made him a Leo. On a whim I phoned Bill, who was then living in Riverdale, and said, "What's your birthdate?"

"August 16," he said. "Why?"

"You're going to laugh," I said, and told him.

But he didn't laugh. He said, "I used to think there was nothing to it, but over the years I've noticed with my groups that the signs have often worked out. Leos do seem to be stubborn. You know," he said, naming a certain bassist whom he had fired, "he's a Leo. And he was always trying to run the group. I told him, 'Look, if you want to lead a trio, form your own.' But it didn't do any good, and I let him go." He paused a second, then said, "I'd never have a Leo in my trio."

I laughed out loud, partly at the sound of it and partly because he had in that generalization illustrated the very quality we were discussing. On the one hand, I cannot imagine Bill rejecting a man solely for his sun sign. On the other hand, as far as I know, Bill was ever afterwards the only Leo in that trio.

BILL'S FORTUNES CONTINUED to rise. He and Ellaine moved into an apartment in Riverdale, and his life took on some of the elements of what is called normalcy.

Creed Taylor left Verve to form his own CTI label. Helen said to me, "Who's going to produce Bill now?"

"You are," I said. And she did, from then until the end, making some of Bill's finest albums.

The rest of the 1960s were good years, very productive years, for Bill, for me, for Helen. I became involved in the fledgling Montreux Jazz Festival in 1967. The next year I arranged for Bill to play it. I had already been there three weeks when Helen and Bill arrived with the rest of his trio, which at that time included Eddie Gomez on bass and Jack deJohnette on drums.

Bill, Helen, and I went to the Chateau de Chillon, just off the Montreux lakeshore, made famous by Lord Byron in the poem so many of us were forced to memorize in our school days. I took a photo of the castle; it became the cover of the album Helen produced from the concert Bill played that night. The three of us prowled the dungeon where Bonivard had been imprisoned, chained to a pillar for four years. We puttered through ancient chambers and examined a secret passage or two and a few beds wherein many a noble affair was doubtless consummated.

I was bitching about the music business.

Bill said, "Well, man, you and I have something most people don't—freedom. And you have more than I do, because you don't have to play a gig every night."

Bill played Montreux several times after that—and Rio de Janeiro and Tokyo and Paris.

The Verve period was followed by a brief one at Columbia Records, neither the most successful nor the most creative time of Bill's life. Clive Davis, president of Columbia, tried to get him to make a rock album. Needless to say, the suggestion got nowhere. Then followed the long association with Fantasy, which is documented in an eleven-album package reissued by Fantasy in 1988.

I did not see Bill often in those years. I had moved to Toronto. Bill would occasionally play there. I realized that he was becoming a legend.

On arriving for a week at the Town Tavern, he called and said he needed a dentist: he had a toothache. I knew, from the Toronto musicians, of a dentist who was not only good at his work but was an accomplished pianist as well. I called him. His nurse said he was busy with a patient.

About six that evening, the dentist called me. He said that he had just finished a busy work day and asked the nurse if there had been any calls. She said someone had called on behalf of a Mr. Bill Evans, who needed a dentist.

"What did you tell him?" he said in alarm.

"I said you were too busy today to see anyone else," she told him.

"What?" he said. "Do you realize you turned down God?"

He packed a kit of tools, met Bill at the Town Tavern, and fixed the ailing tooth in the kitchen.

Bill had pianist friends in cities all over the world. When he was in Toronto, he would spend a lot of time with Doug Riley, a superb pianist who was strongly influenced by him. Doug's little boy heard Doug talk so much to his wife, also a musician, about Bill that when Bill was visiting them, he looked up adoringly and said, "What's your first name, Billevans?"

I followed Bill's Fantasy albums as they came out, marveling as always at the grace and intelligence of the playing. One track of one of them shattered me. This was Bronislau Kaper's tune "Hi Lili Hi Lo," which Bill recorded with Eddie Gomez in the duo album titled *Intuition*. The song bore a dedication on the album cover: "for Ellaine." The tune is happy-sad in character; in Bill's treatment, it had a profound melancholy. I realized I hadn't spoken to Bill in many months and phoned him in New York. I told him how much I liked the album, we talked for a while, and then I said, "Give my love to Ellaine." There was a crushing silence on the line. Then Bill said, "Didn't anyone tell you? Ellaine took her own life."

I blurted, helplessly, "How?"

"She threw herself under a subway train."

Instantly I thought of that ghastly cold night in the subway with her. That she should have died there was a thought I found almost unendurable. I can hardly listen to that performance of "Hi Lili Hi Lo," her favorite song. And I can only guess what Helen went through at the time: Bill was out of town, and she had to identify the body.

Bill went back on heroin for a while, then got into a methadone treatment program in 1970. For the next ten years or so, he was free of it. He remarried. I met his second wife, Nenette, once or twice, but I never really knew her. Friends described a very troubled marriage. They had a son, whom Bill gave the very Welsh name Evan Evans. Bill moved out and took an apartment in Fort Lee, New Jersey.

After I moved to California in 1974, Bill and I remained in loose touch by telephone, and once I heard him at Howard Rumsey's Concerts by the Sea at Redondo Beach. Philly Joe Jones was the drummer with him at the time, and in the dressing room they were telling funny stories about their junkie days.

Around 1980, I began to hear on the musicians' grapevine that Bill was back on dope, but not heroin. He was shooting cocaine. He came to Los Angeles for an engagement. One of the musicians went to hear him, then urged me to go to see him the following night. "How is he playing?" I said.

"Brilliantly."

"How does he look?"

"Awful."

"I don't want to see him," I said. "I can't go through that again." Hal Gaylor told me sometime later, "Cocaine is far worse than heroin, because you have to do it again a couple of hours later. It's deadly."

Joe LaBarbera, the drummer, was with Bill at the end. Bill was taken with severe stomach pains in his apartment in Fort Lee. Joe drove him to the hospital. "The funny thing is," Joe said several years later, "that he was in control of the situation even then. I didn't know where the hospital was, and he was directing me."

Joe took him to Mount Sinai Hospital and checked him in. Bill died there.

IF I CAN remember vividly my discovery of Bill's playing, I can similarly remember the moment when I learned of his death. I went home to Canada to see my mother, who was dying of cancer. I walked into her house in Kingston, Ontario, and looked down a hall toward the kitchen, where she stood in a pale blue bathrobe. She seemed so frail and old. I had hardly had time to embrace her when the telephone rang. It was the Canadian Broadcasting Corporation in Toronto. How they even knew I was there, I don't know. But they told me of Bill's death and asked me to do a network interview about him. I agreed. I managed to suspend all feeling about his death: I had to contend with my mother's pending departure.

A few days later in Toronto, I did the interview. The engineer played Tony Bennett's record of "Waltz for Debby," the version he made with Bill—Tony has recorded it three times. I thought of the cities I had been in with Bill: Los Angeles, Toronto, Chicago, Paris, Montreux, New York. I remembered writing the "Waltz for Debby" lyric in Helen's living room. (Jobim always calls it "The Debby Waltz.") It hit me that Bill was really gone, and I think this awareness was getting into my voice. It was at this point that the lady producer of the show asked possibly the most tactless question I have ever had in an interview. She said, "Can you tell us any funny stories about him?" I didn't know whether to laugh or cry. Or maybe it was a clever question, a good one, to pull me back from the brink. I talked about Woody's blazer.

After I finished the interview, the one person I wanted to be with was Oscar Peterson. As I drove out to his house in Mississauga, I remembered an evening in New York when Bill and I went to hear him. I had suggested that they make a two-piano album together, and they were both interested in the idea, which, for various contractual and logistical reasons, never happened. When we entered the club, Oscar brought whatever he was playing to an early close and then played, beautifully, "Waltz for Debby." Bill said, "I don't thing I'll ever play it again." He did, of course.

Oscar too had heard the news of Bill's death, and the banter and insult in which we usually indulge were suspended that day. He knew what I was feeling.

Two or three years later, I was having dinner with Oscar's former wife Sandy, with whom he had remained friends. "I think," I said, "Oscar was much more affected by Bill's death than he would admit to me that day."

"You better believe it," she said.

Oscar almost always plays "Waltz for Debby" in his concerts now.

After Oscar and I had talked of all manner of other things that afternoon, we at last got around to discussing Bill, including his drug habit.

"Maybe," Oscar said gently, "he found what he was looking for."

IN 1984, GROWING curious about the actual status of various pianists with other pianists, I did a survey of the sixty-odd well-known pianists who subscribed to the *Jazzletter*. The forty-seven respondents included pianists such as Alan Broadbent, Dave Brubeck, Kenny Drew, Dave Frishberg, Dizzy Gillespie, Roger Kellaway, Junior Mance, Nat Pierce, and Billy Taylor. I asked them to name, in no particular order, five pianists in three categories: those they considered the "best," those they thought the most influential, and their personal favorites. The results were startling.

As best, Art Tatum garnered 36 votes, Bill Evans 33, and Oscar Peterson 27. As most influential, Tatum 32, Bill 30, Bud Powell 24. Among personal favorites, Bill won: Bill 25, Tatum 22, Oscar 19.

While this was by no means a "scientific" survey, it gave some idea of the respect in which he was held by pianists. I think if you surveyed musicians on all instruments, the results would be similar.

And yet not everybody gets it. A friend of mine wrote to ask, "What is the source and meaning of the rarified (important, influential, virtually deified) position occupied by Bill Evans in the world of jazz—in both the large world of listeners and critics as well as in the community of jazz musicians? I've listened to Evans's music, both his performances and his compositions, for fifteen or twenty years, and he has moved me frequently. But no more than many other pianists, none of whom achieved the influence or reputation associated with a cult. [While] I can well understand why Thelonious Monk became a seminal and vastly influential figure in jazz, I can't quite comprehend Evans's comparable status."

My friend says elsewhere in his letter that Oscar Peterson "has greater range and technical facility." Not so. If you're talking about sheer speed, go back and listen to the runs Bill plays on the "Spartacus" track of *Conversations with Myself*. He's as fast as Oscar, fully as facile. But he doesn't use his speed in the same way that Oscar does. And the flow of tones from one chord to another is part of "technique." That night we went to hear Oscar, I asked Bill why Oscar didn't use some of the voicings Bill had brought into jazz. Bill said, "It wouldn't be appropriate to what he does." Both of them were blessed with a sense of the fitting. And in time of course Oscar did embrace certain things that Bill had brought into jazz.

These comparisons—which are one of the curses of the jazz world—are wasteful. In jazz, more than any form of music I know, you are listening to individual expression. You may listen to a Frenchman for what his philosophy of life contributes to your own; to an American Indian or an Australian aborigine or a Swede for the insight he offers. But you are not going to get the same thing from all of them, nor should one want to. Therefore to compare them on some sort of competitive scale is foolish, and meaningless. You accept them for what they are. Jazz fans, perhaps encouraged by all the polls that have plagued the art, too often ask who's "best"—and excoriate one pianist or trumpet player for lacking what another one has. It is like derogating Lester Young for not having Ben Webster's tone. *My favorite pianist is better than your favorite pianist, my favorite tenor player is better than your favorite tenor player.*

Bill was strikingly individual. Anyone who knew his work well could turn on a car radio, catch a jazz piano track, and know he was hearing Bill within two bars, because of his use of chord scales, his tone, his attack, and his rhythmic sense. His rhythmic placements were unique—much emulated but never successfully captured by anyone else. His sense of the balance of chords and of the linear motions within them was wonderful. He introduced into jazz certain voicings, and a use of inversions, that captivated and then captured a generation of pianists to the point that some among them have consciously sought ways out of the trap of sounding like him. He changed the tone character of jazz piano. Tone was a negligible element in previous jazz playing. For all his brilliance, Bud Powell had a painful tone. Nat Cole began the change, producing crystalline sound, Oscar Peterson took it further, and Bill brought into jazz the kind of tone appropriate to Debussy and Ravel and modern harmonic function and obvious in the classical world in the playing of Walter Gieseking and Emil Gillels. Everyone else picked it up from Bill. Bill's tone, or variations of it, spread all over the world. Jazz pianists everywhere touched the keyboard differently after Bill came along. Finally, there is his control of dynamics. In any given thirty-two bars of a Bill Evans solo, there are infinite gradations of intensity, dozens, maybe even scores of levels of loudness, all contributing not to technical dazzle but to the intense feeling in his work. I have gathered that not everyone's ear detects this.

His imagination was enormous. Though he had, as I say, his personal vocabulary, his clichés if you like, his bag of tricks, just like everyone in jazz, which is not as totally improvised a music as some of its champions pretend, he was genuinely one of the most imaginative, inventive, and adventurous improvisers the art has known.

Maybe Martin Williams said it best: "The need to know what he was doing, intellectually and theoretically, was one pole of the dichotomy of the remarkable combination of careful deliberateness and intuitive spontaneity, of logic and sensitivity, of mind and heart, that was Bill Evans the musician."

WHEN MODIGLIANI DIED, the prices of his paintings shot up overnight and now are astronomical. In a delicious example of funereal opportunism, his hometown of Livorno, Italy, which ignored him when he was alive, began in the early 1980s dredging its canal in search of sculptures he deep-sixed there one night in 1914 in disgust with this aspect of his own work.

That an artist's work rises to "value" with his death is inevitable, but the record industry is outstanding in the exploitation of necrophilia, as witness the cases of Janis Joplin, John Lennon, and Elvis Presley. Nor has jazz been free of this kind of avarice.

If it is true that an artist has a right to be judged by his best work, it is only just that in most instances the recordings a jazz musician has rejected be left in obscurity. He clearly did not want to be represented by them. To issue flawed or interrupted takes to milk a few more dollars out of the departed is despicable.

No such unfortunate story attached to the two albums that Helen derived from tapes of two concerts played in Paris November 26, 1979, by Bill's last trio. They are not only not inferior Evans. They are, to me at least, the best and highest examples of his art to be found on record.

What those albums, recorded less than ten months before his death, prove beyond question is that he had begun to evolve and grow again, which is unusual in artists in any field. Artists tend to find their methods early and remain faithful to them, which sometimes leads in actors to the kind of mannered and self-satirizing performance so sadly typified by John Barrymore at the end. It is rare to see sudden growth in older jazz musicians, as in the case of Dizzy Gillespie after he changed his embouchure in his late sixties. Bill, on the clear evidence of those Paris albums, was in his most fertile period when he died.

Bassist Marc Johnson and drummer Joe LaBarbera, who were with him at the end and in these Paris recordings, were beautifully sympathetic to Bill. Characteristically, he gave them much credit for what had happened in his playing, suggesting a direct relationship between this final trio and the one with LaFaro and drummer Paul Motian.

The two Paris albums consist almost entirely of material he had recorded before, which gave me a chance to compare his early and late work. The first,

Elektra Musician 60164-1, comprises "I Do It for Your Love"; "Quiet Now," a Denny Zeitlin composition of which Bill was particularly fond; "Noelle's Theme"; "My Romance"; "I Love You Porgy"; "Up with the Lark" (a Kern tune; Bill had a flair for reviving forgotten gems); "All Mine"; and "Beautiful Love." The second, Elektra Musician 60311-1-E, contains "Re: Person I Knew"; "Gary's Theme," a Gary McFarland tune; three of his own tunes, "Letter to Evan"; "34 Skiddoo"; "Laurie"; and the Miles Davis tune "Nardis."

"My Romance" was in that first Riverside LP, *New Jazz Conceptions,* made when he was so young and uncertain of his worth and uncomfortable with the praise that was being poured on him. He truly believed he didn't deserve it, as he said to me once in a long letter I lost in a fire in Toronto, which is all the more unfortunate in that it was one of the most remarkable examples of self-analysis by an artist I have ever encountered. He was explaining why he had become a heroin addict. He said that the acclaim he was receiving by the time he was with the Miles Davis group—February to November of 1958—made him acutely uneasy. He didn't feel he deserved it. I remember the next line of that letter verbatim: "If people wouldn't believe I was a bum, I was determined to prove it."

That early "My Romance" is two choruses long, ballad tempo, without intro. He simply plays the tune, twice, solo, with minimal variation. But already there is that enormous control of the instrument, and those intelligent voice leadings. To go from that version to the one in Paris twenty-two years later, is fascinating, and somewhat disturbing. The later version opens with a long intro that has only the most abstract relationship to the tune. Bill moves through a series of chords that float ambiguously (to my ear at least) between A-flat and E-flat, then goes into the tune itself, in C, up-tempo, with rhythm section. It is like a sudden sunburst, so bright, and the audience applauds. C, incidentally, is the key of the early Riverside version. Bill was very fussy about keys. When he was taking on a new tune, he would try it out in all the keys—and such was his influence on other pianists that Warren Bernhardt learned Bill's "My Bells" with Bill's voicings in all twelve keys, as a discipline. In any case, "My Romance" stayed in C for all those years, but the last version is profoundly different, a distillation of years of musical wisdom, quite abstract, exploding with energy and life.

But the most striking thing to me about the Paris albums is that Bill seems to have struck the perfect balance between his intuitive lyricism and deliberative intelligence, to have resolved the dichotomy of which Martin Williams perceptively wrote. Without any loss of the worldly wisdom he had accumulated, his work at last is filled again with that indefinable something that he and others recognized as the essence of the *Everybody Digs* album.

It is said that all men go in search of their youth. The Paris albums suggest that in the end, Bill found his.

Not long after Bill died, Phil Woods went into a fury when he read a critic's comment that Bill didn't swing. "Swing" is a tricky verb as applied to music. What swings for one person may not swing for another, since the process involves a good deal of the subjective. It is impossible to state as an objective "fact" that something "doesn't" swing. What Bill did not do was swing obviously. If you want to hear Bill swing obviously, go back to the first Riverside album. The influence of Bud Powell was, it seems to me, not yet internalized, and Bill goes bopping happily away, backed by Teddy Kotick and Paul Motian, banging out the time in a way that only the deaf could miss. But like Turner making the implicit assumption that you don't need obvious waves and horizon and clouds to know what the sea looks like and giving you only his heightened perception of them, Bill often in his later years didn't hit you over the head with the time. He assumed you knew where it was.

He once explained to me how he felt about it, and I do not know whether he ever told anyone else. He drew an analogy to shadow lettering in which the letters seem raised and you see not the letters themselves but the shadows they apparently cast. That's how Bill played time, or more precisely played with it.

Finally, there is an ineffable quality in Bill's playing that I am more and more inclined to see as mysticism, whether Russian or something even more Oriental. Bill had extraordinary powers of concentration. He told me once that you should be able to focus your mind on a single tone for as much as five minutes. That would have been an uncanny feat, possible to yoga adepts but few others in this world. Yet that is how Bill thought, and his total involvement with the tone or the chord or the scale happening *now* was very deep indeed. All this is beyond my powers to describe, as for that matter all music is beyond my powers to describe. But I hear it, and I am moved by it. And I can't say or do anything to help or instruct those whose neurological organization and life conditioning do not predispose them to its perception. I would tell them that a certain famous arranger told me he went through a long period of being unable to hear what the fuss was all about. And then one day Bill's work hit him.

I don't think music is accessible through explanation, in any case, although explanation may deepen one's appreciation of it. It has to be discovered, and no musician's work more than Bill's. I discovered it, Alan Broadbent discovered it, countless others discovered it. And now Bill is being discovered by a new generation. I got a letter from a young man just out of graduate school. He named as his favorites the three pianists so admired by the pianists I polled—Tatum, Peterson, and Evans.

He said he listens to them in the dark.

Bill would like that.

Black Like Him

Francis Davis

Bobby Short a jazz pianist? Yes, and a jazz singer, too, according to this appreciative piece by one of today's most admired younger jazz critics, Francis Davis, who sees beyond (or around) the political incorrectness of Short's performing for—in fact, entertaining—an elite audience at the elite Hotel Carlyle. From his 1990 collection Outcats.

With its Victorian banquettes and pastel murals of fat wood nymphs striking fey poses (by the forgotten pseudo-Frenchman Marcel Vertès), the Café Carlyle is a dowdy relic from a time when a hotel's amenities were understood to be for the local gentry rather than for conventioneers. The Carlyle's waiters, busmen, and wine stewards are like the supercilious house servants you see in old movies; they go about their business as though invisible, demanding in return the sort of peel-me-a-grape insouciance it takes generations of inherited wealth to pull off. Anything more than that is an affront.

But which is more humiliating: to think of yourself as rude for not acknowledging services rendered, or to be thought gauche by others for not recognizing when expressions of gratitude are inappropriate? My companion and I were trying to be invisible, too, but we were making ourselves conspicuous by thanking someone each time a dish or piece of silverware was brought or removed. Our parents taught us that good manners would make us appear gracious, but what did they know of such things? When you're around people who take service for granted, you realize that good manners are a dead giveaway of humble beginnings.

What were we doing at the Carlyle if we felt so out of place? We wanted to hear Bobby Short in his natural habitat, but (speaking for myself) Short was only the half of it. I grew up believing, as many working-class Irish Catholics do, in an inverted Protestant ethic: heaven was reserved for have-nots like for me and my family, because wealth was conclusive evidence of corruption somewhere along the line. (This is still the creed I live by, and it's a good one to cling to if you plan on being a jazz critic.) But encouraged by the drawing-room musicals of the thirties and forties that I watched on television, I also grew up equating adulthood with limos, penthouses, luxury liners, and sinfully expensive supperclubs like the Café Carlyle (it didn't occur to me till later that none of the adults I knew in real life enjoyed any of these plums). Was the Carlyle as I imagined it would be? Yes and no. Remember the scene in *Hannah and Her Sisters* when Woody Allen drags Dianne Wiest to the Café Carlyle? She does coke right there at their table as they listen to Bobby Short. "They wouldn't know the difference!" she protests when Allen scolds her. "They're embalmed!" Just my luck. I finally make it to the Carlyle and nobody who's anybody goes there anymore. The Bright Lights in the Big City are somewhere else now, panting for more lurid thrills.

The Carlyle is the sort of room in which the entertainment is generally as unobtrusive as the rest of the help. But Bobby Short, who's synonymous with the place, is the antithesis of such a whispering performer. Befitting his past as a child vaudevillian, Short is a belter who spends a surprising amount of time on his feet, away from the piano (which, given his sub–Erroll Garner effusions, is just as well). He claps his hands together *hard* every so often, as though realizing that the room itself is his competition. His extravagance transforms a bandstand tucked away against a wall into center stage.

"The audience has so much to distract their attention," Short remarked during a brief conversation I had with him in his tastefully appointed Sutton Place apartment the afternoon following my visit to the Carlyle. "They have a drink or dinner or a cigaret in front of them, and someone very important to them, either romantically or in terms of business, across the table. The idea is to go out there and grab their attention as quickly as you can and maintain it until you go off. You see, I can't give the audience a chance to resume their conversation.

"Before my arrival, the Café was a place where not only guests and residents of the hotel went for dinner, but also people from the neighborhood. The girls from Finch College would have their beaus take them there, and dine there with their parents, who would stay at the hotel when they came to visit." With his pampered moonface and rounded, townhouse diction, Short is the only man I have ever heard use the word "beaus" without sounding sarcastic. No, he wasn't wearing a monogrammed smoking jacket, but his dark blue jumpsuit looked as elegant on him. As he spoke, he sat in front of open shelves of African art objects. From time to time, his Dalmatian, resting glumly on a divan, attempted to jump on his lap. "Jealous thing," he scolded, rubbing the dog's neck. "That's what he is, you know.

"The Carlyle was, and still is, the kind of upper-crust, Upper East Side hotel," he continued. "The Café had always held its own financially, but it had never been that important a part of New York social life. I'm sure that many of the people who frequented the Café were unhappy with the changes that my presence brought about. On the other hand, people from all over started coming and liked me, which is why I'm still welcome there."

SHORT HAS HELD forth at the Carlyle at least six months a year since 1968. His current twentieth-anniversary engagement follows on the heels of his best record ever—the record that, to be frank about it, made me take him seriously. *Guess Who's in Town* is an homage to the late Andy Razaf, a prolific black lyricist best remembered for his collaborations with Fats Waller, although (as the album demonstrates) he also wrote memorable songs with Eubie Blake, James P. and J. C. Johnson, and the white transplanted Englishman Paul Denniker, among others. *Guess Who's in Town* is unusual for Short in that it exposes rather than disguises his lineage from Ethel Waters and other black vaudevillians. It's his *Black Album,* as it were.

The album's four Waller tunes are an unexpected pleasure, in light of Short's admission (to Whitney Balliett in *The New Yorker,* almost twenty years ago) that he felt "inadequate" to sing Waller. "I was probably thinking of Waller's bubble, and how impossible it would be to capture," Short said, when I reminded him of the quote. "But I feel quite comfortable singing the ballads he wrote with Razaf, because when Waller chose to sing a serious song, he often had a difficult time overcoming his comic image." A case in point is "How Can You Face Me?" one scoundrel's admonishment to another in Waller's interpretation, but a wounded reverie of seduction and abandonment in Short's.

Razaf's witty but down-to-earth lyrics rescue Short from the chichi that is sometimes his downfall, and he returns the favor by washing away the implied blackface that too many contemporary singers of both races seem to feel is necessary to interpret vintage black pop. He gives these songs the same respect he would Gershwin or Porter, and they deserve it. Recognizing that Waller's "Black and Blue" is as much a protest against a black pecking order based on skin color as it is against white oppression (Spike Lee thinks he discovered something new?), Short finds a poetry in Razaf's lyric that even Louis Armstrong barely touched. ("It's right there in the verse," Short told me. "'Browns and yellows, lucky fellows, ladies seem to like them light.' It's especially touching when you remember it was originally written to be sung by a woman [in the 1929 revue *Hot Chocolates*]. Coal-black women have always had a hard time of it in black society.") The late Phil Moore's arrangements frequently put a good horn section—featuring the trumpeter Harry "Sweets" Edison, the trombonist Buster Cooper, the alto saxophonist Marshall Royal, and the baritone saxophonist Bill Green—to trivial uses, most noticeably on an over-syncopated "Honeysuckle Rose," and an aimless pastiche of big band themes on Denniker's *Make Believe Ballroom.* But Moore's setting for "Ain't Misbehavin'" is refreshingly modern, with moody counterpoint between Short's piano and John Collins' guitar in advance of the horns. There are sprightly arrangements of Denniker's "S'posin'" and Blake's "Tan Manhattan" (an ode to Harlem's cultural self-sufficiency, although uncharitable ears might hear it as just another darky song), and a stark reading of J. C. Johnson's "Lonesome Swallow," featuring only Short's voice and piano, in faithful evocation of the classic 1928 version by Waters and James P. Johnson. The only one of the album's eleven tracks that backfires is William Weldon's "I'm Gonna Move to the Outskirts of Town," because Short, with his dainty elocution, sounds ludicrous shouting the blues.

IN AMERICAN LEGEND, café society has always been where the white and the black folk meet, but in reality, the black folk are usually there to do their jobs. In his twenty years at the Carlyle, Short has sung himself practically hoarse. His baritone is so split with phlegm that he sounds some of his low notes in two different keys. (Thankfully, *Guess Who's in Town* was recorded during one of his vacations, when he was well rested and in relatively strong voice.) But age has done Short an unintentional favor in slowing down his vibrato, and in a space as confined as the Carlyle, he has propinquity working in his favor: the lavaliere microphone he wears on a string necklace allows him to fill the room without sacrificing intimacy. His between-numbers anecdotes are charming and full of information about what year and movie or show each song is from. He lavishes attention on obscure introductory verses, not as a pedantic exercise, the way thirtysomething cabaret show-offs like Michael Feinstein and Andrea Marcovicci do, but as a way of injecting suspense into overfamiliar material (and, in some cases, as a way of replicating the easy transition from narrative to song that the verses originally provided on stage or screen).

Accompanied by the bassist Beverly Peer and the drummer Robbie Scott, Short did a dozen songs the night I heard him, including two that have become unaccountably obscure—Kurt Weill's and Ira Gershwin's "You've Only One Life to Live" (from *Lady in the Dark*) and Harold Arlen's and Leo Robin's "Hooray for Love" (from the 1948 film *Casbah*). He revitalized Cole Porter's "I Get a Kick Out of You," giving it an unexpected twist by performing it as a ballad, phrasing the "You obviously don't adore me" line with genuine poignance instead of the customary Ethel Merman pizzazz. And he sang "Bye Bye Blackbird" with such feeling and style that I no longer doubted the legend that Miles Davis decided to record his classic version of this tune as a direct result of hearing Short's. (Miles voted for Short in a 1956 "Musicians' Musician" poll that Leonard Feather conducted for *The Encyclopedia Yearbook of Jazz*.)

To my regret, the set included nothing from *Guess Who's in Town*. But toward the end of the show, Short sang "Princess Poupouly Has Lovely Papaya," a piece of fluff from the public domain. With his shoulders thrown back in a characteristic pose that reflected his pride in being a self-made man, he told the audience that this was a song their parents used to hear as they drifted from nightspot to nightspot in the naughty twenties. I don't think I'm attaching too much importance to the fact that he didn't say *our* parents. For me, the key to Short's appeal is in the delirium with which he delivers the opening lines of "Make Believe Ballroom": "Away we go, by radio, to realms of sweet delight. . . ." This is a song Short has lived. Now in his sixties, he grew up wanting in on the good life he heard about on the radio and in the movies. So did I, but white boys don't have to answer to anyone for dreaming beyond their means.

A shocking number of both blacks and whites find something incongruous about a black man in bibbed shirt and cummerbund singing Cole Porter and Noel Coward to white swells, as though getting funky was what a black man had to do to certify his blackness. (And as though the race was too impoverished to accommodate variety—too isolated from the white majority to share any of its values.) Short has his own kind of soul. The ninth of ten children born to a Danville, Illinois, domestic who considered the blues too vulgar to permit in her house (and who allowed her son to enter vaudeville only because the family needed the income during the Depression), Short reminds us that black America has its own traditions of gentility and aspiration, by no means limited to its bourgeoisie. "I am a Negro who has never lived in the South," he wrote in *Black and White Baby*, his 1971 memoir, ". . . nor was I ever trapped in an urban ghetto." He's not a native of the high society he's bought into, either. But neither were the upwardly striving small-town midwesterners and sons of Jewish immigrants (all of them black and white babies themselves, in terms of what they absorbed from jazz) who wrote the songs that have become smart-set anthems. The Republicans think that ours is a trickle-down economy, but the truth of the matter is that our culture trickles up. Like the money we slave for, these songs about the finer things in life are too valuable to be entrusted solely to the rich. Which is why it's comforting to know that the man currently doing the best job of singing them in a supperclub knows what it's like to sing for his supper.

The House in the Heart

Bobby Scott

Reprinted in A Lester Young Reader *(1991; edited by Lewis Porter), this moving remembrance of Young by the composer/pianist/singer Bobby Scott appeared originally in Gene Lees's* Jazzletter *in September 1983.*

"We the whores, Socks," said the worn-out mouth. The bent shoulders, old before their time, fought to maintain a balance that the weight of the tenor saxophone hanging around his neck precariously played with. Lester always seemed to be leaning like that edifice in Italy, a topple imminent, never to realize itself but seconds away at all times. I swear the crepe soles of his boot-style shoes bore an equalizing agent. Prez *teetered* in those last years.

He was without a sense of the time dimension, like waves lapping one into another on a beach, each so much a part of what was before and will be after that no discernment is possible. You don't count waves unless you are prepared for madness. I do not mean that his playing straddled time and eras, as we've come to catalogue them. No, his mind did. The style of Lester was fashioned within time and imprisoned by it. You knew where he was. But there was so much more to Prez than the notes that crept out of his horn.

"We the whores, Socks."

I was the right proper young fool in the autumn of 1955, when I went on tour with Jazz at the Philharmonic. Full of himself, as the Irish say. But at the time I thought I had a decent reason to make an ass of myself: I was playing with first-class musicians, and I was eighteen years of age. In fact I had been playing with pros since I was twelve, earning a livelihood, and had even recorded my first album, for Savoy, at fifteen. Now I see myself playing then as an exercise in flailing around I still won't listen to any of the records I made in that period of my life.

I had been hired by Gene Krupa (who turned me onto Delius, by the way) to fill the spot vacated by Teddy Napoleon. Krupa had added a bass player to bail out the one-handed piano players of the new generation. I certainly was one of those.

It's not clear to me where we started. I seem to remember Hartford,

Connecticut. I came away from the tour with changed opinions and musical values, although this was not obvious in my own playing. Sadly, the experience lowered my estimates of some of the men and their music. But in some cases it raised them. I'd heard very little of Buddy Rich, certainly not enough to make a proper judgment. But his technical prowess alone was mind-boggling. Krupa said to me one night, in an odd matter-of-fact tone, "No one ever played like that before, chappie, and no one will ever play like that again." We were standing in the wings, watching Bud play one of his fabled solos, and Gene—I remember this vividly—didn't share my wide-eyed amazement. I was made to understand that Buddy was Buddy, and that was that. I think the old man envied me my newness of eyes and ears.

All the men on tour had played too much and too long. I felt the frayed nerves on the plane flights, saw the drawn faces when certain hotels were mentioned, could almost weigh the years of singing for their suppers.

But I think of that time as the fall I met Prez.

"We the whores, Socks."

Lester Young was the first person I had known who was outside my ken. He was a visitor from a small planet. Everything that I'd imagined to be way out and bizarre was living reality in Prez. And he gave me more food for thought than anyone I'd met, excepting my music teacher, Edvard Moritz, and a Lutheran minister named Jacob Wagner. But neither of them had the totality of Prez's person. His was a world, fully constructed with all the loose ends tied up, that created reality could not and did not puncture, not even slightly. Prez reminded me that there was such a state as St. Paul spoke of when he said categorically, "We are *in* this world but not *of* it."

I wondered about his spectral being every second I was in his company. It cut through every tidy notion I had formulated about the meaning of this existence. That he was upsetting to many people is an understatement. His voice did nothing to relieve a searcher's quandary. As it was in him, buried deeply, that to impose himself was somehow not fitting, the converse occurred. St. Anselm says that theology is "faith seeking understanding," the intent of intellectual exercising being the effort to create a "religion" or overt practice, the exercise of one's faith making it into a fortress that can stand up easily to the assaults of Reason. However, faith creates its own brand of counterreason and couches itself in felt words, rather than legalistic scientific terms. That leads me to phrases like "You don't find God. You lose yourself until God finds you." That is the quality of understanding Lester required, if in your search for him you eventually noticed that he had found you.

What struck me most was his openness to younger musical talent. It wasn't patronization, a tip of the hat to the coming generations. It was genuine, and his interest constant.

Norman Granz that year presented every member of the touring party with a battery-operated record player. It could be set on one's knees and gave a decent reproduction, considering the tiny speakers. I ran out and purchased some records, one of which was a wonderful album by Jimmy Giuffre on Capitol, which featured a trumpeter then unknown to me, one Jack Sheldon. Prez didn't cart his own phonograph about with him, for the compelling reason that he could only apply himself to the care of his clothes, his whisky, and his horn. I had no notion then of the virtue of paring down one's duties in life. Prez, unlike myself, knew what he could and could not handle. So my phonograph was shared with him. But only in the measure that he listened, for never once did he ask me to play a recording he knew did not delight me.

Prez fell in love with Jack Sheldon's tone production and melodic invention. Sheldon played a solo on "I Only Have Eyes for You" that Prez found so agreeable—and I, too—that we damn near wore the cut out. Prez tried repeatedly to get one of the trumpeters on the tour to take an interest in this young man's talent, to no avail. As the man was in Lester's age group, Prez used him as a measure of what one should not become: deaf to the newer generations. I became acutely aware of the differences in how Prez and his colleagues looked at life through the microcosm of music. His playing might be imprisoned by the years of his youth, but his hearing was not.

I was looking upon an actuated illumination. Other people perceived that illumination incorrectly. The uninitiated might think that what one saw in Prez was the defeat of the human spirit, or the surrender to alcoholism. Some no doubt thought they were seeing an expression of homosexual dislocation. The puzzle of Lester Young. An alcoholic he might have been; homosexual, no.

I came to think his was the exquisite loneliness that comes of a splendid type of isolation. His heart was an Islandman's heart, the heart of one unhappy on a mainland. It put him outside the temporal stream of life, much like an Aran Islander, judging tides with his eyes before trying twenty-foot waves of the ocean in a curragh made of skins and sticks and spit that no sane boater would take out on a quiet mountain tarn in northern California. And the most shocking thing, in gaining knowledge of where Prez was at, was the wholesale misunderstanding of everyone who crossed his path. He was half to blame for it, to be sure. But it was his dearest, his most precious fault, this almost inherent obfuscation.

Being black in America produces its own survival mechanisms. The most obvious and necessary is a facade. But I am not sure that Lester's behavior can be so easily explained. He was born in a time when "race relations" in the Deep South had indeed formed separate communities—separate worlds, really. To hear him speak of his childhood was to be treated to experiences wherein the outer white community wasn't even mentioned. It is quite possible that in a place such as Woodville, Mississippi, the two never met. Yet he gave no indication of a general condemnation of any group of people. In his words he expressed many attitudes—but never contempt. In fact, his moral posture was refreshing and, surprisingly, rang of a pure Christian view in which offenders are seen as pathetic. It was as if he were more concerned with *how* an offensive person "got that way." But he was pragmatic enough to know that there are junkyard dogs and junkyard dog mentalities. I think what made him almost sympathetic to bigots was his deepest understanding of what they had paid for their hatred and how unrewarding the whole exercise must be.

But he had his own fiction and had transfigured it into the beautiful solos all of us who loved him are familiar with. That some people couldn't exorcise their demons as he did, I'm sure, led him to his sympathetic posture. It wasn't with condescension that he looked upon offensive people. That would have taken him where his heart wouldn't allow him to go. So he pitied, felt bad for such misguided souls. I'd call him Gandhi-like, except that Lester was more perceptive than that overrated ascetic.

If Prez was made to feel he wasn't wanted, he left long before he had to be asked to. I remember him saying wistfully, as he looked down at the passing acres of American heartland from a DC-3, "Sure as hell is enough room for everybody, ain't there, Socks?" Thus he summed up the overstuffed cities as culprit.

I always felt he was *visiting* pockets of urban discontent, bringing a message. He often looked at the city we had just played and were flying away from with eyes that brought to mind the words of the Carpenter about shaking the dust of a town off one's sandals.

Dusting off one's sandals and blessing the unfriendly congregation was, in his case, initially effected by Scotch and marijuana. As he spoke less than almost anyone I have ever known, I came to read his silences, hoping to see what it was that he wasn't saying. He once said to me, "The best saxophone section I ever heard is the Mills Brothers." That made me laugh, and made me think. The Mills Brothers, a vocal quartet, had a blend one rarely heard in the sax section of a band. This kind of indirectness, the very hallmark of his verbal expression, enhanced the misguided ideas about him. Not that he gave a damn. It bothered me, though. Truths become throwaways if life deems that they emanate from an eccentric.

By his late years Prez was more revered than taken seriously. This was to everybody's loss. For his judgments on music had risen from the same source as his unique musical improvising. Oh, I can't say that hearing him live in 1955 was as invigorating as his recordings of the 1930s and 1940s. He had become debilitated and, worse, bored. But not with music. More with his own making of a contribution.

AT EIGHTEEN I found nothing sacred. I still am not a hero worshipper, believing Admiral Halsey's evaluation that "there are no great men, only little men who do great things." I do lay claim to an understanding, a historical one, of just where Lester fit into jazz, and how tall the shadow he had cast. One had only to listen to Zoot and Stan, or Art Pepper and Paul Desmond, to hear Prez's voice, his heart, hurdle a generation. I leave out the obvious players like Brew Moore who more imitated Prez than were stoked by him. Once, told of a player who "plays exactly like you" and was even called the Something Prez, Lester said, "Then who am I?"

In fact, I think Lester was tickled by my sacrilegious attitude toward giants. He chuckled and chortled at my teenage mind's evaluations. He saw jazz, as I did, as a counterculture, knowing that whatever the critics tried to make of it, it would remain inaccessible to people more disposed to swim in the broad river of Culture than in a streamlet.

Like all good things, jazz is inherently at odds with what is around it. Like philosophy, it contends for ears and hearts and minds. It will never rule, for its nature is to subvert.

One of the great poetic voices of the twentieth century, Padraic Pearse, went to his death relatively unknown and largely unpublished but secure in the knowledge that he had fathered the Irish Republic. (He led the Easter uprising of 1916.) In a poem called "The Fool," he said, "Oh, wise man, riddle me this. What if the dream come true? What if millions shall dwell in the house shaped in my heart?"

When a man is miscast and talented, he of necessity builds a house in his heart to live in. Some men, like Pearse, though dead, build dwellings that others live in. Jazz players are miscasts, too—my mother quite seriously considered them social mutants—and in their case there are further difficulties in that their houses are not discernible to the casual listener. Their playing then remains—to the large audience—noise from reeds, bent brass, and wind columns. Even noise of course can serve a simple purpose. God forbid that the majority had no noise at all. What then would drown out their own hearts' voices? Mantovani has halted countless important discussions, stayed the dissension in all too many breasts. It is as if Andy Williams typified Voltaire's "best of all possible worlds." (Aaron Copland once bitched about hearing Brahms on Muzak in his bank. The manager said he thought it better than pop music. He didn't understand Copland's reply that he liked to "prepare" himself for Brahms.)

We're all like Pearse. We all try to build houses inside ourselves. Some, like Pearse and Prez, have their houses recognized and the dream becomes a reality that someone can dwell in; and some insinuate the dream and themselves into the main flow of time and culture. They're oftimes whole communities, as in the cases of Bach and Beethoven. And the most alienated has the greatest need to build a house in his heart, so that he may find a home. From this perspective it is easy to see Kafka's work in an understanding way—or a projectionist like Bradbury. The physical disability of deafness, in the cases of Beethoven and Fauré, might have affected their ordering food in a restaurant, but little else. When told that he was deaf, Beethoven shouted, "Tell them Beethoven hears!" He had long since taken up residence in the house he shaped in his heart.

A talent has a design. The walls are its totality, not its limitation. Within them are color and decor, shades or venetian blinds, tissuelike curtains filtering light. And these houses are filled with other voices, soft compelling ones, abrupt rhetorical ones, often angry voices seeking more than an ear.

The visiting of such a house can impel the guest to go about building his own or, at the very least, cultivating an interest in esoteric architecture. I have always seen my own heart as a door. But it has no knob on the outside. It can be opened only from the inside. If you have been following this rather oblique line of reasoning, you'll know we have arrived at the second phase of the search.

What would make a Lester Young open his door and let us in?

TEN YEARS OR so ago a prominent tenor saxophonist with a reputation of giant proportions needed a rhythm section for a gig. Another pianist asked whether I'd do the job. I didn't know the saxophonist personally, so I went to hear him with the players he was using at the moment. I came away confirmed in my mind that the man had no intention of pleasing *any* audience. The evening was a study in antisocial behavior, back-turning included. I am not talking about an off night. We all have those. All this man's nights were "off" nights.

I pondered the reason for his display, knowing I was going to take a pass on the gig, truly wondering why a mature person would be doing something that so obviously pained him. When I remembered Pascal's warning that the brain is a cul-de-sac, I realized that the man was probably trying to open his heart and not succeeding, and I felt sympathy. His heart was locked, from fear of critical judgments. I was made to evaluate the enormous weight of character and balance required for the successfully lived life. Most important of all in his case was the absence of courage. Pure courage. The kind only lovers know of. The kind of giving that opens one's whole person to scrutiny and judgment. And criticism.

Lester had no such problem. He was never touched by such a fear. The point is rather simple. Prez exhibited the bravery of the human spirit.

The remarkable aspect of his offering informational aids to my young self was the way he made me absorb them by osmosis. He seemed to be engaging himself in conversation and allowing me to sift through the points made by both sides. He didn't sell me. "It's all in the *way* you look at it, Socks," he'd say, reminding me how powerful were the fictions of life, and how the *way* in which you viewed them altered them for good or ill.

I don't want you to get the idea that Prez was a fountain, gushing forth knowledge. If you had asked Prez a ridiculous question like, "Do you hate Pollacks?" he'd have answered, "I don't know them all." He had an ability to see through many fictions ("Walter Cronkite and the seven o'clock white folks' news," he called it.) [I don't think Cronkite was hosting the seven o'clock news until after Young died, so it was probably his predecessor, but the point still holds.—Ed.] And often his own questions ended as answers! He didn't presume to possess intelligence, either. That alone was refreshing, considering that he was forty-five and could have cried out his empiric gatherings. But he didn't even trust himself. He was in every way an outsider, vigilant and artfully suspicious.

That fall of 1955 saw a dream boxing match that made partisans of everyone on the tour. Archie Moore was challenging Rocky Marciano for the championship of the world. Archie was the overwhelming favorite among the musicians. I call him Archie, familiarly, because on several occasions he sat in on bass with my trio. He was no player, of course, but he did thump his way through some blues.

Buddy Rich and Birks, as Dizzy Gillespie was called by friends, led the voices for Moore. All the musicians wanted to lay bets, but they all wanted Moore. Only Prez was for the Rock. So, dutifully, he bet "thirteen of my motherfuckin' dollars" with every musician who was hollering for Moore. Lester never did explain to me why he always bet no more and no less than thirteen dollars on anything.

When they had firmed the bets, saying, "You're on, Prez," Lester whispered to me, "Who they think bein' sent in there with Moore? Little Lester?" (He referred to his own son.) "The Rock knocked Joe Louis's ass *through the ropes!*" he chuckled, hearing Buddy and Birks proclaiming Moore's virtues and Marciano's failings. Being a fight fan myself, and having boxed in the amateur, I saw it as a toss-up with a slight edge to Marciano. The Rock had a cast-iron jaw that had been tested and a resilient nature that he had proved against Jersey Joe Walcott. Marciano's fight with Ezzard Charles saw him hit about as hard as a man could be, and still he came away a winner. And he took just a bit better than he could give.

The fight is history. Marciano put the challenger away, but not before Moore provided some first-class moments of his own. He came close to dropping Marciano, but you don't get paid for *close*. Marciano topped off the falling Moore with a hammer blow to the top of the head that would drive someone of my weight through the canvas.

And Prez gloated.

"Give me my motherfuckin' money," he taunted, at the referee's last count, digging into his colleagues' sensibilities in an unkind way, which surprised me. Later he said to me, "*You* should have bet a lot o' money, Socks. They got off too easy." It dawned on me that in laying it into him for his prediction of the outcome, they had offended him. And it seemed that it didn't matter to some of them that they had, as if Prez were not a part of the family, if that's what it was.

Even the respect shown him was often perfunctory, and too many musicians seemed merely to suffer him. (Illinois Jacquet was an outstanding exception.) I was suffered, too, reminded by the musicians in an exquisitely subtle way that at my age I was not entitled to an opinion. I've often thought I came by Lester's friendship as a result. We were both suffered.

In his early years, Prez told me, he'd had trouble at jam sessions. His playing had put more people off than it turned on. He said it was his aversion to gymnastics and the "big" sound. Although he thoroughly enjoyed some of his colleagues—Bean, Byas, and Ben Webster to be sure—he wasn't influenced by them. He mentioned, rather, solos by the Louis Armstrong of the 1920s more than he did his fellow tenor players. Prez didn't arpeggiate in the style of his age. His was a more horizontal linear expression, more in keeping with the approach of a trumpeter, trombonist, or adventurist singer. That distinction is the key to his heavy influence on later players.

It doesn't take a speculative genius to surmise that Getz, Pepper, and Desmond did not like the natural sound of the saxophone. Possibly the enigma of the bastard quality of the instrument—half reed, half brass—nettled them to soften and neutralize it. Prez did the laboratory work for all the successive players and pointed the *way*. Nor do I mean to minimize their accomplishments.

Prez was less harmonic than Coleman Hawkins. His preoccupation with the pentatonic scale sang more of his Mississippi folk roots than it did of his later big-city life. It evoked a country preacher more than a streetwise tart. Zoot often makes me feel Prez is in the room, when he's playing a piece that allows for that brand of proselytizing. Peculiar it is, too, for it makes less use of the blues than it does rural folk elements. That Zoot plays in that manner, coming as he does from a suburb of Los Angeles, can only mean to me that he didn't merely stay in the foyer of the house Prez shaped in his heart. Prez has become a *Tao*, a way, a path. Few artists in the twentieth century have had so many surrogate vicars.

OK, you may say, you've got a point, but I think you're making a mountain out of a molehill. The man played "simple," easily digestible solos. His facility wasn't in a class with the other giants I can name.

I give that argument its due. There's much sense in it and a modicum of truth.

But once I asked Prez why he didn't play certain licks, which everyone I knew did, knocking out a few of them on the piano for him. His face took on a great incredulity, and he fired back, "That's the way Bird played!" He paused, and then he said, "He plays those licks, I play my licks, you play your licks." I nearly fell off the piano bench from the weight of his truth. I had been raised in the high noon of bebop, and wherever I went in those days, I was judged by how well I had adapted myself to the Holy Writ of Bird, Bud, Monk, and Birks.

I am always amazed at how well Prez *wears*. His expression is not one of *immediate* importance, like Charlie Parker's was, nor so energetic in the rhythmical sense. (Bird suffered terribly from rhythm sections that were a decade behind him in understanding.) Bird was subjective and biting, Prez more sedate and objective. Bird's playing was locked into the range and the character of the alto. That is why the bit of tenor playing he did on record is nondescript. In contrast, I am forced to remember how interesting Lester's clarinet playing was. Lester could move into a new setting—export himself, as it were. Was it because his playing was so organic? Was his conception more melodic, of its very nature?

I remember walking into a nightclub where he was performing with a local rhythm section. "Oh, Socks, baby, I'm glad to see you here! This boy playin' piano plays *very well*. But he puts eight changes where there oughta be two! You know me, Socks. Somethin' like 'These Foolish Things,' I mean, I like the E-flat chord, the C-minor, the F-minor seventh, the B-flat nine. You know. Shit. I can't play when there are eighty-nine motherfuckin' changes in the bar!"

I spoke with the pianist, who wasn't as yet aware what Prez liked to hear behind him. Whether he followed my suggestions or not, I never learned, because for Prez every job ended sooner than later. I mentioned the incident to him at Birdland one night a month or so later, and he was puzzled: it was ancient history by then, and he couldn't raise up a memory. All he remembered of my visit in fact was my outrageous show business silk suit, required by the straight-up singing act I was doing at the time. A stranger he remained, alienated from the moving parts of watches and never noting the differing structures of cities or the many faces he would pass.

For those who became his intimates—alas, a surprising few—he took on a Lewis Carroll dimension. At times his innocence was baffling. Lester could say, "I don't believe it!" and *mean* it. Most of what we see in life is so destructive, so bizarre, that most of us experience a confusion not unlike Prez did. I still have not adjusted to the notion that there are best-selling diet books, going at fifteen or twenty dollars a pop, in a world in which ten thousand human beings are starving to death *each week* in the Horn of Africa. It was only when I realized how hard it was for Prez to commit himself to understanding the unrepentant world out there that I connected a hidden portion of him with the rest of his behavior.

You could call him superstitious, though not to the degree that it froze him. Willie Smith, he once told me, was a "number" person. Prez said that if Willie came up with the wrong numerical position on boarding a plane, he was apt to get off it. Lester felt a huge surge of anxiety if a very ill person—or worse, one in a wheelchair—got onto our flight.

"God damn it, Socks," he'd groan, "it's a Johnny Deathbed!" His eyes would remain fixed on the plane's entrance—until he saw a child, or an infant, board. If it was an infant, he eased immediately, noticeably. Although he never talked about religion, Prez let me know that the Deity was to be taken for granted. He obviously believed in the fair mercy of God, for the presence of the infant on our flight ruled out any chance that God would take out the entire flight to collect the Johnny Deathbed. The implications that vibrated outward from this view amused, and stimulated, me greatly. It was Lester's conviction that people about to take the Big Journey ought to be in their "cribs" waiting, not out here where innocents might have to share their fate. He felt we shared responsibility with the Deity and had to "get our shit together."

I always felt that I must have said something or done something that *signaled* Prez. He was a believer in such things, always open to the unspoken, the unexpected, even to the unwelcome sign. It is told that he had two weeks left of a gig in Europe in 1959 when he upped and flew back home to his almost immediate death. A sign, no doubt, danced before his eyes in Paris.

There was a brilliance to Lester's otherworldliness that made me weigh what is called *educated*. Lincoln defined learning as telling ourselves what we knew all along to be the truth but were afraid to tell ourselves. Prez *sensed* everything. He was somehow aware that the gray matter in the cranium is a first-class deceiver and relied on intuition. Once, when we were looking for a restaurant in a city new to both of us, he said too comfortably, "One more block, Socks, and we'll eat." He was right! I've since credited a good deal of his obliqueness to a preoccupation with inner voices he let lead him. Often people thought they had run up against an alcoholic mist too thick to penetrate. But that was rarely the case. He just wasn't listening, for there were moments when his lucidity was remarkable, although his intake of grass and booze had been his usual.

His day-to-day existence was like a pendulum. Besides, he was a night person. The day for him was a many-houred awakening of a long-toothed spirit. He *entered* the evening. Even the quantity of his words increased as the light of day waned. It was as if he'd climbed a ridge of small hillocks, then settled into a golden period, a span of bewitched time. In a very real sense, his day was ushered in by the pushing of air columns through instruments, the heartbeat of a walking bass, the glistening punctuations of a ride cymbal. His sticklike body, so worn by his utter disregard for its health, straightened to its limit only during those hours of music. And the music turned on his capacity for camaraderie and humor.

For a reason I have never been able to isolate, he shouldered the burden of being resident jester on that 1955 tour. And he was good at it. His brand of storytelling was unique. It was littered with so many "motherfuckers" that it was shushed down, and out, when we found ourselves in the company of the general public. But when we traveled in quarantine, he was allowed to stretch out, and never since then have my sides ached so much.

He would have mock fights with Roy Eldridge and other "shorter" fellows who would grab his arms as if to do him up. "Midget motherfuckers!" he would cry in pretended desperation. "Lawyer Brown, Lady Pete!" he would call to Ray Brown and Oscar Peterson. "Socks! You gotta help me with these midget motherfuckers!" Only Prez could carry it off. For minutes afterwards, he'd mumble to himself, still in his fiction and dramatic mockery, "Those . . . *midget . . . motherfuckers!*" And he would say, "Socks, I could take 'em—one at a time! But the midget motherfuckers gang up on me! They gang up on ol' Prez!"

Nobody ever made so much fun so consistently, so hard, so freely. Sometimes, when he was on a roll, it went on for days. Not jokes or one-liners, although he had a few of those. No, it was always situational and personal. As I'm writing this, I can *hear* him again, hear the fake dramatic pauses, the ham acting, the truncated exclamations he was known for and, most of all, the disarming sweetness. The bastard!

It takes a considerable amount of confidence to laugh at one's self. "Dr. Willis Wiggins," as he referred to himself, had it. He knew all about what Rodney Dangerfield has turned into a science. Prez tripped that thin line between self-deprecation and wholesome abandon. To my eye, unseasoned at the time, there was a truth I couldn't see.

He had the courage that makes for *self*. The quality of bravery that never asks dumb questions or looks for conspiracy in honest words. The great danger of *becoming* your musical expression was one to which Lester never succumbed. It set him apart from other musicians, made less by their inability to be something other than their music. No one who knew him would call him a "regular guy." Not ever. But he *could* be, if he so chose. That in itself broadens his humanity.

Most players of note get used to applause, as they do to the growth of their vanity. Prez acted upon Solomon's assessment that *all* is vanity. He never promoted himself to me, or anyone, in any way. It was odd. Most of the musicians I've spent time with always touch that base, either quietly or with trumpeting.

I got behind the wheel of my car yesterday, and the radio was on with ignition, automatically. The exquisite lyrical tones of Paul Desmond jumped out at me, and my first thought, if sweet Paul will forgive me, was Dr. Willis lives!

A LOT OF things seem to have changed since 1955. Even memories are refurbished. I find myself reevaluating friends and family, thinking of collisions of Will and Personality, the packets of wrong words we have all let slip at one time or another.

But Prez never changes.

He alone makes me look to my "gate receipts," as he called all bottom lines, and check out the bases of all social comings-together I deemed important over the years.

That he is gone, and has stopped, frozen in time, has only strengthened the outline of his self in my memory. A handful of people I've known have a near degree of his definition. But no more than a handful.

He never spoke of his lineal roots, but there was no mistaking his being a product of woodpile philanderings. His skin was off-white, a light coffee alabaster, and his hair an obvious auburn that was darkened by a conk. When it was in need of a conk, Roy Eldridge would whisper to me, "Call him a big red motherfucker, Socks. He'll jump up and down."

His clothes draped his frame. I took it that he'd lost weight and simply wouldn't waste money playing at being a fashion plate. There was something rumpled, but not disheveled, about his appearance. His walk, which was more a shuffle than an honest walk, had something Asiatic about it, a reticence to barge in. He sidled. It was in keeping with the side-door quality of his nature. He was punctual. He started early and left later than most of us, maintaining his cool and living rhythm, but his pace was that of a sleepwalker. I think that Prez thought there was nothing worth hustling for.

The two of us, like old Pick and young Pat, shilly-shallied most of the time, rapping. He liked to draw on the romantic liaisons that littered his youth, hoping I'd learn something from the retelling. While he was living with one aggressive and hostile lady, he said, he took to putting his horn, in its case, into a garbage can outside her house before he entered, never knowing how she'd react to his absences, catting. So he took no chances with the "Green Horn-et," as he called the case.

One night, though, he'd had enough of her "beatin' up my ass." So he decided to do a little number himself. "You oughta've seen the bitch . . . drop t' her knees, Socks. Bitch hollerin', 'Don't make a fist, Prez, please don' make a fist!' Shit, I tol' the bitch, 'You been using your goddamn nails on ol' Prez for a year now!'" He'd pause, the light that made the bloodshot eyes seem so alive going down, and he'd look me square in the face. "You *gotta* be a man 'bout some things, Socks."

There was, of course, a lot of comic bravado in his kiss-and-tell stories. But I took away from them an idea of what I might expect if I continued being a gypsy with a song that had to come out.

He was too gentle to have kicked ass. I couldn't imagine him doing it. I might get into a fight, but not Prez. Yet he harped on taking a stand. The late Jack Dempsey said to me, "Don't ever let people use the name you had to fight for, kid. Never." He said it in a restaurant called Jack Dempsey's, which he did not own. And he echoed Prez.

Lester was inclined to remind me that music was a universe and that I ought not to sit only in a corner of it. His own attitude was one of discovery. I once asked him what would most knock him out, and he answered, "My own big band, with Jo Stafford and Frankie-boy as my singers." The few feet between us became a revelation ground as he touched on things no interviewer ever asked him about. His tastes were catholic, and when he liked something, you couldn't run it down to him.

He forced me to think of *music*, not just jazz, and I thank him for it. In fact I had to watch out for his underselling, or I might have come to the conclusion that jazz was no more than an aberration. It's not that he downgraded it. He just took the edge off my idolatry. I thought of jazz as my life's breath; he thought of it as second nature.

It wouldn't have surprised him that a man like Leonard Bernstein would have liked to play jazz. Lester would have encouraged him, regardless of the fact that Bernstein wasn't a first-class jazz talent. For Prez it was unthinkable that the joy he had known would not be of interest to a fellow countryman with musical ability. I suspect that Lester believed no one owned music. Not even a part of it. I welcomed that openness. Few players have earned a niche like his, but there he was, sundering the very notion of the proprietorial.

"You can't own . . . what ain't, Socks."

How could someone "own" what those still unborn might say on a horn twenty years hence? Once I mentioned a talented bass player of real stature who was a rabid racist. A despairing look came into that quiet-eyed face as I told him a story of a man's unkindness, saying that none of us is responsible for the tone of his skin. Prez then told me a story about a man who thought he had lost something valuable, only to remember in his panic that he'd left it at home. "Ain't no truth there, Socks. That's the only good thing about mirrors. They make you look at yourself."

And then he said that a fool makes the other man pay for his inadequacies. And because he doesn't take the loss himself, "he loses the chance to find out who the fuck he is." Prez said that such people hungered for something they had never given themselves. Trouble was, he sighed, "nobody else *can* give it to them."

He was dying then.

I knew he was. I dreamed, and I rationalized. But there were moments when our eyes met and the weariness in his told me. Like an old maid, I counseled him to take better care of his health. It occurs to me now how I bored the shit out of him by doing that.

Prez had come to me, to life, from out of nowhere, really, and it seemed he'd always been around, like the wind in October and the weeping clouds of March. Where would he go, in any case? A person such as Prez *is*. But there were signs. A few shallow-sounding laughs. Twice, quite remarkably, he referred to himself in the past tense and didn't seek to rectify the mistake.

The bottle of Scotch he carried in a red plaid bag was always in his lap. It took priority over his horn and clothing. I began to see that his juicing had gone through the worst form of transubstantiation. Booze was medicine now, and I wasn't fooled by his excuses, good as they were. I remember the sadness that came from that lonely face—that of a kid whose candy had fallen into the dirt. He'd been dealt a low blow, his greatest pleasure having been turned into an anesthetic imperative.

TWO "SANCTIFIED" OLD ladies lived behind Prez on Long Island, their yards abutting his. They had never conversed with him, indeed did not know him or anyone else who didn't belong to their church congregation. As Lester dressed rather zoot-suity, drank, and played jazz, they had reached their own opinion of him.

One summer afternoon, while the ladies were back-porching and gossiping, Mr. Young and his son, Little Lester, sauntered into the yard and commenced to toss a ball around. The ladies couldn't but start revising their opinion of their neighbor. "Isn't that nice?" they chirped, watching father and son.

They were still watching when Prez decided he'd had enough ball tossing. He and Little Lester walked to the back door. Prez tried the knob. He turned his face down toward Little Lester and said, "*There*, you dumb motherfucker, you done locked us both out the house!"

The ladies never recovered.

Prez used profanity—and *all* language—creatively. And he had the oddest gentle way of saying *motherfucker*.

In a Texas airport he came under the scrutiny of some Texas Rangers. They looked at him as if he were a Martian, in his crepe-soled boots and porkpie hat with the wide brim, forgetting of course their own western headgear. Prez elbowed me and whispered, "Go tell them I'm a cowboy, Socks."

In the winter of 1956, I made a vocal recording that became number one on the Hit Parade. The "success" it brought ruined the quality of my life and sent me off doing an "act" in nightclubs that, thank God, I never did carry off well enough to be marketed like a bar of soap.

During that time I ran into Lester. After the greetings and questions about immediate family, he said, pointedly, "They say your hat don't fit no more, Socks." I was taken aback. I told him, "That ain't the story, mornin' glory."

He smiled and said, "Letter A, then, Socks," meaning of course, back to the top.

There were entire conversations like that. Countless people said to me, after hearing us talk for a few minutes, "What the hell was he talking about, Bobby?" In the 1980s his behavior would be regarded as mild. So, too, Lenny Bruce's. But being inaccessible didn't help Prez.

Lester was very aware of how people broke hearts with their tongues. A man misjudged as often as Prez was, and offended so easily, would know about that. Accordingly, his own observations were couched in "unknown" terms, that he might not give offense. I saw it as very responsible behavior. In any case, Prez wasn't a presumptuous man and considered his judgments no more important than anyone else's. He was sensitive but not touchy. He took the ribbings of his colleagues well. For instance, every few nights, with much aplomb and mock assurance, Oscar Peterson would lay in those "extra" chord changes during Lester's solo in the Ballad Medley. During a concert in the Montreal Forum, Prez sidled back to the nine-foot grand piano, unaware that just below him and inside the instrument was an open microphone. Turning to Oscar his puzzled, pleading face, he said, "Where are you motherfuckers at?"

The audience's laughter sounded like Niagara Falls.

Norman Granz told Lester to stay after the concert. I found him sitting cross-legged, his face as forlorn as the head of a cracked porcelain doll.

"What are you waiting for, Prez?" said his worshipping eighteen-year-old friend.

His eyebrows raised, in acknowledgment of his faux pas. "Lady Norman's gonna give me a reading." He winked. "I bought it, Socks," he said, as I walked slowly off the stage, looking back and thinking how much he seemed like a kid kept after school.

He never said he thought Norman was wrong about the incident, and he credited Granz with bailing him out of many predicaments.

He had names for everyone, or almost everyone. For some reason he never invented one for Herb Ellis, who, like Lester himself, is a very gentle man. But Lester hung "Sweets" on Harry Edison, and now everyone knows him by that name. And he gave the title Lady to men—Lady Pete, Lady Norman, Lady Stitt, Lady Krupa. And he gave me my name. Because I was the youngest member of the troupe, Bobby Scott became Bobby Socks, and then just Socks.

As a vehicle for his high humor, he conjured up a conspiracy against the two of us. Often, if we boarded a flight at the last minute, the seats we got were served dinner last. Too often we were just digging into our food when the plane began its descent. Lester trotted out his paranoia, blaming everyone from the midget motherfuckers to the White House. I couldn't eat for laughing. He'd squinch up his face in a deviltry that could bring me near to wetting myself, and mumble, "You see this shit, Socks? You see *this?*" He would shake his head, glancing furtively toward the back of the plane where "the enemy" sat. His voice, still softly clandestine, would push out. "They're tryin' to *get* us, Socks." And I of course had to go along with him or let the splendid humor of it die.

The quiet that surrounded and covered Lester was of a contemplative nature and origin. If he allowed me to "divert" him, he did it out of an interest in, and a love for, me. He didn't need diversion. Small things could and would draw his interest and attention.

Whatever he was in his totality, and no one is privy to such knowledge of another, the one observation I could make about him was that the peace that emanated from him was a glowing proof of a *balanced* personality.

Happiness depends, it has always seemed to me, on the health of one's moral condition. Lester was a happy person, no more besieged than the rest of us. But he had the conviction that gives a fighter staying power. He never gave up what was consistent with his values. He skirmished frequently, as sensitive people do, with becoming a number instead of a name, a figure rather than a living person, a reputation instead of a producer of beautiful music.

He knew what made him happy and what he would have to tolerate, and his baleful puss told you how hard it was sometimes to keep apart the rights and the wrongs in the affray.

At the time, I found his complaints nothing but griping. Now that I am a man and have, as the Indians say, walked a mile in his moccasins, I have become an echo of those gripes. He experienced doubts of tremendous size and often converted them before my eyes into something else.

When I arrived at the airport apron one morning, I made my way through the small group of passengers and found Prez with a perplexed and doom-filled face, eyeing our aircraft. It was a DC-3, slightly worn-looking but otherwise apparently fit.

"Socks baby, it's a *two-lunger!*" Prez felt much safer in a four-engine craft. "We gotta have a *four*-lunger, Socks! Shit! You lose one, you still got *three!* One of *these* motherfuckers goes, an' we only got *one* lung left!"

Moments later, having accepted the inevitable, he was sitting next to me, back in his groove, snapping his fingers at the engines outside the window, and hollering (to the chagrin and embarrassment of the tour members): "Get it! Get . . . *it!* God . . . damn . . . IT!"

He talked to the engines, shouting his encouragement as we barreled down the runway. He was still hollering, to the shushing sounds of Ella Fitzgerald and Norman Granz, when the creaking weight of metal lifted up out of the un-Cloroxed clouds into the sunshine.

He smiled then. He had fortified himself with Dewars. He whispered, "It's only gettin' here that bothers me, Socks." I told him I had no inclination to be a bird, either. And yet he trusted the pilots implicitly. "They got their shit together," he said.

I have never enjoyed traveling as much since then.

NOR HAVE I ever met anyone who wore aloneness as forthrightly as Prez.

St. Augustine offers us this: God created man that man might seek God. The implication is that even God cannot escape loneliness. Nietzsche quips, not untruthfully, that crying is the same as laughing, except that it is at the other end of the same rainbow, differing only in intensity, not character. Why is loneliness the major tone quality of large cities, where millions congregate? Is Augustine right? Or is what we call "loneliness" an outgrowth of personal dislocation, inasmuch as we are among the multitude? Are we, as the bishop of Hippo implies, made in the image of our Maker, and marked by the loneliness of His own dispersal?

One can safely say that the groundbreakers in the arts are nearly always testaments, monuments, to loneliness. What the artist seeks to offer to others he must hone by himself. Does he then give us his solitariness? Are not the solitary and the lone one and the same? And why is it most likely the source of all the world's joys?

I trust Augustine and believe that loneliness is the glue and ether of existence. Further, how one handles it marks one's life as successfully lived or as a failure. The friendship I developed with Prez was marked by the reeking exquisiteness of his loneliness. What confounded me, and still does, was what made him confident enough to lower the weir that damned his precious solitariness and allowed me to join with it, in concert.

When music is not pedantry, as in Buxtehude, or gymnastics, as in Varèse, or structure, as in the canons of Bach, it is the transfiguration of the loneliness its creator has come to acknowledge and live with. Lester's sound was profoundly beseeching. It sought out the tired residue of the greatest war a human being wages, the one with and inside himself. Prez echoed his own despair, raising it miraculously until it took on a new aspect. What better way to serve one's brothers in loneliness? To be able to express one's own deepest feelings of limitation and incertitude, breaking the fetters and raising up the specter in others so clearly that they begin to see the silhouette of their own solitariness, is a reward unto itself.

For me the best moment of each evening was Lester's solo in the Ballad Medley. That year he played "I Didn't Know What Time It Was." I never became bored with it. I realized that it was his sound production and phrasing that seduced me. And there was, to my ears, a reverent quality that he instilled in the notes. Although he couldn't help but sound labored and worn, it was the voice of a sage, and there was no shooting from the hip in it. He had to work harder than the other players. They were healthier. He was deceptive, though. I swore I heard hectic winds when he looked me squarely in the eyes. On those few occasions I did indeed see defeat there. But I could do nothing that would alter the situation. At eighteen I wouldn't take it upon myself to inform the powers that be that he might be unable to perform. But on he'd trudge, miraculously, his crepe-soled shoes scraping . . .

He plays the melody so well that it is a bit of a shock to me. Me, who learned three-quarters of the tunes I know purely harmonically. Prez won't play a tune if he doesn't know the lyric—the entire lyric. Knowing the lyric, he makes the shape of his offering more organic, his phrasing elegant. Ultimately Lester shows me *who* and *what* I am; he makes it come to life in his playing. In among the notes I find my recognizable shape and identity.

The tired figure of a man who befriended a boy walks on and points the bell of his horn upward in a strange supplication.

Then come the tones of wonder.

THE BIG BANDS

GEORGE T. SIMON

The Big Bands, *George Simon's panoramic survey of the Swing Era, is a basic book—and as such has been revised and reissued many times since its original publication in 1967. In these opening pages of his magnum opus, Simon—a prolific writer and important editor—sets the Big Band scene.*

THE SCENE

Do you remember what it was like? Maybe you do. Maybe you were there. Maybe you were there in New York two-thirds of the way through the 1930s, when there were so many great bands playing—so many of them at the same time. You could choose your spots—so many spots.

You could go to the Madhattan Room of the Hotel Pennsylvania, where Benny Goodman, the man who started it all, was playing with his great band, complete with Gene Krupa.

You could go a block or so farther to the Terrace Room of the Hotel New Yorker, and there you'd find Jimmy Dorsey and his Orchestra with Bob Eberly and Helen O'Connell . . . or to the Blue Room of the Hotel Lincoln to catch Artie Shaw and his band with Helen Forrest . . . or to the Green Room of the Hotel Edison for Les Brown's brand-new band.

Maybe you'd rather go to some other hotel room—like the Palm Room of the Commodore for Red Norvo and Mildred Bailey and their soft, subtle swing . . . or to the Grill Room of the Lexington for Bob Crosby and his Dixieland Bobcats . . . or to the Moonlit Terrace of the Biltmore for Horace Heidt and his huge singing entourage . . . or down to the Roosevelt Grill for Guy Lombardo and his Royal Canadians and their extrasweet sounds.

And then there were the ballrooms—the Roseland with Woody Herman and the Savoy with Chick Webb. Not to mention the nightclubs—the Cotton Club with Duke Ellington, or the Paradise Restaurant, where a band nobody knew too much about was making sounds that the entire nation would soon recognize as those of Glenn Miller and his Orchestra.

Maybe you didn't feel so much like dancing but more like sitting and listening and maybe taking in a movie too. You could go to the Paramount, where Tommy Dorsey and his band, along with Jack Leonard and Edythe Wright, were appearing . . . or to the Strand to catch Xavier Cugat and his Latin music . . . or to Loew's State, where Jimmie Lunceford was swinging forth.

And if you had a car, you could go a few miles out of town . . . to the Glen Island Casino in New Rochelle to dance to Larry Clinton's music with vocals by Bea Wain . . . or to Frank Dailey's Meadowbrook across the bridge in New Jersey to catch Glen Gray and the Casa Loma Orchestra with Peewee Hunt and Kenny Sargent.

Of course, if you didn't feel like going out at all, you still were in luck—and you didn't have to be in New York either. For all you had to do was to turn on your radio and you could hear all sorts of great bands coming from all sorts of places—from the Aragon and Trianon ballrooms in Chicago, the Palomar Ballroom in Hollywood, the Raymor Ballroom in Boston, the Blue Room of the Hotel Roosevelt in New Orleans, the Mark Hopkins Hotel in San Francisco, the Steel Pier in Atlantic City and hundreds of other hotels, ballrooms and nightclubs throughout the country, wherever an announcer would begin a program with words like "And here is the music of ——!"

The music varied tremendously from style to style and, within each style, from band to band. Thus you could hear all types of swing bands: the hard-driving swing of Benny Goodman, the relaxed swing of Jimmie Lunceford, the forceful Dixieland of Bob Crosby, the simple, riff-filled swing of Count Basie, the highly developed swing of Duke Ellington, and the very commercial swing of Glenn Miller.

Many of the big swing bands were built around the leaders and their instruments—around the clarinets of Goodman and Artie Shaw, the trumpets of Harry James and Bunny Berigan, the trombones of Jack Teagarden and Tommy Dorsey, the tenor sax of Charlie Barnet, the pianos of Ellington and Count Basie and the drums of Gene Krupa.

And then there were the sweet bands. They varied in style and in quality too. Some projected rich, full, musical ensemble sounds, like those of Glen Gray and the Casa Loma Orchestra, Isham Jones, Ray Noble and Glenn Miller. Others depended more on intimacy, like the bands of Hal Kemp and Guy Lombardo and of Tommy Dorsey when he featured his pretty trombone. Others played more in the society manner—Eddy Duchin with his flowery piano and Freddy Martin with his soft, moaning sax sounds. And then there were the extrasweet bandleaders. Lombardo, of course, was one. So was his chief imitator, Jan Garber. So was the Waltz King, Wayne King.

And there were the novelty bands, generally lumped in with the sweet bands—Kay Kyser, with all his smart gimmicks, including his College of Musical Knowledge and his singing song titles; Sammy Kaye, who also used singing song titles and introduced his "So You Wanna Lead a Band" gimmick; and Blue Barron, who aped Kaye . . . and so many others who aped Barron, who aped Kaye, who aped Kyser, who aped Lombardo.

There were so many bands playing so many different kinds of music—some well, some adequately, some horribly—all with their fans and followers. The *Metronome* poll, in which readers were invited to vote for their favorite bands in three divisions (Swing, Sweet and Favorite of All), listed almost three hundred entries in each of the four years from 1937 through 1940. And those were merely the bands that the readers liked most of all! There were hundreds more all over the country that didn't even place.

Why were some so much more successful than others? Discounting the obvious commercial considerations, such as financial support, personal managers, booking offices, recordings, radio exposure and press agents, four other factors were of paramount importance.

There was, of course, the band's musical style. This varied radically from band to band. A Tommy Dorsey was as far removed from a Tommy Tucker as an Artie Shaw was from an Art Kassel or a Sammy Kaye was from a Sam Donahue. Each band depended upon its own particular style, its own identifiable sound, for general, partial or just meager acceptance. In many ways, the whole business was like a style show—if the public latched on to what you were displaying, you had a good chance of success. If it rejected you, you'd better forget it.

Generally it was the band's musical director, either its arranger or its leader or perhaps both, who established a style. He or they decided what sort of sound the band should have, how it should be achieved and how it should be presented, and from there on proceeded to try to do everything possible to establish and project that sound, or style.

Secondly, the musicians within a band, its sidemen, played important roles. Their ability to play the arrangements was, naturally, vitally important. In some bands the musicians themselves contributed a good deal, especially in the swing bands, which depended upon them for so many solos; and in the more musical bands, whose leaders were willing to listen to and often accept musical suggestions from their sidemen.

But the musicians were important in other ways too. Their attitude and cooperation could make or break a band. If they liked or rejected a leader, they would work hard to help him achieve his goals. If they had little use for him, they'd slough off both him and his music. The more musical the band and the style, the greater, generally speaking, the cooperation of its musicians in all matters—personal as well as musical.

Salaries? They were important, yes, in the bands that weren't so much fun to play in. But if the band was good musically and if the musicians were aware that their leader was struggling and couldn't pay much, money very often became secondary. Pride and potential, and, most importantly, respect usually prevailed.

Thirdly, the singers—or the band vocalists, as they were generally called—often played important roles in establishing a band's popularity, in some cases even surpassing that of the band itself. A good deal depended upon how much a leader needed to or was willing to feature a vocalist. Most of the smarter ones realized that any extra added attraction within their own organization could only redound to their credit. Even after many of those singers had graduated to stardom on their own, their past relationships with the bands added a touch of glamour to those bands and their reputations.

Thus such current stars as Frank Sinatra and Jo Stafford still bring back memories of Tommy Dorsey, Doris Day of Les Brown, Ella Fitzgerald of Chick Webb, Peggy Lee of Benny Goodman and Perry Como of Ted Weems.

And there were many others who meant very much to their leaders—Bob Eberly and Helen O'Connell to Jimmy Dorsey, Ray Eberle and Marion Hutton to Glenn Miller, Dick Haymes and Helen Forrest to Harry James, Kenny Sargent and Peewee Hunt to Glen Gray, Bea Wain to Larry Clinton, Ivy Anderson to Duke Ellington, Mildred Bailey to Red Norvo, Anita O'Day to Gene Krupa, June Christy to Stan Kenton, Ginny Sims to Kay Kyser, Dolly Dawn to George Hall, Wee Bonnie Baker to Orrin Tucker, Amy Arnell to Tommy Tucker, Jimmy Rushing to Count Basie, Al Bowlly to Ray Noble, Eddy Howard to Dick Jurgens, Bon Bon to Jan Savitt, Skinnay Ennis to Hal Kemp and, of course, Carmen Lombardo to brother Guy.

But of all the factors involved in the success of a dance band—the business affairs, the musical style, the arrangers, the sidemen and the vocalists—nothing equaled in importance the part played by the leaders themselves. For in each band it was the leader who assumed the most vital and most responsible role. Around him revolved the music, the musicians, the vocalists, the arrangers and all the commercial factors involved in running a band, and it was up to him to take these component parts and with them achieve success, mediocrity or failure.

The Leaders

Some were completely devoted to music, others entirely to the money it could bring.

Some possessed great musical talent; others possessed none.

Some really loved people; others merely used them.

Some were extremely daring; others were stodgily conservative.

Some were motivated more by their emotions, others by a carefully calculated course of action.

And for some, leading a band was primarily an art; for others, it was basically a science.

That's how much bandleaders varied—in their ambitions, their ideals, their motivations, their talents and their personalities, as well as in their musical and ethical standards and values. They were as different personally as their bands were musically. Yet, with varying degrees of intensity, each sought success in one form or another—from the most purely artistic to the most crassly commercial.

Their approaches varied with their personalities and their talents. Highly dedicated and equally ambitious musicians like Glenn Miller, Benny Goodman, Artie Shaw and Tommy Dorsey approached their jobs with a rare combination of idealism and realism. Well trained and well disciplined, they knew what they wanted, and they knew how to get it. Keenly aware of the commercial competition, they drove themselves and their men relentlessly, for only through achieving perfection, or the closest possible state to it, could they see themselves realizing their musical and commercial goals.

Others, equally dedicated to high musical standards but less blatantly devoted to ruling the roost, worked in a more relaxed manner. Leaders like Woody Herman, Les Brown, Duke Ellington, Gene Krupa, Count Basie, Harry James, Claude Thornhill and Jimmy Dorsey pressured their men less. "You guys are pros," was their attitude, "so as long as you produce, you've got nothing to worry about." Their bands may have had a little less machine-like proficiency, but they swung easily and created good musical and commercial sounds.

Other leaders, often less musically endowed and less idealistically inclined, approached their jobs more from a businessman's point of view. For them music seemed to be less an art and more a product to be colorfully packaged and cleverly promoted. The most successful of such leaders, bright men like Guy Lombardo, Kay Kyser, Sammy Kaye, Horace Heidt, Shep Fields, Wayne King and Lawrence Welk, were masters at creating distinctive though hardly distinguished musical styles; men respected more for commercial cunning than for artistic creativity. They might have been faulted by *Metronome* and *Down Beat* but never by *Fortune* or *The Wall Street Journal*.

At the other end of the bandleading scale were those not nearly wise or calculating enough to realize that they never should have become bandleaders in the first place. Among these were some of the most talented and colorful musicians on the scene, to whom the music business meant all music and no business. Their lives were undisciplined and so were their bands. They swung just for the present, for a present filled with loads of laughs and little acceptance of their responsibilities as leaders. Unfortunately, almost all of this last group wound up as bandleading failures. For no matter what they would have liked to believe, leading a band was definitely a business, a very competitive, complex business consisting of almost continuous contacts—and often difficult and crucial compromises—with a wide variety of people on whom not merely the success but the very life of a dance band depended.

The leaders were called on to deal daily and directly—and not only on a musical but also on a personal basis—with their musicians, their vocalists and their arrangers, directing and supervising and bearing the responsibilities of each of these groups. But that wasn't all. For their survival also depended a great deal on how well they dealt with all kinds of people outside their bands—with personal managers, with booking agents, with ballroom, nightclub and hotel-room operators, with headwaiters and waiters and busboys, with bus drivers, with band boys, with the press, with publicity men, with music publishers, with all the various people from the radio stations and from the record companies and, of course, at all times and in all places—and no matter how tired or in what mood a leader might be—with the ever-present, ever-pressuring public.

No wonder Artie Shaw ran away to Mexico!

Homage to Bunny

George Frazier

George Frazier is said to have been among the first jazz writers to appear in a daily paper, and this "homage" to Bunny Berigan, which appeared as an obituary in the Boston Herald *in June 1942, certainly exemplifies the high-flown yet endearing approach of certain journalists—particularly sportswriters—of that period.*

Bunny Berigan (*ave atque vale*) died at the age of thirty-four.

Now the apocrypha will begin to take shape, constantly expanding, constantly gaining credence. Now the stories will begin to be told and retold, the I-know-for-a-fact stories mushrooming in the gray hours before dawn when musicians gather and tell the gallant tales. A story here and another story there, until presently the legend will be born. It was that way with Beiderbecke, and it will be that way with Berigan, too. Because both of them died young.

But legend or no legend, there will always be that horn. It's there on the records and it's unforgettable. It is there in the "Sometimes I'm Happy" and "King Porter Stomp" out of the splendor of the early days of the Goodman band. The tone big and rich and coming at you suddenly, and singing so magnificently that you're screaming with jazz. It is there in his own Okeh recording of "I Can't Get Started," which is one of the most memorable trumpet performances ever cut into wax. It is there in the Tommy Dorsey "Marie," which is just about as good Dorsey as you'll ever hear. It is in a lot of things. In "Honeysuckle Rose" and "Squeeze Me," behind Mildred Bailey; in "Find Me a Primitive Man" and "Hot House Rose" and "Let's Fly Away," behind Lee Wiley; in "Billie's Blues," behind Billie Holiday.

And it is always something wonderful. Something that seems to come down out of the sky (which is precisely the way it seems with Bix) and all of a sudden bursts into something so eloquent that you will never forget it until the day you die.

But now he is dead, this big, shaggy bear of a man, this sandy-haired man with the watery eyes and the thin huskiness in his voice. He is dead and people are mourning him. He went to the University of Wisconsin, played with

Hal Kemp, Paul Whiteman, Tommy Dorsey, Benny Goodman, and, finally, with his own band.

He was as barrelhouse in his private life as he was in his playing. He just didn't care whether or not school kept. But those things are of no moment. The thing that counts is the music that he blew and that will forever remain fresh and beautiful and exciting.

In his brief time on this earth, Bernard (Bunny) Berigan (1908–1942) handled a trumpet so flexibly and with such enchantment that he earned the right to be numbered among the truly great jazz musicians of all time.

Inevitably, the stories about him will be born in a thousand and one backrooms, because it is always that way when an abundant talent expires early. The portrait of the artist as a dead young man is not likely to be the most faithful of portraits.

So men will stretch out on iron beds in squalid hotel rooms, staring at the ugly scars where the enamel has flaked from the posts and nurse their drinks and stroll in their talk down all the yesterdays of their own and Bunny Berigan's life. In the rooms of college dormitories on spring evenings, the undergraduates will squat before phonographs and listen to the man's records and retell the stories of his life and hard times. In finishing schools, in cubicles to which the fragrance of perfume clings, the rich, well-born girls will spin the web of legend about this man Berigan. On buses roaring through the everlasting night . . . in booking offices . . . on bandstands in Boston and Pottstown and Atlanta . . . everywhere people will talk about him, and some of what they will say will be fact, but most of it will be merely fiction.

But when the data is all in—all the data and a good deal that is less than that—there will still be that horn and the glory it put onto records. And about that, there can never be any arguing. Because as long as there is a Bunny Berigan record left and a machine to play it on, there can be no denying the grandeur of his accomplishments.

It may well be that on some tomorrow this Bunny Berigan will be a more hallowed man than Leon Bismarck Beiderbecke. For one thing, he has had the advantage of decent recording. That, and the benediction of some good bands playing behind him. This is no attempt to belittle Bix, but simply an impartial consideration of the facts. Beiderbecke was wonderful, but it was his sad fortune to have played with some of the raggedest, most hopeless groups you ever heard. He is like a voice crying in the wilderness, a full-throated singing voice fighting every minute to overcome the drawback of some of the most illustrious bums who ever carried union cards. Bix was all right, but I never cared much for the company that he kept on records.

Berigan, on the other hand, recorded with some lofty talents. He recorded with the Goodman band, for example, at a time when Benny and his men were fresh and unspoiled by too much acclaim. He recorded with Mildred Bailey, too, and in a wonderful small band that included Johnny Hodges and a Teddy Wilson who had not had his head and talent turned by excessive praise. He was, at one time or another, in the studio with Bud Freeman and Billie Holiday and Eddie Miller and a lot of other people who had something to say and the equipment with which to say it. Bix, for all his genius, never participated in as wholly satisfying a recording as Goodman's "King Porter" or Holiday's "Billie's Blues" or Bailey's "Squeeze Me."

But aside from this, there is the indisputable fact that, band or no band, Berigan was one of the greatest trumpet players who ever lived, with power and majesty and slashing attack and nervous vibrato and something that was fire rather than merely warmth.

The last will and testament of Bunny Berigan is the music he put on the sound track of the motion picture *Syncopation*. It is as unforgettable a document as any man ever left behind him.

Now that Berigan is dead, the kids, as well as people like myself who haven't been kids for a long, long time, will dig out his records and play them and replay them until they, and we, are dead, too. As to which is the greatest of these records, no one can say with any certainty, because Bunny made some awfully good ones, and the rest is a matter of personal taste.

The one that suggests itself immediately, of course, is "I Can't Get Started" (which is better on Okeh than on his subsequent Victor). That—a Follies tune by Vernon Duke—was his theme song and it will always be associated with him. He used to play it back in the vagrant nights when he and Red McKenzie had a hole-in-the-wall on West 52nd Street that was charitably called a night club. The fact that, between them, they used to drink up the slim profits didn't disturb them one iota. The joint was jazz, and jazz was all that they cared about. Jack Teagarden would drop by for a nightcap or seven and end up by playing the blues for a half hour solid. And every other trombonist who happened to be in the house at the time would wonder why, sweet, dear Lord, he hadn't studied oboe, or something else which provided less competition. Because Jack was absolutely matchless when he stepped up onto that tiny bandstand and the guys decided E-flat was the key.

And then Bunny Berigan would get up on the platform and raise his horn to his lips. The notes would swell across the room in all their ruggedness and the tune would be "I Can't Get Started." That was really a majestic thing—the most impassioned torch song anyone ever heard. It was a concerto for trumpet. Later on, it got onto a record, of course, and every kid from Brunswick, Maine, to Palo Alto, California, and back to New Haven, Connecticut, could hum it note for note—and doubtless did. Which shouldn't have disturbed anyone, because the record has all Berigan's virtues and none of his defects. It has his magnificent sense of construction. It has a beginning, a middle, and an end. It tells a story, and it tells it in that massive, brooding style, building note by note into one of the greatest solos on or off records. It has dignity and as long as the record of it is to be heard, no one can dismiss jazz as specious.

Actually, Berigan had two styles—one for small groups and the other for large, organized bands (although the splendor in either case is identifiable as the product of the same genius). In things like Goodman's "King Porter" and "Sometimes I'm Happy" he gives the impression of unbelievable power. He is that way, too, in Tommy Dorsey's "Marie" and "Song of India." His notes are like massive chunks of granite, and the sum of them is anything but shapeless. He knew how to utilize a reed section as a cushion for the bite of his notes and how to get the most out of the arrangements that framed his solos. Listen to "Marie," just where the vocal ends. Suddenly there is an explosive announcement from Berigan's horn and the record has taken fire, and it is jazz, but the best.

But you shouldn't neglect the things he made with small bands either. For example, what he plays after Johnny Hodges' solo in Mildred Bailey's "Honeysuckle Rose," where his vibrato is at its most typical. Or the stuff he plays behind her in "Squeeze Me," where his tone is beautifully clouded and his imagination is almost flirtatious. Or what he plays in Bud Freeman's "Tillie's Downtown Now," where he is the most casual guy in the world, fooling around with the melody as if he had nothing to do, until suddenly he lashes out, like a boxer who has been waiting for an opening.

But Bunny Berigan made a lot of records. These happen to be merely what one man prefers among them.

The Spirit of Jazz

Otis Ferguson

Otis Ferguson, better known as one of America's finest film critics, also wrote about jazz for The New Republic *in the mid-thirties. (He was killed in World War II.) This vivid appreciation of Benny Goodman appeared in December 1936.*

Benny Goodman was born in what he now refers back to as the Chicago ghetto twenty-seven years ago, and about twelve years later showed up in knee pants on one of the riverboats, to play in a small jazz band with Bix Beiderbecke, dead now and immortal (Go away, boy, Bix is reported to have said. Don't mess around with the instruments). But Benny Goodman had with him a clarinet of his own, which at that time must have been as long as he was, and he had a superior sense of music; he played with the band, all right. He played around all the time in those first days, studying under good men, mastering his difficult instrument, and going to high school a little, and after that forming a band with a few boys from some sort of conservatory he attended—historic names now, Bud Freeman, Dave Tuft, Muggsy Spanier. And at the age of sixteen he went to the West Coast to join the Ben Pollack orchestra, which is as historic as the deuce. He stayed with the organization about four years, playing it out every night, working alongside such men as that force on the trombone, Mr. Jack (Big Gate) Teagarden, learning. When he left Pollack, he worked here and there in New York, in pit and stage and radio bands, recording and later getting up a band of his own.

But that is all an interim period for most of us. The general public must have heard his music at one time or another, but there was no ballyhoo to announce where it was coming from. Then, less than two years ago, he started going to town for the general public, and reports came back from the Palomar in Los Angeles that you could not get within fifty yards of the stand, and afterward you could hear over the Congress Hotel's wire in Chicago that this might have been a sedate enough ballroom before, but now Benny was in and blowing the roof off, and they were yelling from the floor.

And this winter he is to be seen in the main room at the Pennsylvania Hotel. The room as you come in is spacious and warm with the air of moderately well-to-do living, people and tables filling the space around the floor and around the raised walk on all four sides, waiters and captains bustling in a quiet efficiency of silver and steam and flourish. But the far side of the room is the main side, where the boys sit high and easy in their chairs and Benny Goodman stands in front, quiet or smiling into the spotlight or tilting his instrument to the rafters as they rise to the takeoff. Sooner or later they will lead into one of those Fletcher Henderson arrangements of an old favorite, and the whole riding motion of the orchestra will be felt even through the thick carpets and the babble of the crowd, and those with two feet under them will move out onto the floor, because the music can be heard best when it is fulfilling its original simple purpose, coming through the ears and the good living wood underneath. As they get along into the later choruses, the boys will let out a little of that flash and rhythmic power which make these separate defined instruments into something indefinable, a thumping big band with the whole room under its thumb ("Got the world in a jug"); the floor will become solid with people, even some of the bare backs and stiff shirts will jolly up noticeably and perhaps do the truck a little (dear, dear).

And then, even with the final blast of the out-chorus still echoing in the hall, everything is suddenly natural and workaday. The men put up their instruments, stretch, look about them, file off at random; Benny stands leafing through his music to give out the numbers for the next set, recognizing as many people as is expedient, later going off to sit at a table somewhere: How's everything? That's fine. Himself, he's on the wagon tonight; he drinks with glum heroism at a glass of plain water. "A Scotch here and a soda there and where the hell are you in the morning? You know?" So now he feels better in the morning. He has a heavy voice coming from well down under the ribs and pleasant with the forthright lively concision of popular speech. Someone comes up, moving with vast importance, and desires that Benny should intervene with the Selmer people. They make clarinets and it seems they've got some conspiracy of imprecise mouthpieces as against the gentleman in question: if she plays good high, then she don't play good low; likewise vice versa. Benny says come around after, he'll see; then presently out of the side of his mouth: Never *was* one of the things that would play right by itself, you have to nurse it. You know a clarinet? What's he think I can do about a damn clarinet, drive me crazy. Benny Goodman looks sadly at the Scotch on the table and drinks his water.

By now a slight and quiet young man has detached himself from the gossip and joshing of the musicians hanging around in the back, and drifted over to the piano—on which he has only time left to run through two numbers, if that. In a place like this, where there are too many dine-and-dancers too sure that a young man sitting at an upright piano can't be anything to hush your mouth about, Teddy Wilson is as fine an artist at starting late and quitting early as he is at his music, which is the finest. He runs through a few chords. Anyone who wants to hear it a little can move over to the piano. Some do. Just playing to amuse myself is all, Teddy says.

Well, how about the Waller tune "Squeeze Me," Teddy; you used to play that pretty nice. Oh that? he says with his fine smile. I believe I forgot that one by now. He feels through the chords with unerring musical sense and listens for the turn of phrase in some backward corner of his mind—like the mind of any good jazz musician, it is a treasury and stuffed catalogue of all the songs the rest of us have thought lovely and then presently put aside for new toys. He finishes, repeats the last phrase. Hm, I *knew* I didn't have that one rightly any more, he says, shaking his head. But the song is back for us, the song never died at all. He starts the first chords over, and this time his right hand is released from concentration and free on the keyboard, and to get the pattern in music of those clear single notes without hearing the phrase as it is struck off, you would have to make some such visual image as that of a common tin plate scaled up into the sun, where there would be not only the flash and motion but the startling effect of flight, the rise and banking in curves, the hesitation and slipping off, and the plunge straight down coming suddenly. Wilson in his best mood of creation is something like that.

These nights he shows to better advantage when he comes out with the quartet. There, with something to work for, he really works and is fine in many ways. Remember that he is a Negro in a white man's world, a jazz player in a world where the thirst for music is so artificial it cannot attend with comfort anything not solemnized. And then see the quiet repose and lack of cocksureness, strut, or show, the straightforward and friendly absence of assumption that comes only from a secure awareness of the dignity of a person and of his work. But even if this were the place for oversolemn pronouncements, there isn't the time. The stand is filling up again, the boys sucking on reeds, limbering up valves—doing whatever it is that musicians do with a sort of happy-go-lucky boredom. There is no more than time to say, as the first pop tune starts to go up in smoke, that memory may fade and the current musical note perish, but that fifty years around the recorded music of Mr. Teddy Wilson (now craftily surprised that the band came back so soon) should have established him where he belongs—not only great in jazz but among the best lyricists of any time or form.

Swing in, swing out, the band is up again and drawing the people out like the sun in the fable. With Krupa, Reuss (guitar), and the inspired quiet Stacy (piano) laying down a thick rhythmic base, it plays on through whatever songs are the demand of the day, making most of them sound like something. This is an organization in the line of the great jazz bands—Jean Goldkette,

Fletcher Henderson, McKinney's Cotton Pickers, Ellington, Kirk, et al.—a little lighter than some of these but more beautifully rehearsed and economical, and with cleaner edges. The reed section, scored as such, is more prominent than in older hot bands, giving a fuller lyric quality; but the section (five men, counting Goodman) has a hard skeleton of attack and swing that supports any relative lightness of brass. The band as a whole gets its lift from the rhythm men and the soloists as they take off; it is built from the ground rather than tailored—thanks to the talent, ideas, and leadership of one man.

The recent spreading of interest in good jazz to some extent made Benny Goodman's current music possible, and to some extent was made possible by Benny Goodman's music. He got good men working together, got some ace arrangements of all the good tunes, new and old, and played them wide open though bands weren't supposed to be successful that way. It wasn't so much that he made the people like it as that he gave them a chance to see what it was like when done well (too many hot bands have sounded like a barnyard until they got going around 2:00 A.M.). And one of the important things about his show is that he went right ahead with the same method of getting good music when it came to the old color-line bogey. He would introduce Teddy Wilson as playing with the trio, and the people would bang hands for more (they say on some nights he even had to send the rest of the band home). So hotel managers would get the point almost painlessly: and could no longer say No beforehand, on the ground that people would not stand for it. And when the trio got Lionel Hampton to play the vibraphone, the balance between black and white was even (two of each), and still no kick. Stand for it?—the people stand up from their tables just to hear it better.

They play every night—clarinet, piano, vibraphone, drums—and they make music you would not believe. No arrangements, not a false note, one finishing his solo and dropping into background support, then the other, all adding inspiration until, with some number like "Stomping at the Savoy," they get going too strong to quit—four choruses, someone starts up another, six, eight, and still someone starts—no two notes the same and no one note off the chord, the more they relax in the excitement of it the more a natural genius in preselection becomes evident and the more indeed the melodic line becomes rigorously pure. This is really composition on the spot, with the spirit of jazz strongly over all of them but the iron laws of harmony and rhythm never lost sight of; and it is a collective thing, the most beautiful example of men working together to be seen in public today.

It isn't merely hell-for-leather, either. Gene Krupa, a handsome madman over his drums, makes the rhythmic force and impetus of it visual, for his face and whole body are sensitive to each strong beat of the ensemble; and

Hampton does somewhat the same for the line of melody, hanging solicitous over the vibraphone plates and exhorting them (Hmmm, Oh, Oh yah, Oh dear, *hmmm*). But the depth of tone and feeling is mainly invisible, for they might play their number "Exactly Like You" enough to make people cry and there would be nothing of it seen except perhaps in the lines of feeling on Benny Goodman's face, the affable smile dropped as he follows the Wilson solo flight, eyes half-closed behind his glasses. There was a special feeling among them the first morning they recorded this piece, the ghost of the blues perhaps; and when the clarinet takes up, you will hear the phrases fall as clear as rain, with a sustained glow of personal essence that starts where command of the instrument (the tension of mouth, delicate fingering, etc.) leaves off. Then Hampton sings a chorus, his vibrant hoarse voice and relaxed emphasis so appropriate to the general color; and when they take up again, the instruments blend so perfectly as to be indistinguishable, singing in unison with a sweet breadth of tone that goes beyond the present place and time to some obscure source of feeling and native belief. The term "swing"—no more definable in words than the term "poetry"—is defined at its best in this piece, where the actual beats are lost sight of in the main effect, so that the inexorable and brute lift of the time signature as carried in Krupa's great drum seems fused in the harmony and melodic line of the song. And you may say of the excitement this thing starts in the blood only that these four men are quite simple and wonderful together, that they are truly swinging.

The quartet is a beautiful thing all through, really a labor of creative love, but it cannot last forever, and as the band starts again, you realize that even in jazz there are several kinds of musical appreciation. For if they'll agree to put on the "Bugle Call Rag" before the end of the evening, I'll be willing to say there's nothing finer. There is some hidden lift to this old band standby, with its twenty quaint notes from the "Assembly" call dropping the barrier to a straight-out progression of simple chords—and they are off, riding it with collective assurance and fine spirit, the men in their sections, the sections balancing, the soloists dropping back with care for the total effect. The guests are presently banked in a half-moon around the stand, unable to be still through it or move away either; and as it builds to the final solid chords, Krupa becoming a man of subtle thunder and Benny lacing in phrases, the air is full of brass and of rhythms you can almost lean on. The music seems more than audible, rising and coming forward from the stand in banks of colors and shifting masses—not only the clangor in the ears but a visual picture of the intricate fitted spans, the breathless height and spring of a steel-bridge structure. And if you leave at the end, before the "Good-Bye" signature, you will seem to hear this great rattling march of the hobos through the taxis, lights, and people, ringing under the low sky over Manhattan as if it were a strange high thing after all (which it is) and as if it came from the American ground under these buildings, roads, and motorcars (which it did). And if you leave the band and quartet and piano of the Goodman show and still are no more than slightly amused, you may be sure that in the smug absence of your attention a native true spirit of music has been and gone, leaving a message for your grandchildren to study through their patient glasses.

The Mirror of Swing

Gary Giddins

And exactly fifty years later, the brilliant and omnipresent critic Gary Giddins sums up Goodman on the occasion of his death. From Faces in the Crowd *(1992).*

While memories are fresh, it won't do to consider Benny Goodman, who died in his sleep on the afternoon of June 13, 1986, at 77, exclusively as a jazz musician. The emotions conjured by his name are unique to those few who transcend the specifics of talent and come to represent an era. If he wasn't the king of a musical idiom called swing, he was surely king of the Swing Era, an agreeable focus for Yankee pride at a time when music counted not only for art, entertainment, and sedative, but as a balm with which to weather terrible storms. Goodman will be remembered for his contributions to jazz, which are manifold, and he occupies an impressive historical niche as the first musician to enjoy hugely successful careers in three discrete fields (jazz, pop, and classical). Yet in his time Goodman was also a blessed and seemingly eternal presence in media culture who, through an unofficial contract between artist and public, reflected the nation's new vision of itself in the arts—earthy, democratic, and homegrown, and at the same time refined, virtuosic, and international.

The enormous sense of loss that attended his death was animated in part by the realization that an age had passed, and not just a musical one. (Other Swing Era titans are still with us, including the great progenitor Benny Carter and the great crooner Frank Sinatra, who inadvertently helped supplant big bands in the public affection.) Goodman came to prominence when America was making major discoveries about the nature of its cultural life, and proved an exemplary figure for national preening. He was in all important respects distinctively American, purveying an undeniably American music with at least the tentative approval of academics and Europhile upper crust, into whose circles he married. His connections put him in Carnegie Hall (a big deal in 1938) five years before Duke Ellington. The public took comfort in him, too. He was white, but not too white, which is to say Jewish, but not too Jewish; and serious, but not too serious, which is to say lighthearted, but sober. At the height of the Depression, he had perfect credentials for entertaining a suffering, guilt-ridden nation. Goodman was one of the 12 siblings born to penniless Russian immigrants in Chicago. He received his first clarinet at 10, in 1919, and had a union card three years later.

Everyone knows this story, or a version of it. As the favorite fable of the 1930s, it was internalized by Depression-bred children who went on to dramatize it for stage, screen, and radio countless times into the late 1950s, and occasionally ever since. It's told of Berlin, Gershwin, and Jolson, and with appropriate variations in ethnicity, of Armstrong, Crosby, Sinatra, Handy, Jim Thorpe, and Presley. Until Vietnam and the civil rights era, it was standard grammar school indoctrination, combining the American dream with melting pot diversity, cheerful tolerance, and a ready willingness to brave new frontiers. If nations were judged by the lies they told about themselves, this one just might guarantee salvation. Small wonder, then, that when an individual appears worthy of the crown, we bow our heads in gratitude. With few exceptions, however, only performing artists and athletes are able to pull this particular sword from the stone.

Few Americans have handled the role of cultural icon as well as Goodman. For more than 50 years, he endured as one of the nation's favorite images of itself. Several weeks before his death, a few musicians were sitting around trading anecdotes about him, causing one to remark, "At any given time somebody somewhere is telling a Benny Goodman story." Those stories are rarely kind, usually having to do with his legendary cheapness, absentmindedness, mandarin discipline, rudeness to musicians, and various eccentricities. But they never dented his media image, nor were they meant to. Americans usually come to resent the entertainers they've deified, yet Goodman remained virtually unblemished. Any real skeletons that may have resided in his closet rattled in peace. It isn't hard to understand why. Everyone could feel good about Goodman. You could send him anywhere, from Albert Hall to Moscow, and rest assured that he would comport himself with quiet dignity and spread Americanism in a manner the world would take to heart. Had he worn striped pants and a top hat, he could not more naturally have embodied everything America wanted to believe about its promise of tolerance and opportunity—those democratic underpinnings insufficiently embraced at home but glamorized for export to the rest of the world.

The *Time/Life* history of all things would have us believe that Goodman helped the country unwind with a new and thrilling music, which is true only in the sense that Columbus discovered America. The music wasn't new, and some of the country had already unwound to it. Goodman, like Elvis 20 years later, adapted black music for white tastes. He toned it down, cleaned it up. Unlike Presley, he was willing to take risks with his celebrity. Perhaps he was so socially unconscious, he didn't realize the implications of those risks. In any case, with the politically astute critics John Hammond (his future brother-in-law) and Helen Oakley spurring him on, Goodman hired Teddy Wilson virtually at the moment he achieved commercial leverage. They first recorded together in the summer of 1935, at two sessions produced by Hammond—the first in support of Billie Holiday, the second the debut of the Benny Goodman Trio. A year later, after the success of his big band, Goodman took Oakley's suggestion to take Wilson on the road, and a bulwark of racism was fatally breached.

Goodman was proud of his musical origins, as witness his many tributes to Fletcher Henderson, whose reputation was fading when Goodman and Hammond conspired to revive it. Henderson's arrangements provided the original Goodman orchestra with a style, and remained Benny's favorite music to play (he especially loved Henderson's arrangement of "Somebody Loves Me") until the end of his life. Beyond the vagaries of race, however, Goodman's superb musicianship indemnified him as an honorable standard-bearer for the art suddenly thrust into his hands. He was, this above all, a nonpareil clarinetist; a bandleader who innovated chamber-sized ensembles; and the sponsor who introduced (again with the help of the ever-alert Hammond) numerous great players, arrangers, and singers.

With his unpretentious air and perpetually puzzled look, his amiable stage manner and nearly country-boy shyness, his strangely aristocratic inflections despite a tendency to mumble, and his unmistakable obsession with music/work, he was all that central casting could ask as the hero of the most celebrated parable in American music. The fabled night during which Goodman was transformed from mere musician to looming eminence is an elaborate morality play, involving the genesis of the Swing Era, the ascendancy of mass-market technology, the hero's conflicting feelings about race, and semi-rugged individualism. Goodman's rise is not unlike the touchingly grotesque 1930 Hollywood version of *Moby Dick* (starring John Barrymore and Joan Bennett), played out as a road story with a happy ending for an agreeably ambivalent Ahab.

Goodman was a 26-year-old fledgling bandleader when he embarked on a promotional cross-country tour in the summer of 1935. Despite six months of weekly appearances on the "Let's Dance" radio program, a library of arrangements by Fletcher Henderson, Edgar Sampson, Benny Carter, and others, and a band that included Bunny Berigan, Jess Stacy, and Gene Krupa, Goodman had cause for misgivings. Big band jazz was still far removed from the mainstream; talented jazz players of Goodman's generation were obliged to work in stuffy ballrooms, playing bland dance music and novelties to earn a living. Jazz was something you played after hours, or sneaked into arrangements as a condiment when no one was looking. Indeed, shortly before leaving New York, Goodman was fired from the Roosevelt Grill for not playing "sweet and low," as he later recalled. Reaction was no better on the road west, and after three dismal weeks at Elitch Gardens in Denver, where he was nearly fired for playing pieces that went on too long and for not offering waltzes, comedy, and funny hats (Kay Kyser was packing them in down the street, Goodman was drawing flies), his bookers suggested he cancel the ensuing engagements in California.

He refused. Tour's end was to be the Palomar Ballroom in Los Angeles. But first there was a Monday night in Oakland, and Goodman was astonished to find the place nearly filled; it reminded him that one reason he had been able to finance the tour was the report of interest in his records in California. Still, he knew the Palomar was a more imposing room, and, chastened by the experience in Denver, Goodman decided to open with stock arrangements and sugary ballads. He continued in that vein for an hour with no response, but by the second set he had made up his mind that if he was doomed to failure he would go down honorably. He called for the Henderson charts and counted off "Sugar Foot Stomp." The crowd roared with approval. He couldn't believe it. *This* was what they had come to hear, the good stuff. The young audience stopped dancing and pressed against the bandstand. On that night, August 21, 1935, the Swing Era was born, because on that night middle-class white kids said yes in thunder and hard currency. Goodman stayed at the Palomar for two months and then moved on to Chicago, his hometown, where he played six months at the Congress Hotel.

It's a good story, and variations on it have been told many times since with different protagonists. *The Buddy Holly Story* offered an almost verbatim reenactment, as the discouraged rock and roller opens a set with country favorites, before—pride of purpose coming to the fore—switching to rock and roll. Inherent in every retelling are two paradigmatic twists that first appear in the Goodman saga. First, the influence of technology: The mystery of California's enthusiasm was solved when Goodman and his booking agent, Willard Alexander, realized the impact of network radio. Through "Let's Dance," Goodman's music had been relayed around the country by 53 stations, with the necessary allowance for different time zones. In New York, he was heard from 10 P.M. until 1 A.M., playing the tame band arrangements of the day. For the Los Angeles market, he had to perform two additional hours, beginning at the outset of prime time, 7 P.M., and finishing around midnight. To fill the larger time slot, he drew on the very jazz numbers that cost him his job at the Roosevelt Grill. He had no way of knowing he was nurturing an audience on the west coast with every Saturday night broadcast.

The second twist was racial. From the days of antebellum minstrel shows to the present, the point at which indigenous American music becomes pop culture is the point where white performers learn to mimic black ones. Many of Goodman's biggest hits were virtual duplications of records that Fletcher Henderson and Chick Webb had recorded months, even years, before. Ellington's band had been declaring "It Don't Mean a Thing if It Ain't Got That Swing" for three years before Goodman reached California, and territory bands had spread the sound of swing throughout the Midwest by 1930. Louis Armstrong's success on records opened the door for everyone. Even before that, the Original Dixieland Jazz Band, the first white band to popularize the New Orleans style, had caused a sensation in New York in 1917, helping to usher in the Jazz Age, with Paul Whiteman reigning as surrogate for the real thing. In one form or another, jazz had been skirting America's consciousness for nearly 20 years before Goodman's triumph.

Goodman himself learned jazz from those musicians, white and black (notably clarinetists Leon Rappolo and Jimmy Noone), who had left New Orleans for Chicago during the teens and early '20s. His borrowings have been held against him. But given the colonialist iniquities of the period—not least the network radio hookups that were closed to blacks—and the emotional prejudices directed at the very foundations of African-American music (the Puritanical distrust of heady rhythms, at least until they were distilled by white precision and decorum), it's no good blaming the symbol of racial favoritism for racism itself, especially when that symbol took an activist stand against it. As Milt Hinton recently observed, Goodman's contribution to dismantling the color barriers was "a daring, daring thing."

Yet by the mid-1960s, when race was a central issue in discussions about jazz, Goodman was often dismissed as though his stature in jazz was as spurious as that of Whiteman. The King of Swing hyperbole, an astoundingly effective public relations ploy in its day, had become an albatross, as did the invidious 1955 movie ("Here, Fletcher, hold my clarinet") *The Benny Goodman Story*, which, frequently broadcast, was a real source of embarrassment to him and did nothing to improve his reputation for insensitivity. The racial animus, matched by envy and personal resentment, not least in the ranks of musicians who had suffered under his withering stare (he was known as "the Ray" by bandsmen) or those who despaired at never getting the chance, resulted in a barrage of contentious carping.

Easy to understand why: In 1963, Goodman was still exhibited as the representative jazz artist for the home viewing and arts center audiences, while Ellington continued on the road playing one-nighters, composing and recording the most extensive body of music ever produced by an American. Musicians of John Coltrane's generation remained relatively unknown to the general public. As late as 1975, a leading classical music critic challenged me with the assertion that Goodman was a more important composer than Ellington. When I told him Goodman didn't compose at all, he was incredulous. Goodman himself had no trouble penetrating the delusions of reputation. I once asked him if he actually composed any of the several riff tunes for which he is co-credited. "Oh, maybe one or two, but I doubt it," he said.

Goodman, like all icons, was an easy target. In the '60s I heard a jazz musician acknowledge him as a great clarinetist who should stick to the classics since he couldn't really improvise, and a classical musician groan that Goodman had murdered Mozart but was a genius in jazz. Other forms of damning praise saluted him as a popularizer or as an ambassador. Even Bud Freeman, who presumably had no racial or high-versus-low-art axes to grind, put a weed in his bouquet. After describing Goodman, at 13, as having "the technique of a master and a beautiful sound to go with it," and recalling the "thrill" of working with him in 1928, he concluded, "I don't mean to imply that he's a creative player; but he certainly is a masterful player." I've heard people who ought to know better argue that Goodman never surpassed his early idol, Jimmie Noone, which is like saying that Louis Armstrong never surpassed King Oliver. In truth, Goodman's instrumental style is so much his own that you can recognize it almost immediately. His playing may ultimately have done more to sustain his reputation than his work as a bandleader. In the latter capacity, Goodman demonstrated an irreproachable taste in arrangers ("good taste in Negroes," one wag observed), but he offered little that was genuinely new until the 1940s, when he re-formed his band to play the modernist music of Eddie Sauter and Mel Powell. As a clarinetist, he was his own man.

GOODMAN'S VICTORY AT the Palomar meant that jazz would no longer be the property of the impassioned few. It now emerged from the underground jam sessions to engulf even the ballroom pioneers—the Whitemans and Pollacks and Reismans—who had tried to limit jazz to an occasional solo or effect. Following the examples of Henderson, Ellington, and Webb, Goodman played music that was jazz from start to finish. He upended the music business. Yet as a major white star, he had to pay the usual price; he was required to water down the original brew. On the surface, that meant recording nearly as many pop vocals as jazz instrumentals; the result was essentially popular music with jazz interpolations (or fusion, as it's known today). Even in this regard, he went his own way. In addition to his regular pop singers, including Martha Tilton and the talented Helen Forrest, he recorded with authentic jazz singers—Ella Fitzgerald, Jimmy Rushing,

Maxine Sullivan, and others. The same little-known studio player who presided over Billie Holiday's first record in 1933 would launch Peggy Lee's career in 1941.

Goodman always kept his balance, refusing to allow his celebrity to dictate essential musical decisions. When he broke all records at New York's Paramount Theater in 1937, and faced the kind of shrieking adulation that was then new to American entertainment, he would sit placidly, waiting for the audience to finish its performance before he started his. By introducing trios, quartets, and other small groups in addition to the big band, he even made the fans sit still for chamber jazz. Yet subtler indications of musical dilution were felt, reflecting Goodman's stringent personality and insistence on precision. He often seemed more concerned with unison execution and projection than with the spirited abandon that typified not only the best black bands but his own early work as a sideman. Paradoxically, his rigidity was a primary reason for his success.

Goodman's soloists didn't compare with those in the Henderson orchestra, but his fastidious ensemble could sometimes get more value from a Henderson arrangement than Henderson's relatively unwieldy band did. If some of Goodman's records are anemic copies of Henderson's ("Wrappin' It Up," for instance), others ("Blue Skies," "Sometimes I'm Happy") are exemplary interpretations, which is undoubtedly one reason Henderson enjoyed writing for him. Despite his apprenticeship in hot jazz, Goodman had a preternatural understanding of what a mass audience would accept. Were the dancers discomfited by brutal tempos? Goodman simmered them down. He knew how to inject just the right touch of excitement into a performance.

Consider his hit version of Edgar Sampson's "Don't Be That Way," originally recorded by Chick Webb. Webb took the tempo way up and climaxed the performance with an explosive eight-bar drum solo. Goodman modified the tempo, streamlined the ensemble parts, introduced a famous fade-down in volume, and reduced the climax to a two-bar drum break by Gene Krupa that, because of its sudden intrusion, jolted the jitterbugs. (Coda: Years later, Krupa's formidable replacement, Dave Tough, completed a performance of "Don't Be That Way" with an extended break that awed everyone in the band but left the audience cold. He asked Goodman to play it again during the second show. This time he mimicked Krupa's relatively simple outburst, and the crowed cheered.)

Goodman was primarily a popularizer of big bands, but he was an innovator of small ones. The Benny Goodman Trio was conceived when Goodman heard Teddy Wilson play "Body and Soul" at a party given by Red Norvo. Shortly afterwards, in the summer of 1935, Goodman, Wilson, and

Krupa recorded four sides for RCA. The combination of clarinet, piano, and drums was by no means new (Goodman had heard others, notably Jelly Roll Morton, use it during his adolescence), but Goodman greatly increased its flexibility and made it the foundation for several variations. A year later, in California, he was advised to visit a disreputable sailors' hangout called the Paradise Café to hear the entertainment—one Lionel Hampton. Goodman returned the next night with Wilson and Krupa to jam and had no trouble convincing Hampton to join them on the road.

The small groups were a popular draw at Goodman's shows, and although Wilson and Hampton were billed as special attractions rather than as members of the orchestra, their presence paved the way for integrated bands. Krupa went the distance when he left Goodman to start his own band and allowed his star soloist, Roy Eldridge, to sit in his trumpet section. (Integrated audiences came later.) The chamber groups also gave Goodman the opportunity to indulge himself as a clarinetist on wistful ballads ("The Man I Love," "Moonglow") and flashy stomps ("Runnin' Wild," "China Boy"), and rekindled the spark of his earlier playing. They gave him the chance to work with favorite musicians without regard to race. In the big band, Goodman's soloists tended to mimic the great stylists assembled by Henderson, especially Coleman Hawkins and Eldridge. Only Goodman himself bested his opposite number—Buster Bailey—in the Henderson band, though the arrangements tended to limit the size and scope of his solos. With the small group, which grew to a sextet by 1939, he could stretch out in the company of the incomparable guitarist Charlie Christian, trumpeter Cootie Williams, whose temporary defection from Ellington wowed the musical community (Goodman also tried to snare, unsuccessfully, Johnny Hodges), and, on records, Count Bassie. Before long, other bandleaders introduced chamber groups, including Webb, Ellington, Artie Shaw, Woody Herman, Tommy Dorsey, and Dizzy Gillespie.

If the combo recordings as a whole stand up better than those by the big band, which today suffer needlessly from the idiot obsession with reissuing complete works in chronological order, the generous playing time accorded the leader is a major reason. On the orchestra's pop sides, his clarinet is often the only solace: In the course of a conventional arrangement worsened by a dire vocal, Goodman's blistering clarinet flashes to the fore and creaky sentiments are momentarily banished. Goodman was a hot player whose adroit blues choruses distinguished him almost from the start during his days in Chicago. His command of every register enabled him to contrive a style of high drama and earthy swing. A student of the Chicago Symphony's Franz Schoep as well as of jazz clarinetists, he never allowed technique to vitiate the rhythmic charge of his music. Artie Shaw had a prettier tone, Barney Bigard a fatter one, but Goodman was unfeigned and lusty. He could growl with bemusement or ardor, according to mood, and when he really let go, leaning back on his chair, feet flailing the air, or hopping around on one leg, he could make anyone's heart beat a little faster. Goodman's rhythmic gait was unmistakable: His best solos combined cool legato, a fierce doubling up of notes, and the canny use of propulsive riffs.

He displayed some of those gifts as early as 1926, when he first recorded, still under the influence of Jimmie Noone. A year later, when Goodman was only 18, an English publisher brought out *Benny Goodman's 125 Jazz Breaks for the Saxophone and Clarinet*. Had he retired in 1935, he'd be remembered now for his rigorous solos on numerous records by Ted Lewis, Adrian Rollini, the Joe Venuti–Eddie Lang Orchestra, Red Nichols, the Charleston Chasers, and others. At his best, he was able to sustain a similar excitement all his life. Forty years after the kingdom of swing had been gentrified almost beyond recognition, he could still provoke the crowd's roar. Last summer, as an unbilled performer at a tribute to John Hammond, he provided the highlight of the Kool Jazz Festival. It was anything but a middle-aged jazz audience that cheered him on when he came out and played "Lady Be Good" with George Benson, and then—seated, both legs levitating—layered climax after climax on "Indiana." Up to that point, the young white-blues crowd had greeted every jazz performer with impatient demands for the man of the hour, blues guitarist Stevie Ray Vaughan. When Goodman finished, that same crowd was on its feet.

When my review of that concert appeared, Goodman's assistant told me the Old Man was pleased and surprised by it, since he'd gotten it into his head that I considered him outmoded. I have no idea why. How could anyone think that? Goodman kept his faith until the end. Ultimately, he mirrored not only a chapter in America's cultural history, but the spirit at the core of a music that can only be enfeebled when nostalgia gets between musician and audience. In 1975, I visited Goodman at his East Side apartment. He had been practicing Gounod's *Petite Symphony* when I arrived, and I asked him if he preferred improvising or playing written music. "Gee," he said, "I enjoy both. Listening to music is emotional. Sometimes you like something a lot, and another time you hate it. The whole goddam thing about jazz is emotional. I like to feel the excitement. If it doesn't come out as a wild endeavor—wild with restraint—it doesn't have it." Goodman had it in 1926, and he had it 60 years later.*

*When I wrote "The Mirror of Swing," a couple of days after Benny Goodman died, I had heard many of the nasty Goodman stories making the rounds, but underestimated the depth of resentment. A few months later, John Lewis, Roberta Swann, and I produced an American Jazz Orchestra tribute to Goodman. More than two-thirds of the AJO had worked with Goodman at one time or other (an extraordinary statistic), and their recollections made the rehearsals memorably hilarious. Yet some stories were related with a naked hatred for what was described as the man's cruelty, cheapness, and vulgarity. Of course, virtually every one of them commenced with a statement of high regard for his musicianship. John Lewis, who does not traffic in gossip, mused one afternoon that throughout jazz history the most innovative and accomplished musicians on every instrument but one were black; his exception was the clarinet and Goodman.

My own limited experiences with Goodman were altogether positive. He graciously met with me in 1975, when I approached him for my own illumination, with no story or publication in mind; and he agreed immediately to lend his name and prestige to the initial board of advisers to the AJO. Still, Goodman was by all accounts a troubled and troubling man, which makes his untouchable status as a celebrity all the more remarkable. Despite the petty jealousies he exhibited and elicited, his private woes remained if not entirely private then confined to the grousing of musicians. I see no reason why they shouldn't be aired now. Yet it would be a shame if the contemporary thirst for pathographies (Joyce Carol Oates's sadly indispensable term) obfuscated Goodman's nearly impeccable public posture and the affection he inspired in the hearts of music lovers for more than half this century.

Jimmie Lunceford

Ralph J. Gleason

Gleason, in Celebrating the Duke *(1975), evokes another of the major bandleaders, Jimmie Lunceford, as well as the experience of being a young fan in the heyday of the big bands.*

They used to appear on blue-label 35-cent discs every couple of weeks at the bookstore on the Columbia campus—two sides, 78 rpm, and you had to be there right on time or the small allotment would be gone and you would have missed the new Jimmie Lunceford record.

If you were lucky you got one, ran back to your room in John Jay or Hartley Hall, sharpened your cactus needle on a Red Top needle sharpener, the little sandpaper disc buzzing as you spun it, and then sat back in ecstasy to listen to the sound coming out over your raunchy, beat-up Magnavox.

True big band freaks, of whom I was one, were absolutely dedicated to the Lunceford band. It had—and still has—a very special place in the memories of those who date back to the Era of Good Feeling of the 30s, when the big bands symbolized a kind of romance and glamour and exotic beauty long gone from the world of entertainment.

You savored those records and, since this was long before the economy of abundance and the discs came one at a time, weeks apart, and albums (packages of 78-rpm singles or, a bit later, Long Play discs) were absolutely unknown, you had time to absorb the records.

There must have been hundreds of vocal trios in the colleges who tried to sing like the Lunceford band's trio and who spent countless hours memorizing the words and the phrasing of "My Blue Heaven."

I first heard them on the radio. A remote broadcast from some long-forgotten ballroom somewhere in the Middle West, a wild, throbbing sound in the night by people I never heard of, absolutely killing me with its subtlety and its insinuating rhythms.

And when I got to the Big Apple and found that you could actually get to see a band like this in person at the Apollo or the Savoy Ballroom or the Renaissance or the Strand or Paramount theaters, I simply couldn't believe it. It was just too good to be true.

The guy who showed me that this nighttime radio music came fully processed on platters was a tall, rangy, premed student named Keery Merwin, who shared busboy chores with me from eight to ten mornings at the John Jay Hall dining room. We got into a conversation early on as we wiped up the spilt maple syrup from breakfast and I found he not only had a phonograph but a box of records. We went straight up to his room at ten, cut classes and played records all day long. When we met, he had all the early Luncefords—"Sophisticated Lady" (that was Decca 129!), "Rose Room," "Black and Tan Fantasy," "Dream of You" and "Rhythm Is Our Business," with that line that haunts me yet: "Mose plays the bass in the band. . . ." We dug them deeply in an era before the verb "to dig" had emerged into the general slang. What I mean is, we hardly listened to anything else.

We went out and found other people to play them to. A chance conversation in the corridor outside Irwin Edman's philosophy class and the lunch hour was spent up in Keery's room with the turntable spinning away.

Two things became immediately apparent. I had to have a phonograph and I had to have the records. I got them both as fast as I could. Later, I conned the editor of *Columbia Spectator* into letting me take over the record column from the departing previous tenant and I was in business.

Now the Lunceford discs came to the door gloriously free, sometimes even before they were available at the bookshop.

It ruined me, of course. I never felt the same about the classroom. I spent more time at the Apollo Theater when Lunceford was there than I did at school. I used to see two shows a day. Then a week or so later I'd repeat the performance at the Strand Theater downtown in mid-Manhattan.

That summer and on until the war interfered (Hitler's war, that is), I raced hundreds of miles at night in my father's car to hear the band at the Roton Point Casino, at the Armory in Saratoga, anywhere I could find it; and finding it, in those days before jazz disc jockeys and *Down Beat* listings, was no small task in itself. Sometimes we'd even call the number listed in the Manhattan phone book for the band and get Harold Oxley's office, where the switchboard gal always acted as if we wanted to serve a summons.

Then there was the wonderful summer of 1939 when the band played for two weeks at a nightclub on the Boston Post Road—the Larchmont Casino—and I worked at Playland nearby, and every night after I closed up the joint at eleven or midnight, I ran over to the club and heard the band till the club closed. One fall they showed up suddenly on Fifty-second Street for a two-week booking—was it at the Bandbox?—and opening night there was no one there but me, my girl and her two roommates. It was a beautiful private concert. The absolute end.

Going back now, after thirty years, to hear these discs, it all comes back. The incredible dynamics of the band, the way it could whisper, and the great roar it got from the brasses and the amazing cohesion of that sax section on "I'm Walking Through Heaven With You" and the whole mystique. Usually we can't return again, but this music, like certain other things, brings back an era and a feeling and an emotion like an instant replay. There was never anything like it.

It's impossible to believe now, after all these years, that this band numbered only fifteen and sometimes sixteen members, plus the leader.

In the mental flashback it seems like many more. And I think the reason is that so much went on there that an illusion of great numbers was created.

It wasn't just "For Dancers Only." It was for listeners and for viewers and for lovers, too. With Jimmie taking that little soprano up sometimes to play lead on a song and the rest of the time standing there—white-suited in summer—waving the baton like a magic wand over the heads of the dancers and smiling, the band produced a variety and volume and an ever-changing tapestry of sound that was really unique.

To begin with, it had character, just as Duke Ellington's band has always had character. It *sounded* like Jimmie Lunceford. You didn't have to wait for the individual voice of some musician, for a particular familiar arrangement or for a well-known number. You coasted down the dial on the car radio late at night and when you hit Lunceford, you *knew* it was Lunceford. Who else could it be? Later, of course, there were little Luncefords, now and then, but in the beginning there was only the one sound and of course that was the way it really stayed because the imitators never made it.

Visually, it was the greatest. No other band put on as much showmanship before or since. They looked good all the time and they made music sound like making it was fun, and they enhanced it with all the tricks, from Russell Bowles or Elmer Crumbley putting the trombone wa-wa mutes on their heads to the flaring sideways and up-and-down motion of the sections in unison.

They would have been great on television. The back row visually going one way, the front row visually going the other, and in the middle of it all, hunched behind that great battery of equipment drummers in those days looked like the center of all things; Jimmy Crawford and Sonny Greer and Chick Webb and Jo Jones had so much equipment you were devastated just by seeing it), the long-jawed James Crawford pounding out that pulse.

The ballroom usually wouldn't let you stand in front of the band. You had to keep dancing (no chore to *that* band), but sometimes you could cluster at the edge of the bandstand or, at Roton Point, stand behind it, outside on the balcony looking at Long Island Sound in the moonlight and feeling the music just the same.

The best place, though, was in front of the band, where you could see and hear it all as you danced along *very* slowly and watch the trumpets twirl and the trombones wave and see those eyes of Earl Carruthers look to his section mates as he rocked backwards in the chair, anchoring the sax section. And where you could see the wisp of mustache on Willie Smith and the sly look in his eyes as he leaned forward to sing and get a good view. Eddie Wilcox, sitting at the piano, extending relaxation to new dimensions. No one else ever equaled the way he could put his legs at an angle to the piano, slump back in his chair and still play! And his only rival for looking blasé was Johnny Hodges!

Lunceford had the quality of projecting excitement instantly. Not in the way he looked, because Jimmie Lunceford looked positively placid. What always puzzled us was how he could *look* so placid standing there in front of all that magic. And sometimes it even seemed as if he listened to a different drummer, from the way that long baton waved.

But the band itself, the totality of it, looked every instant as if it was about to do something you had better not miss. And it usually did. How it could is still a mystery to me. Probably only the Casa Loma band (twelve years of one-nighters, legend has it) spent more time on the road. That was what was so remarkable about the two weeks at the Larchmont Casino. Later, of course, just before the wartime pressure began to get bad, there were other location jobs, but in those days there was a terrible fact of life which none of us even thought of. Where would a Negro band work, aside from the Howard and the Royal and the Apollo, if it didn't have the Cotton Club or some other special place? No hotel hired Negro bands in those days. It was as simple as that. And we never thought then about the rest of it, the lack of everything from a place to sleep to a hamburger, that marked even those one-nighters and the bus rides.

I think now those men were heroes. Then I only knew they were magicians. What a terrible thing I thought it was for Sy Oliver to even want to leave the band! The miracle, of course, now that hindsight clears the view, is that they stood it as long as they did.

It was a young world then, an unsophisticated one by today's standards, and glitter and tinsel and flash could add up to glamour. But I still think the Lunceford band had much more than that. They had class as well. They walked and they talked and they played like men who had been touched with a very special thing. Duke's men had it and, later, Basie's. They looked regal. That's the only word.

And of course, they were.

The Lunceford band didn't play the blues very often. Its repertoire leaned towards ballads and novelties and certain other kinds of original material, such as "Yard Dog Mazurka."

They played the sentimental songs and the cute ones and the tricky ones. And the thing that was so impressive then and remains so now, hearing the music again, is the way in which they could take the most trivial material, the most banal of pop songs in an era when a pop song was by definition banal, and make something of it.

They did it by the arrangements of Sy Oliver and Eddie Wilcox, basically, and then of Eddie Durham, Jesse Stone, Gerald Wilson, Roger Segure, Don Redman and Chappie Willet. You had to have a band that remained the same, month in and month out—and Lunceford's band remained basically the same unit for many years—in order to develop the kind of group skill that made it possible to play complicated things.

But it wasn't the complicated arrangements that did it. What made the Lunceford band was its wonderful way with ballads. The slow, sleepy "Charmaine" and the delightful "My Blue Heaven," and then the novelties, the insinuating "Organ Grinder's Swing" and "Sleepy Time Gal" and "Hittin' the Bottle."

Those tunes became part of the culture of their time, imbedded in the consciousness of all who heard them. In a way, Lunceford made them into folk music. Certainly in "I'll Take the South," to be specific, there was and is social comment.

The songs were all played, regardless of their simplicity or complexity, for dancers, basically. And they were programmed in the sets to serve that function. After all, these *were* dance bands and, except for its one brief tour of Europe just before World War II broke out, I doubt if the Lunceford band ever played a concert. They played dances and they played stage shows; the concert era for big bands came a good deal later.

The dance, of course, was the fox-trot and its acrobatic extension, the Lindy Hop. Lunceford programmed those sets to take care of the dancers. They began with the slow, dreamy ones and they ended with the up-tempo stomps, and periodically towards the end of the night the whole house would be rocking and rolling to "Running Wild" or "White Heat," after an interim period of the middle-tempo groovers like "Pigeon Walk."

They would set up the whole evening with swinging versions of "Annie Laurie" or "Four or Five Times" and then cut loose with a screaming version of one of their flag-wavers. Or maybe they would do "For Dancers Only" for half an hour, grinding down the blues-ish sound and feeling in the growls and the riffs and making the whole audience meld together into one homogenous mass extension of the music.

Dance tempos are themselves an extension of basic body tempos, of the rhythm and speed of walking, and tempos and beats that fit with them work into easy dance music. Everything the Lunceford band did fitted into half-time or double-time and so was a perfect base for dancing.

The era of the Lunceford band was the era of the silly pop song, of "Organ Grinder's Swing," of "I'm Nuts About Screwy Music" and "The Merry

Go Round Broke Down." What these artists did—and the Lunceford band was not alone in this; Louis Armstrong's great discs of that period have the same thing and, of course, Fats Waller was the prototype—was to take the silliest song and transform it. Over and over, the Lunceford band proved, as a later Lunceford song was to make famous, that "Tain't What You Do" ("it's the way hotcha do it!"). Style, in a pre-McLuhan world, was it.

The dreadful syrupy ballads of the time, sung endlessly by male and female vocalists in special quarter-hour radio shows on the Saturday night Hit Parade and with innumerable silly hotel bands, were all that the foes of pop or Mickey Mouse music said they were. Until Lunceford's band got hold of them—and then "The Love Nest," "Honest and Truly," "The Best Things in Life Are Free" and the others became music, interesting, as well as danceable, music.

Henry Wells and Dan Grissom could sing the sentimental songs and Sy Oliver and Willie Smith and later Trummy Young could handle the novelties. It worked. It worked so very well that a whole generation of America loved their music and will, I think, find it just as delightful today as in those lost but well-remembered years when it all began.

Jimmie Lunceford died on August 13, 1947, on a tour of one-nighters in the Pacific Northwest at the beginning of the postwar boom.

The band had barely survived the war years. The draft took key men, and inflation and the high cost of operating on the road made it difficult to keep going. With Lunceford gone, the band struggled on for a while and then died.

The question, of course, is whether if Lunceford had lived the band would have kept abreast of music and remained, as Ellington and Basie have, a constant verité in a musical world of flux.

The answer, I think, is unequivocally yes.

In the beginning, the Lunceford band synthesized the influences of Ellington and Armstrong and soloists such as Chu Berry into a style of its own. Then, as Sy Oliver and Gerald Wilson developed as arrangers, it began to offer music that was much more original in concept. There are passages in "Yard Dog Mazurka" and in "Hi Spook" and other later Lunceford numbers that really presaged the musical revolution that transformed jazz in the 50s.

Proof, if you need it, of the way in which Lunceford's music—and by that I mean the music played by the band and arranged by the arrangers; I'll pass by the question of how much Lunceford himself was responsible for, but at the very least he hired the men and bought the arrangements—influenced the course of jazz can be found in several things.

Stan Kenton, for one, is deeply indebted to Lunceford. It is generally forgotten now, but Kenton's first trip to the East Coast in the mid-40s was with a band that did its best to be a white Lunceford, and at one time Kenton even hired James Crawford away from Lunceford.

Then there is, of course, the almost classic case of Sy Oliver and Tommy Dorsey. Much of the success of the later Dorsey period dates to Sy Oliver's joining the Dorsey band to write its book.

The Lunceford trumpet section opened up the sky for the screamers, making Armstrong's earlier high notes seem modest indeed. And the deft employment of dynamics and the strength of the descending chord at the end of a tune were unusual then, though commonplace now.

Of the bandleaders who were strong then and who remain on the scene today, only Goodman has failed to keep abreast of the times.

To be a successful bandleader in the 30s, it seems to me, it was necessary to be acutely responsive to the changes of the times. Lunceford obviously was. He was not afraid of new names and new blood. Paul Webster, a highly important man in the early days of modern jazz, was an early recruit to the band. My intuition tells me there would have been more and more over the years, and had Lunceford lived, the band would have developed into another breeding ground for young talent with a bent for experimentation. Lunceford was certainly not averse to it.

Also, I think the Lunceford band could have been easily the biggest thing to hit television. It was such a visual band and so entertaining that it's hard to see how it could have failed in a medium that has rewarded so well so many with so little visual talent.

Technical brilliance, humor, entertainment, perfect dance tempos and a variety of excellent soloists (Eddie Tompkins, Eddie Durham, Willie Smith and Joe Thomas were just four of the first-class soloists in the original band) gave the Lunceford band all the necessary equipment. The arranging talents of Wilcox, Durham and Sy Oliver, and later Gerald Wilson, would have provided the framework.

The speculation is idle, of course. The war came, the men left, Lunceford died, and the strange, living but impersonal organism that is a band disappeared. We don't know and can't know what would have happened.

But the music is still there. The nostalgia, of course, but more than that. The invigorating sound, the special feeling, the fresh ideas and, above all, the vitality.

It was a band to have a good time to, to love to, to dance to, to enjoy. It still is and I'm so glad these sides can once again be set out there for the world to hear.

If you missed Jimmie Lunceford, you missed something great, and the opportunity to catch up is present with this set, luckily. They were part of my life and I want them to be part of everyone's.

Two Rounds of the Battling Dorseys

Tommy Dorsey and Jimmy Dorsey

The sibling rivalry of bandleader brothers Tommy and Jimmy Dorsey was played out on a national stage. This exchange of comments on each other by the battlers themselves first appeared in Esquire's 1947 Jazz Book.

Jimmy by Tommy Dorsey

My being the younger of the Dorsey boys puts me in rather a spot. But, being the bigger of the Dorsey boys puts Jimmy in rather a spot. I wouldn't want anyone to think I was picking on my older brother.

That difference in age, however, seemed to ride right through our careers with the brother always having a slight head start. I won't say I was particularly envious. Shall we say I was just determined to catch up?

Once when I was lagging behind the brother as a mere youth, our father chastised me with, "Thomas, look at your brother. A lot of people would like to be in his shoes."

Instead of looking at the brother, I looked at his shoes and answered, "A lot of people could get in his shoes!"

Can you blame me for getting sore at him? Do you know one time he had me scooting all over the country trying to establish my own orchestra after brother Jim had taken *our* band to the Coast to go on Bing Crosby's Music Hall.

Of course, he didn't exactly *take it away* from me at Glen Island Casino. We'd had a few words, or something, about the tempo of a tune, or something. The next thing you know, we had our own separate bands, Jimmy featured on the Music Hall, Tommy knocking down from two to three hundred dollars a night (for the whole band, including transportation and commissions.)

Most of our fights about the Dorsey Brothers Band took place after hours at a midtown gymnasium named Plunkett's. I remember I got so mad at him in Plunkett's one day that I went over to his room and smashed all his saxophones on the radiator. I guess that fight started over who was going to stand in front of the band at Glen Island.

I couldn't tell you what we fought about most of the time. I remember once in a surge of brotherly affection I went down to the pier to meet Jimmy on the *Ile de France*. Jimmy had been touring Europe with Ted Lewis in an orchestra that included Muggsy Spanier and George Brunies. We hadn't seen each other for months, but within five minutes we were fighting again.

Plunkett's was a wonderful place with a roster more exclusive than any Union League Club. This membership had reserved seats at some of the best battles the Dorseys ever staged. Late in the afternoon you'd see Bix Biederbecke and Frank Teschemaker, napping in one of the booths in the back room after a tough record date. Of course, they'd wake up as soon as the Dorsey fights began.

Chances are that Josh Billings, Jack Bland, Eddie Condon and Red McKenzie would be tuning up for an evening's engagement of the Mound City Blue Blowers. Of course, they'd stop tuning at the drop of a Dorsey. Josh used to play a suitcase with two whisk brooms and the heel of his foot. With that unique equipment, he could top most drummers.

There was a big icebox at Plunkett's, the kind with a door that you could open and walk into. Eddie Condon used to keep his entire wardrobe in the icebox and before the Mound City Blue Blowers' job he used the icebox as the star's dressing room.

I remember another icebox just like the one at Plunkett's when Jimmy worked at the Greystone Ballroom in Detroit with Gene Golkette's orchestra. There was a prize fighter–jazz fan around Detroit at that time who dogged Jimmy's footsteps. Jimmy just couldn't lose this fan, until one evening he locked him in the icebox. I often thought of locking Jimmy in the Plunkett icebox but it seems I could never jockey him into position.

Arnold Johnson had the big band at the Paramount Hotel back in the Plunkett days and you'd see his drummer, Sid Jacobs and his piano player, Harold Arlen, there on their way to work. (That's right, the same Harold Arlen that wrote "Stormy Weather.") Johnny Williams came down from Boston to play the drum for Leo Reisman at Jimmy Walker's Central Park Casino (ah, there, Majestic records). Joe Venuti, Eddie Lang, Jerry Colonna, Artie Shaw and Harry Goodman would drop in from time to time between radio shows just to keep track of the Dorsey fight marathon.

I guess we got older because after the days at Plunkett's we just didn't seem to fight much any more.

The brother carved a niche on the Coast and on Decca records; I carved mine in New York and on Victor.

Since then we've gone our separate ways to what is commonly recognized in this business as "moderate success." And, much to the surprise of the New York Athletic Club, the Boxing Commission and a few hecklers from Madison Square Garden and 52nd Street, completed with nary a cross word exchanged.

Some of our staunchest fans don't like this. They claim we're getting old and soft.

A music critic for a swing magazine put the blame for the recent slump in the band business on our shoulders.

"The lull in the band business," he screamed, "is due to the Dorseys not fighting. There's no interest any more."

That puts the brother and myself in a very embarrassing situation. Despite the pleas of the trade, along with the natives of Shenandoah Valley who always counted on "those Irish brothers" for a good show, we've made a solemn promise to remain good boys.

And not only that, I like the brother. Not just because he's a Dorsey, but he's a whale of a musician, has a nice, easygoing manner and, well, he's good to his mother.

Tommy by Jimmy Dorsey

Tommy Dorsey? It's a good thing Tom stuck to the trombone. He'd never make much of a fighter. I know, because I used to whip him daily myself. There used to be a little trap called "Plunkett's" where I took the duke from Tom in numerous contests.

The name of Plunkett's in the telephone book was "The Trombone Club." That was on account of Tommy Dorsey was the best customer. That is to say, he owed the till the most money. One time that I know of he owed $850 in cash to Jimmy Plunkett and the barman philosopher, Gene O'Byrne. Neither Jimmy nor Gene could afford to be mad at Tommy; he owed them too much money.

Whenever Tom walked into Plunkett's he would say, "How's the damper?" "O.K.," Gene might reply, "we took in $23 tonight." That would be Tommy's cue to say, "Well, now, let's see. You'd better give me the twenty-three."

Tommy and I staged more battles in Plunkett's than in any other spot in the metropolitan district. Arthur Schutt, the baron of the piano, was forever trying to keep peace among the Dorseys. This was because Arthur wanted a few moments of peace himself as he had plenty of battles of his own with his wife, Virginia. Arthur, a fine musician and one of the cleverest of all arrangers, was about that time a constant host to Eddie Condon, the eminent conductor.

Arthur had about 35 radio shows a week and a fancy apartment at the

Park-Vendome on 57th Street. I know Arthur's apartment had a hardwood floor. Eddie often mentioned it. You see, he was sleeping on it those days. If my kid brother, Tommy, had only let Arthur write the arrangements things would have been fine with the Dorsey Brothers Orchestra. But Tommy's man wrote most of them and if you ask me that is probably the reason why the band broke up.

Funny thing though, even as kids those Dorsey battles were mainly about music. In the short-pants days back in Scranton they concerned who played cornet better. At that time both of us were on the cornet. With the accent on the first syllable. That's why Pop switched us to saxophone and trombone, I guess. Being the older of the two brothers, I had an advantage, but being the smaller of the two I also had a disadvantage. That made us about even.

I guess the best times the brother and myself had in the band business together were the real early days. We're all familiar with that early struggle to get somewhere and it's always a good thing to look back upon. Of course, it was no fun then trying to "break it up" with the Dorsey Brothers' Wild Canaries. But we learned a lot of tricks from those early local Pennsylvania tours that served us in good stead years later.

When finally we did make the grade and rated some national recognition for the Dorsey Brothers name, slightly more than a decade later—at Sands Point, the Palais Royale, the Riviera and that never-to-be-forgotten Glen Island Casino—we were in different brackets, fighting (as a team, this time) stronger competition, mixed up in the very complicated business of big-time music. The pressure of trying to do big things as brand-new band leaders under those conditions kind of showed up on both of us. Ask any patron of Glen Island Casino who was there on May 30th, 1935.

However, in the interim, between the Wild Canaries and Glen Island, there was a very pleasant interlude when the brother and I served as side-men, sometimes together, sometimes separately. Generally we angled to get in the same bands because Mom and Pop wanted it that way. We thought we did a pretty fair job together, minding our own parts and sticking to our own sections. Of course, one of our ex-bosses, like Paul Whiteman, might have other ideas on this. That's for Paul to write about, not me.

In the long run, it's hard to say who won what battle. We just went our separate ways, built up our separate followings (we do share some fans; probably those are the ones who championed a Dorsey Brothers Orchestra), and put our pennies in our separate piggy banks.

Tommy has his musicians, I have mine and never the twain shall meet.

Only once was that rule upset. Three years after the split-up, Ray McKinley, the drummer of the Dorsey Brothers outfit, had voiced some idea of leaving my band. The brother got wind of it, called Ray and offered him a job. I didn't like it and the boy at the bell rang the gong to start another round. It was a short round, though. McKinley settled it as a draw by forming his own orchestra and leaving us both on a limb.

As for the brother, he has a lot of qualities I strongly admire. I suppose all fellows brag about their kid brothers that way. We're always glad to see them get ahead. My kid brother, for instance, is a helluva fine musician, a shrewd businessman and one of the most untiring packages of energy I've ever seen. As far as the trombone goes, who can operate one any better?

Oh, I guess we'll fight again, we always have, but it'll never seem as much fun as it did at Plunkett's when Jack Bland, Vic Burton, Johnny Williams and Max Kurtzman would be holding me down, while Sid Jacobs, Red McKenzie, Miff Mole and Muggsy Spanier were hanging on to Tommy trying to keep us apart.

JAZZ ORCHESTRA IN RESIDENCE, 1971

CAROL EASTON

In Straight Ahead: The Story of Stan Kenton *(1973), Carol Easton reports on the always controversial Kenton in 1971—late in his career and life but as driven as ever.*

"MAGIC IS WHEN YOU'VE BEEN RIDIN' THE BUS ALL NIGHT FOR FOUR HUNDRED MILES AFTER DOIN' A ONE-NIGHTER, AND THE OLD MAN'S DRINKIN' WITH YOU, AND WE'RE ALL HAVIN' A BALL. YOU WAKE UP IN THE MORNING AND HE'S IN THE FRONT OF THE BUS AND HE'S HAD THE SAME SUIT ON ALL NIGHT, BUT HIS SUIT LOOKS LIKE IT'S IMMACULATELY PRESSED. HIS HAIR IS COMBED, AND HE SMILES. AND HE'S OLD ENOUGH TO BE ALL OF OUR FATHERS—EVEN WILLIE MAIDEN'S! AND YOU WALK OFF THE BUS HUNG OVER AND DRAGGIN', AND YOU'RE LIKE TWENTY-FIVE, THIRTY YEARS OLD, AND THERE HE IS, HANDING YOU YOUR SUITCASE. THAT'S MAGIC!"

—DICK SHEARER, *LEAD TROMBONE*

He enters the small concert hall from the back, unannounced, while the band is tuning up. Assuming the hunched posture characteristic of men who pass the six-foot mark at an age when it can only be embarrassing, he makes his way to the stage. Signs of physical strain are painfully evident. The face, a ravaged relief map charting thirty grinding years on the road, looks flaccid and sallow. Faded, sunken blue eyes peer wearily, warily out from above frighteningly dark circles of fatigue. He looks overweight and undernourished, unhealthily bloated and cadaverous, all at the same time. The profuse perspiration could simply be the August heat, but more likely it's weakness; after all, the man is almost sixty, he's had major surgery twice within a few months' time, he's still got a drainage tube sticking out of an incision in his gut—should he even be ambulatory, let alone conduct an orchestra in this hundred-degree-plus oven?

Stiffly and gingerly, in deference to that obscene tube, he seats himself at the piano. Those gargantuan hands that can reach chords as lush and full as any ever heard on this earth begin the intro to "Artistry in Rhythm" with a sincerity that belies thirty years of repetition. Impossibly, the skin takes on tone and color. The eyes begin to sparkle like a lover's. A radiant smile erases ten years from the face. And when he rises to his full six feet four inches to conduct the body of the piece, you get the unforgettable, powerful, all-stops-out, larger-than-life impact of STAN KENTON, head high, shoulders back, juices flowing, arms flailing convulsively, projecting vibrations of vitality, authority and sexuality that flood the room like a searchlight. Involuntarily, you respond.

Years ago, a young Stan Kenton discovered that music could ease a persistent internal ache, and he willingly became its prisoner for life. Music gave him the realization of his generation's classic success fantasy: fame, fortune, creative satisfaction. It gave him the power to turn on an entire generation, and gratified his voracious ego by making him a legend before he reached forty. In return, it occupied his life like a conquering army, displacing three wives, two daughters, a son, the warmth and companionship of innumerable good people, a college education, well-loved homes, boats and a list of simple, everyday pleasures too painful to recount. Not to mention his youth and his health.

Undoubtedly, Stan considers it a fair exchange. Separated from his music, the man exists only as a frustrated fragment in search of wholeness—a wholeness made possible by a charter bus with STAN KENTON ORCHESTRA on the outside and nineteen musicians on the inside, whether en route to a one-nighter at the Burlington, Iowa, Elks Lodge or a sold-out concert at Carnegie Hall. For him, those moments on the bandstand, sandwiched joyously between his music and his audience, are everything. All the rest is waiting.

THIS IS STAN'S twelfth full-time band, and the last he intends to build. In a business so abrasive to the sensitive personalities it attracts that a notoriously large number of them shatter under its pressures, the price of survival defies the Straight imagination. What nine-to-five mind can begin to grasp the cumulative effect of thirty years on the road? *Thirty years!* Representing how many punishing one-night stands? How many interchangeable hotel rooms, indigestible meals, interminable interviews? How many loadings of buses, trains, planes, taxis and private cars? How many packings and unpackings of clothing, shaving gear, travel clock? How many timetables, itineraries, schedules, maps, miles, poker hands? How many hands outstretched to be shaken or tipped? How many 3 A.M. revelations and regrets?

How many fifths opened at midnight and emptied by dawn? How many fans demanding to be stroked with a word or a smile? How many mornings of waking unsure of the day, the time zone or the town? How many sleepless nights in a bus seat designed for short-term occupancy? How many sneak attacks of heartburn, backache, boredom, piles, insomnia, allergies, migraine, depression? How many unobserved birthdays, anniversaries, Christmases? How many requests for "Eager Beaver"? How many choruses of "Peanut Vendor"? How many downbeats?

Knowing this to be Stan's last band, its members share a heavy sense of responsibility. They see the band as a kind of institution that began before most of them were born, and to judge from the way they're playing, they're determined to give the Old Man's career on the road one hell of a finish. In casual conversation, they come across more like disciples than employees. "The people out front all remember the big tall gray-haired fellow with the long arms," says bass trombonist Graham Ellis, "with his beautiful music that we're playing. To the guys in the band, he is a person to worship—because he's so dedicated, so devoted, such a beautiful person."

At thirty-five, Ellis is one of the oldest members of the band. The average age is thirty, a statistic skewed somewhat by Stan's fifty-nine years. Many are barely old enough to vote. And on this sweltering night at the University of Redlands, next door to the Mojave Desert, they present a motley image of hairy faces, colorful and mismatched shirts and physiques that reflect the most sedentary occupation next to proofreading.

The audience consists of a hundred and fifty music students, average age seventeen. Most are attending this week-long music clinic, formally designated "Jazz Orchestra in Residence," at the behest of a persuasive schoolband director. Others are here courtesy of scholarships, or their parents' largesse; and for a few, the tuition and travel expense represent a substantial personal investment in terms of dishes washed, lawns mowed, papers delivered, short-term loans negotiated. The majority are Southern Californians, but many are from as far away as Phoenix, Oakland, Seattle—and one piano student has motorcycled all the way from New York. But their attitude during registration this afternoon was curiously indifferent. Asked what they thought of Stan Kenton's music, nine out of ten responded with a vague shrug or fakeout, "Oh, he's okay, I guess." Born after Korea, weaned on rock 'n roll, raised on hard rock and in all probability never exposed to a big band any hotter than that of their local college—what would they know of Balboa, of Progressive Jazz, "Artistry in Rhythm," "Eager Beaver," "City of Glass"? Who are Maynard Ferguson, Anita O'Day, Gerry Mulligan, Lee Kontiz, Bob Graettinger, Shorty Rogers, Art Pepper, Shelly Manne, June Christy, Stan Getz, Zoot Sims to them? Stan Kenton? An unknown quantity. Someone whose music their parents once listened to in a Neanderthal, pre-

TV world totally outside their never-look-back frame of reference. If the name connects at all, it's only because they've seen it on their school-band arrangements. And how could it be otherwise? To these children of electronics, if you haven't made it on the tube (or at least the top forty), you haven't made it. Lawrence Welk may be a musical joke to them, but at least they know who he is and what he stands for. But . . . Stan Kenton? Shrug.

Now that he's got their attention, Stan steps to the microphone and in a voice emanating from some subterranean source delivers a few brief, low-keyed words of welcome. One oblique allusion to his illness—"I guess you all know I've just gotten out of the nuthouse"—and flashing that dazzling smile, he gives the downbeat for "Rainy Day."

"Rainy Day" is a ballad that begins like a dirge, with the five trombonists playing slower than trombonists were ever meant to play, thus requiring a degree of control that sends all the trombone students in the room into paroxysms of awe. As the full band joins in and the number gains momentum and intensity, the students' eyes begin to widen and their jaws to drop. And by the time the arrangement builds and swells and climaxes, without ever perceptibly picking up tempo, the audience is beginning to levitate right out of its collective seat. "Ooooooooh," moans a seventeen-year-old trombonist in the front row, "that does my heart good!"

As a concession to his physical condition, Stan delegates the conducting of the next number, "Chiapas," to its composer, Hank Levy. Levy is a musician's musician whose particular genius lies in musical prestidigitation—unorthodox time signatures. To the untrained ear, his work evokes images of cyclotrons gone berserk, sending shattered melodies and countermelodies somersaulting crazily over each other in dynamic, driving rhythms with no apparent pattern. What does a layman know of 5/4, or subdivided rhythms? But these students know something of the intricacies of writing, playing and *thinking* in such literally offbeat time signatures; hearing such a piece performed with the full virtuosity and power of the band for which it was written gives them a mind-blowing, exhilarating glimpse of the hoped-for result of all those practice hours, and the sudden and subdued ending of "Chiapas" leaves the kids turned on like strings of Christmas-tree lights.

Saxophonist Willie Maiden conducts the next number, shamelessly milking the last drop of theatricality out of his arrangement of "Hey, Jude." He cues each solo with a broad flourish—a jive game, Willie calls it. But the kids love it, particularly the six flashy horn solos. By the time the band reaches the pretentious big finish, the eyes of Kenton's trombonists are bulging out of their sockets; the kids are cheering, whistling and exchanging hushed "Wows." And in the makeshift wings, for all the world like an adulation junkie getting a fix, Stan Kenton, resident Legend, smiles.

Redlands is less than a hundred miles away from Balboa, where it all began—but for Stan, it's been a matter of thirty years and God knows how many miles. When his first band opened at the Rendezvous Ballroom, it was the most exciting thing to hit Balboa before or since that summer of 1941. The gangling, painfully self-conscious young man who led that band was idealistic to the point of fanaticism; he *believed,* and his fierce enthusiasm carried musicians and audiences along with it like a tidal wave. Every performance was an exercise in sustained hysteria. His intensity, his total commitment to the music was awesome to behold. The vulnerability on his face was like a public confession. Had Stan appeared on the stand stark naked, with a bag over his head, he would have been less exposed.

That young man has undergone considerable changes in the intervening years—but in the rarefied atmosphere of this music clinic, he lives again. No wonder Stan prefers these clinics to all his other endeavors, even though the financial rewards are nil. In this environment, reality gracefully withdraws. Surrounded by eager students who approach him with just the proper mixture of respect and adoration, he feels young. They ask, he answers. He gives, they take. There is much exchanging of bits and pieces of evidence indicating a resurgence of jazz, maybe even of big bands! Rapport is expedited by a vocabulary with built-in exclusivity: embouchures, charts, chord progressions, phrasing, triplets, time signatures, section work, intonation, improvisation, chops. For this brief time, music is all there is.

To an impressionable young musician, a week of studying and performing with this band is the experience of a lifetime. For most of them, this is the closest they'll ever come to a professional band—although music as something less than a lifetime calling may still bring them tremendous gratification. For a few, this may be the first serious step toward a vocation. One or two may even possess sufficient promise to warrant a job offer from Stan. He has hired a number of sidemen out of these very clinics. Their enthusiasm almost makes up for their lack of experience, and it keeps operating costs down; and operating costs constitute the basic fact of life for a road band these days.

"Jazz Orchestra in Residence" means precisely that. Musicians and students live on campus for the duration of the clinic. The musicians make themselves accessible not only during the scheduled classes and rehearsals, but at virtually any waking hour—and students aren't shy about requesting private lessons.

On the surface, the interaction between Kenton and kids is an ideal teacher-student relationship, in which Stan and all the members of his band willingly share everything they know about technique, theory, composition, arranging, improvisation and, basic to all of this, professionalism of approach. To both teachers and students, the experience is rewarding.

On a deeper level, there is a strong feeling of *family*— an almost exclusively male family, to be sure—with all the hierarchy thereof. Stan is apparently incapable of saying "Good morning" without involuntarily projecting a quality that inspires instant allegiance. No effort is spared to win his approval. In this father role, he is perfectly cast.

The musicians function as older brothers to the students. Other clinic staffers, administrators and such, are stern but helpful uncles. At the pyramid's base are the student-sons. There are a few favorites, a few scapegoats. Sibling rivalry is intense but controlled. The family appears to be totally self-sufficient. Everyone has his clearly defined role to play, his assigned work to do. Life is simple, clear-cut, black and white—just like a sheet of music.

On the final afternoon of the clinic, parents begin arriving to reclaim their children and appraise their investments. The students are in a last-day-of-camp mood, charged with nervous energy, anticipating the loss of something precious but ephemeral. All assemble in the concert hall for a marathon demonstration of what the week has wrought.

Each of eight student bands performs two numbers. The students, sweaty but starry-eyed, blow as they've never blown before. The last group to play is the "head band," so called because unlike the other bands that played standard Kenton arrangements, its music is improvised. Their wildly spontaneous performance is aptly critiqued by an excited alto player: "It sounds like shit, but it sure is fun!"

By the time the Kenton band takes its place to conclude the concert and the clinic, a representative (read "middle-aged") group of Redlands citizens has joined the audience. Along with the parents, they make up an interesting generational cross-section. Members of the respective age groups respond, as though programmed, to the elements of the music that push their respective buttons. The students turn on to the immediacy, as well as the mechanics, of the more demanding, experimental concert numbers, while most of the oldsters remain irrevocably in the "Artistry" bag. The latter group applauds politely enough for the Hank Levy charts, but it's "Peanut Vendor" that sends their eyes rolling back in their heads, accompanied by sighs of, "*That's* the Stan Kenton I remember!" It's not necessarily a reflection of their musical sophistication; it's a simple matter of nostalgia, an emotion Stan abhors. Never Look Back is his credo; the past is best forgotten. Period. And yet . . . Stan Kenton provided the background music for the coming of age of a generation. And if the reprise of that music recalls a time when idealism was high, options open and responsibilities minimal—who can resist the pull of *that* Paradise lost? And so the yellowing sheets of "Peanut Vendor" remain in the book.

In the wake of the exhausting decibel volume created by the students, Stan shrewdly shifts the mood. "We're going to assume that you, the audience, collectively, is a beautiful woman," he announces, "and we're going to go about the process of making love in a very easy and quiet manner." Screaming brass may be his trademark, but nobody can get the emotional mileage out of a sentimental ballad like "Love Story" or "MacArthur Park" that Stan can. So that the final encore leaves the audience satisfied, relaxed, ready for nothing more taxing than a good night's sleep. While the band faces the prospect of loading the bus and getting under way, hopefully by midnight, toward tomorrow night's job in San Francisco, four hundred fifty miles away.

Barring blowouts, mechanical failures and acts of God, they'll get a few hours' sleep on the bus and check into a San Francisco motel "on the day sheet," saving the price of a room for tonight. The unprecedented two weeks in Redlands (for two consecutive clinics) has left them bored, restless, anxious to get moving. The first few days were a welcome relief from the pressured pace of one-nighters (they've been known to do seven straight months of them). Only a musician who ran out of clean socks a week ago can know the joys of catching up on his laundry, as well as his sleep. And the respite from one-nighters provides an opportunity to take care of other personal matters for which there's simply no time on the road. For Mike Vax, lead trumpet player, Redlands will be forever memorable as the town where he (1) bought a new sports car, and (2) got engaged. But the novelty of unpacking your bag, of sleeping in the same bed for more than two consecutive nights, begins to pall surprisingly soon. Exiled from the familiar insulation of the bus, there are too many reminders of the deprivations built into the bizarre lifestyle of a road band, and only constant psychological vigilance can guard against questioning the validity of the bus as a surrogate home, the other band members as surrogate family, Stan as surrogate father. Saxophonist Chuck Carter cannot afford to dwell on thoughts of his wife and five children in Indianapolis, and Willie Maiden must at all costs maintain the fiction that he and his chick in Chicago communicate via ESP.

Sexually, one-night stands are infinitely safer than two-week engagements, during which a relationship can develop sufficient potential to deflect a lonely sideman from his single-minded dedication to the band. Once his mind swivels in the direction of a real home and family, his enthusiasm begins to erode and his resignation is just a matter of time.

The members of this band wile away countless hours on the bus weaving elaborate fantasies of a time when they'll have their own road bands. Musicians who put in their time on the road with Stan years ago and have since put down roots in New York, Chicago or Los Angeles view such ambitions dubiously. The road is a young man's scene. Some adapt to it better than others, but all succumb eventually to its merciless pace.

BUD SHANK, *saxophonist:* "I wouldn't ever want to do it again. No home life. No sleep. Too much drinking. No chance for study. No home. No wife. No home."

MILT BERNHART, *trombonist:* "I developed a chronic cold. All that jostling around, long jumps up to five hundred miles, eating quickly and dangerously, not getting enough sleep. I never felt terribly good, so I was always looking for the time I could break away."

LAURINDO ALMEIDA, *guitarist:* "I like to see the country . . . going through the misty trees at dawn in Oregon, meeting my first snowstorm in New York, seeing the sunrise, beautiful things. But it's so tiresome. Many times we'd vote if we stay in that town or if we go ahead and travel two hundred or three hundred miles that night after the concert. If enough people vote yes, you have to go."

MEL LEWIS, *drummer:* "The bus gets to stinking of dirty clothes, sweat and booze and cigarette smoke and cigar smoke, and the guys have their shoes off and everybody's wearing their socks for two and three days, because we don't always have a chance to get them washed. There comes a time when you have to make up your mind. And my wife had put up with five years of road with me."

JUNE CHRISTY, *vocalist:* "We worked seven nights a week, in a different town every day with no time to rest. If we did have a night off, we'd spend it traveling on the bus. I finally became very ill, and Stan wasn't at all sympathetic because he was holding up and he felt if he was, everyone else should be, too."

GERRY MULLIGAN, *saxophonist:* "Life on the road is murder. It's as though life begins and ends when you have your horn in your mouth. It's like the loneliness of the long-distance runner."

In Stan's straight-ahead view, no allowances are made for those who forsake the road for the comforts of home, family and in many cases a substantially higher income. "They've lost their love for music," is the way he puts it. "When a guy comes in the band and he shows potential, I always feel that maybe there's a possible chance of him developing into a leader himself. And there have been just dozens and dozens of wonderful musicians in the band. And usually when they leave the band, I'll have high hopes of them maybe doing something with their music. But it seems like the majority of them just kind of fall by the wayside and go the path of least resistance. New York is full of them. Hollywood is, Las Vegas, too—guys that've just kind of sold out.

But even Stan admits that it's not that simple. The dilemma has accompanied him through three broken marriages; a basic ambivalence underlies the rationalizations. "The road is our out because when we play, we play our way, without restrictions. Entirely free. And we couldn't be that way if we stayed in one place. So when a musician settles down—and usually they settle down because of family problems; *marriages are the thing that hang musicians up the most*—it's only right that the wife doesn't want her husband wandering around the world and she's left to raise the kids. So they *have* to compromise. They'll go into television [he's tried it] or into recording [that, too]. And most of them are miserably unhappy, but they just can't seem to do anything about it. . . . Sometimes wives will destroy a guy, and don't even know they're doing it! That's one good thing about this band; I think there are only three or four guys out of the whole band that are married.

"Mike Vax told me yesterday that his marriage is not going to affect our relationship whatsoever. He feels that's the way it's gonna be. But it's not gonna be that way. She's not gonna be able to stand bein' away from him; she's gonna want him with her, and she should have him with her. Husbands and wives should be together. And when things keep them apart, there's a great risk of the relationship falling to pieces."

Mike Vax is in love, and his reality is structured accordingly; but Stan's feelings on the subject are no secret, and when Mike broke the news to the Old Man it was with trepidation. "I was almost scared to tell him I was engaged. I felt he might think that I wouldn't do as good a job because I had a woman on my mind—which was part of the reason our last first trumpet player left the band. His wife pressured him. But Sandy would never want me to quit. She fell in love with a musician, and she knew it when she did it."

But Sandy has only just turned twenty, and Mike's self-delusion is colossal. "The only difference between me and a guy who works from nine to five every day," he says coolly, "is that Sandy'll see me once in awhile for a lot of time, whereas that guy's wife never sees him from nine to five anyway, and half the time she never sees him at night because she's at a bridge club or he's bowling, so they say a few words to each other at dinner and that's it. I'm going to stay with Stan until he retires, but after that I'll probably start my own band and Sandy'll just come on the road with me, for as long as she wants to." Never mind the complication of children, or the possibility that Sandy may find a lifetime of waiting, interspersed with road trips which for her will lack even the mitigating satisfaction of playing music, less than fulfilling. Mike and Sandy met three weeks ago in Iowa, where Sandy was the reigning Miss Burlington. Mike is twenty-eight, and has never married. And Stan shrugs and says, "Sure, Mike, your marriage won't affect our relationship whatsoever."

Sandy and Mike take off for San Francisco in their shiny new red Datsun, waving good-byes to the rest of the band members gathered around the bus outside the Redlands dorm. In the vast darkness of the parking lot, the amber lights inside the bus are inviting; the motor throbs, a reassuringly familiar sound. Stan, with his incision hopefully on the mend, supervises the loading—a conscientious father getting his boys off to camp.

Loading the bus is a ritual so familiar that its participants could perform it in their sleep—and have done so on numerous hungover occasions. In the well-established order of priorities, essentials come first. Luggage, instruments, music stands, all the paraphernalia of the business end of the band is stowed in the luggage compartment, deep in the belly of the bus. What goes into the passenger section is considerably more varied. Everyone has his own seat, and there's a special significance in its location. The back of the bus is reserved for those who want to *cak* (sleep). The front of the bus is Insomnia City, the scene of all-night discussions and drinking bouts. Stan's seat is the second behind the driver.

The last items to be loaded are the most personal. Everyone has his own cassette recorder with tiny earphone, to accommodate his particular musical taste (most prefer the classics to jazz, which creates endless arguments). Trombonist Dick Shearer stashes the self-improvement book he's currently reading. Willie Maiden must have his orange security blanket. Trombonist Mike Jamieson, the only member of the band who appears capable of running around the block without collapsing (and a thrower perpetually in search of a catcher), checks on the baseball and mitt, football, Frisbee and other token sporting gear that he breaks out during food stops, gas stops, booze stops and breakdowns. Like adaptable animals, each man converts his seat into a customized nest, equipped with his particular antidote for boredom: booze; cards; booze; magazines; booze; tapes; booze. Along with such vital accessories as paper cups and ice.

It's almost 1 A.M. Seat backs are adjusted, bodies settled, shoes removed. The door hisses shut. The interior light is switched off, replaced by pencil-thin reading lights. The transmission grinds into gear. The tires crunch through the gravel of the parking lot toward the highway. Moving through the night, the men breathe a collective sigh of relaxation.

They're home.

Flying Home

Rudi Blesh

One of the great innovators—and tragic heroes—of jazz was Charlie Christian (yet another John Hammond "discovery"), who revolutionized jazz guitar playing before his death, at twenty-three, in 1942. This narrative of his life and career is by Rudi Blesh, himself an innovator as a jazz writer and educator, in his 1971 book, Combo: U.S.A.

Deep Second was the street where the music was. Deep Second was way over east, across the Sante Fe tracks. On Deep Second were dance halls like Slaughter's and Hall's Hall—that's right: A. Hall ran a hall. In those years—the late twenties and early thirties—the bands came into Oklahoma City from all over the Territory, which no longer referred to the Indian Territory—that was gone—but to the entire area of Missouri, Kansas, Arkansas, Oklahoma, and Texas.

When I was young we all heard Territory jazz bands like Alphonso Trent's, George E. Lee's, and Terence Holder's—his band became Andy Kirk's Twelve Clouds of Joy. We had a band of our own there, one of the best: Walter Page's Blue Devils. Page was originally from Missouri but his band was in Oklahoma City so much of the time that we thought of it as our band. Partly this may have been because he had a local singer, Jimmy Rushing or Mr. Five-By-Five, who sang real blues with a slight urban accent.

Jimmy Rushing is a good example of the involvement of black Oklahoma City with music of all kinds. His father played trumpet—his brass band gave Sunday concerts in the park down on the river. Jimmy's mother and brother were singers, too, and all of them participated in the operettas staged at the high school. Jimmy, in addition, had violin training, and played piano by ear.

There was soul music and legitimate music, side by side. Both could be heard in the streets: the black serenading groups that played all spring, summer, and fall, particularly in northwest Oklahoma City, the better middle-class white residential district. One of these groups had my friend Charlie Christian in it.

Ralph Ellison was talking about black Oklahoma City, where he was born, about music there, and, especially, about his friend, Charlie Christian. Christian was a genius of the guitar, who went from a cigar-box instrument to a blues guitar, who created a new role for the guitar in jazz, and who pioneered the electrically amplified guitar, now the mainstay of rock, blues, and pop. Christian did all of this in less than four years on the big time, before dying at the age of twenty-three.

A quiet boy, Charlie did most of his talking on the guitar. His words have not survived his youthful death. So it is Ralph Ellison, who once planned to be a trumpet player and, instead, became one of the great American novelists, who is the one to tell the story of a young Christian's years in Oklahoma City.

> The serenading groups were two to four pieces. You would hear guitar and perhaps mandolin, generally some kind of bass, either a real string bass or the kind called a "tub bass" which is made from an inverted washtub and a broom handle, with one string. There might be a violin—in fact nearly any kind of portable instrument might show up. All of the players could sing. They would wander over town, especially on warm (read "hot") evenings, stopping to play requests and then passing the hat around. On summer nights their sounds—raggy or blue—would blend with the bells of the ever-near ice-cream cone wagons. In cooler weather—fall or spring—the ice cream part of the street polyphony would change to the call of the Mexicans with their small pushcarts fashioned from perambulators: "Hot tamales! Hot tamales! Get your hot tamales!"

Ellison even recalled the going prices in those days: an ice-cream cone, a nickel; the small "finger" tamales, a cent apiece or a half dozen for a nickel.

Besides the wandering serenaders there were similar groups based at the barbecue stands where a pig would be roasting in a hot pit and Martha Washington pies would be frying in deep fat. The pies were dough turnovers filled (and really filled) with fresh (and really fresh) fruit—apples, red cherries, or Elberta peaches. Barbecue stands were all over town in strategic spots, like the one on Classen Boulevard between 17th and 18th, where an old inter-urban railway station had been. The "resident" groups, like the strolling serenaders, played and sang ragtime, current popular songs, the blues, and, by request, could comfortably move on into the light classics.

The funky blues and the dark, rolling boogie were there, of course. But it was from a musical climate almost as diversified as that of New Orleans that the artist, Charlie Christian, came. But New Orleans is, or was, an old city with a rich and ancient cultural heritage. Oklahoma was brash and new—a mushroom metropolis of a hundred thousand people where only forty years before had been prairie, with Indians camping on the buffalo grass. In Oklahoma City—black Oklahoma City—there was a special reason named Mrs. Zelia N. Braux.

> We were strongly, almost obsessively, oriented to music. That's where Mrs. Braux came in. She had a theater of her own, the Aldrich, on Deep Second near Central. Ma Rainey, Bessie Smith, Ida Cox, Mamie Smith—all the great blues women—sang there. Bands played there, like King Oliver's—that's what first brought Lester Young to Oklahoma City.
>
> But where Zelia Braux had a decisive role was in the schools. She was musical director, or supervisor, for the whole public system from the elementary grades through high school. That meant, you understand, the black schools, for there was rigid segregation. In actuality, it meant one school; for grade school and high school were both crowded into one building. But in music at least, due to Mrs. Braux, separate and unequal meant unequal for the white students, not the black ones.
>
> Music instruction in the white schools, I've been told, was perfunctory—mainly pupils being taught to sing "Three Blind Mice" and "Flow Gently Sweet Afton." Not so with Mrs. Braux! She personally trained and conducted the band and the orchestra, staged complete operettas with school talent. She herself gave instruction to all the pupils, talented or not. And that instruction would have been amazing in any general school system, anywhere. It included four years of harmony—beginning in the eighth grade—and a considerable amount of theory. And four years compulsory music appreciation!
>
> So when Charlie Christian would amuse and amaze us at school with his first guitar—one that he made from a cigar box—he would be playing his own riffs. But they were based on sophisticated chords and progressions that Blind Lemon Jefferson never knew.

All members of Charlie's family were musical. Before leaving for Oklahoma City (when Charlie was two), Mr. and Mrs. Christian had provided all the music in a silent movie theater in Dallas; she on piano, he on trumpet. Mr. Christian, Ellison says, had become blind sometime in those years after moving to Oklahoma, but he still played, strumming a guitar or a double-necked mandolin. Charlie had two brothers, Clarence, and the eldest, Edward, who was about four years older than Charlie. Mr. Christian and his three sons made up a strolling quartet with Mr. Christian and Charlie on guitars, Edward on string bass, and Clarence doubling on violin and mandolin. By that time Charlie had acquired a real guitar. They all sang and the relative pitches of their voices blended into a male quartet. They played opera or blues, but even on some sentimental ballad they would insinuate some rather sophisticated chords into the orthodox "barbershop" harmony.

I sometimes think of all those wonderful sounds, all lost, now: the high, buzzing drone of the cicadas (we called them locusts), the ice-cream bells down the block, the voices of children, the rustle of cottonwood leaves in the light evening breeze, and those soft chords being hummed over the pulsing strings.

Douglass School, exclusively for blacks, was at Walnut and California, well into the black area. Ellison was playing upright alto, known as "peck horn." His teacher was Charlie Christian's father. Soon he was getting trumpet lessons from a barber next door, Joseph Meade. Everyone was getting music lessons from someone.

Music was in the air; no special thing in itself but, rather, a bright thread in the fabric, a part of daily life. That life, which included the basics—working, eating, sleeping, playing, going to church, making love—was interwoven, like all those "lost" incidental evening sounds, with an organ point of music. There was, for example, baseball.

Charlie was a baseball player—a good one. Clarence could have been a major leaguer, if it had been in the post-Branch Rickey period . . .

(It was Rickey, of course, who as owner of the Brooklyn Dodgers, had signed first baseman Jackie Robinson and broken the color line in professional baseball.)

. . . but he didn't want to sign with the Black Yankees. So he went into professional music, instead. Edward preferred football and he, too, if the time had been later, might well have made it as a pro.

But you should have seen the Christian brothers at pool! I used to play with them and I know! We didn't have to go to a pool hall to play—even if we had the money. We played at the Christians. They lived around Philips, between Grand and California Avenues.

I had better explain this. Oklahoma City, Main Street, running east-west, was a kind of dividing line. The Santa Fe tracks were a north-south one. The tracks are east of Broadway. So, going east of Broadway on Main, First, or Second, you would first hit the better white whorehouses and then, soon, you would be in black Oklahoma City. Now, south of Main the parallel streets, called Avenues, are, in this order: Grand, California, and then Reno. Each street south of Main took you a step down the financial, social, and, certainly, the moral ladder. You went from second-rate white "houses" to third-rate and then to the black brothels. Interspersed was other illegal entertainment: gambling and the liquor places which were always beyond the law, anyway, because Oklahoma went dry long before national prohibition.

Down in that southeast part of town, clustered beyond this protective "moral moat," was the poorest part of the black area. It was deep in that ghetto, over east of the tracks, that the Christians lived, near the North Canadian River. There was a block of three-story tenements—almost shacks. They ran from Grand Avenue nearly to the middle-of-the-block dirt alley, back to back with similar ones that faced on California Avenue. They had small backyards on the alley. It was in the Christians' backyard that the pool table was.

Somewhere, somehow, they had gotten hold of a discarded pool table. It was full size, dilapidated when they got it, I suppose, and its legs were missing. They fixed up the playing surface and set it up on four uncemented brick piers. They had good pool balls and cues. I would not conjecture where these might have come from.

Those pool games with the Christians would make a believer out of you. I do really think that some of those ragtime pool sharks—like Jelly Roll Morton and Eubie Blake—would have run down in Charlie Christian's backyard.

Somehow, in that poor life that was so rich and warm and unified, it all fitted together: baseball and pool, "Choc" beer and "White Lightning," Mrs. Braux's dicty "harmony chords" and the wailing blues along the Santa Fe and Katy (MK and T) tracks.

From the unity of a poor family it would be tempting to infer a kind of happy tribal life throughout the black inner cities like that in Oklahoma City. Then, or now, it would be a false extrapolation, a self-serving myth like the "happy darkies on the plantation." The black community had its splits, a deep one following cultural lines: basically, whether to follow the white culture or to develop the already existing black one. Success, status, the possibilities of financial reward, and the chance for eventual racial integration, all seemed to be on the white cultural side. It became identified with respectability, even basic morality. Bach (or Victor Herbert) was "nice;" the blues (except, perhaps, Handy's) were "lowdown." Not white America alone, but a goodly segment of black America, consigned ragtime, jazz, and the blues to the wine shops and the bordellos. As Ralph Ellison writes:

> Charlie Christian . . . flowered from a background with roots not only in a tradition of music, but in a deep division in the Negro community as well. He spent much of his life in a slum in which all the forms of disin-

tegration attending the urbanization of rural Negroes ran riot. Although he himself was from a respectable family, the wooden tenement in which he grew up was full of poverty, crime and sickness. It was also alive and exciting, and I enjoyed visiting there, for the people both lived and sang the blues. Nonetheless, it was doubtless here that he developed the tuberculosis from which he died.

. . . jazz was regarded by most of the respectable Negroes of the town as a backward, low-class form of expression, and there was a marked difference between those who accepted and lived close to their folk experience and those whose status strivings led them to reject and deny it. Charlie rejected this attitude, in turn, along with those who held it—even to the point of not participating in the musical activities of the school. Like Jimmy Rushing, whose father was a businessman and whose mother was active in church affairs, he had heard the voice of jazz and would hear no other. Ironically, what was perhaps his greatest social triumph came in death, when the respectable Negro middle class not only joined in the public mourning, but acclaimed him hero and took credit for his development. The attention which the sheer quality of his music should have secured him was won only by his big-town success.

Fortunately for us, Charles concentrated on the guitar and left the school band to his brother Edward, and his decision was a major part of his luck. For, although it is seldom recognized, there is a conflict between what the Negro American musician feels in the community around him and the given (or classical) techniques of his instrument. He feels a tension between his desire to master the classical style of playing and his compulsion to express those sounds which form a musical definition of Negro American experience. In early jazz these sounds found their fullest expression in the timbre of the blues voice, and the use of mutes, water glasses and derbies on the bells of their horns arose out of an attempt to imitate this sound. Among the younger musicians of the thirties, especially those who contributed to the growth of bop, this desire to master the classical technique was linked with the struggle to throw off those nonmusical features which came into jazz from the minstrel tradition.

Ralph Ellison had a foot in each of the two black worlds. Bent on becoming a legitimate trumpet player, he left Oklahoma City in 1933 for Tuskegee Institute in Alabama. He came back after two years and found the scene really jumping.

We jammed in back at Hallie Richardson's. Hallie's shoeshine parlor sold a lot of things, from shines to tobacco to pot, and from Cokes to corn to Choc beer. I'd better explain a couple of these things. Corn wasn't green corn on the cob but bootleg corn whiskey. Unaged and clear in color it was sometimes called "White Lightning," though it definitely could strike twice in the same place. Choc beer—really "Choctaw" beer—was not regular beer but a fermented potable made by the Indians out along the Canadian River east of town. Choc was not unlike the Mexican pulque made from cactus. I have no idea whether Choc beer was made from cactus or, indeed, from what—but it was a comparatively gentle intoxicant. It patted you on the head instead of kicking you in the pants.

My last trip back to Oklahoma City I got nostalgic and asked for it. I got vague looks and a trailing-off question: "Choc beer? . . ." It, too, was gone.

The jam sessions at Hallie's attracted men from the visiting Territorial bands. Charlie Christian and other locals jammed with the stars from the Trent, Lee, Kirk, and other reigning groups. There were fantastic pianists, like Count Basie who joined up with the Blue Devils in Oklahoma City, and some phenomenal women ragtimers like Kansas City's Julia Lee, sister of bandleader George E. Lee, and Mary Lou Williams, pianist and arranger for Kirk's Clouds of Joy. There were great trumpeters, like Lips Page from Dallas, fine trombone men, and a whole raft of saxophone players.

Regional styles, both ragtime and the blues, crossed and hybridized; individual ideas went into a golden pool, the capital building funds of a great, growing style, the child of ragtime and the blues, later—and restrictively—to be called "Kansas City Style."

In those years, Oklahoma City was one of the true germinal points. A little earlier, in the 1920s, it was somewhat like the Sedalia, Missouri, of the 1890s—a railroad center where not only lines but creative ideas crossed. In Sedalia, ragtime came from the crossing of two main lines: black African polyrhythm and white harmony and melody. In Oklahoma City, so recently laid out on virgin prairie, it was a new kind of jazz coming from the crossing of the main lines: ragtime and the blues.

The sequence ragtime to blues is a measure of a cruel social retrogression. Why should the blues, song of sorrow, follow ragtime, the dance of joy?

It is a musical sequence expressing a sequence of events: first, the slavery spirituals, joyful or sorrowful but full of faith; next, Emancipation, with its promises bringing hope; then, the cynical reversal of Emancipation, with the Civil War turned into a Southern victory. Ragtime had come at the height of the post-Emancipation hope, a salute to a future that the ragtimers, and their people, thought they saw. With the dashing of hope, the blues began to surface.

If ragtime is a dance, the blues are a song. They are the voice of the spirituals, darkened; blind faith—even if not all hope—gone. So the Southwest guitar—always remote from the blackface banjo—became a voice, first the "other voice," answering the wandering evangelist's voice, and then the "other voice" answering the wandering blues singer's wail.

It had to be in the Southwest that jazz would get the guitar voice that it needed—a voice to replace the chopping 4/4 chords of the banjo and the early, subservient rhythm guitar. New Orleans-born Lonnie Johnson first brought the singing single-line guitar countermelodies into jazz. It was natural for him to do so: he was a blues singer. Eddie Lang followed in Lonnie's footsteps. The voice was there, needing now the power to hold its own with brass and reeds.

Lonnie, even though tried out by Ellington, did not get the chance to continue in jazz. Eddie Lang died in 1933. The new guitar role they had tried to open up might very well have gone no further. Jazz guitar, in fact, reverted to the old chopped chords. In the big-time pool of jazz talent there was no one in sight to advance the new idea. There were players capable of doing so, out in the boondocks—or one at least in Oklahoma City. Charlie Christian, however, might very well never have had the chance. That he did get the chance must be counted as largely pure luck. The precarious touch and go of jazz development has been well expressed by Ellison:

> . . . the musical contributions of these local, unrecorded heroes of jazz are enjoyed by a few fellow musicians and by a few dancers who admire them and afford them the meager economic return which allows them to keep playing, but very often they live beyond the period of youthful dedication, hoping in vain that some visiting big band leader will provide the opportunity to break through to the wider spheres of jazz. Indeed, to escape these fates the artists must be very talented, very individual, as restlessly inventive as Picasso, and very lucky. Charles Christian . . . was for most of his life such a local jazz hero.

In 1935, Charlie was only sixteen. His break would not come for four years. He was getting ready, whether consciously or unconsciously makes little difference—especially when dealing with genius. Thinking as he was, in melodic terms—the voice of spirituals and blues—it was the jazz horns that he was listening to, not other guitarists.

> The man who had musicians in Oklahoma City going was Lester Young. To us he was the future. As, indeed, he was. That melodic line, so swinging, so sinuous, so unpredictable! And a line so clearly—as you could hear—based on chords, but far-out chords that could lift a blues or a ballad out of sight!

Lester first came to Oklahoma City sometime in 1929, a tall, intense young musician in a heavy white sweater, blue stocking cap and up-and-out-thrust silver saxophone. He left absolutely no reed player, and few young players of any instrument, unstirred by the wild, original flights of his imagination.

It should be said that Lester Young didn't bring Charles Christian out of some dark nowhere. He was already out in the light. He may only have been twelve or thirteen when he was making those cigar-box guitars in manual training class, but no other cigar boxes ever made such sounds. Then he heard Lester and that, I think, was all he needed.

Charlie digested the advance musical road maps from Lester. He was ready. He went out on the road with Alphonso Trent, at "Fonnie's" invitation. The Trent band was "class." It had been the first to play the top white hotel in Dallas, the Adolphus. Now, in the mid-1930s, Trent had a sextet. To go with Trent, Charlie had to switch to string bass. He is said to have handled the giant, unwieldy instrument as if it were a guitar. If so, he anticipated the later double-bass pathbreakers, Jimmy Blanton and Charles Mingus.

Charlie had now broken out of the local vise and was making the territory. Musicians were talking about him. With Trent he was heard in all the Territory towns—Tulsa, Little Rock, Fort Worth, Dallas, Kansas City—all the links in the one time cheap theater and tent show circuit, the Theatre Owners' Booking Association, known professionally as "Toby," or, as Ralph Ellison noted, "Tough On Black Asses."

With Trent, Charlie even broke out of the Territory limits, visiting the northwest. Sometime in that period he was also with a band headed by Anna Mae Winburn and also with the Jeters-Pillars Orchestra in St. Louis. James Jeters and Hayes Pillars had left the Trent saxophone section to form their own group, more a commercial outfit than a jazz band, but good experience for young Charlie.

Rejoining Trent, Charlie was given the guitar seat, and they headed for the Dakotas. In Bismarck he was heard by a young girl guitarist. Seventeen-year-old Mary Osborne's reactions to the sound of nineteen-year-old Charlie Christian's guitar were later reported by Al Avakian and Bob Prince:

> . . . on entering the club she heard a sound much like a tenor sax strangely distorted by an amplification system. On seeing Charlie, she realized that what she was hearing was an electric guitar playing single line solos, and voiced like a horn in ensemble with the tenor sax and trumpet. She says, "I remember some of the figures Charlie played in his solos. They were exactly the same things that Benny recorded later on as 'Flying Home,' 'Gone With What Wind,' 'Seven-Come-Eleven' and all the others."

At that time Christian's prominence was established locally to the extent that a Bismarck music store displayed the latest electric guitar model "as featured by Charlie Christian."

For a year, since 1937 with his own small combo in Oklahoma City, Charlie had been playing electric guitar. The electronically amplified guitar had been recently developed. Most guitarists were at first afraid of it, and many spurned it as an "illegitimate" instrument. Charlie embraced it and quickly probed its possibilities. There was no doubt that electric guitar was a guitar *plus*—in fact, a new instrument.

There is more than mere amplification—making the tone louder—involved. There is the sustaining of tones far past the normal point of acoustic "decay," so that former inaudibles are now audibles. Tone qualities are changed, too, in different ways at different stages of amplifications, so that the guitar voice becomes many different voices.

Charlie had the new style. His guitar had the new volume. He was ready for the big time. But, to paraphrase famous entertainer Jimmy Durante, Was the big time ready for him?

John Hammond saw to answering that question—in the affirmative. Now a Columbia executive, Hammond had not lost his interest in new talent or his steamroller activism when he wanted the new talent to be given a chance. He recently recalled the Charlie Christian affair:

> In the summer of 1939 Mary Lou Williams kept talking to me about Charlie Christian, who at that time was playing with his brother's band at the Ritz Café in Oklahoma City. This was about the time that I was recording Mary Lou with Mildred Bailey, and we had many discussions about Floyd Smith and the ghastly sounds he made with his electrified Hawaiian guitar, which was being featured with Andy Kirk's band. Mary Lou assured me that Charlie played a regular six-string guitar, amplified, and that he was essentially a blues man. Consequently, around August 2, 1939, I booked myself on a plane to Oklahoma City.
>
> It was a ghastly trip in a non-air-conditioned plane which included a five-hour stopover in Chicago at the airport, to pick up a local flight that had ten stops between Chicago and Oklahoma City. But when I got to the airport I found six delightful black musicians waiting for me at the airport in a 1926 Buick sedan (which was on its last legs) waiting to take me to the fourth-best hotel where Charlie's mother was working as a chambermaid on the eleventh floor.
>
> At the Ritz Café the guys played Wednesdays, Fridays and Saturdays and salaries for each guy were $2.50 a night. Since I arrived on a Wednesday, they were playing that night and I went over to the Ritz and heard

them. I guess it was one of the most exciting days of my life, and the impact of hearing Charlie was similar to the first time I heard Bessie Smith, or the Basie band in Kansas City in 1936. Charlie was superlative in the band. The rest of the guys were merely semipros.

At that time Benny Goodman had a weekly radio show, *Camel Caravan,* with a $300 budget for guest artists. I flew to L.A. the next morning and somehow was able to persuade Benny to take on Charlie, using the $300 radio fee to cover Charlie's expenses for the trip. He arrived in L.A. on August 10 and came over to the Columbia studios on Western Avenue where Benny was making his first Columbia recordings, which I was supervising. He was really a sight to see—a nineteen-year-old, scared kid with a big broad-brimmed Texas hat, very pointed yellow shoes, a green suit and a purple shirt with an outlandish tie. He might be in style now. He wasn't then.

Benny refused even to listen to him with an amplifier, but at the end of the session I persuaded Benny to let Charlie play. Charlie played straight guitar and Benny asked him to run through "Tea for Two" and for about two minutes they played together, at which point Benny left the studio thoroughly annoyed and convinced that it was another of my "pointless enthusiasms."

My best friend in the world at that time was Artie Bernstein, who played bass with Benny and had once played with me in a string quartet when he was a cellist. Artie heard enough to be impressed, so he and I cooked up a scheme whereby the music world and Benny could hear Charlie that night at the Victor Hugo Restaurant in Beverly Hills. The band hit at 7:30 P.M. for a dinner set, and between 9:00 and 10:00 P.M. there was a break, after which the Benny Goodman Trio and Quartet were to be featured in a one-hour concert before the big band came on again.

During the dinner break Artie and I sneaked Charlie Christian in through the kitchen and set him up on the bandstand—amp and all. Benny, needless to say, had no idea this was happening because he was busy talking to publishers and other celebrities during the dinner break. I had also called about twenty of my friends in L.A. to come to the bar and be a kind of claque, so that Charlie's efforts should not go unnoticed.

When Bennie got on the stand and saw Charlie sitting there I thought he was literally going to kill me since he had told me there was no possible way he could use him. He got back at me, however, by calling for "Rose Room," a tune he was sure Charlie didn't know. Benny was mistaken because Charlie did know it, and on the third chorus he signaled Charlie to take a chorus. He took over twenty. The whole room was electrified, and the entire tune took forty-three minutes on my stopwatch. Benny even persuaded Charlie to sit in with the big band, after the quartet was finished, much to the disgust of Arnold Covey (Covarrubias), his regular guitar player.

Benny kept Charlie over until the *Camel Caravan* broadcast the following week, when Charlie came up with the riffs of "Flying Home" which erroneously is listed as being composed jointly with Benny and Lionel Hampton.

The rest, I guess, is history.

The rest *is* history but a history in which Charlie Christian's live part would be tragically short. From that day, August 16, 1939, it would be hardly two and a half years until the young guitar genius from Oklahoma would be dead. Into that short span of days would be crowded all his innovative work in the big-time mainstream of jazz. In that short span he would change not only guitar development but that of jazz and would lead directly into bop, cool, funky, Free Jazz, and Rock and Roll. The voice of his guitar, a whole third of a century later, is still modern. Musically, it still fulminates. But being a voice, it is also a message. Charlie Christian's message, like that of that other Southwest Charlie, "the Bird," is not yet wholly decoded. And yet they were both saying something so simple: freedom.

But, again, the message—like Garcia's—might never have gotten delivered. Charlie's mission to Los Angeles was, actually, aborted when the young man that Benny dubbed "an impossible rube" walked into the studio interrupting the recording of a new Fletcher Henderson arrangement of a "pop" tune—"Spring Song," by Jakob Ludwig Felix Mendelssohn-Bartholdy. But for an aroused and determined Hammond, Charlie Christian would have gone back to the sticks, his amplified guitar still unheard by the captious powers. When Benny, despite himself, got with those new sounds, Charlie was in.

Bill Simon later described how, at the Victor Hugo, "Charlie just kept feeding Benny riffs and rhythms and changes for chorus after chorus. That was Benny's first flight on an electrically amplified cloud . . . in future months, that 'impossible rube' was to inspire and frame the most fluid, fiery, interesting and human sounds that Goodman has ever produced."

For Benny Goodman it meant a new direction: the Sextet was formed, with a composer-in-residence. For Charlie Christian it meant the proper field at last (and just in time) for his genius. On the most practical level it meant that his weekly wage now jumped from the Oklahoma City level of $7.50 a week to the new figure of $150.00, a jump of 2,000 percent! And, on the level of Charlie's human appetites, it meant ample funds for his chief interest outside music—chicks. Life became an around-the-clock ball. He became a high-gear after-hours playboy.

As to the type of judgment implied in Benny's epithet of "impossible rube," Ralph Ellison speaks with a certain justifiable annoyance:

> Charles Christian was an unsophisticated rustic about as a Watusi lead drummer is a barbarous primitive. Charlie's sophistication lay where his life really was: in his music. It would have to be proven to me that a green suit and purple shirt crippled his art, or that spats and a derby would have made it greater.

With Goodman, Charlie, like Wilson and Hampton, played publicly only with the small group. The impromptu quintet of the Victor Hugo was enlarged to a sextet by the inclusion of Artie Bernstein. Before recording with Benny, Charlie took part in an all-star Lionel Hampton session at Victor, together with a rising young trumpeter, Dizzy Gillespie, and a formidable battery of saxophones: altoist Benny Carter and tenors Ben Webster, Chu Berry and the perennial Hawk. The four-side session was on September 11, 1939, and the title of the first waxing to catch the Christian message was a Hampton vibraphone *tour de force,* "Hot Mallets."

Two days later, at Columbia, with Hammond supervising, Charlie recorded five sides with the full Goodman band. Then, on October 2, the Sextet made its first recordings. The first side was "Flying Home" which opens with Charlie and Lionel doing the Christian riffs in unison and B.G. taking the bridge. The second chorus—thirty-two bars—is all guitar, racing single notes hopping sudden chop-chord hurdles. Hamp's vibes take the next chorus, and the ride-out is on the opening unison riffs, Benny again taking the bridge.

The label credit, as Hammond observed, only partly introduced Charlie as composer (and thus established an invidious precedent). But he was introduced as a soloist, startling, beautiful, wholly formed, and from nowhere. "Flying Home" is notable, too, as prefiguring (or, more accurately, establishing) what was soon to be the standard bop "form" or routine: the opening and closing unison theme with solos in between. This would be the structure utilized by Dizzy and "the Bird" to frame their solos, the form that a young jazz student once called "improvisation between book ends." It was Christian who brought this format into bop only a year later when the new jazz began incubating uptown at Minton's, with Charlie in the center of the jam combos.

The companion side to "Flying Home" was, interesting, "Rose Room." Benny did not get a twenty-chorus ride on an "electronically amplified cloud" this time. Benny may have been willing, and Charlie, too, but Columbia, with its three-minute record fetish, certainly was not.

In the sixteen weeks remaining in the year, Charlie participated in ten recording sessions. One was a follow-up, all-star Victor date with Hamp, two were with Lips Page, backing up blues-singer Ida Cox. Four sessions, to the continued annoyance of the displaced Covarrubias, were with the full Goodman band; two were devoted to Sextet cuttings; and one was a date on which both band and Sextet did sides.

The joint session, which was on November 22, produced two sides owing much to Christian. One is the full-band "Honeysuckle Rose"; the other is "Seven Come Eleven," based on the chords of Gershwin's "I Got Rhythm" and with the unison opener and closer. Jointly credited to B.G. and Charlie as composers, it is, of course, one of the riff originals that Mary Osborne recalled Charlie's having played in Bismarck a year before he joined Goodman.

Now the scene opened up: road trips, after-hours jam sessions in the good jazz towns, and always the new chicks. "Everybody loved Charlie. The chicks mothered him, and the musicians kidded him good-naturedly. He was the Willie Mays of jazz."

But Charlie Christian did not have the rugged constitution of Willie Mays. The ghetto days in Oklahoma City had been times of deprivation. There might have been pool games in the back yard, yet not enough food in the kitchen. The warning signals began to come, times when Charlie's energy would suddenly give out. Goodman, finally, sent him to his doctor who found t.b. scars in Charlie's lungs. He advised rest. Charlie went on balling.

In New York in 1939 and early in 1940, the uptown after-hours jam scene was Puss Johnson's on St. Nicholas Avenue. Bassist Milt Hinton recalls:

> Everybody would come in there, all the guys from the bands downtown. We'd go to the Savoy to hear Chick Webb. That was the band that really swung. Then, after the Savoy, we'd go to Puss Johnson's . . . this particular place was for Sunday nights, that was the off-night around New York. . . . It would start about three in the morning and last to about nine or ten A.M. It was always bright daylight when we came out. It just blinded you.

Then, later in 1940, came Minton's. Minton's Playhouse was in the Hotel Cecil on 118th Street. Ex-bandleader Teddy Hill was manager. Though an "ex," Teddy was not soured on jazz. He was both ex-pro and perennial fan of the new. He sent out word: *Come to Minton's and jam.* It immediately became *the* spot.

"When Teddy took over," says drummer Kenny Clarke, "Minton's changed its music policy. Teddy wanted to do something for the guys who had worked with him. He turned out to be a sort of benefactor since work was very scarce at that time. Teddy never tried to tell us how to play. We played just as we felt."

Minton's pieced out the jazzmen's schedule. Monday night had now become the "dark" or "off" night. Minton's filled out the evening and night hours until Clark Monroe's Uptown House would open to run until dawn. Monroe's was on 138th Street and, at 4:00 A.M. the trek on foot would begin, musicians with their instrument cases, trudging the twenty blocks in the dark.

"Minton's," as singer Carmen McRae says, "was just a place for cats to jam . . . you'd see cats half stewed who weren't paying much mind to what was happening. But the musicians were."

Minton's, mainly, was the place where the new thing was happening. Like ragtime and early jazz, in its beginnings it had no name. It had first to be discovered. Then it could be named. Ragtime had begun (or at least, developed) in saloons and bordellos. The earliest jazz had sprung up in the streets. This new jazz began in a room that Mary Lou Williams has described:

> . . . not a large place but . . . nice and intimate. The bar was at the front, and the cabaret was in the back. The bandstand was situated at the rear of the back room, where the wall was covered with strange paintings depicting weird characters sitting on a brass bed, or jamming, or talking to chicks.
>
> During the daytime, people played the jukebox and danced. . . . It seemed everybody was talking at the same time; the noise was terrific. Even the kids playing out on the sidewalk danced when they heard the records.

A regular group—salaried but jamming—coalesced at Minton's: players from various bands, young men dissatisfied with jazz as it then was, and all looking for something new. Some of them had played in Hill's last band. Twenty-three-year-old Dizzy Gillespie was one. "He was getting his style together," as Kenny Clarke remembers. Kenny himself, with revolutionary ideas about drum rhythm, held the charter at the drums. Hill inadvertently gave him his nickname, "Klook." Listening to Clarke's broken, offbeat rhythms on the bass drum, he asked, "What is that klook-mop stuff?"

A weird and genuine character held forth at the piano: Thelonious Sphere Monk, a devotee of wild hats and wild chords. Chords, or "changes," were a big obsession with the young jazzmen both at Minton's and elsewhere.

Beyond the freeing of rhythm from the 4/4 straitjacket, a new harmony of extended, modern chords was the key to what was going on. They were the necessary basis for the new, anticliché melodic developments. The young men felt that all of the improvisational possibilities on the old basic triads had been worked out. Further struggle with them would only be a restirring of cold broth.

The "new" chords—long ago explored by Chopin and later, Debussy—were extended, or augmented, chords that ran on up from the fifth degree of the ordinary triad, and beyond the accustomed seventh, to the ninth, eleventh, and even thirteenth degrees. From the ninth degree on, the chord begins to incorporate a second key and polytonality enters. For example, the triad in C major, extended through the diminished seventh to the ninth, brings in the tonic note of another key, D. Add the eleventh and the thirteenth and you have superimposed the D major triad over that of C major.

Now, working on the known triads of an old standard—"I Got Rhythm" for example—by thinking of these upper polytonal intervals, the improviser could use notes that were apparent discords and yet that had a strange logic in their unaccustomed but not unpleasant dissonance. They seemed to upset traditional musicians more than the public. Louis Armstrong, first hearing them, called them "clinkers."

The first advantage from this new harmonic procedure was a practical one. Outsiders—the usual crowd of would-be jammers—could be kept off the stand out of the regulars' hair. The new chords dumbfounded "the no-talent cats who," as Dizzy said, "couldn't blow at all but would take six or seven choruses to prove it."

The head "crazy chord" man was Monk. Mary Lou recalled that "when Thelonious Monk first played at Minton's there were few musicians who could run changes with him. Charlie Christian . . . and a couple more were the only ones who could play with Monk then. Charlie Christian and I used to go to the basement of the hotel where I lived and play and write all night long. I still have the music of a song he started but never completed."

Klook recalled that Christian and Monk were hand in glove:

> We used to look forward to Charlie coming in. We used to wait for him to come in after finishing work with Benny Goodman. Charlie was so sold on what we were doing he bought an extra amplifier and left it at Minton's. Charlie used to talk about the music at Minton's so much, Benny Goodman even used to come. He was all the rage at the time. . . . We used to convert our style to coincide with his, so Benny played just the things he wanted to play.

Thus tactfully, as Klook subtly infers, the new secrets were kept from B.G. who obviously did not need them anyway. There was, indeed, the idea in the air that a new music might be developed, so complex and difficult that the imitators and exploiters—especially the white ones—could not grab it as they had grabbed the black man's ragtime and, to a certain extent, swing. Mary Lou has told how the idea started:

> Thelonious Monk and some of the cleverest of the young musicians used to complain, "We'll never get credit for what we're doing." They had reason to say it. . . . Monk said, "We are going to get a big band started. We're going to create something that they can't steal because they can't play it."
>
> There were more than a dozen people interested in the idea, and the band began rehearsing in a basement somewhere. . . . Everyone contributed to the arrangements, and some of them were real tough. . . .
>
> It was the usual story. The guys got hungry, so they had to go to work with different bands.

It would not have succeeded anyway. Any art form—music, painting, architecture, literary style—can be imitated once it has been conceived and created.

There might be the "leeches"—as Mary Lou Williams called them—at Minton's. And the indifferent ones—the "half-stewed cats." There were also devoted followers, nonmusicians, who realized that something, unnamed but momentous, was happening up there at Minton's. It is ironic—in view of the total situation—that one of these followers was a young white man and that to him we owe, not only some of the finest solo recordings that Charlie Christian ever made, but the only records ever made of a jazz style in the very moments of its birth.

> Jerry Newman, a young jazz fan, and then amateur engineer, became a regular at the place and night after night would record the happenings with his own semipro equipment. He recalls that Charlie most of the time would electrify the crowd with his riffing and his long-lined solos and his powerful drive, but that sometimes the stand would become jammed with battling no-talents, and Charlie would simply sit there and strum chords.

Newman treasured his perishable Minton acetate discs (this was before the advent of tape). He realized that they were unique documents. The first to be released for public sale were six sides in 1947, in a three-pocket 78 rpm Vox album. "Charlie's Choice, I, II, & III," is some twelve minutes of mainly Christian creation on the chords of "Topsy." "Stomping at the Savoy" gets a similarly extended treatment with Charlie flying home free of the Goodman ballast. The group playing on the Vox release were the regulars considered as the Minton house band: Charlie, Monk, and Klook with trumpeter Joe Guy and bassist Nick Fenton.

Subsequently the Newman acetates have been more fully released, first on Newman's label, "Esoteric," and later on the labels Archive of Folk and Jazz Music and "Counterpoint." They are the sort of documents of the real American history that the Establishment—foundations, universities, learned societies, and the appropriate branches of business—should do and never do. It is always some lone "nut," like a Jerry Newman, who does it if it is done at all. God bless them all!

Some place along the line, before it moved downtown to 52nd Street, the Minton's mintage got its name, "bop"— actually "bebop" to begin with. There are many theories as to its specific origin. It may have come from a song current in the early 1940s, "Hey Baba Rebop." It may, as many believe, have come from phrases hummed by the players—similar in intent to the phrases Gene Krupa used to get drum tones. There was Leo Watson's wild scatting; Mary Lou Williams' coinages like "oo-bla-dee" and "tisherome"; and Dizzy's surrealist polysyllables like "oop-bop-sh'-bam." Barry Ulanov, in his *History of Jazz in America,* credited Charlie Christian's "humming of phrases as the onomatopoeic origin of the term."

Anyway, bop got its name and to no good purpose. The name, like "ragtime" (poor, ragged music) and "jazz" (sexual intercourse), only served to belittle the music in unreflective or preprejudiced minds. Christened with a triviality, bop moved downtown to Swing Street to begin its brief moment in the white spotlight.

Charlie Christian, one of the bop creators, would not live to share even this brief moment. He blazed on through 1940, touring with Goodman, recording two-score sides, all but four with B.G., helping to put bop together after hours, and then in the after-after hours, having a ball. He had discovered one usable, unhackneyed triad: chicks, pot, and the dark hours.

As an artist he was at, or nearing, his peak. As a physical entity he was far past it. In the spring of 1941 it all caught up with him at last. He was hospitalized in the municipal sanitarium, Seaview, on Staten Island. He never quit Seaview alive.

There were numerous visitors. Basie came, then sent his own physician, Dr. Sam McKinney, to supplement the routine sanitarium care. Teddy Hill came every Sunday, taking the long, elevated-plus-ferry ride both ways from Manhattan. Generally he would bring a baked chicken and a chocolate layer cake, prepared for Charlie by one of his "mothers," Mom Frazier who ran an uptown restaurant that was a musicians' hangout. Bill Simon reports that "when Hill would try to pay her, she'd shrug him off with, 'Now you take this to my boy and tell him to hurry out of that hospital.'"

John Hammond, in California at the time, had a guitar sent to Charlie. And there were other visitors:

> Charlie, in his new-found "high-life" had acquired another set of friends, and that's how he happened to die at the tender age of twenty-three; TB was only part of it.
>
> There are stories of some of the boys from the Goodman and other bands dropping over to the Island for visits and spiriting Charlie out of the hospital for "parties" with combustible tea and chicks. These parties had their comic moments—if one can forget their tragic consequences.
>
> There was the time, for example, when the Germans had just begun to overrun Western Europe. This one bass player, who was more concerned than most of his colleagues with current events and politics, buttonholed Charlie for an intense one-way discussion. Charlie was "stoned," and he loved everybody and would agree with anybody about anything.
>
> "And Charlie, those German planes roared over and dropped all those bombs and leveled just about every building in Rotterdam. And thousands of people—women and children—got wiped out. How about that, Charlie?"
>
> Charlie cut through his haze and answered emphatically—"Solid!"
>
> He had a couple of other "friends"—a guitar player and a tap dancer; the latter a well-known character around the bands. They brought over the pot and they also brought chicks. Charlie was getting better—in fact it looked as though he would be getting out soon, and he was feeling his oats. But it was winter and Charlie sneaked out late one special night and got excited and overheated.
>
> Dr. McKinney learned of these extracurricular activities and made sure they were stopped, but it was too late. Charlie had pneumonia.

Hammond was notified and hurried east. He went right over to see Charlie. It was a Saturday. The next day, Teddy Hill was the last friend to see him alive. That night, March 3, 1942, Christian died at the age of twenty-three.

He had revolutionized an instrument, helped to revolutionize a music. At his death only ninety-six record sides by this pathfinder had been issued. He was not the titular leader on a single disc. The ninety-six have since been supplemented by a few more: the Jerry Newman acetates; eight sides from Hammond's second "Spirituals To Swing" concert at Carnegie Hall, which was on Christmas Eve, 1939; and some previously unissued things from a 1941 Goodman Sextet session.

The sides issued during Charlie's lifetime—besides being the textbook of all guitarists since—would alone establish him as one of the giants along with Louis, Sidney, Lester, Lady Day, and a very few others. The posthumous addenda, however, bring us a more complete Christian. With Benny, Charlie often simply lapsed into the old chopped-chord style he himself had made obsolete, spreading out only when his solos came.

At Minton's, Newman captured him winging with his own flock. When Vanguard issued the Hammond concert sides on an LP, we heard a Charlie relatively subdued in the Sextet bind (frozen entirely out of a solo in "Stomping At the Savoy") except for his own "Flying Home" and a sensational, Minton's-like, chain-bursting thirty-two bars in "Honeysuckle Rose" that got the sextet to clapping hands and really flying home. In the concert sides where Charlie sits in with the Kansas City Six, he is deferent to his idol Lester Young. Yet, following Prez in "Pagin' the Devil," he quietly and modestly shows both the Prez and the Christian in his own playing.

One of the unissued takes from Columbia lets us hear Charlie Christian in the very act of creating a riff number. We hear just what it was that he made of the guitar: an instrument as complete as the piano. In ragtime and jazz the piano can be both singer and accompaniment. That is to say, the treble (right hand) can sing and the bass (left hand) can accompany—fill out the harmony and supply the pulsing basic rhythm. (The roles of the hands can be reversed, of course.)

Before Charlie Christian, the guitar had barely touched its possibilities of filling both roles: singer and accompaniment. Christian created singing single lines of melody in the blues way while giving them a ride on his rhythmic chord riffs.

The number in which we can hear this happening as he creates a new number, is in the Columbia LP album, *Charlie Christian,* where it is given the title, "Waitin' For Benny." Al Avakian ant Bob Prince, who rescued this previously unissued—and not even titled—item, produced the album. In their liner notes they tell what happened at the session:

> Before Benny arrived at the session that produced "Air Mail Special" and "A Smo-o-o-oth One," the musicians were jamming for their own pleasure. The engineers were testing equipment. Fortunately, the disc on which the jamming was recorded was preserved. In "Waitin' For Benny" Charlie, in the process of warming up, builds simple riffs, one leading into another, until he comes to a logical conclusion . . . then he rhythmically feeds Cootie Williams chords à la Basie, then riffs behind the trumpet, and Cootie proceeds with the only free, jamming swing-era trumpet he has ever recorded. Before the end of his improvisation, Charlie is briefly heard reaffirming his simple riffs.

At the end of the jamming the engineer can be heard off mike calling, "Stand by." The boss has arrived and now business will begin. The first number, which was cut shortly thereafter, was the tune, "A Smo-o-o-oth One," the tune Charlie had just riffed into being, with composer credit being given solely to Benny Goodman who wasn't even there when it happened.

Charlie did not live to need the royalties. Mislabeled credits could not take from him what he had created. And premature death did not come soon enough to cut off his creativity before his work was substantially complete.

Like Charlie Parker, who died at thirty-five—a "Bird" apparently still able to fly a little—and Lester Young, who died inside long before his final dissolution, Charlie Christian found the time to tell it like it was.

An "impossible rube" from Oklahoma, he may have been a doomed and tragic young man but he was a supremely great artist. There are many artists from bad to good to great. But even among the great ones, the true original is rare. Charlie Christian was a true original.

There was only one Charlie Christian. Yet he came from a dark and teeming multiplicity, from the flat, wide prairie, out of the crowded, black shacks. He came out of that vast, one-time anonymity of the blues—a man, a hick, an artist—the Easy Rider with his song.

The Fabulous Gypsy

Gilbert S. McKean

This profile of Django Reinhardt, the one undisputed jazz master from Europe, appeared in Esquire *in 1947. It serves both as a valuable contemporary glimpse of Reinhardt and as a high-level example of a kind of writing that may seem somewhat dated but that projects an appealing energy and immediacy.*

The last time I saw Django, his heart was warm and gay; the last time in London, that is. His costume looked as if it had been picked out of *Esquire*—one piece per issue over a period of years. From under a wide-brimmed, gray felt hat long strands of jet-black hair were visible—hair so long that it made the average American musicians look as if they had just been crew-cropped for Cornell. Around his neck was loosely knotted a multicolored silk scarf, looking not unlike an Air Force escape map. The suit he was wearing could not have had a more suave, conservative cut had it been styled on Lenox Avenue. His feet were shod in bulky, rugged ski boots.

As he walked down Piccadilly toward the Circus he caused such consternation that he disrupted two ration queues, and it was reported in fairly unreliable circles that a Bond Street tailor was stricken with apoplexy at the sight. The amazing part about the whole thing was that the unconcerned gypsy air with which he wore the outfit made it look *right!* You almost wondered why everybody else was dressed so stupidly.

This sartorial apparition is considered by many to be the greatest of all jazz virtuosi, certainly the greatest creative soloist ever to develop outside the United States.

Django is a character. To brand a musician as a character is as redundant as, say, the statement that Harry Truman is President of the United States. (Upon rereading that last clause, I am not sure the point was properly driven home.) But Django is the genuine article—a character with a capital "C," in neon lights. He is unreliable, unreasonable and inordinately vain; at the same time he is sincere, generous, lovable. The appellation "genius" is being flung about considerably these parlous days and there is no valid reason for ignoring the fabulous gypsy. He is a genius. There.

Django's life is as incredible as his music, the latter being described as a sort of flat-foot-floogie with the frou-frou. It's a long way by gypsy caravan from the shantytown at the gates of Paris where he spent his childhood to Carnegie Hall and Café Society, but our hero made it. He always knew he would. The word *django* is doubtless the French equivalent of the American infinitive *to horatio alger.*

America has always been the good earth, the land of dreams, to Reinhardt. As a child he used to slip into the neighborhood movie theaters where he could commune with the daring cowboys and insidious redskins racing across our cinematographic wild and wooly West. Later on this land of action attracted him as the only country cut to his own heroic size, a place where an artist would be properly recognized, where palms grew calloused not from manual labor but from being constantly crossed with silver.

For Django is a mercenary soul. He knows that the fiddler must be paid but he is primarily interested in a guitarist. Not that he is a miser in any sense of the word; he is generous and loves spending money even more than making it. And he is supremely contemptuous of the pittances doled out by many French entrepreneurs. Rather than accept a sum he considers beneath his artistry, he will decline offers that would make many another French musician gasp. He chucks the whole show, takes to his gypsy train and strums his costly chords gratis to the four winds.

When the impresarios agree to pay Django his enormous demands, the money lasts only a few days. He fancies himself the *grand seigneur,* the 18th-century French equivalent of the big operator, and yearns to be considered King of the Gypsies. The Reinhardt table usually groans with succulent cheeses, tasty sausages, French bread and plenty of good *vin rouge;* at any hour of day or night "The Man" is surrounded by dozens of his gypsy "cousins" who come to break bread and to gossip.

Gambling is his chief extravagance. He will say *blanc* is *noir* if the odds are decent and has been known to leave Monte Carlo several hundred thousand francs light after a few evenings' differences of opinion with the croupiers. No matter how much money he makes with his music, he is always forced to borrow from his old friends. They have endeavored to reason with him to be prudent even to the extent of citing the parable of the grasshopper and the ant.

"*Eh, mon vieux,*" they tell him. "It is not necessary that you support the casinos as if they are your own private charity. Let them look elsewhere for their rent!"

But Django is incorrigible. He is still a gypsy at heart—a rather willful gypsy, too. His youth was that of a caravan nomadic—until he was twenty he had never worn a suit nor lived in a house. But out of a welter of backward gypsy tribes with many almost medieval customs, the illiterate floating slum of the wagon train, has come this guitarist of gigantic creative stature—an instrumentalist to set the "peasants" (which is the gypsies' derisive term for all outsiders) on their ears. For the past twelve years he has been idolized by jazz fans, first in France and then all over the world. One of his greatest admirers and sponsors, Charles Delaunay, head of the Hot Club du France, has written the gypsy's biography upon which this article is based.

Django was literally born to the sound of applause. His mother, billed as La belle Laurence, was the star of a group of itinerant gypsy players touring France and Belgium. While the rest of the troupe was giving its show in the little Belgian town of Liverchies on the night of January 23, 1910, she was giving a more important performance in the trailer outside. The baby was baptized Jean, but they called him Django from the first.

By the time the boy was fifteen he was a widely traveled man—all over France, Italy, and Belgium, and he saw action with the Algerian Dead End kids in the Casbah. But the charms of music began to soothe his savage breast about the age of ten. His hard-boiled playmates eyed him somewhat askance when they saw his preference for the music of gypsy guitars, violins and mandolins—instead of pursuing the manly art of raiding pushcarts and vineyards. At the tender age of thirteen his guitar had been heard in professional appearances in various Apache hangouts in the slums of Paris. La belle Laurence called for him each night to collect his pay lest he wager it away.

By 1928 his good fortune and talent had given him a place in the European limelight. Lady Luck not only smiled at him, she gave him the key to her apartment. But all the good things went up in smoke early one November morning that year.

Returning home, Django found his gypsy trailer full of artificial flowers to be sold at the cemetery next day. There was a rustling noise under the flowers.

"*Nom d'un nom!* Those accursed rats again!" He raised the candle sleepily. It was almost burned through and crumbled in his hand, the burning wick falling on the celluloid flowers below. There was an immediate explosion and the place became an inferno.

With stunning rapidity he was almost surrounded by flames. In desperation he clutched a blanket in his left hand to use for a shield as he fought his way out. His life was miraculously saved, but as he ruefully contemplated his injuries he wondered if it was worth saving.

"*Regardez donc!* My left hand!" It was a shapeless mass of seared flesh. And the surgeon recommended amputating his right leg. It developed that the leg stayed on, but it was a year and a half before he learned to walk again. And the hand? Well, nobody expected him ever to play again.

By sheer will power Django trained himself to use first one finger, then another. Not only did he regain his skill but he capitalized on his disability to become an even greater guitarist. Compensating for the paralysis of his fourth and fifth fingers, he developed a new method of chording which made his style completely new and distinctive.

Following his recovery the old wanderlust hit Django. He and his brother traveled through the south of France, earning their way by passing the hat after playing guitar duets in sidewalk cafés.

Credit for "discovering" Django, or rather rediscovering him, should go to Emile Savitry, one of the typical *avant-garde* artists of prewar Montparnasse. While he was spending a few days in Toulon, he ran into two wandering minstrels. One of the motley duet played surpassingly fine guitar, so the intrigued Emile invited them to his apartment for a record bash. On tap were classical records, Hawaiian selections and finally *le jazz hot.* In this little furnished room in the port area of Toulon, Django first heard the orchestra of Duke Ellington, the great artist who was to feature him at Carnegie Hall some fifteen years later. He was so overwhelmed by the torrents of *hot* pouring from the phonograph that he burst into tears. This jazz evoked a profound response in the gypsy. From now on he got his kicks from Louis Armstrong and the Duke, not from the waltzes, tangos and popular French ditties which had previously formed his repertory.

It was only a question of a few months before Savitry had got Django enough jobs to get him up the ladder to Paris. There he impressed Jean Sablon, who was singing in a swank night club and wanted Django for his personal accompanist. This was agreeable, but the guitarist with typical Gallic insouciance neglected to show up for work half the time. Swallowing his pride, Sablon sent his car to the outskirts of Paris each evening to get the musician out of bed and to work on time.

Before this door-to-door delivery system went into effect, the ever-practical Django had another means of transportation. In the gypsy camp where he lived just outside the Paris wall, a sector known as the *Zone,* there were no streets. It was unthinkable for his shoes and clothes to become soiled on his way to work. The problem was solved each evening with a most engaging expedient.

"*Attention,* my little cabbage," he would exclaim to his wife. "My sweet, it is time for me to go to the job of music."

"*C'est bien.* I am ready, my love," she would reply. Then she would bend forward, Django would mount her shoulders and off they would go through the mucky ways. When the pavement was reached he would tax her strength no longer, gallantly dismounting to walk the rest of the way toward Montmartre.

The next important step in Django's development was the formation of the Quintet of the Hot Club of France. This club was an organization of French lovers of American Jazz music which got together at first to enjoy records, but soon was running concerts of its own featuring the best French musicians and such visiting American stars as Coleman Hawkins and Benny Carter.

By 1934 the HCF had reached the point where it was looking for a band to uphold the banner of France in the jazz world. They found what they wanted in a group drawn mostly from Louis Vola's band which, in the past, used to jam between sets in a back room at the Claridge. Personnel consisted of Stephane Grappelly (violin); Django Reinhardt, Joseph Reinhardt, Roger Chaput (guitars); and Louis Vola (bass).

With their first concerts the Quintet became the rave of Paris and their records enabled the world to share this music. American fans were delighted to hear a European band catch the spirit of jazz music, yet remain unique; many who found blaring trumpets, bleating saxes and obtrusive drums a bit strenuous on the ears were captivated by the delicate improvisations of this ensemble.

Few in this country who avidly followed their Victor and Decca releases realized what a volatile little package this combination was. In the two stars, Grappelly and Reinhardt, there was enough explosive temperament to supply the Metropolitan Opera and a ballet company for a complete season, including matinees. This petty rivalry constantly threatened to split the combination; not only were they bickering over top billing, but they were personally antipathetic toward each other. Grappelly, elegant though penny-pinching and somewhat superficial, was Django's opposite in nature, although they were perfect complements musically. Some of the trouble arose because their records were variously issued for contractual reasons, as Django Reinhardt and the Quintet of the Hot Club of France or Stephane Grappelly and his Hot Four.

The situation came to a head during the Quintet's first broadcast to the United States in 1937. On their bandstand in the Big Apple cabaret on Rue Pigalle (known as Pig Alley since the 1944 American invasion) the musicians grew tense as the time approached. The seconds ticked away and at the "On the Air" signal, the American announcer went confidently into his introduction. . . .

"From Paris we now bring you the music of Stephane Grappelly and his Hot Four."

Django turned white with rage, jumped to his feet and began to stalk out of the studio. Only the humblest of apologies and a promise to correct the error before the end of the program induced him to return. He has not forgiven Grappelly to this day, but the fault was not the violinist's.

The group was playing in England when war broke out in 1939. Stephane chose to remain in England as he is part Italian and was technically a non-belligerent. All the others returned to France where Django formed a considerably successful big band. After the lull of the phony war, the Germans unleashed their blitzkrieg and Django took to the road with countless thousands of panic-stricken Parisians. On the run his gypsy experience served him well and he fared much better than the hapless city dwellers.

After the Pétain maneuver, things returned to "normal" and Django returned to Paris and greater fame than ever. The rebellious youth of France subtly expressed their hostility toward the Nazis in this fad for American music. A new Quintet was formed with Hubert Rostaing replacing the missing Grappelly. For once Reinhardt's extravagant salary demands were useful; every time the Germans wanted him to play he would ask an impossible figure.

Among his engagements during this period was a two-week stint in North Africa in 1942. Lady Luck looked the other way when he sailed back to France on November 6. Two days later the Allies invaded Africa, missing a terrific USO recruit by a matter of forty-eight hours.

The next year, tiring of Nazi-occupied France, Django attempted to escape to Switzerland. A German patrol happened upon the café where he was to rendezvous with the guide. A search of his person revealed a letter from a Swiss impresario and a membership card from the British equivalent of ASCAP—the Performing Rights Society. Arrested immediately for espionage, he was taken for interrogation before a German major. The officer took one look, as the story has it, and said, "Reinhardt, old chap! What are you doing here?" It seems the major was an old German jazz fan who collected the Quintet's records before the war. Probably one of the more esthetic Nazis who wouldn't think of handling a record without first washing the blood off his hands.

It will be a surprise for many to learn that, while he can read no music, Django has done considerable writing for the symphony orchestra. His *Boléro* was performed on the same program as the more famous Ravel composition and did not suffer by comparison. An organ Mass composed by him especially for the gypsies to play during their annual pilgrimage to Sainte-Marie-de-la-Mer prompted the organist of Sacré Coeur Cathedral to remark that he had never heard a better-conceived Mass, original yet fully respecting the traditions and harmonies. He has even attempted a symphony, but it is so daringly modern that no orchestra has yet programmed it. He dictated his serious work to Gerard Leveque, a young musician who lived in an apartment next to him. Whenever inspiration seized Django, he would bang on the wall until Leveque came rushing in with his paper and pencil.

The war years in France were about the same for Django as for the other Frenchmen, with the exception that he fared better than many because he earned good pay in the night clubs of Paris. Of course, there was the soul-sapping uncertainty shared by all. You never knew whether the occupation was a sometime thing or whether you were part and parcel of the Nazi Thousand Year Plan.

When the Allies swarmed into the barricade-ridden "City of Light," they liberated jazz and Django, incidentally, along with the *mademoiselles, vin ordinaire* with exotic and expensive labels, nonvintage champagne, and immature Calvados. He was very popular with the Yanks from the first, making several appearances with Special Services, Armed Forces Network broadcasts and performances with the Air Transport Command band. Any jazz *aficionados* who were lucky enough to make Paris spent much of their time searching the night clubs of Montmartre for the guitarist. One eighteen-year-old G.I. arrived in Paris one morning and, rushing to the Hot Club headquarters, demanded the whereabouts of The Man. It seems he was playing in Marseilles at the time. "Well, when does the next train leave?" the soldier asked. "I'm a guitarist and I enlisted in the Army just so I could come to France and see Mr. Reinhardt." (This little episode is documented by reliable authorities and is offered without charge to the Army Recruiting service.)

In the latter part of 1945, he came to London for a reunion with Grappelly. Call it sentiment, call it patriotism—at any rate, when the two first sat down to improvise a bit, there was something of a psychic cue from somewhere. The first selection played was the Marseillaise—once through in a slow and noble march tempo and then swung joyously. It was so superb that it was included in the first recording session at His Master's Voice studios, where the Quintet needled wax for the first time since the war. Four sides were also cut for British Decca *ffrr* records. These selections, "Belleville," "Liza," "Muages" and "Love's Melody" are now available in America.

When Django returned to France, he amazed everyone by coolly disregarding all offers and played a return engagement of his famous disappearing act. He mounted his sturdy trailer, joined his gypsy caravan and vanished into the French countryside. Several American booking agents who had been negotiating for an American appearance promptly began growing another ulcer. Finally a letter and a contract from Duke Ellington caught up with him—it sounded *formidable* so he boarded a plane for the promised land.

On tour with the Duke, Django enjoyed considerable success despite the fact that someone had the brilliant idea of giving him an unfamiliar, electrically amplified guitar. He has always played a guitar without amplification.

At his Carnegie Hall appearance with Ellington, he also suffered from the world's most ineptly balanced sound system, but managed to play more inventive jazz than any other soloist on the program.

Last year, a few days before Christmas, New York jazz devotees received an early Yuletide gift in Django's appearance at Café Society's Uptown Branch. (The phrase "Yuletide gift" is used to inject a holiday flavor into the statement and, in view of the astronomical tariffs prevalent in Gotham bistros, is used loosely.) The William Morris Agency Svengalis still persisted in the electric guitar, but the balance and amplification were immeasurably better than at the mildly unfortunate Carnegie affair. Lionel Hampton, Paul Whiteman, King Cole and many others came, saw and went sent.

Some time ago, our hero learned that Dorothy Lamour owned some of his records. This started a lovely daydream which had him playing the male lead opposite her in a film. This wish will probably never be fulfilled, but Django has talents and a life story which Hollywood may well use some day.

It is devoutly hoped, however, that Django never becomes as popular as, say, Frank Sinatra. Reinhardt is almost illiterate and can sign his name only with great difficulty. If he ever were cornered by a hundred autograph hounds, it would take him a week to sign his way out of the trap.

MINTON'S

RALPH ELLISON

Minton's Playhouse—where bebop was more or less born; where Charlie Christian did his most important work and where Dizzy, Monk, and Parker could fully develop. Here, Ralph Ellison—already quoted at length in Blesh's Christian profile—meditates on Minton's, in a piece that appeared first in Esquire, *in 1959.*

It has been a long time now, and not many remember how it was in the old days; not really. Not even those who were there to see and hear as it happened, who were pressed in the crowds beneath the dim rosy lights of the bar in the smoke-veiled room, and who shared, night after night, the mysterious spell created by the talk, the laughter, grease paint, powder, perfume, sweat, alcohol and food—all blended and simmering like a stew on the restaurant range, and brought to a sustained moment of elusive meaning by the timbres and accents of musical instruments locked in passionate recitative. It has been too long now, some twenty years.

Above the bandstand there later appeared a mural depicting a group of jazzmen holding a jam session in a narrow Harlem bedroom. While an exhausted girl with shapely legs sleeps on her stomach in a big brass bed, they bend to their music in a quiet concatenation of unheard sound: a trumpeter, a guitarist, a clarinetist, a drummer; their only audience a small, cockeared dog. The clarinetist is white. The guitarist strums with an enigmatic smile. The trumpet is muted. The barefooted drummer, beating a folded newspaper with whiskbrooms in lieu of a drum, stirs the eye's ear like a blast of brasses in a midnight street. A bottle of port rests on a dresser, but it, like the girl, is ignored. The artist, Charles Graham, adds mystery to, as well as illumination within, the scene by having them play by the light of a kerosene lamp. The painting, executed in a harsh documentary style reminiscent of W.P.A. art, conveys a feeling of musical effort caught in timeless and unrhetorical suspension, the sad remoteness of a scene observed through a wall of crystal.

Except for the lamp, the room might well have been one in the Hotel Cecil, the building in 118th Street in which Minton's Playhouse is located, and although painted in 1946, sometime after the revolutionary doings there had begun, the mural should help recall the old days vividly. But the décor of the place has been changed and now it is covered, most of the time, by draperies. These require a tricky skill of those who would draw them aside. And even then there will still only be the girl who must sleep forever unhearing, and the men who must forever gesture the same soundless tune. Besides, the time it celebrates is dead and gone and perhaps not even those who came when it was still fresh and new remember those days as they were.

Neither do those remember who knew Henry Minton, who gave the place his name. Nor those who shared in the noisy lostness of New York the rediscovered community of the feasts, evocative of home, of South, of good times, the best and most unself-conscious of times, created by the generous portions of Negro-American cuisine—the hash, grits, fried chicken, the ham-seasoned vegetables, the hot biscuits and rolls and the free whiskey—with which, each Monday night, Teddy Hill honored the entire cast of current Apollo Theatre shows. They were gathered here from all parts of America and they broke bread together and there as a sense of good feeling and promise, but what shape the fulfilled promise would take they did not know, and few except the more restless of the younger musicians even questioned. Yet it was an exceptional moment and the world was swinging with change.

Most of them, black and white alike, were hardly aware of where they were or what time it was; nor did they wish to be. They thought of Minton's as a sanctuary, where in an atmosphere blended of nostalgia and a music-and-drink-lulled suspension of time they could retreat from the wartime tensions of the town. The meaning of time-present was not their concern; thus when they try to tell it now the meaning escapes them.

For they were caught up in events which made that time exceptionally and uniquely *then,* and which brought, among the other changes which have reshaped the world, a momentous modulation into a new key of musical sensibility; in brief, a revolution in culture.

So how *can* they remember? Even in swiftly changing America there are few such moments, and at best Americans give but a limited attention to history. Too much happens too rapidly, and before we can evaluate it, or exhaust its meaning or pleasure, there is something new to concern us. Ours is the tempo of the motion picture, not that of the still camera, and we waste experience as we wasted the forest. During the time it was happening the sociologists were concerned with the riots, unemployment and industrial tensions of the time, the historians with the onsweep of the war; and the critics and most serious students of culture found this area of our national life of little interest. So it was left to those who came to Minton's out of the needs of feeling, and when the moment was past no one retained more than a fragment of its happening. Afterward the very effort to put the fragments together transformed them—so that in place of true memory they now summon to mind pieces of legend. They retell the stories as they have been told and written, glamourized, inflated, made neat and smooth, with all incomprehensible details vanished along with most of the wonder—not how it was as they themselves knew it.

When asked how it was back then, back in the forties, they will smile, then, frowning with the puzzlement of one attempting to recall the details of a pleasant but elusive dream, they'll say: "Oh, man, it was a hell of a time! A wailing time! Things were jumping, you couldn't get in here for the people. The place was packed with celebrities. Park Avenue, man! Big people in show business, college professors along with the pimps and their women. And college boys and girls. Everybody came. You know how the old words to the "Basin Street Blues" used to go before Sinatra got hold of it? *Basin Street is the street where the dark and the light folks meet*—that's what I'm talking about. That was Minton's, man. It was a place where everybody could come to be entertained because it was a place that was jumping with good times."

Or some will tell you that it was here that Dizzy Gillespie found his own trumpet voice; that here Kenny Clarke worked out the patterns of his drumming style; where Charlie Christian played out the last creative and truly satisfying moments of his brief life, his New York home; where Charlie Parker built the monument of his art; where Thelonious Monk formulated his contribution to the chordal progressions and the hide-and-seek melodic methods of modern jazz. And they'll call such famous names as Lester Young and Ben Webster, Coleman Hawkins; or Fats Waller, who came here in the after-hour stillness of the early morning to compose. They'll tell you that Benny Goodman, Art Tatum, Count Basie, and Lena Horne would drop in to join in the fun; that it was here that George Shearing played on his first night in the U.S.; of Tony Scott's great love of the place; and they'll repeat all the stories of how, when and by whom the word "bop" was coined here—but, withal, few actually remember, and these leave much unresolved.

Usually, music gives resonance to memory (and Minton's was a hotbed of jazz), but not the music then in the making here. It was itself a texture of fragments, repetitive, nervous, not fully formed; its melodic lines underground, secret and taunting; its riffs jeering—"Salt peanuts! Salt peanuts!" Its timbres flat or shrill, with a minimum of thrilling vibrato. Its rhythms were out of stride and seemingly arbitrary, its drummers frozen-faced introverts dedicated to chaos. And in it the steady flow of memory, desire and defined experience summed up by the traditional jazz beat and blues mood seemed swept like a great river from its old, deep bed. We know better now, and recognize the old moods in the new sounds, but what we know is that which was then becoming. For most of those who gathered here, the enduring meaning of the great moment at Minton's took place off to the side, beyond the range of attention, like a death blow glimpsed from the corner of the eye, the revolutionary rumpus sounding like a series of flubbed notes blasting the talk with discord. So that the events which made Minton's *Minton's* arrived in conflict and ran their course, then the heat was gone and all that is left to mark its passage is the controlled fury of the music itself, sealed pure and irrevocable, banalities and excellencies alike, in the early recordings; or swept along by our restless quest for the new, to be diluted in more recent styles, the best of it absorbed like drops of fully distilled technique, mood and emotion into the great stream of jazz.

Left also to confuse our sense of what happened is the word "bop," hardly more than a nonsense-syllable, by which the music synthesized at Minton's came to be known. A most inadequate word which does little, really, to help us remember. A word which throws up its hands in clownish self-depreciation before all the complexity of sound and rhythm and self-assertive passion which it pretends to name; a mask-word for the charged ambiguities of the new sound, hiding the serious face of art.

Nor does it help that so much has come to pass in the meantime. There have been two hot wars and that which continues, called "cold." And the unknown young men who brought a new edge to the sound of jazz and who scrambled the rhythms of those who used the small clear space at Minton's for dancing are no longer so young or unknown; indeed, they are referred to now by nickname in even the remotest of places. And in Paris and Munich and Tokyo they'll tell you the details of how, after years of trying, "Dizzy" (meaning John Birks Gillespie) vanquished "Roy" (meaning Roy Eldridge) during a jam session at Minton's, to become thereby the new king of trumpeters. Or how, later, while jetting over the world on the blasts of his special tilt-belted horn, he jammed with a snake charmer in Pakistan. "Sent the bloody cobra, man," they'll tell you in London's Soho. So their subsequent fame has blurred the sharp, ugly lines of their rebellion even in the memories of those who found them most strange and distasteful.

What's more, our memory of some of the more brilliant young men has been touched by the aura of death, and we feel guilty that the fury of their passing was the price for the art they left us to enjoy unscathed: Charlie Christian, burned out by tuberculosis like a guitar consumed in a tenement fire; Fats Navarro, wrecked by the tensions and needling temptations of his orgiastic trade, a big man physically as well as musically, shrunken to nothingness; and, most notably of all, Charlie Parker called "Bird," now deified, worshiped and studied and, like any fertility god, mangled by his admirers and imitators, who coughed up his life and died—as incredibly as the leopard which Hemingway tells us was found "dried and frozen" near the summit of Mount Kilimanjaro—in the hotel suite of a Baroness. (Nor has anyone explained what a "yardbird" was seeking at that social altitude, though we know that ideally anything is possible within a democracy, and we know quite well that upper-class Europeans were seriously interested in jazz long before Newport became hospitable.) All this is too much for memory; the dry facts are too easily lost in legend and glamour. (With jazz we are not yet in the age of history, but linger in that of folklore.) We know for certain only that the strange sounds which they and their fellows threw against the hum and buzz of vague signification that seethed in the drinking crowd at Minton's and which, like disgruntled conspirators meeting fatefully to assemble the random parts of a bomb, they joined here and beat and blew into a new jazz style—these sounds we know now to have become the clichés, the technical exercises and the standard of achievement not only for fledgling musicians all over the United States, but for Dutchmen and Swedes, Italians and Frenchmen, Germans and Belgians, and even Japanese. All these, in places which came to mind during the Minton days only as points where the war was in progress and where one might soon be sent to fight and die, are now spotted with young men who study the discs on which the revolution hatched in Minton's is preserved with all the intensity that young American painters bring to the works, say, of Kandinsky, Picasso and Klee. Surely this is an odd swing of the cultural tide. Yet Stravinski, Webern, and Berg notwithstanding, or more recently, Boulez or Stockhausen—such young men (many of them excellent musicians in the highest European tradition) find in the music made articulate at Minton's some key to a fuller freedom of self-realization. Indeed, for many young Europeans the developments which took place here and the careers of those who brought it about have become the latest episodes in the great American epic. They collect the recordings and thrive on the legends as eagerly, perhaps, as young Americans.

Today the bartenders at Minton's will tell you how they come fresh off the ships or planes, bringing their brightly expectant and—in his Harlem atmosphere—startlingly innocent European faces, to buy drinks and stand looking about for the source of the mystery. They try to reconcile the quiet reality of the place with the events which fired, at such long range, their imaginations. They come as to a shrine; as we to the Louvre, Notre Dame or St. Peter's; as young Americans hurry to Café Flore, the Deux Magots, the Rotonde or the Café du Dôme in Paris. For some years now, they have been coming to ask, with all the solemnity of pilgrims inquiring of a sacred relic, to see the nicotine-stained amplifier which Teddy Hill provided for Charlie Christian's guitar. And this is quite proper, for every shrine should have its relic.

Perhaps Minton's has more meaning for European jazz fans than for Americans, even for those who regularly went there. Certainly it has a *different* meaning. For them it is associated with those continental cafés in which great changes, political and artistic, have been plotted; it is to modern jazz what the Café Voltaire in Zurich is to the Dadaist phase of modern literature and painting. Few of those who visited Harlem during the forties would associate it so, but there *is* a context of meaning in which Minton's and the musical activities which took place there can be meaningfully placed.

Jazz, for all the insistence of the legends, has been far more closely associated with cabarets and dance halls than with brothels, and it was these which provided both the employment for the musicians and an audience initiated and aware of the overtones of the music; which knew the language of riffs, the unstated meanings of the blues idiom, and the dance steps developed from and complementary to its rhythms. And in the beginning it was in the Negro dance hall and night club that jazz was most completely a part of a total cultural expression; and in which it was freest and most satisfying, both for the musicians and for those in whose lives it played a major role. As a night club in a Negro community then, Minton's was part of a national pattern.

But in the old days Minton's was far more than this; it was also a rendezvous for musicians. As such, and although it was not formally organized, it goes back historically to the first New York center of Negro musicians, the Clef Club. Organized in 1910, during the start of the great migration of Negroes northward, by James Reese Europe, the director whom Irene Castle credits with having invented the fox trot, the Clef Club was set up on West Fifty-third Street to serve as a meeting place and booking office for Negro musicians and entertainers. Here wage scales were regulated, musical styles and techniques worked out, and entertainment was supplied for such establishments as Rector's and Delmonico's, and for such producers as Florenz Ziegfeld and Oscar Hammerstein. Later, when Harlem evolved into a Negro section, a similar function was served by the Rhythm Club, located then in the old Lafayette Theatre building on 132nd Street and Seventh Avenue. Henry Minton, a former saxophonist and officer of the Rhythm Club, became the first Negro delegate to Local 802 of the American Federation of Musicians and was thus doubly aware of the needs, artistic as well as economic, of jazzmen. He was generous with loans, was fond of food himself and, as an old acquaintance recalled, "loved to put a pot on the range" to share with unemployed friends. Naturally when he opened Minton's Playhouse many jazzmen made it their own.

Henry Minton also provided, as did the Clef and Rhythm clubs, a necessity more important to jazz musicians than food: a place in which to hold their interminable jam sessions. And it is here that Minton's becomes most important to the development of modern jazz. It is here, too, that it joins up with all the countless rooms, private and public, in which jazzmen have worked out the secrets of their craft. Today jam sessions are offered as entertainment by night clubs and on radio and television, and some are quite exciting; but what is seen and heard is only one aspect of the true jam session; the "cutting session," or contest of improvisational skill and physical endurance between two or more musicians. But the jam session is far more than this, and when carried out by musicians, in the privacy of small rooms (as in the mural at Minton's) or in such places as Hallie Richardson's shoestring parlor in Oklahoma City—where I first heard Lester Young jamming in a shine chair, his head thrown back, his horn even then outthrust, his feet working on the footrests, as he played with and against Lem Johnson, Ben Webster (this was 1929) and other members of the old Blue Devils orchestra—or during the after hours in Piney Brown's old Sunset Club in Kansas City; in such places as these with only musicians and jazzmen present, then the jam session is revealed as the jazzman's true academy.

It is here that he learns tradition, group techniques and style. For although since the twenties many jazzmen have had conservatory training and were well-grounded in formal theory and instrumental technique, when we approach jazz we are entering quite a different sphere of training. Here it is more meaningful to speak, not of courses of study, of grades and degrees, but of apprenticeship, ordeals, initiation ceremonies, of rebirth. For after the jazzman has learned the fundamentals of his instrument and the traditional techniques of jazz—the intonations, the mute work, manipulation of timbre, the body of traditional styles—he must then "find himself," must be reborn, must find, as it were, his soul. All this through achieving that subtle identification between his instrument and his deepest drives which will allow him to express his own unique ideas and his own unique voice. He must achieve, in short, his self-determined identity.

In this his instructors are his fellow musicians, especially the acknowledged masters, and his recognition of manhood depends upon their acceptance of his ability as having reached a standard which is all the more difficult for not having been rigidly codified. This does not depend upon his ability to simply hold a job but upon his power to express an individuality in tone. Nor is his status ever unquestioned, for the health of jazz and the unceasing attraction which it holds for the musicians themselves lies in the ceaseless warfare for mastery and recognition—not among the general public, though commercial success is not spurned, but among their artistic peers. And even the greatest can never rest on past accomplishments for, as with the fast guns of the old West, there is always someone waiting in a jam session to blow him literally, not only down, but into shame and discouragement.

By making his club hospitable to jam sessions even to the point that customers who were not musicians were crowded out, Henry Minton provided a retreat, a homogeneous community where a collectivity of common experience could find continuity and meaningful expression. Thus the stage was set for the birth of bop.

In 1941 Mr. Minton handed over his management to Teddy Hill, the saxophonist and former band leader, and Hill turned the Playhouse into a musical dueling ground. Not only did he continue Minton's policies, he expanded them. It was Hill who established the Monday Celebrity Nights, the house band which included such members from his own disbanded orchestra as Kenny Clarke, Dizzy Gillespie, along with Thelonious Monk, sometimes with Joe Guy, and, later, Charlie Christian and Charlie Parker; and it was Hill who allowed the musicians free rein to play whatever they liked. Perhaps no other club except Clarke Monroe's Uptown House was so permissive, and with the hospitality extended to musicians of all schools the news spread swiftly. Minton's became the focal point for musicians all over the country.

Herman Pritchard, who presided over the bar in the old days, tells us that every time they came, "Lester Young and Ben Webster used to tie up in battle like dogs in the road. They'd fight on those saxophones until they were tired out, then they'd put in long-distance calls to their mothers, both of whom lived in Kansas City, and tell them about it."

And most of the masters of jazz came either to observe or to participate and be influenced and listen to their own discoveries transformed; and the aspiring stars sought to win their approval, as the younger tenor men tried to win the esteem of Coleman Hawkins. Or they tried to vanquish them in jamming contests as Gillespie is said to have outblown his idol, Roy Eldridge. It was during this period that Eddie "Lockjaw" Davis underwent an ordeal of jeering rejection until finally he came through as an admired tenor man.

In the perspective of time we now see that what was happening at Minton's was a continuing symposium of jazz, a summation of all the styles, personal and traditional, of jazz. Here it was possible to hear its resources of technique, ideas, harmonic structure, melodic phrasing and rhythmical possibilities explored more thoroughly than was ever possible before. It was also possible to hear the first attempts toward a conscious statement of the sensibility of the younger generation of musicians as they worked out the techniques, structures and rhythmical patterns with which to express themselves. Part of this was arbitrary, a revolt of the younger against the established stylists; part of it was inevitable. For jazz had reached a crisis and new paths were certain to be searched for and found. An increasing number of the younger men were formally trained and the post Depression developments in the country had made for quite a break between their experience and that of the older men. Many were even of a different physical build. Often they were quiet and of a reserve which contrasted sharply with the exuberant and outgoing lyricism of the older men, and they were intensely concerned that their identity as Negroes placed no restriction upon the music they played or the manner in which they used their talent. They were concerned, they said, with art, not entertainment.

But they too, some of them, had their own myths and misconceptions: That theirs was the only generation of Negro musicians who listened to or enjoyed the classics; that to be truly free they must act exactly the opposite of what white people might believe, rightly or wrongly, a Negro to be; that the performing artist can be completely and absolutely free of the obligations of the entertainer, and that they could play jazz with dignity only by frowning and treating the audience with aggressive contempt; and that to be in control, artistically and personally, one must be so cool as to quench one's own human fire.

Nor should we overlook the despair which must have swept Minton's before the technical mastery, the tonal authenticity, the authority and fecundity of imagination of such men as Hawkins, Young, Goodman, Tatum, Teagarden, Ellington and Waller. Despair, after all, is ever an important force in revolutions.

They were also responding to the non-musical pressures affecting jazz. It was a time of big bands and the greatest prestige and economic returns were falling outside the Negro community—often to leaders whose popularity grew from the compositions and arrangements of Negroes—to white instrumentalists whose only originality lay in the enterprise with which they rushed to market with some Negro musician's hard-won style. Still there was no policy of racial discrimination at Minton's. Indeed, it was very much like those Negro cabarets of the twenties and thirties in which a megaphone was placed on the piano so that anyone with the urge could sing a blues. Nevertheless, the inside-dopesters will tell you that the "changes" or chord progressions and the melodic inversions worked out by the creators of bop sprang partially from their desire to create a jazz which could not be so easily imitated and exploited by white musicians to whom the market was more open simply *because* of their whiteness. They wished to receive credit for what they created, and besides, it was easier to "get rid of the trash" who crowded the bandstand with inept playing and thus make room for the real musicians, whether white or black. Nevertheless, white musicians like Tony Scott, Remo Palmieri and Al Haig who were part of the development at Minton's became so by passing a test of musicianship, sincerity and temperament. Later, it is said, the boppers became engrossed in solving the musical problems which they set themselves. Except for a few sympathetic older musicians it was they who best knew the promise of the Minton moment, and it was they, caught like the rest in all the complex forces of American life which comes to focus in jazz, who made the most of it. Now the tall tales told as history must feed on the results of their efforts.

Minton's Playhouse

Dizzy Gillespie

This section of To Be or Not to Bop *by Dizzy Gillespie (1979; with Al Fraser) also takes us back to Minton's—in Gillespie's voice primarily, but with sidebars by Thelonious Monk, Mary Lou Williams, and other prime witnesses.*

In those days we had several means of access to experience: big bands were one, jam sessions were another. I tried to get plenty of both. Musical happenings at that time were an excellent reason to want to stay around New York. Amongst musicians when I came up, we had a very close feeling of camaraderie. We were all trumpet players together—Charlie Shavers, Benny Harris, Bobby Moore, and I—and we were unified socially; not just trumpet players, other musicians too. We traded off ideas not only on the bandstand but in the jam sessions. We had to be as sensitive to each other as brothers in order to express ourselves completely, maintain our individuality, yet play as one. Jam sessions, such as those wonderfully exciting ones held at Minton's Playhouse, were seedbeds for our new, modern style of music.

Monk'd be asleep on the piano. To wake him up, I'd mash the quick of his finger and wake him up right quick. He'd say, "What the fuck're you doing, muthafucka!" He'd wake up and go into his thing.

I first met Monk during the early days, 1937 and 1938. Monk used to be with Cootie Williams up at the Savoy, and then, in 1939, he got the gig down at Minton's. I learned a lot from Monk. It's strange with Monk. Our influence on one another's music is so closely related that Monk doesn't actually know what I showed him. But I do know some of the things that he showed me. Like, the minor-sixth chord with a sixth in the bass. I first heard Monk play that. It's demonstrated in some of my music like the melody of "Woody 'n You," the introduction to "Round Midnight," and a part of the bridge to "Manteca."

There were lots of places where I used that progression that Monk showed me. You see, I give people credit; I don't try to take nothing from nobody. If I get something from someone, and I expand on it, I give them credit for it.

Now in my ending of "I Can't Get Started," there's an expansion of a minor-sixth chord going to the first chord of the ending of that song and also to the introduction of "Round Midnight." It's the same progression. Those are two of my most well-known solos on ballads, and the first time I heard that, Monk showed it to me, and he called it a minor-sixth chord with a sixth in the bass. Nowadays, they don't call it that. They call the sixth in the bass, the tonic, and the chord a C-minor seventh, flat five. What Monk called an E-flat-minor sixth chord with a sixth in the bass, the guys nowadays call a C-minor seventh flat five. C is the sixth note of an E-flat chord—the sixth in the bass—the bass plays that note. They call that a C-minor seventh flat five, because an E-flat-minor chord is E-flat, G-flat, and B-flat. So they're exactly the same thing. An E-flat-minor chord with a sixth in the bass is C, E-flat, G-flat, and B-flat. C-minor seventh flat five is the same thing, C, E-flat, G-flat, and B-flat. Some people call it a half diminished, sometimes.

So now, I extended that into a whole series of chords. B minor, E seventh, B-flat-minor seventh, E-flat seventh, A-minor seventh, D seventh, A-flat-minor seventh, D-flat seventh, and into C. We'd do that kind of thing in 1942 around Minton's a lot. We'd been doing that kind of thing, Monk and I, but it was never documented because no records were being made at the time. There was a recording ban.

The union wanted a trust fund for the musicians and wanted the record companies to pay for it, but they refused to pay. So the union stopped us from making recordings. I don't think it was a question of stopping the new style of music from coming out. They just wanted some benefits for the musicians. It was a good move for the musicians trying to get some of the money that was being made by these people who were making records. The recording ban lasted three or four years, I think 1942, 1943, and 1944. I was recording again by 1945.

The only reason some of the new things we were doing musically were never documented is because there were no records made at the time to show what we were doing. So later, when I recorded "I Can't Get Started," I didn't play the regular progressions. I went E seventh to E-flat seventh, D seventh to D-flat seventh, to C. And then we'd do the flatted fifths inside of that. Tadd Dameron used to do those kinds of things too.

I asked Monk one time, "Hey, man, show me something that you learned from me that you used countless times in other works."

Monk said, "A Night In Tunisia."

"Not a tune." I said, "I'm talking about progressions." Then I showed him what I'd learned from him the first time, that one particular thing that opened up a whole new trail for me. But he couldn't remember one particular thing that he'd heard me do. I was always a piano player, so I was always finding things on the piano and showing them to the guys. I'd show Monk.

And I know that there are hundreds of things, because we used to get together. I'd say, "Look, here . . ." and show him something. But Monk is the most unique musician of our crowd. He was the one least affected by any other musician, unless he's affected by piano players like James P. Johnson and Fats Waller or Duke Ellington. I never heard him play like Teddy Wilson. I never heard him play like that. When I heard him play, he was playing like Monk, like nobody else.

Also, by that time, I was getting my chops together. And Roy used to come by Minton's. Roy is the most competitive musician. Roy used to just shower trumpet players with chops and speed. I'll never forget the time, the first time, Roy heard me make an altissimo B-flat. Boy, his eyes went up. I always had my speed, but didn't have too much chops. But I was getting them together at that time. One time, we were playing "Sweet Georgia Brown," in A-flat. I played about two choruses and hit a high B-flat. Roy looked!

"Look, you're supposed to be the greatest trumpet player in the world," Monk used to tell him, "but that's the best." And he'd point at me. Monk will tell you that. Ha! Ha! "You're supposed to be the greatest trumpet player in the world," Monk said, but that guy is. He'll eat you up." Monk'll tell anybody. He'd tell Coleman Hawkins. Anybody. Monk would tell anybody how he feels about his playing. Monk'll tell you the truth, whatever he thinks about it. He's not diplomatic at all.

* * *

Thelonious Sphere Monk (piano)

I first met him at the Rhythm Club.

How did he sound when you first heard him?

He sounded good.

Was it different from what you'd been used to hearing?

Yes, I mean it sounded original.

Did you hear anything of his that you especially liked?

I heard a lotta things.

Which things?

Well, I don't know all his tunes, so I can't say which one I like the best.

If there's any great contribution that you think Dizzy's made to our music, what do you think that contribution would be?

I mean that is hard to answer. That's hard to say, you know.

Are there any incidents you can recall, let's say from the days at Minton's or the Savoy when something Dizzy did or said to you struck you as particularly unique, that really knocked you out?

I don't know what you mean when you say "knocked you out." Well, he was amusing to the people on the stage.

What do you like most about him as a person?

His musicianship. That's what.

MONK'S CONTRIBUTION TO the new style of music was mostly harmonic and also spiritual, but Kenny Clarke set the stage for the rhythmic content of our music. He was the first one to make accents on the bass drum at specific points in the music. He'd play 4/4 very softly but the breaks, and the accents on the bass drum, you could hear. Like, we called them, dropping bombs.

The most distinctive bass player among us was Oscar Pettiford. Ray Brown came on the scene afterwards, but Oscar Pettiford was the bass player for our music. I can't talk about what happened on bass before Oscar because I never did play with Jimmy Blanton too much. But Oscar was a great devotee of the guitarist Charlie Christian. He played a lot like Charlie Christian; his style was based on Charlie Christian's. A lotta bass players, when they play a solo, are always thinking in terms of tonics. Jimmy Blanton was the first one that I heard playing differently, but they tell me Oscar was playing the new way in Minneapolis before he came to New York. He'd picked up on Charlie Christian and was playing melody on the bass, like a soloist, like a trumpet, or any other melody instrument. A lotta bass players, right now, when they play a solo, you can hear them always, boom, the tonic. Then they go and play a little something, and then they jump back when the chord changes. They change on the melody because they feel a need to play a supportive role. You don't need the tonic when you're playing solos. You don't need the tonic. A lotta bass players, except the new bass players, don't understand that.

Charlie Christian was baaad! He knew the blues, and he knew how to do the swing. He had a great sense of harmony, and he lifted the guitar up to a solo voice in jazz. But he never showed me a total knowledge of the harmonic possibilities of the instrument. His harmonic sense wasn't on a level with a guy like John Collins. John Collins practiced hours and hours, man, different variations of chords. John Collins is about the most, the deepest of the guitarists because he knew a thousand ways to play one thing. And you have to practice like that; you just can't get that on the guitar because of the positions on the instrument. You've gotta find out where the positions are, where the best positions are, and once you've learned that, you can go on and get a new one, and another one, and another one. That's how John Collins played.

Other musicians came to Minton's in the early days (1939–42) such as Kermit Scott, a saxophone player, and Nick Fenton, a bass player. Kermit Scott had his own little style going. He lives in California now and came out on the stage with me in Monterey, in 1974, and played "Manteca." He went right on out there and took care of business. I introduce him every time I go out to California as one of the founders of our music. He gets a little play behind that. He used to play with Coleman Hawkins too.

A whole group of tenor players came to Minton's—Don Byas, Lucky Thompson, Horace Hoss Collar, and Rudy Williams. A lotta trumpet players came too, and pianists; but these were the ones who impressed me most in the very early days at Minton's. Some great musicians would come afterward, and certain ones who were there at the beginning didn't make the transition with us. Clyde Hart played a lot of gigs and record dates with us, but Clyde Hart had developed as a piano player along the same style as Teddy Wilson. So he didn't play like us, but he knew what we were doing, and he was right along with us all the time, you know. He adapted himself, but he never broke away from the older style of playing the piano. Bud Powell never played at Minton's. Bud was inspired first by Billy Kyle and then Charlie Parker. You see, Bud Powell didn't play the piano like a piano player, he played like a saxophonist, like Charlie Parker, a-diddle-de-diddle-de-diddle-a-diddle.

My own contributions to the new style of music at this point were rhythm—Afro-American and Latin—together with harmony. I built most of the harmonic structure and showed the piano players how to play comp with the soloists and generally whatever was needed with our music for accompaniment. As far as my own style of playing was concerned, I always went for effect. Whatever the effect was for me at the moment was what I played. Now, a lot of things are played when music is written, and if you play every note that is down there, it will become involved and stiff. So rather than bother myself with that stiffness, I eliminate those notes and make it so that the note will be heard without being played. I see some guys try to transcribe my music on paper but if you play it like that, sometimes you'll sound real corny. That's because they hear notes that I didn't even play. It's there, without being there. It's implied. And although people can't really hear it, they feel it. It's an auditory illusion.

What happened down at Minton's anyway? On Monday nights, we used to have a ball. Everybody from the Apollo, on Monday nights, was a guest at Minton's, the whole band. We had a big jam session. Monday night was the big night, the musician's night off. There was always some food there for you. Oh, that part was beautiful. Teddy Hill treated the guys well. He didn't pay them much money—I never did get paid—but he treated the guys nicely. There was always some food there for you. He had a kitchen, you know, and you could eat there.

We had a lot of fun. Hoss Collar (who was really an alto player) and I used to have this routine. Let's see, you'd hold out your hand and say, "I'm hitting. You're an ass." No, that wasn't it. Now I've got it. When you held out your hand, he'd say: "I'm hitting. You're an ass." You'd reply, "That's what *you* is." And he'd say: "That's what you *want* me to be." Right now, I walk up to some of the cats and say: "That's what you want me to be," and they go to pieces. Me, too.

Then there was a guy they used to call the Demon. He came to play, but he never did. Couldn't play to save his life. But he played with everybody—Lester, Charlie Parker. He was the first freedom player—freedom from harmony, freedom from rhythm, freedom from everything. The Demon was from Newark, and he never stopped playing.

Johnny Carisi was the only white boy up in Harlem playing at Minton's. He'd learn all the tunes. Played all of Thelonious Monk's tunes, all of mine. I'd play a chorus. He'd be right behind me. Roy? Right behind Roy. Right behind everybody. He was welcome so long as he could blow the way he did.

Jerry Newman, among many others, recorded us in Minton's with Charlie Christian. He had a wire recorder. He just brought it down there and went home and put out a record.* He never gave any of us a dime, not me, Joe Guy, Don Byas, Chu Berry, Charlie Christian, Nick Fenton, Ken Kersey, nor Kenny Clarke.

There were big fines for playing jam sessions, and the union had "walking" delegates who would check on all the places that were frequented by jazz musicians. So we were taking a big risk. One guy in California would follow you around to see if you were going to a session. He belonged to the "colored" local out there at first, and then they merged and put him in charge as "walking" delegate for places where the "colored" musicians would be playing. He'd follow you around just waiting to see you pick up your horn without a contract, and fine you a hundred to five hundred dollars. We were somewhat immune from this at Minton's because Henry Minton, who owned the place, was the first "colored" union delegate in New York. Unfortunately, to the young jazz musician, the union has always been just a dues collector. On our level we never saw it as being of any real benefit, and sometimes it kept us from gaining experience. The union benefited the classical musicians and created things for them, but the jazz guys got nothing. There wasn't much help you could expect from the union. Guys were saying, even back then, "You don't do anything for jazz musicians. You do

*"The Men from Minton's," May 1941.

everything for classical musicians." That was under the "unity" program which still exists now, every election. We've always had movements within the union to kick out the officials, but they've never made any headway. In the first place, they controlled the composition of the membership through regulations like the three-month waiting period to keep "foreign" musicians out. That meant anybody, even from next door in New Jersey. A lot of situations like the one I mentioned at the World's Fair in 1939 arose with the musicians, and from my angle, it looked like the union was siding with the employer instead of employee. The president of our local now, Max Aarons, has been a very close friend of mine and has done a lot of things for me, personally. I'm not saying that the union hasn't done anything for anybody. But I can't remember one thing the union has done to benefit jazz musicians generally. As far as jazz musicians are concerned, the union is still only collecting dues.

Though the tale is told that somehow we all wound up in Minton's, gigging, that isn't really true. I never worked at Minton's. I went there to jam. Charlie Parker never worked at Minton's either; only Monk and Kenny Clarke, who had the house band, actually *worked* at Minton's. The sessions were nightly, and I couldn't go to Minton's when I was playing with Benny Carter on Fifty-second Street because we worked at the same time. I wasn't working with anybody when I was going to Minton's to blow, unless I was working with Cab at the Cotton Club or someplace else where we got off early.

After hours, I'd go to the Uptown House to jam. There was as much creativity going on at Monroe's Uptown House as they had at Minton's. That's where we all used to go after hours, until daylight, to play. Clark Monroe had a warm feeling for musicians, and he also used to feed us. He didn't pay you any money, but you could eat and he had a band there, a non-union band, a "scab" band, they called it. Charlie Parker played in that band after he came to New York.

What we were doing at Minton's was playing, seriously, creating a new dialogue among ourselves, blending our ideas into a new style of music. You only have so many notes, and what makes a style is how you get from one note to the other. We had some fundamental background training in European harmony and music theory superimposed on our own knowledge from Afro-American musical tradition. We invented our own way of getting from one place to the next. I taught myself chords on the piano beginning at Laurinburg because I could hear chords in European music without anybody telling me what they were. Our phrases were different. We phrased differently from the older guys. Perhaps the only real difference in our music was that we phrased differently. Musically, we were changing the way that we spoke, to reflect the way that we felt. New phrasing came in with the new accent. Our music had a new accent.

Kenny Clarke

The leaders of it were Diz and Bird.

You wouldn't include yourself?

KC: I'm thinking from a modest . . .

Please don't be overly modest.

KC: Well, the overall thing . . .

DG: Everybody had a part to play, and he had a big role. His part was just as important a contribution as mine or Charlie Parker's or Monk's. His contribution is on the same level. No one is more than the other. I'd think of something and bring it, and say, "Hey, look, Klook, look at this, here, man," and show him on the piano.

He'd say, "Yeah, lemme try that." And in trying it, he'd do something else, something to aid this; and by him doing that, I'll think of ten other things to do.

This new style was something free, definitely, something that was flowing naturally from you, but at the same time, it required a great deal of technical study. Some of the older guys I talked to said, "Well, after Diz and them, just anybody couldn't play, you had to be a technician." Why?

KC: Well, it's like I said in the first place. It was the most intelligent phase of our music. It was the most intelligent, before or after, and up until now. If we had remained on that same plane, it's no telling what we'd be playing today, instead of deviating into something else.

Yeah, they were coming along, everyone. It became almost a cult after a while, and the ones who felt themselves musically strong enough would enter it. I mean, later, Miles came here to New York to attend Juilliard. I mean everyone was studying. Max was studying over at the New York School of Music. These young guys that were coming up under us, we were teaching them that whatever you do, get an education. Then you can do whatever you wanna do.

Speaking about the social aspects of this era, Kenny, you were also known to be one of the more militant of the men who were creating this new musical style.

DG: The word is vociferous. . . .

What kind of statement, if any, were you making about the social scene around you?

KC: It was an economic thing because we were already together socially.

But were you making any statement about the world around you?

KC: Yeah, in a way. The idea was to wake up, look around you, there's something to do. And this was just a part of it, an integral part of our cultural aspect. It was just more musician, to respect somebody that's doing something. And somebody'd say, "Yeah, that Dizzy, man, sure gave us the word." Things like that.

What was the word?

KC: Wake up.

"Bebop" was later publicized as a "fighting" word. Was this a "fighting" music?

KC: No, no, by all means no!

DG: It was a love music.

KC: "Bebop" was a label that certain journalists later gave it, but we never labeled the music. It was just modern music, we would call it. We wouldn't call it anything, really, just music.

Did this music have anything special to say to black people?

DG: Yeah, get the fuck outta the way. . . .

KC: Yeah, like I said it was teaching them. I mean people who you idolize. It was nice when you'd see a brother, ballplayer on the field, and you knew that he'd just finished college. You'd have a certain amount of respect for him, more than you'd have for some dumb cat outta the cornfield, and because he can play baseball, they put him on the team. There was a message in our music. Whatever you go into, go into it *intelligently.* As simple as that.

Can you think of anything amusing that happened between you two during those early years jamming at Minton's?

KC: Well, I think that we've known each other for forty years, and I don't remember us passing one harsh word. And I think about that often. I say, "Here's a man I never disputed with, never had any contrary thoughts about." Seems like what he was thinking, I was thinking too. Never one harsh word. The thing he didn't like—I knew he didn't like—was when he was playing, and I'd drop a stick. That was hell to pay then.

DG: Muthafucka, do you want your sticks glued to your hands? Get some Elmer's Glue and . . . Ha! Ha!

KC: Anything else but that. That was unpardonable.

Milton Hinton

I made many sessions up at Minton's. I thank Diz for that. What really happened there for me was the outcome of this thing on the roof, where Dizzy showed me these new changes. Everybody used to come to Minton's to blow at night. I lived right across the street from Minton's, so I was kind of like the house bass player. I was the handiest one, just because I lived there and eventually wound up living in the Cecil Hotel. But so many kids from downtown, kids that couldn't blow, would come in and they would interrupt. Monk would be there, and Diz would be there, and I'd be there, and kids would come in there that couldn't blow, just bought a horn. And we're getting ready to blow, "How High the Moon," and these kids would jump in and they would just, you know, foul up the session.

So Diz told me on the roof one night at the Cotton Club, "Now look, when we go down to the jam session, we're gonna say we're gonna play, 'I Got Rhythm,' but we're gonna use these changes. Instead of using the B-flat and D-flat, we're gonna use B-flat, D-flat, G-flat, or F and we change." We would do these things up on the roof and then we'd go down to Minton's, and all these kids would be up there. "What're y'all gonna play?" We'd say, "I Got Rhythm," and we'd start out with this new set of changes, and they would be left right at the post. They would be standing there, and they couldn't get in because they didn't know what changes we were using, and eventually they would put their horns away, and we could go on and blow in peace and get our little exercise.

Johnny Carisi (trumpet)

About me being the only white guy at Minton's, I think I lucked up on getting in there at the beginning of it, because later on a lotta cats came, mostly because I told them, Kai Winding and a coupla guys.

The only "thing" I ran into was really a backhanded kind of compliment, in a way. There was a lotta getting loaded there. I remember one time we took a walk outside, and Joe Guy was pretty stoned. I guess the previous set I'd managed to keep up with them, whatever they were doing, and Joe Guy, half-hostile, and half-familiar, family kinda style, grabbed me and says, "You ofays come up here, and you pick up on our stuff." And the other cats were saying, "What're you doing, Joe?" They cooled him out. He was loaded and everything. But it was kind of a compliment, because he was really saying, "Man, you're doing what we're doing." I wasn't anywhere near the player I could be as far as the sax was concerned, but I guess I had good instincts as far as, like, what to play. Never mind how I played it.

At Minton's there was a lotta getting loaded. As a matter of fact, Monk taught me how to drink. At the end of a set, he'd say, "Come on, come to the bar." I'd say, "Monk, I don't drink much." He insisted. He'd say, "What? Call yourself a jazz player . . ." And the next thing you know he had me drinking double gins. It was very funny.

Illinois Jacquet (tenor saxophone)

The first time I met John Birks Gillespie was in Chicago, I think, in 1940 when I was appearing at the Grand Terrace with Lionel Hampton's band, and he was, I think, at the Sherman Hotel with Cab Calloway. They would get off a little earlier than the place we were working on the South Side of Chicago. We went until four o'clock, and I think the Sherman Hotel got off at like one. So he got a chance to come out and hear the Hampton band, and afterwards, he and I went out. He came up to my room at the Ritz Hotel and started playing his trumpet, right in the mute. And I thought that was just phenomenal, you know, that a musician could just pick up his horn and want to play, any time of night or any time of day. That's how I first met him.

Most people will hear about a musician like Gillespie before they probably even meet him. His playing, the way that he'd convert chords, and his progressions were different from the trumpet players at that time. His style was completely different than anyone I'd ever heard. And then you could hear one change in his playing in 1940, when I first heard him. I could hear the whole concept of the changing of the trumpet, the style was changing. I could tell that there was gonna be some difference.

I could tell that he knew what he was doing. It was just that it was so different, his technique. You could tell that it was a well-developed brain, jazz music wise. You know when you study music, and you play this type of music, you can almost tell if a person has studied his instrument or if he's just, like, gifted and he can go along with certain things. And I could tell that he was well developed with progressions of chords and the fundamentals of taking a solo. You tell a story, and I could tell that his story was already written before it was told, you know.

Working in the bands, that was your college. If you played music, the big bands were your college. Cab Calloway's band, Duke Ellington, Count Basie, the late Jimmie Lunceford, and all those big bands. And most of those people in the bands, the musicians, were college graduates or started out to be doctors and started playing music. But they were all educated musicians, mostly, in their field. You got in a band, the discipline was there. The band itself was a school. Maybe a lot of them didn't finish college, but most of those guys had been to colleges. So when a youngster like me would join a band like Lionel Hampton or Basie, everybody was like professors.

Nobody else would be acting a fool and drinking. Everybody was so busy reading their music, some of that would rub off on you. And after a year or two of that, you would begin to act that way, live that way, play that way, and get more ambition about your music, your job, you know. And it made a better musician out of the individual. See, you need a lot of discipline out here too; all that is required in being a better musician. And I think this is what is missing today. A lot of the younger musicians today don't have the outlet of being able to join some of the big traveling bands. Most of the big bands, today, a lot of the big names are gone. They're no longer with us, some of them; and the economy is different. There are different changes; times have changed, prices are higher. To have a big band today costs a fortune in hotels and what not. So they are missing something by not being able to get the experience out of the big bands. Before, when you were able to leave the big bands, you could go out on your own, because you had been with the band, you had the experience. That's why Dizzy is still going strong today, because he's been with a lotta big bands. That was a school for him. He couldn't have gotten that in school. He couldn't have gotten it nowhere. That's the only school he could've gotten it from—the school he went to.

During the time in the forties when Minton's was operating, we used to go up there and jam. I was with the bands at the time, and I would come in and out of town. When I was in the city, we were appearing at the Apollo or downtown at the Paramount or the Strand. After the last show we'd go to Minton's and sit in or listen to some of the guys play.

It was sorta like a free-for-all. People that could play would wanna sit in. They could get up and play. Take a chorus or join the session. Sometimes these would be guys that couldn't play as well as some of the other guys. Still they had the opportunity to get up there and play. But sometimes they would be a little off key. They would think that Monk would be in the key of B-flat, and he would be in the key of F-sharp or D natural. And then these guys wouldn't stay on the stand too long because they could never find the keys that Monk was playing in. So right there he knew that they would probably not be qualified to take up all that time with those long undesirable solos. And like Monk and the others would get into some weird keys sometimes, and while they'd be changing keys, things would be getting modern all the time, because the keys were sorta hanging *them* up a little bit too sometimes. But a lotta guys just wanted to get up there tried to get into another key when they saw them coming. You'd modulate into another key, and they wouldn't stay up there *too* long. Then when they disappeared, the regular guys would come up that could really play, and they'd go on and finish what they were trying to do. So, like, you would get a chance to play things that you would ordinarily play in B-flat, in D natural, see. But you were schooled enough to play in those keys because you knew when you were in a different key.

There were many, many giants that would come in there to play. People like Dizzy, Charlie Parker, Denzil Best, Harold West, Shadow Wilson. Sometimes the late Sid Catlett would come in. Monk, Sir Charles Thompson, Bud Powell, Freddie Webster, Don Byas. It was just like a jam, somewhere to go and play. There was not any strain on being a cutting session or anything like that. Nothing like that. People just came to play. The musicians came to play, late at night, because it seemed like the music would sound better that time of morning. They didn't have nothing to do but go to bed. They didn't have to make no shows or be between shows. The job was over.

So the music would be sounding good. If you could play and the guys knew it, they would ask you to play. You know, "Come on, man, take your horn out and play something." But, I mean, there would be a lotta other musicians that would be there who weren't qualified to get up there, but still, they would have their horns. They were trying. So to not be no drag, we would let them up there, but it would be kinda tough when they'd get up on there, and they thought they were in B-flat. Sometimes they would think and they would go home and woodshed and come back and they would know how to play in all the different keys. That would make a change, right there, because they thought that if you could play in B-flat, you had it made. You'd see guys up there trying to tune up because they'd be in B natural. It would make them think twice if they were in the wrong key, and they'd go home and woodshed. And if they ever came back, they'd be ready to play in all the keys. And that made them better musicians. That changed a lotta musicians into better musicians. That is one way there was a change in music, in jazz music, during that period.

The major difference in the new music was the chord changes. You see, in Louisiana, where I think that jazz was born—I was born in the state of Louisiana, so quite naturally ever since I can remember, we've been listening to jazz music—from the times when they played right from the ear, because there was no time for people to study music, I imagine, they just played. Pick up any instrument, and if you had some kind of a soul for music, you'd just learn it sideways, any kinda way. Learn that song, learn it fast, learn it slow, play it in waltz time. It was the same song, you know. There was nobody to teach you. And so quite naturally when you heard those bands back there, they were just all playing together. You hear a Dixieland band playing today, everybody's playing together. They're going for themselves, you know. And I think what happened was that people started playing on the chord line, and started getting more progressive, then they started to realize that all those people didn't have to play together, like solos. If one was good enough, then he could play without all that interruption, like Louis Armstrong. That means when you hit Coleman Hawkins, you'd hear just the saxophone and the piano and the rhythm section. Because now they were getting together, and they were playing on chord lines. So it was sorta like you knew where you were going, and you knew who you were playing with, and you knew what they knew. Say, for an instance, your piano player. You're listening to him, and you know he knows what he's doing because he's running what you're playing. He's listening to you. If you two don't co-ordinate together, somebody's worried, and your piano player says, "Man, what was that you were playing? Because I wanna play that with you."

So people started playing together and chord changes became more understandable to soloists. And then they start to hearing people like Roy, before Diz, and then Diz. Dizzy started changing the progressions, and started playing the whole chord instead of the melody. Play the melody too, but you can play the chords, and you don't even hear the melody. And you could take the chord changes and make other songs out of the same melody. You wouldn't even know your own song after they got through with the chords, and wouldn't play your melody. We started doing that later in the forties, Charlie Parker, Dizzy, and myself—all of us were doing it that way. And that changed the pattern from Dixieland to swing, and from swing to the progressive era. The music was progressing into chord changes, and if you didn't know your chords, well then, you couldn't play certain songs with these guys. They weren't playing the melody to the songs. So, like, it went from playing just with the ear to where a person would tell you just what he's gonna play. And if you're playing with him, that's what he wants to hear on the guitar, on the piano, the bass line. Most drummers at the time were hip enough to know what was happening anyway, because they could hear. The change was away from the old pattern of solos in Dixieland style into more of a studious musician's sureness, someone who had studied a little deeper into what had already been done. And then they took it and started to play the chord changes, the correct changes, and that helped change the style of music. Diz and the others were well schooled in that change. They were well schooled, knew where they were going with it. Because today, I mean, you have to be accomplished on your instrument to play with Dizzy now, today. He would know right away if you were not capable of playing the piano with him, or the guitar, because you're involved in chord changes. Just any gifted musician could not sit there, unless he was able to hear everything. And it's hard to be that gifted. You have to put it together a little bit.

Sometimes you have to go into the woodshed. You have to get into the books. It's good to have talent, but you must put something with it. And I think that's what Dizzy has done. He has the talent, and he always had it, but he put something with it. He put some knowledge with it.

And then they called it bebop. Well, people give things all kinda names, you know. But it is music, and it's progressive music, music that has moved from where it began to where it is today. Now, there is not much change in progressions, because that's always gonna be there, the foundation. But it's how you play it. How you're gonna write for it. How are you gonna play? Are you gonna play like Coleman Hawkins? Are you gonna play like Louis Armstrong? Or are you gonna get your own creation, your own painting, or your own style? And this is what Dizzy has contributed to the world of music—his own style. And that is one of the hardest things to do in music, to be an individual stylist. We have to give him that edge, because he really worked for it, and I saw the development. I saw him develop it. I saw him developing a style from the early forties up until now. And he has not changed, spiritually, from the time I met him up until now. And this is one great thing that I admire in him. That he has maintained dignity and discipline as a jazz musician, as a trumpet player, and as a man.

Mary Lou Williams

After I had left the Andy Kirk band, I think it was around 1940 or 1941, we were working in Kelly's Stables, and I decided to stay here in New York. During that period, I was living at the Dewey Square Hotel, and that was the beginning of what they later called 'bop.' I used to go around the corner to Minton's and I met Dizzy there.

Well, you know he had that name—Dizzy—and so when people hear such a name, they actually think the person corresponds to the name. But I thought he was wonderful; he's always been great to me and he was very charitable, even then, you know. He knew that I was in New York and wasn't working, and he began to give me some of his gigs. And most of them were non-union gigs. He sent me on a gig up here, on 149th Street, to play a ballroom for him. He left and went with another group to play, and he put me in charge of his group. Illinois Jacquet was there, and Oscar Pettiford, and Klook, Kenny Clarke, was on drums. Just one horn, Illinois Jacquet, the rhythm section, and myself.

And so they featured me at this ballroom, and they had a big placard out front, "Mary Lou Williams, blah, blah, blah." About how I'd just left Andy Kirk's band. We were very popular. Andy Kirk's band had quite a few followers in New York. So I went to this gig, and the place was jammed and packed. And these little gigs that Dizzy was getting weren't paying too much money, only five or six dollars per man. I saw this big crowd there, and I told the guys, "We're not gonna play any more. Let's take intermission," I said. And I told the manager, "We can't play for this kinda money; you'll have to give us more money." I think he gave me $20 as the leader but the big surprise was that the delegates from the union happened to be there that night. I guess that was about the biggest crowd they'd ever had. This was the first time union delegates had ever been there; it was such a big crowd. And we didn't know what was happening until about a week later; the Board called me downtown to the union for playing a non-union gig. They talked about it, and they were saying that I really was an asset to the union. "You know what she did?" the musicians said. "She stopped the boys from playing, and she wouldn't play any longer until they gave them more money."

And that's actually how I got into the union. Otherwise, I would have had to wait three months or six months, you know, whatever the time. That was one of the good things that he did for me. He always looked out for me, and I never realized how wonderful he was until years later. Anytime he thought I wasn't working, or something wasn't happening right, he'd always come to my rescue.

I went to Minton's every night. When the thing started, Thelonious Monk and the others had a little band going. They were afraid to come out because they were afraid that the commercial world would steal what they had created. So they stayed in Harlem, at Minton's, and the downtowners began to come up, writing their notes on their little pieces of paper and everything, you know. I detected that in the club. It finally got downtown about this new music that was going on in Minton's. And these sessions were really terrific. The cats would come in around nine-thirty or ten o'clock at night, and even later, and they'd jam there all night. The house only paid for maybe a small trio, and the place was jammed. And in no time, the commercial world from downtown was coming in on it, and they tried to learn it. I heard some of the guys speak about not wanting to play downtown or play in the open so everybody could take it from them. Because you know the black creators of the music have never gotten recognition for creating anything. The music is so heavy. I don't think anybody is looking for any big applause or anything about what they've created. But after a while, you get kinda really disgusted and dried out because everything you create is taken from you, and somebody else is given recognition for it. But the music is so great, I think half of them could care less, except they have to eat and sleep, you know. But Minton's was really a good scene, and it all started there until they began to play on Fifty-second Street.

Dizzy did not receive a warm, open reception when he was coming up. He came up the hard way. And I know of at least ten musicians that have become bitter, and they're just not doing anything, you know; they're working off an ego and all that. Well, he doesn't. He's just a nice guy. He's so nice to everyone else until it added to his power as far as being the greatest in the world. He is, in fact, and you can't deny it. And I've seen him go all the way out for someone in order to make them a success, and continually do it. I've gone out when he has asked me to come and help him to do things, and he'll sit there patiently—he has a lotta patience—and he'll teach musicians how to play. Someone made a remark once that every musician that was playing with him during this period should be paying him two or three hundred dollars a week because he teaches all of them. He'll sit there patiently with them until they learn what he wants them to learn. And he'll keep people; seems like he just hates to fire them if they're not good. I've never seen such a great giant like him before in my life.

Oh, I forgot to mention the number of jobs Dizzy has gotten for people, people who are now big movie stars, writing for the movies and everything else. Yet, he goes along just being nice, playing his instrument. The rest, they'll just go on their way and think about what *they* wanna do in life, you know.

I played through all the eras. I changed. In the "modern" era, there were more notes, you know, like, the 1930s era was the feeling. You see, the blues stayed in it from the beginning of the spirituals. The blues feeling has always been there, even with Coltrane. I could hear that in his music, although he went way out, but I could still hear that feeling in his music. Well, it was still in bop except it was just millions of notes. You know, when we first heard it during the forties, it sounded like a musician, like *Dizzy was playing a million notes in one bar.* See, and that was the change, and they still had their own beat going; you could still move your head or your body with it. That was the only change; and the phrasing every other note. That was the big change for that era, but the other era was practically all swing. During the swing era, as far as a pianist goes, you had to have a great left hand. You could play all the notes you wanted to play, but if you didn't have a great left hand, or two hands, you weren't considered a great pianist. And it was practically all swing, you know, like a Basie kind of a thing. But bop came along with a more modern thing, and the blues and the swing part, but it was just more colorful.

Oh, yeah, and the harmony structure of the blues changed from the plain old C seventh, and what not, to major seventh and many other beautiful modern harmonies. But they were beautiful, like riding around and taking in the scenery, rather than just having a steady beat going.

* * *

CHARLIE PARKER deserves special mention because he was not actually here at the beginning. When Charlie Parker came to New York, in 1942, the new style of music had already begun, but he made a gigantic contribution, which really added a new dimension to the music. It's hard to describe it exactly, he contributed so many different elements. A lotta guys played fast. Rapid! I mean *in one,* these cats. But they didn't play the notes that Charlie Parker played. His modus operandi was different, how he attacked and how he swung. I was always a piano nut, from a little boy; I'd show "Yardbird," too, things on the piano and how our music was structured. But Charlie Parker played very syncopated and sanctified. There was nobody playing like that in our style. I always thought like that too, though most guys went more straight and evenly from one note to another because I, also, aside from my piano playing, was always the teacher of the drum. So I'd hear that in the drums, and I played like that, with accents. But Charlie Parker, when he came on the scene, had it down to a T personified.* Charlie Parker's contribution to our music was mostly melody, accents, and bluesy interpretation. And the notes! "Bird" has some notes in his melodies, the lines that he wrote, that are deep, deep notes, as deep as anything Beethoven ever wrote. And he had little things that he used to play inside. He'd play other tunes inside the chords of the original melody, and they were always right. The little inside tunes that he played were always on the right chords of the original melody. The press, when we later started getting some notice, always tried to pretend we were angry with each other, envious, jealous, and things like that, but that's absolutely false.

My wife used to tell me all the time, "I like the way that Charlie Parker puts them other little numbers in there. Why don't you do something like that? Play 'O Solo Mio' in the middle of 'Dizzy Atmosphere' or something like that."

Yes, Charlie Parker was something else, and he jammed with us at Minton's too.

---

*Charlie Parker's bluesy, syncopated style is often attributed to the influence of "Old Yardbird," Buster Smith, a saxophonist out in Kansas City. I never heard "Old Yardbird" play, but I've heard about him.

At the Hi-De-Ho

Hampton Hawes

Everyone who spent time with Charlie Parker seems to have written about it. Here, from Hawes's Raise Up Off Me *(see p. 306), is some convincing testimony to Parker's overpowering influence.*

One of the great tracks in jazz is Charlie Parker's "Parker's Mood." It begins with a three-note figure contained in a G minor triad—in this sequence: Bb-G-D—and whenever you heard someone whistling those notes in L.A., you knew you were in the presence of a friend. It signified you were using but cool, and when you went to buy dope late at night (which was the usual time to cop) if the bell wasn't working or you didn't want to jar the Man out of a sound sleep or there might be someone uncool on the premises, you went Bb-G-D in that fast, secret way and the cat would pop his head out the window. When Bird first played his "Parker's Mood" I think those notes might have been drifting around somewhere in his head and they just flew right out.

In 1947 I graduated from Polytechnic High School, split out the back of the auditorium (thinking, *Damn, I'm free, got my diploma and didn't fuck up, can sleep till twelve tomorrow*), threw my cap and gown in the back of the Ford and made it only fifteen minutes late to The Last Word where I was working with the Jay McNeely band. A few months later I joined Howard McGhee's Quintet at the Hi-De-Ho. Bird had worked his way back from the East Coast and joined us. When I had first heard him at Billy Berg's in 1945 I couldn't believe what he was doing, how anyone could so totally block out everything extraneous, light a fire that hot inside him and constantly feed on that fire. Now at the time there were maybe ten people in the neighborhood of 50th and Western who knew there was a genius playing alto. Most people who had heard him thought he was crazy. His playing was too free and blazing and pure; it could be dissonant and harsh on the ears if you weren't accustomed to the sound. He had already recorded those early classics with Dizzy but you couldn't find the records on any jukeboxes. Today the DJ's can take a new sound and spread it like flash fire; before you know it you're on television beaming to thirty million people. But this was before TV, and jazz was years away from reaching the concert halls. The only people in the vicinity of 50th and Western who were hip to him were a few of the street people, one or two chicks at the house where he was staying—the woman who owned it, a madame with a whorehouse on the east side, was a good friend of his and put him up whenever he was in town—and, of course, other musicians. When word got around where he was playing they came to check him out. Motherfuckers peeked and backed right up. Those of us who were affected the strongest felt we'd be willing to do anything to warm ourselves by that fire, get some of that grease pumping through our veins. He fucked up all our minds. It was where the ultimate truth was.

As with anyone that heavy and different, some people were awed or afraid of him and kept their distance. Others pursued him, would drop by his pad and hang out, figuring if they were around him long enough some of his shit was bound to rub off on them. I watched motherfuckers write down his solos note for note, play them on their own gigs and then wonder why they didn't sound as good. And if they had to follow Bird's solo with their own stuff, that would really leave them exposed—like standing naked and wet in a cold wind. Bird would take advantage of these dudes, borrow money and burn them in various ways. It wasn't that he was a bad cat, any junkie would do the same thing. It was a matter of dope or no dope; survival. Bird was out and he was strung, and in order to be around him you had to contend with that.

I never crowded or bothered him. I was busy trying to figure out my own life and I sensed that aside from his music it wasn't going to do me any good to be spending a lot of time around Bird. But he was the best player in the game, and on the stand when he'd sometimes look around at me and smile I knew I had played something good.

He was a sad driver—when his two-year-old car fell apart he left it in the street; borrowed mine once and tried to shift without using the clutch—so I'd pick him up every night at the madame's house in my '37 Ford, take him to work and bring him back. When I came home early one night he motioned me to follow him to his room. I waded through piles of sandwich wrappers, beer cans and liquor bottles. Watched him line up and take down eleven shots of whiskey, pop a handful of bennies, then tie up, smoking a joint at the same time. He sweated like a horse for five minutes, got up, put on his suit and a half hour later was on the stand playing strong and beautiful.

For two weeks he never said a word to me—going to the club, on the stand, or driving home. But it wasn't an uncomfortable silence; he was either stoned, froze, or just off somewhere else, and I respected whatever trip he was on and whatever distant place it carried him to. It was never an ego trip. If someone were to ask him who he liked better on alto, Henry Prior or Sonny Criss—it was the sort of thing a young player starting to come up would ask—he'd shrug and say, Both. They're both cool. Shooting down other players was as foreign to his nature as a longing for sharp clothes and a Cadillac or whether or not he had a white woman, which were the black badges of success in those days. He had plenty of white women but it never interfered with his music.

Sometimes I'd pull up in front of the club and he'd be too high to get out of the car. Howard McGhee would ask me where Bird was. I'd say, Sittin' in the car. No point in trying to pull him out, he wouldn't have been able to play anyway. After a while he'd get himself together, walk in and start blowing—even before he reached the stand, weaving his way through the tables playing in that beautiful, fiery way.

At the end of the second week of the gig he spoke his first words to me. It was close to three in the morning when I left him off at the madame's house. He got out, started walking toward the house, then stuck his head back in the window and said, "I heard you tonight."

The next day I told the guys in the band I was going to drop by Bird's place and see if he wanted to go to a movie. Everybody said, That's a dumb idea, he isn't going to want to go to any show. That's too square for him, too bourgeois. I dropped by anyway. He came to the door in a T-shirt and the same pin-stripe suit he wore on the stand. Said it was a nice day and a show sounded like a good idea. We went to a newsreel playing nearby. As I was buying my ticket I realized Bird was no longer with me. Looked up and down the street and saw him coming out of an alley halfway down the block. He wandered up to the box office and laid out his money, not saying anything about the little side trip. Afterwards we ate a hot dog and drove around downtown in my Ford, enjoying the spring day. When I dropped him off back at the house he said, "I had a nice time."

That weekend I smoked my first joint, some light green from Chicago Bird pulled out as we were driving down Avalon Boulevard to get a hamburger and a Coke. Didn't feel anything till after we ate and I started driving home. I said, Man, why are all these horns honking at me? Bird said, You're driving backwards. I stopped and let him take over the wheel. He made it back to his place, stripping gears all the way. I walked the ten blocks to my house and was weaving up to the door when I saw a tiny old lady from my father's church staring at me. Watched me trying to make it to the door and said, "Young man, are you behaving yourself?" I made it up the stairs, lay down under the bed, and getting a flash from the old church days asked God aloud to deliver me from the devil.

Next day Bird phoned me and said, "That was some powerful light green."

His uncle was Bishop Peter E. Parker and maybe he was close to God. I know he was damn near like a prophet in his music. He scared a lot of people over the years and died of pneumonia, so they say, in Baroness Nica Rothschild's Fifth Avenue living room when he was thirty-four. But as long as I knew Bird, I was never awed or afraid of him. I loved him. And how can you be afraid of somebody you love?

Bird

Miles Davis

And from Miles Davis's Autobiography *(see p. 243), this atypically modest, if somewhat ambivalent, view of Parker.*

Bird could be a lot of fun to be around, because he was a real genius about his music, and he could be funnier than a motherfucker, talking in that British accent that he used to use. But he still was hard to be around because he was always trying to con or beat you out of something to support his drug habit. He was always borrowing money from me and using it to buy heroin or whiskey or anything he wanted at the time. Like I said, Bird was a greedy motherfucker, like most geniuses are. He wanted everything. And when he was desperate for a fix of heroin, man, Bird would do anything to get it. He would con me and as soon as he left me, he would run around the corner to somebody else with the same sad story about how he needed some money to get his horn out of the pawnshop, and hit them up for some more. He never paid nobody back, so in that way Bird was a motherfucking drag to be around.

One time I left him in my apartment when I went to school and when I got back home the motherfucker had pawned my suitcase and was sitting on the floor nodding after shooting up. Another time, he pawned his suit to get some heroin and borrowed one of mine to wear down to the Three Deuces. But I was smaller than he was so Bird was up there on the bandstand with suit sleeves ending about four inches above his wrist and suit pants ending about four inches above his ankles. That was the only suit I had at the time, so I had to stay in my apartment until he got his suit out of the pawnshop and brought mine back. But man, the motherfucker walked around for a day looking like that, just for some heroin. But they said Bird played that night like he had on a tuxedo. That's why everybody loved Bird and would put up with his bullshit. He was the greatest alto saxophone player who ever lived.

Anyway, that's the way Bird was; he was a great and a genius musician, man, but he was also one of the slimiest and greediest motherfuckers who ever lived in this world, at least that I ever met. He was something.

I remember one time we was coming down to The Street to play from uptown and Bird had this white bitch in the back of the taxi with us. He done already shot up a lot of heroin and now the motherfucker's eating chicken—his favorite food—and drinking whiskey and telling the bitch to get down and suck his dick. Now, I wasn't used to that kind of shit back then—I was hardly even drinking, I think I had just started smoking—and I definitely wasn't into drugs yet because I was only nineteen years old and hadn't seen no shit like that before. Anyway, Bird noticed that I was getting kind of uptight with the woman sucking all over his dick and everything, and him sucking on her pussy. So he asked if something was wrong with me, and if his doing this was bothering me. When I told him that I felt uncomfortable with them doing what they was doing in front of me, with her licking and slapping her tongue like a dog all over his dick and him making all that moaning noise in between taking bites of chicken, I told him, "Yeah, it's bothering me." So you know what that motherfucker said? He told me that if it was bothering me, then I should turn my head and not pay attention. I couldn't believe that shit, that he actually said that to me. The cab was real small and we all three were in the backseat, so where was I supposed to turn my head? What I did was to stick my head outside the taxi window, but I could still hear them motherfuckers getting down and in between, Bird smacking his lips all over that fried chicken. Like I said, he was something, all right.

So I looked up to Bird for being a great musician more than I liked him as a person. But he treated me like his son, and he and Dizzy were like father figures to me. Bird used to always tell me that I could play with anybody. So he would almost push me up on stage sometimes to play with somebody who I didn't think I was ready for, someone like Coleman Hawkins or Benny Carter or Lockjaw Davis. I might have been confident in my playing with most people, but I was still only nineteen and felt that I was too young to play with certain other people—though there weren't many that I felt that way about. But Bird used to build up my confidence by saying he had gone through the same bullshit when he was younger back in Kansas City.

I did my first recording date, in May 1945, with Herbie Fields. Man, I was so nervous about making that date that I couldn't even hardly play. Even in the ensemble playing—I didn't get to play no solos. I remember Leonard Gaskin on bass on that date, and a singer named Rubberlegs Williams. But I tried to put that record out of my mind and I forgot who else was on that date.

I also got my first important nightclub gig at that time. I played with Lockjaw Davis's group for a month at the Spotlite on 52nd Street. I had been sitting in with him a lot up at Minton's, so he knew how I played. Around that time—maybe a little bit before this, I don't exactly remember—I started sitting in with Coleman Hawkins's band at the Downbeat Club on 52nd Street. Billie Holiday was the star singer with the group. The reason that I got to sit in a lot was because Joe Guy, Bean's regular trumpet player, had just gotten married to Billie Holiday. Sometimes, they'd be so high off heroin and be fucking so good that Joe would miss his gig. So would Billie. So, Hawk would use me when Joe didn't show up. I used to check with Hawk down at the Downbeat every night to see if Joe had shown up. If he didn't, then I would play the set.

I loved playing with Coleman Hawkins and behind Billie when I got the chance. They were both great musicians, really creative and shit. But nobody played like Bean. He had such a big, huge sound. Lester Young—Prez—had a light sound and Ben Webster used to be running all kinds of funny-ass chords, you know, like a piano, because he also played piano. And then there was Bird who also had his own thing, his sound. But Hawk started liking me so much that Joe got his act together and stopped missing sets. Then the gig with Lockjaw came around.

After the gig with Lockjaw was over, people started using me a lot on The Street. What was happening was that white people, white critics, were now beginning to understand that bebop was some important shit. They began talking and writing a lot about Bird and Dizzy, but only when they played on The Street. I mean, they wrote and talked about Minton's, but only after they had made The Street the place for white people to come to and spend a lot of money to hear this new music. Around 1945 a lot of the black musicians were playing down on 52nd Street, for the money and the media exposure. It was around this time that the clubs on 52nd—like the Three Deuces, the Onyx, the Downbeat Club, Kelly's Stable, and others—started being more important for musicians than the clubs uptown in Harlem.

A lot of white people, though, didn't like what was going on on 52nd Street. They didn't understand what was happening with the music. They thought that they were being invaded by niggers from Harlem, so there was a lot of racial tension around bebop. Black men were going with fine, rich white bitches. They were all over these niggers out in public and the niggers were clean as a motherfucker and talking all kind of hip shit. So you know a lot of white people, especially white men, didn't like this new shit.

There were a couple of white music critics, like Leonard Feather and Barry Ulanov, who were co-editors of *Metronome* music magazine and who understood what was going on with bebop, who liked it and wrote good things. But the rest of them white motherfucking critics hated what we were doing. They didn't understand the music. They didn't understand, and hated, the musicians. Still, the people were packing into the clubs to hear the music, and Dizzy's and Bird's group at the Three Deuces was the hottest thing in New York.

Bird himself was almost a god. People followed him around everywhere. He had an entourage. All kinds of women were around Bird, and big-time dope dealers, and people giving him all kinds of gifts. Bird thought this was the way it was supposed to be. So he just took and took. He began missing sets and whole gigs. This was fucking with Dizzy's head, because though he might have acted a little crazy, he was always organized and took care of business. Dizzy didn't believe in missing gigs. So he would sit down with Bird, beg him to pull his act together, threaten to quit if he didn't. Bird didn't, so finally Dizzy quit, and that was the end of the first great group in bebop.

Dizzy's quitting the group shocked everybody in the music world, and upset a lot of musicians who loved to hear them play together. Now, everybody realized that it was over and we weren't going to hear all that great shit they did together no more, unless we heard it on record or they got back together. That is what a lot of people hoped would happen, including me, who took Dizzy's place.

When Dizzy left their band at the Three Deuces, I thought Bird was going to take a band uptown, but he didn't, at least not right away. A lot of club owners on 52nd began asking Bird who his trumpet player was going to be since Dizzy quit. I remember being with Bird one time in a club when the owner asked that, and Bird turned to me and said, "Here's my trumpet player right here, Miles Davis." I used to kid Bird by saying, "If I hadn't joined your band, *you* wouldn't even have a job, man." He would just smile, because Bird enjoyed a good joke and one-upmanship. Sometimes it didn't work—me being in the band—because the owners liked Bird and Dizzy together. But the owner of the Three Deuces hired us in October of 1945. The group had Bird, Al Haig on piano, Curly Russell on bass, Max Roach and Stan Levey on drums, and me. It was the same rhythm section that Bird and Dizzy had right before Dizzy quit. I remember the gig at the Three Deuces being for about two weeks. Baby Laurence, the tap dancer, was the floor show. He took four and eights with the band and was a motherfucker. Baby was the greatest tap dancer that I have ever seen, or heard, because his tap dancing sounded just like a jazz drummer. He was something else.

I was so nervous on that first real gig with Bird that I used to ask if I could quit every night. I had sat in with him, but this was my first real paying gig with him. I would ask, "What do you need me for?" because that motherfucker was playing so much shit. When Bird played a melody I would just play under him and let him lead the fucking note, let him sing the melody and take the lead on everything. Because what would it look like, me trying to lead the leader of all the music? Me playing lead for Bird—are you kidding? Man, I was scared to death I was going to fuck up. Sometimes I would act like I was quitting, because I thought he might fire me. So I was going to quit before he did, but he would always encourage me to stay by saying that he needed me and that he loved the way I played. I hung in there and learned. I knew everything Dizzy was playing. I think that's why Bird hired me—also because he wanted a different kind of trumpet sound. Some things Dizzy played I could play, and other things he played, I couldn't. So, I just didn't play those licks that I knew I couldn't play, because I realized early on that I had to have my own voice—whatever that voice was—on the instrument.

That first two weeks with Bird was a motherfucker, but it helped me grow up real fast. I was nineteen years old and playing with the baddest alto saxophone player in the history of music. This made me feel real good inside. I might have been scared as a motherfucker, but I was getting more confident too, even though I didn't know it at the time.

But Bird didn't teach me much as far as music goes. I loved playing with him, but you couldn't copy the shit he did because it was so original. Everything I learned about jazz back then I learned from Dizzy and Monk, maybe a little from Bean, but not from Bird. See, Bird was a soloist. He had his own thing. He was, like, isolated. And there was nothing you could learn from him unless you copied him. Only saxophone players could copy him, but even they didn't. All they could do was try to get Bird's approach, his concept. But you couldn't play that shit he played on saxophone with the same feeling on trumpet. You could learn the notes but it won't sound the same. Even great saxophonists couldn't copy him. Sonny Stitt tried, and Lou Donaldson a little later, and Jackie McLean a little later than both of them. But Sonny had more of Lester Young's style. And Bud Freeman used to play a lot like Sonny Stitt played. I guess Jackie and Lou came the closest to Bird, but only in their sound, not in *what* they played. Nobody could play like Bird, then or now.

Waiting for Dizzy

Gene Lees

Another superb profile from Lees—this one of Dizzy Gillespie in 1989, and of a recording session involving Art Farmer, Phil Woods, and Benny Golson, among others. Collected in Lees's Waiting for Dizzy *(1991).*

It felt strange, going out there. And we got lost. "This isn't it," Benny Golson said, as the driver of the van pulled into a parking lot by an office building in Englewood Cliffs, New Jersey. Art Farmer concurred. It looked unfamiliar to me, but then I hadn't been to Rudy van Gelder's recording studio in twenty-five years and was disoriented by the new buildings along what once was a country highway. I had last come out here for the *Bill Evans with Symphony Orchestra* session that Creed Taylor produced for Verve. That was in 1965.

We left the parking lot and traveled a little farther. Benny said, "I think this is it," and the driver pulled into a lane among trees, running in an S-shape in a mini-woodland and strewn with puddles from last night's rain, and suddenly there was the cement block building with a high-peaked roof that Rudy van Gelder had built a good thirty years ago to capture some of the acoustic qualities of a church. A sign affixed by the door advised all ye who entered here that there was to be no smoking or drinking within these walls. Rudy said cigarette smoke penetrated and damaged recording equipment. Everyone who had ever recorded here knew Rudy's quirks, and one of them was that you never touched his equipment.

"You know," Art Farmer said, in his low slow voice and with a somewhat grave and almost frowning expression he takes on when he is about to lay something funny on you, "Jim Hall and Red Mitchell have the classic story about Rudy. Red went to high school with Rudy. Red and Jim were here doing a duo record. They talked about the sound they wanted, and Red was in the control room with Rudy, and Red said, 'You know, Rudy, maybe if we just put a little more of this in there,' And he touched one of those faders, and Rudy said, 'That's it. You don't owe me anything. Just pack up and get out.' "

Benny laughed. "He pushed friendship a little too far."

"That was it," Art said. "If you touched anything in his control room . . ."

We went into the building. The studio was immediately familiar: the peaked wooden ceiling, the cement-block walls, the recording booth. Rudy still wore cotton gloves when he left the booth to adjust a microphone in the studio. I asked him why he did it. He said, "I'll tell you why I do it. Because it doesn't leave fingerprints on the microphones."

Rudy looked much the same. So did Creed Taylor, youthful—almost boyish—at sixty. A Southerner with family roots in New Orleans, he is actually Creed Taylor V, a fact I uncovered after reading that another Creed Taylor had participated in the first battle of the Alamo, when the American forces took the church from the Mexicans. That earlier Creed Taylor—who complained of the way the American forces treated the Mexicans—was a direct ancestor of the present Creed Taylor.

Creed's sandy hair had thinned a little at the back, and he wore slightly tinted glasses after retinal surgery. But he showed no sign of the strain of his eleven-year legal battle with Warner Bros. Records, a battle he had won in Santa Monica after the longest civil suit in the history of the California Superior Court.

One thing was different, though: the studio was filled with television equipment, high floodlights shining down from suspended tubes of black cloth and making pools of light on the floor around music stands and microphones, and cameras, including a monstrous instrument mounted on a boom. The crew was getting set up.

Creed won eleven million dollars in that suit; his lawyers had advised him that he could get much more if he wanted to fight further, but he'd said, No, he'd had enough; he wanted to get on with his work, get back to his career, get back to making records. This first session for his CTI label was to be something extraordinary: the first high definition (or hi-def, as it is already being called) jazz video in America and, probably, the world. High-definition television is already on the air an hour a day in Tokyo, and some form of it will probably be in use in America sooner than anyone thinks. With double the number of lines to the screen, it looks like color photos in motion. The vividness is startling. Outside, crews were getting ready for the sessions in a huge video truck next to a generator truck. These cameras were prototypes, and one of them alone was costing Creed $27,000 a day. The mere thought of the cost of this recording made me uneasy, and only the more so when I mused that this was Creed's own money.

It was a typical Creed Taylor move: daring and original. Like the *Bill Evans with Symphony Orchestra*, which must have been an expensive album; or Bill's three-piano *Conversations with Myself*, which got Bill his first Grammy; or the Freddy Hubbard *Red Clay* album; or *The Individualism of Gil Evans*, made when nobody in the world thought Gil was "commercial" and which Creed made only because he loved Gil's writing. Or the great Jimmy Smith albums. Or the George Benson recordings. Warner Bros had swiped Benson from Creed, who had a contract with him. That's what he sued them for. And now he was suing CBS records to get back the masters of his CTI records.

Creed had called me in California and asked me to come east and work on this hi-def video project. He wanted me to interview some of the musicians, capture if possible some of their personalities and histories on film in segments to be spaced among the musical numbers. It sounded a little nuts to me, but I have great faith in Creed's imagination. He will take chances, go into things with only a faint idea of how they will come out, putting his faith in the people he's working with. And he had ordered up a varied, to say the least, crew of musicians: among them Art Farmer, Phil Woods, Bob Berg, Anthony Jackson, Charlie Haden, Tito Puente, Airto Moreira and his wife Flora Purim, and Dizzy Gillespie. Creed idolized Dizzy, still remembering in awe the first time he saw him, fronting his big band back when Creed was an undergraduate in psychology at Duke University. He was looking forward to Dizzy's arrival. And he was treating everyone like royalty.

In the past few days, we had discussed the project at length. Creed said, "How do we keep it out of the record-store bins marked 'various artists'? What's the unifying principle?"

"Dizzy," I said. Because of the breadth of his influence, which goes far beyond bebop. Creed agreed that it certainly was one of the principles. Dizzy was to come in on the last day and record two pieces of material.

BENNY GOLSON AND I had been talking about Dizzy in the van on our way out here from Manhattan. We were to pick Art Farmer up on the way. Art lives in Vienna now, and he was staying in the apartment of a friend; Benny had recently moved back to New York after many years of writing film scores in Los Angeles.

"Dizzy was talking about Art last night," Benny said. "Dizzy said, 'Did you hear Art's recording of *U.M.M.G.?*'" I assumed he meant *Upper Manhattan Medical Group*. "The first recording of it I heard was Dizzy's, that he did with Duke. He just happened to come by the studio that day, when they were recording, and he just happened to have his horn. Duke said, 'Take your horn out.' He didn't quite understand the tune, and so Swee'pea, Billy Strayhorn, said, 'Well look, this is the way it goes.' And he played and it was fantastic.

"Dizzy and I talked about an hour on the phone last night. I called him in Atlanta. I told him that many people can follow those who are already taking the lead. But when he came along, he was stepping out into dark places, at some personal risk, I guess—risk of being ridiculed. Louis Armstrong said something like, 'They play like they're playing with a mouthful of hot rice.' Where's the melody? The bass drum is dropping too many bombs. There were all kinds of derogatory things said about them. And now today, it's the standard.

"When John Coltrane and I—we were together every day during that time—went to the Academy of Music to hear Dizzy in 1945, and they started to play, we almost fell off the balcony. Because we had been playing with local bands. And we all were used to playing . . ." He sang an example of swing era riffing. "And all of a sudden, Dizzy was playing other things, things we had never heard, and you can't imagine the impact it had on me. I told Dizzy last night that that moment changed my whole life, and I've spent the rest of my life trying to comprehend what it's all about. It's so limitless. It's perpetual. Of course, Dizzy is so modest, I could hear the embarrassment coming through the phone."

Benny said, "He was always didactic. Really. He was a teacher without even intending to be. And Art Blakey, too! All of us who came through Art's band, we would do anything for him. Freddy Hubbard and I were talking about that the other day. When I left that band, I was in trouble. I could not play with another drummer. I was irritated, I was annoyed, I would get angry, because I wasn't hearing what I was used to hearing. When I joined his band, I was playing soft, and mellow, and smooth, and syrupy. By the time I left I was playing another way, because I had to. He would do one of those famous four-bar drum rolls going into the next chorus, and I would completely disappear. He would holler over at me, 'Get up out of that hole!'" Benny laughed. "He taught us a lot."

We pulled up in front of a building on the West Side. Art Farmer emerged and we shook hands and embraced. Benny said to him, "Did you bring your box of chops?" Art laughed. Benny explained, "That's Curtis Fuller's line."

"They're on their way. They'll be here by tomorrow," Art said.

We got into the van and the talk turned back to Dizzy. "He makes no claims whatsoever for himself," I said.

"He gets embarrassed," Benny said. "Like a little boy. I was telling Gene about that *U.M.M.G.* thing that he recorded with Duke, and then you recorded. You know, I was talking to Dizzy last night about the time when he and Charlie Parker were together. He said, 'Do you know what Charlie Parker brought? Charlie Parker brought the rhythm. The *way* he played those notes.'"

"The accents," Art said.

"It's the *way* he played it," Benny said. "It was really a combination of the two. I said to him, 'You were so far ahead that when you first recorded, you had Clyde Hart, who was a stride piano player, and Slam Stewart. It took a while for the rest of the instrumentalists to catch up with what you were doing, and the trombone was the last.'"

I said, "Bobby Scott said, 'The rhythm sections were ten years behind Bird and Dizzy.'"

"That's true," Benny said. "They were playing boom-chank boom-chank." Art chuckled. "Art," Benny said, "you know more than I do, because I never really got to know Charlie Parker and you played with him."

"You've seen the movie, I presume," I said.

"I didn't see it," Benny said.

"Yeah," Art said. "I saw it. It didn't get him, but it's not a crime. Because somebody that big, they should either have more input from somebody who knew him, or else do it fifty or a hundred years later. There are too many people around who knew Bird who are disgusted with the movie. If you didn't know him, well then it wouldn't make any difference. And the guy in the picture is nothing like Dizzy. Dizzy is a guy—and Bird was too—when these people walked into the room, you knew there was a presence there. The guy who played the part of Dizzy was very quiet, almost meek, a mousy kind of guy. And Dizzy is nothing like that at all." He and Benny laughed at the discrepancy. "And everyone who knew Bird recognizes that he was very strong intellectually, and had a very strong personality. This guy in the movie came across as somebody who was a little boy, child-like, and never knew what he was doing. Not to take anything away from the actor—he was a good actor. But he didn't know what he was dealing with. The guy in the movie came across as too much of a victim, a sad guy. Bird had a sense of humor. He wasn't going around crying all the time.

"I remember that when we were living in Los Angeles, there was a little black weekly newspaper called the Los Angeles *Sentinel* that came out with a review of Bird. I read it and I was so surprised that I took it over to where he was staying, and woke him up, and said, 'Hey, man! Read this!' The lady who wrote it said, 'This saxophone player carries himself with the air of a prophet. And he's got a little wispy black boy who plays the trumpet and a bass player with an indefatigable arm.' She said, 'He carries himself with the air of a prophet, but there's really not that much going on.' Bird was sitting up in the bed, reading it, and he said, 'Yeah, well, she's probably okay, but the wrong people got to her first.' She was the girlfriend of a trumpet player out there who wasn't into anything."

Benny said, "One of the most ridiculous things I have heard recently was by a female critic who said Kenny G is very much like Charlie Parker. I couldn't believe it. I'm not taking anything away from Kenny G but he's nothing like Charlie Parker.'" And Benny and Art laughed.

* * *

FOR ME, TOO, it was the rhythm in the playing of Charlie Parker and Dizzy Gillespie. Having grown up with Wagner and Debussy and Ravel in my ears, the harmony was not startling. There is little in bebop harmony that wasn't in use in European concert music by the end of the nineteenth century. It was the rhythmic shifting to which Bird and Dizzy were prone that startled me. I had grown up loving Edmond Hall and Trummy Young and George Wettling and Big Sid Catlett and the Goodman small groups, and in them the solos tended to fall into comparatively neat bar divisions, two or compounds of two. Even Coleman Hawkins and Charlie Christian had not prepared me for this swift evolution in jazz. Charlie Parker said once in an interview that he and Dizzy and Don Byas and Kenny Clarke and their friends were not rebelling against anything: they simply thought this was the logical way for the music to go.

I never was able to accept the story that they "invented" bebop at Minton's as a thing the "white boys" couldn't steal. It is at odds with Dizzy's character, his spirituality and unfailing kindness. And anyone who credited that story simply doesn't know how skilled musicians hear. Once I was sitting in Jim and Andy's with Marion Evans, the arranger, when a Les Brown record came on the jukebox. There was a particular smoky sound in the brass that the band occasionally used. I mused vaguely that I wondered what it was. Marion said, "Trumpets voiced in thirds, with trombones doubling it an octave down," and he told me what mutes they were using. He'd never heard the record before. Another time I was at the rehearsal of a large orchestra in Los Angeles, as they prepared to perform Alfred Newman's score for *Captain from Castille* at a concert. There is a particular chord in that music that has always caught my ear, and I expressed my curiosity about it to Dave Raksin, who was standing near me. Dave told what the chord was, its inversion, and spelled it all the way up, including what instruments were on the parts. During World War II, Robert Farnon used to listen to short-wave radio from the U.S., to get the latest pop tunes. He'd write them down as fast as they went by, line and changes. I don't hear that well, but I know any number of people who do. The ears of Billy Byers are legendary. So there was no way that, in those early days of bebop, people like Mel Powell or Eddie Sauter or Ray Conniff—any number of people—could be baffled about what was going down on the bandstand at Minton's. In any case, art is never created out of such petty motivations. And if Bird and Dizzy actually didn't want the "white boys" to know what they were doing, why did they so generously show it to people like Stan Levey, Red Rodney, Teddy Kotick, and Al Haig, and hire them to play with them? I hardly ever remember a time when Dizzy didn't have someone white in his group, whether it was Phil Woods in the mid-1950s or, later on, Lalo Schifrin or Mike Longo on piano.

By all reports, Johnny Carisi was always welcome on that Minton's bandstand, because he knew the tunes. If anything—and this was always true in jazz—the idea was to blow anybody off the bandstand who couldn't keep up. One of the men they consistently stomped on was a black tenor player. Dizzy called him the original freedom player—free of melody, free of harmony, and free of time.

Those rhythmic displacements on the first bop records—those starts and stops in funny places in the bar structure, so exciting and surprising finally, weren't what I was used to, and when what Bird and Dizzy were doing began to make sense to me, it was a revelation. My God, such fresh and inventive musical minds.

I FIRST KNEW Dizzy in 1959, or maybe 1960. I was putting together an article for *Down Beat* that in time took the title *The Years with Yard*. Charlie Parker's nickname was, of course, Yardbird, ultimately shortened by most people to Bird. But I have always heard Dizzy refer to him as Charlie Parker, the name in full, or, sometimes, Yard. Dizzy was playing Minneapolis at the time, and I went up there from Chicago with my photographer friend Ted Williams to take the notes and the pictures for the article that would appear over Dizzy's byline. For some reason now forgotten, we were to meet him in a little park somewhere. As Ted and I approached, we paused to watch him for a minute. Lost in some musical thought, Dizzy was softly dancing, all alone there in the sunlight. I never forgot it; it was one of the most poetic things I have ever seen.

I asked Dizzy about his humor on the bandstand, the jokes, the gestures. He said that if he could do anything to set a sympathetic mood in an audience, for his music, he would do it, and if humor would accomplish that end, he had no intention of giving it up. Even then he was announcing that he would like to introduce the members of his group after which he introduced them all to each other. He still does it. It still gets laughs. But sometimes the humor is quite spontaneous.

Once in the 1970s, he appeared in Los Angeles on a bill with Carmen McRae at a hotel that had decided to "try" a jazz policy. Everything went wrong. The sound system was poor, the piano was out of tune. Partway through Carmen's opening half of the concert, the pedals fell off the piano, and her accompanist was thereafter unable to move well through the chords in her ballads. Dizzy grabbed his horn and rushed on-stage to help her, filling the spaces in her phrases. Intermission came. A crew set up the bandstand for Dizzy's half of the performance.

His microphone stand was high, to pick up the sound of his uptilted horn. But whoever had put it there had left the cord spiralled around the stand.

Dizzy came out and looked at it. He shares with the late Jack Benny a curious ability to walk onto a stage and stand there doing absolutely nothing and somehow making the audience laugh. He pretended, as is his wont, that he was unaware that they were there as he examined the problem of the microphone stand. He set his horn on the stage, standing on its bell, its body tilted at a forty-five-degree angle. And he studied that mike stand and the cord coiled around it from several angles. The audience had begun to giggle softly. Suddenly he picked it up, held the weighted foot of the stand high in the air, and spun it, so that the cord uncoiled itself. The audience exploded in laughter, and at that point Dizzy affected surprise, as if taken aback by the discovery that he was not alone in the room. He took the mike off the stand, and looked back and forth in mock shock, and then said, "It is twenty years since Charlie Parker and I played Los Angeles." Pause. "It still ain't shit."

The laughter became a roar.

A few years ago, Dizzy changed his embouchure, and now he gets a bigger, fatter tone than he used to. It has acquired a rather velvety quality. I think he paces himself. I doubt that, at seventy-two, he could sustain entire evenings of blazing solos as he did in the late 1940s in front of his big band. But he knows how to handle it.

Someone pointed out to me a while ago that many, perhaps most, of the earlier generation of jazz trumpeters and some of the trombone players sang. Louis Armstrong, Red Allen, Hot Lips Page, Ray Nance, Jack Teagarden, and others would do occasional vocal choruses. Clark Terry still does. Partly it was because they were of a generation that considered they were in show business, they were there to entertain. But I suspect they did it as well as a way to rest their chops. I heard Dizzy in a university concert in Chicago a year or two ago. He played superbly. And then he did two numbers in which he didn't play at all. He clowned a little, and sang—one of the numbers being, inevitably, "Swing Low, Sweet Cadillac." And then he went into the closing number, a long burning solo at a fast tempo. He was at the absolute peak of his form, full of surprises, simple melodic phrases alternating with those cascades of notes. And I concluded he had sung those two tunes to give his lip time to rest up for this finale.

He is, aside from being one of the major figures in modern musical history, a very shrewd showman.

THE FIRST DAY of the session was devoted to setting up the sound and the cameras. The musicians ran the material down. Phil Woods had been engaged for the session, but he was on his way back from Europe and Jerry Dodgion subbed for him. The material Benny had written was tough, and Creed realized it was going to be hard on Art Farmer's lip. He wanted Art more for his solo value than as a lead player, and set Amy Landon, his assistant, to checking on several potential players to ease Art's burden. There is a softness about Creed that causes him to be very reserved, as if to protect himself from the importuning world; I once took it for coldness. I was wrong.

The summer of 1989 was viciously hot in the northern east coast United States. It rained every second day, at most every third day, and the humidity between rains was almost unendurable, particularly in Manhattan. Those powerful television lights completely overcame the air conditioning in Rudy's studio and turned it into a sauna.

We were all drained at the end of the day, when I rode back to the Omni Park hotel—where Creed had put most of us up—with Airto Moreira and his wife, Flora Purim. Flora reminded me of something: that when she and Airto arrived in New York from Brazil in the mid-1960s, they stayed in my apartment for a week or so until they found a place of their own. I had completely forgotten about it.

The van crossed the George Washington Bridge. The buildings of Manhattan receded to the south in layers of aerial perspective, at last to disappear in the pale humidity.

Airto said, "We were in Europe for two weeks at Ronnie Scott's club with our band, every night, two sets, very late—we would start at 10:45 P.M., first set, second set one o'clock to two something. We did that for two weeks, then we went all over Europe for almost three weeks with Dizzy Gillespie and an all-star United Nations band. So it was pretty heavy: flying every day, waking up at 6:30 in the morning, going to the airport, the plane leaves at nine, baggage outside the room at six o'clock. Got my luggage stolen, two big bags."

Flora said, "It was great working with Dizzy. Dizzy is one of the greatest teachers, without teaching you. He shows you ways of handling life. When he goes onstage, and the music changes, it's so easy, so humorous. Everything is a laugh, it's fun, and if it's not fun, he doesn't want to do it. He's been a big inspiration to us lately. The last year, we've been working on and off with him.

"We're losing a lot of players who are the center, and Dizzy Gillespie is one of the last of them. If Dizzy hadn't come up with his bebop, we wouldn't be here."

Airto said, "He made the fusion of Latin music and jazz. He was the first one who understood it and tried to play with those guys, and did it."

"He's still doing it," Flora said. "Dizzy is still behind the fusion of Latin and jazz music."

Airto said, "He just blew our minds on the road for three weeks in Europe. Flying every day, as I said. We were so tired, we couldn't even rehearse the sound any more. Dizzy would just come in and play, and then everybody felt good, and thinking if this man is playing like this, at least we should play *something*. And very strong. I don't know how he does that, at seventy-two."

Flora said, "His energy level is very high, and what he stands behind is very strong, even though he's very shy to say it. We've done some interviews together, and sometimes people would ask him why he was still doing it, and he would come off with things like, 'For the money.' Which is not true. He doesn't need the money at all. He's a rich man."

"He's made some good money," Airto said.

"He's there," Flora said, "because this is life. This is life to him, and to us. There are different kinds of musicians. There are musicians who make their livelihood emotionally, not just financially. I believe Dizzy is one of them. Art Blakey is another one of them. We look up to them as examples."

THE NEXT MORNING, I rode out to Rudy's with Phil Woods, who'd just got in, and was weary. In Paris, he and Dizzy and a number of other American jazz musicians had been honored by the government of France. Phil's wife, Jill Goodwin—she's the sister of Bill Goodwin, Phil's drummer; and they are the children of announcer Bill Goodwin, whom older readers will remember from the network radio days—said to me once, "Phil's angry at all the right things." It's a remarkably apt description.

Phil said: "Just come back from Paris where François Mitterand presented Milt Jackson, myself, Stan Getz, Jackie McLean, Percy Heath with medals, made us *Officers* of the Order of Arts and Letters, which is one step above the *Chevalier*, and Dizzy had already been named Chevalier and Officer, so he was named Commandant. It was neat, man. Danielle, the president's wife, a lovely lady, came to two concerts. Some cats were saying that she understood the changes, she was singing along. She loves 'A Night in Tunisia' and all that stuff.

"I was trying to relate that to my country, Bush coming up with a polka band or something.

"But how wild. You go to France and they recognize American jazz. It was kind of neat. I'll show you the medal." He pulled it out, displaying it in its velvet-lined case. "I wore it all the way home on the plane. It didn't impress customs at all. Isn't that something? I got a lot of salutes from the police in France. It helps with your parking tickets. This and two dollars will get you a beer at Jim and Andy's. It's amazing, isn't it, how other cultures accept our music so readily, and here, it's hard to get arrested?"

"Where did you first meet Dizzy?" I asked.

"I met Dizzy in 1956, when we did a State Department tour, first stop Abadan, Iran; next stop Aleppo, Syria; Damascus, Bayreuth. All the trouble spots, all the places that are now on fire, the State Department sent Dizzy. I think if they'd sent him one more time, he could have cooled it all out. But obviously the State Department knew something. That's what always bugs me. When there's trouble in the world, our government recognizes jazz. But the rest of the time, we have troubles with the subsidies and all that. We get the roach, what's left over. The National Endowment for the Arts disseminates huge amounts of money. A category called Folk, Ethnic, and Jazz, splits about ten or twenty million—a pittance. Most of the money goes for blue-haired ladies listening to Mahler, conducted by some cat from Israel or somewhere else. You go to France and they give you medals, and wine, and dine you, and treat you like an artist.

"I was with Dizzy for the Mideast tour, and then South America. I had known Dizzy before, but only peripherally. When you work with him, you get to know him. But going to Iran first, that was a killer. And they loved the music. They didn't understand the jazz part, but Dizzy has such an important thing. The rhythm, that grabs people immediately. If you don't know anything about bebop. Dizzy is such a master of rhythm, the Afro, the South American. He was the first cat to fuse the jazz and the Cuban and the South American. Dizzy is the cat who discovered that, the first cat who used conga drums and all that, with Chano Pozo. That's a real big contribution of Diz, which is sometimes overlooked—not by musicians, of course. A lot of people know about the bebop part, but not the rhythm. He loves to play drums.

"When we were in the Mideast, he was out there playing with snake charmers. He'll sit in anywhere—Carnival in Rio, any drummer, any rhythm. He has an uncanny ability to memorize it or feel exactly what they're doing, and then fitting it into the jazz mode, without prostituting either one of them. He's a rhythmic genius.

"That stick he carries—did you ever see that, that thing he made out of a stick and Coca-Cola bottle caps?"

"Yes, I have. In fact, I suggested to Creed that he use it as a visual motif. He called Dizzy, and Dizzy had lost it, so Creed had one made for him." There's no name for this instrument of Dizzy's invention. It is a pole with a rubber pad on the bottom. He mounted bottle caps on nails on a stick. He can stand in a room and bounce that thing and kick it with his toe and stomp a beat with his foot or shake this thing in the air, setting up the damnedest swing you ever heard, all by himself. I just call it Dizzy's rhythm stick.

Phil said, "I once flew back with him on the Concorde. When you travel with Dizzy, it's incredible. He was carrying that stick, right through the metal detector at the airport. The detector flips out with a hundred Coca-Cola caps rattling. And all the control people cheer and applaud: here comes Dizzy with that silly thing! The big stick. He plays it all the way through the airport; you can hear him come a mile away. He gets away with it."

"There was a time," I said, "when we all thought nobody in other countries could play jazz, but not any more."

"No no," Phil said. "That's no longer true at all."

I reminded him of the group he once led, during his long residence in France, called The European Rhythm Machine.

He said, "We used to call it the European Washing Machine. The cleanest band in the West. Look at the people you've got today. Niels-Henning Ørsted Pedersen. All the way back to Django Reinhardt, Grappelli, René Thomas, Daniel Humair. The list is long. They used to say that the horn players were okay, but the line went that the drummers didn't swing, the rhythm sections were inferior to ours. That's no longer the case. It's all over now. There are some Japanese bands that sound great. There's a cat in Japan who copies Miles so closely that when Miles fired his piano player, he fired *his* piano player in Japan. And the jazz clubs of Russia are flourishing."

A few days before this, the crackdown on the Tiananmen Square protesters had begun, and the executions were under way. Phil said, "We were supposed to go to China, but I told my agent to cancel the tour—and I'd love to go to China. My band is a natural since we don't use microphones. We're not a fusion band. We play Porter, Gershwin, and what have you. But for the moment I think we'll hold back on that. That's about the only country I've missed."

WE REACHED RUDY'S. Phil and Art Farmer embraced. Art told us a story. Some years ago, late at night, Grady Tate had left Baron's in Harlem. As he was getting into his car, a man pointed a gun at him and demanded his money. Grady emptied his wallet and handed the money over. The man said, "Hey, ain't you Grady Tate?"

Grady admitted that he was.

The holdup man said, "Hey, I've got all your classics."

Grady said, "I've got a new album. I've got some in the back. I'll give you some."

The man said, "No, that's cool, man. I'll buy my own."

Phil and Art and Benny and the others went into the studio and began to rehearse. The tenor player was Bob Berg, from Brooklyn. His playing was hot, hard, and beautiful. Flora and the band rehearsed a complex piece by Gilberto Gil called "Quilombo," which called for her to spit out the words at incredible speed and make them swing. She did it, too, and I was astonished by her. Astonished, too, by how much she had grown since Creed and I first heard her in the 1960s. Airto was cooking all over his complex of rhythm instruments, some of which he invented, working closely with Tito Puente. Airto's beard is now flecked with gray; Tito's full head of curly hair is now white. I talked to him during the lunch break, as most of the musicians and the crew gathered at trestle tables in the shadows of trees to consume the catered food Creed had laid on for them. Though Tito speaks fluent Spanish, his English is without accent—or rather, it is that of New York City.

"When I went to Juilliard," Tito said, as leaf-shadows made by a hazy sun played on his handsome face, "I came from the navy. I was in the navy during the war. They paid for the lessons. I went to study arranging and composition and conducting—not percussion. Nothing to do with Latin music. I went to the old school, the one that was on Manhattan Avenue at 124th Street.

"I studied trap drumming when I was seven years old. In the neighborhood in which I lived, in Spanish Harlem, there was a band that I used to sit in with, and a man named Montecino, who is still alive, showed me how to play the timbales. I already had the execution of the drumming, and that helped me to get into the timbales, which I'm very happy I did now.

"Dizzy was probably the first one to bring the Latin rhythms into jazz—with Chano Pozo. That was '46 or '47. His was the first big jazz orchestra to really utilize these Latin rhythms. Then after that we had Stan Kenton and Duke Ellington, and Woody Herman. I wrote some charts for Woody Herman and we did an album together. I've known Dizzy forty years or more—not longer than Mario Bauza, of course.

"The band that really started what we now call Latin jazz was the great Machito, who passed away about five years ago. He developed the influences of Cuba, Haiti, Santo Domingo, Puerto Rico, and Brazil.

"I grew up with a lot of drummers around me in Spanish Harlem. That's where I learned a lot about the rhythms, thanks to Machito—he was my mentor—and Mario Bauza, who is still around today and is one of the greatest maestros of our music and knows everything about the Cuban music. He's responsible for a lot of our music being played today."

Mario Bauza plays a significant role in the life of Dizzy Gillespie. Born in Havana in 1911, he is one of the many refutations of the idea that jazz and classical music have always been separate and unrelated streams. He played bass clarinet in the Havana Symphony Orchestra, and then, after moving to the United States, played trumpet with Chick Webb, Don Redman, and Cab Calloway. It was Bauza who brought Dizzy into the Cab Calloway band, where his national reputation began to catch hold. That was in 1939, a year before Dizzy met Charlie Parker in Kansas City, and we may assume that Dizzy, then twenty-two, was introduced to the rhythms of Caribbean music at least that far back.

Later that afternoon, during a break, I heard Romero Lubambo, an excellent young guitarist from Brazil, talking to one of the camera crew. He is tall, with a full face and sandy hair. He said, "The whole time I was in Brazil, I liked to listen to American musicians to learn how to improvise, how to play jazz. Now I am playing with the greatest musicians in the world, I think. For me it is fantastic. We used a lot of the American know-how of doing jazz improvising. What I did in Brazil, and what I am doing here, is playing Brazilian music together with the American. For me it is very close, American and Brazilian. Jazz is very influential in Brazilian music and vice versa.

"Until thirty years ago, we didn't have many improvising in Brazilian music. I'm not so old, but it was singing. But not with many improvisations, and then we borrowed the jazz know-how. This is from what I understand.

"Dizzy through his seventy-something years made everybody be happy when they heard his name. Everybody here is happy already, to see him tomorrow. Everybody is looking forward to seeing him laughing and playing, always great. It's nice."

AT NEWARK AIRPORT the next morning, I waited. Dizzy was playing an engagement in Washington, and flying in for one afternoon of this three-day recording. I was thinking about Dizzy's essential character, about the title of one of his finest tunes, "Con Alma," which is Spanish, meaning with feeling or with soul. It is a wonderfully appropriate title for a tune by Dizzy.

How did this boy, with that curiously elegant natal name John Birks Gillespie, son of a father who abused and beat him in his childhood, who grew up in a society that committed unspeakable acts of racism all around him, and many of them upon him and on his friend Charlie Parker, grow up to be so loving? It has always seemed to me a triumph of the human spirit that anyone born black in America can even bear the company of white people, and for Dizzy, who years ago took up the B'hai religion, to have such love for his fellow man amounts to a miracle. It is not that he is unmindful of the abuses of his people. But he has found laughter even in that. Lalo Schifrin, who was his pianist in the early 1960s, told me of walking up a street with Dizzy in Glasgow or Edinburgh. Occasionally, affecting that very proper English he can turn on or off at will, he would stop someone on the street and say, "Pardon me, my name is Gillespie, and I'm looking for my relatives." He would leave some baffled Scot looking after him as Lalo fell apart with laughter.

His antic humor has been part of his life apparently since he was very young. It dates at least as far back as his early twenties, when he was working in a band in Philadelphia, because someone there named him Dizzy. He no longer remembers who put the name on him, "but," he says, "I'm glad he did." I first heard of him when he got fired from the Cab Calloway band, purportedly for firing spitballs at Cab. But that not only illuminates his life off-stage: it is used very shrewdly on-stage. One of my most vivid memories is of an incident in which his laughter, his clowning, his shrewd showmanship, and above all his kindness, came together on a stage in Canada.

It happened this way.

I was asked to do an evening of my songs at one of a series of concerts sponsored by the Canadian Broadcasting Corporation at a place called Camp Fortune in the Gatineau Hills, outside Ottawa. I was told I could use a large orchestra, which meant arrangements had to be written. I chose Chico O'Farrill to write them, because I love his work, and we were neighbors and friends. When Chico agreed to do the concert, the producer, Peter Shaw, asked him to perform his *Aztec Suite*. It had been written for and recorded by Art Farmer. Peter asked us to track Art down and ask if he would join us in the concert, but Art had moved to Europe and we had trouble finding him. Chico said, "How about Dizzy?"

And I said, "Why not? We can always ask him."

We called Dizzy and he agreed to do it—which meant that he had to read and learn a by no means simple piece of music in one or two rehearsals. But this presented me with a problem. I am essentially a writer, not a performer. Performance takes certain highly honed skills that I lack. And there is no more brilliant *performer*, questions of music aside, than Dizzy. I told Peter, "There is absolutely no way I'm going to follow Dizzy Gillespie on a stage. I'll open; he can close." But, Peter suggested, this would set up an imbalance. So Chico and I wrote a new song, in long form, that we could do with Dizzy as a closer.

Dizzy, as it happened, got delayed by weather in St. Louis and missed the first rehearsal. Chico rehearsed the orchestra, with Mike Renzi playing the trumpet part in transposition on the piano, no mean feat in itself. Dizzy got there in time for the final rehearsal, and seemed to be memorizing the *Aztec Suite* as fast as he was reading. That was the afternoon I came to appreciate his consummate musicianship, questions of jazz quite apart.

Well, the evening came, and terrified or not, I sang my half of the concert, apparently not disastrously. The audience was warm, and at the end I said something to the effect that I had never before sung my lyrics in the country in which I was born, and I was very glad to be there. Then I said something like, "Now, ladies and gentleman, it is my privilege to introduce one of the great musicians of our time, Mr. Dizzy Gillespie."

Birks came out on the stage, looking (as is his wont) as if he was startled to find people there—and there were five or ten thousand of them, I would guess, blanketing the hillside of a natural amphitheater in front of the stage. He took the mike from the stand, gave a long Jack Benny pause, and said,

"Damn! I'm glad I'm a Canadian!" The audience roared, and as usual he had them in his hand before he'd played a note. And then he and Chico and the orchestra sailed into the *Aztec Suite*.

He played brilliantly—this piece he had never played before. There is a gesture he has, a motion, that always reminds me of a great batter leaning into a hit. He has a way of throwing one foot forward, putting his head down a bit as he silently runs the valves, and then the cheeks bloom out in the way that has mystified his dentist for years, and he hits into the solo. When that foot goes forward like that, you know that John Birks Gillespie is no longer clowning. Stand back.

And that foot went forward a lot that night. At the end of the suite, the audience went crazy. They were screaming. Backstage I said to Peter Shaw, "I'm not going out into that. I'm not that nuts."

But Chico and the orchestra and Dizzy were setting up for the number I was to do with them. Now Dizzy's part was a long one, written out on accordion-folded music paper. He started to put it on his music stand—and dropped it. It spilled at his feet, and the audience tittered a little. Setting his horn down on his bell, he got down on his knees and started to fold it, like a man trying to put a road-map back the way he found it. When he had it neatly together, he stood up; and dropped it a second time. He did this three times, until Chico and the orchestra and the audience and I were helpless with laughter and the mood at the end of the *Aztec Suite* had faded into the past. he let the laughter die down. And then he introduced me. He handed that audience to me. I couldn't believe the generosity of this; or the cleverness, the canny sense of show.

And we finished the concert and went to a party. It was probably that night that he told me he had never in his life walked onto a stage without feeling at least a little nervous, and that humor helped to break the feeling.

I got thinking about the last time I'd seen Birks. We'd been guests on one of Steve Allen's TV shows in Los Angeles. Three of these shows were shot that day. We were on the first of them, and one guest on the second show was to be Doc Severinsen. Dizzy said he wanted to stick around after we'd finished and hear Doc play. One of the girls in makeup heard him say it, and passed it along to Doc. I heard Doc reply, "Oh boy! That's all I *need*—Dizzy Gillespie listening to me." A little later he came to our dressing room, and Dizzy greeted him warmly, and they fell immediately into the camaraderie of men in the same profession. They didn't talk about music. They talked about lip salves and medications. Birks said, "I've got something great! Freddy Hubbard turned me onto it." He opened his trumpet case and gave a small package to Doc. "Try it," he said.

It came time for Doc to do his show. Dizzy stood in the shadows, listening. Doc played with a small group. There were none of the high notes, none of the flourishes, you hear during his usual television appearances. He played a ballad, mostly in the middle register, the notes sparse and thoughtfully selected. He sounded a lot like, of all people, Bix Beiderbecke. "He's beautiful," Dizzy said, and if Doc in the spotlight had been able to see the smile of John Birks Gillespie in the shadows, he would have felt compensated for all the dismissals of his jazz playing by critics.

I have a very deep love for Dizzy Gillespie. He has contributed immeasurable joy to our troubled era. And to me, he has contributed insight.

THESE THOUGHTS WERE in my mind as he got off the plane, carrying the big, square, black case that accommodates his idiosyncratic trumpet, and wearing sandals and a short-sleeved safari jacket.

He grinned, greeted the driver of the van, and our cameraman and sound technician, and got into the back seat. I was in the front seat, leaning over its back, and I suddenly had a wave of emotion. "Hey, Birks," I said, "I'm awful glad to see you."

He went serious. He tapped the middle of his chest, indicating his heart. His goatee is gray now, and so is his head. He said, "Me . . . too!"

I told him Creed had ordered a new version of his rhythm stick made for him; Dizzy had misplaced the last one, made with pop-bottle caps. This one was de luxe: made not with bottle caps but the tiny cymbals you find in tambourines. I said it was at the studio, waiting for him. "Where'd you find that thing originally?" I said.

"I made the first one," he said, and I remembered the first time I'd seen it. He demonstrated it to Jerome Richardson and me, and we were astonished at the polyrhythms he could set up with it. "I made two or three after that." He chuckled. His voice is low and a little thick in its texture, with a touch of the south in its accent. He is one jazz musician whose speech is not like his playing; in fact they are radically different. "That stick was something. I could be at one end of the airport and be walking with that stick, and all the guys knew where I was, from the rattle. Every now and then I would do it, and they'd know where to find me."

I said, "Everybody I've talked to, Phil Woods, Benny Golson, Art Farmer, said you have always been the great teacher. I remember Nat Adderley said once, 'Dizzy's the greatest teacher in the world if you don't let him know he's doing it.'"

"Is that true? I don't know about that," he said, and I saw that embarrassment Benny Golson had described. This was no affectation of modesty; this was genuine humility. "But what little I do know, I'll give it, any time. So I guess it's not actually someone with a whole lot of knowledge giving it out to people. But anything I learned, I'll tell somebody else. So that's what they mean by that. I will tell anything that I've learned."

"Miles said to me once, 'I got it all from Dizzy.' Art Farmer said that you came in to hear him one night and he realized that everything he was playing, he'd learned from you."

"That's a good question, about those guys. One example is Art Farmer," he said, trying to steer the conversation away from himself. "I made a record with Duke, a Duke Ellington party. I wasn't called to make the record, but I just went by the record date to see all the guys in the band I hadn't seen in some time. And when I walked in, Duke pulled out this *U.M.M.G.,* and said, 'I want you to try this.' So he gave me the part and they played it. And then Strayhorn was there. Strayhorn had to show me a couple of things. There were some very big surprises in that number—the resolutions at certain parts. Out of a clear blue sky, boom! A-flat minor seventh. And how it got there, you don't know. So Strayhorn came over to the piano and showed me and then I didn't have any trouble.

"But Art Farmer!" The sound of South Carolina was in the way he said it: Aht Fahmuh. Driving in South Carolina two or three years ago, I was slightly startled by a sign on the highway that indicated the direction to Cheraw. It looked so matter of fact. I vaguely thought it should say under the name: birthplace of John Birks Gillespie. "Boy!" Dizzy said. "I heard Art Farmer do it. I just happened to have the radio on, and boy! This guy! He must have spent some time on this number, because he knew every in and out of the progressions, he knew all of the resolutions. Boy, he really operated on that. Like a surgeon. Art Farmer is some fantastic musician. He's so pretty. Some guys can play all the changes, and you don't get the significance of the resolutions going from one to the other. But Art Farmer, he's so gentle. Just beautiful. I'm sorry I made the number. But if I hadn't made the number, Art wouldn't have made it, because he liked the record I made with Duke, and he said, 'I want some of that,' and he went and got it.

"Art Farmer. Nat Adderley. There's some good trumpet players around. I think there are more than in the early days. Because we had a hard core of young trumpet players, like Charlie Shavers, Kenny Dorham, Fats Navarro, and of course Miles is in there and, let's see—Dud Bascomb. He was a very tasty trumpet player. We used to talk when I was at the Savoy with Teddy Hill's band and Dud was with Erskine Hawkins. We used to say, 'Man! I wonder what it would be to be with someone like Duke Ellington and Cab Calloway.' And he wound up with Duke Ellington and I went with Cab Calloway. So we got two of the best jobs in New York. But that Dud Bascomb!

"And then there was a trumpet player named Little Willie, who played with Buddy Johnson. He was very talented, too. He didn't get a chance to play too much on records."

"Birks, I want to talk to you about the Caribbean, and the Afro-Cuban, and the Brazilian. It's like Phil Woods and others say, you were the first jazz musician to get into that music, to combine jazz with these various Latin influences."

"And I'll tell you something," Dizzy said, "the Latin guys play jazz better than the jazz guys play Latin." That was something to think about.

He said, "I was always interested in that music. All of my compositions have a Latin tinge. Every one of them. And that means that I am a lover of Latin music. I remember the first time I went to Argentina, I composed a piece that sounded like their music, called *Tango-rene*. I recorded it with the big band. That was a nice trip. I like Argentina very much.

"This year I was in Budapest. In my hotel they had a gypsy band, with a guy who played violin. He was *bad*, boy. I was supposed to come back after our performance in the theater and play a little bit with them. But that's where the tango comes from—that area of the gypsies.

"Which reminds me of a time in Africa. I went to Kenya for the State Department for the tenth anniversary of independence for Kenya. They took me to a dance one night. And I heard these guys playing. And I closed my eyes, and it sounded like calypso, the West Indian guys. So when the musicians asked me how I liked the music, I said, 'To tell you the truth, it sounded very similar to West Indian music.' And one of the guys, he say, 'You know, *we* were here first!' I said, 'Thank you very much.'" And he laughed at the memory.

I asked him what caused that immediate affinity between them when he first heard Charlie Parker in Kansas City, during his time with Cab Calloway.

"The method and music impressed me, the more I heard him play. Because it was so much the way that I thought music should go. His style! The style! Was perfect for our music. I was playing like Roy Eldridge at the time. In about a month's time, I was playing like Charlie Parker. From then on—maybe adding a little here and there. But Charlie Parker was the most fantastic . . . I don't know. You know, he used to do tunes inside of tunes. He'd be playing something and all of a sudden you'd hear 'I'm in the Mood for Love' for four bars. Or two bars. Lorraine told me one time, 'Why don't you play like Charlie Parker?' I said, 'Well that's Charlie Parker's style. And I'm not a copyist of someone else's music.' But he was the most fantastic musician."

WHEN WE GOT to Rudy van Gelder's, the camera crew asked Dizzy to wait a few minutes so they could get shots of his arrival. He waited a little, then began to get impatient. He said he wanted to get out and warm up his lip. He waited some more, finally got out, and went directly into the studio, where Benny Golson was rehearsing one of the numbers Dizzy was to record. Everything stopped, and the mood in the place became reverent. Various of the musicians shook his hand, or hugged him, and he wore that great embracing grin. Art Farmer beamed; his hair too is gray now. Phil Woods, in a red polo shirt and a small leather cap, grinned, and shook hands: "Sky King," he said. It's his nickname for Dizzy, because he is always in an airplane, going from one gig to another. In fact, though he lived only a short walk from this studio, he wouldn't even have time to go home to see his wife Lorraine before flying back to Washington later today.

"Hey!" Dizzy said, when he saw the rhythm stick Creed had had made for him. "Beautiful!" And he gave it a few experimental shakes.

He left the studio, went out to one of the trailers that were standing by, took out his horn, and began to practice. After a while he came back, and the recording began. Dizzy played on two tunes, both Latin, and both rhythmically powerful. In each case he mastered the material quickly, and soared off into solos, the notes cascading down from his horn. The takes were interrupted repeatedly. What began to be apparent is that the compound rhythms weren't bothering Dizzy, but the polyrhythms he was piling on top of them were bothering the band. One tune, "Wamba," kept breaking down at the same point, and Benny Golson, in a red shirt, would start it again. Dizzy's every solo was totally fresh, unrelated in any way to his solos in the previous takes. The studio grew hotter. Dizzy opened the safari jacket and played barechested, always with that uncanny concentration he brings to bear.

The rhythm . . . the rhythm!

I was in the booth with Creed and Rudy; I couldn't bear the heat of the studio, and didn't know how the musicians were doing so. Dizzy kept playing. "That man is a miracle of neurological organization," I said to Creed.

"That's a good way to put it," Creed said.

The tune kept breaking down; I kept looking at the clock. This was the last day of shooting, with that one camera alone at $27,000 a day. . . . And Dizzy had to return late in the afternoon to Washington. There could be no extensions of the date. The suspense was getting to me. Creed showed nothing; not a flicker of anxiety. He is always like that. I don't know how he does it. Maybe the training in psychology . . .

And at last it was over. Dizzy did his two brilliant takes. The musicians applauded. Creed went into the studio to thank him. Dizzy packed up his horn. A limousine took him back to the airport.

I said to Creed, who is never ever demonstrative, "Well, are you happy?"

"No," he said with a trace of a smile. "I'm ecstatic."

All the musicians were packing up. Soon the studio was empty. Across a chair lay Dizzy's rhythm stick, the new one Creed had had made, and that Dizzy loved. Creed planned to send it over to his house, a minor gift. The light from above flooded the stick, Dizzy's music stand, and the microphone, set high for his uptilted horn. It was as if the ghost of this colossus were still there.

THROUGHOUT THOSE DAYS, I was forcefully struck by the diversity of America that is represented in jazz. When I was a teen-ager, listening to bands and dazzled by the solos of Ray Nance, Cootie Williams, and so many others, some of them—Zoot Sims, for example—not much older than I, I wondered if this music was just a job to them, one that got boring from doing it night after night, or if it was a genuine passion.

I learned very early that it is the latter.

Charlie Haden said it as well as I have ever heard it expressed after the last session.

He said: "It's very rare in the recording industry for a producer to place such importance on creative values. Jazz, for so many years, has been treated as a tax write-off for most big record companies. And now, more and more, conglomerate corporations that are in the record business are just looking to sell many many records and make a lot of hits and a lot of money. Which is okay, but it's kind of sad that the art forms and the deeper values are forgotten about.

"That's sad for the jazz musician, and other artists dedicated to their art forms, film-making, poetry, dance, painting.

"I feel it is the responsibility of every one of us to improve the quality of life; to make this planet a better place; to bring deeper values back to the society, which are taken away from the people by the conditioning of mass media, of society's profit-oriented racist-sexist values. People are taught by the mass media what they should like, what they should wear, what they should listen to. And then they are sold these things.

"It's very sad that this music is put on the side, and not many people know about the importance of this art form we call jazz. And the other sad thing is that whenever someone has an opportunity to educate people in film about this art form, they always miss the mark. They never show the brilliance of improvisation and what it really is. They show a romantic story, or a story about drugs, or a story about alcohol, or the perennial image of the jazz musician as a child who hasn't grown up; who cares only about sex and alcohol and drugs and music, and really doesn't have any feelings or opinions or ideas or interests about any other things in life. Which is very sad, because it's not true.

"I think that Creed has done a great thing here, by making this record and also making it a video, so that people can see what we're all about, and what we love, and why we're doing what we're doing: we're actually fulfilling a calling to a responsibility to the universe. And that is to make beautiful music, and bring beauty and deeper values to people's lives, so that they can touch the deeper parts inside themselves. And there will be more of us.

"If the leaders of all the countries of the world were able to sit down and think about these things and to bring this music and these values to the people of the world, there would be a different mentality. The governments of different countries would be concerned about life. They would have reverence for life, instead of placing importance on weapons.

"It's all included in this music, the beauty of all those things. Because improvisation teaches you the magic of being in the moment you're living in. You get a different perspective about life. And you see yourself in relation to the universe in a completely different way. There's no such thing as yesterday, there's no such thing as tomorrow. They're only right now, when you're improvising. The spontaneity is there. When you're touching music, you see your extreme unimportance.

"The reason it hasn't been given more to the public, there's no vested interest, there's no profit being made. Since the beginning of this country, if there's no profit being made, they won't give it to the people.

"That's why government subsidy is really difficult. In Europe, you have a lot of countries that subsidize jazz concerts and musicians. It doesn't happen in the United States and it's very sad. The only thing that is similar to subsidization is the National Endowment for the Arts, which isn't nearly enough.

"People should be able to turn on television and see beautiful music. If I were an alien from another planet, and I landed in Queens one night, and I walked to the nearest house and looked in the windows and I saw the kids sitting on the floor, looking at MTV, I would say to myself, 'My God, is this the best that this country's popular artists have? Are these the best values they have to give to their young people?'

"Values of sequins, limousines, wealth, perpetuated every day with the whole superstar structure of the music industry. And every time that you bring music with deep values to people, it touches somebody.

"It's the people who have corrupted the music that we have to worry about, that we have to try and change, and one of the ways of doing this is to just keep playing, and to present the music to as many people as possible, because the more people hear this music, the more people are going to be attracted to it.

"And, hopefully, more endeavors will happen like we just did, because it brings great musicians together who usually don't have a chance to play music with each other, and it allows them to feel comfortable and relaxed in improvisation. And, when music is presented on the same level that the music is played, that's the thing that's really meaningful. When it's presented on a level of reverence and respect.

"People have lost their appreciation for beauty. The great thing about this art form is that musicians care about beautiful sound. They want to make their instruments sound really really beautiful. It's so important, beautiful sound—to be able to hear the beauty of the musician's soul. Every musician . . . they learn their favorite notes, they discover their favorite notes, their favorite sound, and they make their music sound as beautiful as they can for the listener, and that's what makes it so great. It's a dedication and an honesty that you don't find very many places. Improvisation and spontaneity are about honesty. It's completely pure honesty. The musician is baring his soul to the people, and hoping he can touch their lives, in a humble way. Every great musician learns that before they can become a great musician, they have to become a good human being. That's the most important thing, to strive to be a good human being, and to have humility.

"It's like the guy in Washington a few years ago. In the middle of winter, an airliner crashed in the middle of the Potomac River. People were on their way home from work. A guy got out of his car. He saw a woman who got out of the aircraft and couldn't reach the lifeline that was being thrown to her. And he didn't think twice, he jumped into the river and rescued her, and disappeared. Finally someone found him, and said, 'What's your name?' And he said, 'It doesn't matter what my name is, I just did what I had to do.'

"And that's greatness to me."

I GOT UP early the next morning in the hotel and called Phil Woods. Phil and his wife had found me a house for the summer near their own. They live in Delaware Water Gap, Pennsylvania. We got into the car. Phil told me the best way was to go out through the Lincoln Tunnel. I hate the New York tunnels. They give me what Woody Herman used to call the clausters. I'm always afraid the roof is going to fall in and, New York being what it has become, probably some day it will. I wanted to go out over the George Washington Bridge.

Phil said the other route was faster. "Only take us an hour and twenty minutes or so."

"You sure?"

"Promise," he said.

But the whole West Side was tied up with traffic because President George Bush was coming to New York for some event or another. And when we got down in the tunnel, the traffic stopped completely.

"Hey, Phil, you promised me," I said.

"It'll be cool," he said.

At last it crawled forward. But hardly had we come out of the tunnel than it stopped cold again on the highway. People shut off their engines and got out and stood around on the cement. I asked a truck driver who had climbed to the roof of his cab to look ahead what was happening. "Ah the president's coming in or something," he said.

Of course. From Newark airport, where I'd picked up Dizzy the day before. The air was as hot and humid as ever. Phil and I stood around on the highway and told music business stories. We were there a half hour or so. The truck driver said, "Next time, I'm voting Democrat!"

And then, on a parallel highway, we saw it, the cavalcade of black limousines with dark glass, the one with the pennant identifying the president's car. How silly. To tie up this traffic like this. Why didn't they fly him in a helicopter to the Pan Am building? What was all this gasoline costing? I wondered if the man in that dark car would ever recognize the contribution of Dizzy Gillespie to the American culture; it seemed unlikely. And if he ever did, it would be for political reasons.

The traffic started moving again; we'd been on our way for an hour and a half. "Phil, you said an hour and twenty minutes!"

Inevitably, we talked more about Dizzy. "The Sky King," Phil said again.

I said, "I think his sense of humor lets him get away with things the rest of us wouldn't have the nerve to try."

"You know," Phil said, "he didn't do any clowning at all on this European trip. Occasionally he likes to do jokes and sing and scat. But when we did the All Star thing, which was Hank Jones, Max Roach, Stan Getz, Jackie McLean, Milt Jackson, boy was he playing. Because he knew he was with the musicians who grew up with him, and there was no funny business. He was alllll serious, man. Some European critics have said, Ah, Dizzy's chops are gone. I hope they were there that night." Phil whistled. "He was hitting high r's.

"Dizzy changed the way of the world. That music means so much to so many people everywhere."

Phil searched the radio dial until he found a jazz station. We heard a superb pianist whom we could not identify. It turned out to be Kenny Barron. The sky darkened. We were in a cloudburst. I slowed to about thirty miles an hour as the sheets of rain swept across the highway and all the crawling cars turned their headlights on. We'd been traveling now more than two and a half hours.

"Phil, you promised me!"

And the sun came out.

An Evening with Monk

Dan Morgenstern

Dan Morgenstern's valuable firsthand witness of Thelonious Monk was published originally in Jazz Journal *in 1960.*

It is perhaps a coincidence that one of Thelonious Monk's favorite tunes is a nineteenth-century Protestant hymn by a composer named William H. Monk. Not only the composer's name, but also the title of the piece, "Abide With Me," seems perfectly fitting for Thelonious. We suspect that Monk himself always knew what he was doing, or at least what he wanted to be able to do. The same can hardly be said for the world around him. Yet, there were always a few who did abide with Thelonious, and made it possible for him to go his own way.

Monk's way was no blind alley, no one-way street. But it was his own way, which in our time must be a hard way. How far he has traveled, and how much undiscovered beauty he has found along this way—that is something we can all hear now if we want to. But rarely could it be heard better, and more succinctly, than at a recent "retrospective" all-Monk concert in New York's Greenwich Village.

Jazz concerts are frequently a dubious proposition. It would not be an exaggeration to say that the Monk concert at a little off-Broadway theater called Circle in the Square was the first perfect jazz concert these ears have witnessed. The setting was unpretentious and informal, the people in attendance had come to hear music, and Monk and his companions wanted to play. The concert started late and ended early, yet no one could have wished for more. In two sets of six numbers, Thelonious Monk demonstrated with supreme authority his right to be numbered among the happy few: those who've "got their own," as the Lady who knew put it so well. We can't know what it cost Thelonious Monk to go his own way so uncompromisingly, but it was worth the price. To himself as well, we hope.

It is unwise to burden a jazz performance with the adjective "retrospective." All art is retrospective, insofar as past experience goes into the creation of it. But whilst it is possible to give a painter a retrospective show, since the painting is finished but remains, it is a different story with jazz. Jazz is captured in time only through the intervention of a machine, but the musician travels on. He cannot recreate, for himself or for others, what once was. So Thelonious Monk did not give his listeners the promised retrospective view of a quarter-century of musical activity. Instead, he gave us something much better. He gave us Thelonious Monk in 1960. Not retrospective, but full of that urgency of the here and now which is a special dimension of a jazz performance. Monk was out to show us not what he was but what he is.

The stage at Circle in the Square is the wooden floor, around which three sections of seats are raised. There were no garish spotlights, and the houselights were off. The atmosphere was neither formal nor sloppy. The performers were in full view, close enough to establish rapport but with no one breathing down their necks. There was a brief and unembellished introduction without "hard sell" or artiness, and then Thelonious Monk, piano, Charlie Rouse, tenor sax, Art Taylor, drums, and Ron Carter, bass, appeared and promptly settled down to business.

Monk has been called an eccentric *ad nauseam.* True, he is not like other people, even other jazz musicians. Yet much that has been labeled eccentricity is quite simply a way of being which seems to be the way Monk wants to be. Sunglasses with bamboo frames may look ridiculous on others but look just right on Monk, which may be why he wears them. There is nothing about Monk, who is a big man, which invites ridicule. You would not pick a fight with Monk if you met him in a bar. You might step aside if you saw him coming, because there is about him the air of a man who knows where he is going. He may not be on your time, but he knows what time it is. He is one of the few musicians of the generation labeled "modern" (what shall we call them in 1980?) who has that quality which Max Weber called *charisma.* It is hard to define this quality, but it can't be faked. It is, perhaps, of metaphysical significance, but it is strongly linked to physical presence. You wouldn't ask Monk for a light, but if he asks you for one, the completion of that brief ritual might well leave you with the feeling that there has been much more than superficial communication. By the same token, Monk always makes you feel that it is a privilege to attend his performances. Not that there is any haughtiness involved. It is just that you are made to know that while it may be nice to have an audience around, it isn't essential, and it's just your good luck that you are there and Monk is in the mood to play. Miles Davis doesn't always make you feel that way, but once he grows up he well might. Perhaps that is because Monk, underneath it all, has a warm and catching sense of humor. When he enjoys himself, he lets you know it, and makes you laugh with him. Never at him.

* * *

THERE MUST HAVE been times when people did laugh at Monk. Not in the beginning, perhaps. As Mary Lou Williams has told us (in *Hear Me Talkin' to Ya,* the best of all books on jazz), Monk played with plenty of technique when he first came around to jam in places like Kansas City. He came into town with "either an evangelist or a medicine show." That ain't Julliard or Berklee, but it is schooling. It was later, around 1939, when Monk used to sit down in Harlem after-hours places to play (by himself; with others he still comped their way) that some listeners pinned the label "zombie music" on his stuff, and called him "Mad Monk." As Teddy Hill has told us in the same book, Monk lived with his family at the time, and thus was able to be "undependable," that is, do what he wanted to do musically without worrying about pleasing the boss, or the customers, or the leader. What he played then, when Teddy Hill sometimes had to plead with him to leave so he could close up the place (named Minton's Playhouse), was very likely a crabbed, introspective, difficult kind of music. It certainly wasn't what Monk plays today. But it was necessary, and it already had the power to communicate as Dizzy Gillespie, Charlie Parker, Kenny Clarke, and Coleman Hawkins soon felt.

It was Hawk who hired Monk in 1944, to play in his band on 52nd Street, and people would ask Coleman why he didn't get rid of "that Chinese pianoplayer." But others dug Monk's language. Of those who could help his career it was first Hawk, then non-musicians like Blue Note owners Alfred Lion and Francis Wolf. And disc jockey Fred Robbins, on whose show we first heard Thelonious and muttered "What the hell is that?" but went out to buy the record and spent hours trying to figure out what the chords were. (We think it's "Somebody Loves Me," but won't bet. The other side, "Suburban Eyes," was easier. It's "All God's Children Got Rhythm.") Still, it took quite some time before night clubs would hire Monk, as a leader. Only a few years ago, at the Five Spot, did a club owner really create a happy environment for Monk to work in. Riverside Records have given Monk a great deal of freedom and many albums. Last year Monk did the Apollo, and there was the fancy thing at Town Hall. And last month the showcase at Circle in the Square. Yet, ironically, Monk, at the height of his popularity, is not able to work a club in New York because he has lost his cabaret card, that disgusting symbol of New York City's arbitrary police power over performing artists. But concerts they can't stop, and Monk's was a sellout.

About the music, then. There was the best of Monk's work in three categories: The ballads, the jump originals, and the essays on standards. In the first category, the lovely "Ruby, My Dear," one with Charlie Rouse showed that he has heard Monk's record with Hawkins; the first success, "'Round Midnight," the only Monk tune with lyrics—by Bernie Hanighen, of whom Billie spoke so well—played a little faster than usual, but haunting as ever; and

"Ask Me Now," on which Monk's one piano chorus was simplicity itself, and yet profoundly moving; all done with a shifting of the accents, like Louis does it, to bring out the natural beauty of the melody. And last but not least, "Crepuscule with Nellie," which is for Nellie Monk, his devoted wife, and which Monk now plays in a formalized version which, brief as it is, is wholly essential: One chorus of unaccompanied piano, not in strict time, but with that unique Monk accent which has an inner swing; then into time with the band coming in with a slow, flowing statement of the theme, under embellishments by Thelonious, and a chorded ending which seems to suspend rather than end the tune, leaving it to echo in the mind. With these slow tunes Monk creates and sustains a mood. It may be the nostalgic, restless longing of "Midnight," the yearning of "Ask Me Now," the warm breath of romance in "Ruby" or the affirmation of peace in "Nellie." All these moods are lyrical, and all are moods of love, and in each one of them not one note is superfluous or imperfectly placed. And they all sing.

The faster numbers Monk has composed are seemingly bare skeletons for improvisation. If you start counting notes, that is. They are phrases, riffs—angular, seemingly abrupt. Yet, when Monk plays them, they become melodies, and they flow. And they create a rhythmic and harmonic climate for the improviser which makes him play Monk's Music. Perhaps that is why some hornmen prefer to have Monk "lay out" behind them. They sound better when they don't. Monk is a disciplined musician, but he gives you plenty of freedom. That duality is one of the keys to good jazz, and one aspect of it is the sense of form. Monk's compositions are the perfect jazz compositions—not suites, or quartets, or sonatas, but short pieces which have definite melody, unique harmonic texture, implicit swing *and* are good to play. These are pieces like "Straight," "No Chaser" (the blues), "Well, You Needn't," "Bemsha Swing," and others that weren't played that night. "Blue Monk," a masterpiece, is just a blues and also an original composition.

In the third category, Monk like Duke, excels. Here he wrote the standard material of jazz. "In Walked Bud" is a variation on "Blue Skies." "Rhythm-a-ning" is "I Got Rhythm." They are also Monk.

Monk played that night. He raised his cohorts to greater heights than they straddle alone. Art Taylor kept perfect time and also got off his own things, which, being in a solid time-context, stood out very well. Carter, the bassist, was new to the group but knew the fundamentals of Monk's musical grammar and swung. Charlie Rouse is not among the leading tenors, but he is one of the most consistent, dependable, and musicianly of his generation. He played well with Tadd Dameron in the late forties, and he plays better today. His sound is not very big but well placed, his technical equipment excellent and his ear sure. He can swing. With Monk, he is better than a stronger individualist might be, because there is no conflict between his and

Monk's intentions. On the night of the concert, Rouse played with inspiration, especially on "'Round Midnight" and "Rhythm-a-ning." He has humor and sincerity. Sincerity, by the way, is a term often used as a pat on the back. We intend it to imply a devotion to musical ends and musical sense rather than naive innocence or lack of sophistication. Monk let Charlie Rouse carry the major part of the solo space, which is in accord with the role of a horn in jazz. It also enables Thelonious to frame his statements perfectly. There was never too much or too little, it was always climactic—it had perfect outer as well as inner balance.

Thelonious played the piano that night, as he is wont to, with his arms and elbows as well as his hands. The sound or "tone-cluster" he wants to get at times can only be created this way. It isn't a whim, but part of a method. When Monk plays, his whole body is involved. There is the characteristic movement of the feet, sometimes quite audible; the occasional finger-snapping, or movements hinting at dancing or boxing, including a Jimmy Cagneyish thumb-under-nose gesture. Sometimes the dance is more than hinted at; Monk gets up and does a few turns. That is either when he is really having a ball or when somebody is blowing hot air only. All concerned know which is which: that night Monk did a little time-step during Rouse's solo on "Rhythm-a-ning." Monk is one of the jazzmen who are fun to watch at work, which is something to think about. If a musician doesn't look good when he plays, chances are he won't sound too good. And if he looks funny, chances are he'll sound that way. The way a man approaches and handles his horn, and himself, will always reveal something about his music. Monk approaches a piano with the air of a man going to work (a work he enjoys) and he handles it as if he was saying: "You'd better behave now and do what I want or I won't come back until you are ready."

Thelonious Monk has reached a point in his musical development which enables him to communicate fully. There is in his work today a clarity and assurance which always has been a component of it but not until now a leading characteristic. The listener no longer wonders how Monk will extricate himself from a musical problem because the problem does not arise. The spontaneity and immediacy of the music are still present, but Monk knows where he is at, and so does the listener. This knowing gives Monk's music that dimension of balance and structure which is so clearly lacking in much contemporary jazz. You can enjoy Monk's music, and absorb its message, because it is whole. And while Monk explores many moods, he leaves you with a feeling of fulfillment rather than frustration. He leaves you happy. There isn't any better way to be left. If Thelonious Monk had to upset a lot of people before they'd let him make them feel happy, or at peace with themselves, that was inevitable. Thelonious Monk, in his music and his being, is one of those things only jazz could have made possible.

Thelonious and Me

Orrin Keepnews

In 1987 the Complete Riverside Recordings of Thelonious Monk *were issued. As part of the accompanying text, Orrin Keepnews, who for many years produced Monk's records, wrote of their relationship, of making the Riverside recordings, and of Monk's music.*

It should be clearly understood that the purpose of this collection is to present to the greatest possible extent the complete results of the six-year association between Thelonious Monk and Riverside Records. This is not at all the same as merely reissuing all the albums he made for that label, or even offering the material from those albums plus a scattering of alternate takes. The intention here is something I consider much more personal, more revealing, more historically and musically significant. This is, basically, all of my work with Thelonious, including several of the accidents and the failures as well as the highly important creative moments. Except only for the tapes that have vanished (and must be assumed to be lost forever, accidentally or unthinkingly destroyed), it is the full and naked truth about several pivotal recording years in the career of a very major jazz artist, which means that it is at times something quite different from the carefully packaged entertainment units that the public is usually allowed to purchase.

Therefore, this is also a very important segment of my lifelong involvement with the creation of jazz records. Monk was the first artist of real consequence with whom I went into the recording studio. Although I have never felt there was any point in comparing one valid artist with others, I must admit that it is entirely possible that he was the most important musician I have ever worked with. Certainly he was the most unusual, probably he was the most demanding. Undoubtedly I learned more from him than from anyone else—at least partly because our association began so early in my career that at the time I knew practically nothing and therefore had almost everything to learn! It was in some respects a most rewarding working relationship, but it was at times extremely frustrating. We last worked together in 1960, and therefore I had two decades before his death in which to think with regret of projects we might have done or should have done.

Above all, however, I will always retain a feeling of satisfaction. Over the years it has come to my personal definition of the role of the jazz record producer that he should serve primarily as a *catalytic agent.* In a literal sense, my dictionary refers to this as something that "initiates a chemical reaction and enables it to proceed under different conditions than otherwise possible." In a jazz sense, I mean that the producer's job is to create, in whatever ways he can, a set of circumstances that will allow and encourage the artist to perform at the very highest level. I first attempted to function in this way on my early sessions with Monk, and I do feel that at least some of the work I helped bring into being was truly different and lastingly valuable, and that without my involvement it might not have been quite the same.

Monk and I first met a very long time ago. It was early in 1948, only a few years after he had been involved in the pioneering bebop sessions at Minton's Playhouse in Harlem. As I like to point out in recalling that initial encounter, it was so incredibly long ago that I was still several years away from producing my first album, and Monk was poised at the very beginning of his recording career. Specifically, Blue Note was preparing to release his first 78-rpm single, and I had just made a formal (although unpaid) entrance into the jazz world by becoming the managing editor of a small and previously quite traditionalist magazine.

It was precisely this combination of roles—Thelonious as a new recording artist and me as a totally inexperienced jazz journalist—that was responsible for our being brought together one evening, thereby setting in motion a chain of events that eventually led to our intense six-year working relationship at Riverside and to the creation of all the recordings that make up this collection. I was twenty-five years old at the time and Monk (if his listed birthdate in 1917 is accurate) was just past thirty, but there was considerable difference between us. Even though the outside world was not aware of Monk, his reputation in certain jazz circles as the eccentric "high priest of bop" was already well established. I, on the other hand, was merely a beginning jazz writer who was editor of *The Record Changer* simply because my former college classmate Bill Grauer (who was later to be my partner at Riverside) had just become publisher of the magazine. But Alfred Lion, the guiding force at Blue Note, had seen an opportunity to influence us newcomers into publicizing his unusual young pianist. So I found myself sitting in Lion's living room, not only meeting this already-legendary musician but attempting to interview him.

My first real problem was to understand what he was saying. In later years I developed the theory that Monk had several different ways of speaking: to strangers, or if his mood was withdrawn, there would be a thick and murky tone that made it necessary to strain for each word. As he came to know you better and to accept you, his speech patterns gradually became clearer. I remain convinced that in speech (as in his music) Thelonious for the most part became easier to comprehend only when and if he wanted to. At our first meeting, facing an intrusive young writer that his record company had thrust at him, he retreated behind a wall of grunts and mumbles and one-word answers.

Nevertheless I kept at it and somehow—possibly because I have always been stubborn, or because I had the arrogance that can come from ignorance and was too inexperienced to be properly frightened of him—I succeeded in putting together what Monk later told me was the first article about him ever to appear in a national publication. He may have been wrong about that: there was a George Simon story in *Metronome* at about the same time, and that magazine certainly had a much larger circulation. But the really important thing was that Thelonious liked what I had to say and remembered it; seven years later, that had a lot to do with my becoming his record producer.

On re-reading that original *Record Changer* piece a great many years later, it is clear that I responded immediately and strongly to this man and his strange music. At that time I was still very much a traditionalist, with virtually no knowledge of the new jazz forms; I had not yet heard anything attractive in the bebop of Gillespie and Parker. As I wrote in that article, I had previously found modern jazz to be "frenetic, emotionless, and rhythmless." Nevertheless, I found myself highly impressed by the test pressings I heard that night from Monk's first Blue Note session. I remember most clearly the original version of the tune called "Thelonious" (which was to be recorded again for Riverside, almost exactly ten years later, in a big-band concert performance). And the total impact of what I heard led me to some initial comments that, quite astonishingly, I would still be willing to affirm today, close to forty years later!

Calling his first records "an outstanding example of unified small band jazz," I used such phrases as "discipline and coherence" and "purposeful and coordinated." I noted his "warmth," his "firm rhythmic sense [and] fertile imagination," and found him "capable of a wry, satiric, humor that has a rare maturity." Most remarkably, when you realize how much of a novice I was back then, I was able to perceive that "he is engaged in developing an essentially original piano style," and that in those first recordings he had "created a band style molded around his own ideas and shaped to his own manner of playing, much as Jelly Roll Morton and Duke Ellington did before him." I continue to feel that to appreciate properly Monk's work and his position in jazz history it is essential to understand that he stands in a direct line of succession from Morton and Ellington. The fact that I grasped this basic point on first hearing him not only speaks well of my jazz instincts but also points up the clarity with which Monk's message has always been delivered—to those who are willing to listen with open ears.

However, for seven years I had no occasion to make use of my early insights. Although I had begun to enjoy a good deal of the new music that was all around me in New York, and by 1953 had become professionally involved in the record business, the young Riverside label at that time was almost exclusively concerned with reissues of early classics by Louis Armstrong, King Oliver, Jelly Roll, and Ma Rainey. Then, early in 1955, we received a momentous telephone call from Nat Hentoff, informing us of the possibility that Thelonious might be available for recording.

Monk's career had not been progressing well. He could not work to any extent in New York clubs; several years after a minor narcotics-related conviction, he was still unable to obtain from the police department the "cabaret card" that was required under the arbitrary regulations that were then in effect. He had moved from Blue Note to Prestige Records a couple of years earlier, but his records were not doing so well with either the critics or the public—perhaps at least in part because of the rather overdone publicity emphasis on the weirdness and obscurity of his music. Monk was quite unhappy with Prestige, and they did not consider him at all important in comparison with the label's top-selling attraction, like Miles Davis and the Modern Jazz Quartet. Prestige, we were informed, could easily be persuaded to release Monk from his contract.

Grauer and I responded with great enthusiasm. We had made the decision to get heavily involved in recording contemporary jazz; to sign Thelonious would not only be a strong starting point, but would certainly let the jazz world know just how serious we were. We met with Monk, and I was very pleased to learn that he knew exactly who I was and remembered quite clearly and approvingly what I had written about him. Having very little to lose, he was willing to take a chance with the fledgling Riverside operation, particularly since it was run by the men responsible for that article. It did take a touch of trickery to free him from Prestige. All that was required was repayment of an absurdly small sum of money that had been overadvanced to him, but the label might not turn the pianist loose quite so casually if they were aware that a rival company was standing by. So I personally lent Thelonious the necessary funds, and I still have on my wall a framed copy of the letter informing him that "with receipt of your cash for $108.27," Prestige was "releasing you of your exclusive recording. . . ." It was the start of a very exciting and significant period, the beginning of the first of my several long-term associations with major jazz artists. It opened the door for our many record sessions together, several of which were of great importance to his career and unquestionably to mine, and to the overall story of jazz in our times.

Signing this genius was not hard; recording him was never easy. When I entered a studio with Monk in 1955, for the first of a great many times, I was quite inadequately prepared for the task. Like many of my colleagues at the independent jazz labels of that era, I was a fan who had become a producer by the simple procedure of declaring that I was one. I was one of the owners of the company, so who could argue with my claim? But I know now that I, as an executive, would never entrust so important, difficult, and sensitive an artist to a producer as thoroughly inexperienced as I was then. I handled a few sessions, with studio musicians and with pianist Randy Weston (who was a disciple of Monk, but has always been one of the gentlest of human beings). Such a background in no way prepared me for working with this erratic, stubborn, basically intolerant, and overwhelmingly talented artist. I was at the beginning of a massive learning experience!

Sonny Rollins, with whom I have often discussed the ever-fascinating subject, shares my belief that Thelonious was a great teacher, and that we both have absorbed very important (although certainly very different) lessons from him—despite the obvious fact that he was undoubtedly the most unorthodox and indirect of teachers and never in his life gave either of us (or anyone else) a formal lesson. Sonny, who has spent some time in India, has referred to Monk as his "guru," and this is perhaps a more accurate term than "teacher," since he functioned less as an instructor than as a guide who helped you bring out the very best qualities within yourself. As examples, I am aware of how he aided Rollins in developing both his musical sense of humor and his ability to play ballads in a way that combines beauty with emotional strength; I also know how greatly John Coltrane's several months with Thelonious at the Five Spot in 1957 accelerated his transition from a rather interesting young bebop tenor player into an unconventional, boundary-extending giant. Above all, I remain deeply conscious of the extent to which my early sessions with this brilliant, difficult, and demanding man literally forced me to learn very quickly under pressure a great many necessary and valuable skills and attitudes and some essential truths about dealing effectively with a great variety of jazz artists.

My first problem—and it was an almost symbolic preview of what my future as a producer would include—came on the scheduled first day of recording with Monk, and involved the absence of a reputedly quite reliable musician. Kenny Clarke and Oscar Pettiford, both already recognized as among the elder statesmen of the new music, were the carefully chosen sidemen for this initial album. We were all to gather at the small Riverside offices in midtown New York and travel together across the Hudson River to the New Jersey studios of Rudy van Gelder, the most celebrated of jazz engineers. I was relieved when Monk arrived almost on time, just after Pettiford, but Clarke was nowhere to be found. We waited with growing impatience and concern; we telephoned everywhere; eventually Thelonious suggested using a substitute. Ironically, his choice was Philly Joe Jones, who in later years was to be Riverside's most frequently used drummer, but I had barely heard of him, and did not want to begin by being pushed into using an unknown in place of an acknowledged master. Van Gelder agreed to give us a one-day postponement; Kenny, when finally located, insisted quite convincingly that Monk had told him the date was scheduled for the next day. It was not the last time that Monk was to indicate a lack of concern for such routine things as time and place and passing on the kind of basic information that is important to ordinary people.

Looking back on that album, I realize that the real problem had begun long before. My partner and I had decided that our initial goal was to reverse the widely held belief that our new pianist was an impossibly obscure artist; therefore, we would start by avoiding bebop horns and intricate original tunes. We proposed an all-Ellington trio date: certainly Duke was a universally respected figure and major composer with (as my 1948 article had noted) a valid musical connection with Monk. He agreed without hesitation, despite claiming to be largely unfamiliar with Ellington's music. I insisted that Thelonious pick out the specific repertoire, and eventually he requested several pieces of sheet music. But when we finally arrived at the studio, he proceeded to sit down at the piano and hesitantly begin to work out melody lines, as if he were seeing the material for the first time! I will never know to what extent he was actually learning on the spot, but I'm certain that at least in part he was deliberately testing, demonstrating that he was in command, and probing at this new producer to see how he would react. (There were a few very strong clues: it is clear from his performance that he was quite aware of the quote from Chopin's Funeral March that forms the coda of Ellington's original recording of "Black and Tan Fantasy." And he turned out to be an unbelievably quick study, moving from fumbling note-picking to intriguing improvisation in very little time—although it may have seemed an eternity to me.)

If this was indeed my first lesson at Monk's "school," I was somehow able to pass the test. I reacted calmly and patiently, although that was not at all how I felt. I was in the process of learning that the most important thing is to get the job done, *not* to be the winner in a clash of wills.

I was also becoming aware of the pervasive, though not entirely universal, attitude among jazz musicians that the operators of record companies (even including producers) are—like club-owners—members of another world. If we are not exactly the *enemy,* we are at least the *opposition*. I have always fought against this attitude, often successfully. I do happen to be one of the few jazz producers who can be found listening to the music in clubs with any regularity, and it remains true that some of my warmest friendships have been with people I work with. Thelonious and I never became close friends, but we had a direct and honest relationship throughout his Riverside years. We could talk at times about matters outside music (we had young sons of almost the same age, and compared notes on the difficulties of fatherhood; at this point in time—early 1986—my son Peter happens to be involved in researching and writing a biography of Monk). Above all, I take pride in the fact that Thelonious actively brought young musicians to my attention on more than one occasion. He was the first to tell me about both Wilbur Ware and Johnny Griffin, who became very important parts of the Riverside picture; and Clark Terry, whom I first met when Monk called him for the final session of the *Brilliant Corners* album, became a vital link in a most important chain—Clark introduced me to the Adderley brothers, and it was Cannonball who first made me aware of Wes Montgomery.

When we moved on from the relative calm of the first trio albums to the hectic sessions involved in the creation of *Brilliant Corners,* the pace of my learning process increased rapidly. Later in these pages I will deal in some detail with the actual circumstances of those and several other tense periods in the recording studio. What I want to emphasize now is that, working with this larger-than-life-size figure named Thelonious Monk, I was going through the most rigorous kind of on-the-job training. I was beginning to learn, under conditions of extreme pressure, the importance of being flexible, of instantly altering plans and schedules, not tightening up when faced with the unexpected, and remembering that a major aspect of the producer's role is to reduce the overall tension. Above all, I was beginning to grasp a fundamental lesson that I suspect many jazz producers never fully appreciate: it is the artist's album, not mine. My *only* objective is to achieve the best possible results, and I must juggle, move, and maneuver myself and everyone else in whatever ways are necessary to reach that goal. It took many more sessions and situations before I thoroughly absorbed these lessons, but my course of instruction most definitely began with Thelonious.

It was during the final day of work on the *Brilliant Corners* album that I first became aware of the value of listening carefully when Monk spoke. (I soon came to realize that he had a remarkable ability to convey deep truths through specific, seemingly casual or even comic comments.) On this occasion, Clark Terry was briefly rehearsing "Bemsha Swing" with the composer. "Don't pay too much attention to what I'm playing behind you now," I heard Thelonious tell him, "because when we record I'll probably be playing something completely different and it'll only confuse you. . . ." It is difficult to imagine a more concise and accurate summation of the fundamentally fluid, ever-changing, improvisatory nature of Monk's approach to music. Similarly, listening to a playback of the blues called "Functional," while making his first solo-piano album, he noted to me: "I sound just like James P. Johnson." Of course he didn't sound *exactly* like the master stride pianist (to whom he had listened often as a teenager; they had lived in the same New York City neighborhood). But it was both an acknowledgement that Thelonious was aware of some of his most important roots and an announcement that he was satisfied with the way he was playing.

That same solo album also was the occasion of our first major confrontation, from which I learned another major lesson: working on behalf of the artist doesn't mean you have to turn yourself into a doormat. The first scheduled session for this album never took place; after a series of phone calls announcing that he was on his way, Monk finally arrived at the studio well over an hour late and unprepared. I had waited in order to deliver a rather heavy-handed speech: there were certain necessary limits to what my self-respect could allow; I could accept perhaps a half-hour's lateness, but after that he needn't bother to show up at the studio; I would have left. We set a new date; I got there about fifteen minutes early—and Thelonious was waiting for me. He gave me one of his big, slow smiles and quietly asked: "What kept you?"

Monk's first contract with Riverside was for three years, which was a usual maximum period in those days. This meant that it ended in the spring of 1958, after his first Five Spot engagement with John Coltrane had thrust him into the spotlight, but actually before there had been enough fame to encourage a major record label to try to entice our artist away. (It was a common enough procedure to let a small jazz company run the risks of early development and then have the giants move in; Prestige, for example, had lost Miles Davis to Columbia, and the Modern Jazz Quartet and Coltrane to Atlantic.) After some not unfriendly negotiation, his advance payments were more than doubled and his royalty percentage increased, and Thelonious began a second three-year span with our live recordings of the 1958 Five Spot quartet. But long before the end of that contract it was clear that a change would take place. His advisors were convinced that it was time to move on; six years *is* a long time with one label, and Columbia, then in one of its active jazz periods, was beckoning.

I did feel badly about not being able to discuss the future directly with Monk, and I have always felt distressed by the fact that I can say, quite immodestly, that nothing in his subsequent recording career really approached the creativity and variety of the best of his work at Riverside. But the only specific unpleasantness associated with his departure derived from the fact that his second contract had called for several more albums than we had been able to make. I was never fully aware of the circumstances, but Bill Grauer had learned of the existence of tapes professionally recorded—perhaps by the concert promoters, perhaps by radio stations—during two major performances on an early 1961 European tour. The musicians' union had already agreed that we were entitled to further albums from Monk before his contract with Columbia could be approved. Since there is really no way to force an unwilling artist into the studio (particularly *this* artist), use of the existing tapes seemed the best possible solution.

Thelonious and I saw each other from time to time in the New York jazz world of the sixties, but our closeness had been tied to work together. By 1973 I had moved to San Francisco, and not long after that he retreated into a period of total inactivity and seclusion that lasted until his death in 1982. My last contact with him came about two years before that. On a sudden impulse, during a trip to New York, I telephoned him; the conversation ran approximately like this:

"Thelonious, are you touching the piano at all these days?"

"*No, I'm not.*"

"Do you want to get back to playing?"

"*No, I don't.*"

"I'm only in town for a few days; would you like me to come and visit, to talk about the old days?"

"*No, I wouldn't.*"

When I repeated this to Barry Harris, who was much closer to him in the last years than almost anyone else, the pianist told me: "You were lucky. You got complete sentences. With most people, he just says, 'No.'"

So I am by no means an expert on the last periods of his life. The Thelonious Monk of the years from 1955 to 1961 is the man I really knew, and learned from, and helped as best I could to express his creativity on records. *That* Thelonious was a very unusual human being and extremely good at what he did; I am glad that I was able to know him and work with him.

John Coltrane

Nat Hentoff

Hentoff—with his typical generosity and grasp—confronts the complexities and ambiguities of Coltrane and his music in this chapter from his 1976 book, Jazz Is.

Coltrane, a man of almost unbelievable gentleness made human to us lesser mortals by his very occasional rages. Coltrane, an authentically spiritual man, but not innocent of carnal imperatives. Or perhaps more accurately, a man, in his last years, especially but not exclusively consumed by affairs of the spirit. That is, having constructed a personal world view (or view of the cosmos) on a residue of Christianity and an infusion of Eastern meditative practices and concerns, Coltrane became a theosophist of jazz. The music was a way of self-purgation so that he could learn more about himself to the end of making himself and his music part of the unity of all being. He truly believed this, and in this respect, as well as musically, he has been a powerful influence on many musicians since. He considered music to be a healing art, an "uplifting" art.

Yet through most of his most relatively short career (he died at forty), Coltrane divided jazz listeners, creating furiously negative reactions to his work among some. ("Antijazz" was one of the epithets frequently cast at him in print.) He was hurt and somewhat bewildered by this reaction, but with monumental stubbornness went on exploring and creating what to many seemed at first to be chaos—self-indulgent, long-winded noise. Some still think that's what it was.

Others believed Coltrane to be a prophet, a musical prophet, heralding an enormous expansion of what it might now be possible to say on an instrument. Consider Art Davis. He is a startlingly brilliant bassist, as accomplished in classical music as in jazz. (Because Davis is black, he has been denied employment by those symphony orchestras to which he has applied, and so he has challenged them to pit him against any classical bassist of their choice. The challenge has gone unanswered.) Anyway, Davis, whom I've known for years, is a rationalist, a keen analyzer of music and of life. He is not given, so far as I have ever known, to giant or even small leaps into faith. Davis requires a sound scaffolding of fact and proof for his enthusiasms.

But here is Art Davis, who played for a time with Coltrane, as quoted in the Fall 1972 issue of the periodical *Black Creation* [Institute of Afro-American Affairs at New York University]: "John Coltrane would play for hours a set. One tune would be like an hour or two hours, and he would not repeat himself, and it would not be boring. . . . People would just be shouting, like you go to church, a holy roller church or something like that. This would get into their brains, would penetrate. John had that spirit—he was after the spiritual thing. . . . You could hear people screaming . . . despite the critics who tried to put him down. Black people made him because they stuck together and they saw—look what's going down—let's get some of this. You know all the hard times that John had at the beginning, even when he was with Miles. And when he left Miles, starting out, everybody tried to discourage him. But I'd be there and the brothers and sisters would be there and they supported him. . . . John had this power of communication, that power so rare it was like genius—I'll call him a prophet because he did this."

Coltrane had another power, a power of self-regeneration that also has to do with that power of communication. One evening in the early 1950s, I saw Coltrane in Sheridan Square, in Greenwich Village. He looked awful. Raggedy, vacant. "Junk," said a musician with me. "He's been hooked a while." But, I noted, he had a bottle of wine in his hand. "That, too," said the musician.

And Coltrane stopped using both. By himself. During his huge musical ascent, which was soon to start. Coltrane was clean and stayed clean. That's power. Like Miles.

Coltrane changed jazz in as fundamental a way as Charlie Parker had before him and Louis Armstrong before Parker. One thing he did was to radically reshape—by the overwhelming persuasiveness of his playing—all previous jazz definitions of "acceptable" sounds and forms.

Obviously, through the decades, jazz had encompassed an extraordinary range of sounds—growls, slurs, cries, guffaws, keening wails. And certainly it had been accepted from the beginning that each player had his own "sound." There was never any one criterion for how every trombone or tenor saxophone or singer should sound. Still, at each stage of jazz history certain kinds of sounds were beyond the pale. Or at least they were considerably downgraded. For years, to cite a pre-modern-jazz example, Pee Wee Russell's rasping tone (which, to its denigrators, veered between a squeak and an access of laryngitis) was mocked by a good many musicians as well as listeners. Yet Pee Wee proved to be among the most inventive and seizingly original of all clarinetists.

Lester Young was in disfavor among some of his peers for quite a while because his sound was too "light" compared to Coleman Hawkins' robust fullness. Nor was Lee Wiley the only appraiser to think of Billie Holiday that she sounded "as if her shoes were too tight." At the advent of Charlie Parker one of the many criticisms of his playing by older musicians and by traditionalist listeners was that his tone was "bad," too acrid by contrast, say, with that of Johnny Hodges.

In the chaos of John Coltrane, a majority of the initial reviews of his recordings in the early and mid-1950s also cited his "strident," "unpleasant" sound. Mine were among them. Later, however, when Coltrane was really underway and pushing his instrument beyond any previous limits of sound possibilities, the intermittent rawness of his tone, the high-pitched squeals, the braying yawps, the screams, generated even more intense hostility along with the denunciation that his extensive solos were structureless, directionless. "Musical nonsense" wrote one critic.

In retrospect, however, it is clear that Coltrane was one of the most persistent, relentless expanders of possibility—all kinds of possibility: textural, emotional, harmonic, and spiritual—in jazz history. And also one of the most totally exposed improvisers in the history of the music.

I was converted, or educated, from listening first to Coltrane with Miles Davis for many nights. This was the Coltrane "sheets of sound" period (a phrase originated by critic Ira Gitler). The term came about, Gitler later explained, "because of the density of textures he was using. His multinote improvisations were so thick and complex they were almost flowing out of the horn by themselves. That really hit me, the continuous flow of ideas without stopping. It was almost superhuman, and the amount of energy he was using could have powered a spaceship."

Miles would sometimes grumble about the constant hailstorms of notes in a Coltrane solo, since Miles himself preferred to work with space, to let his notes breathe. And the length of the solos also occasionally annoyed him. "Why did you go on so long?" he once asked Coltrane after a particularly lengthy flight by the latter.

"It took that long to get it all in," said Coltrane, and Miles accepted the logic of the answer.

Actually, Miles Davis was much intrigued by the sheer will to creativity of Coltrane on his better nights. "Coltrane's really something," Miles told me one afternoon in 1958. "He's been working on those arpeggios and playing them fifty different ways and playing them all at once. However," there was a glint of triumph in Miles, "he *is* beginning to leave more space—except when he gets nervous."

It was important for Coltrane to work with Miles. For one thing, of course, he received attention, with the Davis imprimatur legitimatizing Coltrane for some of those who up to that point had considered Trane either incompetent or a charlatan or both. Miles, it was agreed by nearly all, could not and would not be conned musically. If he hired the man, the man must have something to say. That imprimatur also gave Coltrane confidence. Feeling set upon by the critics, he had passed a far more severe test by being considered worthy of a place in the Miles Davis band.

Even more valuable to Coltrane, however, was his stay with Thelonious Monk—in between stints with Miles Davis in the late 1950s. That collaboration at the Five Spot Café in New York's East Village was a key historic event—of the musical order of Louis Armstrong playing second cornet to King Oliver at the Royal Garden Café in Chicago in the 1920s. I was there nearly every night all the weeks Monk and Trane played the Five Spot, and it was there I finally understood how nonpareil a musician, how dauntless an explorer Coltrane was. The excitement was so heady that soon musicians were standing two and three deep at the bar of the Five Spot nearly every night.

Monk creates a total musical microcosm, and for musicians who play with him the challenge is to keep your balance, to stay with Monk, no matter where his unpredictably intricate imagination leads—and at the same time, play yourself, be yourself.

"I learned new levels of alertness with Monk," Coltrane said, "because if you didn't keep aware all the time of what was going on, you'd suddenly feel as if you'd stepped into a hole without a bottom to it." He learned other things as well. "Monk was one of the first to show me how to make two or three notes at one time on tenor. It's done by false fingering and adjusting your lips, and if it's done right you get triads. He also got me into the habit of playing long solos [longer than with Miles] on his pieces, playing the same piece for a long time to find new conceptions for solos. It got so I would go as far as possible on one phrase until I ran out of ideas. The harmonies got to be an obsession for me. Sometimes I was making jazz through the wrong end of a magnifying glass."

As a teacher, one of the most liberating teachers in jazz, Monk had another kind of impact on Coltrane, as on practically all the musicians who have played with him. Monk kept insisting that musicians must keep working at stretching themselves, at going beyond their limitations, which really were artificial limitations that came from their having absorbed conventional—and thereby gratuitously constricting—standards of what can and what cannot be done on an instrument.

Before Coltrane came with the band, Gigi Gryce had learned this lesson: "I had a part Monk wrote for me that was impossible. I had to play melody while simultaneously playing harmony with him. In addition, the intervals were very wide besides; and I just told him I couldn't do it. 'You have an instrument, don't you?' he said. "Either play it or throw it away." And he walked away. Finally, I *was* able to play it. Another time I was orchestrating a number for him, and I didn't write everything down for the horns exactly as he'd outlined it because I felt the musicians would look at the score and figure it was impossible to play. He was very angry, and he finally got exactly what he wanted. I remember the trumpet player on the date had some runs going up on his horn and Monk said they were only impractical if they didn't give him a chance to breathe. The range was not a factor "because a man should be flexible on all ranges of his horn.'"

Then came Coltrane. The story, told by Art Blakey, is in J. C. Thomas' *Chasin' the Trane:* "I played drums on the *Monk's Music* album for Riverside, where Monk expanded his group to a septet with both Coleman Hawkins and John Coltrane on tenor. Naturally, Monk wrote all the music, but Hawk was having trouble reading it, so he asked Monk to explain it to both Trane and himself. Monk said to Hawk, 'You're the great Coleman Hawkins, right? You're the guy who invented the tenor saxophone, right?' Hawk agreed. Then Monk turned to Trane, 'You're the great John Coltrane, right?' Trane blushed, and mumbled, 'Aw . . . I'm not so great.' Then Monk said to both of them, 'You play saxophone, right?' They nodded. 'Well, the music is on the horn. Between the two of you, you should be able to find it.'"

Coltrane kept looking and finding, and, never satisfied, looked some more. His audience was growing, especially among musicians, but more nonmusicians were finding that if they *actively* listened to his music, their whole way of hearing jazz might well be changed. This did not mean, however, that they had to listen analytically. In the liner notes for Coltrane's album, *Om,* for example, I suggested that those who were finding Coltrane "difficult" start again, but this time without "worrying about how it is all structured, where it's leading. Let the music come in without any pre-set definitions of what jazz *has* to be, of what *music* has to be.

"If you find yourself responding—and I don't mean necessarily with conventional 'pleasure,' but rather with any strong feeling—listen on. In this music, just as textures are themselves shapes and motion is by colors as well as by time"; so, in the listening, I should have gone on, ingress is by routes that will unexpectedly come upon you in guises other than the usual ways to get into a piece of music. A link of pitches perhaps, an a-rhythmic phrase that will lead to a strong subterranean pulsation.

For the last seven years of his life Coltrane continued to make more demands of himself musically than any jazz musician, except perhaps Cecil Taylor, ever has. None of this, so far as I could tell, was done as an act of competition. It was himself, and only himself, Coltrane kept pressuring to hear more, feel more, understand more, communicate more. At home he would practice for hours, sometimes silently—just running his fingers over the keys—and pick up new instruments and meditate and listen to recordings of Indian music and the music of South African Pygmies. Possibilities. Always more possibilities. He decided he wanted two drummers working with him. Then, on an album, he fixed on two bass players. I asked him why. "Because I want more of the sense of the expansion of time. I want the time to be more plastic."

Time. Vast, fierce stretches of time. The music sometimes sounding like the exorcism of a multitude of demons, each one of whom was mightily resisting his expulsion. Yet at other times Coltrane could sound his probes with such gentle luminescence as to fool the voracious spirits, but soon the shaking, smashing, endless battle would begin again.

At nightclubs there were scores, hundreds of exhilarating, exhausting nights during which the listeners, along with the musicians, had no resting space but had to keep emotional pace as best he could with the ferociously wheeling, diving, climbing Coltrane.

For better or worse, and that depended on the inventiveness of the musicians who followed him, Coltrane more than any other player legitimated the extended jazz solo. As Archie Shepp, a tenor saxophonist befriended and influenced by Coltrane, said, "That was his breakthrough—the concept that the imperatives of conception might make it necessary to improvise at great length. I don't mean he proved that a thirty- or forty-minute solo is necessarily better than a three-minute one. He did prove, however, that it was possible to create thirty or forty minutes of uninterrupted, continually building, continually original and imaginative music. And in the process, Coltrane also showed the rest of us we had to have the stamina—in terms of imagination and physical preparedness—to sustain those long flights."

I once tried out on Coltrane my theory that one reason he developed such long solos was in an attempt to create and sustain a kind of hypnotic, dervishlike mood so that the listener would in time become oblivious to distractions and end up wholly immersed in the music with all his customary intellectual and emotional defenses removed.

"That may be a secondary effect," Coltrane said, "but I'm not consciously trying to do that. I'm still primarily looking into certain sounds, certain scales. Not that I'm sure of what I'm looking for, except that it'll be something that hasn't been played before. I don't know what it is. I know I'll have that feeling when I get it. And in the process of looking, continual looking, the result in any given performance can be long or short. I never know. It's always one thing leading into another. It keeps evolving, and sometimes it's longer than I actually thought it was while I was playing. When things are constantly happening the piece just doesn't feel that long."

Always looking, Coltrane always tried to be ready for the unexpected revelation, "that feeling." Alice Coltrane told me that "when John left for work he'd often take five instruments with him. He wanted to be ready for whatever came. That was characteristic of John. His music was never resigned, never complacent. How could it be? He never stopped surprising himself."

He was a man who spoke of universal, transcendent peace—becoming one with Om, "the first vibration—that sound, that spirit which set everything else into being." And yet his music, to the end, although sometimes almost eerily serene, remained most often volcanic. Ravi Shankar, who had come to know Coltrane, said: "I was much disturbed by his music. Here was a creative person who had become a vegetarian, who was studying yoga and reading the *Bhagavad-Gita,* yet in whose music I still heard much turmoil. I could not understand it."

Marion Brown, the alto saxophonist and composer, was one of the musicians assembled by Coltrane for his almost unbearably intense set of "free jazz," *Ascension,* and Brown recalls: "We did two takes, and they both had that kind of thing in them that makes people scream. The people in the studios were screaming."

Perhaps Om, the first vibration, is a scream. Perhaps Coltrane wished so hard to transcend all of what he regarded as his baser, antispiritual elements, that he was doomed, from the time his ambition became so otherworldly, to always feel desperately imprisoned. Hence the scream. But part of the scream may also have been the pain, the difficulty, of self-purgation, a process that had become the normative conundrum of thorns in his life.

Whatever the explanation—if there is a discernible matrix of explanations for the phenomenon of Coltrane—by the time he died of cancer of the liver in 1967, he had helped shape a new generation of jazz musicians. He didn't like the term "jazz," by the way, since he felt all music to be one, without labels.

In musical terms Trane's contributions have perhaps been most succinctly described by David Baker, who has long taught black music, and other music, at the University of Indiana. Now that Grove's *Dictionary of Music and Musicians* has at last decided to admit articles on jazz musicians, Baker is writing an entry on, among others, John Coltrane. And the achievements of Coltrane he will cite are: "using multiphonics, playing several notes or tones simultaneously; creating asymmetrical groupings not dependent on the basic pulse; developing an incredibly sophisticated system of chord substitutions; and initiating a pan-modal style of playing, using several modes simultaneously. I've transcribed some of his solos for teaching my students at the University of Indiana. I think all musicians should study Coltrane solos the way we now study the études of Bach and Brahms."

Coltrane, who read theory as well as biographies of the creative (Van Gogh, for instance), might have been pleased to hear that. But at night, on the stand, there would be no abiding satisfaction for him in what he had done in the past. "You just keep going," he told me once. "You keep trying to get right down to the crux."

He even frustrated himself—in addition to knowing the crux would always be beyond him or anyone else—by yearning for yet another impossibility. "Sometimes," Coltrane said to me one afternoon, "I wish I could walk up to my music as if for the first time, as if I had never heard it before. Being so inescapably a part of it, I'll never know what the listener gets, what the listener feels, and that's too bad."

Looking at Coltrane's early background—born in Hamlet, North Carolina; schooling in Philadelphia; rhythm-and-blues work with Eddie "Mr. Cleanhead" Vinson; gathering experience with Dizzy Gillespie, Earl Bostic, Johnny Hodges, Miles Davis, and Thelonious Monk—there would have been no way to predict (before Miles and Monk, anyway) the singular, unyielding questioning force that was to revolutionize much of jazz. There never is any way to predict the coming of the next jazz prophet. And that's why nearly all speculation, learned or otherwise, about the future directions of jazz is always futile. The future of jazz has always depended on unexpected individuals with radical (though at first seemingly opaque) questions to ask—questions they eventually proceed to answer: Louis Armstrong on the nature of the jazz solo; Duke Ellington on the nature of the jazz orchestra; Charlie Parker on the obsolescence of the rhythmic and harmonic language that preceded him; and John Coltrane on all manner of jazz constrictions that antedated *him*.

In spending himself on trying to answer the questions that consumed him, Coltrane eventually developed what in jazz terms could be called a large audience. As Martin Williams has pointed out, "It was almost impossible for a man to be as much of a technician, artist, and explorer as Coltrane and still have the kind of popular following he had. What did he tell that audience? In what new and meaningful things did his music instruct them?

"I don't know, of course," Williams continued. "And perhaps as a white man I can't know. But I would venture a suggestion. I don't think Coltrane spoke of society or political theory. I think that like all real artists he spoke of matters of the spirit, of those things by which the soul of man survives. I think he spoke of the ways of the demons and the gods that were always there, yet are always contemporary. And I think that he knew that he did."

Some months after Coltrane died, I was visiting a black college in Delaware. It had been a year during which I had lectured at many colleges—mostly on education and civil liberties. When music had come into the discussion, the emphasis invariably was on rock sounds and players. Only at this black college did the students talk of Bird and Ornette Coleman, and especially of Coltrane.

"You know," one of the black students said, "when Trane died, it was like a great big hole had been left. And it's still there."

In one sense that hole is indeed still there and will continue to be. Obviously, certain artists do leave great big holes when they die, for they are irreplaceable in the size and scope of their originality. Louis Armstrong. Duke. Lester Young. Coleman Hawkins. Billie Holiday. And on and on. As this book is being written, there has yet been no successor to Coltrane in terms of having dominant, pervasive influence on the jazz of the 1970s.

On the other hand, as pianist Keith Jarrett said of Trane's death, "Everyone felt a big gap all of a sudden. But he didn't intend to leave a gap. He intended that there be more space for everybody to do what they should do."

And there *is* more space for further generations of seekers. In one way or another they are all children of Coltrane. And, of course, of all those who shaped him. The legacy is long and rich and demanding.

Bessie Smith: Poet

Murray Kempton

In 1987, in New York Newsday, *the journalist Murray Kempton marked the half-century since Bessie Smith's death with this account of the powerful impression she made on him as he watched her perform in 1933.*

"Woke up this morning when chickens was crowing for day."

—"Young Woman's Blues"

Woke up yesterday morning where there is not a chicken to crow for day and remembered that on September 27 next Bessie Smith will have been dead for fifty years.

She was killed a few miles from Clarksdale, Mississippi. The gods could not have selected a more appropriate place to close her epic, because Clarksdale is not very far from the railroad tracks where the Southern used to cross the Yellow Dog and where Miss Susie Johnson's Jockey Lee had gone.

September is a while away. But what fitter day for filing an advance notice of this special occasion could there be than July 4, which is sacred to the falling-short but undiscouragable pursuit of happiness that is most of what the works of Bessie Smith are about. Most but, as usual with great subjects, by no means all.

The rising sun ain't gonna set in the East no more.

—"Hard Time Blues"

To distill a complexity into the sparest of direct statements and still preserve intact its paradox was among the subtler of Bessie's arts. We have no way to know the source of most of her lyrics; she must have picked up a good many in the carnivals and others were written for her by hands more practiced. But a lot of these words have to be her very own and they bring us the sense of being in the company of the last of the Anglo-Saxon poets.

There are, as an instance, those lines in "Lost Your Head Blues" that have been authenticated as pure improvisation: "Once ain't for always and two ain't but twice." I have puzzled over them off and on through my conscious life and am yet to be sure precisely what they mean. All that I know with certainty is that they are entirely beautiful.

If I ever get my hands on a dollar again,
I'm gonna hold on to it till the eagle grin.
—"Nobody Knows You When You're Down and Out"

Or "My heart's on fire but my love is icy cold." No generation is long enough to produce more than one writer who can bring off this cadence so perfect that, when you think you remember it and look it up, you find that you were wrong because you had allowed some bit of dross—say an adverb—from your own literary baggage to intrude and spoil the rhythm and taint the purity of the original. Those of us who learned to write from the blues are to be envied, and those of us who have since forgotten the lesson are to be pitied.

Thirty days in jail and I got to stay there so long.
—"Jailhouse Blues"

"Jailhouse Blues" was her first record and the first of hers I ever owned, which is to say that it was the one I have played most and thus the one I have loved most, because the record of Bessie's you have heard most often ends up the deepest in your heart.

I also saw and heard her once at the old Howard Theater in Baltimore in 1933, and was too overwhelmed for any coherent recollection. Witnesses to the apparitions of creatures from another world are seldom useful for details. I have only two memories. One is the shock of the recognition of how faintly even her records conveyed the immensity of her actual presence.

The other involves one of my companions, who was far from having conquered his baby fat and was indeed huge enough to be the most conspicuous figure in the house except of course Bessie herself. At one point she descended from higher things to "One-Hour Woman," one of the requisite dirty songs her grandeur somehow always kept from being quite disgusting, and then she noticed Freddy and, like giantess calling out to giant, she began singing that she had found in him her one-hour man.

He turned turkey red and fled the theater. Long afterward I ran into him and wondered as tactfully as I could if he remembered that afternoon we had gone to hear Bessie. He replied that he had and that, even though dozens of women had since bruised his heart, it was the supreme regret of his life that he had not held his ground and heard the whole set.

"Is it true," he asked, "that she sang 'Muddy Water'?" I answered that she had and his sigh had resonances of sorrow and loss not unworthy of her own. We would still have no more used for her any name except the bare and stately "Bessie" than we would have spoken of Juno as Mrs. Jupiter. Goddesses do not have last names.

Awhile back I fell into one of those tiresome discussions where the other party says you take Julius Erving and I'll take Larry Bird and you take Sarah Vaughan and I'll take Ella Fitzgerald. There was no disposing of such nonsense except to observe that the years have taught me to be grateful for having them all, but I had to say that Sarah Vaughan is the greatest jazz singer I have ever heard. "What about Bessie Smith?" a bystander inquired. I could only answer that I had concluded that there could never have been a Bessie Smith; the molds where they stamp out human beings are just too small for stuff of those proportions.

MAHALIA JACKSON

GEORGE T. SIMON

The supreme gospel singer Mahalia Jackson may not have sung jazz, but in this jaunty encounter with George Simon—published in Metronome *in 1954—it becomes clear that she thought about jazz a great deal and was happy to share her views.*

It was an incongruous setting. It was an Indian Summer's day in New York. It was World Series time and the Columbia Records public relations man was holding a portable radio to his ear, trying to hear above the swank Madison Avenue din, when I met him outside the fashionable hotel.

I had heard Mahalia Jackson and I had heard about Mahalia Jackson. But I had never met her. I'd never even seen her, and I was wondering what she was like. "Let's go right on upstairs; she's expecting us," said the Columbia man, as he switched off his radio and left the Indians in the lead, for the time being. (Such a sacrifice I considered almost beyond the call of duty.)

In the elevator I wondered even more. I knew that Gospel Singers didn't usually stop at such chic East Side hotels. But I'd been told that Mahalia was something quite different. I recalled her picture on the front of an Apollo Record album, complete with flowing gown, and I pictured some sort of a flowery setting and interview.

The maid met us at the door to the suite and took our hats. In the living room three men were busy talking business. The Columbia man introduced us, and we'd just started discussing what the Giants had been doing during our elevator ride, when Mahalia came in the room.

She wore a different dress this time. It was a simple cotton house dress, the kind any wife might wear any morning. And from her warm, straightforward greeting, I sensed immediately that Mahalia was as simple and as disarming as the garment she wore. Her frankness in the interview that followed complemented my initial sensory perception.

From listening to her records, I knew that Mahalia had a real, honest, old-fashioned feeling for real, honest, old-fashioned jazz. I knew, too, that she was actually more of a religious singer than a jazz singer, though, of course, the two have a good deal in common. So I hit her directly. "What do you think of jazz today?" I asked.

She looked at me—a little startled at first, I thought, and then almost condescendingly. "It ain't jazz," she answered simply. "It's nothing much—just a lot of noise. You know, when you take a real jazz player, like a trombone, he's supposed to sound like a real voice. They don't sound that way now.

"It hurts me. I was brought up in the South. I know sound. I knew Louis and Papa Celestin and King Oliver. It's a bring-down up here in the North. Louis is great, of course, and I liked that Bob Crosby band, but most of the stuff that's supposed to be Dixieland is just plain hideous. It sounds like the way some of the English did when they first tried to play jazz years ago. It's terrible.

"Good jazz has to have a soul and feeling, like the blues. If it has to be loud, let it sound round and full . . . But maybe I shouldn't be talking about all this, because I'm a Gospel Singer. I sing Divine songs and they have more to offer than jazz does."

I asked her to elaborate further. She hesitated a bit because she didn't want to hurt anybody—and, anyway, jazz wasn't exactly her field. She was, after all, primarily a Gospel Singer, she kept insisting. I asked her if the two really weren't almost the same thing.

"Well, they are and they aren't," she said. "The blues and spirituals are closely related, but the big difference is that a spiritual has hope, whereas the blues is sad all the way through and stays that way. Another thing about jazz—it makes people happy on the surface, but when it's over, it's through. But a Gospel Song lasts—it penetrates much deeper and stays with you."

Gospel Singing and jazz have one common factor, however, according to Mahalia. Both depend greatly upon the performer's emotional projection. "You can't write jazz, and when I sing I don't go by the score. I lose something when I do. I don't want to be told I can sing just so long. I make it 'till that passion is passed. When I become conscious, I can't do it good."

Mahalia, who has just been signed by Columbia Records (she is also doing a radio show for the CBS network), feels that her singing has never been captured properly on records because she has had to pay too much attention to timing, etc. "It all disgusts me. You don't really get my feeling 'till you hear me in person." CBS gave her a press party at a swank Park Avenue apartment recently, and they say that when Mahalia really let loose, many people many floors below on the street stopped, and stood enchanted at the awesome sound that emanated from far above.

Recording session restrictions also hamper jazz performances, she feels. "Jazz is all in the bounce. All that production is all wrong."

She likes most of the jazz singers of today. Ella, Billie, Sarah, "they all come from Ethel Waters. Dinah Washington's like Mamie Smith. Annie Laurie, she *really* sings the blues, the old kind of blues, primitive, in a sulky, mournful voice."

There are others she likes. Kay Starr was the first one of all she named. Then, surprisingly, came Jo Stafford, "soulful, deep feeling." Then, among the men, were Billy, Nat and Perry and another surprise "that Tennessee Johnny, or Ernie—he's good, too!"

The hint that she had had enough interviewing for the time being came when she brought out her Bible and started to read through it. First it was a bit to herself. "There's something here that tells how I feel about all this," she said. "It's from the sixty-sixth Psalm where David said 'Make a joyful noise unto the Lord.' And then he said, 'Sing with a loud voice.'

"That's how they sing in the cotton fields. They sing for faith and for courage to go on, for deliverance for freedom."

She didn't say it, but the implication was obvious. Mahalia Jackson doesn't sing to fracture any cats, or to capture any Billboard polls, or because she wants her recording contract renewed. She sings the way she does for the most basic of singing reasons, for the most honest of them all, without any frills, flourishes, or phoniness.

Sounds sort of incongruous in this day and age, doesn't it? But there's nothing incongruous about it when Mahalia Jackson tells it.

I left the chic East Side hotel with the Columbia man and for a while I'd forgotten all about the Indians and the Giants. There are, after all, giants in other fields, too!

Lady Day Has Her Say

Billie Holiday

Blindfold tests, conducted by Leonard Feather, were a leading feature of Metronome *for many years. In February 1950 the column was host to Billie Holiday, who—unsurprisingly—pulled no punches.*

The main problem in conducting a blindfold test with Billie Holiday, or with anyone of her musical stature, is that of limiting the records to a small but comprehensive selection. Personally, I was so interested in investigating Billie's views that a marathon test involving several hundred records seemed mandatory. Considerations of time and space, however, reduced the project to a round dozen discs, on which Billie commented as follows.

The Records

1. It's "I Got Rhythm," isn't it? Sounds like Jacquet . . . and now *it doesn't* sound like him. Is that some concert or something? Well, it jumps, it's very exciting at times, but I don't care too much for the rhythm section. Under the circumstances, not a bad record, but this kind of thing is according to the atmosphere you're in. If I had my choice of records I wouldn't pick this. Two stars.
2. Duke! . . . I always loved this—it gets four right now! I've always wanted a band to play under me like that when I sing; they don't mess around or noodle, they just help you. I've wanted it all my life! I almost got that with Gordon Jenkins, on "You're My Thrill," but that was pretty music. This has bounce, too. You know, the only ones who can take a solo while I'm singing and still not interfere with me are Lester Young and Teddy. I always like Hibbler, but he has some tricks I don't care for. And Hodges is always my man. This is an all around great record. Four.
3. Peggy, isn't it? . . . I always loved Peggy—loved her when she first started, and she's been very fortunate; she's always had the kind of background every singer needs . . . That clarinet sounds very fa-

miliar. I like it. Sounds a lot like Goodman. Don't tell me it is, I'll die! Three stars.

4. Who's that guitar? . . . The piano is the kind of bop I like; it makes sense. I don't know the alto; he's trying to play like Charlie, whoever he is. I like the tenor; he's nice and even and smooth. And I like that unison in the last chorus. I call this bop, and I like it *very* much. Three stars.
5. This is Ruth Brown, and you don't have to play it, I know all about this. I can't stand copycats, and this girl copies Miss Cornshucks note for note. She looks a little better but she hasn't got a damn thing; I just do not like her. I'd like to get 'em both together with a good piano player and have 'em both sing; if Cornshucks' *So Long* isn't twice as good, I'll eat my hat. When Cornshucks sings this style, she *means* it. Sure, I copied Bessie Smith and Louis Armstrong—but not note for note; they *inspired* me . . . I don't care if she hates me for saying this, it's my opinion!
6. That's Teddy Wilson . . . no, wait . . . yes, I still say it's Teddy, I won't take that back! Bud Freeman on tenor, maybe Joe Marsala on clarinet. I'm not much on this Dixieland; I mean I don't recognize them too well, but they're all swinging and it's a good record. Do I like good Dixieland? Damn right I do—three stars!
7. That's Sarah . . . this is the best record I've heard of hers in a long time. She sticks to the melody—maybe she has to, because of the vocal background. You know, on "The Man I Love" she goes so far out, it stinks; she got so that even musicians couldn't understand what she was doing. That sort of stuff is for an instrument, not for a voice. Maybe I'm old-fashioned, but I just don't like or understand it. But this one is worth three stars.
8. That's whatshisname, "Mr. Blues"—Wynonie. He has the best backgrounds on his records of any blues singer of his type. That's Tab Smith on alto. The tenor sounds like Lester . . . It *is* Lester! . . . No, it isn't . . . yes, it is! Nobody in the world does that but Lester! . . . I like this kind of blues singing; I love T-Bone Walker too. Four stars!
9. That could be anybody; they all sound alike to me . . . the girl that used to be with Krupa—Anita—or any of them. I guess the band is Stan Kenton . . . June Christy? I liked "Willow Weep for Me," but I haven't heard many of their things. This is just fair; the tune, the band and the singing, all fair. Didn't move me. Two stars.
10. That's Jimmy Rushing . . . he never killed me . . . it's Basie's band and the tenor sounds a little like Lucky Thompson. This is just fair, very fair . . . tell the truth I'm ashamed of them. That band—I

could just cry for what's happened to it, when I think how great it used to be. Two stars.

11. I don't know who the hell this is but it sure is great. The piano player's wonderful! This sounds awfully familiar—is it Woody's band? Now this is what I call bop—the real thing! It doesn't heckle your ears—you get right up to a pitch with it, come right down—it moves you. The soloists? *Everybody's* great! Four stars.
12. I believe this has my girl on it—Jackie Cain. She's the greatest for this kind of thing; she's made a business, made a life out of perfecting it. I think she and her husband are great . . . That's that girl on 'cello and the girl on drums. The group has a marvelous sound; all they need is a break. At Bop City they didn't have a chance, because their music is soft and not exciting—no clowning, no funny bow ties. They should be able to work in any good hotel, any theater—anywhere; they're the best. Bop like this is here to stay!

Records Reviewed by Billie Holiday

Following were the records discussed in Billie Holiday's blindfold test. She was given no advance information about them either before or during the test.

1. Jazz at the Philharmonic. "Endido," Part I (Mercury). Jacquet, tenor; Hank Jones, Jo Jones, Ray Brown, rhythm.
2. Duke Ellington. "Don't Get Around Much Any More" (Columbia).
3. Benny Goodman Orch. & Peggy Lee. "For Every Man There's a Woman" (Capitol).
4. Lennie Tristano. "Sax of a Kind" (Capitol). Tristano, piano; Billy Bauer, guitar; Lee Konitz, alto; Warne Marsh, tenor.
5. Ruth Brown. "So Long" (Atlantic).
6. Mel Powell, "Muskrat Ramble" (Capitol). Powell, piano; Don Lodice, tenor; Gus Bivona, clarinet.
7. Sarah Vaughan. "Make Believe" (Columbia).
8. Wynonie Harris. "Come Back Baby" (Aladdin). Tab Smith, alto; Allen Eager, tenor.
9. Stan Kenton. "He Was a Good Man as Good Men Go" (Capitol). June Christy, vocal.
10. Count Basie. "Walking Slow Behind You" (Victor). Rushing, vocal; Paul Gonsalves, tenor.
11. Woody Herman. "That's Right" (Capitol). Lou Levy, piano.
12. Roy Kral–Jackie Cain. "Ever-Lovin' Blues" (Atlantic).

The Untold Story of the International Sweethearts of Rhythm

Marian McPartland

The exuberant, highly literate pianist and broadcaster Marian McPartland, in a piece written in 1980 and reprinted in her 1987 book, All in Good Time, *remembers a triumphant all-girl jazz band, and the world of the thirties and forties in which it flourished.*

The theater was ablaze with lights that proclaimed—THE INTERNATIONAL SWEETHEARTS OF RHYTHM. The Sweethearts, an all-woman sixteen-piece band, were familiar to the tough, show-wise audience, and a long line of eagerly expectant people stretched down the street and around the corner, waiting for the doors to open. Known to the audience as the finest all-girl jazz band in the country, the Sweethearts had in seven years attained a reputation equal to that of the great male bands of the period, those led by Jimmie Lunceford, Count Basie, and Fletcher Henderson. The year was 1945; the place, the Apollo Theater in Harlem.

A hot attraction, the Sweethearts were then at the height of their fame, although to some they were merely a novelty—sixteen pretty girl musicians led by an extravagantly beautiful young woman, Anna Mae Winburn. They played with assurance, discipline, and excitement, reflecting the expert teaching of their director, Maurice King. There were some fine soloists, including Violet (Vi) Burnside, a driving, gutty tenor sax player with more than a suggestion of Coleman Hawkins in her style. The star soloist of the trumpet section was Ray Carter, whose muted sound was colorful and technically brilliant. The hard-swinging drummer, Pauline Braddy, inspired by her idol and mentor Big Sid Catlett, whipped the band along with a strong rhythm. Her foot beating on the bass drum pedal matched exactly the time-keeping of the bassist, Margaret (Trump) Gibson, and together they gave solid, dependable backing to the soloists.

The main attraction was roly-poly Ernestine (Tiny) Davis, billed as "245 Lbs. of Solid Jive and Rhythm." A compelling personality, she had a distinct flair for comedy and a humorous way with a song. Her comic dancing, rolling eyes, and funny rendition of "Stompin' the Blues" broke up the audience; and she played a strong, forceful trumpet on "I Can't Get Started," another crowd-pleaser.

The band played at the beginning of each show (four a day), and again later in the show. There were other name acts on the bill, but the Sweethearts opened and closed the program.

This band was truly unique in that it was a racially mixed group, a phenomenon unheard of even in blasé New York City. They were known to have traveled widely in the South and Midwest, many miles from their starting point, the Piney Woods Country Life School near Jackson, Mississippi, where the original band was formed in 1938. The members of that first band were all approximately fourteen or fifteen years old, high-spirited, naive youngsters who enjoyed playing for dances in small towns within driving distance of the school.

Between 1938 and the present date at the Apollo, the band's personnel had changed many times. Ione and Irene Gresham, who both played sax with the original band, had decided to stay at Piney Woods when the band turned professional; this was a decision reached by several of the girls. Others had concluded that life on the road was not for them; still others had left the band to get married. However, some of the members of the original group remained—Helen Jones and Ina Belle Byrd, trombone; Willie Mae Lee Wong, baritone sax; Edna Williams, trumpet and vocals; Johnnie Mae Rice, piano; and Pauline Braddy, drums. Inside the theater the girls were dressing and warming up on their instruments. Tiny Davis practiced high notes on the trumpet, getting ready for her feature numbers. Anna Mae Winburn gave final touches to her sleek, upswept hairdo. She wore an exquisite, tightly-fitted sequin gown, while the band members were dressed in decorous black skirts and jackets, with white blouses. Each girl wore a flower in her hair, which added a feminine touch to their rather severe attire. Mrs. Rae Lee Jones was the manager of the band, a tall, imposing woman and a disciplinarian reminiscent of a boarding school matron. She walked among the girls, adjusting a neckline here, tucking in a stray hair there, checking the girls' lipstick and eye makeup. "That'll do; off you go," she ordered. With a last-minute flurry of practice notes, the girls filed out of the dressing room to take their places on stage.

The huge curtain parted as strains of the Sweethearts' theme song, featuring Rosalind (Roz) Cron on alto sax, filled the theater. Next, a solid, swinging arrangement of "Tuxedo Junction" kept the audience snapping their fingers. Among the several outstanding soloists featured on the program was diminutive Evelyn McGee, who drew whistles of appreciation for her singing of "Candy" and "Rum" and "Coca Cola." Anna Mae Winburn put aside her baton to sing "Do You Want to Jump, Children?" "Yeah, yeah," shrilled the band, answering her musical question in childlike voices. Following this was a wild, frantic version of "Sweet Georgia Brown" taken at an impossible tempo, with Vi Burnside free-wheeling in and around the melody, playing a shower of notes on her tenor sax that took one's breath away. When the show was over, and with the echoes of the cheers and applause still ringing in their ears, the girls could now look forward to a quick snack between shows, visits from friends, and the heady excitement of being back in New York City.

Few white people ever saw the Sweethearts. At that time the Apollo and other theaters like it—the Howard in Washington, the Regal in Chicago, the Paradise in Detroit—catered to black audiences, and the small number of whites who ventured there were the real jazz aficionados. Among them was record producer John Hammond, who thought the band was "just marvelous; a great band." It might even have been, as one of the fans remarked, "the world's greatest girl dance band." Pianist Earl "Fatha" Hines had high praise for the group—"a wonderful swinging bunch of gals"—but there were negative comments, too. Huffed one well-known woman player when asked if she had ever worked with the Sweethearts, "You wouldn't catch me anywhere near *that* band." And the typical remark from male musicians was, "You certainly couldn't consider them in the same league as any good *male* band." Yet musical director Maurice King was enthusiastic. "You could put those girls behind a curtain and people would be convinced it was men playing." The group was often likened to the Lunceford band, and Jimmie Lunceford himself had high praise for the girls.

It had taken stamina, long hours of practice, dedication, and experiences both rewarding and frustrating to bring the International Sweethearts of Rhythm all the way from Piney Woods, Mississippi, to the Apollo Theater in New York. The newer band members were all aware of the pioneering spirit that had helped the first schoolgirl band to pave the way for the present group's highly acclaimed reputation.

RESEARCH INDICATES THAT the principal of Piney Woods Country Life School, Laurence C. Jones, was a most unusual man—well-educated (University of Iowa), charming, knowledgeable in the ways of the world, and totally committed to raising money for the betterment of his school. Money was constantly needed to take care of the thousand boys and girls, many of them orphans, who lived at the school.

Mr. Jones believed in keeping everybody working. The bell rang at 5:00 A.M.; at six the children had breakfast; and by seven they were all busy with schoolwork or some other activity. There was a farm—boys were taught farming and furniture-making among other things—and the girls learned domestic skills such as cooking and dressmaking. The football team bested everyone in the area, and there were two marching bands, one of boys, one of girls. The school had everything—there never had been a place like it for blacks in the South. At that time they were held back, yet Mr. Jones's powers of persuasion were so strong that he was able to convince the white businessmen that he met that his idea of teaching every child a trade was of prime importance. He knew the right people to approach, and money flowed into the school from many sources.

There was a great deal of musical activity before the formation of the Sweethearts. In addition to the forty-five-piece marching bands, there was a group called "The Cotton Blossom Singers," who were at that time the main fund-raisers for the school. Mr. Jones personally supervised all these activities.

This was the burgeoning swing era—the great bands of Ellington, Hines, Basie, and Lunceford were developing unique stylings from their jazz heritage. A new kind of jazz, jazz people could dance to, began to flourish, and it burst forth all over the country, inspiring white musicians—the Dorsey Brothers, Benny Goodman, Artie Shaw, Glenn Miller—to form their own bands. It was inevitable that someone would think of putting together a different type of show business package, one that was bound to succeed—an all-girl (white) swing band, Ina Ray Hutton and Her Melodears. Irving Mills, mentor of the Ellington band, did just that.

According to Helen Jones, who had been adopted at the age of three months by Laurence Jones and his wife and brought up at Piney Woods, Mr. Jones heard Ina Ray and her band in Chicago, and his fertile mind instantly grasped the possibilities and advantages of establishing such a group to raise funds for Piney Woods. As soon as he returned, he set about selecting girls for the band. There were many who had musical talent and who, with training, would develop into competent musicians. Helen Jones recalls that Mr. Jones wanted her to play the violin, but she begged for a chance to learn the trombone, because she "loved to watch that slide going in and out." This was a fortunate decision, because Helen's strong, full tone enhanced the Sweethearts' trombone section from the formation of the group until they disbanded.

No one remembers who was the first director of the band. After Laurence Jones had assembled the group, they were rehearsed for a short time by a teacher named Lawrence Jefferson. Then Edna Williams, a talented young pianist and trumpet player not much older than the band members themselves, took over. It seems that Edna Williams, or someone like her, taught the girls their first tunes, which were, according to drummer Pauline Braddy, "Baby, Don't Tell On Me," "How Long, Baby," "720 in the Books," and "Star Dust." Some of the girls were given half notes or whole notes to play, while others played the melody. A few learned the tunes by reading the music, while the others would imitate notes and phrases sung or played by the teacher. She also taught them breath control and how to produce a tone. Gradually they became proficient enough to move on to "stocks"—sheet music copies of popular tunes of the day. Finally, they were ready to set forth on a fund-raising trip in the area, as Mr. Jones had envisioned. Sixteen in all, the girls rode in a special bus to play dates in armories, halls, and high school gymnasiums. Mr. Jones thought of everything. He even hired a chaperone, Mrs. Ella P. Gant, who traveled along with the girls.

As the girls gained in experience and proficiency, the band blossomed. The plain blouses and dark skirts the girls wore gave them a fresh appearance. Their neatly combed hair and well-scrubbed faces emphasized how young they were (14–15) to be on the road. Soon the trips became longer, and Mr. Jones hired Vivian Crawford as tutor for the girls, and Mrs. Rae Lee Jones (no relation) to replace Mrs. Gant. Mrs. Jones was a social worker from Omaha, whom Laurence Jones had met on one of his fund-raising trips. She kept order among the girls and brooked no disobedience, but was concerned enough about their health to see that they all ate well and drank plenty of milk.

By now the band was beginning to sound more professional. Some of the original group had dropped out, and others took their places. Evelyn McGee, a talented youngster from Anderson, South Carolina, joined the band as a vocalist. Mr. Jones had an uncanny way of spotting talent. On a trip with the band to Bolivar, Mississippi, he espied a very beautiful girl, Helen Saine, playing basketball, and invited her to come to Piney Woods and join the band. "But I can't play an instrument," said Helen. "We'll teach you," Mr. Jones replied. Something in his approach must have made the invitation seem worthwhile to her parents, because Helen Saine was allowed to leave immediately for Piney Woods and was soon learning to play tenor and alto sax.

Then came Grace Bayron and her sister, Judy. While on a trip to New York the year before, Laurence Jones had noticed Gracie carrying her saxophone case on an East Harlem street. He followed her home and asked her parents if they would relocate their family to Piney Woods—Mr. Bayron to teach Spanish, Gracie and Judy to play in the band. The parents declined the offer, but by some strange quirk of fate both died within the same year. Remembering Laurence Jones's invitation, Gracie Bayron telephoned him soon after her parents' death. Arrangements were made, and a few days later a chaperone arrived to escort the girls to Piney Woods. "Gracie started playing in the band right away," Judy Bayron recalls. "I was just given a guitar to hold so I could sit in the rhythm section. But eventually I learned to play trombone."

The band began to take on an air of professionalism that Rae Lee Jones helped to bring about with her constant supervision and strict rules. She had insisted that each girl wear a flower in her hair on stage. Now she started buying costumes for them that gave them a more sophisticated appearance.

Hotel accommodations for a racially mixed group were impossible to find, so trips were made in a bus filled with bunk beds so that the group could travel all night and wake up refreshed. They ate on the bus, practiced, prepared their lessons, got dressed and, as the bus pulled into town, were ready in their costumes for their performance. It would seem as if the Sweethearts led an exciting life, traveling from town to town, playing to packed houses and appreciative audiences, but in fact it was a hard, rugged existence, with no chance for social life. The girls looked glamorous on stage, but, says Helen Jones, "We were the biggest bunch of virgins in America."

The band's fund-raising endeavors took them farther and farther afield, and in October 1939 they played Chicago, Des Moines, Omaha, and Kansas City in the space of a week. Their Chicago appearance was sponsored by the Chicago-Piney Woods Club, and a review of their performance at the Romping Earl's Club House read in part:

"Sixteen girls, best known in music circles as the 'International Sweethearts of Rhythm' who hail from Piney Woods, Mississippi, right in the heart of the Delta, invaded Chicago Saturday night and gave jitterbugs, swing fans and hep cats something to talk about.

"They beat out a bit of mellow jive, sang the latest song hits, then started a swing session that caused the dance lovers to stop in their tracks and listen to the hot sounds that blared out from the instruments played by these Mississippi girls.

"Together for two years, these girls handle their instruments like veterans and can rightfully take a place among the leading male aggregations."

Perhaps reviews such as this helped to pique the interest of a talent promoter from Washington, D.C., for Daniel M. Gary suddenly appeared on the scene, approaching Mrs. Jones with the suggestion that he take over the bookings for the band. It seems that after consulting with Laurence Jones, Mr. Gary did indeed start booking the band, and they embarked on their most successful tour thus far, playing major cities in the South and Midwest.

However, as their musicianship improved and their successes increased, so in direct proportion did their problems—problems that would soon lead to a decision that would drastically affect the future of the band and its members.

It appears that Laurence Jones thought he was losing control of the band, primarily because Rae Lee Jones was encouraging the girls to question his judgment in financial and other matters. He therefore confronted her with the threat of dismissal. When the girls decided to stand by her, he informed them that they would not receive their high school diplomas unless they returned to Piney Woods immediately. To his dismay, the girls refused to change their minds; even his adopted daughter, Helen, defied him. Perhaps they had already been influenced in their decision by thoughts of the bright future Dan Gary had promised them.

It was a momentous decision, especially since everyone knew they were virtually running away from Piney Woods, taking with them the uniforms and instruments belonging to the school, as well as the bus. Perhaps the consequences of such a decision had not yet dawned on them—that Mr. Jones, hurt and furious at what he thought was a betrayal, would later have Rae Lee Jones arrested for theft. Even this did not stop the forward movement of the band, because Dan Gary, through his various political connections, managed to secure her release, on the condition that the bus, uniforms, and instruments be returned to Piney Woods.

At this point, having lost Piney Woods as home base, the band needed a new headquarters. Property records show that Rae Lee Jones, as Trustee of the International Sweethearts of Rhythm, Inc., purchased a ten-room house at 908 South Quinn Street, Arlington, Virginia. The girls believed they were members of the corporation and that they owned shares in the house, as they had been told that a portion of their salaries would be used to help pay the mortgage. It was a beautiful idea—their very own house where they could rest and relax. To girls who had started in the band with nothing, the prospect of having their own house was thrilling indeed.

Once settled in Arlington, the girls rehearsed every day, sometimes for as long as six hours at a stretch, and consequently their playing became more polished. They began to believe that their dreams of hitting the big time would come true when they were plunged into the exciting, fast-moving, sometimes sinister web of black nightclubs, while continuing to play at well-known ballrooms and theaters. There were more changes in the band personnel—stronger, more experienced musicians were brought in. Anna Mae Winburn, who had once led a group of her own, was hired to front the band; her beauty and stage presence were a definite asset. She brought down the house with her rendition of "Blowtop Blues," a song written for her by jazz critic Leonard Feather.

It was becoming quite evident that despite the many changes and improvements in the band, their repertoire was too limited for the bookings Dan Gary had scheduled for them at theaters such as the Apollo, the Howard Theater in Washington, D.C., the Regal in Chicago and other top-rated theaters across the country. It was time to bring in an arranger, and Mrs. Jones was advised to hire Eddie Durham, who had been prominent in the Count Basie Band and who was also well-known as a songwriter, guitarist, and trombone player. He had to his credit a hit song, "I Don't Want To Set the World on Fire," and other original tunes. His arrangements of "St. Louis Blues" and "At Sundown" were simple, but effective. He also arranged a beautiful Harold Arlen song, "When the Sun Comes Out," as well as some of his own compositions, "Moten Swing" and "Topsy," for the Sweethearts. Durham had his own all-woman band, so he knew the best approach to take in teaching the Sweethearts. Knowing that there were few improvisors in the band, he wrote out solos for them that sounded as if they were improvised on the spot when played.

Durham had high regard for the Sweethearts, and he enjoyed working with them. "People couldn't believe it was women playing," he commented, "so sometimes when the curtain opened I'd make off that I was playing and the girls were just pantomiming. Then I'd stop, and people could see they really were playing. I simplified things for them as much as possible. You structure arrangements for people . . . you write for what you've got. I had to train the Sweethearts, but at the Apollo nobody believed girls could play that way."

Durham showed considerable sensitivity in allowing for the girls' technical limitations while stressing their strong points. He played an important role, as a teacher as well as an arranger, in the development of the band. Through his efforts they were beginning to know where they were going musically.

None of the surviving members of the band's early days recalls exactly when their romantic fantasies of success ran head-long into reality. They were becoming aware that real life was turning out to be not only places like the Apollo, but also endless and grueling one-nighters, tedious rehearsals, and long nights on the bus. They sometimes had to eat in dirty restaurants, where often they were handed their food through a back window, typical treatment for blacks in the South at that time. (Anna Mae Winburn recalls screaming angrily at one restaurant owner, "My brother is overseas fighting for people like you, and you're treating me this way?")

Most of the time the girls slept on the bus because it was too risky for mixed groups to stay in black hotels. On the rare occasion that they did, there was always the danger that the police would question the hotel owner, trying to find out if some of the girls were white. Ironically, the white girls, and those who looked white, suffered as much from Southern racism as the black band members.

The girls were harassed in hotels and restaurants, and even while on stage. Policemen would roam the clubs, trying to spot the white band members. Often they succeeded, despite the heavy, dark makeup the lighter-skinned girls used in an attempt to disguise their pale complexions, and the wigs they wore to hide their light hair. When this happened, Mrs. Jones was ready with false credentials to prove the girls were Negro. It was a constant worry in the minds of the girls that, despite all their precautions, one of their number might be taken away at any time, not for any wrongdoing but simply because of her color.

Harassment of another sort was experienced by some of the black band members. During a performance in a nightclub, Anna Mae Winburn tripped while stepping onto the stage. When a white man rose to help her, he was immediately forced back into his seat by a nearby policeman who ordered, "You sit down and let that nigger woman help herself."

(A few years later Anna Mae and her husband, Duke Pilgrim, fared better in a confrontation with Southern police. While driving through town with two white members of the band they had formed, their car was stopped by a policeman. "You know you're not supposed to have them white women in the car," rasped the officer. Pilgrim, with a look of innocence, replied, "I know that, officer, that's why I've got them sitting in the *back* seat." He drove away, leaving the befuddled policeman standing there.)

The band kept improving, kept moving ahead. They had seen their names on theater marquees and billboards, and they had heard the warm applause of audiences all over the country.

Their next big milestone musically was the hiring of Jesse Stone as the band's coach-arranger. Like Eddie Durham, Stone was a highly respected and successful figure in the world of topflight Negro swing bands. He had written several well-known songs, "Idaho" and "Smack Dab in the Middle" being the most familiar.

Jesse Stone made many changes and improvements in the band. He brought in several new musicians, among them Lucille Dixon, bass; Marjorie Pettiford (Oscar's sister), alto sax; Johnnie Mae (Tex) Stansbury, trumpet; Amy Garrison, sax; and Roxanna Lucas, guitar. The addition of these talented women, whose reading and playing skill was at an advanced level, raised the caliber of the entire group. He made a special point of teaching the girls how to improve their intonation, how to listen to each other in order to achieve a smooth blend and a sharp attack. Some of his new arrangements were more challenging than anything the girls had attempted thus far, and therefore special coaching was necessary.

The major innovation that Stone made was the formation of a singing group drawn from the band. Helen Jones recalls, "We had some numbers where a group of us went down front and sang. Evelyn, Ella Ritz Lucas, somebody else and myself had a quartet. We went down front after we played part of the show and we sang and everybody liked it. Jesse is really the one who did that. In fact, we sang some of his numbers."

During Jesse Stone's first year with the band the Sweethearts made considerable musical progress. The overall sound was smoother, the musicianship improving. It was a rough life, but a free one to the extent that the girls had broken loose from familial ties, from school and similar restraints. Also, the earlier camaraderie had grown into a bond of friendship that had been strengthened by the many experiences, good and bad, that the girls had shared.

But not only did the band members learn more about music from Jesse Stone, they also became fully aware through him that they were performing for less than adequate wages.

Evelyn McGee recalls, "Jesse would fight with Mrs. Jones about how she was taking advantage of the girls. For example, we played five shows a day in Baltimore during Christmas week. The lines were unbelievable, the audiences fantastic—but at the end of the week Mrs. Jones gave each girl less than $100.

"Jesse hit the ceiling, and gave his notice. But Mrs. Jones held him to his two-year contract, so he stayed on another year. When he finally left, it wasn't because he was dissatisfied with the band. It was because of the treatment we were getting from Rae Lee Jones."

The girls were becoming disenchanted, and some of them left. Those who stayed on seemed to have a more philosophical attitude about things. "It's funny, when you're young and don't know anything, you do a lot of things without thinking," Helen Jones reflected recently. "You believe a lot of things people tell you when you're 'country' and don't know much about the world. I can see how certain people kept control of our destiny then. Deep down, we knew we weren't making much money, and we knew the hotels were dirty and the food was bad. But we didn't think about that so much—we were enjoying ourselves."

The year was 1944; the Americans had been involved in the Second World War for three years. Perhaps because many male musicians had been drafted, all-girl orchestras proliferated and flourished. Among them the groups directed by Phil Spitalny, Ina Ray Hutton, and Ada Leonard were best known, but all the girls bands were more in demand than they had ever been before.

Not only were the Sweethearts busy, they were perhaps more stable, since there were fewer changes of personnel that year. One notable change was replacement of Marge Pettiford as lead alto by Rosalind (Roz) Cron, a Jewish girl from Boston, Massachusetts. Roz had been with Ada Leonard's band for some time. There were violins in that band, and the music was more sedate. Consequently Roz, a high-spirited girl who was an extremely good player, relished the freer, more swinging style of the Sweethearts.

"I remember something about the difference between working for Ada Leonard and being with the Sweethearts," Roz says. "In all the theaters, when the Sweethearts started playing the audience would come in, dancing down the aisles to their seats. Black audiences were always like that. But if you'd go to hear Tommy or Jimmy Dorsey, or Ada Leonard, people just *walked* to their seats and sat down."

Shortly after Roz Cron joined the band, Maurice King arrived from Detroit to replace Jesse Stone as musical director. He had a cataclysmic effect on the band. Roz Cron in particular was impressed. "Maurice immediately put us through the most grueling rehearsals. It was a tough struggle, but we made it. 'Tuxedo Junction' turned into a really polished thing."

Maurice King recalls, "When I worked with the girls I would show them a passage in an arrangement and how to phrase it, four bars at a time. We'd keep on going over it, and finally, when it jelled, you could see their little eyes beam. It was like putting an erector set together."

King obviously enjoyed teaching and working with the girls. He began writing specialty numbers for the band, and his "Vi Vigor," "Slightly Frantic," "Don't Get It Twisted," and "Diggin' Dirt" became part of the Sweethearts' book. "'Diggin' Dirt' was what we called a dance stopper," said King. "We'd end the tune, pause, and then start it all over again. We'd do this several times. It was a big number."

En route to California, where they were scheduled to record for the Armed Forces Radio Network, the girls spent their days playing, rehearsing, and sleeping on the bus. Finally, they reached Texas, where they were booked on a series of nightclub dates. One afternoon in Austin a policeman who was watching them rehearse asked King, "Isn't that a white girl over there?" "What makes you think she's white?" King replied. Looking right at Roz Cron, the policeman said, "Well, she looks white to me." At this point King answered piously, rolling his eyes heavenward, "Well, our girls are not responsible for what one of their parents may have been forced to do." He then turned back to the band and continued the rehearsal, while Roz, red as a beet, had a difficult time keeping quiet.

Once in California the girls were plunged into a round of new activities. They were taken to various Hollywood studios to make short films which would later be used as "fillers" in movie theaters. Most of these are now in the collections of jazz buffs.

At this time the Sweethearts also recorded several shows live at the Club Alabam for the GIs in Europe and the Pacific, each show featuring a big star. It was thrilling for the Sweethearts to work with such people as Ethel Waters, Lena Horne, Jerry Colonna, Phil Harris, and Jimmy Durante. Recently portions of these programs have surfaced in a collection of women's jazz performances on a small, independent label. Many of these "air checks" are also being sold on the open market, so there is no telling where the music of the Sweethearts may be heard next.

After playing the Club Plantation, one of the best West Coast jazz clubs in Los Angeles, the group set forth once again for Arlington, Virginia. A whole new chain of events was beginning. The State Department had become interested in the band, because there had been a demand for it from the GIs in Europe who had heard the broadcasts over the Armed Forces Radio Network. This resulted in a tour of Europe with USO Camp Shows for the Sweethearts.

Attired in their brand new USO uniforms, the Sweethearts sailed for Europe on July 15, 1945, reaching Le Havre on July 22. They were chaperoned by Maurice King, as Rae Lee Jones had become ill and couldn't make the trip. In the European Theatre the war was already over, but there were still thousands of GIs in the Occupational Forces to be entertained. When the girls arrived, they were ecstatically received, and, every time the band performed, the audiences went wild. The program varied somewhat from the routine they used in nightclubs. Tunes were added that the GIs knew and liked, but basically it was the same show that had excited the Apollo audience earlier that year.

They were all living together in a hotel, and Maurice King was required to conduct a room check at 10:30 P.M. every night, because of the curfew. He would make the room check and leave, knowing full well that some of the girls would sneak out afterwards. "I should have received a medal for bringing back that band intact," King has said with a mysterious smile. Piney Woods seemed a million light-years away.

When the band returned to the States after Christmas 1945, the girls had money in the bank for the first time in their lives. As financial guardian of the band, Maurice King had seen to it that most of the money the girls earned was deposited in U.S. banks to await their return from Europe. Only Helen Jones had elected to have Rae Lee Jones hold her money for safekeeping, instead of depositing it in a bank.

The controlling factors of the band were still the Washingtonians, Dan Gary and his partner, Al Dade. Gary was still the president of the corporation, and Rae Lee Jones was still the trustee, although she had left Arlington to return to her hometown of Omaha, seriously ill.

The band went on. More and different projects were being undertaken. Leonard Feather, who has always admired women musicians and done his best to further their careers, now prepared to record for RCA Victor, using different women's groups. The Sweethearts recorded two numbers for Leonard Feather—"Don't Get It Twisted" and "Vi Vigor," both written by Maurice King. They also made two sides for Guild Records, with one side featuring Tiny Davis singing and playing "Stompin' the Blues." The reverse side spotlighted Anna Mae Winburn singing "Do You Want to Jump, Children?" The culmination of all this activity was a short film, *That Man of Mine,* which starred Ruby Dee and featured the Sweethearts. Maurice King wrote the theme song, and the Sweethearts played it.

At last the Sweethearts had realized some of their earlier dreams. They had played to audiences of thousands in the United States and abroad, recorded overseas broadcasts with big-name Hollywood stars, had made records and films. What was left for them?

For some it seemed a good time to leave the band and go back to school. Others had already met their future husbands, and they left to get married. A few stayed on, but there were many new girls coming in. Some remained for a while, but others left after only a week or two, so it is impossible to document all the band members during the last years the group was together. Nevertheless the band continued to grow in stature. Some of the musicians were the best the band had ever had, and this is confirmed by the following enthusiastic review carried in the July 27, 1946, issue of *Billboard.* Noting the band's appearance at the Million Dollar in Los Angeles, the review read in part:

"The joint is jumpin' again this week with a solid bill headlined by the International Sweethearts of Rhythm . . . Anna Mae Winburn fronts the Sweethearts (all-gal ork) in smooth and easy style. Fem musikers are top instrumentalists and dish out a polished brand of music, offering such widely titled concoctions as 'Don't Get It Twisted' and 'Just the Thing.' Instrumental breaks fall to Pauline Braddy on the skins and a sensational sax tooter, Vi Burnside. Latter socked 'em between the eyes with 'After You've Gone' and 'I Cover the Waterfront.'

"In the vocal bracket, featured thrush Mildred McIver does 'Day by Day' and 'Mr. Postman Blues' well . . . Surprise vocal shot was guitarist Carline Ray doing 'Temptation.' Gal has a deep voice and knows how to peddle a tune."

The band was to continue until the end of 1948, playing brilliantly and getting excellent reviews. And yet, something was missing now that virtually all the original Sweethearts had left.

Helen Jones was on her way back to Omaha to visit Rae Lee Jones, now desperately ill. It was a shock to Helen to see her so obviously near death, but just as shocking was the admission Mrs. Jones made—that she had spent all the money Helen had entrusted to her. She begged Helen's forgiveness. "I didn't realize the magnitude of it until years later," Helen reflected recently. "I felt so sorry for her. There she was, down and out, in this little old house that she had bought for her parents. And when she died she left it to me, but I didn't take it. Her parents were still there, and I didn't want to put them out. So there was nothing I could do. At that time I was young, and I didn't know anything, so whatever came up, I just accepted it. That's life—everyone learns one way or another."

Somehow, in spite of the mystery surrounding the management of the band, Rae Lee Jones had been the life force that held it together. When she died, the band also died.

But memories and dreams do not die easily. They still flourish in the hearts and minds of these women, who open their scrapbooks and point with pride to the fresh-faced group of girls with whom they once had shared so much. No matter that their moment in the spotlight was brief. Their spirit and courage has been passed on to a new generation of talented young women, who are seeking their own dreams.

A Starr Is Reborn

Gary Giddins

Kay Starr is always being rediscovered. In an appreciation wrtitten in 1985 and collected in Faces in the Crowd *(1992), Gary Giddins paid tribute to this extraordinary singer, who could—and did—sing country, jazz, gospel, pop, and show tunes, all superbly. Her admirers include Lester Young, Bud Powell, and Mahalia Jackson (see p. 632), yet when most people remember her, they think of her pop hits like "Wheel of Fortune" and "Bonaparte's Retreat." Such are the penalties of commercial success.*

In a 1958 interview, writer Chris Albertson asked Lester Young if he thought "anybody nowadays" could sing like Bessie Smith. He got a surprising response: "Yeah . . . sometimes you think upon Kay Starr and listen to her voice and play one of Bessie Smith's records and see if you hear anything." A similarity? "Yes, very much," Young said. Kay Starr, best known in those days for the oxymoronic "Rock and Roll Waltz," had other admirers in the jazz world, including Dinah Washington, Helen Humes ("I think she swings from way back"), and Bud Powell, who voted her best female singer in a 1956 poll. Five years before that, the traditionalist readers of *Record Changer* voted her number six among female vocalists in its "All-time" poll (after Bessie Smith, Ma Rainey, Billie Holiday, Mildred Bailey, and Ella Fitzgerald). By the time of the Young interview, however, Starr was hardly ever discussed or reviewed in jazz circles; in subsequent years, as she and her best records dropped from sight, she was remembered chiefly for a few hits ("Side by Side," "Wheel of Fortune," "Rock and Roll Waltz") that all too neatly embodied 1950s whitewashed pop—the stuff rock and roll was supposed to puncture and sink.

My interest in Starr was roused a year ago, in Amsterdam, where I found reissues of records she made for Capitol and RCA in the fifties. When I discovered other reissues, pressed in Japan and England, turning up as imports in New York stores, I decided to write a column about her—a historical account of a neglected (and presumably retired) singer, whose most enduring work had been overshadowed by her ephemera. Then a press release arrived, announcing a three-week engagement at Freddy's Supper Club. I attended opening night with some trepidation, wanting her to recapture the prodigious zest and savvy blues-colored phrasing of the radiant and largely forgotten jazz records she made between 1945 and 1961, but fearful of hearing no more than an extended sop to lifeless nostalgia. All doubt was eclipsed about ten seconds into her opening set.

Starr is an electrifying performer, thoroughly in command of her talent. I don't hear much Bessie Smith in her, but I can understand why Young and many others did in that decade when white girl singers tended to be cool as menthol and cute as high-buttoned shoes. She holds the stage like someone who paid her dues in tent-shows, red-hot and earthy, enthralled to a sinewy beat, unafraid to belt, jolt, wag her finger, shimmy, and tell bad jokes. Nor is there anything faded or ersatz about her exuberance, wit, and musicality. Starr has an open, lucent quality, accentuated by a wide, sexy smile and glittery eyes. For me, she represents a "new" addition to the very small pantheon of great working jazz singers.

Starr is so unabashedly consumed with the pleasures of singing, it's hard to imagine her in premature retirement: She's sixty-three, the age Helen Humes was when she returned to duty a decade ago. Nor has she been entirely inactive. She has sung for corporations, appeared with the Summer Symphony in Los Angeles, and toured for more than two years with the nostalgia revue, *4 Girls 4* (along with Helen O'Connell, Rosemary Clooney, and Martha Raye). In every instance, she was locked by a large band into a rigidly rehearsed repertoire. Her decision to "do something for myself" followed an experience in London two summers ago, when she appeared as part of a Kool Jazz package. She explained, in characteristically breathless fashion, "It was a one-nighter in a little jazz club and when I said I would do it, I didn't know I'd have only three or four musicians. I almost had cardiac arrest. But I was able to get the drummer touring with us, Jerry White, and of course I had Frank [Ortega, her music director of nineteen years], and how much trouble can you get into if you've got a good drummer? I sat there singing and before I realized what was happening to me, I felt like I'd been released or something. Just felt so free, singing and soaring and having the best time, and I didn't have anybody in my way. When I came back and started doing the normal kinds of dates, with the eighteen- and twenty-five-piece bands, I suddenly was boxed in, and I thought, 'What's happening here?' And I sat down with myself and said, 'Look, what's happening is you really want to sing with a smaller group.' So I let it be known and pretty soon I got a bite from Frank Nolan, who owns Freddy's. I was anxious about it, but I don't like to talk about what a good time I'm having—I *really* am."

Except for an appearance in Brooklyn seven years ago ("does that count?"), she hasn't appeared in New York in at least fifteen years. The show mirrors her anxiety only in its politic variety, though she abstains from a medley of hits. Backed by Ortega on piano and a pick-up trio (guitarist John Bassili, bassist John Ray, drummer Ronnie Zito), she leads off with a jaunty version of "Love Will Keep Us Together," replete with half-time interludes and the unblushing blues notes that are a Starr speciality. She slides in and out of pitch like a trombone. When I asked her about the song, she said, "That was Toni Tennille. I think Fats Waller or somebody did it first and she found it." As Starr sings it, Waller doesn't seem an unlikely source, but actually Neil Sedaka wrote it. She does the two strongest songs from her *Just Plain Country* album of twenty-three years ago, "I Really Don't Want to Know" and "Crazy," but with more feeling and invention than in her previous versions. Taking the former as a blues (it isn't), she slows it down to a deliciously sensual plea, twanging upper-register notes against chesty mid-range phrases, and underscoring musical conceits with histrionic ones—expressive mask, imploring hands. The ease with which she switches from country laments to "Honeysuckle Rose" or "Hard-Hearted Hannah" is startling. Like Joe Turner, whose blues style is equally at home in jazz, r&b, r&r, Starr uses Oklahoma drawl and superb time to democratize all genres.

Starr still sings Pee Wee King's "Bonaparte's Retreat," her big hit of 1950, because she found it herself in Dougherty, Oklahoma (where she was born), convinced Capitol to let her do it, and credits its success with the company's decision to hand her the aptly named "Wheel of Fortune." It's a trite piece, notwithstanding a hootchie-cootchie middle-strain that lets her sashay. She slows "For the Good Times" to a crawl, paced by Ortega's tremolos, and colors an occasionally stagy interpretation with serpentine portamentos that resemble tailgate glides. Then she rests her chops by turning the stage over to the pianist, who plays a medley of five Ellington tunes, the highlight of which is "Mood Indigo" strummed harplike on the strings.

Starr invariably chooses the right tempo and melodic embellishments, investing her songs with a voluptuous huskiness that can give the illusion of abandon, as on a dramatic "I'm Through with Love," complete with half-yodeled cries and stop-time release. She doubles the tempo on "Lazy River," takes an Armstrongian break, and makes the last note a perfect descending triad. The set begins to unravel toward the end with a travel medley that disappoints because her single choruses of "Going to Chicago" and "Kansas City" make you want to hear more; instead, they're just teasing preludes for the exceedingly anticlimactic "New York State of Mind." She closes with her chartbusters, the insidious "Rock and Roll Waltz" and the inevitable "Wheel of Fortune," rendering them palatable with self-mocking zeal.

STARR'S BRASSY FUSION of urban swing and country twang fixed the attention of several bandleaders in the thirties and forties and later established her as a "utility singer" (her phrase) able to indemnify almost any kind of song against banality. Yet her versatility offended chroniclers of every genre. Though she has recorded some of the most effective swing band vocal albums of the past thirty years, as well as notable efforts in country, gospel, and r&b, she isn't listed in any of the standard encyclopedias for those fields. Her remarkable collaborations with arranger Van Alexander in 1960 were ignored by most jazz magazines. In books on American popular or jazz-related singers she is mentioned parenthetically or not at all. She is listed in Hardy and Laing's *Encyclopedia of Rock,* ironically enough, but is grouped with the likes of Pat Boone and Gale Storm as one of "those whites with no feeling for r&b," who were guilty of "undercutting black performers." Which is triply absurd: Starr had little to do with rock; she's one of the rare "white" singers (she's actually three-quarters Native American) with a profound feeling for rhythm and blues; and her one notorious "cover" was of a white performer. The moral of all this is a variant on Gresham's law: A performer's good records will be driven out of circulation and memory by the bad ones that yield immediate and staggering profits.

When I visited her in the penthouse that Freddy's provided for her stay in New York, Starr was completing a photographic session ("Some photographers make you pose till you feel like drugstore lettuce," she noted) and preparing Vodka collinses. The radio was playing singers of her generation, and I was trying to think of a polite way to say that she reminded me of a white Dinah Washington, when she threw up her hands and said, "*There's* my favorite singer." I turned to the radio, and of course it was Washington. "I stood up at her wedding to Night-Train Lane. I think I've known Dinah about half my adult life. I got to meet her on Central Avenue in L.A. when I was with Charlie Barnet, and she'd come to hear me with Charlie's band, and we became really good friends. We'd laugh because she was one color and I was another but we were the same." One of the numbers Starr recorded with Barnet in 1944 was "What a Difference a Day Makes," which became Washington's signature song years later. Could Starr's recording have influenced her? "I don't think so, I don't think she listened to *anybody.* She just had it and knew what to do with it." Minutes later: "And that's my other favorite singer"—Ella Fitzgerald, whom Starr slightly resembled on her first recordings, made in 1939.

The question of influence is always nettlesome, and never more so than in the instance of a singer who violates all the usual pigeonholes. Starr was born Katherine La Verne Starks in Oklahoma, in 1922, to a full-blooded Iroquois father and a mother who is Cherokee, Choctaw, and Irish. Since three of the most individual "white" women jazz singers—Mildred Bailey, Lee Wiley, and Starr—are American Indians, I asked if she thought there was an ethnic connection. "I don't have any idea, but it's interesting, isn't it?

Red Norvo and Mildred used to come to my house at the beach, but we never talked about it. If you were on a reservation, which is government run, they have Presbyterians and Methodists and people telling you your religion—in order to get subsidized you had to go to church. But those of us who *weren't* brought up on some kind of reservation don't really belong to a church. I go to everybody's church, why not? God is everywhere. But most of us believe in elements, in wind and trees and the earth, and I think we're just children of the soil. I think we three Indians, if you've researched the other two, you've found they've always been honest: They weren't trying to prove anything in particular, they were just doing what came naturally, and rolled with the punches. That's the personality Mildred had, it was mine, and the little bit I knew of Lee Wiley, it was hers. Of course, Indian music has a hell of a beat—it's all drums and chanting. There is not a whole lot of melody to our music."

As a child, she pretended her mother's chicken coop was an amphitheater and was satisfied to entertain the roost until her aunt entered her in a contest. She won third prize for simultaneously singing and working a yo-yo. Most of her childhood was spent on the move: "My daddy worked for a big sprinkler company and was foreman when they put automatic sprinklers in big buildings all over Texas. I've said that I lived in every town in Texas for fifteen minutes, because it seemed like that to me. I never really got to know anybody, and my mother was my playmate all my life—she's still the best girlfriend I've got—so it was easy for her to go on the road with me as my sister because we did everything together." She performed on radio with Bill Boyd and his Cowboy Ramblers in Dallas, and the Light Crust Doughboys in Fort Worth. When the family finally settled in Memphis, she repeatedly won a local radio contest and was offered her own fifteen-minute show three times a week. She was thirteen. Shortly afterwards, the great jazz violinist Joe Venuti and his orchestra came through Memphis.

"Joe's contract called for a girl singer, and he didn't have one. He thought he could bluff his way through with a boy singer, but towns like Memphis, Tennessee, going through growing pains, weren't having it: The contract called for a girl singer, and where *is* she? They wouldn't let him open. Joe's road manager heard me on this radio show, just me and a piano player, pop songs and a few rhythm songs, because it's hard to sing rhythm songs with just rum-ching rum-ching, but when you're young you're invincible and think you can do anything. So I was trying to do anything, and he heard me and didn't have any idea how old I was. My voice hadn't started to grow up—I sounded like Dolly Dawn, Bonnie Baker, and those other young voices. But I had the feel, and so he called the station and wanted to talk to me about joining Joe Venuti's band. I said, 'Gee, I'm sorry, you're going to have to talk to my mother and dad.' He said, 'WHAT?'—he thought I was at least a young adult.

"So he went up to the house, and my father said okay, because I was going to cry, I was going to throw a fit if they didn't let me. But I had to be off the stand by twelve, so I could go to school. They had to buy me two evening dresses, and at thirteen I weighed about 165 pounds. Joe thought I was wonderful and took me under his wing, and every summer after that I used to sing with his band. But we had to tell everybody my mother was my sister because those hotels could have been closed with everybody having alcoholic drinks and a thirteen- or fourteen-year-old kid on the stage. I guess the person I give the most credit to for anything I've done or ever will do is Joe Venuti. He taught me to sing with authority. He said, if you make a mistake make it loud. When we played places like a hotel in Toledo or Memphis, if someone like Menuhin or Kreisler was in town, they'd be in the dining room to listen to Joe play quiet things like 'Estralita' that are good for the digestion, and I'd sing quiet songs. But after dinner, when they left, he went back to playing jazz, and he played great jazz."

I asked if she had listened to Bessie Smith. "Not until later when musicians made me conscious of her, because I think they could feel that once in a while I had a tendency towards the blues. But in the part of the country I came from there is a great deal of gospel, so I was exposed to all this stuff. The guys in the band used to take me to Beale Street, to those churches and, my God, those holy rollers. You never heard anything like it in your life. I mean those people would start singing and would sing until their voices disappeared, and they broke out in a sweat and fell to the floor, writhing and foaming at the mouth—the goddamnedest thing you ever saw. The holy rollers would start at midnight and sing until noon on Sunday. The worshipers came and went, but the singers just stayed there. It was sobering, I'll tell you that, and all-encompassing, and if you had that kind of feel about you anyway and you didn't know where you were going, it could sure help you get there. So I loved it."

In 1939, Gil Rodin heard Starr on a Venuti broadcast and recommended her to Bob Crosby, who had just signed with the Camel Caravan. She sang "Memphis Blues" (Crosby's sidekick Johnny Mercer introduced her) on the first show and was pulled. She and her mother returned to the Plymouth Hotel to get their things, when someone from the Glenn Miller band walked in, complaining that Miller's singer, Marian Hutton, had collapsed on stage and a replacement was needed. A musician pointed out "that little round-assed girl" getting in the elevator, and Starr soon found herself doing two weeks at the Glen Island Casino and recording two selections with the Miller band—in Hutton's key. "I sound like Alfalfa," she says. She certainly doesn't sound like Kay Starr on the sappy "Love with a Capital You," though on "Baby Me," an Eddie Durham rhythm tune, she suggests a Fitzgeraldian lilt. If you place all of Starr's early recordings in chronological order, from the Crosby number to her solo sessions in 1945, you can hear her style come into focus incrementally. In five performances with the Barnet band, which she joined in 1944, another with Wingy Manone, and four more with Ben Pollack, you hear her refining her vibrato, dynamics, and time. But the personality isn't there, the husky edge, the rhythmic assurance.

That would come a year later, and seems to have developed at least in part from an inflammation of the throat. Starr contracted pneumonia while touring army camps on transport planes. Forced to leave the Barnet band, she learned that nodes had formed on her vocal chords. Rather than have them snipped off, which, she was warned, might change her range and sound, she agreed to have them frozen for three months. "Every two days they were sprayed, and if you can believe anybody as gabby as me didn't utter a sound for three months, and couldn't even taste what I was eating—well, it was weird. The keys I sang in stayed the same, but it might have made me a little raspier. Everybody seems to think it did."

In March of 1945, producer Dave Dexter called her for a record session at Capitol. "I thought I was in the wrong room and started to back out before anybody saw me. Dave called me, 'Come back, Okie, you're in the right place.' There was Nat Cole, Coleman Hawkins, Benny Carter—I thought I'd died and gone to heaven." She sang on two sides with the Capitol International Jazzmen ("If I Could Be with You" and "Stormy Weather") and at last demonstrated a style that was unmistakably her own. During the next two years, she recorded a series of records for small labels, accompanied either by a band with Vic Dickenson and Barney Bigard or one with Joe Venuti and Les Paul; the rhythm section for both included Red Callendar and Zutty Singleton.

These are the records on which her early reputation as a jazz singer was based, and most of them hold up marvelously well. Performances such as "Sunday," "After You've Gone," "Frying Pan," "I'm Confessin'," "There's a Lull in My Life," and "All of Me" find her phrasing with unaffected proficiency, taking tempo changes and breaks in stride, fully abreast of the demanding rhythms. A 1946 big-band session for Rondolette offers a fully matured "Them There Eyes," and a 1947 Just Jazz concert (with Charlie Shavers and Willie Smith) includes her sensuous "What Is This Thing Called Love?" and a version of "Good for Nothin' Joe" that was withdrawn because she sang the phrase "beats the hell out of me" (you can hear the audience gasp). At the same time, as a direct result of the Dexter session, she embarked on her first, long association with Capitol Records.

In those years, Capitol had a near monopoly on pop singers, and used different color labels for different musical categories. Starr appeared on every color. "I was a utility singer because I had tried country, blues—I could sing with Ernie Ford ["I'll Never Be Free" was a big hit] or I could do Dixieland. They figured that the rest of the girls were so stylized—except Jo Stafford, no matter what she did it was still Jo Stafford. But someone like me could do anything, and they used me as such." The degree to which Starr's country cry and worldly swing confused the company's staff producers resulted in 78s like the one that paired "Bonaparte's Retreat" with "Someday Sweetheart." Consider two imports that anthologize material from the early years at Capitol: *The Fabulous Favorites!* and *The Kay Starr Style.* The first is a collection of relentlessly gimmicky hits that stultify and date the singer; the second offers straight-ahead arrangements of standards, usually in a big-band context. Even when the standards aren't any good, the settings elicit an improvisational spark that makes her performances timeless.

The record that made her a major star and sealed her fate was "Wheel of Fortune," a classic story of a cover of a cover. During Starr's first week at Freddy's, George Weiss, who wrote the song with Ben Benjamin, dropped by to meet her for the first time (they thanked each other for buying each other's homes). He described the genesis of their hit. The song was originally crafted for Johnny Hartman at RCA, whose record went nowhere. In December 1951, Eddie Wilcox, the former Jimmie Lunceford arranger, produced a version for Sonny Gale on the Derby label, which seemed likely to take off. Weiss, however, disappointed with the Hartman record, revised the song and sent it to Voyle Gilmore at Capitol.

The week the Gale record hit the stores, Starr was awakened at night and told to come over to the studio. "I didn't realize there was this big conspiracy going on," she says. "They forced me to learn the song and said it had to be recorded that night. My record was out a week after Sonny's Gale's. Her record company was smaller, so mine became the hit. She don't like me one bit, and I'd be afraid to meet her." Starr's million-seller was covered by other singers, including Dinah Washington, whose version was number three on the r&b chart that year. The "drugstore" version was recorded by Marilyn Horne: "She did it to keep herself in vocal lessons, and it's spooky how much she sounds like me. We used to do it together at parties."

In 1955, Starr left Capitol for RCA. "Capitol had been like a family, but then they wouldn't let me have any say. So RCA came along and, though my heart wasn't in it, my heart wasn't in staying at Capitol either. Well, at the first session they gave me 'Rock and Roll Waltz' and I thought it was a joke, because I don't read music and all I could read were the lyrics and I thought, 'Oh, my God, look at this—one, two, and then, rock, one, two, and then roll.' I said to Hal Stanley, who was my manager and who had introduced me on Central Avenue, 'Is this a joke?' He said, 'No, this is what they want to do.' I thought, 'Oh, I've left Capitol Records for this!' Because I was used to doing blood and guts, those kinds of songs, and this looked to me like a nursery rhyme. I really was incensed, but Stan said, 'What the hell do you care? Do it.' So I said okay, and the whole time I did it I thought to myself, 'What if this becomes popular? How in the hell am I ever going to present this?' I mean I almost had to take a Dramamine to do it. And oddly enough, nobody ever requested it. Yet I was told that it was the quickest single record to ever go a million at RCA. A writer once called me and said, 'Do you know you had the first rock hit at RCA, the first with rock and roll in the title?' I thought, he thinks that's rock? I don't know *what* it was, but it sure wasn't rock."

Starr's RCA albums are another story—long out of print and deserving of a fresh hearing. Superficially, they fall into categories: jazz (*The One—the Only Kay Starr*), gospel (*I Hear the Word*), blue ballads (*Blue Starr*), and rhythm and blues (*Rockin' with Kay*). In fact, they are of a piece. The arrangements combine a male choir with Ellingtonian brass comments, efficient band riffs, and effective if brief solos, and Starr is riveting. The 1957 *Blue Starr* is perhaps the strongest, from the trombonelike melisma she applies to the word *you're* in "It's a Lonesome Old Town (When You're Not Around)" through the five-minute tour de force version of "I Really Don't Want to Know" to the impeccably modulated "Blue and Sentimental." Like all great interpretive singers, she has a cache of unlikely material that she brings alive by dint of her ingenuity and charm, ranging from Ink Spots hits ("We Three," "Do I Worry") to Hoagy Carmichael's southern cycle ("Lazy Bones," "Rockin' Chair," "Georgia on My Mind"), to which she supplies a definitive tang.

She returned to Capitol in 1959, and during the next three years recorded an extraordinary series of albums mostly in collaboration with Van Alexander. Largely ignored at the time of their release, they were probably her most satisfying achievements. Alexander first made his mark writing for Chick Webb's band in the 1930s (he arranged Ella Fitzgerald's milestone hit with the band, "A-Tisket, A-Tasket") but subsequently busied himself in movie work. The Starr sessions gave him an opportunity to strut his stuff, and he took full advantage of it; these records don't have the usual Capitol gloss, a sound created chiefly by Nelson Riddle and Billy May. "Van Alexander was the sweetest man to work with," Starr says, "but sometimes you'd hear things in his music, raunchy things, and I told him, 'There's a side to you you don't let anybody see, but it's in the music.' The record company people would find new songs—all they thought about was being commercial—but we'd all put in lists for the old standards."

Although Alexander worked with a full orchestra, balancing reeds and brass in standard Basie-out-of-Henderson style, his chief forte was voicing saxophones. On *Movin'*, he uses them for swooning jazz textures and raucous r&b riffs, anticipating Starr's phrasing on "Lazy River" with neatly scored portamentos, and her oscillating between registers on "Night Train." The texture of reeds is alternately rough and smooth on a version of "Swinging Down the Lane" that rivals Sinatra's. For contrast, "Indiana" is swung over a trombone riff. Starr has never sounded more exuberant, leaning into consonants in a way that propels the rhythm, finding just the right blues groove to make the most of "Going to Chicago" and "Sentimental Journey," and driving "On a Slow Boat to China" and (surprisingly) "Around the World" with steamy embellishments and bright tempos.

Movin' on Broadway is in some ways even more impressive. "I decided to do all the songs different than they were usually done—like getting a low, earthy phrasing for 'On the Street Where You Live.' Van said, 'How are we gonna do this?' I said, 'Don't worry, leave it to me.' " "(You Gotta Have) Heart" becomes a blue ballad, complete with sexy reeds, guitar obbligato, piano tremolos, and Harry Edison's pungent trumpet. "Get Me to the Church on Time" is done Basie-style. "I Love Paris," with its vocalized brass, suggests Ellington (only Starr can make the word *sizzle* sizzle). "All of You" is worked out over a sax riff that might be played—no joking—by the World Saxophone Quartet. On *Jazz Singer,* organ is scored with the orchestra, and though most selections are jazz standards, many of them from the twenties, the irresistible ringer is a deep blues rendition of Skillet Licker Riley Pucket's "I Only Want a Buddy Not a Sweetheart," with tenor sax and organ accompaniment. The last in the series, *I Cry by Night,* has Starr making a rare appearance with a quintet—four-man rhythm section plus either Ben Webster (one of his few sessions in this period) or Mannie Klein. The obvious restraint imposed on the musicians is regrettable, but Starr and the material ("Lover Man," "Baby, Won't You Please Come Home," T-Bone Walker's "I'm Still in Love with You") are first-rate, and her interaction with the surprisingly ethereal Webster on "More Than You Know" is sublime.

STARR CURRENTLY DIVIDES her time between Los Angeles and Honolulu, and much of her attention in recent years has focused on Indian affairs. In 1967, she was named to the Advisory Board of the Los Angeles Indian Center, which raised $2 million. In the early seventies, she helped found a scholarship fund and, with Grace Thorpe (Jim Thorpe's daughter), a university in Davis, California, called DQ (for Desanawidah Quetzalcoatl), which recently graduated the first American Indian dentist. Starr and her husband own a tile business, "so if anything happened to me and I couldn't sing, I wouldn't be alone, somebody would take care of me." Presumably she will be sunning herself in the spotlight for some time to come. Now that she's past her commercial prime, she can concentrate entirely on the attributes that make her art an enduring one.

Needless to say, she isn't signed with a record company: "I'd love to record, but it's a different world today, and I'm not really a business-minded person." It seems unlikely that an American record company will present her with opulent band arrangements, but as her engagement at Freddy's demonstrated, she doesn't need more than a good rhythm section and maybe a couple of soloists. That was the setting for much of her best recorded work in the past; it was also the setting for Helen Humes's comeback albums and for the ones with which Rosemary Clooney has been braving new musical heights in the eighties. Starr is in her prime right now; there's no reason she couldn't make some of her best records in the next few years. A retrospective of her past accomplishments, matched by a rash of new ones, will probably define her place once and for all as one of the incomparables.*

*Despite subsequent tours and exceptional press, Kay Starr was unable to revive her recording career.

Moonbeam Moscowitz: Sylvia Syms

Whitney Balliett

In 1974, in The New Yorker, *Whitney Balliett profiled the nightclub and musical-comedy (and jazz) singer Sylvia Syms, whose long and elegant career ended recently, as she would have wanted it to, when she died on stage, at the Algonquin, acknowledging applause. Collected in Balliett's 1988 book,* American Singers: Twenty-Seven Portraits.

Excellence generally parries neglect with bitterness, stoicism, or a brave and judicious narcissism. Sylvia Syms has long since chosen the last of these weapons. She has said of herself, with her wide smile, "I have no desire to be a superstar. I don't think I could stand the responsibility of having to prove myself every single day. If you don't make it, you have a ball trying. But I've made it. I don't know by whose standards, but I've made it by mine. So the only person I have to satisfy now as far as my singing is concerned is me." During the forty or so years of her career, she has sung in almost every notable nightclub in the country. When the nightclub business began faltering, in the mid-fifties, she turned to the theater, were she has appeared on and off Broadway in *Diamond Lil* with Mae West, in innumerable productions of *South Pacific,* in which she has perfected the part of Bloody Mary, in *Dream Girl* with Judy Holliday, in *Thirteen Daughters* with Don Ameche, in *Funny Girl* with Carol Lawrence, in *Flower Drum Song* and *Camino Real,* and as the lead in *Hello, Dolly!* And along the way she has made recordings, one of which, a daring up-tempo version of "I Could Have Danced All Night," became a hit for Decca in 1956. But time and again, just as she has appeared ready to swim into the lagoon of recognition and financial comfort, she has foundered. The causes have been myriad—an operation; a female rival; her own intransigence toward working conditions, managers and bookers, and clothes; an automobile accident; her physical construction; the twists and turns of her private life; and the tricks of fashion. But she continues to work well as both an actress and a singer. Here is the singer in two different settings—a rehearsal for a concert appearance with the composer Cy Coleman, a sitting-in at The Cookery with her friend Barbara Carroll.

IT WAS A SLEEPY New York Saturday, and Sylvia Syms was in Cy Coleman's sumptuous living room. They were rehearsing a dozen Coleman songs for the concert, which was to take place the next day. She was wearing one of her many djellabahs, and she looked tiny in the high-ceilinged room. She is barely five feet tall, and is plump and shapeless. Her legs, both broken in the accident, look spindly, as does her left arm, which was also broken. Childhood polio has left her with a curvature of the back. But her presence is immediately commanding, and on first meeting her one is surrounded by her rich voice, her frequent laughter, and her rhythmical, dramatic motions. Her moon-shaped face lights up whatever it is aimed at. Her wide mouth is almost always smiling; she has large, slightly slanted eyes, elfin ears, and an aquiline nose; and her broad forehead ends in a helmet of short, coppery hair. She is an impulsive, long-syllabled talker who is apt to sail into any subject *in medias res,* and she did when Coleman excused himself to make a phone call: "Mr. Sinatra sent me his newest single this morning," she said. "I don't know why I call him Mister when I've known him as Francis for so many years. I guess it's my profound respect for him. I don't remember when we first met, but *he* would know. I've watched him greet by name without hesitation someone he hasn't seen in twenty-five years. He's a quiet man, articulate and well-informed, and he's been a gracious friend. When I was in the hospital after my operation, he called every day, or had someone call if he couldn't, and when it became clear I'd need a respirator to take with me wherever I went, he had the best one there is sent to me. I still use it an hour every day. He has a good sense of humor. After my automobile accident, he sent me a pair of skates with the message 'Try these next time,' and I returned the gesture when he opened a tour at Caesar's Palace by sending him an antique silver ear trumpet. I've never once watched him sing and not come away with something new. I'm grateful to have been alive during his era. All of which explains why, when I was a guest at his home in Palm Springs and he asked me to sing at some inn we had gone to after dinner, I couldn't. I just couldn't get up there knowingly in front of him and sing. All he said was, 'Sylvia, you're nuts!'"

Cy Coleman sat down at the piano again and loosed a couple of booming chords. "God!" he said. "The sound of the piano is frightening this early." Sylvia Syms put on a pair of granny glasses. They decided on "Witchcraft." By the third measure, her body had begun to reflect her singing. She bounced slowly up and down, rocked her shoulders from side to side, and swung her hips. She has a powerful contralto, but she controls it effortlessly. Her diction is bell-like, but she does all sorts of subtle rhythmic things with the words—sometimes piling them together, sometimes letting them drift. The next number was a slow ballad. Her voice became soft, she stretched out her hands, palms up, and raised her shoulders. The number was full of crooning turns of phrase, and one heard slow breezes and early stirrings. Then she and Coleman went into a buoyant duet of "Hey, Look Me Over" and a ringing version of "The Best Is Yet to Come," which they did in unison, in harmony, in alternating passages, and as a round.

Sylvia Syms laughed and leaned against the piano. "My! They're going to get a warmed-up lady out at the theater in New Jersey. What time is it, Cy? I have *no* sense of time and I spend all day at home calling for the time. We have two shows of *South Pacific* today, and they're picking me up at three." Cy Coleman said it was just after one, and he suggested a final rehearsal at noon the next day. Sylvia Syms walked the ten blocks to the small apartment she has long had on Lexington Avenue. She took short steps and swayed from side to side, as if she were shouldering her way through the press of her talk. "For some reason, I got to reminiscing about my childhood with Cy before we started today, and it was painful. I was born the oldest of three children in Manhattan but grew up in Flatbush. My maiden name was Blagman and when I started out I called myself Sylvia Black. Then I saw the name Syms with a 'y' somewhere and I liked it and took it. My mother was a New York girl and so was her mother, but my father came from Russia. It was a great love affair between my father and mother. He yelled a lot at me, but I never heard him yell at her. My mother still lives out there. She's intelligent and funny and articulate, and she still points that finger at us children when we visit her and says do this or do that, but now we just laugh and tell her to jump in the lake. She's very into her Judaism, and I suppose she wishes I were, too. I've always been aware of being a Jewess, but my religion is people. My father designed clothes, and he died when I was seventeen, but I didn't know him as much else than a strict, hardworking family man. I was a very removed child, and it started when I sang with a full and beautiful voice before I'd learned to talk. I sang in my carriage, and later I'd sit on the front stoop and sing at the top of my lungs. But my parents didn't know how to cope with my singing. They were poor and their backgrounds had taught them that the life of a singer or actress led directly to the gutter. My father was sensitive in all areas except the one I was interested in, so I got no help, no formal training. I was born a heavy child, and I grew heavier because I was unhappy. Very soon I created a complete fantasy world. I got a reputation, and I'd hear parents tell their kids to keep away from that crazy Sylvia. I'd stay awake all night listening to music on the radio, and when I was in my mid-teens I started sneaking out of the house after everyone was asleep and going down to New York. I'd get on the subway and go to Fifty-second Street. My father got hysterical when he found out, but that didn't stop me. I had long red coppery-chestnut hair tied in braids and parted in the middle, and I had absolutely no fear of going out in the middle of the night. Who wanted to make passes at a fat Jewish girl from Brooklyn? I became the first of the groupies, and I began learning about the momentary, joyful noises of jazz. And I had the greatest people to teethe on. I got to know Fats Waller. He had bad feet, and I remember him playing the organ in a little church uptown and pumping it with his bare feet. And I got to know Art Tatum. He called me Moonbeam Moscowitz, the Jewish Indian. He'd take me uptown after work to the Log Cabin or Tillum's, where he would play with a tenderness and warmth he never showed downtown. Sometimes Jerry Preston, who owned the Log Cabin, would call my mother and tell her everything was O.K., and around seven or eight in the morning he'd send me home in a limousine. Or else Tatum would take me even further uptown to a grits-and-fried-chicken place, and after we'd eaten we'd walk down the street and watch the sun come up. On my twenty-first birthday, he gave me a little glass piano with his initials on it, but it eventually broke. And three years before he died he had Van Cleef & Arpels make a gold piano with a keyboard of sapphires for the black notes and freshwater pearls for the white notes. But I don't have that anymore, either. Erroll Garner pestered me about it so much I finally gave it to him, and he took it everywhere, in its original little felt bag.

"Billie Holiday became my mentor, and I copied everything she did, excluding the drugs and booze. She said to me once, 'You know what's wrong with you, Sugar? You love me.' She was a beautiful, dignified lady, with an innate sense of good taste. She was drawn to singing songs you knew she understood. She had a kind of animal relativity to the songs she sang. I have no concept of living within a budget, but once I saved twenty-five dollars and bought her a print gown for her birthday, and she was so pleased you'd have thought I'd given her the moon on a stick. I can remember her in the gown at the Onyx Club, coming down those little stairs in the back and the lights softening and the room becoming silent and her moving onto the stage and looking just like a panther. She began wearing gardenias in her hair because of me. One night when she was working at Kelly's Stable, she burned her hair with a curling iron just before show time, and I ran down the street to the Three Deuces, where Ada Kurtz had the checkroom. Checkroom girls sold flowers then, and I bought a gardenia and Billie put it in her hair to hide the burned place. Of all the men she married or knew, I think she loved Buck Clayton the most. We were sitting around at the club on the Street where Billy Eckstine had his big band, and B said to Billie, 'Ain't I pretty?' 'Yeh,' she said, 'but you ain't the prettiest.' 'Well, who is the prettiest, then?' B asked her. 'Buck Clayton's the prettiest man in the world.' I got to know Lester Young through Billie. In fact, she used to tell me when I started singing that I sounded just like the way he played. He was the first person I ever heard say to his piano player, 'Just play vanilla, man. Just play vanilla,' which meant cut out the embroidery and play the proper chords behind solos. I still use the phrase when I run into an accompanist who thinks he's Niagara Falls. Lester was a quiet, inside-himself man, and he'd always tell me, 'It's hard, Baby, it's hard.' I don't recall how I met Duke Ellington, but he called me Lady Hamilton. He made every woman in the world feel beautiful. Once, when I was working in Chicago, Bentley Stegner, who was a music writer for the *Sun-Times,* took me to hear Duke. It was snowing and blowing and there weren't any cabs, so we walked and walked through knee-deep snow, and I had on an old babushka and my mascara ran all over my face, and when we got there Duke took one look at me and said, 'Lady Hamilton, I don't know where you just came from, but please save a few dried-up bones for me.' I hung out with Mildred Bailey, too. She was a wild lady, and she had a rapier tongue. I'd go to hear her at Café Society, and I went to her little house on Sniffen Court. She was a domestic lady and she loved to eat, and so did I. She thought I looked like her and she'd tell people I was her little sister. She told me I'd be a star but I'd be very unhappy getting there."

Sylvia Syms arrived at her door and pulled a key out of her bag. "Before I moved in here, I lived with the comedienne Pat Carroll in a loft right over the Fifty-fifth Street Playhouse, near Seventh Avenue. When we opened the fridge, film music came out, and we could lie on the floor and look through a little hole and watch the pictures." She put her key in the lock and waved, her stubby fingers spread like a child's.

IT WAS EIGHT-THIRTY on a Monday evening. Sylvia Syms was still in *South Pacific,* but Monday was her day off, and she was in a cab headed for The Cookery, where she was planning to sing with Barbara Carroll. As was her wont, she had spent most of the day at Elizabeth Arden getting the week's accumulation of "Texas dirt" she used for makeup as Bloody Mary removed from her face and arms. She was wearing a black-and-white cotton knit suit, and her hair was arranged tightly around her face and she looked radiant. She leaned into a corner of the seat, and her legs lifted from the floor. "I met my great friend Barbara in 1946. I'm not a woman's woman, and Barbara and Judy Holliday and Pat Carroll have been my only women friends. When I first met Barbara, it was like seeing my reflection in a mirror. We've been through just about everything together, including the automobile accident. I was about to go back to California to audition for the mother in the television series *Bridget Loves Bernie,* and I'd been visiting Barbara at her country place in South Salem. We were being driven back to New York in her little car, and Barbara insisted she sit in the front, so I got in the back with her daughter, Susie. We were coming to a toll gate and Susie and I were playing some kind of game, and the brakes failed and—whammo! I threw myself on top of Susie and she was unhurt. Barbara looks as beautiful as ever, but I don't know how many operations she's had on her face. I was in and out of a wheelchair for a year and a half. But, please God, I'm in fine shape now. I consider that I've come through smelling like a rose, which is why I spend every available minute finding out what the rest of the garden is like."

At The Cookery, Barbara Carroll finished her set, and she and Sylvia embraced. Barbara asked her if she would sing during the next set, and Sylvia said yes. Sylvia examined her face in her compact mirror. "It doesn't matter if I'm Sarah Schlepp during the day. But when I perform I have to wear the best. As a result, I've turned into a not-half-bad-looking woman. In the broadest sense, I like me. I even enjoy the things about me I'm not too crazy about. But I didn't feel that way during my first singing job, which was at Kelly's Stable. I went in there one night with a couple of Brooklyn friends and auditioned with Benny Carter's group for Ralph Watkins, the owner, and he offered me a job for the summer. I'd met dear Benny one night at Nick's, and his daughter and I hung out a lot. It was 1940, and Ralph Watkins paid me twenty-five dollars a week. The Nat Cole Trio was the intermission group and Billy Daniels was the star. The job worked out O.K., but I didn't have the right clothes and I must have looked awful. I didn't work again for five years, and then I went downtown into the Little Casino. I was there a whole year, and Ram Ramirez, who composed 'Lover Man,' was my accompanist. Mike Levin wrote about me in *Down Beat,* comparing me with Billie Holiday and Lee Wiley. I was a buxom, sharp broad, but I was stupid enough to resent the comparisons. I guess I thought I was Topsy and had just grown all by myself. But on the strength of the piece I was hired at the Club Troubador for two hundred dollars a week. Louis Jordan and his Tympany Five were there, and so was Georgie Auld's big band. Another singer, who shall remain nameless, was starred. Well, I was breaking it up, and she wasn't, and one night after work Mike Colucci, who ran the place and was a nice gent, told me, 'Sylvia, I have to fire you.' He wouldn't tell me why, and I was crushed. I found out later what had happened. The other singer's manager handled all sorts of big acts, like Nat Cole and Stan Kenton, and when he heard I was hurting his act he called Colucci and said, 'Get rid of Sylvia Syms.' In the fifties, when I was working in New York, this great big man came in to hear me five nights in a row, and finally he introduced himself and told me I was the best singer he'd ever heard. It was the same gent who had had me fired, and I was flabbergasted. All I could say was 'Oh yeah, how come you did what you did to me at the Troubador?' and all he said was 'She was my act and you were killing her. If you had been my act and someone else was killing you, I'd have protected you in the same way.' I had a gossamer vision of the business. I romanticized it, and I guess in some ways I still do.

"In 1946, I got married for the first time. Actors have always been my downfall, and I married Bret Morrison, who was doing *The Shadow* on radio. He's one of the nicest men I've ever known, and he's probably the only man I'd marry if I ever married again. Anyway, I was a rotten wife. I had my head in too many places. We lived in an elegant duplex on West Sixty-seventh Street, but it was a mausoleum, and it turned me off. We had all the right linen, the right china, the right crystal—and all the wrong ingredients for a good marriage. We were together until 1953. In the mid-fifties, I married Ed Begley—the dancer, not the actor—but it's not a part of my life I like thinking about.

"My being fired at the Troubador gave me a mysterious quality. It was O.K. to be fat if you were exotic. I have some pictures of myself from the mid-fifties when I reached two hundred and forty-two pounds. I looked Chinese. People didn't know what to make of me, and because of my dark complexion they started asking me if I was black. In fact, a lady television interviewer asked me the same question a while ago. I started working in every upholstered joint in New York, and I began to create a nice following. I was in the Ruban Bleu in 1951 with the Norman Paris Trio, and I worked off and on for several years at the Village Vanguard. People like Orson Bean and Robert Clary and Harry Belafonte came and went there, but I stayed on forever. I worked at the Show Spot with Barbara when Mabel Mercer was upstairs in the Byline Room. But I have always been just another name on the lists of the various managers who have handled me—mostly, I think, because they haven't known what to do with me. I even had one once who told me I should be grateful I was working because I was such a mess, which did its little damage. I was never good-enough-looking to sing with a band, and in a lot of the rooms I worked you were required to mix with the patrons, and I just didn't know how. But in 1954 the managers Pete Cameron and Monte Kay came into my life, and they got me a recording contract with Decca. Nothing much happened until 1956, when, at the end of a session, Milt Gabler, who was the A. & R. man, reluctantly let me record 'I Could

Have Danced All Night.' Reluctantly! They were dead set against it. Rosemary Clooney had had a hit version on Columbia for a couple of months, and on top of that I wanted to do it at double tempo, which nobody had done. But a month later my version took off and became a hit, and so did other tunes I recorded, like 'In Times Like These,' 'Dancing Chandelier,' and 'It's Good to Be Alive.' The upshot was I got job offers all around the country in hotels and nightclubs, and it nearly destroyed me. They expected Miss America but they got me. I still didn't know how to dress, and the clothes I wore made me look like the 'Beer Barrel Polka.' It got so if Ed Sullivan wanted someone to sing 'I Could Have Danced All Night' on his show, he asked Julie Andrews and not me. But I've finally discovered that your wardrobe can be one of your most important assets. There are women in every audience who spend the first twenty minutes of a singer's performance counting the sequins on her dress."

Barbara Carroll stopped at the table and said she'd play a few numbers before Sylvia Syms sang. After she had run through five or six, she smiled at Sylvia and announced her. Barbara moved to the far end of the piano bench, and Sylvia sat down beside her. They looked like girls sharing a swing. Sylvia warmed up with Sammy Cahn's "Can't You Just See Yourself?" She smiled broadly, lifted her head, and slowly rotated her shoulders. When the number was over, she eased into Harold Arlen's "As Long As I Live." Her head bounced up and down, and she snapped the fingers of one hand. She moved right inside the song, and, heating up the words, poured them out through the runnel of the melody. Then she sang an exquisite version of Billie Holiday's "Easy Living," and that created a peculiar sensation. The way Billie sang the song ran along behind her, and the two seemed to be singing a duet. She moved with a deliberate, almost heavy ease from word to word, and her voice echoed Billie's. She finished, and, crossing one knee over the other, folded her hands on her raised knee. Her voice dropped into a low buzz, and in a gentle, staccato fashion out came the opening words of "Imagination." The staccato passage eased away, and Sylvia went into a legato bridge. The deceptive ease with which she sang made her softest phrases ring. She considers herself a narrative singer, a storyteller who happens to sing her stories, and it was easy to see why. The room was in thrall and when she was done there was a long moment before the applause. She stood, bobbed quickly several times, and returned to the table. Barbara Carroll laughed and clapped; the swing had stopped.

Sylvia Syms looked in her mirror, and ordered more coffee. People came over to the table and told her how beautiful she sounded, and she replied with a round of pleased "Thank-you-darling's." "Being a performer is like suffering a chronic condition," she said after they had gone. "Performing is also the most dominating mistress in the world; I'd never have been able to give so much to a human being. Singing for me is my total cleansing. It's what keeps Mabel Mercer young and full of the gorgeous juices and adrenalin, and it does the same for me. I have to have a personal, almost physical relationship to the songs I sing, so I paraphrase them in my head for my own understanding. I can't sing 'The Boy Next Door,' nor can I sing Cy Coleman's 'Big Spender,' because it's about a prostitute. And I don't understand singers who make a swinging thing out of a tragic song like 'Love for Sale.' So lyrics are terribly important to me. My notes follow the words and they generally land in the right places, but if they don't I invariably know it. If you laugh when you're singing, an audience will laugh with you, but if you cry, the audience won't cry with you. That is Mr. Sinatra's secret: his joy, his emotion never overreach; they always stop just in time. There has to be a certain amount of improvisation in my singing. I almost always breathe a song in the same way, but the notes are given a different emphasis. I perform in a one-to-one way. I have to *see* a face in the audience, and then I'll sing to that face. It's a very personal thing, to sing *to* people and not at them. I *need* my audience, which is why I never sing to myself at home.

"Before I leave for the great beyond, I'd like to do an album of all the songs I've done before, the songs I did first and kind of feel I own. I'd like Gordon Jenkins and Don Costa to do the arrangements, and I'd sing Sammy Cahn's 'Guess I'll Hang My Tears Out to Dry' and Harold Arlen's 'As Long As I Live.' And there'd be James Shelton's 'I'm the Girl' and his 'Lilac Wine,' which only singers like me sing. And I'd do 'Mountain Greenery' and 'Imagination' and all the Jimmy Van Heusen and Rodgers-and-Hart songs I've done before. I'd call the album 'On Second Thought.' I think it would be an important thing. When you ask as much as I have of this world, you have to leave something in exchange."

The Lindy

Marshall and Jean Stearns

In their important book Jazz Dance *(1966), Marshall and Jean Stearns write of the Lindy, the Jitterbug, and the famous Savoy. Marshall Stearns was the founder of the Institute of Jazz Studies at Rutgers.*

For nearly a decade the Lindy—more widely known as the Jitterbug—remained the sole possession of a small group, a kind of folk *avant-garde,* consisting of amateur dancers in a few big cities. As far as the general public was concerned, the dance arrived out of nowhere around 1936 to go with a new music called swing that was played by a man named Benny Goodman.

There were youngsters "jitterbugging in the aisles," as Benny Goodman played the Paramount Theater in New York City and made headlines from coast to coast. (The fire department was called in, and the balconies were checked for safety.) Commentators treated the event as another in a series of inexplicable phenomena produced by somebody else's teenagers. The swing era, with its own music and dance, had officially begun.

Simultaneously, the public began to see—in the movies, in vaudeville, at nightclubs, in ballrooms, and in Broadway musicals—groups of dancers tossing each other around with what appeared to be fatal abandon. To the uninitiated it looked like mass suicide. And yet, no matter how high a dancer soared, he hit the deck right on the beat and swung along into the next step. These were teams of newly professional Lindy Hoppers.

When the average teenager who liked to dance looked carefully, he saw that these couples were doing a step together—when they were on the ground—which was not too difficult, and which some of the older, more worldly kids in his own neighborhood were already doing in a comparatively mild fashion. So he tried it. The girls quickly evolved their own uniforms—saddle shoes, full skirts, and sloppy sweaters—while across the land, at high school proms, young ladies in evening gowns began to jitterbug, presenting a happily incongruous spectacle.

Writers have referred to the Lindy as "the only true American folk dance," but it is more than that. The Lindy is a fundamental approach, not an isolated step, used in later dances from the Afro-Cuban Mambo to the rock-

and-rollers' Chicken. The Lindy caused a general revolution in the popular dance of the United States.

The decisive nature of this revolution is partly explained by a member of an older generation, George Wendler, who recalls sadly how the Lindy hit Detroit: "The Lindy Hop reached here about 1929 as the Jitterbug . . . it became the foundation for all sorts of eccentricities from my old-fashioned point of view. It seemed to gobble up and incorporate every novelty that followed it.

"Looking back at it, though, it did eventually open up dancing for white people. The sophisticated mask was discarded, you were permitted to get with it and be carried away. The girls' pleated skirts, billowing and whisking this way and that as they reversed their pivots, added a new beauty. Then when partners became separated, they would 'truck' or strut or maybe improvise something of their own.

"We old-timers had what I might call a bread-and-butter style, always dancing close to our partners, and performing variations on the Waltz and Fox Trot, sometimes with real style and grace. We could do a few novelties like the Charleston, but not, of course, as a steady diet. We just went back to our bread-and-butter steps. We felt this way about the Lindy—a novelty that wouldn't last.

"But then the Lindy became the bread-and-butter style of all the following generations, and we died on the vine, replaced everywhere by some kind of Lindy Hoppers. I don't recall any conservative style of dancing making a hit since the Lindy revolution." The Lindy became the first step youngsters learned, and it remained the foundation of most of their dancing.

The influence of the Lindy, and the more flowing style of dancing that was a part of it, spread swiftly and surely. It went deep as well as far. For example, a youngster named Ernie Smith, who later became a top executive in a New York advertising firm, lived in a white middle-class suburb of Pittsburgh and felt the tremors in 1939 when he was fifteen years old. The girls at high school had taught him to dance, and his interest in jazz was awakened. But there was something missing.

Smith went to hear the big white bands at the Westview Ballroom and the big Negro bands at the Stanley Theater. As his appreciation grew, he found himself irresistibly attracted to a ballroom in Hill City, the Negro section of Pittsburgh: "I lived a kind of Jekyll-Hyde existence. In the daytime I went to high school and got along fine with my friends there. At night I'd sneak over to Hill City and study the dancers from the balcony of the ballroom. I found what I'd been missing." Smith imported his own version of Hill City dancing at the next high school prom, shocking and impressing his friends in a very satisfying fashion.

The fundamental lesson of Hill City was to dance smoothly. Hopping and bouncing around the dance floor, while pumping your partner's arm—the hitherto approved style—was corny: "The hardest thing to learn is the pelvic motion. I suppose I always felt that these motions are somehow obscene. You have to sway, forwards and backwards, with a controlled hip movement, while your shoulders stay level and your feet glide along the floor. Your right hand is held low on the girl's back, and your left hand down at your side, enclosing her hand. At this time, the girls at high school wouldn't or couldn't dance that way."

Smith soon mastered the Lindy, which was known in Hill City as the jitterbug, and perfected his own versions of the breakaway, improvising variations on the Boogie Woogie, Suzie-Q, Shorty George, and Camel Walk, in a manner mildly reminiscent of Snake Hips Tucker. The response at high school became more and more gratifying, but he realized that he could no longer attend such childish dances.

Instead, Smith became a member of a pretty rough gang of white kids, who went dancing to jukeboxes at nearby mill towns, picking up partners on location. These boys had never attended high school, and they wore their hair cut long and one-button, rolled-lapel suits with peg-trousers. They even walked alike—a sort of catlike bounce, shoulders hunched and head bobbing up and down, with arms held close in front of the body and fingers snapping. In those days they thought of themselves as "hep" (later "hip").

On these excursions, Smith found girls who could dance. They were the first white girls who could move in the authentic, flowing style: "I suppose you'd call those mill-town girls lower class. They were poorer and less educated than my high-school friends, but they could really dance. In fact, at that time it seemed that the lower class a girl was, the better dancer she was, too. I never brought any of them home."

Because they had more opportunities to see Negro dancers, or because they were simply less inhibited—or both—these mill-town girls were the first white girls in that area to dance the Lindy. It was one stage in a process taking place here and there across the country.

MEANWHILE, THE SAVOY Ballroom set the pace. Bands, vaudeville, nightclub performers, and dance acts were booked in New York: phonograph recordings, musical shows, and radio programs originated there. Although other parts of the country favored other steps at other times, the Savoy's influence was all pervasive and conclusive. Harlem, with its rapidly increasing population from the deep South, had the talent and the tap-root connections with a dance tradition that could nourish a fine art.

John Martin, writing about the Savoy Ballroom in *The New York Times,* was one of the few dance critics to realize—later—the importance of what had happened:

> The white jitterbug is oftener than not uncouth to look at . . . but his Negro original is quite another matter. His movements are never so exaggerated that they lack control, and there is an unmistakable dignity about his most violent figures . . . there is a remarkable amount of improvisation . . . mixed in with . . . Lindy Hop figures.
>
> Of all the ballroom dancing these prying eyes have seen, this is unquestionably the finest.

The point at which a Lindy dancer became a real professional is difficult to determine, because the stars of the Savoy danced for the fun of it without a thought of turning pro. By the late thirties, however, contests were frequent, and a good dancer could make a little pocket money. Members of the Savoy group went downtown to enter contests at the Roseland Ballroom, giving their hometowns as Detroit, Chicago, or Toronto, and danced off with the prizes. (The champion Lindy Hopper at Roseland was a white boy named Lou Levy, who later married one of the Andrews Sisters.)

With swing music the rage and jitterbugging the dance to go with it, Herbert White, still head bouncer at the Savoy, became the agent of all the Lindy groups who proceeded to appear in vaudeville, nightclubs, Broadway musicals, and the movies. (Shorty Snowden was the first and last dancer to defy Whitey openly and leave the group to tour with the Paul Whiteman orchestra—a decision that took considerable courage.) Whitey employed around seventy-two dancers—the equivalent of a dozen troupes—under such names as "The Savoy Hoppers," "The Jive-A-Dears," and "Whitey's Lindy Hoppers."

He also managed to turn a pretty penny every step of the way. When the contract called for transportation by train, Whitey sent the dancers by bus and pocketed the difference. No matter how much the act earned, they continued to be paid the small amount Whitey had offered in the beginning. The dancers never objected. They knew nothing about show business, and they were being paid, however poorly, for doing what they loved to do.

"Those Lindy Hoppers made it tough for everybody," says Pete Nugent grimly. "With their speed and air steps they made all the other dancers look like they were standing still. They never made any money, and Whitey treated them like slaves, and they dressed like a little-league baseball team, but they stopped the show wherever they appeared."

Whitey had a monopoly. In 1939 Mike Todd hired seven teams of Lindy dancers to perform in *The Hot Mikado* at the New York World's Fair. (Six teams were needed, but Whitey persuaded Todd that an extra couple should stand by.) When a backstage argument arose—for the dancers were an undisciplined and clamorous group—Todd fired them. He then discovered that no other dancers were "available"—Whitey had them all booked. Todd flew all the way to Chicago in search of Lindy Hoppers and could find none good enough for the show. On his return he decided he had never fired the original group, and the show continued.

Making the best of an old stereotype, the male dancers in the troupe, who wore tight jersey trousers, padded their supporters with handkerchiefs (a trick that has been known to happen in ballet) and executed an occasional slow, stretching step facing the audience. It was a private joke. Eventually even Mike Todd noticed it with horror. "If this isn't stopped, I'll never be able to put another show on Broadway." He ran to the wardrobe mistress to ask whether the dancers were wearing supporters. When assured that they were, he decreed that thenceforth each must wear *two* supporters.

Whether or not they knew show business, the Lindy Hoppers proved to be a big draw. When rehearsals for *The Hot Mikado* began, nobody spoke to them, and the star of the show, the great Bill Robinson, took it upon himself to refer to "that raggedy bunch of crazy kids." In their ignorance they sassed Bojangles and got in bad with everybody.

When the show opened, however, all was forgiven and they became the darlings of the cast. Even Bojangles changed his mind and announced at a backstage party in Pittsburgh: "Nobody had better mess with me or the Lindy Hoppers—*they* take care of the first act and *I* take care of the second."

Some kind of a climax in the diffusion of the Lindy occurred during the late thirties at Radio City Music Hall. The Music Hall, of course, prides itself on the dignity of its stage shows and takes great pains to make its mammoth productions impressive. During the swing craze, however, somebody at the Music Hall lost his head and hired a troupe of Whitey's Lindy Hoppers.

The widely advertised film at Radio City was *Jezebel,* featuring Bette Davis and George Brent, while the management dreamed up the complementary theme, *The World of Tomorrow,* for the stage show. Toward the end of a long and involved stage presentation, six Lindy Hoppers—three boys and their partners—danced resolutely all the way to the center of the great stage. Al Minns remembers it with horror: "Everybody backstage was so polite, too polite, and then going out on that great expanse was terrifying. Why, dancing there is like dancing inside an enormous cave, you can't see the audience at all, it's just solid black out there, but you can hear a quiet restlessness or breathing." The Music Hall was a far cry from the Cats' Corner at the Savoy Ballroom.

Supporting the dancers with what the management considered much better than the real thing, Erno Rapee stood solemnly upon the podium, conducting a very square symphony orchestra. A hundred-voice male choir costumed like jolly tars lined the back of the stage, performing a stationary

Truck, with one finger pointing limply skyward. The entire aggregation was plodding through a nonrhythmic version—amplified beyond endurance—of "I'm Just a Jitterbug."

At the end of exactly three minutes of dancing, precisely planned by the director, the Lindy Hoppers quietly withdrew and giants emerged on both sides of the stage and hammered two big gongs. They were stripped to the waist as if they were introducing a J. Arthur Rank movie. At this moment, right on cue, ballet dancer Patricia Bowman ascended briskly on a rising platform through a trapdoor in the center of the stage, posed like a butterfly, ready to swoop about.

After several days and nights of this careful routine, the Lindy Hoppers rebelled. One evening without warning they reverted to form, ignoring the accompaniment and clapping their hands and stomping their feet to give themselves some kind of beat. They even screamed and hollered encouragement to each other. In fact, they forgot where they were, and their dancing improved astonishingly. Whereupon the huge audience forgot where it was, too, and began to clap, stomp, scream, and holler, but more loudly.

The dancing seemed to be over before it started, and at the correct moment, the giants strode out to hammer the gongs and Patricia Bowman started rising. But nobody could hear the gongs and everybody was yelling "More! More! More!" demanding an encore and wondering for a moment, who is that woman coming through the floor and messing things up? When the audience showed no signs of stopping, Miss Bowman descended slowly out of sight.

Backstage, as the Lindy Hoppers were returning to their dressing rooms on the fourth floor, the intercom started to bellow "Lindy Hoppers back onstage to take a bow! Lindy Hoppers back onstage to take a bow!" and they ran back five times to bow and cool off the audience so the show could continue. Each time, meanwhile, the giants had been wearing out the gongs, and Patricia Bowman was bobbing up and down without being permitted to swoop about.

As they ran back onstage for the last time the Lindy Hoppers heard a Rockette exclaim: "At last, show biz comes to the Music Hall!" The foundations of Radio City trembled, and the next day the group received a check and a polite note saying their particular type of act was not the kind needed at that precise moment. No real Lindy dancers appeared there again.

(Tap dancer Bill Bailey reports similar difficulties at Radio City. "Those violins gave me a hard time, swooping and sliding all over the place," he says, "but I finally got them to quit playing until I finished, and then I told them they could play whatever they wanted.")

Herbert White died wealthy in the forties. The Savoy Ballroom was torn down in 1959 to make way for a housing development. In the same year *Ballets Africaines,* "direct from Africa" (via Europe), was playing to sell-out crowds on Broadway, with a finale composed, according to critic Douglass Watt, of "a thoroughly expert Lindy Hop." Perhaps the Lindy had come full circle and influenced one of its sources.

Like other old-timers—the doctor made him quit dancing in 1938 because his feet had been pounded shapeless—Shorty Snowden has his reservations about what is happening today: "Lindy Hopping today seems to be mostly acrobatic tricks. The kids don't stop to learn the fundamentals first, they just start throwing each other around. To be done right, the Lindy was mostly footwork, and now there's no real footwork anymore. And they don't do it fast, they have to dance half-time." By 1950 Al Minns and Leon James were working in factories.

Today, a mild version of the Lindy has penetrated the length and breadth of the land. The director of a coast-to-coast chain of dance studios describes the Lindy as "our national dance" and is prepared to teach an emasculated version of it to anyone in a very short time. (The youngsters accepted a watered-down sample of it in the late fifties for a rock-and-roll dance called the Chicken.) In a small number of ballrooms, in a limited number of big cities, we are told that a few young dancers are still capable of an inspired Lindy.

A Night at the Five Spot

Martin Williams

From Williams's collection Jazz Changes, *this evocative account of another renowned jazz locale—New York's famous Five Spot—written in 1964.*

The Five Spot Cafe in New York City sits at the corner of Cooper Square and St. Mark's Place. The address may sound a bit elegant unless one knows that St. Mark's Place is an extension of Eighth Street into the East Side and that Cooper Square is the name given a couple of blocks along Third Avenue at the point where Third Avenue ceases to be called the Bowery. All of which means that the Five Spot Cafe is at the upper reaches of New York's now dwindling skid-row area.

It was once a pretty sordid stretch of sidewalk, this Bowery, but since the city removed the Third Avenue elevated train tracks and let the sunshine in a few years ago, the street has been given something of a face-lift, or at least a wash-up, and the number of alcoholics who stagger along, panhandle in, or recline on its sidewalks has declined constantly.

This current paucity of winos along the Bowery is only one indication of fundamental changes taking place in the general area of the East Side below 14th Street. There are, for example, about six prospering off-Broadway theaters there. And some of the old pawnshops and secondhand clothing stores have disappeared, to be replaced by collectors' bookshops, paperback-bookstores, and even a music store.

Right across the street from the Five Spot, an old greasy-spoon lunch room has been transformed into one of those chi-chi hamburger palaces, the kind where the counter is made of unfinished wood and the menu reads "beefburgers, seventy cents."

The area was once the upper end of New York's Lower East Side. But now it is being called the East Village. And that nominal aspect of its transformation is coming about because a little more than ten years ago, the artists and writers and painters moved there from across town to escape the spiraling rents and the increasingly middle-brow atmosphere of Greenwich Village on the West Side. The Five Spot owes its existence as a jazz club to these transplanted artists and the cultural interests they brought with them.

The current Five Spot Cafe is a fairly large room as New York jazz clubs go. One enters it under a neat sidewalk canopy, which reaches from the front door to the gutter. One walks through a short vestibule, with its hat-check booth to the right, and into a square, dimly lit room. The walls are painted a warm red, and the effect of contemporary decor is spoiled only by a couple of square columns in the center of the room that are encased in mirrors and look rather like surplus props from a 1936 Ruby Keeler musical.

A bar takes up almost the length of one wall on the right as one enters. To the left, at right angles to the bar, is a slightly raised platform, the club's bandstand. The wall behind the bandstand contains three archways, leading to a kind of patio area where patrons are seated behind the musicians on crowded evenings.

9:30 P.M. The bar is full, although the relief group, the Roland Hanna Trio, is not due to start playing until ten and Thelonious Monk's quartet not expected till eleven. The bar looks familiar; it was moved from the original Five Spot, once a few blocks down the Bowery but now demolished for another of those grim, hazardous institutions known as modern housing.

According to the New York Fire Department's notice posted on a back wall, the club's occupancy is limited to 223. There are about thirty-five persons now at the tables and more arriving. It is mostly a young crowd, the kind one would expect during a holiday weekend. The red walls are covered with posters and flyers for artists' showings and gallery openings and for jazz concerts dating back a year or so—just like the walls of the old Five Spot.

Across the room, a lone man sits in a corner table. A waiter, dressed in a neat, red jacket that almost matches the paint on the walls, says politely, "Sorry, sir, this is a table for four." The waiter looks like a college student on a part-time job, and he is.

A couple come in and are escorted to a table near the bandstand. She is wearing a mink, and he doesn't look old enough to have bought it for her.

In the patio area, there is a jukebox. To judge from its listed contents the clientele's taste runs to the Marvelletes, Brook Benton, Nina Simone, and (for goodness sake!) Moms Mabley. It isn't playing, however, but there is a piano LP being quietly piped through the house public address system. The recorded pianist is heaping up currently hip block chords at a great rate.

It isn't very much like the old Five Spot. It is cleaner, neater, bigger, yet younger, more prosperous, and business-like but still very comfortable and easy as clubs go.

Behind the bar, Iggy Termini, a stocky, blond man of medium height, and co-proprietor with his brother Joe, is polishing glasses when he isn't filling them or checking some small account books he keeps back there. He and the bar itself are the familiar sights in a relatively unfamiliar atmosphere.

* * *

THE ORIGINAL FIVE SPOT was a neighborhood bar and had been in the Termini family for more than twenty-five years. It was not particularly a Bowery bar, for there are many such that cater almost exclusively to the thick tastes and thin pockets of the skidrow clientele. When the Termini sons, Joe and Iggy, came out of the army, the father Termini gradually turned the place over to them. They in turn found themselves getting as customers more and more of the Village expatriates who had moved into the neighborhood. These included sculptor David Smart and painter Herman Cherry, both of whom hounded the management to put in some live entertainment—specifically, some live jazz. The Terminis finally capitulated.

The honor of being among the first musicians to play jazz in the Five Spot belongs to the David Amram–George Barrow group, to Cecil Taylor's quartet with Steve Lacy, to Randy Weston, and to Charlie Mingus. By that time, the future had clearly been decided, and this small East-Side bar was a going New York jazz club.

It was rather a relaxed scene in those early days. There was no cover or minimum charge, relatively inexpensive beer, and a lot of attentive listening. Too much listening in a sense; in order to handle the increasing crowds, Joe and Iggy had to take on some help and made the mistake of hiring a few younger jazz fans and hippies to tend the customers at the tables. As a result, something like the following scene was played with minor variations several times a night:

Customer: "Waiter, could I have another. . ."

Waiter: "Shush, man! Don't you dig—Jackie is soloing? Wait a minute!"

It soon became house policy to interview a prospective employee carefully, and if he admitted the slightest interest in jazz, he probably wouldn't get the job.

The Terminis soon went after the then-legendary Monk for the Five Spot. They finally got him, and it was Monk's extended stays at the club that had as much as anything else to do with his rediscovery by musicians and critics as a major jazzman. The most celebrated of the several Monk Five Spot gigs was the first, in the summer of 1957, with Monk, tenor saxophonist John Coltrane, bassist Wilbur Ware, and drummer Shadow Wilson, a group and an occasion important enough to have become fabled within six months of its existence. And it was at this point that Joe Termini would acknowledge, in one of his relatively guarded moments, "Well, we're in show business now."

And after the triumphs with Monk? Well, the second most celebrated booking was surely the first New York appearance of saxophonist Ornette Coleman (who was also something of a fixture for a while), and there was a return engagement for pianist Cecil Taylor too.

Meanwhile, the Terminis had temporarily branched out with a second and larger club, the Jazz Gallery, a promising but ill-fated enterprise a few blocks up and across town.

Then, Charlie Mingus was back to close the original Five Spot before the wrecking crews moved in to demolish it.

Iggy and Joe acquired a corner cafeteria and tobacco shop a few blocks up the street, redesigned it, and applied for a license to operate a cabaret. They didn't get it at first, and for a while it was touch and go at the new Five Spot with legally allowable pianists, without drummers, and with some weekend sessions. They took in Hsio Wen Shih, the son of a Chinese diplomat, the former publisher of *The Jazz Review,* writer on jazz, and architect by profession, as a part of the organization. Finally there came the license and an official opening with the current Thelonious Monk Quartet, an engagement which continued for seven months.

9:55. A male voice, young, drifts up from somewhere in the crowd that is drinking, chatting, and waiting for the music to start: " . . . swimming in the nude and that sort of thing, but they've clamped down on it." Roland Hanna, looking like a kindly but officious banker who is about to explain an overdraft to a befuddled dowager, enters the clubroom through the kitchen, crosses the floor to the area behind the bandstand (this patio area is the section that used to be the cigar store), and chats with his bass player, Ernie Farrell.

Behind the bar, Iggy says softly to an old customer, "This is a quiet place. I mean there're no problems." (He probably has in mind the Bowery drunks who used to wander into the old place and try for a handout before Joe could grab them and usher them out, thrusting them firmly among the crowd of fans that usually filled the sidewalk outside the club.)

A few feet down the bar, a young man who has been nursing a beer for about an hour says to his companion, "How about that rent strike in Harlem?"

10:05. Hanna moves out of the patio area, through an archway, and onto the bandstand. He sits down on the piano bench and warms up by running through the middle octaves of the keyboard. Farrell is in place. Drummer Albert Heath also looks ready. They begin, and Hanna's banker's demeanor continues through the thick chords of his opening chorus of "On Green Dolphin Street." The crowd continues to buzz and chat. But then Hanna is interpolating a phrase from "Solar" and waggling his head, and the banker is a forgotten person.

There is applause as the pianist segues into a bass solo, and it is followed by a sudden burst of irrelevant laughter from someone enjoying a private joke at the bar. A young man in a heavy, black turtleneck sweater and olive-drab corduroys crosses the room earnestly searching for the men's room door, snapping his fingers as he goes.

Hanna's right hand travels up the keyboard, and the number is over. Scattered applause.

Through the front windows of the patio, a city bus visibly grinds down the side street. At the canopy, a lone panhandler approaches a couple of arriving jazz fans.

The place is filling up, and the late arrivals are not so young as the earlier crowd.

10:20. Heath, in a long drum solo, has the eyes and ears of the crowd. At the end of the bar, a middle-aged woman looks on admiringly, and as if she knew exactly what was happening. She has a copy of *The New Yorker* and a half-empty martini glass on the bar in front of her. To her right, her escort looks noncommittal.

10:40. Hanna, into a fast blues, laughs about the tempo during Farrell's long solo. At the front door a waiter takes down the rope for a couple in their late thirties and for four youngsters on a double date. The older couple ends up at the bar, and the foursome gets a table.

10:50. Frankie Dunlop and Butch Warren have arrived, but so far no Monk and no Charlie Rouse. Hanna finishes his set and announces into the mike that he is turning over the bandstand to "Mister high priest, Thelonious Monk." Shades of 1947 press agentry! A waiter confides to a customer at a back table that Hanna tongue-tangled it into "the high beast of prebop" a few nights back.

Various beards, bulky sweaters, and Brooks Brothers suits begin shuffling around the room, table-hopping, men's-rooming, and telephoning, as silence follows Hanna's departure from the stand.

Nobody turns up the lights between sets, and the red walls smolder on the right and left, to the front and rear.

"Did you ever see Monk's drummer?" asks a fellow at the bar, loudly for some reason.

A woman at a back table giggles constantly.

"Yes, Germany and Japan were *allies* during the war—you mean you didn't *know* that?" says her to her at a table by one of the mirrored columns.

"Ya, but ze Americans zey. . .," says she, a young, blond girl looking earnestly at her escort.

11:20. "Look out!" someone shouts to a waiter near the center of the room. Behind him the dark figure of Monk is rushing down an aisle between the tables, singular of purpose and unmistakable in his tweed hat and heavy tan jacket. He is quickly through the kitchen door at the back end of the club, headed for the dressing room beyond.

11:27. Monk comes through the kitchen door and moves toward the stand, a little more slowly this time but no less purposefully. He is hardly in front of the piano before he is playing "Don't Blame Me" solo. A burst of hard applause covers his opening notes, but almost immediately the room is silent. He plays with unrelenting and uncompromising emotion, and there is simply nothing to do but listen. Then a sudden, hard succession of clusters of tones in the bass. What did he *do*? Ah, anyway Monk is still growing. The second chorus begins with wild, sardonic trills, played partly with the inside fingers of the right hand while his outside fingers carry the melody notes. An unexpected alignment of ten notes ends the piece abruptly.

"Thank you. . . ." He taps the microphone and then slaps it lightly with three fingers. Is it on? "Thank you, ladies and gentlemen. . . ." A deep voice, followed by more tapping. "Thank you, ladies and gentlemen, and good evening to you. Now Butch Warren will play a bass solo for you." Monk goes hurriedly off the stand with a couple of right and left lunging movements that seem to contradict each other but which end him up on the patio behind the bandstand.

Warren plays a cleanly articulated "Softly, As in a Morning Sunrise." As he begins, Charlie Rouse arrives and ducks quickly behind the bandstand. Monk paces erratically.

"And now Frankie Dunlop will warm up with a number."

About two minutes later, Monk and Warren are back on the bandstand, and Monk offers his brittle, out-of-tempo opening chorus to "I'm Getting Sentimental Over You." Just before the bridge, Monk leans to his left and looks under the piano, almost as if the next notes were down there somewhere. Then a break takes them into tempo for the second chorus, with tenor saxophonist Rouse walking onto the bandstand as he plays, and Monk really working behind him with a clipped distillation of the melody in support.

Halfway through the chorus, Monk gets up, leaving his instrument to undertake his swaying, shuffling dance. Half the crowd seems to be nodding knowingly about his eccentricity. But a few in the audience seem to realize that, besides giving his group a change of texture and sound by laying out, Monk is conducting. His movements are encouraging drummer Dunlop and Warren, particularly, to hear, not just the obvious beat, but the accent and space *around* the one-two-three-four, the rhythms that Monk is so interested in.

Warren solos, and Monk and Rouse leave the stand. Then Dunlop is there alone. He articulates the four eight-bar divisions of the piece very clearly on his drums for two choruses. The group reassembles. Anybody who can't dig the music will probably like the show.

Monk's well-known bass figure leads him to a fast "Epistrophy," his theme. They give it a full performance. Monk accompanies Rouse with accents that are dazzling, although he isn't playing so demandingly of his theme. Then he signals musically for Rouse to come back for the out chorus.

"Midnight." The piece ends; the set is over. Monk leads the way off the stand, and for a moment the piano sits empty, bathed in an amber spotlight.

At the door, two couples arrive and ask, "When will Monk be on again?"

"He should be back in an hour. Roland Hanna will be on in a few minutes."

"You wanna wait? You wanna go in now or come back?"

You Dig It, Sir?

Lillian Ross

The first Newport Jazz Festival took place in 1954, and Lillian Ross was on hand to report on it for The New Yorker *with her caustic eye and deadpan prose. Jazz writing has many virtues, but humor is not conspicuous among them; this may be the funniest piece on jazz ever written.*

When, earlier this summer, Mr. and Mrs. Louis Livingston Lorillard, a young and adventurous couple who spend their winters in Capri and the warm-weather months in Newport, Rhode Island, decided to put on an American Jazz Festival at the Newport Casino, they invited sixty-five of their neighbors at the famous old resort to join them in sponsoring it. They received only two acceptances—and only one from a long-established member of the community; that was Mr. George Henry Warren, of New York, who has summered in Newport practically all his life. Undismayed, the Lorillards went ahead with their project. As a token of good faith and to help ease the rest of the summer colonists into the spirit of the occasion, Mr. Warren and his wife decided to give a dinner party on the Friday of the weekend the Festival was scheduled to be held and invite the sixty-three reluctant neighbors. The invitations, which were sent out a fortnight or so before the party, were unanimously accepted. Suddenly, the prevailingly chilly mood changed, with the result that more than fourteen thousand people turned out for two brassy, four-hour concerts that were held on Saturday and Sunday nights on the neat, spacious grass courts of the nineteenth-century gabled Casino, perhaps best known as the birthplace of lawn tennis in this country, and another thousand attended a Sunday-afternoon forum on the subject of "The Place of Jazz in American Culture."

To promote the affair, the Lorillards and some jazz-loving friends set themselves up as Newport Jazz Festival, Inc. (Official purpose: "To encourage America's enjoyment of jazz and to sponsor the study of our country's only original art form.") They got permission to use the Casino for the nominal fee—approved without dissent by the Casino's board of governors—of three hundred and fifty dollars. They also found a producer for the Festival—a Boston jazz impresario named George Wein. Associated with the Lorillards and the Warrens in Newport Jazz Festival, Inc., were, among other sponsors, a number of leading jazz musicians from various dives across the nation; Leonard Bernstein, the composer and conductor; John Hammond, the jazz critic and scholar; Cleveland Amory, the author of *The Last Resorts*; Marshall Stearns, associate professor of English at Hunter College and director of the Institute of Jazz Studies, who organized the Festival's forum; and Father Norman O'Connor, chaplain of the Newman Club of Boston University, who is known as the Jazz Priest and served as the forum's moderator. Much to the surprise of the sponsors, after two nights of good, solid jazz, ranging from Dixieland to very modern and played by sixty-five musicians, a number of whom had never before seen the surf beating against the rocky shores of old New England, they emerged with the sure and not inconsiderable profit of more than eleven thousand dollars. Mr. Lorillard, who, when he is not sponsoring jazz festivals, owns and directs a Newport travel agency, and who underwrote the event, plans to use the money to promote the study and development of modern American music.

The Warrens' dinner party was held in the garden of their house, which is near the Old Stone Mill, known to local historians as the most controversial building in America because it has never been determined who built it or when. I was fortunate enough to be invited to the party, and a few minutes after I checked in at the Hotel Viking on Friday evening, Mrs. Lorillard telephoned to see if I had arrived. "Everybody's here, and they're all talking about the *Festival!*" she said in a tone of wonder. "They're warming up!"

When I got to the party, I found the guests in the garden, casually grouped around a singer named Lee Wiley, a pretty blonde in a shell-pink décolleté gown, who was being accompanied by Teddy Wilson on an upright piano. Miss Wiley is a specialist in singing songs by George Gershwin, Rodgers and Hart, and Cole Porter; Wilson is one of the nation's leading jazz pianists. Miss Wiley was singing, "We'll go to Yonkers, where true love conquers . . . We'll go to Coney and eat bologny . . ." in a soft, low voice, and her audience, finely tanned and formally dressed, looked rapt. They applauded vigorously when she finished, and there were many cries of "Bravo!"

Mr. Warren, a gracious, jolly, pink-cheeked man wearing tortoise-shell glasses and a tuxedo, who used to be a financier and now devotes most of his time to philanthropic activities, led me to a chair next to Mrs. Lorillard. "Newport is not on the skids, no matter what anybody says," he assured me. "Have you ever seen anybody more alive than this crowd?"

"I'm still uneasy," said Mrs. Lorillard, an attractive, titian-haired woman in a sapphire-blue satin gown. "It could be Guy Lombardo, and they'd act just as enthusiastic."

"Thank heavens it *isn't* Guy Lombardo!" said a woman who had on an evening wrap of white ostrich feathers.

"Thank heavens it isn't *Meyer Davis!*" said a third woman, who, somewhat older than the others, was wearing a black lace dress with a high collar. "I've been getting Meyer Davis for nineteen years, and now I'm enjoying that nice Mr. Wilson at the piano. George, I must say it's a change. Mr. Wilson is musically somehow or other more frolicsome."

Mrs. Lorillard said in an undertone to me, "Things are really looking up. Yesterday morning I was at my lowest ebb. I was on a radio program being interviewed about the Festival, and all they kept asking me was what I thought of Liberace! Actually, I come from a long-hair family. My great-aunt was Lillian Nordica, the famous Wagnerian opera singer, and I was brought up on classical music, but I believe that jazz is an art, too. Oh, there's Mrs. Harold Brooks! She broke her ankle last night, but she's here anyway. She's *really* moral support! Her luncheons are always being described in *Vogue.* And she's bought a box for the Festival. Boxes are a hundred dollars apiece."

Miss Wiley started singing "I've Got a Crush on You." A tall, ruddy-faced man moved forward, sat down on a gravel walk beside her, and, hugging his knees, looked up at her.

"Oh, my!" said Mrs. Lorillard to me. "That's Barclay Douglas. You know—the stockbroker. He's president of the Clambake Club. The most exclusive private club in Newport."

Mrs. Warren tiptoed over to Mr. Douglas and asked him if she could get him a cushion.

"Oh, don't get me a cushion!" Mr. Douglas exclaimed, his eyes fastened on Miss Wiley. "Your gravel is so soft!"

A small, bright-eyed, elderly gentleman with white hair, a white mustache, and a red carnation in his lapel came over to Mrs. Lorillard and took her hand. "Is it true that you've bought tickets for the Jazz Festival?" she asked him.

He gave a dignified nod. "My wife and I went over to the Casino to purchase tickets for what we thought was going to be a symphony concert—the kind you had last year," he said, plainly enjoying every one of his words. "The young lady there said it was a *jazz* festival this year. My wife asked, 'What is a *jazz* festival?' and the young lady said that all those nightclub musicians would come and play, and my wife turned to me and said, 'You know, this just might be *fun.*'" He laughed heartily, and pressed Mrs. Lorillard's hand between both his own.

"We'll have a narrator doing a running commentary on the various kinds of jazz and the jazz musicians who play at each concert," Mrs. Lorillard said eagerly. "Our narrator is Stan Kenton, the *avant-garde* bandleader. He's a very strong fighter for the cause of modern jazz, but he knows everything about all the schools, and he'll make everything clear."

"Dear, dear, are there *schools?"* the man said, his eyes twinkling. He squeezed Mrs. Lorillard's hand again.

"I just can't wait till tomorrow, when I can introduce you to Pee Wee Russell, the clarinetist," Mrs. Lorillard said throatily. "You'll appreciate Pee Wee, and Pee Wee will appreciate you. Each of you, in your own way, is a traditionalist."

As the older of the two traditionalists bowed again and turned away, Mrs. Lorillard said to me, "Now I'm sure that all the members of the old guard in the colony here are with us. We'll get their moral support, anyway. I guess they didn't want to be sponsor because it might mean investing money. Last year, we got them to sponsor bringing the New York Philharmonic to Newport for a classical-music festival, and they all lost sixty-seven cents on every dollar, even though the state gave us a grant of five thousand dollars for it. It really was a flop, so these people are cautious now. I suppose it's simply a matter of money. This year, when we asked the state for a grant for the Jazz Festival, the people up in Providence said no. I guess they didn't want to risk any more money, either. The only other Newport sponsor, in addition to George Henry Warren, is a man named Edward Capuano. He's a newcomer from Providence. He's a successful businessman, and I guess when he got our letter, he figured we were some kind of good investment. You know, it's a strange thing, but the only people who are opposing the Festival are a few members of the younger set. They're the *most* cautious."

Mr. Lorillard, a serious-looking man with a round face, whose great-grandfather, Pierre Lorillard, helped found the Casino in 1879 and built The Breakers, one of Newport's earliest mansions, made his way over to his wife and said out of the corner of his mouth, "Just heard that the Carl Haffenreffers bought *two* boxes."

Mrs. Lorillard gave me a significant look. "You know—beer," she said.

"So far, so good," said Mr. Lorillard.

The next morning, in the lobby of the Viking, I ran into a man named Nat Hentoff, who is the New York editor of *Down Beat,* a magazine of the jazz world. He told me that he was waiting for Stan Kenton, who was going to collaborate with him on the narration for the concerts. "They want to give the Festival a kind of academic flavor," Hentoff said. "It's George Wein's idea. He plays piano himself, and he's opened a couple of jazz nightclubs in the Boston area. He's energized Boston in jazz almost singlehanded. Hi, Stan," he said, greeting a tall gray-haired man with a watchful manner who was ambling across the lobby.

"Hi," Kenton said, in a deep narrator-type voice. He told us he had just been seeing the sights of Newport with Russell Jalbert, a member of the Festival staff. "Very interesting place," Kenton said. "They've got the oldest synagogue in America here. It's called the Touro. For a minute, I thought that might have been where Muggsy Spanier wrote 'Relaxin' at the Touro.' But Jalbert set me straight. Seems that a branch of the Touro family built a sanitarium outside New Orleans, and that's where Muggsy was at when he wrote the number. Nice fellow, Jalbert. But he told me somebody named Oscar Pettiford had called up and asked for tickets, and Jalbert wanted to know, 'Who's Oscar Pettiford?' I told him Oscar is the greatest jazz cellist in the world. You know, we're exchanging educations here, all right. Hey, there's George."

Wein turned out to be a stocky man of twenty-eight who seemed to be filled with controlled frenzy. He told us that there had been a sudden rush of buying tickets for the Festival, and that Newport's two biggest hotels were completely booked. At the moment, Festival workers were polling year-round Newport residents to see if they had any spare rooms to rent. "I don't even know where *I'm* sleeping tonight," Wein said. "Can you imagine that? At the moment, they're setting up emergency cots right in the Casino. Well, let's get started on the program." We adjourned to a small lounge off the lobby, and Wein started things off by saying that for the first concert, that night, about fifty musicians were expected. Among those he named, while Hentoff took notes, were Eddie Condon, Ralph Sutton, Wild Bill Davison, Lou McGarity, Peanuts Hucko, Buzzy Drootin, Milt Hinton, Vic Dickenson, Pee Wee Russell, Bobby Hackett, Cliff Leeman, Jack Lesberg, Lee Wiley, Kenny Clarke, Percy Heath, Horace Silver, Milt Jackson, Dizzy Gillespie, Lee Konitz, Ray Brown, Oscar Peterson, Gerry Mulligan, and Ella Fitzgerald. "We want to throw modern, swing, and Dixieland together—even have the guys playing them together," Wein said. "As long as there's a common beat, every guy can play solo his own style. One big happy family."

"You don't think there'll be trouble?" Kenton asked anxiously.

"No," said Wein.

"It's hardly ever done, and almost never successfully," Kenton said.

"I'm convinced this will work," said Wein. "All they need is a beat."

"I don't want any honkers," Kenton said.

"We don't *have* any honkers," said Wein. "We've got nothing but top jazz artists, and we'll put them on one after the other. After more than three hours, of course, it'll get to be a beat thing, but I want people leaving that Casino saying, 'Whew! That was a little too much!' That way, they'll remember the night. Like giving them three Bach cantatas in one concert."

"I'd like to see Stan playing piano behind Pee Wee Russell," said Hentoff. "Progressive Prototype behind Old Conservative. What dramatic contrast! A capsule history of jazz."

"You can't tell," Kenton said. "We might find something together. And I'll be just as happy to introduce Eddie Condon as I will be to introduce Dizzy Gillespie."

"No matter what happens, we'll do this again next year," Wein said. "We're trying to do in two days what should take a week, but we'll give an all-round presentation of jazz, and it will be remembered. Artists from all branches of jazz. All getting together and blowing."

The three men were silent for a moment and looked at each other soberly. Then Kenton said, "Well, we'd better get this thing organized," and they settled down to work on the program. It was decided to have the Eddie Condon Dixieland group play first, and follow it with a swing group made up of Vic Dickenson on trombone, Pee Wee Russell on clarinet, and Bobby Hackett on trumpet.

"Good!" Wein said. "That way, Hackett will get a chance to warm up his chops before he accompanies Lee Wiley."

"Now, there's a good combination," said Hentoff. "Good musicians all appreciate Lee Wiley. She's a musicians' singer. She sings from within the song."

"Put it down in the notes," Kenton said to Hentoff. "I want to be sure to tell the crowd that."

After the intermission, it was decided, they would have Dizzy Gillespie, and he would be followed by Oscar Peterson.

"You don't think Oscar will get bugged about going on second?" Hentoff asked.

Wein said no, he didn't. "Oscar is the sweetest guy," he added. "He'll do anything."

"Oscar blows fine piano," said Kenton.

An elderly lady wearing a large white picture hat and carrying a white lace parasol came into the room and knocked timidly on the back of a chair. "Pardon me, gentlemen," she said. "What time is the jazz-music lecture?"

The three men looked startled. After a brief silence, Wein stood up and bowed. "Four o'clock tomorrow afternoon," he said.

"I'll be there," the lady said.

Wein sat down heavily. "We're in!" he said. "The only thing that can make things rough now is if it should rain."

A couple of hours later, I walked over to the Casino to pick up my tickets for the concerts. Wein went along with me to find out whether a bus bringing Eddie Condon and some other musicians from New York had arrived yet. The street was clogged with clamoring automobiles, and Wein looked at them affectionately. "All these people may not be able to get into any place to eat or sleep, but they're going to hear a lot of good music," he said. "This town will never be the same again. What I want is to get Doris Duke's aunt or somebody else here with a big mansion to give us their place and let us turn it into a school of modern music. Maybe we could get the Perry Belmont estate, with all those stables. We could make Newport the jazz center of the world. What Salzburg is to Mozart! What Bayreuth is to Wagner! What Tanglewood is to classical music! That's what we could make Newport be to jazz!"

At the Casino, we were joined by one of Wein's assistants, a young man named Charlie Bourgeois, who was wearing a T-shirt, Army suntans, and sneakers. He told Wein that workmen were beginning to set up folding chairs on the grass courts out back. "They're fixing the chairs so that each blade of grass curls around each chair leg," Bourgeois said. "That's what we get for putting on a show on sacred grounds. And the head greenskeeper wants us to take the chairs off the lawns after the concert and put them up all over again tomorrow."

Wein said he would have a talk with the head greenskeeper. "There's our shell," he said proudly as we walked out onto the courts. He pointed to a crescent stage that had been built at one end. Several workmen were setting up loudspeakers on it, and others were gently placing folding chairs on the grass. "The sound is going to be good," Wein said. "The local Unitarian Church lent us the rostrum free, but that stage cost us twelve hundred dollars. The total nut of this Festival, counting the musicians' fees and transportation costs, is going to come to something like forty thousand dollars. I get scared when I think of it, but then I tell myself *maybe* we'll break even."

A young lady named Terri Turner, who was acting as Wein's production manager, came running over to him and reported breathlessly that Lee Konitz, a very-modern saxophone player, had just telephoned from New York to say that he had missed the Eddie Condon bus. Wein hit himself on the head with his fist, but then quickly pulled himself together. "Tell him to take a plane, train—anything," he said. "He can't goof off! He's got to be here!"

"Maybe he's subconsciously bugged about riding up with Dixieland musicians," Bourgeois said.

Wein looked at his wristwatch. "It's only two o'clock," he said. "Musicians are never themselves till four in the afternoon."

As I was leaving my hotel for the Saturday-evening concert, the desk clerk handed me an engraved invitation to attend a reception and supper party for the musicians that Mr. and Mrs. Lorillard were giving at their home, Quatrel, on Bellevue Avenue, after the performance. I arrived at the Casino half an hour before the scheduled starting time of the concert and found the grounds packed with paying customers. Refreshment stands dispensing both hard and soft drinks had been set up on the sidelines and were doing a lively business. Backstage, musicians of all schools were milling about and pounding one another on the back.

"What, *you* here?" Jo Jones (drummer, swing) cried out to Buzzy Drootin (drummer, Dixieland).

"Hey, I hear Dizzy Gillespie's challenged Stan Kenton to a tennis match during intermission!" another musician shouted.

I came upon Wein standing off to one side of the shell, studying the people in the audience. It wasn't a typical jazz audience, he told me, and he figured that the average age was forty-five. "They look like a lot of people who know nothing about jazz," he said. "It's a social thing with them. That's the way it should be."

A man wearing a white dinner jacket and a maroon bow tie came up, introduced himself to Wein as John J. Sullivan, the Mayor of Newport, and told him apologetically, "I was asked to say a few words."

"O.K., but make it short," said Wein. "We've got a long program, and this'll get to be a beat thing."

Bourgeois, still wearing sneakers, hurried up and said that the Eddie Condon bus had just pulled in, three hours late. "Eddie really knows his timing," Wein said as he hurried off to meet the bus. The Mayor turned to me. "Not a store front in town doesn't have a Festival poster in the window," he said. "This is the greatest thing that's happened to Newport in years. I was the city treasurer two years ago, and I'm in a position to know. But we're humming now! Restaurants overcrowded! People hunting for rooms! Now maybe we'll get that new hotel we've been waiting for for thirty years. You know, I'm not the public-speaking type. We've never had a public affair like this. This will be the biggest crowd I've ever talked to. I'd better study my speech." He took a couple of typewritten pages from his pocket and read softly to himself, "Distinguished jazz lovers: Today jazz is known throughout the world . . ."

A few minutes later, Wein returned and said that over seven thousand people were on hand—four thousand more than anybody had even hoped for—and that Casino workmen were trying to scare up extra chairs for them. Mayor Sullivan gallantly commissioned some of his policemen and firemen to pitch in and help. Wein passed the back of his hand over his brow. "The greenskeeper gave us a special dispensation to leave the chairs on the lawn all night, thank God," he said.

Only half an hour late, the festivities were opened by the Mayor, who spoke rather lengthily on the importance of jazz to our national culture and to Newport's economy. Next came a Boston disc jockey named John McLellan, who said briskly that never before in history had so many of the major artists in jazz been assembled for a series of concerts. As I joined the audience, McLellan announced that there could be "no more appropriate narrator for the first important jazz festival to be held in the United States than the man who has based his life on his belief in jazz—Stan Kenton." The occupants of the hundred-dollar boxes—all of them looking radiant in formal dress—gave Kenton a big hand. The Lorillards looked unbelieving.

"Perle Mesta is here," Mrs. Lorillard said in a tremulous whisper as I stopped by for a moment.

"Count and Countess Reventlow are in somebody's box," Mr. Lorillard said. "They don't even *like* jazz."

"How nice of Perle Mesta to come!" Mrs. Lorillard said. "And our senator—Theodore Francis Green." She indicated an elegant, white-haired old fellow, who waved to her and called out, "Magnificent undertaking! Bold enterprise!"

Mr. Lorillard cleared his throat nervously and said out of the corner of his mouth, "Here we go."

Onstage, Kenton, looking distinguished and silvery-haired under the stage lights, was saying that the earliest form of jazz was the music that grew out of the spirituals, the work songs, the field hollers, and the blues of the American Negro, and that a new kind of music had been born in the South, especially in New Orleans, where it had been played by brass bands in parade and funeral processions. The music had moved out of New Orleans, Kenton went on earnestly, to St. Louis and then to Chicago, and musicians of all races and backgrounds had been influenced by it. It was a free music, a music that called for self-expression and allowed the closest possible communion with other musicians. "This New Orleans jazz came to be called Dixieland in the form in which it was taken up by young men in Chicago and throughout the Midwest and Southwest," Kenton said. "These men kept the small band that was characteristic of New Orleans jazz. They kept the free interplay of melodic voices—a kind of counterpoint, several melodies playing at once—they kept the beat, the regular pulsation that was the rhythmic identification of jazz. And I would like to introduce to you some of the men who are happy experts in this idiom . . . to illustrate for you the freewheeling pleasures to be found in the extrovertish land of Dixieland."

A couple of elderly, powdered ladies near me laughed softly. "Isn't he charming?" one of them said.

Her companion agreed. "I wonder if he knows Meyer Davis," she said.

Kenton introduced the Dixieland group, called them "fiercely independent artists," and said that one of the most remarkable figures in the history of jazz would lead them. "The Sir Thomas Beecham of jazz—Eddie Condon!" Kenton said.

Condon—diminutive, hollow-cheeked, and sallow—took a bow and turned to his musicians. He raised his arms, and then, as he let them fall, at

9:05 P.M., the first chord was finally struck. All at once, bass, piano, clarinet, trombone, trumpet, and drums pierced the quiet that had suddenly descended, and a tremor went through the crowd. The musicians were playing a standard Dixieland number called "Muskrat Ramble." Condon picked up his guitar and joined in with the others. The audience leaned forward expectantly.

As the evening progressed, the audience seemed to approve of everything that was played and everybody who played it. A full yellow moon rose opposite the shell, and the musicians squinted uneasily at it. The intermission was canceled, and Kenton, with his listeners vigilantly attentive, plowed straight ahead through Dixieland and swing into an introduction to the latest in jazz styles—"The product," he said, "of the most recent experiments, of the attempts that have been constant throughout the history of jazz to extend the range and the communicative powers of jazz and of each instrument as well." He then presented the Milt Jackson Quartet (drums, bass, piano, and vibraphone) as "an example of modern-jazz chamber music." The four musicians, looking young, intense, and intellectual, played a few numbers, and the audience listened solemnly to their subtly swinging beat, characterized by off-beats and cross-rhythms. After that, introduced by Kenton as a man who has "a knowledge of the roots of jazz and the whole history of the form that is as complete as anyone's" and as "one of the great figures in the evolution of jazz," Dizzy Gillespie came bouncing onstage, trailed by four plaid-coated musicians. A murmur went through the audience. Gillespie, wearing a wrinkled brown suit and the ever-present tuft of hair on his chin, held a trumpet in his hand. The bell of the trumpet had been bent up at an angle—"so I can hear myself play," he explained to the audience. Then he gravely introduced the members of his unit to each other, as if they had never met before. The two powdered ladies exchanged glances. "He *is* an amusing gentleman," one of them said.

Wein came scurrying over to me. "I goofed off and lost my own speech," he said hoarsely. "I'm looking for Hentoff to write me another one."

A *Down Beat* photographer, who was sitting nearby, told Wein where to find Hentoff, and then said, "Is Dizzy bugged or something? He's so subdued."

"I don't imagine Dizzy ever played Newport before," Wein replied. "He'll get more like himself with time."

Gillespie put down his trumpet and, taking a small camera from the pocket of his jacket, started photographing his musicians.

"Dizzy blows fine camera," the photographer said.

Bourgeois waved to Wein from the sidelines and called out that Lee Konitz, the man who had missed the bus, had turned up, just in time to go on.

When the Oscar Peterson Trio came on (Peterson, piano; Ray Brown, base; Herb Ellis, guitar) and started playing modern jazz in the direct, hot tradition, the audience let itself go with abandoned gaiety. Then Gerry Mulligan, a baritone saxophonist with a freckled boyish face and a forward-jutting crew cut, led a quartet playing complex modern style again.

"First one, then the other—one, then the other," a man behind me said. "I'm exhausted. And the only room I can get tonight is up somewhere on Cape Cod."

Ella Fitzgerald, whom Kenton introduced as a "vocal genius," came on next, and then Wein took the stage to read a short speech about the now hopeful future of an annual American Jazz Festival in Newport. The concert wound up with a twenty-minute jam session conducted with Toscanini-like motions by Eddie Condon (assisted by Gerry Mulligan, in charge of riffs), in which all the musicians—Dixieland, swing, modern, and very modern (including Stan Kenton at the piano)—seemed to find a common beat, and blew.

On my way out, I ran into Mayor Sullivan, who was beaming at the crowd. He nodded happily to me. "Saviors of Newport," he said.

Senator Green was pumping Mr. Lorillard's hand. "Enthusiastic congratulations!" he said. "Magnificent success! Bold, bold enterprise!"

The Lorillards' party was going strong when, shortly after one-thirty, I drove up to their eighty-five-year-old, French-style, ocean-front mansion. Most of the musicians were there, along with most of the box-holders, and all were helping each other to large servings of scrambled eggs, sausages, hot rolls, and champagne. The Lorillards stood at the entrance, feverishly shaking hands with the guests. Cleveland Amory congratulated the host and hostess. "Tonight Newport went back to its beginning," he said. "Back to the time when it hummed with artists, writers, schoolteachers, ministers, and freedom."

A scholarly-looking young man in the doorway said, "Jazz has made the grade—from Storyville to Newport in fifty years."

The Lorillards thanked everybody and looked happy.

Mrs. Amory was saying to Wild Bill Davison, "My husband used to play the trumpet. How do you get that sound?"

"All you got to do is feel good," Davison told her.

In a corner, a tall woman, dressed in a flowered chiffon gown and wearing a jeweled comb in her hair, was explaining to Percy Heath (bass, modern) and Peanuts Hucko (clarinet, Dixieland) that in the old, lush days in Newport, when every house had a large staff of liveried servants, the wives of the multimillionaires used to plan entertainments on a competitive basis. "A favorite trick was to let a hostess go ahead and announce her party, and then a stronger rival would announce a party for the same night," she said.

"There was one attempt to give a rival party tonight, but I've heard it was a dismal failure. As a matter of fact, the entire rival party, including the hostess, decided to come *here*." Heath and Hucko nodded sympathetically.

Another woman joined the group and said in a strong British accent, "There may be a small amount of local criticism from some stick-in-the-muds, but I've seen exactly the same attitude at the Edinburgh Festival. Some people in Edinburgh shut up their houses and take to the rocks for the whole three weeks, groaning about 'the mob.' But the Edinburgh Festival is a huge success, and the Newport Festival is a duplicate."

"You bet," said Peanuts Hucko.

"I understand they're saving the best for tomorrow night—Gene Krupa," the woman went on. "I'm a grandmother and about to become a great-grandmother, but I don't mind saying it's always been my ambition to play the drums."

"You bet," said Peanuts Hucko.

Nearby, Pee Wee Russell was being presented by Mrs. Taylor Chewning, a vivacious, deeply tanned woman with long blond hair, to another guest—the Argentine Ambassador, Hipolito J. Paz. "I've been told that Mr. Russell has played with the greatest jazz musicians," Mrs. Chewning said. "He played with Mr. Bix Beiderbecke."

Russell and the Ambassador shook hands.

"Chum, I don't boast, you know," Russell said, with a self-deprecating gesture. "But a couple of times tonight I played all right."

"Superb," said the Ambassador.

In another corner, Eddie Condon (guitar, Dixieland) was carrying on a friendly conversation with Gerry Mulligan (baritone saxophone, very modern). Between them stood Professor Stearns, the organizer of the forum. "Never thought I'd see the day come when you two would be playing together," Stearns said.

"Well, I'm not exactly hysterical about kids playing saxophones bigger than they are," said Condon.

"Anybody who still chooses to play a four-stringed instrument is practically prehistoric," said Mulligan.

"We're all one big happy family," said Stearns.

James H. Van Alen, president of the Casino, came up and announced that he was something of a songwriter himself. He produced a piece of sheet music entitled "Good Evening, Mr. President," and handed it to Condon. Below the title was the inscription, "Respectfully Dedicated to Dwight D. Eisenhower. Words and Music by J. H. Van Alen (Rhode Island)."

"It was played at the inaugural ball," Mr. Van Alen said.

Condon started reading the words of the song aloud:

"Believe us, Mr. President,
We're glad it's you, not we,
Who have got the job of keeping
Our great country safe and free . . ."

Condon looked up from the music. "What did you say you played there at the Casino?" he asked.

"Tennis," said Mr. Van Alen.

Condon shook his head sadly. "After what they heard at the Casino tonight, tennis will never be played there again," he said.

"You fellows certainly had the crowd giving our lawn a workout," Mr. Van Alen said. "All that steady, undulating motion."

In another part of the room, a trombone player was conversing with a group of Newporters. "Europe from now on is just like Des Moines, Iowa," he told them. "They really go for jazz over there. And Australia is opening up. Ella Fitzgerald is going out on a seven-day tour, and Gene Krupa for fourteen."

One of the Newporters said that it was the first time he had heard Miss Fitzgerald, but that he believed he had once heard Krupa play.

"Gene's been around for a long time," the trombone player said. "He's still plenty big. After all these years."

Wein joined the group, his energy and enthusiasm undiminished. "Wait till tomorrow," he said. "We'll have Billie Holiday. One of the greatest. Billie is a real queen!"

"Pres will be here," the trombone man said to Wein. "Billie doesn't talk to Pres. Pres," he went on for the information of the Newporters, "is Lester Young. He's president of all the saxophone players, and that's why we call him Pres. Pres and Billie are bugged with each other. They haven't spoken for five years."

"Oh, do try to get them to make up," a lady in the group said.

The next day, at the Lorillards' invitation, I stopped in at their cabaña at the clubhouse of the Spouting Rock Beach Association, at Bailey's Beach. Mr. and Mrs. Amory were there.

"Got to bed at seven A.M.," Mr. Lorillard was saying. "Used up thirty dozen eggs. Five cases of champagne. What a ball!"

Amory said, "I asked Wild Bill Davison to go swimming, but he says he never takes off his clothes on Sunday. I didn't ask him why."

At the cabaña next door, Mrs. James Banks, a gentle-looking, gray-haired woman who was wearing a long-sleeved print dress, turned around and said, "It was a lovely party. I got to bed at five this morning."

"Thank you, Mrs. Banks," said Mr. Lorillard.

That afternoon, the forum on "The Place of Jazz in American Culture" was conducted by a panel consisting of Dr. Alan Merriam, instructor of anthropology at Northwestern University; Professor Willis James, of the Music Department of Spelman College, in Atlanta; Henry Cowell, composer and professor of music at Peabody Institute; and Professor Stearns. As moderator, Father O'Connor called his colleagues together for a brief meeting just before the forum began to tell them that he didn't think the audience wanted to hear a lot of boring talk. "We don't want to sound like a bunch of long-hairs," said the Jazz Priest.

The members of the panel agreed. "I'm supposed to talk about the influence of jazz on classical music, whatever that means," Cowell said.

"You can tie that up in five minutes," Father O'Connor told him.

"I slept in the most fantastic place last night," Cowell said. "It was a very old mansion owned by Mrs. Peyton Van Rensselaer. I had a door opening out from my second-floor bedroom into nothing. Space."

"I slept in the same house," Stearns said. "My closet had a staircase in it."

"People don't want to hear serious jabber," Cowell said. "Let's try to stir up questions among ourselves. Even arguments."

"Anything goes," Father O'Connor said. "It has to. Why, a couple of the musicians came up to greet me this morning and said, 'Hi, Dad!'"

At the forum, I took a seat next to Maxim Karolik, a Bostonian and patron of the arts who has spent his last twenty-five summers in Newport and who with his late wife donated the M. and M. Karolik Collections of Eighteenth- and Nineteenth-Century Furniture and Painting to the Boston Museum of Fine Arts. He was sitting with Gerry Mulligan.

"Jazz is no longer only for cabarets," Karolik said. "No question about it."

"You dig it, sir?" Mulligan asked.

"It's something to ponder," said Karolik. "Rachmaninoff spoke about it. It is an established fact. Jazz is America's contribution to music."

The forum started with a brief talk by Dr. Merriam on the relation of African music to jazz; there was no direct connection between the two, he said, but there had been a certain amount of blending. Then Professor James gave examples of field hollers and street cries that became the basis of the blues. He was followed by Professor Stearns, who defined jazz as the blending of African and European music in the United States over a period of three hundred years. "Jazz leads from rigidity toward mobility," he said. "It is anti-Puritan and inimical to all regimentation. It may be in the groove, but you can hop in and out of it."

Cowell said that, as a classical composer, he envied jazz musicians who didn't know how to read notes. "Jazz musicians are free, and they have it all over us," he said.

Karolik whispered, "No question about it. This Festival is the strongest vitamin Newport ever had."

It rained heavily for a solid hour before the second concert. It was still raining intermittently when the concert began, but six thousand people sat sturdily in the audience, raincoats pulled up over their heads, and stared patiently at the stage. They were not disappointed. Again McLellan introduced Kenton. Again Kenton gave a brief lecture before calling on the musicians. Again the musicians were of various schools and of various degrees of temperature. Billie Holiday sang, "Love will make you drink and gamble . . . stay out all night long . . ." while Buck Clayton played a mournful obbligato on the trumpet. Teddy Wilson, introduced by Kenton as one of the first of the "cool" musicians, meaning musicians whose emotions are controlled and ordered, played, and so did George Shearing (modified cool), Ruby Braff (neither cool nor non-cool, but himself), Lennie Tristano (ultra-cool), Lee Konitz (ultra-cool), Jo Jones (swing), Milt Hinton (swing), Lester Young (pres of cool, non-cool, swing, and modern), Gil Mellé (ultra-ultra-cool), Gene Krupa (immortal). . . .

After the final number, Tony Corey, the head greenskeeper at the Casino, waited until most of the audience had left, and then signaled for the removal of the folding chairs from his lawn. He said he would soak his grass with water continuously for three days. "Got to keep the alcohol from eating away at it," he explained. "I'll take it slow and bring it back gradually. We've done a lot of suffering, but I guess it was worth it."

Johnny Green

Fred Hall

"Body and Soul" may be the most recorded and admired of all American popular songs, but its composer, Johnny Green, is rarely celebrated. This extended excerpt from an interview with Green comes from More Dialogues in Swing *by Fred Hall (1991).*

See p. 1006 for Gary Giddins on various recorded versions of "Body and Soul."

Of all the great standard American popular songs, "Stardust" and "Body and Soul" are likely the most recorded. Everyone knows Hoagy Carmichael wrote the "Stardust" melody and almost everybody knows Hoagy from his many recordings and films. But the composer of "Body and Soul" was Johnny (later dignified to John) Green, certainly no retiring, self-effacing fellow, but not a performer whose face the general public could identify as a star. But a star he was. Composer of "Out of Nowhere," "I Cover the Waterfront," "Coquette," "I Wanna Be Loved," "Easy Come, Easy Go" and many more evergreens, Johnny was a very fine pianist, who led his own orchestra on radio, for movies, and in the great hotels for many years. He was a formidable conductor of symphony orchestras and for MGM studios where he was the Executive-in-charge-of-music for many years, winning five Academy Awards for such films as *An American in Paris* and *Easter Parade*.

Johnny was a companion, an associate, and a favorite of musical royalty. His career is a microcosm of the most creative, glamorous, and productive period in American musical history, from the late twenties to the late sixties. As a businessman, Johnny Green led the powerful American Association of Composers and Publishers (ASCAP) through some of its fiercest conflicts with broadcasters, recording companies, and other major users of music. He could also deliver a half-hour speech for an hour or two hours at the drop of a half-note and with the greatest of charm.

In the spring of 1988, as I finalized plans to produce a "Tribute to ASCAP Composers" for my summer jazz series at the Ranch House in Ojai, California, I telephoned Johnny. He was an ASCAP past-president and I wanted him to be our guest of honor. "I'll be there if I can drag myself out of this bed," he told me. I learned he was gravely ill, and died before the concert could be staged. This interview, however, took place in happier times beside his pool at his gracious home in Beverly Hills in January of 1986. As we began, I noted that Johnny, unlike so many fellow hit-makers such as Harry Warren and Sammy Fain, was not self-taught but instead was a Harvard graduate and had received an extensive musical education.

JOHNNY: Don't forget, I had my first big number one national hit while I was still in college. By that time I had written a large quantity of the world's worst chamber music, when I wrote "Coquette." So, of the two ways that I burst—maybe burst is a little bloated—emerged on the scene in a kind of national sense, one was as an arranger. . . .

FRED: This was for Guy Lombardo?

JOHNNY: That was my first paid professional job. And I hasten to add, I had nothing to do with formulating the style of that band; not that I didn't love working with the Lombardos, 'cause I did. But in those days there was the Gold Coast Orchestra at Harvard and there was the Barbary Coast Orchestra at Dartmouth and the Casa Loma Orchestra was a college orchestra. The Gold Coast Orchestra at Harvard, of which I was a founding member and the chief arranger, was so good that it made some records for Columbia, you know. So, my emergence into where people said, "Who is this fellow Green?" was by way of a popular song and arranging for dance bands. I think my point of view is not all that foreign from when you mention Harry Warren and Sammy Fain. Harry and Sammy are two of the most musically gifted men I have ever known in my life. It isn't important whether Harry Warren could give you the anatomical structure of a chord that he used. Nobody who sings "About a Quarter to Nine "or "Atchison, Topeka and Santa Fe" or "You'll Never Know" or any of those great Harry Warren songs gives a continental damn if Harry knows the difference between an appoggiatura and a Neopolitan six.

And as far as Sammy is concerned—funny you mention Sammy—because my first job, as they say in the movies, and I was a hot twenty years old, because as long as we're talking about me (my favorite topic), I graduated from Harvard when I was nineteen, so at the age of twenty I was working for Paramount at their studios in Astoria, Long Island, and Sammy Fain was working there. As the chips fell, I became two things; I became Sammy's orchestrator and musical secretary. I never found either job beneath my dignity. I loved working with Sammy and I'll tell you one of the proud small medals that I wear is that the first time the American public ever heard "You Brought a New Kind of Love to Me" by Sammy and Irving Kahal; they heard it in my arrangement and orchestration in a picture called *The Big Pond* starring Maurice Chevalier. That's what Sammy wrote songs for. I was the orchestrator of that picture.

FRED: You wrote "Coquette" before you were with Lombardo. Did he introduce the song?

JOHNNY: Yes, he did. It was just a tune that I brought with me when I went to Cleveland. I came to Lombardo by way of those very Columbia recordings that I mentioned earlier. Guy heard them and was intrigued with what he heard and made it his business to find out who had written those orchestrations and who was "little old me." Guy got in touch with me at Harvard and asked me if I'd like to work for him that coming summer, which was the summer between my junior and senior years. A close, close, close friend of the Lombardos was the king of popular lyricists, Gus Kahn. I had a lot of melodies that I took with me to Cleveland, and one of them was the one that we are talking about, and the Lombardo boys liked it. But Carmen (Lombardo) thought there were things about it that should be different. That's why you see Carmen's name on the music. That's the only song of mine in which I ever had a collaborator, but "Coquette" is by Johnny Green and Carmen Lombardo. The song took its shape, its form, in which you know it, during that summer of 1927 and Gus Kahn was out there visiting the Lombardos and Gus fell in love with the tune. Gus gave it the title "Coquette." Gus was the king of Leo Feist. You may remember—I hate to date you, Fred, but you remember the logo, "You can't go wrong with a Leo Feist song." Well, they were my first publishers, thanks to Gus Kahn. The song was published in September of my senior year and by January it was number one.

FRED: Your song "Body and Soul" arguably is the best song you've ever written, but you may not agree with that.

JOHNNY: Well, I ain't ashamed of it.

FRED: I understand that it was difficult to convince publishers and performers in this country to use the song. They felt that perhaps it was a little too complicated, so you went to England with it?

JOHNNY: What happened was this, Fred. During the period that I wrote "Body and Soul" with Eddie Heyman, I was Gertrude Lawrence's accompanist, or if you'd like it a little more earthy, I was Gertrude Lawrence's piano player. Maybe a few of our audience would drop a quick, "Who was Gertrude Lawrence?" Gertrude Lawrence was the first lady of the British stage from [the] mid-twenties through the initial run of *The King and I* in which she played Anna in New York. Well, I had met Gertie Lawrence while I was still in high school, and that's a long story. I fell out with my father, who didn't want me to be a musician, which is why I'm a graduate Harvard economist (may the dear Lord help me). I went to work in a Wall Street bond house when I graduated from college, all of this to please my dad whom I loved very much, a brilliant man. I didn't agree with him about much but I loved him and I recognized his great brilliance. In any case, I walked out of that Wall Street bond house job after six months and said, "What am I doing here, this isn't what God wanted me to do with my life." That caused a big rift with my old man and I needed a job. And who gave me my job? Gertie Lawrence! And just as today, if Ann-Margret's going to have a new act in Las Vegas, Marvin Hamlisch writes the new act.

Gertie Lawrence in those days not only appeared in musical comedy and in legitimate theater, but she appeared in what the British called cabaret and she appeared in what the British called the wireless and she made what the British called gramophone records. She wanted some special material so she commissioned Eddie and me to write four special pieces. Well, if you were writing a clump of four pieces of special material for that kind of a performer, what would you write? You would write a rhythm song, you'd write what we call a comedy number but the British call a point number. You'd write a lovely (God willing) ballad, and in those days, the inevitable torch song.

FRED: Which was, of course, "Body and Soul." I know the show opened in England and it seems to me that the first big hit was by the famous Bert Ambrose Orchestra.

JOHNNY: Bert Ambrose was home dressing to go to the evening session at the Mayfair where he played with the Ambrose Orchestra. He had his wireless on and he heard Gertie Lawrence singing this song he'd never heard before. He rushed to the phone and got Gertie on the phone and said, "What is that song? That 'Body and Soul,' who wrote it?" She said, "Johnny Green." He said, "Our Johnny Green, our 'Coquette' Johnny Green?" She said, "Yes, the same." He said, "Well, how do you come by it?" She said, "He wrote it for me." Well, I will make it very brief from here, she gave him a manuscript copy that she had—overnight he had one of his guys do a "scratch," as we call them. The next night he started playing it at the Mayfair and it was unprecedented. Every band in London, every artist in London was coming in and taking it down—that is literally true. It spread like wildfire and the next thing, I got a call from the late Henry Spitzer at Harms. He said, "Did you and Heyman write a song called 'Body and Soul'?" I said, "Yeah, we wrote it for Gertie Lawrence." He said, "Are you aware what a smash it is in England?" I said, "Well, I heard that she did it and that some people were playing it." You know, I was so naive at that point, it's hard to believe, but I was. Anyway, he slapped a contract on Eddie Heyman and me and it was published in England, not in this country. It became, I don't mean to sound egotistical, it became the anthem of Europe. As a result, Max Gordon bought the American rights to a song written by an American composer and American lyricist that had become an English song. He bought the

American rights for Libby Holman in the show *Three's a Crowd* which starred Fred Allen, Libby Holman, and Clifton Webb and opened in 1931. Libby Holman introduced it to this country.

FRED: If I had to choose a favorite recording of that song it would have to be Coleman Hawkins' "Body and Soul" without any singing. What would you say, Johnny? With all the records made, it's probably the most recorded song of all time.

JOHNNY: Well, it's one of the most recorded songs of all time, one of the, I guess, three or four of all time. Coleman and I were good friends and you know, that recording, that treatment of "Body and Soul" is a classic and I loved it. On the other hand, it is a jazz treatment and the very essence of jazz is improvisation; that's the heart of jazz, that's it's motivation, that's it's genre, that's why it exists. So what you have on the Coleman Hawkins record is very little of the theme and an awful lot of the variations, if you want to use the nomenclature of the classic form of theme and variation.

FRED: But the changes are intact and the song is unmistakable on that account.

JOHNNY: There's no question about it, but it's Coleman Hawkins superimposed on Johnny Green, if you will. I would think even though Ella Fitzgerald also goes off into other spheres, she really states the song and she sings the lyric. I think maybe that's my favorite recording.

FRED: Let me jump around a little bit. I guess my second favorite of yours is "I Cover the Waterfront." Did that come out of a picture also, Johnny?

JOHNNY: No, it went *into* a picture. I'm being only a little facetious. You know that picture came into being as the result of a series of stories in *The New Yorker* magazine by a waterfront reporter by the name of Max Miller. Max Miller wrote this series of articles or stories in *The New Yorker* and the byline of his column in whichever New York paper it was, was, "I Cover the Waterfront." He was a maritime reporter and also a great short story writer. That was the inspiration for the picture. I don't remember who did the screenplay. Edward Small produced the picture and it was called *I Cover the Waterfront* and it starred Claudette Colbert and Ben Lyon. There was a guy, a very enterprising, bright, bright young man with United Artists by the name of Monroe Greenthal and we are talking 1933. Eddie and I by that time, you'll forgive me, were hot as a pistol. We were very famous, we had "Out of Nowhere," we had "Body and Soul," we were doing nicely, and Monroe Greenthal wanted an exploitation song for the picture. This was very early in the days of exploitation songs.

So he called Eddie and me in and offered us a very handsome stipend to write this exploitation song. Well, to be an exploitation song for the picture it had to have the title of the picture. He had ordered a ballad because he figured that it had to be a ballad because it was a love story and he wanted it to reach the hearts of the public. I didn't want to do it. I said, "What kind of a title is that for a love song? 'I Cover the Waterfront and That's Why I Love You'?" But my beloved Eddie Heyman, he said, "I think I can lick it." That was enough for me, if Eddie thought he could lick it. I said, "Eddie, you're the doctor." And did he ever. I mean, you only have to think of the first couple of lines of that verse that Eddie wrote: "Away from the city that hurts and mocks, I'm standing alone by the desolate docks, in the still and the chill of the night." Do I have to go any further? It's one of the great song poems ever written. In the refrain, the chorus: "I cover the waterfront, I'm watching the sea. Will the one I love be coming back to me?" That's it!

FRED: So he did the lyrics first in this one instance.

JOHNNY: He came up with the first line of the verse and the first quatrain of the chorus, I then went away and wrote the music and we worked together from there. But I mean, it's sheer poetry, but I wouldn't have done it and it was one of the biggest songs I ever had.

FRED: Again, what's your favorite recording?

JOHNNY: I think Sinatra's, I really do.

FRED: There's a great instrumental on it, of course, Artie Shaw.

JOHNNY: Artie and I were talking—sitting here talking on the eighteenth of January. Less than a month ago. I had a long, long talk with Artie. If Artie likes you, you can't have a short talk with Artie.

FRED: Artie's a friend of ours and Gita (my wife) has been working on some of his songs. She said, "Writing lyrics to some of his tunes, he'll call up and say, 'Look, I've only got a minute here and I've got eighty-nine things to do,' and an hour and a half later . . ." As Mel Tormé said, "The trouble is that you take a breath when you're talking to Artie, forget it, you'll never speak again."

JOHNNY: Oh yeah, but he's fascinating. The first record that I made for Columbia with my first band called "A New Moon Is Over My Shoulder," well you know every record, opens with a long clarinet solo by whom? Artie Shaw.

FRED: That's a record I wish I had. The only records of your big band I really have or that I can get my fingers on are the ones with Fred Astaire.

JOHNNY: Well, I'll settle for that.

FRED: Those were records you can say were perfect in every detail.

JOHNNY: What an extravagant compliment! Well, they are archival. I'm very, very proud because they're all my arrangements, you know.

FRED: And featuring your piano.

JOHNNY: Yes, and one of the very proud things in my life, Fred, is the number of treatises about those recordings, that have been written around the world, in Germany, France, and England. They really are a block of archival stature. And, of course, I loved working with Fred.

FRED: And you worked with him a lot. Didn't you do the Packard Hour with him on radio?

JOHNNY: I did the Packard Hour on radio and I worked with him at Metro, of course.

FRED: I made a note of two of those records that I liked best, "They Can't Take That Away from Me" and "The Way You Look Tonight."

JOHNNY: Those are two of that series of recordings that are very close to my heart for very sentimental reasons. Don't forget that those records were made at a time when we still recorded on the big, thick, soft wax and on a slave turntable and instant acetate was turning. Those acetates really shouldn't happen to Hitler, they were so awful, but there was no such thing as tape, so there was no editing. You started with groove one and it went through the last cutoff. That was that take. Both George Gershwin—my life was infinitely blessed because both George and Jerome (Jerry) Kern were close, close friends of mine. When I got the rough pressing, it was two days after we had done the recording on "The Way You Look Tonight," I rushed out to Jerry's house (Beverly Hills) with it and said, "Here" (I'm going to choke up). He sat there and cried like a baby and came across the room and put his arms around me and gave me such a hug, and exactly the same thing happened with George in "They Can't Take That Away From Me." But it was the same scene and I can still feel those two hugs and I can still see those two guys with the tears coming down their faces. I feel blessed that God gave it to me to write those arrangements because I adore those two songs.

FRED: You worked with Fred on at least two movies that I know of. I wonder how it was to work with Irving Berlin? I've always heard that he was on the set all of the time and had his finger in everything that happened.

JOHNNY: Irving was a professional curmudgeon, you know. I had a great experience with him on *Easter Parade* because our contract with him at Metro called for him to write four new songs for the picture. We had the rights to all of the Berlin catalog. By we, I mean MGM. You know nobody ever created a note for Irving Berlin, you take my word for it, but on the other hand, he was a complete illiterate musically. He can only play in one key, depending on which way you are looking at the piano, it's either F-sharp major or minor, or G-flat major or minor. You know about his piano where he could clamp the keyboard around—why did he want that piano? Because his ear is so sophisticated that he hears other keys, he hears the entire spectrum of the harmonic language. He's brilliantly gifted.

His musical right hand is a guy called Helmy Kresa, who worked with Irving on everything for years. Helmy was sick at the time. I mean not a cold, he was seriously ill, at the time that we did *Easter Parade* and unavailable to help and Irving was beside himself. He was frantic because he had to write these four songs and somebody had to put them down 'cause he didn't know how. So I was music director of the picture and I said, "Irving, who can be Helmy Kresa? If you would accept me I would be delighted to *try* to be Helmy Kresa." Irving was so darling about this, "Holy Christmas, the great Johnny Green is going to sit and take down while I play?" I said, "The great Johnny Green could learn something. Please, Irving, it would be a privilege." He couldn't get over that and he slapped his knee—you know the great Berlin gesture. I did learn and I learned plenty.

I have to tell you an anecdote which you will love. In one of the songs I took down, I sat there in a chair and he's at the piano playing in F-sharp. I sat down with my pad of manuscript paper and I took the song down. I said, "Gee, that's a nice song, Irving, this song, you know. I have one thought." He was avidly interested, he wanted to know. I said, "In such and such a bar, Irving, you played the third in the bass and it has a somewhat muddy sound." I hadn't gone near the piano yet, and I figure we'd be better with a fifth in the bass in that particular spot. He said, "Let me hear it, let me hear it, I want to hear it." So I went to the piano and he said, "Now play it my way first." So I played it his way. "Now play it your way." I played it my way. "Play it my way again." So I played it his way again. "I like my way." And that was it.

FRED: What is it about harmonic structure of your songs, the songs that we've talked about here, that appeals to jazz musicians so much? Can you put a finger on it?

JOHNNY: I can't answer that modestly.

FRED: Wait! Nobody asked you to answer it modestly.

JOHNNY: Well, the dear Lord gave it to me to be inventive, tasteful, and practical at the same time, harmonically speaking. I say so frequently, Fred, and I do want to get this in, I say, "Thank God." I don't do these things alone, Fred, none of us does. I mean, gifts come to us from the Almighty, I've always believed that, I just wanted to get that in. But people make such a big hullabaloo, you know, about the impossible difficulty of the middle of "Body and Soul." Well, I didn't invent inharmonism. Inharmonism is when the key-tone of an outgoing musical statement becomes the leading tone into a new key a half-tone higher. I wrote "Body and Soul" in D-flat major, so that the key-tone of D-flat is obviously D-flat. The middle strain starts out in D-natural major which is a half-tone higher. Therefore, the key-tone of D-flat becomes what is called the leading tone, becomes a C-sharp leading to D-natural. I didn't invent inharmonism, but I happened to be the first pop songwriter to use it in a pop song. And then everything that happens throughout that middle is perfectly natural. It lies under the fingers.

I happen to be a saxophone player myself. You know about saxophones, you know about the thumb keys and the octave key and all. You don't have to go through any of those gyrations. Everything lies naturally, you see. So you say, "Why do jazz musicians like the way I write harmonically?" They also like another composer, harmonically as much as or better than I, that's Harold Arlen. He has the same gift, the same type of gift only much greater than mine. What we write is inventive but it's also in good taste. It's natural, it's musical. It is not, you know, putting your left elbow in your right ear. Or as we used to say, you don't go from New York to Boston by way of Philadelphia. You go up to Boston Post Road. That's the way my harmonies go.

FRED: Looking back at a career so full of so many different things, what part of it gave you the greatest satisfaction? What do you look back on with the greatest pleasure or sense of accomplishment? Writing songs? Leading a band? Playing the piano? Conducting? Scoring?

JOHNNY: I don't think I can be exclusive about that. I love making music and when I'm doing any one of the things that my so-called versatility makes it possible for me to do, that's what I love most, when I'm doing it. And when I'm writing, I love writing most. When I'm conducting, I love conducting most. I love the theater. I love any time that what I'm doing musically is in the ambience or environment of the theater. And the theater means everything from a concert hall to the screen to the musical theater. I love being where there's a live audience that can applaud. I'm the world's biggest ham.

Jazz in America

Jean-Paul Sartre

The French have always taken jazz seriously. Sartre romanticized both jazz and America in this entry from his book Les Cahiers America. *Translated by Ralph de Toledano, it first appeared in America in the* Saturday Review of Literature *in 1947.*

Jazz is like bananas—it must be consumed on the spot. God knows there are recordings in France, and some sad imitators. But all they do is give us an excuse to shed a few tears in pleasant company. Like everyone else, I really discovered jazz in America. Some countries have a national pastime and some do not. It's a national pastime when the audience insists on complete silence during the first half of the performance and then shouts and stamps during the second half. If you accept this definition, France has no national pastime, unless it is auction sales. Nor has Italy, except stealing. There is watchful silence while the thief works (first half) and when he flees there is stamping and shouts of "Stop, thief" (second half). Belgium has its cockfights, Germany vampirism, and Spain its *corridas.*

I learned in New York that jazz is a national pastime. In Paris, it is a vehicle for dancing, but this is a mistake: Americans don't dance to jazz; instead they have a special music, heard also at marriages and First Communions, called: Music by Muzak. In apartments there is a faucet. It is turned on and Muzak musics: flirtation, tears, dancing. The faucet is turned off, and Muzak musics no more: the lovers and communicants are put to bed.

At Nick's bar, in New York, the national pastime is presented. Which means that one sits in a smoke-filled room among sailors, Orientals, chippies, society women. Tables, booths. No one speaks. The sailors come in fours. With justified hatred, they watch the smoothies who sit in booths with their girls. The sailors would like to have the girls, but they don't. They drink; they are tough; the girls are also tough; they drink, they say nothing. No one speaks, no one moves, the jazz holds forth. From ten o'clock to three in the morning the jazz holds forth. In France, jazzmen are beautiful but stupid, in flowing shirts and silk ties. If you are too bored to listen, you can always watch them and learn about elegance.

At Nick's bar, it is advisable not to look at them; they are as ugly as the musicians in a symphony orchestra. Bony faces, mustaches, business suits, starched collars (at least in the early part of the evening), no velvety looks, muscles bunching up under their sleeves.

They play. You listen. No one dreams. Chopin makes you dream, but not the jazz at Nick's. It fascinates, you can't get your mind off it. No consolation whatsoever. If you are a cuckold, you depart a cuckold, with no tenderness. No way to take the hand of the girl beside you, to make her understand, with a wink, that the music reflects what is in your heart. It is dry, violent, pitiless. Not gay, not sad, inhuman. The cruel screech of a bird of prey. The musicians start to give out, one after the other. First the trumpet player, then the pianist, then the trombonist. The bass player grinds it out. It does not speak of love, it does not comfort. It is hurried. Like the people who take the subway or eat at the Automat.

It is not the century-old chant of Negro slaves. Nor the sad little dream of Yankees crushed by the machine. Nothing of the sort: there is a fat man who blows his lungs out to the weaving motion of his trumpet, there is a merciless pianist, a bass player who tortures the strings without listening to the others. They are speaking to the best part of you, the toughest, the freest, to the part which wants neither melody nor refrain, but the deafening climax of the moment. They take hold of you, they do not lull you. Connecting rod, shaft, spinning top. They beat you, they turn, they crash, the rhythm grips you and shakes you. You bounce in your seat, faster and faster, and your girl with you, in a hellish round.

The trombone sweats, you sweat, the trumpet sweats, you sweat some more, and then you feel that something has happened on the bandstand; the musicians don't look the same: they speed ahead, they infect each other with this haste, they look mad, taut, as if they were searching for something. Something like sexual pleasure. And you too begin to look for something. You begin to shout; you have to shout; the band has become an immense spinning top: if you stop, the top stops and falls over. You shout, they shriek, they whistle, they are possessed, you are possessed, you scream like a woman in childbirth. The trumpet player touches the pianist and transmits his hypnotic obsession. You go on shouting. The whole crowd shouts in time, you can't even hear the jazz, you watch some men on a bandstand sweating in time, you'd like to spin around, to howl at death, to slap the face of the girl next to you.

And then, suddenly, the jazz stops, the bull has received the sword thrust, the oldest of the fighting cocks is dead. It's all over. But you have drunk your whisky, while shouting, without even knowing it. An impassive waiter has brought you another. For a moment, you are in a stupor, you shake yourself, you say to your girl: Not bad. She doesn't answer, and it begins all over again. You will not make love tonight, you will not feel sorry for yourself, you will not even be surfeited, you won't get real drunk, you won't even shed blood, and you'll have undergone a fit of sterile frenzy. You will leave a little worn out, a little drunk, but with a kind of dejected calm, the aftermath of nervous exhaustion.

Jazz is the national pastime of the United States.

DON'T SHOOT—WE'RE AMERICAN!

STEVE VOCE

Some comic relief, in this account of the hardships encountered by jazz musicians touring Britain—from the food to the fans. From Just Jazz 4, *edited by Sinclair Traill and the Hon. Gerald Lascelles (1960).*

The man with the tenor-saxophone got down to business right away. Without any words of introduction he cruised smoothly into an up-tempo exploration of "How About You?"

With unbelievable precision and an articulation which left the audience boggling at one chorus while he swept on through the next, the James Dean of the saxophone cast his pearls of sound around the cinema.

Stan Getz was making his provincial debut.

BUT THE PEARLS of sound bore no relation to the chunks of indigestible gristle, the glutinous mass of pastry which, an hour before, had been a transport café meat pie and which were now fighting inside him to overthrow the Getz circulatory system.

THE HAZARDS WHICH beset the American musician on tour in Britain are such that it is only by great fortitude that he survives his visit. The fact that he manages to maintain high musical standards in his concerts is quite inexplicable. Contributory causes are certainly not plastic fried eggs and meat pies that would bring a U-2 from 12,000 feet to ground level in a matter of seconds.

Away from his natural habitat of all-night bars, drinks with meals in cafés, apple pies out of the slot machines, he becomes a forager in desperate need. He finds, with furious incredulity, that the pubs closed at 10 P.M. and that all the restaurants are shut. His hotel won't serve anything after seven and the bun-enclosed sausage that he buys from the street-vendor is no more edible than a stuffed penguin. In answer to his question "Well, where are the birds at, man?" he is told that English young ladies get the hell out for home and family when the sun goes down. "Hell, man! How do the English stand it? I mean I heard about the guys on the *Mayflower,* but I didn't know they was still running the joint!"

DURING THE COURSE of many encounters with visiting Americans I have had the chance to observe the different ways in which they react to the various off-stage situations in which they embroil themselves—from the regal aplomb of Duke Ellington to the awe-inspiring bawdiness of Wild Bill Davison.

Their attitudes vary from mute disbelief to a brusque aggressiveness that implies that if somebody doesn't do something about this pretty damn' quick the offended person will overthrow the government singlehanded.

THE EDDIE CONDON mob arrived in town at the unappropriate time of eleven o'clock on a Sunday morning. They kicked and stumbled their way off the train through a pile of empty whisky bottles—"travellin' high" is the phrase, I believe—and began soliciting the porters for directions to the nearest bar. They were told that all bars were closed, and their bleary faces paled as though the Wall Street Crash had just been announced.

Finally we persuaded them to bridge the gap until opening time with lunch at a Chinese restaurant, although this was an obvious breach of etiquette—Wild Bill pointed out that he never took food on an empty stomach.

Once inside the restaurant Condon and Davison each produced a half of Scotch (how the bottles survived the journey is a mystery). Bill placed his on his table with great deliberation, causing much concern to the management. "No drinking please, yes?" asked the manager hopefully. "No," agreed Bill, opening the bottle. "You got glasses?"

After a lot of argument glasses were provided ("You drink water, yes?" "No," agreed Bill politely) and the contents of the bottles began to disappear into the well-oiled systems of Messrs. Condon and Davison.

The restaurant was fairly crowded and we had been unable to get adjacent tables. I was seated with Bill while Condon and his associates were at the other end of the room.

Bill ordered a fruit salad as a concession to the management to show that he hadn't simply come to use their glasses. I believe he did actually eat some of it, but don't remember. I do remember the whisky disappearing with an impressive swiftness, and from the other end of the room the voices of Condon and George Wettling were raised in mortal debate over who was going to finish the bottle. Finally the Davison meal was concluded.

Bill wiped his mouth with the back of his hand and got to his feet. "A lot of people think Eddie Condon is an ***-hole," he announced loudly. The diners fell silent. The manager, with commendable tact, dropped behind the cash-desk as though he had been poleaxed.

Condon, looking like a miniature but very angry bull, slowly lifted himself from his chair at the other end of the room. "How's that again?" he asked.

"I said a lot of people think Condon's an ***-hole." A Chinese waitress stopped in full flight with two dishes of chow-mein. "But it's not true," Bill continued. Condon began to sit down. "He's *two ***-holes.*" He sat down beaming.

ONE OF THE gifts that American musicians seem to possess is the ability to handle waiters—especially the kind in evening dress. These people have a certain protocol which always frightens me, and rather than upset it I will move down the road and eat in the snackbar, or even go without. Not so our American guests who have a no-nonsense way of short-circuiting the grandest of Grand Hotel staff. I have seen drummer Barrett Deems paralyze an offending waiter just by looking at him.

There was some trouble over an Irish pound note. The Louis Armstrong band had just returned from an Irish tour and had been paid in Irish currency. When trombonist Trummy Young offered the Irish note the Hungarian waiter embarked on a tirade of mid-European abuse which implied that he had never before been so insulted.

Barrett Deems turned round in his chair and impaled the waiter upon his death-ray stare—quite sufficient to put Flash Gordon and a whole army of Dhreens in bad trouble. The waiter, who was really only a man, blanched and reeled off with the pound note, mewing and mouthing like a tortured cat. "That guy looks unhealthy," said Deems sourly, adding his favorite two-word phrase.

The service improved remarkably after that and the waiter's colleagues couldn't do enough for us. Deems let up on them and when he was going out distributed half-smoked packets of cigarettes amongst them. "Poor guys, I feel for them," he said. "It must be hell for anyone having to live in this place."

This endearing ritual of the cigarette packets was carried out with magnificent impartiality. During the afternoon and evening which I spent with him he handed packets to most of the people he met. I still have a couple lying about in a drawer somewhere. Deems explained as he reached in his pocket: "I try all the brands, but I ain't found one that I like yet. I think maybe I'll kick the habit," he added, passing over a packet of mentholated king-size filter-tip monsters.

JIMMY GIUFFRE AGREED to be interviewed with pleasure, providing we didn't mind if he ate while we talked. Was there a good hotel nearby where he could get a meal?

We went to one of those select chrome-and-glass places which only employs waiters with public-school educations. Dick Huddart, the Rugby League international forward (he plays Rugby the way Wild Bill Davison plays cornet) came with us, Giuffre, who is a quiet, immaculate man, took a lot of trouble selecting the right table. We were favored with the personal attention of the headwaiter, a formidable man who managed to convey the impression that he had just come out of conference with the Prime Minister. He looked over his nose disdainfully at the rugged bulk of Dick Huddart (uneasy in a dainty little chair) and across the table at me. His nostrils quivered with distaste as he took note that I was wearing a green shirt. Giuffre was in evening dress, so the headwaiter figured that he was the one who could read. He handed him the menu, a piece of cardboard approximately the size of an average single-bed sheet.

"I believe I would like some orange juice to start with," said Jimmy, "and just two coffees for my friends. They've already eaten."

The headwaiter jumped as though he had been slapped in the face. "No sir," he said firmly, "you can't do that."

"I can't do what?"

"Your friends must have a meal."

"But I just got through telling you, they already ate."

"I'm afraid the rules of the hotel don't permit guests to make use of the dining-room unless they intend to have a meal, sir."

"Well I am making use of the dining-room and I am having a meal. You go get those coffees."

The headwaiter's face reddened. Obviously the Prime Minister never spoke to him like this. Sensing impending disaster, Dick and I got to our feet. "Never mind, Mr. Giuffre," I mumbled, "We'll see you afterwards."

"In a pig's valise you will." Mr. Giuffre was roused. "Sit down," he rapped out.

We sat.

"I want a glass of orange juice to begin with, and two coffees for my friends who already ate. Would you please go and get them?"

"But sir, if I did that it would be establishing a precedent." This was to be a fight to the death.

"In that case I wish to establish a precedent. If you find yourself incapable of taking my order, will you please bring the manager."

Muttering to himself and with very bad grace, the headwaiter beckoned to one of his underlings and gave the instructions. ". . . and two pots of coffee for these . . . gentlemen," he said scornfully.

The waiter returned with the coffee and a large glass of orange squash. "One moment," Giuffre held up the glass and looked at it curiously. "This is orange juice?"

"No sir, that is orange cordial." The waiter looked embarrassed.

"Well look, I want orange juice. You know, like you go out in the back and jump on an orange." Giuffre was prepared to draw a picture.

The coffee wasn't very good. The meal was worse. However, to Giuffre went the final victory. When we were leaving he tipped the waiter. The headwaiter was standing by the door, still glaring threateningly at the person who had dared to challenge his authority. Giuffre noticed him and called the waiter back.

"Oh, and give this to the red-faced guy who establishes the precedents," he said loudly. The redness increased. He handed the waiter a sixpence. "Is that enough?" Giuffre turned to me.

"It's enough," I croaked.

ONE OF THE most consistently good-humored groups of musicians to visit Britain has been that of Count Basie. Generally addressed by his musicians as "Base" (to rhyme with Maize) the Count is perhaps the most easy-going and unorthodox of bandleaders. While other men are martinets or suffer from "star" temperament, Bill Basie mixes in with the boys in the band.

On a coach trip with the band, trumpeter Thad Jones and I were sitting behind the Boss, who was dropping off to sleep. Wanting to attract his attention Thad reached over and pulled Basie's hat firmly down over his head. While the unfortunate Count struggled with both hands to get it off, Thad beat him mercilessly with a rolled-up newspaper.

After a second house concert the whole band was starving, none of them having eaten since breakfast. Suddenly the stage door burst open and a phalanx of variously bearded men (there are more different types of beards in the Basie band than there are obsolete British rockets) forced their way through the crowd of autograph hunters in search of food.

Dick Huddart and I, who once again had already eaten, had joined Billy Mitchell, Benny Powell, and Sonny Cohn. It was after ten and the pubs had closed, and at the best of times Liverpool on a Sunday night is not a good place to eat.

After some ten to fifteen minutes of driving round in Huddart's car looking for a café, Billy Mitchell began making comments from the backseat.

"Man," he said, adjusting his heavily-framed glasses. "I sure do like the way this town is laid out. The fellow who laid this town out sure knew what he was doing." We passed two or three more restaurants which had the blinds drawn. "I don't know how long it's been dead, but I sure like the way it's laid out."

Finally we decided on a Chinese restaurant in the town center. It was evidently a popular decision, because by the time we arrived practically the whole band was there. A hint of what was to follow was given by the picture that presented itself at the door.

Joe Williams and Charlie Fowlkes were standing up at their table and shouting at a Chinese waiter. By various gestures and threats they were trying to make him understand what they wanted. The waiter, true to the characteristics of his race, remained inscrutably silent. He seemed to be working on the principle that it was only a matter of time before they discovered that he didn't speak English, and that nothing he could say could add any enlightenment. The situation was made more comic by the fact that the waiter was about five feet high, and Williams and Fowlkes are both of giant stature.

However, he had nothing on the waiter who finally came to serve us. Our waiter could understand a few words of English but, apparently from deliberate malice, brought the antithesis of any order that was given him. Consequently Sonny Cohn's chicken chow mein appeared in the shape of a Spanish omelette, Benny Powell's lobster salad became chop suey and rice. In Billy Mitchell's case the waiter really excelled himself. I don't remember what Billy ordered, but I'm sure the fiendish-looking concoction which was finally laid before him could never have been envisaged by anything but the most intensely oriental mind.

"I'll knife him! I'll murder him!" Sonny Cohn, who had no thought of pouring oil on troubled waiters, embarked on a detailed catalogue of what would be the fate of the waiter if left to Sonny Cohn. Billy Mitchell was more positive. He hurriedly swallowed the tragedy on his plate, recalled the waiter and placed his original order again. This time the waiter brought him a plate of fried rice. Billy gently began to explain to the waiter what he had originally wanted. He went into great detail, but the waiter had him licked. He just stood there impervious to everything. Gradually Billy's explanation built up into a crescendo of invective which had Huddart and I gasping with admiration. But the strain was too much and finally he sat down exhausted and asked the waiter quietly for a glass of water. The waiter brought him a coffee.

Meanwhile Charlie Fowlkes and Joe Williams were still having trouble.

"For God's sake," Williams was saying. "You mean to say you work in a

Chinese restaurant and you don't know what Soya sauce is?" Like his colleague, the waiter let Williams beat his brains out against an unruffled silence.

"Boy, I need a drink after this lot." Billy Mitchell mopped his brow.

It was then that I realized the fact that the pubs had closed an hour before.

Thoroughly beaten and suffering from various stages of chronic indigestion, the Count's men returned sadly to their hotel (no bar) for an early night.

THE ELLINGTON METHOD of eating on tour is, as one might expect, more regally eccentric. In the dressing-room Duke will produce from his pockets the various parts of a large dismembered chicken, elegantly draped in silk handkerchiefs. He offers the limbs around with graceful elegance: "Does anyone wish to dine?"

Later in the evening we drove by taxi, in company with clarinettist Jimmy Hamilton and his wife, Jimmy Rushing, Clark Terry, and a varied assortment of Ellingtonians, to a club in Liverpool's Upper Parliament Street. Upper Parliament Street approximates to a 1960 equivalent of old Storyville, albeit a little quieter and less colorful.

The reason for the visit was that Mrs. Hamilton had heard from somewhere that red beans and rice were on the menu and, tired of egg and chips, she felt that red beans and rice were essential to her continued well-being.

We were all comfortably seated (Jimmy Rushing in characteristic pose with napkin tucked in collar) and ready to eat when the waitress informed us that red beans and rice had never been and would not ever as far as she knew be on the menu.

I could see one of those incidents looming up, and when Jimmy Rushing stood up and offered to instruct the cook on the preparation of the dish, I reached for my hat.

However, Little Jimmy made the journey to the kitchen and in a moment returned with the assurance that the red beans and rice would not be many minutes.

When it finally came it turned out to be West Indian red beans and rice which, so I am told, is just not the same as American red beans and rice. Nevertheless the incident does demonstrate the potential of a native American with his back to the wall in a serious situation—especially Jimmy Rushing's back.

EARL HINES HAS the elegance and confidence which kills crises before they arise. When satisfied he moves his cigar to the other side of his mouth (Earl is seldom without a cigar in his mouth—I believe he has one there while he sleeps) and compliments the waiter with "Good deal, Jack."

When Earl has been directed to the bathroom, when a porter holds the door for him, the reply always is the same: "Good deal, Jack."

In fact, if told that he had been chosen to be the first man into space, I know what his reply would be.

Woody Herman has a similar elegance in his dealings with waiters who seem to look upon him as being the man they were born to serve.

WAITERS AND HOTEL staff combine with American musicians to make a highly combustible mixture, but not all the ensuing pantomimes can be laid at the door of the caterers. Not by a long way.

Paul Desmond, altoist with the Dave Brubeck Quartet, is probably the most mild-mannered and retiring American one could envisage. Nervous and haunted, he is a man who would go to any lengths to preserve the sanctity of privacy and, like the retiring but well-intentioned Bill Harris, is much liable to be misunderstood.

During the Quartet's first tour he decided to catch the midnight train back to London (the rest of the group were staying overnight)—a decision which gave us ninety minutes to kick our heels in a station waiting-room full of tramps and drunks.

It was February and very cold outside. The waiting-room was smothered in that stifling British Railways heat which knows no moderation. Sweat and beer fumes contributed to produce a sticky jungle humidity. Occasionally the drunks convulsed into two or three bars of song. Every so often one would fall off a chair and lie, still asleep, sprawling on the floor. The whole impression was that of a prison camp during the height of the Indian mutiny.

Paul and I squeezed into a corner and after about ten minutes had become a part of the scenery, rendered partially unconscious by the atmosphere and the fact that we were both wearing overcoats—there was hardly room to take them off.

From outside came sounds of approaching turbulence and discordant voices yelled the lyrics of one of Mr. Presley's current million-sellers.

Finally the door burst open and three teenage girls rioted into the room, causing instant chaos and enforced reshuffling amongst the drunks and layabouts.

For some reason we attracted their attention, and one of them came across and tried to pick up Paul's alto case. He snatched it back with a quick movement and smiled at her nervously. He held the case on his knee, apparently to protect it and himself from further onslaught.

"Hey mister," the hoyden shrieked accusingly, "you're a caveman, aren't you?"

"Huh? Who me? No, I guess not. I guess not." Desmond's voice cracked as he shrank back in his chair.

"He is. Isn't he?" she turned accusingly to me. It was all rather like a denunciation in the French Revolution.

"Isn't he a caveman?" She turned to her two colleagues who were eagerly closing in. "Doris! You come and look at this feller. Isn't he a caveman?"

Without hanging around for further enlightenment we picked up our things and, pursued by the accusing cries, fumbled our way out into the cold. The harridans showed every sign of joining in pursuit, so we ran.

Paul's train had by now arrived at its platform, so I saw him onto it. He huddled into a corner seat, swathed in coats and scarves, looking miserable enough to convince me that he wouldn't sleep so well during the journey.

It wasn't until I was on the bus going home that I found the solution. Looking through the window I saw a poster lit momentarily by the lights from the bus. It advertised the show at the local music-hall, and in big letters at the top it said:

TOMMY STEELE AND THE CAVEMEN.

I often wondered how Desmond figured it out.

BIG BILL BROONZY was a mighty man, and while I can only relate the following incident at secondhand, I'm pretty sure of its truth.

Bill was being driven by car from one city to another, and he and his driver stopped en route at a transport café for a meal.

Bill pored over the menu which contained the usual heady variety of exotic dishes:

Sausage and Chips
Egg and Chips
Egg Sausage and Chips
Pie and Chips
Egg Pie and Chips

Bill scratched his head and asked the man behind the counter: "Is everything you got with chips?"

"Yes, mate."

"Well, I guess that's it then. Bring me a double whisky and chips."

GOFFIN, *ESQUIRE*, AND THE MOLDY FIGS

LEONARD FEATHER

British-born Leonard Feather was one of the leading figures in jazz writing, promotion, and production for many decades. An acute reporter if in this case hardly a disinterested bystander, he here salutes the role of Esquire *and its famous editor, Arnold Gingrich, in popularizing jazz, and recalls the jazz wars of the mid-forties, when issues of modern vs. traditional and black vs. white were already looming large.*

Robert Goffin, passed over briefly or ignored in most analyses of jazz historiography, deserves to be remembered for his several auspicious contributions to jazz.

Born in 1898 near Waterloo, Belgium, he wore so many hats in his long life (he died in 1984) that *Down Beat* once called him "the world's most versatile jitterbug." He was one of his country's foremost criminal lawyers, a draughts champion, author of books on legal finance, gastronomy, poems, rats, spiders, eels, history, and jazz, and a former vice-president of the Brussels Ice Hockey Club.

Around 1927 he took over direction of *Music,* the Belgian counterpart to *Metronome,* and liberalized its policy towards jazz. He wrote a subjective, somewhat melodramatic book, *Aux Frontières du Jazz,* published in 1932 but never translated into English. It showed a reasonably sensitive understanding at a time when most critics, particularly in America, equated jazz with Paul Whiteman (Goffin's *bête blanche*) and Bing Crosby.

In the vanguard of Belgium's anti-fascists, he had to leave hurriedly when his country was invaded, saying goodbye to his 3,000 78s, his Renoirs and Gauguins and Modiglianis. Escaping to France and Spain, he sailed from Portugal and arrived in New York in July 1940.

Goffin was an imposing figure, over six feet tall and weighing more than 250 pounds. His big, beaming smile, zestful love of life and down-to-earth manner seemed, to some, at odds with his serious record of cultural achievements. His only frustration was a failure to master the English language.

We met just days after his arrival in New York and became good friends, making the rounds together often to visit the Savoy, Kelly's Stable, and the Apollo. One night, after attending a screening of the movie *Blues in the Night,* then catching the Basie band at the Famous Door, Goffin told me about a plan on which he had been working: he wanted to give a full, officially sponsored course on the history of jazz at the New School for Social Research in the Village, on West 12th Street. Because he still spoke a somewhat hilarious fractured English (friends imitated his standard greeting, "Ow you feel?"), and because of my fluency in French, he suggested that I collaborate with him, translating his scripts and giving separate lectures.

Aside from a few isolated lectures by visiting bandleaders, there had never been any attempt to offer a serious history and analysis of the music, as part of a regular curriculum. Goffin's initiative would set an important precedent. I agreed eagerly to take part.

The lectures, fifteen in all, were set to begin February 4, 1942. We agreed on a series of topics: the blues, ragtime, Louis Armstrong, Duke Ellington, boogie-woogie, Chicago style, and so on. In addition to using records, we planned to persuade musicians to help us with live performances. Because of the unique nature of the project we had no trouble in attracting them: at the first lecture our guest speaker-performers were Louis Armstrong, Benny Goodman, and Benny Carter. For a New Orleans session we had Red Allen and Sidney Bechet; to illustrate the blues, our live vocalist was Helen Humes. The African Student Group from Columbia University arranged to send Liberian musicians to demonstrate the origins of rhythmic concepts that were said to have laid the foundations for jazz. Other guests were Pete Brown, Mel Powell, and Bobby Hackett.

One of our main problems in assembling the series was that there was virtually no literature on jazz. Even Goffin's own book and Panassié's *Le Jazz Hot,* published in 1934, were already somewhat outdated. The only other books of any consequence were the very superficial ghost-written autobiography of Louis Armstrong, a somewhat better Benny Goodman autobiography, *The Kingdom of Swing,* written by Irving Kolodin, and Charles Edward Smith's *Jazzmen,* which dealt almost exclusively with the New Orleans aspect of jazz origins. *The Jazz Record Book,* of which Smith was co-editor, was more recent and a little broader in scope.

We were obliged to depend mainly not on books but on our own knowledge and firsthand experience. Occasionally I would illustrate a point at the piano; often we would rely on our fairly substantial collections of 78s for demonstrations. (By now some of my own collection had been shipped over from England.)

The course was successful, attracting close to 100 evidently serious stu-

THE NEW SCHOOL
FOR SOCIAL RESEARCH
66 W TWELFTH ST NEW YORK

SWING MUSIC

15 weeks. Tuesdays, 8:20-10 P.M. $12.50. **Robert Goffin** and **Leonard Feather**

Beginning September 29. The course deals with the background and development of jazz, musically and historically. The lectures are illustrated by recordings and by musical demonstrations in the form of weekly "jam sessions," featuring outstanding white and Negro musicians from the leading swing bands.

Sept. 29	Before jazz in New Orleans
Oct. 6	Ragtime and the pioneers
Oct. 13	First period of Negro jazz
Oct. 20	From New Orleans to Chicago—King Oliver
Oct. 27	Jazz from America to Europe
Nov. 3	Original Dixieland
Nov. 10	White pioneers
Nov. 17	Louis Armstrong
Nov. 24	From Fletcher Henderson to Duke Ellington
Dec. 1	Chicago style
Dec. 8	Big white bands
Dec. 15	Benny Goodman
Dec. 22	Outdated and small Negro bands
Jan. 5	Big Negro bands
Jan. 12	From spiritual to boogie-woogie

The series: $12.50

Each lecture: $1.10

ROBERT GOFFIN. Docteur en Droit, Brussels. Editor, La Voix de France; formerly editor, Alerte, anti-Nazi weekly, Brussels; Music, first jazz magazine. Secretary, P.E.N. Club; former president, association for jazz studies in Europe. Author, Jazz Band; Aux Frontières du jazz; Empress Carlotta; Rimbaud vivant; other books.

LEONARD FEATHER. Conductor of WMCA jazz quizz program, Platterbrains; writer of lyrics, music and arrangements for Count Basie, Duke Ellington and other band leaders. Formerly director, Rhythm Club, London; BBC jazz programs; special recording bands for Decca, Columbia and Victor recording companies in London and New York. Public relations counsel for Louis Armstrong, Lionel Hampton, et al. Contributor to New York Times, Down Beat, Music and Rhythm, and leading music publications; to Melody Maker, and Radio Times, official BBC journal, London.

dents; we repeated it in the autumn. In a sense we had given birth to jazz education, but this accomplishment was not enough for Goffin, who had even more ambitious ideas. One night in 1943 we sat in the Hurricane, listening to the music of Duke Ellington's orchestra. With us was Arnold Gingrich, the editor of *Esquire*. As the evening progressed, Goffin's unquenchable enthusiasm was directed towards a new and daring end. Because he knew of Gingrich's intense interest in jazz, he sensed that the moment was right.

"Jazz has never had any continuous, serious exposure in any national American magazine," he said. "Why can't you have a jazz poll, print the results in your magazine, and run a series of articles?"

Gradually a plan crystallized. We did not want our poll to wind up like those conducted in *Down Beat* or *Metronome,* in which, typically, Charlie Barnet or Tex Beneke would be the leaders on "hot tenor," followed by Coleman Hawkins and Ben Webster; Ziggy Elman would win for "hot trumpet" and Alvino Rey for guitar; Helen O'Connell or Dinah Shore would be elected No. 1 female jazz singer while Billie Holiday went unhonored.

"The only way out," I said, "is to put together a panel of experts, rather than rely on the readers."

"Right," Goffin said, "and we know who the real experts are."

That Gingrich agreed enthusiastically did not surprise me for, like Goffin, he had long counted jazz among his seemingly endless range of intellectual concerns. He had helped to found the magazine in 1933, establishing it as a publication of the kind that did not feel the need to translate any French or Latin references in its pages. Ernest Hemingway, an early contributor, led Gingrich to John Dos Passos, Ring Lardner, and scores of others. (Gingrich had published "The Snows of Kilimanjaro" in *Esquire,* paying Hemingway $1,000, twice his regular fee.)

Sitting in Arnold's office, as I occasionally did during the next thirty years, I was never surprised when a discussion we were having about the relative merits of Roy Eldridge and Red Allen would be interrupted by a phone call from Tennessee Williams, Truman Capote, or Hemingway. He would then pick up the conversation exactly where we had left it.

Balding and thin-faced, with a heavy moustache, Arnold smoked powerful and repulsive French cigarettes, which I refused regularly, and drank Irish whiskey, which I accepted willingly.

He attracted a seemingly limitless circle of friends and took joy in his every interest, from jazz, about which he wrote occasionally with authority and passion, to fishing, which was his abiding love. He was considered one of the world's greatest fly fishermen.

When Gingrich told David Smart, then *Esquire*'s publisher, about our ideas for a jazz adventure, Smart not only agreed, but took it one step further. "Let's not just announce the winners," he said. "Let's get them all together and put on a concert—the *Esquire* All Americans."

In assembling our board, Goffin and I ensured that it was racially integrated. At one time or another while the polls were held, our panelists included E. Simms Campbell, the black *Esquire* cartoonist and author of a couple of articles on jazz; Dan Burley, the writer for Associated Negro Press and a competent jazz pianist; and Inez Cavanaugh, a singer and writer who had contributed to *Metronome* and *The Crisis.*

Our first panel, voting in late 1943, comprised George Avakian, Campbell, Goffin, Feather, Abel Green of *Variety* (included, against my wishes, for political reasons, and dropped the following year); Elliott Grennard of *Billboard;* John Hammond; Roger Kay, an Egyptian critic then writing for *Orchestra World;* Harry Lim, from what was then known as Java, conductor of jam sessions; Paul Eduard Miller, the Chicago-based writer who, along with me, became a regular contributor to *Esquire;* Bucklin Moon, author of *The Darker Brother;* Timme Rosenkrantz, who had edited a swing magazine in Copenhagen; Charles Edward Smith; Frank Stacy, then the New York editor of *Down Beat;* Bob Thiele, editor of *Jazz Magazine,* and Barry Ulanov, editor of *Metronome.*

A patriotic motive was involved; plans were set up to present the evening as a benefit for the Navy League. Additionally, our concert coincided with the opening of the government's fourth War Loan Drive; seats were sold for war bonds, with the house scaled from $25 to $100. Station WJZ set up a bond booth in its building to sell tickets. With the help of large donations from several very wealthy fans, we were proud to be able to announce afterwards that $600,000 worth of bonds were sold.

Because the power of *Esquire* and the importance attached to the venture enabled Smart and Gingrich to pull some strings, the winners were set to appear in the first jazz concert ever given at the Metropolitan Opera House. As for the poll results, they reaffirmed our faith in the voters and our preference for this method over the system of drawing on the public's relatively limited knowledge.

The winners were: First Choice (Gold Award): Louis Armstrong, trumpet; Jack Teagarden, trombone; Benny Goodman, clarinet; Coleman Hawkins, saxophone; Art Tatum, piano; Al Casey, guitar; Oscar Pettiford, bass; Sid Catlett, drums; Red Norvo and Lionel Hampton, tied for miscellaneous instrument; Louis Armstrong, male vocal; Billie Holiday, female vocal; Artie Shaw, best musician in the Armed Forces.

Second Choice (Silver Award): Cootie Williams, Lawrence Brown, Barney Bigard, Johnny Hodges, Earl Hines, Oscar Moore, Milt Hinton (tied with Al Morgan), Cozy Cole, Leo Watson, Mildred Bailey; Willie Smith (the saxophonist) and Dave Tough tied for Armed Forces.

Soon after the votes were tabulated, I set about organizing a record session with a group of the winners. The entire Gold Award rhythm section was available (Tatum, Casey, Catlett, Pettiford), as were Coleman Hawkins, Cootie Williams and, on clarinet, the third-place winner, Edmond Hall.

All were eager to participate, even though only union scale was to be paid and, in Tatum's case, it meant working as a sideman for the first time since he had arrived in New York many years before as Adelaide Hall's accompanist.

Bob Thiele, of Signature Records, had agreed to produce the session, but after all the musicians had been booked a crisis arose: Thiele could not be reached on the phone and had not signed the contract. Desperate, I called Milt Gabler to ask if he would be willing to take over the session for his Commodore label. His affirmative decision was one he never regretted, since the four tunes we made on 4 December 1943 turned out to be, with the possible exception of Billie Holiday's "Strange Fruit," the most successful records ever to appear on the label, and have been reissued several times.

As soon as *Esquire* sent out a press release announcing the winners' names, the Negro press gave our undertaking massive support. A four-column streamer headline in the New York *Amsterdam News* read: "20 of 26 Winning Musicians in *Esquire* Band Poll are Negroes; Winners at Met Opera House January 18." The Pittsburgh *Courier* announced: "'Ace' Negro Musicians Sweep *Esquire* Mag's Jazz Band Poll. All American Jazz Band Top Heavy with Race Stars; Set for Historic Debut in Sacred Confines of Famous Metropolitan Opera House."

This enthusiasm was not unanimous. A small magazine called the *Jazz Record,* edited by the pianist Art Hodes and by Dale Curran, published a savage attack under the byline of Jake Trussell, Jr., who called the results a "foul and dismal smirch" on our reputations as critics. Breaking the votes down by race, he found that "only one [critic] awarded the white musicians higher than 42.9% of the total votes: this was George Avakian." He concluded that, "This Avakian proved himself a really big man amongst jazz critics." Next highest, he declared, was Charles Edward Smith, "who gave the whites fifteen out of a possible thirty-five points . . . Feather, Harry Lim and Timme Rosenkrantz were low men, with all awarding less than seven points . . . to white players. If this isn't inverted Jim Crow, what on earth is?"

Trussell made his stance clearer by avowing that: "The top men for small hot-jazz-band work today are predominantly white men!" He went on to single out his own dream band, with such members as Yank Lawson, Georg Brunis, Pee Wee Russell. But the most memorable statement was Trussell's complaint that Jess Stacy, Joe Sullivan, and Art Hodes received only four, three, and two votes respectively. "These men," he wrote, "are the three greatest small-band piano men on contemporary wax. *To mention Art Tatum in the same gasp with them is blasphemous!*"(my italics).

Such was the state of jazz criticism, at least in the *Jazz Record* and other small publications, in 1944.

Not all the objections to *Esquire*'s efforts had such a flagrantly racial basis. What bothered the offended critics most often was their equation of "the real jazz" with the older New Orleans musicians, principally Bunk Johnson and George Lewis, *vis à vis* the artists they dismissed as "swing musicians" while categorically denying that swing music was jazz. In an article titled "Featherbed Ball" in the *Record Changer,* Ralph J. Gleason took this position in an impassioned attack on what he called "the Feather-Miller-Goffin-Ulanov axis," branding us as "the exponents of big-band jazz, or the small bands like Norvo and Wilson."

Gleason praised the independent record labels through which "you and I get more George Lewis and Bunk and James P., and we can skip the Norvo and the Basie." He pointed out the necessity "to make firms like Decca agree to record Bunk Johnson instead of King Cole," and suggested that "the way to combat the nonsense spewed out by the Goffin-Feather-Ulanov axis and its satellites is not to get mad and talk to the boys and write letters to each other, but to get mad and write articles for *Down Beat* . . . and *Esky* . . . there is no answer but to usurp the fountainheads of information ourselves and attempt, by using the word jazz to mean the music of Bunk and Oliver, to erase, in time, the damage already done by Feather-Miller-Goffin-Ulanov and their ilk."

In the same publication one Jazzbo Brown suggested that "the so-called experts of *Esquire,* by keeping good jazz safely hidden from the public while forcing upon them the Eldridges, the Tatums and the Pettifords, have created in the minds of intelligent music followers a totally false impression of real American jazz music."

The first *Esquire* concert was held 18 January 1944 in an atmosphere of extraordinary excitement. It was as if, after so many years underground, jazz was about to be apotheosized. Gold and Silver "Esky" statuettes were awarded to the winners. Never did I observe, backstage, any sense of rivalry or jealousy among the musicians. Louis Armstrong and Roy Eldridge worked side by side; Billie Holiday and Mildred Bailey took their turns, as did Lionel Hampton and Red Norvo, who also played a vibes duet on a single instrument when Hampton's broke down. With Teagarden, Bigard, Hawkins, and the gold-star rhythm team rounding out the personnel, it was a night not merely to remember, but to commemorate, logically, in an album.

Recordings of the concert were, in fact, released on V Discs, for use only by the Armed Forces. Over the years I tried persistently, through Joe Glaser (who managed many of the artists) and Milt Gabler at Decca Records, to arrange for the release of a live album. As the artists died off the matter of obtaining clearances from the estates became more complicated and the idea, though never actually shelved, went on the back burner. Inevitably, many years later, the entire concert showed up mysteriously on an album pressed in Japan; I had to send to Tokyo to obtain a copy.

Aside from the poll and the concert, jazz enjoyed ancillary benefits. Paul Eduard Miller edited *Esquire*'s *1944 Jazz Book,* a 230-page volume with a knowledgeable introduction by Gingrich, bio-discographies of anyone who had received any votes in the poll, articles by Miller, Smith, Campbell, Goffin, George Hoefer, and me among others, and numerous illustrations.

In the magazine itself, Goffin contributed a "desert island discs" feature that appeared in September of 1943, listing a dozen records chosen to accompany various musicians and critics in the event of involuntary isolation. Starting in the June 1944 issue, Miller and I began what was known as "The Rhythm Section," in which we would alternate in conducting a jazz symposium and contributing features and record reviews.

Despite (or possibly because of) the initiative taken by *Esquire,* no other national magazine gave jazz regular coverage. I had been able to secure a few bylines in the *New York Times* starting in 1941, and several writers, notably Hammond and George Frazier, continued to find outlets, but *Esquire* essentially remained an oasis.

For our second annual celebration the concert was transferred to Los Angeles, where many of the winners gathered at the Philharmonic Auditorium. Again the concert was a benefit, this time for the Volunteer Army Canteen Service. Hollywood celebrity flourishes were added: Lionel Barrymore presented Duke Ellington with his Esky; Lena Horne, in one of the evening's most touching moments, paid tribute to her friend Billy Strayhorn and gave him his award. Billie Holiday was particularly moved to receive her Esky from Jerome Kern (it was one of Kern's last public appearances; he died later that year), and Judy Garland made the presentation to Anita O'Day. Danny Kaye was the master of ceremonies.

A new dimension this year was a three-way radio hookup, with segments from New Orleans, Los Angeles, and New York. Under the auspices of the National Jazz Foundation in New Orleans, Louis Armstrong was presented, leading an all-star group. Nesuhi Ertegun, editor of the *Record Changer,* had scarcely a good word to say even about this segment ("Higginbotham playing horribly, Armstrong playing badly and Bechet playing superbly"), though the rhythm section with James P. Johnson, Richard Alexis, and Paul Barbarin came in for a little faint praise. Leon Prima's band, despite the presence of Irving Fazola on clarinet, drew almost none.

The New York segment presented Benny Goodman. From Los Angeles were heard the Duke Ellington orchestra (giving Ertegun a chance to observe: "I have never heard the Ellington band sound as bad as when they played a composition by Leonard Feather"), Art Tatum and Anita O'Day backed by some Ellington men and Sid Catlett. For a finale the three cities merged for a collective Armstrong-Ellington-Goodman blues, a live experiment comparable to the overdubbing that would later be a common practice in the recording studios.

There was a bonus for me in this California visit: I fell in love. Invited to dinner by Peggy Lee, I met Jane Leslie Larrabee, a singer I had heard but not known on 52nd Street. Jane had all the right qualities for me: she was attractive, affable, sweet-natured and glad to keep me company as we went, the following evening, to hear Gerald Wilson's new band at Shepp's Playhouse. I proposed that night. A few weeks later, after thinking it over, Jane came to New York, and soon after that I remember calling Red Norvo: "Have you got a dark suit? OK, put it on; I want you to be the best man at my wedding." Over forty years later, Jane and I are still married, proud of our daughter and son-in-law, and glad that I had acted somewhat impulsively in 1945.

During my Los Angeles visit in January for the concert, I made several radio appearances to promote the event and talk about this year's poll. The board of voters had been expanded to twenty-two, and the number of winning categories slightly increased.

The Gold Award winners were Cootie Williams, J. C. Higginbotham (Ertegun's "horrible" trombonist), Johnny Hodges, Coleman Hawkins, Benny Goodman, Teddy Wilson, Al Casey, Oscar Pettiford, Big Sid Catlett, Red Norvo, Louis Armstrong and Mildred Bailey (vocal), Ellington (arranger and band), Buck Clayton, Armed Forces. Silver winners were Roy Eldridge, Lawrence Brown, Benny Carter, Lester Young, Edmond Hall, Art Tatum, Oscar Moore, Slam Stewart, Dave Tough, Harry Carney (miscellaneous instrument), Joe Turner and Billie Holiday, Billy Strayhorn, Count Basie and Willie Smith (Armed Forces).

Added this year was a New Stars division, for which bronze Eskies were given to Dizzy Gillespie, Bill Harris, Herbie Fields, Flip Phillips, Aaron Sachs, Eddie Heywood, Remo Palmier, Chubby Jackson, Specs Powell, Ray Nance (violin), Eddie Cleanhead Vinson, Anita O'Day, Johnny Thompson (arranger), Lionel Hampton (band), and Mel Powell for Armed Forces.

Once again *Esquire*'s efforts were lauded by musicians, by the public, by everyone but the traditionalist critics. Along with Ertegun, Rudi Blesh of the *New York Herald Tribune* found fault with almost everything. Reviewing the first thirty minutes in the ninety-minute broadcast, he complained that Bunk Johnson, "this perennially great player," was lost and inaudible in the noise of inappropriate swing. "Thus ended thirty minutes which presented only a travesty of the original and still vital jazz which was to have been presented."

The New York portion gave Blesh a chance to take a swipe at Benny Goodman (whose "flashy virtuosity has fooled so many into thinking him a great player and a creative personality; in spite of great commercial and popular success he is, of course, neither") and to insult Mildred Bailey, "the white woman who imitated the wrong Negro singers."

During the final portion: "Duke Ellington played a puerile, moronic riff tune, composed—if that is the term—by one of *Esquire*'s jazz critics. The effect was that of waterlogged saxophones snoring in a welter of sound effects." Later came "a trite Ellington tune, dished out in successive choruses by the Duke in a turgid turmoil, by Armstrong in a clipped, imaginative, masterful variation, and by a fumbling piece of Goodman embroidery." Blesh concluded that *Esquire* has "missed the opportunity and disavowed the responsibility to present true cultural values."

At the suggestion of Arnold Gingrich, for the third year we placed the New Stars voting in the hands of musicians: specifically, all who had been winners in previous polls, and all those on the board of experts who also were currently active as musicians. Not all the potential voters could be reached; however, a total of forty-one musicians fulfilled their obligations by participating in this New Stars selection.

The 1946 list showed a few changes, three of them prompted by the achievements of Nat King Cole, whose trio included Oscar Moore on guitar. The Gold winners were Cootie Williams, Bill Harris, Benny Carter, Hawkins, Goodman, Cole, Moore, Tough, Jackson, Norvo, Ellington (arranger and band), Armstrong and Ella Fitzgerald/Mildred Bailey (tied). Silver awards went to Charlie Shavers, Vic Dickenson, Hodges, Don Byas, Bigard, Wilson, Palmier, Krupa, Stewart, Stuff Smith, Strayhorn, Herman (band), Cole (vocal), Holiday.

The New Stars, selected by the jury of their peers, were Pete Candoli, J. J. Johnson, Charlie Parker, Charlie Ventura, Jimmy Hamilton, Erroll Garner, Bill De Arango, J. C. Heard, Junior Raglin, Ray Perry (violin), Ralph Burns (arranger), Herman, Eckstine, Frances Wayne.

The celebration this time took the form of an hour-long broadcast on the ABC network, from the Ritz Theatre on West 46th Street, with Orson Welles as narrator and featuring the Ellington and Herman orchestras, along with the King Cole Trio. With Ellington supplying a gentle piano obbligato, Welles delivered a sensitive tribute to jazz. Later I made the Esky presentations, among them one for Welles, honoring his contributions to jazz (he had been involved with a series of broadcasts presenting traditionalist musicians). The finale found Herman's vocalist, Frances Wayne, joining with the

Ellington orchestra to sing Duke's "I'm Checkin' Out, Goombye" [*sic*] and the two bands teaming up for "C Jam Blues."

I was delighted to see Woody Herman honored. I knew of no other bandleader more respected by his sidemen, and none who worked harder to keep his standards high. This was a spectacular year for him: he had his own sponsored radio series on the ABC network, with a segment in which I interviewed a different member of the orchestra each week. In 1986, the year of his fiftieth anniversary as a leader, Herman still had his unique reputation and still fronted a band of brilliant youngsters.

By now it was evident that the *Esquire* undertaking had met with unprecedented approval almost everywhere; but the *Jazz Record* was still on the warpath. An article by Sergeant John Broome in the August 1945 issue was headed "On the Feather in *Esquire*'s Bonnet" and subheaded "Cult of Shining Mediocrity Takes All Meaning out of Jazz Criticism and Reduces It to Profitable Trade." In the November 1946 issue a piece by one Carter Winter informed us that:

> Every single year there's a new crop of phoneys—black and white—trying to pervert or suppress or emasculate jazz. This year it's Diz Gillespie . . . a few years ago it was Cab Calloway . . . before that it was Whiteman and Grofe . . . On the one hand you have the professional vipers—the real mad [*sic*] cats—headed by Diz Gillespie who try to cut the heart out of the real main line jazz and twist it into something like one of Carmen Miranda's hats because they want to be frantic . . . On the other hand you've got those characters who are convinced . . . that jazz is dead or dying . . . Their groove is just as crappy as Gillespie's.

Even in *Esquire* an occasional critical voice would be heard through the letters-to-the-editor department. Typically, one such letter read:

> We have been taken aback by the opinions of your chief critic Leonard Feather, who is, we feel, either completely incompetent or thoroughly dishonest. We feel that some of his ideas may influence some of your readers . . . to prefer . . . the sentimental, affected honkings of Coleman Hawkins or the shrill "I-can-blow-higher-and-louder-than-you-can" shriekings of Roy Eldridge to the simple, honest playing of Bud Freeman or the incomparable Muggsy Spanier . . . Nor do we feel that such examples of Mr. Feather's type of jazz as his Commodore recordings with the Esquire All Stars are worthy of the name . . . If Mr. Feather wants to write of his "jump boys," let him, but please have someone else around who can write of Dixieland or New Orleans, of the music that is real, that is jazz.

It was in June 1945, in the *Esquire* letters column, that the term "Moldy Fig" originated. Wrongly attributed to me (and often spelled Mouldy Figge), it was actually coined by Sam Platt, a member of the U.S. Navy whose letter to the editor so characterized the supporters of the older jazz. It was, of course, picked up by me, by Barry Ulanov, and eventually by many others on both sides of the schizoid jazz world.

That artists of the calibre of Hawkins and Eldridge, along with Tatum, Ellington and the rest, could be sneeringly dismissed as the "jump boys" was typical of one aspect of the mid-1940s *Zeitgeist*. (Yet the same issue carried a letter from a GI in Italy who welcomed the Rhythm Section department of the magazine, and who declared that "Tatum, Casey and Hawkins were never better" than in my "*Esquire* Bounce.")

Beyond doubt, however, the venom flowed in both directions. Take, for instance, this quote from the September 1945 issue of *Metronome:*

> Just as the fascists tend to divide group against group and distinguish between Negroes, Jews, Italians and "real Americans," so do the moldy figs try to categorize New Orleans, Chicago, swing music and "the real jazz." Just as the fascists have tried to foist their views on the public through the vermin press of *Social Justice,* the *Broom* and *X-Ray,* so have the Figs yapped their heads off in the *Jazz Record, Jazz Session* and *Record Changer.* The moldy figs are frustrated by their musical illiteracy, just as they are frustrated by their inability to foist their idiotic views on the public, and frustrated by the ever-increasing public acceptance of the critics and musicians they hate.

These mean-spirited, clumsily written words were my own. Having been virtually branded as a musical fascist, a pseudonymous writer for the *Record Changer,* calling himself Bilbo Brown, responded in kind. He took the names of *Metronome*'s editors and altered them to resemble those of prominent Communists: we became William Z. Feather, George Browder Simon, and Barry U. Leninov. This was unfair to Simon, who was really not involved in the battle of words, but Barry Ulanov and I continually asked for trouble by assuming that the best defense was attack. If the writers in both camps had moderated their tone and concentrated on trying to advance the cause of the musicians they believed in, without denouncing those they opposed, much of the ill feeling could have been avoided.

In one of the best researched and less hysterical articles attacking me, Hugues Panassié rightly pointed out that my holier-than-thou attitude, and my assumption that as a musician I was *ipso facto* a better critic, were unjustified. Critics who are musicians disagree among themselves just as often as those who have no empirical background. As Panassié also wrote, it is possible, through selective quotation, to pick out opinions that agree with one's own and contradict those of the critics with whom one disagrees. I was certainly vulnerable in this area, having often quoted remarks by musicians whose views coincided with mine. Later, when I began the "Blindfold Test" series in *Metronome,* my conscience was clear, since I never edited the subjects' views regardless of their divergence from mine.

That the pervasive bitterness in the jazz community would lead to trouble of a more consequential nature should not have surprised us, but in 1947 shock waves were felt in our world with the publication of the latest *Esquire Jazz Book.* What happened, or how it came about, was never made entirely clear. Somewhere along the way Arnold Gingrich left *Esquire* and moved to Switzerland and the editing of the *Jazz Book* fell into the hands of Ernest Anderson, a promoter best known for his close association with Eddie Condon, whose very name was anathema to the modernists.

Under Anderson's guidance the book was quite unsubtly transformed into a virtual publicity outlet for Condon and his associates, while the space devoted to the poll and the winners was conspicuously restricted.

If the attempt to capture the book for Condon and his friends had not been so blatantly opportunistic, perhaps the uproar that ensued might have been avoided, but the tone and intent of the book left room for no reaction but anger on the part of the musicians who had been given short shrift, along with the panelists whose votes previously had been the *raison d'être* of both the books and the concerts.

The black press was particularly outraged. "Musicians Squawk Over Omissions in *Esquire Jazz Book* Results," one headline read in the *Amsterdam News.* It was complained that the book had:

> a bare listing of the winners, with none of the details about the musicians and the scientific tabulation of the voting of the critics as in former issues. The book . . . carries thirty-seven photos of white musicians with only seventeen of Negro musicians and singers. At least twenty of the pictures are of musicians . . . with the Eddie Condon outfit. [The book] carries an article by Eddie Condon's booking agent . . . articles are printed by such close Condon pals as Art Hodes and others. There is a series of about twenty pictures of the Condon group in an eight-page spread and not a single Negro face appears among them. It reeks of "Dixieland" and "white supremacy" music . . . While Sarah Vaughan is listed as the award winner for female vocalist, there's nothing in the book about her save her name. On the other hand, however, there is a full-page spread on Lee Wiley, a white singer who has appeared with Condon.

The story went on to complain about the absence of a photo of Art Tatum, the failure to list the specific findings of the critics, failure to include articles by any of the voters, and failure to detail the musicians' own choices for the New Star listings.

These are the musicians whose achievements were downplayed in the book: Gold Award: Armstrong, Harris, Carter, Hawkins, Goodman, Wilson, Moore, Buddy Rich, Jackson, Norvo, Ellington (band and arranger), Armstrong (vocal), Holiday. Silver Awards: Gillespie, Dickenson, Willie Smith, Lester Young, Bigard, Tatum/Cole (tied), Barney Kessel, Tough, Ed Safranski, Carney, George Handy (arranger), Herman, Cole (vocal), Fitzgerald.

The *Esquire* New Stars for 1947 were Miles Davis, Trummy Young, Sonny Stitt, Lucky Thompson, Rudy Rutherford, Dodo Marmarosa, John Collins, Shadow Wilson, Ray Brown, Milt Jackson, Tadd Dameron, Boyd Raeburn, Al Hibbler, Sarah Vaughan.

What had been meaningful in the *Esquire* adventure was not only that national attention had been brought to the Tatums and Norvos and Holidays, but also that many of the winners, particularly in the New Stars category, had never before been singled out for recognition; in many cases it would be years before they would be similarly acknowledged by *Down Beat* or *Metronome,* and in too many instances, such as Lucky Thompson and John Collins, even Billy Strayhorn, this was the only award they ever won. Consequently, the lack of any special attention given to them in the *1947 Year Book* was doubly deplorable.

Word traveled fast during that disputatious era. The resentment among the *Esquire* winners, past and present, was unanimous. A letter was drawn up and addressed to David Smart. It read as follows:

> Dear Sir:
>
> We, a group of musicians who have won awards in the *Esquire* All American Jazz Polls, hereby protest against the treatment given to the poll in *Esquire's 1947 Jazz Book.* We wish to know the answers to the following:
>
> 1) Why was the book edited by the personal manager of Eddie Condon, who has nothing to do with jazz today, and why did it devote much of its space to publicity stories and pictures of musicians who work for Condon and for the editor?
> 2) Why were our individual votes (which are widely read by musicians) not printed in the book?
> 3) Why is there not a single story or picture, anywhere in the book, on any of this year's New Star winners?

4) Why does the list of the year's so-called "best records" ignore practically every record made by the younger jazz musicians, including the *Esquire* winners, while devoting most of its space to records made by older musicians of the Dixieland clique?

We regard the entire book as an insult to the musical profession and to the jazz musicians who have helped *Esquire* by taking part in its jazz activities.

As long as the present unfair set-up continues, we do not wish to vote in any future polls, and we will refuse to accept any future awards.

The top copy of this letter was not sent to David Smart; instead, he received a duplicate, for a simple reason: the original, still in my possession, is a unique and valuable document. It carries the signatures of Louis Armstrong, Coleman Hawkins, Roy Eldridge, Red Norvo, Buddy Rich, Charlie Shavers, Dizzy Gillespie, Willie Smith, Boyd Raeburn, Charlie Ventura, Miles Davis, Al Casey, Flip Phillips, Pete Candoli, Shadow Wilson, Trummy Young, Tad [*sic*] Dameron, Sarah Vaughan, Aaron Sachs, Billie Holiday, Buck Clayton, Big Sid Catlett, Johnny Hodges, Harry Carney, Oscar Pettiford, Cootie Williams, Teddy Wilson, Ella Fitzgerald, Duke Ellington, Ray Nance, Nat King Cole, Chubby Jackson, and J. C. Heard.

That, of course, marked the end of the *Esquire* era. The entire board of twenty, with the exception of Dave Dexter and Charles Edward Smith, served notice on *Esquire* that they were severing all connections with the magazine. It was probably the first and only time in the history of jazz criticism that so many experts, representing such a wide span of opinions, had come so close to unanimity on anything.

Possibly the revolt was inevitable and the poll doomed. The writing had already been visible on the wall: *Esquire* had dropped its regular feature coverage, Gingrich was not around to help us, and as a devastating postscript Robert Goffin sued the magazine, claiming that he had been frozen out of the picture. That I refused to testify on behalf of *Esquire* undoubtedly helped his case. Among the promises he supposedly received in the course of a settlement was that *Esquire* would never again run a jazz poll.

It was a melancholy ending to a glorious four-year ride. What Goffin and Gingrich and I had concocted, that night at the Hurricane with a live soundtrack by Ellington, survives not only in memory, but in the statuettes still proudly displayed by those lucky few who were in the right place, with the right talent, at the right time.

The end of our *Esquire* collaboration did not connote a break with the Gingriches. Jane and I continued to see Arnold and Helen Mary, who was

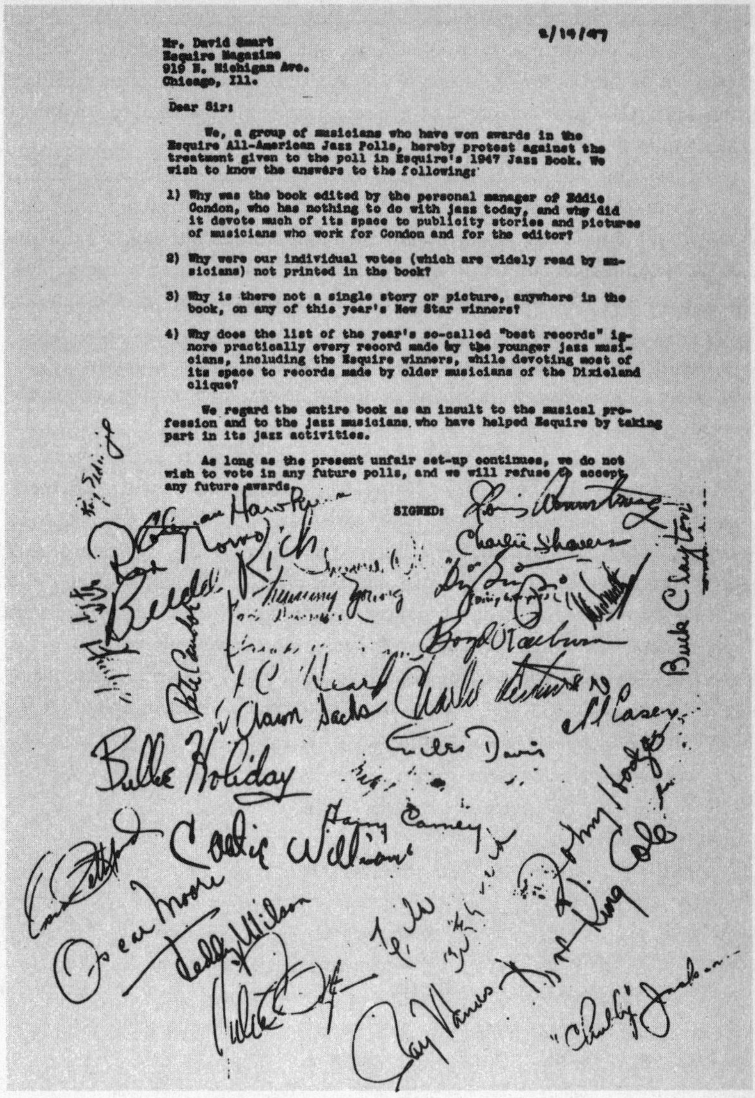

2/14/47

Mr. David Smart
Esquire Magazine
919 N. Michigan Ave.
Chicago, Ill.

Dear Sir:

We, a group of musicians who have won awards in the Esquire All-American Jazz Polls, hereby protest against the treatment given to the poll in Esquire's 1947 Jazz Book. We wish to know the answers to the following:

1) Why was the book edited by the personal manager of Eddie Condon, who has nothing to do with jazz today, and why did it devote much of its space to publicity stories and pictures of musicians who work for Condon and for the editor?

2) Why were our individual votes (which are widely read by musicians) not printed in the book?

3) Why is there not a single story or picture, anywhere in the book, on any of this year's New Star winners?

4) Why does the list of the year's so-called "best records" ignore practically every record made by the younger jazz musicians, including the Esquire winners, while devoting most of its space to records made by older musicians of the Dixieland clique?

We regard the entire book as an insult to the musical profession and to the jazz musicians who have helped Esquire by taking part in its jazz activities.

As long as the present unfair set-up continues, we do not wish to vote in any future polls, and we will refuse to accept any future awards.

SIGNED:

both his first and his third wife (there was a brief second marriage in between). We visited them in Switzerland, met them often after Arnold returned to New York and became editor of the short-lived *Flair* for Fleur Cowles. Soon he rejoined *Esquire* and in 1952 became publisher and a vice president. I wrote for the magazine a few more times, but our friendship long outlasted the business relationship. After Smart died, Arnold reached the mandatory retirement age of seventy but stayed on as editor-in-chief. Helen Mary died in 1955; later we saw Arnold in the company of his last wife, Jane. Our mutual interests in jazz, social issues, and a spectrum of other topics never abated.

The last time I saw him, a few months before his death, he was still following the daily routine: up at 4 A.M., fishing for an hour in the river that flowed behind his New Jersey home, changing clothes and flagging down a bus with a lantern around 5:30 A.M., studying music books en route to New York, practicing the violin at the office from 7 to 8 A.M. before starting work.

I doubt that he ever gave up those foul French cigarettes; in July 1976 I picked up a newspaper in Nice and read that he had died of lung cancer. He was seventy-two.

In *Nothing But People*, his book of memoirs recalling the early days at *Esquire*, he wrote: "Looking back, I suppose I got more personal enjoyment out of the jazz promotions than out of any other single thing the magazine ever did." Then, typically, he proceeded to disclaim credit: "This whole jazz hoopla was about one tenth my idea and nine Dave's." He neglected to point out that since Dave Smart knew and cared nothing about jazz, his suggestion that we stage the concerts would not have come about but for that indispensable one tenth. The starting points, without which the whole enterprise would never have been born, were Arnold Gingrich's lifelong affection for jazz, and Goffin the catalyst standing close by.

3

CRITICISM

Bechet and Jazz Visit Europe, 1919

Ernst-Alexandre Ansermet

This article, by the great conductor (he led the first performance of Stravinsky's Rite of Spring*) appeared in 1919 in the* Revue Romande *as "Sur un orchestre nègre." Translated by Walter Schaap for the bilingual French magazine* Jazz Hot *and anthologized in 1938, it became famous for proclaiming the interest jazz could hold for classical musicians and for its early perception of Sidney Bechet's remarkable talent.*

This is not about African Negroes but about those of the Southern states of the U.S.A., who have created the musical style commonly known as the rag. Rag music is founded essentially on rhythm and in particular on the qualities of syncopation in rhythm. Rag music first came to Europe in the form of the cake-walk, as I recall, and then with the one-step, two-step, fox-trot, and all the American dances and songs to which the subtitle of rag-time is applied. America is full of small instrumental ensembles devoted to rag-time, and if the national music of a people is none other than its popular music, one can say that rag-time has become the true national popular music of America. I remember having traveled by railroad between Berne and Lausanne with a group of young Americans. One of them began to hum a piece of rag-music, whereupon they all joined in, marking the rhythm, by beating their hands on the wooden benches, just as the Swiss in a foreign land, yodel in remembrance of the homeland. Today, rag-time has conquered Europe; we dance to rag-time under the name of jazz in all our cities, and the hundreds of musicians who contribute to our popular music are all applying themselves at this very moment, to adapt this new art to the taste for the insipid and the sentimental, to the coarse and mediocre sensuality of their clientele.* Rag-time is even passing into what I will call for lack of another

*Permit me another anecdote on this point. One day, while seeking some examples of rag-time at an American publisher's I found one which I rejected because of its dullness and lack of character. Slightly hesitant, the publisher offered me another which he designated as the model of the first; it was a remarkable thing whose accent and force of character seized me at once, but which his clientele would not have, declaring it too trying. The publisher had then made the sugary replica which he had shown me at first, and had withdrawn the original from circulation.

name, the field of learned music: Stravinsky has used it as material for several works, Debussy has already written a cake-walk, and I well believe Ravel will lose no time in giving us a fox-trot. But, under the name of Southern Syncopated Orchestra, there is an ensemble of authentic musicians of Negro race to be heard in London. Instrumentalists and singers, they present us pell-mell with all sorts of manifestations of their art, the old with the new, the best with the worst. It's a mysterious new world which we were acquainted with only through its more or less distant repercussions, and which finally reaches us in its living reality. One can hardly imagine a more opportune manifestation, and it is to be hoped, for our common edification, that the British metropolis will not alone reap its benefits.

THE FIRST THING that strikes one about the Southern Syncopated Orchestra is the astonishing perfection, the superb taste, and the fervor of its playing. I couldn't say if these artists make it a duty to be sincere, if they are penetrated by the idea that they have a "mission" to fulfill, if they are convinced of the "nobility" of their task, if they have that holy "audacity" and that sacred "valor" which our code of musical morals requires of our European musicians, nor indeed if they are animated by any "idea" whatsoever. But I can see they have a very keen sense of the music they love, and a pleasure in making it which they communicate to the hearer with irresistible force,—a pleasure which pushes them to outdo themselves all the time, to constantly enrich and refine their medium. They play generally without notes, and even when they have some, it only serves to indicate the general line, for there are very few numbers I have heard them execute twice with exactly the same effects. I imagine that, knowing the voice attributed to them in the harmonic ensemble, and conscious of the role their instrument is to play, they can let themselves go, in a certain direction and within certain limits, as their heart desires. They are so entirely possessed by the music they play, that they can't stop themselves from dancing inwardly to it in such a way that their playing is a real show, and when they indulge in one of their favorite effects which is to take up the refrain of a dance in a tempo suddenly twice as slow and with redoubled intensity and figuration, a truly gripping thing takes place, it seems as if a great wind is passing over a forest or as if a door is suddenly opened on a wild orgy.

The musician who directs them and to whom the constitution of the ensemble is due, Mr. Will Marion Cook, is moreover a master in every respect, and there is no orchestra leader I delight as much in seeing conduct. As for the music which makes up their repertory, it is purely vocal, or for one voice, a vocal quartet, or a choir accompanied by instruments, or again purely instrumental; it bears the names of the composers (all unknown by our world) or is simply marked "Traditional." This traditional music is religious in inspiration. It is the index of a whole mode of religion and of a veritable religious art which, by themselves, merit a study. The whole Old Testament is related with a very touching realism and familiarity. There is much about Moses, Gideon, the Jordan, and Pharoah. In an immense unison, the voices intone: "Go down, Moses, way down in Egypt land. Tell old Pharoah: Let my people go." And suddenly, there they are clapping their hands and beating their feet with the joy of a schoolboy told that the teacher is sick: "Good news! Good news! Sweet Chariot's coming."

Or else a singer gets up, "I got a shoes (pronouncing the *s* to make it sound nice), you got a shoes, all God's children got a shoes. When I get to heaven, gonna put on my shoes, gonna walk all over God's heaven." And the word *heaven* they pronounce in one syllable as *he'm,* which makes a long resonance in their closed mouths, like a gong. Another time, a deep bass points out the empty platform to one of his companions and invites him to come and relate the battle of Jericho, and it's a terrible story which begins with the mighty deeds of King Joshua and all sorts of menacing fists and martial treads; their hands are raised and then lowered, and the walls come tumbling down. In a lower tone, but with such a tender accent, the quartet also sings "Give me your hand" or sometimes "Brother, give me your hand." There is another very beautiful thing in which a female voice sings the ample sweeping melody (wavering between the major and minor) and of those who are going away towards the valley of the Jordan to cross the river, while the choir scans with an ever more vehement motif, "Nobody was heard praying."

In the non-anonymous works, some are related to a greater or lesser extent to these religiously inspired works, others sing the sweetness of Georgia peaches, the perfume of flowers, country, mammy, or sweetheart; the instrumental works are rags or even European dances. Among the authors, some are Negroes, but these are the exceptions. The others are of European origin, and even when this is not true of the author, it is of the music; most rag-time is founded on well-known motifs or on formuli peculiar to our art,—there is one on the "Wedding March" from *Midsummer Night's Dream,* another on Rachmaninoff's celebrated *Prelude,* another on typical Debussy chords, another simply on the major scale.*

The aforementioned traditional music itself has its source, as could

*Some time ago, I met in New York, one of the most celebrated rag-time composers, Irving Berlin. A Russian Jew by origin, he had, like Cesar-Napoleon Gaillard, been a jack-of-all-trades, and known all kinds of fortune before becoming rich in writing Negro music. Devoid of any musical culture, incapable of writing his notes, hardly knowing how to play the piano, he told me himself how he used to pick out the notes on the piano with one finger, or whistle to a professional who noted down these melodies which entered his spirit, and how then, he'd have the professional seek out the harmonies until he was satisfied. Having assimilated the Negro style perfectly, it is to this style that he applies his gift of musical invention, which is indeed remarkable.

doubtless be easily rediscovered, in the songs the Negroes learned from the English missionaries. Thus, all, or nearly all, the music of the Southern Syncopated Orchestra is, in origin, foreign to these Negroes. How is this possible? Because it is not the material that makes Negro music, it is the spirit.

The Negro population of North America is African in origin. I am acquainted with the music of the African Negroes. They say it consists in work-songs and ritual dances, that it is based on melodic modes differing from ours, and that it is particularly rich in its rhythm which already practices syncopation. In losing their land, have the Negroes carried off to America lost their songs as well? (One shudders in conjuring up such an image.) At least, they didn't lose the taste for them. In their new villages by the cotton fields, the first music they find is the songs which the missionaries teach them. And immediately, they make it over to suit themselves.*

The desire to give certain syllables a particular emphasis or a prolonged resonance, that is to say preoccupations of an expressive order, seem to have determined in Negro singing their anticipation or delay of a fraction of rhythmic unity. This is the birth of syncopation. All the traditional Negro songs are strewn with syncopes which issue from the voice while the movement of the body marks the regular rhythm. Then, when the Anglo-Saxon ballad or the banal dance forms reach the Dixieland land of the plantations, the Negroes appropriate them in the same fashion, and the rag is born. But it is not enough to say that Negro music consists in the habit of syncopating any musical material whatsoever. We have shown that syncopation itself is but the effect of an expressive need, the manifestation in the field of rhythm of a particular taste, in a word, the genius of the race. This genius demonstrates itself in all the musical elements, it transfigures everything in the music it appropriates. The Negro takes a trombone, and he has a knack of vibrating each note by a continual quivering of the slide, and a sense of glissando, and a taste for muted notes which make it a new instrument; he takes a clarinet or saxophone and he has a way of hitting the notes with a slight *inferior appoggiatura,* he discovers a whole series of effects produced by the lips alone, which make it a new instrument. There is a Negro way of playing the violin, a Negro way of singing. As for our orchestra tympani, needless to say with what alacrity the Negro runs out to greet them, he grasps all the paraphernalia instantaneously including the most excessive refinements, to set up an inexhaustible jugglery.

The banjo itself (string instrument strummed with a pick) is perhaps not the invention of the Negro, but the modification for his use of a type of instrument represented elsewhere by the mandolin.

*It's me, Lord, who needs Thy benediction. It's not my brother, it's not my sister, it's me, Lord.

By the grouping of these chosen instruments, following the most diversified combinations, a more or less definite type of Negro orchestra constituted itself, of which the Southern Syncopated Orchestra is as the first milestone,—an attempt at a synthesis of great style. Composed of two violins, a cello, a saxophone, two basses, two clarinets, a horn, three trumpets, three trombones, drums, two pianos, and a banjo section, it achieves by the manner in which the instruments are played, a strangely fused tonal sonority, distinctly its own, in which the neutral timbres like that of the piano disappear completely, and which the banjos surround with a halo of perpetual vibration. Now the fusion is such (all brasses muted) that it is difficult to recognize the individual timbres, now a very high clarinet emerges like a bird in flight, or a trombone bursts out brusquely like a foreign body appearing. And the ensemble displays a terrific dynamic range, going from a subtle sonority reminiscent of Ravel's orchestra to a terrifying tumult in which shouts and hand-clapping is mixed.

In the field of melody, although his habituation to our scales has effaced the memory of the African modes, an old instinct pushes the Negro to pursue his pleasure outside the orthodox intervals: he performs thirds which are neither major nor minor and false seconds, and falls often by instinct on the natural harmonic sounds of a given note,—it is here especially that no written music can give the idea of his playing. I have often noticed, for example, that in [their] melodies the A-sharp and the B-flat, the E and the E-flat are not the sounds of our scale. It is only in the field of harmony that the Negro hasn't yet created his own distinct means of expression. But even here, he uses a succession of seventh chords, and ambiguous major-minors with a deftness which many European musicians should envy. But, in general, harmony is perhaps a musical element which appears in the scheme of musical evolution only at a stage which the Negro art has not yet attained.

All the characteristics of this art, in fact, show it to be a perfect example of what is called popular art,—an art which is still in its period of oral tradition. It doesn't matter a whit, after all, whether Negro music be written by Russian Jews, German Jews, or some corrupted Anglo-Saxon. It is a fact that the best numbers are those written by the Negroes themselves. But with these as with the others, the importance of the writer in the creation of the work is counterbalanced by the action of tradition, represented by the performer. The work may be written, but it is not fixed and it finds complete expression only in actual performance.

Nevertheless, some works in the repertory of the Southern Syncopated Orchestra mark the passage from oral tradition to written tradition, or if you choose, from popular art to learned art. First we have a number for choir, soprano, and orchestra, inspired by the traditional works, and signed

Dett. On a Biblical text, "Listen to the Lambs," which Handel too has treated in the *Messiah,* this musician has written a very simple yet very pure and beautifully enraptured work. Or we have some works of Mr. Will Marion Cook including a very fine vocal scene entitled "Rainsong." Perhaps one of these days we shall see the Glinka of Negro music. But I am inclined to think that the strongest manifestation of the racial genius lies in the blues.

The blues occurs when the Negro is sad, when he is far from his home, his mammy, or his sweetheart. Then, he thinks of a motif or a preferred rhythm, and takes his trombone, or his violin, or his banjo, or his clarinet, or his drum, or else he sings, or simply dances. And on the chosen motif, he plumbs the depths of his imagination. This makes his sadness pass away,—it is the blues.

"These great blue holes which the naughty birds make."

But, for the bitterness of this line, the most refined poet and the Negro coincide here in their expression.

There is in the Southern Syncopated Orchestra an extraordinary clarinet virtuoso who is, so it seems, the first of his race to have composed perfectly formed blues on the clarinet. I've heard two of them which he had elaborated at great length, then played to his companions so that they are equally admirable for their richness of invention, force of accent, and daring in novelty and the unexpected. Already, they gave the idea of a style, and their form was gripping, abrupt, harsh, with a brusque and pitiless ending like that of Bach's second *Brandenburg* Concerto. I wish to set down the name of this artist of genius; as for myself, I shall never forget it—it is Sidney Bechet. When one has tried so often to rediscover in the past one of those figures to whom we owe the advent of our art,—those men of the seventeenth and eighteenth centuries, for example, who made expressive works of dance airs, clearing the way for Haydn and Mozart who mark, not the starting point, but the first milestone—what a moving thing it is to meet this very black, fat boy with white teeth and that narrow forehead, who is very glad one likes what he does, but who can say nothing of his art, save that he follows his "own way" and when one thinks that his "own way" is perhaps the highway the whole world will swing along tomorrow.

Harpsichords and Jazz Trumpets

Roger Pryor Dodge

This relatively early (1934) attempt to negotiate the relationship between jazz and classical music first appeared in Lincoln Kirstein's innovative and influential magazine, Hound and Horn. *Dodge's criticism has recently been collected in a book called* Hot Jazz and Jazz Dance, *edited by his son, Pryor Dodge.*

In the history of Jazz we find that the immediate result of the bringing together of the four-part hymn and the Negro, was the Spiritual. The Spiritual, though concededly the most original any one thing the Negro has contributed *outright,* seems to me chiefly significant as containing the first seed of Jazz. Unfortunately a great deal more critical interest is expended on the Spiritual out of the *church,* than on the Jazz out of the *dance hall.* In fact, quite aside from my personal conviction that Jazz is by far the most important music of the two, the Spiritual is so well taken care of that new collections are constantly appearing, whereas Jazz, taken for granted as contemporary dance music is scarcely acknowledged, let alone notated. For we can hardly consider a popular song publishing company's issue of the simple Ground Bass, or harmonic vamp accompaniment with occasional uninspired instrumental suggestions, as the written counterpart of that extraordinary and highly developed music. This present lack of adequate notation can be compared very simply to the similar musical situation in Europe during the sixteenth, seventeenth, and even eighteenth centuries. In this connection a few lines from a letter written by a certain Andre Maugars in 1639 upon the occasion of a visit to Rome, give an exciting picture of the times:*

> I will describe to you the most celebrated and most excellent concert which I have heard . . . As to the instrumental music, it was composed of an organ, a large harpsichord, two or three archlutes, an Archiviole-da-

*Vide, Arnold Dolmetsch's: *The Interpretations of the Music of the XVIIth and XVIIIth Centuries.*

> Lyra and two or three violins . . . Now a violin played alone to the organ, then another answered; another time all three played together different parts, then all the instruments went together. Now an archlute made a thousand divisions on ten or twelve notes each of five or six bars length, then the others did the same in a different way. I remember that a violin played in the true chromatic mode and although it seemed harsh to my ear at first, I nevertheless got used to this novelty and took extreme pleasure in it. But above all the great Frescobaldi exhibited thousands of inventions on his harpsichord, the organ always playing the ground. It is not without cause that the famous organist of St. Peter has acquired such a reputation in Europe, for although his published compositions are witnesses to his genius, yet to judge of his profound learning, you must hear him improvise.

He also adds "In the Antienne they had . . . some archlutes playing certain dance tunes and answering one another . . ." (Which, by the way, helps bear out the theory that all great music, even church, leans upon and is developed by the dance.) Now, as then, there is such a musical bustle and excitement in the air that no Jazz musician needs more than a harmonic base or a catchy melody, to play extempore in solo or in "consort." Improvised Jazz is comparable to such music as Maugars heard at St. Peters, and though the distorted (to our ears) dynamics and instrumental tone quality of the Negro brass and woodwind sound harsh and fantastic at first, like Maugars, one gets "used to this novelty" and finally takes "extreme pleasure in it." Moreover its start and development occurring during our lifetime, we should feel its power tremendously and have a definite emotional reaction; a purely contemporary enthusiasm, which can never be experienced for a bygone music, no matter how great it was.

When we consider that not only Frescobaldi but Handel, J. S. Bach, Haydn, Mozart, and even Beethoven, were all great improvisers, we realize it was intellectual superiority which made them write down what they could improvise more easily—not the limitations of a modern academic composer. We realize that such individuals who could improvise the most difficult and inventive counterpoint and fugue on a keyboard, needed only to push their minds a step further to dispose parts to an orchestra. On the other hand when we consider that the Negro instrumentalist is apparently uninterested and incapable of writing down his own real improvisations, that his inspiration is absolutely dependent upon harmonic progressions provided by other instruments than his own and that though he takes great pleasure in it, his counterpoint is the happy accident of a confrère "getting off" at the same time, then, we can understand perhaps, why this structure of Jazz, this musical development by the instruments themselves (and the different musical styles that implies) is at a standstill as far as native, written composition for solo or symphony goes.

To appreciate the significance of the act of improvisation, we must not overlook the fact that improvisation is absolutely imperative to the development of an art form such as music and dancing. On the other hand we must not overvalue the ability itself, as at the time, this resource must be so commonplace that every performer can avail himself of it with perfect ease. It is when the spirit of a folk school of music so excites the folk artist that it is the most natural thing in the world for him to make variations on every melody he hears, or to invent new melody on a familiar harmony or to extemporize in general, that we find a real freedom of invention. It isn't essential that the whole group experience the same improvisatory spirit. This is the only way, in my opinion, to ensure telling change and growth. When this atmosphere does not prevail, the creations of the solitary individual, no matter how revolutionary, always will lack the force of those of a much less important man who has the basic, group impetus back of him. The creations of the former, after the first shock, become more old-fashioned than the most common material of folk improvisation. Richard Wagner is a good example. Moreover it must be understood that by group feeling I do not mean the will to organize a group. A Dalcroze, a Mary Wigman, Les Six, or a Picasso may impose rules on a train of satellites, but instead of receiving back new force and inspiration from contemporary fellow artists, on the contrary, they are run into the ground by a coterie of pupils and imitators. Also it must be understood that what passes for improvisatory art in our exclusive little studios of both dancing and music, where the girls and boys find new freedom in expressing the machine-age or the dynamic release of the soul, or in musical combinations in the manner of the written works of Liszt, Scriabin, Milhaud, or Gershwin, is not the art of improvisation that I discuss.

Whereas the academic child prodigies of today content their masters and their public with nothing more than a mature reading of a score, even a child in early days was expected to improvise, and the quality of his extemporaneous playing was the criterion by which he was judged. When Mozart held an audition for the child Beethoven, he fell half asleep listening to what he presumed were prepared pieces. When Beethoven, greatly vexed, for he had been improvising, insisted the Master give him a theme and then made countless variations on it, Mozart is reported to have jumped up crying, "Pay attention to him: he will make a noise in the world some day." And when Mozart as a child had played for Papa Haydn, he had shown the same prodigal invention. And remember Haydn, Mozart, and Beethoven were at the close of a great musical period and were improvising as that tradition had demanded, even though they themselves were the founders of the Romantic Virtuoso movement. It is for that involuntary, impersonal connection with the past that I mention them, not for the new avenue they opened up for the nineteenth century.

If we turn to the musical literature of the seventeenth and eighteenth centuries we find that no two artists were supposed to play identical variations and ornaments on the same piece; on the contrary, the artist was expected extemporaneously to fill in rests, ornament whole notes, and rhythmically break up chords. The basic melody, as in Jazz, was considered common property. If the player exactly imitated somebody else or faithfully followed the written compositions of another composer, he was a student, not a professional. However, to the student we owe the inspiring textbooks written by such masters as Couperin, Ph. E. Bach, Geminiani, Mace, Quantz, etc. This is a literature which from all sides presses the fact that if the pupil has no natural inspiration and fantasy in melody, no feeling as to how long to trill, or where to grace notes, or in what rhythm to break up a figured bass, he had better give up all hope of pleasing his contemporaries. It was not the contemporary virtuoso, professional or semi-professional musician who benefited by the few notations in circulation. It was the student. The fact is, that in a healthy school of music it is a drawback to have to read music. It is unnecessary to write it for your own convenience and too much trouble to take the infinite pains necessary to notate a fellow artist's daily compositions. In such a school it is the well-balanced composer not depending on written notes himself, but with an eye on posterity or with pupils to interest, who takes the pains to notate more than the simple harmony or melody.

At that time one listened first, as one does now to Jazz, for the melody, then recognized the variations as such and drew intense enjoyment from the musical talent familiarly inspired. Instead of waiting months for a show piece to be composed and then interpreted (our modern academic procedure), then, in one evening, you could hear a thousand beautiful pieces, as you can now in Jazz. Instead of going to a dance hall to hear Armstrong, in earlier times you might have gone to church to hear Frescobaldi; or danced all night to Haydn's orchestra; or attended a salon and listened to Handel accompany a violinist—with his extemporaneous variations so matter of course; or sneaked in on one of Bach's little evenings at home, when to prove his theory of the well-tempered clavier he would improvise in every key, not a stunt improvisation in the manner of someone else, but preludes and fugues probably vastly superior to his famous notated ones. Academicians of today can improvise in the styles of various old schools but the result is commonplace, not only because of the fact of improvising in a school that is out of date, but because such an urge is precious and weak in itself, limiting the improviser to forms he has already seen in print. Even in contemporary modern music, the working out is so intellectual that the extempore act does not give the modernist time to concoct anything he himself would consider significant.

Contrary to the modern academician and similar to the early composers, Jazz musicians give forth a folk utterance, impossible to notate adequately. For even if every little rest, 64th note, slide, trill, mute, blast, and rhythmic accent is approximately notated and handed back to them, it is impossible to get them to read it. To read with any facility these extremely difficult improvisations takes a highly developed academic training, a training which is not general, usually, till the best part of an improvising period is past. The great Negro musicians are not pianists or harpsichordists consciously contrapuntal. The very range of the keyboard which stimulated the seventeenth- and eighteenth-century European mind to great solo feats of combined polyphonic and harmonic invention only suggests to them, for the most part, a simple harmonic, rhythmic accompaniment. The Negro is par excellence an instrumentalist: a trumpeter, a trombonist, a clarinetist. He is still musically unconscious of what he has done or what he may do. But, do not conclude from this that Jazz music is still at the simple folk-tune stage. Far from it. For though the birth of the Spiritual was the birth of a new folk song containing the seed of Jazz, Jazz itself is something more than just another folk tune. Jazz has reached the highest development of any folk music since the early Christian hymns and dances grew into the most developed contrapuntal music known to history.

To understand even better the source of Jazz, remember the Spiritual is a song, a highly developed hymn if you will, compared to which the Blues, the seed manifestation, is really a step backward in the direction of the Chant: a step altogether natural and necessary for a new art form to take, as witness the retrogression of early Christian music surrounded by Greco-Roman culture. Although the simple sing-song monotonous way of both Blues and Spirituals reveals a lack of depth, comparatively foreign to the old Chant, this is to be explained, I think, by an appreciation of the vast difference in direct antecedents. The Negro received his little bit of the greatness of a Choral, from the Protestant Hymn mixed with Moody and Sankey. Whereas the Gregorian Chant came out of the austere Greek modes mixed with the passionate Semitic plain song. Also, the tunes which skimmed along in the drawing-rooms and music halls during the whole of the nineteenth century, were principally polkas, Irish reels, jigs, or the schottische. These the Negro was quite naturally exposed to. So as he was breaking down the four-part hymn into the Spiritual, so was he, through his own heritage of *rhythm,* twisting this music of the marches and jigs into first, a cake-walk, later—

Ragtime. To play this early American dance music he had to accustom himself to the white man's musical instruments; and it was this familiarization which laid the foundation for his extraordinary instrumental development into Jazz.

Ragtime, we now perceive, was the rhythmical twist the Negro gave to the early American dance tune. Here, the different instruments were finding their places in the musical pattern and already daring to add their own peculiar instrumental qualities. But—suddenly, the whole breadth of melodic and harmonic difference between the folk-tune stuff Ragtime was made out of, and the Chant stuff the racial Blues were made out of, touched something very deep in the Negro. He found himself going way beyond anything he had done so far. For he had now incorporated his own melodic Blues within his own syncopated dance rhythms and miraculously created a new music—a new music which moved him so emotionally that Jazz bands sprang up like mushrooms all around him. The Blues, retrogressed hymn, secular Spiritual, had fathered itself by way of the clarinet, trumpet, trombone, banjo, drums, and piano into a rebirth, and christened itself JAZZ!

Now, the many things that go into making a *playing style* suit one instrument rather than another, are usually taken for granted. As a matter of fact they are the result of an experimental development which takes time and is very interesting to trace. The playing style of the harpsichord was not evolved in a day and neither was the playing style of the Jazz valve trumpet. Both started by emulating the human voice (the harpsichord by way of the organ); that is, they took their melody from the singers; and both twisted this song into a stronger instrumental form. Taking these two examples as broadly representative of their respective cultures, we can see of what little importance, after the first vital impulse, the human voice was in the development of these two musics. I doubt if the voice could ever carry the development of a music very far without the advent of a composer, as there always seems to be such satisfaction for a folk singer in repeating verse after verse and letting the words alone be inventive. Though the harpsichord seems a very complicated instrument to compare alongside the single-noted valve trumpet, or a slide trombone, nevertheless I feel more of a true basis of comparison here than with, say, the trumpet and violin. We moderns only know the present virtuoso violin, an instrument without any real inventive playing style of its own—an instrument merely swinging back and forth between the imitative sweet singing of a tune and the highly developed musical figures lifted out of keyboard music. But a careful, lively carrying out of all the turns and graces of old music on the harpsichord, can give us a fairly clear outlook on the playing style two or three hundred years ago; and only the extreme artificiality of the harpsichord has made this possible. Any instrument with the dynamic range of the modern piano and violin, possesses, possibly, a clean crystallized style at the outset, but the traditional playing style can be absolutely swept away by one little wave of romanticism. The mechanical construction of the harpsichord itself has stood in the way of any such collapse into smooth and suave decadence.

If in the harpsichord music of the seventeenth and eighteenth centuries we find crystallized the various styles of the other instruments, it is due to the fact that while that instrument lasted, a fairly traditional way of playing persisted. Since the birth of the augmented symphonic orchestra, one hundred years or so ago, we have been listening to lukewarm instruments, some forgetful of a playing style originally belonging to them and others unaware of a playing style possible to them. They have no bite in performance. They are completely swamped under the arbitrary dictum of a conductor reading the arbitrary dictum of a composer. Such a clever, dramatic juxtaposition of instruments, as indicated by Stravinsky, seems to me no more than clever, and absolutely no more than one man can do without help from the instruments themselves. And I think, whatever his followers may be still doing, he himself is aware of this in some sort of a way and feels that he is tired of exploiting the folk tune, horizontally, vertically, atonally, seriously, or comically. I do not call intellectual messing around with the tone colors of atrophied, academic conservatory instrumentalists, composition in significant instrumental playing style. And I know, merely intellectually, one could never invent such a style. A *playing style* does not spring out of subjective interpretation or subjective composition. It springs out of primitive group feeling spreading itself deliriously, growing and feeding upon itself. Out of this feeling may or may not appear conscious, composing artists. Their appearance is, however, the beginning of the end, for from then on the group tends towards *listening,* not *participating,* and it is not long before the composer becomes one of a small class, forced to fall back on himself and his kind for nourishment. In this connection consider the most natural of instruments, the human body. In seventeenth- and eighteenth-century ballet, we know there existed a highly significant and artificial movement and posture. Now we see its complete romantic disintegration—the brief spurt of modern ballet being more of a healthy modernist criticism than actual healthy, artificial dancing. Of the old technique of ballet all we have left is disintegration; and a revolt against disintegration as intellectually manufactured as Schonberg's revolt against harmonic accord.

The shaping of melody by the instruments involved is something I feel accounts not only for the character of old European music but for the character of Jazz; and the development of the latter I have had the opportunity of observing. First, the trumpet, piercing and high pitched, dominating the whole orchestra as it could, took over the principal presentation and variations of the melody, something hitherto left to the violins. So the importance of the first violinist vanished, the first trumpeter taking his place. In a limited way the trumpeter already held this position in the military brass band, but there he was either traditional *cor de chasse, cor de bataille,* or simply playing violin or voice music relegated to the trumpet. In a Jazz orchestra he is inventing his own music and doing things previously considered impossible on such an instrument. In order to satisfy a wild desire to play higher and higher he blew harder and harder and in the process made unavoidable squawks and fouled notes. These not only surprised but delighted him, and now, though he has a trumpet technique inferior to none, he still blasts and blows foul notes in beautiful and subtle succession, and with his extraordinary manipulation of mutes gets a hushed dramatic intensity that entails harder blowing than ever before. This difficulty of performance has kept the trumpet, so far, melodically inventive in the hands of the inventors, plus a few white imitators. But lately even the great artist, Louis Armstrong, has fallen into a florid cadenza style, induced, I fear, by excess technical ease. Armstrong has always favored the "open" manner of trumpet playing and a melody of the wide, broken chord variety, seemingly impossible in range. Even when he sings he is really playing trumpet solos with his voice.

The natural playing style of the slide trombone quite obviously would be dictated by the rhythmic movement of the arm sliding back and forth, something no trombonist has been allowed to feel heretofore. The Negro trombone player has become a sort of dancer in the rhythmic play of his right arm. He makes this instrument live, by improvising solos as natural to a trombone as the simplest of folk tunes are to the voice. This cannot be said of the trombone in any other music save Jazz. However, as important as this instrument is, I find because of its low register and a certain cumbersomeness in size, that the trumpet has gone beyond it in inventiveness, even carrying further the trombone's own newly created rhythmic and melodic twists. This copying of one another's style we meet constantly, and in order not to detract from the original creative importance I wish to distribute amongst the various instruments, it is well to understand how that which one instrument creates another may incorporate to more complete advantage. In other words, many trumpets can play in trombone style but I've heard only one trombonist create trumpet melodies, and he is Joseph Nanton (Tricky Sam) of Duke Ellington's orchestra. Theirs is a lazy style, which the trumpeter has seized upon with the rhythmic instinct of his mind and transposed to the trumpet for variety's sake, but which they, having conceived, are confined to. At this stage of the game if we had to choose between trumpet and trombone we would find the trumpet more of an all around instrument.

The faculty of imitation is possessed to a high degree by the pianist and almost to the exclusion of originality. This of course has not tended to make him an important contributing factor to Jazz. The piano has been pretty generally relegated to the position of harmonic and rhythmic background and its occasional excursions into the foreground are not noticeably happy in inspiration. Owing to the conspicuous commonplaceness of our virtuosi, the Negro pianist only too easily slips into the fluid superficialities of a Liszt cadenza.* This tendency of the Negro to imitate the florid piano music of the nineteenth century which he hears all around him, has kept the piano backward in finding its own Jazz medium. It takes a very developed musical sense to improvise significantly on the piano; a talent for thinking in more than one voice. The counterpoint that Jazz instruments achieve ensemble is possible to a certain extent on the piano alone, but this takes a degree of development Jazz has not yet reached. The best piano solos so far, in my opinion, are the melodic "breaks" imitating trumpet and trombone. Lately the pianist has found some biting chords, and felt a new desire to break up melody, not only rhythmically as inspired by the drum, but rhythmically as a percussion instrument fundamentally inspired by its own peculiar harmonic percussion. This perhaps will lead him to contribute something no other musician has. Claude Hopkins is a notable example of such a pianist, but on the other hand Bix Beiderbecke (white) is doing this, and seems to have lost all sense of melody in the process. His intellect has gone ahead of his emotion, instead of keeping pace with it. That is the main trouble I find with our "hot" white orchestras. All they have they got from the Negro, and they are a little too inclined to fling back the word "corny." Until their own output proves more truly melodic or the Negro has completely succumbed to the surrounding decadence, they are still melodically "catching up" to the Negro.

The clarinet has been the instrument of very inventive players but somehow its facile technique has inspired florid rippling solos only too often. The saxophones have found their place, playing the background harmony in threes and taking the "sweet" choruses. Though I dislike the way the saxophone is generally played, it can be as "hot" as the clarinet when it is "jazzed up"; however, it is mostly used for soft, sentimental passages. The drums on occasion have qualified the playing style of the entire orchestra, as in the old washboard bands. Nobody who has heard a clarinetist used to playing in conjunction with a washboard, can have missed noticing the persistently syncopated and galloping style induced by the incessant rubadubadubadub of the washboard. Amazing things have been done with kettledrums, and

*Dodge had at this time obviously not discovered boogie-woogie piano (Editor's note, *Hound and Horn*).

any good drummer can take a "break" and off-hand crowd into it more exciting rhythms than a Modernist can concoct after the lengthiest meditation. The violin has not been favored by the hot Jazz bands although when "jazzed up" it falls in very readily with the spirit. Here again we can see the same musical result of the arm movement as in the case of the trombone, although not quite as pronounced. The style of playing, I should judge, is similar to that in vogue before the advent of the tight bow. They even get an effect of the old bow by loosening the hair and wedging the violin in between the hair and the bow and then playing all the strings of the violin at once. The remaining instruments, bass fiddle, guitar, banjo, and tuba are in very versatile hands but for the most part contribute solos in styles similar to the ones I have already discussed. They have contributed, however, a few individual elements such as the "slap" of the bass or the contrapuntal, inventive accompaniment of the guitar.

A Jazz composition is made up of the improvisations of these players, and although the arranger is coming more and more into prominence, his work is still very secondary. The arranger takes a fragmentary rhythm from an improvisation on a given melody, and applies this rhythm over and over again throughout the natural course of the melody. Maybe this rhythm is given to the three trumpets, and a counter theme given to the other musicians; but in any case it is usually musically very uninteresting and only saved by the piercing interpretation of the men in the better bands. Though most written music of Moderato Tempo or faster, from Haydn on, has had such rhythmic patterns applied throughout, the composers have been conscious of their best melodic phrases and have woven them into the piece with intellectual skill. But this being one of the last stages in folk development, the Jazz arrangers are not equal to the task and their output is very tiresome. Even if any highly inventive improvisation should be orchestrated into the score it would lose its original appeal through the self-consciousness of the reader, for the actual melodic richness is unappreciated both by the Jazz player as well as the listeners, only the robust playing style of the instrumentalist exciting their admiration.

It is a fact that the many Jazz orchestras playing under the name of a star performer or leader, mislead the public into thinking that the leader or performer creates the music. This brings up the question as to how we should rate benefactors, managers, impresarios and the like, of all large organizations promoting art, whether opera, ballet, symphony, or Jazz orchestra. The Diaghilev ballets are a good example, for these productions included not only the dancers and choreographers, painters and musicians, but Diaghilev, upon whom depended everything from the securing of backing to the choice of ballets. He managed the financing, he controlled and selected the great artists, smoothing out their differences, and he proved himself a rare man; probably more rare than any single one of the artists. But important as he was to the life of the organization, students will always pick out the important separate creators and give them their due credit, for these were the people who were the backbone of the organization and upon whom all lasting significance depends. To attribute their art significance to Diaghilev is as foolish as it would be to attribute a Beethoven symphony to any one of his benefactors. I think the Jazz orchestra is placed in about the same situation. There are players, arrangers, and a personality in every orchestra, and the leader can be anything from the best player to no practicing musician at all. He can be everything from a great personality to a shrewd businessman, and whether he is a musician or not he is always able to take the role of a master of ceremonies. He usually sets the policy of the orchestra, and is responsible for the quality of players and arrangements. Also we find the leader, more often than not, employs orchestrators. As a rule he *can* orchestrate, but because of the tiresome routine of public performance and the running of the organization, he employs, let us say, the saxophonist to do this tedious job, though since all except a few pieces are simply arrangements of passing popular tunes, any outsider does just as well. When we see the names of two composers on a piece of music, one well known and the other unknown, we can guess who did the composing. Always look for this other name before attributing the work to the well-known name. And of course on a record of this piece where the melody is entirely changed into a new vastly more important synthesis by an unknown individual in the orchestra, we see only the name of the original composer, as no musical importance is attached to these variations. In Jazz as in Ballet, the public must discover for itself who is responsible for the various works.

The four solos that follow are notated from records made by Bubber Miley. He said they were variations on a Spiritual his mother used to sing, called "Hosanna," but the Spiritual turns out to be a part of Stephen Adams' "Holy City" commencing at the seventeenth bar. There the tune is in four-four time and eight bars long, but Miley's version has but two bars taken out next to the last bar and the remaining six bars drawn out to twelve by dividing each bar into two. In the composition "Black and Tan Fantasy" this theme is announced in the minor, but his hot solos (variations) are on the original major. As he improvises these solos the orchestra simply plays a "vamp" rhythmic accompaniment. I have written them out under each other as in an orchestral score, with the theme on top, in order to facilitate intercomparison; but it must be understood that these are pure improvisations out of a folk school, with no idea of adequate notation. All of these solos are by Bubber Miley except the first twelve bars of No. 2, which is by Joseph Nanton, a trombonist in Duke Ellington's orchestra. As I have said, Negro improvisations are either on the melody or on the harmony, and it would appear that

Miley paid no attention to the melody, so far removed are his variations; but by playing certain parts of the theme, then the corresponding part in any one of the hot solos, you will find that many times he did have the theme in mind.

In No. 1, all through the first twelve bars, there is a vague resemblance to the theme. The thirteenth and fifteenth bars are exactly the same as the theme but his treatment of these bars takes the startling form of blasts. In No. 3, if we play the fifth and sixth bars of the theme, and then his corresponding variations, we again see a melodic resemblance, but it is curious how this is his first melodic attack after the four-bar hold; that is, instead of continuing with the melody, he is starting one.

In the thirteenth bar of No. 3 he wonderfully distorts the B-flat in the

theme, to an E-natural. Here is a take-off of the most extreme kind, and accordingly he followed the harmony until he could catch up with the melody. This he did at the twenty-first bar, finishing with a jazzed-up version of the theme.

A typical jazz distortion of the given melody is to lengthen the time value of one note by stealing from another, thereby sometimes reducing the melody to an organ point. Though this was practiced prior to Miley, it is interesting to see how the whole note in the first bar of the theme is held longer and longer until in No. 4 he is holding it seven bars. Notice how the improvisations do not have any break between the twelfth and thirteenth bars, that is, where the theme begins its repeat.

It seems to me the little phrases in bars eight, nine, and ten of No. 1,

where he plays with his melody at either end of the octave, can only be found elsewhere in such music as Bach's *Goldberg Variations.* For example:

Joseph Nanton's twelve-bar variation in No. 2 seems to be on the harmony. It is followed by Miley's beautiful entrance, a slow trill on the original B-flat. In No. 4, which he made for me, the little coda to the long note is the purest music I have ever heard in Jazz. I speak of purity in its resemblance to the opening of the Credo for soprano voices in Palestrina's *Missa Papae Marcelli*. You will observe that the thirteenth bars of both No. 3 and No. 4 are the same. The freedom leading up to the C in the fifteenth bar is amazing and the A-flat in the nineteenth bar, after all the agitation, is no less surprising.

There were two elements essential for this freedom of thought; harmony and rhythm. Miley told me he needed the strictest beat and at least a three-part harmony. Though the piano could give him this, he was always better, however, with the orchestra and its background of drums, etc. Whereas the academy now might be able to compose parts like this, write them down and with a little shaping make something very inventive, no folk artist could do so, as his improvising in such a manner that rhythm and melody are torn apart, really demands these two elements. We can now understand how a person like Duke Ellington was indispensable to Miley—"When I get off the Duke is always there." The Duke's cooperation, in fact, inspired Miley to the best work he ever did and neither of them sustained very well their unfortunate parting of the ways. The Duke has never since touched the heights that he and Bubber Miley reached in such records as "East St. Louis Toodle-O," "Flaming Youth," "Got Everything But You," "Yellow Dog Blues," etc., etc.—and of course the many "Black and Tan Fantasies." The sudden and tragic death of Bubber Miley put a stop to his career before he was thirty—though without the guidance of the Duke, who is a real Diaghilev in a small way, perhaps he would have slipped backward too.

In an article I wrote seven years ago entitled "Negro Jazz" I held out high hopes for the art, though at the time those critics who deigned to notice Jazz were in no undecided terms announcing its complete extinction. Since that time Jazz has not only persisted but advanced way beyond my expectations. It is only now that I have my doubts; it is the present tendencies that seem to be spelling doom in the near future. For the Negro is tired of the Blues and likes to write the popular tunes which are a sort of compromise between his former music and Tin-Pan Alley, and fairly eats up any like compromise of a white person. There are few real Blues singers left like Bessie Smith. Her inventive way of singing does not seem to have been contagious. When I hear an early record of Bessie Smith's and then listen to a Cab Calloway and see how much more the Negro now enjoys the latter, I realize that the Blues have been superseded and white decadence has once more ironed out and sweetened a vital art. At the moment, through the arrangers and the more conscious players, Jazz is in process of being crystallized into a written music, but the gulf is too great between this and what I consider good Jazz, for such a crystallization to have any significance in the future.

One would suppose that academic composers would jump at this medium, but the little that has been done in the field is of less value than those arrangements I have spoken of. With the awareness of an academic education, the composers have combined the simple side of Jazz with the complex side of modern music and the public, with a similar viewpoint towards the treatment of such music, finds it interesting. But even for them this music does not seem to wear well and probably is no more than their standard of novelty. Our composers may have the craftsmanship of Bach still sticking in their craws, but they lack even a taste of his melodic significance—it is an already embellished melody of the seventeenth and eighteenth centuries which Bach has so vitally mixed with his craftsmanship. These Moderns give us musical mathematics and acrobatics applied to any and every folk tune, but their work lacks as true a line of melody as we might find in the most obscure trombone solo. As I am in complete accord with other Moderns who theoretically object to using Jazz, it must be understood that I am not urging composers to *use* it in the same sense that Dvorak *used* folk tunes. What I propose for consideration is, that as this whole period is permeated with Jazz, it cannot be such a precious or out-of-the-way attitude to become *part of it*. Though a fine Modern-Jazz music may still be written, frankly, the best I think we can hope for is that this eating decadence of Jazz be a slow process, and that in the meantime the Negro will crystallize more of his work on records, such work as Duke Ellington and Bubber Miley turned out in the old days.

Of the many American writings on Jazz, both pro and con, few are knowledgeably critical, none of any instructive value. There are magazines and articles in Europe with an attitude towards Jazz as serious music that we haven't approached. And there is Prunières, the one important critic, to my knowledge, who has an appreciation of the improvised solo in Jazz. The American criticisms on the subject seem confusedly to hover around on the one hand, the spirit of America, the brave tempo of modern life, absence of sentimentalism, the importance of syncopation and the good old Virginia cornfields; and on the other hand, the monotonous beat, the unmusical noises, the jaded Harlem Negro, alcoholism and sexual debauch. These solos in the "Black and Tan Fantasy" may not have the significance I attribute to them but they could at least be a premise for criticism. As notated music it certainly is not just noise, squawks, and monotonous rhythm: nor do vague favorable praises seem appropriate. Such solos as I have printed, demand musical investigation.

CONCLUSIONS

WINTHROP SARGEANT

The crotchety Winthrop Sargeant was The New Yorker*'s critic of both classical music and jazz for many years, and his book* Jazz, Hot and Hybrid *was both startling and influential when it appeared in 1946. In the concluding chapter he tried to anatomize the relationship between his two fields of expertise—neither the first nor the last critic to attempt this difficult (impossible?) task.*

Sometime ago in a speech the late James Weldon Johnson remarked sardonically that where music and dancing are concerned, Americans are always "doing their best to pass for colored." The presence of African idioms in the bulk of our popular music, the instinctive manner in which even the White American musician turns to jazz improvisation, the spontaneous response of the average American to jazz as something that "speaks his own language," something that "feels" even more akin to him than the prim songs of his European forebears—these things all hint at profound ethnological questions that the present writer is scarcely qualified to tackle.

It is obvious, nevertheless, that jazz does respond in several ways to what is loosely spoken of as the "American psychology"; that while its ancestry may be African and European, it is none the less a peculiarly American form of musical expression. The spontaneous, improvisatory aspect of jazz is remarkably adapted to the musical needs of a pragmatic, pioneering people. Like the typical American, the jazz musician goes his own syncopated way, making instantaneous and novel adjustments to problems as they present themselves. He is an individualist. He prefers making his own kind of music to interpreting the compositions of sanctified masters. He is little concerned with precedent and is inclined to respect what "works" rather than what is laid down in theory books. The discipline of tradition "cramps his style." He cannot abide the idea of foregone conclusions: an art form that demands a beginning, a middle, and an inevitable end is alien to his psychology. His greatest "kick" is gotten out of feverish activity; his goal is usually somewhat indefinite.

It is not surprising that a society that has evolved the skyscraper, the baseball game, and the "happy ending" movie, should find its most characteristic musical expression in an art like jazz. Contrast a skyscraper with a Greek temple or a medieval cathedral. Where each of the latter gives forth a sense of repose, of acceptance, of catharsis, the skyscraper thrusts unrestrainedly upward. Its height is not limited by considerations of form—but by the momentary limits of practical engineering. Where the Greek temple and the cathedral are built for permanence, the skyscraper is soon torn down and replaced by taller and better skyscrapers. The individual skyscraper is merely a tentative makeshift. Another generation will probably relegate it to the junk heap, a fact of which its designers and builders are fully aware. Like the jazz "composition" it is an impermanent link in a continuous process. And, like jazz, the skyscraper lacks the restraint and poise of the classical tradition. The skyscraper has a beginning (i.e., a foundation) and perhaps a middle, but its end is an indefinite upward thrust. A jazz performance ends, not because of the demands of musical logic, but because the performers or listeners are tired, or wish to turn to something else for a change. It lacks entirely the element of dramatic climax. As far as form is concerned it might end equally well at the finish of almost any of its eight-bar phrases. A skyscraper ends its upward thrust in a somewhat analogous way. It might be stopped at almost any point in its towering series of floors. It must, of course, stop somewhere. But the stop is not made primarily for reasons of proportion. Nor does it carry that sense of inevitableness that attaches to the height of the Greek temple. It stops simply because its builders didn't have money enough, or energy enough to make it still higher, or because the practicalities of big city life made greater height inadvisable.

The same analogy can be carried over into the field of popular drama where the American preference for "happy endings" is found in more than nine out of ten movies and radio scripts. What is the "happy ending"? A kiss, a vague promise of future joy—in other words, no ending at all. The typical American does not like endings. He is an incurable progressive. He does not like to bother his head thinking about doom and destiny. There is something about inevitability that runs contrary to his conception of life. And because of this his most characteristic arts—the comic strip, the skyscraper, journalism, jazz, the tap dance, the "happy ending" movie—all lack the element of "form" that is so essential to tragedy, to the symphony, to the novel, to the opera, to monumental architecture and even to some of the less pretentious arts of other nations. These remarks are not made in any spirit of belittlement toward what are, after all, America's popular "lowbrow" arts. The lowbrow arts of other lands are often less interesting and less vital than America's. The point is that America's lowbrow arts seem to be her most characteristic ones. Her novels, symphonies, plays, and churches are all more or less closely related to European prototypes. Her popular art is not.

The difference between a jazz performance and a classical "composition" is not only a difference in musical substance. It reflects a difference in national psychology. The European "composition" is a complex structure of organized sound, fixed more or less immutably as to form. It perpetuates the message of a creative mind through generations, even centuries. The understanding of this message presupposes a tradition—a guarantee that men will, to some extent, think and feel alike from generation to generation. The form in which this message is cast is subject to a process of intellectual development. Its composers themselves are highly trained professionals, the greatest of them capable of extraordinary feats of technique which average people marvel at but can scarcely hope to duplicate.

Jazz lacks these conditions and attributes. It relies on suspense, on sudden adjustments to the unexpected, for its essential vitality. The best of it is created impulsively, and is forgotten almost instantly afterward. Its tradition is not a carefully guarded intellectual heritage, but a simple matter of musical instinct. From its listeners, jazz invites not contemplation or applause, but participation. It is a "get together" art for "regular fellows," a breaker down of social and psychological barriers, an expression not of aristocratic craftsmanship but of mass good fellowship.

A great deal of recent writing about jazz has assumed for it the status of a fine art. The eloquent defenders of *"le jazz hot"* have held jazz concerts in the most impressively conservative American concert halls, and have discussed these concerts in lofty critical language. They have written books and published magazines dealing solemnly with the aesthetics of jazz and the artistry of the popular virtuosos who play it. They have even argued that the great musical issue of the day is that of jazzism vs. "classicism," that jazz is in some way the American successor to the venerable art of concert music, its tunesmiths and improvising virtuosos the latter-day equivalents of so many Beethovens and Wagners. Bach, after all, used to improvise too.

The enormous popularity of jazz, coupled with the prevailing decadence of concert and operatic music, has given this view a superficial appearance of weight. Considered merely as a social phenomenon jazz leaves its unfriendly critics in the position of King Canute. You can't ignore an art that makes up seventy percent of the musical diet of a whole nation, even if its primitive thumps and wails fail to fit the aesthetic categories of refined music criticism. Jazz has often been innocently described as a "folk music." And, considered purely as music, it is one. But its powers over the common man's psyche are not even vaguely suggested by that term. No other folk music in the world's history has ever induced among normal people such curious psychopathic aberrations as the desire to wear a zoot suit, smoke hashish, or jabber cryptic phrases of "jive" language. None, probably, has ever produced waves of mass hysteria among adolescents like those recently associated with the swing craze. Nor has any folk music ever before constituted the mainstay of half a dozen nationwide publishing, recording, broadcasting, and distributing industries.

Yet when you try to approach jazz from a critical point of view, you are immediately struck by a curious split which divides almost every aspect of jazz from any real correspondence with so-called "classical" music. For all the attempts of Paul Whiteman, Benny Goodman and others to bridge the gap, it still remains generally true that jazz players can't play "classical," and that "classical" players can't play jazz. Not one jazz *aficionado* in a thousand has any interest in "classical" music, and very few serious concertgoers feel anything more cordial than mild irritation when they listen to jazz. Attempted mixtures of the two idioms invariably act like oil and water. Jazzed classics and symphonies with jazz themes have a tendency to ruffle tempers in both camps. Even the impartial critic is at a loss for any similar scale of standards in the two arts. Though many a jazz aesthete has tried to, you can't compare a Louis Armstrong solo to a Josef Szigeti sonata performance, or a Bessie Smith blues to an aria from *Rigoletto.* There isn't any common ground.

The disregard of this distinction among jazz critics has led to some curious concert ventures and to a vast amount of amazing aesthetic double-talk. Jazz concerts in Carnegie Hall and the Metropolitan Opera House have been hailed as cultural milestones when, in fact, they only proved that jazz can be played in uncongenial surroundings especially designed for the wholly different requirements of *Traviata* or the New York Philharmonic—if that needed proving. Ever since the pundit Hugues Panassié discovered *le jazz hot* in a French chateau full of phonograph records, the world of intellectual jazz addicts has been calling a spade a *cuiller à caviar.* The ebullient, hit-or-miss ensemble of a New Orleans stomp is reverently described as "counterpoint"; the jazz trumpeter's exuberant and raucous lapses from true pitch are mysteriously referred to as "quarter tones" or "atonality." Jazz, as an art with a capital A, has become something to be listened to with a rapt air that would shame the audiences of the Budapest Quartet. To dance to it (which is just what its primitive Negro originators would do) becomes a profanation.

Highbrow composers have also tried bridging the gap. The idea that an amalgamation of jazz with such traditional forms as the sonata or the symphony might result in an American style of concert music is too attractive to be ignored. American composers have repeatedly written jazz symphonies, jazz concertos, and jazz fugues. But they usually discard the idea after a few experiments, and they never succeed in using jazz as anything but a superficial ornamental embellishment, as they might, say, use a Balinese or Algerian tune for local color. Their so-called jazz composition is not jazz at all—as any jitterbug can tell from the first note. Its rigid highbrow musical structure prohibits the very type of improvisation that makes jazz fun to listen to. It remains a "classical" composition with jazz-style trimmings, something about as American and about as homogeneous as a Greek temple with a shingle roof. The outstanding exception to this rule is probably Gershwin's mildly jazzy opera *Porgy and Bess,* which came close to artistic success. But Gershwin's opera is saved, as far as the appropriateness of its music is concerned, mainly because it is a folk opera with a Negro setting. It is, in other words, a highly specialized type of opera, if, indeed, it can properly be considered an opera at all. The use of the same idiom in connection with the generality of operatic drama would be unthinkable.

Why does this peculiar split exist? The answer, I think, will be found by clearing away the pseudo-classical verbiage of the jazz critic and looking at the aesthetic nature of jazz itself. Jazz, for all the enthusiasms of its intellectual *aficionados,* is not music in the sense that an opera or a symphony is music. It is a variety of folk music. And the distinction between folk music and art music is profound and nearly absolute. The former grows like a weed or a wildflower, exhibits no intellectual complexities, makes a simple, direct emotional appeal that may be felt by people who are not even remotely interested in music as an art. It is often beautiful to listen to, whether it is jazz, or Irish or Welsh ballad singing, or Spanish *flamenco* guitar playing, or New England sea chanties, or Venetian gondolier songs. But it is not subject to intellectual criticism, for it lacks the main element toward which such criticism would be directed: the creative ingenuity and technique of an unusual, trained musical mind.

Art music, on the other hand, is an art as complicated as architecture. It begins where folk music leaves off, in the conscious creation of musical edifices that bear the stamp, in style and technique, of an individual artist. Its traditions—the rules of its game—are complicated and ingenious. They are the result of centuries of civilized musical thinking by highly trained musicians for audiences that are capable of judging the finer points of such thought. Art music is no field of wildflowers. It is a hothouse of carefully bred and cultivated masterpieces, each one the fruit of unusual talent and great technical resourcefulness. You may prefer the open fields of folk music to the classical hothouse. That is your privilege. But if so, you are simply not interested in music as a fine art. And it is no use getting snobbish about your preference and pretending that your favorite musical wildflower is a masterpiece of gardening skill. It isn't.

Thus, the remarks "I prefer early Chicago-style jive to *Tristan and Isolde,*" or "I prefer Kirsten Flagstad to Ethel Waters" are not really critical or evaluative statements. They are like the saying "I prefer percherons to race horses"—an understandable preference, but one that would be meaningless to a racing enthusiast. "But after all, hasn't jazz got melody, rhythm, and harmony, and aren't these attributes of concert music?" Of course. But the uses to which these materials are put differ greatly in the two arts. Jazz harmony . . . is restricted to four or five monotonous patterns which support the florid improvisations of the soloist like a standardized scaffolding. These patterns never differ, never make any demands on creative ingenuity. Virtually every blues, and every piece of boogie-woogie pianism, uses precisely the same harmony as every other blues or boogie woogie piece. Rhythmically, jazz is somewhat more ingenious, but not much more varied. It is limited to four-four or two-four time, and its most interesting effects are the result of blind instinct rather than thought.

Melodically, jazz is often strikingly beautiful and original. But jazz melody, like all folk melody, is of the amoebic rather than the highly organized type. Jazz melody, unlike most highbrow melody, consists of tunes rather than themes. These tunes are as simple and self-contained as one-cell animals. They can be repeated, sometimes with embellishments and variations, but they are incapable of being formed into higher musical organisms. Cell for cell, or melody for melody, they often compare favorably with the themes of highbrow music. The melody of Bessie Smith's "Cold in Hand Blues," for example, is a much more beautiful tune than the "V for Victory" theme of Beethoven's Fifth Symphony. But when you have played it, that is all there is—a beautiful, self-sufficient amoeba. Beethoven's crusty little motif is a cell of a different sort, almost without significance by itself, but capable of being reproduced into a vast symphonic organism with dramatic climaxes and long-range emotional tensions.

The jazz artist, like all folk musicians, creates his one-cell melodies by instinct and repeats them over and over again, perhaps with simple variations. The composer of art music, on the other hand, is interested in one-cell melodies only as raw material. His creative mind begins where the instinct of the folk musician leaves off, in building such material into highly organized forms like symphonies and fugues. It is the technique and ingenuity with which he accomplishes this job that is the main subject of music criticism, as it applies to composition. And this is why music criticism is apt to sound pompous and miss its mark when it is applied to the creative side of a folk art like jazz. There is, to be sure, a large amount of concert music and of opera that is related to folk-music sources, and that sometimes scarcely rises above the folk-music level. Chopin waltzes, Brahms Hungarian dances, Tchaikovsky ballet tunes, Grieg songs, old-fashioned Italian operatic arias, and so on, sometimes fall under this heading. But the sophisticated music world has long thought of these items as belonging to a special, "semi-popular" category. They are not the backbone of symphonic or operatic art. And they are seldom the subject of serious music criticism.

One of the most striking features of jazz as compared with art music is its lack of evolutionary development. Aside from a few minor changes of fashion, its history shows no technical evolution whatever. The formulas of the jazz musical language that we have analyzed were nearly all used in the earliest of jazz and still constitute, with minor modifications, the basis of jazz technique. Occasionally, as in the piano rag, these formulas have taken on a special character due to the popularity of certain instruments or combinations of instruments. But the formulas themselves have remained constant. Jazz today remains essentially the same kind of music it was in 1900. Its simple forms—the blues, the eight-bar barbershop phrases—have been characteristic of it from the very beginning. This lack of evolution, which is an attribute of all folk music, is another of the main differences between jazz and concert music. The history of the latter shows a continuous development of structural methods. Few important highbrow composers have left the technique of music where they found it.

Considered as performance, jazz has more impressive claims to critical attention. Its virtuoso performers are often gifted with extraordinary technique of a sort, and are nearly always differentiated by interesting individualities of style. Jazz performance has its own type of excitement. But it is a totally different type of excitement from what one feels when listening to a performance of concert music. In the concert hall or opera house, music is not only an art but a kind of game. The soprano singing the most hackneyed coloratura aria (or the conductor leading the profoundest symphony) sets about overcoming certain prearranged obstacles of which the audience is aware. There is a special exhilaration (more or less independent of purely musical pleasure) in noting the ease with which the soprano hits her high notes, or the suavity and polish with which she turns her melodic phrases. It is like watching a crack shot on a complicated target range, making an extraordinary number of bull's-eyes. This particular exhilaration is completely lacking in jazz. There are no obstacles, no precise tests of technical mastery. Inspired by his mood, the improvising jazz player may launch into quite remarkable feats of virtuosity. But the virtuosity all appears on the spur of the moment, some of it the result of sudden emotion, some even the result of accident. Since he is improvising, one is never quite sure what the player set out to do in the first place. One doesn't know which target he is shooting at.

The much-discussed element of improvisation, too, has been greatly overrated in recent writing about jazz. A false impression has been given that the jazz artist, when he is "in the groove," creates an entirely new musical composition extemporaneously. Actually this is never the case. Only a small portion of the jazz heard today is improvised. And even in that small portion improvisation affects only a few elements of rhythm and melody. The two most intellectually complex features of music—harmony and form—are never improvised even in so-called improvised jazz. They conform in every case to well-worn standard patterns.

Perhaps the most artistically significant peculiarity of jazz as opposed to "classical" music, however, is the extremely limited nature of its emotional vocabulary. As a musical language, jazz is graphic and colorful, but in poetic resources it is about as rich as pidgin English. A great deal of it appeals exclusively to the motor impulses without affecting the emotions at all. When it does affect the emotions, it is limited to the expression of a few elementary moods—sexual excitement, exhilaration, sorrow (in the blues), and a sort of hypnotic intoxication. Its vocabulary does not encompass religious awe, tragedy, romantic nostalgia, metaphysical contemplation, grandeur, wonder, patriotic or humanitarian fervor—all of them more or less stock-in-trade emotions conveyed or embellished by highbrow symphonic or operatic music. A jazz finale to Beethoven's Ninth Symphony, a jazz *Funeral March* in *Götterdämmerung* or a jazz *Pélleas et Mélisande* would impose considerable strain on the expressive powers of jazz, not to speak of the artistic sensibilities of the listener.

These comparisons between jazz and the traditional art of the concert hall and opera house may strike the musically sophisticated reader as being somewhat obvious. But the confusion they attempt to clarify has befogged a tremendous amount of contemporary journalism. The more you analyze the aesthetic peculiarities of jazz the more you realize that it is completely unlike any other type of music that has ever existed. Musically, it is really something new under the sun. Its perennial growth from shantytown and the canebrakes to Hollywood and the music factories of the industrial era is something peculiar, apparently, to the kind of civilization we live in. It seems to sprout in cycles. Every twenty years or so the American intelligentsia discovers the primitive music of the American Negro, gives some manifestation of it a new name (ragtime, jazz, hot jazz, swing) and begins hurling gauntlets and breaking lances in its defense. As a rule, the type or facet of jazz that causes this flurry is soon absorbed into the main body of commonplace, commercial popular music and is imitated and repeated until the intelligentsia itself gets tired of it. Then, a few years later, some aesthete comes across the obscure wellspring of jazz again, calls attention to it, and the process is repeated. The cycle is usually the same. It begins with the discovery that the obscure, uneducated Negro is playing a wonderfully engaging type of music. It passes from discovery to exploitation. The musical

Negro is written about, moved from his humble surroundings into the limelight, made into a self-conscious artist, paid homage and given, if he is lucky, something in the way of commercial success. With success comes wholesale imitation by the popular music business, which always knows a good thing when it sees it. The Negro's music becomes a national fad. But this commercialization always seems to end by cheapening and standardizing the product, and by killing the fresh, exuberant quality that the Negro originally gave it. The cycle closes in decadence and atrophy. The Negro, like as not, goes back to working in a garage or a cotton field, and the commercial music business goes on manufacturing the sort of pseudo-Negroid music that "sells" to the uncritical mass of American listeners.

If this cycle proves anything, it is that folk music is still created by a "folk"—that is, by a humble, uneducated group of peasant-like people who have been denied access to the benefits of modern civilization. It can be lifted out of its folk *milieu* and exploited commercially. But in the process it takes on a mass-production finish and loses the hand-hewn quality that gave it its original charm. It ceases to be a folk music, properly speaking, and becomes a "popular" music instead. This distinction between folk and "popular" music would have been incomprehensible to the peoples of Europe a century ago. "Popular" music is a distinctly democratic, and pretty distinctly an American, phenomenon. The age-old European class distinctions entailed a more or less permanent proletariat, or peasant class. Folk music was the music of the peasants. Art music was for the upper classes. Democracy has somehow changed this picture. It has brought about the new category of "popular" music. Popular music is mass-produced music, created, like bathtubs, automobiles or Grand Rapids furniture, to fill the needs of the average bourgeois American. Like most of the things created to fill this need, it is efficient, standardized, sometimes inspired, but usually lacking in individuality and artistic distinction. It usually gets its artistic coloring, as does most Grand Rapids furniture, by nostalgically imitating various established styles. This imitation often takes a nationalistic turn. Popular music imitates primitive Negro jazz, for example, very much as popular furniture imitates American "antiques," and with much the same result. The original primitive music of the American Negro, however, is not an antiquarian style. It is still with us. And it is so largely because the Negro, in America, still occupies the position of a small, peasant proletariat, in the old European sense. This peasant proletariat happens to have astonishing musical gifts, and, being a peasant proletariat, it is incessantly creating a true, modern folk music. We have other small regional proletariats—Tennessee hillbillies and Southwestern cowhands, for example. All of them create folk music. But it happens that the Negro is the largest and most sharply defined of all these groups.

The type of music he creates is directly related to his position in American society.

The folk dialect of jazz, like any verbal dialect, was developed originally by people who were isolated from standardized education. One of its most important ingredients has been the rather colorful awkwardness—the lack of technical polish—with which it has been played. What the jazz aesthete admires in early Chicago jazz is something analogous to the naïveté of primitive painting. And this naïveté, when genuine, is the fruit of ignorance. No amount of "blackface" imitation by sophisticated musicians can really reproduce it. Jazz appeared in the first place because the poor Southern Negro couldn't get a regular musical education, and decided to make his own homemade kind of music without it. As his lot improves, and with it his facilities for musical education, he may well be attracted by both the greater slickness of American "popular" music, and the greater technical and emotional scope of "classical" music. The Negro, after all, has already proved that he can sing opera as well as blues, and compose symphonies as well as boogie woogie. It is not at all unlikely that the education of the mass of American Negroes will sound the death knell of the type of primitive jazz that the aesthetes most admire.

In spite of pure aesthetic thinking, art has a way of fitting itself to the needs of society, and society is changing pretty rapidly. Three hundred years ago, most important highbrow music (aside from the opera) was performed in churches, and the dominant forms of highbrow music were the mass and the sacred oratorio. When the concert hall supplanted the church as a place to listen to music, new forms—the symphony, the sonata, and the concerto—were evolved to fill the new need. Today the future of the concert hall is in doubt. The radio and the phonograph have enormously changed the way in which the majority of people listen to music. The day of the symphony may possibly be drawing to a close, and new forms better suited to broadcasting and recording may now be in process of evolution. Already the flexible idiom of jazz has found a strong foothold in the technologically changed situation. The phonograph has made possible for the first time the preservation of composerless music. Improvisation may now be recorded in wax just as permanently as deliberately composed music was ever recorded in printed notes. Hot jazz, the composerless art, has flourished under the new dispensation.

Jazz, as I have tried to point out earlier in this chapter, has not proved itself an art of sufficient poetic or intellectual scope to take the place in civilized society occupied by the great art of concert and operatic music. But in both its "folk" and its "popular" forms, it is an art to be reckoned with. It has the quality of vitality that characterizes music designed to fill a real and thirsty demand. It has more of this vitality than a great deal of contemporary highbrow music has. Even the popular tunes of such commercial tunesmiths as Irving Berlin and Vincent Youmans convey human emotion; not as profoundly, perhaps, as Beethoven did, but clearly and understandably nevertheless. At a time when most highbrow symphonists seem conspicuously unable to convey this sort of emotion with any freshness or originality, jazz has shown a remarkable capacity for ingratiating itself with a widening musical public. Humanity will no more do without music than it will do without speech. The musical talent that produced jazz is not likely to die out. Perhaps it will someday express itself in a great art of American music. Meanwhile jazz, as a rip-snorting stimulant to the social life of a restless, energetic people, need offer no apologies. It is rapidly becoming the world's most universally welcomed popular art form. And there can be no doubt that the world is the richer for it.

Has Jazz Influenced the Symphony?

Gene Krupa and Leonard Bernstein

In Esquire's 1947 Jazz Book *appeared this unlikely but pointed exchange between the famous drummer and the not yet famous conductor—not yet famous as a conductor, anyway. The two prodigies, of course, are gnawing at the same old bone—the relationship between jazz and classical.*

Emphatically No! Says Gene Krupa

Gene Krupa lives in Yonkers in a handsome house he designed himself. From the time charming Mrs. Ethel Krupa meets you at the door until you leave, you'll hear music at the Krupas'. But, surprisingly, it is all symphonic music. Every hour or so, Robert, the Krupa butler, puts another stack of albums into the Capehart—albums of music by Delius, Ravel, Milhaud, Stravinsky, Debussy, by Gene's friend, Leonard Bernstein, and by other classical composers. In a half a dozen visits to Gene's house your editor has yet to hear jazz there.

A discussion between Gene and David Broekman, the symphonic conductor, at the 400 Club where the Krupa orchestra was currently playing, prompted the debate on these pages. George Carhart, for many years Gene's close friend, and incidentally, the man who first brought Dave Tough and Bud Freeman to Europe, talked to Gene in a series of interviews at Columbia record dates, and backstage at the Capitol Theatre in New York. Gene's opinions were reverently transcribed and submitted to him for approval. The result is this article which Gene feels explains his point of view.

Plans for his concerto for swing band and philharmonic orchestra are moving forward rapidly as we go to press. It is expected that the work will be completed early in 1947. Later in the year he will have a chance to prove his findings in the music laboratory called Carnegie Hall.

My good friend Leonard Bernstein says that symphonic music, "serious" music written for performance by the full orchestra, has been influenced by jazz. The jazz influence is said by some critics to be especially apparent in Leonard Bernstein's own compositions.

I disagree. I have never heard anything genuinely and honestly derivative of jazz in any such music, even, maybe especially, in such works as Igor Stravinsky's Ebony Suite, which Woody Herman, with his usual swing instrumentation, brilliantly performed last season in Carnegie Hall and several other places. I've never heard it in a single one of the "serious" pieces of George Gershwin, who, anybody will tell you, was preeminently "the American jazz composer."

But, then, I've never heard it, as has John Hammond, in the works of Darius Milhaud, for all that during his American visit in the early thirties, Milhaud listened, entranced, to the unsurpassable jazz virtuosity at the hot piano of such great artists as Fats Waller, Earl Hines, and Jimmy Johnson. I watched Maurice Ravel, at the old Sunset in Chicago, marvel at Jimmy Noone's transcendent clarinet—an instrument which seems to have a special meaning for the French. Jimmy could fly over a clarinet like no one before him or since—ask Benny Goodman—and it was undoubtedly Noone's technical virtuosity, not the music itself, which obsessed Maurice Ravel. For all his preoccupation with rhythm, I've never heard the least echo of that music, or any music like it, in his compositions.

Leonard Bernstein and others profess to hear traces, echoes, derivations of jazz in Frederick Delius, John Alden Carpenter, Manuel De Falla, Honegger, Prokofiev, even Shostakovitch.

The influence of jazz has been found by someone or other, unnecessarily eager to make out a case for jazz that it doesn't need, anxious perhaps to endow it with reflected "respectability" so that he won't need to make excuses to himself and others for liking it, in the works of every one of these composers. But, in my opinion, it isn't there.

Let's pay a little more attention to two of the composers mentioned earlier, Stravinsky and Gershwin. They are reputed to show the most jazz influence. The contention might well stand or fall with them.

Stravinsky did evince preoccupation with jazz music. He talked about it. He wrote a series of compositions with titles referring to "ragtime," but no evidence of that preoccupation appears in the actual music, honestly examined, honestly listened to. That preoccupation was purely verbal. Although apparently able to sense, to feel, the jazz tempo, he has been unable to express it. For all his tremendous musical vitality, that vitality did not encompass the peculiar rhythmic, driving, let us say American quality which is the essence of jazz.

Nor is that essence to be found in the more pretentious work of George Gershwin. It exists in the blues feeling of some of his popular songs, particularly when played in the authentic jazz spirit by authentic jazz instrumentalists. But it does not exist in his Concerto in F—even if in some passages he did use derbies to mute the trumpets.

His "Rhapsody in Blue," which too often has been labeled "The Jazz Symphony" is much more—as is Gershwin's serious work as a whole—in the tradition of Claude Debussy. And I don't believe the opening of *L'Après-midi d'un faune* is reminiscent of Jimmy Noone's clarinet work.

Does this mean that I believe that jazz can never and will never form part of the mainstream of America's and of the world's music? To say it can't is to say that America, out of itself, has nothing to contribute musically to the world. Jazz is the United States' own native, original musical idiom.

Jazz can be the basis of great music to be written by an American composer just as much as, say, Czech folk tunes were the basis of the music of Smetana and Dvořák.

But jazz can only make its proper contribution to the whole of music, will only make that contribution when both its composition and performance of the music which is developing out of it, are executed by musicians who are completely at home in the idiom. Music must be both conceived and performed. It must be both composed and played.

And jazz cannot be approached from outside. It cannot be approached synthetically and artificially Above all, it cannot be approached unsympathetically.

Too many "good," "pure," and "serious" musicians, and let's admit that, composing and playing in the idiom to which they are accustomed, are *good* musicians—approach the native American idiom, the jazz idiom, with intolerance, even with condescension. They stoop, but not to conquer. And so, they almost invariably make an unholy mess of their attempts. Then, of course, they sneer at jazz. They tell anyone who will listen that the stuff wasn't music in the first place, but naturally. However, the failure was with them, and all the name calling in the world cannot disguise that fact.

Are there in existence musicians who can compose and, equally important, play this music? A generation ago my answer would have had to be no. The traditional "great men" of jazz, Johnnie Dodds and Frank Teschemaker on the clarinet, Joe Oliver, Louis Armstrong and others on the trumpet, Earl Hines and James P. Johnson, Jesse Stacy and Fats Waller at the piano, Chick Webb and Baby Dodds at percussion, were not such, even if it is almost blasphemy to say so. It wasn't their fault. They were great musicians in spite of it. But they came up the hard way. They played for dough, played professionally, most of them, while they were still in short pants. They never had the chance to get highly technical classical training. And, essentially, they were performers, virtuosos, not creators. At most, they were improvisers. They achieved a certain measure of greatness in performance because they'd never been told that this or that was "impossible." They achieved, through very lack of classical training, effects which transcended themselves and their instruments. Don't misunderstand me. I'm not questioning their inherent musicianship. Louis Armstrong, "Satchmo," one of the very greatest of jazz trumpeters, could stand up in front of the New York Philharmonic and improvise a brilliant contrapuntal concerto flawless in color and tone against anything they might play.

But the great jazz masters didn't and don't have what musicians must have to achieve the kind of music we hope to achieve in America—musical discipline and a comprehensive musical background. They were locked within their limitations, and they were utterly unable to understand anything beyond the one segment of music which they *were,* the music they sensed rather than knew. They could only play what they *felt* inside themselves. Consequently, the music they played, as *they* played it, was limited by their own limitations.

Most jazzmen, at any rate a lot of them, were never at ease with musical notation. If they attempted to *learn* something musical, some passage, some effect, they sweated it out in rehearsal. Their music, and I must repeat again, as *they* played it, was caged in, locked in. It couldn't go much beyond its start. Within their own field, they showed genius, but the field was narrow and specialized.

But those limitations are not, I must emphasize again, inherent in jazz, natural to the idiom itself. Once the fetters are removed, America's own musical idiom is capable of limitless development.

A trumpet player in my band today is a case in point. I refer to young Red Rodney. Red was brought up in a musical family, his father being a famous symphony musician. Naturally, Red's first training and influence were thoroughly classical. But Red's musical interest these days is all jazz. (As I write these lines the young man is in the middle of a Dizzy Gillespie period. Nevertheless, he has a powerful degree of respect for Bobby Hackett. Beiderbecke to him right now is just a three-syllable name.) Perhaps Red is typical of today's young musicians who may soon be able to bridge the gap between jazz band and symphony.

Let me pass along a word, with great respect, to Mr. Stokowski and Mr. Koussevitzky and their august brethren:

> Gentlemen, if you should sometime in the future schedule for performance a work based on jazz, containing jazz passages, when such music is written, don't entrust its execution entirely to the regular members of your organizations. They are highly competent musicians—but this is not for them.
>
> The most skilled Cordon Bleu would look silly beside a Rhode Island cook at a shore dinner, or a Texas ranch-hand at a barbecue.

American music, jazz music, must be played by men who were brought up to drink rye and Coke in juke joints. A lifetime of blond beer in Munich or Torino Vermouth isn't quite the same thing.

So, when you present American music, music growing out of jazz, make sure it is played by American musicians brought up in its tradition.

There are such musicians, men who feel jazz and who are the musical equals otherwise of the regular members of your orchestras. There weren't a generation ago. But there are now.

Try them.

That's the only way, Maestros, you will ever find out what American music has to offer you and to offer the world.

Some of the top men today, and a great many more of the musicians coming up, have the greatness of jazz's legendary figures. They were brought up in the idiom, they feel it, it's part of them and they are part of it, just as much as in the cases of Teschemaker and Dodds and Beiderbecke and the rest of them.

They have the same greatness, and even though it sounds somehow irreverent to write it down, they have a lot more. Sentiment aside, they have a whole lot more. They have all the background, the knowledge, the education and training their predecessors lacked. In them, the idiom, the jazz technique, the native music of America, enters into the mainstream of music. These musicians are part of jazz. They are also part of the world's musical tradition.

They are the ones who will write and play the new music, the American music that has its roots in and flows from jazz, flows from the trumpets of Bix Beiderbecke and Louis Armstrong and the piano fingers of James P. Johnson, from Eddie Condon's guitar and from Pee Wee Russell's clarinet.

What will the American music developed out of the jazz idiom be like? I don't pretend to know what Bix's answer might have been, had he lived. But I have, for what it's worth, an answer of my own.

Top priority on my time is now being given to a musical experiment, an experiment in composition, the result of which I hope you'll hear sometime in 1947.

It will be a composition, in concerto form, written for my swing band, with the usual brass, rhythm and reed sections, and for a seventy-man symphony orchestra. The melodic contrapuntal line, the hot solos and jazz rhythms, will be played by musicians who know how to play them. The broad masses of harmony, the swelling legatos, will be played by musicians, the symphony musicians who know how to play them. In its present outlined form my tentative concerto for "swing band and symphony" has three movements. First is a moderate tempo blues. Second is the drag, the tragic slow blues. And last is a frenzied, wild boogie. It will take, as I plan it now, about twenty-five minutes to play.

Even if my particular experiment is not too successful, it will represent what I think will be the coming American music. And it is the kind of music I want to hear. I want to hear a jazz solo weaving its intricate, dynamic melodic line across the powerful harmonies of a full symphony orchestra. I want to hear a quartet or trio of horns improvising against the background of fifty violins. That's when the symphony will meet jazz as far as I'm concerned.

Positively Yes! Says Leonard Bernstein

Leonard Bernstein lives in a penthouse on eastside New York City. Still a bachelor, Leonard is perhaps the hardest working of all contemporary composers. His days, and many of his nights as well, are full of studying, composing, writing. But when it's time to relax, Leonard shares the interest of his close friend, symphony composer David Diamond, in le jazz hot. *Parties in the Bernstein apartment seem to be accompanied exclusively by music from a long procession of favorite jazz records. You hear band music by Leonard's friend, Gene Krupa. You hear songs by Billie Holiday, piano playing by Teddy Wilson and Bix Beiderbecke. And you hear Commodore classics by Bud Freeman, Pee Wee Russell, Max Kaminsky, Gene Schroeder, George Wettling, Dave Tough, and Bernstein's fellow conductor, Eddie Condon, who seems to be present at most Bernstein taffy pulls. When the evening gets late, Leonard is apt to turn off his record player and sit down at the keyboard to play his conception of boogie woogie and the blues.*

This season he will conduct the New York City Symphony in a series of twenty concerts. Especially selected by the conductor to head the bass section was Jack Lesberg, the Dorchester, Massachusetts, bass player featured in Eddie Condon's jazz band.

THERE IS NOTHING more provocative and challenging than participating in a debate when one is convinced that both sides are wrong. In this spirit I heartily submit the thesis that serious music in America would today have a different complexion and a different direction were it not for the profound influence upon it of jazz.

When I say that both sides are wrong, I am maintaining that those who separate serious music from the influence of jazz are either ignoring profound musical trends, or else have an axe to grind, and should take the matter up with Aldous Huxley; and that those, on the other hand, who point with pride to the "jazzy" works of Stravinsky, Milhaud, and Walter Piston have mistaken "influence" for "fad," and should talk it over rather carefully with Humphrey Bogart.

I am not sure whether it is permissible to be didactic in an *Esquire* jazz book, but I shall have to risk a little preliminary historical information in order to make the point clear. Actually, if I am supposed to be representing the voice of serious music against that of jazz, I must confess an unfair advantage. Having started out with a Beethoven sonata in one hand and an Archie Bleyer arrangement in the other, I have kept a rather ambidextrous grip on both. So if I appear to live on the other side of the tracks, I do keep a little shack handy on this side too. I therefore take the liberty of being somewhat historical.

To begin with, American music in the nineteenth century was anything but American. Our country was a brand-new one, comparatively speaking, but a full-grown baby, like Minerva springing adult from Jupiter's brain. As such, America was faced with the great and delicate problem of being a pioneer society, dedicated to revolutionary and daring propositions, but with no traditions except European ones. Anyone who was really anyone in music had first to prove it by studying in Europe, and then coming home with a big Lisztian piano concerto or a Wagnerian tone-epic under his arm. Yet the nineteenth century was the greatest nationalistic cauldron of all A.D. history. To use only musical examples, it was the century when Russian music was being glorified by Moussorgsky, Norwegian music by Grieg, Spanish music by Albeniz, Hungarian music by Liszt, Bohemian music by Dvořák.

It was this same Dvořák who arrived on these shores and pointed out to the bewildered and unnationalistic American composers that they, too, could be nationalist glorifiers. He saw a wealth of indigenous folk material latent in America, unused, and ever so usable. Indian and Negro melodies in particular seemed to him to be crying for symphonic transfiguration. And to prove it, he wrote a *New World* Symphony, based on some of these self-same tunes, and a more beautifully Bohemian symphony was never written.

Immediately the American composers got the point; and there ensued such an outpouring of Indian and Negro operas, suites, cantatas, and tone-poems as I can give an idea of only by refraining from listing them. They are mostly forgotten now, or to be dug for in the dustiest back rooms of the dustiest used-book shops. Out of every movement, however it is based, does emerge some positive asset; and in this case it is the music of MacDowell (Indian school) and of Henry Gilbert (Negro school) which remains with us today; genial, sometimes inspired, European music trying its best to be American.

Why did this movement fail? For fail it did, in the sense of a healthy, historical construction. After all, it was large, it was active, it was earnest, it was sincere. But it was unnatural. It was trying, however sincerely, to be something it was not. A national music is national in direct proportion to how close to its home audiences feel. And when such an audience was presented with an Indian lament, they could think it all very pretty and even touching, but it wasn't *their* music. The fact remained that they were not Indians, any more than we are today. Or, to make the case complete, any more than they were all Poles or all Irish. They were, and we are today, a tough audience. For to what indigenous folk-material could they all respond in common?

Our swift survey has carried us approximately to the point of World War I, when a great many things stopped happening, and at the conclusion of which a great many new things began to happen. Most of us recall that wild postwar era with mixed feelings; and those of us who are too young to remember it, all have probably been, or will shortly be, delightfully enlightened by *Billion Dollar Baby.* The reflection of that decade in American music was brilliantly clear. There was a necessity to be original at all costs, to be chic, and to be American. But now no Dvořák was needed to promulgate a movement. Something new had been added. Jazz had come to stay.

The really remarkable thing about jazz for the serious composer was that it solved simultaneously the two problems of being original and of being American. For here at last was a musical material which was everybody's bread and butter. No real American could fail to understand a symphonic work which sounded like jazz. Now everyone would feel at home and hurray for the Big City Hearthrug.

Something new had been added: but something old had been omitted—the element of the unconscious. If we accept the principle that what we call "inspiration" in music is an impulse that springs from the unconscious and attains fruition through the medium of conscious manipulation, then it simply won't do for a composer to seat himself at his table and decide that he is going to be American or anything else. His output should be the natural expression of his psyche, or his soul, or his collected experiences, or his frustrations, or his adjustment, or whatever you choose to call it. If he is American, the music will be American in terms of his place in the development of American history. Thus the composers of the twenties were American in a different sense from, but on about the some plane as, the Indian school of earlier decades. Both groups were trying too hard.

I think I have already said that some positive asset emerges out of every movement, however it is based. The man who gave this postwar movement life, controversy, and real genius was George Gershwin. His aim, in contradistinction to that of the "serious" composers, was to make of the materials of jazz, with which he was so intimate, a sort of symphonization in the tradition of the European masters, rather than to paste jazz onto already crystallized personal styles and forms, as did Stravinsky and Ravel. Gershwin approached this great merger from the left, so to speak, from the realm of wah-wah mutes and ga-ga chorus girls. Stravinsky approached it from the bulwark of European musical strength, backed up with orchestras with woodwinds in fives, and the guardian spirits of Debussy and Rimsky-Korsakov. Neither really reached the middle: Stravinsky's jazz was really Stravinsky *plus* jazz; Gershwin's concert music was Gershwin plus everyone else under the sun. In neither case was a real integration attained.

Came the crash. Again, many things stopped happening, and many new things began to happen. Again, a new decade ran itself out, this time at a far slower and wearier pace. Musically, it meant a new conservatism, a new reflectiveness, a reconsideration of traditional values. It was just at this point, that, for the very first time, the moment arrived for the sober absorption of all that had happened, and the consequent opportunity for the development of a real, unconsciously derived, American style. And it is the music of this decade which I feel owes the greatest debt to jazz.

We must first take a strong stand on what we mean by "jazz." Avoiding all the lengthy discussion that usually accompanies attempts to define the word, let us make the simple distinction between the commercial song, as we understand the term on Broadway, and the freely improvised jazz of Negro origin, which we know usually in the few formal variants of the Blues. The "popular song" has had, and can have, no influence whatsoever on serious music. It is created for money, sung for money, and dies when the money stops rolling in. It is imitative, conventional, emotionless. This has nothing to do with the fact that there are many such songs of which I am very fond. I wish I had written "I Get a Kick Out of You"; but I must insist that Mr. Porter has no influence on serious music. I love a Gershwin or a Rodgers tune; but the same truth still holds. There are those who show, for example, the influence of a song like "Fascinatin' Rhythm" on symphonic music. Well and good, but the influence is not original with "Fascinatin' Rhythm." Those charming, truncated phrases of Gershwin's go back to the improvised jazz, the real source. It is this jazz, then, that we have to take into account.

My old piano teacher, Heinrich Gebhard, used to say that music was divisible into melody, harmony, rhythm, form, counterpoint, and color. To be at all complete I should devote a chapter apiece from here on to considering these six elements. For jazz has influenced our composers on all six counts. But perhaps one will stand for all, and a short discussion of *rhythm,* the most important influence, may give you some idea of what I have meant all along by "unconscious."

One invariably associates the word "syncopation" with jazz. Literally it means a shortening, or cutting off. Musically, it means putting an accent on a weak beat, or in an unexpected place; or bringing in a note a little earlier or a little later than would seem indicated. For instance, if we consider a conventional musical bar, of 4/4 meter, we see easily that the strongest beat is always the first, the next strongest the third, then the second and fourth (weak beats). Putting special accents on 2 and 4 (either or both) would amount to a simple syncopation. (They all did it over a century ago.)

But that is too simple. Let us go further. If we break this bar up into eighth-notes (eight to the bar), we find we have even weaker beats, and many more of them. For if 2 is a weak beat in a group of four quarter-notes; how much weaker, then, is the second half of this beat alone in a group of eight eighth-notes! Now put a special accent on this unsuspecting member:

1234′5678

and you begin to get a suggestion of jazz. It was this innocent act, merely the replacing of an accent, which caused the Charleston, the Rhumba, the Conga, and many a bump and grind to happen.

Now let us take the rhumba pattern as we know it most simply:

123/456/78.

We see at once that these eight eighth-notes now seem to divide themselves into smaller groups of threes and twos. One might rewrite the pattern as follows:

123/123/12.

Thus, a passage of music in 4/4 time which used to run smoothly in this way:

1234/5678/1234/5678

can now become:

123/123/12/123/123/12,

or if juggled accordingly to the composer's whim:

12/123/12/12/123/123/12,

or any other variation of this pattern. This simple procedure opens up new vistas for the serious composer. In the twenties, when he borrowed overtly from jazz, he used these rhythms as jazz used them, over a steady and monotonous bass which kept the old reliable quarter-note constantly beating. But now that he does not consciously borrow from jazz, these rhythms crop up in a non-jazzy context, without a meter-bass necessarily holding them up, but with a life of their own. They have acquired personal qualities—not always hard and percussive, but sometimes graceful, sometimes singing, sometimes even nostalgic. The whole procedure has unconsciously become common usage among American composers. And the startling thing is that very rarely does this music ever sound like jazz! The scherzo movement of my symphony *Jeremiah* would certainly not bring any connotation of jazz to mind; and yet it could never have been written if jazz were not an integral part of my life.

For those of you who are further interested I recommend careful listening to and study of the works of Copland, Harris, Sessions, Schuman, and Barber, to name only a few. For those of you who are not, don't worry about it. Just listen to the best in jazz and the best in serious American music, and enjoy it. For analyses and diagnoses notwithstanding, the great synthesis goes irrevocably on.

No Jazz Is an Island

William Grossman

In the first issue (October 1956) of the much admired magazine Jazz Review, *William Grossman began a series of articles on the history of jazz. This opening section is particularly useful in its reminders of jazz's religious and spiritual roots.*

The story of jazz is a miniature history of the modern mind. From the New Orleans jazz of King Oliver, Jelly Roll Morton, and Bunk Johnson to the current divergent trends, one can trace a telescoped repetition of the major developments in Western thought during the past two hundred years. To do this, one must concentrate not on technical musicology but on what the music expresses, i.e., the "content" of the music. After all, this is the ultimately significant thing. Methods, forms, and techniques are an indispensable means by which the content is communicated, but they are nothing in themselves. Their whole importance lies in what they succeed in expressing.

Traditional New Orleans jazz provides a logical starting point. The first thing one notes about this music is its immense vigor and vitality. Some consider it a childish vitality, belonging only in the kindergarten of life and fortunately superseded by the sophistication of more recently developed types of jazz. Others welcome it as whole-souled, honest earthiness in contrast to the preciousness and emotional apathy of some modern jazz. But almost no one who knows the music will deny that, for better or worse, it expresses vitality in abundance.

There is another basic element in the content of New Orleans jazz: a profoundly religious feeling. It is not merely religious but specifically Judeo-Christian. Persons who question this will be found, in almost every instance, to be unfamiliar with the music or to be unreceptive to the communication of Christian feeling by any medium. The underemphasis on this element in most of the literature on jazz doubtless reflects its underemphasis in the worldview and critical standards of most of the writers on jazz.

If the reader accepts the existence of a strong religious element in New Orleans jazz, he may as well skip this paragraph, which is intended to indicate some of the objective evidence of that element. Among the several sources that contributed to the creation of New Orleans jazz, church music, including the spirituals, is outstanding. According to the late Bud Scott, "Each Sunday, Bolden went to church and that's where he got his idea of jazz music." Scott added that he himself had derived the four-beat jazz guitar style (which he claimed to have originated) from the hand-clapping in church. The original repertory of the Negro country brass bands consisted entirely of church music; these bands are known to have exercised a great influence on the New Orleans brass bands. The striking similarities in both form and feeling between New Orleans jazz and gospel singing (with its accompaniment) leads one to conclude either that there is a strong religious element in both or in neither, and to deny it in the gospel singing would of course be absurd. Most of the creators of New Orleans jazz have been believers, some of them—including Oliver and, surprisingly, Morton—with persistent faith even in time of extreme adversity. Such fundamental attitudes in a musician are likely to get into the music he creates. The Reverend Alvin Kershaw, whose profundity of insight is almost unparalleled among speakers and writers on jazz, finds a pronounced Christian element in traditional jazz and has had George Lewis' New Orleans band play in his church. There is plenty of additional evidence.

The combination of abundant vitality and Christian feeling characterizes not only New Orleans jazz but also certain music in the European tradition—most notably that of Johann Sebastian Bach. The conspicuousness of both elements in his music has been frequently remarked. As a consequence, several learned writers have likened him to a *preacher.* Unlike a monk or a mere theologian, a preacher must have not only religiousness but also vigor in order to put his message across and some degree of earthiness in order to link a man's daily struggles with the Christian's eternal aspirations. The preacher analogy is therefore appropriate for a creator of music that combines these qualities, such as Bach or the various traditional jazz musicians who have also been called preachers.

The Renaissance in Europe had introduced a respect for earthy vitality which, combined with an already pervasively Christian ethos, gave rise to the state of mind or emotional attitude that could produce music like Bach's. It has often been remarked that music lags behind the other arts in the reflection of successive changes in prevailing attitudes or ways of thinking. Thus the Christian element had already been on the wane in literature and the fine arts even before Bach's time. In an irregular way, and subject to occasional reversals of direction, music since then has reflected the increasing secularization and the weakening of Christian feeling.

What has this side-glance at history to do with jazz? Just about everything. For the Negroes who created New Orleans jazz were part of an ethnic group to which Christianity had only recently been introduced. Their faith had the fervor associated with earlier periods in the history of Christianity. Their music, like Bach's, was a sort of anachronism, an expression of old and, to some extent, discarded (by others) attitudes. It is interesting to observe that in New Orleans jazz the synthesis of Christian feeling and abundant human vitality led to much the same optimism and healthful good humor—and (in the blues) to the same miraculous transformation of sadness into a source of rich comfort—as in Bach. Writers have noted certain technical resemblances between traditional jazz and Bach's music, but they have neglected the far more important resemblance in emotional attitude.

As time moved on, however, jazz went the way of post-Bach European music—and of Western man. What have been the dominant trends in modern European and American thought? One, amply attested, has been a continuation of the movement away from a Judeo-Christian orientation. In jazz, too, this tendency is plainly discernible. It is a long road from the almost devout way in which a New Orleans jazz band performs a spiritual to Dizzy Gillespie's rendition of "Swing Low, Sweet Chariot"—or, as he has sung it, "Swing Low, Sweet Cadillac." A milestone on this road is Louis Armstrong, whose Reverend Satchelmouth joshing, very significantly, marked the period in which he departed from the New Orleans norm.

The words spoken or sung by Louis or by Dizzy are only symptomatic; so is the virtual elimination of spirituals in the modern-jazz repertory. The important change is in the content of the music. This change cannot be demonstrated with scientific irrefutability, but it is nevertheless obvious. Not that the religious element has wholly disappeared in nontraditional jazz. Along with the vitality of the old music, it is especially conspicuous in the blues, even when played by a nontraditional group. The funkiness of the blues, and their association with the mood of religious music, generally manage to come through. But emphasis on alien elements has been added. Even in Bird, who was closer to the tradition than most bopsters and moderns, the blues contain not only the traditional blues feeling but also undercurrents of despondence and even, at times, of desperation, elements inimical to the fundamental confidence and optimism of the Christian believer. In less blues-minded moderns, the religious element generally becomes considerably weaker. The tendency among bopsters and modern-jazz musicians to turn away from the Judeo-Christian tradition—to turn from all religion in the conventional sense or to Mohammedanism or some other exotic religion—is consistent with the change in the content of the music.

Another powerful influence on the development of Western thought and attitude in the past two hundred years has been romanticism. This is, in essence, a revolt against the restraints of conventional society and against the self-discipline of both the classical humanist and the Christian. In place of these, it embraces naturalistic emotional expansiveness and indulgence. Here again the development of jazz parallels that of Western thought, and here again Louis Armstrong stands at the crossroads. In place of the emotional discipline that characterized the music of King Oliver's Creole Jazz Band, in which he had played second cornet, Louis gave the world the persuasive eloquence of his personal barbaric yawp. The polyphony of classic jazz impeded this emotional expansiveness, so Louis played it down and gave new emphasis to the solo, an emphasis that has characterized jazz ever since.

The undisciplined naturalistic expansiveness or indulgence of the romantic, whether in jazz or any other area of human activity, tends to take either or both of two main directions. One leads to nervous excitement, frenzy, or savageness. Such content was extremely rare in Western music prior to the nineteenth century, but is found in works by Berlioz and several later composers, some of whom have influenced modern jazz. However, the frenetic element found its way into jazz chiefly as a direct result of the general breakdown of classic values in favor of naturalistic expansiveness rather than through the influence of European music. This element and its consequences can be readily traced from Louis and the white Chicago school to the bop vein in modern jazz.

In this connection, it seems curious that devotees of Charlie Parker so rarely talk or write about the expressed content of his music. Commenting on, say, his much-admired recording entitled "Ko-Ko," they write about his "new world filled with unheard-of sounds," his "tremendous facilities for improvisation," etc., although the most important and striking (to a person whose interests are exclusively musical) fact about his brilliant performance in this recording and in various others is the pitiful, disoriented desperation, close to frenzy, in the content of the music. Much of Bird's music exemplifies Charles M. Fair's characterization of the content of bop as "jangled sadness" and a "frantic, almost desperate emotion." Leading to a revolution of form and method—its *musicological* significance—such music has a far greater *human* significance, for it represents a breakdown of the spiritual and emotional attitudes underlying the classical, conventional worldview on which our civilization (and traditional jazz) was founded. Greater issues than those of musical talent or form are involved in the jazz revolution of the 1940s and 1950s. Musicological analysis is useful, but in the case of bop and modern jazz it, together with extravagant praise of technical innovation, have tended to obscure the much more earth-shaking change in emotional attitude and the crucial issues involved in the acceptability of that change. One sometimes gets the impression that these issues are being deliberately sidestepped. They are the issues on which modern jazz is most vulnerable.

The other romantic direction leads to languor and revery. This is the course taken by crooning and by sweet dance music. It finds its *reductio ad absurdum* in the lethal syrup of mood music. This direction in European music is typified by Debussy, to whom some modern jazzmen look as a source. In so doing, they tend to reject profundity, for in Debussy's music, as Hugo Leichtentritt says (*Music, History, and Ideas*), "there is no passion, no deep feeling, no real emotional art, but rather the cult of suggestive, enchanting sound . . . His is an altogether sensuous art, without any marked moral quality, without religious feeling or metaphysical overtones." Modern-jazz musicians can make no more serious mistake than to attach themselves to the tradition of modern European music, which, to quote Leichtentritt again, shows "prodigious skill and emptiness of soul, great ingenuity wasted on paltry conceptions." Does not modern jazz often exhibit exactly the same combination of ingenuity and spiritual emptiness?

The two directions—frenzy and languor—are apparently opposites, but they are alike in their denial of the vital balance and emotional discipline that characterize classic (as opposed to romantic) art products in jazz, in "serious" music, in painting, and in every other medium. Their respective denials of genuine vitality converge in a deadly meaninglessness. The frenzy of jazz becomes almost indistinguishable from the fast-solo gibberish that modern jazz inherited from bop. The languor of popular ballads and of syrupy dance or mood music merges into the coolness or emotional apathy of much "modern" jazz. It is significant in this connection that contemporary nontraditional jazz scrupulously avoids the hot classic repertory ("Milenberg Joys," "Sister Kate," etc.) but sometimes joins forces with the crooners and with sweet dance music by performing pop tunes in a languidly sentimental mood. Examples are probably unnecessary, but some that happen to come immediately to hand are George Duvivier's arrangements of "What Is There to Say" and of "We'll Be Together Again," recorded by the Chico Hamilton Trio, and the Modern Jazz Quartet's recorded version of "Autumn in New York."

Frenzy or nervous excitement and coolness or emotional apathy are not only reconcilable but actually complementary, as indicated by their combination in the manic-depressive personality. A listener whose orientation is religious in the Judeo-Christian sense will find both of them inimical to his fundamental worldview. Even without such an orientation, a person in search of whole-souled, valid experience will find them irrelevant to his quest. Almost equally irrelevant will be some of the peripheral elements—cuteness, preciousness, lyricism without depth—so often discernible (often there seems to be nothing else) in the content of recent music, whether jazz or "classical."

A far-reaching but ambivalent development in Western thought is the popularization of classic values, the effort to present them in a way that will attract a mass audience. By way of illustration, one has only to mention the work of Norman Vincent Peale in religion or of Andre Kostelanetz in "serious" music. Mass popularization generally entails some change in the values themselves, often a change that makes their new form or embodiment unacceptable to the elite. The triumph of mass-man as an aesthetic and moral arbiter has nevertheless made this development almost inevitable.

Like other recent tendencies, mass popularization has its counterpart in the area of jazz. Swing, which swept the country in the late 1930s and more recently has subtly reinfiltrated the jazz ranks, and rock 'n' roll today, may be considered mass-man's hot jazz. So may most of Louis Armstrong's music in his pseudo-traditional vein. Their derivation from traditional, classic jazz is clear, but so also is their broadening and concomitant weakening of the original values. Both swing and rock 'n' roll, and much of Louis's music, are primarily homophonic. They do not demand the emotional control and intellectual acumen necessary for full enjoyment of classic-jazz polyphony. Nor do they require emotional profundity of any sort.

And yet the best examples of swing and of rock 'n' roll may at least suggest to a listener who is fed up on hit-parade that music in the jazz idiom can be something more than sentimental or peppy or cute or "inspirational." The original values, however weakened and distorted, are sometimes perceptible in these popularizations, which may therefore stimulate the interest of a discerning listener or performer and may lead him to demand something closer to those values. That he cannot readily find this in modern or "progressive" jazz is evidenced by the rapidity with which the music (apart from what Bill Coss calls the "bop doldrums") shifts its ground. Some rhetorical questions by Turk Murphy on this subject, from his preface to *The Heart of Jazz,* bear repeating: "It [progressive jazz] is always moving, apparently. Could this be reason to believe that it moves because it so quickly becomes boring to the performers? If progressive jazz stood still, might one wonder if it could stand the scrutiny given, over the years, to traditional jazz?"

Any importance that may be attributed to the traditional-jazz renaissance of the past sixteen or seventeen years must rest upon its ability to satisfy the demand for aesthetic experience based on classic values. Persons who reject the "modern" emotional attitudes generally reflected in nontraditional jazz are likely to look upon the renaissance as the most wholesome of the current jazz trends. But it, too, represents a development in Western thought extending far beyond the realm of jazz. This is the twentieth-century reaction against the extremes of modernism. Here in America it has given us such substantial art products as Samuel Barber's *Adagio for Strings* and Andrew Wyeth's paintings. In the field of criticism and aesthetic theory, its leaders in the United States were Paul Elmer More and Irving Babbitt. In its more profound reaches, it carries its search back to the mainstream of balanced wisdom from which nineteenth-century romanticism and even eighteenth-century rationalism were departures. Thus it becomes associated with the recent revival, among intellectuals, of a lively interest in Judeo-Christian values. Very naturally, its manifestation in jazz is a renewed interest in the type of jazz that has most nearly expressed the emotional attitudes induced by that wisdom and by those values. One suspects that the haste with which some performers and some writers brush aside the traditional-jazz renaissance reflects their understanding of the devastating effect that an insistence on the traditional values would have upon the world of modern jazz to which they belong.

No jazz is an island. All jazz is part of the mainland of Western spiritual development. Personal preferences among types of jazz, when not based on the listeners' musical limitations, represent adherence to one or another of the tendencies in that development. To an outsider, the aggressiveness with which the aficionados of one school of jazz attack another school may appear silly, a tempest in a teapot. It is far from this. Below the surface it is a defense, whether well- or ill-advised, of an attitude toward life.

The Unreal Jazz

Hugues Panassié

The highly regarded French critic and enthusiast Hugues Panassié reacted violently to the main direction jazz took in the postwar world. Here he inveighs against the confusing (as he sees it) of real with "unreal" jazz. From the collection The Real Jazz *(1960).*

Bop is no love-child of jazz . . .

—Charlie Parker

It is amazing to note that so many years after the birth of "bop," there still are critics who keep the public misinformed by calling it "jazz" or "modern jazz."

That some people could have hesitated, at the beginning of bop, is very understandable—in their first records, Charlie Parker and Dizzy Gillespie were playing with jazzmen such as Sidney Catlett, Don Byas, Trummy Young, Clyde Hart, Slam Stewart and others. The music still had several jazz characteristics. Besides which Parker and Gillespie had been playing for years with jazz orchestras and were inspired, in their formative years, by great jazz musicians.

When they had disciples and started playing with them, however, it was a different proposition—the disciples, instead of being formed by jazz musicians, started right away on the bop formula and were not raised on the jazz tradition. Drummers started "dropping bombs," piano players forgot that they were supposed to feed the soloists and were only interested in playing their own fantastic parts; in fact, in the bop orchestra, the bass player, with his regular four beat, was the only swinging musician, the only reminder of the jazz tradition; but one man could not make up for a whole orchestra.

The music degenerated at an incredible speed. A few years after the still virile and a little jazz-like playing of Dizzy and Parker, we had the emasculate sounds of Miles Davis, Lee Konitz, Paul Desmond, Gerry Mulligan, Chet Baker, etc.: the music had lost its last link with jazz: dynamics. Today, people have to call "hard bop" (one of the most comical formulas ever) the music of the few progressive instrumentalists who try to get some power back into their playing.

How anybody can call this music jazz is beyond my understanding.

A tepid, nauseous cliché, chewed up to seasickness, would have the public believe that there have been three kinds of jazz: New Orleans—Mainstream—Modern Jazz. It would be hard to distort the facts more.

It is well known that jazz is born of the blues and religious singing of the American Negroes; that it is the instrumental transposition of the vocal style of blues and sacred singers; and that it is built on the same pulse-beat.

Now, when you hear any New Orleans' style musicians, for instance Louis Armstrong, Joe Oliver, Tommy Ladnier, Kid Ory, Johnny Dodds, Jimmy Noone, Barney Bigard, you immediately notice that they play the blues (and other numbers) on their horn exactly the way that blues singers sing them. The words are not there any longer, so there are more notes, longer phrases, but the horn playing has this typical "singing" quality: a vibrato like the human voice, long held notes, many inflections or glissandos, etc.

If you come to what is currently referred to as "Mainstream," and which is, in fact, *all* post-New Orleans jazz, you find the very same characteristics. Great tenor sax players like Coleman Hawkins, Ben Webster, Buddy Tate,—trumpet players such as Buck Clayton, Cootie Williams, Ray Nance, Cat Anderson, alto saxes like Johnny Hodges, Earl Bostic, trombonists like Trummy Young, Higginbotham, guitarists like Tiny Grimes, Billy Mackel—all use expressive vibrato, holding notes, lots of inflections, etc.

But when you come to the so-called progressive jazz, nothing is left, nothing recalls the music of the blues singers: it's a no-vibrato sound, endless runs with no sustained notes, hardly any inflection at all, to say nothing of the harmonic climate of the blues which is sadly distorted.

In the hands of the boppers, the blues have the same lugubrious atmosphere as an arrangement of "My Funny Valentine" written by one of those "progressive" arrangers.

The assertion according to which "modern jazz would have been influenced by Negro church music" is also deprived of any foundation whatever. I just read several articles which pretend to prove it, written by Mimi Clar in *The Jazz Review* (November and December, 1958). It's really amazing! Every time this lady quotes a musical example to show the similitude between jazz and Negro church music, the example chosen is from *jazz* musicians, not boppers: for instance, from Count Basie's "The Comeback" ("here the guitar chords function in parallel fashion to the church drum; the brushed snare drum occupies the place of the church hand claps"); from

Charlie Shavers, whose chorus in Lionel Hampton's "Star Dust" contains—according to Mimi Clar—an effect similar to the "'holy-laugh' heard in present day churches." Where could be found the bop trumpet player using the holy-laugh effect? In the few cases when boppers are quoted as an example of similitude with Negro church music, the example given has nothing to do with the bop itself. For instance, Mimi Clar mentions Charlie Parker's break in "Night in Tunisia," Art Blakey's break in Horace Silver's "Quicksilver." Then she adds "Breaks are part of Negro church music too"!!! Weren't they also part of jazz—long before bop was born?

In fact, every important essential element of Negro church music which is quoted by Mimi Clar and others, has its equivalent in real jazz—never in bop or progressive music. For example, church hand-clapping has its counterpart in a drum—jazz style. That is, the one which favors a strong accentuation of the after-beat. Nothing of the sort can be found in bop drumming. "The rhythmic exchange between one or more instruments or voices" which Mimi Clar quotes as "fundamental to both modern jazz and Negro church music" can easily be found in big band riffing (Count Basie, Erskine Hawkins, Fletcher Henderson) but is never used in bop, in fact, Mimi Clar quotes Count Basie's "Cherry Point" as an example of it!

Any accurate analysis of the musical characteristics of both jazz and bop will show that the former is deeply rooted in the blues and the Negro religious music, or even better to say it is its orchestral equivalent; while bop has nothing to do with it, has separated itself from it.

In fact, that is what all jazz musicians think. I have never met one of them who considered bop the same music as the one he was creating and performing. Several of them have even publicly stated it: Louis Armstrong, Milton Mezzrow, Zutty Singleton, Lionel Hampton, Buck Clayton, among them.

Moreover the most famous of all bop musicians, Charlie Parker, agreed that "Bop is no love-child of jazz, it is something entirely separate and apart."

Now, during the later years, some boppers have insisted that their music was jazz; but this new attitude came from the fact that the music known to the public as "be-bop" was so much disliked that, in order to be commercially successful, the only way out for the boppers was to get under the "jazz" banner. And this explains to the uninitiated why the word "jazz" has been used so eagerly by progressive musicians to name their orchestras during the later years: Jazz Messengers, Jazz Lab, Modern Jazz Quartet, etc. . . . , while real jazz orchestras like Louis Armstrong's, Duke Ellington's, Count Basie's, Johnny Hodges's, etc., never had the need of announcing themselves as "jazz": their music would clearly speak for itself.

The same phenomenon can be observed with other words. For years boppers were laughed at, people objecting to their poor tone and lack of emotional power of their playing. "We don't care about tone and soul" they would answer, "we only care about technique, speed," etc.

Today, while keeping their cold, unemotional approach, the progressives (and/or their followers) have "soul" on their lips every other word. LPs come out titled *Plenty plenty soul, Soultrain* (an execrable play of words made with the tenor sax Coltrane), *Soul Brothers,* etc.

Another word just as misused is "funky." In the last year or two, the number of progressive musicians who pretend to be "funky," and the number of progressive critics who imagine their heroes are "funky," would, if they all met, make a quite considerable army. Anyone with the slightest knowledge of jazz knows that "funky" is a slang word synonymous with "low down," "gut bucket" or any similar term previously used. In fact, it refers to the rough, unsophisticated music best typified by Kid Ory, Tricky Sam, Johnny Dodds, Lips Page, or Bubber Miley when they play the blues. It is a way of playing in which the musician uses comparatively few notes and puts a lot of expression into every one of them, "working" at length a note or a couple of notes by a large inflection, maybe adding some "growl" to it, etc. Nothing could be further removed from the style of the progressive musicians, which consists of runs, long phrases with hardly any notes being stressed, or worked on. I don't know if a progressive ever *really* tried to be "funky"; if he did, he probably failed so miserably that nobody noticed.

We would only be too glad to leave the boppers and the coolers alone but as long as they have the intolerable presumption to present themselves as jazzmen, it is impossible for us to ignore them. The way in which progressive critics insist that their heroes are great *blues* players is the most absurd affirmation imaginable. Great blues playing is almost synonymous with "funky" playing. To play good blues, progressive musicians should forget all about their technical runs, their "changes" and everything: that is precisely what they never do, except maybe for a couple of bars.

It has been said many times that Charlie Parker was a great blues player. He certainly *could* have been one. When he was playing in the Jay McShann orchestra, he was really playing the blues. Some basic quality of the blues remained in his playing and could be felt from time to time during a few bars. But most of the time Charlie Parker was not playing the blues at all. Take "Parker's Mood," for instance: the first bars of the opening chorus are played in the blues idiom but, right in the middle of the chorus, Charlie Parker starts bopping and all the blues flavor fades away.

Now, do not misunderstand me: Charlie Parker and his disciples are entitled to play as they like, to make the kind of music they think is the best. If Parker wanted to create that style of variations on the 12-bars blues formula, all right: it might be good music of its kind, but do NOT call it jazz, and do NOT say that Charlie Parker and some of his progressive imitators are great BLUES players.

In other words, my quarrel with the progressive people is not about the value of their music—I do not judge it. But I do know that it is not the same music as the one named "jazz," and I do not want the two kinds of music to be confused, for very important reasons.

One reason is that the large public, who started not so long ago to appreciate the real jazz music and its most famous musicians, such as Louis Armstrong, Duke Ellington, Fats Waller, Lionel Hampton, Count Basie, etc., just cannot take the so-called progressive jazz. This is not the time to debate whether the public is right or wrong in its rejection of the bop and cool sounds. What matters is that by offering the public progressive music and calling it "jazz," the danger is they may develop a keen dislike of the genuine article. I know what I am talking about. Six or seven years ago, in France, some good (although not too well known) jazzmen could come from the States, tour all over the country and draw enough people to the concert halls to pay all the expenses even if not to make a fortune. Today, after years of "progressive" musicians on the air, on records, on tours, an important part of the public gave up attending "jazz" concerts. It is virtually impossible, nowadays, to cover expenses for the same bands which were doing good enough business at the end of the forties and the beginning of the fifties. That is what I mean when I say that the pseudo "modern" jazz is killing the real jazz.

Another reason which makes it absolutely necessary to avoid confusion between the two musics is the prejudice that this same confusion causes among jazzmen. Ignorant people mix them (on recording dates or concerts) with boppers, and jazz musicians cannot play well in such circumstances. They also have to suffer another injustice: by claiming that the so-called "modern jazz" is an improvement on the older one, great jazzmen of preceding decades are left out in the cold: they are not booked in the main clubs, at jazz festivals, they no longer appear on records, etc. Not only that: the *young* musicians who prefer to get their inspiration from Louis Armstrong, Earl Hines, Coleman Hawkins, etc., are victims of a conspiracy of silence. As long as one does not play in the "modern" idiom, one is called "old-fashioned." Young jazzmen of great value such as Wallace Davenport (trumpet), Plas Johnson, King Curtis (tenor sax), Roy Gaines (guitar) hardly get any publicity. Had he not participated in Jimmy Rushing's Vanguard LP, Roy Gaines would still be unknown to jazz lovers. Wallace Davenport proved himself to be a great trumpet player in Mezzrow's last recording date for the Vogue label. Yet as with Mezz, whom the progressives hate, and stupidly dismiss as a bad musician (despite the fact that so many jazz greats such as Louis Armstrong, Fats Waller, Lionel Hampton have openly stated their appreciation of him), scarcely anyone made mention of this date and, particularly, of the extraordinary trumpet playing in it. However, anyone with any real knowledge of jazz cannot but marvel at the amazing trumpet solos in "Moonglow" and "Serenade to Paris" which are to be found in this Mezzrow LP (on which, by the way, both Mezz and Jimmy Archey play some of their best music ever recorded).

Now, if those young jazz musicians are not given a chance, what will happen? They will have to quit music, or learn to play a music which they don't feel and like instead of playing the way they want to (just as that fine piano player Hank Jones has had to do too often); and in years to come—when the older generation of jazzmen have gone—there will be no jazz.

It is important and urgent that something should be done. Young musicians who want to play jazz should have the right to do so. They should not be limited, on records, to a few bad "rock 'n roll" dates on which they cannot express what they want to.

A couple of years ago, Ruby Braff—a fine trumpet player who prefers the Armstrong idiom to bop—stated, "I can't get any bookings unless I change my style—lose my identity and play like Miles Davis." And if you think he was exaggerating, read these few words on Ruby Braff—written by Dom Cerulli in *Down Beat* (January 8, 1959, page 38): "Ruby Braff hasn't worked more than a few weeks in 1958 and the outlook for 1959 isn't much brighter."

Just as long as real jazz lovers and critics allow bop to be presented to the public as "Jazz" or "Modern Jazz," it is very unlikely that the situation will get any brighter.

All What Jazz?

Philip Larkin

Larkin, Britain's most famous postwar poet and misogynist, was for several years jazz critic for the Daily Telegraph. *In 1970 he reprinted his reviews in a book called* All What Jazz?, *the introduction to which appears below. No one who knows Larkin's work will be surprised at his biting contempt for jazz's latest directions.*

Introduction

1

I have rescued these articles from their press-cuttings book because for all their slightness and superficiality they contain occasional sentences that still amuse me or seem justified. Moreover, as I read them I discern a story which, though ordinary enough, it might be entertaining to bring out into the open.

To tell it means going back some way. Few things have given me more pleasure in life than listening to jazz. I don't claim to be original in this: for the generations that came to adolescence between the wars jazz was that unique private excitement that youth seems to demand. In another age it might have been drink or drugs, religion or poetry. Whatever it happens to be, parents are suspicious of it and it has a bad reputation. I can tell adolescents don't feel like this about jazz today. For one thing, there are so many kinds that to talk about jazz as such would leave them puzzled as well as cold. Then again, it has become respectable: there are scholarly books on it, and adult education courses; it's the kind of interest that might well be mentioned on a university entrance form. And there's so much of it: records, wireless, television, all dispense it regularly. In the thirties it was a fugitive minority interest, a record heard by chance from a foreign station, a chorus between two vocals, one man in an otherwise dull band. No one you knew liked it.

Nevertheless, it had established itself in my life several years before I consciously heard anything that could properly be called real jazz. This happened by way of the dance band, a now-vanished phenomenon of twelve or fourteen players (usually identically uniformed) that was employed by a hotel or restaurant so that its patrons could dance. Their leaders were national celebrities, and had regular time on the radio: five-fifteen to six in the afternoon, for instance, and half-past ten to midnight. They were in almost no sense "jazz" bands, but about every sixth piece they made a "hot" number, in which the one or two men in the band who could play jazz would be heard. The classic "hot number" was "Tiger Rag": it had that kind of national-anthem status that "When the Saints Go Marching In" had in the fifties. Harry Roy had a band-within-a-band called The Tiger-Ragamuffins. Nat Gonella's stage show had a toy tiger lying on the grand piano. Trombonists and tuba-players became adept at producing the traditional tiger growl. I found these hot numbers so exciting that I would listen to hours of dance music in order to catch them when they came, in this way unconsciously learning many now-forgotten lyrics. Those hot numbers! When the bands began to visit the local Hippodrome, I was able actually to see them played, the different sections suddenly rising to play four bars then sitting sharply down again; the shouts of "Yeah man," the slapped bass, the drum breaks. It was the drummer I concentrated on, sitting as he did on a raised platform behind a battery of cowbells, temple blocks, cymbals, tomtoms and (usually) a chinese gong, his drums picked out in flashing crimson or ultramarine brilliants. Even the resident Hippodrome drummer, a stolid man with horn-rimmed glasses, excited me enough for me to insist that our tickets were for his side of the house, so that I could see what he was doing. I wanted to be a drummer. My parents bought me an elementary drum kit and a set of tuition records by Max Abrams (that will date the anecdote), and I battered away contentedly, spending less time on the rudiments than in improvising an accompaniment to records.

I recount this simply to show that I was, in essence, hooked on jazz even before I heard any, and that what got me was the rhythm. That simple trick of the suspended beat, that had made the slaves shuffle in Congo Square on Saturday nights, was something that never palled. My transition to jazz was slow. The first jazz record by an *American* band I ever owned was Ray Noble's "Tiger Rag" (it had a drum break). The second, rather surprisingly, was The Washboard Rhythm Kings' "I'm Gonna Play Down by the Ohio." The third was Louis Armstrong's "Ain't Misbehavin'." After that they came thick and fast. Sitting with a friend in his bedroom that overlooked the family tennis-court, I watched leaves drift down through long Sunday afternoons as we took it in turn to wind the portable HMV, and those white and colored Americans, Bubber Miley, Frank Teschemaker, J. C. Higginbotham, spoke immediately to our understanding. Their rips, slurs, and distortions were something we understood perfectly. This was something we had found for ourselves, that wasn't taught at school (what a prerequisite that is of nearly everything worthwhile!), and having found it, we made it bear all the enthusiasm usually directed at more established arts. There was nothing odd about this. It was happening to boys all over Europe and America. It just didn't get into the papers. It was years before I found any music as commanding as Jimmy Noone's "The Blues Jumped a Rabbit," Armstrong's "Knockin' a Jug" or "Squeeze Me," Bessie Smith's "Backwater Blues," or the Chicago Rhythm Kings' "I Found a New Baby."

At Oxford my education grew. I met people who knew more about jazz than I did, and had more records, and who could even parallel my ecstasies with their own. The shops, too, were full of unreturned deletions, some of which have never been reissued to this day (the Sharkey Bonano Vocalions, for instance, or Louis Prima's "Chasin' Shadows"). I wish I could say that we could recite Black Swan matrix numbers, or knew what was available on Argentine HMV, or played instruments and formed a band, or at least had enough musical knowledge to discuss the records we played intelligently. Only one of our circle could read music: he played the saxophone, but his taste didn't really accord with mine: he was too fond of phrases such as "not musically interesting" or "mere rhythmic excitement." True, our response to Fats Waller's "Dream Man" or Rosetta Howard's "If You're a Viper" was a grinning, jigging wordlessness, interspersed with a grunt or two at specially good bits. For us, jazz became part of the private joke of existence, rather than a public expertise: expressions such as "combined pimp and lover" and "eating the cheaper cuts of pork" (both from a glossary on "Yellow Dog Blues") flecked our conversations cryptically; for some reason, Kaminsky's plaintive little introduction to "Home Cooking" became a common signal, and any of us entering the steam-filled college bath-house would whistle it to see if it was taken up from behind any of the bolted partition doors.

If I say that on leaving Oxford I suffered a gap in my jazz life I am probably reporting a common experience. Most jazz enthusiasts found the war a compulsory hiatus in their devotion. If they were not away in the services, and their collection broken up, the American Federation of Musicians' recording ban of 1942–44 descended on them, together with the general shortage of consumer goods, including records, that hostilities brought increasingly as the war went on. For my part, I was in a series of provincial lodgings where jazz was not welcome, and when I was united with my collection in 1948 and had something to play it on there followed a period when I was content to renew acquaintance with it and to add only what amplified or extended it along existing lines—new records by old favorites, replacements of discs previously abandoned or broken. When the long-playing record was introduced in the middle fifties, I was suspicious of it: it seemed a package deal, forcing you to buy bad tracks along with good at an unwontedly-high price. (The dubbing or remastering of 78s as LPs, too, was regarded as a damaging practice.) This deepened my isolation.

All this is not to say that I was ignorant of the changes taking place on the jazz scene. I knew, for instance, that what I had known as one music had now bifurcated into trad and mod. In Britain one heard a good deal more of the former, thanks to the revivalist boom, but I don't know that I went overboard about it; I liked Lyttelton, and later on the energetic little Barber band that could pack any concert hall between Aberdeen and Bristol. I heard it in Belfast in 1954: a thousand people squashed into the smallish Plaza dance hall, and a thousand more milled outside, the more enterprising getting in through a small square window in the men's lavatory. This was the pre-Ottilie period, when after "Panama" and "Chimes Blues" and "Merrydown Rag" Lonnie Donegan would come forward with his impersonation of Leadbelly. There was no bar: I went and stood on the landing, pursued by the high nasal Glasgow-American version of some incident from transatlantic railway history. All the same, there seemed an element of slightly-unreal archaism about much of the trad of the period, particularly from California, and I could never bring myself to take these grunting and quavering pastiches seriously. On the whole, therefore, I thought it best after the war to suspend judgment, out of an almost-academic shyness about going into a "new period." For modern jazz I was even less well briefed. What I heard on the wireless seemed singularly unpromising, but I doubt if I thought it would ever secure enough popular acceptance to warrant my bothering about it.

2

WHAT I AM doing, I suppose, is demonstrating that when I was asked to write these articles I was patently unfitted to do so and should have declined. The reason I didn't was that I still thought of myself as a jazz lover, someone unquestionably on the wavelength of Congo Square, and although I knew things had been changing I didn't believe jazz itself could alter out of all recognition any more than the march or the waltz could. It was simply a question of hearing enough of the new stuff: I welcomed the chance to do so, feeling confident that once I got the feel of it all would be made clear. Secondly, I hadn't really any intention of being a jazz *critic*. In literature, I understood, there were several old whores who had grown old in the reviewing game by praising everything, and I planned to be their jazz equivalent. This isn't as venal as it sounds. Since my space was to be so limited, anything but praise would be wasteful; my readers deserved to be told of the best of all worlds, and I was the man to do it. It didn't really matter, therefore, whether I liked things at first or not, as I was going to call them all masterpieces.

But there came a hitch. When the records, in their exciting square packages, began obligingly to arrive from the companies, the eagerness with which I played them turned rapidly to astonishment, to disbelief, to alarm. I felt I was in some nightmare, in which I had confidently gone into an examination hall only to find that I couldn't make head or tail of the questions. It wasn't like listening to a kind of jazz I didn't care for—Art Tatum, shall I say, or Jelly Roll Morton's Red Hot Peppers. It wasn't like listening to jazz at all. Nearly every characteristic of the music had been neatly inverted: for instance, the jazz tone, distinguished from "straight" practice by an almost-human vibrato, had entirely disappeared, giving way to utter flaccidity. Had the most original feature of jazz been its use of collective improvisation? Banish it: let the first and last choruses be identical exercises in low-temperature unison. Was jazz instrumentation based on the hock-shop trumpets, trombones, and clarinets of the returned Civil War regiments? Brace yourself for flutes, harpsichords, electronically-amplified bassoons. Had jazz been essentially a popular art, full of tunes you could whistle? Something fundamentally awful had taken place to ensure that there should be no more tunes. Had the wonderful thing about it been its happy, cake-walky syncopation that set feet tapping and shoulders jerking? Any such feelings were now regularly dispelled by random explosions from the drummer ("dropping bombs"), and the use of non-jazz tempos, 3/4, 5/8, 11/4. Above all, was jazz the music of the American Negro? Then fill it full of conga drums and sambas and all the tawdry trappings of South America, the racket of Middle East bazaars, the cobra-coaxing cacophonies of Calcutta.

But, deeper than this, the sort of emotion the music was trying to evoke seemed to have changed. Whereas the playing of Armstrong, Bechet, Waller, and the Condon groups had been relaxed and expansive, the music of the new men seemed to have developed from some of the least attractive characteristics of the late thirties—the tight-assed little John Kirby band, for instance, or the more riff-laden Goodman units. The substitution of bloodless note-patterns for some cheerful or sentimental popular song as a basis for improvisation (I'm thinking of some of the early Parkers) was a retrograde step, but worse still was the deliberately-contrived eccentricity of the phrasing and harmonies. One of the songs I remember from my dance-music childhood was called "I'm Nuts About Screwy Music, I'm Mad About Daffy Tempos," and I've often meant to look it up in the British Museum to see whether the rest of the lyric forecast the rise of bop with such uncanny accuracy. This new mode seemed to have originated partly out of boredom with playing ordinary jazz six nights a week (admittedly a pretty grueling way of earning a living), and partly from a desire to wrest back the initiative in jazz from the white musician, to invent "something they can't steal because they can't play it." This motive is a bad basis for any art, and it isn't surprising that I found the results shallow and *voulu*. Worst of all was the pinched, unhappy, febrile, tense nature of the music. The constant pressure to be different and difficult demanded greater and greater technical virtuosity and more and more exaggerated musical non sequiturs. It wasn't, in a word, the music of happy men. I used to think that anyone hearing a Parker record would guess he was a drug addict, but no one hearing Beiderbecke would think he was an alcoholic, and that this summed up the distinction between the kinds of music.

What I was feeling was, no doubt, a greatly-amplified version of the surprise many European listeners felt when, after the war, records of Parker and his followers began to arrive across the Atlantic. "America has gone mad!" wrote George Shearing on reaching New York during this period (it didn't take him long to follow suit), and whereas Shearing was (presumably) taking only Parker and Gillespie on the chin, I was taking everything up to 1961—Monk, Davis, Coltrane, Rollins, The Jazz Messengers, the lot. I was denied even the solace of liking this man and disliking that: I found them all equally off-putting. Parker himself, compulsively fast and showy, couldn't play four bars without resorting to a peculiarly irritating five-note cliché from a pre-war song called "The Woody Woodpecker Song." His tone, though much better than that of some of his successors, was thin and sometimes shrill.* The impression of mental hallucination he conveyed could also be derived from the pianist Bud Powell, who cultivated the same kind of manic virtuosity and could sometimes be stopped only by the flashing of a light in his eyes. Gillespie, on the other hand, was a more familiar type, the trumpeter-leader and entertainer, but I didn't relish his addiction to things Latin-American and I found his sense of humor rudimentary. Thelonious Monk seemed a not-very-successful comic, as his funny hats proclaimed: his *faux-naif* elephant-dance piano style, with its gawky intervals and absence of swing, was made doubly tedious by his limited repertoire. With Miles Davis and John Coltrane a new inhumanity emerged. Davis had several manners: the dead muzzled slow stuff, the sour yelping fast stuff, and the sonorous theatrical arranged stuff, and I disliked them all. With John Coltrane metallic and passionless nullity gave way to exercises in gigantic absurdity, great boring excursions on not-especially-attractive themes during which all pos-

*I fancy, however, that Parker was improving at the time of his death, possibly as a result of meeting Bechet in France (Bechet was always ready to instruct the young).

sible changes were rung, extended investigations of oriental tedium, long-winded and portentous demonstrations of religiosity. It was with Coltrane, too, that jazz started to be *ugly on purpose:* his nasty tone would become more and more exacerbated until he was fairly screeching at you like a pair of demoniacally-possessed bagpipes. After Coltrane, of course, all was chaos, hatred and absurdity, and one was almost relieved that severance with jazz had become so complete and obvious. But this is running ahead of my story.

The awkward thing was that it was altogether too late in the day to publicize this kind of reaction. In the late forties battle had been joined in the correspondence columns between the beret-and-dark-glasses boys and the moldy figs; by the early sixties, all this had died down. Setting aside a qualification or two I should like to make later, one can say only that to voice such a viewpoint in 1961 would have been journalistically impossible. By then Parker was dead and a historical figure, in young eyes probably indistinguishable from King Oliver and other founding fathers. There was nothing for it but to carry on with my original plan of undiscriminating praise, and I did so for nearly two years. During this time I blocked in the background by subscribing to *Down Beat* again (there was none of the FRISCO CHIRP'S VEGAS DEBUT headlines I remembered from my schooldays), and read a lot of books. I learned that jazz had now developed, socially and musically: the postwar Negro was better educated, more politically conscious and culturally aware than his predecessors, and in consequence the Negro jazz musician was more musically sophisticated. He knew his theory, his harmony, his composition: he had probably been to the Juilliard School of Music, and jazz was just what he didn't want to be associated with, in the sense of grinning over half a dozen chords to an audience all night. He had freed his music as a preliminary to freeing himself: jazz was catching up with the rest of music, becoming chromatic instead of diatonic (this was the something fundamentally awful), taking in other national musical characteristics as the American Negro looked beyond the confines of his own bondage. Practically everyone was agreed about all this. It was fearful. In a humanist society, art—and especially modern, or current, art—assumes great importance, and to lose touch with it is parallel to losing one's faith in a religious age. Or, in this particular case, since jazz is the music of the young, it was like losing one's potency. And yet, try as I would, I couldn't find anything to enjoy in the things I was sent, despite their increasing length—five, seven, nine minutes at a time, nothing like the brilliant three-minute cameos of the age of 78s. Something, I felt, had snapped, and I was drifting deeper into the silent shadowland of middle age. Cold death had taken his first citadel.

And yet again, there was something about the books I was now reading that seemed oddly familiar. This *development,* this *progress,* this *new language* that was more *difficult,* more *complex,* that required you to *work hard at appreciating it,* that you *couldn't expect to understand first go,* that needed *technical and professional knowledge* to evaluate it *at all levels,* this *revolutionary explosion* that *spoke for our time* while at the same time being *traditional* in the *fullest,* the *deepest* . . . Of course! This was the language of criticism of modern painting, modern poetry, modern music. *Of course!* How glibly I had talked of modern jazz, without realizing the force of the adjective: this was *modern* jazz, and Parker was a modern jazz player just as Picasso was a modern painter and Pound a modern poet. I hadn't realized that jazz had gone from Lascaux to Jackson Pollock in fifty years, but now I realized it relief came flooding in upon me after nearly two years' despondency. I went back to my books: "After Parker, you had to be something of a musician to follow the best jazz of the day" (Benny Green, *The Reluctant Art*). Of course! After Picasso! After Pound! There could hardly have been a conciser summary of what I don't believe about art.

The reader may here have the sense of having strayed into a private argument. All I am saying is that the term "modern," when applied to art, has a more than chronological meaning: it denotes a quality of irresponsibility peculiar to this century, known sometimes as modernism, and once I had classified modern jazz under this heading I knew where I was. I am sure there are books in which the genesis of modernism is set out in full. My own theory is that it is related to an imbalance between the two tensions from which art springs: these are the tension between the artist and his material, and between the artist and his audience, and that in the last seventy-five years or so the second of these has slackened or even perished. In consequence the artist has become over-concerned with his material (hence an age of technical experiment), and, in isolation, has busied himself with the two principal themes of modernism, mystification and outrage. Piqued at being neglected, he has painted portraits with both eyes on the same side of the nose, or smothered a model with paint and rolled her over a blank canvas. He has designed a dwelling-house to be built underground. He has written poems resembling the kind of pictures typists make with their machines during the coffee break, or a novel in gibberish, or a play in which the characters sit in dustbins. He has made a six-hour film of someone asleep. He has carved human figures with large holes in them. And parallel to this activity ("every idiom has its idiot," as an American novelist has written) there has grown up a kind of critical journalism designed to put it over. The terms and the arguments vary with circumstances, but basically the message is: Don't trust your eyes, or ears, or understanding. They'll tell you this is ridiculous, or ugly, or meaningless. Don't believe them. You've got to work at this: after all, you don't expect to understand anything as important as art straight off, do you? I mean, this is pretty complex stuff: if you want to know how complex, I'm giving a course of ninety-six lectures at the local college, starting next week, and you'd be more than welcome. The whole thing's on the rates, you won't have to pay. After all, think what asses people have made of themselves in the past by not understanding art—you don't want to be like that, do you? And so on, and so forth. Keep the suckers spending.

The tension between artist and audience in jazz slackened when the Negro stopped wanting to entertain the white man, and when the audience as a whole, with the end of the Japanese war and the beginning of television, didn't in any case particularly want to be entertained in that way any longer. The jazz band in the nightclub declined just as my old interest, the dance band, had declined in the restaurant and hotel: jazz moved, ominously, into the culture belt, the concert halls, university recital rooms, and summer schools where the kind of criticism I have outlined has freer play. This was bound to make the reestablishment of any artist-audience nexus more difficult, for universities have long been the accepted stamping-ground for the subsidized acceptance of art rather than the real purchase of it—and so, of course, for this kind of criticism, designed as it is to prevent people using their eyes and ears and understandings to report pleasure and discomfort. In such conditions modernism is bound to flourish.

I don't know whether it is worth pursuing my identification of modern jazz with other branches of modern art any further: if I say I dislike both in what seems to me the same way I have made my point. Having made the connection, however, I soon saw how quickly jazz was passing from mystification ("Why don't you get a piano player? and what's that stuff he's playing?") to outrage. Men such as Ornette Coleman, Albert Ayler, and Archie Shepp, dispensing with pitch, harmony, theme, tone, tune, and rhythm, were copied by older (Rollins, Coltrane) and young players alike. And some of them gave a keener edge to what they were playing by suggesting that it had some political relation to the aspirations of the Black Power movement. From using music to entertain the white man, the Negro had moved to hating him with it. Anyone who thinks that an Archie ("America's done me a lot of wrong") Shepp record is anything but two fingers extended from a bunched fist at him personally cannot have much appreciation of what he is hearing. Or, as LeRoi Jones puts it, "Listening to Sonny Murray, you can hear the primal needs of the new music. The heaviest emotional indentation it makes. From ghostly moans of spirit, let out full to the heroic marchspirituals and priestly celebrations of the new blackness."

By this time I was quite certain that jazz had ceased to be produced. The society that had engendered it had gone, and would not return. Yet surely all that energy and delight could not vanish as completely as it came? Looking round, it didn't take long to discover what was delighting the youth of the sixties as jazz had delighted their fathers; indeed, one could hardly ask the question for the deafening racket of the groups, the slamming, thudding, whanging cult of beat music that derived straight from the Negro clubs on Chicago's South Side, a music so popular that its practitioners formed a new aristocracy that was the envy of all who beheld them, supported by their own radio stations throughout the world's waking hours. Perhaps I was mistaken in thinking that jazz had died; what it had done was split into two, intelligence without beat and beat without intelligence, and it was the latter which had won the kind of youthful allegiance that had led me to hammer an accompaniment to Ray Noble's "Tiger Rag" when I was twelve or thirteen. Beat was jazz gone to seed, just as "modern jazz" was: B. B. King or Ornette Coleman? A difficult choice, and if I were to come down (as I should) on the side of the former, it wouldn't be under the illusion that I was listening to the latterday equivalent of Billie Holiday and Teddy Wilson, Pee Wee Russell and Jess Stacy, or Fats Waller and his Rhythm.

3

My slow approximation through these articles to the position just stated is the story I promised lay in them, and the amusement—at least, for me—is watching truthfulness break in, despite my initial resolve. As I said, it's an ordinary tale, and perhaps hardly worth telling. On the other hand, once I had worked out to my own satisfaction what had happened to postwar jazz, I couldn't help looking round to see who, if anyone, had anticipated me. Jazz writers as a class are committed to a party line that presents jazz as one golden chain stretching from Buddy Bolden to Sun Ra, and their task is facilitated by the practice jazz magazines have of employing several reviewers (the trad man, the mod man, the blues man) to ensure that nobody ever has to write about anything they really detest. This is good for trade, lessens the amount of ill-will flying about the business, and gives the impression that jazz is a happy and homogeneous whole. But was there no one among them who had realized what was going on, apart from myself?

I don't mean to suggest that there are not many knowledgeable critics to whom the party line is a sincere reality, nor to imply that they are given to mendacity. When a jazz writer says, "You can hear Bessie in Bird," or "Shepp's playing pure New Orleans street marches," I'm quite prepared to believe he means it, as long as I have permission to mark his mental competence below zero. I also take leave to reflect that most of them are, after all, involved with "the scene" on a commercial day-to-day basis, and that their protestations might be compared with the strictures of a bishop on immorality: no doubt he means it, but it's also what he draws his money for saying. Would any critic seriously try to convince his hearers that jazz was dead? "Jazz dead, you say, Mr. Stickleback? Then we shan't be wanting next month's record stint, shall we? And don't bother to review 'Pharoah Saunders: Symbol and Synthesis' for the book page. And—let's see—we'd better cancel that New Wave Festival you were going to compère. Hope you make the pop scene, daddyo." And so they soldier on at their impossible task, as if trying to persuade us that a cold bath is in some metaphysical way the same as a hot bath, instead of its exact opposite ("But don't you see the evolutionary development?").

But of course there was Hugues Panassié, the venerable Frog, who matter-of-factly refused to admit that bop or any of its modernist successors was jazz at all, simply adducing their records as evidence. It was a shock to find myself agreeing with Panassié: back in 1940 I had considered him rather an ass, chiefly because he overvalued Negro players at the expense of white ones ("the natural bad taste of the Negro" was a favorite phrase of the time), in particular the forcible-feeble Ladnier. But in appealing to the ear, rather than regurgitating the convoluted persuasions of the sleeves, he was producing the kind of criticism I liked, and I had to take back much of what I had thought of him in consequence. Then there was Brian Rust, authoritative discographer, who in his introduction to *Jazz Records 1932–1942* claimed that by 1944 "jazz had split, permanently, the followers of the bop cult demanding—and getting—music in an ever-freer form till (at least in the writer's opinion) it ceased even to be recognizable as jazz at all." He also said that if he played Charlie Parker records to his baby it cried. And it was amusing to find Benny Green, who had made very merry with the bewilderment of old-style fans at the chromatic revolution, devoting the last pages of his book to sarcasms about Ornette Coleman and "some nebulous lunacy called Free Form": nothing is funnier than an upstaged revolutionary. Now and then, too, a reviewer got the wrong record, as in 1961 when the editor of *Down Beat,* Don De Micheal, took off on Ornette in heartwarming style ("the resulting chaos is an insult to the listener"), ending "If Coleman is to be a standard of excellence in jazz, then other standards might as well be done away with." Only once (August 1967) did I let fly in this way, and then it was like hitting the stumps with a no-ball: the piece wasn't printed.

Such examples* could indeed be multiplied, but might only seem added strokes to a self-portrait of the critic as ossified sensibility. To say I don't like modern jazz because it's modernist art simply raises the question of why I

*To which should certainly be added Henry Pleasants, author of *Serious Music—And All That Jazz!* (1969).

don't like modernist art: I have a suspicion that many readers will welcome my grouping of Parker with Picasso and Pound as one of the nicest things I could say about him. Well, to do so settles at least one question: as long as it was only Parker I didn't like, I might believe that my ears had shut up about the age of twenty-five and that jazz had left me behind. My dislike of Pound and Picasso, both of whom pre-date me by a considerable margin, can't be explained in this way. The same can be said of Henry Moore and James Joyce (a textbook case of declension from talent to absurdity). No, I dislike such things not because they are new, but because they are irresponsible exploitations of technique in contradiction of human life as we know it. This is my essential criticism of modernism, whether perpetrated by Parker, Pound, or Picasso*: it helps us neither to enjoy nor endure. It will divert us as long as we are prepared to be mystified or outraged, but maintains its hold only by being more mystifying and more outrageous: it has no lasting power. Hence the compulsion on every modernist to wade deeper and deeper into violence and obscenity: hence the succession of Parker by Rollins and Coltrane, and of Rollins and Coltrane by Coleman, Ayler, and Shepp. In a way, it's a relief: if jazz records are to be one long screech, if painting is to be a blank canvas, if a play is to be two hours of sexual intercourse performed *coram populo,* then let's get it over, the sooner the better, in the hope that human values will then be free to reassert themselves.

*The reader will have guessed by now that I am using these pleasantly alliterative names to represent not only their rightful owners but every practitioner who might be said to have succeeded them.

The Musical Achievement

Eric Hobsbawm

Hobsbawm, one of Britain's leading historians, first published his classic book The Jazz Scene *in 1959 (under the name Francis Newton). This chapter, from the recently republished and expanded edition, is as persuasive and disinterested as any of the myriad attempts to identify the value of jazz and place it in proper relation to the rest of the world's music.*

The first thing to do when considering the musical achievement of jazz is to forget that of classical Western music. The two are non-competitive, in spite of the efforts of stubborn adversaries of jazz among the classicists, and of some jazz and classical modernists, to establish that they are not. If we ask: has jazz produced anything like the Beethoven Ninth, or the Bach *B-Minor Mass,* or *Don Giovanni,* the answer must be a flat no. Nor is it likely to produce music to compete with the Western classical art tradition, except conceivably in the field of opera. If we judge jazz by the standards of Western art-music, we can say that it has produced a number of beautiful melodies—but no more beautiful ones than Western art, or even light and pop music,* a particularly successful genre of accompanied *lieder,* in the vocal blues, a few suites of the late romantic type, a great variety of formally uncontrolled, but imaginatively most fertile "variations on a theme," and a few exercises in such forms as fugues and canons. The achievement is a minor one, in terms of absolute and architectural music.

If we judge jazz playing by the standards of Western art-playing, the balance-sheet is more impressive, for not even the most stubborn classicist will deny that jazz has vastly extended the range and technical possibilities of every instrument it has touched, with the exception of the smaller stringed ones; and few will even deny that, man for man, the finest jazz players are—perhaps with the exception of the pianists—considerably superior to their classical opposite numbers. But we are, after all, here considering jazz not as

*Let us not be superior about light and pop music. Utterly feeble in every other way, it has at its best, and even at its top-level average produced numerous splendid melodies, as witness Stephen Foster, George Gershwin, and others. That some of us prefer other melodies is another matter.

a pioneer of novel instrumental combinations and colors and new instrumental possibilities, but as a music with self-contained achievements.

It has achievements but not in terms of art-music, the very concepts of which are alien to it. This does not mean that jazz may not influence art-music, or fuse with it. Indeed it has shown a marked tendency to do so of late. But when it does it will no longer be jazz, but jazz-based art-music, just as Bizet's *Carmen,* and even de Falla, are not Spanish popular music, but Spanish or Spanish-tinged art-music. Jazz already has its Bizet: George Gershwin's *Porgy and Bess,* the finest American contribution to opera so far, bears the same sort of relation to jazz as *Carmen* does to Spanish music; indeed, a rather closer relation, since a diluted form of jazz belonged to Gershwin's musical idiom.* It has not yet developed its de Falla, or more exactly, its Bartók or Mussorgsky, but there is no *a priori* musical reason why one day it should not.

The fundamental unit of the orthodox arts is the "work of art" which, once created, lives its life independently of all but its creator; sometimes, as when critics object to a Yeats or Auden revising their own verses, even of him. If it is a picture, it has merely to be preserved; if a book, to be produced. Music and drama have to be performed, but in our academic generation this has increasingly come to mean "interpreted as nearly as possible in the way intended by its original producer." Virtually all historic-musical scholarship is no more than an attempt to recapture this original, authoritative authenticity: there are men who regret that we cannot hear our Handel exactly as Handel meant us to because, unfortunately, we no longer castrate boy singers. The "work of art" which is particularly appreciated we call a masterpiece, a category wholly independent of performance. No one thinks less of Figaro because the Lesser Wigston amateur operatic society murders him.

Now jazz simply does not function this way. Its art is not reproduced, but created, and exists only at the moment of creation. The nearest orthodox parallel is in those arts which have never been quite able to get rid of their popular, not to say vulgar, origins: on the stage. For actors, and indeed for most of us part of the time, drama is what the actors and other stage people make it. A play, however poetic, which is not at the same time a "vehicle"—i.e., which does not allow actors to act—is dead. A great drama abominably acted is merely potential drama. A Henry Irving, who probably never in his life acted in a good unspoiled play, produced a greater emotional catharsis more often than Mr. X who has never acted except in the most authentically produced Shakespeare, because Irving was a greater artist. When it comes to music-hall artists, we admit this freely: a Chaplin or a Marie Lloyd pro-

*Thus the melody of "Summertime" is a literal, and doubtless unintentional, copy of the well-known spiritual "Sometimes I Feel Like a Motherless Child."

duces great art, even when their subject-matter is, by orthodox standards, minor art or no art at all.

This is the way jazz works—though its supreme contribution to the popular arts is a combination of individualism and collective creation, which has long been forgotten in our orthodox culture. It happens that, thanks to the gramophone, bits and pieces of that continuous process of joint creation which is the life of the jazz musician in employment are separated out as "works," even as "masterpieces." But they are not finished works, even if they are "composed" or "arranged." A Louis Armstrong may say to himself on hearing a play-back of his 1928 "West End Blues": "That's a good version, I'll stick to it whenever I play this piece in future at three-minute length," and a Duke Ellington or John Lewis may say of a recording: "That is about how it ought to sound." But if we could hear every "West End Blues," "Across the Track," or "Django" ever played, even by Armstrong, the Ellington band, and the Modern Jazz Quartet themselves, we should hear an unending series of re-creations and modifications, a life-long flux. Moreover, the individual piece is not, for the jazz musician or the jazz-lover, the real unit of the art. If there is a natural unit of jazz, it is the "session"—the evening or night in which one piece after another is played—fast and slow, formal and informal, the whole gamut of emotions. Continuous creation is the essence of this music, and the fact that most of it is fugitive troubles the musician no more than the ballet dancer.

If there is no authenticity and no permanence in the sense of our orthodox arts, neither is there the sharp distinction between the genius and the rest. It is not the object of jazz to produce works, or even performances, which can be classed in a special category of critical excellence, but to enjoy the music, and to make others enjoy it, while creating it. There are, of course, geniuses: Armstrong, Bessie Smith, or Charlie Parker for example. But the essentially collective and practically-minded character of the music means that the value of the music, even of a particular piece, is largely independent of them, so long as there is a sufficiently large body of professional craftsmen of adequate competence and creativity. Nobody can draw up a list of the twenty best recorded instrumental blues. After one or two obvious choices, there are hundreds of records (and in real life, thousands of performances) which would be, in their way, equally good. Good jazz, like a good cook or couturier, is not judged by producing works which, even in memory, stand out as the best ever, but by the capacity to produce constant variety at a high level of excellence. Jazz, in fact, is "music for use," to use Hindemith's phrase, not museum music or music for ranking by examiners.

None of this means that jazz is minor art in the way in which light and pop music is; merely that it gets its effects as major art in a different, and formally more economical, way from art-music. Stephen Foster's or George Gershwin's songs are pretty and enjoyable, but nobody would expect to get the emotion out of them that we draw from Schubert's *Erlkönig* or *In diesen heil'gen Hallen.* But from Bessie Smith's "Young Woman's Blues" we can draw this emotion. Kreisler playing *Caprice Viennois* merely shows off a dazzling technique in a pleasant tune; but Louis Armstrong playing "It's Tight Like This" takes us into the emotional realms of Macbeth's soliloquies. Even Johann Strauss's *Emperor Waltz,* perhaps as high-grade a piece of light classical music as has been composed, merely gives us a great deal of pleasure and satisfaction, but it is well worth swapping it, even as recorded by the Vienna Philharmonic, for "Parker's Mood." Admittedly the relatively small scale on which jazz operates as art limits its scope: after all, a single speech of *Phèdre* is quite within the compass of jazz whereas the whole tragedy is not. But what there is of jazz at its best is heavy stuff: it is small, but made of uranium.

The pleasures of jazz are therefore first and foremost in the emotion it generates, which cannot be isolated from the actual music. This may be illustrated by the persistent prejudice of everybody connected with the music—players, critics, and fans—in favor of improvisation. There is no special musical merit in improvisation, which is merely spur-of-the-moment composition, and therefore likely to be less good than considered and revised composition.* For the listener it is musically irrelevant that what he hears is improvised or written down. If he did not know he could generally not tell the difference. But improvisation, or at least a margin of it around even the most "written" jazz compositions, is rightly cherished, because it stands for the constant living re-creation of the music, the excitement and inspiration of the players which is communicated to us. There is very little doubt that the most powerful effects of jazz lie in the intensified communication of human emotion. That is why the primitive sung blues has retained its unchallenged place in it, and why the technically imperfect and primitive discs of New Orleans jazz hold their own, so long as they "blow out," while the orchestrations and compositions often date. This is true even of modern jazz, in spite of the claims of some of its supporters. What survives in Parker, and has conquered even many of those who were originally most repelled by his innovations, is its "tortured, searing, blasting beauty, reminiscent of the shouting gospel congregations of the South." (Marshall Stearns) His innovations belong to history, and if there had been nothing more to him than this

*Of course the jazz composer—i.e., every creative player—does consider and revise, but in the process of playing his parts over and over again, and, as it were, working them slowly into their finished form; that is, assuming he does not change his ideas and want to turn an elaborated piece into something else.

he would be no more important than W. C. Handy, who first wrote down the blues.

Jazz is thus players' music and music directly expressing emotions, and its technical forms of creation and musical possibilities reflect both facts. For instance, it does not depend on a "composer"—for we can hardly call the collection of simple themes which make up the general jazz repertoire (the so-called "standards") compositions. They may be good tunes or bad, folk blues or pop ballads, or some other themes, but their merit is irrelevant. If their harmonies lend themselves to jazz development, they will do. The blues always do, and fortunately they are good music, but the only lasting merit of "All the Things You Are" or "How High the Moon," which have become "modern" standards, or "I Can't Give You Anything but Love, Baby" and the other standards of the 1920s is that they are good pegs on which to hang jazz. The original jazz "composition"—i.e., performance—emerged simply from the interplay of various musicians on a given theme, according to certain rough rules of convenience or tradition. A "new" composition could come into being in three ways: by playing a different theme, by getting together a different group of players—provided always they knew one another well enough to cooperate smoothly—and by playing the same theme with the same musicians another time, when one or more of the players had different ideas. The result was a mass of varied "compositions" of the same scope and in the same idiom. It is obvious that accident plays a great part in such musical creation which is, in a sense, like good talk or a good football match, in which anything—the combination of a particular group of people, the presence of one particularly stimulating person, a good audience, or just one of those good moods—can make all the difference. (The old-established tendency for some players to take drink or marihuana, or some other drug, is merely an attempt to eliminate this fortuitousness by artificially establishing the "good mood" in which the musician creates freely. How far it does so is a matter of debate.)

This accidental factor remains strong, even when jazz composition becomes somewhat more systematic with the "arrangement." The most intelligent jazz composers have always recognized that jazz is not composed with notes or instruments but with creative men and women. As M. Hodeir, the best of the classically trained critics has put it, in jazz the "fusion of individualities" takes "the place of architecture." The good jazz composer-arranger either imagines his sound and then looks for particular individual players whose personal voice comes nearest to his ideas, or derives his ideas from the personalities of his actual team. The greatest of the Creole composers, Jelly Roll Morton, seems to have chosen the first course, a relatively easy matter in so unified a style of playing as that of New Orleans. The young Duke Ellington generally leaned more towards the second: we can actually observe him "discovering" the "growl" sound of his brass from Charley Irvis (trombone) and the late Bubber Miley (trumpet), and later building some of his most characteristic orchestral effects on it. In his earlier works the "composition" is often little more than the assembling and shaping of the ideas spontaneously produced by the players. This is why the successful jazz composer has almost invariably been a band-leader, or at least permanently attached to a band; and why the most elaborate jazz compositions (for instance Ellington's) have rarely been taken up—except as straight imitations—elsewhere. As soon as they are played by other players they change. Conversely, the composer himself is limited by having to find musicians who have his house style, or else he is obliged to modify his own style. Thus Ellington has been visibly troubled by the loss of Barney Bigard in 1942, for his liquid Creole clarinet had become part of his musical palette, and subsequent replacements have not been wholly successful. Of course capable musicians entering a band with a marked house style of its own can very often adapt themselves to it. Jazz composition has only slowly emancipated itself from this dependence on the individual personalities of its players. Perhaps this is a major reason why so far no full-scale jazz composition, e.g., a jazz opera, has emerged. Gershwin, who has brought off the nearest thing to it in *Porgy and Bess,* was used to working in the orthodox tradition, i.e., to writing in terms of notes on paper and not of specific men. Ellington, whose idea of a "concerto"—and a highly successful one too, as witness the marvelous "Concerto for Cootie"—was to write a piece bringing out the special qualities of each of his soloists, has undoubtedly found the step to impersonal composition hard to make.

If jazz composition is limited technically by the need to compose men rather than notes, it is equally limited by the nature of jazz creation, as we have sketched it above. To put it in a word, it stands or falls by the human emotions it generates, and not by its qualities as "pure" music. It is, to quote the sagacious M. Hodeir again, "precisely the kind of music that can be listened to without burying one's forehead in one's hands . . . in jazz 'sensorial interests' greatly outweigh 'intellectual passion' . . . a sharpened sensuality takes the place of loftiness, and the fusion of individualities takes the place of architecture." The most intelligent jazz composers have instinctively recognized these limitations. Jelly Roll Morton gave New Orleans music deliberate shape and elegance, but did not attempt to change it. Duke Ellington is almost exclusively a composer of pieces expressing moods, or re-creating sense-impressions, as the titles of his records indicate: "Mood Indigo," "Misty Mornin'," "Creole Love-Call," "A Portrait of Bert Williams," "Such Sweet Thunder." Modern jazz composers have found their most fruitful field in incidental music to films, in which the jazz gift for mood-expression and music-painting is used to great effect, as in Chico Hamilton's music for *Sweet*

Smell of Success and John Lewis's for *Sait-on jamais?* And why not? It is a long time, even in the classical arts, since anyone has objected to Hugo Wolf because he illustrates poems in song, or to Bizet, because a concert selection of *Carmen* does not sound so well as a Beethoven quartet, or to Prokofiev's *Cinderella,* because it is intended to go with a ballet. There is plenty of precedent for serious music which buttresses its own architectural weaknesses by leaning on other arts, and strengthens these in turn. In the composite work of art—the ballet, the opera, the film—there is wide scope for jazz, and indeed this seems the most natural way of further development for a music which emerges from the popular arts, whose more elaborate achievements have always been in the nature of "mixed" entertainments—"variety" at the lowest level, the composite pantomime-allegory-ballet-opera at its highest.

Jazz certainly possesses a "natural" bent towards "pure" music, but even this must not be confused with the tendencies of art-music. It emerges from the ordinary player's pride in his technical expertise, which makes good players vie with one another to play increasingly "difficult" things. Modern jazz is largely the product of such technical experimenting. Technical, but not architectural. Left to themselves, jazz players or composers formed in jazz will experiment with everything except musical forms. If they play fugues or canons it is because they are trying to imitate classical music. Anyone anxious to tell the difference between a "pure" jazz composition and a jazz composition borrowing from classical music should compare, say, *Brilliant Corners* by Thelonious Monk with, say, John Lewis's *Concorde.* In the first we will find experiments in tempo, and in the combined sound of saxophones, such as vibrato explosions in unison. In the second we shall find an orthodox, relatively simple, fugue. Not that architecture is lacking in such "pure" jazz compositions; but, as might be expected in a players' music, it is the architecture of the instrumental solo.

This is not a criticism of the increasingly numerous attempts to marry jazz and classical music. In the first place, there is no law against it. In the second place it is a perfectly reasonable thing, both for classical composers and for jazz musicians with ambition for more complex things, to break through the technical limitations of jazz. After all, it may be plausibly held that a genuine American classical music will emerge only when American composers have assimilated the idiom of their native folk-music (i.e., of jazz) as Spanish, Hungarian, Russian, Czech, Finnish, and English composers have in their own time assimilated theirs. In the third place, it is no doubt a good thing for the self-respect of jazz musicians (especially of black ones) that their music should prove its ability to satisfy even the intellectually more ambitious listener. I merely wish to establish the important distinction between the sort of jazz which evolves toward more elaborate and "legitimate" music in its own way, and the sort which results from the crossing of jazz and "straight" music: the distinction between Jelly Roll Morton's "Deep Creek Blues" and Paul Whiteman's "symphonic jazz" in the 1920s, or between Thelonious Monk and Dave Brubeck in the 1950s. So far, of these two types of jazz, the first has produced better and more fruitful results than the second, though it is quite conceivable that this might one day cease to be the case.

What then, are the musical achievements of jazz? Its major, perhaps its only real achievement, is that it exists: a music which has rescued the qualities of folk-music in a world which is designed to extirpate them; and which has so far maintained them against the dual blandishments of pop music and art-music. Taken in isolation, no recorded version of the blues "How Long" is a great work of art, in the serious sense, though many of them are extremely moving, and though the tune is beautiful and the poetry good.

How long, long, has that evening train been gone
How long, how long, baby how long?

I've got a girl who lives upon the hill
If she don't love me, I know who will
How long, how long, how long?
If I could holler like a mountain jack
Go up on the mountain and call my baby back,
How long, how long, how long.

The important and artistically valid thing is that this theme should produce works as different as Count Basie's orchestral-cum-vocal version, the late Jimmy Yancey's beautiful piano solo, or Joe Turner's shouting blues, and that it should remain alive, and capable of stimulating every group of players who touch it to produce their own music: some good, some mediocre, some poor, but, given a certain competence and feeling, all of it genuinely touching the genuine music. Whatever other and higher merits it has or may acquire, its chief merit is that of proving that genuine music, even in the twentieth century, can avoid both the blind-alleys of commercial pop music, which establishes its *rapport* with the public at the expense of art, and *avant-garde* art-music, which develops its art at the expense of cutting itself off from all but a chosen public of experts.

It has produced a great deal more, as M. Hodeir has demonstrated for the rare readers who possess both a good knowledge of jazz and of orthodox music, in his excellent book. (Note especially the chapters on "The Romantic Imagination of Dickie Wells," "Concerto for Cootie," "Charlie Parker and the Problem of Improvisation.") There are artists of superb caliber and overpowering genius, works of permanent value, which may be played with equal or greater enjoyment thirty years after their original performance, and a crop of technical innovations of which orthodox music has so far made practically no use, perhaps because of the deficiencies of both its composers and its players. However, the very attempt to express the achievements of jazz in terms of art-music must, as I have already suggested, distort the nature of that achievement.

Admittedly, all this is small-scale work. Jazz is little music and not big music, in the same sense as lyrics are little poetry and epics big poetry; pottery little art and cathedrals big art. Limitation of scope and relative smallness of scale do not make an art less good or true or beautiful. They do, however, put certain artistic achievements out of its reach: a sports car is not a worse vehicle than an airplane, but one designed for different purposes. Jazz has many merits, and a large number of people have derived from it consistent and intense and self-respecting pleasure, and have been profoundly, and justifiably, moved by it. But there are things which jazz cannot do (as conversely, there are things which modern classical music cannot do), and no purpose is served by pretending otherwise, except to butter up the self-esteem of people who are too lazy or ignorant to understand the more complex forms of art. Jazz, like Keats's definition of poetry, is "simple, sensuous, and passionate," though, unlike Keats's definition, it can also be technically highly sophisticated and demanding, while the apparent simplicity of its emotions often conceals very great complexity. Of course, so do apparently simple emotions in real life. But there are other things in life and the arts than these, and jazz does not supply them.

Nevertheless, its place in the musical not to mention the general cultural history of our century is already assured. It has demonstrated the vitality, and the possibilities of evolution, of a people's music; and if ever a way is to be found out of the impasse into which the orthodox arts have penetrated in our age, it may well be found by studying the nature of jazz, its creators, and its public. (This no more implies that the orthodox arts are to be saved by imitating jazz than the study of the aerodynamics of birds means that planes have to be constructed to look like seagulls.) It has been increasingly unavoidable. However little orthodox musicians have done with it, they have not escaped its presence. And it has been pretty certainly the most important musical achievement of the United States of America to date; and quite certainly the only one to win international acceptance. No orthodox American composer is a genuinely international figure, as the great classical composers were in their day; all are provincial figures blown up by local pride, and perhaps enjoying a limited appreciation or a *succès d'estime* among the musically better-informed international public. But Louis Armstrong, Bessie Smith, Charlie Parker are accepted without question all over the world, wherever there is a public for jazz, and indeed wherever American culture is discussed; and so is jazz itself.

King Oliver

Larry Gushee

Larry Gushee is not a prolific critic, and his work remains uncollected, but Martin Williams included several examples of his very perceptive reviews in the anthology The Art of Jazz. *This consideration of a King Oliver collection first appeared in* Jazz Review *in 1958.*

Louis Armstrong 1923: WITH KING OLIVER'S CREOLE JAZZ BAND,
Riverside RLP 12-122. Joe (King) Oliver, Louis Armstrong, *cornets*; Honore Dutray, *trombone*; Johnny Dodds, *clarinet*; Lil Hardin Armstrong, *piano*; Bill Johnson, *banjo*; Baby Dodds, *drums*.
Chimes Blues; Just Gone; Canal Street Blues; Mandy Lee Blues; Weather Bird Rag; Dippermouth Blues; Froggie Moore; Snake Rag.
Add Stomp Evans, *saxophone:*
Mabel's Dream; Southern Stomps; Riverside Blues.

The title of this album may be commercial good sense; musically, however, it is simply nonsense. There have been blessed few bands that have ever played together like Joe Oliver's, and Louis' presence is but one of many elements responsible. And his contribution is, in a sense, a negative one, for he is rarely heard in the role in which he found real greatness, that of genial, poignant, triumphant soloist, set off by subordinate, if not run-of-the-mill, musicians. Here and there we hear a phrase, sometimes only a single tone, played with the warm, slightly irregular vibrato so different from Joe Oliver's. We know it is Louis and are thankful for that knowledge.

If a band can be said to have a clearly recognizable and highly original sound, it must consist of something more than the arithmetic sum of a certain number of individual styles. I suspect that the *sine qua non* is discipline, which chiefly finds expression as consistency and limitation. Individual talent and skill do not even come into question here, at least as they are generally thought of, for one of the paradoxes of style is that poor musicians can create a fine sound (Unconscious Poetry of the People Dept.). Begin with a group of musicians out of the common run, and who are guided by some dominant principle or personality, and the resultant sound will be truly unique, pleasing to the ears because it is musical, to the soul because it is integral. This is what makes the first records of Charlie Parker and Dizzy Gillespie, the Mulligan Quartet, the Original Dixieland Jazz Band, stylistically great as well as musically pleasing.

And so these recordings, in their way, are a norm, and object lessons of what a jazz band needs to be great. Unfortunately, it is not quite possible to say to the infidel, "Listen and believe," for so much of the music escaped the acoustical recording technique. Happily, the imagination will gradually supply much of what the ear cannot perceive, much as it can fill in (indeed, is expected to fill in) the gaps in a figure incompletely sketched.

Our idea of how this band *really* sounded, however, will always contain one element of uncertainty, barring the discovery of time travel, since the recorded sound of the Creole Band depended to so great an extent on the company that recorded it. On this reissue the sides made for Gennett (all except 3 on side 2) must have been cut in marshmallow—with Johnny Dodds crouched inside the recording horn. It seems to me that the Paramounts (the above-mentioned exceptions) must sound more like actuality: clarinet is toned down, cornets are strong, with the second part actually being heard, the piano chording does not run together in an amorphous droning, and the bass line is generally clearer, the more so since it is reinforced by Stump Evans's bass sax.

Still, the Gennetts are in the majority here, and assisted by Riverside's remastering, they sound fine. Chiefly they sound fine because Oliver, like Jelly Roll in his happiest days, knew the sound he wanted, and had the brass and the guts and the prestige to run a band his way. Whether the tempos, so often felicitous, were Joe Oliver's independent choice, or determined by prevailing dance style I cannot know. The fact remains that the Creole Band (and the New Orleans Rhythm Kings) played a good deal slower than bands like the Wolverines and the Bucktown 5, which recorded only a year later. The tempos they chose never exceeded their technical limitations, while, for instance, the Wolverines and, especially, the later Chicagoans often played too fast for comfort (theirs and ours). I am sure that this accounts for much of the superb swing of the Creole Band.

But even more important is the manner in which the separate beats of the measure are accented. Here we tread on thin ice, the subjective conditions of hearing being difficult to verify objectively. Different people must hear the relative amplitudes of the beats differently—how else to account for the fact that many contemporary emulators of this style seem, to my ears, to accentuate the secondary beats far too much, rather than playing a truly flat four-four as did Oliver's rhythm section? You see, though, that I already beg the question. On the other hand, some of the so-called revival bands manage to reproduce the effect of the Creole Band's rhythm, while failing in other respects. The trouble is, I suspect, that the horns sound as if they are working too hard, and any suggestion of laboriousness immediately sets a band apart from the relaxed assurance and ease of the older group.

The truly phenomenal rhythmic momentum generated by Oliver is just as much dependent on *continuity* of rhythmic pulse—only reinforced by uniformity of accentuation in the rhythm section and relaxed playing. One never hears the vertiginous excitement of Bix, or Tesch; one never feels that, with a little less control, a break or an entire chorus would fall into irrationality or musical *bizarrerie*. Oliver's swing is exciting after a different fashion: it is predictable, positive, and consistent. Only rarely is the total effect *manqué,* as in "Froggie Moore," where the stop-and-go character of the tune makes consistency more difficult to achieve.

Its consistency is, as I have said, largely the result of Oliver's personal conception of a band sound. How much he molded the musicians to fit the ideal pattern of his own imagination, or how much he chose them with the knowledge that they would fit in, without trying to change their personal styles, is something we can't determine since we lack recordings by New Orleans bands before 1923. We have no record of how Louis sounded before he came to Chicago—we know he is full of the spirit of King Joe, although their ideas of instrumental tone were divergent. Dodds's rare gift of phrasing, his ability to bridge the gap between trumpet phrases (generally those of the tune itself) and to place the final note of his own phrase on the beginning of a trumpet phrase, we know from many other records, but none of them antedate these sides. And the rhythmic approach, too, is initiated by the Creole Band, with due note taken of Ory's 1921 "Sunshine" date; we hear it again but infrequently, perhaps a bit in NORK, certainly in the Tuxedo Band, in Sam Morgan's Band, and in many of Bunk's records, and other more recent ones in that tradition.

The impression of consistency is made all the stronger by the refusal of the musicians to permit themselves too much freedom. In successive choruses of a tune Oliver's sidemen often play the same part note for note, or with only slight variation—notice Dutray in "Froggie Moore," especially; Dodds in the same tune and in "Snake Rag." The ODJB did this too, but there is always an undertone (overtone to some) of the ludicrous—visions of tiny mechanical men playing chorus after chorus identically come to us, and one wonders how or why they go on. . . . Dutray, to be sure, often plays a pretty strict harmony part, as if from an orchestration, but there is a good deal more besides, and his mannerisms, his agility and grace, are strictly his own and not from the public domain.

A riff produces somewhat the same kind of excitement as does Oliver's "consistency," stemming ultimately from the irritation born of sameness, and expectation of change unfulfilled by the riff itself, but heard in a superimposed solo. The excitement of riffs, however, is bought too cheap, and works best in the immediacy of ecstatic suspension of our normal listening habits, most effective in the physical presence of a band. The Creole Band's way is less obvious, more complex, and, in the long run, makes a *record* that remains satisfying for year after year.

All these words will never convince someone against his will, and perhaps some will never feel or know why the Creole Jazz Band is so great and sets the standard (possibly, who knows, only because of an historical accident) for all kinds of jazz that do not base their excellence on individual expressiveness, but on form and *shape* achieved through control and balance.

My panegyric tone admits of modification in some instances. The Paramount's "Mabel's Dream" is too slow—in fact, the tempo is an exception in the group of tunes on this record, neither as slow as the *andante* "Southern Stomps" and "Riverside," nor as fast as the rather relaxed "Chimes Blues." The latter is too relaxed for its own good, the tricky chimes effects are dated and special, and Louis solos better elsewhere ("Riverside" and "Froggie Moore").

But all of this is trivial. I love this band and its myth, the perfection it stands for and almost is, its affirmation and integrity, the somber stride of "Riverside Blues," the steady roll of "Southern Stomps," the rock of "Canal St. Blues," the head-long sprint of "Weather Bird"; I love the musicians in this band, too, although my affection is tinged with sadness to think that, with the exception of young Louis, already himself but not yet complete, none of them ever again realized himself so well within a band. This is no reproach to them; it is only the result of the paradoxical fact that this band, recorded only a generation ago and marking the beginning of consistent recording of jazz, was one of the very best that jazz has ever known.

Bix Beiderbecke

Benny Green

A full-scale and judicious examination of Bix—his life, accomplishment, and legend—by Benny Green, unquestionably the finest critic among active jazz players. From his superb 1962 book, The Reluctant Art.

. . . which is the right man,
Walt Whitman or Paul Whiteman? . . .
—Cole Porter

The curse of jazz music is its hagiography, perhaps only to be expected in an art form possessing so much surface flamboyancy. The apparent glory of the spectacle of a lone soloist pitting his inventive powers against the world every time he stands up to play, combined with the element of the picaresque in so many gifted musicians, has been the supreme misfortune of the music. Popular journalism has found it easy to tack on to the body of jazz a spurious romanticism tending to obscure the art that lies beyond. There has been a surfeit of what Walter Sickert once called "the recourse to melodrama to which the disinclination for real critical work drives some critics."

Not all the journalism was meant to have this effect. Some of the very worst critics had the very best intentions. The effect has been deadly nonetheless. Artistic prowess has been neglected in favor of what the twentieth century refers to as "human interest," a phrase which implies that poking one's nose into other people's business is more edifying than poking one's soul into other people's art.

Now the effect of magnifying the artist's personal foibles at the expense of his creative output is to create a sourceless mythology, an order of saints without divine inspiration of any kind, which is precisely what has happened to jazz all through its history, and precisely why the world at large is consistently baffled by the spectacle of a bohemia seemingly peopled only by eccentrics and degenerates producing music which doesn't sound like music at all. It is as though for every genuine lover of painting there were fifty who knew only that Toulouse-Lautrec frequented bawdy houses.

That Buddy Bolden should be immortalized as a barber and scandalmonger whose trumpet could be heard at a range of one, five, or ten miles, depending on the degree of fanaticism to which one adheres to his particular legend, is understandable, for no recordings of Buddy Bolden exist. That Freddie Keppard should be remembered for covering his trumpet valves with a handkerchief to hide his fingerings from covetous rivals is a little less sane, though it may well be aesthetic justice. That Frank Teschemaker should be mourned as an incipient genius cut down by a premature death is hardly acceptable in the light of his recorded work. That Lester Young should be deified as The Man in the Pork-Pie Hat and Charlie Parker fondly recollected as an attempted suicide is quite unforgivable, for by now the legend is devouring the art from which it sprang.

With Bix Beiderbecke the position is already impossible. Sanity long ago fled in wild disorder from the task of interpreting his career. The damage was done many years ago by two agencies, the mawkish contemporaries who grabbed prestige from accidental associations with him, and the disgracefully inept journalism over the years which encouraged the process because it made what was called "very good copy," which always means very bad copy. Bix is jazz's Number One Saint, and any attempt at a rational analysis of his talent usually invokes the bitterness of a theological dispute.

Today Bix is a kind of patron saint of Improvisation, a beatific figure before whom the idolators kneel in reverence, and at whom the debunkers heave giant brickbats. Of course the circumstances were ideal for this process of deification. The exquisite talent, the weakness for bathtub gin, the seraphic smile, the artistic frustration, the premature death, all played out against the backdrop of the Roaring Twenties. The façade has been building up, brick upon critical brick over the years, until today the man is equated with all kinds of people, objects, and causes with which he has only the most tenuous connection. Today, when anybody mentions Bix Beiderbecke, a confused vision is conjured up of all the variegated symbols with which he has been juxtaposed, from Capone to Gatsby, from the crude fact to the artistic synthesis of the fact. The dismal truth awaiting the earnest student of Bix is that his vision will become impaired the moment he breathes Bix's name, and that instead of one figure he will see half a dozen, all interesting enough, but only one of which has much to do with music. The five spurious Beiderbeckes feed on the single reality, the hard core at the heart of the myth, the creative artist. There is the cardboard martyr of the Bixophiles who concoct biographies with acknowledgments to the Princeton dance programs of the Jazz Age; there is the marvelous boy one critic talked of "with wisps of genius swirling around in his brain"; there is the whimsy-whamsy superman of the Condon–Carmichael anecdotes; there is the baby-faced apotheosis of the Jazz Age, with glib parallels drawn between the Bix Crash and the Wall Street Crash—" . . . like the stock markets, he was riding high but shaky by 1929"; there is the actual jazz musician, the one-sixth of the legend which has supported the parasitic growth of the other five-sixths; and, finally, and in some ways the most fascinating of all facets of the legend, there is the fictive Bix projected by Miss Dorothy Baker in her novel *Young Man With a Horn,* a book so perfectly symptomatic of the failure of the writer of fiction to perceive the quintessence of the Jazz Life that the discrepancies between it and the reality of Bix's experience should serve as an invaluable guide to the aspiring writer of jazz fiction.

Fragments of the Bix myth are quite true of course. Bix Beiderbecke really is a key figure in the development of jazz. His dilemma really was a new one for the improvising musician, and he really was the first, perhaps the only, white musician to contribute something completely original to the jazz art which was not artistically suspect. Digesting the bare facts of his life one is soon convinced of the peculiar lovability of this amiable goofer Bix Beiderbecke, with his frightful *naïveté* in a worldly environment and his helplessness or irresponsibility which made a man like Frank Trumbauer desire to father him even at the expense of his own career. But Bix offered up as a martyr on the altar of fine art is more difficult to swallow. Bix's death, by no means the outcome of a self-destructive lust, seems rather to have been, like everything else in his life except his music, a confused accident, the aimless drift of an unsophisticated young man who was hardly aware at any time of what was happening to him.

There were huge blanks in his musical education, and he evidently became increasingly aware of them. He must also have realized the comic ineptitude of many of the musicians with whom he worked. No great jazz musician ever kept worse musical company than Bix Beiderbecke. He seems to have spent most of his career working with lame dogs and most of his energies in helping them over a stile. This apparent indifference to the poor quality of his companions is one of the surest indications of his amazing lack of awareness as a creative artist. To him, the dedicated ruthlessness of the creator would have seemed mere churlishness. Pee Wee Russell once said, "His disposition wasn't one to complain. He wasn't able to say, 'I don't like this guy, let's give him the gate and get so-and-so.' He was never a guy to complain about the company he was in." It is in that last sentence of Russell's, and not in the idiotic talk of selling his soul to Paul Whiteman, that the only real indictment of Bix lies. "He was never a guy to complain of the company he was in." No more deadly accusation could be leveled at any artist.

Sensational as Bix's arrival must have seemed to those who witnessed it, it is clear on reflection that nothing could have been more inevitable. Of all the things that had to happen to jazz, Bix had to happen to it more certainly than all the others, and when jazz has finally run its course and its development seen for what it is, a single continuous process, even the time at which he appeared will seem to have been predictable almost to the year. The jazz Bix heard as a boy was born of a sociological phenomenon whose total effect on the history of man has yet to be charted. Jazz was the musical expression of an oppressed minority dumped on an alien society, and in its beginnings was therefore not respectable, certainly not to the kind of middle-class immigrants the Beiderbeckes typified.

By the time Bix was old enough to understand what he was hearing, jazz had already begun its advance north. He was only one of thousands of white youths intrigued by it. And just as surely as jazz was the result of the transference of African native culture into the melting pot of the Deep South, so was the Bixian dilemma of the last years born of the contrast between the hybrid music Bix played and the sensibilities of the essentially European mind which conceived that music, for although Bix is always nominated as the All-American Boy of his period (the notes to the Memorial album on American Columbia begins "The Bix Beiderbecke Story is the great romantic legend of American jazz"), Bix was the son of German immigrants aware of European music who tried to school the boy in what they thought they knew.

There is indeed a sense in which Bix was a martyr, but it has nothing to do with all the puerilities about marijuana nights and bathtub gin. Bix was the first jazz musician who felt obliged to attempt a widening of the harmonic scope of jazz by grafting on to it some of the elementary movements of modern harmony, the first improviser to try to take the patterns beyond the primitive shapes of New Orleans and give them a tint of the subtleties of the Impressionist composers of Europe.

By the end of his short life he had become less interested in the cornet, and obsessed instead by the piano and the half-formulated pieces he composed for it, a change of attitude with the most profound implications. The added harmonic dimensions of the piano, on which he was able to strike several notes simultaneously, were obviously better suited to his purpose. By that time the early days with the Wolverines only seven years before, days when he was a mere boy carrying the entire band on his shoulders, must have seemed far distant indeed, uncomplicated days before his own developing sensibilities forced him far beyond the point for which his training and experience had equipped him.

The body of legend dimly appreciates that a tension of this kind existed somewhere in Beiderbecke's life, but interprets it with unfailing lack of perception. The Bix legend goes very briefly as follows—"Innocent young white boy with jazz gift. Becomes recognized and records masterpieces in the Big City. Starts to drink. Reaches peak around 1927. Sells his soul to commercialism. Falls ill. Half-recovers. Dies. End of life, beginning of legend." It will be perceived that this framework leaves convenient gaps for the insertion of gangsters, the Right Woman, the Wrong Woman, and the rest of the clumsy farrago which takes the music for granted and delivers a kind of affectionate rap on Bix's posthumous knuckles for being naughty enough to join a band as corrupted as Paul Whiteman's, a band whose only contribution to jazz was the money it poured into the pockets of those who sat in its elephantine ranks.

This artistic defection of Bix's is the one big blot on his copybook, the sole act for which posterity finds it difficult to forgive him. Indeed some criticism cannot find the heart to forgive him at all, being possessed of no heart in the first place, nor a brain nor an ear. Rudi Blesh once wrote with tight-lipped resolution, "Bix's playing is weak. He just pretended to be a jazz musician because his weakness permitted him to play in the commercial orchestras of Whiteman and Jean Goldkette. Bix was neither a tragic nor an heroic character, he was a figure of pathos." Leaving aside the curious defective logic of Blesh's second sentence, I am obliged to admit that there is a whole school of this criticism which discounts Bix, and throughout this school great stress is laid on the fact that Bix finally went for the fleshpots when he should have been preserving his innocence.

Now all this kind of plot stands up very well when it is transferred to an idiom as crass as itself, for instance Hollywood and the fourpenny library romantics. But as an evaluation of Beiderbecke the artist it is so wildly inept that no deliberate parody of authentic criticism could ever get further from the mark. The truth about what happened to Bix and the motives behind his apparently irresponsible behavior are obvious to any thinking jazz musician who has himself experienced, even if to a far less vital degree, the process which took hold of Beiderbecke. Educated by his own worldly experience as an artist, the jazz musician looks at the great mound of rubbish which has accumulated about Bix's figure and chuckles in wonder to himself, thinking perhaps that after all it is hardly reasonable to expect much better from such a parcel of fools.

The Artist-Who-Sold-His-Soul-For-A-Hip-Flask theory is useful in one way, because it is so completely, utterly hopelessly wrong that all one has to do to get to the truth of the matter is to reverse all its main propositions. After all, the man who is consistently wrong is just as sure a guide to conduct as the man who is consistently right.

The one significant thing about Bix is not that he sold his soul to Paul Whiteman for three hundred dollars a week, but that he refused to sell his soul, no matter what the consequences, and that he would have been prepared to sacrifice everything, even the one priceless gift he possessed, his jazz gift, rather than compromise musically so much as a semiquaver. The conventionally accepted story of Bix's growing artistic lassitude, which finally destroyed him, may be neatly reversed to arrive at the truth. Bix embodies the case of artistic irresponsibility and unawareness which imperceptibly evolves into a growing wonder at the glory of music and a desperate attempt to create something worthy of that glory. It is a process half-aesthetic, half-intuitive, and all the more peculiar for the fact that throughout his adult years Bix remained intellectually unaware of the process that had taken hold of him, unable to rationalize its effects, unable to help the process along, unable even to opt out for the simple reason he was hardly aware he had ever been opted in. Iain Lang struck miles nearer the target than Blesh when he remarked that there was no hard core of intelligence or character in Bix to enable him to cope with his unwieldy fame, although he too goes on to describe the Whiteman episode as a compromise.

What did, in fact, happen to Bix had to happen to somebody as soon as jazz started to travel north into the nation at large where middle-class whites like Bix could hear it and be stirred by it. About Bix's reaction to the tremendous strains imposed upon him by his unique experience at the hands of music, there is something which borders, not on the heroic, but on the comic, and the fact that neither intellectually nor morally was he equipped to cope with that experience does make some belated sense out of Blesh's word "pathetic." The most comical thing of all about this battered reputation of Bix Beiderbecke is that there is little opposition to the Sale-of-Soul theory. Instead of opinion being divided between the Bleshes on one hand, who believe that as Bix knew he couldn't play jazz anyway, he joined the highest-paid band in the country and made the best financially out of his own shortcomings, and those like myself who can see quite clearly that joining Whiteman was artistically the only honest thing Bix could possibly have done, the field is divided between those who know Bix joined Whiteman and despise him for it, and those who know he joined Whiteman and forgave him for it. Both the Bixophobes and the Bixophiles miss the point.

IN 1923 A BAND called the New Orleans Rhythm Kings was playing in Chicago. It was the first important white band in jazz history and it was among those which brought to Chicago the authentic source-music of New Orleans. Bix Beiderbecke, enrolled at a nearby military academy for the sons of middle-class families, spent his weekends listening to them. By the end of the year, he was already propping up his comrades in the Wolverines, the first white band to be composed wholly of non-New Orleans musicians.

These "firsts" are more important than they might appear to the casual reader, for they chart minutely the spread of jazz across the Continent. The Rhythm Kings were significant because they were the first convincing proof (with apologies to the Original Dixieland Jazz Band) that white musicians could generate effectively the spirit of jazz. And the Wolverines were just as significant because they proved, though far less effectively, that this spirit could be acquired at second-hand, that jazz was not merely a local dialect, but that those with a sympathy for it and some musical endowment might come to acquire its nuances. The New Orleans Rhythm Kings and the Wolverines are the first and second premises in the proof of the proposition that jazz, like more formal kinds of music, is universal.

The incident of the young Beiderbecke catching up with the rare spectacle of the Rhythm Kings in full cry is not so extraordinary. There were thousands like Bix who sensed that something unusual had happened to music. For those thousands, the piquancy of the experience must slowly have faded away, finally achieving the status of an adolescent love affair, as indeed it was in a way, fondly but faintly remembered. Bix did not react in this way for the very good reason that he was abnormal. Perhaps only slightly so, but enough to transform what was for others a casual incident on the road to maturity into an event of shattering import. Bix was that rare bird, the natural or born musician, the kind who unnerves the layman when he reads about him and tempts him to embrace half-baked theories of reincarnation or demoniac possession to explain away his own mediocrity. Bix's musical gift as a small child even won a brief local fame. His mother later said that at three years he could pick out with one finger on the piano the melody of Liszt's Second Hungarian Rhapsody. Later the Davenport press referred to "this prodigy who at seven could play any selection he heard."

We now come to the first significant point in Bix's development. An attempt was made at formal musical instruction. The attempt failed. It failed because, as George Hoefer wrote in one of the few rational essays on Bix which exist, "The teacher gave up, realizing he couldn't teach the boy anything and that the talent was one which lay deep within." In fact, time was to prove that it lay so deep within that nobody, Bix included, ever really succeeded in digging it out.

Now the failure at formal instruction represents the kind of impasse which is reached in almost all attempts of parents to educate their children musically. The comedy of the Piano Lesson looms large in the childhood of countless people whose musical potential proved to be negligible. Someone notices in a child what he thinks is an obvious gift for music, at which the middle-class vision sees the concert halls of Europe, tailcoats, and floral tributes. The lessons, if they are given at all, are usually given very badly, and the collapse of the scheme quickly follows, bringing down with it whatever might have been of the original talent. The precosity is half-forgotten and over the years is gradually reduced to the proportions of a family reminiscence . . . " . . . you should have heard Bixie when he was a kid. Play anything and couldn't read a note. That kid really had an ear for music. . . ."

As it happened, Bixie had more than just an ear for music, he had something much more serious, a soul which hungered for it. Evidently when the teaching began, Bix was too young and too immature to sense any dynamic in what he was being shown, but in his teens he had a fresh encounter with music in the one form capable of galvanizing him into positive action. He needed something bright and gaudy to attract his adolescent sensibilities, something with immediate appeal and not too much depth, something with an aura of excitement about it, above all something free enough from tradition to appeal to his undisciplined, unschooled musical faculty. The recordings of the Original Dixieland Jazz Band and later the New Orleans Rhythm Kings filled the bill to perfection.

Of Bix's progress up to and including the Wolverines episode there is no evidence of any conflict in his mind about what he was doing. The Wolverine's music was crude and naïve and, Bix apart, mediocre jazz even for the period. Even Bix is no more than promising, despite the retrospective hysteria of the Bixophiles. Jazz was a goodtime music and the Wolverines were a goodtime band. Any talk of self-expression or aesthetic morality would have meant little to its members, a collection of nondescript college boys with very questionable gifts for jazz or any other kind of music. Years later some of them confessed that Bix finally left them because the gulf between his potential and theirs had become ludicrous. The point is that while he was with the Wolverines the horizons of jazz were Bix's horizons too.

It is in the next phase of Bix's career that one can see the first signs of the dilemma which was to envelope him. The young cornetist leaves the Wolverines and eventually joins Charlie Straight's band in Chicago. But before this a most curious sequence of events occurs. In February 1925, already a professional musician of three years standing, Bix enrolls at the University of Iowa, registering for English, Religion and Ethics, Music Theory, Piano Lessons, and Music History. At his first interview with his freshman adviser, Bix asks to drop Religion and take more music instead, as neat a summation of his life as anybody could make. The request is refused and instead Bix is ordered to enroll immediately for Military Training, Physical Education, and Freshman lectures. Four days later Bix and the University of Iowa part company forever.

The incident certainly appears comical in retrospect, but to do justice to the University of Iowa, which is more than it did to Bix, its behavior was no more fatuous than that of most educational institutions. That a place of instruction should refuse to teach music to a brilliant natural musician like Bix, and instruct him instead in the art of cleaning a dummy rifle may look like a parody, but to Bix at the time it must have been a nasty shock. Reality is the most merciless satirist of all.

This astonishing interlude in his career is the first outward sign of what was happening to Bix the musician. A glance at the subjects he named and the additional ones he requested, reveals the process. What he was attempting to do at the University of Iowa was to revoke his own decision of years before when he refused to cooperate in the matter of his own musical education. The fiasco in the Davenport front parlor was the first crisis and the fiasco at the University of Iowa the second, and they are closely related. In some way the passion for formal knowledge and instruction, dormant since early adolescence, was awakened. The months of playing with the Wolverines were evidently months of self-revelation, months in which Bix became aware for the first time as an adult of the power of music in his life. The attempt to enroll at the University of Iowa was the first stage in the blind stumble towards orthodoxy which is the story of Beiderbecke's artistic life. The embryo-student in Bix is one of the facets of the man which fascinated Dorothy Baker when she came to write her novel about him, although the misreading of the social background and the hero's relation to music made nonsense of the whole experience, as we shall see.

The Bix legends begin to date from his time. From now on, two things impress those who talk about him, his inborn musical gift and his personal eccentricities. That master-purveyor of Bixian whimsy, Hoagy Carmichael, has claimed that his soul was so disturbed on first hearing Bix that he instantly fell off a davenport,* which may or may not have been intended as an oblique reference to Bix's origins.

Carmichael worked zealously on the Bix legends, from the Princeton dance dates with the Wolverines, right through to the last days of the summer of 1931. It is difficult to know how much to take of Carmichael's anecdotage, for there is no doubt that enthusiasm for his subject and his gift for savoring a good sentimental story are apt to run away with Carmichael's tongue when Bix is being discussed. The only time I ever met Carmichael, he had half a dozen Bix stories at his fingertips, stories I had never heard before, and I confess I found myself wondering whether Carmichael had either.

The catalog of Bix's vagueness in everyday life is the conventionally unconventional one. Forgetting personal belongings, having no money in his pockets, forgetting to go to bed, leaving his instrument in a succession of

---

*Not the most idiotic reaction to music ever recorded. "The Ellington brass section arose and delivered such an intricate and unbelievably integrated chorus that the late Eddie Duchin, usually a poised and dignified musician, actually and literally rolled on the floor under his table in ecstasy." *Hear Me Talkin' to Ya.* Hentoff and Shapiro.

bars and speakeasies. Some of these stories may have exaggerated the whimsicality of the man, but they are hardly misleading in a consideration of the musician.

Music was the only thing that had any reality for him. Iain Lang's descriptive phrase, "a playing fool," sums up Bix perfectly. He was indeed a playing fool in the idiomatic sense of the phrase, in that to play came first, last, and everywhere for him, that to play was the only function which had any true meaning, that nothing which was not directly connected with playing was worth half a thought.

Every action in Bix's life from the time he left home points to this conclusion. And yet there are men grown in years if nothing much else who glance hastily at the sums of money Bix earned and deduce as the reader of a dime magazine deduces, without wit or integrity. They make the discovery that Paul Whiteman paid Bix more than anyone else did, and that therefore Bix's joining Whiteman was a more heinous crime than his joining, say, Charlie Straight, Jean Goldkette, or even the University of Iowa. I wonder how jazz critics would react were their integrity assessed in the same way.

As early as 1922 Bix had what was for the jazz musician of the time an unusual interest in what for lack of a better phrase might be termed non-jazz harmonies. One ex-student of Chicago University who worked a date with Bix around this time said that during intermissions Bix would "park on the piano bench and improvise, much to the consternation of the other musicians, who thought he was playing nothing but a progression of discords . . . he was playing sixth, ninth and thirteenth chords which later became common in dance arrangements. In those days dance numbers were played with only the simplest harmonies."

Victor Moore, the drummer with the Wolverines, testified that Bix attended concerts even in the Wolverine days, and of later times he says, "In 1929, when I made my first visit to New York in four years, I met Bix downtown, and almost the first thing he said to me was, 'Come on, I've got seats for the symphony tonight.' After the concert we went backstage, where Bix was enthusiastically received by the musicians, who considered him a genius and were proud of his friendship."

Moore's remark about the reaction of the legitimate musicians is intriguing and very possibly true, for by 1929, Bix, besides having become something of a connoisseur of modern classics, was beginning to evolve into a confused embryo of a composer himself, although the process was taking place despite his conscious efforts rather than because of them. Before this period, however, Bix had met a musician who was to have a profound effect upon his career and finally ended his own in either dedication or disillusion. Frank Trumbauer is unique in jazz history, for he is the only musician known to have suffered artistic death at second hand. It is as though when Bix was buried Frank Trumbauer was vicariously buried with him, for from the day of Bix's death, Trumbauer ceases to play much active part in a musical world where he had been most prominent.

Trumbauer was the diametric opposite of Bix in many ways. As a musician, he was a minor talent although he is said, because of his drastic tonal amendments, to have become a figure of great interest and some inspiration to Lester Young. Trumbauer was an excellent executive musician by the standard of the jazz world of the late 1920s, and even more important, he was a practical man. It was Trumbauer who procured for Bix regular jobs and recording sessions from the days when they first worked together in Trumbauer's band in St. Louis in 1925. From then till Bix's death Trumbauer contrived to work in the same band as Bix whenever possible. He got them both the Goldkette and the Whiteman jobs and was also partly responsible for the pattern of the great Bix recordings of the period. For these reasons he is sometimes depicted as the villain of the piece, the man who seduced Bix away from the path of virtue, the agent who handed Whiteman Bix's head on a plate. In fact, if Bix had never met Trumbauer, most of his great recordings might never have been cut at all.

The Bix–Tram recordings were the best Bix ever made, though the reason had nothing to do with Trumbauer's organizing ability. By 1927 Bix had reached the point of perfect balance between his inborn jazz gift and his artistic awareness of European music. The acquisition by an unschooled musician of a more conventional and literate taste may eventually lead to a kind of ossification of the jazz spirit, as the career of a player like Benny Goodman testifies. But before that stage is reached when the musical limb becomes atrophied from the overtaxing of its muscles, great benefits may accrue. By 1927 Bix had reached this stage. His jazz ability had matured, and his sensibilities were now highly refined through his contact with modern classical music. Before 1926 he was far cruder. After 1928 he suffered partial and inexorably advancing paralysis because of the relentless advance of those same sensibilities. The point of balance was reached in the handful of recordings he made with Trumbauer in 1927–28.

The really significant thing about Bix's solos in "Singing the Blues," "I'm Coming, Virginia," and "Way Down Yonder in New Orleans" is that the playing is the product of a completely confident and lucid mind. The advance on the boyish enthusiasm of the Wolverines is immeasurable. For the first time the unbiased listener can dispense with the five ghostly Bixes and come to grips with the reality of Beiderbecke's greatness. Only now does the student, till now floundering in the quicksands of the unwieldy Bix legend, find himself on firm ground.

Like *Hamlet,* "Singing the Blues" is full of quotations. It is the most plagiarized and frankly imitated solo in all jazz history. For trumpeters of the same school, like Bobby Hackett and Jimmy McPartland, it has become a set piece, a tiny fragment of improvisation that has come to achieve the unexpected dignity of a formal composition.

When a musician hears Bix's solo on "Singing the Blues," he becomes aware after two bars that the soloist knows exactly what he is doing and that he has an exquisite sense of discord and resolution. He knows also that this player is endowed with the rarest jazz gift of all, a sense of form which lends to an improvised performance a coherence which no amount of teaching can produce. The listening musician, whatever his generation or style, recognizes Bix as a modern, modernism being not a style but an attitude. At this point some explanation may be required, for we have arrived at another of the apparent contradictions in Bix. If he was so poised a musician on his great recordings, what of all the talk of the days with Whiteman when the arrangers left blanks in the score for Bix's solo, and the troubles Bix had reading simple parts which his fellows could read with ease? Was Bix illiterate or wasn't he?

Bix may not have been a very proficient sight-reader, but that does not mean he did not understand the nature of harmonic progression. Sight-reading bears the same relationship to improvising on a chord sequence as reciting doggerel does to the composition of light verse. So much for the legend of Bix's illiteracy, nurtured in a critical climate which finds incapacity of any kind romantic, and artistic shiftlessness picturesque. Whether or not Bix could read the meticulous drivel written for the Whiteman book is quite irrelevant to the issue of his literacy. Literacy in music can be achieved only by the use of the two appendages stuck on either side of the human head in rough symmetry. Bix's solo in "Singing the Blues," with its formal logic, its subtlety, its sureness of movement from cadence to cadence, and its characteristic implication of a deep sigh in place of the extrovert passion of his colored contemporaries, is musical literacy of the rarest kind.

The Bix solos of this period are museum pieces because they are the first peak reached by the white musician in his pursuit of what had been exclusively a colored muse. In the person of Beiderbecke the contact of the white races with jazz blossoms for the first time into minor works of art, and naturally the character of these works is quite different from the nature of the great colored jazz of the period. In Bix, the racial exuberance of Louis Armstrong has been distilled through an alien temperament. There is melancholy in Bix's playing, but it is not the extrovert melancholy of the blues. It is something unmistakably bittersweet, a quality which once led Francis Newton to draw the comparison with Watteau rather than with Bessie

Smith. In Bix's day racial segregation was one of the facts of life in the jazz world, at least so far as the public was concerned. There were no mixed bands which appeared officially in public, and even mixed recording sessions still seemed an un-American activity. Because of this phenomenon, people often see the musicians of the period in hermetically sealed compartments. There appears to be far less social contrast, for instance, between Basie and Kenton than there does between Trumbauer and Fletcher Henderson, but it is wise to remember that this segregation was not nearly so rigid outside working hours. The dependence of the knowledgeable jazz lover on recordings may tend to obscure the fact that apparently antipathetic figures like Bix and Louis played together and had a healthy mutual regard.

In November 1927, at the end of the year of "Singing the Blues" and "I'm Coming, Virginia," Bix joined Paul Whiteman. The Bixophobes say he did it because he liked the sound of the salary. The Bixophiles, on the other hand, see his recruitment by Whitman through Trumbauer as the fatal mistake which was to lead to his death, the turning point in a tragedy of Attic proportions. But in view of the way in which Bix had been reacting to music for the past five years his acceptance of the Whiteman job was a perfectly logical and artistically justifiable thing to do, keeping in mind, of course, the fact that Bix was neither a moralizing bystander nor a clear-headed adult. The casual breeze with the Wolverines had been followed by a dawning interest in classical music which led to an unsuccessful attempt to be a student. Then came the Charlie Straight Band, where some ability as a sight-reader was probably required. After that came Goldkette, where Bix met full orchestrations for the first time.

Furthermore, there were associated with the Whiteman circus two men for whom Bix in his *naïveté* had tremendous admiration, Grofé and Challis. To get into the Whiteman band appears to be lots of different things to different people. To the layman who has never known the reality of artistic activity it seems like a final artistic giving up the ghost. To the professional dance band musician with his eye on suburban respectability it seems like the crowning of a career, the procurement of the top-paying job in a financially insecure profession. To a romantic jazz fan it seems like a tragic error. True, perhaps, but to Bix Beiderbecke it seemed like the largest single step he had yet taken on the quest for knowledge, musical profundity, legitimacy, organized activity or whatever else one cares to call it. Those who can listen to the Whiteman band's dreadful travesties of musical art may find this hard to believe, but they should remember that Bix possessed neither the worldliness which twenty-five years of studying jazz has given to many of us since, nor the critical coherence to assess exactly how valuable Whiteman's music was. He knew only that there were men working for Whiteman musically literate in the conventional sense, and that to work with them must surely enrich his experience and help him towards the mystical ultimate in musical expression.

The point has been made by the carpet knights that in the Whiteman band the finest talent on earth might wither if left there long enough. If Bix had been fit enough in mind and body to continue, then would not his artistic vitality have begun to ebb? Very possibly, but although this issue may be vital to us, it meant nothing to Bix. Musicians have a disconcerting habit of doing what they want to and not what critics think they ought to do. Preserving his jazz gift was not what Bix was after. He was stalking bigger game, although stalking it with a misguided folly which appears ludicrous thirty years after.

To have warned Bix that a prolonged spell with Whiteman might have spoiled his jazz gift would have been as pointless as telling a fretting prisoner that the security of his cell is more relaxing that the chaos of the world outside. What Bix desired was some experience which would enrich him in the broad musical sense, and the fact that he was a poor enough judge of intrinsic values to think Whiteman's band could give him this experience indicts his judgment but not his motives.

So far from being a moral coward who sold out to the highest bidder, Bix was the blind unreasoning artist who followed his advancing sensibilities as only a blind unreasoning artist can, completely oblivious of the consequences. To the critics unable to appreciate the kind of musical compositions which had so fascinated Bix, this issue of his advancing sensibilities is an inconvenient fact to be pushed hastily out of court on the grounds of lack of proof. Bix was not a conveniently prolific letterwriter or diarist who chronicled his development for the edification of posterity. He was not even a conscious artist at all. Nonetheless the truth is as self-evident and as irrefutable as if he had left a signed statement. It is implicit in his movements from band to band, in the development from the Wolverines through Whiteman to his death, and above all in his later compositions for the piano.

It is the supreme irony of Bix Beiderbecke's stay with Whiteman that he came to the orchestra seeking after a state of musical grace, unwittingly endowing Whiteman as he did so with the only real musical grace that clumsy group ever possessed. Bix in the Whiteman band looking for pearls of wisdom was like Tarzan at a Keep Fit Class. To any intelligent jazz fancier the one letter Bix actually did write, the one to his mother telling how frightened he was at the thought of joining a band as renowned as Whiteman's, may seem comical enough to make even a Blesh laugh. Here is this gifted musician about to bestow on a mediocre vaudeville act his own talent, a musician so far above the jazz standards of almost all his contemporaries that today we only tolerate the horrors of Whiteman's recordings at all in the hope that here and there a Bixian fragment will redeem the mess. And here is that musician telling his mother that the Whiteman band overawes him.

The summation of the whole Bix–Whiteman paradox is contained in the Whiteman recording of "Sweet Sue." Every indelicacy that might conceivably be crammed into a four-minute performance is included in what the sleeve notes to the American Columbia Memorial album describe with some restraint as "a real period piece." Quacking brass, lumbering tubas, the tinkling of bells and the clashing of cymbals, portentous slow movements and dashing fast movements, comically bogus profundity, saccharine harmonies, teashop violins, and what sounds like a deadly parody of every singer, male, female, and neuter, who ever sat in the ranks of a dance-band. In the midst of this farrago, the listener may discover a single chorus by Bix Beiderbecke which momentarily dispels the nonsense as though by magic. There is no clucking interference from the rest of the band. The rhythm section merely accompanies Bix for thirty-two bars, and everyone else, from Whiteman to the lowest menial on his orchestrating staff, leaves it to him.

The result is that Bix, playing casually enough, never at any time approaching the intensity of "I'm Coming, Virginia," or "Way Down Yonder in New Orleans," still reaches his own level of invention, and by the effortless ease of his creativity, reveals the pitiful gulf between his own mind and the minds which conceived the holocaust preceding and following the solo. It is a telling illustration of the truth that the natural jazz player will create, without even stopping to think about it, phrases which the merely literate orchestrators will never think of simply because the scope of their training and experience does not include that kind of inventive resource.

Bix's solo in "Sweet Sue" is in no way untypical of the time, 1928. To refer to the text of this particular solo is in no way loading the dice. For a Bix solo it is commonplace enough, but it contains at least four instances of the peculiar Bixishness of the man's style. The phrase linking the end of the first eight bars with the start of the second eight contains no rhythmic complexities of any kind, although the precision and attack with which it is played creates the illusion of rhythmic force. After climbing the chord of the major sixth, the phrase descends in the ninth bar with three notes which are archetypal for the curious elusive quality of wistfulness one finds occurring so consistently in Bix's jazz. To say that these three notes belong to this chord or that mean nothing. It is in their context in the time and space of the solo, and the manner in which they are executed, that their effectiveness lies.

In the movement from the twelfth to the thirteenth bar occurs a quaver of silence in a run of quavers. The momentary break is totally unexpected because it occurs off the beat, where one's sense of rhythm has not led one to expect it, instead of on the beat, where it might have sounded ordinary enough. The result is a skipping effect which brings a gaiety of spirit giving the solo fresh impetus, and causing a subtle change of mood from the melancholia of the ninth bar.

In bars nineteen and twenty the conception of the phrasing becomes far bolder than hitherto. The time values change from quavers to minim triplets striding across the harmonies with a freedom of tonality comparatively rare in those earlier days of jazz. In bars twenty-one and twenty-two occurs a phrase which appears to be leading on from itself but which surprisingly evolves into a sequential echo of itself in the following two bars. The solo ends with rather more dependence on the fifth and tonic than is usual for Bix.

Now this kind of observation is mere quackery if it is to be used to prove that Bix had a profound mind, if for instance I were to suggest that Bix consciously played off the melancholia of the ninth bar against the jollity of the skip three bars later. When he played Bix was consciously thinking, as all jazz musicians do, no matter what the psychoanalysts may say, only of the movement of the harmonies from resolution to resolution. Whatever emotional or dramatic effects we may care to observe in the result are the product of the intuitive powers of the soloist, not his reasoning intelligence at work.

But examples like this do illustrate Bix's curious individuality as a jazz musician, and his rare ability to evoke in the listener a range of emotions not so common in jazz as one might think. The very nature of the melancholia he conjures is distinctively Bixian, sensitive and reflective, quite devoid of the element of self-pity which obtrudes in so much later jazz aiming consciously at the same effects Bix produced instinctively. The "Sweet Sue" solo is superbly musical. It has been conceived by a born musician, and that such a man could ever have seen any virtue in the feverish goings-on in the preceding and subsequent choruses, is only further proof of the mess in which the intuitive artist can land himself when he lacks the normal reasoning powers.

AT THE END of 1928 Bix collapsed, after a prolonged spell of heavy drinking and keeping his nose to Whiteman's commercial grindstone. Whiteman sent Bix on a cure for the drinking, and gave him a holiday with pay from the orchestra. Throughout this period of Bix's absence the band is said to have worked with his chair empty on the stand, an anecdote which may help to redress the balance of the evidence against Whiteman as the villain of the piece. Of course there was no villain. Whiteman can hardly be blamed for not pensioning Bix off with enough money to keep him in booze and seeing that he got the most salutary kind of musical experience. Whiteman was just a businessman and Bix one of his employees. He did all he could reasonably be expected to do for Bix and more. He did let Bix record solos like "Sweet Sue," even if they shattered the lunatic symmetry of his scores. He paid Bix his full salary throughout an absence lasting some months. He paid for Bix's cure, and made no attempt to replace him till it was quite clear Bix was never coming back.

The fleshpot theory, having been severely battered by the story of Bix's evolving sensitivity, and broken into small pieces of the evidence of Bix's letter to his mother, finally gets ground into dust by the story of Bix's reactions to his own breakdown. The shock of being no longer able to hold his place in Whiteman's band did, to quote Hoefer, "contribute a great deal to his poor physical and mental condition during the last years of his life." Of course it did. The golden door was being slammed in his face, and for the rest of his life Bix seems not to have cared very much what else happened to him. But the loss to the jazz cause was largely hypothetical. The jazz world, had it but known it, had already lost Bix before he left Whiteman. And music had gained a hopeless convert.

Carmichael and Jimmy McPartland have both referred to Bix's disappointment at not rejoining Whiteman, and indeed the facts of Bix's behavior after his first, partial recovery comprise a pathetic record. He insisted on courting Whiteman, trailing in the wake of this lumbering great orchestra, trying to persuade Whiteman and himself that everything was as it had always been.

Bix returned to the band, in February 1929, to find that Whiteman, up to his neck in commercial radio commitments, was demanding the kind of program that even Bix knew was unworthy either as jazz or as the light program music which had once seemed so attractive to him. In September Bix collapsed again, returning to his home in Davenport in an effort to recover himself. Throughout this convalescence, Bix thought of this mythical recovery in terms of a return to Whiteman. In April 1930 he was back in New York, looking for his job. But Whiteman no longer needed the kind of talent that Bix possessed. The Wall Street disaster had been followed by economies everywhere in the entertainment business, and jazz musicians generally found themselves hard put to earn a reasonable living.

Bix's friends, solicitous as always for the welfare of their hero, tried to persuade him to take a job with the Casa Loma Orchestra, but Bix, perhaps better educated by now as to what was music and what was an unwitting lampoon of itself, declined. Sometime in September 1929 Bix made his last recordings, and in November he returned to Davenport. The three months he spent there must have produced comedy of classic proportions. Apparently Bix pottered about his hometown doing a few gigs, playing at a local hotel, and so sick in body and spirit that he was barely able even to fulfill even these modest obligations. Dorothy Baker turned her back on a delicious situation when she ignored this episode in Bix's life, perhaps stranger in its way than anything else in the record.

I suspect the crowning irony must have been the sheer ignorance of the town as to who Bix Beiderbecke was anyway. The local musicians must have known and wondered. Some old acquaintances might have shaken their heads. But the real satire of the situation must have arisen from the fact that generally jazz musicians are celebrities only to each other.

In February 1931, Bix returned to New York for the last time, by now the inspiration for a full-sized legend. Throughout his absence in Davenport people had wondered what was wrong with him and how long he might be away. Rumor circulated about his sudden death, his remarkable recovery, his imminent return, his lost talent, his newfound talent. The process of deification began months before he died.

Bix remained in New York all that summer, doing some radio work, staying at home for days at a time. The story of his swift decline and death in August has many variations, and for an example of the alarming way in which his friends insisted on waxing dramatic about him at all times, there is Hoagy Carmichael's unabashed version of a day he once spent with Bix in the summer of 1931:

> I went by Bix's room one day. I met a maid in the hall. "What's the matter with that fellow anyway?" she asked. "Who is he? He hasn't been out of his room for three days."
>
> Tell the maid. Who is he? I looked at the maid's black face. "Just a guy," I said, and went on to his room.
>
> "Hi, Hoagy." Bix was lying on the bed. He looked bad, there was something missing, as if part of him were already in the dark.
>
> "Hi, Bix." I sat down. I was uneasy. "How's it going, fellow?"
>
> Bix smiled wanly. "What are you doing?"
>
> "Been listening to the Publisher's theme song: It's not commercial." Bix looked away and then I heard his voice. "Don't worry, boy, you're . . . ah . . . hell . . ."
>
> "Get your horn out. Let's doodle a little."
>
> He shook his head. "Ran into a girl the other day," Bix said. "She's going to fix me up in a flat out in Sunnyside."
>
> "Swell, get out of this dump and you'll feel better. You might eat something."
>
> He looked at me and the veil went from his eyes for a moment. "How's for bringing her over some night?"
>
> "Sure, any time," I said.
>
> And Bix brought the girl and came to my apartment one night. We

> didn't have a drink, we didn't talk music, and it soon became apparent that this girl had no idea who Bix was. And then the terrible thought struck me. I didn't know either.

From a literary point of view Carmichael made two bad mistakes in the construction of his short story. A best friend doesn't ask a languishing hero to play the trumpet at a time like that. The introduction of a symbolically mysterious woman who, like the population of Davenport, had no idea who Bix was, is an excellent box-office ending ruined by Carmichael's maddening last sentence.

It would be too much to hope that the incidental circumstances of Bix's death would be clearly defined for posterity. In fact the stories contradict each other so violently that to accept them all would be to conclude that each of the six Beiderbeckes the student comes to know, all died separate and independent deaths. For many years the stock story was the one about the Princeton dance date. Bix had a chill but went through with the gig because the promoter insisted on the condition that no Bix, no gig. But then, quite recently, it occurred to one of Bix's biographers that Princeton didn't run college dances in the middle of August. The story Carmichael once told me involved a visit to the bank, and sounded at least as credible as all the other tales.

But what is more important than the actual manner in which Bix died is the way he behaved when he sensed he was about to die. And here most of the witnesses corroborate each other. The one thing Bix took any real interest in over the last months was his piano-writing. For years he had been pottering with some half-defined compositions which he had never written down and, indeed, never really finished. The pieces were well-known to his intimates, and the most famous of all, "In a Mist," he had recorded as far back as September 1927.

The general impression seems to have been that Bix was anxious to leave these miniatures behind him in some permanent form, and with this end in view he recruited the help of Whiteman's arranger, Buddy Challis. "In a Mist" itself epitomizes the extraordinary conflict which raged inside the man. It is a bewildering amalgam of barrelhouse thumping and Debussyian subtleties which illustrates more pointedly than any facts or any anecdotes how the sensibilities of a jazz musician were stimulated by the impact of modern impressionist music. That is why Bix's piano pieces have remained for more than thirty years what they were when he first conceived them, curiosities. No other jazz musician underwent Bix's musical evolution in quite the same way or under quite the same conditions, and the piano pieces are essentially a product of these factors in Bix's life.

"In a Mist," "Candlelight," "In the Dark," are the most valuable clues we have as to what Bix would have done had he lived on into the era of the commercial big bands, or, more important, what he might have become had the campaign in the Davenport front parlor succeeded, had Bix never heard the Original Dixieland Jazz Band or the New Orleans Rhythm Kings. It seems at least possible that he would have emerged as a minor composer of some distinction, perhaps a creator of unconsidered trifles, but at least trifles conceived and written with a true musical faculty. The more one considers this possibility, and the more one remembers that for all his unqualified success in the jazz world, Bix gravitated despite himself back to the world of formal sound, the more one is tempted to the hair-raising conclusion that he only became a jazz musician at all because of the unique circumstances of his life and background. Fortunately for the art of jazz, Bix happened to have an instinctive appreciation of the spirit of the music. It was this sympathetic understanding of an unschooled idiom, combined with his genuine musical endowments, which created the classic fragments bequeathed to us on gramophone records.

Now there are the bare bones of the story of Bix Beiderbecke, and their implications are patently obvious to all those not determined to transmute every episode of artistic activity into *grand guignol* pastiche. A natural musician with a middle-class background becomes declassé through his inability to ignore his own powers. He drifts into an artistic cul-de-sac, drinks too much and dies still attempting to educate himself in the subtleties of a music which make the subtleties of his own sound gauche in the extreme. As a vehicle for fiction nothing more stimulating could be wished for. But what, in fact, did happen when the inevitable attempt was made to transmute Bix into fiction?

Dorothy Baker is the least bad novelist who ever attempted to fictionalize the jazz life, and her *Young Man With a Horn,* the least bad jazz novel so far written. Once that has been acknowledged, there remains little to say of *Young Man With a Horn* which is not violently critical. In the edition of the novel which I first read, though not in later editions I possessed, there were printed on the introductory page the words, “A novel based on the music but not the life of Bix Beiderbecke.” This remarkable statement prepared me for the worst, and I was not disappointed. It became instantly apparent that the mind which conceived the novel knew nothing of any real significance about its hero. Bix’s life and Bix’s music were one and the same thing, no more divisible than Candide’s disfigurements and the philosophy those disfigurements inspired.

Here the novelist was presented with a ready-made theme of overwhelming poignancy and dramatic power. An unschooled man caught up in a tremendous aesthetic experience his training and experience have left him woefully ill-equipped to control, a man who stumbles into a new kind of artistic activity and imposes upon it an influence as alien to it as his own social and racial background, a man whose sensibilities have outstripped his temperament so completely that in the final reckoning the man suffers complete physical and artistic collapse. Above all, a man whose life is utterly without interest the moment it is divorced from his music.

But this evidently was too awkward a theme for Miss Baker to handle, or perhaps even to notice at all. What did she give us instead? A twaddling tale of a musician with a gift "equal to, say—oh, Bach's," who is unhappy in love and dies of dissipation. Bix was obviously the greatest white jazz musician Miss Baker had heard about, so she grafted on to him the hack figure of the artistic genius who is romantically frustrated.

That was not all. Worse was to come, much worse. Miss Baker understood as little of the nature of Bix's musical talent as she did of the nature of his life and the real dramatic element in it. The romantic tragedy of his life was not contained in the kind of silly footling romance with the extraordinary Amy North whom Miss Baker dreamed up, but with the music itself.

In place of Bixian subtlety we get nonsensical talk of going for notes so high they do not exist, " . . . at least, not on a trumpet," Miss Baker belonging to that layman society which religiously believes that ability in a jazz trumpeter is related directly to how high he can blow. And worst of all, instead of the symptomatic decline after leaving Whiteman, we get a deathbed scene in an ambulance of such excruciating sentimentality that even Hoagy Carmichael would never have dared.

The extent to which Miss Baker misread the case is best illustrated by her manipulation of the sociological facts to make her hero more sympathetic to the reader. (More sympathetic than Bix Beiderbecke, if you please!) She ruthlessly demotes our hero in class, so that where Bix was the son of comfortable immigrant parents, Rick Martin is a downtrodden member of a shiftless proletariat with no parents, no home life, no help from anybody, a character to whom music is evidently a refuge from loneliness rather than an impulse too strong to resist, as it was for Bix.

There is no mention of the middle-west, no mention of the European strain in the family, so vital a factor in the history of Bix, no mention of the unsuccessful attempt to redeem a lost musical situation at Iowa University. People sometimes suggest to me that such facts are no concern of the novelist bent only on portraying a fictitious character. But in the special case of Bix Beiderbecke the facts cannot be rejected because without them there would have been no hero in the first place. Bix was a product of the middle class and so was his music. The refinement and the Europeanization were no accidents, which is why it is courting artistic disaster to take Bix's musical prowess as the inspiration for a novel, and abandon all the contributory factors. The result will be not a man but a cardboard effigy propped up with a few cliches, which is exactly what Rick Martin turns out to be. That is why Bix was a fascinating man and a beguiling artist while Rick Martin is a silly cipher who never once gives the impression of intuitive greatness which any sketch of Bix, no matter how casual, ought to give. I wonder what Bix himself would have made of Amy North with her pathological jealously, of the comically hackneyed drummer Smoke, who pays our hero the supreme compliment of permitting him, Rick, to befriend him. And above all, which particular dirty word would Bix have uttered when he came to that high note nonsense?

What Dorothy Baker did in fact do with *Young Man With a Horn* was to consummate, once and for all, in a permanent form, all the misconception, all the vulgarity, all the spurious romanticizing, all the distortions of the figure of Bix which have been so prominent a feature of jazz journalism for the last thirty years. *Young Man With a Horn* summarizes the whole process. It is an anthology of everything crass and cheapskate ever written by an outside world which lacked the wit and the energy to come to a true understanding of his gift and his dilemma.

One can get too solicitous about Bix. He is almost too pathetic. He was the victim of his own artistic fecklessness, and even in his best jazz performances a victim of the irony of the jazz musician's predicament, which is that he is uncompromisingly individualistic and yet chained by the sheer mechanics of his art to the limitations of whoever he is obliged to play with. Perhaps that is why my favorite among all the Bix stories I ever read suggests that perhaps his ordeal was not quite so painful all of the time as writers like Miss Baker would have us believe. The sheer detachment of the man seems at times to be enviable. The bandleader Russ Morgan tells this story. "I remember one time three of us went out to play golf early in the morning and we came across Bix asleep under a tree. The night before he had decided to play some twilight golf and had lost all his golf balls. So he just laid down and went to sleep. We woke him up and he finished the course with us."

James P. Johnson

Max Harrison

This careful and useful consideration of one of the greatest jazz pianists appeared first in Jazz Monthly *in 1959. Harrison was one of Great Britain's hardest working critics, editors, and popularizers of jazz. Reprinted in Harrison's* A Jazz Retrospect *(1976).*

Perhaps jazz was born in New Orleans, but New York soon was up to something different. One way of explaining the divergence would be to suggest that the influence of vocal blues on phrasing and instrumental timbre was crucial in the South, not in the North. During the early decades of this century New York was to a considerable extent a piano town, highly competitive in this as in other respects, and it is said that when Jelly Roll Morton passed through in 1911 his normally well-nourished ego received a considerable blow from the executive skills of the best local players. His transformation of ragtime into jazz was a matter of the blues, plus greater sophistication in the handling of contrasted themes and, later, of the small, collectively improvising band. For the New Yorkers it involved almost everything except the blues, but it happened mainly—or at any rate first—on the piano keyboard.

The example of ragtime and the possibility of improvisation were common to both North and South—also to the Middle West—yet the special point about the New Yorkers was their musical curiosity. James P. Johnson best illustrates how this operated on several levels at once. His imaginative, beautifully organized, but finally inappropriate accompaniments to—or rather duets with—Bessie Smith may demonstrate his failure to grasp the blues, yet this was essentially a creative misunderstanding in that it left him open to other influences of perhaps still earlier origin. As Dick Wellstood wrote, "James P. is the focal point. The rags, cotillions, mazurkas and all those other unknown phenomena came together in him and he made jazz out of them." Unlike most of the other New York pianists, such as his pupil Fats Waller, or Willie "The Lion" Smith, Johnson, despite his wide-ranging interests, never lost contact with those country-dance fiddle-tunes, banjo music, hymns, marches, folksongs, etc., from mid-nineteenth century, as is confirmed by some of the piano solos, like "Mule Walk," "Blueberry Rhyme," or "Arkansas Blues," which he recorded in late middle-age. At the other extreme, he is said to be the sole old-timer who, in 1947, had a word to say in favor of Dizzy Gillespie.

Of course, Johnson was luckier than most jazz musicians in his early background. Born in New Brunswick, N.J., probably on February 1, 1891, he initially learned from his mother, and when the family moved to Jersey City, near New York, he continued with a local musician named Bruto Giannini. This man had considerably more vision than the average piano teacher, for he appreciated the uncommon bent of his pupil's exceptional ability. Johnson was allowed to go on with his stomps and rags—with the fingering corrected—but he was made to work intensively at scales, arpeggios, and all the other basics of a well-rounded technique. Giannini also taught him harmony and counterpoint, and, perhaps most important, he studied the classics of European keyboard literature. This latter was an interest he was able to pursue in New York, to which the family next moved. Johnson began appearing as a musician while still at school there, and performed in a wide variety of circumstances, sometimes in the lowest of dives, but he also attended orchestral concerts and piano recitals.

This balance of earthiness and sophistication remained characteristic, but the point of Giannini's four years of training at this stage of Johnson's career was that it equipped him to learn still more. Interviewed decades later, he was quite clear as to what he had got from each of the dominant Harlem pianists of an older generation such as Fred Bryant ("He invented the backward tenth. I used it and passed it on to Fats Waller") or Sam Gordon ("He played swift runs in thirds and sixths, broken chords, one-note tremolandos"). Johnson also had the taste, technique, and knowledge of the classical repertoire to benefit from the European tradition's long harvest, and he mentions adapting procedures from Beethoven and Liszt in particular. The latter is the significant name because for Johnson and the other most advanced New York pianists, as for Liszt, Alkan, Chopin, and other Romantic piano composers almost a century before, the point of virtuosity was not the chances it offered for display but that it was a catalyst, a means of extending the instrument's scope and hence their music's range of expression. The audience could be dazzled if it liked, yet what mattered to the pianists was bringing fresh resources—rather literally—into play. The Harlem keyboard men of Johnson's generation formed the first school of jazz virtuosos of whom we have real knowledge, and the exploratory drive was still active when, many years later, it led one of his contemporaries, Eubie Blake, to begin studying the Schillinger system of composition at the age of sixty-six.

It had been active much sooner in the piano rolls that Johnson, Blake, and several others began to cut during 1917 and which are our earliest evidence of their work. This method of recording eliminates some of the most personal aspects of execution, but items such as "Baltimore Buzz" convey Johnson's exultant joy in playing, a feeling which comes only from having conquered one's instrument (*cf.* recordings by the young Hines, the young Gillespie, etc.). "Gypsy Blues" or "Don't Tell Your Monkey Man" speak clearly, too, of his knowledge of pianistic resource, of his technique, and of an imagination which finds its most apt expression on the keyboard. These and several other rolls are almost incessantly inventive, and communicate not only instrumental mastery but a personal gaiety, even optimism, of which only the sourest intellectuals would disapprove.

Because of the better Harlem pianists' classical links it is not surprising that these pieces are fully worked-out fantasies on given melodies rather than jazz improvisations. The archetypal case, Johnson's rather later piano roll of excerpts from *Running Wild,* an all-Negro musical, is in direct descent from the kind of treatment nineteenth-century virtuosos gave to operatic melodies; the rhythms are different, but little else. Such items remain delightful to hear yet sound like a beginning, not an end, because the demands of a mode of expression centered on the piano, the types of resource and kinds of formal organization that go with it, can be heard on these rolls, especially "Vamping Liza Jane" or "Railroad Man," supplanting the requirements of the original melody, which finally is dissolved in the texture. Sure enough, having broken with ragtime's static syncopations and rather formal expression of mood, as well as its emphasis on thematic melody, in favor of a more developed pianism and all it implied, many other things followed, not least the necessity of a smoother rhythmic flow.

We cannot be absolutely certain about such details with piano rolls, of course, but Johnson's first gramophone recording, "Harlem Strut," dating from 1921, though basically a piece of 2/4 ragtime, does have a tendency toward a 4/4 pulse. This is more apparent in "Carolina Shout" and "Keep Off the Grass" done later that year, although here the flowing forward movement is by no means supplied by the left hand alone, each piece having various ternary patterns superimposed on the underlying 4/4 to offset any possibility of rhythmic squareness. This was eventually taken up by orchestral jazz, as in Don Redman's 1927 scores of "Whiteman Stomp" (a piece composed by Waller) and "Tozo" for Fletcher Henderson. Other bands caught up later—e.g., Lloyd Hunter's "Sensational Mood" of 1931—but Johnson and his friends were doing it in 1921. As Wellstood wrote, "He had an almost architectural way of handling rhythm, of placing pulses like building blocks, and a wonderfully subtle manner of allowing different rhythmic conceptions to exist simultaneously in both hands." This is literally true, and in, say, "Keep Off the Grass" we find the beats of one two-bar unit grouped 3+3+2 in one hand against 3+2+3 in the other, and then these patterns reversed between the hands in the next two bars.

During the 1920s Johnson was extremely active in the world of Negro showbusiness and it is remarkable that he retained mastery of this sort of playing. In fact he did more, developing his compositional skill and executive control to the points shown in "Riffs" (1929) and "Jingles" (1930), which channel great rhythmic zest through airy, prancing trebles and resonantly-spaced basses, marking almost—though not quite—the summit of his achievement as a jazz pianist. So far as recordings are concerned, the peak came at a surprisingly later date with the magnificent group of solos he set down for the Blue Note and Signature labels during 1943, including "Carolina Balmoral," "Blues for Fats," "Caprice Rag," "Improvisations on Pinetop's Boogie," and the items mentioned in the second paragraph. These performances, besides preserving the simple happiness of country-dance tunes within the lucid complexities of Harlem piano at its ripest, were an achievement in quite another sense for they came after the stroke Johnson suffered in 1940, from which he only recovered slowly, and which marked the start of the slow decline in his health that resulted in his death in 1955.

Despite the long-matured brilliance of this and much other music, however, Johnson remained a neglected figure, except among his fellow pianists. They had a just appreciation of his apparently inexhaustible inventive power and, in most cases, beautifully disciplined playing. We can savor these, too, on the several versions he recorded (on piano roll or disc) of each of his most famous pieces, where the thematic material is always varied in new ways, with chanting lyricism and spry elegance. Yet *Jazz Hot and Hybrid* or *Jazzmen*, books which exerted a largely undeserved influence in their day, made not a single mention of him. Or consider two groups of recordings he cut in 1944, one of solos on Waller melodies, the other of compositions of his own accompanied by an inept drummer. Among the latter's more gross solecisms is that he plays straight through the recurring breaks of pieces such as "Over the Bars," thereby considerably diminishing their effect. It is typical of the misunderstandings to which Johnson has been subject that these ill-matched duets—or rather duels—have repeatedly been praised at the expense of the sensitive, manifestly affectionate solo improvisations in memory of his recently-deceased pupil.

As if to console him, and arising directly, of course, out of the admiration of his fellow professionals, Johnson's influence was very considerable. It would not be quite true to say that his followers "constitute the elite of the jazz piano tradition" because several highly significant figures like Earl

Hines, Bud Powell, and bluesmen such as Jimmy Yancey were untouched by him. Yet one still could devote a whole essay to his formative rôle in the playing of others, and, aside from obviously related stylists like Willie "the lion" Smith, Johnson's concern with resources hitherto untried in jazz had a marked, possibly crucial, effect on the attitudes of Duke Ellington and Art Tatum. Even Thelonius Monk, on one celebrated occasion, thought he sounded like Johnson, and if his two versions of the blues "Functional" be juxtaposed with the older man's two "Blue Moods" pieces the idea appears less far-fetched. Waller might seem the obvious example of Johnson's influence, yet the similarities between these two are less revealing than the differences. Thus, remembering the attention he gave to the European classics, Johnson's harmony is rather disappointingly conventional, whereas on the very few occasions in the recording studio that Waller gave something like full rein to his talent he produced music of considerable harmonic interest, as in "Clothes Line Ballet" or "Beale Street Blues." Rhythmically, however, it is the younger man who is conservative, and, with a few exceptions like the 1923 "Snake Hips" piano roll, which is in an even 4/4, his playing often has a rather old-fashioned 2/4 feeling, whereas Johnson's left-hand parts show far more variety and exorcise the rhythmic ghost of ragtime with a consistent four-to-the-bar. Pianistically they were quite different, too, with Johnson's delicacy, precision, and grace answering Waller's power and warmth.

If this last comparison suggests greater subtlety on Johnson's part, that is correct. Items like "Scouting Around" or "Crying for the Carolines" use the same type of folk material and draw on the same European tradition of virtuoso keyboard writing as did Louis Moreau Gottschalk, the New Orleans-born composer who attempted this sort of fusion far ahead of jazz. If Johnson's pieces have a more complex impact than "Le Banjo" or "Bamboula" (subtitled "Danse des Negres"), if, too, they seem more personal statements than ragtime with its slightly mechanical cheerfulness—itself the reverse image of the nostalgia and insecurity of Stephen Foster's Negro dialect songs—it may be that in Johnson both the folk roots and the aspirations to cultural status went deeper.

Though he played an important rôle in freeing jazz from the ragtime influence, his attitudes remained in some respects closer to those of the rag composers than to those of jazz musicians. Although their music was descended in part from the sardonic parodies of the cakewalk, they wanted their formal, fully notated compositions to be considered as art, not entertainment. Hence Scott Joplin's attempt at opera with *Treemonisha,* hence Johnson's attempt with *The Organizer,* which had a libretto by Langston Hughes. Rare exceptions like Bix Beiderbecke aside, it was many years before jazzmen began to reflect the Harlem pianists' wide interest in non-jazz musics, but Johnson's attempts at large-scale composition were virtually inevitable. *Tone Poem,* completed in 1930, *Harlem Symphony,* which followed in 1932, Suite in Sonata Form on "St. Louis Blues" (1936), and the Jasmine Concerto for piano and orchestra all had a few performances and then were dropped by performers and audiences who were unprepared for the sort of fusion they attempted, whether successfully or otherwise. More accomplished composers than Johnson—such as the nineteenth-century Russians—met almost insoluble difficulties in matching folk material to symphonic processes, and we may doubt whether he, any more than Ellington, would be able to control long-duration forms. Perhaps his orchestral pieces, whatever their status, are best regarded as part of an intrinsically healthy movement to remove the divisions between "serious" and "popular" art. Their continuing unavailability in print or on disc must be regretted, however, for in our present state of enforced ignorance we shall always be uncertain of how Johnson fared.

Coleman Hawkins

Dan Morgenstern

Morgenstern, winner of an almost embarrassing number of Grammy Awards for his liner notes, did justice to the great saxophonist in 1973 and won yet another Grammy when he wrote these notes for the album The Hawk Flies.

Even among the chosen few, the extraordinary men and women who make up the peerage of jazz, Coleman Hawkins stands out.

To begin, there is his sound, a thing of beauty in and of itself. Hawkins filled the horn brimful with his great breath. Sound was his palette, and his brush was the instrument that, for jazz purposes, he invented—the tenor saxophone.

In this post-Coltrane age, the tenor sax is so prominent a feature of the landscape that it's hard to imagine it wasn't always there. Lester Young once said, accurately, "I think Coleman Hawkins was the President first, right?," here meaning "president" in the sense of founding father. Which wasn't the sense in which Billie Holiday had laid "Pres" on Lester—at a point in time when the president of the United States was a great man, Number One in all the land.

Tenor time in jazz begins in 1924, when Coleman Hawkins joined Fletcher Henderson's band. In a decade there, he first mastered, then established the instrument. While trumpet still was king, it was due to Hawk that tenor became president. Thus jazz became a republic in the Swing Era. King Louis was peerless by definition, but his powerful message unlocked the magic in other noble souls. If we hear young Coleman Hawkins both before and after Armstrong joined Henderson, the point is clearly made.

The saxophone family of instruments had been invented by Adolphe Sax to mirror the range and variety of the strings; he wanted his instruments to sing, to have the warmth of wood and the power of brass, and thus created a hybrid of wind mouthpiece and brass body, unlocked by a new system of keys. He did this in the 1840s, but with the exception of Bizet, Debussy, and later Ravel, no major "serious" composer knew what to do with the new arsenal of sound. Until it was discovered and mastered by jazzmen in the early

1920s, the saxophone remained a brass band and vaudeville instrument—a novelty.

Coleman Hawkins's first instruments in St. Joseph, Missouri, were piano and cello. (Of all the saxophones, the tenor most resembles the cello in range and color.) As a boy, he heard and saw The Six Brown Brothers in vaudeville. They used the whole range of saxes, from sopranino to contrabass, and with all their clowning really knew how to play. Young Coleman began to explore the saxophone.

Exactly when this occurred is not entirely clear. Hawkins, like so many other performers, prevaricated about his age. It was widely accepted that he was born on November 21, 1904; a date he unsuccessfully tried to adjust to 1907. Still, underneath incessant joking and good-natured teasing about age with his friends (Ben Webster: "I was in kneepants when my mother first took me to hear you." Hawkins: "That wasn't me; that was my father. I wasn't born then!") there ran a current of doubt, and when Charles Graham, doing biographical research, obtained a copy of Hawkins's birth certificate, it read 1901!

By the time the Father of Tenor Saxophone left for Europe in March 1934, he had already created the two prototypical tenor styles in jazz: the fast, driving, explosive riff style and the slow, flowing, rhapsodic ballad form. He made the mold, he was the model: already, Ben Webster, Herschel Evans, Chu Berry, Budd Johnson, and many more had sprung, fully armed, from his high forehead.

To Europe, where the greatness of jazz had been felt mainly through records, Hawkins brought it in the flesh. Sidney Bechet had spent time there back in the twenties, and Louis Armstrong himself had flashed like a comet through England, Scandinavia, the Low Countries, France, Italy, and Switzerland earlier in the thirties. But Hawk came and remained; the first fixed star of magnitude.

WHEN HIS ERSTWHILE Henderson colleague, Benny Carter, that master of the alto sax, clarinet, trumpet, and arranger's pen, crossed the Atlantic a bit later and also decided to stay, the two often hooked up. Together and individually they put their stamp on European jazz for decades.

The process was reciprocal. Hawkins's love for certain of the better things in life—good food, good drink, good clothes, pretty women, fast cars—was apparent before he left his homeland, but Europe sharpened and deepened his tastes. His sense of his own dignity and worth also expanded in the warmth of European appreciation and adoration. From here on in, Hawk was a cosmopolitan.

Meanwhile, there were not just contenders to his crown back home, but a whole new tenor style, introduced by Lester Young. Only a few of Hawk's great European recordings had made their way into the hands of American musicians during his absence. The climate seemed right for battle and the tenor brigade was ready for Bean (as musicians then called him, "bean" being a synonym for head, i.e., brainpower) when he came home in late July of 1939, just before the outbreak of World War II. Chu Berry, Ben Webster, Don Byas, and Lester himself were gathered to greet Hawk at a Harlem after-hours spot called Puss Johnson's (there were many such music spots; the reputation of Minton's is all out of proportion). The master arrived without horn (but with a striking lady), listened, and refused to be drawn into battle. A few days later he returned with horn and reestablished his sovereignty.

Hawk's victory became official with the release, late in 1939, of the biggest record of his career: "Body and Soul." Consisting of just two choruses—framed by a brief piano introduction and short tenor cadenza—it stands as one of the most perfectly balanced jazz records ever made. After more than three decades it remains a model of flawlessly constructed and superbly executed jazz improvisation, and is still the test piece for aspiring tenorists.

Although young tenor men in increasing numbers were taken with Lester's cooler sound and unorthodox phrasing, the Hawkins approach remained firmly entrenched (as the newfound popularity of Ben Webster with Duke Ellington and Don Byas with Count Basie proved in the early forties). There also arose a school of tenors equally influenced by both: Illinois Jacquet, Buddy Tate, Gene Ammons, and Dexter Gordon are examples.

Furthermore, that leader of the new style soon to be labeled bebop, Charlie Parker, symbolized the possibility of a Hawkins–Young fusion. Though fashionable jazz criticism has emphasized only Young's influence on Parker, there can be no doubt that Hawkins, especially in terms of harmony, approach to ballads, and use of double time, also profoundly touched Bird's conception.

The influence was a two-way street. Hawkins was the first established jazz figure of major stature to not only accept but *embrace* the new music, which he rightly saw as a logical development. Consider this: Hawk was the *only* name leader to hire Thelonious Monk, the strange piano player from Minton's house band, for a downtown gig (on 52nd Street) and to use him on a record date (the earliest music heard on this remarkable collection, and Monk's studio debut). And this: for a February 1944 date with a larger band, Hawkins hired Dizzy Gillespie, Max Roach, Leo Parker, and other young modernists to back him. And this: at the end of 1944, Hawk took to California a pioneer bop group that included Howard McGhee and Denzil Best. As early as 1947, Hawk used Miles Davis on a record date; a few years later, he had him in his band. The 1947 date on this album clearly reflects Hawk's commitment to the new sounds, and his ability to fit himself into it. (Note also the inclusion of a Monk tune, perfectly interpreted.)

Hawk didn't just adapt to bop; profoundly touched by Parker, he entered a whole new phase of musical development at an age when most players have settled permanently within a given framework.

The new Hawk was most clearly visible in the blues. Prior to the mid-forties, Hawkins rarely played blues, and never with much of what we now call "funk." But Bird brought a new blue stream into jazz, and Hawk was nourished by it (hear him here on "Sih-sah" and "Juicy Fruit"). And Bird's song in Hawk's ear didn't end with the blues. You can feel it throughout the 1957 session, and in the magnificent "Ruby, My Dear" which stems from a Monk–Hawkins reunion album that co-starred John Coltrane. (The rest of that date, by the way, can be heard on *Monk/Trane.*)

For many years they had affectionately called him "The Old Man." But he still looked, felt, and played young and it was the Old Man's pride that he could keep up. No resting on laurels for him; virtually everything new was a challenge. But for a while, when Lester's way of playing tenor dominated the scene, and bop had little time to look back, Hawkins fell somewhat out of favor. When producer Orrin Keepnews gave him *carte blanche* to pick his own men for the 1957 date reintroduced herewith, the result was the first loose, modern jazz date for Hawk in some time. It compares most interestingly with the session of ten years before, and not only for the work of Hawk himself and repeaters J. J. Johnson and Hank Jones. (It is also interesting that Hawk did not choose a bop rhythm section for himself.)

Throughout the fifties, with Norman Granz's Jazz at the Philharmonic and also on his own, he frequently teamed with old friend Roy Eldridge, ten years younger but a fraternal spirit. From 1957 on, the Metropole in New York's Times Square area became their home base. Most jazz writers (except visitors from Europe) shunned the place, but musicians did drop in to hear Roy and Hawk: among them, Miles Davis, Sonny Rollins, and John Coltrane.

AT THE SOULFUL establishment across the street, The Copper Rail, the players and their friends congregated to eat and drink. Even when they were three-deep at the bar, you could hear Hawk's laughter, or his voice emphasizing a point, from anywhere in the house. Though he was not a large man, his voice had a presence remarkably similar to his saxophone sound. Hawk was strong in those days. The new tenor voices, significantly that of Sonny Rollins, seemed closer in conception and sound to him than to Lester, and his star was once again in ascendance. He and Roy made periodic tours abroad. Recordings were again fairly frequent. His personal life was happy. His health seemed robust.

"You have to eat when you drink," he used to say, and he was still following his own rule. A girl I knew thought nothing of cooking him eight eggs for breakfast, and he could go to work on a Chinese dinner for two or a double order of spareribs in the wee hours of the morning with the gusto of a hungry lumberjack. In the course of a working day, he'd consume a quantity of Scotch even Eddie Condon would have deemed respectable, but he could also leave the booze alone when it got to him. When Lester Young died in 1959, not quite fifty, the Old Man told me how he used to try to make Pres eat when they were traveling together for Jazz at the Philharmonic. "When I got something for myself, I'd get for him, too. But I'd always find most of it left under his bus or plane seat when we got off."

Hawk liked Lester very much, but the only tenor player I ever heard him call "genius" was Chu Berry. Other musicians he bestowed this title on were Louis, Bird, Art Tatum, Dizzy Gillespie, and Monk—the latter a personal favorite.

At home, Hawk rarely listened to jazz. His sizable collection was dominated by complete opera sets (Verdi, Wagner, and Puccini) and also included a lot of Brahms and Debussy. Bach and Beethoven were there as well, and some moderns, but Hawk liked music with a big sound and romantic sweep best of all. With his luxurious hi-fi setup, he could fill his comfortable Central Park West apartment with sound, and the commanding view of the park went well with the music. Sometimes he'd play the piano, which he did surprisingly well—always music of his own.

In the final years, which his friends would rather forget but can't, Tommy Flanagan would sometimes drop by and make Hawk play the piano and try to copy down some of the tunes. Hawk was always a gifted composer—even with Henderson—but never had the patience to write the stuff down. By then, the expensive hi-fi equipment had fallen into disuse, the blinds were often drawn to shut out the view, and the sound most frequently heard was that of the TV—on around the clock to keep the insomniac company. As often as not, there'd be food defrosting in the kitchen—chicken, chops, ribs, or steak—but "by the time it's ready for me to fix," he once told me, "I've lost my appetite from this whiskey." He knew exactly what he was doing to himself, but some demon had hold of him.

It had nothing to do with the socio-psychological clichés of art and race so often applied to "explain" jazz artists, but it did have much to do with the fact that he was living alone now, and that his aloneness was of his own making. His last great love gone because in his jealousy he could not accept that a woman could love a man much older than herself, he now chose to accelerate the aging process he had previously hated and successfully fought off. He let his grizzled beard and hair flow freely, and let his once immaculately fitting suits hang from his shrunken frame.

ONLY WORK COULD shake him out of his depression, but now it seldom came. He'd never been one for managers and agents; if people wanted his services, they could call *him*. But only a few employers—mainly the loyal Norman Granz, sometimes George Wein, a club owner here or there—would still come through. My friends and I got him some gigs. It was a vicious circle: because he didn't work much, he was rusty when he did play (he had always disdained practicing, and lifelong habits don't change), and because he was rusty (and shaky), he wasn't asked back. Even quite near the end, a few nights of work, leading to resumed eating, could straighten him out, and he'd find his form. But there was no steady work to make him stay on course.

Perhaps it would have been too late; he hated doctors and hospitals and refused all suggestions of medical attention. And since his voice, incongruously, remained as strong as ever and his ego just as fierce, it was difficult to counteract him. He welcomed company but never invited anyone. His daughters would come by to visit and straighten up the house when they were in town. Frequent visitors included Monk and the Baroness Nica de Konigswarter, but the closest people near the end were Barry Harris and drummer Eddie Locke.

Monk was at Hawk's bedside when it had finally become necessary to take him to a hospital. Monk even made the Old Man laugh—but it was for the last time.

Coleman Hawkins was a legend in his own time: revered by younger musicians, who were amazed and delighted at his ability to remain receptive to their discoveries; loved by his contemporaries, who were equally astonished by his capacity for constant self-renewal. He was one of those who wrote the book of jazz.

The art of Coleman Hawkins transcends the boundaries of style and time. Fortunately, it is well documented. The great sound and mind that is one of the landmarks of jazz lives on, as in these grooves, awaiting your command to issue forth once more.

Even among the chosen few of jazz, Coleman Hawkins stands out. Hear him well.

Not for the Left Hand Alone

Martin Williams

This considered evaluation of Art Tatum by the eminent Martin Williams appeared in his critical history, The Jazz Tradition, *first published in 1970.*

When Louis Armstrong first arrived in the early twenties, the reaction of his fellow musicians was generally positive. His elders, most of them, and particularly if they were from New Orleans, heard him as a fulfillment of what they had been working on. And younger players seem to have felt that here was someone who could serve as an inspiration and guide, from whom they could take at least a part if not all, and go on to develop something of their own.

When Art Tatum arrived about a decade later, the first reaction of many musicians seems to have been one of delight and despair. If this is where it's going, they seemed to say, I can't follow. And then some of them decided, perhaps temporarily, to hang up their horns.

What they heard in Tatum was, first of all, an exceptional musical ear, and beyond that, an unequalled capacity for speed and for musical embroidery. And those things remained for years a source of frustration to many a musician. But not so (one learns with gratification) to Coleman Hawkins, who heard something more, perhaps even something else, and found inspiration in it.

The speed and embroidery were dazzling of course. Tatum played with an array of ascending and descending arpeggio runs, octave slides and leaps, sudden modulations, double-third glissandos—a keyboard vocabulary in which swift, interpolated triplets were a small matter. His left hand could walk and it could stride; he also liked to use a kind of "reverse" stride, the chord at the bottom, the note on top. And he could execute all these at tempos that most players could not reach, much less sustain. Indeed, his early "Tea for Two" seemed to be a textbook summary of what one could learn from Earl Hines; "Tiger Rag" all one could get from Fats Waller; and by "Get Happy" in 1940, more than Waller was ever likely to get to.

Was Art Tatum then, as has been said, only a kind of superior, jazz-oriented cocktail pianist who borrowed the styles of certain leading players and elaborated them with cool keyboard showmanship?

From the beginning, Tatum's rhythmic sense was absolutely sure, and over the years it seemed to grow to even lighter and more flexible. One might say that, by the late forties, Art Tatum's command of musical time and tempo was rare by any standard, rare for a player of any genre of music. Beyond that, his swing was infallible. Yet it is so subtly and perfectly assimilated to all aspects of his art that a listener will often find himself responding to it, not with his feet or his head, but inwardly, with his feelings. That subtlety was also an aspect of a keyboard touch that seemed capable of evoking endlessly varied sounds from the piano without ever seeming to strike its keys—and this on a percussive instrument in a music which tends to treat all musicians percussively.

Tatum's repertory tended to remain stable, but it was added to over the years, and the additions were mostly medium-tempo ballads. That fact seems to me indicative. Also, by the late forties, "Tiger Rag" and "I Know That You Know" were less often heard; "Get Happy" had slowed down; "Tea for Two" was slower and had become a succession of chromatic modulations, some of them delivered a bar at a time. The newer pieces contained some unusual harmonic challenges (the stark simplicity of "Caravan," for one example; the relative complexity of "Have You Met Miss Jones?" for another). The inflated "light classics" ("Humoresque," "Elegie") lay relatively neglected, and there were no additions of their kind.

Art Tatum's capacities for melodic invention were limited. Indeed, given a solo chorus on "Mop Mop," with nothing but the chord progression of "I Got Rhythm" to work with, he could come up with a building succession of pianistic platitudes whose dexterity could not disguise their essential emptiness. But Art Tatum's harmonic imagination was so challenging that a performance could include fluid, altered voicings, unexpected passing chords and substitutions, left-hand counter-melodies—toward the end of his career he seemed capable almost of providing his ballads with whole substitute progressions every eight measures.

An Art Tatum bass line is a paradox of absolute dependability and rhythmic sureness, lightness, and deftness of touch, and at the same time harmonic and rhythmic adventure and surprise. Has any other jazzman reached the level of integration of rhythm and harmony that was Art Tatum? In him they could become inseparable, in identity, integrated also with his touch, his momentum, and his swing. And there are those sublime moments when he moves from an ad lib section into a sustained tempo—or sometimes only apparently ad lib. If I cite "Tenderly" or "There'll Never Be Another You" or

"Someone to Watch Over Me" or "I Gotta Right to Sing the Blues" or "What's New," I necessarily neglect many such ravishing transitions.

By calling Tatum's melodic imagination limited, and denying him the ability to sustain spontaneous, invented melodies, I risk denying him one of the most gratifying aspects of his work. He was basically an artist of the arabesque, true, but he also functioned in that middle ground which André Hodeir has called paraphrase, where fragments of the original theme take their place beside invented phrases, to form allusive structures in variation. And there, Tatum's choice and placement of terse transitional phrases can be all verve and elegance. Art Tatum's best harmonic and melodic adornments help us discover what is potentially beautiful in a popular song; his invented, passing phrases subdue what is not.

Tatum's maturity came in the late 1940s, and it is worth remarking that it came after the modernists of Charlie Parker's generation had established themselves, and after Tatum had largely abandoned the trio format with bass and guitar which brought him the only public popularity he ever had—and which, like any role but that of solo pianist, inhibited Tatum's inventive powers. That maturity was announced in a series of recordings he made for the Capitol label in 1949.

The Capitol performances display a heightened harmonic imagination and a firm confirmation of Tatum's always evocative touch on the keyboard—"My Heart Stood Still" or "Dancing in the Dark," or, for simpler structures, "Blue Skies," "Willow, Weep for Me" or "Aunt Hagar's Blues." And, again, there is firm command of tempo, of musical time, and a growing use of rhythmic suspense and surprise evident everywhere, but particularly on "I Gotta Right to Sing the Blues" or "Someone to Watch Over Me."

If there is a masterpiece of the series it would have to be either "Willow Weep for Me" or "Aunt Hagar's Blues." Both offer in abundance the Tatum paradox that all surprises quickly assume an inevitability as one absorbs them. Indeed this Capitol "Aunt Hagar's" seems so perfect in its overall pattern and pacing, with every short run and every ornament appropriate and in place, that it may be the masterpiece of all his recorded work.

Pianist Dick Katz has written that Tatum approached each piece in his repertory through a kind of loose arrangement, and the general patterns of opening ad lib (if there was one), of movement into and out of tempo, of certain ornaments and frills tended to be there consistently—or, rather, versions of them did. (Even Tatum's interpolated "quotes" tended to be consistent: "In a Sentimental Mood" usually contained a fragment of "Swanee River" and ended on "My Old Kentucky Home"; "Somebody Loves Me" glanced at "Pretty Baby"; "Indiana" ended wryly with the traditional "Funky Butt"; "Blue Skies" with "In and Out the Window"; and over the years

"Sweet Lorraine"'s Sousa allusion was joined by a fragment of Paderewski's minuet and a quote from "Narcissus.") But the patterns were all loosely held, and, like the pieces themselves, always a basis for spontaneous rephrasing and paraphrase, reharmonization, reaccentuation, and elaboration. If the Capitol recordings are the best introduction to Tatum, the second best might be a successive listening to all versions of one of his often-recorded standards, "Sweet Lorraine," say, or "I Cover the Waterfront" or "Tenderly," or such widely separated, early-and-late pieces as "Sophisticated Lady," "Moonglow," or "Ill Wind."

The series of 1953–56 extended solo recordings which Tatum did under Norman Granz's auspices (issued on Clef, Verve, and more recently collected on Pablo) are a singular documentation of a remarkable musician. To expect each performance of each piece to be definitive is perhaps to misunderstand the nature of the improviser's art and the pleasures and rewards of attending him. And to pick, let us say, thirty excellent titles from that series (as one easily could) is perhaps to provide the listener with the kind of guide he might prefer to arrive at for himself.

I will single out "Jitterbug Waltz" for its overall design, for its control of tempo and movement, and for its particular grace in the countermovements in Tatum's bass line. I will cite "Have You Met Miss Jones?" for its high adventure in modulatory risk and daring, and for its mastery of musical time both in its "free" and its in-tempo sections. And there is the ease and daring of "Tenderly," a kind of triumphant climax to his several versions of that piece—indeed, Tatum's art might almost be defined through his surviving versions of "Tenderly."

The series does have its failures, of course: it has further examples of Tatum's wasting his time on puzzling material ("Taboo," "Happy Feet," "Blue Lou"), and of Tatum's finding relatively little where one might have expected more ("Star Dust"). And I cannot say that for me Tatum's taste in free tempos, or his choice of ornaments always avoids the pompous and vulgar ("All the Things You Are").

To be sure, to raise the question of vulgarity is to raise the question of taste, and the question of opposing Tatum's taste to one's own. But it is also to raise the important question of Tatum's sly, redeeming, pianistic humor. Time and again, when we fear he is reaching the limits of romantic bombast, a quirky phrase, an exaggerated ornament will remind us that Tatum may be having us on. He is also inviting us to share the joke, and heartily kidding himself as well as the concert hall traditions to which he alludes.

Opposing one's own taste to Tatum's is ultimately the critic's business, of course. But raising the issue here can also serve to remind us of the aesthetic miracle that was Art Tatum. For somewhere among the melodies he chose, the ornaments with which he enhanced them, the lines he altered, the phrases he added, the sense of musical time and momentum he evoked in us, the unique harmonic adventure he brought us each time, and each time differently, somewhere among all these, the alchemy of a great jazzman brought his performances to the highest levels of compositional solidity, integrity, and strength.

As with many other major jazz artists, the revelation of broadcast and privately recorded material enlarges our image of Art Tatum. The so-called "discoveries" recordings, taped at an informal evening [in 1950] in the home of a prominent Hollywood musician, offer a generally heightened Tatum, and in "Too Marvelous for Words" we have probably the supreme example of Tatum's wending his adventurous way into an absolutely "impossible" harmonic corner, and then dancing free on his bass line, while executing a fluid treble line to ornament the feat.

Was Tatum, as a master of ornament and paraphrase, out of the mainstream in a music whose emphasis fell increasingly to harmonically oriented invention? I think that Tatum's influence, although it may have been somewhat indirect, has been crucial. I have mentioned Coleman Hawkins, and Tatum was Hawkins's second great influence after Armstrong. What Hawkins heard in Tatum was the core concern, and harmonic impetus, and Hawkins, probably helped by his own early training on piano, understood. Hawkins's arpeggio-based style and his growing vocabulary of chords, of passing chords and the relationship of chords, was confirmed and encouraged by his response to Art Tatum.

Similarly, Charlie Parker. We learn with delight that Parker once took a kitchen-help job in a club where Tatum was working in order to absorb him live. And Parker proved to be the pianist's equal in the imaginative use of harmony. The saxophonist proved to be a superb, inventive melodist as well, but we should also acknowledge the clear effect that Tatum's rhythmic language, his patterns of accents, his speed with short notes—his melodic rhythm—had on Parker.

The final effect of Art Tatum has to be between his keyboard and his listener, of course. One can return to a familiar Tatum recording and discover something new, or delight in something previously unnoticed, or discover that what we already thought we knew still seems surprising. Or one can come upon an unfamiliar version of any Tatum standard and discover that, as anticipated, it truly does offer something new.

For the listener, the Tatum adventure seems unending.

Time and the Tenor

Graham Colombé

This generous account of Lester Young's artistic progression—a much-debated subject—first appeared in Into Jazz *in 1974 and was reprinted in* A Lester Young Reader *in 1991.*

It has been a common attitude to see Lester Young's career as a steady artistic decline after the departure from Basie's band, so I must make it clear at once that I do not accept this view. The evident decline in the early forties was followed by a struggle to pull himself together after his army service and come to terms with bop; there was then a settling down about 1948 and 1949 into an unstrained, totally personal style that was related to the earlier one but had its own identity and merit. A similar view was expressed but with insufficient detail and evidence by Burnett James in his *Essays on Jazz,* and the case for decline was put with rather more specific comments by Benny Green in a chapter in *The Reluctant Art,* to which I shall refer later.

While considering Lester's music in the fifties, I shall deal only with studio sessions under his own name, except in 1957, when these give too one-sided a picture. In 1950 Lester signed a new recording contract with Norman Granz, whose company produced (again excepting 1957) at least one album a year for the rest of Lester's life. The first date (March 1950) was not a complete success because of the presence of Buddy Rich, but it does make clear certain aspects of Lester's style. On the medium fast "Up 'n' Adam," it's obvious that Rich's heavy, inflexible drumming doesn't suit Young at all, although he struggles against it and manages to produce some soaring, floating phrases that glide above the heavy ground rhythm. More relaxed work from the rhythm section (including Hank Jones and Ray Brown) improves the other four performances, and two of them are exemplary of a number of later recordings. "Too Marvelous for Words," at an easygoing medium tempo, has the theme played in a stealthy, subdued manner in the lower register but changes to a more forceful mood in the upper register for the second chorus. This very effective practice dramatizes Lester's solemn, almost respectful attitude to the tunes he played and their words, and then his feeling of freedom as he takes over with his own stream of melody. "Polka Dots and Moonbeams" shows the nature of Lester's ballad playing for the rest of the decade and also makes clear why certain listeners have been unable to come to terms with this later music. On this track Lester drops his guard and plays not just with an emotional depth equaled by only a few but with an extreme frankness rare even in jazz. His solo here has beauty, tenderness, and sadness, but these can all be found elsewhere. What is unique here is Lester's expression of his vulnerability. His approach to this song is an admission that life can be painful and dreams can be shattered, and the only solace for what has happened is here and now in the beauty of music. This mature tragic awareness is what distinguishes Lester in the fifties from Lester in the thirties, and with the advantage of hindsight it's easy to understand how the magical, buoyant optimism of the early years could not last, given the man Lester was and the society he lived in. His later music is therefore sometimes disturbing and confusing, but it does tell a certain emotional truth about what the United States did to Lester Young. Many people like listening to jazz as a simple, refreshing, uplifting experience, and I can understand why this music may not appeal to them; Benny Green, in his essay on Billie Holiday, showed he was prepared to go further than that into the music, so it's with reluctance that I accuse him of a superficial response when he compares Lester's "bland virtuosity" of the thirties with the later "weary sentiment." To me it seems that neither phrase does justice to the strength and depth of Lester's music.

Mr. Green rightly draws attention to the saxophonist's uncertainty in the lower reaches of his horn, and this is an inescapable characteristic of his later work. But I don't see why listeners who can accept the fluffs on some of Armstrong's and Davis's classic recordings should not accept this fault also. The comparison is not made lightly, because I think there are tracks in the fifties that are classic performances in the Young canon. "Count Every Star" from Lester's next session is an excellent track that allows a number of observations about Lester's style. The rhythmic approach may at first suggest the advent of diminished technique, or a lack of alertness, but, since certain very lively phrases make it clear that was not the case, we must accept, as we do with Monk, that Lester has chosen to play this way, and we must try to acclimatize ourselves to it. We can discover then that, although Lester may now lag even further behind the beat than before, his music still swings, again like Monk, in a very personal way. Apart from the fast "Neenah" this session (July 1950), with John Lewis, Joe Shulman, and Bill Clark, has four medium to slow tracks where Clark's drums are barely audible, producing a sound that foreshadows the later Jimmy Giuffre Trio and underlines the beauty of Lester's tone. This has certainly changed, but the husky vibrato is hardly "grossly sensual," as Benny Green calls it. Lester, in fact, displays a delicate control over his tone, and the subtle variations he employs are usually appropriate to his phrases, which often form a pattern of sudden contrasts. Legato, mournful figures, drawn out over the rhythm, are followed abruptly by exhilarating, rising patterns, fingered with extreme rapidity.

The next two sessions (January 16, 1951, and March 8, 1951) were made with the rhythm section Lester was using at Birdland—John Lewis, Gene Ramey, and Jo Jones. Lewis's personal, elegant simplicity blends well with the tenor and encourages the gentler side of Lester, so that in spite of the lift that Jo Jones gives the rhythm section, Lester does not fully reveal the drive of which he was still capable, preferring to float along in a blithe, sometimes almost gay, mood that shows that his melancholy was not yet pervasive. Nevertheless two of the best tracks are the slow "Undercover Girl Blues" and the even slower "Slow Motion Blues" (prophetically titled because his playing actually acquired a feeling of slow motion a few years later). Lester was a great blues player, and in the fifties his playing of slow blues, as with the ballads, took on a deeper involvement. The surprising achievement of his blues playing is to retain the blues feeling yet to convey, usually by employing the ninth and thirteenth extensions of the chords, a sublime lyricism at the same time. Bechet is the only other person who comes to mind as managing this blend, though of course in a more forceful manner. The lyricism is also there naturally in numbers like "A Foggy Day" and "Let's Fall in Love," which Lester rescued from oblivion, and it is particularly striking, as Lester moves from the tune to his improvisation, that there is, so to speak, no loss of melody. His own inventions are frequently as memorable as the tune.

The following year Lester attended a lengthy session with Oscar Peterson, Barney Kessel, Ray Brown, and J. C. Heard [November 28, 1952]. It began with four extended tracks, and the busy, prodding drive of this group at first had the effect of inhibiting Lester and restricting his phrasing to small intervals and simple patterns. By the time the third track—a fast "Tea for Two"—was recorded, he had adjusted to the situation, and he plays two solos that, though less inventive than those with Lewis, exceed them in drive and momentum and demonstrate Lester's continuing technical ability. Among the shorter tracks recorded later, "I Can't Get Started" and "These Foolish Things" are very moving performances in the mood of "Polka Dots and Moonbeams," and the melodic quality of the improvising is again impressive. By the time "On the Sunny Side of the Street" was played, Lester was at home enough to indulge himself. The theme statement starts straightforwardly but suddenly jumps to a definitely post-Parker, double-time phrase before reverting to a decorated version of the tune, descending to a throbbing low note, after an unexpected pause, and returning deviously to the tonic to complete the first sixteen bars; the middle eight begins with a simple, declamatory, Armstrong-like phrase and develops in this way until another double-time run leads back to a masterly paraphrase of the tune in the last eight bars. The sheer variety of phrasing available to Lester at this time is quite astonishing.

This variety is underlined on the next two sessions, by Lester's regular band (December 11, 1953, and December 10, 1954), where he has Jesse Drakes on trumpet as frontline partner, and the square, rigid, limited nature of the trumpet's phrasing emphasizes the opposite qualities in the saxophone lines. When Connie Kay told me that Drakes was in the band as straw boss as well as trumpeter, the musical incompatibility was at last explained. He is an anonymous "modernist," technically competent enough but lacking Lester's warmth and melodic invention. In fact Lester's involvement makes Drakes sound cynical, and I wish Charles Fox, who wrote in a recent *New Statesman* that Lester himself was "often cynical-sounding" at this time, would listen to these records and reconsider. From the 1953 session two interesting tracks are a fast "Jumpin' at the Woodside" and an even faster "Lady Be Good," which are actually the last examples of Lester in command at up-tempo. He is in command in that he produces satisfactory solos without struggling, but he is not capable, at this tempo, of invention to match what he can do when he has more time. The session a year later included an Ellington tune, "It Don't Mean a Thing," and "Rose Room," another melody associated with the Duke, and it's intriguing to wonder what music might have resulted if Lester had ever joined the Ellington band, particularly as the sound of Paul Gonsalves's off-mike playing of "Happy Reunion" at the Rainbow in 1973 was the nearest thing I've heard to Lester's thin, husky, passionate tone on much of his later ballad playing. This sound and passion are evident on two beautiful ballads from this date, "I'm in the Mood for Love" and "Come Rain or Come Shine," where the tone seems slightly thinner than before but the feeling more intense.

For the next session (December 1, 1955), Granz decided to choose the players himself, and he obviously hoped to stimulate Lester by a reunion with Harry Edison, supported by a rhythm team of Peterson, Ellis, Brown, and Rich. Naturally enough the first number was a fast "One O'Clock Jump," and Peterson develops a very swinging groove in his opening choruses. When the tenor comes in, it's at once obvious that something is wrong. The tempo is too fast for Lester, and he's in trouble, neither brain nor fingers can cope. In fact this is the first really weak solo in the Young discography, and it was due to his lack of concern for his health having finally caught up with him. Very soon after this date he went voluntarily to the hospital for treatment and rest. Nevertheless on the slow tracks that followed

"One O'Clock Jump," he played valid, moving solos with an entirely new atmosphere, and I cannot refrain from quoting W. B. Yeats in an attempt to explain it:

An aged man is but a paltry thing,
A tattered coat upon a stick, unless
Soul clap its hands and sing, and
louder sing
For every tatter in its mortal dress.

What Lester somehow conveys now is an impression of a man in totally exceptional circumstances, perhaps even a man who knows he has not long to live because he is not going to make much effort to stay alive. For the rest of his life there is a haunting quality in his music that can transcend technical failings and reach straight inside the right listener. Charlie Parker's first "Loverman" had the same quality. On this 1955 record Lester floats in slow motion over the rhythm, some of his runs relating to Coltrane's "sheet of sound," in that it's hard to pin down their relation to the beat though it's undeniably there. His tone, now wispier then before, becomes even more distinctive, and his gentle lines are sometimes interrupted by louder, piercing phrases of an almost heartrending quality. However, the logical sequel to this record did not occur for another year and a half, and the two sessions that took place less than two months later present a Lester transformed.

Granz's second attempt to stimulate him with fresh companions must have succeeded beyond his wildest dreams. After some weeks in the hospital, Lester came out refreshed and ready to play, and the three men who I think encouraged him most on the *Jazz Giants '56* date (January 12, 1956) were Roy Eldridge, Teddy Wilson, and Jo Jones. Well though Edison had played six weeks before, Eldridge had the edge over him in his ability to rise to an occasion, or even initiate one, and this was an occasion everyone rose to. As the music is fortunately available on Verve, I need not emphasize the excellence of the solos by Eldridge, Wilson, Jones, and Vic Dickenson or the invaluable rhythm work of Freddie Green and Gene Ramey. What is important here is to understand Lester Young's contribution. Most striking at first is his tone, which has changed yet again. In fact the tone he plays with here and on the following day has an identity of its own, which clearly separates it from both earlier and later recordings. His sound is broader and warmer, as if, after confronting a vision of his own end, Lester was able, through the support of people who mattered to him both as musicians and as friends, to find again in music, if only temporarily, the hopes of personal fulfillment it had offered him at the beginning of his career. His solos are simpler than those of a few years before, but more confident; it seems he has blended an earlier style with the Armstrong-inspired mode that had preceded it, though retaining an occasional, almost shyly inserted, double-time figure derived from the language of bop. The obliqueness of earlier times has all but vanished, and Lester has extended the impression of total openness that emanates from "Polka Dots and Moonbeams" to his medium tempo solos (perhaps not the fast "Gigantic Blues"), so that this session, though not representing him at his artistic peak, is unique in showing him competing successfully in terms of unconfined, rhapsodic passion (terms that he had replaced in the thirties with his own dry, contained economy) with Bechet, Armstrong, and Hawkins (and of course with Eldridge, who was actually there).

The next day Lester recorded a further seven titles (also on Verve), with Wilson, Ramey, and Jones. These retained the mood of the previous day, but with an occasional lessening of intensity and a hint of awareness that this was only a temporary recovery. "Pres Returns," the medium-tempo blues that was the first number recorded, is one of Lester's best recordings (with excellent drums from Jones), and it points the way to his final phase, where feeling and sound were to become so touching that they could make concern for technique and imagination seem almost irrelevant.

The following year Lester recorded with Harry Edison again, and it was as if the 1956 session had never existed. This date (July 31, 1957) is the weakest available on record from Lester's entire career. Apart from Lester's tenuous grip on himself, it sounds at times as if the octave key on his saxophone is not working properly. The first track recorded, a blues called "St. Tropez," features Lester on a new metal clarinet, and the tone he obtains is very reminiscent of the Kansas City Six session. Unfortunately he seems to be having technical problems on this instrument, too; in three separate solos he plays a total of sixteen choruses, of which a few are coherent but several are disastrous, with harsh squeaks and places where he blows but no note comes out. Nevertheless on other tracks where he plays tenor ("Flic" in the Jepsen discography is really "Waldorf Blues" and the sleeve details on American Verve MGV 8298 are inaccurate), Lester manifests the ability mentioned before to communicate in spite of technical difficulties. Toward the end of "Sunday" he suddenly produces, after a number of slow, slurred, legato phrases, an abrupt, leaping figure that astonishes with its sudden suggestion of hidden life and agility. This session must have represented a particularly bad day for Lester, because at a Los Angeles concert with JATP three months later, he produced some nimble phrases in the up-tempo "Merry Go Round" and a finely controlled "Polka Dots and Moonbeams" in the ballad medley. The famous *Sound of Jazz* television program in December of the same year showed on the recording made at the rehearsal a tantalizing snatch of Lester playing an obbligato to Billie Holiday on "Fine and Mellow." This fragment gives a breathtaking insight into the new rapport that could have developed between Lester and Billie, and the mystery of why Granz did not record them together in the fifties, when he had them both under contract, is something somebody should ask him about.

Early next year (February 7, 1958) there was another date with Edison that produced a medium "Flic" ("Waldorf Blues" in Jepsen) and a slow "You're Getting to Be a Habit with Me" to complete the album begun a year before. Lester is in better health, and his tone is a little rounder and slightly less husky. The haunting quality mentioned earlier dominates, and his spare, legato phrases spread like oil over the waves of the rhythm giving a feeling of timeless tranquility. The next day Hank Jones replaced Lou Stein, and, more important, Roy Eldridge was added to the group. The album recorded that day was called *Laughin' to Keep from Cryin'* and has on the cover a quite exceptional photograph of Roy leaning toward Lester, whose face is creased in laughter presumably at what Roy is telling him. Without detracting from Edison's playing, which is by his own standards excellent, I would say that only Buck Clayton could have equaled the sensitivity with which Roy matches Lester's fragile probing here, and he would not quite have distilled the emotional intensity that Roy and Lester bring to the music. I find this is a very good session, but I realize that others may not agree as willingly as they would over the 1956 recordings. There is no other music in jazz to relate to this final style of Lester's, and the emotional response of the listener can be, as it is in my case, so powerful that it's impossible for me to imagine how the music comes across to those who hear it more objectively. Lester plays clarinet again on two tracks, happily with more success than on "St. Tropez," and the sound of the thirties is uncannily recaptured. Although certain phrases that the richness of the tenor would have supported come over as rather too simple, his playing on the opening chorus of "They Can't Take That Away from Me" is so tremendously affecting that Edison's solo, which follows, sounds cold and shallow in comparison (though actually it's not), and it is not until Roy's muted entry that Lester's mood is regained. On the other three tracks Lester is back on tenor, and the solo that finishes the long blues called "Romping" is a triumph in making simple phrases moving and meaningful.

Lester's last studio session was in Paris [March 2, 1959] less than a fortnight before his death. Although his tone is slightly thinner, he is a little more lively than he was the previous year. (An intriguing aspect of these later recordings is that Lester's sound is never quite the same in any two years, and one comes to distinguish the different vintages.) The rhythm section is dominated by the magnificent drumming of Kenny Clarke, who fills the gaps in Lester's lines with intelligence and swing. Lester plays a dozen of his favorite tunes, and the resulting album provides a clear summation of his final style and a convincing demonstration of how his musical spirit survived the physical wasting away. His tone may be tattered here, but "soul claps its hands and sings." Whether in the intense melancholy of "I Can't Get Started" or the surging swing of the final "Tea for Two," Lester's music still had beauty right up to the end of his life.

In conclusion I would suggest that Lester's later music has been considered suspect because rigid concepts of sex roles make some people expect men to play jazz with "virility." Lester was an opponent, consciously or otherwise, of "machismo." Surely his personal and musical communion with Billie Holiday was a result of his willingness to accept aspects of himself that many men would consider feminine. In his last ten years he had the courage and the honesty to express those aspects in music, and for that, as for his earlier pioneering achievements, he deserves our profound gratitude.

Bop

LeRoi Jones

From Jones's important book Blues People *(1963) comes this telling analysis of how jazz reacted to bebop: with "traditional," "progressive," and, finally, hard bop.*

If bebop was an extreme, it was the only kind of idea that could have restored any amount of excitement and beauty to contemporary jazz. But what it perpetrated might make one shudder. Bebop was the *coup de grâce,* the idea that abruptly lifted jazz completely out of the middle-class Negro's life (though as I have pointed out, the roots of this separation were as old as the appointment of the first black house servant). He was no longer concerned with it. It was for him, as it was for any average American, "deep" or "weird." It had nothing whatsoever to do with his newer Jordans. And as I mentioned, the music by the mid-forties had also begun to get tagged with that famous disparagement *art* (meaning superfluous, rather than something that makes it seem important that you are a human being). It had no "function." "You can't dance to it," was the constant harassment—which is, no matter the irrelevancy, a lie. My friends and I as youths used only to emphasize the pronoun more, saying, "*You* can't dance to it," and whispered, "or anything else, for that matter." It might not be totally irrelevant, however, to point out that the melody of one of Charlie Parker's bebop originals, "Now's the Time," was used by blues people as the tune of an inordinately popular rhythm & blues number called "The Hucklebuck," which people danced to every night while it was popular until they dropped. No function, except an emotional or aesthetic one—as no Negro music had had a "function" since the work song. I am certain "Ornithology," a popular bebop original of the forties, would not be used to make a dance out of picking cotton, but the Negroes who made the music would not, under any circumstances, be willing to pick cotton. The boogie woogies that grew, and were "functional" in the house parties of the new black North were no more *useful* in any purely mechanical sense than bebop. But any music is functional, as any art is, if it can be put to use by its listeners or creators. A man might be right in thinking that bebop was useless to help one clear the west 40 (though I cannot see why, except in terms of one's emotional proclivities); nor was it really good to wear dark glasses and berets if one wanted to work in the post office or go to medical school. But the music was a feast to the rhythm-starved young white intellectuals as well as to those young Negroes, uncommitted to the dubious virtues of the white middle class, who were still capable of accepting emotion that came from outside the shoddy cornucopia of popular American culture.

In a sense the term *cultists* for the adherents of early modern jazz was correct. The music, bebop, defined the term of a deeply felt nonconformity among many young Americans, black and white. And for many young Negroes the irony of being thought "weird" or "deep" by white Americans was as satisfying as it was amusing. It also put on a more intellectually and psychologically satisfying level the traditional separation and isolation of the black man from America. It was a cult of protection as well as rebellion. The "romantic" ornamentation of common forties urban Negro dress by many of the boppers (and here I mean the young followers of the music, and not necessarily the musicians), they thought, served to identify them as being neither house niggers nor field niggers. Granted, it was in a sense the same need for exoticism that drove many young Negroes into exile in Europe during these same years, but it was also to a great extent a deep emotional recognition by many of these same Negroes of the rudimentary sterility of the culture they had all their lives been taught to covet. They sought to erect a meta-culture as isolated as their grandparents', but issuing from the evolved sensibility of a modern urban black American who had by now achieved a fluency with the socio-cultural symbols of Western thinking. The goatee, beret, and windowpane glasses were no accidents; they were, in the oblique significance that social history demands, as usefully symbolic as had been the Hebrew nomenclature in the spirituals. That is, they pointed toward a way of thinking, an emotional and psychological resolution of some not so obscure social need or attitude. It was the beginning of the Negro's fluency with some of the canons of formal Western nonconformity, which was an easy emotional analogy to the three hundred years of unintentional nonconformity his color constantly reaffirmed.

The overemphasized, but still widespread, use of narcotics, not only among musicians and those similarly influenced but among poorer Negroes as well, should thus become understandable. Narcotics users, especially those addicted to heroin, isolate themselves and are an isolated group within the society. They are also the most securely self-assured in-group extant in the society, with the possible exception of homosexuals. Heroin is the most popular addictive drug used by Negroes because, it seems to me, the drug itself transforms the Negro's normal separation from the mainstream of the society into an advantage (which, I have been saying, I think it is anyway). It is one-upmanship of the highest order. Many heroin addicts believe that no one can be knowledgeable or "hip" unless he is an addict. The terms of value change radically, and no one can tell the "nodding junkie" that employment or success are of any value at all. The most successful man in the addict's estimation is the man who has no trouble procuring his "shit." For these reasons, much of the "hip talk" comes directly from the addict's jargon as well as from the musician's. The "secret" bopper's and (later) hipster's language was the essential part of a cult of redefinition, in terms closest to the initiated. The purpose was to isolate even more definitely a cult of protection and rebellion. Though as the bare symbols of the isolated group became more widely spread, some of the language drifted easily into the language of the mainstream, most of the times diluted and misunderstood. (There is a bug killer on the market now called "Hep.")

THE SOCIAL AND musical implications of bebop were extremely profound, and it was only natural that there should be equally profound reactions. One of these reactions, and one I have never ceased to consider as socially liable as it was, and is, musically, was the advent and surge to popularity of the "revivalists."

"At about the same time that the first little bop bands were causing a sensation on Fifty-second Street, New York suddenly became conscious of New Orleans music and found itself in the middle of a 'New Orleans revival.' In doing research for the first historical study of jazz, *Jazzmen,* published by Harcourt, Brace and Company in 1939, the editors, Frederic Ramsey, Jr., and Charles Edward Smith, with the help of jazz enthusiast William Russell, had found an elderly New Orleans trumpet player named Bunk Johnson working in a rice field outside of New Iberia, Louisiana. There had been a series of semiprivate recordings of Bunk with a New Orleans band and they finally decided to bring Bunk to New York. On September 28, 1945, a seven-piece New Orleans band led by Johnson opened at the Stuyvesant Casino, on the Lower East Side of Manhattan. . . . If the writers and critics who were responsible for bringing him to New York had simply advertised that here was a New Orleans band which represented the jazz style of perhaps thirty years before, there would have been no trouble. . . . Instead the writers, not all of them, but a very clamorous group of them, said very openly that this was the last pure jazz band, the only one playing 'true jazz' and that newer styles were somehow a corruption of this older style."

Bunk Johnson's "rediscovery" was only one development in the growth of the revivalist school. Lu Watters and his Yerba Buena Band, Bob Crosby and his Bobcats, and the many Eddie Condon bands in New York playing in residence at Condon's own club were already popular in the late thirties. By the forties the popularity of "Dixieland" bands was enormous at colleges throughout the country, or at any of the other places the young white middle class gathered. The "revived" Dixieland music was a music played by and for the young white middle class. It revived quite frankly, though perhaps less consciously, the still breathing corpse of minstrelsy and blackface. Young white college students trying to play like ancient colored men sounded, if one knew their intention, exactly like that, i.e., like young white college students trying to play like ancient colored men.

". . . the Castle Band began to record Jelly Roll Morton's arrangements; the Frisco Jazz Band imitated Lu Watters; the early Bob Wilber band (associated with Scarsdale High School) copied King Oliver . . ."* The Tailgate Jazz Band even began to imitate the Yerba Band's imitations of the old Oliver Band. There were Dixieland revivalist groups all over the country, thriving like athletic antique dealers. A few of the old Negro musicians like Johnson and Kid Ory were re-recorded or rediscovered, but for the most part Dixieland was a kind of amateur "white jazz" that demonstrated more than anything the consistency of the cultural lag.

Whole bodies of criticism grew up around the senseless debate about "which was the real jazz." Jazz criticism had grown more respectable around the early forties; also, there had been a great deal more legitimate research into the origins and diverse developments of the music, though much of it was still in the "gee whiz" or hobby stage. Many of the men who wrote about jazz were middle-class white men who "collected hot" (the term for collecting jazz records), and there is no body of opinion quite as parochial as the hobbyist's. Quite a few "little magazines," devoted to "collecting hot" and dedicated to the proposition that no one under fifty could play "the real jazz," sprang up all over the country. Usually there were only two or three kinds of features in these magazines: articles castigating the "moderns" (which many times meant swing musicians); articles praising obscure Negroes who had once played second cornet for the Muskogee, Oklahoma, Masons; or discursive investigations of the "matrix numbers" of records issued by defunct record companies. Many of the critical writers in these magazines canonized the cultural lag by writing about jazz as if they were trying to discredit Picasso by reconstructing the Pyramids: "In a sense, the New Orleans revival demonstrated that a good portion of the white world had caught up with and was enjoying—frequently to the point of active participation—an imitation of the music that the American Negro had played twenty to thirty years earlier."†

**The Story of Jazz.*

†*Ibid.*

* * *

BY THE FORTIES the "mixed group" had become a not uncommon phenomenon. Jelly Roll Morton had recorded with the New Orleans Rhythm Kings in the twenties, and during the thirties Benny Goodman had various mixed groups, and a few of the other white swing bands had also hired single Negro musicians or arrangers. Also, perhaps, there were more informal sessions where both white and black musicians blew. In the forties, however, these sessions grew very numerous, especially in New York. And many of the small bop recording groups were mixed, not to mention the groups that played around Fifty-second Street. In fact, by the time the recording ban was lifted, and more bebop records could be heard, a great many of the most significant releases featured mixed groups. To a certain extent these mixed groups reduced the cultural lag somewhat, and many white musicians by the mid-forties were fluent in the new jazz language.

By 1945, the first really bop-oriented big white band had formed under clarinetist Woody Herman, and by 1946, Herman had one of the best big bands in the country. The band was made up both of swing musicians, liberated swing musicians, and after its break-up and remodeling, many young white beboppers. Right up until the fifties many of the best young white musicians in the country had played in the various Herman "Herds." Men like Chubby Jackson, Neal Hefti, Ralph Burns, Bill Harris, Flip Phillips, Billy Bauer, Dave Tough (a swing retread), Stan Getz, Terry Gibbs, Urbie Green, Red Mitchell, Zoot Sims, Al Cohn, Jimmy Giuffre, all passed through these Herman bands, and they were among the white musicians who had grown impressed with, and then fluent in, bebop phrasing.

Herman's bands played a useful mixture of wide open swing style with varying amounts of solid boppish accents. They had good soloists and in Neal Hefti and Ralph Burns, better than competent, though sometimes overambitious, arrangers. However, there were two other large white bands coming into their own around this same period, whose music in some ways was much like the Herman band (some of the same musicians played in all three bands), though they later began to use arrangements and compositions that were even more ambitious than anything the Herman band wanted to do. These two bands, Stan Kenton's and Boyd Raeburn's, were the central figures (though Kenton for much longer) in the ascendancy of a new reaction, *progressive jazz*. Again, this was a music created for the most part by young white musicians, many of whom had had a great deal of experience in the large white swing organizations of the forties. Unlike Dixieland, this music did not conjure up any memories of minstrelsy or blackface; in fact, quite the opposite, progressive jazz was probably the "whitest" music given the name *jazz* to appear up until recent times. It was a music that was at its best vaguely similar to what contemporary classical composers were doing.

It was a self-consciously "intellectual" and intellectualized music, whose most authentic exponent was Stan Kenton, with compositions like Bob Graettinger's "Thermopylae," "City of Glass," and "House of Strings." (Raeburn's music, for all his ambitions toward a "serious popular music," as titles like "Boyd Meets Stravinsky," "Yerxa" or "Dalvatore Sally" would indicate, still sounded quite a bit like bucolic mood music; "Mickey Mouse music" is a musicians' term for it.)

Not so strangely, the term *progressive jazz,* as it became more used in America, came vaguely to denote almost any jazz after swing except Dixieland. That is, any jazz that Americans could call, if they had an opportunity, "weird" or "deep." In fact, even today there are many people who speak knowingly of the progressive jazz musician, to mean, I suppose, anyone who does not play swing, "traditional" jazz, or Dixieland. In an ironic sense, Kenton's ideas were not much different from Paul Whiteman's; even the term *progressive* carries much the same intention of showing how much "advance" jazz had made since its cruder days when only Negroes played it. (Also, any term that denotes progress or advance even in the arts, can be used quite comfortably in the post-Renaissance West. Kenton was at least as smart as Whiteman.) So two very apparent reactions resulting from the emergence of bebop, revivalist Dixieland and progressive jazz, both the inventions of white musicians, shot off violently in two extremely opposite directions. One, toward the reproduction of a vanished emotional field, whose validity was that it removed its participants from the realization of the sterility and nonproductiveness of their contemporary emotional alignments; the other, an attempt to involve unserious minds in a *Kitsch* of pseudo-serious artistic "experience." (Some of Raeburn's records were packaged in jackets with imitation "surrealistic" covers, with explanations of the "symbols" on the back of the jackets. The symbols were numbered for easy identification.) Both were essentially "college boy" musics, since it grows increasingly more difficult as one gets older to delude oneself about one's legitimate emotional proclivities. But the polarity and grim significance of these two "movements" is quite clear with only the advantage of twenty years' history. In either case, these twin reactions involved the white middle class; and the peculiar nature of each reaction seems as formal as would a political reaction caused by some similarly disrupting source (as bebop, and the social orientation concomitant with it). However, the *fact* of bebop and the attitudes that had engendered it could not be affected by white middle-class reactions to them. The Negroes these reactions could affect were just as outraged by the "meaningless" music of the forties as their white doubles. Stan Kenton was a big favorite at Howard University, though a young pre-medical student once told me how terribly hostile he thought Charlie Parker was.

* * *

What was called "cool jazz" cannot be placed simply as "reaction," that is, not as simply as progressive and Dixieland can be. In many ways cool was a legitimate style of jazz music, if the definition of the music can be widened a bit to include obvious innovators and masters who might not be ordinarily identified as members of the "cool school." Cool was not the obvious reaction progressive and Dixieland represented, but in its final use as a "public" music, it did serve to obscure the most precious advances Parker and the other boppers had made. Except for individuals like Miles Davis, who is always cited as the innovator of the post-bop cool approach, most of the musicians readily associated with the style were white musicians who abandoned (or didn't properly understand) Parker's rhythmic innovations, and put to dubious use his melodic and harmonic examples. The recordings that Davis made in 1949 and 1950 ("Israel," "Boplicity," "Jeru," "Godchild," "Move," "Venus De Milo," "Budo," "Darn That Dream") with two groups of nine musicians that included Kai Winding, Lee Konitz, Gerry Mulligan, Max Roach, J. J. Johnson, John Lewis, Kenny Clarke (only Davis, Mulligan, and Konitz played on both sessions), are generally looked upon as the beginning of the cool style. All of the men named, with the exception of the drummers Roach and Clarke, both of whom were bop innovators, went on as leaders in the cool movement to one degree or another. These recordings also gave popularity to a new term, *chamber jazz,* and made the cool sound ubiquitous in a couple of years.

Miles Davis played with Parker very often, and is featured on several of the best records Parker ever made. At that time, Davis was still trying to find his own voice, first of all by discovering that he wasn't Dizzy Gillespie. (An obvious analogy is Gillespie's finding out he wasn't Roy Eldridge before he found his own voice.) Davis's rhythmical freedom and phrasing mark him as a bopper, even though he was regarded as a sort of leader of the cool movement. But his splendid lyricism and almost solipsistic tone, played almost exclusively in the middle register, put him very close to the cool sound that identified the new style. Also, his penchant for playing popular ballads followed a practice the other cool instrumentalists were very fond of. But Davis always made his versions of any popular ballad exclusively his own in terms of the emotional weight he would give them, while most of the other instrumentalists identified with the style would play the ballad straight, seeking to make only the improvised choruses sound completely extemporaneous.

Most of the reed men associated with the cool style owed more allegiance to Lester Young, having forgotten or not having been interested, it seemed, in what Charlie Parker had done. And in copying Young's melodic approach, they also went straight back to his rhythmic attack as well. What was prized most of all in Young was his completely relaxed, anti-frenetic approach, as well as the languid, evanescent, almost alto-like tone that made his tenor saxophone so singular during the thirties. The majority of the cool instrumentalists never sought to further define Young's melodic and rhythmic accomplishments. The uses they made of them, with the cautious abandon that some fluency with bop accents supplied, were generally overly predictable and flat.

The nucleus of arrangers (Gil Evans, Mulligan, Carisi) and musicians Davis used for the 1949–50 recording dates (and also in an ill-fated band that made a couple of club dates) were out of the Claude Thornhill band, a white dance band. In fact, Evans was one of the first arrangers to do big-band arrangements of any of Charlie Parker's compositions. And there is small doubt that Davis did, and does, have a deep admiration for the purple lushness of the Thornhill sound, as can be readily attested by many of his own records, especially those on which Evans is the arranger. But for Davis, his small vibratoless tone was only a means rather than an end. He had a deep connection to the basic blues impulse, and he could insinuate more blues with one note and a highly meaningful pause than most cool instrumentalists could throughout an entire composition.

Perhaps the cool timbre was much more suitable for most white musicians, who favored a "purity of sound," an artifact, rather than the rawer materials of dramatic expression. Davis, too, for all his deep commitment to the blues, often seems to predicate his playing on the fabrication of some almost discernible object. And in this he seems closer to Bix Beiderbecke than Louis Armstrong. There were other Negro musicians before Davis who seemed as deeply persuaded by the beauty of the "legitimate" artifact-like sound, rather than by the classic open stridency of most jazz instrumentalists. Lester Young comes to mind immediately, but men like Teddy Wilson, Benny Carter, Johnny Hodges, seem obvious examples, also the many Negro saxophonists influenced by Young in Davis's own generation. Davis himself became the most copied trumpet player of the fifties, and because of the apparent simplicity of his method, his style is even now one of the most ubiquitous in jazz.

The period that saw bebop develop, during and after World War II, was a very unstable time for most Americans. There was a need for radical readjustment to the demands of the postwar world. The riots throughout the country appear as directly related to the psychological tenor of that time as the emergence of the "new" music. Each response a man makes to his environment helps make a more complete picture of him, no matter what that response is. The great interest in the Muslim religion by Negro musicians in the forties (many of them actually changed their names to Muslim ones) adds to the image of the Negro in America at that time as much as our knowing how many more Negroes were able to buy homes in Scarsdale adds to that image. Knowing that a Negro musician felt like changing the name of a popular song from "Honeysuckle Rose" to "Scrapple from the Apple," or that he would call one of his compositions "Klactoveedsedstene" helps clarify his attitudes and even further, the attitudes of a great many Negroes responsible to the same set of emotional alternatives.

The "harshness" and "asymmetry" of bebop was much closer to the traditional Afro-American concept of music than most of its detractors ever stopped to realize. But it is easy to see that the "harshness and asymmetry" of the music (or ideas) of one period might seem relatively mild and regular in another, maybe only a few years later. If "Livery Stable Blues" seemed crude and unsophisticated to Paul Whiteman, it is relatively easy to see why Stan Kenton might think the same of most bebop and seek a similar solution. Though by Kenton's time and during the years when cool jazz came into vogue in America, the lateral exchange of cultural reference between black and white produced an intercultural fluency that might have made such a misunderstanding, or lack of feeling, on Mr. Kenton's part impossible. It was the Negro's fluency with the technical references of Western music that made bebop (and all jazz, for that matter) possible, and it was certainly a fluency with these same superficial references of Negro music that produced, with whatever validity, the white cool style (or any jazz that white musicians played). What was not always attained in the case of the white jazz musician was the fluency of attitude or stance. And as I have said before, Negro music is the result of certain more or less specific ways of thinking about the world. Given this consideration, all talk of technical application is certainly after the fact.

Cool jazz is not as clearly a "white style" as Dixieland or progressive if Lester Young and Miles Davis can be placed within the definition. Yet Lee Konitz, a leader of the cool school and one of the most gifted white musicians to play jazz, cannot be linked to Davis or Young, except in the most superficial ways. In the case of Davis and Konitz, even though they have played together on several occasions and are together responsible for some of the best cool music (the eight recordings made in 1948–49), their basic approaches are entirely dissimilar, despite the fact that they both, within the demands of the instrument, favor light, pure tones with almost no vibrato. There the resemblance ends. John Lewis, the pianist and leader of the Modern Jazz Quartet, and pianist Lennie Tristano, a white leader of one of the most exciting branches of the cool style, are both considered to be equally involved with this style; however, it would be difficult to find two more dissimilar instrumentalists and composers. Even though both men have shown deep interest in extended forms and the use of contrapuntal techniques in jazz, their methods are very different. Lewis, for all his persistence in drenching his compositions with the formal dicta of European music, is one of the most moving blues pianists in jazz, while it is hard to think of Tristano playing a blues.

During the late forties and right up until the middle fifties, the cool style was very popular. Long-playing albums by many of the musicians associated with the cool style (or "West Coast jazz," as it came to be called, with the great popularity of musicians like Shorty Rogers, Gerry Mulligan, and Dave Brubeck on the Coast) sold fantastically all over the country. The soft, intimate sound and regular rhythms of such groups, along with their tendency to redo popular ballads like "Spring Is Here" or "My Funny Valentine" with just a vague bop accent, made them listened to everywhere by white and black college students and young-men-on-the-way-up who were too sophisticated to listen to Dixieland. Also, many of the cool stylists maintained a healthy attitude toward the innovations that progressive jazz was supposed to have made; *contrapuntal jazz* and *jazz fugue* became standard terms that could be applied to a music whose name had once been a transitive verb unutterable in polite society.

There are many important analogies that can be made between the cool style and big-band swing, even about the evolution of the terms. *Swing,* the verb, meant a simple reaction to the music (and as it developed in verb usage, a way of reacting to anything in life). As it was formalized, and the term and the music taken further out of context, *swing* became a noun that meant a commercial popular music in cheap imitation of a kind of Afro-American music. The term *cool* in its original context meant a specific reaction to the world, a specific relationship to one's environment. It defined an attitude that actually existed. To be *cool* was, in its most accessible meaning, to be calm, even unimpressed, by what horror the world might daily propose. As a term used by Negroes, the horror, etc., might be simply the deadeningly predictable mind of white America. In a sense this calm, or stoical, repression of suffering is as old as the Negro's entrance into the slave society or the captured African's pragmatic acceptance of the gods of the captor. It is perhaps the flexibility of the Negro that has let him survive; his ability to "be cool"—to be calm, unimpressed, detached, perhaps to make failure as secret a phenomenon as possible. In a world that is basically irrational, the most legitimate relationship to it is nonparticipation. Given this term as a consistent attitude of the Negro, in varying degrees, throughout his life in America, certain stereotypes might suddenly be reversed. The "Steppinfechit" rubric can perhaps be reversed if one but realizes that given his constant position at the bottom of the American social hierarchy, there was not one reason for any Negro, ever, to hurry.

The essential irony here is that, like *swing,* when the term *cool* could be applied generally to a vague body of music, that music seemed to represent almost exactly the opposite of what *cool* as a term of social philosophy had been given to mean. The term was never meant to connote the tepid new popular music of the white middle-brow middle class. On the contrary, it was exactly this America that one was supposed to "be cool" in the face of.

THE COOL STYLE, like arranged big-band swing, inundated America and most Negro musicians (bop or swing) who did not master the cool approach. (Actually, it did finally have a narrower definition, since even Miles Davis went into a virtual eclipse of popularity during the high point of the cool style's success. In part, this might have been caused by Davis's personal problems, but I read in print more than a few times during the early fifties that Davis was "a bad imitation" of a white West Coast trumpeter, Chet Baker. If anything, the opposite was true; but Baker fitted in more closely with the successful syndrome of the cool. His barely altered renditions of popular ballads in a cracked, precious middle register were the rage of the mid-fifties, and Baker sang as well.) Like commercial swing, the music created a term of success and fame for its best-known stylists, who were inevitably white. Miles Davis and John Lewis were not the "Kings of Cool," as Basie and Ellington were not the "Kings of Swing"; instead, quite predictably, the "kings" during the height of the cool rage were white musicians like Gerry Mulligan, Chet Baker, Dave Brubeck, or Paul Desmond. In fact, the Dave Brubeck Quartet, which featured Paul Desmond on alto saxophone, was perhaps the perfect fifties cool success story. Brubeck, a pianist, had studied (though quite briefly, I believe) with the contemporary French composer Darius Milhaud, and it was he who, to a large extent, popularized the idea of using fugues, rondoes, and other such consciously affected pickups from European music. This was a natural for college-bred audiences who liked a little culture with their popular music. (A student at the University of Oregon suggested in an article in the *Northwest Review,* quoted in the *Jazz Review,* that Brubeck also played the alma mater of any college he happened to be visiting, "when the audience is beginning to drag.") Finally, Brubeck and his music formally entered the American mainstream when his picture appeared on the cover of *Time* magazine. Jazz had at last made it up the river from New Orleans (with the help of Paul Whiteman, Benny Goodman, and Dave Brubeck), right into the waiting room of Henry Luce's office.

Perhaps the Korean War, like the other two "major" wars before it, helped bring about changes in jazz. I am almost certain that the fifties took on their own peculiar foreboding shape because of the grim catalyst of the Korean War and the emotional chaos that went with it. The Negro could not help but be affected; neither could his music. Cool was not a style that could outlast the fifties, and as in the case of commercial swing, most Negro musicians were never committed to it anyway. But the Japanese soldier in the racially significant Hollywood film had been changed to a North Korean or Chinese soldier, and now he asked the Negro soldier in the integrated Armed Forces questions, too. One question in the movie *Steel Helmet* was, "Black boy, why you fight this war . . . you can't even sit in the front of the bus?" And soldier James Edwards's answer was pitifully inadequate.

Korea and what historians are calling "the legacy of the cold war" proposed even harsher realities for America than World War II. The greater part of these are just now, in the 1960s, beginning to be felt in something like their real measure. But even in the mid-fifties America was a changed place from what it had been only a decade and a half before. Two hot wars and wedged between them and coming after them, a cold one, plus the growing significance of the atomic bomb as a force that had suddenly transformed the world into a place that was "no longer a series of frontiers, [but] a community which would survive or perish by its own hand" were only the impersonal parts of an American's experience of the contemporary world that had changed him and his society perhaps radically in the fifteen or so short years since 1940. The heroic wars "to make the world safe for democracy" had dwindled grimly into "police actions," the nature of which many American soldiers did not find out until they were captured. Even the term *democracy* was blackened by some ambitious, but hideously limited, men who thought that it meant simply "anti-communism." These phenomena are all legacies of the cold war era; the fifties were their spawning ground, and the generation who would have to be fully responsible for them was not yet fully grown. Perhaps they were in college, as I was, listening to Dave Brubeck.

The Supreme Court was trying to answer James Edwards's interrogator, with its 1954 decision, to integrate the schools "with all deliberate speed." Now in 1963, nine years later, integration has not been fully accomplished, and in a great many cases where it has been, there is mere token integration. But the internal strife in the United States between black and white has at least been formally acknowledged as a conflict that might conceivably be legislated out of existence, though again it is the sixties that must test the validity of this desperate hypothesis. The fifties was a period of transition, in many aspects, of beginnings and endings. For one thing, Charlie Parker died in February of 1955, at thirty-five.

Perhaps it is good to use that midpoint of the fifties as an arbitrary point where the counterreaction called "hard bop" began to be noticed. An analogy between this development and the ending of the swing era by the beginnings of bebop in the forties is obvious, though the situation was not as extreme as it had been in the forties.

Amidst the cellos, flutes, fugues, and warmed-over popular ballads of the cool, there was evident, mostly among Negro musicians, a conscious, and many times affected, "return to the roots," as it has been called so often: "It was Horace Silver as musical director of Art Blakey's Jazz Messengers who first announced it, of course, and obviously he and the rest had turned to church and gospel music and the blues as sources of renewed inspiration. If these men were reluctant to listen to King Oliver and Bessie Smith, they heard Ray Charles and Mahalia Jackson with a kind of reverence" (Martin Williams).

The hard-bop reactions were loudest in the East, i.e., New York, which led quite predictably to the new style's being called "East Coast Jazz," to place it within the immediate reach of the press agents and jazz critics. *Funky* (a word with as dubious a place in polite society as *jazz*) became the treasured adjective, where once *cool* had been, with *soul* (as a quality of expression, probably found only in Negroes wearing Italian suits) following closely behind. The harsher, rawer, more classic timbres of older jazz were restored. Most of the melodies in hard-bop tunes were very simple, however, founded usually on some basic riff, usually much less complex than the jagged lines of the classic bop melodies. Pianists like Silver played fewer chords than the bop pianists, though their style was impossible without the innovations of bop pianist Bud Powell. But the soloist's dependence on chords was, if anything, made greater. The hard boppers sought to revitalize jazz, but they did not go far enough. Somehow they lost sight of the important ideas to be learned from bebop and substituted largeness of timbre and quasi-gospel influences for actual rhythmic or melodic diversity and freshness. The hard bop groups utilized rhythms that are amazingly static and regular when compared to the music of the forties. (And merely calling tunes "Dis Heah" or dropping *g*'s from titles is not going to make the music more compelling.)

Hard bop has by now become little more than a style. The opportunities for complete expression within its hardening structure and narrowly consistent frame of emotional reference grow more limited each time some mediocre soloist repeats a well-chewed phrase or makes of the music a static insistence rather than an opening into freer artistic achievement. It has become a kind of "sophistication" that depends more on common, then banal, musical knowledge, instead of truth or meaning suddenly revealed. What results, more times than not, is a self-conscious celebration of cliché, and an actual debilitation of the most impressive ideas to come out of bebop. One has the feeling, when listening to the most popular hard-bop groups of the day, of being confronted merely by *a style,* behind which there is no serious commitment to expression or emotional profundity.

But what is most important about hard bop and the shape it took as a reaction to the growing insipidities the cool style had pushed on jazz is the change of stance which had to occur in order for the Negro musician to be able to react as he did. Again, this change, becoming apparent in the mid-fifties, had further implications that are only just now beginning to be fully understood. "Soul" music, as the hard-bop style is often called, does certainly represent for the Negro musician a "return to the roots." Or not so much a return as a conscious reevaluation of those roots. Many times this reevaluation proved as affected and as emotionally arid as would a move in the opposite direction. The shabbiness, even embarrassment, of Hazel Scott playing "concert boogie woogie" before thousands of white middle-class music lovers, who all assumed that this music was Miss Scott's invention, is finally no more hideous than the spectacle of an urban, college-trained Negro musician pretending, perhaps in all sincerity, that he has the same field of emotional reference as his great-grandfather, the Mississippi slave. Each seems to me merely burlesque, or cruder, a kind of modern minstrelsy.

The direction, the initial response, which led to hard bop is more profound than its excesses. It is as much of a "move" within the black psyche as was the move north in the beginning of the century. The idea of the Negro's having "roots" and that they are a valuable possession, rather than the source of ineradicable shame, is perhaps the profoundest change within the Negro consciousness since the early part of the century. It is a reevaluation that could only be made possible by the conclusions and redress of attitude that took place in the forties. The feelings of inferiority which most Negroes had and still have to a certain extent were brought to their lowest valence up until the present time in the forties. The emergence then of a psychological stance based on the emotional concept of "equality of means" meant that finally all the "barriers" against useful existence within the American society could be looked at by Negroes as being only the inventions of white Americans. The form and content of Negro music in the forties re-created, or reinforced, the social and historical alienation of the Negro in America, but in the Negro's terms. The Negro jazz musician of the forties was *weird*. And the myth of this weirdness, this alienation, was sufficiently important to white America for it to re-create the myth in a term that connoted not merely Negroes as the aliens but a *general* alienation in which even white men could be included. By the fifties this alienation was seen by many Negro musicians not only as valuable, in the face of whatever ugliness the emptiness of the "general" culture served to emphasize, but as necessary. The step from *cool* to *soul* is a form of social aggression. It is an attempt to place upon a "meaningless" social order, or order which would give value to terms of existence that were once considered not only valueless but shameful. *Cool* meant nonparticipation; *soul* means a "new" establishment. It is an attempt to reverse the social roles within the society by redefining the canons of value. In the same way the "New Negroes" of the twenties began, though quite defensively, to canonize the attributes of their "Negro-ness," so the "soul brother" means to recast the social order in his own image. White is then not "right," as the old blues had it, but a liability, since the culture of white precludes the possession of the Negro "soul." Even the adjective *funky,* which once meant to many Negroes merely a stink (usually associated with sex), was used to qualify the music as meaningful (the word became fashionable and is now almost useless). The social implication, then, was that even the old stereotype of a distinctive Negro smell that white America subscribed to could be turned against white America. For this smell now, real or not, was made a valuable characteristic of "Negro-ness." And "Negro-ness," by the fifties, for many Negroes (and whites) was the only strength left to American culture.

This form of cultural arrogance was certainly useful in defining the emergence of the Negro as an autonomous human factor within American society. But it could not sustain its weight as a means to artistic expression without an added profundity that would give it a fluency within the total aspect of the society. This strength had to be returned, as it were, to the culture that had given it shape. Its secrecy had been a form of protection and incubation; but for it to remain secret or exclusive at this point in American social history would make it as sterile as the culture from which it was estranged. Secrecy had been the strength of the Afro-American culture when it was dependent largely on folk sources for its vitality, but now it had to be reinterpreted in terms of the most profound influences in the open field of *all existing* cultures, or it would retreat to the conditional meaningfulness of the folk or the final meaninglessness of the popular. Hard bop did the latter.

On Bird, Bird-Watching, and Jazz

Ralph Ellison

In 1962, Ellison wrote this typically large-minded piece on Charlie Parker for the Saturday Review of Literature. *It is available today in the collection of Ellison's essays* Shadow and Act.

Bird: The Legend of Charlie Parker, a collection of anecdotes, testimonies, and descriptions of the life of the famous jazz saxophonist, may be described as an attempt to define just what species of bird Bird really was. Introduced by Robert Reisner's description of his own turbulent friendship and business relations with Parker, it presents contributions by some eighty-three fellow Bird watchers, including a wife and his mother, Mrs. Addie Parker. There are also poems, photographs, descriptions of his funeral, memorial and estate, a chronology of his life, and an extensive discography by Erik Wiedemann.

One of the founders of postwar jazz, Parker had, as an improviser, as marked an influence upon jazz as Louis Armstrong, Coleman Hawkins, or Johnny Hodges. He was also famous for his riotous living, which, heightened by alcohol and drugs, led many of his admirers to consider him a latter-day François Villon. Between the beginning of his fame at about 1945 and his death in 1955, he became the central figure of a cult which gloried in his escapades no less than in his music. The present volume is mainly concerned with the escapades, the circumstances behind them and their effect upon Bird's friends and family.

Oddly enough, while several explanations are advanced as to how Charles Parker, Jr., became known as "Bird" ("Yardbird," in an earlier metamorphosis), none is conclusive. There is, however, overpowering internal evidence that whatever the true circumstance of his ornithological designation, it had little to do with the chicken yard. Randy roosters and operatic hens are familiar to fans of the animated cartoons, but for all the pathetic comedy of his living—and despite the crabbed and constricted character of his style—Parker was a most inventive melodist; in bird-watcher's terminology, a true songster.

This failure in the exposition of Bird's legend is intriguing, for nicknames are indicative of a change from a given to an achieved identity, whether by rise or fall, and they tell us something of the nicknamed individual's interaction with his fellows. Thus, since we suspect that more of legend is involved in his renaming than Mr. Reisner's title indicates, let us at least consult Roger Tory Peterson's *Field Guide to the Birds* for a hint as to why, during a period when most jazzmen were labeled "cats," someone hung the bird on Charlie. Let us note too that "legend" originally meant "the story of a saint" and that saints often identified with symbolic animals.

Two species won our immediate attention, the goldfinch and the mockingbird—the goldfinch because the beatnik phrase "Bird lives," which, following Parker's death, has been chalked endlessly on Village buildings and subway walls, reminds us that during the thirteenth and fourteenth centuries a symbolic goldfinch frequently appeared in European devotional paintings. An apocryphal story has it that upon being given a clay bird for a toy, the infant Jesus brought it miraculously to life as a goldfinch. Thus the small, tawny-brown bird with a bright red patch about the base of its bill and a broad yellow band across its wings became a representative of the soul, the Passion and the Sacrifice. In more worldly late-Renaissance art, the little bird became the ambiguous symbol of death and the soul's immortality. For our own purposes, however, its song poses a major problem: it is like that of a canary—which, soul or no soul, rules the goldfinch out.

The mockingbird, *Mimus polyglottos,* is more promising. Peterson informs us that its song consists of "long successions of notes and phrases of great variety, with each phrase repeated a half-dozen times before going on to the next," that the mockingbirds are "excellent mimics" who "adeptly imitate a score or more species found in the neighborhood," and that they frequently sing at night—a description which not only comes close to Parker's way with a saxophone but even hints at a trait of his character. For although he *usually* sang at night, his playing was characterized by velocity, by long-continued successions of notes and phrases, by swoops, bleats, echoes, rapidly repeated bebops—I mean rebopped bebops—by mocking mimicry of other jazzmen's styles, and by interpolations of motifs from extraneous melodies, all of which added up to a dazzling display of wit, satire, burlesque, and pathos. Further, he was as expert at issuing his improvisations from the dense brush as from the extreme treetops of the harmonic landscape, and there was, without doubt, as irrepressible a mockery in his personal conduct as in his music.

Mimic thrushes, which include the catbird and brown thrasher, along with the mockingbird, are not only great virtuosi, they are the tricksters and con men of the bird world. Like Parker, who is described as a confidence man and a practical joker by several of the commentators, they take on the songs of other birds, inflating, inverting and turning them wrong side out, and are capable of driving a prowling ("square") cat wild. Utterly irreverent and romantic, they are not beyond bugging human beings. Indeed, on summer nights in the South, when the moon hangs low, the mockingbirds sing as though determined to heat every drop of romance in the sleeping adolescent's heart to fever pitch. Their song thrills and swings the entire moonstruck night to arouse one's sense of the mystery, the promise and the frustration of being human, alive and hot in the blood. They are as delightful to eye as to ear, but sometimes a similarity of voice and appearance makes for a confusion with the shrikes, a species given to impaling insects and smaller songbirds on the points of thorns, and they are destroyed. They are fond of fruit, especially mulberries, and if there is a tree in your yard, there will be, along with the wonderful music, much chalky, blue-tinted evidence of their presence. Under such conditions be careful and heed Parker's warning to his friends—who sometimes were subjected to a shrike-like treatment—"you must pay your dues to Bird."

Though notes of bitterness sound through Mr. Reisner's book, he and his friends paid willingly for the delight and frustration which Parker brought into their lives. Thus their comments—which are quite unreliable as history—constitute less a collective biography than a celebration of his living and a lamentation of his dying, and are, in the ritual sense, his apotheosis or epiphany into the glory of those who have been reborn in legend.

Symbolic birds, myth and ritual—what strange metaphors to arise during the discussion of a book about a jazz musician! And yet, who knows very much of what jazz is really about? Or how shall we ever know until we are willing to confront anything and everything which it sweeps across our path? Consider that at least as early as T. S. Eliot's creation of a new aesthetic for poetry through the artful juxtapositioning of earlier styles, Louis Armstrong, way down the river in New Orleans, was working out a similar technique for jazz. This is not a matter of giving the music fine airs—it doesn't need them—but of saying that whatever touches our highly conscious creators of culture is apt to be reflected here.

The thrust toward respectability exhibited by the Negro jazzmen of Parker's generation drew much of its immediate fire from their understandable rejection of the traditional entertainer's role—a heritage from the minstrel tradition—exemplified by such an outstanding creative musician as Louis Armstrong. But when they fastened the epithet "Uncle Tom" upon Armstrong's music they confused artistic quality with questions of personal conduct, a confusion which would ultimately reduce their own music to the mere matter of race. By rejecting Armstrong they thought to rid themselves of the entertainer's role. And by way of getting rid of the role they demanded, in the name of their racial identity, a purity of status which by definition is impossible for the performing artist.

The result was a grim comedy of racial manners; with the musicians employing a calculated surliness and rudeness, treating the audience very much as many white merchants in poor Negro neighborhoods treat their customers, and the white audiences were shocked at first but learned quickly to accept such treatment as evidence of "artistic" temperament. Then comes a comic reversal. Today the white audience expects the rudeness as part of the entertainment. If it fails to appear, the audience is disappointed. For the jazzmen it has become a proposition of the more you win, the more you lose. Certain older jazzmen possessed a clearer idea of the division between their identities as performers and as private individuals. Off stage and while playing in ensemble, they carried themselves like college professors or high church deacons; when soloing they donned the comic mask and went into frenzied pantomimes of hotness—even when playing "cool"—and when done, dropped the mask and returned to their chairs with dignity. Perhaps they realized that whatever his style, the performing artist remains an entertainer, even as Heifetz, Rubinstein, or young Glenn Gould.

For all the revolutionary ardor of his style, Dizzy Gillespie, a co-founder with Parker of modern jazz and a man with a savage eye for the incongruous, is no less a clown than Louis, and his wide reputation rests as much upon his entertaining personality as upon his gifted musicianship. There is even a morbid entertainment value in watching the funereal posturing of the Modern Jazz Quartet, and doubtless, part of the tension created in their listeners arises from the anticipation that during some unguarded moment, the grinning visage of the traditional delight-maker (inferior because performing at the audience's command; superior because he can perform, effectively, through the magic of his art) will emerge from behind those bearded masks. In the United States, where each of us is a member of some minority group and where political power and entertainment alike are derived from viewing and manipulating the human predicaments of others, the maintenance of dignity is never a simple matter—even for those with highest credentials. Gossip is one of our largest industries, the President is fair game for caricaturists, and there is always someone around to set a symbolic midget upon J. P. Morgan's unwilling knee.

NO JAZZMAN, NOT even Miles Davis, struggled harder to escape the entertainer's role than Charlie Parker. The pathos of his life lies in the ironic reversal through which his struggles to escape what in Armstrong is basically a *make-believe* role of clown—which the irreverent poetry and triumphant sound of his trumpet makes even the squarest of squares aware of—resulted in Parker's becoming something far more "primitive": a sacrificial figure whose struggles against personal chaos, on stage and off, served as entertainment for a ravenous, sensation-starved, culturally disoriented public which had but the slightest notion of its real significance. While he slowly died (like a man dismembering himself with a dull razor on a spotlighted stage) from the ceaseless conflict from which issued both his art and his destruction, his public reacted as though he were doing much the same thing as those saxophonists who hoot and honk and roll on the floor. In the end he had no private life and his most tragic moments were drained of human significance.

Here, perhaps, is an explanation, beyond all questions of reason, drugs or whiskey, of the violent contradictions detailed in Mr. Reisner's book of Parker's public conduct. In attempting to escape the role, at once sub- and super-human, in which he found himself, he sought to outrage his public into an awareness of his most human pain. Instead, he made himself notorious and in the end became unsure whether his fans came to enjoy his art or to be entertained by the "world's greatest junky," the "supreme hipster."

Sensitive and thoroughly aware of the terrifying cost of his art and his public image, he had to bear not only the dismemberment occasioned by rival musicians who imitated every nuance of his style—often with far greater financial return—but the imitation of his every self-destructive excess of personal conduct by those who had in no sense earned the right of such license. Worse, it was these who formed his cult.

Parker operated in the underworld of American culture, on that turbulent level where human instincts conflict with social institutions; where contemporary civilized values and hypocrisies are challenged by the Dionysian urges of a between-wars youth born to prosperity, conditioned by the threat of world destruction, and inspired—when not seeking total anarchy—by a need to bring social reality and our social pretensions into a more meaningful balance. Significantly enough, race is an active factor here, though not in the usual sense. When the jazz drummer Art Blakey was asked about Parker's meaning for Negroes, he replied, "They never heard of him." Parker's artistic success and highly publicized death have changed all that today, but interestingly enough, Bird was indeed a "white" hero. His greatest significance was for the educated white middle-class youth whose reactions to the inconsistencies of American life was the stance of casting off its education, language, dress, manners, and moral standards: a revolt, apolitical in nature, which finds its most dramatic instance in the figure of the so-called white hipster. And whatever its justification, it was, and is, a reaction to the chaos which many youth sense at the center of our society.

For the postwar jazznik, Parker was Bird, a suffering, psychically wounded, law-breaking, life-affirming hero. For them he possessed something of the aura of that figure common to certain contemporary novels, which R. W. B. Lewis describes as the "picaresque saint." He was an obsessed outsider—and Bird was thrice alienated: as Negro, as addict, as exponent of a new and disturbing development in jazz—whose tortured and in many ways criminal striving for personal and moral integration invokes a sense of tragic fellowship in those who saw in his agony a ritualization of their own fears, rebellions and hunger for creativity. One of the most significant features of Reisner's book lies, then, in his subtitle—even though he prefers to participate in the re-creation of Bird's legend rather than perform the critical function of analyzing it.

Reisner, a former art historian who chooses to write in the barely articulate jargon of the hipster, no more than hints at this (though Ted Joans spins it out in a wild surrealist poem). But when we read through the gossip of the accounts we recognize the presence of a modern American version of the ancient myth of the birth and death of the hero. We are told of his birth, his early discovery of his vocation, his dedication to his art, of his wanderings and early defeats; we are told of his initiation into the mysteries revealed by his drug and the regions of terror to which it conveyed him; we are told of his obsessive identification with his art and his moment of revelation and metamorphosis. Here is Parker's own version:

> I remember one night I was jamming in a chili house (Dan Wall's) on Seventh Avenue between 139th and 140th. It was December, 1939 . . . I'd been getting bored with the stereotyped changes that were being used all the time, all the time, and I kept thinking there's bound to be something else. I could hear it sometimes but I couldn't play it. Well, that night, I was working over "Cherokee," and, as I did, I found that by using the higher intervals of a chord as a melody line and backing them with appropriately related changes, I could play the thing I'd been hearing. I came alive.

From then on he reigns as a recognized master, creating, recording, inspiring others, finding fame, beginning a family. Then comes his waning, suffering, disintegration, and death.

Many of the bare facts of Parker's life are presented in the useful chronology, but it is the individual commentator's embellishments on the facts which create the mythic dimension. Bird was a most gifted innovator and evidently a most ingratiating and difficult man—one whose friends had no need for an enemy, and whose enemies had no difficulty in justifying their hate. According to his witnesses he stretched the limits of human contradiction beyond belief. He was lovable and hateful, considerate and callous; he stole from friends and benefactors and borrowed without conscience, often without repaying, and yet was generous to absurdity. He could be most kind to younger musicians or utterly crushing in his contempt for their ineptitude. He was passive and yet quick to pull a knife and pick a fight. He knew the difficulties which are often the lot of jazz musicians, but as a leader he tried to con his sidemen out of their wages. He evidently loved the idea of having a family and being a good father and provider, but found it as difficult as being a good son to his devoted mother. He was given to extremes of sadism and masochism, capable of the most staggering excesses and the most exacting physical discipline and assertion of will. Indeed, one gets the image of such a character as Stavrogin in Dostoievsky's *The Possessed,* who while many things to many people seemed essentially devoid of a human center—except, and an important exception indeed, Parker was an artist who found his moments of sustained and meaningful integration through the reed and keys of the alto saxophone. It is the recordings of his flights of music which remain, and it is these which form the true substance of his myth.

Which brings us, finally, to a few words about Parker's style. For all its velocity, brilliance, and imagination there is in it a great deal of loneliness, self-deprecation, and self-pity. With this there is a quality which seems to issue from its vibratoless tone: a sound of amateurish ineffectuality, as though he could never quite make it. It is this amateurish-sounding aspect which promises so much to the members of a do-it-yourself culture; it sounds with an assurance that you too can create your own do-it-yourself jazz. Dream stuff, of course, but there is a relationship between the Parker *sound* and the impossible genre of teenage music which has developed since his death. Nevertheless, he captured something of the discordancies, the yearning, romance, and cunning of the age and ordered it into a haunting art. He was not the god they see in him but for once the beatniks are correct: Bird lives—perhaps because his tradition and his art blew him to the meaningful center of things.

But what kind of bird was Parker? Back during the thirties members of the old Blue Devils Orchestra celebrated a certain robin by playing a lugubrious little tune called "They Picked Poor Robin." It was a jazz community joke, musically an extended "signifying riff" or melodic naming of a recurring human situation, and was played to satirize some betrayal of faith or loss of love observed from the bandstand. Sometimes it was played as the purple-fezzed musicians returned from the burial of an Elk, whereupon reaching the Negro business and entertainment district the late Walter Page would announce the melody dolefully on his tuba; then poor robin would transport the mourners from their somber mood to the spirit-lifting beat of "Oh, didn't he ramble" or some other happy tune. Parker, who studied with Buster Smith and jammed with other members of the disbanded Devils in Kansas City, might well have known the verse which Walter Page supplied to the tune:

Oh, they picked poor robin clean
(repeat)
They tied poor robin to a stump
Lord, they picked all the feathers
Round from robin's rump
Oh, they picked poor robin clean.

Poor robin was picked again and again and his pluckers were ever unnamed and mysterious. Yet the tune was inevitably productive of laughter—even when we ourselves were its object. For each of us recognized that his fate was somehow our own. Our defeats and failures—even our final defeat by death—were loaded upon his back and given ironic significance and thus made more bearable. Perhaps Charlie was poor robin come to New York and here to be sacrificed to the need for entertainment and for the creation of a new jazz style and awaits even now in death a meaning-making plucking by perceptive critics. The effectiveness of any sacrifice depends upon our identification with the agony of the hero-victim; to those who would still insist that Charlie was a mere yardbird, our reply can only be, "Aint nobody *here* but us chickens, boss!"

Why Did Ellington "Remake" His Masterpiece?

André Hodeir

One of the most inflammatory pieces of jazz criticism is this 1962 attack on the later Ellington by the distinguished French writer André Hodeir (from his book Toward Jazz). *The battle over Ellington's later accomplishments rages on.*

Duke Ellington holds a privileged position in the history of jazz. He was its first composer in the strict sense of the term, and for a long time he was its only composer. Fats Waller was not a composer, he merely wrote tunes. Ernie Wilkins is an arranger who works with other people's ideas. A composer is a musician who makes full use of a capacity which neither the tune writer nor, with very few exceptions, the arranger possesses, a capacity which might be defined as that of endowing jazz with an additional dimension. This dimension, which gives a work new depth and greater possibilities for development, is form. Jazz history may be summed up as follows: Armstrong created jazz, Ellington created form in jazz; Parker and Davis re-created jazz, while Monk is trying to re-create form in jazz.

In order to create his music, the Duke forged himself a double-edged tool. On the one hand, he had a flair for orchestration and handled tone color imaginatively; by working on these natural gifts he was able to transform them into an orchestral language. On the other, he benefited by that respect which a band leader can earn by combining a smiling authority with an indisputable musical superiority; he used it to build an orchestra which, for fifteen years, was absolutely unique in jazz. His musical language was as integral a part of his orchestra as his orchestra was of the works he produced. There may have been other jazzmen with the equipment necessary to equal the Duke as a composer, but if so they lacked the organizational flair necessary to create a means of expressing themselves. Anyone can bring a score to a bandleader; the only way to be really creative in jazz is to have an orchestra at one's disposal. And if one has built that orchestra all by oneself, one may be in a position to make a substantial contribution to the language of jazz. Having an orchestra at one's disposal is not sufficient, however. Don Redman, Fletcher Henderson, Sy Oliver, and several others have attempted to break new ground in the field of form, which had been by-passed by the early jazzmen. Their praiseworthy efforts, however, lacked any deeply felt inspiration. It was thanks to Duke Ellington that we have been able to avoid doing the same spade work over again today. Single-handed he changed the face of a desert and brought forth the first fruit of that multidimensional music which may one day supplant every other form of jazz; and though at times the fruits were bitter, at others they were sweet indeed.

Duke Ellington was a brilliant precursor, though he hit his full stride in only a few, rare instances, as against hundreds of errors (errors which were nevertheless full of original touches and partial achievements); the Duke was once a great musician, but now fatigue seems to have gotten the best of him.

I understand the reasons for this fatigue, but I must also observe its effects. What I cannot bear is to watch Ellington the middle-aged bandleader debase the work of Ellington the artist. The fact that for the past ten years he has written nothing worthwhile—has so declined, in fact, that there have been doubts that he actually wrote certain pieces of trash signed Ellington—would not in itself be very exceptional. Composers as great as Stravinsky, Bartók, and Schönberg each reached the point in their careers where they mysteriously seemed to lose their best creative powers forever. With Ellington, however, one would have thought that even after the creator in him had succumbed to the exhausting life he has led, the musician would survive. The Duke had been the only composer; we would still have liked to regard him as the greatest orchestra leader.

And yet two years ago . . . but this is a sorrowful tale. The directors of a large recording firm persuaded Ellington to record a set of pieces taken from his past. The idea was a rather poor one to begin with, but did have a positive side which might have deserved serious thought. After all, works as rich in sound textures as "In a Mellotone" or "Ko-Ko" might well reveal new dimensions when enhanced with the glamour of high fidelity.

I wish to call the reader's attention to the last-named piece. As he must know, the original version of "Ko-Ko" was recorded in 1940; it constitutes the most perfect example of Duke Ellington's language (then at the height of its development) and remains one of the undisputed masterpieces of orchestral jazz. Every jazz fan knows the 1940 "Ko-Ko" by heart.

This is where our story takes a preposterous turn, for as it happens there was at least one man who had forgotten that unique moment of beauty in the history of jazz, and that man was Duke Ellington himself! So far as I know, neither Rembrandt nor Cézanne ever did a watered-down copy of an early painting containing a vision that was already perfect in itself. Great works of architecture have, it is true, been altered, but the architects were already dead when this was done. The Duke has done "Ko-Ko" over again, and the result is a hideous copy which makes a mockery of his own masterpiece. Moreover, he has allowed this new version to be issued on a record, the mere title of which—*Historically Speaking*—is an insult to his great name.

The whole thing is so unthinkable that I am assailed by a doubt: perhaps he did it purposely, in a conscious effort at self-debunking. In that case this article would be ludicrous, and there would be nothing left for me but to crawl into a hole for having written it. But then, who has ever attained such a summit of greatness? Not even Nietzsche. No, I'm afraid that the obvious explanation of this desecration is not a credit to Ellington. There is only one possible alternative: either the Duke has simply lost the remarkable musical sensibility which lay at the heart of his genius, or else he was never really conscious of the beauty of his music.

My love and respect for Duke Ellington and his music make me inclined to doubt this last hypothesis. The contemporary artist has one anguishing advantage over his predecessors, and this is a sense of historical perspective which enables him to situate himself with regard to the past. Duke Ellington is not a pure creature of instinct like Armstrong or Parker; whether we like it or not, every composer is an intellectual, a person capable of meditation. I should hate to think that Ellington never knew *who he was.* And if he did know, how can he have forgotten? Can he have lost, not only his creative powers, but his musical awareness as well, becoming oblivious to his own mistakes—I should say, his *crimes?*

But the hardest part of my task remains undone. I hope no one will think I am performing it with the bitter gusto that one can take in pulling down minor idols; Jimmy Noone and Mezz Mezzrow are mere straw men; we are dealing here with something that was once very important. I was a very young musician when I first heard Ellington's "Ko-Ko" sixteen years ago, and I immediately succumbed to the magic spell of that long-awaited vision. Suddenly I saw jazz in a new light; Ellington's music had reached fulfillment at last, and there was reason to hope that this achievement foreshadowed the revelation of an even more exciting musical universe.

The years have passed and the Duke's music has failed to keep its promise, but it would be unfair to hold this against him; the important thing, after all, is the tremendous contribution he did make. (I cannot help smiling when I think of the indignant article I published after the Duke's stay in Paris in 1950; my anger at his decline was justified, but in giving vent to it, I lacked proper perspective. This is not the case today, however, for the matter at hand is far more serious.)

The 1940 version of "Ko-Ko" was splendidly strange and violent. The introduction seemed to come from another world, while Tricky Sam's (Joe Nanton) solo had a wail that was more than merely exotic, and even the

Duke's piano had an unearthly sound to it. Above all, this was the first time that anyone had really *written for a jazz orchestra;* the beauty of Blanton's famous break was due entirely to the rigorous conception that had guided the Duke's hand throughout the previous choruses.

Listening to the 1956 version of "Ko-Ko" is one of the most painful ordeals imaginable to anyone for whom jazz and music are *living* experiences. Nothing is left of the qualities I have just mentioned (very briefly, I'm afraid, but then every jazz fan, I hope, will know what I'm talking about), nothing save an atrocious caricature. What was once magnificent becomes grotesque, the epic spirit gives way to stupid gesticulation, and the sense of mystery to mere vulgarity. Yet scarcely a note of the score itself has been changed. Never have two *versions* of a single piece constituted two such different *works;* only in jazz, I feel, is such a distortion of creative concept possible. What is unbelievable is that both versions should be the work of one and the same musician. One may object that Ellington no longer had the same musicians at his disposal. Tricky Sam and Blanton are dead. But in that case he shouldn't have re-recorded "Ko-Ko"! Whichever way you look at it, the Duke alone is responsible. In 1956 he had good material at his disposal. Quentin Jackson is a very respectable trombonist. The burden of his disgraceful, buffoonish interpretation of a solo which constituted one of the high points of Tricky Sam's career, must be borne by the Duke as well, for it was he who put Jackson in an impossible situation from the very moment when he snapped his fingers for the down-beat.

This is the crucial point. The reader does not realize, perhaps, that this moment of a performance, which does not appear on a recording, determines in one out of two cases the quality of the work about to be played. If the leader does not hit the right *tempo,* if his finger-snapping is a bit too slow or a bit too fast, his musicians will be thrown off balance with little hope of recovery. A bandleader worthy of the name almost always sets the right tempo at the very outset. In 1940 the Duke had a marvelous intuitive grasp of his composition; the tempo chosen was just right and his orchestra, which didn't always "swing it" ("In a Mellotone" was one of many pieces spoiled by a drummer who sounded like a frustrated drum major), immediately hit the right pace. The 1940 version of "Ko-Ko" remains one of the most swinging records of the swing era. As for the "Ko-Ko" of 1956 . . .

What can possibly have happened? I don't think this disaster can be explained by practical considerations. Had recording techniques shrunk as they developed, making it necessary to play the arrangement in a shorter space of time, the Duke's decision to speed up his tempo would have been understandable, though not acceptable. If the Duke had not had the old recording at his disposal, one might think he had simply made an equally inexcusable error of judgment. Why this insane choice? Perhaps the Duke wanted to prove that his present orchestra had greater technical virtuosity than the earlier group; I find this unbelievable, but if it is true, what a dismal failure for the sake of such a trivial demonstration!

None of these explanations is satisfactory. No, there is only one possible reason for this choice, and that is a *diminution of musical sensibility;* it would not be the first time I have encountered such a thing.* How can a great musician have become so insensitive? I cannot carry this explanation any further, for the truth is that the whole thing is as puzzling to me as it is painful. I can only observe the results of the Duke's choice and these are disastrous.

Not only is Quentin Jackson's solo made *impossible* (as against Tricky Sam's, which we cannot avoid hearing "in our head"), but the whole arrangement is *inevitably* performed in a jarring, jerky style devoid of any swing. Ellington's broad phrasing can no longer draw its deep, even breath, but gasps and pants laboriously; once lovely figures are now twisted and contorted, a veil of ugliness has fallen over the work as a whole.

What did the Duke have to say about all this? Did he stand helplessly by, watching this farcical desecration of what ought to be his favorite score? Did he rush into the studio to put a stop to it, begin again from scratch, or even . . . call the whole thing off? Not a bit of it. He had already accepted—or even suggested—two "improvements" on the original, two changes which could not fail to disfigure it: a ridiculous introduction on the drums, and an affected clarinet solo which now dominates that stupendous fourth orchestral chorus (which, in the earlier version, was punctuated by percussive piano work of a splendidly aggressive character). After that, what was to stop him from ruining his own music completely with a bad choice of tempo? And why should he object to the record being issued?

For me the title *Historically Speaking* means "The Duke Judged by His Past." I'll never forget the musician who did the original "Ko-Ko," but now I can never forget the one who agreed to sign this new version. I hope I've made myself clear. This is not just another bad record, it is the sign of a dereliction which confirms once and for all the decadence of a great musician.

We have the right to demand a great deal only of those who have done great things. There should be no doubt about it; the present article constitutes an unprecedented tribute to the Duke in his golden age. But it is also meant to put the reader on his guard against the enticements of a once glorious name which now represents only an endless succession of mistakes. This was the most ghastly mistake of all, for nothing can ever redeem it.

*Does anyone remember what happened to Trummy Young's famous trombone solo on "Margie" (which he once recorded with Jimmie Lunceford), when he played it last year [1957] at the Olympia with Louis Armstrong? Here again the notes were exactly the same, but the tempo was such that what had once been a supple play of ambiguities now became a mere skeleton, devoid of any musical meaning. True, it was only Trummy Young.

On the Corner: The Sellout of Miles Davis

Stanley Crouch

The much-admired Crouch, disciple of Ralph Ellison and Albert Murray, tears into the later Miles Davis in general and Davis's autobiography in particular. From the 1995 collection The All-American Skin Game.

The contemporary Miles Davis, when one hears his music or watches him perform, deserves the description that Nietzsche gave of Wagner, "the greatest example of self-violation in the history of art." Davis made much fine music for the first half of his professional life, and represented for many the uncompromising Afro-American artist contemptuous of Uncle Tom, but he has fallen from grace—and been celebrated for it. As usual, the fall from grace has been a form of success. Desperate to maintain his position at the forefront of modern music, to sustain his financial position, to be admired for the hipness of his purported innovations, Davis turned butt to the beautiful in order to genuflect before the commercial.

Once given to exquisite dress, Davis now comes on the bandstand draped in the expensive bad taste of rock 'n' roll. He walks about the stage, touches foreheads with the saxophonist as they play a duet, bends over and remains in that ridiculous position for long stretches as he blows at the floor, invites his white female percussionist to come, midriff bare, down a ramp and do a jungle-movie dance as she accompanies herself with a talking drum, sticks out his tongue at his photographers, leads the din of electronic clichés with arm signals, and trumpets the many facets of his own force with amplification that blurts forth a sound so decadent that it can no longer disguise the shriveling of its maker's soul.

Beyond the terrible performances and the terrible recordings, Davis has also become the most remarkable licker of monied boots in the music business, willing now to pimp himself as he once pimped women when he was a drug addict. He can be seen on television talking about the greatness of Prince, or claiming (in his new autobiography, *Miles*) that the Minneapolis vulgarian and borderline drag queen "can be the new Duke Ellington of our time if he just keeps at it." Once nicknamed Inky for his dark complexion, Davis now hides behind the murky fluid of his octopus fear of being old hat, and claims that he is now only doing what he has always done—move ahead, take the music forward, submit to the personal curse that is his need for change, the same need that brought him to New York from St. Louis in 1944, in search of Charlie Parker.

BEFORE HE WAS intimidated into mining the fool's gold of rock'n'roll, Davis's achievement was large and complex, as a trumpet player and an improviser. Though he was never of the order of Armstrong, Young, Parker, or Monk, the sound that came to identify him was as original as any in the history of jazz. His technical limitations were never as great as commonly assumed, except when he was strung out on drugs and didn't practice. By January 1949, when he recorded "Overtime" with Dizzy Gillespie and Fats Navarro, he was taking a backseat to nobody in execution. By May 1949, when he traveled to France and was recorded in performance, he was muscling his way across the horn in molten homage to Navarro and Gillespie, the two leading technicians of the bebop era; he was three weeks short of his twenty-third birthday and already had big-band experience with Billy Eskstine and Gillespie, already had stood next to Charlie Parker night after night on bandstands and in studios.

The conventional idea that Davis discovered that he couldn't play like Gillespie, and proceeded to develop a style of stark, hesitant, even blushing lyricism that provided a contrast to Parker's flood of virtuosic inventions, is only partly true; a methodical musician, Davis systematically worked through the things that were of interest to him. Eventually he personalized the levels of declamation, nuance, melodic fury, and pathos that are heard, for example, in Parker's "Bird of Paradise." But first he examined Gillespie's fleet approach and harmonic intricacy, which shaped the dominant approach to bebop trumpet. From Gillespie, he learned bebop harmony and was also encouraged to use the keyboard to solve problems; he even took from Gillespie an aspect of timbral piquancy that settled beneath the surface of his sound. But Davis rejected the basic nature of Gillespie's tone, which few found as rich or as attractive as the idiomatic achievements of the Negroid brass vocabulary that had preceded the innovations of bebop. Davis grasped the musical power that comes of having a sound that is itself a musical expression.

He moved in the direction of a refined *and* raw understanding of tonal manipulation based in the blues. His early problems with pitch demanded that he focus first on the quality, the weight, and the accuracy of his sound. Once he established control over his tone, Davis's work began to reflect his affection for the resources of color and nuance heard in Armstrong, Freddy Webster, Harry Edison, Buck Clayton, Rex Stewart, Navarro, Dud Bascomb, and Ray Nance. But his extraordinary discipline led him to strip everything away, striving for a sound that was direct in its clarity, almost pristine in its removal from the world of Negro trumpet tone. On that clean slate, Davis later added dramatic timbres and attacks.

Next Davis chose to work out a style that was superficially simple, that was rarely given to upper-register explosions or to the rhythmic disruptions that the boppers had built upon the droll games that Lester Young played with the beat. On his first recording as a leader in May 1947, Davis already had the dark, warm sensuousness that he later extended and refined. By using Charlie Parker on tenor, rather than on his customary alto, Davis got a richer texture, the sort of thickness that he favored in his later quintets; and a number of writers have heard premonitions of the tonal concerns, the phrasings, and the moods of *The Birth of the Cool,* the highly celebrated but essentially lightweight nonet sessions that Davis steered a few years later.

But the essential influence on Davis's first recordings as a leader was still Parker. The saxophonist's 1946 recording of his "Yardbird Suite" with Davis as a sideman shows precisely the ease that characterizes the playing and the writing of the trumpeter's own session, especially "Half Nelson" and "Milestones." On that first date, Davis not only plays quite well himself, but uses the mood of the material to inspire Parker to reach for an emotional projection that the saxophonist rarely called upon. Davis resides comfortably in the middle register as he improvises through the difficult harmonies of his compositions, sailing and swinging in almost seamless legato eighth notes on "Little Willie Leaps" and inventing a meticulous thematic improvisation on "Half Nelson." Harmonically his notes say bebop, and he works toward the layered sound that has a top, a middle, and a bottom, all the while understating a thoroughly felt joy as he nearly swings the ink off his tail.

Equally important were a number of other recording dates under Parker's leadership. There are examples in the ballad sessions of the winter of 1947 of the softer approach to sound and ensemble, as when Parker plays delicate and soaring obligatos behind Davis on "Embraceable You," "Out of Nowhere," and "My Old Flame." Even earlier, as the flutist and composer James Newton points out, the contrapuntal Parker writing of "A-Leu-Cha" and "Chasin' the Bird" brought to bebop qualities that Davis's "cool" nonet explored. By "Marmaduke" in 1948, Davis is much closer to the almost purely melodic style of quiet but calling intensity that became an important aspect of his musical signature.

Then came *The Birth of the Cool*. Davis's nonet of 1948–50 played little in public and recorded only enough to fill an album, but it largely inspired what became known as "cool" or "West Coast" jazz, a light-sounding music, low-keyed and smooth, that disavowed the Afro-American approach to sound and rhythm. This style had little to do with blues and almost nothing to do with swing. That Davis, one of the most original improvisers, a man with a great feeling for blues, a swinger almost of the first magnitude, should have put "cool" in motion is telling. Indeed, it is the first, premonitory example of his dual position in jazz.

Heard now, the nonet recordings seem little more than primers for television writing. What the recordings show us, though, is that Davis, like many other jazzmen, was not above the academic temptation of Western music. Davis turns out to have been overly impressed by the lessons he received at Juilliard when he arrived in New York in 1944. The pursuit of a soft sound, the uses of polyphony that were far from idiomatic, the nearly coy understatement, the lines that had little internal propulsion: all amount to another failed attempt to marry jazz to European devices. The overstated attribution of value to these recordings led the critical establishment to miss Ellington's "The Tattooed Bride," which was the high point of jazz composition of the late 1940s. Then, as now, jazz critics seemed unable to determine the difference between a popular but insignificant trend and a fresh contribution to the art.

Davis began making his truest contributions as a leader in the 1950s. The Prestige recordings from 1951 to 1956 have been reissued in a single package, and it constitutes one of the richest bodies of work in small-group jazz. One hears Davis consolidating influences, superbly cross-weaving improvisational styles and instrumental approaches, in his own playing and in that of the musicians he brought together. The quintet included John Coltrane and a rhythm section that was nearly as important to jazz of the fifties as Basie's was to that of the thirties.

In the early fifties, inspired by Monk, Armstrong, Young, and Holiday, Davis learned to strip away everything not essentially musical. He maintained the harmonic sophistication of the bebop school, but picked only the most telling notes for the construction of his melodic lines. He recognized that the smooth swing of Basie and the territory bands used pulsations that, for all their flirtations with the beat, were never jerky. In this work Davis sublimely combined the unsentimental detailings of tone, emotion, and attack of the blues; the joy and the surprise of Armstrong and Young that melodically rose up over the tempo and meter of ensembles in the thirties; and the idealistic but earthy sensuousness of the romantic balladeer.

One of the more interesting things about Davis during these years is that he brought together musicians with varied tastes in sound. As early as 1946, when he recorded "Yardbird Suite" and "Ornithology" with Parker, the smooth, vibratoless sound of Parker was contrasted by the heavier Coleman Hawkins–derived tone of Lucky Thompson's tenor. Davis himself had worked with Hawkins, and used tenor players rooted in Hawkins's work (such as Thompson and Sonny Rollins) until he hired Coltrane. But his alto choices were always Parker derived, such as Jackie McLean and Davey Schildkraut. Just as he was interested in bringing together the essences of blues-based trumpet and ensemble swing with the lessons of the bebop movement, Davis also seemed to want to fuse the tones of those different schools in his ensembles.

Thus, in 1951, he brought McLean and Rollins together for a sextet recording, the instrumentation foreshadowing the six-piece group he later led with Cannonball Adderley and Coltrane. Davis played with confidence on the blues, gave poignance to the ballads, swung with very individual articulation on McLean's "Dig." But perhaps the high point of the session was Rollins's tenor on "It's Only a Paper Moon," where his gruff and ghostly sound reached startling levels of lyricism and fresh phrasing. For the next three years he was playing marvelously, with J. J. Johnson, Jackie McLean, Jimmy Heath, Horace Silver, Gil Coggins, Percy Heath, Kenny Clarke, and the Art Blakey on Blue Note Records. And in 1954 Davis reached one of his first peaks as a bandleader and a player. In March he recorded a version of "Old Devil Moon" that had an arranged and recurring vamp that anticipated the sound of the Coltrane rhythm section of the 1960s.

In April he brought together trombonist J. J. Johnson, tenor saxophonist Lucky Thompson, pianist Horace Silver, bassist Percy Heath, and drummer Kenny Clarke. According to Silver, Thompson had written arrangements that didn't come off, and they did two blues numbers, a fast and a slow blues, "Walkin'" and "Blue and Boogie," to avoid a failed day in the studio. The results were signal achievements. The weight of the ensemble sound is perfectly balanced and darkened, Davis's and Johnson's broad brass tones melding in unison with Thompson's thick, breathy tenor; Silver's percussive attack and the ideal mesh of Heath's bass notes with Clarke's cymbals and drums form perhaps Davis's first great rhythm section. On the swift "Blue and Boogie" the trumpeter moves over the horn with grace and pride, his last two choruses a response to the emerging challenge of Clifford Brown.

In December Davis used Heath and Clarke again, but instead of horns he brought Monk's piano and Milt Jackson's vibes. The overtones of Davis's trumpet and the ringing of Jackson's metal keys achieved another superior texture (this one foreshadowed the electric piano on *Filles de Kilimanjaro,* the trumpeter's last important jazz record some fourteen years away), Davis's abstraction of the melody of "The Man I Love" reached back in conception, but not in execution, to Parker's classic transformation of "Embraceable

You." Because of the trumpeter's problems with Monk's style—contrapuntal, icily voiced, given as much to ongoing improvised arrangements as to chordal statement—Davis asked the pianist to "stroll," or lay out, during his improvisations. The musical effect is systematically wonderful, however much Monk was irritated. Monk's improvisations are easily the highest expressions of originality and profundity in all of the Prestige sessions.

They are also the peak of piano playing on any Miles Davis recording. Monk brings a motivic brilliance, a command of inflection and timbre, and an idealistic lyricism that are unexpected in their purity. His playing is as far from European convention as bottleneck guitar work. His melodic response to Davis on "The Man I Love" is startling. And on "Swing Spring," Davis pulls off what must be one of his best spontaneous decisions. Featured first with just bass (Percy Heath) and drums (Kenny Clarke), he jumps back in after Jackson has finished his improvisation and Monk is about to play. Monk stops immediately, and Davis plays again with Heath and Clarke, choosing to use a patented Monk phrase for his last chorus. He builds upon it and finishes. Monk then picks up the phrase and invents one of his most masterful recorded performances. It is, quite simply, one of the high points of jazz.

As Davis developed into the next phase of his bandleading and his improvising, he continued to expand on blues, pop songs, Kansas City swing, and the conceptions he personalized from Parker, Monk, and Ahmad Jamal, whose 1955 arrangement of Gould's *Pavane* provided the structure for Davis's 1959 "So What" and the melody for Coltrane's 1961 "Impressions." When he formed his great quintet in 1955, with Coltrane, pianist Red Garland, bassist Paul Chambers, and drummer Philly Joe Jones, Davis not only improvised marvelously eight times out of ten, but also wrote particularly imaginative arrangements. Much of the praise that this quintet has received is deserved. It was a unit that had invincible swing at any tempo, that utilized the possibilities of group color with consistent intelligence, that stoked fire as ably as it crooned. No small part of Davis's achievement was his rhythm section, an ongoing, spontaneously self-orchestrating unit of piano, bass, and drums that delineated the forms of the tunes, responded to the improvisation of the featured horns, loosened and tightened the beat, and swung with an almost peerlessly precise attention to color and the varied possibilities of harmonic-percussive drama. Still, what made this band so wonderful was Davis's breadth of emotional expression. His sensibility drew on the entire sweep of jazz feeling, from the playful to the tender to the pugnacious to the aloof to the gutbucket-greasy and the idealistically lyrical.

When he moved to Columbia Records in 1957 and *'Round About Midnight* was released with the same musicians, Davis was on the verge of becoming a star, a large influence, a matinee idol, and a man destined to sink down in a way no one—himself least of all—could have imagined. Columbia Records, with its distribution and promotion networks, its record club, the air play its products received, and the ink it could generate outside the jazz press, started the most significant leg of Davis's march to celebrity. The trumpeter soon saw his performances and his recordings become emblems of taste in contemporary art.

With Nat Cole and Sidney Poitier, moreover, Davis became part of an expanding vision of American glamour in which dark-hued Negroes were admitted into precincts of romance and elegance that had previously been almost the exclusive province of light-skinned Afro-Americans like Billy Eckstine. As Betty Carter observed of Davis's matinee-idol appeal, "Miles wasn't a power trumpet player, he was a stylist. He had a soft, melodic approach that made him very popular with women. Women really liked him the way they liked Dexter Gordon, Gene Ammons, Ben Webster, Johnny Hodges, and all of those guys who knew how to play things that had some sweetness in them."

Davis also benefited from a shift in audience taste that harked back to the popularity of the glowering, sullen, even contemptuous nineteenth-century minstrel characters known as Jasper Jack and Zip Coon, who sassed and sometimes assaulted the plantation white folks. Davis's bandstand attitude originated in the bebop generation's rejection of Armstrong's mugging and joking, in a trend of aggression that opened part of the way to what became blaxploitation ten years later (and now causes whites who confuse their own masochism with sensitivity to celebrate Spike Lee). The result was superbly described by Ralph Ellison:

> . . . a grim comedy of racial manners; with the musicians employing a calculated surliness and rudeness, treating the audience very much as many white merchants in poor Negro neighborhoods treat their customers, and the white audiences were shocked at first but learned quickly to accept such treatment as evidence of "artistic" temperament. Then comes a comic reversal. Today the white audience expects the rudeness as part of the entertainment.

A story about Davis from this period may be apocryphal, but it has poetic truth. It has been related that one night a European woman approached Davis at the bar in Birdland to tell him that she loved his music, that she bought all his records, even though they were quite expensive in her country. Davis is said to have replied, "So fucking what, bitch?" As the stunned woman walked away, the musician with Davis said, "Miles, you really are an evil little black sonofabitch, aren't you?" And the trumpeter replied, "Now the bitch will buy *two* of every one of my records. When you have stock in Con Edison and make all the money I make, you have to act the way people expect you to act—they want me to be their evil nigger, and that's what I'm ready to be."

These first developments in ugliness aside, Davis's achievement in those years was genuine. It drew not only on the detailed idiomatic thought of his own musical conceptions, but also on his interaction with his musicians. Just as Davis had been deeply impressed by the spare side of Monk's decidedly Afro-American approach to instrumental technique, and by Monk's immaculate sense of thematic variation, so Coltrane, when he left Davis to work with Monk in the summer of 1957, was inspired to push beyond his superior bebop art; Monk remade Coltrane substantially, and even the sixteenth-note rhythms that the saxophonist worked on until the end of his career were introduced by the pianist's formidable "Trinkle Tinkle." Thus, when Coltrane returned to Davis's band in 1958, he brought materials that elevated the intellect, the surprise, and the fire of the group. In fact, as the 1960 Stockholm recording shows, the saxophonist was blowing the trumpeter off his own bandstand.

But Davis understood how to use Coltrane. By now he was fully his own man. The album *Milestones* shows how well he understood that a jazz recording should emulate a strong forty-minute set in a nightclub. Though the under-recorded piano greatly reduces the power of what is quite mighty swing, the recital shows just how much of a bopper Davis still was, and how strongly he believed in the blues as an organizing tool for the overall sound of a recording. Four of the six pieces are blues numbers; each is approached differently, utilizing varied tempos, big-band effects, saxophone exchanges of entire choruses, drum breaks, harmonization, unisons, antiphony. With the title work, moreover, Davis began his exploration of modal materials—limited harmonic structures that relied on scales—and pointed toward *Kind of Blue,* perhaps his most influential album and certainly one of his finest achievements.

In the interest of accuracy, however, it is important to recognize that Davis's publicity, and the cult that has grown up around him, inflated his work out of proportion. As a trumpeter, Davis was constantly challenged by Clifford Brown, who died, at the age of twenty-five, in an automobile accident in 1956. By 1953 Brown was being hailed as "the new Dizzy." His extraordinary technique, his large sound, his unlimited swing, and his heroic combination of melancholy and grandeur brought an Armstrong-like bravura to the bebop trumpet. Brown's recordings show that he possessed qualities of beauty that Davis would never equal. Had Brown lived, Davis would have had to deal with another force of unarguable potency. It is the influence of

Brown, not Davis, that has dominated the instrument, from Donald Byrd and Lee Morgan through Freddie Hubbard and Booker Little, and now Wynton Marsalis.

Other strengths of Davis's have been overstated too. His idea of the small group was, finally, no more sophisticated than John Lewis's, Charles Mingus's, or Horace Silver's, and he was rarely as imaginative in his arrangements. Though his fame grew, he had yet to explore the kinds of metric innovations that obsessed Max Roach. And as the Dizzy Gillespie–Sonny Rollins–Sonny Stitt sessions of December 1957 reveal, especially in the playing of Rollins and Gillespie on "Wheatleigh Hall" and of all three on "The Eternal Triangle," the Davis group on *Milestones* was far from the last word in swing or fire.

As for formal innovations, both George Russell and Mingus examined modal forms before Davis, and each made use of pianist Bill Evans (who became important to the next stage of Davis's development). Rollins's *Freedom Suite,* from the summer of 1958, exhibits a much more provocative and successful conception of group rhythm and extended form than anything Davis had produced. (What Rollins did with tenor saxophone, bass, and drums has still to receive the critical recognition it deserves.) And compare Davis's much-lauded improvisation on "Sid's Ahead" from *Milestones* of 1958 with Louis Armstrong's "Wild Man Blues" of 1957: you will hear a vast difference in subtlety, nuance, melodic order, and swing. As fine a player as he had become, Davis could not even approximate Armstrong's authority.

Still, of all the trumpet players who came to power during and after the first shock waves of Parker's innovations, Davis seemed the one who would eventually come the closest to Armstrong's emotional gravity. As he proved with his eerie, isolated, and mournful playing for the score of the murder thriller *Escalator to the Scaffold,* and in the better moments of his collaborations with the arranger Gil Evans (*Miles Ahead, Porgy and Bess, Sketches of Spain*), he had a talent for a transfixing musical logic and a scalding melancholy. It is true that those albums with Evans also reveal that Davis could be taken in by pastel versions of European colors (they are given what value they have in these sessions by the Afro-American dimensions that were never far from Davis's embouchure, breath, fingering); if Davis's trumpet voice is removed, in fact, a good number of Evans's arrangements sound like high-level television music. But these infirmities pale before the triumphant way that Davis summoned a range of idiomatic devices far richer in color and in conception than those of any of his fellow beboppers.

In the liner notes of *Porgy and Bess,* Davis noted a movement in jazz away from harmonic complexity toward simpler structures that emphasized melodic invention. In early 1959—the watershed year in which Ellington recorded *Jazz Party;* Coleman, *The Shape of Jazz to Come;* Coltrane, *Giant Steps;* Monk, *Orchestra at Town Hall;* and Mingus, *Blues and Roots* and *Ah Um*—Davis made *Kind of Blue.* Here the modal movement reached a pinnacle, precisely because Davis understood that blues should be the foundation of any important innovation in jazz. The record, which uses his sextet with Coltrane, Cannonball Adderley, and Bill Evans, has the feeling of a suite. It is dominated by the trumpeter's compositions. (On one piece where straight-out swing was called for, Davis used Wynton Kelly instead of Evans; but on the softer pieces the things that Evans had learned from Debussy, George Russell, and Mingus issued in voicings of simple materials with intricate details.) The set realized all of the possibilities of cool jazz without sinking into the vacuous, the effete, and the pretentious.

By 1960 Coltrane and Adderley had left to lead their own bands, and Davis began to cope with a jazz scene of expanding technical and emotional means. Davis's playing continued to grow in power and intensity, but for all his success he was no longer the center of the discussion. The centers, instead, were Coltrane and Ornette Coleman, who were inspiring charlatans as well as serious musicians. It seemed possible that the crown would slip from Davis's head, that he might be relegated to the neglect experienced by many of the older masters. Former Davis sidemen were leading the most imposing small bands of the day—Coltrane, Silver, Blakey, Adderley, Rollins. Musicians he had been associated with, such as Monk and Mingus, were either refining, or adding to, the art, especially to its formal scope. In terms of pure bebop, Gillespie's quintet with James Moody was playing extraordinarily well, as was the Modern Jazz Quartet, with its lyrical use of percussion and harmony instruments. When his second great rhythm section of Wynton Kelly, Paul Chambers, and Jimmy Cobb left him in 1963, Davis had to rebuild for what became his last great period.

He soon found the musicians who provided the foundation for his final creative years. With *Seven Steps to Heaven,* Davis introduced George Coleman on tenor, another of the fine tenor players who had followed Coltrane into the band, and the rhythm section of Herbie Hancock, Ron Carter, and Tony Williams, the force that was to shape the orchestration and the propulsion of his next phase. The band with Coleman made its finest music in concert performances, released as *Four,* and *My Funny Valentine.* Wynton Marsalis has noted that on the many fast numbers of *Four,* Davis produced unorthodox phrases that are technically challenging and demand unique fingerings. *My Funny Valentine,* by contrast, and particularly the title tune, captured Davis in a moment of heroic intimacy that he rarely reached again.

When Wayne Shorter joined him in the fall of 1964, Davis had what has been considered his best group since the *Milestones* ensemble. In January

1965 the band recorded *E.S.P.,* and the music still sounds fresh. The trumpeter was in superb form, able to execute quickstep swing at fleet tempi with volatile penetration, to put the weight of his sound on mood pieces, to rear his way up through the blues with a fusion of bittersweet joy and what Martin Williams termed "communal anguish." The rhythm section played with a looseness that pivots off Williams's cymbal splashes and unclinched rhythms, Carter walking some of the most impressive bass lines of the day, and Hancock developing his own version of the impressionism that Evans was making popular.

Shortly afterward, Davis went into the hospital for surgery and didn't return to work until late in the year, when he recorded *Live at the Plugged Nickel* in Chicago. At the Plugged Nickel he and his musicians were staring right in the face of the period's avant-garde, spontaneously changing tempi and meters, playing common or uncommon notes over the harmonies, pulling in harsh timbres, all the while in a repertoire that was roughly the same as the trumpeter had been using for a decade. Again, as with *My Funny Valentine,* the pieces were remade. Shorter was in such startling form that his improvisations remained influential through the 1980s. Davis himself seemed to be having trouble with his instrument; his authority on *E.S.P.* is rarely heard. His "Stella by Starlight," however, with its masterful touches of brass color, is one of the supreme late efforts: it swells with intimacy, voices an elevated bitterness that seems to argue with the human condition, then rises to a victorious swing.

The remainder of Davis's studio recordings with that band drew on the chromaticism of Warne Marsh and Lennie Tristano, who influenced Shorter and Hancock—and, to the surprise of almost all concerned, on popular dance music, on rhythm and blues and rock 'n' roll. Though the albums vary in quality, though they sometimes lack definitive swing or cohesive fire, even the weaker ones have at least a couple of first-rate performances. The range of ideas heard from the rhythm section put it in line with the best of the day, and Shorter wrote many fine compositions, especially on *Nefertiti.* But the clues to Davis's course were in his own pieces, in "Stuff" and in much of the work for *Filles de Kilimanjaro.* His extended "Country Son," which features perhaps Shorter's finest studio improvisation with Davis, revealed that he was capable of a flirtation with pop rhythms. He was headed, in fact, in the direction of Motown, the English bands, and the black rock of Sly Stone and Jimi Hendrix.

"Mademoiselle Mabry," on *Filles,* is a brilliant example of Davis's ability to elevate pop material. An innovation in jazz rhythm, it is an appropriation and an extension of Hendrix's "The Wind Cries Mary," and proof of what Davis might have done had he kept control of his popular sources, rather than succumb to them. The borrowing was in perfect keeping with the tradition begun by Armstrong's alchemical way with banal popular songs. In fact, what Davis does with popular influences throughout this recording shows off his sophistication and his ability to transform yet another universe of music in his own image.

That Davis was able to initiate what became known as fusion, or jazz rock, and with it to inspire musicians as different as Hancock, Rollins, Hubbard, and Coleman, shows what a powerful position he had in the minds of Afro-American jazzmen. Jimmy Heath described his position this way:

> Miles led the way for a lot of people because he was one of the ones who got through. He had the fine clothes, the expensive cars, the big house, all the magazine articles and the pretty girls chasing him. He seemed like he was on top of *everything.* Then you had all of this rock getting all of the press and it was like Elvis Presley all over again. Miles stepped out here and decided he was going to get himself some of that money and a lot of musicians followed his lead. It was like if Miles had led the pack for so long they didn't know how to stop following him, even if the music wasn't any good.

And then came the fall. Beginning with the 1969 *In a Silent Way,* Davis's sound was mostly lost among electronic instruments, inside a long, maudlin piece of droning wallpaper music. A year later, with *Bitches' Brew,* Davis was firmly on the path of the sellout. It sold more than any other Davis album, and fully launched jazz-rock with its multiple keyboards, electronic guitars, static beats, and clutter. Davis's music became progressively trendy and dismal, as did his attire; at one point in the early 1970s, with his wraparound dark glasses and his puffed shoulders, the erstwhile master of cool looked like an extra from a science fiction B-movie. He was soon proclaiming that there were no Negroes other than Sonny Rollins who could play the saxophone, and that musicians like Ornette Coleman and Mingus needed to listen to Motown, which was "where it was at." Many hoped that this would be only a phase, but the phase has lasted twenty years. In his abject surrender to popular trends, Davis sank the lowest in 1985 in *You're Under Arrest,* on which one hears what is supposed to be the sound of cocaine snorting. His albums of recent years—*Tutu, Siesta, Amandla,* and the overblown fusion piece that fills two records on *Aura*—prove beyond any doubt that he has lost all interest in music of quality.

As usual, where Davis led, many followed. His pernicious effect on the music scene since he went rapaciously commercial reveals a great deal about the perdurability of Zip Coon and Jasper Jack in the worlds of jazz and rock, in the worlds of jazz and rock criticism, in Afro-American culture itself. The cult of ethnic authenticity often mistakes the lowest common denominator for an ideal. It begets a self-image that has succumbed to a nostalgia for the mud. What we get is the bugaboo blues of the noble savage, the surly and dangerous Negro who will have nothing to do with bourgeois conventions. (This kind of Negro has long supplied the ammunition for the war that many jazz and rock critics have waged against their own middle-class backgrounds.)

Davis's corruption occurred at about the time that the "Oreo" innuendo became an instrument with which formerly rejected street Negroes and thugs began to intimidate, and often manipulate, middle-class Afro-Americans in search of their roots, and of a "real" black culture. In this climate, obnoxious, vulgar, and antisocial behavior has been confused with black authenticity. This has led to blaxploitation in politics, in higher education, and in art—to Eldridge Cleaver, Huey Newton, and the Black Panthers; to black students at San Francisco State demanding that pimps be recruited to teach psychology classes; to the least inventive and most offensive work of Richard Pryor and Eddie Murphy; to the angry cartoonish coons of Spike Lee and the flat, misogynist, gutter verse of Ice-T and racist rap groups like Public Enemy.

Davis provides many unwitting insights into such phenomena in his autobiography, *Miles,* written with Quincy Troupe. His is, at least in part, the story of a jet-black Little Lord Fauntleroy attracted to the glamour and the fast life of the jazz world during the period when heroin was as important to the identity of the bebop generation as LSD was to the youth culture of the late 1960s. The book draws a number of interesting portraits—of Dexter Gordon, of Sugar Ray Robinson, of Philly Joe Jones—but it is overwhelmingly an outburst of inarticulateness, of profanity, of error, of self-inflation, and of parasitic paraphrasing of material from Jack Chambers's *Milestones.* Would Simon and Schuster publish such a book, without sending the manuscript to any number of experts for evaluations and corrections, if it were written by a white man? Perhaps the editors assumed that since Quincy Troupe is a Negro, he should know.

Davis's book is divided against itself. His sensitive and lyrical recollections of experience are constantly overwhelmed by his street corner poses. The trumpeter's desire to be perceived as the hippest of the hip has destroyed his powers of communication. This is particularly unfortunate, since his story falls far outside the clichés of jazz and racial lore. His father was a successful dentist and a gentleman farmer who reared his children to have a high sense of self-worth. Davis recalls riding horses and living on a 300-acre estate; there was a cook and a maid. It was a world as full of sophistication as it was of superstition, as full of privilege as prejudice.

Davis tells of what he heard about the St. Louis Riot of 1917, of his father's looking with a shotgun for the man who called his son a nigger, of a preference Negro bands had for light-skinned musicians that blocked a young friend of his from working with Jimmie Lunceford, of the way women started throwing themselves at him as he grew into his late teens. His involvement with music is well described, as are the personalities of many musicians he grew up with, some of whom fell by the wayside. There are powerful evocations of certain aspects of the times: of how drugs took over the lives of musicians, of the difficulties musicians had negotiating the territory between the cult world of bebop and the more general kind of success enjoyed by Ellington. And some of what is probably Troupe's best writing has nothing to do with music; the brief sections on Sugar Ray Robinson sheds unexpected light on the influence of boxing on Davis's playing. If one listens to Davis's jabbing, suspenseful, aggressive improvisation on "Walkin'" from the 1961 Black Hawk recording, one hears not only Monk, but also, we can now say, Robinson:

> Sugar Ray Robinson would put an opponent in four or five traps during every round in the first two or three rounds, just to see how his opponent would react. Ray would be reaching, and he would stay just out of reach so he could measure you to knock you out, and you didn't even know what was happening until, BANG! you found yourself counting stars. Then, on somebody else, he might hit him hard in his side—BANG!—after he made him miss a couple of jabs. He might do that in the first round. Then he'd tee-off on the sucker upside his head after hitting him eight or nine more times hard in the ribs, then back to the head. So by the fourth or fifth round, the sucker don't know what Ray's going to do to him next.

Once our memoirist gets to New York, however, the book begins to lose itself in contradictions and obscenities. On one page Davis will say that Parker was "teaching me a lot about music—chords and that shit—that I would go play on the piano" when he went to Juilliard, and then a few pages later that "Bird didn't teach me much as far as music goes." Davis claims that he became the musical director of Parker's group, but Max Roach, who was also in the band, vehemently disputes the claim. (It is proof, he says, that the trumpeter has "become senile.") Davis recalls being taken to Minton's in Harlem for the great jam session by Fats Navarro, whom many considered second only to Gillespie, but then says, "I would tell him shit—technical shit—about the trumpet." Jimmy Heath has a rather different memory of what Davis did or did not learn from Navarro: "Fats ate Miles up every night. Miles couldn't outswing him, he couldn't outpower him, he couldn't outsweet him, he couldn't do anything except take that whipping on *every* tune."

On things racial, it's impossible to figure out from this book what Davis really felt. "I could learn more in one session at Minton's than it would take me two years to learn at Juilliard. At Juilliard, after it was all over, all I was going to know was a bunch of white styles: nothing new." But only one page later he says:

> I couldn't believe that all of them guys like Bird, Prez, Bean, all them cats wouldn't go to museums or libraries and borrow those musical scores so they could check out what was happening. I would go to the library and borrow scores by all those great composers, like Stravinsky, Alban Berg, Prokofiev. I wanted to see what was going on in all of music. Knowledge is freedom and ignorance is slavery, and I just couldn't believe someone could be that close to freedom and not take advantage of all the shit that they can. I have never understood why black people didn't take advantage of all the shit that they can.

Of the interracial couples that he saw in the clubs on Fifty-second Street, Davis observes:

> A lot of white people, though, didn't like what was going on on 52nd Street. . . . They thought that they were being invaded by niggers from Harlem, so there was a lot of racial tension around bebop. Black men were going with fine, rich white bitches. They were all over those niggers out in public and the niggers were clean as a motherfucker and talking all kind of hip shit. So you know a lot of white people, especially white men, didn't like this new shit.

And then, explaining why he didn't want to do an interview for *Playboy,* he declares, "All they have are blond women with big tits and flat asses or no asses. So who the fuck wants to see that all the time? Black guys like big asses, you know, and we like to kiss on the mouth and white women don't have no mouths to kiss on."

Davis's treatment of women is disgusting. He details the way he destroyed the career of his first wife, Frances Taylor, who was a dancer, and later, claiming that black women are too bossy, he cites Taylor as an example of the way a good colored woman ought to be. He volunteers tales of slapping Cicely Tyson around, though she was probably responsible for his not dying from a binge of cocaine that spanned nearly six years.

The cavalier way that Davis imputes drug use to black musician after black musician is no less objectionable. (He claims repeatedly that the white jazz press didn't start paying attention to white guys being junkies until Stan Getz was arrested, but Leonard Feather has shown that in fact white musicians got the bulk of the attention for using drugs.) And the morality of the trumpeter's memory is oddly selective. About a woman who helped him during his time as a drug addict, Davis says, "I was seeing this same rich white girl who I'd met in St. Louis; she had come to New York to check me out. Let's call her 'Alice,' because she's still alive and I don't want to cause her trouble; plus she's married." And the customers of a white call girl were "very important men—white men mostly—whose names I won't mention." It seems that militant Inky respects the privacy of those mouthless, gluteus minimus white women and those white johns more than he does the dignity of his fellow musicians, some of whom were his very close friends.

One of the most disturbing things about *Miles* is its debt to Jack Chambers's *Milestones,* a critical biography written in two parts between 1983 and 1985 and now available in one volume from Quill. Pages 160–61 of *Miles,* for example, look alarmingly like pages 166–67 of *Milestones.* (There is even a cavalier reference to Chambers as "some writer.") Davis and Troupe:

> Bird had an exclusive contract with Mercury (I think he had left Verve by then), so he had to use a pseudonym on record. Bird had given up shooting heroin because since Red Rodney had been busted and sent back to prison at Lexington, Bird thought the police were watching him. In place of his normal big doses of heroin, now he was drinking an enormous amount of alcohol.

Chambers:

> . . . the man behind the pseudonym was Charlie Parker. Parker was under some pressure, not only because he had an exclusive contract with Mercury, but also because the trumpeter in his band, Red Rodney, had been arrested and committed to the federal prison in Lexington. Parker believed that he was being watched by narcotics agents, according to Ross Russell, and he had given up narcotics for the time being and was consuming large quantities of alcohol instead.

Much of the material used in *Milestones* and again in *Miles* comes from interviews done over the years. Troupe denies using any of it, then says that "the man can quote himself," then blames the publisher for "messing up" by omitting a discography and a bibliography, and by not checking facts.

But the important point, finally, is that *Miles* paints the picture of an often gloomy monster. It is full of stories that take the reader down into the sewers of Davis's musical, emotional, and chemical decline. Once the rage at his cruelty and his self-inflation has passed, we are left aghast at a man of monumental insecurity who, for all his protests about white power and prejudice, is often controlled by his fear of it, or of any other significant power. (One example of many: Davis asserts that he never listens to white music critics, and blames many of the woes of the music business on them, but then he admits that once they had him worried that he sounded inferior to Chet Baker, who was his imitator.) Obsessed with remaining young, and therefore willing to follow any trend in pop music, Davis is now a surly sellout who wants his success to seem like a heroic battle against the white world.

To that end, this former master of musical articulation often reduces himself to an inarticulate man. Davis has worn the mask of the street corner for too long; he thinks, like Pryor and Murphy and Lee, that his invective gives him authenticity. Gone is the elegant and exigent Afro-American authenticity of the likes of Ellington, at ease in the alleys as well as in the palace, replaced by youth culture vulgarity that vandalizes the sweep and substance of Afro-American life. The fall of Davis reflects perhaps the essential failure of contemporary Negro culture: its mock-democratic idea that the elite, too, should like it down in the gutter. Aristocracies of culture, however, come not from the acceptance of limitations, but from the struggle with them, as a group or an individual, from within or without.

Space Is the Place

Gene Santoro

In a piece written in 1987 and reprinted in his book Dancing in Your Head, *the critic Gene Santoro pays admiring attention to the self-declared "tone scientist" Sun Ra and his "impossible-to-classify" music.*

You've never seen a show quite like it, except maybe for the Neville Brothers, Jimi Hendrix, the Grateful Dead, Sunny Ade, James Brown. It's certainly not like any other jazz performance. The musicians snake onto the stage in a long line, stepping in time, chanting a tune like "Space Is the Place" to handheld percussion, wearing spangled headgear and flowing, colorful robes that suggest an extremely foreign origin. Settling in with their instruments, the dozen or more players segue with an easygoing sense from old big-band tunes to ultra-free jazz, sometimes jump-cutting to keep the audience on its toes. A few numbers later, the leader himself ambles out, takes his place behind a bank of acoustic and electronic keyboards, and starts calling tunes from the immense repertory his group has built up during the thirty-odd years the core musicians have been working together. Ellington and standards careen into spacey blowouts with no beats dropped by onstage or offstage crowds. They know that with Sun Ra, Ruler of the Omniverse and leader of the Omniverse Arkestra, you can only expect the unexpected. Nothing seems alien to him.

And yet, according to him, everything here is alien to him. "I've never been born. I *arrived,*" is how he opens the conversation we're having in a two-room suite in Time Square's Edison Hotel. He's sitting on the sofa sporting a straw fedora atop his red hair, a blue chasuble-style robe, and boxer shorts, while we watch the five-minute segment a local news show has pieced together from footage shot the night before at New York's Sweet Basil.

> There are some very powerful forces, an unknown force more powerful than God, Satan, Lucifer, the Devil. It's not written in any books, and it's never been spoken on this planet. That's what's kept me all of these years: I've been knowing ever since I've been a child about these forces. It's the reason I've got a band, 'cause they keep sending me

> people so I can keep on moving like I've got to. The Creator is using me, 'cause people are ready for something better. I do what The Creator tells me: I'm not a man—I'm really an angel. I'm not a minister, a preacher, or a politician. There is no classification for what I am here to do. Sun Ra is the only name that can help the planet Earth, now that words have gone bad from the Tower of Babel. I don't want anyone to worship me or my people. I just want to get this planet back on its feet.

Musical crackpot, self-deluded weirdo, hypocritical self-promoter—just a few accusations that have dogged Sun Ra and his freewheeling yet highly disciplined sounds ("I prefer to call myself a tone scientist rather than a musician") for the generation he's been making them. Along the way, he's also explored directions that, if they seemed off the map at the time, are now firmly and indelibly etched into the jazz world. Electronic keyboards, for instance, which he took up in the late fifties ("I bought one of the first electric pianos Wurlitzer made," he claims) to nearly universal ridicule, using them to create the offbeat, spacey textures his vision required. Free blowing, which took him and the Arkestra so far outside the pale when they began trying it in the early sixties that they stayed confined to a handful of venues like New York's Slug's. Using light shows and dancers and mimes and outrageous costumes as part of the celebratory swirl and vaudeville ritual that constituted, then and now, the extravaganza of a Sun Ra Arkestra performance. Reviving big-band standards and section work while good-naturedly skewering and updating the stylistic and harmonic assumptions inherited from the Swing Era and bop alike. However you trace through the past three decades, you're bound to see Sun Ra's footprints.

As he does in his impossible-to-classify music, so too in his conversations Sun Ra circles around a widening gyre of motives and topics, returning time and again to touchstones. "You don't have to turn the tape machine on or take notes right now. I'll get back to it. I always get back to it," he smiles at one point, then reiterates. "There isn't a birth certificate, 'cause I wasn't born." But the story goes that he first appeared as Herman Blount seventy or so years ago, in Birmingham, Alabama. "The first instrument I played was a kazoo," he says offhandedly, "and I came home one day and found a piano and just knew how to play it. I've always been that way: all I have to do is feel it in my heart, and I can play it. No one has ever had that talent on earth before, because the spirit couldn't find nobody who was willing to give up *every*thing, including their life, including their death—everything." Trained in high-school bands and at Alabama A&M, he continued his musical career by working as a sideman with the likes of blues belter Wynonie Harris and fiddle master Stuff Smith as well as in society bands. "Bands I was in played everything from Dixieland on up," he shrugs.

Moving to Chicago in the late thirties, he did the music for the floor shows at the Club DeLisa, that way hooking up with trailblazing big-band arranger Fletcher Henderson (his charts put the Benny Goodman Orchestra over), whose band also performed there. For about a year in the late forties, in fact, Sun Ra was Henderson's pianist. "There aren't that many people left who know how Fletcher and Jimmie Lunceford and those leaders worked out what they did, how they led their bands. Not everybody can play their music. I can and I do, because I was there, so I can write what the old people were playing off the records."

When his tour with Henderson was up, Sun Ra began to lead his own orchestra. "I first was introduced to Sun Ra by a drummer name of Robert Barry after I had gotten out of the Air Force," recalls longtime tenor mainstay John Gilmore.

> He was playing down at Shep's Playhouse on 43rd St. in Chicago. Sun Ra and Pat [Patrick] had been working regularly, and he had used another substitute tenor playing for Pat, and Barry said I might get the gig if I came out. I brought my horn, he say come back the next night, and that was it (laughs). So we built the band from three pieces on up: added Richard Evans the bass player, Dave Young on trumpet, Jim Herndon on tympani, and Bob Barry was on drums. We had about eight pieces: Johnny Thompson was on tenor for a while, Von Freeman played alto for a while, Lee O'Neill—his son is playing drums with us now.

Even then the seeds for the Arkestra were sown: the group often wore exotic costumes and played an array of African and Eastern percussion instruments. By the early fifties they were known (among myriad names) as the Solar or Myth/Science Arkestra, and on their gigs at Chicago venues like the Pershing Hotel wore beanies and white gloves and blazers. Gilmore continues,

> So we built it up to about eight pieces and started working in a place called Budland, the equivalent to Birdland in New York. Stayed there a long time, about a year. Ahmad Jamal was working upstairs, used to come downstairs and steal Sun Ra's stuff. Every Monday for about an hour he'd be in the phone booth listening, right, Sunny? A whole lot of people came that year, everybody who'd come to town would stop in. Ray Charles came in one time, says, "I can't see these dudes but whoever they are they sure are smoking." (laughs) Sonny Rollins came through, all of the cats who lived in Chicago. It was a moving city at that time, people always in and out, a lot of things going on. We backed up all kind of people, like Dakota Staton and Sarah Vaughan, Johnny "Guitar" Watson, all kind of people.

By the late fifties the core octet had moved from being a backup band to intensive rehearsals and its own gigs.

The music they made during this period has been compared to hard-bop style of contemporaries like Art Blakey and his Jazz Messengers, but its idiosyncratic twists and turns seem more in line with what Charles Mingus was doing then: shredding big-band and bop tactics and reweaving them into something distinct by dint of his acute, probing sensibility. Like Mingus (who also accumulated long-term allegiances from key players), Sun Ra rerouted the path of the large-ensemble tradition in jazz, and thus became a precursor of younger musicians leading big groups today, like Henry Threadgill, David Murray, Craig Harris, and Olu Dara. (Harris, in fact, toured with Sun Ra for about three years, mostly in Europe, and recorded with him on *Strange Celestial Road.*) Among the cues Sun Ra's work offers this growing movement is how to harness the explosive language of free jazz to a larger group's more organized, rhythmically centered charts—since he is one of free jazz's inventors and has led a big band for over thirty years, there are few better places to begin that course of study.

"Sun Song" and "Sound of Joy" were cut in the mid to late 1950s, when, as the liner notes point out, Trane was an unheralded sideman and Ornette Coleman was still unrecorded. Listening to them now, after two generations of jazz experimenters have passed through the scene, is still a revealing and charged experience. Recognizable in outline as bop-influenced, the music stretches and warps that genre.

One key element Ra changed was the rhythms: layering interlocking polyrhythms via his multitudes of percussionists, shifting tempos within tunes, he reached beyond the abilities of even a sophisticated trapsman like Blakey to suggest the African underpinnings for his music. His harmonic structures more and more avoided the repeating chord cycles jazzmen borrowed from popular tunes and substituted modally based, recurrent, open-ended melodies. (That approach would later lead Miles Davis and his then sidemen John Coltrane and Bill Evans to produce classic LPs like 1959's *Kind of Blue,* which helped shift jazz's focus. Trane's self-confessed admiration for and derivations from Gilmore's tenor work are well documented.) Rather than using the piano as a polyphonic horn, the attack that dominated jazz keyboards from the days of Eubie Blake on, Sun Ra would move from boogie and stride stylings to percussive poundings ("Transition"), generating dense tone clusters and sonic bursts à la Thelonious Monk or Henry Cowell or Harry Partch.

By 1959, Sun Ra's compositions had become naked displays of hammering percussion and wildly varied instrumentation that unsheathed a new, rawer edge. At roughly the same time that Ornette Coleman and John Coltrane and Albert Ayler and Cecil Taylor were blasting free of bop's conventions, Sun Ra was leading his Arkestra into the stratosphere, helping launch free jazz. (The Arkestra of this period was captured on film, *The Cry of Jazz,* in the same year that saw the release of *Kind of Blue.*) They also abandoned Chicago for a small town outside Montreal, where a gig turned into an extended stay. A tour in Spain followed, and they landed back in New York in 1960.

Gilmore and Allen and especially Pat Patrick (who'd preceded the rest of the band to the Apple on his own, working there while they were in Canada and Spain) lined up a host of outside gigs, doing everything from jingles to pop sessions, to help support the communally housed Arkestra. According to Sun Ra, one key session found him, Gilmore, and Allen together: "We was all there to do the theme for the *Batman* TV show, but nobody ever give us no credit. And I did a record with Chief Ebenezer Obey then that the company never put out, and one with James Moody." But if they managed to hustle work, credited or released or not, the city was, as always, an extremely expensive place to live, especially for a large commune, and there were other inevitable problems. "Our neighbors started complaining about us practicing," explains Sun Ra, "and we couldn't find anyplace where they didn't complain." In 1971 they did, in the Germantown section of Philadelphia, where the Arkestra is still housed today. As Sun Ra puts it, "Our neighbors there *like* us to rehearse, they enjoy it, they say it helps them sleep." Maybe it's better to just imagine their dreams.

Like the eternal present of a dreamscape, the music of the Arkestra has never "evolved" in the sense that their current sounds abandon their past; in what they do, all periods and styles coalesce simultaneously. "I can play everything," says Sun Ra. "I'm a Gemini; I get bored with one thing, but I have to play everything, 'cause otherwise I get bored. Whatever I'm doing, the part of me that's a Gemini be saying, Enough of that. I have to follow that. That's one reason I have the big band: I want to hear the alto, then I want to hear the tenor, then I want to hear the trumpet, then I want to hear the rhythm, then I want to hear me—keep moving, that's my nature. As long as I'm doing that, everything is harmonically balanced with me."

The early sixties found the Arkestra veering into unexplored territory. A cut like "Beginning" on 1961's aptly titled *We Are in the Future* points the way: dense percussion overlays support the mournful, vaguely Eastern modalities Gilmore pulls from his bass clarinet in conversation with Allen's chirping, quavering flute. At the same time, "Tapestry from an Asteroid" swoons like an Ellington ballad whose lushness has gone slightly awry, and "Jet Flight" romps like uptempo bop, reminding us that nothing disappears in Sun Ra's cavernous musical cosmos.

The big band is Sun Ra's self-described ideal vehicle; he has no use for small combos, explaining,

> I always played in big bands, I know how to take a band and create for it. The bigger the band, the better. Every time my band rehearses they learn something. I'll write something they can't read, and they have to study for about six months, something very simple, maybe a fingering that they got to work out a solution. On a lot of my tunes, like "Jet Flight," they don't have to miss but one note and they'll never get back in. I always have my own style, play it differently every night. The band has to be accustomed to some strange chords. They have to play the same things that are written on somebody, but then I might think of something else to add, so I'll play it real quick and then I want somebody in the band to catch *that.* That's how it becomes deeper, more profound, and more in keeping with the exact psychic pitches of people. One Sun Ra LP is called *Cosmic Tones for Mental Therapy.* It works, it works all the time. I'm reaching a part of people, I don't know whether it's the soul or what you call it, it's the part of them that science don't know about. I *do* know about it. That's when the soul starts to wake.

In his entire approach Sun Ra demonstrates what he means when he says, "I know the whole history of jazz, the whole history of music. My [music] equations tell me all that." As with his music for the Arkestra, his solo keyboard work encapsulates a panorama of styles and periods. Gilmore puts it this way: "It's such a joy to hear Sun Ra play, it's like history on the bandstand: bits of Jelly Roll Morton, Fats Waller, James P. Johnson. I mean, where could you go that you could hear all that in one night—on the gig [laughs]. He's covering some territory." Then there are the echoes of Ellington himself, and Monk as well. Nor is jazz the only musical link to Sun Ra's peculiar keyboard stuff, as *John Cage Meets Sun Ra* (Meltdown Records MPA-1) indicates, connecting Sun Ra with the Ives/Cage axis that runs through American "classical" music.

And so Sun Ra and the Arkestra ("Next Stop Jupiter") continue to endure, if not exactly prosper, despite real and imagined persecutions. "I've been bypassed for a lot of things. That's why they sent the Art Ensemble to Europe before they sent me. They've invited Ornette Coleman to write symphonies and things but not me, because I talk about space and things so they think I'm a kook. That's what they think. I think so too for ever bothering to explain it. We do not disagree."

Easy to Love

Dudley Moore

These enthusiastic remarks by the actor (and sometime pianist) Dudley Moore appeared as liner notes for Easy to Love, *a 1988 collection of previously unreleased cuts—all recorded in the early sixties—by Erroll Garner.*

Listening to this selection of Garner's recordings was a chilling experience—chilling in the sense that one knows one is listening to an exception—one is listening to a phenomenon. No matter what the rational opinions are, one comes to the conclusion that here is a uniqueness that is almost unbearably strong. They say that certain types of genius are the result of untiring practice and application—terms which of course double to mean enthusiasm or passion—but what exactly Garner had to do to acquire this unique tonal vocabulary is hard to understand completely. Suffice it to say that his persona is streaked in bold and subtle flashes across his music. You didn't have to know the man to feel, what is certainly for one very brief moment in history, a unique singing voice. To achieve this at all on a piano is no mean feat, but it is not the technical aspect of his playing that astonishes, although that is one thing to knock one off one's feet. It is the fact that the technical aspect evaporates in this spectacular contact that is made through a music that is entirely Garner's own.

Mind you, there are parts of Garner that I don't appreciate at all or find particularly remarkable. I don't think his wayward introductions are necessarily an extraordinary feature of his work. Or, that the sentimentality he sometimes allows himself in unabashed ballads is particularly interesting. However, when he plays a ballad with that combination of deep feeling and caressing rhythm, I sag with the burden of gratitude. I may be getting purple with my prose at this point, but what can one do in the face of this gift that is extended to us all. Not everyone knows, realizes, or understands the importance of Erroll Garner. He understood it, I'm sure, but also would probably have been too reticent to admit it. Criticism was sometimes blind to it, although his public acceptance was always gigantic. He once said, "Some people know what life's about and some people don't." The spontaneity and relaxed growth in his music pleads a knowledge of life and I guess if you don't get it, you don't get it. This does not imply membership in some darkly exclusive club, but merely the futility of describing a feeling. I love music that lives and breathes and encourages life. I hate music that conjures up an apparition of death. That doesn't mean to say that I don't love music that is inspired by requiems or death itself. However, the outcome of even such potentially morbid music has to be joy. The optimism of life, of being alive, of feeling alive, of communication, of love . . . that's what Garner is and what he does for me and will always do for me. That's why I love to try and play like him. His music has got into my veins and I wish that everyone could be as drugged as I am with this particular non-chemical. Long live Garner. I bless that day in 1957 when I heard him for the first time. I shall always treasure the experience and I am able to relive it, listening to this music today. I never met the man to say hello and thank you. I didn't have the nerve to do that, even though I did spend a couple of times in a club close to his arm and at several of his concerts in London. One day he came into a club where I was playing and I was so nervous,—I so wanted to share my love for him and how he had affected me—that my panic allowed me to spill a bottle of Coca-Cola on the middle of the keyboard to the point where all the keys stuck together and I could only play on either side of this sticky log.

Garner brought to the piano an element which I don't think anyone else had previously provided—the element of sensuality. It was engendered by a true rubato in the sense that Chopin understood—that is, a left hand which is ostensibly regular and a right hand that moves freely against it, "the result of momentary impulse," as the great pianist Josef Hofmann said. (He also maintained, rightfully I think, that . . . "Perfect expression is possibly only under perfect freedom.") This rubato is a rarity in any music and finds its true fruition in Garner's playing,—a smooth, undulating arm that floats and caresses sweetly above a gently pulsing bass. Garner must be one of the very few who can soothe our souls with this most elusive of arts. There's no doubt in my mind that his unique and enlivening rhythmic approach is an irrefutable addition to musical language, nourished as it is by the poignant, passionate, or pagan palette (!)—if you'll once again excuse my purple prose—of his harmony.

It is interesting to note that often after a passage or phrase of considerable rubato where the melody notes hit just behind the basic beat, Garner will, in the last couple of bars (generally of an eight-bar phrase), get right on to the beat again—not to steady himself like a tightrope walker using the bar, but just because it feels good in the style. I've never known Garner to need to put out a hand to steady himself, as it were. There's never a moment when one says, "Whoops!"

It is extraordinary that this man, who did not read or write music, could have produced such richness of rhythm and harmony, even a latent counterpoint—for his two hands enjoyed the sweetest, cooperative marriage. Jazz can, in one way, resemble painting by numbers. The chordal system that emerged from its roots, which was then enriched by the advent of impressionist harmony, has been organized into a figured bass concept like that of former times (the sixteenth and seventeenth centuries). The result is a system that is relatively easy to learn wherein chordal inversions are left to the individual taste of the pianist, who has the advantage of being able to play more than one note at once. All I can say is, thank God Garner chose the piano as his means of expression, since he would not have been perhaps quite as remarkable on a one-line instrument. We would not have had the glory of the interplay between his two hands or the piquant structure of his chords and textures.

Although Garner seemed to hit a few clankers now and then in terms of melody, these are never really wrong notes so much as moments of intense creativity that have spiralled off. Rhythmically he never fails us and that is probably the most remarkable thing. He really doesn't, not even when he seems to be even remotely strapped by the sheer physical stuff that one encounters on a piano from time to time. Relaxation was of total importance to him. Lesser artists like to mystify us with claims of difficulty. When Garner decides to *combine* his many colors we are most nobly fed—an infectious notion of rhythm and sensual swing with a flirtatious and coquettish melodic gift, an ability to take us with him into areas of sweet contentment where our heads all bob gently and thankfully like mesmerized turkeys.

It is more than great octave work that he indulged in. It succeeds without apparent effort and he even seems to be trying new things as he plays without being at all perturbed at the prospect of keeping things in rhythm. Everything is always within the style even when the actual notes may not perhaps be exactly what he wanted. But, then again, everything *sounds* right because it *swings* and because his spirit leaps out to us.

His endings almost seem nonchalant, as if to say "I've done this one—let's get to the next." This spontaneity is paralleled in his almost exclusive love of the first take; his enthusiasm ran hot and he knew he would not be able to give the same spirit out again, whatever notes had hit the floor. This did not mean of course that he was unwilling to play the same tune more than once in quick succession. he could do so, but often chose to do so in different styles and tempos, refreshing the tune each time with new invention.

Garner often seems to bend notes, sliding, as he does, with his right hand from black to white keys. Thus he favors the keys based on flats, where such opportunities abound, notably the keys of D♭, E♭, G♭, A♭, and B♭, as appear in these selections. The result is melody which has the liquidity of a singer's portamento. He gives us much succulent ornamentation and gentle repetition of little motifs to gladden the heart. Sometimes, as in "Somebody Loves Me," he slows the tempo down as he digs in with more voluptuous rhythm as the choruses continue. He often jokes with us, as in the staccato-octave opening chorus of "Taking a Chance on Love" with its typical midkeyboard sax-section-like accompanying "woofs." He often plays his own Garner riff, as in "Lover Come Back" or "Easy to Love"; there are quotations from other melodies and often, dotted eighth-notes in the bass which bestride the beat merrily like a child, plonking about in seven-league boots, tugging gaily-fluttering kites gently and playfully in his right hand. And sometimes, he will delay the emergence of the melody as in the reckless beginning of the third chorus of "Somebody Stole My Gal" and then make us grin with his wonderful octave work in the last chorus. These are all expressions of a humor that pervades his work almost constantly—a humor that is often so much more telling than graver utterances of other jazz performers. Humor is intrinsic to Garner's nature and is a companion to his feeling for life, to the joy and sensuality of his playing. Humor resides in the flesh of his music in both perky and witty guise.

To my mind, Erroll Garner is probably the most important pianist that I have ever heard—and that includes classical pianists. The problems in his music are different from those facing a classical pianist; the answers are complex. He may sort of know what he's going to play to a greater or lesser degree from a vocabulary that expands gently and continuously. But—we are always delighted with the freshness and the originality of approach, a desire to communicate. He cultivated his garden wonderfully, completely, roundly. For those people who don't hear or feel his soul, I am sorry. I don't know how one could explain the feeling to anyone. However, I think he speaks to the heart of all of us, even to those who only feel what he says, subconsciously.

In the long run, who cares if his right hand was always lagging at just the perfect point behind the left. In the long run, who cares if his right hand runs were always structurally impeccable; they actually were an infallible feature of his relaxation, plunging us into happiness and wild enthusiasms. The feeling that that particular technique exuded was one of being alive. In the long run, who cares that his sense of texture was extraordinarily original; it was, more importantly, rich. Who cares that his hands were big and could cover this or that interval with ease; they delighted us with unparalleled, unchangeable octave work. Ultimately all these *"things"* gave us more—*pleasure*. The technique cannot be separated from the music, but the music is infinitely more important. Passion . . . that's what he had . . . passion. And that's what all great artists have. A sprinkling of the demonic, a yearning for the tender, and a straight line to joy.

Bessie Smith

Humphrey Lyttelton

From another of the exemplary British critics and enthusiasts of jazz, Humphrey Lyttelton, this consideration of the prodigious Bessie Smith. From The Best of Jazz *(1979).*

When Bessie Smith came to record it, "St. Louis Blues" had already been popularized by other singers on the theater circuits, one of whom, Ethel Waters, had made it her own speciality. As usual, Bessie ran over this obstacle like a steamroller. Her version became definitive, putting back into the song the essence of the real blues which had originally inspired Handy to write it. With her in the studio that day in January 1925 was Fred Longshaw, a competent and diligent musician with no jazz pretensions who elected to play harmonium on the occasion, and young Louis Armstrong who had arrived in New York some four months before to join Fletcher Henderson's Orchestra. By this time, Bessie had been a recording star for a full two years, and there is little reason, in view of her temperament, to disbelieve the legend that she was far from pleased by the booking of Armstrong in place of her preferred Joe Smith who was out of New York at the time. Musical considerations apart, the prospect of sharing the limelight with a young and no doubt bumptious musician who was currently being hailed as a phenomenon was hardly likely to appeal to her.

In the event, Louis approached most of the numbers which they recorded at the session with great seriousness and restraint (the only dubious exception being some jokey, out-of-place playing in a vaudeville song called "You've Been a Good Ole Wagon," which Bessie converts into a solemn blues). These were, after all, two already great artists with an instinctive awareness of their own transcendent artistry. Whatever was said on the surface—and Louis himself claimed to prefer the records he made with a much lesser singer called Maggie Jones—it would have been surprising if they had failed to find a common artistic meeting ground.

That common ground is located in the very opening bars of "St. Louis Blues," which they transposed into the key of E-flat. It is easy to be derisive about the contribution of Fred Longshaw and his asthmatic harmonium. If the quality of swing belongs to the angels, then the devil must have invented the harmonium expressly to destroy it. And yet, like a great many odd noises from the primaeval days of recording, its sound has become woven into the very atmosphere of the piece to the extent that, were technology to find a way of expunging it and substituting a crisply-recorded rhythm section, I should be loath to see it go. What carefully-contrived arrangement could be better than the husky and sombre B-flat major chord which replaces Handy's tango introduction and, as it were, opens the curtain on Bessie's performance?

Fresh in my memory is a conversation about Louis Armstrong with the British trombonist George Chisholm, a Louisphile of long-standing. He made the point that Louis was one of the very few musicians who possessed such innate swing that he could establish a tempo with the shortest of phrases—sometimes even with one note. Bessie Smith shared this faculty. While Fred Longshaw is hard at work trying to establish coordination between foot-pedals and keyboard, she makes plain within the span of the words "I hate to see . . ." exactly the tempo which she intends to maintain. It is significant, in the light of Sam Wooding's comments earlier about her slow, drawn-out style, that this blues tempo is much slower than anything to be heard in instrumental jazz at that period. It was not until well into the thirties that musicians started tackling this sort of slow-drag blues. If we listen again to some of the famous instrumental blues that traditional jazz bands take at a crawling pace today—King Oliver's "Riverside Blues," the Armstrong Hot Five's "Savoy Blues," Jimmy Noone's "Apex Blues" or Ellington's "Creole Love Call"—we find that they trot along at what we now consider a medium tempo, presumably to give the dancers what they wanted. Bessie, used to singing to motionless or at any rate swaying audiences, could afford to set her own dramatic tempo—and she was lucky in an accompanist for whom music held very few surprises to which he could not instantly adapt.

No words about the rapport and musical understanding between Bessie Smith and Louis Armstrong can do justice to the opening chorus of "St. Louis Blues." In a mood of experiment I once learnt off by heart the vocal and cornet lines so that I could play them on trumpet as one continuous melody. The result came as near to a perfect *instrumental* blues chorus as one could conceive. It is not just in inventive talent that the two principals were evenly matched. Passion is an elusive quality in music, often impersonated by a sort of spurious frenzy, a simulated hysteria that is all too familiar in contemporary pop music that boasts a black gospel-song influence. I have sometimes said that the great jazz giants whom I have hard in person—Louis Armstrong, Sidney Bechet, Coleman Hawkins, John Coltrane—have all made the same striking impression that, were the instrument to be suddenly wrenched from their lips, the music would continue to flow out of sheer creative momentum. Such is the great wave of passion on which "St. Louis Blues" is carried that I am similarly rather surprised that it doesn't continue to well out of the speakers when the amplifier is suddenly switched off or the needle lifted.

Each one of Louis Armstrong's responses is worthy of analysis. I will be content to pick out three. At the very beginning, in answer to Bessie's opening line "I hate to see that evenin' sun go down," he reacts without hesitation to the dramatic mood which she has set by starting a descending phrase with seven E-flat notes hammered out with great intensity. The whole phrase is imbued with a beauty and melancholy that disguise the fact that all Louis is doing in terms of structure is playing the straight five-note scale from E-flat down to A-flat that ushers in the subdominant chord of the second four bars. In this, he is bound by the meticulously correct but deadeningly unadventurous harmonies churned out by Fred Longshaw on the harmonium. Louis spent much of his musical career overcoming, and indeed glorifying, unimaginative backing, and this recording is a fine example. At the end of the first verse, Armstrong's feeling for harmony enables him to play a neat trick as he follows Longshaw's chord progression doggedly with a note pattern that changes only at the last moment, when it seems on the very verge of mockery. And then, in the very last verse of all, following a veritable clarion call to action by Bessie on the word "Nowhere" that ends the minor tango section, Louis responds to the line "I got the Saint Louis Blues just as blue as I can be" with a complex fill-in that almost comes a cropper. The snatch of melody that Louis plays, phrasing it recklessly across the beat, is one which crops up elsewhere in music related to New Orleans. It sounds as if its inspiration was the trio section of the famous march "National Emblem" which . . . was always quoted by Louis Armstrong in his versions of "Tiger Rag" and may possibly have had connections with that tune itself. In the tune "Clarinet Lament" by Duke Ellington's Orchestra, featuring the New Orleans clarinetist Barney Bigard, the same phrase is elevated to the status of an introductory cadenza. Whatever its origins—and it is not inconceivable that Louis invented it himself—it fills the bill admirably in this instance, providing a fitting response to Bessie's stirring lament and showing, in passing, Louis Armstrong's uncanny, catlike ability to recover from a bad mistake and continue on his way without the missing of a beat.

As for Bessie Smith herself, this is one of her masterpieces. Having said that, I shall not, to the reader's relief and certainly to mine, be following up with pages of detailed analysis. It was central to Bessie Smith's art that she simplified rather than elaborated her themes. In modern times the quality in black music popularly known as "soul"—expressed in techniques directly borrowed from Negro church music—has been progressively exaggerated to the point where a simple blues becomes a positive fireworks display of shrieks and moans and wild vocal contortions. Neither the classic female singers nor the country bluesmen who preceded them went in for such antics. Bessie's way, taken up and carried forward right into the rock 'n' roll era by the great Kansas City blues singer Big Joe Turner, was to restrict the range of a song to no more than five or six notes and to construct her phrases so economically that a change in direction of just one note could have a startling dramatic or emotive effect. One example stands out in "St. Louis Blues." The first two twelve-bar blues verses begin with identical phrases, sung to the words "I hate to see that evenin' sun go down" and "Feelin' tomorrow like I feel today" respectively. Bessie starts the second verse, as Handy intended, with a melody line that begins in exactly the same way as the first. But where the word "see" in "I hate to see . . ." descends to the E-flat keynote as in Handy's original melody, the last two syllables of "tomorrow" hover indeterminately in the "blue note" area between the second and third notes in the scale, eventually making a little upward turn which creates an unimaginably desolate effect. Indeed, if I wanted examples to illustrate my earlier definition of "blue notes" I need do no more than point to these two lines and to the words "sun" in the first and "feel" in the second.

There is another characteristic of Bessie Smith's style which goes a long way to explaining why many commentators, myself included, choose to regard her, not as the culmination of a tradition of blues singing, but as the beginning of a new tradition of jazz singing. Since a jazz critique developed a long time after the music itself had begun, we have had the luxury of making many of our definitions in retrospect. Thus the jazz singers to us are those who, like the musicians, have enhanced their chosen themes with a blend of insight, blues feeling, and creative variation, whether improvised or not. A singer who sang "St. Louis Blues" note for note from the sheet music as Handy had written it down would not sound to us like a jazz singer, however sincere the interpretation. For one thing, much of Handy's phrasing is symmetrical, with matching phrases following hard on each other like flower patterns on a wallpaper. And this sort of tightly-knit symmetry is the very antithesis of the broadly-sweeping and imaginative composition which we recognize in the best of jazz. Bessie Smith shared with Louis Armstrong a sort of built-in musical radar which steered her unerringly away from approaching symmetry. Since the words of popular songs were often harnessed to fairly jerry-built construction, we find both Bessie and Louis often making a dog's breakfast of the lyrics in the interests of improved musical architecture. A famous example of Bessie's cavalier treatment of the words occurs in the song "Cake Walkin' Babies" where, in order to deliver a superbly rhythmic and swinging musical phrase, she sings "The only way to win is to cheat 'em." Less extreme are the occasions in "St. Louis Blues" where, for purely structural ends, she inserts a breathing point right in the middle of a verbal phrase, knocking its grammar sideways. In the first verse, she sings "It makes me think I'm / on my last go-round," emphasizing the point by letting her voice fall off the syllable "I'm" in a characteristic way. Likewise in the last verse, while Louis and Fred Longshaw faithfully reproduce Handy's repetitive melody to the words "I've got the Saint Louis Blues just as blue as I can be," Bessie will have none of it. To turn the line into musical sense, she makes a dramatic pause on the second "as," dropping off it in two steps in another of her striking mannerisms and cutting it off completely from the rest of the sentence. Paradoxically, this apparent sacrificing of the literary sense to musical construction actually deepens the emotional content of the song, a point to which I will return later.

The second Bessie Smith performance that I have chosen comes from a period, four years after the recording of "St. Louis Blues," when times had changed. Recording technique had made the giant stride into electrical reproduction, and singers no longer had to bellow into the cavernous mouth of a receiving horn as if aiming for the back row of the stalls. True, theaters continued to demand powerful voice projection—the era of whispering crooners was several years away. But the new recording methods could cope with subtler nuances now, and Bessie had plenty of these in her musical armory. Unhappily, her career was moving rapidly towards a crisis. After almost a decade since Mamie Smith first opened up the blues market, the sales of blues records were beginning to decline. In an effort to boost sales, the managers of "race" recordings began to stuff the lists with material in which "blue" rather than blues was the operative word. Bessie Smith almost always managed to imbue the most relentless double entendres with a certain melancholy dignity, but nevertheless it is a sad experience to play through her output of this period and hear the great voice, fraying somewhat at the edges under the stress of furious living, applied to a succession of songs in which the same old harmonic progressions—and sometimes the same melody—are trotted out to prop up a string of double meanings.

And then suddenly, a gem appears. In view of the imminent collapse of Bessie Smith's career, it is tempting to read some sort of autobiographical significance into her recording of "Nobody Knows You When You're Down and Out." She had recently been involved in a disastrous Broadway debut, and her records were not selling as briskly as they once did. But she was still very far from down and out. What is more, her uncertain and dangerous temperament had long put such tenuous friendships as she acquired at risk without applying the test of poverty. Bessie Smith rarely treated a song with anything less than total commitment, as witness the impassioned, almost tragic, overtones which she lent to songs such as "Alexander's Ragtime

Band" and "There'll Be a Hot Time in the Old Town Tonight." Written by an entertainer called Jimmy Cox, "Nobody Knows You When You're Down and Out" teeters on the razor's edge that separates the lyrical from the maudlin, but with a firm embrace Bessie guides it on to safe ground. She has the assistance of a five-piece band led by Clarence Williams but dominated by the fine cornet-playing of Ed Allen, who backs her in a manner reminiscent of Joe Smith.

With benefit of greatly improved recording, we can hear in this performance more characteristics that stamp Bessie Smith as a supreme jazz singer. The manipulation of tone—or more accurately, timbre—is one attribute which distinguishes the jazz musician from his "straight" dance-band colleague. A melody line will be given all kinds of contrasting nuances through a great repertoire of thin notes and thick notes, sweet notes and sour notes, clear notes and hoarse or "growled" notes. These are used purely as materials in the musical construction, without particular reference to the theme or mood of the song that is being played. The fact that Bessie is singing words does not deter her from deploying her tonal resources in a manner quite independent of the general portent of the lyric. We have an example of this at the very outset of "Nobody Knows You . . ." The opening two lines—"Once I lived the life of a millionaire/Spending my money, I didn't care"—seem on paper to demand a wistful interpretation, tinged with regret. And no doubt from a "straight" cabaret singer they would have got it, complete with a dollop of self-pity. Bessie is clearly not too concerned with a literal reading of the words. She takes her inspiration from the melody to which they are attached, treating those opening lines as two matching phrases, built on major and minor chord sequences respectively, which follow each other like great breakers on a seashore. One can imagine Louis Armstrong or Sidney Bechet—or, much later on, Ben Webster—giving the second line the same majestic swell.

A few lines later, something equally unexpected happens. The words "I carried my friends out for a good time . . . ." are shouted like a full-blooded blues, with a poignant flattening of pitch on the word "friends." And then, with the phrase "buying bootleg liquor," Bessie suddenly lets her voice drop away so that the words are virtually spoken, with a profoundly melancholy inflection. The moment brings vividly to life guitarist Danny Barker's recollection that, in performance, "she was unconscious of her surroundings. She never paid anybody any mind." Heaven knows what emotion prompted Bessie to lapse into soliloquy on those words. We learn from Chris Albertson that Bessie always preferred homemade liquor, maintaining that anything sealed made her sick. So far as we know, there was nothing in her often riotous relationship with bootleg liquor to prompt such sudden sadness. Once again, it transpires that there is a compelling *musical* reason for the device. For after building steadily for three lines, the melody suddenly collapses feebly on those words "Buyin' bootleg liquor, champagne, and wine." It is the kind of weak, one-note phrase for which jazz players have become adept at improvising an alternative. Bessie's does not merely bridge the gap, it endows the line with great emotional strength. The point is made again most forcibly when, after the beautifully apt cornet solo by Ed Allen, Bessie returns to the chorus but, this time, hums the first bars of each line, in the words of Chris Albertson, "expressing the feeling behind the song more effectively than any words do." This is the standard which Bessie Smith set for all jazz singers to follow, using improvisation in its fullest sense on the melody of a song to express a deeper meaning than that of the words on their own. It was an example which, a decade later, enabled Billie Holiday to make remarkable music out of popular ditties of the caliber of "I Cried for You" and "Back in Your Own Back Yard," not to mention "Ooooooh, What a Little Moonlight Can Do."

We cannot leave Bessie Smith without referring to the rhythmic aspect of her music. Elsewhere in this book, I make the point that, of all the musicians who recorded in the early twenties, only three—Louis Armstrong, Sidney Bechet, and Bessie Smith—seemed to possess the instinct to overcome and, indeed, change the rhythmic conventions of the day. Of these three, I would put Louis and Bessie together in the very top bracket. In some ways, Bessie had the more difficult task, since she had to handle words which were often harnessed to melodies conceived in the even quaver, eight-to-a-bar rhythm which ragtime bequeathed. I have already spoken of her habit of altering the words or the sentences to conform to her rhythmic notions. "Nobody Knows You . . ." is full of such adjustments. For instance, Jimmy Cox's original words in the song's second line are "Spending all my money, I didn't care" to match the syllables of "Once I lived the life of a millionaire." Recoiling from symmetry as ever, Bessie drops the word "all," which enables her to sing the phrase across the beat, stringing the words "Spending my money I" into one phrase. In several instances, her unerring rhythmic instinct, based like Louis Armstrong's on an underlying rhythm of twelve eighth notes (or four quaver triplets) to the bar, gets her out of difficulty with the lyrics. The very opening line, for instance, is almost impossible to sing in a "straight" fashion without distorting the word "millionaire." If an even-quaver style is used, giving the notes of "Once I lived the life . . ." equal value, then undue emphasis has to be put on the last syllable—"million-*aire*" to make it scan. If the quavers are dotted in more lilting style, then it is the first syllable—"*mill*-ionaire"—that has to be stressed. Free of both tight conventions, Bessie is able to drape the sentence loosely over the two bars so that "millionaire" comes out exactly as it is spoken.

I hope I have made the case for regarding Bessie Smith, not simply as an exalted blues singer, but as one of the greatest of all jazz performers. Unfortunately for her, technology inflicted upon singing styles in the thirties the kind of radical changes which instrumental jazz was not to suffer until the arrival many years later of electronics. Bing Crosby, like most of his jazz associates a great fan of Bessie's, was to develop an intimate use of the newly-perfected microphone from which "crooning" emerged. Bessie Smith's career had already suffered two setbacks by the end of the Jazz Decade. The blues on which her early triumphs had been built had lost their popularity and, with the dramatic slump of 1929, the bottom fell clean out of the recording industry. In 1933, at the instigation of John Hammond (a young enterpreneur endowed happily with both money and taste, who, three days later, was to introduce a newcomer called Billie Holiday to the studios), she made a recording comeback after two years' absence. At her own request, no blues were involved, but the rowdy vaudeville songs which she sang on this occasion seem to be a throwback to the rorty atmosphere of the twenties rather than a presage of the new mood of the thirties. Nevertheless, Bessie was in fine voice and apparently good spirits, and there has been much intriguing speculation as to how she would have fared had not her life come to its abrupt and violent end on a Mississippi road in 1937.

With the wisdom of hindsight we can understand why Hammond's courageous gamble with her in 1933 bore no immediate fruit. The singers who came to fame in the thirties—among them Billie Holiday, Connee Boswell, Mildred Bailey, Ella Fitzgerald, and, on the male side, a late-developing Louis Armstrong—all cultivated a light, confidential style well-suited to the improved sound techniques in both studios and theaters. Never in a million years could Bessie have trimmed her voice or her personality to the intimacy of the living-rooms into which rapidly developing coast-to-coast radio pumped popular music. But, in the very year of her death, the discovery of a legendary New Orleans musician called Bunk Johnson, who had played with Buddy Bolden at the beginning of the century and whom many believed to be long dead, instigated a revival of interest in early forms of both jazz and blues which was soon to grow into something of a craze. There is little doubt that Bessie Smith would have been sought after in the early stages of the New Orleans Revival. Whether her down-to-earth nature, deeply suspicious of anything smacking of the phony, would have put up for long with the movement's inherent nostalgia and sentimentality, is another matter. Sidney Bechet's awful verdict makes such speculation appear trivial. "It was like she had that hurt inside her all the time, and she was just bound to find it."

Billie Holiday

Benny Green

In another chapter of The Reluctant Art, *Benny Green offers the finest (to me) account of the art of Billie Holiday.*

MOM AND POP WERE JUST A COUPLE OF KIDS WHEN THEY GOT MARRIED. HE WAS EIGHTEEN, SHE WAS SIXTEEN, AND I WAS THREE.

—BILLIE HOLIDAY

By a fluke of circumstance I came across the recordings of Billie Holiday under conditions I suggest were unique. To the ordinary jazz fancier songs like "Mean to Me," "I Can't Get Started," "Body and Soul" and "More Than You Know" are merely melodic shapes used as springboards to creative improvisation. They are songs without words or sentiments. Their titles are mere labels of convenience by which they may be identified in the crowded world of musical themes, exercises in musical abstraction whose personal characteristics consist purely in the style of their harmonic nuances. This is doubly true of the practicing musician, whose relationship towards them is precisely that of the aspiring sculptor towards a block of uncut stone. He is all too aware of their texture, their shape, and the tempos their construction implies, so that when he comes across a vocal performance of them he will often find them pedestrian and even unfamiliar.

But when I first encountered Billie Holiday's recorded version of "Mean to Me" I possessed none of the questionable experience of the adult round which might have debased the currency of my critical faculties. Until I heard Billie Holiday sing "Mean to Me" I was unaware that the song existed. This innocence had a curious effect. For several years I accepted these songs in the form in which Billie Holiday had introduced them to me. I sensed they were great jazz performances without knowing why, although looking back on it, I was no doubt charmed beyond all resistance by the salty appeal of the diction, the tactful poise of the accompaniments, and above all by the exuberance of the rhythm. The Teddy Wilson–Lester Young–Benny Goodman pick-up groups were my first experience of art potent enough to induce me to try my own hand. It was their virtues which tempted me to enter the jazz world, to aspire towards the kind of musical expression which in the end was never achieved because it meant being as good as Lester Young.

The jazz of the Wilson–Holiday groups was obviously related to the earlier jazz with which I was familiar, but it had about it a quality too subtle for me to have then defined. Had I known it, recordings like "Laughing at Life," "Sugar," and "He Ain't Got Rhythm" represented a stage in jazz development when the instrumental sophistication of its soloists was in perfect sympathy with the more adventurous harmonic conventions of the day. The imbalance between these two factors was more delicately poised than ever before or since in jazz, now approaching the stage when all the possibilities of diatonic harmony were being realized, the end product of an evolution as natural and as inevitable as the growth of an amoeba.

But the day I heard Billie Holiday for the first time I knew nothing of all this. All I was aware of was the fact that this jazz was texturally richer than any small-group jazz I had heard before, that it had managed in some impalpable way to ignore the impasse of the Chicagoans as though the impasse had never existed, which of course for musicians like Young and Wilson, Webster and Carter, it never had, and that somehow the brave piping voice of the singer lent the music an ironic edge which seemed suddenly to bring it much closer to external realities than it had ever seemed before. Some years went by and I became a musician. The songs I had learned from Billie Holiday went, lamentably, out of fashion, apart from a few timeless pieces like "On the Sunny Side of the Street" and "Pennies From Heaven." "I Can't Get Started" was certainly popular in the scrambling, inchoate days of the New Jazz, but it was the "I Can't Get Started" of a harmonic adventurer like Dizzy Gillespie, not the "I Can't Get Started" of a soloist like Lester Young, whose inner quietism came from an instinctive understanding that his style, by the time he recorded the tune with Billie Holiday, was now an artistic constancy, beyond the petty considerations of acceptance and rejection.

The jazz of the later 1940s was the direct opposite of the pick-up music of ten years before, because it was vainly ambitious, self-consciously revolutionary, and somehow nervously aware that, arriving at a time when there were a few signs that the outside world might one day sit up and take notice, it was playing for higher stakes than any the Chicagoans or the Swing Kings had ever dreamed of. Too much of it was unrelaxed and therefore the direct antithesis of what Billie Holiday had already achieved.

All of this was quite understandable. It was precisely because of the mastery of men like Young, Wilson, Carter, Eldridge, Hodges and the rest of the sidemen of the Wilson–Holiday recordings that the generation succeeding them was inspired to dump the entire legacy of the 1930s, at least for a while, and seek the broader harmonic license that alone could enable them to escape from definitive solo patterns like Hawkins's "Body and Soul" and Lester Young's "Twelfth Street Rag." It is a process repeated in all the arts periodically. The Youngs and the Hawkinses had exhausted the form for the time being, and the only alternative to stagnation was extension of the form.

There were several unfortunate byproducts of this upsurge of activity. One of them was the eclipse of the Wilson–Holiday era, its leading figures, its conventions, even its repertoire. Practically the whole of Billie Holiday's recorded output consisted of songs which were now considered by very young men to be distinctly passé. The last word in vocal profundity was considered to be "Lover Man," a record which flattered only to deceive, for it seemed to promise the modern equivalent of Billie Holiday's vocal formula of the 1930s. On the surface the formula was indeed the same, with Parker and Gillespie playing the roles of Lester and Buck Clayton. The performance was still built around the singer. As time proved, Sarah Vaughan was soon to turn her back on this kind of jazz record, while the nearest thing to a replacement for the vintage Billie was Billie herself, now ten years older and an artist of an entirely different character, as we shall see. But when modernism first burst upon the astonished ears of a generation of jazzlovers bred on the resolving felicities of Benny Carter and Benny Goodman, the casual masterpieces of the Vocalion sessions seemed quaint in their *naïveté*.

Modernism slowly became part of the *status quo*. As the necessity for the ruthless anarchy slowly faded away, the New Jazz became absorbed into the main body of the music, as inevitably it had to be. It was no longer an outrageous joke for the new masters to borrow the material of the old ones. Miles Davis could record "Bye, Bye, Blackbird," with a perfectly straight face, even perhaps too straight a face. Once the revolution became respectable, it could afford to become reasonable too, and acknowledge officially what its leading lights had always acknowledged privately, that there was a great deal worth salvaging from the generation it had opposed so violently.

The enlightenment permeated every stratum of jazz activity, until the inevitable happened. I was working in a sextet one night in a London jazz-club when somebody produced an orchestration of "Mean to Me," complete with chord symbols. It was then, twelve years after, that it dawned upon me exactly what it was Billie Holiday had been doing with such material. The tune itself now sounded like the work of a dullard, its harmonies uninspiring, and its melody fraudulently sequential. I realized that when she recorded it in 1937, Billie Holiday had produced a version so rich in creative resource that it had instantly become for me the definitive edition, without my realizing that I had rejected anybody else's. "Mean to Me," to do it justice, is really quite a charming song, skillfully constructed and reasonably helpful to a jazz musician, but it is something vastly removed from Billie Holiday's recording of the same name.

I cannot exaggerate the shock to my musical system this one harmless orchestration caused. My emotions were a confused mixture of the indescribable rapture the professional feels when his innocence, long since forgotten, is suddenly handed back to him on a plate, and genuine bewilderment that I should have ever joined in the wholesale renunciation of the 1930s my own generation seemed to think was obligatory for playing modern jazz.

From then on my enthusiasm for Billie Holiday became a rational as well as an emotional thing, for I was now able to understand with the wisdom of hindsight what I had only vaguely sensed many years before. Of course the experience with "Mean to Me" repeated itself with many other songs in the Holiday repertoire. I had literally to learn these tunes all over again. Sometimes the wrench was too much. I never could, for instance, reorientate my thinking far enough to accept the written line of "I'll Get By," because Billie's version had for too long been the true one for me, the first version of any musical performance being the one which for obvious reasons makes the deepest impression.

And the conclusion I eventually came to was that Billie Holiday is one of the most significant jazz artists who ever lived, more significant by a thousandfold than many of the mimetic artisan craftsmen whose nuances we all strove to acquire as fashion changed, that she was one of the most remarkable natural musicians jazz has seen, so natural in fact that it is very doubtful whether she was ever fully aware of it, and that in being obliged to use words at certain pitches instead of just the pitches themselves, her unqualified artistic triumph was all the more remarkable because it required her, almost inadvertently, to prove the universality of jazz in a way no instrumentalist could possibly have done.

THE PRIMARY FACT about the career of Billie Holiday is its purity. This is a truth so obvious and so unconditional that it often tends to be overlooked, or worse, taken for granted. It is an astonishing truth when considered in the context of the musical world in which Billie Holiday lived and worked. For a woman to sing for nearly thirty years without once bowing to the demands of the world of commercial music surrounding her sounds literally impossible when we remember that most of her material was borrowed from that very world, a world that has never regarded jazz as anything much more than an undefended treasurehouse to be pillaged at leisure, with vast sums of money to be made out of sickly, bowdlerized versions.

It may, on the face of it, appear unpardonable to claim as a virtue in the jazz art an integrity taken for granted in most others. After all, to claim respect for a singer merely because she refused to commit artistic suicide seems like a very negative compliment. But it must be remembered that Billie Holiday's position was unique in that she had either to borrow the songs written for the popular market or elect not to sing anything at all. Because she had to use these songs, it was remarkable that she never succumbed to the stylistic outrages to which many of them so obligingly lend themselves. Billie Holiday was chained by circumstance to the jingles of Tin Pan Alley, explaining the perception of Charles Fox's remark that while Bessie Smith drew on the poetry of the blues, Billie Holiday had largely to create her own. It raises a vital point, this dubious material. It was the price that people like Billie Holiday had to pay for the handicap of not being household words, like Shirley Temple, Kate Smith, and Rudy Vallee. The companies for which Billie Holiday recorded required some bait to catch the unenlightened eye of the record-buying public, for Billie was never issued in the Race series of recordings that followed a prescribed racial pattern. Her work was thrown into the open market, yet another musical result of a sociological phenomenon, the urbanization of the American Negro as he moved into the industrialized areas and fought for the same fruits of city life as his white counterpart. Billie was cut from the rich poetic imagery of the blues on two counts, the lack of demand for it among the audiences on which companies like Vocalion had their eye, and her own environment. There were no cotton fields in Baltimore, but there were plenty of clubs and dance halls.

That was how Billie Holiday came to record tunes like "If You Were Mine" and "Me, Myself and I," which, left to the kind of performers for whom they were probably intended, would have been forgotten long ago. But Billie rose far above these limitations, making the instinctive adjustment between the triviality of the material and the grandeur of her own conception. It so happens that "Me, Myself and I" is one of the great vocal masterpieces of jazz.

The first Billie Holiday recording sessions may be described as a false start. They typify the levity of approach that riddles jazz history in all its phases. Of the countless songs she might have sung, Billie works over one dismal little piece called "Riffin' the Scotch," whose only virtue is its limitation to three minutes duration. Consider the situation. A young girl appears who possesses the rarest of all jazz gifts, the ability of a singer to hold her own with outstanding instrumentalists. She gets the chance to record, with musicians as distinguished as Benny Goodman and the Teagarden brothers.

The result is a lyrical outrage like "Riffin' the Scotch." It was Goodman's tune and Goodman's invitation to record, but it is depressing to think that the same man who could appreciate Billie's gifts well enough to ask her to the studio should then saddle her with some inane concoction of his own. Another instance of Goodman looking for the main chance, another phase in the campaign to "ride out the worsening depression."

The session is interesting in another way, for it was the only time Billie ever got mixed up with the older generation in a recording studio. Not that Goodman or the Teagarden brothers were old men, but they favored a style that was already in the process of being superseded. Billie was essentially a child of the Swing Age, a purveyor of art music rather than the folk poetry of Bessie Smith. Her aura was essentially that of witty stylists like Teddy Wilson. In "Riffin' the Scotch," the accompanying group represents the tail-end of a dying era rather than the early flourishes on an emergent one. The jolly extroversion of the whole accompaniment made quite the wrong setting. Jazz was passing out of the brash stage. Billie required the poise of a group more sophisticated than a Chicago ensemble with a few scored passages thrown in. It is a depressing reminder of the realities of the jazz life that the greatest singer of her generation should make her recording début with a cheapjack lyric whose final cadence is the excruciating jocosity of a cork being pulled out of a bottle.

This episode occurred in December 1933, and it was not for another eighteen months that the first masterpieces began to appear. In the summer of 1935 she recorded four sides much closer in spirit to the work she was to produce over the next ten years. Indeed these tracks are already typical of the vintage Billie Holiday. Not all of them were pitched in quite the same stylistic key, because one of them was virtually by the Benny Goodman Trio with a few extras thrown in. "Miss Brown to You" opens with brilliant interplay between Goodman and Teddy Wilson, typical of the small-group series beginning to appear about this time. The rest of the session was rather different and established a pattern for all the successful Holiday recordings of the next few years. "What a Little Moonlight Can Do" and "I Wished on the Moon" allowed great freedom of movement to the front line of Goodman, Roy Eldridge, and Ben Webster, and the result was vastly different from the background Goodman and the two Teagardens had provided for "Riffin' the Scotch." And in at least one of the four songs, "I Wished on the Moon," there was that kind of melodic literacy and lyrical imagination that the singer's talent merited.

Now the formula for this session, being typical of all those that followed in the next three or four years, is worth examining in some detail. The first important point is that usually the songs were not those one would normally expect to find in the repertoire of the jazzman of the period, due, of course, to the insistence by the business interests involved that at least the titles should mean something to a public which had never heard of Billie Holiday or Teddy Wilson. So that songs like "I Wished on the Moon" would have to be mugged up in the studio, there being no orchestration to hand upon which either the musicians or the singer cared to waste any breath.

In her autobiography, *Lady Sings the Blues,* Billie gives her own description of how these sessions were conducted. There are few more revealing passages in any book on jazz. The musicians arrived at the studio, sometimes not entirely sure who else was going to be there, but confident there would be no passengers. The selected song copy would be handed round, the chord sequence digested, and the solos meted out. There was no music and very little plan. In other words, the recordings were quite plainly jazz performances which were different from the normal live session only in that they had to be restricted to three minutes playing time. In a most touching paragraph Billie bemoans the passing of the madcap days without seeming to realize why they were gone forever:

> On a recent date I tried to do it like the old days. I'd never seen the band or the arrangements, and I didn't know the songs they had picked for me, and they wanted me to do eight sides in three hours. We were doing all standards but nobody could read the stuff; the drummer did nothing but sit there grinning; the music had wrong chords; everybody was squawking. We pushed out about nine sides like they wanted. But not a damn one of them was any good.

The clue to the difference, not only between the early Billie sessions and the later albums, but between the entire jazz scene of, say, 1937 and 1957, is contained in that remarkable phrase of Billie's, "the music had wrong chords." In the sense in which Billie evidently meant it, there is literally no such thing as a wrong chord. I am not talking now of obvious solecisms like a major third in a minor triad, or the inclusion of the major seventh in a dominant seventh chord, but of altered chords, amended chords, substituted chords and the rest of the chromatic virtuosity which colored the whole of jazz from the moment Parker and Gillespie forced themselves on to a world whose ear at first was too bigoted to listen.

The reason why the session Billie refers to was a failure had nothing to do with the ineptitude of the arrangers or indeed the grin of the drummer. It was linked to the fact that the kind of recordings for which Billie Holiday is now revered, required for their creation an implicit assumption on the part of the musicians taking part that no prearrangement was necessary because the harmonic conventions to which they were adhering were sufficiently limited to preclude any possibility of clash or confusion. The men who supported Billie in the early days were the most talented jazz musicians of their era. In such a situation, written arrangements would have been folly. The Swing Age was the last time in jazz history that the music was still free enough not to require the strategems of prearrangement. Ten years later Sarah Vaughan could not do the same thing because by now the music had lost its innocence and demanded planning of the most detailed nature.

After the "I Wished on the Moon" session, the recordings occurred regularly. A glance at the titles reveals that in theory both the singer and the instrumentalists should have been hamstrung by the mediocre quality of many of the songs. "If You Were Mine" has a chord sequence well enough suited to the diatonic days of jazz, but the lyric is only passable. "One, Two, Button Your Shoe" is a similar case, a reasonable harmonic structure but a lyric that is no more than an excuse for the counting-house gimmick. "Me, Myself and I," "If Dreams Come True," "How Could You," were none of them bad tunes, but hardly the kind of material to inspire a great artist to great performances.

Sometimes her luck was better. "These Foolish Things," "Body and Soul," "More Than You Know," "You Go to My Head," and "Easy Living" represent the higher musical reaches of the Holiday discography. But when one listens to all these recordings indiscriminately, the skillful songs and the average jingles, the peculiar truth emerges that for some reason they were all more or less as good as each other, that apparently Billie Holiday was independent of the material she used. Songs came to her as competent minor products of the popular music machine of the day, went through the treatment, and emerged as the touching expression of thoughts and emotions their composers had never dreamed of. "Me Myself and I" sung by anyone else would be no more than the slightly cretinous but not objectionable expression of the infatuation of one person for another. The Billie Holiday recording is positively joyous. It abounds with the expression of a happy, helpless love, so that the triteness of the lyric disappears to be replaced by a wit of expression whose incongruity with the original tune is almost comical.

The process is even more impressive when it takes place in a worthier song. Billie Holiday's "Summertime," recorded with an Artie Shaw struggling desperately and not quite successfully to a big bad jazzman, possesses a quality of worldliness which no other recording of the song remotely approaches. The poesy of Ira Gershwin is transmuted into the realist expression of something more resilient. "Your daddy's rich and your ma is good lookin'" has a mature felicity about it that somehow enhances the phrase beyond all measure, reducing the conventional pseudo-operatic interpretation of the song to mere pap.

The same is true of "Body and Soul" which, although it departs from the small jazz group formula of the other records, is identical in its vocal freedom. When Billie sings the words, she invests them with an intensity achieved by the childishly simple device of singing them as though she meant them. The fact that she chooses to sing the lesser-known alternate lyrics on the last middle eight, the lines that begin, "What lies before me, a future that's stormy?" suggests that she must have given close thought to the meaning of the words before singing them.

The woman herself was inclined to be a little disingenuous about this autobiographical facet of her art. "I've been told that nobody sings the word 'hunger' like I do. Or the word 'love.' Maybe I remember what those words are all about." What she means is that she knows very well that the overtones of a tragic personal life obtrude into every performance, but the curious thing is that these are not the only overtones. In some way suggestions of sweetness and light also become noticeable whenever she approaches a certain phrase or cadence.

There are two recordings from this period alive with optimism and bravery of spirit. Neither "Without Your Love" nor "Laughing at Life" sounds like the kind of song to defy the years. The lyrics in each case are competently constructed, and "Without Your Love" has a few couplets easier to criticize than they are to compose. However, anyone who looked through the song copy would expect no more than a passable vocal performance. Billie Holiday invests it with an astonishing vitality that cannot be explained away by technical analysis. Her first chorus is comparatively subdued, and gives way to solos by Teddy Wilson and Buck Clayton. But when Billie returns for the last middle eight, the performance builds to an emotional climax in which the voice transforms the melody into a exultant cry. "I'm like a plane without wings," sings Billie, and the written melody is almost abandoned. "A violin with no strings," she continues, and the performance becomes a triumphal statement.

"Laughing at Life" is a valuable performance for rather different reasons. It demonstrates the nebulous process whereby an unplanned recording magically grows out of itself, so that in the end it does indeed have a form no less firm because apparently accidental. During the first vocal chorus Lester Young complements the vocal line with a certain phrase which later appears in the last chorus as a formal riff behind the voice. When it first appears, in Lester's first-chorus accompaniment to Billie, it appears to exist for a fleeting moment before subsiding. But the idea evidently stayed inside the head of Lester, because at the end he repeats the phrase after trimming it down. The other members of the band join in and the effect lifts the vocal up on its shoulders, so to speak. Had an orchestrator attempted something similar, the phrase would have lacked the light spontaneity of the version of "Laughing With Life" we actually do possess. A successful jazz performance of this kind always lives on a knife-edge of failure until the very last cadence has been struck. The riff effect fitting so happily behind the vocal is one of those thousand-to-one shots which come off more than once with Billie Holiday because of the superlative quality of the men supporting her.

Some of these recordings from Billie's early days rank as the best jazz of their era. If the lay world, so readily fobbed off with imbecile corruptions of the term "jam session" really wants to discover something true about jazz, it has only to give a few hours of its time to the Wilson–Holiday recording of "I Must Have That Man," a side which contains the very quintessence of the jazz of the period. The sentiment of Dorothy Fields's lyric is ideally suited to the tender disillusion of Billie's delivery, so constrained as she opens the first chorus. The vocal is followed by solos from Benny Goodman, Lester Young, and Buck Clayton, which brings us to the most remarkable fact of all about this remarkable recording. Billie completes the first chorus, then retires in favor of the solosits. Depsite the greatness of the musicians involved, the listener finds himself awaiting the return of the voice, a return that on this recording never comes. It is one of the most impressive tributes to her ability that Billie Holiday was able to form a link in a chain comprised of the most gifted musicians of the period without ever allowing the tension of the performance to sag. The essence of this whole group of recordings is that the voice, besides being preoccupied with second-class light verse, is also elevated to the status of featured instrumentalist. As soon as Billie changed the formula, as in time she did, something of the integrated purity of performance was lost.

Why was the formula ever changed at all? Presumably because the professional status of the artist herself was changing. The "Summertime" session was the first to appear under the name "Billie Holiday and Her Orchestra," a studio fiction no doubt, but still some slight indication of the rising tide of recognition. That was in the summer of 1936, and by the spring of the following year, another session under the same official heading is beginning to show signs of an evolution away from the small informal jam session of earlier days. On "Where Is the Sun" and "I Don't Know If I'm Coming or Going," the instrumentation is almost identical but the musicians are cast in a far more subservient role. There is little solo time for any of them, for the performance begins and ends with the vocal, now the chief attraction.

But the change was gradual and did not become the rule for some time yet. Indeed, the greatest triumphs of the informal sessions were still to come. January 25, 1937, was a key date in jazz history because it was the first time that Billie Holiday and Lester Young recorded together. So monumental were the achievements of this partnership that we are now half-inclined to regard this whole pre-war era as one in which Billie and Lester were perpetually working together in the studios. In fact, it was not till Billie had been recording for three years that Lester made his appearance in her discography, by which time the formula for the unrehearsed method had already been evolved. Lester was not always available, possibly because of the touring commitments of the Basie band, but from now on, whenever it was possible, he appeared on every Wilson–Holiday recording date. It is worth remembering that recognition of Lester's talent was still rare in those days, another hint as to the instinctive musical acumen of a woman with no formal training or instrumental experience.

On the very first session they shared, the results were outstanding. Apart from "I Must Have That Man," so typical of the best jazz of the day, there was "He Ain't Got Rhythm," a little-known song of Irving Berlin's, on which Lester played one of the most cunningly wrought solos of his life. The lyric happened to possess just that degree of piquancy that Billie's voice could express so naturally. The time values she gives to the word "equator" and her slightly unusual pronunciation of "aviator" with which it rhymes, makes the whole phrase sound far wittier than it really is. Billie's insistence that her phrasing was strongly influenced by Lester's instrumental mannerisms is borne out by another track from the same session, "This Year's Kisses," where Lester states the melody with that bland elegance reflected later when Billie starts to sing.

From then on, the Billie–Lester antiphonies flowed from the studios with astonishing consistency. "I'll Never Be the Same" is one of the most skillful of all because it demonstrates a facet of the Holiday style that may have been born of either of two factors, or perhaps a combination of both. Instead of singing the written melody over the first two bars of the second half of the first chorus, Billie dispenses with the phrase, which is unexpectedly chromatic, employing instead a simple device of her own. The whole impact of the first phrase is changed. In the original the line "I'll never be the same" contains a furious activity, but Billie amends it to a single note repeated to accommodate the syllables of the phrase. It was a similar gambit to the one she used in "I'll Get By," recorded earlier the same year, although the latter was so drastically amended that for a bar or two one is not quite sure she is not singing a different song from the one named on the label.

Now this paraphrasing of the written melody in a instrumental manner was sometimes due to the limitations of her range. "I'll Get By," for instance, has unusually generous intervals spanning its opening few bars, and it is very possible that Billie Holiday, always very much a middle-of-the-register singer, felt more comfortable compressing the range of the song rather than impose upon herself the slightest element of the wrong kind of strain, or have the musicians fishing around for appropriate keys. On the other hand, I believe that the kind of paraphrase to be found in "I'll Never Be the Same," which typifies all her work, has artistic rather than technical origins. Billie Holiday was removing the odium of a slightly precocious phrase, replacing it with one that is alive with all the candor and apparent simplicity of much of the best jazz.

There is one recording from this period where the considerations of range really did cause her some hard thinking, so that on "I Cried for You," encompassing a jump of a major ninth in its first three bars, the group plays jazz first. Johnny Hodges gives a masterly statement of the theme which departs from the written line without ever ceasing to pay it deference, before Teddy Wilson plays an impeccable four-bar modulation taking the key down a minor third for the convenience of the singer. Somebody like Sarah Vaughan would never have to resort to such tactics, which is why she is able to sing a tune like "Poor Butterfly," again with a demanding range, without resorting to the anti-climactic device of dropping down an octave to avoid a crisis of pitch. But what handicap is a restricted range when the act of compression can achieve such felicities as the remolding of the first phrase of "I'll Never Be the Same" or the complete recasting of the melodic line of "I'll Get By"?

Much later in her career, when the ravages of a desperately unhappy life were beginning to tell, her range shrank much more seriously, so that in singing old standbys like "Body and Soul" and "These Foolish Things," she dropped her key by a tone or sometimes more. But by then her voice had changed so profoundly in character that she was a different kind of artist altogether. The great virtue of the recordings from the first period was their heart-lifting optimism, a certain buoyancy of spirit which made the listener feel an affinity for a disembodied sound whose owner he might never have heard of before. I am convinced that for much of the time Billie was not consciously aware of what she was doing while she was doing it. To her, singing was not so much the exercise of an artistic function as the natural means of expression towards the world. This relationship involving the mechanics of making music is common enough among the best instrumentalists, but certainly no singer since Bessie Smith could be said to need to sing as desperately as Billie Holiday. The casual effects she threw off would be psychological masterstrokes had they been thought out and planned ahead. As it was, they remained emphatic triumphs of intuition.

One of the most affecting examples occurs in the Holiday recording of "What Shall I Say?," a deceptively simple-sounding little melody with one of those invisible dynamos built into it so that one has only to play it as written with a modicum of rhythmic understanding to produce a reasonable jazz performance. In the lyric the following lines occur:

What shall I say when the phone rings
and somebody asks for you?
They don't know I ask for you too.
What shall I say?

The vowel sounds at the end of the second and third lines could be awkward to sing. The word "you" is included twice, but with obviously different stresses, and at very different points in the line. Moreover, the second "you" occurs immediately before the word rhyming with the first "you." It is not a clumsily written lyric, but it might have been constructed with rather more consideration for the singer than the writer has shown. There are a dozen ways round the problem. Billie Holiday's is the best, as well as the simplest of all. She pronounces the first "you" in the normal way, doing the same with the word "too" which rhymes with it. The second "you" she simply changes to "ya," thus eliminating any danger of idiotically echoing vowel sounds.

But the mere technical process is not what is important. Probably Billie never even considered it. She must have come to the amendment of the second "you" by an entirely different path, and when we listen to the recording it is very obvious where that path lay. When the second "you" occurs, changed to a "ya," the whole performance suddenly stops being a formal musical exercise and instead confronts the listener with a human statement, directed specifically at whoever happens to be present. There is an amazing colloquial candor about that second "you," born of the ability of the woman singing it to make the tritest lyric a valid statement of emotional experience. When "ya" appears, one suddenly realizes with a disturbed shock of surprise, that Billie is experiencing the lyric dramatically as well as musically, so that the finished product has a depth of sensitivity unknown to other women singers since Bessie Smith.

Sometimes the ability to make a certain phrase, or word, or perhaps just a syllable, shine with a fresh luster, seems to be a lucky shot in the dark, but it is really part of a system no less comprehensive because it happens to be subconscious. Billie Holiday, who never suggested she might know of factors in a poetic performance like manic overtones, had an infallible instinct for evoking these overtones every time she stepped up to a microphone. In "Blame It on the Weather," an obscure pop song recorded in January 1939, with Wilson, Benny Carter, and Roy Eldridge, she sings the phrase, "they'll see through me like glass," delivering the last word in such a way as to rehabilitate it, investing it with all its translucent qualities. The word flashes and shimmers with a crystalline brilliance, transmuting a commonplace simile into a shaft of genuine poetry. This ability to restore to tired words the vitality they once had, abounds throughout her work and is the key to several truths about her style, especially its inimicability.

There are surprisingly few instances where she actually creates a specific melodic phrase of the kind one used to find in the quaint old series, "Fifty Hot Licks." Her improvisations can hardly ever be torn out of context because they are rather affairs of stresses of syllables, subtleties of phrasing, regrouping of notes. None of her inventions are as elaborate or as ambitious as, say, Sarah Vaughan's celebrated version of "Body and Soul," which is better compared with instrumental versions like those of Hawkins and Red Allen than it is with Billie Holiday's. The Sarah Vaughan "Body and Soul" is highly ingenious rather than inspired. It accepts the challenge of modern harmony with brilliant resource, but it reeks of the midnight oil in a way that none of Billie Holiday's performances ever did. The difference between them is the difference between a perfect abstraction and a slice of humanism.

Now and then a whole phrase does leap out of its context into the memory purely as a fragment of musical invention, like the rephrasing of the notes of "a telephone that rings" in the 1952 version of "These Foolish Things," recorded with one of the JATP concert parties. More typical is the way she remolds an entire song, flattening a phrase here, stretching a time value there, reducing the arpeggio phrases to the very bone, slipping in a grace note which just so happens to be one of the most important harmonies of the chord.

In "One, Two, Button Your Shoe," made in the vintage days with Bunny Berigan and Irving Fazola, she virtually abandons the written line completely, using the harmonies whose names she did not know, to build a new, sleeker melodic line which reduced the number of pitches by more than half, until a phrase like "tell me you get a thrill," originally linked syllable by syllable to the arpeggio of the major seventh with the major sixth thrown in to make up the number, emerges through the voice simply as the actual note of the major seventh and not its arpeggio, repeated four times, exactly as Lester Young might have played it, or any competent jazzman of experience. The next phrase is identical except that the major seventh chord now becomes the dominant seventh, whereupon Billie promptly performs the same trick a semitone lower, giving form to her variations just as though she had swotted up the harmonies from the textbooks the night before, when really she is trusting to her ear and her taste.

No jazz musician, whether he uses his vocal chords or an instrumental keyboard, can be taught this kind of invention. It is the fruit of instinct wedded to experience, and therefore remains exclusively the possession of the man who spends most of his life weaving instrumental patterns round chord sequences. From people with no instrumental training it is unfair even to expect it, which is why Billie Holiday is unique in all the annals of jazz.

Because of the apparently nebulous nature of this art of making jazz, a process impossible to convey by teaching or by writing down in congruous terms, or even recognizable without a certain sympathy in the mind and heart of the observer, there are very few technicalities by which the theorists can blind us with their science when discussing Billie Holiday's singing. M. Hodeir may potter about indefinitely preaching to be converted and terrifying everybody else by the diabolonian cunning with which he computes the mathematical processes which go into the making of a jazz record, but his method founders in the face of a performance by Billie Holiday. There is nothing to compute, no inversions to detect, no daring passing chords to recognize by name, none of the contents of the usual box of vocal tricks which may easily be defined according to the rules of discord and resolution. There are a few Holiday mannerisms reducible to academic terms, but far less than in the case of the two contemporaries whom most people mistakenly regard as her closest rivals, Ella Fitzgerald and Sarah Vaughan.

One habit in particular of Billie's has a wry relevance to her art because many people who know of it misconstrue it as a serious deficiency and even a source of embarrassment. On recordings spanning her entire career, Billie has a habit of falling away from the pitch of a note soon after she arrives at it. I have heard this device cited as proof of her inability to hold a note long enough to establish its pitch. But the musician who listens carefully to these falls soon notices that far from being technical solecisms, they are musically correct effects enhancing the dramatic impact of the lyric. It is not by accident that every time Billie falls away from these notes, she allows the fall to continue just so far and then arrests it—at the next note down in the arpeggio of the relevant chord. She was especially partial to this effect when the chord in question was a diminished seventh, probably because her instinct told her that the intervals between the notes of that chord, all minor thirds, were not so broad that they might sound too protracted. This fall is one of her devices in the transmutation of "I'll Never Be the Same," on the phrase, "a lot that a smile may hide."

However, this description of what is after all an elementary trick of improvisation does not do justice to the artist, because once again the device was a means to an end, the end being the expression of a kind of fatality in the world she sang about. The fall would express a wry sense of philosophic despair, as though even the happy songs were wise in the knowledge of sadder lyrics and sadder lives. There is a profound difference between this kind of stylistic sophistication and the harmonic dexterity of Ella Fitzgerald which, being an end in itself, finally reduces the art of singing to the decadence of gibberish. Instead of aspiring to establish the voice as a second-class instrumental keyboard, the singer should attempt to raise it to the highest jazz level because of its potential value in expressing specific ideas and emotions rather than the impressionistic gestures of most instrumental jazz. The gibberish vocal makes a mockery of communication instead of exalting it. The thought of Billie Holiday indulging in such antics is too far from reality to be considered for more than a moment. It is useless your analysts telling you that Ella Fitzgerald or Sarah Vaughan can follow the most intricate chord sequence through to the ultimate flattened fifth in the final tonic chord, hitting resolution after resolution with the same correctitude as any suburban music teacher. When the emotional content is nil, all the correctitude in the world will not save the performance from artistic damnation, an observation that applies more than ever in the world of modern jazz, with its daunting harmonic complexities and its pathetic pursuit of legitimate acceptance.

In the early 1940s Billie Holiday's career entered on the second of its three phases. Gradually the small-group formula was cast aside, being replaced by an accompanying orchestra playing decorous arrangements, neatly rehearsed and carefully tailored to meet the demands of the singer. The implication was quite clear. Billie Holiday was now the star. No longer was she one of a group of jazzmen creating variations on written themes. The voice was now the focal point, apart from a few fragments thrown the way of the soloist, like Roy Eldridge's masterly eight bars in "Body and Soul," used as a buffer between the end of the first chorus and the introduction into the performance of the alternate lyrics to the middle eight. From the purist point of view these recordings have nothing like the value of the earlier masterpieces, which had Billie to offer and half a dozen others besides. But judged strictly as vocal performances they show no noticeable decline from the sessions of the middle 1930s.

I mention "Mandy Is Two" because it bears such forcible testimony to Billie's talent for endowing any old jingle with the grace of art. The lyric is a piece of sentimentality of the worst kind, difficult to endure without resort to rabelaisian noises. Its conquest by Billie Holiday is symbolic of her whole career. By showing she could make such songs valid in the jazz context, she was demonstrating in the most dramatic way that there is no material that cannot be used as jazz material if the artist involved is gifted enough, and that triteness itself, pitifully inferior to the realist beauty of the words Bessie Smith sang, may be invested with an emotional depth to move the most hardened of cynics.

Billie, was, in fact, annexing a huge area of musical experience on behalf of jazz. She was reclaiming all the land of the popular song. Of course she was not the first to attempt this. Musicians had been borrowing silly jingles and making great jazz out of them for two generations. She was not even the first singer to do this. Louis Armstrong had actually made "Song of the Islands" sound something like the real thing. But Billie was the first figure in jazz whose entire career was concerned with this type of performance of this type of material. She was dealing in the medium of words all the time, so that no matter how prejudiced you might be towards jazz, no matter how indifferent you were to the pathos of its cadences, you could at least understand what it was this woman was singing about.

Usually she was singing about love, one of the two subjects in the world about which everybody in the world professes to be an expert. (The other is music.) She took these songs far more seriously than anyone else dreamed of doing. To other singers they were the excuse for standing up and simulating a few emotional platitudes. To audiences they bore no relationship to reality at all, being the incidental music of a dream world where unrequited love wept crocodile tears, all expressed in mediocre verse. To the men who wrote the songs, they were factory products, designed to live for a few moments and then be cast aside, so that their component parts might be broken down and redesigned in fresh permutations. When Billie Holiday hit upon songs like "I've Got a Date with a Dream" or "Please Keep Me in Your Dreams" the tunesmiths of Tin Pan Alley got more than they had ever bargained for and certainly more than they deserved.

The use of more formal musical settings for her recordings raises a point about Billie Holiday which may never effectively be answered. In 1941 Lester Young made his last recordings with her. Many factors must have contributed towards this split. It was the period when Lester was severing his connections with the Basie band. It was also the time when Billie was sufficiently established, at least with a small coterie audience, to record under her own name. And possibly more important than either of these factors, the Swing Age was slowly grinding to a halt. In retrospect we can see quite clearly that during the early 1940s the Wilson–Young–Eldridge axis was gradually being replaced as the advance guard of jazz. The arrivistes Parker and Gillespie were soon to make the work of the Wilson generation so quaint in its comparative innocence that its eventual appeal was destined to be the elusive charm of a period piece. The era of the small jazz group busking away in the recording studio without much of a plan to guide the musician, was slowly becoming no more than a glorious chapter of the past.

However, the assessment of these factors soon becomes impossible, because the most dominant fact of all is one which by its very nature cannot be measured with any accuracy. The romance between Billie and Lester is one of those rare exquisite moments when melodrama and prosaic reality reach out and touch for a while. It is a truism of jazz history that the partnership with Lester Young, personal as well as professional, was the most vital association of Billie Holiday's career. It proved to be a working romance which was unusually fruitful, as connoisseurs well know. Were its two central figures artists of the same magnitude in any other sphere, then the task of the biographer would be eased considerably. But the mature approach to this kind of situation is consistently lacking in the jazz world, almost as though in the final reckoning the musicians were too self-conscious about the artistic possibilities of what they were doing to accept their own place with complete *savoir-faire.* It is understandable enough that nobody will ever read *The Collected Letters of Billie Holiday* or *The Private Correspondence of Lester Young,* so it is left for the curious to wonder about the possible clues to the nature of the close friendship of the period's most remarkable singer and instrumentalist.

It is too tempting to draw the obvious conclusions, to say that the two careers became one and were therefore never the same after the parting. Or that Lester's uncanny knack of complementing Billie's vocal phrases with his own aphorisms was the result not just of musical instinct, but of musical instinct enhanced by the passion of a love affair. There is a remarkable parallelism in both the rate and nature of their artistic declines that might be more than coincidence. But, then, Lester's oblique instrumental comments on a vocal performance may just as easily be found behind Jimmie Rushing as Billie Holiday, and nobody has suggested that Lester ever felt unduly romantic about Jimmie Rushing. What failure there was in the careers of each of them seems to have been a failure of temperament, not the failure to meet a romantic crisis.

Neither Lester nor Billie said anything very substantial about the effect of their relationship on their work together. Each one bore for the rest of his professional career the nickname the other concocted, and Billie did say, several times, that she always felt happier about a session when she knew Lester would be present. In her own words:

> For my money Lester was the world's greatest. I loved his music, and some of my favorite recordings are the ones with Lester's pretty solos. . . . Lester sings with his horn; you listen to him and can almost hear the words. People think he's so cocky and secure, but you can hurt his feelings in two seconds. I know, because I found out once that I had. We've been hungry together, and I'll always love him and his horn.

Her reference to the vocal overtones of Lester's style establishes beyond reasonable doubt that there was some artistic as well as emotional interdependence. Lester's whimsy about always thinking of the lyrics to a song when you were improvising on it, is worth considering also. It is fair to assume that on recordings like "Laughing at Life," "Without Your Love," "Me, Myself and I," "Mean to Me," and "Time on My Hands," on all of which Lester displays an instinct of what Billie is going to sing that is almost psychic, there were moments where the warmth of a private liaison spilled over on to the grooves of the record. Whatever anyone cares to imagine, the antiphony they created remains unmatched in all jazz, ranking among the rarest delights the music has to offer.

The tragic decline of Billie Holiday's fortunes in the last years of her life is another of those commonplaces of jazz criticism about which nothing new of any relevance to the music can be said. The same element of self-destruction that shadowed the life of Charlie Parker is evident in Billie's career. Nobody has any illusions about the terrifying inroads on her talent made by the way she chose to live.

Because her recognition, like Lester's, was a belated one, there is a tendency to revere anything she did in the last years of her life, to ignore conveniently the fact that by the middle 1950s she had hardly any voice left at all. This decay may be charted in every detail throughout the recordings she has left us, but before it began to be serious, and after the break with Lester, she cut several more outstanding tracks, in some of which can be noted a brave attempt to behave as though time were not racing ahead at all. The sessions with Eddie Heywood are a case in point. "How Am I to Know" shows her amending arpeggio phrases once again into a flatter line while still suggesting the framework of the original tune by stressing the more prominent of the harmonies. "I'll Be Seeing You" shows how she could take a popular ballad, admittedly of a superior kind, and transform it into something so touching that nobody who knows the recording can take anyone else's version very seriously.

"On the Sunny Side of the Street," recorded with a rhythm section led by Heywood in April 1944, demonstrates the instrumental nature of her thought. The opening phrases of the first theme, containing the words, "Take your coat and take your hat," and "Can't you hear that pitter pat?," make use of only three notes in the diatonic scale, and are reminiscent of the remarkable phrase Lester played in his Aladdin recording of the same song a little later, when he makes a fall of an octave in the most unexpected place.

Throughout the 1940s Billie continued to make records which although they were distinct in character from the pre-war hit-or-miss classics, were unmatched in their field, then and now. The more commercial nature of the orchestral backing may have won them a slightly wider fringe audience than she usually commanded, but the songs themselves compromise not a single crochet in their suitability to her style. "Good Morning, Heartache," with its rise from minor to major in its first eight bars, is typical Holiday material. But the side I usually associate with this period and this type of recording is "Crazy He Calls Me," which, besides having an amusing lyric and an unusual melodic line, happens to possess a certain relevance to Billie's attitude towards her lovers in private life. In "Lady Sings the Blues," there is more than one echo of the futile devotion of this song.

The divine spark died very hard. Almost to the end she was capable of producing the kind of vocal vitality that can carry an entire accompanying group, as she did in a heroic version of "All of Me," recorded with one of the earliest JATP groups. As late as 1955 in "Please Don't Talk About Me When I'm Gone," she eclipses Benny Carter, Harry Edison, and Barney Kessell in the buoyancy of her delivery, producing another colloquial effect that lends an unexpected edge to the words. At the opening of the second eight she sings "listen," dropping the second syllable an octave in a manner so casual that for a moment the performance ceases to be vocal and becomes speech instead. Both these tracks revive to some extent the glories of earlier times, with their rough insistence that jazz is a down-to-earth affair, making a strange contrast with the tonal felicities of Sarah Vaughan's commercial output and Ella Fitzgerald's faithful deadpan transcriptions of the Songbooks.

In the last two or three years of her life the songs she chose to record were usually sad ballads whose lyrics time and again forced even the most objective of listeners to see parallels with her private life, for by now her technique was so ravaged by physical decline that she was by all the normal rules no longer qualified to sing any song demanding sustained notes and skilled control. But the normal rules applied to her no more at the end of her life than they had in the beginning. Whatever shortcomings there might now be in her breathing, her range, and her pronunciation, she had retained, because it was a very real part of her personality, this unfailing ability to wrest out of every lyric the last drop of significance, and even to insert her own where the lyricist had failed to include it. As this was the very core of her art, the last recordings overcame their own technical limitations in a miraculous way.

The British edition of *The Billie Holiday Memorial* issued by Fontana, inadvertently demonstrates this. The album is made up of recordings from the pre-war period, except for the last track of all, made within a year of her death. "For All We Know" is yet another song whose lyrics might be a personal statement as well as a vocal recitation. At first the contrast between this croaking, middle-aged voice and the purity of the young hopeful girl of "On the Sentimental Side" is truly frightening. It all sounds like a clinical demonstration of the suffering and unhappiness of a woman whose life ended in circumstances as wretched as any person's could. There seems to be nothing left of a wonderful talent. But more detailed listening suggests that in its way, "For All We Know" is the most moving statement on the whole album, not simply the grisly evidence of the decline and fall of a once-great artist.

All the ballad performances of these last years must be approached in the same way. They must not be evaluated according to the normal rules of the vocal game, because to Billie Holiday it never was a game. Whether or not she was able to curb her mannerisms of style, now becoming parodies of themselves, whether or not she was aware she might be making a public confessional of her own decay, whether or not her breath was too short and the bar-lengths too long, or the control of her now drunken vibrato painfully ineffectual, she knew she was echoing the same lyrical sentiments she had expressed twenty-five years before. The raw material of the words had maintained their constancy, while the most vital facet of her art, the ability to make those lyrics sound profound, had not deserted her.

Performances like "For All We Know" must therefore be accepted as recitative with musical accompaniment rather than as ordinary singing. This is admittedly special pleading but it is entered on behalf of a very special jazz musician, and is in fact perfectly justified. It is always disastrous to present a record like "For All We Know" to somebody who, being unaware of the details of the life and career of the singer, merely accepts it as another song by another crooner and finds, quite naturally, that the performance is excruciatingly bad, just as a prospective furniture buyer seeking polished walnut would recoil in horror from the trunk of an oak tree. By the criteria of that person, Billie's voice would impress only by its complete inadequacy to cope with technical problems that half the technicolored sopranos of Hollywood could master without a thought, and usually do.

But Billie's technical decline did not matter. In a way it actually made her one supreme virtue more evident than ever. At the very end she was barely capable of singing at all in the conventional sense. Her range had shrunk to unmanageable proportions. Her diction unconsciously parodied the girlish delights of the 1930s. Her breathing was labored. Of actual tunefulness, melodiousness, or whatever we care to call the beguiling rise and fall of the line of a melody, there was almost none.

The trappings were stripped away, but where the process would normally leave only the husk of a fine reputation, it only exposed to view, once and for all, the true core of her art, her handling of a lyric. If the last recordings are approached with this fact in mind, they are seen to be, not the insufferable croakings of a woman already half-dead, but recitatives whose dramatic intensity becomes unbearable, statements as frank and tragic as anything throughout the whole range of popular art.

In view of this, it is understandable that the more ambitious the lyric, the more effective its delivery by Billie Holiday was likely to be, and that any song involving the pathos of pastness, the relentless advance of time and nostalgic understanding of the transient nature of experience, would sorely tempt us to equate it with the facts of Billie's life. Thus, "Speak Low," a song of rare sensitivity in its approach to the subject of the transience of love, takes on a further dimension when Billie sings it, becoming an authentic statement by the middle-aged on the brevity of youth. Each of the phrases, "Everything ends, the curtain descends," "love is pure gold and time a thief," "our summer day withers away," "our moment is swift," and above all the reiteration of the phrase "too soon" spring to life as they do under the touch of no other singer. So does one come across Don Pedro's words, "Speak low if you speak love" from *Much Ado About Nothing,* through the medium of jazz music and a dying woman. The depth of the performance is here indisputable, as we forget for a moment about singing in its conventional technical sense and hear instead someone using the jazz idiom to convey, subconsciously or otherwise, the story of a life which, for all its towering artistic achievements, was ravaged by self-indulgence and finally destroyed by drug addiction.

Billie Holiday's gift of treating a lyric leads us finally to the most daunting speculation of all. If her touch was infallible, as it certainly seems to have been, what might have happened had the songs of her life been cast more artistically, or written with a finer sensitivity, or dealt with a range of subjects a little broader than the encroaching horizons of unrequited love? Naturally there must have been a limit to the range and depth of her expression, which was no doubt suitably employed when singing of the love of a woman for a man. Such themes were the very quiddity of her personality. But there is one incident in her career that gives us a strong hint of what might have been, where the lyric moves away for a moment from the boudoir and the "two-by-four" she sings of in "He's Funny That Way," and concerns itself with one of the crucial themes of the twentieth century.

Most of Billie's best-known songs concern the inhumanity of men towards women. "Strange Fruit" deals with the inhumanity of men towards man. It is a bitter and ironic comment on a race murder, worlds removed from the asinine demimonde of gay amours and faithless lovers to which most popular singers are committed. Much is written about jazz as the music of social protest, but it is sometimes difficult today to see how it is protesting, or what it is protesting about, and to whom, especially now that it has purchased, at the price of its own blood, an evening dress suit, swopping its candor for respectability. In "Strange Fruit" the mask is off and for a few minutes jazz is being specific.

I do not know whether, according to the peculiar lights of the purists,

"Strange Fruit" by Billie Holiday is a jazz record. I do not know, or care, whether there are those who will shuffle uncomfortably and point out that "Strange Fruit" is politically "committed," and therefore no work of art at all. What I do know is that it would have been lamentable had a woman of her talent not grappled at least once in her life with so universal a theme. In so doing, she proved yet again that jazz music can extend its boundaries far wider than many of its patrons realize, and that there is literally no subject not fair game for the jazz singer provided she happens to be a Bessie Smith or a Billie Holiday.

For the whole point about Billie's "Strange Fruit" is that the effectiveness of the performance lies not in the lyric but in its expression by a jazz singer. The effect could only have been gained by an artist steeped in the very quintessence of the jazz art all her life. The rise and fall of the phrases, the shaping of the words, the feeling for a dying cadence and the occasional slight amendment or variation of the melody, these are the exclusive weapons of the jazz artist. No other musician can possibly have access to them. They are, indeed, all that the jazz musician has to offer the world of music at large, and they cannot be acquired to quite the same degree in any other kind of musical environment. Certainly they cannot be reduced to a formula and sold at a guinea an hour, as some musicians attempt to do. If the jazz musician, in his preoccupation with the conquest of harmony, forfeits these weapons, then he is behaving like the ship's captain who tore up the keel to make fuel for the engines.

I believe that when Billie Holiday sings the phrase "pastoral scene of the gallant South," civilization has said its last word about the *realpolitik* of racial discrimination in all its forms and degrees. The resigned bitterness and contempt with which Billie throws out the phrase, leaves nothing else to be said. And the bitterness and contempt are rendered by someone who knew the hard truth of discrimination, even in its less deadly forms.

There was once a film produced in Hollywood called *New Orleans.* It was no better and no worse than all the other films from Hollywood involving jazz music in one way or another. In other words, it was an insult to reasonable intelligence, a slur upon the artistry of every jazz musician who ever strode from the dominant to the tonic without falling flat on his face, a lie sold to gullible audiences at two and threepence a throw. The plot has passed into merciful oblivion, where it came from in the first place, but one well-remembered detail is that the heroine was a great singer who had a ladies' maid. The great singer had a voice like an understudy at a suburban operatic society. The ladies' maid was played by Billie Holiday. The incident is humorously recounted in *Lady Sings the Blues,* and ends with the comment, "I never made another movie. And I'm in no hurry."

Her death occurred within a few months of the death of Lester Young, and since then the best work of both of them has been made available in memorial albums. Valuable as these collections undoubtedly are, there is only one way to appraise Billie's career with any justice, the same way as one appraises Lester Young's, in strict chronological order. And at each stage of the journey, the listener should administer upon himself the corrective of the corresponding work of contemporaries like Goodman, Ellington, Hawkins, and Basie.

This kind of diligence reveals the fairly natural division of the Holiday career into three parts; the first, covering roughly the pre-war period, produced infinitely the best jazz, largely because the conventions of the day were in perfect harmony with the talents of the musicians expressing them; the second saw Billie emerging as the leading attraction of each performance, eliminating a great deal of the instrumental virtuosity going on in the background; the third traced her melodramatic fall into a premature grave during a time when she recorded a series of vocal performances, hardly vocal performances at all, which, despite their academic crudities, stand as heart-searing evocations of the jazz spirit.

Throughout this career the material is drawn almost exclusively from outside the jazz world, which is essentially an instrumental world and cannot by its very nature produce good vocal material, any more than a Beethoven can induce a trombone to deliver verbal addresses. For the strange truth is that theoretically there is no such thing as a jazz singer. The very phrase is a contradiction in terms. The reason is the same one as the reason why there is no such thing as a two-hundred-year-old man. It takes too long. Life is too short for the production of either phenomenon. The jazz singer, were she to exist, would have to have all the intimacy with the abstract world of harmonic patterns which only a practicing instrumentalist can ever acquire. She must be able not only to sense the dramatic beauty of the resolution of the dominant seventh chord built on the mediant of the scale, as Billie does when she reaches the second bar of "On the Sunny Side of the Street," but to understand how such an effect is achieved, when it is grammatically permissible to achieve it, and how best to adjust the time-values of the syllables of the lyric, if and when she meets the other requirements. For it is the grossest fallacy to regard a girl who sings merely as an instrumentalist who happens to be using her vocal chords instead of a keyboard. Singing of that kind, which Duke Ellington used to set up for Kay Davis, belongs in an entirely different category, one of relatively minor importance, by the very nature of the fact that the Kay Davis effect possesses neither the resonance of an instrument nor the ability to convey specific ideas through the medium of language.

In a way the singer has a far harder task than any instrumentalist. The player who would improvise is limited only by the movement of harmony from bar to bar. He can use as many or as few notes as he pleases, so long as he lives by the inexorable rules of resolution governing whichever convention of jazz he happens to have been raised on. Not so the singer who, in addition to her subservience to the harmonies, has also to pay tribute to the number of syllables in each bar. If she decides to defy the syllabic content, she finds herself faced with one of three dilemmas, each more terrifying than the other.

She may find herself obliged to stretch out a vowel sound like a piece of elastic, repeating it at several pitches until the time duration for that vowel sound is fulfilled. Ella Fitzgerald often does this, and although she does it with technical expertise, the point of the matter has not the remotest connection with technical expertise. If a singer indulges in the Elastic approach, she may, when singing "All the Things You Are," find herself confronted with the awkward fact that the first word of the lyric, "You," occupies the first four beats of the song, the whole first bar, so that if she is to attempt the same skill as the musician does, at shaping phrases based on a harmonic underpinning, she is going to have to keep saying the word "you" until the first bar is over. If, as is likely, she discovers that the chord which gives light and shade to that word is the relative minor common chord of the key, she will very likely sing the three notes of that triad, top them off with the root an octave lower, allow one crochet to each note, thus filling in the correct time value of her first bar, and intone the sound "Yoo-Hoo-Hoo-Hoo." As instrumental jazz the effect is poor. As vocal jazz it is even worse, because it is placing an inoffensive little vowel sound on the rack of protraction and keeping it there until the metronome sounds the moment of release.

Very often the singer, who works her way into this beguiling but deadly trap, makes a desperate attempt to work her way out of it again by finally refusing to acknowledge the sovereignty of words at all. Now she is free. Now she can create patterns in no way inferior to the creations of musicians, except that, lacking the experience and craftsmanship which comes with the struggle for mastery over a tangible keyboard, she will lack also the good taste that usually comes with this ability. But at least she is now free. At what cost? A hair-raising one, reduction of the English language to absurdity, all on the pretext of making the human voice sound like an instrument. Singers who really desire the status of an instrument should stop making life difficult for themselves and everyone else within earshot, and learn to play one, just as the reactionaries who insist that every instrumentalist ought to simulate the sound of the human voice should have their vocal chords removed and a trombone rammed down their gullets instead.

Gibberish vocals are the price the singer has to pay for this freedom to move about the realms of discord and resolution without the attendant drudgery of keyboard practice. No matter whether the gibberish is grammatically correct as with Ella Fitzgerald, or positively ingenious, as with Sarah Vaughan, it will still be gibberish whose emotive content is roughly nil, because it is hampered by all the drawbacks of the voice in jazz while abandoning its one great advantage, the achievement of catharsis through the use of familiar words and familiar combinations of words.

There is a third way by which the singer might grant herself this limitless freedom without resorting to gibberish, and that is to sing original lyrics to her own improvisations, always keeping in mind the distinction between the authentic jazz vocal and all other variations, from the recitation of jazz-with-poetry to nonsensical shooby-dooby tongue-wagging. The distinction is this. The jazz vocal, if it is not to deliquesce into a gooey pool at the singer's feet, must for most of the time have one verbal sound for each note. The first bar of "All the Things You Are," which has one note, has only one syllable, while the first bar of "Carolina in the Morning," whose number of beats is the same, comprises not one semi-breve but eight quavers and has therefore been provided, most thoughtfully, by Gus Kahn with the eight vowel sounds, "Nothing could be fi-ner than to."

It is now that the enormity of what Billie Holiday was attempting begins to become apparent. For the last of the three alternatives, the composition of the singer's own words to match the movements of her own improvisations, has two painful riders. First, she must take care never to be maneuvered into an impromptu performance, because she must always be limited to the number of verbal compositions she has managed to complete. Second, she had better have the skill of the lyricists whose words she is superseding, if she is not to be jeered out of court for vandalism. Annie Ross half-managed to do this, but her best recordings were not wholly self-supporting because the starting-point was always somebody else's solo, in its way more disastrous than trying to improve on Ira Gershwin and Lorenz Hart. There can have been few more telling exhibitions of inadvertent musical folly than John Hendrick's diseased-hip lyrics to Charlie Parker's solo on "Now's the Time." Anita O'Day will be remembered as the brave spirit who attempted a jazzbo-doggerel edition of Cole Porter's lyrics to "You're the Top." The double-talk marathons of Ella Fitzgerald and Sarah Vaughan, amusing and skillful though they may be, have nothing to do with the art of remolding a melody without at the same time strangling its lyrics.

What has all this to do with Billie Holiday? Everything, because she happens to have been the only woman singer of the past thirty years who achieved the impossible. Unless we understand what she was attempting, we cannot attempt to decide whether she succeeded and whether it was worth succeeding at. By a fortuitous combination of natural endowment and accidental circumstance, of environment and heredity, she actually did possess this rarest of all jazz instincts, the sense of form. She may have acquired it through early indoctrination with the work of Louis Armstrong and Bessie Smith. She may have inherited it from her father, Clarence Holiday, who once worked in the Fletcher Henderson Orchestra. Probably she was born with it. She was that freak thing, the born or natural musician. Had she been a man, she would surely have taken to instrumental improvisation as naturally as Teddy Wilson did, or Lester Young or any of the rest of her early collaborators. It is impossible to teach a girl what Billie could do, and even if it were it would take a lifetime to teach it. She just happened to have the natural musician's ear for harmonic movement combined with the actor's aptitude for word combinations. Plunged as she was, virtually from birth, into a jazz environment, her singing possessed an extraordinary validity intensified by the fact that throughout a tempestuous life she experienced on a personal level all the situations used as themes in the lyrics of the songs she sang.

That is why it is artistic suicide for any other singer to attempt a facsimile, even were she to possess the same musical instinct. Billie Holiday's great performances are the fruit of her experience of her own life. The performances of her imitators are the fruit of their experience of Billie Holiday.

Cult of the White Goddess

Will Friedwald

Friedwald's 1990 book Jazz Singing *is the fullest and finest consideration we have or are likely to get of the art of jazz singing. This chapter deals primarily with the three major white women singers of the thirties and early forties: Mildred Bailey, Connee Boswell, and Lee Wiley.*

You sing . . . the way Bix played.

—Bud Freeman to Lee Wiley (as reported by Wiley in an interview with Richard Lamparski)

White goddesses were as essential to the big-band era as brass, reed, and rhythm sections. They decorated the fronts of swing bands like the figureheads on a ship, and no bandleader who wanted to fill dance halls or sell records dared go on the road without one.

As late as 1929, however, no such creatures existed. Men sang on dance-band records and you might go through two dozen sides before you found one with a girl singer. A few vocalists in the late twenties used small, sometimes hot bands to back them, but of these only Annette Hanshaw herself sang anything resembling jazz. The classic blues singers would eventually influence later generations of singers (and Bessie Smith was even making a comeback shortly before her death), but as a genre, they were never deader than they were in the early thirties. The double onslaught of Crosby and Armstrong had pushed women aside, and the earliest ones to assimilate the new style were men.

How, then, did it get to the point where it is now—where singing has become women's work almost exclusively, where female musicians are inevitably asked if they sing and male singers are expected to also play an instrument? One feminist point of view suggests that women who had an interest in music were forbidden by the dominant patriarchy to play instruments and were instead encouraged to sing. (The only instrument deemed acceptable for women was the piano. There were so many lady pianists in New Orleans; as Jelly Roll Morton remembered, "When a man played the piano, the stamp was on him for life, the femininity stamp." Although it's ridiculous to suggest that Billie Holiday, Carmen McRae, and Peggy Lee are nothing more than thwarted trombonists, this makes more sense than Jimmy Rushing in a backless evening gown.)

The real harbinger of the species of female jazz-and-band singers was the virtually simultaneous appearance of three women, the Three White Goddesses, who invented and defined the canary tradition in the early thirties: Mildred Bailey, Connee Boswell, and Lee Wiley.

The age of the girl singer began on September 15, 1931, when Jack Kapp put Mildred Bailey in front of the Casa Loma Orchestra for four songs. Kapp was then developing the theory that would later put Decca Records on the map, that of combining names—or good band plus good singer equals a doubly strong record and extra sales. Two other major vocalists appeared in the same year: Lee Wiley recorded her first vocal refrain with Leo Reisman's very-much-listened-to society orchestra in June, and two months later, Connee Boswell, who had only recently become the dominant voice in the Boswell Sisters trio, began recording as a soloist both on her own releases and in tandem with name bands.

Then, a record called "Rockin' Chair," by Mildred Bailey with a group of Paul Whiteman sidemen, became one of the year's major records and established the band canary for all time. Though Whiteman's name wasn't on the label, bookers, agents, and other bandleaders knew it was a "Whiteman Production" and started aping it. If Whiteman, still the central figure in American popular music, had scored a hit using a spoon player, doubtless all the other bands would have gone out and hired spoon players. As it happened, they started hiring girl singers.

Immediately, the status of Boswell and Wiley went up along with Bailey, and with them a new flock of songbirds suddenly began turning up on band records. Helen Rowland sang with Fred Rich's band in 1931, and then joined Freddy Martin in 1933. Jean Bowes fills up thirty-two bars with the Dorsey Brothers studio group in 1932, and when the Dorseys took to the road they brought along Kay Weber in the chirping department. Ben Pollack, whose bands will always be remembered for their excellent jazz musicians, modulated from hot to sweet by adding a skirt to the payroll, and similarly, Hotel Taft bandleader Georgie Hall knew his unit could never hit the big time unless they were behind the behind of a "chantootsie" (Earl Wilson's term), and always made sure he had one who had one. Most importantly, Duke Ellington annexed Ivie Anderson—temporarily jettisoning his "female voice-as-orchestral instrument" concept—to His Famous Orchestra in 1931, and Benny Goodman, in premiering his ground-breaking white swing band in 1934, brought along Helen Ward. After the following summer, when Goodman made white swing the prevailing mode of popular music, the waves of new bands that modeled themselves after BG made these gowned, bejeweled creatures as inevitable a part of the scenery as batons and music stands.

It's ironic that the woman most responsible for the whole phenomenon should be Mildred Bailey, and as we'll see, irony is the stuff of Mildred Bailey's life. Both her career and her music are shot through with it, like a Cole Porter lyric. It's the comic irony of the big woman who wants nothing more than to be perceived as dainty and petite; it's the dramatic, almost tragic irony of the artist who never really learned who she was and what she wanted, so instead she spends her life in a fruitless pursuit of what Artie Shaw calls $ucce$$, love, money, fame, and popular approval, which continually elude her like the Lost Chord.

At the time of "Rockin' Chair" in 1932, the twenty-nine-year-old Bailey was on the verge of her third marriage, husband number two having given her the name Bailey. Born Mildred Rinker in Spokane, Washington, she shared an early passion for hot music with her three brothers (all of whom wound up in the music business: Al in vocal groups and then as a radio producer, Charles in song publishing, and Miles as a booking agent) and Bing Crosby, then a local lad who hung around with brother Al. Bailey's mother died when she was fourteen, and she went to live with family in Seattle, later working as a song demonstrator and singer in Los Angeles. When Al and Bing gained some local success as a vocal duo, Bailey encouraged them to come to Hollywood and obtained work for them through the same agency she dealt with (Crosby later credited Bailey with giving him his "start"). Bailey went to work on radio station KMTR at about the same time Crosby and Rinker joined Paul Whiteman. Fortunately, not long before they left the Maestro's entourage, they were able to help Mildred on to the bandstand of the "King of Jazz."

Though Whiteman would later get the credit for using the first steady girl band singer, he very nearly missed the boat where Bailey was concerned. Even though he brought her along on tours and occasionally gave her a spot on his broadcasts, he didn't take her seriously enough to use her on any of his records for two whole years—and probably never would have recorded her at all had Kapp not first shown Whiteman her potential. (She did appear on records by two satellite bands of Whiteman personnel, Eddie Lang's and Frank Trumbauer's.)

When she finally did record with the Whiteman band proper, in the last ten months of her tenure with "Pops," the result was twenty of the limpest entries on her entire discography. Whiteman's 1932–33 orchestra played far less jazz than his earlier bands with Beiderbecke, Trumbauer, and Crosby, or his later ones with Berigan and then the Teagarden Brothers, so it's not surprising that her ten sides with this elephantine orchestra should be so stiff and unswinging (although she does get a little funky on "We Just Couldn't Say Goodbye" and toward the end of the bridge of "Can't You See?"). The other ten—made with Mildred feted by small though not especially hot groups of Whiteman men—fare little better: "Too Late" has an unbelievably corny (in both arrangement and performance) bridge, and when she tries to phrase a little farther out in the last eight bars of "Lies" and "Dear Old Mother Dixie," an intrusive vocal group defeats her purpose. Of the Whiteman-era performances, only "Concentratin'," with its adventurous though unsure rhythmic liberties, and the remarkable "Rockin' Chair" (which would be replaced by a superior remake) can be called satisfying.

Bailey sings "I'll Never Be the Same Again" on one of her last Whiteman sides, and sure enough, when she resumed recording a few months later—this time under the aegis of Jack Kapp—everything changed. "Harlem Lullaby" and "Is That Religion?" reveal the oversize Whiteman organization as the culprit holding Bailey back. These two art-deco minstrel numbers, one a mammy tune and the other a mock hymn, call for Bailey to rock, moan, and preach, without the timidity and self-consciousness that mar her earlier work. Bailey's nine sides with the Dorsey Brothers (1933) not only prove that she had solved most of her rhythmic problems (they would never go away completely), but that she's working on her tone as well. The early voice sounds uncomfortably dark and deep, influenced in equal portion by the classic blues singers and the white belters of the acoustic twenties. Typically, when we describe a singer as achieving tonal maturity, as in the case of Crosby, Armstrong, and Sinatra, we mean their voice shifts from the light whimpers of their first recordings to the lower, fuller sound of their grown-up work. In Bailey's case, we mean the opposite. As she got better her voice grew lighter and lighter until it became delicate and paper-thin but nevertheless solid. Bailey apparently figured it was easier to swing a clarinet than a tuba, and later told *Time* that "I couldn't sing *big* if I wanted to."

In addition to her work with Kapp, Bailey began working with jazz-oriented producer John Hammond. Hammond's idea was that you were not a "jazz singer" until you recorded with Negroes, so he organized a date for Mildred and an early Benny Goodman band with Coleman Hawkins, and then a series of small-band sessions, one of which used the inspired idea of recording her without a drummer in the classic blues tradition. These four numbers, made with Berigan, Johnny Hodges, bassist Grachan Moncur III, and Bailey's favorite accompanist, Teddy Wilson, thankfully did not attempt to re-create the Clarence Williams Blue Five idea but rather to update it, with some modern prefigured background riff scoring and a less formalized interaction between all five participants. Though Hammond accurately assessed these four tracks as "among the most beautiful that I ever made," he never got greedy for seconds. Instead, over the next four years, he put Bailey in front of a series of semiorganized jam sessions. These records bounce amiably and boast a colorful supporting cast (especially Chu Berry and Roy Eldridge). But her recorded legacy would be so much poorer if it consisted *only* of these.

The best thing that ever happened to Mildred Bailey was Red Norvo, her third and last husband and her most important collaborator. They met in Whiteman's ranks (he played vibes behind her on "Rockin' Chair") and were married in 1933—the same year Kapp stupidly prevented Norvo from putting his advanced ideas on wax—and organized a touring band together in 1936, appropriately christened "Mr. and Mrs. Swing." Together with the young arranger Eddie Sauter, they created three years' worth of the most beautiful vocal records ever produced, each a perfect blend of written ensemble passages, vocal refrains, and instrumental improvisations and each a minor classic of shading and dynamics that would have a profound influence on many singers, including Frank Sinatra, and even more arrangers. Making these years all the more remarkable for Bailey was the fact that she still did the small-group dates for Hammond. The two radically different kinds of records, the earthy blowing sessions on the one hand, the masterfully scored orchestral works on the other, compliment each other beautifully, in much the same way Duke Ellington alternated between big- and small-band sessions throughout his career.

On Sauter's superior 1937 remake of "Rockin' Chair," Bailey's now mature and secure, featherlight voice emotes for two slowly rocking choruses over a choir of saxophones that suit her far better than any "genuine" vocal group ever did (such as her 1931–32 Victors with the King's Jesters and her 1941–43 efforts with the Delta Rhythm Boys). "Smoke Dreams," another 1937 triumph, represents the three-way collaboration at its zenith: The arranger second-guesses the future with a dissonant, amelodic ensemble of brass and reeds; Bailey speaks for the past with her highly individual rhythmic patterns; and Norvo's vibes both lead them and hold them together as the dominant voice in the score.

Quixotically, Sauter did not develop into a great jazz arranger, although he was much praised by critics who confused his classical leanings for what they called "progressive" jazz. Sauter's charts for Benny Goodman today sound cold, hollow, and occasionally pretentious, and his later Sauter–Finegan Orchestra disavowed jazz (and, one might say, music) entirely (to give him credit though, his last significant work was *Focus,* a stunning album-length creation for strings, rhythm, and Stan Getz's tenor). Sauter's later work with Bailey brings home dramatically that the Bailey–Sauter combination signified nothing without Norvo.

Unfortunately, Mr. and Mrs. Swing did not get along as well financially and personally as they did musically. Their band broke up in 1939 and their marriage followed early in 1940. Bailey, suffering from one of her first serious illnesses (brought on by constant touring), which had contributed to the disintegration of the band, looked around for something new to do. She tried chirping with Benny Goodman's band on a few cold-sounding Sauter arrangements that were not up to her classic collaborations with either man. She indulged a penchant for commercialism by Europeanizing her accompaniments, first using a pretentious chamber octet piloted by Alec Wilder (which also backed her on a season of Bob Crosby's radio show), and later with a pitiful pitfull of pseudo-symphonic strings. She made a series of sides for Decca with the Delta Rhythm Boys and others, which went nowhere.

Finally, in 1944, she got her last break. CBS put her in front of one of the major jazz radio shows of the war era in which she performed a mixture of ballads, up-tempos, and blues with Paul Barron's sympathetic swing band, which, though not as idiosyncratically perfect for Bailey as the Norvo group, suited her fine nonetheless. Importantly, a roster of big-league players from the jazz world came with the package as guest stars.

Too bad there were only thirty-four shows and only a handful of the airchecks have ever been released, because apart from one last good session with Hammond for Majestic, which resulted in two terrific takes of "Lover, Come Back to Me," and numerous novelties and dates with strings, and a good, completely overlooked Victor session, that was about it for Mildred Bailey. Illness had been a serious problem for her since 1938, and she was hospitalized then and again in April 1943 and yet again in 1949, after which she went into retirement on a farm she owned in Poughkeepsie, New York. She made it to Los Angeles in the spring of 1950 for a final recording session and a long-overdue appearance on the Bing Crosby show (their duet was a marvelous "I've Got the World on a String"). Back in New York, she did a Saturday morning radio show with the dreaded Morton Downey, Sr., and in the fall of 1951 played Detroit with Ralph Burns as accompanist. Becoming seriously ill around Thanksgiving, she checked into the Poughkeepsie Hospital, where she died on December 12, 1951.

The first of the canaries was dead. The tragedy wasn't her death but that in life she was only able to produce her greatest art by accident when the circumstances were right, with the same kind of chance results that define jazz itself. From the evidence of those who knew her, she had little idea of what made her special. "Mildred thought that the big-band sound, often with choirs, was essential for popular appeal," said John Hammond, and when he proposed the Berigan–Hodges–Moncur–Wilson session, "Mildred thought I was crazy." According to Bucklin Moon, she considered her *Time* review (of a gig at Cafe Society) a major triumph even though the anonymous critic was an ignoramus who not only made several insulting remarks about her "mountainous girth," but went on to insinuate that the only thing she could sing was "Rockin' Chair."

But the most revealing description of Bailey's personality comes from her close friend and fellow artist, Lee Wiley. "In going out" of Wiley's apartment, she told Richard Lamparski, "Mildred fell on the floor and by God I really talked her into living, because she apparently [wanted to be] dead. Well, what I did was to use some of her own language. I said, 'Mildred! Now you get your ________ off of this floor! You can't go on being like this! Stop! Get up your ________!' Or something like that, and do you know that pretty soon a smile came over her face [and] she got up."

Rhythmically, Bailey comes out of the classic blues approach, specifically Bessie Smith's a cappella phrasing, and this in spite of Bailey's sweet and unblue tone. Norvo has spoken of Mildred's friendship and adoration of Bessie, and Eddie Condon reported that when Smith played one of her final shows in New York, Mildred was present but refused to follow her, such was her respect for the empress. As it happened, she never outgrew the twenties approach to rhythm, and never fully absorbed the new rhythmic language of Crosby and Armstrong. By 1935, when the official coming of swing made 4/4 *the* standard time of popular music and jazz, Mildred must have seemed increasingly anachronistic.

Today, if the 1960s has taught us anything, it's not to be concerned with what time signature (or lack of it) a performer picks out for himself so long as he "swings" within that idiom. But in the late forties Mildred had a tough time finding critics and audiences—not to mention accompanists—who knew what she was going for. For her entire life Mildred would never be truly comfortable with the "four heavy beats in a bar and no cheating" (the words are Count Basie's) that characterize swing.

The most recent standard in Bailey's repertoire, "Almost like Being in Love" (recorded with a string orchestra in 1947 on Majestic), makes her rhythmic thinking crystal clear, and is accentuated by a shortness of breath caused by illness and middle age. She takes the tune as written, in standard post-Crosby ballad time (that is, legato), and staccato-izes it into little tiny pieces, breaking it down into the strong/weak pulses characteristic of Dixieland. To try to capture her meter on the typewriter: "*What* a *day* (pause) / *This* has *been* (pause)."

Armstrong might have given these notes equal weight, probably pausing just before and not after that last syllable, "been." Crosby would have filled in what Armstrong only suggests, extending the last note and likely throwing in one of his characteristic satellite notes halfway through this last word to break up the time a little. Frank Sinatra, who recorded "Almost like Being in Love" two months before Bailey, also fills in the pauses within the line (only taking a breath between lines) but would never use one of Crosby's grace notes here, thereby only according the absolute difference in the weight of each note.

All this helps explain why Mildred needed Norvo so badly. As the man who brought the xylophone* to jazz, Norvo had to master every jazz rhythm style, his career serving as an outline of the history of the music. From the 2/4 of Whiteman-era dance bands to the 4/4 of swing, from the double time of bebop (he led one of the pivotal Charlie Parker sessions in 1945) to the free time of his collaborations with third-streamers and prototypical avant-garde men like Bill Smith, Jack Montrose, and Charlie Mingus, there is nothing that Norvo didn't play. Both as a great musician and as her husband, Norvo knew exactly how to make Bailey comfortable, what kind of backing would produce the most from her. She suffered without him in more ways than one, and was fiercely envious of his second, successful marriage to Shorty Rogers's sister Julia.

Sadly, that dainty and delightful powderpuff bounce (bounce as distinct from straight swing) that makes her so special today came across as antiquated in her own life. No wonder she resented Bing Crosby so much; although Crosby (as John Hammond has confirmed) repeatedly bailed her out of rough financial waters, she never came close to equaling his chameleonic rhythmic mastery, which allowed him to fulfill Jack Kapp's prophecy of the ultimate pop music patriarch. She could never, as Crosby did, land a Hawaiian hit in 1937 and a country-western best-seller six years later; instead, she struggled vainly to keep her career and life together. That she and Crosby were born a few months and a few miles apart, and grew up with the same influences and advantages (and the same Guinness book achievements, the first full-time male and female singers with a band, the same band no less), must have really made her gnash her teeth. Forty years since her death it seems ironic, but then "ironic" is a word that pops up quite a bit when the subject is Mildred Bailey.

On the other hand, being born in New Orleans doesn't ensure jazz greatness, but the Crescent City's musicians have traditionally enjoyed a rhythmic advantage over those from other locales. Importantly, the only major popular singer (after Armstrong, Louis Prima, and a few other doubling instru-

*As Norvo played it, the xylophone was a tunable percussion instrument that belonged in the front line as much as it did in the rhythm section.

mentalists) to come out of New Orleans was Connee Boswell, who was so much a part of that city, and vice versa. Though we hear a considerable amount of Bing Crosby in her work, and something of Bessie Smith and a few of Caruso's techniques, the overwhelming influence is that of Louis Armstrong and, going deeper into the roots of both Boswell and Armstrong, New Orleans itself. But Boswell had the most commercial success of the three original White Goddesses—in spite of her unswerving allegiance to the great New Orleans jazzmen, sharing their wildly swinging beat; a raw, earthy voice; and her delightful disrespect for "proper" enunciation. Boswell epitomizes the New Orleans musician's directness and open emotionality.

Born in 1907 in Kansas City, Missouri, Connee, a cripple since early childhood, grew up the most musical child of one of the most musical families in the most musical city in the world. She studied several instruments, primarily cello, and later claimed to have a classical background, which is likely since we don't know how much Negro jazz a middle-class white girl would have been able to hear. "We liked jazz music and swing music and even some of the ragtime music that they played in those days," she told Rich Conaty later. "But we bought virtually every type of record that came out. . . . I loved Caruso and the way he used to be able to take a deep breath and then sing on that deep breath. But also I used to listen to Mamie Smith and then to Bessie Smith."

Apart from the previously mentioned Dixie rhythm style, Boswell structures her 1931–35 Brunswick recordings according to the New Orleanian tradition as codified by Armstrong. The first chorus is sung relatively straight, the second turns much looser, and if there is an instrumental break, the out chorus (or half-chorus) will be wilder still, climaxing and then resolving the performance. Even on these "straight" first choruses Boswell gets endearingly playful: On a tune with a basic three-line construction, for instance, she'll drop way behind the beat on the first two lines and then jump back on top of it on the third—an elaboration of an idea from the Armstrong–Crosby vocabulary that on one ever did as well as Boswell. She does it to make the harmony, which will generally resolve to the tonic chord at this point, the rhythm, and she "resolves" back to the top of the beat, and drama, which "resolves" as the title line is repeated, all parallel to each other.

Kapp believed that Boswell's frisky embellishments would deter sales (he told the same thing to Crosby) and you can almost hear Kapp shouting "sing the melody" at the top of his lungs in the recording booth. He temporarily conventionalized both Connee's and the trio's work and, as Connee put it, "Those records just didn't come out right."

These disappoint at first, because songs like "Clouds" and "Chasing Shadows," which have relatively little melodic development, require Connee's deluxe treatment to make them special. But without rhythm to play with and without the opportunity to do her own arrangements (as she always preferred to do), Connee focuses our attention on her tone—and what a tone it is! Unlike Bailey's thin, delicate wisp, which, though charming, represented a coy middle-American attitude toward sex, Boswell's is a more directly sensual, genuinely vaginal instrument, something else she picked up in New Orleans. That isn't fur on her voice, honeychile, that's pubic hair. Bailey may elaborate on Bessie Smith's rhythm, but Boswell picks up on her attitude.

When Goodman legitimized swing music and made it marketable, Kapp no longer had any excuse to hold Connee to straight numbers. She waxed a lot of sides with a Crosby-derived schottische beat, and also got to work with jazz units such as Woody Herman's, Ben Pollack's, and a rhythm section that followed her through four jazzed-up ballads (two standards, "Nobody's Sweetheart" and "Dinah," and two new songs destined to achieve that status, "Blueberry Hill" and "The Nearness of You").

However, nothing matched the empathy she shared with the homeboys in Bob Crosby's Bobcats. They had already made one satisfactory session together (which produced the fine "You Started Me Dreaming") when, on the heels of Maxine Sullivan's hit "Loch Lomond," they reteamed to swing four other ancient numbers, the folk "Home on the Range," two Victor Herbert operetta pieces—"Gypsy Love Song" and "Ah! Sweet Mystery of Life"—and another "Ah!" number, "Ah! So Pure," from von Flotow's *Martha*. Kapp, who at first wanted to cash in on another label's hit, showed a middle-brow streak about a mile wide. In an interview with Michael Brooks, Boswell said Kapp "nearly fainted at the playback. Said von Flotow would turn over in his grave." He considered the Boswell–Bobcats record, which they called "Martha," a desecration, or at least a mean parody of the semiclassical stuff he was raised on. Actually, Boswell consummated a perfect marriage of jazz and the Euro-pop tradition, realigning von Flotow's melody to the demands of swing but retaining its recitative/aria structure to alternate Connee's vocal passages with choruslike chanting by the band and superb solos by Eddie Miller's hard swinging tenor and Yank Lawson's trumpet. It worked beautifully.

But Kapp was livid. "He wouldn't issue it at first and only consented after I said if the record didn't reach a certain number of sales I'd take full-page ads in *Variety* absolving him and the company from any blame." (If he was willing to "betray" the music he loved to make a buck, why should we be shocked at what he did to music he didn't particularly care about—meaning jazz?)

Anyhow, "I didn't need to place the ads," Boswell concluded, since "Martha" quickly became her biggest seller. In the late thirties she headlined at least one major New York nightclub, spent a season of singing overdone Meredith Willson charts on the big-money "Maxwell House Good News" show, and then a more musically satisfying year as the first regular femme thrush on Crosby's radio program, and, in spite of her handicap, an off-and-on movie career that sustained itself deep into the television era. The years leading up to the war became rewarding ones for Boswell, and not only career-wise: Her voice grew deeper, her rhythm freer, her abilities as an arranger more skillful, and her command of a lyric more mature.

Next to none of Boswell's postwar performances have been made available in my lifetime, but the few I've heard (mostly airchecks) indicate that just as Annette Hanshaw's postretirement disc of "You're a Heavenly Thing" reflects a more modern Connee Boswell influence, Boswell's own later work shows that one of her own disciples, Kay Starr, was rubbing off on Connee, leading to a more "mannish," harder-swinging approach. But other vocalists, emerging in the postband era, among them many Boswell "students" such as Ella Fitzgerald, Doris Day, and Starr, gradually usurped the older woman's popularity. The big-time appearances became fewer and fewer until she retired in the late fifties, by then a victim of rock 'n' roll. She claimed later that her husband-manager's sickness had caused what she described as her "temporary retirement."

But there were to be a few more records with Bing Crosby (specifically "That's A-Plenty"), a few LPs for minor labels, and two important albums. Sy Oliver's small-band arrangements on *Connee* demonstrate a common failing of Boswell's later work, that of being too tightly arranged. Without enough blowing, the idea of Connee singing a standard melody over an Oliver riff works for a couple of songs and then becomes predictable. (Only "Lullaby in Rhythm," which started life as an Edgar Sampson riff, seems suited to its quasi-R&B setting.)

But after the partial success of the Oliver album, Boswell created her last important work, the apex of her entire career: *Connee Boswell and the Original Memphis Five in Hi-Fi.* It began as a project to record the ailing jazz giant Miff Mole. "He was a great trombonist of the twenties," she told Rich Conaty; he "had been very sick and they didn't expect him to live. Finally, he got a little bit better and [Victor] finally decided . . . to call and ask me if I'd like to do this Dixieland album. They were going to get as many [of the Original Memphis Five] as they possibly could."

They decided on a format of half Boswell vocals and half band instrumentals, which consisted of the three remaining active Memphis Fivers, clarinetist Jimmy Lytell, pianist Frank Signorelli, and Mole, filled out by the great trumpeter Billy Butterfield, bassist Gene Traxler, and Tony Sparbaro, the New Orleans drummer who'd been there on the first jazz records ever made. "It was up to me which tunes I wanted to do and all that," Connee reminisced, "When I did 'Say It Isn't So,' I didn't write out a solo for Miff to play. I said, 'I want you to play a solo on this.' He said, 'I don't think my lip will hold out.' So I said, 'Miff, come on and try it.' And so I talked him into it. Miff played the solo on that, and if you listen to the solo he does, it's really very beautiful."

In addition to the lovely ballads ("Say It Isn't So") and jazz standards ("All of Me" and "The Saints"), the album's pinnacle is Boswell's very worthy sequel to "Martha," a jazz adaptation of Rudolf Friml's "Giania Mia." Instead of the usual solos from her sidemen—there are plenty of those on the other tracks—Connee re-forms the Boswell Sisters through overdubbing and shows her Ukelele Ike roots with a vocal trumpet imitation. Again, her translation of classical effects into the jazz idiom, such as the substitution of a perfectly timed rest for the original's high-note climax, makes it work on a level beyond parody.

The rightness of the total album that makes it a classic, the perfect balance between vocals and instrumentals, the fast and slow numbers, the solos of Boswell and the musicians underscore another difference between Boswell and Mildred Bailey: Connee instinctively knew what would work for her and what wouldn't, while Bailey's own judgment did her more harm than good and she floundered like a fish out of water without worthy collaborators, a Norvo or a Hammond. In a telephone conversation shortly before his death in 1972, Jimmy Lytell said that of the thousands of records he'd made, "that one with Connee Boswell" was easily his favorite.

After this final triumph, a 1958 B-movie called *Senior Prom,* in which she sang "The Saints" again, was her last major gig. She always spoke of a comeback, but those who knew her in her sixties describe her as having gotten quite silly in her last years. She died in 1976, within a year of two other stars of the Kraft Music Hall, Bing Crosby and bandleader John Scott Trotter.

Boswell's pairing with the Memphis Five was only one of the records that made the late fifties the richest period in the history of vocal jazz. Not only were the giants associated with that era doing their greatest work (Frank Sinatra's *Only the Lonely, Mel Torme Swings Shubert Alley*) and newcomers making significant debuts (Carmen McRae and Betty Carter), but many major artists of the thirties created their most satisfying efforts, like the Boswell album, Crosby's *Bing with a Beat,* Armstrong's *Satchmo: A Musical Autobiography,* Jimmy Rushing's *The Jazz Odyssey of James Rushing, Esq.,* and perhaps the best of all, Lee Wiley's *West of the Moon.*

Even before Wiley opens her mouth on the first song of *West of the Moon,* the rocking first notes of Ralph Burns's introductory vamp let us know that we're in for something special. Then, when Wiley enters on the first few bars of the neglected Irving Berlin tune "You're a Sweetheart," we know at once that she and Burns will make good that promise. Never on any of the twelve songs on this album does either one let us down. *West of the Moon,* like the other records I've mentioned, still astounds me with its natural perfection, translucent mist atmosphere, flawlessly selected (and sequenced) tunes, and tasteful organization—all of which display the highest possible level of craftsmanship.

But Wiley herself elevates *West of the Moon* into a work for the ages by being simply the most naked of all singers. There's a muscular, internally strong quality to Crosby, Armstrong, and Sarah Vaughan that allows them to be vulnerable yet never leaves them completely defenseless. Even Billie Holiday, who learned a thing or two from Wiley, will respond to pain with invective and the sharp-edged wit of the blues. Bailey and Boswell find protection in rhythm, but Wiley extends no defenses, no walls, no barriers between her heart and her audience.

Where Boswell swings hard and Bailey bounces, Wiley blows smoke rings, each note a puff that melts into wisps of vibrato. Rhythm is second to tone here, her burnished, bittersweet instrument dominating where the beats will fall in a much freer way than had ever been done before. Bud Freeman told her, "When you sing, you remind me of the way Bix played." Although she didn't agree, the comparison suggests why she had to wait until the "cool" fifties to find her most perfect accompanist in Ralph Burns, the modernist arranger associated with Woody Herman's Lester Young–influenced band, and indirectly points up Wiley's similarities with Holiday, who had also picked up on the Beiderbecke influence by way of Lester Young.

In fact, Burns gives the entire orchestra a Wiley sound by emphasizing the slightly spacey intervals she loved, and by creating a floating, tranquil ensemble sound that makes you think Wiley is somehow playing all the instruments herself. Unlike many arrangers who'll try to sweep a singer's shortcomings under a carpet of distractions (strings, choirs, loud brass), Burns's writing is as honest as Wiley herself. Realizing that a woman in the thinnest of negligees is sexier than one completely nude, his strings don't cover Wiley but further expose her nakedness (a lesson Nelson Riddle learned on Sinatra's *Close to You* and Marty Paich on *Tormé*).

The story of Wiley's life and career would be easier to tell if it were one of triumph after triumph leading up to 1956's *West of the Moon,* but that masterpiece climaxes nearly fifty years of stops and starts. Like Boswell and Bailey, she lied or let others lie about her age, claiming 1915 as a birth date when the maturity of her voice in 1931 (and Vince Giordano's discovery that she recorded a demo for Victor in the late twenties) points to a date a few years earlier. Her brother recently admitted 1910 to Gus Kuhlman. (Wiley was also supposed to be part Indian, something they used to say about Bailey, Kay Starr, Keely Smith, and even Jack Teagarden, even though his sister flatly stated that there was never one drop of Indian blood in their veins.) Like Boswell, Wiley had an instinctual sense of what would work for her musically and what wouldn't, and her talent for songwriting (she always claimed to have written "Ghost of a Chance") paralleled Boswell's gift for arranging. Unfortunately, like Bailey, Wiley allowed herself to be the victim of her own destiny rather than the master of it, like the heroine of a forties film noire like *Detour:* "Someday, fate or some mysterious force can put the finger on you or me for no reason at all."

Originally from Oklahoma (born in Fort Gibson, although John Hammond remembers her as being from Muskogee, raised in Tulsa), Wiley discovered the blues early on. "I used to sit in school and dream about being a singer," she told Richard Lamparski many years later. "I had a boyfriend who would skip school with me and we would go over to the local store and play records . . . they called them 'race records,' and they were sold only in a certain part of town, the colored part . . . like Bessie Smith and Clara Smith, but especially Ethel Waters." She added, "Mildred Bailey used to come on WPW every night around dinnertime. It was so wonderful, I couldn't wait until she would come on." To hear Wiley tell it, her life was a rags-to-riches story from the Tony Bennett records : As a teenager she sings on an Okie radio station where a music publisher hears her and says there's a big future for her in New York. So, not yet twenty, she runs away to the big town (working at station KNOX in St. Louis en route) where big-time bandleader Leo Reisman signs her immediately for his broadcasts and Victor recordings. From the band she graduates to her own program, "The Pond's Cold Cream Hour Starring Lee Wiley," and her own records—once again, Kapp—backed by the Dorsey Brothers, Casa Loma, and Johnny Green's orchestras. At this time she also guest stars with Paul Whiteman and appears on the covers of radio fan magazines.

Suddenly the first of several serious illnesses hit her and shook her off her perch at the top. "I got out of the doctor's office and I walked down Central Park West. . . crying all the way," she said. The hospital suspected she had a touch of tuberculosis, and even though they turned out to be wrong (fortunately), she had to stop singing and recuperate in Arizona for a year. The scenario was repeated sometime later: Shortly before she was scheduled to do a screen test in Hollywood she caught an eye disease that left her temporarily blind and disfigured. Still, she carried on—or off-and-on. After the public deserted her, the jazz community took her under its wing. In 1963 a TV executive made Wiley's life into a telefilm with Piper Laurie playing the lead and Benny Carter directing the music.

Wiley's early "popular" sides interest us more for archeological reasons than musical ones. Though Leo Reisman claimed to dislike jazz, he didn't let that keep him from such great hot musicians as Bubber Miley, Max Kaminsky, Adrian Rollini, and Wiley, and his band has a rhythmic lilt that complements its musical comedy affiliations. On Wiley's own song, "The South in My Soul," the band substitutes concert aggrandizing for black feeling (Don Redman recorded it with Harlan Lattimore, "The Colored Crosby," handling the refrain), but with her help they pull it off with conviction. Don't mind that she didn't have everything down pat during this prelude to her fifteen minutes of fame, but rather be amazed that she shows any trace at all of her later advanced style so early on.

When Wiley stepped up from canary to chanteuse and the selective audience replaced the mass one, everything about her work improved, not just her voice itself but the caliber of her sidemen and repertoire. In a phenomenon we'll explore in greater detail later on, Wiley may have been the one to introduce the idea of the "standard." In the thirties performers did whatever tunes music publishers hoped would sell, there being such a limitless flow of good and sometimes great songs that it never became necessary to do anything that was even six months old. The only exceptions were jazz musicians, who, much to the song plugger's chagrin, frequently recorded old numbers out of the New Orleans or blues tradition or that Louis Armstrong had transformed into jazz perennials. But Wiley made a series of sessions for Liberty, then a high-class music shop that catered to an upper-crust clientele of sophisticated showgoers, in which she waxed albums of the works of Cole Porter, Rodgers and Hart, and the late George Gershwin. (Recently, Merritt Records issued one of the Porter sessions complete with breakdowns and alternate takes, providing a fascinating window into Wiley's creative process.)

With their all-star accompaniment (Bunny Berigan, Fats Waller, Pee Wee Russell), these sides and Wiley's five-year marriage to pianist Jess Stacy (their union consummated musically in a Commodore recording) served as her ticket into the semiunderground world of jazz. First the musicians and then the critics picked up on her, even more than they had on Mildred Bailey, who once said to Wiley, "You know, Lee, it's an interesting thing about you and me. We have certain audiences and they seem to be the same type of people." Wiley played Wendy to that ragtag group of drunkards, geniuses, and lost boys whose Peter Pan was Eddie Condon. Though this combination resulted in only a few recordings—and those marred by Jack Kapp—she was given at least one specialty at each Condon concert or broadcast, and dozens of excellent live performances have been preserved on tape.

Finally, Mitch Miller of Columbia saw fit to give her one final shot at the big-label big time and, by way of the songbook package, reacquaint her with the musical comedy crowd. They used twin piano backing to steal some of Mabel Mercer's thunder, which, to my ears, wears pretty thin after one or two songs (and she committed no less than eighteen songs to wax with this accompaniment). The record bombed, but the idea worked. Wiley became virtually the only artist in history to be equally admired by devotees of both Louis Armstrong and Bobby Short; the combination of jazz and cabaret patronage made one of her albums, the 1950 *Night in Manhattan,* go legitimately gold after thirty-five years in record-shop racks.

Night in Manhattan, the better of the two CBS albums, combines two ten-inch LPs, one with the proto-Ferrante-Teicher-type pianos, the other with an extension of Bessie Smith's cornet-piano-voice format. Wiley had first experimented with this instrumentation on her Commodore disc and then added bass and drums on her Berigan–Cole Porter date for Liberty to modernize the idea for her own needs without sacrificing its vitality, *Night in Manhattan* goes a step farther, covering Wiley, trumpeter Bobby Hackett, and the rhythm section with a shimmering silk stocking of strings. Wiley's "I've Got a Crush on You" remakes Sinatra's rendering of that Gershwin classic from three years earlier, using the same arrangement and the same scrumptious Hackett introduction, obbligato, and solo.

The two Victor albums, *A Touch of the Blues* and *West of the Moon,* followed an underpar group of Rodgers and Hart numbers for George Wein's Storyville label (with the same instrumentation and Ruby Braff assuming Hackett's role). The charts are generally overbaked on *A Touch of the Blues*—except for an exquisite "Melancholy Baby" with that great trumpet and rhythm idea, this time it's Billy Butterfield—but thankfully only a temporary lapse of taste for arranger Al Cohn. The previously mentioned *West of the Moon,* however, is great enough for two albums; my only regret is that it's over too quickly and that Wiley and Ralph Burns didn't make another fifty albums together. Like Boswell, she chose to let these Victor albums close her third act, and thereafter retired—coming back only briefly, on the insistence of Johnny Mercer, to do a final album for Monmouth-Evergreen. She died on December 11, 1975.

The three women had more in common than that long walk down the thirteen miles of bad road that too often separates musical artistry from commercial marketability. For one thing, there was the relationship with Crosby: Bailey being a hometown friend, Wiley recording with him on Decca, Boswell sharing his mike on countless discs and programs. Even more important, each exerted an important influence on Billie Holiday, an influence that revealed itself more in each of the three white goddesses of the immediate post-Holiday generation—Peggy Lee, Kay Starr, and Anita O'Day—than in Holiday's own work. Though all three have their deepest roots in Holiday, the only thing in jazz that foreshadows O'Day's vibratoless tone is Bailey's; what Starr gleaned from Boswell has already been mentioned. Peggy Lee's debt to Lee Wiley may be the greatest of all.

As Bill Borden, producer of Lee Wiley's last album, put it, "Decades in jazz are generations as the classicists count." Peggy Lee sings the way I like to think Wiley would have had she been born ten years later: a notch or more free in her rhythm and fluffier in her tone. Think of Wiley's phrases as jagged lumps of sugar floating in dark coffee—sharp but sweet nonetheless. With Lee, the edges are softer and more streamlined, and the liquid flows right along with the lumps. On Lee's best record, the well-titled *Black Coffee,* she uses Wiley's favorite setting—voice, trumpet, and rhythm. The Wiley influence so pervades Lee's "Call It a Day" (mid-fifties, Capitol) that it's hard to believe she wasn't trying to copy Wiley's 1933 performance of the song—the kicker is that Wiley's was unissued (rejected by Kapp because of harmonic noodling in the climax), and there's no way Lee could have heard it.

What Mildred Bailey, Connee Boswell, and Lee Wiley added to the jazz vocabulary would vastly outlive their own careers; though each was more than a torch singer, each died with the knowledge that the torch had been passed on.

Ella Fitzgerald

Henry Pleasants

And then there is Ella, about whom critics have surprisingly little to say, other than to state that she is the ultimate jazz singer or to denigrate her in favor of Billie Holiday (see Benny Green) or Sarah Vaughan. Her situation is not unlike that of Art Tatum—there's no way to ignore the technical and musical genius of these two, or their immense and joyous fecundity, even if you prefer your art less Olympian. This is taken from Pleasants's The Great American Popular Singers (1974).

Gerald Moore, the English accompanist, tells about the time Dietrich Fischer-Dieskau, following a matinee recital Moore and the German Lieder singer had given together in Washington, D.C., rushed to the National Airport and took the first plane to New York in order to hear Duke Ellington and Ella Fitzgerald at Carnegie Hall.

"Ella and the Duke together!" Fischer-Dieskau exclaimed to Moore. "One just doesn't know when there might be a chance to hear that again!"

The story is illustrative of the unique position that both Ella Fitzgerald and Duke Ellington occupy in the musical history of our century. More than any other artists working in the Afro-American idiom, they have caught the attention and excited the admiration of that other world of European classical, or serious, music.

Ella's achievement, in purely musical terms, is the more remarkable of the two, if only because she has never ventured into the no-man's-land of semi-classical or third-stream music separating the two idioms. Duke Ellington is a familiar figure on the stage at symphony concerts, as both pianist and composer, in his jazz-flavored symphonic suites. Ella has ranged widely between the ill-defined areas known as "jazz" and "popular," but not into classical, although she has sung the songs of the great American songwriters—Arlen, Gershwin, Porter, Rodgers, for example—with symphony orchestras. Many classical singers, however, like Fischer-Dieskau, are among her most appreciative admirers.

Unchallenged preeminence in her own field has had something to do with it, along with consistent performance throughout a career that has already extended over nearly forty years. Although she has never been, in her private life, a maker of headlines, her honors have been so many that word of them has filtered through to many who never saw a copy of *Billboard* or *Down Beat* and never will.

To enumerate those honors would be tedious. Suffice it to say, citing the entry under her name in Leonard Feather's *New Encyclopedia of Jazz,* that, between 1953 and 1960 alone, she was placed first in *Metronome, Down Beat,* and *Playboy* polls in either the "jazz singer" or "popular singer" categories, or both, no fewer than twenty-four times. She had been a poll winner long before that—she won the *Esquire* Gold Award in 1946—and she is heading the polls in both categories to this day.

With Frank Sinatra and Peggy Lee, she shares the distinction of having achieved a nearly universal popularity and esteem without sacrificing those aspects of her vocal and musical art that so endear her to fellow professionals and to the most fastidious of critics and lay listeners. Not even Frank and Peggy are admired so unanimously. The refinements of their art often fall on unappreciative or hostile ears. But with Ella, the exclamation "She's the greatest!" runs like a refrain through everything one reads or hears about her. One is as likely to hear it from an opera singer as from Bing Crosby ("Man, woman and child, Ella Fitzgerald is the greatest!").

Of what does her greatness consist? What does she have that other excellent singers do not have? The virtues are both obvious and conspicuous, and there is general agreement about them. She has a lovely voice, one of the warmest and most radiant in its natural range that I have heard in a lifetime of listening to singers in every category. She has an impeccable and ultimately sophisticated rhythmic sense, and flawless intonation. Her harmonic sensibility is extraordinary. She is endlessly inventive. Her melodic deviations and embellishments are as varied as they are invariably appropriate. And she is versatile, moving easily from up-tempo scatting on such songs as "Flying Home," "How High the Moon?" and "Lady Be Good" to the simplest ballad gently intoned over a cushion of strings.

One could attribute any one, or even several, of these talents and attainments to other singers. Ella has them all. She has them in greater degree. She knows better than any other singer how to use them. What distinguishes her most decisively from her singing contemporaries, however, is less tangible. It has to do with style and taste. Listening to her—and I have heard her in person more often than any other singer under discussion in these pages—I sometimes find myself thinking that it is not so much what she does, or even the way she does it, as *what she does not do.* What she does not do, putting it as simply as possible, is anything wrong. There is simply nothing in her performance to which one would want to take exception. What she sings has that suggestion of inevitability that is always a hallmark of great art. Everything seems to be just right. One would not want it any other way. Nor can one, for the moment, imagine it any other way.

For all the recognition and adulation that has come her way, however, Ella Fitzgerald remains, I think, an imperfectly understood singer, especially as concerns her vocalism. The general assumption seems to be that it is perfect. That she has sung in public for so many years—and still, when on tour, may do two sixty-minute sets six or seven nights a week—with so little evidence of vocal wear and tear would seem to support that assumption. Her vocalism is, in fact, as I hear it, less than perfect. "Ingenious" and "resourceful" would be more appropriate adjectives.

She has, as many great singers in every category have had, limitations of both endowment and technique. But, also like other great singers, she has devised ways of her own to disguise them, to get around them, or even to turn them into apparent assets. Ella's vocal problems have been concentrated in that area of the range already identified in the case of earlier singers as the "passage." She has never solved them. She has survived them and surmounted them.

She commands, in public performance and on record, an extraordinary range of two octaves and a sixth, from the low D or D-flat to the high B-flat and possibly higher. This is a greater range, especially at the bottom, than is required or expected of most opera singers. But there is a catch to it. Opera singers, as they approach the "passage," depress the larynx and open the throat—somewhat as in yawning—and, focusing the tone in the head, soar on upward. The best of them master the knack of preserving, as they enter the upper register, the natural color and timbre of the normal middle register, bringing to the upper notes a far greater weight of voice than Ella Fitzgerald does. Even the floated *pianissimo* head tones of, say, a Montserrat Caballé should not be confused with the tones that Ella produces at the upper extremes of her range.

Ella does not depress the larynx, or "cover," as she reaches the "passage." She either eases off, conceding in weight of breath and muscular control what a recalcitrant vocal apparatus will not accommodate, or she brazens through it, accepting the all too evident muscular strain. From this she is released as she emerged upward into a free-floating falsetto. She does not, in other words, so much pass from one register into another as from one voice into another. As Roberta Flack has noted perceptively: "Ella doesn't shift gears. She goes from lower to higher register, the same all the way through."

The strain audible when Ella is singing in the "passage" contributes to a sense of extraordinary altitude when she continues upward. In this she reminds me of some opera tenors who appear to be in trouble—and often are—in their "passage" (at about F, F-sharp, and G) and achieve the greater impression of physical conquest when they go on up to an easy, sovereign B-flat. The listener experiences anxiety, tension, suspense, relief, and amazement. It is not good singing by the canons of *bel canto,* which reckon any evidence of strain deplorable. But it is exciting, and in the performance of a dramatic or athletic aria, effective.

Both this sense of strain in that critical area of Ella's voice, and the striking contrast of the free sound above the "passage" may help to explain why so many accounts of her singing refer to notes "incredibly high." Sometimes they are. The high A-flat, A, and B-flat, even in falsetto, must be regarded as exceptional in a singer who also descends to the low D. But more often than not they sound higher than they are. Time and again, while checking out Ella's range on records, I have heard what I took to be a high G or A-flat, only to go to the piano and find that it was no higher than an E or an F. What is so deceptive about her voice above the "passage" is that the *sound* is high, with a thin, girlish quality conspicuously different from the rich, viola-like splendor of her middle range. It is not so much the contrast with the pitches that have gone before as the contrast with the sound that has gone before.

In purely vocal-technical terms, then, what distinguishes Ella from her operatic sisters is her use of falsetto; what distinguishes her from most of her popular-singer sisters is her mastery of it. One may hear examples of its undisciplined use in public performance and on records today in the singing of many women, especially in the folk-music field. With most of them the tone tends to become thin, tenuous, quavery, and erratic in intonation as they venture beyond their natural range. They have not mastered falsetto. Ella has. So has Sarah Vaughan. So has Ella and Sarah's admirable virtuoso English counterpart, Cleo Laine.

The "girlish" sound of the female falsetto may offer a clue to its cultivation by Ella Fitzgerald, and to some fundamental characteristics of her vocal art. It is, for her, a compatible sound, happily attuned to her nature and to the circumstances of her career. She entered professional life while still a girl. Her first hit record, "A-Tisket A-Tasket," was the song of a little girl who had lost her yellow basket. The girl of the song must have been a congenial object of identification for a young singer, born in Newport News, Virginia, who spent her childhood first in an orphanage, later with an aunt in Yonkers, New York, who drifted as a young dancer into Harlem clubs, and who fell into a singing career in an amateur contest at the Harlem Opera House when she was too scared to dance.

"It was a dare from some girlfriends," she recalls today. "They bet me I wouldn't go on. I got up there and got cold feet. I was going to dance. The man said since I was up there I had better do something. So I tried to sing like Connee Boswell—'The Object of My Affection.'"

According to all the jazz lexicons, Ella was born on April 25, 1918, and entered that Harlem Opera House competition, which she won, in 1934, when she would have been sixteen. She became vocalist with the Chick Webb band the following year, was adopted by the Webb family and, following Chick's death in 1939, carried on as leader of the band until 1942. She would then have been all of twenty-four, with ten years of professional experience behind her.

According to Norman Granz, who has been her manager throughout the greater part of her career, she was younger than that. Granz says that she was born in 1920 and had to represent herself as older, when she first turned up in Harlem, to evade the child-labor laws. She was adopted by the Webbs because a parental consent was a legal prerequisite for employment.

It should hardly be surprising, then, that her voice, when she began with the Chick Webb band, and as it can be heard now on her early records, was that of a little girl. She was only fourteen. She was a precocious little girl, to be sure, and probably matured early, as other black entertainers did—Ethel Waters and Billie Holiday, for example—who grew up in the tough clubs and dance halls of Harlem while other girls were still in secondary school. What mattered with Ella, however, and affected her subsequent career, was that the little girl could also sound like a young woman—and was irresistible.

The sound worked, and so did the little girl. Ella has never entirely discarded either the girl or the sound. She was, and has remained, a shy, retiring, rather insecure person. To this day when, as a woman of matronly appearance and generous proportions, she addresses an audience, it is always in a tone of voice, and with a manner of speech, suggesting the delighted surprise, and the humility, too, of a child performer whose efforts have been applauded beyond her reasonable expectations.

Nor has Ella ever forsaken her roots in jazz. George T. Simon, in *The Big Bands,* remembers watching her at the Savoy Ballroom in Harlem when she was with Chick Webb:

> When she wasn't singing, she would usually stand at the side of the band, and, as the various sections blew their ensemble phrases, she'd be up there singing along with all of them, often gesturing with her hands as though she were leading the band.

The fruits of such early enthusiasm and practice may be heard today in Ella's appearances with the bands of Count Basie and Duke Ellington, when one or more instrumental soloists step forward to join her in a round of "taking fours," with Ella's voice assuming the character and color of a variety of instruments as she plunges exuberantly into chorus after chorus of syllabic improvisation (scatting).

Ella owes at least some of her virtuosity in this type of display, or at least the opportunity to develop and exploit it, to Norman Granz and her many years' association with his Jazz at the Philharmonic tours. Benny Green, the English jazz critic, thus describes the importance of this association to the shaping of Ella Fitzgerald's art and career:

> When Ella first began appearing as a vocal guest on what were, after all, the primarily instrumental jazz recitals of Norman Granz, it might have seemed at the time like imaginative commercial programming and nothing more. In fact, as time was to prove, it turned out to be the most memorable manager-artist partnership of the post-war years, one which quite dramatically changed the shape and direction of Ella's career. Granz used Ella, not as a vocal cherry stuck on top of an iced cake of jazz, but as an artist integrated thoroughly into the jam session context of the performance. When given a jazz background, Ella was able to exhibit much more freely her gifts as an instrumental-type improvisor.

Elsewhere, reviewing an appearance by Ella with the Basie band in London in 1971, Green has described as vividly and succinctly as possible the phenomenon of Ella working in an instrumental jazz context:

> The effect on Ella is to galvanize her into activity so violent that the more subtle nuances of the song readings are swept away in a riot of vocal improvisation which, because it casts lyrics to the winds, is the diametric opposite of her other, lullaby, self. And while it is true that for a singer to mistake herself for a trumpet is a disastrous course of action, it has to be admitted that Ella's way with a chord sequence, her ability to coin her own melodic phrases, her sense of time, the speed with which her ear perceives harmonic changes, turn her Basie concerts into tightrope exhibitions of the most dazzling kind.

It was her activity with Jazz at the Philharmonic that exposed and exploited the singular duality of Ella Fitzgerald's musical personality. Between 1942, when her career as a bandleader came to an end, and 1946, when she joined Granz, she had marked time, so to speak, as an admired but hardly sensational singer of popular songs. With Jazz at the Philharmonic, she was back with jazz.

The timing was right. Bop had arrived, and Ella was with it, incorporating into her vocal improvisations the adventurous harmonic deviations and melodic flights of Dizzy Gillespie and Charlie Parker. Indeed, according to Barry Ulanov, in his *A History of Jazz in America,* the very term "bop," or "bebop," can be traced to Ella's interpolation of a syllabic invention, "rebop," at the close of her recording of "'T'ain't What You Do, It's the Way That You Do It" in 1939.

She has cultivated and treasured this duality ever since, and wisely so. Singers who have adhered more or less exclusively to an instrumental style of singing, using the voice, as jazz terminology has it, "like a horn," have won the admiration and homage of jazz musicians and jazz critics, but they have failed to win the enduring and financially rewarding affections of a wider public. Others have stuck to ballads and won the public but failed to achieve the artistic prestige associated with recognition as a jazz singer. Ella, more than any other singer, has had it both ways.

Norman Granz, again, has had a lot to do with it. When Ella's recording contract with Decca expired in 1955, she signed with Granz's Verve label and inaugurated, in that same year, a series of Song Book albums, each devoted to a single songwriter, that took her over a span of twelve years through an enormous repertoire of fine songs, some of them unfamiliar, by Harold Arlen, Irving Berlin, Duke Ellington, George Gershwin, Johnny Mercer, Cole Porter, and Richard Rodgers.

These were the first albums to give star billing to individual songwriters, and they served the double purpose of acknowledging and demonstrating the genius of American composers while providing Ella with popular material worthy of her vocal art. "I never knew how good our songs were," Ira Gershwin once said to George T. Simon, "until I heard Ella Fitzgerald sing them."

As a jazz singer Ella has been pretty much in a class by herself, and that in a period rejoicing in many excellent ones, notably Billie Holiday, Peggy Lee, Carmen McRae, Anita O'Day, Jo Stafford, Kay Starr, and Sarah Vaughan, not to overlook, in England, Cleo Laine. I am using the term "jazz singer" here in the sense that jazz musicians use it, referring to a singer who works—or can work—in a jazz musician's instrumental style, improvising as a jazz musician improvises. Ella was, of course, building on the techniques first perfected, if not originated, by Louis Armstrong, tailoring and extending his devices according to the new conventions of bop.

There is a good deal of Armstrong in Ella's ballads, too, although none of his idiosyncrasies and eccentricities. What she shared with Louis in a popular ballad was a certain detachment—in her case a kind of classic serenity, or, as Benny Green puts it, a "lullaby" quality—that has rendered her, in the opinion of some of us, less moving than admirable and delightful. In terms of tone quality, variety, and richness of vocal color, enunciation, phrasing, rhythm, melodic invention, and embellishment, her singing has always been immaculate and impeccable, unequaled, let alone surpassed, by any other singer. But in exposing the heart of a lyric she must take second place, in my assessment, at least, to Frank Sinatra, Billie Holiday, Peggy Lee, and Ethel Waters.

This may well be because she has never been one for exposing her own heart in public. She shares with an audience her pleasures, not her troubles. She has not been an autobiographical singer, as Billie and Frank were, nor a character-projecting actress, as Ethel Waters and Peggy Lee have been, which may be why her phrasing, despite exemplary enunciation, has always tended to be more instrumental than oral, less given to the *rubato* devices of singers more closely attuned to the lyrical characteristics of speech.

What she has offered her listeners has been her love of melody, her joy in singing, her delight in public performance and her accomplishments, the latter born of talent and ripened by experience, hard work, and relentless self-discipline. Like Louis, she has always seemed to be having a ball. For the listener, when she has finished, the ball is over. It has been a joyous, exhilarating, memorable, but hardly an emotional, experience.

Also, like Louis, she has addressed herself primarily to a white rather than a black public, not because she has in any sense denied her own people, but rather because, in a country where blacks make up only between ten and twenty percent of the population, white musical tastes and predilections are dominant. They must be accommodated by any black artist aspiring to national and international recognition and acceptance. In more recent years, younger whites have tended to favor a blacker music. A B. B. King has been able to achieve national celebrity where a Bessie Smith, fifty years earlier, could not. When Ella was a girl, what the white majority liked was white music enriched by the more elemental and more inventive musicality of black singers and black instrumentalists.

Ella's singing, aside from the characteristic rhythmic physical participation, the finger-popping and hip-swinging, and the obviously congenial scatting, has never been specifically or conspicuously black. It represents rather the happy blend of black and white which had been working its way into the conventions of American popular singing since the turn of the century, and which can be traced in the careers of Al Jolson, Sophie Tucker, Ethel Waters, Mildred Bailey, and Bing Crosby.

When Ella was a girl, black singers—those in organized show business, at any rate—were modeling themselves on the white singing stars of the time, and many white singers were modeling themselves on the charmingly imperfect imitation. It is significant that Ella's first model was Connee Boswell. A comparison of the records they both made in the late 1930s shows again how perceptive an ear Ella had from the first. But it is just as significant that Connee Boswell belonged to a generation of jazz-oriented white singers—others were Mildred Bailey and Lee Wiley—who had been listening to Bessie Smith and, above all, to Ethel Waters.

Again like Louis Armstrong, Ella Fitzgerald has achieved that rarest of distinctions: the love and admiration of singers, instrumentalists, critics, and the great lay public. But while she may be for the jazzman a musicians' musician, and for the lay public the First Lady of Song, she has always been more than anything else a singers' singer. John Hendricks, of Lambert, Hendricks and Ross fame, has put it well, responding to an Ella Fitzgerald record on a *Jazz Journal* blindfold test:

> Well, of course, she's my favorite—she's tops! I just love her. She's Mama! I try and sing my ballads like she does. I was working in a hotel in Chicago, and Johnny Mathis came in to hear me. I had just finished singing a new ballad I was doing at the time, and he came up to me and said, "Jon, you sure love your old Fitzgerald, don't you?"
>
> "Yes," I replied, "and don't you, too?"
>
> "We all do!" he said.
>
> And that's it. Everyone who sings just loves little old Fitzgerald!

The Divine Sarah

Gunther Schuller

This overwhelming tribute to Sarah Vaughan preceded a Vaughan concert at the Smithsonian Museum in 1980. Not surprisingly, Schuller—certainly the jazz authority most deeply rooted in classical music—places Vaughan in the entire context of twentieth-century singing. Perhaps it is surprising that he finds her superior to every great opera singer of this period, but he makes every effort to substantiate his claims, not merely assert them. From the collection Musings.

What I am about to do really can't be done at all, and that is to do justice to Sarah Vaughan in words. Her art is so remarkable, so unique that it, *sui generis,* is self-fulfilling and speaks best on its own musical artistic terms. It is—like the work of no other singer—self-justifying and needs neither my nor anyone else's defense or approval.

To say what I am about to say in her very presence seems to me even more preposterous, and I will certainly have to watch my superlatives, as it will be an enormous temptation to trot them all out tonight. And yet, despite these disclaimers, I nonetheless plunge ahead toward this awesome task, like a moth drawn to the flame, because I want to participate in this particular long overdue celebration of a great American singer and share with you, if my meager verbal abilities do not fail me, the admiration I have for this remarkable artist and the wonders and mysteries of her music.

No rational person will often find him or herself in a situation of being able to say that something or somebody is *the best.* One quickly learns in life that in a richly competitive world—particularly one as subject to subjective evaluation as the world of the arts—it is dangerous, even stupid, to say that something is without equal and, of course, having said it, one is almost always immediately challenged. *Any* evaluation—except perhaps in certain sciences where facts are truly incontrovertible—any evaluation is bound to be relative rather than absolute, is bound to be conditioned by taste, by social and educational backgrounds, by a host of formative and conditioning factors. And yet, although I know all that, I still am tempted to say and will now dare to say that Sarah Vaughan is quite simply the greatest vocal artist of our century.

Perhaps I should qualify that by saying the most *creative* vocal artist of our time. I think that will get us much closer to the heart of the matter, for Sarah Vaughan is above all that rare rarity: a jazz singer. And by that I mean to emphasize that she does not merely render a song beautifully, as it may have been composed and notated by someone else—essentially a *re*-creative act—but rather that Sarah Vaughan is a composing singer, a singing composer, if you will, an improvising singer, one who never—at least in the last twenty-five years or so—has sung a song the same way twice: as I said a *creative* singer, a jazz singer.

And by using the term jazz I don't wish to get us entrapped in some narrow definition of a certain kind of music and a term which many musicians, from Duke Ellington on down, have considered confining, and even denigrating. I use the word "jazz" as a handy and still widely used convenient descriptive label; but clearly Sarah Vaughan's singing and her mastery go way beyond the confines of jazz.

And if I emphasize the creativity, the composer aspect of her singing, it is to single out that rare ability, given, sadly, to so few singers, including, of course, all those in the field of classical music. It is my way of answering the shocked response among some of you a few moments ago when I called Sarah Vaughan the greatest singer of our time. For it is one thing to have a beautiful voice; it is another thing to be a great musician—often, alas, a *truly* remote thing amongst classical singers; it is still another thing, however, to be a great musician with a beautiful and technically perfect voice, who also can compose and create extemporaneously.

We say of a true jazz singer that they improvise. But let me assure you that Sarah Vaughan's improvisations are not mere embellishments or ornaments or tinkering with the tune; they are compositions in their own right or at least re-compositions of someone else's material—in the same manner and at the same level that Louis Armstrong and Charlie Parker and other great jazz masters have been creative.

You can imagine that I do not say these things lightly, and that I do not make so bold as to make these claims without some prior thought and reason. For I am, as many of you know, someone who played for fifteen years in the orchestra of the Metropolitan Opera, loved every minute of it, and during those years heard a goodly share of great singing—from Melchior to Bjorling and DiStefano, from Flagstad to Sayao to Albanese and Callas, from Pinza to Siepi and Warren. Before that, as a youngster, I thrilled to the recordings of Caruso, Rethberg, Ponselle, Muzio, Easton, and Lawrence. So I think I know a little about that side of the singing art. And yet with all my profound love for those artists and the great music they made, I have never found anyone with the kind of total command of all aspects of their craft and art that Sarah Vaughan has.

I do not wish to engage in polemical discussion here. Nor am I Sarah Vaughan's press agent. I would claim, however—along with Barbara Tuchman—that though my judgment may be subjective, the condition I describe is not. What is that condition? Quite simply a perfect instrument attached to a musician of superb musical instincts, capable of communicating profoundly human expressions and expressing them in wholly original terms.

First the voice. When we say in classical music that someone has a "perfect voice" we usually mean that they have been perfectly trained and that they use their voice seemingly effortlessly, that they sing in tune, produce not merely a pure and pleasing quality, but are able to realize through the proper use of their vocal organs the essence and totality of their natural voice. All that can easily be said of Sarah Vaughan, leaving aside for the moment whether she considers herself to have a trained voice or not. As far as I know, she did study piano and organ, but not voice, at least not in the formal sense. And that may have been a good thing. We have a saying in classical music—alas, painfully true—that given the fact that there are tens of thousands of bad voice teachers, the definition of a great singer is one who managed *not* to be ruined by his or her training. It is better, of course, to be spared the taking of those risks.

There is something that Sarah Vaughan does with her voice which is quite rare and virtually unheard of in classical singing. She can color and change her voice at will to produce timbres and sonorities that go beyond anything known in traditional singing and traditional vocal pedagogy. (I will play, in a while, a recorded excerpt that will show these and other qualities and give you the aural experience rather than my—as I said earlier—inadequate verbal description.)

Sarah Vaughan also has an extraordinary range, not I hasten to add used as a gimmick to astound the public (as is the case with so many of those singers you are likely to hear on the *Tonight Show*), but totally at the service of her imagination and creativity. Sarah's voice cannot only by virtue of its range cover four types of voices—baritone, alto, mezzo soprano, and soprano, but she can color the timbre of her voice to emphasize these qualities. She has in addition a complete command of the effect we call *falsetto,* and indeed can on a single note turn her voice from full quality to *falsetto* (or, as it's also called, head tone) with a degree of control that I only heard one classical singer ever exhibit, and that was the tenor Giuseppe DiStefano—but in his case only during a few of his short-lived prime years.

Another thing almost no classical singers can do and something at which Sarah Vaughan excells is the controlled use of vibrato. The best classical singers develop *a* vibrato, of a certain speed and character, which is nurtured as an essential part of their voice, indeed their trademark with the public, and which they apply to all music whether it's a Mozart or Verdi opera or a Schubert song. Sarah Vaughan, on the other hand, has a complete range, a veritable arsenal of vibratos, ranging from none to a rich throbbing, almost at times excessive one, all varying as to speed and vibrato and size and intensity—at will. (Again, my recorded example will demonstrate some truly startling instances of this.)

Mind you, what Sarah Vaughan does with the controlled use of vibrato and timbre was once—a long time ago—the *sine qua non* of the vocal art. In the seventeenth and eighteenth centuries vibrato, for example, was not something automatically used, imposed, as it were, on your voice. On the contrary, it was a special effect, a kind of embellishment—an important one—which you used in varying degrees or did not use, solely for various expressive purposes and to heighten the drama of your vocal expressivity. It is an art, a technique which disappeared in the nineteenth century and is all but a lost art today, certainly amongst classical singers, who look at you in shocked amazement if you dare to suggest that they might vary their vibrato or timbre. They truly believe they have *one* voice, when potentially—they don't realize it—they could (should) have several or many.

Here again, I think Sarah learned her lessons not from a voice teacher, but from the great jazz musicians that preceded her. For among great jazz instrumentalists the vibrato is not something sort of slapped onto the tone to make it sing, but rather a compositional, a structural, an expressive element elevated to a very high place in the hierarchy of musical tools which they employ.

Another remarkable thing about Sarah Vaughan's voice is that it seems ageless; it is to this day perfectly preserved. That, my friends, is a sign—the only sure sign—that she uses her voice absolutely correctly, and will be able to sing for many years more—a characteristic we can find, by the way, among many popular or jazz singers who were *not* formally voice-trained. Think of Helen Humes, Alberta Hunter,* Helen Forrest, Chippie Wallace, Tony Bennett, and Joe Williams.

SO MUCH FOR the voice itself. Her musicianship is on a par with her voice and, as I suggested earlier, inseparable from it. That is, of course, the ideal condition for an improvising singer—indeed a prerequisite. For you cannot improvise, compose extemporaneously, if you don't have your in-

*Alberta Hunter sang remarkably well until her death in 1984.

strument under full control; and by the same token, regardless of the beauty of your voice, you have to have creative imagination to be a great jazz or improvising singer. Sarah's creative imagination is exuberant. I have worked with Sarah Vaughan, I have accompanied her, and can vouch for the fact that she never repeats herself or sings a song the same way twice. Whether she is using what we call a paraphrase improvisation—an enhancement of the melody where the melody is still recognizable—or whether she uses the harmonic changes as the basis of the song to improvise totally new melodies or gestures, Sarah Vaughan is always totally inventive. It is a restless compulsion to create, to reshape, to search. For her a song—even a mediocre one—is merely a point of departure from which she proceeds to invent, a skeleton which she proceeds to flesh out.

There are other singers—not many—who also improvise and invent, but I dare say none with the degree of originality that Sarah commands. She will come up with the damndest musical ideas, unexpected and unpredictable leaps, twisting words and melodies into new and startling shapes, finding the unusual pitch or nuance or color to make a phrase uniquely her own. When one accompanies her one has to be solid as a rock, because she is so free in her flights of invention that she could throw you if you don't watch out. She'll shift a beat around on you, teasing and toying with a rhythm like a cat with a mouse, and if you're not secure and wary, she'll pull you right under. She is at her best and her freest when her accompaniment is firmly anchored.

Perhaps Sarah Vaughan's originality of inventiveness is her greatest attribute, certainly the most startling and unpredictable. But unlike certain kinds of unpredictability—which may be merely bizarre—Sarah's seems immediately, even on first hearing, inevitable. No matter how unusual and how far she may stretch the melody and harmony from its original base, in retrospect one senses what she has just done as having a sense of inevitability—"Of course, it had to go that way, why didn't I think of that?" I go further: in respect to her originality of musical invention I would say it is not only superior to that of any other singer, but I cannot think of any active jazz instrumentalist—today—who can match her.

If it is true, as has often been stated through the centuries, that one way of defining high art is by the characteristic of combining the expected with the unexpected, of finding the unpredictable *within* the predictable, then Sarah Vaughan's singing consistently embodies that ideal.

LASTLY, I MUST speak of the quality of Sarah's expressiveness, the humanism, if you will, of her art. Sarah has a couple of nicknames, as some of you know. The earliest one was Sassy. Next, around the early 1950s, she came to be called "the Divine Sarah," and more recently simply "the Divine One." Now that's a lovely thing to say about anyone, and I would not argue about Sarah's musical divinity, except in one somewhat semantic respect. What I love so in her singing is its humanness, its realness of expression, its integrity. It is nice to call her singing divine, but it's more accurate to call it human. Under all the brilliance of technique and invention, there is a human spirit, a touching soul, and a gutsy integrity that moves us as listeners.

HOW DOES ONE measure an artist's success? By how much audience they attract? By how much money they make? By how many records they sell? Or by how deeply they move a sophisticated or cultured audience? Or by how enduringly their art will survive? Sarah has been called the musicians' singer—both a wonderful compliment and a delimiting stigmatization. What seems to be true for the moment is that her art, like Duke Ellington's, is too subtle, too sophisticated to make it in the big—really big—mass pop market. God knows, Sarah—or her managers—have tried to break into that field. But she never can make it or will make it, like some mediocre punk rock star might, because she's too good. She can't resist being inventive; she can't compromise her art; she must search for the new, the untried; she must take the risks.

And she will be—and is already—remembered for *that* for a long time. To some like me—I've been listening to her since she was the very young, new girl singer with the Billy Eckstine Band in the mid-1950s—she is already a legend. I invite you now to listen to the promised excerpt—only *one* example of her art—a stunning example indeed, taken from a 1973 concert in Tokyo, during which Sarah Vaughan sang and recomposed "My Funny Valentine." Listen!!

(record played)

It is now my privilege to exit gracefully and to invite you to listen to the one and only Sarah Lois Vaughan!

The Blues as Dance Music

Albert Murray

The magisterial Murray, in his influential book Stomping the Blues *(1976), reminds us of the primal relationship of jazz to dance.*

Sometimes you get the impression that many of the articles and books about blues music were written by people who assume that the very best thing that could happen to it would be for it to cease being dance-hall music and become concert-hall music. Over the years most of these writers themselves have been show-biz-oriented entertainment-page reporters and reviewers, whose contact with the workaday environment of blues musicians is somewhat similar to that of the movie reporter and reviewer with the world of movie actors. So much so in fact that many have spent a considerable amount of time grinding out movie-fan-magazine-type articles on the personal lives of the more prominent performers, whom they glamorize and condescend to at the same time.

Many also overlard their copy with downhome and uptown slang expressions, such as *dig* for *understand* and *appreciate, bad* for *excellent, taking care of business* for *performing in an outstanding manner,* and so on, as if to prove that their contact with the idiom is that of a very hip which is to say sophisticated insider. But sometimes the results are even more exasperating than ludicrous. Item: The use of the word *funky* to mean earthy and soulful. The insider's traditional use is synonymous with foul body odor and connotes the pungent smell of sweat-saturated clothes and unwashed bodies, undeodorized armpits, improperly wiped backsides, urine-stained and fart-polluted undergarments. To the ever-so-hip reporter *funky* seems to suggest earthy people-to-people euphoria. To the insider it suggests asphyxiation. As in a version of Jelly Roll Morton's "Buddy Bolden's Blues":

I thought I heard Buddy Bolden say
Nasty, dirty, funky butt take him away.
I thought I heard Buddy Bolden shout
Open up the window and let the bad air out.

But with all their pseudo-inside wordplay, all the gratuitous redundancies about jazz which is to say blues music being an art form indigenous to the United States, and indeed with all their ever ready lipservice to the element of swing as a definitive factor of the idiom, when these very same reporter/reviewers give their evaluations of actual performances, whether live or on records, it is almost always as if they were writing about the concert music of Europe. They condone as well as condemn on assumptions that are essentially those of the European Academy. Not that they themselves seem to be basically hostile to any of the indispensable elements of the idiom. On the contrary, they seem to be personally fascinated and delighted by them. But even so they almost always write as if about concert-hall music rather than dance music.

Some have even written that blues musicians should not have to play in honky-tonks, dance halls, nightclubs, variety shows, popular festivals, and the like. As if downright oblivious to the literal source as well as the intrinsic nature and function of the idiom, some have gone so far as to represent the experience of playing in Storyville, or the dives and dance halls of Memphis, Chicago, Kansas City, and Harlem as a most outrageous form of injustice! There are those who even as they used to declare Duke Ellington to be the greatest of American composers immediately began wringing their hands and shaking their heads over what struck them as being the cruel state of affairs that forced him to spend most of his time on the road with his orchestra playing in nightclubs, ballrooms, and theaters. The fact that Duke Ellington had already become Ellington the Composer by writing music for such places long before his first Carnegie Hall concert seems to have escaped them at such moments, as did the fact that as important as formal concerts came to be to Ellington, he never expressed any desire to take his orchestra off the circuit. As he said one night during an intermission in a dance at the Propeller Club at Tuskegee to a young literary type who was concerned about an article that had reported him (Ellington) as having said that he continued to write dance music mainly to win more people over to his longer concert pieces:

> Don't pay any attention to those guys, sweetie. When you get so goddamn important you can't play places like this anymore you might as well give it up, because you're finished. We try to play everything. We're always very happy when they ask us to play proms, weddings, country clubs, ballparks. You see, this way we get to have most of the fun, because the dancers are not just sitting there watching; they're having a ball.

There is nothing at all ironic about "Stomping at the Savoy" and "Moten Swing" being written by musicians for whom the Saturday Night Function was as much a part of what life is all about as is the Sunday Morning Service. Nor does there seem to be any compelling reason why the audiences for whom such music was written and performed in the first place should not continue to be able to enjoy it in its natural setting simply because another audience now exists in the concert hall.

Not that the function of the concert hall is not also fundamental. It provides a showcase for the new and serves as a permanent gallery, so to speak, for the enduring. Moreover, as in the case of the great masterpieces of European church music, it affords opportunities for the music to be heard on its own apart from its role as an element in a ritual, in other words as a work of art per se. Thus the concert-hall recital at its best is in a very real sense also an indispensable extension of the dance hall. It can serve as a sort of finger-snapping, foot-tapping annex auditorium, where the repertory includes not only the new and the perennial but also such classics as, say, "Grandpa's Spells," "Sugar Foot Stomp," and "Potato Head Blues," that some dancers may be too fad-conditioned or otherwise preoccupied to request. Also, inasmuch as all occasions and circumstances seem to generate musical responses sooner or later, there is nothing intrinsically inauthentic about blues music which is composed specifically for concert recital.

But then the phonograph record has served as the blues musician's equivalent to the concert hall almost from the outset. It has been in effect his concert hall without walls, his *musée imaginaire,* his comprehensive anthology, and also his sacred repository and official archive. Many blues-idiom composers use the recorded performance as the authorized score. Jo Jones and Eddie Durham have said that the first written arrangement of Count Basie's "One O'Clock Jump" was copied from the record by Buck Clayton. Historians and critics of the idiom also use the recorded performance as the official score. What Martin Williams, for example, refers to in his discussion of Jelly Roll Morton, Duke Ellington, and Thelonious Monk as outstanding composers is not their collected scores but their recorded performances. Williams's book *The Jazz Tradition* is based primarily on recorded performances, and the same is true of Gunther Schuller's *Early Jazz.*

Nor is that all. For much goes to show that it may have been precisely the phonograph record (along with radio) that in effect required the more ambitious blues musicians to satisfy the concert-oriented listeners and Bacchanalian revelers at the very same time; long before the first formal concerts. Even as Chick Webb kept them stomping at the Savoy Ballroom on Lenox Avenue in Harlem, and Earl Hines kept them shuffling at the Grand Terrace on the South Side in Chicago, their orchestras were also playing what to all intents and purposes was a finger-snapping, foot-tapping concert for listeners huddled around radios all over the nation. (Not a few dance parties all over the nation were also geared to the radio, but that is another story.) Moreover most of the program was either already available on records or soon would be. When any of the orchestras that had made recordings of merit went on tour, musicians found other musicians and laymen alike in almost every town who were not only as familiar with their styles as with the mannerisms of a favorite athlete but also could recite their solos note for note.

Anytime a band pulled into town early enough before the engagement it was always the same story no matter where it was: *"Hey, here's that Goddamn Lester, man. Goddamn. What say Lester? This my man, cousin.* Dogging Around, *man, you know that record? That's my record. Right after old Count gets through cutting his little old diamond, here come my natural boy: Doo dooby dooby dooby daba doodadoo. . . . Say what you drinking Lester? You want something to eat? You can't spend no money in this town, Lester. You know that, don't you?*

"Man, here that bad Mr. Johnny Hodges. Man, here the Rabbit, in person all the way from the Cotton Club in the Heart of Harlem. Hey, Johnny, you know that thing you did called Squaty Roo? Man I played that record and some cats around here started to give up blowing. Then they borrowed my record and like to wore it out. You got them working, Johnny."

Louis Armstrong had so many musicians working like that on his records in so many places that people used to say all he had to do to play a dance in any town of any size was just turn up with his horn, because all he needed was a couple of hours and he could round up enough local musicians who knew his records note for note to make up any kind of band he wanted to work with for the occasion. They also used to like to tell about how sometimes when the people got there and saw all the hometown musicians on the bandstand they started grumbling, and then old Louis would thread it all together with his trumpet as if with a golden needle and everybody would settle down and have a good time. Whether that part was true or not the way they used to like to tell it, you could see old Louis with his trumpet case and his manager with a briefcase, and maybe a piano player with a folder full of music, being met at the local train station in the middle of the afternoon by the hometown promoter, who already had all the musicians waiting for him at the dance hall. Then, as they used to tell it, all old Louis would do was sit off to one side on the bandstand stripping and cleaning his horn piece by piece while the piano player held the audition and ran through a quick rehearsal. That was all it usually took, because what happened was that they spent the whole dance playing for old Louis, while the rest of the local musicians (along with a number of radio and record fans and hipsters) clustered around the stage in what Count Basie has referred to as the bandstand audience and which is the ballroom equivalent of the traditional Second Line that dances and prances along beside the marching bands in the New Orleans street parades.

In other words, although it may not have been possible for the masterpieces of Mozart, Bach, and Beethoven to have been composed had not music been released from the restrictions of its secondary role as an element in a ritual to become an independent art form as such, it does not follow that the concert hall is therefore indispensable to the extension, elaboration, and ultimate refinement of the intrinsic possibilities of blues music. For one thing, the great body of European Art Music was already in existence and already a part of the heritage of blues musicians. It was already there to be played with, and blues musicians did just that, as they did with everything else in earshot that struck their fancy. And the dancers loved it.

But what is at issue is the primordial cultural conditioning of the people for whom blues music was created in the first place. They are dance-beat-oriented people. They refine all movement in the direction of dance-beat elegance. Their work movements become dance movements and so do their play movements; and so, indeed, do all the movements they use every day, including the way they walk, stand, turn, wave, shake hands, reach, or make any gesture at all. So, if the overwhelming preponderance of their most talented musicians has been almost exclusively preoccupied with the composition and performance of dance music, it is altogether consistent with their most fundamental conceptions of and responses to existence itself.

And besides, as little as has been made of it by students of culture, not to mention assessors and technicians of social well-being, the quality of dance music may actually be of far greater fundamental significance than that of concert music anyway. Dance, after all, not only antedates music, but is also probably the most specific source of music and most of the other art forms as well. It is not by chance that poetry, for instance, is measured in feet, and that drama was originally mainly a combination of poetry and choreography performed not on a stage but in the orchestra, in other words, a dancing place! Furthermore, dance, according to impressive anthropological data, seems to have been the first means by which human consciousness objectified, symbolized, and stylized its perceptions, conceptions, and feelings. Thus the very evidence which suggests that the pragmatic function of concert music is to represent the dancing of attitudes also serves to reinforce the notion that dance is indispensable.

Local Jazz

James Lincoln Collier

The prolific Collier, critic and biographer, has found himself at the center of the current jazz wars (see Dan Morgenstern's attack on his book on Louis Armstrong; *p. 1034**). But Collier's inflammatory political incorrectness shouldn't obscure his dedication to jazz and the usefulness of much of his work. Here, from his 1993 book* Jazz, *is a consideration of a rarely acknowledged aspect of jazz performance.*

I have been saving for last the discussion of a phenomenon in jazz that is little remarked, but that may be more important to the vitality of the music than other aspects I have talked about. It is, in any case, one of the happiest ones. That is what might be called the "local" jazz scene.

Jazz criticism and jazz history have always concentrated on the big names, the stars, and the famous clubs and dance halls where they worked. In fact, jazz history is usually written around a chain of major figures—Oliver, to Armstrong, to Beiderbecke, to Ellington, to Goodman, to Parker, to Davis, to Coltrane, to Coleman—to the point where it might appear to the outsider that these great players *were* jazz history.

But, in fact, perhaps ninety percent of the music has always been made by unknown players working in local bars and clubs for audiences drawn from the surrounding neighborhood, town, and country. Right from the beginning, all over the United States, there have been thousands of jazz bands manned by people who, in the main, play the music only part-time. Some of these are outright amateurs offering a very rough version of the music for the amusement of their friends at tailgate parties, anniversaries, or fraternity beer busts. Others are semi-professionals who play for money on some more or less regular basis in restaurants, bars, lake cruises, clubhouses, campus lounges, community centers—almost anywhere that it is possible to make music. Many are high school music teachers. Still others are professional musicians who make the bulk of their living playing club dates in their area, but keep together trios and quartets that find jazz work two or three times a month. Finally, a fairly considerable number of full-time professional jazz musicians dip into the local jazz scene from time to time when they have nothing else booked, in order to "keep their chops up," as a favor, or because they would rather be out playing than sitting home watching television. I have seen notables like Al Haig, Max Kaminsky, Wild Bill Davison, and Eddie Gomez playing with semi-pros, and even Armstrong, Goodman, and Parker have been known to sit in with such groups on occasion.

It should be borne in mind that this "local" jazz scene exists in big cities as well as small towns and suburban communities. New York, Chicago, Boston, Philadelphia, San Francisco, and other cities have their contingents of part-time players who find bars and restaurants where they can work regularly for modest sums.

It is difficult to calculate how extensive this local jazz scene is. The Horowitz survey gives us some clues, however. It reports that about .8 percent of Americans play jazz in public from time to time—about 1,300,000 adults. There are about 144,500 members of the American Federation of Musicians, which most full-time professional jazz musicians belong to; and as many of these people are not jazz players, it is clear that, as Horowitz says, the 1,300,000 jazz players aforementioned are "largely amateur performers."

My own experience suggests that there is some sort of regular local jazz activity in most cities with populations of 50,000 and above. There are about 500 such cities in the United States, and as the larger cities will have several—even dozens of regularly constituted jazz bands working part-time—the total number of such bands must run into the thousands, and the players in them to the tens of thousands

But it is not just in the cities, large or small, that these local jazz bands are found. Startling numbers of them are to be found in suburban restaurants, and even roadhouses in rural areas. I have repeatedly been astonished to find in a local barroom in a rural backwash a jazz musician of the first quality playing for an audience of working people out for a little fun. (It often turns out that such players were once "on the road with Woody.")

To this must be added the 20,000 college, high school, and even junior high school stage bands and jazz units that rehearse regularly and give occasional concerts. Admittedly, the audience for most of these student groups is artificial, consisting of parents and fellow students dragged out two or three times a year to dutifully applaud the carefully rehearsed version of "Little Darlin'." Nonetheless, it is a jazz experience for everyone involved.

Thus, even though we can only put rough numbers to this local jazz scene, we can be sure that in bulk it vastly outweighs the big-time professional arena in any terms we wish to use—numbers of musicians involved, numbers of gigs played, the size of the live audience. At this moment *The New Yorker* lists nine well-known jazz clubs in New York City that usually feature name jazz musicians. I can think offhand of at least twice that many clubs in Manhattan alone that use semi-professional jazz bands several nights a week. And this is in the heart of the supposed jazz capital of the world, where every night the unsung must compete with the likes of Phil Woods, Barney Kessel, and Gerry Mulligan, all of whom are playing in Manhattan as I write. In most small cities and suburban towns, there are *no* locations that regularly hire big-name jazz musicians: the Mulligans and Kessels appear at such places only for occasional concerts. Here the locals dominate by a factor of at least ten to one, and perhaps many times that: there are thousands of towns in which the appearance of a star jazz musician is a rare event, but that offer local jazz bands on a weekly basis.

This is especially true of Dixieland. With the recent deaths of the last of the Dixieland veterans, like Wild Bill Davison, there are virtually no professionals left playing in this style. There are a few exceptions, like the Jim Cullum Happy Jazz Band, but almost all of the some one hundred bands that show up at the Sacramento Dixieland Festival each year are manned, in the main, by part-timers. It is one of the paradoxes of jazz that this basic form has virtually disappeared from the repertory of the professionals: it is kept alive by the local players.

These local jazz players come from everywhere in the society and include every class and ethnic group. Nonetheless, a disproportionate number of them are middle-class, both black and white, many of them from the higher end of the socioeconomic spectrum. We would not be surprised to find among them a fair number of writers, painters, or college professors, for whom jazz is part and parcel of the intellectual or semi-bohemian lifestyle many of them adopt. It is more surprising to find in this group a large number of doctors, lawyers, dentists, and captains of industry, many of them political conservatives, a strain not generally thought to be widespread in jazz. This phenomenon is important to note, for it contradicts the stereotype of the jazz player as outsider or political radical. It is simply true that there are plenty of skilled, sensitive jazz players around who vote for conservative candidates, oppose gun control, and believe that welfare cheats are responsible for the present federal budget deficit.

Part of the explanation for the disproportionate number of upper-middle-class professionals in the ranks of the part-time players is that there were two paths open to them other than music. Most of them, black and white, came from middle-class homes where it was taken for granted that they would go on to college and have professional careers. Despite that, many of them considered careers in music, some even trained at it, and a fair number actually tried it for a few months or even years. But most quickly began asking themselves why they should settle for the risky, even marginal lives most musicians lead, when they could be doctors, lawyers, government officials, and upper-level corporate executives, with the prestige and money that go along with such careers. For these people, the critical decision to give up music usually followed the realization that they would be spending the bulk of their lives in music playing club dates, or if they were lucky, working in the studios or in pit orchestras. For a kid from a working-class home who may have dropped out of high school to go out on the road, a lifetime of club dates sounds a good deal better than thirty years in the canning plant or the post office. To the young adult with a college degree, there are other alternatives: if you are not going to be playing jazz in any case, why not aim for a professional career and play jazz on the side?

But it is hardly the case that the part-timers among the local players are all surgeons with half-million-dollar annual incomes. The local scene is very democratic. Any local jazz band is likely to include a high school music teacher, a mail carrier or cab driver, one or two full-time club date musicians, as well as a doctor, lawyer, or college professor. They frequently include a retiree who finally has the time to work at his music. Most revealingly, the pecking order on the bandstand forms up along musical, rather than occupational, lines. The clarinet-playing bank president will take his cues from the club-date pianist who earns a fraction of the banker's income but knows Bird's changes to the bridge to "Cherokee."

One factor that keeps the local jazz scene in good health is the fact that the players come cheap. To a few the money is important; some bands of part-timers develop local reputations and can work a hundred or more gigs a year, often for seventy-five, a hundred, or more dollars a man, and for some players the extra five thousand dollars a year is significant. But most of the gigs local bands of this kind work pay twenty-five to fifty dollars a man, and many are what the musicians call "freebies." For many local players, the earnings do not cover their expenses—travel costs, reeds and strings, and instrument repair, to say nothing of the between-set beers, which may not always be on the house.

What matters to these people is the chance to play jazz, and especially to play it in public, and that is as true of the working club-date musician as it is of the rank amateur. There are many busy professional musicians who will give up a Sunday afternoon and travel an hour or more each way, to play a jazz gig with agreeable companions for nominal money. Exactly why it is important for them to play in front of a real audience is difficult to know; obviously, the experience of playing, of itself, is no different in a basement den or a rehearsal hall from what it is in a club. But it does matter to the local players to work before an audience. For the part-time musician this is to some extent a matter of credentials: a player who is working in public for a fee, however small, can savor the idea that he is a jazz musician, in the same way that a schoolteacher who occasionally places a short story with a little magazine can think of himself as a writer.

But I think there is more to it than that. Ordinary local jazz players, whether they work in jazz full-time or not, lead the same sort of daily life that most Americans do: a routine job, marriage and family life with the normal ups and downs; births, deaths, commuting trains, vacation trips, the flu, office parties. The experience of playing jazz in the local gin-mill, however seedy, is the plus, the added factor that lifts them out of their daily lives and enables them to accept more easily the graying hairs, the children's failures, the grind of the job. It heals the battered ego, provides a sense of being on the inside of something, a feeling of doing something wholly worthwhile for a change.

Beyond this, the experience of playing regularly with the same people is like belonging to a bowling league. There is a genuine camaraderie among people who play jazz together frequently. This sense of good fellowship is an important aspect of their gig, especially where the musicians have been working together for a period of time, as is likely to be the case with local groups, who do not have the vast pool of first-rate jazz musicians to call on that exists in big cities. A sense of good feeling on the bandstand is an attraction for audiences, too, who notice the players kidding each other about mistakes, cheering each other on, and indulging in a certain amount of good-natured banter. Good spirits like these are infectious. It is common to hear audiences say, "You all seem to have such a good time playing."

Having a good spirit on the bandstand is more important to local players, who are not doing it for money or prestige, than it is for professionals who more frequently have something to prove—a reputation to uphold, a leader to impress. As a consequence, big egos and domineering personalities are not well tolerated among the locals, and such people are likely to find themselves excluded, no matter how good they are, in favor of less adequate musicians who are more personable, more willing to play the supporting roles that a jazz band, like a football team, requires. Most jazz musicians—and that includes professionals as well—feel a *responsibility* for the music. You don't cheat, you don't look for the showy effect, you don't push yourself forward at the expense of others. You remain humble in the face of the difficulty of playing jazz well, and the example of the great players who manage to do so consistently. Local players generally have little use for musicians who lack this humility.

It is probably here that the line between the full-time jazz player and the part-timer is most clearly drawn. Professionals are working in a very tight market and are perforce more competitive than those who are not dependent on jazz for their living, or just as important, a place in the world. They are more likely to endure the abrasive but gifted player who draws audiences, and to tailor their playing to the demands of the market in order to keep the gig. Local jazz players—and once again we remember that they include a lot of professional club-date musicians—are not immune to commercial pressures, because they, too, want to keep their gigs. But their attitude is more likely to be, "I'm not doing this for the money; why am I driving all the way over here just to play this stuff?" The nonprofessional has the luxury of principle, which the professionals do not always have.

Jazz critics have usually looked down on the nonprofessionals with, at best, amused condescension, and, at worst, outright scorn. They have written virtually nothing about the local jazz scene, one exception being John S. Wilson of *The New York Times,* who occasionally reports on clubs where the unsung groups play. To the average critic, this local jazz scene, with its tens of thousands of players and its huge audience, does not exist.

Professional jazz musicians take a far more tolerant view. As I have pointed out, most professionals, even very big names, find themselves from time to time working with local groups, and they are almost always very accommodating in such circumstances. Rarely do they pull rank or try to dominate the proceedings. As a rule they try to fit themselves into the circumstances as best they can in order to make the gig go smoothly.

It is important for us to keep in mind that "part-time" or "local" is not synonymous with poor musicianship. Among the local players are many who could have had careers in music if they were so impelled, and who from time to time are asked to work with name jazz players. As a rule, the professionals tend to hire other professionals, in part because they need the gigs more than the part-timers do, in part because other pros are more likely to be hiring people for their own gigs. But the professionals usually keep in their books the phone numbers of a certain number of part-timers whose work they respect, and call them on occasion. In fact, the line between the part-timer and the full-time jazz player, the professional and the semi-pro, is fluid. Not only are semi-professionals often hired to work with established musicians, but more frequently than is realized, professionals accept jobs with local players. Professionals get married, have families, find day jobs, and become local players working once or twice a week to bring in a little extra money and to remind themselves that they are, really, musicians. Part-timers take early retirement and attempt to establish themselves as professional. The line is regularly crossed.

But it must be admitted that the majority of the part-time jazz musicians who make up the local bands do not play at a professional level. Many of them are strictly avocational players who like to get out one evening a week and bang around on "Lady Be Good" or "Bernie's Tune" in the best way they can. Others with some training will make a better showing—can indeed sound very professional when they are working in the genre they are most at home in. And this, really, is the point. It is characteristic of the part-time player to be musically limited one way or another. Many of them cannot read very well, and some cannot read at all. Many have only an intuitive grasp of theory, enough to work for them in their genre, but not beyond it. Most have one or another technical weakness—good tone but a poor upper register, a lot of speed but questionable intonation at moments, a fine inventive mind but inconsistent, a big ear and no chops. And it is therefore not surprising that many of them have little experience playing other kinds of music: they cannot sit down in the local concert band and produce the legitimate sound called for; cannot walk into an ordinary club date and play the Latin tunes, recent pop hits, or ethnic specialties such jobs require. They are specialists in jazz who know the jazz standards and the conventions of the music, and can frequently produce an acceptable, even exciting, level of jazz. But they are not—most of them—broad-based musicians.

It could hardly be otherwise. It is very difficult to play a musical instrument well, especially at the level expected of musicians today, when the woods are full of young music school graduates who fly around their horns and read anything in seven clefs. It takes thousands upon thousands of hours of practice, over many years, to reach a competitive level, and it takes constant playing to keep the skills sharp. Many professionals, even after they are well established, continue to practice several hours a day: Benny Goodman practiced obsessively long after he was able to frighten most of the people around him with his technical skills.

The most dedicated of the part-timers make a point of picking up their instruments regularly if they can, if only for fifteen minutes a day. But blessed with regular jobs, commuting time, family responsibilities, and community obligations, they often find themselves going for days at a stretch without touching their instruments. Some make it a point to keep their instruments unpacked so they can practice for a few minutes while waiting for a spouse to finish dressing, or for the children to get out of the bathroom. That is no way to improve.

Some of these local jazz players, especially the younger ones who are making their livings on the club date circuit in Evanston, Marin, or Westchester, have ambitions to move onto a larger stage. Someday they will "get to New York," start playing with the big names, make records under their own name, work in the well-known clubs. But most no longer dream those dreams. They know enough about the music business to be shy of it; they recognize their limitations; they realize that they could play music full-time only by sacrificing their families. Maybe some day—when the kids are older, when they retire—they will woodshed, take some lessons, get their theory together, and see what happens. But for now, it is enough that they can get out once or twice a week, once or twice a month, and play the music.

Nonetheless, these local, part-time jazz players are a far more important part of jazz than has been generally recognized. For one thing, anyone sufficiently devoted to music to endure the often painful struggle to play it as well as they can in constrained circumstances, is bound to care for jazz with something of the fervor of an acolyte. These tends of thousands of local players constitute an important audience for jazz. They listen regularly to the jazz radio programs; they buy tapes and CDs; they tape scores and even hundreds of hours of music for their personal jazz libraries; they go to clubs and concerts when their favorites are appearing.

Moreover, they are an extremely knowledgeable audience. They can hear, to one degree or another, what is going on in the jazz they listen to. They know how So-and-so's version of a tune differs from the standard way of playing it, because they have played it a hundred times themselves. They know which technical stunts are easier to bring off than they sound, and which lazy passages are actually very difficult to play. They are more appreciative of the *musicianship* required of a particular performance, even where the jazz content is not very important. Their experience over the years of playing from time to time with solid professionals, even big-name players, gives them a very clear idea of what goes into a first-rate jazz performance. They are likely to be better critics of the music than many of the well-known jazz writers whose pieces they frequently read. In sum, they make up the best kind of audience jazz musicians have, because they know what is going on in a performance, they approach their art with humility, and they respect those who can do it well.

For another thing, they make available to the public a tremendous amount of live music that otherwise would not exist. Big-city music clubs today often charge customers as much as twenty-five dollars admission, and may require a minimum as well. A couple can easily spend fifty dollars to hear a set or two by a big-name musician, and few people can afford this very often.

The local players, on the other hand, mainly work in places that charge at most a five-dollar music fee, and the majority of them do not charge anything beyond the price of a couple of beers. Furthermore, where a lot of the stars working the big-name clubs are not scheduled to start until ten at night, and may not actually get going until well beyond that, the local bands will start at eight or nine and quit by midnight, simply because many of the musicians have day jobs to get to the next morning. This schedule makes it possible for ordinary people who happen to like jazz to go out to the neighborhood Italian restaurant for a couple of hours to hear the local band, have a couple of drinks and the pizza, and be home in bed at a reasonable hour.

In fact, these local players provide a lot of free music, for they are frequently asked to play concerts for retired people on small incomes, the weddings and anniversaries of friends and relatives, school concerts meant to educate children about jazz, political rallies, and, inevitably, memorial services for other musicians. In some cases, a well-known jazz band will be seen as a community resource, and will find itself being asked to provide free music at community functions—the opening of the new library, the Christmas party for the indigent, the block association's annual fund-raiser. As such, these local groups are integrating jazz into the community in a more real and personal way than the professionals do, who by and large resent being asked to perform for nothing on the reasonable grounds that they ought not be required to compete with themselves.

Jazz stopped being a folk music long before it escaped New Orleans. But in the hands of the local players, jazz remains, in a certain sense, folk music. They are providing for nominal sums, or indeed for nothing, functional music to people who share this aspect of a common culture. And this is why these players are so important to the music: they are not playing jazz for fame and money, but sheerly because they love the music. They are the pure in heart, and they should be condescended to by critics no more than we condescend to the club tennis player who gets onto the court every Sunday for the love of the game.

These local players are essential in jazz. They are the foot soldiers in the army, and in the end it is the foot soldiers, not the generals, who win wars. If the record companies suddenly stopped recording jazz, the radio stations stopped playing it, the jazz clubs switched to hip-hop, and the name players disappeared into the studio, jazz would endure, because these foot soldiers, the local musicians, would go on playing it in neighborhood taverns, high school auditoriums, tailgate parties, or if need be, in their own basement game rooms. As long as these, the true acolytes, go marching on, the music will live.

Fifty Years of "Body and Soul"

Gary Giddins

In 1980, Gary Giddins celebrated the fiftieth anniversary of the omnipresent "Body and Soul" *by tracing the song's recording history.* *See also p. 701 for an interview with its composer.*

In this year of its fiftieth anniversary, let us now praise a song—the most recorded American popular song of all time (nearly 3000 versions). Few songs have survived as long or as well, and none have inspired as many durable interpretations by successive generations of musicians. "Body and Soul" first became famous as the showstopper in a 1930 Broadway revue called *Three's a Crowd,* starring Libby Holman, Clifton Webb, and Fred Allen. Ironically, Arthur Schwartz and Howard Dietz, the show's chief songwriters, tried to have it cut. According to Robert Sour, who collaborated with Edward Heyman on the lyric, the song was actually deleted from several performances at the tryout in Philadelphia, where they wrote several sets of lyrics in a plea to save it. Fortunately for everyone, Libby Holman sang it in New York, and thus was born the ballad that earned its twenty-two-year-old composer, Johnny Green, a grateful footnote in the annals of jazz.

It's hard to imagine jazz without "Body and Soul." Excepting the blues and those songs (such as "I Got Rhythm," "Honeysuckle Rose," and "How High the Moon") that were transformed by jazz musicians into untethered chord progressions, no other piece has been interpreted as frequently or with such consistently rewarding results. Yet it's an unusually difficult example of the thirty-two-bar AABA song, with three key changes in the chorus (and three more in the rarely performed verse), intricate major/minor circuitry, and a wide range; moreover, it has a cloyingly powerful melody. Jazz musicians favor "Body and Soul" not because the harmonies provoke vivid new variations, as is the case with Jerome Kern's "All the Things You Are," but because they like the tune.

Ironically, the improvisation that secured the song's place in jazz—Coleman Hawkins's 1939 masterpiece—suspended the melody almost entirely. Yet even his most demonic and irreverent descendants, including Charlie Parker and John Coltrane, found it difficult to shuffle off Green's imposing melodic coils. Basically, there have been three interpretive approaches: (a) personalized recitation; (b) whimsical variation employing fragments from other songs; and (c) genuine melodic variation. Perhaps only Hawkins, Teddy Wilson, and two or three others have achieved the last, which is a fairly commonplace goal in jazz improvisation. And yet performances of "Body and Soul" continue to proliferate, and several artists have recorded it repeatedly.

Johnny Green has spent most of his life writing movie music in Hollywood. His songs are few, but of high quality: "Out of Nowhere," written in 1931, became as much a part of the bop era (thanks to Charlie Parker, Tadd Dameron, and Fats Navarro) as "Body and Soul" was of swing, and "Coquette," "I Cover the Waterfront," and "I'm Yours" have also enjoyed the respect of jazz musicians. But "Body and Soul" is in a class by itself. Within a period of about eight weeks in the fall of 1930, at least eight versions were recorded, including those by the three torchiest ladies of the era—Libby Holman, Ruth Etting, and Helen Morgan. Louis Armstrong transformed it from a lament of unrequited love to a ballad with greater interpretive potential, and established it as a jazz standard. In trying to trace its progress during the past fifty years, and the progress of jazz as reflected in approaches to that one song, I listened to over ninety versions.

I encountered not only dozens of first-rate performances, but several milestones indicative of the development of jazz itself: the first fruits of what would be the most influential keyboard style of the thirties (Wilson), the long-meter approach to ballads (Eldridge), the culmination of the vertical style of improvisation (Hawkins), the rise of virtuosity in jazz bass (Blanton), the initial explorations of Charlie Parker, and the fullest realization of talented stylists (Chaloff, Cohn, Betty Carter, and others). The magical qualities of "Body and Soul" lay in its ability to inspire musicians to plumb the depths of their own creativity. I've narrowed the list to my favorites, plus a few interesting curios. Two sets of lyrics from the song's Philadelphia tryout are in circulation; Billie Holliday recorded the second set, but almost everyone else sings the first. Also, three writers are officially credited with the occasionally ungainly words ("my life a wreck you're making"). The ringer is Frank Eyton, a staff arranger at Chappell & Co., which offered to publish the song on condition that he work on the lyric. Eyton was cut in, but according to Sour, "He didn't even change a comma." Incidentally, the best "straight" recording is the 1947 rendition by Frank Sinatra (Columbia), who except for dotting one quarter note at the expense of another, sings it just as Green wrote it, thereby demonstrating that the song is pretty wonderful to begin with. I've dated the entries that follow not by the artist's first record but by the one that seems to me most indicative.

1930: LOUIS ARMSTRONG (COLUMBIA). No one translated more pop into jazz than Armstrong, and though his effort with the Les Hite orchestra isn't as prepossessing as some of his other gems from the period, its feeling and drama make the torch singers sound like holdovers from a previous century. His trumpet swings the turnbacks and heats up the last eight bars, but his vocal, seemingly tenuous in its determination to rethink every phrase, is what you remember.

1935: BENNY GOODMAN TRIO (BLUEBIRD). The trio's first record, and one of Teddy Wilson's most celebrated solos—a sixteen-bar variation that sounds almost like an inversion of the melody. But it's a mistake to isolate Wilson's contribution. The record is gripping because of the constant colloquy between Wilson's melancholy provocations (in accompaniment as well as solo) and Goodman's straightforward recitation. Wilson offers a somewhat different paraphrase in the trio's 1938 version (Columbia), and reworks some of the same ideas in his 1941 solo performance (Smithsonian/Columbia).

1937: DJANGO REINHARDT (CAPITOL). The guitarist's superb solo includes a rubbery stop-and-go phrase at the first turnback, a folkishly plucked release, and lightning strumming, as well as a doubletime passage in the third chorus. His 1938 version (EMI) with Larry Adler is charming, but less adventurous.

1938: CHU BERRY AND ROY ELDRIDGE (COMMODORE). After Hawkins, Eldridge has the most claims to B&S, and it's his technical brilliance rather than Berry's rather decorative statement that makes this a classic, the epitome of swing. Eldridge was the first to play the song in long meter (each measure is doubled), a practice that is still widely imitated. He merely embellishes the melody—but what embellishment, and what velocity. Note Catlett's drumming during the release and when Roy returns to the original tempo. Among other Eldridge versions are a 1939 fragment (Jazz Archive), an amazing, extended blitz from a 1941 jam (Xanadu), a 1944 studio version in which a stunning reading is foreshortened by a piano solo (Decca), and a moving 1967 concert without long meter (Pumpkin).

1939: COLEMAN HAWKINS (QUINTESSENCE/RCA). One of the most celebrated improvisations in music, and a gauntlet tossed at every other saxophonist in jazz. There is nothing to compare with it. For two choruses and a brief coda, Hawkins rhapsodizes over the chords, never even hinting at Green's melody after the first seven notes, and the profusion of ideas, the sustained tension, the incomparable rhythmic authority build dynamically, phrase after phrase. Incredibly, it was a huge hit—Hawkins's variations became as much a part of jazz as the original melody; Benny Carter orchestrated part of it, Eddie Jefferson wrote lyrics to it, Hawkins used his improvisation as the basis for subsequent improvisations. In 1948, Hawkins recorded "Picasso" (Verve) after eight hours of preparation; it was the first unaccompanied tenor solo in jazz, and based on the changes of B&S. Of his many other versions, a 1959 concert reading (Verve) was outstanding.

1940: JIMMY BLANTON AND DUKE ELLINGTON (SMITHSONIAN/RCA). A milestone in virtuoso bass playing. Blanton's arco is notable for its warmth, rudely attacked low notes, and glissandos, but his pizzicato half-chorus shows how remarkable an improvisor he was.

1940: BILLIE HOLLIDAY (COLUMBIA). She made all kinds of subtle alterations in the melody, and Eldridge took eight memorable measures. I slightly prefer her 1946 version (Verve), in which the phrasing is more legato and the alterations braver. She always sang, "My life a hell you're making."

1940: CHARLIE PARKER (ONYX). Bird's first recording, from a Wichita broadcast transcription, is a curio—but note how confidently he toys with Hawkins's phrases in bars 9-14. A 1950 concert (Sonet) found him flying high, yet not beyond the tune's gravity.

1942: LESTER YOUNG (PHOENIX). Naturally, he had to try his hand at it, and he's wistful and sure; Nat Cole's famous solo routine is here in embryonic form. Young's deeply considered 1950 version (Savoy) is an often overlooked gem.

1944: JAZZ AT THE PHILHARMONIC (VERVE). Les Paul plays a comical Django solo and J. J. Johnson pays homage with a couple of Hawkins's phrases, but Nat Cole's whimsy just about wins out. His solo consists almost entirely of cleverly juxtaposed quotations, which he'd refined in his trio version (Capitol) earlier that year.

1944: COZY COLE (SAVOY). Ben Webster's turn. He's sensuous and breathy for the first chorus, and ardent to the point of violence when he tips his hat to Roy Eldridge for the long-meter chorus.

1944: ART TATUM (COMET). He left more than a dozen versions, including broadcast and army recordings, but his first try—with his 1937 Swingsters—was inconsequential. A 1940 after-hours gem (Onyx) shows that he viewed the tune with irony similar to Nat Cole's—he alternates Monkian asceticism with flighty asides and makes the release a potpourri of off-the-wall quotes. This propensity came to fruition in the 1944 trio gambol with Tiny Grimes and Slam Stewart, which is to all previous versions what *Animal Crackers* was to drawing-room comedy. Here, and in his 1953 solo (Pablo), he showed greater ingenuity in long meter than at ballad tempo.

1946: DON BYAS (PRESTIGE). Yet another ravishing tenor seduction of the melody, virtuosic and ardent. A more relaxed but no less impassioned reading was captured after-hours in 1941 (Onyx).

1946: BOYD RAEBURN (SAVOY). George Handy's sumptuous arrangement is outerspace schmaltz with swirling harp, punctuating French horns, and a Ginny Powell vocal.

1947: TEDDY EDWARDS (ONYX). I think this is the first bop version. B&S didn't appeal to the boppers right away, probably because its melody demanded attention, while the soloists were looking for new melodies. Edwards broadened his vibrato to suggest Hawk, but his nifty triplets and the injection of Latin rhythm are signs of the times.

1949: JAMES MOODY (PRESTIGE). He ejects from the melody by the second bar, doubletimes his pet licks (while avoiding long meter), and swings with relentless creativity. Not quite up to "I'm in the Mood for Love," but Eddie Jefferson wrote lyrics to this solo too. Moody's 1956 version (Chess) is notable for a splendid Johnny Coles long-meter trumpet solo that coolly navigates the major/minor changes.

1955: SERGE CHALOFF (CAPITOL). Perhaps no other recording demonstrates the full dynamic range of the baritone sax for such emotional effect. Chaloff, suffering from spinal paralysis, cut this from a wheelchair, and though "Thanks for the Memories" and "Stairway to the Stars" are contenders, this may well be his masterpiece, and is certainly one of the most compelling ballad performances in jazz. It's been out of print for nearly twenty-five years.

1956: HANK JONES (SAVOY). Among the bebop piano versions are those by Erroll Garner, Bud Powell, and Barry Harris, but this is the most beautiful—lush chord modulations and a fanciful second chorus (until the release). How did we allow this man to disappear into the studios for so long?

1957: GERRY MULLIGAN AND PAUL DESMOND (VERVE). A four-part ricercar, though the saxophonists encircle the melody and each other so limpidly (the heat rises subtly but steadily) that you might forget that bass and drums also play "parts."

1958: SONNY ROLLINS (VERVE). For his second attempt at an unaccompanied tenor solo, Rollins turned to tradition, and played two choruses plus an intro and coda (built on a single motif). Its chief interest is rhythmic, and though the playing is often magnificent, a comparison with the abstractions of Hawkins's "Picasso" makes the Old Man look godlike.

1960: JOHN COLTRANE (ATLANTIC). He plays long meter throughout, and gives B&S a new character with minor-key alterations. But he never gets beyond the surface, and the most interesting solo is McCoy Tyner's burrowing chorus. Interestingly, Coltrane played a better solo on a rejected alternate take, where Tyner's solo was relatively dull.

1961: BUCK CLAYTON (INNER CITY). A personalized, melancholy statement with authentic drama, and a vividly Armstrongian open-horn finish.

1962: THELONIUS MONK (COLUMBIA). Studious stride in the left hand, and slapdash minor seconds in the right, and all the alterations in the world can't keep the ancient lament from shining through.

1966: HENRY RED ALLEN (IMPULSE). The superbly eccentric New Orleans-born trumpeter-vocalist first recorded the song in 1935 (Columbia), but this version, his solo feature from a concert with the compatibly eccentric Pee Wee Russell, is looser and more inventive. He plays two trumpet choruses, over slow and fast rhythms, and sings with bellicose conviction.

1969: BETTY CARTER (BUSH). From her famous medley with "Heart and Soul" (in which she "lost control . . . yes I lost it"); there is no more sultry or heartrending ballad performance than her chorus and a half of B&S. She reprises Billie's "hell" and does the last eight bars a cappella.

1970: BUDDY TATE (MPS). There is a jaunty after-hours version from 1941 (Xanadu), but this is close to definitive, although I've heard him do it even more effectively in concert. It's a beautifully controlled, piercingly vocalized recitation.

1970: DEXTER GORDON (PRESTIGE). The performance is shaped in part by Tommy Flanagan's minor-key vamp and the subtle long-meter manipulations of Alan Dawson, while Gordon moseys into fantasyland, combining methods B and C (see intro above). His 1978 version (Columbia) overdoes the vamp, and after a good beginning, he gets bogged down.

1973: AL COHN (MUSE). In which all the distinctive aspects of Cohn's style came together in two masterful, immensely communicative choruses—the second, especially, is a straight-from-the-heart marvel, in which hollow moans footnote the compelling sureness.

1977: BENNY CARTER (PABLO LIVE). He plays the first chorus fairly straight on trumpet, but his prolix alto chorus skirts through the chords with admirable independence, the melody peeking through and amplifying his own take.

1978: ARCHIE SHEPP (HORO). The most recent extravaganza by an uneven tenorist, accompanied only by guitar. There's no escaping the melody for Shepp, who rummages through it songfully, ultimately taming it with his penetrating tone (his cries recall Buddy Tate) and acerbic asides.

1978: SARAH VAUGHAN (PABLO). Her 1946 performance (Everest) was merely flawless, the one from 1954 (Emarcy) expertly poised, as she imbued every syllable with nuance and worked in a long-meter section. This version, a duet with Ray Brown, starts with a long-meter release and circles back through the ballad for a creative tour de force.

1978: THE HEATH BROTHERS (COLUMBIA). Percy Heath's "In New York" is a rarity—a bop line composed on B&S changes, inspired by Blanton's last half-chorus with Ellington. Jimmy Heath plays a chorus, but his real confrontation with the tune came in 1975 (Xanadu).

1978: BILL EVANS (WARNER BROS.). This bears comparison with the Goodman trio, since Toots Thielemans dominates with a locked-in harmonica solo, and the real breakthrough is a romantic and highly inventive half-chorus of piano; it's something of a disappointment when Thielemans returns.

1979: HELEN HUMES (MUSE). What a surprise!—proof that a good singer can still invest the song with emotional fortitude and make it work anew. It's startling to hear her riff the second chorus, and take risks throughout. The allure of B&S continues.

Everycat and Birdland, Mon Amor

Francis Davis

In 1986, critic Francis Davis reviewed Bertrand Tavernier's movie 'Round Midnight, *starring Dexter Gordon, and two years later he wrote about the next major jazz film, Clint Eastwood's* Bird *(Forest Whitaker as Charlie Parker). Tavernier wins by default. From Davis's collection* Outcats.

Everycat

In jazz circles, the early word on *'Round Midnight,* the French director Bertrand Tavernier's nicotine-stained valentine to bebop in European exile in the late fifties, went roughly as follows: critics would loathe the movie for its trivialization of jazz history, but musicians—flattered to see one of their own on the big screen—would adore it for validating their existence (the "I'm in Technicolor, therefore I am" impulse that made longhairs embrace *Easy Rider* in late sixties, and black urban audiences embrace *Shaft* and *Superfly* a few years later). Musicians for, critics against, is indeed the way the sides are lining up, now that *'Round Midnight* has opened. You can probably guess which side I'm on, but I'm not saying that musicians are wrong.

'Round Midnight—starring the tenor saxophonist Dexter Gordon as Dale Turner, a fictional composite of Lester Young and Bud Powell—is about jazz as a religious experience, with all the stigmata and stations of the cross presented in jumbled, vaguely sacrilegious fashion. Gordon's Dale Turner is a tortured black innovator who, like Young, memorizes the lyrics to songs before interpreting them instrumentally, addresses even male acquaintances as "Lady," and spent some time in the stockade during World War II for carrying a photograph of his white wife. Like Bud Powell, Turner was once beaten repeatedly on the head with billy clubs, and like many musicians of Powell's generation, he is easy prey for obsequious drug pushers and sleazeball promoters (typified here by Martin Scorsese, in a distracting cameo). He has an old sidekick nicknamed Hersch (presumably Herschel Evans, Young's sparring partner in the Count Basie Orchestra), a daughter named Chan (after Chan Richardson, Charlie Parker's common-law wife), a lady

friend called Buttercup (just like Powell's widow), and another who sings with a white gardenia pinned in her hair (just like you-know-who, though the buppie princess Lonette McKee is unlikely to remind you of Billie Holiday). When the man standing next to Dale at the bar passes out, Dale says, "I'll have what he's been drinking," just as legend has it Young once did. And like Young, he calls someone shorter than himself "half-a-motherfucker"; the only problem is that Lester was talking to Pee-wee Marquette, the midget master of ceremonies at Birdland, whereas Dale is addressing the normal-sized Bobby Hutcherson.

You get the point: Turner is Everycat, less a character than an accumulation of fact and lore. Despite this, *'Round Midnight,* in its meandering middle stretches, is less a jazz film than another buddy-buddy flick, replete with unacknowledged homoerotic undertones (one scene in which Turner is writing music at the opposite end of the table from his French graphic-designer roommate and benefactor—played by François Cluzet and faithfully modeled on Powell's keeper, Francis Paudras—plays like an inadvertent parody of the successful two-career marriage). The only difference is that one of the buddies is a black, dypsomaniacal, six-foot-seven *Down Beat* Hall-of-Famer.

Even so, it's easy to understand why musicians are pleased with *'Round Midnight.* Clichés and all, it's as sympathetic an account of the jazz life as has ever been presented in a feature film, erring on the side of compassion rather than exploitation, guilty of sentimentality but not sensationalism. The uncertainty of Gordon's line readings betrays that he's no actor and that he was given no real character to work with. But his presence and dignity—his paunch-first stagger, his big-man's daintiness, his rasped expletives, and his vanquished Clark Gable good looks—rescue the movie from banality. A former alcoholic, drug abuser, and longtime expatriate himself, he's obviously drawn from personal experience to give a performance that one suspects would have been beyond the ability of a more experienced actor. His peers will recognize themselves in him, and they can be proud of what they see.

Oddly, the drawback to casting Gordon in the lead role was musical. When he's in peak form, Gordon's tone is as bracing and aromatic as freshly perked coffee. But he was recovering from assorted illnesses and an extended period of inactivity during filming, and as a result, his solos have a spent, desultory air. In dramatic terms, this may be just as well, inasmuch as we are given to understand that Dale Turner is a man slowly snuffing himself out, capable of summoning up his former brilliance only in flashes, convinced that death is nature's way of telling him to take five. (You wonder what Francis is using for ears when he says that Turner is playing "like a god."*) But a sub-par Gordon makes the soundtrack album pretty tough

* You also wonder what Tavernier is using for ears, because, contrary to what our own ears tell us, Francis is supposed to be telling it like it is. It's worth passing along an astute comment that the pop critic Ken Tucker made

going. Gordon isn't the only culprit; the soundtrack's supporting cast is made up of musicians ten to twenty years his junior, for whom bebop is little more than a formal exercise, and Herbie Hancock's incidental music is flat and uninvolving when divorced from the film's imagery. Gordon deserves the plaudits he's winning as an actor, but it would be a pity if the lay audience now discovering him accepts the music from *'Round Midnight* as characteristic.

Although *'Round Midnight* is the only recent movie to star a jazz musician, it's not the only one with a jazz soundtrack. Spike Lee's sleeper hit *She's Gotta Have It* boasts a fine soundtrack by his father, the bassist Bill Lee, which has just been released on Island. The elder Lee's modest, by turns moody and frolicsome small-band score goes awry only once, exactly where the black-and-white movie does: in the too-sweet Ronnie Dyson vocal accompanying an oversaturated Technicolor ballet. But in its mix of disciplined composition and footloose improvisation, Lee's music recalls earlier film scores by such jazz composers as Duke Ellington (*Anatomy of a Murder*), Miles Davis (*Frantic!*), Sonny Rollins (*Alfie*), John Lewis (*Odds Against Tomorrow*), and Gato Barbieri (*Last Tango in Paris*). It also brings to mind Henry Pleasants's conjecture that the collaborations between composers and film directors have the potential to become the modern equivalent of lyric theater. Writing before the corporate takeovers of both film and record companies, and before the success of *Easy Rider, The Graduate,* and *Saturday Night Fever* made soundtrack albums little more than K-Tel greatest-hits collections in disguise, Pleasants had no way of knowing that film composers would eventually rank lower than the music-acquisitions lawyers in the overall scheme of things. It's become more and more unusual to hear a score like Bill Lee's, brashly original and homogenetic to the film it serenades. If Dexter Gordon's haunting portrayal in *'Round Midnight* suggests that jazz musicians can be riveting onscreen subjects, Lee's score confirms that they also have plenty to offer behind the scenes. Here's hoping that more film producers take them up on the offer.

Birdland, Mon Amor

Charlie Parker assured himself of immortality when he recorded "Ko-Ko" for Savoy Records, on November 26, 1945. This wasn't the first time

---

about this sketchily drawn character, after the screening we both saw. Francis is a commercial artist; we see one of his posters for an American film starring Jeff Chandler. Tucker pointed out that such a Frenchman would almost certainly be obsessed with American popular culture in general, not just jazz. But when Francis accompanies Dale to New York, he doesn't go looking for paperbacks by Erskine Caldwell or movies by Nicholas Ray. For that matter, he doesn't even hear any live jazz, except for Dale's.

that bebop was performed in a recording studio, nor was "Ko-Ko" the first jazz "original" extrapolated from the chord sequences of an existing tune—a practice that didn't begin with bop, contrary to popular belief. For that matter, Parker wasn't the first improviser to recognize that despite the nondescript melody of Ray Noble's "Cherokee," its fast-moving chords held the potential for tour de force; Charlie Barnet had beaten him to it by six years. Yet there was really only one historical precedent for "Ko-Ko": Louis Armstrong's 1928 recording of "West End Blues." As Armstrong had done (and as John Coltrane would later, with "Chasin' the Trane"), Parker with one performance reshaped jazz into his own image by establishing an exacting new standard of virtuosity. Listeners encountering "Ko-Ko" for the first time are likely to be astonished by Parker's faultless execution at a tempo that starts off reckless and seems to speed up as it goes along. But the most remarkable aspect of "Ko-Ko" is Parker's reconciliation of spontaneity and form—the impression of economy despite the splatter of notes; the surprising continuity of suspenseful intro, staccato bursts, pulsating rests, and phrases so lengthy they double back on themselves at the bar lines. Parker's contemporaries faced the challenge not only of matching his technique, but also of emulating his harmonic and rhythmic sophistication, and his successors still face the same challenge.

Parker's innovations—and those of Dizzy Gillespie and Bud Powell—are today so ingrained in jazz that it's difficult to remember that bebop was initially considered so esoteric and forbidding that only its originators could play it. "Ko-Ko" would seem to prove the point. Stimulated by Parker, Max Roach made a breakthrough of his own on "Ko-Ko," with an unyielding polyrhythmic accompaniment that amounted to a second melodic line. But Gillespie, who had been forced into service as a pianist in relief of Sadik Hakim (listen to Hakim's disoriented intro on "Thrivin' on a Riff," recorded earlier at the session, and you'll know why), also had to spell Miles Davis on "Ko-Ko." Davis, then still in his teens and making his recording debut, declined even to try to his luck on the piece.

Parker was twenty-five but already addicted to heroin; he would be dead in less than ten years. Two weeks after recording "Ko-Ko," he traveled with Gillespie to Hollywood for a nightclub engagement that lasted almost two months, despite the generally hostile reaction of Southern California audiences to bebop (the new style had been nurtured in secret on the East Coast, its dissemination hindered by a musicians' union ban on new recordings and by wartime restrictions on materials needed to manufacture discs). Parker didn't return to New York with his bandmates; instead, he cashed in his airline ticket to buy drugs. He found himself stranded in Los Angeles during a time when police crackdowns on heroin sent street prices soaring and often made the drug unavailable at any price. In August 1946, Parker was confined at Camarillo State Hospital after being arrested for setting fire to his hotel room in the aftermath of a disastrous recording session.

Parker spent six months at Camarillo, returning to New York in April of 1947. He then began a period in which he could do no wrong, at least in the recording studio, where he produced an unbroken succession of masterpieces for Dial and Savoy, including his most memorable ballad performance, a harmonic tangent on George Gershwin's "Embraceable You." Already married and divorced twice, he wooed two women almost simultaneously, marrying one in 1948 and setting up house with the other two years later, without bothering to divorce the first. In 1949, he scored a triumph at the International Jazz Festival in Paris, and a year later made the first of several records on which he was accompanied by woodwinds and strings, the format that brought him his greatest popular success.

But he never kicked his drug habit for good, and he drank to such excess that his weight ballooned to more than two hundred pounds. Despite his drawing power, nightclub owners became increasingly reluctant to book him, for fear that he'd show up in no shape to perform, or not show up at all. At one point, he was banned from Birdland, the Broadway nightclub named in his honor in 1950. Although he somehow eluded arrest for possession (there were rumors that he pointed detectives to other users in order to save his own skin), the cabaret card he needed in order to perform in New York City nightclubs was taken from him without due process, at the recommendation of the narcotics squad, in 1951. The incident that is said to have finally broken him was the death from pneumonia of his two-year-old daughter by his common-law wife, Chan Richardson, in March 1954. Later that year, he swallowed iodine in an unsuccessful suicide attempt. He died of lobar pneumonia on March 12, 1955, while watching television in the New York apartment of the Baroness Pannonica de Koenigswarter, a wealthy jazz patron. He was thirty-four, but physicians estimated his age at fifty to sixty.

Forest Whitaker plays Parker in *Bird,* a film produced and directed by Clint Eastwood and written by Joel Oliansky. Miming to Parker's actual solos, with his eyes wide open and his shoulders slightly hunched and flapping. Whitaker captures the look we recognize from Parker's photographs and the one surviving television kinescope of him (a 1952 appearance on Earl Wilson's *Stage Entrance,* which is featured in the excellent jazz documentaries *The Last of the Blue Devils* and *Celebrating Bird: The Triumph of Charlie Parker*). Unfortunately, even though he's been outfitted with a gold cap over one incisor to make his smile shine like Parker's, Whitaker is less convincing offstage, where most of *Bird* takes place. On the basis of his brief but effective turn as the young, possibly psychotic pool shark who spooks the master hustler played by Paul Newman in Martin's Scorsese's *The Color of Money,* Whitaker was the right choice to play Parker—a master con, among other things. But Whitaker's performance is too tense and pent-up to bring Parker to life, and by the end of the movie, the actor seems as much the victim of heavy-handed writing and direction as the character does.

Why is it always raining in jazz films, and why are the vices that kill musicians always presented as side effects of a terminal case of the blues? It merely drizzled throughout *'Round Midnight,* and though the movie was false in other ways, the mist was in keeping with the slow-motion music performed by the ailing Dexter Gordon. The music in *Bird* is supposed to be defiant and ebullient, but the *mise en scène* is downbeat, with rain gushing against the windows of melodramatically underlit interiors. (You come out of the theater squinting, just like Eastwood.) Like Milton's Lucifer, whither this Bird flies is hell. He brings rain and darkness with him wherever he goes. His unconscious is haunted by symbols—or, to be more specific about it, by a literal cymbal that flies across the screen and lands with a resounding thud every time he drifts off or nods out. The vision is based on a (perhaps apocryphal) incident to which Eastwood and Oliansky have given too much interpretive spin. As an untutored seventeen-year-old in Kansas City, Parker is supposed to have forgotten the chord changes to "I Got Rhythm" while playing at a jam session with the drummer Jo Jones, who, legend has it, threw one of his cymbals to the floor as a way of gonging the teenager off the stage. Except for overwrought conjecture by Ross Russell in a purple passage toward the end of *Bird Lives!,* there is nothing in the voluminous literature about Parker to suggest that this public humiliation haunted him for the rest of his life. To the contrary, it's usually cited as the incident that strengthened his resolve to become a virtuoso. But in *Bird*'s retelling, the echo of that cymbal deprives Parker of all pleasure in his accomplishments. *Bird*'s Parker wants to rage but can only snivel, even when hurling his horn through a control-room window in abject frustration. You don't believe for a second that this frightened sparrow could have summoned up the self-confidence to make a name for himself in the competitive world of jazz in the 1940s, much less set that world on its ear with "Ko-Ko." Parker was a compulsive, which is another way of saying that he was a junkie, but he was also obsessive, which is another way of saying that he was an artist.* Parker's torment is here, but not his hedonism or his genius or the hint of any connection between them.

* Charlie Parker to Paul Desmond (as quoted by Stanley Crouch, in *The New Republic,* February 27, 1989): "I put in quite a bit of study into the horn, it's true. In fact, the neighbors threatened to ask my mother to move once when I was living in the West. They said I was driving them crazy with the horn. I used to put in at least eleven to fifteen hours a day. I did that for over a period of three or four years."

* * *

MUCH OF WHAT *Bird* tells us about Parker is hooey, and at least one of its inventions is an abomination—a character, a slightly older saxophonist who knew Parker as an upstart in Kansas City, who becomes jealous when he finds out that Parker is the talk of New York. A final encounter with this saxophonist seals Parker's doom. Parker stumbles down Fifty-second Street, dazed to find that the jazz clubs that were the settings for his early triumphs have given way to strip joints. (The excuse for his surprise is having been holed up in the country with Chan for a few months, but anyone who knows anything about jazz during this period has to wonder if he's been on the moon—articles in the national press were bemoaning the departure of jazz from "The Street" as early as 1948, and this is supposed to be 1955.) Told by another acquaintance that he hasn't seen anything yet, Parker wanders into a theater where his old Kansas City rival is knocking 'em dead with a greasy rhythm 'n' blues *à la* King Curtis. This triggers Parker's final breakdown. Even assuming that it was necessary to invent a fictional nemesis for Parker, why name that character "Buster," which the filmmakers should have known was the name of one of Parker's real-life Kansas City mentors, the alto saxophonist Buster Smith? And why pretend that Parker, who reportedly found good in all kinds of music, would have been shocked into a fatal tailspin by the advent of rock 'n' roll?*

Jazz fans appalled by the fraudulent portrayal of Parker won't be the only moviegoers displeased with *Bird.* It's a mess. Even at the epic length of two hours and forty-five minutes, the narrative feels hurried and absentminded, with more flashbacks within flashbacks than any movie since Jacques Tourneur's 1947 *noir, Out of the Past.* You're never sure who's remembering what, what year it is, how famous Parker has become, or how long he has to live—Whitaker has the same puppy-dog look no matter how far gone he's supposed to be, so the only way of telling is by the hair style on Diane Venora, the actress who plays Chan Richardson (she gives up her bohemian bangs and braids after becoming a mother). In terms of explaining to an audience that knows nothing about jazz (most moviegoers, in other words) what made Parker's music so revolutionary, *Bird* is about as much help as *The Ten Commandments* was in explaining the foundations of Judeo-Christian law—you almost expect someone to point to Parker and proclaim, like Yul Brynner as Pharaoh, "His jazz *is* jazz." The script primes us for ironic payoffs it never delivers; as when, for example, Parker hears his blues "Parker's

---

* Gigi Gryce on Charlie Parker (as quoted by Orrin Keepnews in *The View from Within,* Oxford University Press, 1988): "We might be walking along and pass someplace with a really terrible rock and roll band, for instance, and he'd stop and say, 'Listen to what that bass player's doing,' when I could hardly even hear the bass."

Mood" sung by King Pleasure, whose lyrics envision six white horses carrying Parker to his grave in Kansas City; he makes Chan promise not to let his body be shipped back to K.C. for burial. What we're *not* told is that, against Chan's wishes, that's exactly what happened—to tell us this would require acknowledging that Parker was separated from Chan at the time of his death, and still legally wed to Doris Snydor, who is conveniently never mentioned in *Bird.* This movie is probably going to be praised in some quarters for its "unsensational" depiction of an interracial relationship. But the relationship between Whitaker and Venora could stand some sensationalizing. The only sparks that fly between them are acrimonious; they bicker from the word go. Although the script makes Chan an awful scold, Diane Venora brings unexpected shadings to the role: you believe in her as a thrill-seeking hipster who's just as glad when motherhood forces her into a more conventional way of life. Venora's is the film's only convincing performance. Michael Zelnicker is affectless as Red Rodney, the white trumpeter who sang the blues in order to pass as a black albino while on tour with Parker in the segregated South in the late forties. Zelnicker wouldn't have had to worry about white sheriffs; black audiences of the period would have hooted this yuppie off the stage. (He and Parker play a Jewish wedding, and when the cute little rabbi says about Parker and the other sidemen, "These boys are not Jewish, but they are good musicians," you feel as though you've witnessed this scene in a hundred other movies. Eastwood and Oliansky are delivering a sermon on the need for unity among oppressed minorities, and what's unbearable about it as that they think they're being subtle.) As the young Dizzy Gillespie, Sam Wright is sanctimonious and old before his time, and (as the jazz critic Bob Blumenthal has pointed out) the audience that knows nothing about the real-life Dizzy is going to wonder how he ever got that nickname. The first time we see Diane Salinger as the Baroness Nica, she's wearing her beret at a tilt that casts half of her face in shadow, and she watches Parker with predatory eyes. She's a shady lady from Grand Guignol. Why this visual insinuation about a woman who made her apartment into a salon for black musicians with whom she maintained platonic relationships, and whose only possible "crime" was that of dilettantism? She had no responsibility—symbolic or otherwise—for Parker's death.

The music in *Bird* has a phony ring to it, even though Parker's recordings were used for most of the soundtrack. There were fans who used to follow Parker around the country, sneaking cumbersome wire recorders into nightclubs to preserve his work and shutting them off when his sidemen improvised. Eastwood and music supervisor Lennie Niehaus go these ornithologists one better (or one worse) by filtering out Parker's sidemen altogether in favor of new instrumental backing. In addition to being unfair to Parker's sidemen, many of whom were indeed capable of keeping pace with him, this removes him from his creative context and gives no sense that bebop was a movement.*

But Parker is out of context throughout *Bird.* The movie would have us believe that he had little curiosity about the world beyond jazz, which in turn showed only oppositional interest in him. In reality, the musicians who worshiped Parker remember him as well-read, with a consuming interest in twentieth-century classical composition. And black jazz musicians of Parker's era had a direct influence on those white artists from other disciplines—the nascent hipsters and beats who people such early fifties novels as Chandler Brossard's *Who Walk in Darkness* and John Clellon Holmes's *Go.* Parker was a source of fascination to these poets, novelists, and abstract impressionists who were beginning to define themselves as outlaws from middle-class convention. They recognized his artistic drive and suicidal self-indulgence as the *yin* and *yang* of a compulsive nature pushing against physical limitations and societal restraints. In *Bird,* few white characters, except those from the jazz underground, seem to know or care who Parker is, and he isn't sure himself.

The pity of all this is that Clint Eastwood is a jazz fan, and *Bird* is supposed to have been a labor of love. In 1982, Eastwood directed and starred in *Honkytonk Man,* the gentle, admirably straightforward story of a Depression-era Okie troubadour called Red Sovine, who succumbs to tuberculosis before realizing his dream of performing at the Grand Ole Opry. Among its other virtues, that film managed to suggest the succor that music can give both performers and audiences. Perhaps believing that Parker was subjected to a harsher reality than Sovine by virtue of being black and a drug addict, Eastwood's tried to find a more insistent rhythm for *Bird,* but the one he's come up with feels choppy, disconnected, and pointlessly arty, with dated experiments in time and point of view forcing him against his best natural instincts as a storytelling director.

Charlie Parker first appeared on screen in the guise of Eagle, a heroin-addicted saxophonist played by Dick Gregory in the forgotten *Sweet Love Bitter* (1967), which was based on John A. Williams's novel *Night Song.* Although Gregory's performance was surprisingly effective, Eagle was a peripheral figure in a civil-rights-era melodrama about a white liberal college professor on the run from his conscience. In the late 1970s, Richard Pryor was supposed to star in a film about Parker that never got made—which is probably just as well, because Pryor brings so much of his own persona to

* When I wrote this, I hadn't yet heard the *Bird* soundtrack. Read on.

the screen that Charlie Parker would have gotten lost. That leaves us with *Bird,* a jazz fan's movie in the worst possible sense—a movie with the blues, a *Birdland, Mon Amor* that wants to shout "Bird lives!" but winds up whispering "Jazz is dead." *Bird* communicates the melancholy that every jazz fan feels as a result of the music's banishment from mainstream culture. In projecting this melancholy on Charlie Parker—whose music still leaps out at you with its reckless abandon, and whose triumph should finally count for more than his tragedy—Eastwood has made another of those movies that make jazz fans despair that mainstream culture will ever do right by them or their musical heroes.

Bird Land

Stanley Crouch

More on Eastwood's Bird, *this time from Stanley Crouch, whose review (from* The New Republic, *in early 1989) also provides us with this book's final response to the dominating presence of Charlie Parker.*

In the red and purple bric-a-brac that often passes for jazz criticism or jazz scholarship, Charlie Parker looms large. He is the rebel speared by the marksmen of the marketplace, and by the grand conspiracy of robed and unidentified klansmen. Parker was truly one of the most mysterious figures in American art. Six years ago I began the bedeviling job of writing Parker's biography. It quickly became clear that much of what was taken for granted about the alto saxophonist was a mix of near-truth, fabrication, and butt-naked lies.

Over the last few years, culminating in Clint Eastwood's very bad film *Bird,* there has been more attention than usual shown to Parker. Almost everything he ever recorded is now available, some of it reworked for sound vastly superior to the original releases. There is a coffee-table book, a video documentary, and a stack of glowing reviews of *Bird* that reveal the extent to which many who would be sympathetic to Negroes are prone to an unintentional, liberal racism. That racism reduces the complexities of the Afro-American world to a dark, rainy pit in which Negroes sweat, suffer, dance a little, mock each other, make music, and drop dead, releasing at last a burden of torment held at bay only by drugs.

It must be that melodramatic notion of suffering that makes Eastwood's film so appealing. Many film critics appear to have the same problem with the depiction of Negro life that many literary critics do. Too quick to prove that they really understand the plight of the caged coon, who would be a man if only the white world would let him, they often fall for condescending, ignorant, bestial images of Afro-Americans, feeling for them as visitors to Dr. Moreau's Island did, where the noble beasts of the jungle were mutilated into bad imitations of human beings in the mad surgeon's "house of pain." In *Bird,* Negro life is such an incredible house of pain that the dying

Charlie Parker summons up, with one exception, only a montage of negative experience.

The exception is his friend Dizzy Gillespie, who proudly asks an audience just served up some sensational saxophone what they think about it. Otherwise Parker on his deathbed summons up a black doctor predicting that he will die from drugs, a black saxophonist laughing at him, a black musician throwing a cymbal at him in disgust during his early, ineffectual efforts at improvisation. All that remains for him, in Eastwood's account, are images of his smiling, vibrant, white lover Chan, and of his white trumpeter buddy Red Rodney. This is a Charlie Parker in no way connected to, in no way the product of, the Afro-American culture filled with the bittersweet intricacies that were given aesthetic substance so superbly in his music.

The movie makes a perfect companion to Chan Parker's *To Bird With Love,* a huge picture book now out of print that was done with the French archivist and producer Francis Paudras. Artfully organized and intimate (it includes bills, love notes, and poignant telegrams), one would never guess from the book that its author was the last of Parker's four wives, the first two black, the last two white. A famous photograph of Parker with his first wife, Rebecca, whom he married when he was fifteen, their son Leon, and her subsequent husband Ross Davis is cropped so that Rebecca doesn't exist. Those are the kinds of croppings that abound in Eastwood's film, which reportedly leans heavily on Chan's unpublished memoir, *Life in E-Flat.* All of the things that Chan knew little about, or preferred to ignore, remain outside the film.

Though Parker was well taken care of as a child, for example, and was quite attached to his mother, whom he called every weekend, she is only referred to once in *Bird,* when the soothsaying doctor tells that boy he better watch out for that dope. Chan is given a monologue about her own childhood and her own father, and asks Parker about his early life, but he tells her in reply only about the day he discovered that he was addicted. So much for the complexity, or the vitality, of *his* past. His second wife, Geraldine, didn't play a large role in his life, and was only married to him a year; but Doris, the third, went to California in 1946 when Parker had a nervous breakdown there, visited him in Camarillo as often as she could, and returned with him in 1947 to New York, where they lived together until 1950. (Though Eastwood's stacking of the deck in Chan's favor elicits a remarkable performance from Diane Venora, there is something distasteful about the film's general slighting of black women, not least in light of Parker's friendships and working relationships with women such as Mary Lou Williams, Sarah Vaughan, and Ella Fitzgerald; only one on-screen speaking part is given to a black female, in a fictitious situation in which Bird recalls being told, when he was working his style out, "Nigger, don't be playing that shit behind me while I'm trying to *sang*.")

This film depicts not Negroes, but Negro props. No wonder, perhaps, in the light of Eastwood's comment to *Newsweek* that because he listened to a lot of rhythm and blues on the radio as a young man, "I think I was really a black guy in a white body." We get the young Parker playing a song flute as he rides on the back of a horse, a teenaged Parker with a saxophone on the porch of an unpainted house, a couple of young Negroes smoking cigarettes near him. Had Parker grown up in New Orleans instead of Kansas City, he would almost certainly have been shown on a cotton bale.

Then the movie flashes forward to Parker in 1945, roaring through the chords of "Lester Leaps In." Forest Whitaker, who plays Parker, has been directed to hump and jerk and thrust his horn outward, exactly as Parker did not. "The thing about Bird," says Art Taylor, a drummer who played with him, "is that he didn't move. He just stood there almost still as a statue, and when he finished, there was a pool of water at his feet." (Whitaker obviously has the talent to get far closer to Bird than he did; but he was not asked to do much more than another version of the Negro manchild.)

Next Parker comes home, high, in 1954, and explains to Chan that he has just been fired from Birdland, the club named for him. As he gives the details, she talks to him as though he is a child who went off without his lock and got his bike stolen. Bird refers to himself as "an overgrown adolescent," angrily taunting her for trying to "work that psychology on him." He swallows iodine, falls to the floor, and Chan stands over him, saying, "That was stupid. Now I'll have to call an ambulance." From that point in the story until its bitter end, despite an outburst here and a joke there, this Charlie Parker is forever under somebody—his wife, his doctors, his agent, the white South, the narcotics police, the court system, the music business. He is always a victim of the white folks, of the iron-hearted colored people, of himself. At best he is an idiot savant, in possession of natural rhythm, with little more than boyish charm and a sense of bewilderment. There is no sign of the sophistication, curiosity, the aggressiveness, the regality, the guile, the charisma of which all who knew Parker still speak. Eastwood's Parker works only at getting high or not getting high.

Even the world of music is presented as something Bird isn't very involved in, other than as a way of making a living. He shows no real love for the saxophone or for jazz. There is no competitive feeling, no sense of threat, no arrogance, no appreciation of any of his predecessors. (As the pianist Walter Davis, Jr. told me, "You can't have a movie about Bird and not have him run over *somebody*. This was a very aggressive man. He took over and made things go *his* way. If you weren't strong, Charlie Parker would mow you down like grass.") He's just a colored man with a saxophone, a white girlfriend, and a drug problem. When he dies, you are almost relieved.

The critics have made much of Eastwood's love of Parker's art, and even more of the technology that he and his music director Lennie Niehaus used to extract Parker's improvisations from their original recordings so that contemporary musicians could overdub them for today's sound. That accomplishment, however, was a catastrophic mistake. The splendid remasterings that Jack Towers and Phil Schapp have done with Parker's own work on Savoy and Verve are vastly superior to this gimmicky, updated sound track. On the CD versions of *Savoy Original Master Takes* and *Bird: The Complete Charlie Parker on Verve,* there are aesthetic details never heard before. Moreover, as Doris Parker said to Eastwood after a screening of *Bird* at the New York Film Festival, "Charlie didn't play by himself. When you take him away from his real musicians, you destroy what inspired him to play what he did." What the musicians play on Eastwood's sound track is often incompatible, in fact, with what Parker's alto is doing; the music is mixed so high that the saxophone almost never rises above the background, and the drummer, John Guerin, does *not* swing.

THE LIFE OF Charlie Parker was a perfect metaphor for the turmoil that exists in this democratic nation. It traversed an extremely varied world, including everything from meeting and talking with Einstein to attending parties with Lord Buckley where Communists tried to turn him. Parker was at once the aristocracy and the rabble, the self-made creator of a vital and breathtakingly structured jazz vernacular and an anarchic man of dooming appetites. He was always trying to stay in the good graces of those stunned by his disorder. His artistic power was almost forever at war with his gift for self-destruction. He was dead in 1955, at thirty-four, his remarkable musical gifts laid low by his inability to stop fatally polluting and tampering with the flesh and blood source of his energy, with his own body.

Those musical gifts made it possible for Parker to evolve from an inept alto saxophonist, a laughingstock in his middle teens, to a virtuoso of all-encompassing talent who by the age of twenty-five exhibited an unprecedented command of his instrument. His prodigious facility was used not only for exhibition or revenge, moreover, but primarily for the expression of melodic, harmonic, and rhythmic inventions, at velocities that extended the intimidating relationship of thought and action that forms the mystery of improvisation in jazz. In the process, Parker defined his generation: he provided the mortar for the bricks of fresh harmony that Thelonious Monk and Dizzy Gillespie were making, he supplied linear substance and an eighth note triplet approach to phrasing that was perfectly right for the looser style of drumming that Kenny Clarke had invented.

THE ANOMALIES ARE endless. He performed on concert stages as part of Norman Granz's Jazz at the Philharmonic, traveling in style and benefitting from Granz's demand that all his musicians receive the same accommodations, regardless of race; but when he was at the helm of his own groups, Parker was usually performing in the homemade chamber music rooms of nightclubs. "One night I'm at Carnegie Hall," he once told the saxophonist Big Nick Nicholas, "and the next night I'm somewhere in New Jersey at Sloppy Joe's." These shifts of venue paralleled the contrasts in his personality. The singer Earl Coleman, who first met Parker in Kansas City in the early forties, said of him:

> You could look at Bird's life and see just how much his music was connected to the way he lived. . . . You just stood there with your mouth open and listened to him discuss books with somebody or philosophy or religion or science, things like that. Thorough. A little while later, you might see him over in a corner somewhere drinking wine out of a paper sack with some juicehead. Now that's what you hear when you listen to him play: he can reach the most intellectual and difficult levels of music, then he can turn around—now watch this—and play the most low down, funky blues you ever want to hear. That's a long road for somebody else, from that high intelligence all the way over to those blues, but for Charlie Parker it wasn't half a block; it was right next door. . . .

It was not Parker's scope, however, but his wild living, and his disdain for the rituals of the entertainment business, that made him something of a saint to those who felt at odds with America in the years after World War II, who sought a symbol of their own dissatisfaction with the wages of sentimentality and segregation. Parker was a hero for those who welcomed what they thought was a bold departure from the long minstrel tradition to which Negroes were shackled. He was, for them, at war with the complicated fact that the Negro was inside and outside at the same time, central to American sensibility and culture but subjected to separate laws and depicted on stage and screen, and in the advertising emblems of the society, as a creature more teeth and popped eyes than man, more high-pitched laugh and wobbling flesh than woman.

* * *

PARKER APPEARED AT a point in American history when that bizarre image of the Negro had been part of many show business successes: minstrelsy itself, the first nationally popular stage entertainment; *Birth of a Nation,* the first epic film and "blockbuster"; "Amos 'n' Andy," the most popular radio program since its premiere in 1928; *The Jazz Singer,* where Jolson's Jacob Rabinowitz stepped from cantorial melancholy into American optimism by changing his name to Jack Robbins, changing the color of his face, and introducing the recorded voice to film; *Gone With the Wind,* Atlanta's plantation paradise lost; not to mention the endless bit parts in all the performing arts that gave comic relief of a usually insulting sort, or that "realistically" showed Negro women advising lovelorn white girls in their boudoirs. Parker offered an affront to that tradition of humiliation.

In fact, the jazzmen who preceded Parker had also addressed the insults of popular culture, and countered those stereotypes with the elegant deportment and the musical sophistication of the big bands. Parker turned his back on those bands, though; and not only because he preferred five-piece units. Manhandling the saxophone and Tin Pan Alley ditties, writing tunes that were swift and filled with serpentine phrases of brittle bravado, arriving late or not at all, occasionally in borrowed or stolen clothes so ill-fitting that the sleeves came midway down his forearms and the pants part way up his calves, speaking with authority on a wide variety of subjects in a booming mid-Atlantic accent, Parker nicely fit the bohemian ideal of an artist too dedicated to his art to be bought and too worldly to be condescended to. (Except, of course, when he chose himself to mock his own identity, as when he stood in front of Birdland dressed in overalls and announced to his fellow players that he was sure they must be jazz musicians because they were so well dressed.)

Historically, Parker was the third type of Afro-American artist to arrive in the idiom of jazz. Louis Armstrong had fused the earthy and the majestic, and had set the standards for improvisational virtuosity and swing; but he was also given to twisting on the jester's mask. Duke Ellington manipulated moods, melodies, harmonies, timbres, and rhythms with the grace of relaxed superiority, suavely expanding and refining the art in a manner that has no equal. Armstrong's combination of pathos, joy, and farce achieved the sort of eloquence that Chaplin sought; and Ellington commanded the implications of the Negro-derived pedal percussion that gave Astaire many of his greatest moments. But Parker was more the gangster hero, the charming anarchist that Cagney introduced in *Public Enemy.* The tommy gun velocity of Parker's imagination mowed down the clichés he inherited, and enlarged the language of jazz, but like Cagney's Tom Powers, he met an early death, felled by the dangers of fast living.

* * *

IN MANY WAYS, Parker reflected the world in which he was reared, the Wild West town of Kansas City, where everything was wide open and the rules were set on their heads. The mayor and the police were in cahoots with the local mob; liquor flowed during Prohibition, and gambling and prostitution were virtually legal. When the musicians went to bed, everybody else was getting up to go to work. Parker's mother was the mistress of a deacon considered an upstanding representative of the life led by those who lived by the Bible. These were, perhaps, the origins of Parker's conviction that finally there was no law; and the double standards of the racial terrain understandably added to that view.

Parker's father was an alcoholic drawn to the nightlife; his mother left him when the future saxophonist was about nine. Convinced that she could keep young Charlie away from the things her husband loved by giving the boy everything he wanted, she reared him as a well-dressed prince who could do no wrong. That treatment is far from unusual in the lives of Negro innovators. It gives them the feeling that they can do things differently from everyone else. But there was also a crippling side to it. As the bassist Gene Ramey, who knew the saxophonist from about 1934, remarks in the excellent oral history *Goin' To Kansas City,* "He couldn't fit into society, 'cause evidently his mother babied him so much, that he . . . was expecting that from everybody else in the world."

But when Parker, who was known for his laziness, became interested in music in the thirties, he quickly discovered that the gladiatorial arena of the jam session made no allowances for handsome brats in tailor-made J. B. Simpson suits at the height of the Depression. He was thrown off many a stage. It was then that he decided to become the best. As Parker told fellow alto player Paul Desmond in 1953, "I put quite a bit of study into the horn, that's true. In fact, the neighbors threatened to ask my mother to move once when I was living out West. They said I was driving them crazy with the horn. I used to put in at least eleven to fifteen hours a day. I did that for over a period of three or four years."

He practiced incessantly, and was in the streets, listening to the great local players. He was drawn especially to Buster Smith and Lester Young, though he told the younger saxophonist Junior Williams that it was when he heard Chu Berry jamming in Kansas City in 1936 that he actually became serious about the saxophone. (So serious, in fact, that he gave his first son Berry's name, Leon.) Berry was swift, articulate, and a great chord player; Smith had deep blues soul; Young preferred a light sound that disavowed the conventional vibrato and invented melodic phrases of spectacular variety and rhythmic daring. Parker was also taken by the trumpeter Roy Eldridge, whom he quotes in an early homemade recording; and studied the harmonic detail of Coleman Hawkins; and he was surely inspired by the unprecedented velocity of the pianist Art Tatum.

VELOCITY WAS ESSENTIAL to Parker's life. Everything happened fast. On the night that Joe Louis lost to Max Schmeling in 1936, fifteen-year-old Charlie Parker proposed to Rebecca Ruffin and married her a week later. He was a morphine addict by the summer of 1937, which suggests that he may have mixed in an upper-class circle, since there was no heavy drug trade in Kansas City at the time. By January 1938, Parker was a father. He was also anxious to see more of the world and "rode the rails" with hobos later that year, stopping in Chicago, then continuing on to New York, where he arrived with a nickel and a nail in his pocket. It was there that Parker found the beginnings of his own style. In 1940 he returned to Kansas City for his father's funeral and joined Jay McShann's big band, becoming the boss of the reed section and the principal soloist. In a few years he headed the movement that added new possibilities to jazz improvisation and was termed, much to Parker's chagrin, "bebop."

It was during Parker's three years with McShann that the intellectually ambitious personality began to take shape. Parker was interested in politics, mechanics, history, mathematics, philosophy, religion, languages, and race relations. He loved to mimic actors like Charles Laughton, was a prankster and a comic. His problems with dissipation became obvious, too; he told his wife Doris that he had never been able to stop, and recalled that his mother would have to come and get him from a hotel where he was using Benzedrine, staying up nights and going over music. These appetites made him unreliable, and McShann had to send him home for rest often, working with his mother to try and help him handle his addiction.

Parker was also, in fine modernist fashion, a man of masks. Gene Ramey, a member of the McShann band, recalled:

> He shouldn't have been nicknamed Yardbird or Bird Parker; he should have been called Chameleon Parker. Man, could that guy change directions and presentations on you! But he also had a gift for fitting in—if he wanted to. That applied to his music most of all. Bird would sit in anywhere we went—Bob Wills, Lawrence Welk, wherever the local jam session was, anybody that was playing. . . . We used to practice together often, just saxophone and bass. We would take "Cherokee," and he would ask me to tell him when he repeated something so he could meet the challenge of staying fresh and fluent. Bird liked to

> take one tune and play it for a couple of hours. Then he would know every nook and cranny of the melody and the chords. He was very scientific about those things. . . . Now he might not talk about it, but don't let that fool you into believing he wasn't thinking about it.

But beneath the masks, beneath the obsession with music, the mimicry, and the involvement in the sweep of life, there was a need. McShann says that Parker had a crying soul that always came out in his playing; and his first wife, Rebecca, observed it when he was in his early teens:

> It seemed to me like he needed. . . . He wasn't loved, he was just given. Addie Parker wasn't that type of woman. She always let him have his way, but she didn't show what I call affection. It was strange. She was proud of him and everything. Worked herself for him and all, but somehow I never saw her heart touch him. It was odd. It seemed like to me he needed. He just had this need. It really touched me to my soul.

The refinement of Parker's rhythm and the devil-may-care complexity of his phrases came to early distinction during those barnstorming years with McShann, in his next job with Earl Hines, and in the laboratory for the new vernacular that was Billy Eckstine's big band. On "Swingmatism" and "Hootie Blues," recorded with McShann in 1941, Parker had already put together the things that separated him from the alto order of the day. His sound is lighter; he uses almost no vibrato; the songful quality of his lines have a fresh harmonic pungence; and his rhythms, however unpredictable, link up with an inevitability that seems somehow to back its way forward through the beat.

When McShann brought his band to New York in early 1942, Parker was able to spend time after hours with the musicians who were stretching the language of jazz uptown in Harlem, usually in Minton's Playhouse or Monroe's Uptown House. "When Charlie Parker came to New York, he had just what we needed," said Dizzy Gillespie. "He had the line and he had the rhythm. The way he got from one note to the other and the way he played the rhythm fit what we were trying to do perfectly. We heard him and knew the music had to go *his* way."

THE IMPORTANCE OF Parker's jamming with Gillespie, Monk, and the others has often been noted; but the importance of his big band experience cannot be overemphasized. In those bands Parker learned not only how to blend with other musicians and how to lead a section, he also became a master of setting riffs, those spontaneous motifs that were repeated as chants. Riffs were what gave Kansas City's jazz its reputation; they compressed the essence of the music into one vital unit of rhythm and tune. By playing for dancers, Parker discovered the world of rhythms that Afro-American audiences had invented. Backing singers as varied as McShann's blues crooner Walter Brown, the romantic balladeer Eckstine, and the unprecedented virtuoso Sarah Vaughan, Parker had three distinctly different approaches to the voice to draw from, all of which were incorporated into the epic intricacy of his melodic inventions. Jazz had always demanded that the player think and play his ideas with exceptional speed and logic, but Parker proved that everything could be done even faster. Unlike Tatum, Hawkins, and Byas, who were excellent technicians given to harmonically sophisticated arpeggios, Parker was primarily a melodist; his work brought lyricism to the chords and made rhythmic variations that matched the best of Armstrong and Young.

BY CASTING ASIDE vibrato, Parker introduced a sound many considered harsh at the time. But the ballad performances on Warner Bros.' *The Very Best of Bird* (the famous Dial sessions of 1946–47) establish that the hardness of his sound was modified by a charming skill for elucidating the riches of romantic fancy in a way that made his music both spiritual and erotic; this was the romantic talent that drew many women to this disordered but beguiling man from whom a high-minded sense of grandeur was delivered with imperial determination. That imperial aspect was also a part of his music's attraction: awesome virtuosity of the sort heard in "Warmin' Up a Riff" or "Ko-Ko" is always a protest against limitations. (Both performances are available on Savoy Original Master Takes.)

The small, curved brass instrument with cane reed and pearl buttons was throttled and twisted, until it allowed him to express a barely stifled cry that was ever near the edge of consuming rage, the pain of consciousness elevated to extraordinary musical articulation. Bird often sounds like a man torn from the womb of safety too soon. He resented the exposure that music demands, and yet he loved it, because there was no other way he could project himself. But this was no primal scream: the fearful force of Parker's music is always counterpointed by a sense of combative joy and a surprising maturity, by the authority of the deeply gifted. Parker brought the violent rage of the primitive blues (of Robert Johnson, for example) to the citadels of art inhabited by the music's greatest improvisors. For Parker, swing and lyricism were some sort of morale, the bars behind which the beast of hysteria was confined.

Will, in sum, was important to the art of Charlie Parker. He was, after all, a heroin addict. Those who know little about intoxication often fail to realize that the repetition of the condition is what the addicted love most. They seek a consistency that will hold off the arbitrary world. If a few glasses of whiskey, or a marijuana cigarette, or an injection of heroin will guarantee a particular state, the addict has something to rely on. As Parker told Doris, "When you have a bad day, there's nothing you can do about it. You have to endure it. When I have a bad day, I know where to go and what to do to make a good day out of it." Doris Parker also notes that the saxophonist often showed the strength to kick the habit, cold turkey, by himself at home. But the temptations ever present in the night world of jazz always overwhelmed him.

Charlie Parker's early fall resulted more from his way of making "a good day" than it did from race, the economic system, or the topsy-turvy world of his art. It was a tragedy played out along a dangerously complex front of culture and politics, something far more intricate than the crude hipster mythology of Eastwood's *Bird.* It was a fully American story of remarkable triumphs, stubborn misconceptions, and squandered resources which tells us as much about the identity of this country as it does about the powers of jazz.

Louis Armstrong: An American Genius

Dan Morgenstern

If one had to choose the two most influential figures in jazz history, they would probably be Parker and Armstrong, so it seems fitting that the last two pieces about individual musicians in this book are about these two giants. Dan Morgenstern's damning review of James Lincoln Collier's Louis Armstrong: An American Genius, *which appeared in the* Annual Review of Jazz Studies 3 *in 1985, a dozen years after Armstrong's death, shows that the greatest of jazz lives—like so many of the world's other great lives—can remain fiercely contested as times, politics, and perceptions change. That the calm and generous Morgenstern should express such a passionately negative view of a colleague's work is a telling symbol of the relentless persistence of the jazz wars—a healthy sign, it may be, since it proves that for many people, jazz is still worth fighting about.*

In spite of its promising title, this critical biography is a deliberate attempt to overthrow the established view of Armstrong. In his preface, the author states that "much of what (has) been published about Armstrong was simply a rehash of the old myths," and some of it "sheer fiction. . . . The body of reliable writing about [him] was surprisingly small."

It is true that book-length studies of the most influential (and arguably the greatest) of all jazz musicians are few in number and less than scholarly in approach. The earliest, Armstrong's own *Swing That Music* (1936; the first biography of a black jazz figure), was heavily ghosted. Next came *Satchmo: My Life in New Orleans* (1947; the first installment of a full autobiography on which Armstrong continued work throughout his remaining years; the fate of the manuscript is unknown). This was definitely by Armstrong himself, if somewhat pedantically edited, and Collier's attitude toward it is revealing. He states that Armstrong "probably" wrote it "in the main," though no one acquainted with Armstrong's writing can doubt that the voice is authentic, and also claims that the book is "unreliable." He quotes much more extensively from Richard Meryman's *Louis Armstrong: A Self-Portrait,* published in

1971 and based on an extensive interview in *Life*. While often revealing, this little book contains frequent mishearings and garblings of Armstrong's transcribed spoken words. Hugues Panassié's *Louis Armstrong,* published in France in 1969 and in English translation two years later, contains much valuable information about the recorded works but can be regarded as idolatrous. Max Jones and John Chilton's *Louis,* published in 1971, is journalistic and not well organized, but contains many interesting facts, prodigious quotes from its subject, and an excellent essay on Armstrong the musician by Chilton, a professional trumpeter. One must agree with Collier that Robert Goffin's *Horn of Plenty* (1947) is fiction rather than biography. There are several Armstrong biographies for the juvenile market (a field in which Collier has been active), but these are of little significance.

Some of the best writing on Armstrong's music, however, is contained in more general works, notably Gunther Schuller's *Early Jazz,* Martin Williams's *The Jazz Tradition,* André Hodeir's *Jazz: Its Evolution and Essence,* and Humphrey Lyttleton's *The Best of Jazz.* While Collier analyzes Armstrong's playing at some length, it can fairly be said that he adds nothing to what can be learned from these sources.

But then, musical analysis is not the focal point of Collier's book, which is biography first and foremost. As such, does it tell us anything new? Collier has organized and presented his considerable research well and gives a detailed account of Armstrong's life and career, bringing together many facts and minutiae hitherto scattered among numerous sources. In this he has performed a valuable service. Unfortunately, he also insists on psychoanalyzing Armstrong at every turn.

In that respect his ideas are decidedly novel. Early on, he tells us that Armstrong was "clearly afflicted with deep and well-entrenched insecurity, a sense of his own worthlessness so thoroughly fixed that he was never to shake it off." Further, Armstrong was driven by an "insatiable, visceral lust [sic]" for applause, and eventually applause became the only balm that could "quench that relentless, sickening interior assault on his self-respect," and, if only for the moment, push "away the feeling that nobody liked him, that he was basically no good."

Strong stuff, more from Adler than from Freud, and a view of one of the most beloved men of our age that is, to say the least, bewildering. If accurate, it would make Armstrong one of the most successful dissemblers in history—a man who craftily managed to hide his true, stunted self not just from the world at large but also from those closest to him. (As if to guard against any nagging doubts, Collier insists that Armstrong had no "truly" close friends.)

To this reader, who knew Armstrong personally and professionally for some twenty-four years, this interpretation of his personality (Collier trots out every cliché regarding absent fathers and neglectful mothers a fan of *Psychology Today* could ask for) seems absurd. But like any writer possessed by a preconception, Collier selects his "facts" to fit the model. Thus he gives us liberal doses of "insights" from Marshall Brown, who for a few days occupied a dressing room adjacent to Armstrong's and only worked with him for a few hours, but fails to consult such close associates as Trummy Young, Armstrong's right arm for twelve years, or bassist Arvell Shaw, whose long tenure with Armstrong, starting with the last big band and stretching over two decades, he totally ignores. And, convinced that Armstrong had no real friends, he didn't bother to look for putative ones.

On the other hand, he presents the negative comments of such New Orleans contemporaries as Pops Foster (whose reliability may be gauged from his straight-faced claim that Jelly Roll Morton employed a second pianist on his solo recordings because he had a weak left hand) and Zutty Singleton, with whom Armstrong had a lifelong, complex relationship. Collier makes much of the conflicts between these proud, stubborn men as seen from Singleton's and his wife's point of view. Clearly, Collier has no understanding of the peculiar ways of elder New Orleans musicians.

Collier's relentless pursuit of his slanted view of Armstrong frequently overwhelms his sense of reality. A revealing example on which I must dwell at some length is his surreal interpretation of the recording sessions made by Armstrong and his band for Victor in January and April of 1933. Twelve sides were cut over a three-day period in January; a further two on April 24 and 26. To Collier, this level of output is evidence that Armstrong was "held in contempt" by "the white men who were overseeing his career," in particular manager Johnny Collins. "It is doubtful," Collier claims, "that any important show-business figure, much less a major artist, has ever been so driven like a pack mule as Armstrong was at this time." Characteristically, he adds that Armstrong "of course should have stood up to Collins."

Collins was indeed an unsavory man, as has been well documented by others, including Armstrong himself, who eventually fired him. But it is nonsense to present these recording sessions as paradigmatic of Collins and others being "callous to [Armstrong's] needs to the point of cruelty." There was nothing unusual about marathon recording sessions, which were scheduled when performers were available in cities with studio facilities; since prolonged touring was part and parcel of any band's working life, the most was made of such opportunities. The all-time record for a single day's jazz output in a studio is held by Benny Goodman, whose band, on June 6, 1935, cut fifty-one tunes—for which the sidemen were paid the munificent sum of one dollar per song!

Having set the stage with such misleading melodramatics, Collier must now find supporting evidence in the records themselves. Of "Dusky Stevedore" he hallucinates that Armstrong "barely gets through" the performance "at all," though that record is filled with trumpet pyrotechnics. Here and elsewhere, a problem seems to be that Collier mishears Armstrong's imaginative use of space and his stretching or contracting of the time-values of notes—stylistic traits especially in evidence at this period—for pauses caused by the need to rest sore lips. Thus he says about "Son of the South" that "Armstrong leaves gaps after each high note . . . to steal a couple of seconds rest," and elsewhere in his comments on these records points to "thin" tone and "faltering upper register." Trumpeter-critic John Chilton, however, has this to say about "Son of the South": "A master of the unexpected, [Armstrong] unites stamina and skill . . . again takes the first trumpet part [Collier fails to state, or cannot hear, that Armstrong plays lead in addition to solo on most of these discs] and tops a fine performance with a spine-tingling coda." Listening to these sessions, Collier works himself up to the point of tears as he fancies how Armstrong "was jamming the sharp circle of steel of the mouthpiece deep into the flesh of his lips to give them enough support to reach the high notes." Collier, a trombonist, at least ought to know that mouthpieces are made of brass.

Collier further imagines that for these sessions, "Victor supplied Armstrong with commercial rubbish: mediocre pop tunes, nonsensical jive songs, and worse," the "worse" being one of Collier's pet peeves—what he chooses to call "coon songs." (In this instance, one such is Hoagy Carmichael's "Snow Ball," also recorded by that notorious Uncle Tom, Paul Robeson.) The "mediocre pop songs" include two brand-new Harold Arlen pieces, which these recordings helped make jazz standards ("I've Got a Right to Sing the Blues" and "World on a String") and a couple of more-than-decent tunes of the day. Almost all the other material is the work of black songwriters and composers, such as "St. Louis Blues," "Mahogany Hall Stomp," and "Basin Street Blues" (the latter an Armstrong masterpiece which Collier inexplicably fails to mention); two songs written especially for Armstrong by the noted Anglo-African composer-arranger Reginald Foresythe ("Son of the South" and "Mississippi Basin"), and other special Armstrong material, including "Laughing Louis," to Collier no doubt a "nonsensical jive song," to others, like Stanley Crouch and this reviewer, a magical performance that must have mystified the Victor executives as much as it does Collier, who evades it. (In any case, humor is not Collier's strong suit, a handicap when it comes to Armstrong). He does pounce on "Don't You Play Me Cheap," but this was written by the drummer in the band, Harry Dial, and recorded by Armstrong as a favor to him. And does Collier really assume that the "viper's chorus" on "Sweet Sue" was mandated by white exploiters?

The incontrovertible fact is that Victor, Collins, et al. had little or nothing to do with choosing this repertory, which was intrinsic to Armstrong and his band, and that the flaws Collier hears in the trumpet playing on these records simply do not exist—esthetic judgments aside.

Collier's incessant harping on Armstrong's presumed failings as a man result in tainting even the praise he frequently (and sometimes fulsomely) heaps on Armstrong's music. He is at home with the Hot Five and Hot Seven series and other works from the 1920s, but finds the mature Armstrong solo style less to his liking. *De gustibus non est disputandum,* but it is peculiar that Collier fails to see that Armstrong's solo architecture and sense of the dramatic stem straight from nineteenth-century vocal traditions, notably Italian grand opera—which also influenced Sidney Bechet. Approval is not required; understanding is.

By the time Collier arrives at Armstrong's post-1946 music, he is as exhausted as he perceives Armstrong to have been on those 1933 sessions. He identifies a few highlights, such as the superb 1957–58 *Autobiography* dates, but omits mention of the significant collaborations with Duke Ellington, Ella Fitzgerald, and the Dukes of Dixieland, among others. His avoidance of the Fitzgerald albums might well be deliberate, since the superior quality of the repertory (the cream of American popular song) and the excellent production values (notably the luxurious original edition of *Porgy and Bess*) contradict his claim that unworthy and/or redundant material and shoddy production marred Armstrong's later recorded work. Since Collier quite clearly comes to the later Armstrong as an outsider, he can't be blamed for merely having skimmed through the enormous recorded output of the All Stars, which he nevertheless dismisses rather cavalierly. He is also puzzled by the great success of the All Star format in live performance, and one cannot avoid the suspicion that he never witnessed one himself—or never encountered Armstrong in the flesh.

Among the many gaffes in the text is the resurrection of the old canard that Don Redman composed the verse to Carmichael's "Stardust." To add spice to the opening of his Chicago chapter, Collier would have us believe that the white clarinetist Don Murray was beaten to death in that city for having associated with a gangster's moll. Murray of course died in Los Angeles, after a fall from the running board of a friend's car. Minor errors often are caused by lack of proper background knowledge: Armstrong did not switch from the Okeh label to Victor due to a dispute with Tommy Rockwell, but because Okeh was going bankrupt; the band that made the *Medley of Armstrong Hits* was not "a pickup group, hastily put together," but the pit band of the Philadelphia theater where Armstrong was appearing when making the record; and he recorded with Chick Webb's band in 1932 during a joint tour with *Hot Chocolates.* For dramatic effect, Collier states that

Armstrong and Zutty Singleton never worked together again after their 1930 parting, but they recorded in 1946, the year they also appeared in the film *New Orleans* (which Collier inexplicably claims starred Bing Crosby).

Technically, Collier seems no more secure. Reams of conjecture concerning embouchure problems rests in the main on wisdom gleaned from the aforementioned Marshall Brown. It is astonishing that, as a brass player, Collier mislabels Armstrong's frequent use of the glissando as "half-valving," which he condemns. Armstrong hardly ever used the half-valve device, yet Collier claims that Rex Stewart picked it up from Armstrong. But then, he is rather weak on Armstrong's influence on specific trumpeters, lumping Bobby Hackett in among "dixieland" players. The statement that Armstrong's direct influence as a trumpeter had ceased by the early 1930s is astonishing, but par for Collier's idiosyncratic course.

Collier makes much of his suspicion that Armstrong was born several years before 1900 and not on the Fourth of July, mainly to set up his subject's "unreliability" as a witness to his own life. But mere suspicion it remains as only circumstantial evidence is offered. (Collier of course ignores Armstrong's remark that his mother called him her "firecracker baby" due to the events surrounding his birthday.) He also intimates that shooting off a pistol loaded with blanks was not the true reason for Armstrong's commitment to the Colored Waifs' Home. Throughout the section on the early life, Collier paints a doleful picture of physical and spiritual deprivation that runs counter to Armstrong's own sunny view of his upbringing.

In doing so, and in (for one telling example) defining the Harlem of 1930 as a "virulent slum," Collier reveals the cultural preconceptions that permeate his book, culminating in the astounding observation that "we cannot perceive Louis Armstrong as we might Ralph Ellison, James Baldwin. He was, by the standards of middle-class America, rough, uncivilized, naive, and ignorant." Clearly, these are also Collier's standards. (Neither Baldwin nor Ellison appears in the index; the reader is referred to p. 74.)

Whose perception of Baldwin, born in Collier's "virulent slum," the son of a storefront preacher and one himself before his teens? And *whose* of Ellison, a jazz trumpeter in the image of Oran "Hot Lips" Page (who idolized Armstrong) long before he became the writer who made Armstrong emblematic of his masterpiece, *Invisible Man*? In Ellison's terms, Collier's book proves Armstrong's invisibility. I recall no references to Armstrong in Baldwin's work. But at the 1958 Newport Jazz Festival, as Armstrong concluded a long set with the National Anthem, Baldwin turned to me and said: "You know, that's the first time I've liked that song."

Perceptions may differ, but Collier's are consistent. He believes that as late as 1929, "many blacks, perhaps the majority, however much they might deny it, truly felt they *were* inferior" (Collier's emphasis). And he goes on: "Even when blacks were beginning to be successful, in show business especially, it was hard to prove that they were 'better' at it than whites." (Note the quotes around "better.")

Prove it to whom? To themselves, as Collier clearly implies? The presumption that black artists and entertainers, at that late a stage of the game, could be unaware of their superiority to the white stars who came in droves to learn and "borrow" from them goes beyond disingenuousness. But it does help us understand Collier's peculiar perception of Armstrong.

Always at pains to place events in their proper context, Collier neatly explains away every forceful act performed by Armstrong on behalf of himself or others by dint of psycho-social rationalization. Even Armstrong's legendary generosity becomes a guilty reflex conditioned by childhood deprivation. Facts that can't be neutered in this fashion are simply ignored. Nowhere does Collier mention that this "ignorant" and "uncivilized" man, who had barely finished fourth grade, was a virtuoso letterwriter. In 1922, he acquired a typewriter, fell in love with it, and from then on produced a ceaseless stream of correspondence with friends and associates, old and new, close and distant, expressing himself in a unique style remarkable for its playful approach to the rhythms, rhymes, and patterns of speech and prose. Conveniently, this omission enables Collier to ignore what the content of the many published (and unpublished but accessible) Armstrong letters might reveal about their author.

But I do Collier an injustice. He does mention that Armstrong wrote letters, if only to dwell on that he signed them "red beans and ricely yours," proof to Collier that he was "obsessive" about food. Armstrong's favorite dish is dismissed by Collier, who has already demolished gumbo and fishhead stew, with "and red beans and rice are—well, beans and rice." Quite so. And wine is fermented grape juice.

In the course of his summation, Collier grapples with larger issues, such as changing perceptions of art and artists. Ultimately, he has to confess that he "cannot think of another American artist who so failed his own talent. What went wrong?"

It is easier to guess what went wrong with Collier. The first thing required of a good biographer is empathy with his subject. In taking what he doubtless considers a hardheaded, unsentimental approach to the legend of Armstrong, Collier succeeds only in creating a phantom. Armstrong, the man, eludes Collier because he is unable, from his white, middle-class, and essentially puritanical perspective, to identify with the culture and environment in which Armstrong's psyche is rooted. Armstrong, the creative artist, remains a puzzle to Collier, whose sober, serious, rational, and essentially classicist esthetic is in constant conflict with Armstrong's passionate, playful, intuitive, and essentially romantic gift for transformation—indeed alchemy—which transcends (or simply bypasses) the bourgeois conventions of Western European "high" culture.

So deep is this gulf that Collier the listener, having arrived at 1947—Armstrong's twenty-fifth year of recording—can't tell Armstrong's playing from that of Irving "Mouse" Randolph, though he is surprised that the solo he thus misattributes is played, uncharacteristically, with a cup mute.

Alas, given our undue respect for appearances, what seems to be the first scholarly book about Louis Armstrong has predictably been hailed as authoritative. Armstrong's music, of course, is the best answer to this attempt to reduce a great artist's humanity to the scale of rat psychology and "explain" his art in terms of socio-cultural stereotypes. In lieu of a vintage Armstrong cadenza, I offer the words—not to be found in Collier—of two great musicians.

First, Teddy Wilson: "Every musician, no matter how good, usually has something out of balance. But in Armstrong's everything was in balance. He had no weak point. I don't think there's been a musician since Armstrong who has had all the factors in balance, all the factors equally developed."

Next, Jaki Byard, on his first meeting with Armstrong: "As I watched him and talked with him, I felt he was the most *natural* man. Playing, talking, singing, he was so perfectly natural the tears came to my eyes."

To Collier, of course, it was all an act.

A Bad Idea, Poorly Executed . . .

Orrin Keepnews

And finally—as a cautionary word, or provocation, or corrective—this long, aggrieved, highly personal, and highly informed attack on the whole idea of jazz criticism, published in 1987 in The View from Within, *by the distinguished jazz producer—and critic—Orrin Keepnews.*

After all these years, I find myself unable to avoid an unhappy conclusion: jazz criticism is a bad idea, poorly executed.

Having opened with a sweeping generalization, it immediately becomes necessary to hedge somewhat. I do not think matters are really appreciably worse than when I entered the jazz world. I am well aware that right now, as has almost always been the case, there are at least a few admirable positive exceptions to my condemnation. And the fault by no means lies entirely with the individual writers. (It definitely is a two-step process: a great deal of the problem must be attributed to the critical concept itself.) But I cannot be dissuaded from a deep conviction that the general performance level among jazz writers is embarrassingly, dangerously low.

I have quite deliberately called this an *unhappy* conclusion: I would much prefer to feel otherwise. Nothing is likely to alter the fact that writing about the arts is a major American activity; as for jazz in particular, the number of words devoted to the subject annually may well exceed the quantity of record albums sold. This being the case, it would be comforting to hope that something valuable, or helpful to the cause of creativity, might come of it now or in the near future. However, since it seems to be a basic fact of jazz life that most new albums will be reviewed and most interviews conducted by young men not especially qualified to do so, there is no real reason to look for much improvement. I cannot be dissuaded from this negative attitude merely by being reminded of writers who may be considered suitably qualified. I am well aware of a number of them, very much including my son Peter Keepnews. More than a few can be capable of cogent analysis, among them (to give some wildly varied examples) Robert Palmer or Stanley Crouch or Gene Lees; the fact that I might disagree with them at least as often as not is certainly not to be held against them. There is a vastly knowledgeable historian like Dan Morgenstern—whom I would probably include as a finalist in any contest for Best of Breed. There is that superlative prose stylist, Whitney Balliett, whose command of the language can be so overwhelming that you might not get around to evaluating the content. Whitney, however, quite often tends to function in a straightforward journalistic fashion, as do such longtime hard workers as Ira Gitler and Leonard Feather. But one can only get into trouble with such indiscriminate and partial name-dropping. It should be clear that my omissions here carry no implications at all; I am not trying to be complete, but merely to indicate that I really am conscious of who is out there.

One problem may be that I have been around too long: the very first jazz writer I read with any consistency was the wonderful pioneer Charles Edward Smith (who, together with Frederic Ramsey, Jr., edited and partly wrote the ground-breaking 1939 book of essays, *Jazzmen*). Charlie Smith was an often turgid and badly organized writer—I edited several of his pieces in the early *Record Changer* days—but he combined encyclopedic knowledge with a passionate love and respect for the music and its creators that make most of his successors seem bloodless. Another problem definitely is that the competent writers (those I have named and as many more as you care to add) are vastly outnumbered by the hordes of shallow, opportunistic, and virtually unidentifiable magazine and newspaper hacks.

A sensible alternative might be merely to ignore what is being written; some of my friends seem able to do that, but I'm afraid it is beyond me. In a recent conversation, saxophonist Joe Henderson referred with a shrug to some negative mention: "You've got to do what you have to do, no matter what they say." It struck me as a slogan suitable for framing. Sonny Rollins quite seriously claims that he never reads any reviews of his work, and I think I believe him. I *know* I envy him. For I am not and never have been sufficiently level-headed, secure, self-protective, incurious—or whatever else might serve as a good enough reason—to ignore the existence of all those writers churning away out there, using their widely varying degrees of competence and their often self-created positions of authority to pass judgment on individual performances or entire careers. Quite to the contrary, critical commentary has always held a horrible fascination for me. I suppose it's something like the feelings of a rabbit for a snake, or the appeal Count Dracula had for his full-blooded victims—I simply cannot turn away. Above all, I cannot resist reviews of records I am directly involved with. Since over the years there have been hundreds of such albums, I must by now have read several thousand conflicting opinions of my own work. Rarely, if ever, have I gained anything thereby.

This is a subject on which I have usually forced myself to remain uncharacteristically silent. Recognizing that I am highly partisan and obviously prejudiced, I have felt that caustic letters to the editors or brilliant essays on the theory of jazz criticism, coming from me, should probably be regarded with suspicion and ruled off-limits. So, except for a couple of rare occasions when I found a comment personally offensive or a fact seriously distorted, I have avoided any form of response. That's how I looked at it for a long time; I now feel I was wrong. Of course I am partisan, but I am also deeply involved, concerned, knowledgeable, and (by nature, training, and experience) more readily articulate on paper than a good many of my equally long-suffering friends and colleagues. A rare opportunity now confronts me. Within this book I am, by definition, primarily a writer and only inferentially a record producer—a position I haven't been in for many years. Having read this far, you have come upon my opinions and comments over several decades on a variety of related subjects. So you already know that I'm capable of being as unkind as any currently active jazz writer, that I can turn out a gratuitously nasty clever phrase with the best of them. This is very possibly my only opportunity to open up on this subject; it would take a much more generous and tolerant soul than mine to pass up the chance.

I must initially establish a couple of personal ground rules. Most people appear to use the terms "reviewer" and "critic" interchangeably, and even standard dictionaries don't clearly support my distinction, yet I have always believed that there's a vast difference. A reviewer provides you with fairly brief and, one hopes, quite specific description and evaluation of a new play, movie, book, or record. The intention is to pass summary judgment, perhaps to condense everything into some arbitrary grading system (B-plus, or two and a half stars); the presumable purpose is to provide trustworthy evidence about whether or not to spend your time and money on the product. A critic, on the other hand, is concerned with the larger and longer view. His territory embraces entire styles and careers; his time-span can be infinite; and if he does deal with specific commodities, it's unlikely to be less than half a dozen albums dissected in terms of some continuing major theme.

Admittedly, the lines of demarcation are not always entirely clear. Some writers routinely assume double duty, turning out their share of capsule reviews and writing a think-piece for the same issue. But the distinction does exist, and as a practical rule of thumb has a lot to do with the status (whether earned or self-proclaimed) of the individual. A critic may really have verifiable credentials or may simply have been around so long that he is accepted as a fact of life, a necessary evil. A reviewer might have a good deal of relevant background, or a little, or just a desire to make a name for himself or to acquire free albums; even after some forty years of reading, it is not always easy for me to figure out which category applies. At least in theory, a reviewer is presumed to be working swiftly and may be excused for being shallow as he strives to meet a deadline: for example, it remains an essential newspaper function to let its readers know the rating of a movie or play within twenty-four hours after it opens (although the significance of that consideration diminishes when various current jazz periodicals take almost a full year before getting around to publishing their definitive word on some "new" releases). It should be clear that my quarrel is largely—although by no means entirely—with reviewers and with the reviewing function as it is now conducted. A full-grown critic, particularly one with a lot of space made available to him in a reputable publication, can do major damage, but it's all those little mosquito bites that really eat you up alive. And by sheer force of numbers, it is the reviewers who turn out the bulk of the words and cumulatively reach the greatest numbers of readers.

(I recognize that these two subdivisions fall short of covering the full range of jazz writing. I am bypassing one segment of the critical community: writers of books which rarely if ever are concerned with the working-level activities that we in the art/business of jazz necessarily deal with on a daily basis, men I think of as basically "cultural historians." Again, there are people who have credentials in more than one category—Gunther Schuller comes to mind, or Stanley Dance—but I am *not* using the term simply to describe those who create entire books from scratch rather than just magazine or newspaper articles. My actual reference is to authors—for the most part, it would seem, inhabitants of universities—whose works advance theories, or offer either relatively straightforward or boldly revisionist histories of the whole subject, and who therefore would appear to be most closely related to those scholars who analyze and footnote other cultural phenomena. In a phrase, men who view the music from an academic tower rather than at street level. There is nothing intrinsically wrong with that position, but it has nothing to do with jazz as I know and live it. Since I do not feel that these people impinge on my reality, I will not be so rude as to disturb theirs—except to point out here that I am deliberately, not accidentally, excluding them from consideration.)

My other ground rule, equally arbitrary, concerns the actual naming of names. I have no personal vendettas in progress at this time, no embarrassing stories I'm anxious to tell. My quarrel is with an entire concept far more than with individuals. Accordingly, my condemnations will remain nonspecific or unidentified. When I do use a name—as I have already demonstrated by strewing a few of them around in an early paragraph—it will either be for description or in praise.

Growing up in New York and paying attention to the popular arts that surrounded me, I rather automatically came to accept and generally to respect the reviewing function as a part of life. Plays, books, movies were analyzed and rated by a small group of usually literate and experienced writers in the daily papers and various magazines; if there were no reviews of jazz records except in obscure and highly specialized sheets, it was quite understandable. Even then I knew that *our* music—which at that time was New Orleans style and its offshoots are opposed to the much more widely popular big-band swing—was a limited-market product. Besides, recorded music was only available in the tiny three-minute units of 78-rpm singles; not until the late 1940s and the coming of the long-play album was the form substantial enough to justify widespread reviewing. (So it should be kept in mind that this whole genre is still comparatively an infant industry, with no real history or tradition.)

But by 1948, and my first serious involvement with jazz at *The Record Changer,* reviews were inevitably an important part of the picture. There actually was still a substantial body of single records around; some were new releases, but a great many were the controversial bootleg reissues of classics and legends owned (and ignored) by the major labels. Forced to take an editorial stand, we elected to publish reviews of the pirate records, on the dual basis of pragmatism (they *did* exist) and idealism (the initial and larger sin remained the anti-cultural policy of RCA Victor and Columbia). We did keep them away from our Number One reviewer, George Avakian, who at the time was working at Columbia, where he eventually did push through a magnificent reissue program. Which brings me quickly to a major point: the experience of working with the early *Changer* reviewing staff was a terribly misleading starting point; that was very possibly the most capable group of its kind ever assembled.

Avakian was thoroughly knowledgeable and experienced; he had been a student at Yale when the remarkable Professor Marshall Stearns (who later founded the Institute of Jazz Studies) was teaching English there, and had been professionally involved with the music since the late thirties as producer, reissue advocate, and executive. He was joined by Bucklin Moon, a talented novelist, essayist, and editor who was a living encyclopedia of traditional jazz—and the one who had to take on all reviewing of bootlegs. Our initial "modern" specialist was the magazine's art director, Paul Bacon. Bill Grauer and I had met him on the evening we first encountered Thelonious Monk at the home of Alfred and Lorraine Lion of Blue Note. A good friend of the Lions, designer of Alfred's earliest album covers and then our first

Riversides, and subsequently a book-jacket designer, Paul never really considered himself a critic. But he was an early and astute observer of the bebop scene, and I'm intrigued at how often his comments on Monk and other pioneers are still quoted. A psychology instructor at Columbia University named Robert Thompson, initially known to us as a traditionalist drummer and bandleader, was another early member of this staff, and by 1953 Martin Williams, then an aspiring young writer from Virginia, came on board. To my recollection, he began by taking on the tricky job of reviewing the very first Riverside albums; even though they were classic-jazz reissues (authorized ones, I must add), the possibilities of ethical and personal conflict were obviously huge.

I have given so detailed a picture of that working group because I have never before been in a position to acknowledge publicly this remarkably literate, concerned, uncruel reviewing team of my youth. Almost equally important is that the majority of them would surely have been disqualified from writing jazz record reviews today. Avakian worked for a major label and, whenever possible, produced reissue albums; Bacon had close ties to a leading independent jazz company; and Thompson was presumably too involved as a working musician to be impartial. But not only did they write a long series of informed and valid reviews, they also remained totally above suspicion. Rabid and fanatical as *Changer* readers could be, I cannot recall a single complaint about any of them. Buck Moon was at an opposite extreme: a dedicated and gifted man who earned his living entirely outside of music. (Jazz was very important to him, but he was a novelist and a book and magazine editor by trade. This surely makes him a great rarity among reviewers of any era—a highly skilled outsider, a nonprofessional who really knew what he was doing.) Only Williams fitted a standard pattern by being young and eager and quite determined to make his mark as a jazz critic; considering that he has been among the most active and respected in the field from then until now, it would seem to have been a good idea to give him his first assignments. He did, it should be noted, write very favorably about those earliest Riversides, but that basically just meant praising Louis Armstrong and Johnny Dodds and Ma Rainey—as well as my notes and Bacon's covers.

So it was not until after (and just possibly because of) the launching of Riverside Records that I began to develop negative feelings about reviewing. Obviously I am often heavily prejudiced in my reactions, but at least I like to think that I function on a somewhat higher level than "favorable reviews are *good,* negative ones *bad.*" I'm actually aware of having produced some albums I now would not defend, and others that may have been overpraised. But down through the years my most frequent reaction has been frustration at having my records at the mercy of people who, for whatever reasons, seem unable to understand them. Being part of a record company means that you get to see a great many different reviews of each album, and I'd suggest that there are few more depressing experiences in life than the consecutive reading of multiple reviews. What you are exposed to could most charitably be described as diversity. More often, particularly when they are read in bulk, the effect is more like total chaos. To one writer a record swings like mad, but another feels that same rhythm section doesn't fit together—why couldn't we hear their obvious incompatability? One reviewer may praise the originality of your well-planned repertoire; the next clipping complains of trite and unthinking tune selection—the difference, of course, is entirely a matter of the writers' own listening backgrounds. What one man hears as too strictly arranged, another finds sloppy; entire albums are rejected or overpraised because of blatant bias against (or in favor of) electric pianos, or female vocalists, or the resurgence of bebop.

My negative conclusions have for the most part been reached gradually, as a result of having been repeatedly hit over the head for a long time. But I think I can actually trace the start of my mistrust back to an oddly matched pair of reviews of the two earliest twelve-inch Riverside jazz albums, both written by the same even then noted writer and appearing in successive issues of *Down Beat* some thirty years ago. The first was a very lukewarm reaction to our initial Monk project—his treatment of eight Duke Ellington compositions. The passage of time has long since validated the concept, which began the helpful process of slightly demystifying Thelonious. But this particular critic spoke of how uncomfortable the pianist seemed with much of this material, and accused us of having "instructed" Monk to deal with music "for which he has little empathy." It's hard to say which baffled and disappointed me more: his belief that my partner and I had been able to "force" Thelonious into an unwanted musical decision, or the failure to grasp the deep and strongly expressed musical affinity between Monk and Ellington.

Then this very same reviewer went on to give highest five-star honors to a Joe Sullivan album we had acquired. While I loved Sullivan, I knew that this specific record was in no way of major stature. So I asked a direct question and, to that writer's credit, got a frank and somewhat embarrassed answer: he had put this album on his turntable at the end of a full afternoon of listening to West Coast cool; as a result, it had at least temporarily sounded like the hardest swinging music imaginable!

From such early experiences I began to get a mental picture of an assembly line moving too fast to permit rational evaluations, and that image has stayed with me over the years. I have come upon many variations and permutations, and in time have developed a tendency to fit them into broad general categories. There is, for example, *The Critical Bandwagon:* when a performer becomes so thoroughly accepted, so deified, that at least for a while you don't have to worry. Everyone will give each of his albums the same top rating for as long as the ride lasts. Then for no discernible reason it becomes time to toss him off the wagon, perhaps simply because some writer decides to attract attention by playing iconoclast and going against the tide of adulation. I've watched this happen very dramatically with Monk, and even with artists who began their careers as critics' favorites and thus for a long time seemed invulnerable, like Wes Montgomery and Bill Evans—although death does tend to restore artistic stature. The quality of the specific record doesn't seem at all relevant to the bandwagon process—a fact that is often grotesquely demonstrated these days by glowing reviews welcoming back the reissue versions of albums that were originally trashed years ago. It's merely that a musician who used to be "out" has now achieved the status of a definitely "in" elder statesman.

There is also the *Prior Premise Review:* the writer begins with a personal conclusion and structures his view of the album to fit. Recently, I have belatedly learned that it was foolish to have had the Kronos Quartet attempt arrangements of Monk and Evans material, because "everyone knows strings can't swing." Many years ago, I read in amazement a destruction of an album involving four-flute charts, by a reviewer who started by making it clear that he did not consider the flute a "legitimate" jazz instrument. The most common use of this category is in defense of the assumption that any commercially successful jazz artist has automatically become aesthetically deficient. (The contention may often be accurate, but it's hardly a routine matter of cause and effect.) I first directly encountered this form of cultural prejudice when I recorded the Cannonball Adderley Quintet in performance at a San Francisco club. Their buoyant and rhythmic repertoire, particularly pianist Bobby Timmons's funky tune, "This Here," struck all sorts of responsive audience chords and the resultant album became a 1960 jazz sales phenomenon. Adderley, a witty and erudite man with a natural affection for the blues, previously respected by critics while a member of the celebrated Miles Davis group that included John Coltrane and Bill Evans, was immediately savaged in print for selling out. *Down Beat* didn't get around to acknowledging the record for several months. When it did, the disparaging review began with a negative reference to its reported sales of close to 30,000 copies, and closed with the quite serious admonition: "If this is the road Cannonball is going to travel, he will only succeed in making money."

The *Assumed Fact Review* can place an undue strain on my temper. I have read that the producer must have "made" the musician play that commercial junk with those electrified sidemen because he wanted to make a lot of money; and on another occasion that the same dictator had "refused" to let an artist play his own compositions. My aggravation in such cases stems from the fact that the evil producer is me. One does just try to rise above it—and I do get beaten on less frequently than certain colleagues who are widely known as studio authoritarians. But there really is no extension of journalistic or critical license that can justify such pseudotelepathic guesswork being passed on to readers as reality. The problem is of course partly a matter of shoddy ethics, but it is also a glaring example of a lack of any knowledge of what actually goes on in the recording process.

Even this, I suppose, is in some respects preferable to the *Immaculate Conception Review,* a sadly prevalent type in which there is no indication that a producer even exists. I don't think this is entirely a matter of my own ego. While his functions and importance may vary greatly—depending on the artist, the nature of the project, and (to a very great extent) the nature of the producer—those functions *do* exist, and do have a bearing on how things turn out. The basic fact is that the role of the producer and his working relationship with the artist are among the most significant elements in the creation of a jazz record. A good deal of what you have read in this book is of course concerned with precisely that. Yet there has always been a vast (although in all probability, even I must admit, unintentional) conspiracy of silence about us. Record reviews, which often seek the praiseworthy goal of listing every single performer, almost never list a producer; most discographies follow the same rule. (In recent years, as my self-assurance has grown and my never-very-large tolerance for anonymity has diminished, I have on occasion taken to describing my own role in the liner notes, particularly if I'm presenting a new artist or if the album concept is one that I've devised. For the most part, however, reviewers still react as if I were invisible.) I have never understood this apparent lack of basic curiosity: if "producer" is a credit that appears on virtually every album liner, shouldn't more reviewers wonder about the degree of credit or blame that might properly be assigned to that person?

Such thoughts inevitably lead me to wonder about the human being behind each review. There is a byline on virtually every one, but who really is the individual bearing that name and why is he (or, very rarely, she) writing as he does? I feel that *identity* is a crucial aspect of criticism. Examine other areas in which new material is automatically examined in print. There are very few new plays in New York in a year, and not many people regularly writing about them. Movies are reviewed in virtually every local newspaper, but there aren't more than a couple of writers handling this job in any given city, and probably only one reviewer in each of the national magazines you read regularly. So as a constant reader you get a pretty good handle on these people; whether or not you fully realize it, you come to know at least something about their tastes, and how their views relate to your own. If eventually you become aware of soft spots and prejudices as well as strengths, you've become better prepared to extract the information that can enable you to draw reasonably sound *personal* conclusions about the subject at hand.

This, however, is not fully comparable to the record-review situation, which is actually much closer in format to book reviewing. While there may be only one regular on the subject in the daily paper, there are dozens of reports in (for example) each issue of *The New York Times Book Review,* just as there are (also just for example) in *Jazz Times.* Each item does carry a byline, but with the jazz reviews how can we be expected to identify all those largely unknown and basically unknowable individuals? All too often they blur into each other, so that hardly anyone is disturbed when all that's remembered or quoted is that an album was given three stars "by *Down Beat.*" Which if course is an anthropomorphic impossibility: the publication itself does no such thing. It was in fact a conclusion reached by one of their all-but-anonymous writers, and how does one go about learning what *that* particular person means by "three stars" or whatever other abstruse rating system is used? Book review sections, on the other hand, traditionally display a certain sense of responsibility: in virtually every such Sunday supplement there's at least an identifying sentence for each writer. We are told whether this is a professor or a lawyer or a published novelist; if there is some special reason, some area of expertise that has led to his being assigned to this evaluation, we are given a clue. Some of us may not think it a particularly good idea to have novels reviewed by novelists, or to turn a work on Freud over to a leading anti-Freudian—but at least we do have that identification to bear in mind while reading the critique.

I have yet to see a jazz publication use this valuable device. Occasionally the reviewer is so well known as a critic or for some other reasons that there is no mystery (on occasion in the past, musicians *have* written record reviews; I recall that both Rex Stewart and Kenny Dorham displayed remarkably good chops in *Down Beat*). But much more often the name means nothing. Perhaps we are not told precisely because there isn't anything to be told: it may be that many of them have no discernible credentials, just a strong desire to write about jazz and a willingness to do so at the very low prevailing rate of pay. Being a fan is really not sufficient, and having been a music student or a disc jockey on college radio is not much better; but if that's all there is to say about a published reviewer, surely we should be told *that.* I am worried by a kind of chicken-or-egg question that is raised by my unfortunately wide range of review-reading. Quite a few of the names found in the national magazines also turn up in the record-review columns of small city newspapers. Which came first? Was writing for his hometown weekly the credential that led to assignments from *Jazziz,* or was the paper awed by the signed reviews in *Down Beat*? And does it really matter? Of course everyone must, by definition, begin someplace, but must they begin at—quite literally—our expense?

For in a performance art like jazz, which in our society has always been forced to exist in the marketplace, critics and reviewers have a special responsibility. They are not merely delivering abstract artistic commentaries; they are messing with a man's ability to make a living. This is not an argument in favor of praising bad merchandise because there's a wife and children to be fed; but it is in opposition to judgments with real economic consequences being arbitrarily disbursed by people who are not qualified to do so. Above all, I suppose, it is a passionate outcry against the smartly turned phrase that is used solely for the benefit of the phrase-turner. I'm afraid I have observed the pattern far too many times to have any tolerance for it: the young writer gets his first chance; being suitably ambitious, he wants to be noticed more than all those other young reviewers. Negatives, he decides, are most likely to turn the trick; brilliant figures of speech in support of something won't register nearly as strongly as the devastating image; being memorably nasty is surely the quickest way to stand out from the crowd. In the long run he may come to realize that venom all by itself doesn't really accomplish that much. For the most part, his predecessors had figured that out; those with sufficient talent or doggedness to continue usually do calm down and mellow out, but there are enough hit-and-run drivers in each generation to create a noticeable amount of destruction.

To some extent my specific attitude about jazz writers has been shaped by the more general feelings I have developed about the role of criticism in relation to any creative art form, and about the particular problems involved in analyzing one medium of expression in terms of another. The second part of that sentence is probably the easier to explain: I have come to believe that language can readily be applied to the explication of a book, a film, a play—anything that is itself directly a product of language—but that *writing* about paintings or dance or music is a much trickier matter. It is in effect a form of translation, and therefore calls for a more than minimal grasp of *both* vocabularies. To write effectively about jazz requires, therefore, some actual facility with English prose in addition to some real understanding of jazz. Neither brisk technical discussion of the music, on the one hand, nor mystical flights-of-fancy verbiage, on the other, is really good enough. True sensitivity helps, and so does experience; but both commodities are usually in short supply, and most writers who have a substantial amount of them to offer—like a Morgenstern or a Gary Giddins—have long since stopped being available for entry-level activities.

As for my major reservations about criticism: to put it most bluntly, I consider it to be with rare exceptions an inhibiting force, simply because it invariably tends to take measurements and give ratings and pass judgment. This may take the form of comparison between particular works or specific artists, leading to the assertion that one is "better" than another. Or it can be more coldly objective, making evaluations in accordance with pre-existing standards. None of this actually has anything at all to do with creativity.

It may be acceptable at the lowest pragmatic level: I admit that I find it hard to read a writer who has trouble handling basic English grammar, and I am uncomfortable when a musician plays wrong notes or fakes the melody line of a standard tune. But there are obviously severe limitations to this approach: it's not very helpful in evaluating a painting by Rousseau or Grandma Moses; and it was of real disservice to many of us when we were first exposed to Ornette Coleman. (I once got around to telling Ornette about my reaction the first time I had heard him play some straight-ahead blues: I had regretted not knowing sooner that he *could* play "normal" changes, that his avoidance of them was entirely voluntary. I do hope I made it clear to him that the knowledge would only have been to *my* advantage. After all, he had always known his own truth; my ignorance, or anyone else's, was quite irrelevant.)

I feel that rules and standards have no valid connection with artistic expression, just as grammar has no specific impact on literary creativity. Actually, I do pay a lot of attention to the "grammar" of various art forms, and find it to be quite important—but only on its own level. Such things have a great deal to do with whether or not you find a work technically competent or properly "professional," which can be very meaningful when writers or musicians are talking to each other (or, perhaps, when I am criticizing a reviewer). But to consider such things to be in any way binding on the artist is decidedly improper.

It seems to me that by now I have done quite enough complaining, and it might be a good idea at this point to become a bit more practical. I do realize that I am not single-handedly going to abolish jazz criticism. Since it is going to continue to be done, how might it be done better? Let me switch, even if only briefly, to a somewhat more constructive approach by attempting to codify some of my personal standards, to indicate some elements that I consider essentials.

To begin with, as a onetime editor who greatly respects the leadership potential of a magazine editor, I have to admit the inequity of dumping exclusively on the reviewers. If I find young jazz writers inexperienced, immature, and indistinguishable, at least some of the blame must be allocated to those who hire them, give them assignments, and presumably read and edit what they turn in for publication. A couple of decades ago, when *Down Beat* was just about the only game in town, I often disagreed with its various editors, but it was certainly true that men like Gene Lees, Don DeMichael, and later Dan Morgenstern were well-defined personalities, who could readily be perceived as giving instruction and a sense of direction to newcomers. I'm not in a position to condemn the current crop of magazine editors, because I just don't know what efforts of that kind they might be making, but the empirical evidence is not reassuring. There are some strong veterans out there now who established their own standards and patterns a long time ago; a Stanley Dance or a Douglas Ramsey is not particularly receptive to—or in need of—guidance. But where are their replacements going to come from—writers whom even crusty insiders like me can at least sometimes read with respect or even agreement? Without some editorial leadership, how can the publications ever begin to tap the vast knowledgeable pool of jazz professionals—the same sort of non-impartial potential reviewers that the book sections always utilize, or that *The Record Changer* relied on almost four decades ago?

Of course I'm aware that musicians have occasionally been spotlighted as writers over the years, usually very recognizable names, often under special circumstances as an attention-getting journalistic ploy. That's not what I'm talking about. I mean regular use of informed, involved, working-level musicians, sidemen and session players, young and old. What about a producer or two, or something as far-out as a jazz-oriented promotion man who might have an intriguing point of view on quality levels in overtly commercial forms of music? What I'm also saying is: where is the editorial courage to take a few chances? Even some really bad choices couldn't hurt that much, and would at least offer an occasional change of pace. And without a little daring, how can we ever hope to break the disgraceful mold that keeps jazz criticism virtually a white male enclave—after all these years, still no women to speak of and so few blacks that an Albert Murray and a Stanley Crouch remain tokens, and a vibrant gadfly like Amiri Baraka is rarely heard from.

I am scarcely making new suggestions. As far back as 1960, the late Bobby Timmons, then a brash young pianist and composer, angrily asked a *Down Beat* interviewer why the roster of critics didn't include "some of the older musicians who know every stage of development young musicians go through." He went on to complain of the "incompatibility" of critics being "predominantly" white: "They don't really know this music. They're interpreting what [we] say and play, and they don't really understand what's happening." There might have seemed an element of irony in the fact that he was talking to Barbara Gardner, a black woman who was then a frequent *Down Beat* contributor and staff record reviewer—but the real irony is that, a quarter-century later, Gardner turns out to have been unique. As for Timmons's remarks, the question of their relative or absolute accuracy seems vastly less important than the undeniable truth that they represent a long-standing and still widespread attitude among musicians. There is something seriously out of alignment when so many who create the music are consistently unable to trust or respect critics as a class.

As for that "constructive" summary of personal criteria, I offer a short list of elements that I hold to be necessary but generally missing in current criticism.

Above all, there is an attitude that I would label *respect for creativity*—which involves the basic realization that the artist is more significant than his critic and which, accordingly, calls for not overvaluing the critical function. In a recent article by Martin Williams, I find this cogent comment: "It's the business of writers like me to say what we think, but I don't like the idea of giving advice to musicians." These are words all critics should strive to live by, for all too often what is called "advice" is merely an attempt to superimpose the writer's values over the musician's. As a major example, there are the years of critical complaints about Sonny Rollins's refusal to return to the way he played in the late fifties. To my direct knowledge, he has not done so simply because he has no interest in retreating to his musical past—in imitating himself. But the answer is actually beside the point; the question should never have been raised. A writer who professes to admire and respect an artist must accept that artist's ability to make a "correct" creative decision for himself. He may not agree with that decision, but he must recognize its primacy. There is a truly immense difference between saying "I prefer" (which is proper critical language) and "he should" (which is not). It is far more difficult for the critic to give the same leeway to a young player—it may be almost impossible to stifle the urge to be a star-shaper, to offer paternalistic words of wisdom—but it is even more important. Rollins, after all, will pay no attention; someone less experienced and less confident may even be swayed.

An essential aspect of this "respect" is the realization that it is not the artist's duty to please a particular writer, and he should not be attacked for failing to do so. Critical evaluation that cannot rise above the level of "I do not like it; therefore it is bad art" is dangerously invalid. This is not a denial of the critic's right to express personal views and reactions, but it is a protest against the kind of pontificating that seeks to present those views as absolute truth. Jazz, as we all like to proclaim, is a long-lived music; accordingly, its history is full of examples of negative reviews being drastically revised and reversed by the passage of time. Once again, an awareness of Monk can be valuable. I would recommend to all beginners the study of early critical comment on his music; it should lead to an appropriate mixture of perspective, humility, and caution.

Secondly, there is *knowledge of the process*—which very much includes some understanding of the realities of recording. There is a great difference between the requirements of club or concert activity and the steps that lead to the creation of a record; failure to appreciate this distinction literally makes it impossible to evaluate a recorded performance. I see no way to state the point at all equivocally; this *is* an absolute truth—and I remain constantly astonished at how rarely any critic has ever sought information on what goes on at a studio session or has asked to visit one. I don't believe they are deliberately avoiding knowledge, or even that they are lacking in curiosity; but I do suspect that, for the most part, they aren't even aware that there is anything unique to be curious about. There isn't time or space enough here to go into the details of what is special, but I assure you that there are a great many quite important distinctions and conventions. Effective recorded sound is quite unlike what you hear in person; the approach to achieving an ultimately satisfactory performance is quite different; and there are of course many occasions that necessitate, for a variety of reasons, editing or combining, or the adding or substituting of overdubbed supplements.

I realize that everyone more or less knows this—or, to be more accurate, knows *about* such things. But a general awareness is not the same as an understanding of the effect that various engineering facts and circumstances have on the art of recording. We who work in the studios are fully aware that only the finished product will be available for the world to judge (and we are frequently very pleased that no one who wasn't there will know just how much sweat and tension and repetition may have gone into it). But we also take for granted the essential fact that our job is to create what is best described as "realism"—the impression and effect of being real—which may be very different from plain unadorned reality. Ignorance of this distinction is surely not helpful to those who choose to pass judgment on the music. I have treasured for years the memory of a review that complained of our stupidity in having used a percussionist: the writer could hear quite clearly how those added rhythms were crowding and disturbing the drummer and throwing him off-stride; why hadn't the leader and I realized this? The only trouble with that criticism was (and there had been no attempt to hide the fact in the album-liner credits) that the "bothersome" percussionist had been added to the tape weeks later and in another studio; he and the drummer had indeed met each other, but not in connection with this project. It is not only to avoid such potential for embarrassment that I recommend knowledge of the process—would a film critic want to avoid all awareness of camera angles and directorial technique?—and I remain willing at any time to conduct a basic course in Studio Realities.

As a close corollary, there is certainly a need for an *understanding of history.* In an earlier period, those with an awareness of the past frequently used a scornful cliché: "When you talk about a jazz pioneer, he thinks you mean Charlie Parker." With the passage of time, Parker actually *is* recognizable as a pioneer; to update the remark you'd probably need to substitute Ornette Coleman or Cecil Taylor. But I suspect the revised version would remain widely applicable. I don't want to overstate the problem: there are many current writers with a strong sense of history; there is no shortage of historical and biographical literature—regardless of how one might evaluate such material, at least the *facts* of jazz are readily available. But I'm not so sure about how widely the lessons of history have been learned.

Having begun as a strict traditionalist, I have always had strong feelings about the continuity of the music. In the fifties, I became aware that contemporary musicians had for the most part very little awareness of the past (Monk, who as a youngster had listened appreciatively to James P. Johnson, was as always an exception). Efforts to bridge the gap had varying results: Randy Weston was fascinated by the incredible right-hand dexterity of Luckey Roberts; Cannonball Adderley began with more background knowledge than most, but was totally broken up by the primitive rhythm section on a Bix Beiderbecke record. It was actually the drastic differences in the rhythmic concepts of traditional jazz forms that presented the greatest problem; now, even though there have been vast changes since the early days of bebop, there is enough of a connective thread to make that forty-year-old tradition important to today's players. So many of them grasp the relevance of the past and feel a deep respect for who and what preceded them; it is in a sense a counterpart of the "second line" tradition in early New Orleans, and it is so strong an element in the mid-eighties jazz atmosphere that I'm sure most writers and many members of the public are aware of it.

But do they understand *what*—in addition to some stylistic mimicry and some pleasant repertoire—the young musicians have learned? One major lesson to be gained from history, for example, is how often time has altered, even reversed, critical judgments. I have already noted how often a reissue of a record that was originally poorly received is now greeted with cheers. I know that many musicians grasp the point that the music exists on its own merits, regardless of initial condemnation or praise, and that time has a way of straightening matters out. I hope that reviewers realize the significance for them of such reversals. They are certainly entitled to their own reactions, uninfluenced by past opinions (although I am sometimes disturbed by the thought that they may also be unaware of them). But do they at least appreciate the implied parallel? For the very same kind of revisionism may well be scheduled to take place when today's records are reconsidered in the future; the key point being demonstrated is that this long-lived music of ours, when it is young, is not necessarily in tune with the critical standards of the moment. Accordingly, it might be wise for the reviewer to try to be a little tender towards something that may strike him as too advanced (or too old-fashioned), to be careful not to choke it off in its infancy with gratuitous harshness.

As a footnote to the subject of understanding history, let me admit that discographers now seem to be an improving breed. I have been aware since my earliest reissue days of the great gaps in this area that will never be filled because paperwork is missing or players have died. I have also long realized that it is both unfair and risky to rely on a performer's memory of one long-past session out of many, and I soon discovered that the most likely answer will be what the musician feels the questioner wants ("That's right, it certainly was Satchmo on that date in Chicago in 1925. . . ."). For such reasons I have for many years—although, unfortunately, not from the very start—tried to set down (and preserve) detailed recording-session logs. For a long time, though, compilers of discographies just didn't seem able to figure out the value of asking people like me. I have some favorite aggravations: notably the celebrated Danish researcher Jorgen Jepsen making blatantly incorrect assumptions in his 1968 volume on Monk. Like deciding that the trio selection which adds John Coltrane and Wilbur Ware to an otherwise solo Monk album, and the only three numbers ever recorded by the original Five Spot Quartet (consisting of those three men plus drummer Shadow Wilson), were all made at the same April 1957 session. It's a tidy thought, but the fact is that the quartet was taped a few months later. And the question is: why not ask the producer? Some sort of barrier seems to have been broken in the early eighties when Michael Cuscuna, preparing a total discography of Thelonious for the Mosaic Records reissue package of his entire Blue Note output, asked me for full, verified Riverside data. Thereafter, a horde of researchers—all of them European, I must note—have probed me for recording truths about Bill Evans, Blue Mitchell, Wynton Kelly, Chet Baker, Kenny Dorham, et al. It can get quite time-consuming, and painfully memory-stirring as well; but of course such specialized, dedicated, and usually entirely nonprofit activities must be encouraged; the creation of an accurate body of information of this kind can be one of our most valuable basic historical tools.

Finally, I consider it essential for writers to have an *awareness of the context* in which the music exists and—to the greatest possible degree—a sense of involvement with jazz and its people. I know an opposite school of thought advocates that the critic keep a suitable distance from the objects of his work; I find that view terribly wrong. A journalist I greatly respect recently admitted, a little sadly, that with only a few unavoidable exceptions he took care to avoid all personal relationships with musicians, for fear of weakening his critical objectivity. I was distressed to hear this; he is a warm human being with a valuable sense of history, and he and a number of artists in his region could learn from each other. I really cannot understand such self-imposed restraint and coldness in as emotional an arena as jazz. Surely an occasional self-disqualification on the grounds of friendly prejudice, or a non-objective interview instead of a review, would take care of the problem.

For there is so much that writers can learn by steeping themselves in the environment of jazz as deeply and directly as possible, by seeking to know the real world that the working musician inhabits. There are many aspects of this world that simply cannot be grasped by detached analysis, that demand a hands-on approach. I have often complained about how seldom I come upon other producers in clubs. Obviously you do find writers in such places quite regularly, usually in the first-night line of duty. But I'd recommend a good deal more attendance at the last set later in the week, without pad and pencil, maybe even buying their own drinks. I am reminded of two very different comments about Ahmad Jamal, an artist who has provoked a wide range of reactions over the years. A particularly visual-minded reviewer (he *was* also the newspaper's art critic) described the pianist as a "pointillist." It sounded meaningful, but when I found in my dictionary that it referred to a method of painting that utilizes small strokes or dots, I understood that it was merely a superficial aren't-I-erudite way of categorizing his rather sparse style. By contrast, Cannonball Adderley, responding to an attempt to dismiss Jamal as merely facile, offered some quite practical advice. Catch him very late at night, and when he knows there are other musicians in the house, he told us; then you'll really hear him play. A very concrete example of why knowing—and caring—is much more valuable than rhetoric.

No one ever said jazz was easy to understand. I'm sure an "easy" music could not have held my attention for so long. You do have to work hard at it. Consider how many faces jazz presents, frequently contradictory ones and often many at the same time. It is high art, and folk art, and a commercial enterprise; heartfelt and a put-on; instinctive and learned. It is above all a matter of individual expression that depends just as heavily on teamwork and ensemble. It exists through the people who performed it in the past and those who play it now, and they are about as varied and hard to categorize a body of artists as the world has ever known—humble, arrogant, clannish, solitary.

Among the things I am most certain about is that jazz cannot properly be perceived in any abstract way. I suppose you can enjoy it by simply sitting there and letting it wash over you. But to have any chance at understanding it well enough to be qualified to comment on the music, you somehow have to make the effort to get inside. No one can draw you a map, and I don't believe you can achieve it by taking courses. Jazz insists on belief, but just being an adoring fan isn't enough. Experience alone doesn't do it; I'm afraid that in my opinion there are writers who have been at it (and making a living thereby) almost forever without actually understanding it at all.

It may even be true that—in approximately the words of Louis Armstrong, or Fats Waller, or whoever is supposed to have said it—if you have to ask, you'll never know. It should be obvious from my comments here that in my view damn few of those who have elected to pass judgment on the music-makers can be considered to know *enough*. Despite my strong misgivings about the concept of jazz criticism, I will grant that the music can use informed, intelligent, articulate, and impassioned commentary; and I'm sure it can survive the other kind. It always has survived, up to now, and so I'll continue to have faith. And now that I've discovered how gratifying it can be to complain and scold, I may even continue to do that.

PERMISSIONS ACKNOWLEDGMENTS

Grateful acknowledgment is made to the following for permission to reprint previously published and unpublished material:

Excerpt from *Mister Jelly Roll* by Alan Lomax. Reprinted by permission of Alan Lomax.

Excerpt from *Satchmo: My Life in New Orleans* by Louis Armstrong. Copyright ©1954, renewed 1982 by Louis Armstrong. Reprinted by permission of Simon & Schuster.

Excerpt from *Music on My Mind* by Willie "The Lion" Smith. Copyright © 1964 by Willie Smith, with George Hoefer. Reprinted by permission of Doubleday, a division of Bantam Doubleday Dell Publishing Group, Inc.

Excerpt from *Music is my Mistress* by Duke Ellington. Copyright © 1973 by Duke Ellington, Inc. Reprinted by permission of Doubleday, a division of Bantam Doubleday Dell Publishing Group, Inc.

Excerpt from *Hot Man: The Life of Art Hodes* by Art Hodes and Chadwick Hansen. Copyright © 1992 by the Board of Trustees of the University of Illinois. Reprinted by permission of the author and University of Illinois Press.

Excerpt from *Hear Me Talkin' to Ya* (Leora Henderson chapter), edited by Nat Shapiro and Nat Hentoff. Copyright © 1955 by Nat Shapiro and Nat Hentoff. Reprinted by permission of Vera Miller Shapiro and Nat Hentoff.

Excerpts from *Buck Clayton's Jazz World* by Buck Clayton, with Nancy Miller Elliott. Copyright © 1986 by Buck Clayton. Reprinted by permission of Oxford University Press.

Excerpts from *Sometimes I Wonder: The Story of Hoagy Carmichael* by Hoagy Carmichael and Stephen Longstreet. Copyright © 1965 by Hoagland Carmichael and Stephen Longstreet. Copyright renewed © 1993 by Dorothy Carmichael, Hoagy Bix Carmichael, Randy Carmichael, and Stephen Longstreet. Reprinted by permission of Farrar, Straus & Giroux, Inc.

Excerpt from *We Called It Music: A Generation of Jazz* by Eddie Condon, narration by Thomas Sugrue (New York: Da Capo Press, Inc.). Copyright © 1947, renewed 1975 by Eddie A. Condon. Reprinted by permission of McIntosh and Otis, Inc.

Excerpt from Mary Lou Williams's autobiographical account (*Melody Maker,* 1954). Reprinted by permission of the Mary Lou Williams Foundation, Inc.

Excerpt from *Of Minnie the Moocher and Me* by Cab Calloway and Bryant Rollins. Copyright © 1976 by Cab Calloway, Bryant Rollins, and Calloway Entertainment, Inc. Reprinted by permission of Calloway Entertainment, Inc.

Excerpt from *Hamp: An Autobiography* by Lionel Hampton, with James Haskins. Copyright © 1989. All rights reserved. Reprinted by permission of Warner Books, Inc. New York, New York, U.S.A.

Excerpts from *John Hammond on Record* by John Hammond with Irving Townsend. Copyright © 1977 by John Hammond. Reprinted by permission of the Estate of John Hammond.

Excerpt from *Good Morning Blues* by Count Basie, as told to Albert Murray. Copyright © 1985 by Albert Murray and Count Basie Enterprises, Inc. Reprinted by permission of Random House, Inc.

Excerpt from *Lady Sings the Blues* by Billie Holiday and William F. Dufty. Copyright ©1956 by Eleanora Fagan and William F. Dufty. Reprinted by permission of Doubleday, a division of Bantam Doubleday Dell Publishing Group, Inc.

Excerpt from *Really the Blues* by Milton "Mezz" Mezzrow and Bernard Wolfe. Copyright © 1946 by Mezz Mezzrow and Bernard Wolfe. Published by arrangement with Carol Publishing Group. A Citadel Underground Book.

Excerpt from *The Trouble with Cinderella* by Artie Shaw. Copyright © 1952, renewed 1980, by Artie Shaw. Reprinted by permission of Artie Shaw.

Excerpt from *Those Swinging Years: The Autobiography of Charlie Barnet,* with Stanley Dance. Copyright © 1984 by Louisiana State University Press. Reprinted by permission of Louisiana State University Press.

"Sonny's the Greatest," "Miles—A Portrait," "Twenty Years with Charlie Mingus" from *Live at the Village Vanguard* by Max Gordon. Copyright © 1980 by Max Gordon. Reprinted by permission of St. Martin's Press, Inc.

Excerpt from *High Times Hard Times* by Anita O'Day with George Eells. Copyright © 1981, 1989 by Anita O'Day and George Eells. Used by courtesy of Limelight Editions, New York.

Excerpt from *Bass Line* by Milt Hinton, with David G. Berger. Copyright © 1988 by Temple University Press. Reprinted by permission of Temple University Press.

Excerpt from *Jazz Spoken Here,* edited by Wayne Enstice and Paul Rubin. Copyright © 1992 by Louisiana State University Press. Reprinted by permission of Louisiana State University Press.

Excerpt from "Milt Gabler Interview" by Dan Morgenstern (with Michael Cuscuna and Charlie Lourie) from the liner notes to *The Complete Commodore Jazz Recordings, Volumes I–III.* Copyright © 1988, 1989, 1990 by Mosaic Records, Inc. Reprinted by permission of Mosaic Records, Inc.

Excerpts (Section I, Chapter 26) from *Miles: The Autobiography* by Miles Davis with Quincy Troupe. Copyright © 1989 by Miles Davis. Reprinted by permission of Simon & Schuster.

Excerpt from *A Call to Assembly* by Willie Ruff. Copyright © 1991 by Willie Ruff. Reprinted by permission of Viking Penguin, a division of Penguin Books USA, Inc.

Excerpt from *Straight Life: The Story of Art Pepper* by Art and Laurie Pepper. Copyright © 1979. Reprinted by permission of Arthur Pepper Music Corp.

Excerpt from *Beneath the Underdog* by Charles Mingus, edited by Nel King. Copyright © 1971 by Charles Mingus and Nel King. Reprinted by permission of Sue Mingus.

Excerpts (Hampton Hawes chapter and "At the Hi-De-Ho") from *Raise Up Off Me* by Don Asher and Hampton Hawes. Copyright © 1974 by Don Asher and Hampton Hawes. Reprinted by permission of Curtis Brown, Ltd.

"How Jazz Came to the Orange County State Fair" by Paul Desmond. Copyright © 1973 by the Estate of Paul Desmond. Reprinted by permission of the Estate of Paul Desmond, administered by Silverman and Shulman, P.C.

"Cecil Taylor" from *The Great Jazz Pianists* by Len Lyons. Copyright © 1983 by Len Lyons. Reprinted by permission of William Morrow Company, Inc.

Excerpt from *Forces in Motion: Anthony Braxton and the Meta-reality of Creative Music* by Graham Lock. Copyright © 1988 by Graham Lock. Reprinted by permission of Graham Lock.

Excerpt from *Remembering Song: Encounters with the New Orleans Jazz Tradition* by Frederick Turner (New York: Da Capo Press). Copyright © 1982, 1994 by Frederick Turner. Reprinted by permission of Frederick Turner and Robin Strauss Agency, Inc., literary agent.

"The Blues for Jimmy" by Vincent McHugh from *Selections from the Gutter: Portraits from the* Jazz Record by Art Hodes and Chadwick Hansen. Copyright © 1977 by The Regents of the University of California. Reprinted by permission of the University of California Press.

"Even His Feet Look Sad" by Whitney Balliett from *American Musicians*. Copyright © 1986. Reprinted by permission of Oxford University Press.

"The Cutting Sessions" by Rex Stewart from *Jazz Masters of the Thirties* by Rex Stewart. Copyright © 1972 by the Estate of Rex Stewart. Reprinted by permission of Simon & Schuster.

"Sunshine Always Opens Out" by Whitney Balliett from *American Musicians*. Copyright © 1986. Reprinted by permission of Oxford University Press.

"The Poet: Bill Evans" by Gene Lees from *Meet Me at Jim and Andy's*. Copyright © 1988. Reprinted by permission of Oxford University Press.

"Black Like Him" from *Outcats* by Francis Davis. Copyright © 1990 by Francis Davis. Reprinted by permission of Oxford University Press.

Excerpt from *The Big Bands, 4th Edition* by George T. Simon. Copyright © 1967, 1971, 1974, 1981 by George T. Simon. Reprinted by permission of Schirmer Books, an imprint of Simon & Schuster Macmillan.

"Homage to Bunny" by George Frazier (*Boston Herald*, June 1942). Reprinted by permission of the *Boston Herald*.

"The Spirit of Jazz" by Otis Ferguson (*The New Republic*, 1936). Reprinted courtesy of *The New Republic*.

"The Mirror of Swing" from *Faces in the Crowd* by Gary Giddins. Copyright © 1992. Reprinted by permission of Oxford University Press.

Excerpt from *Celebrating the Duke* by Ralph Gleason. Copyright © 1975 by the Estate of Ralph J. Gleason. Reprinted by permission of Jean R. Gleason and Jazz Casual Productions, Inc.

"Two Rounds of the Battling Dorseys" from Esquire*'s 1947 Jazz Book*. Copyright © 1947 by The Hearst Corporation. Reprinted by permission of The Hearst Corporation.

"Jazz Orchestra in Residence, 1971" from *Straight Ahead: The Story of Stan Kenton* by Carol Easton. Copyright © 1973 by Carol Easton. Reprinted by permission of The Mitchell J. Hamilburg Agency.

"Flying Home" by Rudi Blesh from *Combo: U.S.A.* by Rudi Blesh. Copyright © 1971 by Rudi Blesh. Reprinted by permission of Harold Ober Associates Incorporated.

"The Fabulous Gypsy" by Gilbert S. McKean, originally printed in *Esquire Magazine.* Copyright © 1947 by The Hearst Corporation. Reprinted by permission of The Hearst Corporation.

"Minton's" by Ralph Ellison from *Shadow and Act* by Ralph Ellison. Copyright © 1954, 1964, renewed 1981, 1992 by Ralph Ellison. Reprinted by permission of Random House, Inc.

"Minton's Playhouse" from *To Be or Not to Bop: Memoirs* by Dizzy Gillespie, with Al Fraser. Copyright © 1979 by John Birks Gillespie and Wilmot Alfred Fraser. Reprinted by permission of Doubleday, a division of Bantam Doubleday Dell Publishing Group, Inc.

"Bird" from *Miles Davis: The Autobiography* by Miles Davis with Quincy Troupe. Copyright © 1989 by Miles Davis. Reprinted by permission of Simon & Schuster.

Excerpt from *Waiting for Dizzy* by Gene Lees. Copyright © 1991. Reprinted by permission of Oxford University Press.

"An Evening with Monk" and "Coleman Hawkins" by Dan Morgenstern. Copyrights © 1960 and 1973, respectively, by Dan Morgenstern.

"Thelonius and Me" by Orrin Keepnews from the *Complete Riverside Recordings of Thelonious Monk.* Copyright © 1987. Reprinted by permission of Oxford University Press.

"John Coltrane" from *Jazz Is* by Nat Hentoff. Text copyright © 1976 by Nat Hentoff. Reprinted by permission of Random House, Inc.

"Bessie Smith: Poet" by James Murray Kempton. Copyright © 1987 by *New York Newsday*. Reprinted by permission of James Murray Kempton.

"Mahalia Jackson" by George T. Simon. Copyright © 1954 by R. Scott Asen, Metronome Archive. Reprinted by permission of R. Scott Asen, Metronome Archive.

"Lady Day Has Her Say" by Billie Holiday Copyright © 1950 by R. Scott Asen, Metronome Archive. Reprinted by permission of R. Scott Asen, Metronome Archive.

"The Untold Story of the International Sweethearts of Rhythm" from *All in Good Time* by Marian McPartland. Copyright © 1980 by Marian McPartland. Reprinted by permission of the author.

"A Starr Is Reborn" by Gary Giddins from *Faces in the Crowd* by Gary Giddins. Copyright © 1992. Reprinted by permission of Oxford University Press.

"Moonbeam Moscowitz: Sylvia Syms" by Whitney Balliett from *American Singers: Twenty-seven Portraits.* Copyright © 1988. Reprinted by permission of Oxford University Press.

"The Lindy" from *Jazz Dance* by Marshall Stearns and Jean Stearns. Copyright © 1964, 1966 by Jean Stearns and the Estate of Marshall Stearns. Copyright © 1968 by Jean Stearns. Reprinted by permission of Schirmer Books, an imprint of Simon & Schuster Macmillan.

"A Night at the Five Spot" from *Jazz Changes* by Martin Williams. Copyright © 1992. Reprinted by permission of Oxford University Press.

"You Dig It, Sir?" by Lillian Ross (*The New Yorker,* August 14, 1954). Copyright © 1954, 1982 by Lillian Ross. All rights reserved. Reprinted by permission of *The New Yorker*.

"Johnny Green" from *More Dialogues in Swing: Intimate Conversations with the Stars of the Big Band Era* by Fred Hall. Copyright © 1991 by Fred Hall. Reprinted by permission of Pathfinder Publishing of California, 458 Dorothy Ave., Ventura, CA 93003.

"Jazz in America" by Jean-Paul Sartre, translated by Ralph de Toledano. Copyright © 1947 by Ralph de Toledano. Reprinted by permission of Ralph de Toledano.

"Don't Shoot—We're American" by Steve Voce from *Just Jazz 4,* edited by Sinclair Traill and the Hon. Gerald Lascelles. Copyright © 1960. Reprinted by permission of the publisher Souvenir Press Ltd., London.

"Goffin, *Esquire*, and the Moldy Figs" from *The Jazz Years* by Leonard Feather. Copyright © 1986 by Leonard Feather (Quartet Books). Reprinted by permission of the Estate of Leonard Feather.

"Bechet and Jazz Visit Europe" by Ernst-Alexandre Ansermet, translated by Walter Schaap. Copyright © 1938 by Walter Schaap. Reprinted by permission of Walter Schaap.

"Harpsichords and Jazz Trumpets" from *Hot Jazz and Jazz Dance* by Richard Pryor Dodge. Copyright © 1995. Reprinted by permission of Oxford University Press.

"Conclusions" from *Jazz, Hot and Hybrid* by Winthrop Sargeant. Copyright © 1946 by Winthrop Sargeant. Reprinted by permission of Jane Sargeant.

"Has Jazz Influenced the Symphony?" by Gene Krupa and Leonard Bernstein from Esquire*'s 1947 Jazz Book*. Copyright © 1947 by The Hearst Corporation. Reprinted by permission of The Hearst Corporation.

Excerpt from *All What Jazz?* by Philip Larkin (London: Faber and Faber Limited). Copyright © 1970. Reprinted by permission of Faber and Faber Limited.

"The Musical Achievement" from *The Jazz Scene* by Eric Hobsbawm. Copyright © 1992 by Eric Hobsbawm. Reprinted by permission of Pantheon Books, a division of Random House, Inc.

"King Oliver" by Larry Gushee (*Jazz Review,* 1958). Copyright © 1996 by Lawrence Gushee. Reprinted by permission of Lawrence Gushee.

"Bix Beiderbecke" and "Billie Holiday" from *The Reluctant Art* by Benny Green. Copyright © 1962 by Benny Green. Reprinted by permission of Benny Green.

"James P. Johnson" from *A Jazz Retrospect* by Max Harrison (London: Quartet Books, Ltd., 1976). Reprinted by permission of Quartet Books Limited.

"Not for the Left Hand Alone" by Martin Williams from *The Jazz Tradition*. Copyright © 1970. Reprinted by permission of Oxford University Press.

"Time and the Tenor" by Graham Colombé. Copyright © 1974 by Graham Colombé. Reprinted by permission of Graham Colombé.

"Bop" from *Blues People* by LeRoi Jones. Copyright © 1963 by LeRoi Jones. Reprinted by permission of William Morrow & Company, Inc.

"On Bird, Bird-Watching, and Jazz" from *Shadow and Act* by Ralph Ellison. Copyright 1954, 1964, renewed 1981, 1992 by Ralph Ellison. Reprinted by permission of Random House, Inc.

"Why Did Ellington 'Remake' His Masterpiece?" from *Toward Jazz* by André Hodeir. Copyright © 1962 by André Hodeir. Reprinted by permission of André Hodeir.

"On the Corner: The Sellout of Miles Davis" from *The All-American Skin Game* by Stanley Crouch. Copyright © 1995 by Stanley Crouch. Reprinted by permission of Pantheon Books, a division of Random House, Inc.

"Space Is the Place" from *Dancing in Your Head* by Gene Santoro. Copyright © 1994. Reprinted by permission of Oxford University Press.

Liner notes by Dudley Moore for "Easy to Love" by Erroll Garner. Copyright © 1988 by Dudley Moore. Reprinted by permission of Dudley Moore.

"Bessie Smith" from *The Best of Jazz* by Humphrey Lyttelton. Copyright © 1979 by Humphrey Lyttelton. Reprinted by permission of Taplinger Publishing Co., Inc.

"Cult of the White Goddess" from *Jazz Singing* by Will Friedwald. Copyright © 1990 by Will Friedwald. Reprinted by permission of Will Friedwald.

"Ella Fitzgerald" from *The Great American Popular Singers* by Henry Pleasants. Copyright © 1974 by Henry Pleasants. Reprinted by permission of Simon & Schuster.

"The Divine Sarah" from *Musings* by Gunther Schuller. Copyright © 1986. Reprinted by permission of Oxford University Press.

"The Blues as Dance Music" from *Stomping the Blues* by Albert Murray. Copyright © 1976 by Albert Murray. Reprinted by permission of The Wylie Agency, Inc.

"Local Jazz" from *Jazz* by James Lincoln Collier. Copyright © 1993. Reprinted by permission of Oxford University Press.

"Fifty Years of 'Body and Soul'" from *Faces in the Crowd* by Gary Giddins. Copyright © 1992 by Gary Giddins. Reprinted by permission of Oxford University Press.

"Everycat and Birdland Mon Amor" from *Outcats* by Francis Davis. Copyright © 1990 by Francis Davis. Reprinted by permission of Oxford University Press.

"Bird Land" by Stanley Crouch. Copyright © 1989 by Stanley Crouch. Reprinted by permission of the author.

"Louis Armstrong: An American Genius" by Dan Morgenstern. Copyright © 1985 by Dan Morgenstern and the Rutgers Institute of Jazz Studies.

"A Bad Idea, Poorly Executed . . ." from *The View from Within* by Orrin Keepnews. Copyright © 1987. Reprinted by permission of Oxford University Press.